ENCYCLOPEDIA OF
BUSINESS
IN TODAY'S WORLD

ENCYCLOPEDIA OF
BUSINESS
IN TODAY'S WORLD

Charles Wankel
St. John's University
General Editor

Volume 1

Los Angeles | London | New Delhi
Singapore | Washington DC

A SAGE Reference Publication

For information

SAGE Publications, Inc.
2455 Teller Road
Thousand Oaks, California 91320
E-mail: order@sagepub.com

SAGE Publications Ltd.
1 Oliver's Yard
55 City Road
London EC1Y 1SP
United Kingdom

SAGE Publications India Pvt. Ltd.
B 1/I 1 Mohan Cooperative Industrial Area
Mathura Road, New Delhi 110 044
India

SAGE Publications Asia-Pacific Pte. Ltd.
33 Pekin Street #02-01
Far East Square
Singapore 048763

Printed in the United States of America.

Library of Congress Cataloging-in-Publication Data

Encyclopedia of business in today's world / Charles Wankel, general editor.
    p. cm.
  Includes bibliographical references and index.
  ISBN 978-1-4129-6427-2 (cloth)
  1. Business--Encyclopedias. 2. Commerce--Encyclopedias. 3. Management--Encyclopedias. 4. International trade--Encyclopedias. 5. International business enterprises--Encyclopedias. I. Wankel, Charles.
  HF1001.E4665 2009
  650.03--dc22   2009002541

This book is printed on acid-free paper.

09 10 11 12 13 10 9 8 7 6 5 4 3 2 1

GOLSON MEDIA
President and Editor   J. Geoffrey Golson
Managing Editor   Susan Moskowitz
Layout Editors   Oona Patrick, Mary Jo Scibetta
Copyeditors   Joyce Li, Barbara Paris
Proofreader   Julie Grady
Indexer   J S Editorial

Photo credits are on page 2010.

SAGE REFERENCE
Vice President and Publisher   Rolf A. Janke
Senior Editor   Jim Brace-Thompson
Project Editor   Tracy Buyan
Cover Production   Gail Buschman
Marketing Manager   Amberlyn McKay
Editorial Assistant   Michele Thompson
Reference Systems Manager   Leticia Gutierrez
Reference Systems Coordinator   Laura Notton

Contents

Volume 1

About the General Editor	*vi*
Introduction	*vii*
Reader's Guide	*xi*
List of Articles	*xxiii*
List of Contributors	*xxxv*
Chronology of Business	*xlv*
Articles A to C	*1–472*

Volume 2

List of Articles	*vii*
Articles D to K	*473–978*

Volume 3

List of Articles	*vii*
Articles L to S	*979–1536*

Volume 4

List of Articles	*vii*
Articles T to Z	*1537–1738*
Glossary	*1739*
Resource Guide	*1783*
Appendix: World Trade Statistics	*1787*
Index	*1927*

About the General Editor

Charles Wankel, Associate Professor of Management at St. John's University, New York, holds a doctorate from New York University. His authored and edited books include *21st Century Management: A Reference Handbook, Reinventing Management Education for the 21st Century, Innovative Approaches to Global Sustainability, The Cutting Edge of International Management Education, Alleviating Poverty through Business Strategy, Global Sustainability Initiatives: New Models and New Approaches, University and Corporate Innovations in Lifetime Learning, Educating Managers with Tomorrow's Technologies, Educating Managers through Real World Projects, New Visions of Graduate Management Education, Innovative Approaches to Reducing Global Poverty, Being and Becoming a Management Education Scholar*, and the bestselling *Management*.

He is the founder and leader of eight scholarly virtual communities for management professors with 8,000 members in 90 nations. He is internationally prominent and has been a Fulbright Scholar and was sponsored by the United Nations Development Program and the Soros Open Society Fund in Lithuania. He has been a visiting professor lecturing around the world including at the Chiba University of Commerce in Japan, and was the 2004 Keynote Speaker at the Nippon Academy of Management Education; Distinguished Speaker at the Education without Borders Conference in Abu Dhabi, United Arab Emirates; and Keynote Speaker at the Association of MBAs Latin America Conference for Deans and Directors.

Dr. Wankel was awarded the Outstanding Service in Management Education and Development Award at the Academy of Management's 2004 meeting. Columbia University's American Assembly identified him as one of the nation's top experts on Total Quality Management. His *Fortune 50* consulting clients include McDonald's Corporation and IBM.

Editorial Advisory Board

David M. Brock, Ph.D.
Ben-Gurion University and Yeshiva University

Sabine Hoffman, Ph.D.
American University of the Middle East

Janice M. Traflet, Ph.D.
Bucknell University

Andrew J. Waskey
Dalton State College

Introduction

Business in today's world is one of increasing diversity. Undertaking commerce even by an individual can mean working globally through a welter of new media with opportunities of all sorts rapidly appearing. The boundaries, scope, content, structures, and processes of a business activity can morph into completely different ones in the course of a project. Contemporary businesses and certainly future businesses find it incumbent upon them to fit with the requirements of environmental and economic sustainability of the others who inhabit our world. Of course the practices, technologies, and tools of business are currently utilized by professional managers in government, education, arts organizations, not-for-profit organizations, political organizations, social service organizations, etc. That is, rather than having an opera company run by a former singer who charms its patrons, what is expected is a former singer who is a professional manager who is adept at grappling with the issues, requirements, and expectations associated with responsible business.

With about 1,000 entries written for this volume by experts from an incredible diversity of fields, this volume provides the opportunity for understanding the landmarks and their interrelationships in the wide domain of business. These volumes indeed enable a person to come to understand what the key issues of a business topic are, and then examine associated topics to emerge with an expanding understanding of any of many areas of business. Thus, users of this encyclopedia may use it as a GPS to navigate them into the language and ideas of the main conceptual terrain of business.

This encyclopedia is designed to include a vast range of different types of entries, including key companies, business policies, regions, countries, dimensions of globalization, economic factors, international agreements, financial instruments, accounting regulations and approaches, theories, legislation, management practices and approaches, ethical and social responsibility issues, legal and contractual structures, professional organizations, technologies, marketing and advertising topics, research and development practices, operations management, and logistics terms, with a global perspective. The wealth of topics included here reflects an integrated vision by the editor of a welter of functions, technologies, and environmental factors. In the past century most business topics were free-standing and mostly of interest to narrow specialists in related departments and organizations. However, the 21st century is one of cross-boundary actions. For example, Amazon incorporates the knowledge of prosumers' book and other product reviews as part of its service to customers. Wal-Mart has suppliers who are alerted by data fed to them by the scanning of RFID tags when the product levels of a particular shelf in a particular Wal-Mart store or in Wal-Mart stores of a particular region or country indicate that it is time to initiate the production packaging and shipping of their products to Wal-Mart. These vendors actually might better understand parts of Wal-Mart's inventory sales, promotions, and requirements better than Wal-Mart managers.

Such new types of partnering create new terms and topics that those wishing to successfully engage and utilize must understand. Increasingly used structural approaches such as outsourcing and offshoring transcend the still important and now classic conceptualization of international business through an understanding of intercultural issues, the political and economic environment of key countries around the world, home country and host country issues, joint ventures, multinational corporations, international negotiations.

Globalization is a by-word of the current business epoch. Today it is normal for a business in a developed country to employ clerks, technicians, salespeople, customer relations agents, and increasingly professionals such as managers, engineers, and researchers in emerging market nations such as India, China, and Vietnam. Increasingly, corporate teams work virtually with team members distributed around the world. New technologies provide interfaces that are coming to replicate and in some ways even improve on the kind of exchanges that traditionally were only available in face-to-face situations.

So, for example, it has been predicted that most people in companies will do part of their work by 2012 using three-dimensional augmented reality interfaces such as that provided by virtual worlds such as Second Life. The need for people in organizations to understand associated newly arising terms and topics such as crowdsourcing, avatars, and teleporting, therefore, is significant.

In the post-Enron, post-Bhopal, post–Three Mile Island, post–Exxon Valdez, and post-9/11 environment, business and society issues and topics refract off each other with new meanings. For example, what in the past might have just been a climate of corruption, bribery, ineptness, and lack of accountability, now in this or that far-flung place today might have global implications. So, the editor of this volume was engaged by Columbia University to teach cutting-edge human resource management (HRM) topics in a Russian oil company in Nizhny Vartovsk, Siberia, where just as in U.S. oil companies, the sharing of cutting-edge management technologies and approaches was proceeding at a rapid rate. Notions such as whistle-blowing, managing stakeholders, alleviating poverty through business strategy, and microfinance are increasingly important for those interested in understanding business to know.

Management information systems are a new universe of technologies, and the terms and topics that encompass them, from just 15 years ago. New applications and functions have proliferated, including e-commerce, the blogosphere, social networking (including Facebook and LinkedIn), digital dashboards, e-learning, executive support systems, internet, intranets, extranets, identity theft, moblogs, privacy, spam, transaction processing systems, virtualization, virtual companies, VoIP, business process reengineering, data warehouses, and customer relationship management (CRM).

Operations management is a field of business that is undergoing many structural and technological changes. The quality management revolution starting in Japan and developing in the mid-80s in the United States and Europe has been overtaken by new issues of global supply chain procurement and distribution. New approaches to designing services take on more import in a service economy. Service blueprinting, front office and back office activities, and servicescapes are among the new by-words. Location analysis, hybrid layout design, and process product and fixed position layouts are increasingly structured in their deployment. Enterprise resource planning (ERP) is increasingly sophisticated with new connectivity and integration issues.

Management strategy has been redefined in the United States by agency theory, the resource-based view of the firm, and such important accounting legislation as the Sarbanes-Oxley Act. New types of financial instruments and their deployment through a wider than traditional spectrum of organizational types resulted from deregulation. The looseness and oversight of this new environment resulted in a looseness in financial dealings. Financial institutions worldwide have been shaken by the great mortgage crisis of 2008. This followed the bailing out of Bear, Stearns, & Co. Inc., a leading global investment banking and securities trading firm, by the American federal government. The world economy is increasingly integrated. The European Union (EU) and NAFTA are just two of many such international structures that foster freer trade. The high price of oil in 2008 reflects the ongoing power of OPEC.

Marketing is no longer just a department in a company; rather it entails the collaboration of many departments, vendors, and even customers working together to market products and services. Today we find companies such as Dunkin' Donuts focusing on the quick provision of inexpensive cups of coffee to go and at the same time other companies such as Starbucks going beyond that to market an entire experience, lifestyle, variety of flavors, and even music to their target market.

We see lateral and vertical marketing, yet the classic mix of the 4Ps of product, price, place, and promotion still frame marketing decisions. Pricing decisions can spring from such varied strategies and focuses as penetration, competition's price, bundling, differential product line pricing across different price-points, psychological selection of price amounts, and premium pricing to exclusive target markets. Advertising nowadays at times includes subliminal or covert messages. Internet advertising is arising in many new varieties. Marketing has gone from international marketing to global marketing, where marketing decisions are made to apply across multiple countries.

This encyclopedia is current and packed with essential and up-to-date information on the state of business in our world. Not only does it reflect where business is, but also conveys the trajectory of business further into the 21st century. The current status of English as the new Esperanto is having a big impact on business around the world. Many business schools in all parts of the world are now offering courses and programs in English. This is creating a need for a reference that will explain English language topics and terms, in university, business, and public libraries. Coverage of the global has not been at the expense of the local. This encyclopedia provides insight into the development and current business situation in a wide spectrum of nations through articles on many individual countries.

Our hundreds of article authors, with their knowledge of a wide range of literatures, provide bibliographic recommendations for those seeking more specific information. Sometimes as in the case of the article on Austria, this might include a link to a Web site that might offer the ongoing updates of the nation's statistical data. The editor hopes that the *Encyclopedia of Business in Today's World* will provide clear overviews of the important business topics of our time.

CHARLES WANKEL
GENERAL EDITOR

Reader's Guide

Competitive Forces

Acquisitions, Takeovers, and Mergers
Competition
Customer Responsiveness
Global Competitiveness Index
Infrastructure
Local Competitors
Patents
Quality
Service Expectations
State-Owned Enterprises (SOEs)

Corporate Profiles

ABN AMRO Holding
Aegon
AEON
Allianz SE
Allstate
Altria Group
American International Group
AmerisourceBergen
A. P. Møller Mærsk Group
Archer Daniels Midland

Assicurazioni Generali
AT&T
Aviva
AXA
Banco Bilbao Vizcaya Argentaria
Banco Santander Central Hispano Group
Bank of America Corp.
Bank of China
Baoshan Iron and Steel
Barclays
BASF
Bayer
Berkshire Hathaway
Best Buy
Bloomberg
BMW
BNP Paribas
Boeing
Bouygues
BP
BT
Canon
Cardinal Health

Caremark Rx
Carrefour
Caterpillar
CEMEX
Chevron
China Life Insurance
China Mobile Communications
China National Petroleum
Citigroup
CNP Assurances
Company Profiles: Africa
Company Profiles: Australia and Pacific
Company Profiles: Central America and
    the Caribbean
Company Profiles: East Asia
Company Profiles: Eastern Europe
Company Profiles: Middle East
Company Profiles: North America
Company Profiles: South America
Company Profiles: South Asia
Company Profiles: Western Europe
ConocoPhillips
Corporate Change
Corporate Codes
Costco Wholesale
Credit Suisse
CVS/Caremark
Dai-ichi Mutual Life Insurance
DaimlerChrysler
Dell
Deutsche Bahn
Deutsche Bank
Deutsche Post
Deutsche Telekom
Dow Chemical
DZ Bank
EADS
Électricité de France
Enel
Eni
E.ON
ExxonMobil
Fiat
Ford Motor
Fortis
France Télécom
Freddie Mac
Fujitsu

Gaz de France
Gazprom
General Electric
General Motors
GlaxoSmithKline
HBOS
Hewlett-Packard
Hitachi
Home Depot, The
Honda Motor
HSBC Holdings
Hudson's Bay Company
Hyundai Motor
Indian Oil
Industrial & Commercial Bank of China
ING Group
International Business Machines
Johnson & Johnson
JPMorgan Chase & Co.
Koç Holding
Legal & General Group
Lenovo
LG
Lockheed Martin
Lowe's
LUKOIL
Marathon Oil
Matsushita Electric Industrial
Merrill Lynch
MetLife
METRO
Microsoft
Millea Holdings
Mitsubishi
Mitsubishi Electric
Mitsubishi UFJ Financial Group
Mitsui
Mittal Steel
Mizuho Financial Group
Morgan Stanley
Motorola
Munich Re Group
NEC
Nestlé
Nippon Life Insurance
Nippon Oil
Nippon Steel
Nippon Telegraph & Telephone

Nissan Motor

Nokia

Novartis

Old Mutual

Pemex

PepsiCo

Petrobras

Petronas

Peugeot

Pfizer

Private Spaceflight Industry

Procter & Gamble

Prudential

Prudential Financial

Renault

Repsol YPF

Reuters

Roche Group

Royal Dutch Shell

RWE

Safeway

Samsung Electronics

Sanofi Aventis

Sears Holdings

Siemens

Sinopec

SK

Sony

Sprint Nextel

State Farm Insurance Cos.

State Grid

Statoil

Sumitomo Mitsui Financial Group

Sunoco

Sysco

Target

Tata Group

Telecom Italia

Telefónica

ThyssenKrupp

Time Warner

Tokyo Electric Power

Toshiba

Total

Toyota Motor Corporation

Tyco International

UBS

UniCredit Group

Unilever

United Parcel Service

United Technologies

U.S. Postal Service

Verizon Communications

Vodafone

Volkswagen

Volvo

Wachovia Corp.

Walgreens

Wal-Mart Stores

Walt Disney

Wells Fargo

Zurich Financial Services

Countries

Africa

Algeria

Angola

Argentina

Asia

Asian Tigers

Australia

Austria

Bahrain

Bangladesh

Belarus

Belgium

Bolivia

Botswana

Brazil

BRICs

Bulgaria

Cameroon

Canada

Central America

Chile

China

Colombia

Costa Rica

Côte d'Ivoire

Croatia

Cyprus

Czech Republic

Denmark

Dominican Republic

Eastern Europe

Ecuador

Egypt
El Salvador
Estonia
Finland
France
Germany
Ghana
Greece
Guatemala
Hong Kong
Hungary
Iceland
India
Indonesia
Industrialized Countries
Iran
Ireland
Israel
Italy
Japan
Jordan
Kazakhstan
Kenya
Korea, South
Kuwait
Latin America
Latvia
Lebanon
Less Industrialized Countries
Libya
Lithuania
Luxembourg
Malaysia
Mexico
Middle East
Morocco
Netherlands
Newly Industrialized Countries
New Zealand
Nigeria
Norway
Oman
Pacific Rim
Pakistan
Panama
Peru
Philippines
Poland

Portugal
Qatar
Romania
Russia
Saudi Arabia
Singapore
Slovakia
Slovenia
South Africa
Spain
Sri Lanka
Sudan
Sweden
Switzerland
Syria
Tanzania
Thailand
Trinidad and Tobago
Tunisia
Turkey
Ukraine
United Arab Emirates
United Kingdom
United States
Uruguay
Uzbekistan
Venezuela
Vietnam
Western Europe
Yemen
Zimbabwe

Cultural Environments

Acculturation
Achieved Status/Ascribed Status
Attitudes and Attitude Change
Bureaucracy
Communication Challenges
Communication Styles
Conformance/Conformity
Confucian Work Dynamism
Context
Cross-Cultural Research
Cultural Norms and Scripts
Culture-Specific Values
Emotion
Enculturation
Entrepreneurship

Ethnocentrism
Feng Shui
Gannon's Cultural Metaphors
Gift-Giving
Global Digital Divide
Guanxi
Hofstede's Five Dimensions of Culture
Individualism/Collectivism
Internal/External
Local Adaptation
Masculinity/Femininity
Monochronic/Polychronic
Multicultural Work Groups and Teams
Negotiation and Negotiating Styles
Neutral/Affective
Persuasion
Power Distance
Schwartz Value Theory
Silent Language of Hall (Nonverbal
    Communication)
Space
Specific/Diffuse
Stereotyping
Time Orientation
Uncertainty Avoidance
Universalism/Particularism
Women in Business
Work/Personal Life Balance

Economics of International Business

Acquisitions, Takeovers, and Mergers
Asian Financial Crisis
Balance of Goods and Services
Bankruptcy
Big Mac Index
Brain Drain
Business Cycles
Capital Account Balance
Capitalism
Capital Repatriation
Centralized Control
Chaebol
Communism
Confidentiality
Contagion
Cooperatives
Cross-Licensing
Current Account

Debt
Development Assistance
Diversity
Economic Development
Economic Indicators
Economic Statistics
Economies of Scale
Economies of Scope
Emerging Economies
Entry Mode
Exchange Rate Volatility
External Debt
Factor Endowments
Franchising
Free Markets
Geocentric
Gini Index
Green Revolution
Gross National Product
Industry Information
Information Systems
Interest Rates
International Capital Flows
Joint Venture
Keiretsu
Licensing
Localization
Macroeconomics
Micro-Multinational
Multinational Corporation
National Accounts
Net Capital Outflow
Neuroeconomics
Open Economy Macroeconomics
Pegged Exchange Rate
Polycentric
Privatization
Purchasing Power Parity
Research and Development
Royalties
Self-Employed Women's Association,
    India
Socialism
Socioeconomic Status
Stock Exchanges
Strategic Alliance
Teams
Technology

Tequila Effect
Terms of Trade
Trade Balance
Underdevelopment
Zaibatsu

Economic Theories of International Business
Absolute Advantage
Chicago School/Chicago Boys
Comparative Advantage
Core
Cross-Hauling
Demonstration Effect
Dependency Theory
Export-Oriented Development
Follow-the-Leader Theory
Heckscher-Ohlin Model
Import Substitution
Infant Industry Argument
Internationalization Model
Leontief Paradox
Linder Hypothesis
Market Imperfections Theory
Modernization Theory
Monopolistic Advantage Theory
Mundell-Fleming Model
Neocolonialism
New Trade Theory
Periphery
Product Life Cycle Hypothesis

Ethics, Corruption, and Social Responsibility
Black Market
Bribery
Copyright Infringement
Corporate Social Responsibility
Corporate Social Responsibility and International
    Business Ethics
Corruption
Foreign Corrupt Practices Act
Industrial Espionage
Intellectual Property Theft
Money Laundering
Opportunistic Behavior
Plagiarism
Reverse Engineering
Sustainable Development
Trademark Infringement

Export/Import Strategies
Agents
Bill of Lading
Certificate of Origin
Countertrade
Direct Export
Distribution
Ex-Factory (Ex-Works)
Export Assistance Program
Export Financing
Export Management Company
Export Trading Company
Indirect Export
Negotiation and Negotiating Styles

Foreign Direct Investment
British East India Company
Concession
Diversifying Investment
Dutch East India Company
Foreign Direct Investment, Horizontal and Vertical
Foreign Portfolio Investment
Hanseatic League
Home Country
Host Country
Hudson's Bay Company
Indirect Foreign Direct Investment
Internationalization
Late Mover
Locational Advantages
Market-Seeking Investment
Multinational Competitive Disadvantages
Multinational Corporation
Resource-Seeking Investment
Royal Africa Company
Tax Holiday
Virginia Company

Globalization and Society
Antiglobalization Movement
Cooperatives
Democratic Globalization
Diffusion of Innovation
Gini Index
Global Capital Market
Globalization
Sustainable Development
Transition Economies

Human Resource Management

Absenteeism
Benefits
Bent Measuring Stick (or Performance Appraisal)
Coaching
Compensation
Cost of Living Allowance
Culture Shock
Education Allowance
Employer–Employee Relations
Empowerment
Ethnocentric Human Resource Policy
Expatriate
External Labor Market
Family Leave
Geocentric Human Resource Policy
Health Care Benefits/Systems
Holidays
Housing Allowance
Internal Labor Market
International Compensation
International Training
Job Enrichment
Local/National
Maternity Leave
Mentoring
Motivation
Overtime
Parent Country National
Payroll Taxes
Pension Systems
Perquisites
Polycentric Human Resource Policy
Productivity
Profit-Sharing
Recruitment
Redundancy
Reentry
Regiocentric Human Resource Policy
Selection
Third Country National
Training
Visa
Working Hours

International Accounting

Accounting Harmonization
Accounting Information Systems
Accounting Software
American Depository Receipt
Auditing Standards
Basel Committee on Banking Supervision
Capital Adequacy
Capital Gains Tax
Compliance
Corporate Accounting
Corporate Governance
Corporate Income Tax
Cost Accounting
Custodians
Disclosure Requirements
Earnings Management
Earnings Quality
Financial Reporting
Financial Statement Analysis
Fixed Costs
Forensic Accounting
Impact Financial Statements
Information Technology Auditing
International Accounting Standards Board
International Financial Reporting Standards
Investor Protection
Nonfinancial Information Reporting
Sarbanes-Oxley
Taxes
Transfer Pricing
Value Added Tax (VAT)
Variable Costs

International Finance

Account Settlement
AEX General Index (Amsterdam)
All Ordinaries Index
ATX Index (Vienna)
Basis Points
Behavioral Economics
Bel-20 Index (Brussels)
Bid/Ask Spread
Blocked Funds
Bloomberg
Bonds
BSE Sensex Index (Bombay Stock Exchange)
Buyout
CAC 40 Index (Paris)
Capital Budgeting
Capital Flight

Cash Management
Chicago Mercantile Exchange
City, The
Clearing House Automated Payment System
Clearing House Interbank Payment System
Clearing Houses
CMA Index (Egypt)
Collateral
Collateralized Debt Obligations
Collateralized Loan Obligations
Commercialization of Space
Credit Ratings
Cross-Border Trading
Currency Exposure
Currency Speculators
DAX Index (Germany)
Debt (Securities)
Debt-for-Equity Swaps
Debt Rescheduling
Deregulation
Discount Rate
Dow Jones Index
Equities
Exchange Rate Risk (or Currency Exposure)
Financial Hedge
Financial Market Regulation
Financial Markets
Fixed Exchange Rate
Floating Exchange Rate
Foreign Exchange Market
Forward Market
FT Index
FTSE
Futures Markets
Gnomes of Zurich
Government Bonds
Hang Seng Index
Hedging
Hostile Takeovers
Initial Public Offering
Interbank Market
Interest Rate Swaps
International Securities Identification
    Numbering
Investment Banks
IPC
ISE National 100 Index
Jakarta Composite Index

KLSE (Malaysian Stock Index)
LIBOR
Liquidity (or Market Liquidity)
Lombard Rate
Madrid General Index
Market Maker
Mark-to-Market Valuation
MerVal
MIBTel Index (Milan)
Microfinance
Microfinance Institution
Money Supply
Mortgage Credit Crisis of 2008
Nikkei Index
NZSE 50 (New Zealand Stock Index)
Option
OSE All Share Index (Oslo)
Prospectus
Public Finance Reform
Real Hedge
Retail Capital Markets
Reuters
Samurai Bond
S&P 500 Index
Securities Financing
Securitization
Seoul Composite Index
Settlement Date
Shanghai Composite Index
Shareholder Activism
Sovereign Borrowing
Spot Market
Spread
Stock Exchanges
Stockholm General Index
Straits Times Index (Singapore)
Structured Notes
Subprime Loans
Swap
Swiss Market Index
Taiwan Weighted Index
TA-100 Index (Tel Aviv)
Too Big to Fail
Trading Volume
Value at Risk
Venture Capital
Wall Street
Wholesale Capital Markets

International Monetary System

Bank for International Settlements
Bretton Woods Accord
Bretton Woods Institutions
Capital Controls
Central Banks
Convertibility
Cross Rate
Currency
Currency Zone
Devaluation
Dirty Float
Dollar Hegemony
Dollarization
Euro
Exchange Rate
Fiat Money
Flexible Exchange Rate Regime
Foreign Exchange Market
Foreign Exchange Reserves
Gold Standard
International Monetary System
Managed Float Regime
Market-Basket Currency
Marshall-Lerner Condition
Monetary Intervention
Monetary Policy: Rules Versus Discretion
Reserve Currency
Revaluation

International Trade

Ad Valorem Duties
Agreement on Trade-Related Aspects of
    Intellectual Property Rights
Arbitrage
ATA Carnet
Banana Wars
Barriers to Entry
Barter
Bill of Lading
Black Market
Business-to-Business
CoCom
Cost, Insurance, and Freight
Countervailing Duties
Country of Origin
Country of Origin Requirements
Customs Broker

Doha Round
Dumping
Duty
Effective Rate of Protection
Electronic Commerce
Electronic Data Interchange
Embargoes
Export
Export Processing Zone
Export Subsidy
Fair Trade
Flag of Convenience
Foreign Sales Corporation
Free Trade
Free Trade Zone
Freight Forwarder
Generalized System of Preferences
Globalization Index
Gray Market
Harmonized System
Import
International Commercial Terms
    (Incoterms)
Internet Domain Names
Invisible Trade Balance
Letter of Credit
Maquiladora
Mercantilism
Most Favored Nation Status
Multi-Fiber Agreement
Neomercantilism
Nontariff Barrier
Quota
Smuggling
Special Drawing Rights
Standard International Trade
    Classification
Subsidies
Tariff
Terms of Trade
Trade Barriers
Trade Liberalization
Trade Pact
Trade Sanctions
Trade War
Uruguay Round
Voluntary Export Restraints
World Customs Organization

Legal and Labor Issues

Antitrust Laws
Arbitration
Child Labor
Choice of Forum Clause
Contracts
Copyright Infringement
International Law
Labor Standards
Legal Environments
New York Convention
Opportunistic Behavior
Patents
Salaries and Wages
Trademark Infringement
Trades Union Congress

Management and Leadership

Accountability
Blame Culture
Board of Directors
Commitment
Decision Making
Global Leadership and Organizational Behavior
   Effectiveness Project
Leadership
Loyalty
Management
Management Development
Management Education
Management Information Systems
Management Research
Management Science
Managerial Accounting
Nepotism
Persuasion
Risk
Status
Vision

Manufacturing and Operations

Bonded Warehouse
Bottleneck
Branch
Carrying Costs
Centralization
Commerce Control List
Concurrent Engineering

Control Systems
Co-Production
Cost Structure
Craft Production
Customization
Deming Model
Distribution
Downstream
Facilities Location Decision
Flexibility
Forecasting
Global Benchmarking
Global Product Divisions
Global Structure
International Division Structure
Intra-Firm Transfer
Inventory
Kaizen
Kanban
Landed Cost
Low Wage Production
Make-or-Buy Decision
Manufacturing
Manufacturing Strategy
Manufacturing Yield
Matrix Structure
Multidomestic Structure
Near-Shoring
Off-Shoring
Operations Management
Optimization
Outsourcing
Procurement
Product Component Model
Product Development
Quality Control
Regional Divisions
Research and Development
Research Methods: Mixed Methods
Research Methods: Qualitative
Research Methods: Quantitative
Risk Management
Robotics
Scheduling
Service Level
Staffing Levels
Standardization
Subsidiary

Supply Chain Management
Supply Chain Risks
Technology Transfer
Transportation
Transport Delays
Turnkey
Upstream
Value Chain
Vertically Integrated Chain
Virtual Vertical Integration
Warranties

Marketing
Advanced Pricing Agreement
Advertising
Back Translation
Branding
Brand Loyalty
Buying Motives/Behavior
Channels
Competitive Market Analysis
Consumer Behavior
Consumer Needs and Wants
Consumer Surveys
Consumption
Customer Relationship Management
Emerging Markets
Focus Groups
Global Brand Strategy
Integrated Marketing Communications
International Marketing Research
Lifestyle Research
Market Audit
Market Development
Marketing
Marketing Research
Market Research
Markets
Market Share
Maslow's Hierarchy of Needs
Media
Media and Direct Marketing
Positioning
Pricing
Promotions
Relationship Marketing
Retail Sector
Sales

Seasonality
Simulation Modeling
SIOP
Wholesale Sector

Political Environments
BERI
Bhopal Disaster
Compensation for Expropriated Property
Contract Repudiation
Country Screening
Environmental Standards
Expropriation
Lobbying
Nationalization
Nongovernmental Organizations
PRINCE Analysis
Regulation
Scenario Analysis
Terrorism

Regional Economic Integration
Bilateral Free Trade Agreements
Candidate Countries
Caribbean Community (Caricom)
Central American Common Market
Common Agricultural Policy
Common External Tariff
Common Market
Cotonou Agreement
Customs Union
Economic Integration
Economic Union
European Coal and Steel Community
European Monetary Union
European Union
Free Trade Area of the Americas
Free Trade Zone
Maastricht Treaty
Mercosur/Mercosul
Monetary Union
North American Free Trade Agreement
Regional Integration
Regional Trade Agreements
Single Market
Trade Bloc
Trans-European Networks
Treaty of Rome

Supranational and National Organizations

Academy of International Business
African Development Bank
Asian Development Bank
Asia-Pacific Economic Cooperation
Association of Southeast Asian Nations
Biodiversity Convention
Department of Commerce
European Bank for Reconstruction
    and Development
Ex-Im Bank
Food and Agriculture Organization (FAO)
General Agreement on Tariffs and Trade
Inter-American Development Bank
International Bank for Reconstruction
    and Development
International Centre for Settlement of
    Investment Disputes
International Chamber of Commerce
International Development Agency
International Finance Corporation
International Labour Office/International
Labour Organization
International Monetary Fund
Kyoto Protocol
Millennium Development Goals
Multilateral Investment Guarantee Agency
National Regulatory Agencies
Organisation for Economic Co-operation
    and Development
Regional Development Banks
Securities and Exchange Commission
Special Drawing Rights
United Nations Centre for Transnational
    Corporations
United Nations Conference on Trade and
    Development
United Nations Industrial Development
    Organization
U.S. Agency for International
    Development
World Bank, The
World Health Organization
World Trade Organization

List of Articles

A

ABN AMRO Holding
Absenteeism
Absolute Advantage
Academy of International Business
Accountability
Accounting Harmonization
Accounting Information Systems
Accounting Software
Account Settlement
Acculturation
Achieved Status/Ascribed Status
Acquisitions, Takeovers, and
    Mergers
Ad Valorem Duties
Advanced Pricing Agreement
Advertising
Aegon
AEON
AEX General Index (Amsterdam)
Africa
African Development Bank
Agents

Agreement on Trade-Related Aspects
    of Intellectual Property Rights
Algeria
Allianz SE
All Ordinaries Index
Alternative Dispute Resolution
Altria Group
American Depository Receipt
American International Group
AmerisourceBergen
Anglo-American
Angola
Antiglobalization Movement
Antitrust Laws
A. P. Møller Mærsk Group
Arbitrage
Arbitration
Archer Daniels Midland
Argentina
Asia
Asian Development Bank
Asian Financial Crisis
Asian Tigers

Asia-Pacific Economic Cooperation
Assicurazioni Generali
Association of Southeast Asian Nations
ATA Carnet
AT&T
Attitudes and Attitude Change
ATX Index (Vienna)
Auditing Standards
Australia
Austria
Aviva
AXA

B

Back Translation
Bahrain
Balance of Goods and Services
Banana Wars
Banco Bilbao Vizcaya Argentaria
Banco Santander Central Hispano Group
Bangladesh
Bank for International Settlements
Bank of America Corp.
Bank of China
Bankruptcy
Baoshan Iron and Steel
Barclays
Barriers to Entry
Barter
Basel Committee on Banking Supervision
BASF
Basis Points
Bayer
Behavioral Economics
Behavioral Finance
Belarus
Belgium
Bel-20 Index (Brussels)
Benefits
Bent Measuring Stick (or Performance Appraisal)
BERI
Berkshire Hathaway
Best Buy
Bhopal Disaster
Bid/Ask Spread
Big Mac Index
Bilateral Free Trade Agreements
Bill of Lading

Biodiversity Convention
Black Market
Blame Culture
Blocked Funds
Bloomberg
BMW
BNP Paribas
Board of Directors
Boeing
Bolivia
Bonded Warehouse
Bonds
Botswana
Bottleneck
Bottom of the Pyramid
Bouygues
BP
Brain Drain
Branch
Branding
Brand Loyalty
Brazil
Bretton Woods Accord
Bretton Woods Institutions
Bribery
BRICs
British East India Company
Brunei
BSE Sensex Index (Bombay Stock Exchange)
BT
Bulgaria
Bureaucracy
Business Cycles
Business-to-Business
Buying Motives/Behavior
Buyout

C

CAC 40 Index (Paris)
Call Center
Cameroon
Canada
Candidate Countries
Canon
Capital Account Balance
Capital Adequacy
Capital Budgeting
Capital Controls

Capital Flight
Capital Gains Tax
Capitalism
Capital Repatriation
Cardinal Health
Caremark Rx
Caribbean Community (Caricom)
Carrefour
Carrying Costs
Cash Management
Caterpillar
CEMEX
Central America
Central American Common Market
Central Banks
Centralization
Centralized Control
Certificate of Origin
Chaebol
Channels
Chevron
Chicago Mercantile Exchange
Chicago School/Chicago Boys
Child Labor
Chile
China
China Life Insurance
China Mobile Communications
China National Petroleum
Choice of Forum Clause
Citigroup
City, The
Clearing House Automated Payments
    System
Clearing House Interbank Payments
    System
Clearing Houses
CMA Index (Egypt)
CNP Assurances
Coaching
CoCom
Collateral
Collateralized Debt Obligations
Collateralized Loan Obligations
Colombia
Commerce Control List
Commercialization of Space
Commitment

Common Agricultural Policy
Common External Tariff
Common Market
Communication Challenges
Communication Styles
Communism
Company Profiles: Africa
Company Profiles: Australia and Pacific
Company Profiles: Central America and the
    Caribbean
Company Profiles: Central Asia
Company Profiles: East Asia
Company Profiles: Eastern Europe
Company Profiles: Middle East
Company Profiles: North America
Company Profiles: South America
Company Profiles: South Asia
Company Profiles: Western Europe
Comparative Advantage
Compensation
Compensation for Expropriated Property
Competition
Competitive Advantage of Nations
Competitive Market Analysis
Compliance
Concession (in Negotiation)
Concurrent Engineering
Confidentiality
Conformance/Conformity
Confucian Work Dynamism
ConocoPhillips
Consumer Behavior
Consumer Needs and Wants
Consumer Surveys
Consumption
Contagion
Context
Contract Repudiation
Contracts
Control Systems
Convertibility
Cooperatives
Co-Production
Copyright Infringement
Core
Corporate Accounting
Corporate Change
Corporate Codes of Conduct

Corporate Diplomacy
Corporate Governance
Corporate Income Tax
Corporate Social Responsibility
Corporate Social Responsibility and
    International Business Ethics
Corruption
Cost, Insurance, and Freight
Cost Accounting
Cost Analysis
Costa Rica
Costco Wholesale
Cost of Living Allowance
Cost Structure
Côte d'Ivoire
Cotonou Agreement
Countertrade
Countervailing Duties
Country of Origin
Country of Origin Requirements
Country Screening
Craft Production
Credit Ratings
Credit Suisse
Croatia
Cross-Border Migrations
Cross-Border Trading
Cross-Cultural Research
Cross-Hauling
Cross-Licensing
Cross Rate
Cultural Norms and Scripts
Culture Shock
Culture-Specific Values
Currency
Currency Exposure
Currency Speculators
Currency Zone
Current Account
Custodians
Customer Relationship Management
Customer Responsiveness
Customization
Customs Broker
Customs Union
CVS/Caremark
Cyprus
Czech Republic

D

Dai-ichi Mutual Life Insurance
DaimlerChrysler
DAX Index (Germany)
Debt
Debt-for-Equity Swap
Debt Rescheduling
Debt (Securities)
Decision Making
Dell
Deming Model
Democratic Globalization
Demonstration Effect
Denmark
Department of Commerce
Dependency Theory
Deregulation
Deutsche Bahn
Deutsche Bank
Deutsche Post
Deutsche Telekom
Devaluation
Development Assistance
Diffusion of Innovation
Direct Export
Dirty Float
Disclosure Requirements
Discount Rate
Distribution
Diversifying Investment
Diversity
Doha Round
Dollar Hegemony
Dollarization
Dominican Republic
Dow Chemical
Dow Jones Index
Downstream
Dumping
Dutch East India Company
Duty
DZ Bank

E

EADS
Earnings Management
Earnings Quality
Eastern Europe

Economic Development
Economic Indicators
Economic Integration
Economic Statistics
Economic Union
Economies of Scale
Economies of Scope
Ecuador
Education Allowance
Effective Rate of Protection
Egypt
Électricité de France
Electronic Commerce
Electronic Data Interchange
El Salvador
Embargoes
Emerging Economies
Emerging Markets
Emotion
Employer–Employee Relations
Empowerment
Enculturation
Enel
Eni
Enron Corporation
Entrepreneurship
Entry Mode
Environmental Standards
E.ON
Equities
Estonia
Ethnocentric Human Resource Policy
Ethnocentrism
Euro
European Bank for Reconstruction and Development
European Coal and Steel Community
European Monetary Union
European Union
Exchange Rate
Exchange Rate Risk (or Currency Exposure)
Exchange Rate Volatility
Ex-Factory (Ex-Works)
Ex-Im Bank
Expatriate
Export
Export Assistance Program
Export Financing
Export Management Company

Export-Oriented Development
Export Processing Zones
Export Subsidies
Export Trading Company
Expropriation
External Debt
External Labor Market
ExxonMobil

F
Facilities Location Decision
Factor Endowments
Fair Trade
Family Leave
Feng Shui
Fiat
Fiat Money
Financial Hedge
Financial Market Regulation
Financial Markets
Financial Reporting
Financial Statement Analysis
Finland
Fixed Costs
Fixed Exchange Rate
Flag of Convenience
Flexibility
Flexible Exchange Rate Regime
Floating Exchange Rate
Focus Groups
Follow-the-Leader Theory
Food and Agriculture Organization
Ford Motor
Forecasting
Foreign Corrupt Practices Act
Foreign Direct Investment, Horizontal
    and Vertical
Foreign Exchange Market
Foreign Exchange Reserves
Foreign Portfolio Investment
Foreign Sales Corporation
Forensic Accounting
Fortis
Forward Market
France
France Télécom
Franchising
Freddie Mac

Free Markets
Free Trade
Free Trade Area of the Americas
Free Trade Zone
Freight Forwarder
FT Index
FTSE
Fujitsu
Futures Markets

G

Gannon's Cultural Metaphors
Gaz de France
Gazprom
General Agreement on Tariffs and Trade
General Electric
Generalized System of Preferences
General Motors
Geocentric
Geocentric Human Resource Policy
Geopolitics
Germany
Ghana
Gift-Giving
Gini Index
GlaxoSmithKline
Global Account Management
Global Benchmarking
Global Branding Strategy
Global Capital Market
Global Competitiveness Index
Global Digital Divide
Globalization
Globalization Index
Global Leadership and Organizational
    Behavior Effectiveness Project
Global Product Divisions
Global Structure
Gnomes of Zurich
Gold Standard
Government Bonds
Greece
Green Revolution
Grey Market
Gross National Product
G20
Guanxi
Guatemala

H

Hang Seng Index
Hanseatic League
Harmonized System
HBOS
Healthcare Benefits/Systems
Heckscher-Ohlin Model
Hedging
Hewlett-Packard
Hitachi
Hofstede's Five Dimensions of Culture
Holidays
Home Country
Home Depot, The
Honda Motor
Hong Kong
Hospitality Sector
Host Country
Hostile Takeovers
Housing Allowance
HSBC Holdings
Hudson's Bay Company
Hungary
Hyundai Motor

I

Iceland
Impact Financial Statements
Import
Import Substitution
India
Indian Oil
Indirect Export
Indirect Foreign Direct Investment
Individualism/Collectivism
Indonesia
Industrial and Commercial Bank of China
Industrial Espionage
Industrialized Countries
Industry Information
Infant Industry Argument
Information Systems
Information Technology Auditing
Infrastructure
ING Group
Initial Public Offering
Integrated Marketing Communications
Integrative Bargaining

Intellectual Property Theft
Inter-American Development Bank
Interbank Market
Interest Rates
Interest Rate Swaps
Internal/External
Internal Labor Market
International Accounting Standards Board
International Bank for Reconstruction and
     Development
International Business Machines
International Capital Flows
International Centre for Settlement
     of Investment Disputes
International Chamber of Commerce
International Commercial Terms (Incoterms)
International Compensation
International Development Agency
International Division Structure
International Finance Corporation
International Financial Reporting Standards
Internationalization
Internationalization Model
International Labour Office/International
     Labour Organization
International Law
International Marketing Research
International Monetary Fund
International Monetary System
International Securities Identification Numbering
International Training
Internet Domain Names
Intra-Firm Transfer
Inventory
Investment Banks
Investor Protection
Invisible Trade Balance
IPC
Iran
Ireland
ISE National 100 Index
Israel
Italy

J

Jakarta Composite Index
Japan
Job Enrichment

Johnson & Johnson
Joint Venture
Jordan
J. P. Morgan Chase & Co.

K

Kaizen
Kanban
Kazakhstan
Keiretsu
Kenya
KLSE (Malaysian Stock Index)
Koç Holding
Korea, South
Kuwait
Kyoto Protocol

L

Labor Standards
Landed Cost
Late Mover
Latin America
Latvia
Leadership
Lebanon
Legal & General Group
Legal Environments
Lenovo
Leontief Paradox
Less Industrialized Countries
Letter of Credit
LG
LIBOR
Libya
Licensing
Lifestyle Research
Linder Hypothesis
Liquidity (or Market Liquidity)
Lithuania
Lloyds TSB Group
Lobbying
Local Adaptation
Local Competitors
Localization
Local/National
Locational Advantages
Lockheed Martin
Lombard Rate

Lowe's
Low Wage Production
Loyalty
LUKOIL
Luxembourg

M
Maastricht Treaty
Macroeconomics
Madrid General Index
Make-or-Buy Decision
Malaysia
Managed Float Regime
Management
Management Development
Management Education
Management Information Systems
Management Research
Management Science
Managerial Accounting
Manufacturing
Manufacturing Strategy
Manufacturing Yield
Maquiladora
Marathon Oil
Market Audit
Market-Basket Currency
Market Development
Market Imperfections Theory
Marketing
Market Maker
Market Research
Markets
Market-Seeking Investment
Market Share
Mark-to-Market Valuation
Marshall-Lerner Condition
Masculinity/Femininity
Maslow's Hierarchy of Needs
Maternity Leave
Matrix Structure
Matsushita Electric Industrial
Media
Media and Direct Marketing
Mediation
Mentoring
Mercantilism
Mercosur/Mercosul

Merrill Lynch
MerVal
MetLife
METRO
Mexico
MIBTel Index (Milan)
Microfinance
Microfinance Institution
Micro-Multinational
Microsoft
Middle East
Millea Holdings
Millennium Development Goals
Mitsubishi
Mitsubishi Electric
Mitsubishi UFJ Financial Group
Mitsui
Mittal Steel
Mizuho Financial Group
Modernization Theory
Monetary Intervention
Monetary Policy: Rules Versus Discretion
Monetary Union
Money Laundering
Money Supply
Monochronic/Polychronic
Monopolistic Advantage Theory
Morgan Stanley
Morocco
Mortgage Credit Crisis of 2008
Most Favored Nation Status
Motivation
Motorola
Multicultural Work Groups and Teams
Multidomestic Structure
Multi-Fiber Agreement
Multilateral Investment Guarantee Agency
Multinational Competitive Disadvantages
Multinational Corporation
Mundell-Fleming Model
Munich Re Group

N
National Accounts
Nationalization
National Regulatory Agencies
Near-Shoring
NEC

Negotiation and Negotiating Styles
Neocolonialism
Neomercantilism
Nepotism
Nestlé
Net Capital Outflow
Netherlands
Neuroeconomics
Neutral/Affective
Newly Industrialized Countries
New Trade Theory
New York Convention
New Zealand
Nigeria
Nikkei Index
Nippon Life Insurance
Nippon Oil
Nippon Steel
Nippon Telegraph & Telephone
Nissan Motor
Nokia
Nonfinancial Information Reporting
Nongovernmental Organizations
Nontariff Barrier
North American Free Trade Agreement
Norway
Novartis
NZSE 50 (New Zealand Stock Index)

O
Off-Shoring
Old Mutual
Oman
Open Economy Macroeconomics
Operations Management
Opportunistic Behavior
Optimization
Option
Organisation for Economic Co-operation and
    Development
OSE All Share Index (Oslo)
Outsourcing
Overseas Private Investment Corporation
Overtime

P
Pacific Rim
Pakistan

Panama
Parent Country National
Patents
Payroll Taxes
Pegged Exchange Rate
Pemex
Pension Systems
PepsiCo
Periphery
Perquisites
Persuasion
Peru
Petrobras
Petronas
Peugeot
Pfizer
Philippines
Plagiarism
Poland
Polycentric
Polycentric Human Resource Policy
Portugal
Positioning
Power Distance
Pricing
PRINCE Analysis
Private Spaceflight Industry
Privatization
Procter & Gamble
Procurement
Product Component Model
Product Development
Productivity
Product Life Cycle Hypothesis
Profit-Sharing
Promotions
Prospectus
Prudential
Prudential Financial
Public Finance Reform
Public Relations
Purchasing Power Parity

Q
Qatar
Quality
Quality Control
Quota

R
Real Hedge
Recruitment
Redundancy
Reentry
Regiocentric Human Resource Policy
Regional Development Banks
Regional Divisions
Regional Integration
Regional Trade Agreements
Regulation
Relationship Marketing
Renault
Repsol YPF
Research and Development
Research Methods: Mixed Methods
Research Methods: Qualitative
Research Methods: Quantitative
Reserve Currency
Resource-Seeking Investment
Retail Capital Markets
Retail Sector
Reuters
Revaluation
Reverse Engineering
Risk
Risk Management
Robotics
Roche Group
Romania
Royal Africa Company
Royal Dutch Shell
Royalties
Russia
RWE

S
Safeway
Salaries and Wages
Sales
Samsung Electronics
Samurai Bond
S&P 500 Index
Sanofi Aventis
Sarbanes-Oxley
Saudi Arabia
Scenario Analysis
Scheduling

Schwartz Value Theory
Sea Piracy
Sears Holdings
Seasonality
Securities and Exchange Commission
Securities Financing
Securitization
Selection
Self-Employed Women's Association, India
Seoul Composite Index
Service Expectations
Service Level
Settlement Date
Shanghai Composite Index
Shareholder Activism
Siemens
Silent Language of Hall (Nonverbal Communication)
Simulation Modeling
Singapore
Single Market
Sinopec
SIOP
SK
Slovakia
Slovenia
Smuggling
Social Contract
Socialism
Social Pact
Socioeconomic Status
Sony
South Africa
Sovereign Borrowing
Space
Spain
Special Drawing Rights
Specific/Diffuse
Spot Market
Spread
Sprint Nextel
Sri Lanka
Staffing Levels
Standard International Trade Classification
Standardization
State Farm Insurance Cos.
State Grid

State-Owned Enterprises
Statoil
Status
Stereotyping
Stock Exchanges
Stockholm General Index
Straits Times Index (Singapore)
Strategic Alliance
Structured Notes
Subprime Loans
Subsidiary
Subsidies
Sudan
Suez
Sumitomo Mitsui Financial Group
Sunoco
Supply Chain Management
Supply Chain Risks
Sustainable Development
Swap
Sweden
Swiss Market Index
Switzerland
Syria
Sysco

T
Taiwan Weighted Index
Tanzania
TA-100 Index (Tel Aviv)
Target
Tariff
Tata Group
Taxes
Tax Havens
Tax Holiday
Teams
Technology
Technology Transfer
Telecom Italia
Telefónica
Tequila Effect
Terms of Trade
Terrorism
Thailand
Third Country National
ThyssenKrupp
Time Orientation

Time Warner
Tokyo Electric Power
Too Big to Fail
Toshiba
Total
Toyota Motor Corporation
Trade Balance
Trade Barriers
Trade Bloc
Trade Liberalization
Trademark Infringement
Trade Pact
Trade Sanctions
Trades Union Congress
Trade War
Trading Volume
Training
Trans-European Networks
Transfer Pricing
Transition Economies
Transportation
Transport Delays
Treaty of Rome
Trinidad and Tobago
Tunisia
Turkey
Turnkey
Tyco International

U
UBS
Ukraine
Uncertainty Avoidance
Underdevelopment
UniCredit Group
Unilever
United Arab Emirates
United Kingdom
United Nations Centre on Transnational
    Corporations
United Nations Conference on Trade and
    Development
United Nations Industrial Development
    Organization
United Parcel Service
United States
United Technologies
Universalism/Particularism

Upstream
Uruguay
Uruguay Round
U.S. Agency for International Development
U.S. Postal Service
Uzbekistan

V
Value Added Tax
Value at Risk
Value Chain
Value Network
Value Shop
Variable Costs
Venezuela
Venture Capital
Verizon Communications
Vertically Integrated Chain
Vietnam
Virginia Company
Virtual Vertical Integration
Visa
Vision
Vodafone
Volkswagen
Voluntary Export Restraints
Volvo

W
Wachovia Corp.
Walgreens
Wall Street
Wal-Mart Stores
Walt Disney
Warranties
Wells Fargo
Western Europe
Wholesale Capital Markets
Wholesale Sector
Women in Business
Working Hours
Work/Personal Life Balance
World Bank, The
World Customs Organization
World Health Organization
World Systems Theory
World Trade Organization

Y
Yemen

Z
Zaibatsu
Zimbabwe
Zurich Financial Services

List of Contributors

Abbeloos, Jan-Frederik J.
Ghent University

Abdallah, Wissam
Lebanese American University

Adams, Laurel
Northern Illinois University

Agarwalla, Sobhesh Kumar
Indian Institute of Management

Al-Ahmad, Zeina
Tishreen University

Anastakis, Dimitry
Trent University

Anderson, Donna M.
University of Wisconsin–La Crosse

Andreeva, Irina
University of Manchester

Andrews, Mitchell
University of Sunderland

Apfelthaler, Gerhard
California Lutheran University

Araujo Turolla, Frederico
Escola Superior de Propaganda e Marketing

Arun, Thankom
University of Central Lancashire Business School

As-Saber, Sharif N.
Monash University

Ayadi, M. Femi
University of Houston–Clear Lake at Texas Medical

Ayadi, O. Felix
Texas Southern University

Baer, Steven D.
Weber State University

Bakir, Caner
Koç University

Balla, Vassiliki
*Athens University of Economics
    and Business*

Ballas, Panagiotis
University of Manchester

Bamber, Greg J.
Monash University

Barker, Michelle
Griffith University

Barrera, Juan Carlos
Elmhurst College

Barrios, Marcelo
Escuela de Dirección de Empresas

Barron, Andrew
ESC Rennes School of Business

Beaulier, Scott A.
Mercer University

Bennett, Kenneth C.
Griffith University

Berg, David M.
University of Wisconsin–Milwaukee

Betschinger, Marie-Ann
University of Münster

Bhasin, Balbir B.
Sacred Heart University

Bodson, Laurent
University of Liège, Belgium

Boehe, Dirk Michael
University of Fortaleza

Bögenhold, Dieter
Free Universitz of Bolzano

Bonin, Hubert
Bordeaux University

Boughey, David
University of the West of England

Bozionelos, Nikos
University of Durham

Braddock, Peter
University of Manchester

Bragues, George
University of Guelph-Humber

Brando, Carlos Andres
London School of Economics

Bristow, Alexandra
Lancaster University Management School

Brock, David M.
Ben-Gurion University

Campbell, Bruce A.
Franklin University

Campbell, Kevin
University of Stirling

Caracciolo di Brienza, Michele
*Graduate Institute of International
    and Development Studies, Geneva*

Carey, Catherine
Western Kentucky University

Carveth, Rodney A.
University of Hartford

Chamberlin, Silas Adam
Lehigh University

Chang, Beryl Y.
European School of Economics

Clements, Brian M. W.
University of Wolverhampton Business School

Connell, Carol M.
City University of New York–Brooklyn College

Connor, Tom
University of Bedfordshire

Corby, Susan
University of Greenwich

Corfield, Justin
Geelong Grammar School, Australia

Cottrell, Marilyn
Brock University

Cox, Mike
Newcastle University

Cuervo-Cazurra, Alvaro
University of South Carolina

Cullari, Francine
University of Michigan

Cumo, Christopher
Independent Scholar

Curran, Louise
Toulouse Business School

Cusiter, Mark
University of Northampton

Dacko, Scott G.
University of Warwick

Dauber, Daniel
*Vienna University of Economics
& Business Administration*

Davies, William
University of London

DeGroote, Sharon E.
Lawrence Technological University

DelCampo, Robert G.
University of New Mexico

Demirbas, Dilek
Northumbria University

Denault, Jean-Francois
Université de Montréal

Dermody, Janine
*University of Gloucestershire
Business School*

Dholakia, Nikhilesh
University of Rhode Island

DiStaso, Marcia Watson
Pennsylvania State University

Dörrenbächer, Christoph
University of Groningen

Drtina, Ralph
Rollins College

Dunlap, Kyle C.
University of Rhode Island

Dupont, Brandon R.
Western Washington University

Egan, Terence R.
Central University of Finance and Economics

Espinosa, Daniel A.
St. Thomas University School of Law

Farrell, Carlyle
Ryerson University

Fellman, Susanna
University of Helsinki

Fenner, Charles R., Jr.
SUNY–Canton

Fernández-Calienes, Raúl
St. Thomas University School of Law

Fischbach, Dirk
Hochschule Harz

Florea, Liviu
Washburn University

Fox, Loren
Independent Scholar

Frederick, Howard H.
Unitec New Zealand

Freire de Lima, Maria Fernanda
Independent Scholar

Froese, Fabian Jintae
Korea University Business School

Fryzel, Barbara
Jagiellonian University

Fullerton, Tom
University of Texas at El Paso

Furst, Sascha
EAFIT University

Gabel, Terrance G.
University of Arkansas–Fort Smith

Gad, Marwa S.
University of Warwick

Garcia-Olmedo, Belen
University of Granada

Gaur, Ajai
Old Dominion University

Gaur, Sonjaya S.
Auckland University of Technology

Gemici, Kurtulus
*University of California
  –Los Angeles*

Georgiou, Ion
Fundação Getulio Vargas

Ghoshal, Animesh
DePaul University

Godden, Christopher J.
University of Manchester

Gomez-Diaz, Donato
Universidad de Almería

Gonzalez-Perez, Maria-Alejandra
EAFIT University

Gordon, Cameron
University of Canberra

Gould, Marie
Peirce College

Gregoratti, Catia
Universty of Manchester

Gregory, Anne
Leeds Metropolitan University

Grigoriou, Nicholas
Monash College Guangzhou

Grønning, Terje
University of Oslo

Guay, Terrence
Pennsylvania State University

Gupta, Sumeet
Icfai University, Dehradun–IBS

Habel, Cullen
*University of Adelaide
  Business School*

Hadjichristodoulou, Celia
European University Cyprus

Haghirian, Parissa
Sophia University

Hall, Joshua C.
Beloit College

Hannif, Zeenobiyah
University of Wollongong

Hansen, S. Duane
Purdue University

Hart, David
Northumbria University

Haynes, Michael
University of Wolverhampton Business School

Hemphill, Thomas A.
University of Michigan–Flint

Higgins, David M.
University of York

Hipsher, Scott A.
Royal Melbourne Institute of Technology

Hodgins, Michael
Northumbria University

Hoffmann, Sabine H.
American University of the Middle East

Holst, Arthur M.
Widener University

Howell, Llewellyn D.
Thunderbird School of Global Management

Hudson, Bradford T.
Boston University

Ibarra-Colado, Eduardo
Universidad Autónoma Metropolitana

Igel, Lee H.
New York University

Insch, Andrea
University of Otago

Iyer, Uma Janardana
Austin Peay State University

Jagd, Søren
Roskilde University

Jain, Arvind K.
Concordia University

Jeffs, Chris
Northumbria University

Jones, Stacey M.
Seattle University

Jory, Surendranath R.
University of Michigan–Flint

Julian, Craig
Southern Cross University

Karlsson, Tobias
Lund University

Kazmi, Azhar
King Fahd University of Petroleum & Minerals

Keeling, Drew
University of Zurich

Kim, Dong-Woon
Dong-Eui University

Kirkham, Elaine D.
University of Wolverhampton Business School

Koehler, Tine
George Mason University

Korotov, Konstantin
European School of Management and Technology

Kosmopoulou, Elena
University of Patras

Kraus, Sascha
Vienna University of Economics & Business Administration

Kte'pi, Bill
Independent Scholar

Kyriakidou, Olivia
Athens University of Economics and Business

Lacktorin, Michael
Akita International University

Lai, Pei-Chun
National Pingtung University
of Science and Technology

Levendis, John
Loyola University New Orleans

Lillevik, Waheeda
The College of New Jersey

Lirio, Pamela
McGill University

Liu, Chengwei
University of Cambridge

Lominé, Loykie L.
University of Winchester

Lugovskaya, Lyudmila V.
University of Cambridge

Ma, Shan
Queensland University of Technology

Machado, Marcelo A.
Kwantlen Polytechnic University

Maloney, Soren E.
University of Cambridge

Malul, Miki
Ben-Gurion University

Manning, Dorothy
Northumbria University

Martins, Miguel
University of Wolverhampton

Mascarenhas, Briance
Rutgers University

Mathur, Ashok C.
Independent Consultant

Matos, Nancy
Esan University

Maura Costa, Ligia
Escola de Administração de Empresas de São Paulo
(FGV-EAESP)

McNulty, Yvonne
Monash University

Mennel, Eva
International Finance Corporation

Metzger, Matthew L.
University of Oregon

Meyskens, Moriah A.
Florida International University

Mishra, Patit Paban
Sambalpur University

Monem, Reza
Griffith University Business School

Morriss, Andrew P.
University of Illinois

Moser, Reinhard
Vienna University of Economics & Business Administration

Mosk, Carl
University of Victoria

Moskowitz, Sanford L.
St. John's University

Mowell, Barry D.
Broward College

Mukhopadhyay, Kausiki
University of Denver

Muñoz, J. Mark S.
Millikin University

Musson, Tim
Napier University

Mykhnenko, Vlad
University of Nottingham

Nadgauda, Seemantinee
Rutgers University

de Nahlik, Carmel F.
Coventry University

Nanut, Vladimir
Università di Trieste–Facoltà di Economia

Nathan, Maria L.
Lynchburg College

Naumi, Fabiha
Independent Scholar

Naveed, Pareesa A.
Rutgers University

Nelson, Patricia A.
Seijo University

Newburry, William
Florida International University

Nisar, Tahir M.
*University of Southampton
    School of Management*

Nye, Christopher D.
University of Illinois at Urbana–Champaign

Ogwang, Tomson
Brock University

Oyangen, Knut
BI Norwegian School of Management

Park, Ji Eun
Saint Louis University

Patten, Lynne A.
Clark Atlanta University

Paul, Helen Julia
University of Southampton

Paul, Pallab
University of Denver

Persaud, Nadini
University of the West Indies

Petrick, Joseph A.
Wright State University

Polley, William
Western Illinois University

Polychroniou, Panagiotis V.
University of Patras

Poon, Irene Hon Fun
City University Cass Business School

Poulis, Efthimios
Bournemouth University

Poulis, Konstantinos
IST Studies, Athens

Puia, George M.
Saginaw Valley State University

Qi Wei, Jean
City University Cass Business School

Quan, Rose
Northumbria University

Rahman, Nafis
Ohio Wesleyan University

Rahman, Noushi
Pace University

Ramoglou, Stratos E.
University of Cambridge

Ran, Bing
*Pennsylvania State University
    –Harrisburg*

Rankaduwa, Wimal
University of Prince Edward Island

Raufflet, Emmanuel
HEC Montréal Business School

Reimers, Jane L.
Rollins College

Rivera, Edwin López
*Universidad de Bogotá
    Jorge Tadeo Lozano*

Rodriguez, Jenny K.
University of Strathclyde

Romero, Esteban
University of Granada

Ross-Rodgers, Martha J.
Independent Scholar

Rothman, Norman C.
University of Maryland University College

Rowley, Chris
City University Cass Business School

Rowley, Jennifer
Manchester Metropolitan University

Roy, Abhijit
University of Scranton

Roy, Mousumi
Pennsylvania State University

Sacks, Michael Alan
Emory University

Salimath, Manjula S.
University of North Texas

Sarfati, Gilberto
Fundação Getúlio Vargas

Sasson, Amir
University College Dublin

Schiffman, Daniel
Ariel University Center

Schneper, William
Florida International University

Schvaneveldt, Shane J.
Weber State University

Scott, Clifford D
University of Arkansas–Fort Smith

Seaman, Claire
Queen Margaret University

Senn, Christoph
University of St. Gallen

Šević, Aleksandar
*Trinity College
    University of Dublin*

Šević, Željko
Glasgow Caledonian University

Shadab, Houman B.
George Mason University

Sharma, Esha
IBS, Jaipur

Sheeran, Paul
University of Winchester

Shoham, Amir
Sapir Academic College

Silberstein-Loeb, Jonathan
University of Cambridge

Singh, Deeksha A.
National University of Singapore

Singh, Satyendra
University of Winnipeg

Sloan, Diane
Newcastle Business School

Smith, Charles
Swansea Metropolitan University

Smith, Jonathan
Anglia Ruskin University

Soltani, Ebrahim
University of Kent

Spangenberg, Sabine
*Richmond, The American
    International University in London*

Spears, Jennifer S.
Emory University

Staber, Udo
University of Canterbury

Stacy, Robert N.
Independent Scholar

Stancil, John L.
Florida Southern College

Stephens, Robert D.
Shippensburg University

Stewart, Ian
Birmingham City University

Suder, Gabriele
CERAM Business School

Sullivan, Timothy
Towson University

Syed, Jawad
University of Kent

Terjesen, Siri
Indiana University

Thoma, Axel
University of St. Gallen

Todd, Patricia
Western Kentucky University

Torres-Coronas, Teresa
Universitat Rovira i Virgili

Traflet, Janice M.
Bucknell University

Trybus, Elizabeth
*California State University
    −Northridge*

Tsahuridu, Eva E.
*Royal Melbourne Institute
    of Technology*

Tsang, Denise
University of Reading Business School

Turgut, Gokhan
HEC Montreal

Turolla, Frederico A.
ESPM, Brazil

Tuttle, Dale B.
University of Michigan−Flint

Umeadi, Michael
Shaw University

Umemura, Maki
*London School of Economics
    and Political Science*

Ural Marchand, Beyza
University of Alberta

Vaiman, Vlad
Reykjavik University

Vasilaki, Athina
*Middlesex University
    Business School*

Velez-Castrillon, Susana
University of Houston

Verousis, Thanos
Aberystwyth University

Vianelli, Donata
Università di Trieste

Viarengo, Martina G.
London School of Economics

Viola, Antonella
European University Institute

Wagner, Ralf
University of Kassel

Waskey, Andrew J.
Dalton State College

Watson, Derek
University of Sunderland

Watuwa, Richard
Cape Breton University

Weatherston, Jamie
Northumbria University

Whaples, Robert M.
Wake Forest University

Williams, Nigel
University of Cambridge

Windsor, Duane
Rice University

Winfrey, Frank L.
Lyon College

Woods, Peter
Griffith Business School

Woodward, David G.
University of Southampton

Woolley, Jennifer L.
Santa Clara University

Wooster, Rossitza B.
Portland State University

Worthington, Andrew C.
Griffith University

Wut, Tai Ming
Independent Scholar

Wymbs, Clifford
CUNY–Baruch College

Xu, Weichu
Old Dominion University

Yalcin, Serkan
Saint Louis University

Yang, Xiaohua
Queensland University of Technology

Zdravkovic, Srdan
Bryant University

Chronology of Business

Fourth Millennium (4000–3000) B.C.E.

The story of how business in today's world came to be begins at the dawn of history. Long before coins were developed, long before records were kept, we nevertheless find physical evidence for which trade is the most likely explanation. Seashells found in inland communities are one obvious example; whether they were used as a currency or bartered for (in addition to decoration, some shells could be used as scraping devices, building materials, and sources of dye), trade is the most likely reason they would wind up there. Other remnants can survive as well: the remains of animals not native to a region, foreign rocks and ores, and worked goods that bear the distinctive signs of other cultures.

During the third and fourth millennia B.C.E., we find these signs of trade among the first settled societies of the Fertile Crescent. Developed urban centers—which depend on trade to a greater extent than agricultural communities where each family could theoretically produce all that they need—appear throughout Mesopotamia, in Sumer, Ur, Susa, and Akkad. Trade always enjoyed a symbiotic relationship with urbanity: urban dwelling required, and trade thrived on and enabled, specialization of labor and production.

As early as 3100 B.C.E., Egyptian goods can be found in Byblos (Phoenicia; now Lebanon), and were likely part of trade of Egyptian grain for Phoenician timber. Around the same time, obsidian was being mined on the Greek island of Mylos, from which it was shipped by traders to various settlements. In this pre-metallurgical age, obsidian was the most reliable cutting tool, but its trade value diminished by the end of the fourth millennium B.C.E., when the alloying of copper with tin ushered in the Bronze Age in the Near East. (The Bronze Age is best thought of as a stage, as opposed to a specific year. The Near East entered it first, about a thousand years before Europe; China followed closely after Europe, with Korea entering the Bronze Age last, around 800 B.C.E.)

2500–2000 B.C.E.

Urban centers in southern Mesopotamia develop metallurgical industries based on copper from the northern Iranian plateau, hundreds of miles away. Other

Iranian imports to southern Mesopotamia include alabaster, marble, turquoise, and obsidian. Artifacts made in Mesopotamia of these Iranian materials are then traded again, and found all over the ancient world, from Syria to the Indus River Valley to Central Asia—travelling over 1,000 miles along ancient trade routes.

2000–1500 B.C.E.

Clearly trade had become vital in Mesopotamia. Just as builders and farmers had developed to answer needs of the community, a professional class of traders called tamkaru develops. Tamkaru combine trading, moneylending, and brokerage. More than just acting as middlemen, the tamkaru offer loans to fund trading expeditions, and local laws develop to deal with the outcome of those expeditions—the proper way to divide profits, to determine what happens if a ship is lost at sea, and so on.

The Code of Hammurabi, organized by the sixth and greatest king of Babylon, is written around 1760 B.C.E. as a code of laws set down in stone so that they would survive the life of any one king, and to divorce the permanence of the law from the transience of the whims of the powerful. Much of the Code is concerned with the Mesopotamian economy—it deals not only with what is and isn't legal, but with fines, inheritance, property, the prices of goods, and trade.

The state did not initiate international trade, but it profits from it through taxes and sets rules for the responsibilities of tamkaru. In addition to the worked goods using Iranian raw materials, Mesopotamia transports pottery, leather goods and textiles, and a wide variety of agricultural goods (fruit and vegetables, grains, fish, beer), taking advantage of the natural resources of the Fertile Crescent. The profit from these goods in turn fund the purchase of goods unavailable locally.

During this same period, trade expands in the eastern Mediterranean, where it is dominated by Minoans and Mycenaeans from Crete and southern Greece. Among the most valuable and most traded goods are timber, Cyprian copper, olives and their oil, grapes and wine, and wheat, a grain cultivated and commodified sometime around 2000 B.C.E. Their trade partners include Anatolia (Asia Minor) and Mesopotamia, but especially Egypt, which has gold from its mines, linen produced from flax, high-quality pottery, and

papyrus, an early form of paper. Because it's a minimally processed plant product, papyrus is susceptible to mold in humid conditions, and so is less useful in climates radically different from Egypt's—but in the right climate, it is so practical and cheap to produce that it still thrives as a commodity. Much of Egypt's gold originates in Punt, acquired via trading expeditions along the Nile and the Red Sea. Caravan trading routes are established to Mesopotamia, Syria, and the Mediterranean Sea.

Unlike in Mesopotamia, in Egypt trade is not the province of private enterprise. The Pharaoh, seen as a divine ruler, controls the economy through a sort of theocratic socialism, and has a total monopoly on international trade, which he delegates to specific traders who work for the state.

1200 B.C.E.

Trade throughout the Bronze Age world is disrupted by violence, as cultures grow large enough to come into prolonged conflict with each other, competing for land, territory, and resources. Greece and Anatolia are invaded by Indo-Europeans, the Hittites and Mycenaeans are wiped out entirely, and mighty Egypt is attacked by various groups they call the Sea Peoples.

There is still a great deal of mystery about who the Sea Peoples were; the Egyptians were never very good at referring to foreign cultures in ways that make it easy for us to identify them now, especially if they made no treaties with them. (Treaties leave us with the names of kings and other leaders, which of course is critical identifying information.) They could have included the Philistines better known from the Bible, the Minoans, or even the Mycenaeans fleeing their own invaders in Greece. Some historians suspect a connection between the Sea Peoples and the Phoenicians.

While trade does not come to a halt, the dropoff is certainly severe, especially relative to the steady growth of the previous centuries.

1000 B.C.E.

The Phoenicians fill the trade gap left by the wars of 200 years earlier. An ancient civilization related to the Canaanites who lived in pre-Hebrew Israel, they were a coastal people who organized in city-states, especially throughout modern-day Lebanon, Syria,

Drawings on the walls of an ancient Egyptian tomb depict the exchange of goods. Egypt had trade and commerce with states throughout the Mediterranean but was under the control of the pharaohs.

and Israel. Their alphabet would later be adopted and adapted by the Greeks, and thence by the Romans and the modern European world. There are many unanswered questions about the Phoenicians, who may have been a culture that included multiple ethnic groups, and who may or may not have seen themselves as distinct from the Canaanites.

From their first appearances in the historical record, they are associated with high-quality timber—the "cedar of Lebanon" which is highly spoken of by Egyptian traders a thousand years before the Phoenicians became the dominant traders of the region—and with sea travel.

It seems very possible that their rise to trade dominance is connected to the Sea Peoples to whom, according to many theories, they are related; they may have learned better shipbuilding or sailing techniques through contact with the Sea Peoples at the time of the Egyptian invasion, or the Phoenician culture of 1000 B.C.E. may in fact be a Sea People culture.

In any case, Phoenicians had been sailing and trading since 1550 B.C.E., and by 1000 B.C.E. they are the principal trade partners of Egypt and the Mesopotamian cultures. Other than timber, they have little in the way of native raw materials, but their trading activity brings them olive oil, wine, dyes, pottery,

glass, metal, and textiles, from all over the Mediterranean coast, as well as fruit from Mesopotamia and gold and grain from Egypt.

Over the next four hundred years, Phoenician trade supremacy encompasses the Mediterranean, North Atlantic, and West Africa—Phoenician traders may have even circumnavigated the African continent. Phoenician colonies are established in Rhodes, Cyprus, Sardinia, Sicily, France, Malta, the Balearic Islands, North Africa, and Spain, in addition to Egyptian and Anatolian trading posts. Cyprian copper, Spanish silver, Anatolian iron, and Mediterranean wine are all part of the Phoenician commercial empire, and they sailed as far as Britain—modern-day Cornwall—to mine tin.

753 B.C.E.
The Kingdom of Rome is founded.

750 B.C.E.
The Phoenician trading empire begins to lose its dominance. Phoenician colonies Carthage (in North Africa), Motya (Sicily), Malta, and Cadiz (Spain) have become independent. Greece begins to emerge from its Dark Ages and establishes strong colonies throughout the Mediterranean.

734 B.C.E.

Greek colonists arrive in Italy from Sparta.

660 B.C.E.

Early coins, possibly the first, are stamped in Lydia, a kingdom in western Asia Minor. Lydian coins are made of electrum, a naturally occurring gold/silver alloy, and are stamped with the royal symbol of a lion's head. Greek historian Herodotus credits Lydia not only with the first coins but with the first retail stores (as opposed to temporary marketplaces and roaming traders). King Croessus of Lydia—whose name is still remembered in the phrase "wealthy as Croessus"—is responsible for one of the seven wonders of the ancient world, the Temple of Artemis at Ephesus, a 120-year project. India and China soon issue coins as well.

594 B.C.E.

Solon, leader of the Greek city-state of Athens, enacts reforms that become the foundation for Athenian democracy.

539 B.C.E.

Phoenicia is conquered by Cyrus the Great, the founder of the Persian Empire, and divided up into four kingdoms given to his loyal vassals. Many native Phoenicians who are able to do so flee to Carthage, which soon begins a long and significant history as a strong maritime power. Phoenician influence over foreign cultures, especially in the Mediterranean region, declines immediately after the Persian conquest. Alexander the Great conquers one of the four Phoenician kingdoms, Tyre, in 332 B.C.E., and distinctly Phoenician culture disappears shortly after, becoming absorbed into Greek culture.

509 B.C.E.

Rome becomes a Republic when its last king is ousted from power after his son rapes the wife of a senator (this, anyway, is the legend; the exact circumstances of the shift in power are unknown). Key to its government over the next five centuries will be its constitution, which establishes a state in which the legislative branch enjoys considerable power and is meant to represent the will of the people. While not a democracy, it is a remarkable leap toward modern governance, espousing ideals that much of Europe won't

adopt for many centuries to come. The office of *pontifex maximus*—high priest—is soon established, and is notable primarily because when the Catholic Church mirrors much of the structure of the Roman Republic, the Pope takes the place of the *pontifex maximus*.

500 B.C.E.

Greek trading dominance extends throughout the Middle East and eastern Mediterranean to the Balkans and southern Russia, and Greek settlement has spread throughout the Black Sea. The trading network exports olives, wheat, and wine for grain from Egypt and Sicily; copper, tin, zinc, and iron from Italy; silver and salted fish from Spain; metals from Asia Minor; and timber from the Balkans. The trade with what is now southern Russia is especially strong, providing Greece with fish, gold, furs, honey, amber, wax, timber, and slaves, who were resold throughout the Mediterranean. Large ships of 1,000 tons and more are for the first time outfitted to sail the seas, and the Greeks' superior knowledge of navigation proves a critical trade advantage, as they can reliably reach ports other cultures would have trouble with.

Indian merchants travel to Ceylon, Indonesia, and Southeast Asia to exchange pearls, cotton, black pepper, and Indian manufactured goods for spices.

411 B.C.E.

After Athens's defeat by Sparta in the Peloponnesian War, and the city-state's resulting loss of maritime supremacy, the democratic government is temporarily overthrown by a coup that blames the defeat on several democratic politicians. Order is restored eight years later.

400 B.C.E.

Goods from India and goods picked from Southeast Asian merchants transported to lands bordering on the Arabian Sea, Persian Gulf, and Red Sea.

347 B.C.E.

Death of Plato, the Greek philosopher whose *Republic* would remain an influence on political philosophy.

336–323 B.C.E.

The conquests of Alexander the Great spread the Greek language from the eastern Mediterranean to the Indus Valley, encouraging its adoption as the language of trade and commerce—and more broadly, the language of travelers throughout the ancient world.

323–146 B.C.E.

The Hellenistic period. The term *Hellenistic* is derived from Hellen, the ancient Greeks' name for themselves. Alexander the Great's conquests brought the known world into contact with Greece, its language and culture, and it enjoys an even greater influence on world culture than Phoenicia had. The Attic dialect of Greek becomes a universal language, with regional dialects becoming much less common, just as radically different English dialects are less common today, with most English speakers in the United States speaking an almost identical language to one another.

Ambitious Greeks migrate to the cities Alexander established in the vast areas between the Mediterranean and the Hindu Kush mountains and between the Arabian desert and the Caucasus mountains. Hellenistic groups establish wine vineyards and olive groves, as well as factories and workshops, and in many places are joined by groups of other ethnicities, especially Jews and Armenians. Hellenistic Greece in general is ethnically diverse, encompassing the many diverse peoples Alexander conquered as well as those who have relocated to do business with Greece and married locals.

322–185 B.C.E.

The Mauryan Empire is established in the Indian subcontinent, the largest empire to rule the region. Under its centralized administration, manufacturing of pottery, metal goods, and luxury goods is encouraged for the purposes of trade, and India begins to participate in the international economy to a greater degree than before.

268–232 B.C.E.

Roads ordered by Maurya's Emperor Asoka encourage trade through Hindu Kush mountains both west to Persia, Anatolia, and the Mediterranean basin and east through China through what eventually becomes the Silk Road. Building on routes previously established by Persian and Macedonian administrations in the previous two centuries, the Mauryan Empire joins those routes and establishes links to the west, and eventually to China. India exported cotton goods, pepper, and gems to China in return for silk.

211 B.C.E.

Rome issues the denarius, the silver coin that becomes the basis for their currency (having previously used cruder bronze coins, as well as the silver drachmae). The denarius is valued at 10 aeses (the aes was a bronze or copper coin). The gold aureus, worth 25 denarii, was rarely used.

Up to this point, the intrinsic value of a coin (the value of the metals it is made of) was the same as the face value. Roman coins have face values set by the state, greater than their intrinsic values—often twice as high, in fact, and sometimes higher, as the silver content of the denarius is eventually reduced in order to prevent shortages as Rome expands. Like letters of credit, a face value higher than an intrinsic value makes wealth more portable.

200 B.C.E.

The Han period begins in China, unifying this vast Asian region into one economic and political unit. The network of roads from the Han capital through Xian, the Tarim basin, Kashgar, and Central Asia becomes joined with the Persian and Indian land routes to become the Silk Road, and China is now part of the economic community that includes Europe and the Mediterranean, the Middle East and the Indian subcontinent, and North Africa. Though called the "Silk Road," the network of routes actually includes sea routes as well.

Chinese silk, lacquerware, ceramics, and paper—more expensive than papyrus but much more practical—soon become important trade goods throughout the west.

146 B.C.E.

The classical Greek heartlands are annexed by the Roman Republic; Hellenistic culture persists, but Greek political independence ends, signaling the dominance of Rome in the ancient world.

140 B.C.E.

The denarius is revalued at 16 aeses, a significant devaluation.

27 B.C.E.

After 500 years, the Roman Republic becomes the Roman Empire with the accession of Octavian, now called Augustus Caesar.

325 C.E.

The first Council of Nicaea establishes the Catholic Church as a unified body, providing Western Europe with a common religion.

400

Sea lanes are established via the South China Sea through the Straits of Malacca to the Bay of Bengal, the Arabian Sea, the Persian Gulf, and the Red Sea to the Mediterranean, expanding the Silk Road.

476

The long-weakened Roman Empire ends in the West when Romulus Augustus is deposed. A descendant of the Roman Empire persists in the East in the form of the Byzantine Empire. Western Europe develops in the shadow of Rome, united by closely related languages and culture, intermarriages, and the oversight of the Roman Catholic Church. As a result, though there is great diversity among European states and peoples, the continent remains more closely connected than it might have been had it not been for the centuries during which Rome courted, conquered, and colonized it.

500–700

After the Roman Empire falls, Jewish and Christian communities continue the trading activity in the Indian Ocean. East Africans including Christians from Ethiopia and, after the 7th century, Muslims on the Somali and Swahili coasts from the Horn of Africa to central Mozambique participate in the trade. This trade occurs through the Arabian Sea to India. Indian traders (mostly Dravidians from Southeast Indian kingdoms) dominate commerce via the Kra peninsula opening in Southern Thailand and the straits of Malacca between Malaya and the Indonesian archipelago.

529–534

Justinian I, ruler of the Byzantine Empire, issues the Corpus Juris Civilis ("Body of Civil Law"). Centuries of imperial Roman law are compiled into three codices, which revive the use of Roman law throughout Europe, influencing civil law.

631

Mohammed, the founder of Islam, dies. By the time of his death, all of Arabia has converted to his faith.

Muslims become a powerful economic and political force through the rest of the Middle Ages.

638

Jerusalem is captured by Muslims.

674–678

Muslim armies face their first serious defeat when they are driven back after a four-year siege of Constantinople, preventing the Islamification of Europe.

718

Muslims are again repelled from Constantinople.

754

Pepin, king of France and founder of the Carolingian dynasty, promises the lands of central Italy to the Pope—thus formalizing the Pope's temporal power as a political force in Europe.

800–1250

Islamic banks, founded to avoid the Koran's prohibitions of certain kinds of banking, offer a wide variety of services throughout the Muslim world, and are instrumental in funding Indian Ocean trade. Among the available services are moneylending, investment broking, and currency exchange.

Lines of credit known as "sakk" are available, from which term we derive the English word "check." Sakks allowed traders to draw letters of credit in one location and cash them in at another, so that the traders did not have to travel with large quantities of gold and silver.

Much of the supply of gold for Europe and the Middle East before the exploration of the Americas comes from various African empires, transported by Arab and European traders across the Sahara desert. Traders arrive by camel and caravan in West African communities, where they trade cloth, salt, metal, and glass for dye, ivory, and especially gold and slaves. Outsiders, emphasizing Arab involvement, sometimes refer to this trade activity as The Silent Trade of the Moors. Such traders leave their products on the riverbank near the mines (usually in the area of the modern-day Ghana and Ivory Coast), and if their trading partners are satisfied with the offering, they leave gold in its place the next morning. If the offering remains, the process is repeated until a trade is made.

The Mosque of Sultan Bayazid in Constantinople. The city was the apex of the Muslim effort to expand the Islamic religion into Europe and was under siege for four years from 674 to 678.

The African empires of Ghana, Mali, and Songhay derive much of their income from the tariffs enacted on these trades, and the routes themselves tend to reflect the dominance of particular states. Ghana is reached via a western trade route from Morocco and Algeria, but the route is abandoned when Muslims sack Ghana's capital; a route from Tunis arises in its place. Muslim traders favor joint ventures in order to avoid sole liability in trading ventures. They pool their resources in several investments in several cargoes on several ships, so that no one's financial well-being can "go down with the ship."

1000–1500
During the classic period of the Swahili city-states of the eastern African coast (where modern-day Kenya, Tanzania, and Mozambique are), there is a thriving market for Asian products such as Indian beads, Chinese porcelain, and Persian pottery, as well as for spices. Textile factories produce cloth both for local demand and export, and copper and gold are mined and traded. Adept shipbuilders, the Swahili conduct their own trade with the outside world until the arrival of the Portuguese in the early 16th century.

1054
The East-West Schism divides the Christian Church into Western Catholicism and Eastern Orthodoxy.

1099
The First Crusade seeks to liberate Jerusalem from Muslims.

1337

The Hundred Years War begins as England and France struggle for dominance of Western Europe.

1434

The Medici family rises to prominence in Florence. Throughout the Renaissance, powerful noble families will be important as patrons of artists and inventors; they and the Catholic Church essentially fund the Renaissance.

1440

The Portuguese establish plantations on São Tomé and the Cape Verde Islands.

1441–1800s

The European slave trade begins, starting with the Portuguese, with other nations soon following. The triangle or transatlantic trade is a symbol of the increasing global nature of trade and business as it ties together the eastern and western hemispheres in a three cornered interaction. The commercial connection can start anywhere. Merchants can carry clothing, guns, and wine south to Africa and trade these items for rhinoceros horn, ivory, grain of pepper, some gold, and especially slaves. The trade extends from Senegal to Angola.

Slaves are especially taken from Dahomey (now Benin) and southern Nigeria (Caribbean and West Indies) and Angola (Brazil). In Africa, this leg is called the firearms trade as merchants located at trading posts (factors) exchange guns for goods, including slaves. The collaborators then use the guns to hunt potential slaves in their "protectorates" and sell them to slavers in return for more guns. The product and human cargo cross the Atlantic in the infamous middle passage by which an estimated 15 million are transported and many die.

The cargo is traded for precious metals from South America and rum, molasses, and sugar from the West Indies and Brazil. The traders then sail up the coast of the Americas, collecting rice and tobacco and later cotton from the American South, wheat from the middle colonies, and naval stores (tar, turpentine, rope, lumber) from New England. The ships then sail back across the Atlantic. The ships could just as easily start from the western hemisphere or Africa. After the slave trade is abolished in the early 19th century, starting with the United States, Britain, and the Netherlands, this trade gradually diminishes.

1453

After the fall of Constantinople to Ottoman Turks, Europeans take to the sea to obtain many of the products available through the Silk Road, and the land routes associated with the Road decline quickly.

1492

Christopher Columbus, seeking a trade route to India, establishes a route to the West Indies instead, introducing Europe to the New World of the Americas. The Columbian Exchange that results from Columbus's repeated trips to the New World, and the trips of other explorers, refers not only to trade but to the exchange of food crops and other plants, animals, and diseases between the continents. Though world population more than doubles between 1500 and 1900, to 900 million people worldwide, the population of the New World is reduced by more than 100 million people in that same time.

1500

After 1500, western European countries facing the Atlantic adopt an economic policy called mercantilism, in which the nation is kept prosperous through government intervention in the private sector. The acquisition of wealth—and for Spain and Portugal, particularly the acquisition of precious metals—is mercantilism's main goal, because stores of such metals are equivalent to a nation's power.

The goal of trade, in essence, is to exchange exports for as much gold and silver as possible—and so Spanish colonialism is fueled in great part by the quest for gold in the New World. Colonies play a major role in mercantilism: they're meant to provide raw materials that their founding nations back in Europe lack, and to serve as captive markets. The English colonies, for instance, provide rum and timber while serving as reliable, predictable customers for English exports; the Dutch take the same approach to their own colonies. Just as those approaches eventually backfire, so too does the Spanish: the influx of precious metals from the New World devalues Spanish currency.

Coffee and sugar are introduced to the New World colonies from the eastern hemisphere, and become cash crops in Brazil, Costa Rica, and Louisiana.

1509

Systemic slave trade begins to the West Indies with Spanish plantations in Hispaniola.

1550

Antwerp (in Belgium) begins its "continuous fair" and becomes the site for the first permanent stock exchange, a meeting place for bankers, merchants, and businessmen. Though no one realizes it yet, this is the first blow to still-nascent mercantilism and a gesture towards modern economic practices, which favor and protect the private sector.

1570

The beginning of Dutch involvement in slave trade.

1577

The Muscovy Company, England's first joint-stock company, is chartered. The joint-stock company, a precursor to the modern corporation, is the chosen instrument of mercantilism. A charter from the state grants the company with a monopoly in a specific region or over a specific trade good. Though trading companies had existed before, these charters came into full flower as mercantilism was adopted, and enable companies to trade all over the world. Many of the New World colonies were founded as joint-stock companies originally.

The Muscovy Company is specifically granted the right to import furs from Russia and the Baltic, and was founded by adventurers searching for a Northeast Passage to China.

1591

The Moroccan defeat of the Songhay Empire marks the end of the Sudanic empires and the decline of the Silent Trade of the Moors. By this time, the flow of specie coming from the Americas and West Atlantic trade had undermined the economic role of Sudanic states.

1600

The British East India Company is granted its charter by Queen Elizabeth I on December 31, 1600, with a 21-year monopoly on British trade in the East Indies (the company persists much longer than its monopoly does). Its main trade was in silk, indigo, opium, tea, and saltpeter, and it was chartered in the hopes of countering some of the Dutch trade superiority in the East Indies. Hostilities with the Dutch East Indies Company (founded 1602) and the Portuguese East Indies Company (founded 1628) are common and sometimes violent. The Dutch dominance in the spice trade is never disintegrated to the extent the crown would like, but inroads are made in the straits of Malacca, originally controlled by the Portuguese.

Its power and economic importance lead the East India Company to a position of political importance and influence, helping to shape history in the generations to come, and the company is the Crown's agent in the British takeover of the Indian subcontinent.

17th Century

New species of animals are introduced into the Americas and Oceania by Europeans settlers and traders, including horses, pigs, sheep, cattle, chickens, cats, dogs, and goats. New industries are begun as a result, and the far more sparsely settled New World has the luxury of providing seemingly limitless grazing space for livestock, leading to thriving cattle (beef, leather, tallow, dairy) and sheep (mutton, wool) industries in the Americas. The horse population is so healthy and has so much room that there is a significant mustang (wild horse) population within generations.

The transmigration of grains and nuts as items of both export and consumption is even more pervasive. The peanut from the New World is introduced in Africa and becomes so important a cash crop that it's instrumental as an excuse to end the slave trade (now arguably no longer the most profitable use for Africa). West Africa also begins to produce cacao, introduced from the Americas, as a cash crop, and the long-staple cotton of the New World replaces the short-staple cotton of Egypt and India as the dominant form of cotton. Manioc (also called cassava) is introduced to tropical Africa and southeast Asia, and is nutritious enough to support dense populations there with relative ease.

Chocolate and maize (corn) become important luxury items in the Old World, and other New World vegetables become so popular that it is difficult to imagine Old World cuisines without them—whether it's the tomato in Italy, the potato in the British Isles and central Europe, the paprika critical to the national dishes of Hungary, or the chile peppers that catch on everywhere but France. Wheat, barley, millet, oats,

Illustration shows a portrait of Pocahantas as Mrs. John Rolfe, from a portrait painting done in London, England, 1616.

rice, and rye introduced from the Old World become important cash crops in the Americas, alongside textiles like flax and hemp.

1607

Jamestown is founded in the Virginia Colony, the first permanent English settlement in the modern-day United States, after the earlier failure of the Roanoke Colony. The original charter of the Virginia Company grants land from the 34th parallel (near Cape Fear, in what is now North Carolina) to the 48th parallel, thus encompassing much of what became New England and the Mid-Atlantic states in America. France and Spain both have claims in this region but are unsuccessful in preventing the English from gaining dominance.

After the death of Elizabeth, who had chartered the Virginia Company, her successor James I granted separate charters to two different branches of the company—the Plymouth and London Companies. War with Spain had financially taxed England at a time when money was sorely needed to fund expeditions to scout out critical trading routes and secure territory, and dividing Virginia between two companies was a way to raise more funds.

The competing Plymouth and London Companies sought to establish settlements as quickly as possible, though were forbidden from doing so within 100 miles of each other.

Plymouth establishes its colony far to the north, in what is now Maine—Popham Colony, which is abandoned a year later when its leader dies and his successor leaves for England upon inheriting an estate and noble title. The London Company establishes its colony further south, named for King James and located on a spot on the water chosen because of the ease of defending it against other European forces.

Unfortunately, the resulting swampiness makes hunting and agriculture infeasible, and the tidal river water is too salty to drink. The colony faces starvation and economic difficulty at every turn in its early years.

1608

The French establish their first settlements in what is now Canada. While the Spanish and Portuguese seek previous metals, the French seek instead to form a monopoly over the New World fur trade, to take advantage of the Little Ice Age that has held sway in Europe since 1400 (and persists until 1800), accounting for exceptionally cold winters.

1609

The first commercial bank is started in Amsterdam for transfer of payments in different currencies.

1612

John Rolfe, a colonist in Jamestown, Virginia, introduces a strain of tobacco that is exported to the Old World, where it is widely successful. The economic outlook of the colony of Virginia takes a quick upturn, and Rolfe marries Pocahontas, the daughter of the Powhatan Indian chief, two years later. When the Rolfes visit England, they are received as celebrities, as in the European mindset Pocahontas is a visiting princess. Their popularity helps to attract further investors to Jamestown's financial concerns.

1619

The first slaves are introduced to Virginia.

1694

The Bank of England opens. The English stock market begins business the following year.

18th Century

Various Navigation Acts passed by the British crown in the 18th century limit the trade its colonies can do with other countries, in order to protect its own economic interests and preserve the status of the colonies as captive markets. By this time, English dominance has been fairly well-established in much of North America, with France and Spain maintaining their respective holdings but the Dutch long gone from New Amsterdam (now New York). The colonies have grown enough that they are no longer happy being subservient to the Crown, but they have no real political power, no advocates in the king's court; the complaint about "no taxation without representation" begins long before anyone contemplates independence.

1720–1734

British "Bubble Acts" are passed to control excessive speculation, by forbidding the selling of stock that the seller does not own.

1764

James Hargreaves redresses the balance between weavers and spinners through the spinning jenny, which allows spinners to keep up with woven cloth.

The Currency Act enacted by the British government forbids American colonies from issuing paper money, and discouraged them from minting coins (in the meanwhile, Britain itself minted no copper or silver coins during this period). Prior to this time, the colonies had issued Colonial Scrip, though it was considered of little long-term value since it wasn't backed by gold or silver. The Act may have accidentally been caused by Benjamin Franklin, who had explained the benefits of the scrip system to the British government, only to be confronted with their horror at his recommendations. In retrospect, Franklin and many others blame the Currency Act for the American Revolution, as it points up a vast difference of economic philosophy between the two countries, and underscores the

British government's determination to keep the colonies powerless.

The Sugar Act enacted around the same time taxes sugar and molasses. Although it is only a renewal of an existing act, and cuts the previous tax in half, that older tax was never successfully enforced in the colonies—and so this is in essence a new tax. The economic impact is severe, on an already depressed colonial economy, adding to dissatisfaction.

1765

The Stamp Act passed by the British government is the first such act to directly tax American colonists, by requiring a tax stamp on any document in order to legitimize it—not simply legal documents requiring the crown's involvement, but commercial contracts, wills, deeds, locally issued permits, even playing cards, pamphlets, and newspapers. The British have grown tired of the expense of their military presence in North America and decided the Americans should be accountable for its funding, even though British economic interests are the principal reason for those militias. Americans bristle at the tax and protest in the streets in many of the colonies, hanging or otherwise abusing effigies of public figures.

Delegates from nine of the 13 colonies (all but New Hampshire, Georgia, Virginia, and North Carolina) meet for the Stamp Act Congress to discuss what should be done. The meeting is held in secret, with no minutes recorded or records kept, and delegates later report that the issues discussed included not only taxation, but conflicts with the British over the right to trial by jury and the existence of the admiralty courts. It is at the Stamp Act Congress that the issue of "taxation without representation" becomes emblematic of the colonists' concerns with their British leaders—Americans are not represented in Parliament and many of them do not feel they should be taxed by it, but instead by local governments who have to live under the same conditions they do. The Declaration of Rights and Grievances produced by the Congress lists 14 points of contention with recent British acts, most of them economic, the rest dealing with human rights. It is delivered to Parliament, which—making matters worse—refuses to discuss the issue or acknowledge the Declaration.

James Watt builds his first working steam engine, pushing water through a cylinder to produce steam which, applied to a piston, turns a wheel. The resulting rotary motion converts a pump into a multiple engine, and by the end of the century, there are over 1,000 such steam engines in use. Human and animal power race toward obsolescence. The use of steam power is a prerequisite for the Industrial Revolution, enabling vast amounts of power to be used that previous methods simply could not have generated.

1767

The Townshend Acts enacted by the British government increase the tax on goods imported into the American colonies, and direct that those taxes be paid directly to the British government, instead of to the local town governments that would usually collect them and use them for their operating expenses. This is another attempt by the British government to collect money from the Americans to fund the British military presence in North America, and it again leads to protests and riots. Dissent is increasing, with less and less time between incidents to let tempers cool down.

1773

The Tea Act enacted by the British government restructures the tax on tea imported to the American colonies, in an attempt to break an American boycott on high-priced British tea. In response, a group of colonists—most likely Samuel Adams and the Sons of Liberty—dress up like Native Americans and destroy a shipment of tea, throwing 342 crates of just-arrived tea into Boston Harbor (the Boston Tea Party). The British government responds with a group of Acts the colonists call the Intolerable Acts, designed both to punish the colonists and to recoup the cost of the destroyed tea. The Boston Port Act, for instance, forcibly closes the port of Boston until the tea is paid for, drawing criticism that an entire city is punished for the acts of a few dozen men, without trial or discussion. The Massachusetts Government Act goes even further, restructuring the colonial government to provide more control to the British, and the Administration of Justice Act allows the British to relocate an officer accused of a crime to another colony—or back to Britain—if it seems that a fair trial cannot be had in Massachusetts. George Washington calls this act the "Murder Act," arguing that it provides extraordinary leeway for the actions of British officers who may

feel free to mistreat locals, knowing they will not face local trials.

1776

The Continental Congress of the United States declares its independence from Britain, a year after war broke out in Lexington and Concord.

1780

Henry Cort invents the pudding furnace, an open-hearth process that cooks molten iron in a great vat. Improvements in the open hearth increase iron production and steel conversion, enabling the heavy industry, shipbuilding, and construction industries worldwide to live up to the promise of the coming Industrial Revolution.

1785

Edmund Cartwright's power loom is the final nail in the coffin of handicrafts, shifting power to industrial workers.

1789

The U.S. Constitution goes into effect, and Revolutionary War General George Washington is elected the first American president.

1793–1794

The Whiskey Rebellion is an insurrection against the new American government, over its tax laws. A tax proposed by Alexander Hamilton on distilled spirits is worded so as to affect small producers more than large ones (which include President Washington). Westerners are especially opposed to the tax since they use whiskey as a barter good, with no cash changing hands—introducing a large tax upsets the balance and its usefulness in barter. Like farming, distilling is not a business one enters into lightly—the start-up cost is significant, and no one wants to abandon it after finally paying off their initial expenses and learning the craft.

Dissatisfaction leads to armed conflict in western Pennsylvania—a disorganized, frustrated rebellion that robs the local mail, tars and feathers a tax collector, and interrupts court proceedings. There are no fatalities, though. Washington declares martial law, and a militia of over twelve thousand soldiers eventually rounds up some twenty prisoners, in a deliberate

"The First Cotton-Gin" drawn by William L. Sheppard depicts African-American slaves using the cotton gin invented by Eli Whitney in 1793. The machine revolutionized the production of cotton, but also enabled the persistence of slavery.

display of federal power. Only two are arrested, one of them dying in prison before his trial, and the other freed by Washington. The whiskey tax has one long-lasting effect on American history: small distillers thrive in Kentucky and Tennessee, which in the late 18th century constitute the American frontier, too wild and sparsely settled for tax collectors to ply their trade effectively. Today, Kentucky is home to most of the world's bourbon producers; Tennessee is the home of Jack Daniels. Both styles of whiskey descend directly from these 18th-century distillers.

Eli Whitney invents the cotton "gin" (engine, meaning simply "machine" at this time). Whitney's machine mechanizes the separation of cotton fiber from seedpods, a job that is difficult to do even for experienced workers. This makes cotton more profitable, and assists in making it the key cash crop of the antebellum American South—it also allows the slavery system to persist at a time when it might have died off due to unprofitability.

Whitney makes little money from his machine, because of poorly handled business practices, but popularizes interchangeable parts in the manufacture of muskets, an idea that is critical to the American system of manufacturing that predominates throughout the Industrial Revolution: interchangeable parts, division of labor, and powered machinery. The system is soon applied to clocks and sewing machines, making them simultaneously more affordable and prized commodities because of the resulting increase in dependability.

1803

The size of the United States is doubled when Thomas Jefferson purchases the Louisiana Territory from Napoleon, who is badly in need of money to fight his wars in Europe. This increases not only the country's territory but the number of its ports, and brings the economically invaluable Mississippi River into the country's territory.

1817–1825

First proposed in 1699, the Erie Canal is built, bolstering the economy of upstate New York (indeed, creating many of the communities there) as well as New York City (by making it easier to transport goods from port). A project considered by many fine minds over the 118 years, including the British government and George Washington, Jesse Hawley finally gets the project off the ground, hoping to turn upstate New York into a bread basket of grain fields which can sell their goods by ship. When Jefferson calls the project folly and refuses to fund it, New York governor DeWitt Clinton agrees to raise the funds, a decision widely considered unwise. It is years before the hundreds of miles of canal are finished, and over 1000 workers die of swamp fever along the way, because of the working conditions in some locations. Leaks develop immediately but are sealed with a new form of concrete that has serendipitously been introduced between the time that construction began and the time it is completed. The canal immediately exceeds the expectations of its builders, and enlargements and feeder canals are begun almost right away, and continue throughout the 19th century. The economy of New York state and city is transformed in a matter of years, inspiring cities like Philadelphia and Baltimore to pursue similar projects.

1819

The Panic of 1819 is the first major economic crisis in American history, though a depression in the 1780s had led to the establishment of the dollar as the American currency. Historians do not all agree on the

causes of the Panic, which results in bank failures, record unemployment and foreclosures, and slumps in both agriculture and manufacturing despite the recent advances of the Industrial Revolution. Some economists paint the panic as part of a normal cycle of boom and bust; others blame the federal government's monetary policy after the debts of the War of 1812.

The Supreme Court case *Dartmouth College v. Woodward* rules in favor of the college, after the state of New Hampshire attempted to alter its charter and turn it into a public school instead of a private one. Renowned orator Daniel Webster speaks in Dartmouth's favor, reportedly bringing tears to the eyes of the justices. It was not a popular decision, because it limited the power of states—but it did so only by holding them accountable to live up to the contracts they made, which in the long run protected both businesses (including institutions like Dartmouth) and individuals. The Woodward in the case name is the secretary of the new board of trustees appointed by the state, though of course the case was really against the state itself.

1820

Textile mills in New England expand. Lowell, Massachusetts, becomes the center of the Industrial Revolution in America, a hub of textile production. In the coming years, industrial production is one factor spurring the construction of railroads for faster transport across the vast and still mostly unsettled continent.

1837

The Panic of 1837 results from rampant speculation on gold and silver, resulting in a five-year depression and the failure of more than a third of the nation's banks.

1857

The Panic of 1857 sees massive business failures when the prosperity of the Gold Rush and the Mexican-American War slows down. Though not as severe as other panics, the Civil War slows down recovery.

1859

The Comstock Lode is discovered in Nevada, on the eastern slope of Mount Davison. This is the first major deposit of silver ore found in the United States, and excavating it provides $400 million in silver and gold over the next 20 years. Not only is the lode instrumental in bolstering the economies of Nevada and California (which was beginning to slow down, a decade after its Gold Rush), but it creates a number of individual fortunes as well—including that of George Hearst, a California prospector who turns his mining interests into the country's largest mining firm and eventually runs for Senate. Hearst's son is William Randolph Hearst, whose family fortune made him the newspaper king and a force in early 20th century American politics.

1861–1865

The American Civil War is fought between an industrial north and an agricultural slave-state south.

1863

The National Bank Act of the United States establishes national charters for banks, basing currency on the bank holdings of U.S. Treasury securities.

1865

After George Pullman lends one of his luxury sleeper train cars for the transport of Abraham Lincoln's coffin, such cars become known as Pullman cars.

1867

The National Grange of the Order of the Patrons of Husbandry—or simply the Grange—is formed, a fraternal organization for American farmers that encourages them to band together cooperatively for their common good. Agriculture is on the decline in the United States; in another generation the country will be mostly urban-dwellers, and that change is already detectable in the air. The oldest agricultural organization in the United States, it remains the most important and powerful through at least the 1950s.

1868

Andrew Carnegie, one of the wealthiest men in history and one of the best-known tycoons in an age of them, founds Carnegie Steel.

1869

Construction of the Suez Canal in Egypt, allowing water passage between Europe and Asia without hav-ing to circumnavigate the African continent. There were canals in use here in ancient times, but the Suez Canal is a modern project excavated by the French. International response is skeptical; the British deride it, but also consider it a threat to their own economic interests. Few outside of France purchase shares in the Suez Canal Company.

But in fact, the effect of the Canal is extraordinary, allowing the world to be circumnavigated in times that would have been unthinkable only a year ago, a boon to trade as well as a factor in Europe's ongoing conquest of inland Africa. Only 20 years later, the British find themselves protecting it during an Egyptian civil war—because it is so necessary to their economic interests.

The first transcontinental railroad in North America is established by the Union Pacific and Central Pacific railroads. The last spike, a symbolic gold spike, is hammered into a special tie of polished laurel wood from California, in a ceremony at the Promontory Summit in Utah—and immediately removed so it could be replaced with a more practical iron spike. The railroad is a vital link for trade and westward travel, and ends the age of the covered Conestoga wagon and the famous searches for safe passage over the Rockies by would-be pioneers. Not coincidentally, a generation later—in 1890—the Census Bureau declares the frontier "closed," meaning that the population density of the United States has reached a point that there is no significant amount of space left unsettled.

Despite the name "transcontinental," the rail line does not traverse the entire continent—it simply makes it possible to traverse the continent by rail, by crossing the Rocky Mountains. The route spans some 1,800 miles, from Sacramento in the west to Council Bluffs, Iowa, in the east, more or less the same route taken by I-80 now.

The railroad made the west more profitable, not only by reducing loss of goods in transit but by shortening the time between production and sale. Westerners with more money to spend could now spend more of it on mail-order goods, which were of increasing popularity—this is the golden age of the Sears catalogue, when everything a person couldn't be expected to make at home, from a new Sunday dress to a crank-operated ice cream maker to snow shoes to shotguns to Franklin stoves, could be ordered through the mail.

1873

The Panic of 1873 leads to a four-year depression, following the crash of the Vienna Stock Exchange and the bankruptcy of the banking firm Jay Cooke & Company. One factor is the outbreak of equine flu, which brings the horse-driven rail industry to a halt, which in turn affects locomotives as coal cannot reach them. Many businesses are forced to have men pull wagons of cargo by hand, and ships stay in port with their cargo untouched, no one available to unload it. Fires rage in major cities with no one able to get to them in time to put them out.

In response to the Panic, the federal government moves to a gold standard, no longer minting silver coins or stocking silver. This reduces the money supply, greatly hurting anyone with a large debt load—which in practice means virtually every farmer in the country, farming being a business which all but the wealthiest men have to fund with loans.

1880s

If the first stage of industrialization emphasized factory production and the mass production of goods on a global basis, the second stage of industrialization emphasizes mass energy as applied to mass transportation and communication on a global basis as well as scientific research with global effects. The combination of steam and locomotion led to the railroads becoming the major form of transportation after 1860. The advance of electrical conversion leads to coal becoming the main fuel until 1900 as well as new mass forms of transportation in the growing urban areas.

The spread of the internal combustion and diesel engines leads to petroleum fuels replacing electricity. As a result, gas and oil ultimately replace coal in the transportation industry, beginning with land and air transport, followed by water transport.

1887

The Interstate Commerce Commission is established in the United States to regulate railroads and ensure fair prices.

1890

The Sherman Antitrust Act is passed to limit cartels and monopolies. The Industrial Revolution created opportunities for national companies to thrive in the United States, but they did so at the peril of smaller companies. The Sherman Antitrust Act actually encouraged businesses that operated in multiple states, by specifically prohibiting certain abusive practices in order to make it unnecessary to outlaw such operation altogether. The ultimate purpose is to encourage competition, keep the market healthy, and prohibit collusive practices between companies at the expense of the consumer, competitors, or the state. The act itself proves to be too vague, and it's refined with further acts and court decisions, but it remains an important statement of legal principle in federal law.

1893

The Panic of 1893 is in many ways a resumption of the 1873 panic, which had been temporarily salved by a speculation-driven expansion during the railroad boom. That speculation led to overextension, which in turn led to the bankruptcy of the Pennsylvania and Reading Railroad.

European investors, foreseeing the panic, accept payment only in gold, which weakens the federal gold reserve and thus the value of the dollar; such fears are justified when the reserve reaches its mandated minimum, at which point notes can no longer legally be exchanged for gold, for fear of bankrupting the federal government of hard currency. This, unsurprisingly, leads to bank failures and a drop in the value of silver, followed by a series of business failures and railroads going bankrupt. Frustrated men in various industries attempt strikes, to little improvement.

President Cleveland and his party, the Democrats, are blamed for the economic troubles, and the following election sees record Republican victories. The depression becomes a key talking point in the bimetallism debate between those who advocate gold and silver standards for currency, and that debate fuels the political careers of pro-silver William Jennings Bryan and (ultimately victorious) pro-gold William McKinley.

Out of frustration, many people seek new lives out west, where the frontier may no longer exist but new opportunities certainly do. From Seattle to Los Angeles, the western cities see significant growth as easterners and Midwesterners arrive seeking a fresh start, a blank slate, the old American promise of a day's wage for a day's work.

1905

The Industrial Workers of the World, or Wobblies, are founded in Chicago at a convention of radicals and socialists who oppose the American Federation of Labor (AFL), finding the AFL too conservative.

1906

The Pure Food and Drug Act is passed by the American government in response to public outcry over the quality of packaged foods and the potential poisonousness of patent medicines. The Meat Inspection Act, similarly, empowers the Department of Agriculture to inspect and destroy any meat found unfit for human consumption.

1911–1913

Henry Ford's Model "T" is the first wildly successful automobile, a product of his assembly line. Though they have been around for decades, after the Model "T" automobiles rapidly shift from luxury items to necessities.

1914

The Federal Trade Commission (FTC) is established in the United States as a further act of antitrust legislation, seeking to protect consumer interests. The FTC is charged with the creation of regulations that further the elimination of anti-competitive practices.

The Clayton Antitrust Act refines the Sherman Antitrust Act, prohibiting anti-competitive price discrimination, mergers and acquisitions that lessen or harm competition, many cases of exclusive dealings and tyings, and one person serving as director of more than one corporation in the same industry.

1929

The New York stock market crash of Black Tuesday on October 29 leads to a lengthy worldwide depression, underscoring the increasing interconnectedness of national economies. Ironically, optimism persists after the crash more than in some previous panics, with many people convinced that the days of severe banking panics are behind them; instead, the Great Depression is the worst depression of modern history, its effects persisting until World War II in the United States—and indeed helping to precipitate that war by making Germany more and more economically desperate.

A portrait of Henry Ford in 1919. He became an icon of the American manufacturing system.

1933–1936

President Franklin D. Roosevelt institutes his New Deal programs to deal with the Great Depression. The First New Deal, enacted in his first year of office, is a series of short-term fixes, emergency relief programs, and banking reforms. The Second New Deal, enacted in 1935 and 1936, more specifically targets the large corporations that the Roosevelt administration holds partially accountable for the Depression.

A number of New Deal programs still exist and have become integral to the federal government, including the Federal Deposit Insurance Corporation that backs banks, the Social Security Administration, and the Securities and Exchange Commission that oversees the securities and stock market.

1944

The United Nations Monetary and Financial Conference, often called the Bretton Woods conference, is held in Bretton Woods, New Hampshire, in the last months of World War II. A group of 730 delegates arrive from all 45 Allied nations, preparing for a postwar world economy.

The conference seeks to accelerate postwar recovery and to preserve political stability by avoiding severe economic panic in any affected nation. An international currency exchange system is established that remains in use through the 1970s. The conference is notably pro-capitalist, and seeks to protect open markets, ending economic nationalism and the use of trade blocks to preserve national economic interests (an idea that remains controversial today).

Bretton Woods also establishes the International Monetary Fund (IMF), an organization that oversees the global economy to promote free trade and economic growth.

1947

When Bretton Woods fails to create its proposed International Trade Organization, the General Agreement on Tariffs and Trade (GATT) is adopted instead. GATT is a treaty that seeks to further the Bretton Woods ideal of ending economic nationalism by reducing or eliminating tariffs, allowing national economies to intermingle without such filters. There are eight rounds of such tariff reductions over the next 44 years, leading up to the establishment of the World Trade Organization.

Dwight D. Eisenhower addresses a North Atlantic Treaty Organization conference in the late 1950s.

1949

The North Atlantic Treaty Organization (NATO) is established with headquarters in Brussels, Belgium. At first a political association of anti-communist nations—Belgium, Luxembourg, the Netherlands, France, the United Kingdom, the United States, Canada, Portugal, Italy, Norway, Denmark, and Iceland—the organization is galvanized by the 1950 outbreak of the Korean War, because of the assumption that all communist nations are working together. NATO becomes a military force from then on, dealing with Cold War conflicts.

1951

The Treaty of Paris creates the European Coal and Steel Community (ECSC), a common market for coal and steel for France, West Germany, Italy, and the three Benelux states (Belgium, Luxembourg, the Netherlands). The goal is to prevent further war between France and Germany. Attempts to create similar European Defense and European Political communities fail.

1955

The Warsaw Pact, a treaty among communist nations, is established in Poland. A response to the formation of NATO, it is originally composed of Albania, Bulgaria, the Czechoslovak Soviet Republic, Hungary, Poland, Romania, and the Soviet Union; East Germany joins in the following year. Like NATO, the Warsaw Pact nations pledge to support each other if any member are attacked; during the next thirty-some years of the Cold War, the Warsaw Pact and NATO member states engage in a number of proxy wars, never fighting directly.

1957

The European Coal and Steel Community countries form the European Economic Community (EEC), also called the European Common Market, to integrate the economies of its member states, dissolving tariffs and other trade barriers.

Euratom, the European Atomic Energy Community, is formed at the same time. Early conflicts among the EEC revolve around the difficulties of establishing a unified agricultural policy and the worries of infringing on the sovereignty of Community member states.

1960

The Organization of Petroleum Exporting Countries (OPEC) is formed, bringing together Iran, Iraq, Kuwait, Qatar, Saudi Arabia, the United Arab Emirates, Libya, Algeria, Nigeria, Angola, Venezuela, and Ecuador, at Venezuela's instigation. Essentially a cartel, OPEC's influence on the oil market has alarmed onlookers from the moment of its inception, and it bears significant responsibility for the oil crises of the 1970s. Advocates point out that before OPEC, and especially before World War II, Western nations regularly exploited the oil-producing Middle East.

1967

The Association of the Southeast Asian Nations (ASEAN) is formed, composed of Thailand, Malaysia, Singapore, and the Philippines, with further involvement on the part of Brunei, Burma (now Myanmar), Laos, Cambodia, and Vietnam.

The ECSC, EEC, and Euratom merge to become the European Community (EC), the precursor to today's European Union.

1973

Denmark, Ireland, and the United Kingdom join the European Community.

1981

Greece joins the European Community.

1986

Portugal and Spain join the European Community.

1989

The Asia-Pacific Economic Cooperation (APEC) is formed as a forum for 21 Pacific Rim nations to discuss common economic and trade concerns. Member states account for nearly half of the world's population and more than half of its gross domestic product, and include Australia, Brunei, Canada, China, Indonesia, Japan, Korea, Malaysia, New Zealand, the Philippines, Singapore, Thailand, the United States, Hong Kong, Mexico, Papua New Guinea, Chile, Peru, Russia, and Vietnam.

The Revolutions of 1989 bring about the fall of the "iron curtain" in Eastern Europe, as many socialist states are dismantled. The Berlin Wall is taken down in October, leading in less than a year to the reunifi-

President Ronald Reagan (right) and Arizona Senator John McCain in 1987. Reagan favored "trickle down" economics.

cation of Germany after two generations. In December, the United States and the Soviet Union officially declare the Cold War to be over.

1991

The Soviet Union collapses amid a resurgence of nationalist sentiment among citizens of its member states and the examples set by the revolutions of 1989.

1993

The North America Free Trade Agreement (NAFTA) is signed amid considerable controversy. NAFTA reduces trade and movement restrictions among the North American nations—Canada, the United States, and Mexico—and in the United States is criticized by both the left and the right wing, as it leads to a significant decline in American manufacturing employment (commonly ascribed to corporations closing American plants and opening Mexican ones with cheaper workers). Though free passage across the borders is foreseen as a second stage of NAFTA, the tightening of American borders after the 9/11 attack postpones this indefinitely.

The Maastricht Treaty goes into effect, forming the European Union (EU), formerly the European Community, which is now one of three pillars of the EU, alongside the Common Foreign and Security Policy and Justice and Home Affairs. Though the name reflects the fact that the EU is no longer a merely economic community, it is the economic effects that are the most profound in both the short- and long-term, as work begins to put the euro into circulation and member states ready themselves for the adjustments of economic unification.

1995

The World Trade Organization (WTO) supercedes GATT, which was perceived as ill-adapted for an increasingly global economy. GATT isn't dissolved, but is under the umbrella of the WTO now; the WTO thus supervises international trade, policing member states to ensure adherence to WTO trade agreements, enforces matters pertaining to intellectual property (a growing concern in an age of computer software and digital media), and so on. WTO member states must grant all other member states most-favored-nation status—or in other words, a member state can favor no other member state more than the others.

Austria, Finland, and Sweden join the European Union.

2001

China joins the World Trade Organization.

2002

The euro is adopted by members of the EU, replacing the national currencies of 12 countries.

2004

In the European Union's (EU) largest expansion—the Eastern bloc enlargement—Cyprus, the Czech Republic, Estonia, Hungary, Latvia, Lithuania, Malta, Poland, Slovakia, and Slovenia are admitted on May

1. Though the largest in countries, population, and landmass, this is the smallest enlargement in gross domestic product (GDP), and brings the per-capita GDP of the EU down severely.

2007

Bulgaria and Romania join the EU, having been unprepared to join as part of the Eastern bloc enlargement.

2008

The mortgage credit crisis in the United States reaches critical mass. The U.S. housing bubble that peaked in 2005 led to declining home values from 2006 on, followed by more and more borrowers becoming delinquent or defaulting. The first effects are confined to the banking and housing industries. Foreclosed properties sell for less than expected thanks to lack of demand, so much of the inflated demand of the bubble having been fueled by speculative purchasing. But the effects on the national and international economies are far more severe than in previous housing slumps. The crisis becomes the focal issue of the presidential election, and the George W. Bush administration and both candidates support an unpopular emergency bailout plan drawing on a $700 billion fund called the Troubled Assets Relief Program.

2009

In response to the ongoing worldwide financial crisis, recently inaugurated U.S. President Barack Obama signs into law the American Recovery and Reinvestment Act ("stimulus plan") on February 17. The largest chunk of the act's $787 billion in expenditures goes to federal programs, including assistance to those most in need (unemployment benefits, food stamp and Social Security increases, school lunch programs and Meals on Wheels, public and low-income housing), infrastructure improvements (including much-needed bridge repair programs and funding for public transportation), and improvements to the country's energy sector. Despite the size of the stimulus plan, it does not represent the whole of the spending expected by the Obama administration.

Norman C. Rothman
University of Maryland University College
Bill Kte'pi
Independent Scholar

ABN AMRO Holding

The parent company of the ABN AMRO consolidated group, ABN AMRO Holding N.V. provides global financial services. In its history of more than one and a half centuries, the company went through a number of mergers and acquisitions. Its origins can be traced back to the Netherlands on March 29, 1824, when Nederlandsche Handel-Maatschappij (Netherlands Trading Society, or NTS) was established. It worked for the Dutch government as a banking concern and also provided finances to industrial houses in the Netherlands and Dutch East Indies. From 1874, the NTS went into banking on a global scale.

In the Netherlands, ABN AMRO's branches increased significantly after World War II. It merged with Twentsche Bankvereeniging in October 1964 and came to be known as Algemene Bank Nederland (ABN). In the same year, there was a merger of the Amsterdamsche Bank with the Rotterdam Bank, with headquarters in Amsterdam. The new name was the Amsterdam-Rotterdam Bank (AMRO).

Talks began between ABN and AMRO about the expansion and strengthening of the two banks, whose capital bases were both strong. ABN AMRO Holding was set up on May 30, 1990, and the legal merger became effective on September 22, 1991.

With headquarters in Amsterdam and a network of over 3,500 branches in 63 countries, ABN AMRO became a premier financial institution providing products, asset management, and a diversified array of commercial, investment, and retail banking services. From 1991 to 2007, ABN AMRO ranked among the largest banks, having total assets of $1.3 trillion at the end of 2006. It employed 102,556 persons and served approximately 20 million clients. Its main area of operations were the Netherlands, the U.S. midwest, and Brazil. ABN AMRO went on an acquiring spree and entered into joint ventures in all three areas.

ABN AMRO acquired the Cragin Federal Bank for Savings in Illinois in July 1993. It began to dominate in the American midwest banking sector after also taking over Michigan-based Standard Federal in 1996. After five years, the takeover of Michigan National Corporation strengthened ABN ARMO's position in the United States even further.

Although ABN AMRO had been making its presence felt in Brazil since 1917, the bank became a more active player after the acquisition of Banco Real in 1998, which was followed by Bandepe and Paraiban. The position was buttressed further after the 2003 takeover of Sudameris bank; ABN AMRO was then the fourth-largest bank in Brazil.

The bank's other international acquisitions included the London stockbroking firm of Hoare Govett (1992), the Scandinavian investment bank Alfred Berg (1995), and the German banks Delbruck and Co. (2002) and Bethmann Maffei (2003). It had also entered into joint ventures with N.M. Rothschild & Sons of London (1996) and Mellon Bank Corporation of Pennsylvania (1998). In 2006 it was able to hold a majority stake only of Italy's Banca Antonveneta.

ABN AMRO undertook an overhaul of its organizational structure and by 2006 it had seven Strategic Business Units (SBUs); two international and five regional. Global clients included rich individuals and about 550 multinationals. Regional clients of the SBUs were from the Netherlands, Europe, the Americas, and Asia. ABN AMRO pursued a very high standard of professionalism, and its business principles are to aim at excellence in its services to business partners and shareholders. ABN AMRO has also done considerable work in contributing to sporting events and projects such as the World Tennis Tournament, the Volvo Ocean Race, and Ajax Football.

RFS Holdings (a conglomerate of the Royal Bank of Scotland Group, Fortis, and Banco Santander) became the owner of ABN AMRO in October 2007. The Dutch government then purchased Fortis's interest in the company on October 3, 2008. It was interested in the SBUs of the Netherlands, private clients, and the International Diamond and Jewelry Group. On October 15, 2008, the finance ministry of the Dutch government appointed its nominee to the supervisory board of ABN AMRO. The Dutch state and the bank would work together for better performance from ABN AMRO. The interim financial report of ABN AMRO Holding ending in June 2008 noted various types of market risks relating to interest, foreign exchange, and equity price. It recorded a profit of about $3,750 million after tax, proving the soundness and vitality of the business. In the present scenario, ABN AMRO Holding has a bright future.

See Also: Acquisitions, Takeovers, and Mergers; Banco Santander Central Hispano Group; Fortis; Netherlands.

Bibliography. "ABN AMRO—Braveheart Two," *Economist* (v.8531/84); ABN AMRO, *The 2007 Guide to SEPA: Becoming a Reality* (Euromoney Publications PLC, 2007); ABN AMRO, www.abnamro.com (cited March 2009); "After ABN AMRO: Three Amigos, Only One Conquistador," *Economist* (v.8589/88); "Banking: ABN AMRO Aims to Be One of Asia's Big Three," *Far Eastern Economic Review* (June 18, 1998); Douglas G. Cogan, *Corporate Governance and Climate Change: The Banking Sector: A Ceres Report* (RiskMetrics Group Inc., 2008); Deborah Orr, "Dutch Colonizers—ABN AMRO's Expansion," *Forbes* (June 14, 1999).

Patit Paban Mishra
Sambalpur University

Absenteeism

Absenteeism can be defined as any failure on the part of the employee to report to work when scheduled to do so. This includes absences that occur for any reason, whether involuntary or voluntary. Here, involuntary absenteeism refers to unavoidable illnesses and injuries that prevent an employee from attending to their work obligations. Voluntary absenteeism, on the other hand, includes unplanned absences to look after sick dependents, but can also be the outcome of boredom and/or low job satisfaction.

Unauthorized absenteeism represents a major cost for organizations all over the globe. Although individual incidents of absenteeism are fairly innocuous, the cumulative impact can be substantial. The impact on the North American economy alone is estimated to be in excess of $60 million. The obvious costs are those associated with the absentees themselves and includes their regular pay and benefits. Beyond this are the costs related to replacement labor, overtime, and lost productivity. There are also several flow-on effects that impact other workers in the organization, including the increased workload and stress experienced by staff members who are required to compensate for the absent coworker. Understaffing or work overload may in turn increase the risk of workplace accidents and reduce the amount of output and the quality produced. There are also additional time and financial costs associated with extra supervision and training of temporary staff. Studies reveal that the costs of absenteeism may in fact be higher than the amount of work time lost due to industrial disputes.

The two key factors attributed to high levels of absenteeism are ability to attend and motivation to attend. The variables that affect an employee's ability to attend work are often beyond the control of organizations. An employee's motivation to attend work, on the other hand, includes variables such as employee morale and satisfaction—factors that are within the control of the organization. A number of studies have shown that organizations that experience high levels of absenteeism also tend to experience issues related to staff morale. Industrial disputes tend also to be greater, as well as the costs associated with workers compensation. Overall, there is an important link between absence and factors such as poor interpersonal communication, job boredom, and poor supervisory skills. Furthermore, there is significant evidence to suggest that a large proportion of absences are potentially avoidable.

A 2005 study on U.S. human resources executives found that personal illnesses accounted for only 35 percent of unscheduled absences from work. Most absences were due to other reasons, including family issues (21 percent), personal needs (18 percent), entitlement mentality (14 percent), and stress (12 percent). Studies also confirm that absenteeism is a low base rate behavior. In other words, absenteeism is most typically associated with a small number of people who are absent often.

Surveys conducted on absenteeism indicate that those on higher rates of pay and with longer length of service are less likely to be absent. Furthermore, absenteeism rates tend to grow as an organization grows. Other statistics relating to absenteeism suggest that women tend to be absent more frequently than men and younger employees are absent more frequently than older employees. When older employees are absent, it tends to be for longer periods of time than younger employees. Absenteeism rates also tend to be much higher in unionized workplaces.

Reduction Strategies

Due to the costs and associated flow-on effects, organizations have pursued many strategies to reduce absenteeism. Most of these measures have been designed to improve employees' quality of work life and levels of job satisfaction, because it is generally accepted that the control of absenteeism depends partly on successfully addressing the physical and emotional needs of employees. These measures are also based on the assumption that absenteeism is the result of employee withdrawal from dissatisfying aspects of the job. The implementation of a high-performance work culture has been one particular strategy utilized by organizations, with a particular emphasis on ensuring employees have an adequate "fit" in the organization.

Other organizations have pursued more flexible work practices that meet the needs of both the organization and its employees. Such measures are based on the assumption that absenteeism is due to the inadequacies associated with existing arrangements, and that the curbing of absences requires providing employees with greater control over when and where they work. The initiatives that have been found to be most successful in reducing levels of unscheduled absences are the implementation of alternative work arrangements, compressed work weeks, job sharing, and telecommuting.

Job redesign has also been the focus of many human resource initiatives aimed at combating absenteeism. Measures such as job enlargement, job rotation, and job enrichment have the impact of increasing the scope of jobs and the skills required to perform them, thus making a typically routine and mundane task more interesting and challenging. Organizations have also implemented more preventative occupational health and safety strategies in order to minimize absences related to workers compensation.

While absenteeism has historically been viewed as an indicator of the adjustment of employees to the workplace, there has been limited attention paid to the social context within which such adjustments occur. The last two decades, however, have been defined by an increased consciousness of the implications of social context on absence behaviors. The emphasis on the social approach has emerged through observations into absenteeism in organizations; in particular, the variations in absence rates across different units and social groups within departments, departments within organizations, and organizations within industries. This has led some researchers to suggest the presence of absence cultures in certain organizational contexts.

See Also: Employer–Employee Relations; Job Enrichment; Motivation.

Bibliography. M. Buschak, C. Cravem, and R. Ledman, "Managing Absenteeism for Great Productivity," *SAM Advanced Management Journal* (1996); R. Isherwood, "The Financial Effects of Absence from Work," *Bulletin of Industrial Psychology and Personnel Practice* (1952); R. M. Steers and S. R. Rhodes, "Major Influences on Employee Attendance: A Process Model," *Journal of Applied Psychology* (1978); J. C. Thomas and M. Hersen, *A Handbook of Mental Health in the Workplace* (Sage, 2002).

ZEENOBIYAH HANNIF
UNIVERSITY OF WOLLONGONG

On American farms, a ton of wheat can be produced with only one hour of labor, versus four hours in the rest of the world.

Absolute Advantage

The argument that countries differ in their ability to produce goods efficiently, and hence one country may have an advantage in the production of a product that is absolute over any other country in producing it is called absolute advantage. Efficiency is defined as producing with a minimum of waste, expense, or unnecessary effort, and therefore includes low cost, fewer resources, and fewer labor hours.

Writing about agricultural trade, Luther Tweeten argues that the United States has an absolute advantage in wheat production because only one hour of labor is required to produce a ton of wheat versus four hours to produce a ton of wheat in the rest of the world. In contrast, elsewhere in the world sugar production requires two hours of labor versus three in the United States to produce one ton of sugar. Because labor supply is limited and transferable between commodities but not between countries, wheat output (elsewhere in the world) is forgone to produce sugar. Similarly, the United States forgoes the expenditure of three hours of labor to produce one ton of sugar to produce three tons of wheat.

While the concept of absolute advantage is closely associated with David Ricardo, the concept actually originated with Adam Smith's 1776 book *The Wealth of Nations.* According to Smith, countries should specialize in the production of goods for which they have an absolute advantage and trade these goods for goods produced by other countries. Smith's argument is that a country should never produce goods at home that it can buy at a lower cost from other countries. Smith demonstrates that, by specializing in the production of goods in which each country has an absolute advantage, countries will benefit by engaging in trade.

Smith was attempting to explain the process by which markets and production actually operate in society. Absolute advantage is an extension of Smith's concept of the division of labor in the production process to a division of labor and specialized product across countries. As Smith observed the production processes of the early stages of the industrial revolution in England, he saw that fundamental changes were occurring. Whereas, in earlier days, a worker performed all stages of the production process, producing enough output for his own needs only, the factories of the industrializing world were separating production into distinct stages. Each stage would be performed exclusively by one individual, hence the division of labor. This specialization increased the production of workers and industries.

David Ricardo expanded Adam Smith's argument to consider the case of a country that has an absolute advantage in the production of all goods. In that case, would such a country derive any benefit from trade? In his *Principles of Political Economy*, Ricardo argued that it made sense for a country to produce those goods that it produces more efficiently and to buy from other countries those goods that it produces comparatively less efficiently. This is the concept of *comparative advantage*, with which Smith's absolute advantage is often confused.

While the industrialized world may have absolute advantage in the production of many commodities, much of the world's natural resources are to be found in developing countries, from which they are mined, quarried, or extracted and shipped overseas for refining and fabrication where high levels of infrastructure (particularly utilities and transportation), skilled labor, and capital are available. Mashaalah Rahnama-Moghadam and colleagues argue that the occurrence of natural resources in the less developed countries might suggest that economic growth had a base in those countries, but the lack of requisite economic resources has made these natural resources little more than export commodities.

Where absolute advantage derives from a unique natural resource, Raineesh Narula and other international trade and business scholars argue that current and future domestic and international investment activity will be focused on those industries related to the exploitation of this resource, often delaying the development of industry in such countries. Countries with an absolute advantage in scarce natural resources, like Norway and Australia, are likely to receive a larger amount of inward investment from home countries that need scarce resources as inputs to higher value production. Resource-poor countries would seek to acquire these resources through outward direct investment. Hence, absolute advantage dictates foreign direct investment strategy.

Vivek Suneya takes this thought further, considering capital itself a scarce resource. He argues that when capital is mobile it will seek its absolute advantage by migrating to countries where the environmental and social costs of enterprises are lowest and profits are highest. While greater productivity and efficiency are a strong argument for offshore outsourcing, Suneya would counter that unrestricted global capital mobility does not serve the needs of society, specifically the preservation of social cohesion and the avoidance of mass unemployment.

See Also: Comparative Advantage; Competitive Advantages of Nations; Economies of Scale; Free Trade.

Bibliography. Panos Angelopoulos and Panos Mourdoukoutas, *Banking Risk Management in a Globalizing Economy* (Quorum Books, 2001); Jeffry A. Frieden and David A. Lake, *International Political Economy: Perspec-* *tives on Global Power and Wealth* (Routledge, 2000); Bruce E. Moon, *Dilemma of International Trade* (Westview Press, 2000); Raineesh Narula, *Multinational Investment and Economic Structure: Globalisation and Competitiveness* (Routledge, 1996); Mashaalah Rahnama-Moghadam, Hedayeh Samavati, and David A Dilts, *Doing Business in Less Developed Countries: Financial Opportunities and Risks* (Quorum Books, 1995); Vivek Suneja, *Understanding Business: A Multidimensional Approach to the Market Economy* (Routledge, 2000); Luther Tweeten, *Agricultural Trade: Principles and Policies* (Westview Press, 1992); Alvin G. Wint, *Corporate Management in Developing Countries: The Challenge of International Competitiveness* (Quorum Books, 1995).

Carol M. Connell
CUNY–Brooklyn College

Academy of International Business

The Academy of Education for International Business (AEIB) is a professional body that was created on November 17, 1958, and became operational in 1959 to foster "the creation and dissemination of knowledge about international business and policy issues." In 1974 the association was renamed the Academy of International Business (AIB).

Today, AIB has more than 3,000 members from 73 countries and is organized into 14 regional chapters geographically: six in Asia and southeast Asia (Australia–New Zealand, China [Beijing], Japan, Korea, Hong Kong, and India); six in North America (one in Canada and five in the United States [midwest, northwest, southwest, southeast, and west]); and two in Europe: Western Europe (Copenhagen) and United Kingdom–Ireland. The Academy is administered by the Dean of Fellows, elected every three years by the body of Fellows of AIB, and the Secretary-Treasurer who is appointed by the Dean "to assist in the affairs of the Fellows Group."

The stated objectives of the association according to its constitution are (1) to facilitate knowledge sharing; (2) to encourage and foster research activities, and bring together professionals from academia, business, and government; (3) to enhance education in international business and through international cooperation; and (4) to promote internationalization. These objectives are pursued through the organization of international and regional conferences and AIB publications that focus on the multicultural background of its participants and the interdisciplinary methodology of its research.

The AIB organizes yearly international conferences. From 1959 until 1985 the conferences were held in North America (two in Canada and 25 in the United States). However, since then, the location has varied significantly (nine in the United States, five in Europe, three in Asia and Canada, and one each in Australia, Mexico, and Puerto Rico). Each regional chapter holds yearly conferences and is responsible for the chapter's publications.

AIB publishes the *Journal of International Business Studies* (JIBS), a highly rated journal according to the Social Science Citation Index. In 2007 it was rated seventh out of 72 in the business category and 10th out of 81 in the management category.

The formation of the AIB Fellows was first brought up in April 1975 by Phillip Grub and Jean Boddewyn (AIB president and vice president at the time) and finally came into existence in 1978 with the appointment of the first president of the AIB Fellows by Richard Farmer, Lee Nehrt. The purposes of the Fellows are "to recognize outstanding contributions to the field of international business, and to provide a forum for discussion among its members," as it is stated in the constitution of the association voted in January 1978. Fellows "shall be international-business teachers, researchers, and administrators—who have significantly helped develop knowledge and practice in the field." The body of the AIB Fellows consists of all past presidents and executive secretaries, full-time teachers and researchers, members of the AIB and non-academic members, "entrepreneurs and managers of private and public organizations mainly devoted to international business." The members are elected by the majority of the Fellows group (since the 1992 amendment) for life.

The original constitution has been amended six times through 2008. These amendments concerned the number, requirements, election process, and structure of the body of Fellows. The most important amendments that are currently applicable to the group of AIB Fellows are two. First, in 1985, the purpose of the Fellows was broadened to include "the exercise of leadership in the field of International Business," and the initial requirement of one-fifth of the body to be nonacademic entrepreneurs and managers was dropped. Second, with the 1997 amendment the number of Fellows was set at 60 under the age of 66 (the number was initially 100, then in 1982 it was limited to 50, excluding the over-70 Fellows). In 2006–07 the maximum of AIB fellows that can be elected each year was (again) raised to five.

See Also: Management Education; Management Research; Management Science.

Bibliography. Academy of International Business, aib.msu.edu (cited June 2008); Jean Boddewyn, *International Business Scholarship AIB Fellows on the First 50 Years and Beyond* (JAI Press, 2008).

Elena Kosmopoulou
University of Patras

Accountability

This concept comprises many alternative meanings and connotations. Although a typical definition would suggest the fundamental notion involved is one of responsibility to someone, or for some action (and both elements could be present simultaneously, of course), there is the added dimension of the need to actually render an account (i.e., of one's conduct) to a superior person or authority so that the adequacy of the level of performance might (retrospectively) be judged.

At a general level, accountability is the basis of agency theory, whereby an appointed agent needs to demonstrate that they have exercised due discretion in the execution of the principal's best interests—although academics for many years have pointed out the implicit encouragement, because of the existence of reward structures that benefit the agent, for that agent to falsify records of activities undertaken on their principal's behalf. The Parable of the Unjust Steward is a classic case here, in which the steward, likely to be dismissed because of his poor performance, encouraged his master's debtors to falsify the amounts owing so as to curry favor with them and thereby achieve the potential for future employment when dismissed from his present job.

At the more specific (i.e., corporate) level, the concept of accountability finds expression in organizational legitimacy theory. This suggests there is a social contract between businesses and the society in which they operate, and that this mandate to exist might be withdrawn should those businesses not be seen as doing things of which society approves. This makes businesses "accountable" and only by rendering an indication of that accountability (and "account" in this context should not be interpreted as necessarily a financial one) is satisfaction achieved.

Not surprisingly, therefore, a thesaurus will suggest "responsibility," "liability," "culpability," "answerability," and "chargeability" as accepted synonyms. Additionally, increasing concern in the early years of the 21st century that good governance should be practiced by governments and nonprofit organizations, as well as by commercial concerns, means that "transparency" is additionally becoming perceived as an essential ingredient in the process—although it has been suggested that while accountability allows for feedback regarding a decision or action only after the event, transparency enables such reporting during, or even before, the relevant event. This has resulted in greater pressure than ever before being put on businesses to be more accountable regarding their actions as they affect both society and the environment.

Many different forms of accountability have been identified, with no less than eight types presently in vogue: moral, administrative, political, managerial, market, legal/judicial, constituency relation, and professional. Although most of these variations on the accountability theme are relatively straightforward, "constituency relation" is potentially obscure. This type of accountability relates to members of agencies representing citizens' interests in a particular domain, and possessing political rights and (more specifically) a government's obligation to empower such members to run for election; or, alternatively, to appoint them to public sector positions such as to hold government accountable and ensure that all relevant constituencies are heard in the policymaking process.

In Britain (as elsewhere in the developed world) accountability has been formally enshrined as a crucial principle of national government since the mid-1990s, at which time it became accepted that holders of public office should perceive themselves as accountable for both their decisions and actions to their public. Additionally, politicians should be prepared to submit themselves to whatever level of scrutiny appears appropriate to the office they hold.

Outside government, business, and nonprofit organizations, accountability has found extension to such things as nongovernmental organizations (NGOs) with their development of the International Non-Governmental Organisations' Accountability Charter, so as to encourage signatory NGOs to work globally in the advancement of human rights, sustainable development, environmental protection, humanitarian response, and other "public goods"; and international aid agencies such as the World Bank and International Monetary Fund (IMF). This last development raises an interesting question regarding to whom a specific body might be considered accountable. While it is the developing nations who receive the beneficence of aid programs, it is the more wealthy nations in the world who provide the wherewithal. So are the World Bank and IMF accountable to the givers or to the receivers?

Various bodies have appeared to promote the accountability agenda, probably most significantly AccountAbility, which for example, produces an annual AccountAbility Rating that measures the extent to which companies put responsible practices at the heart of their business (with the 2007 "winner" being the British petroleum giant BP). AccountAbility is also concerned with specific countries' efforts to advance global competitiveness based on responsible business practices (in which endeavor it has recruited the expertise of Nobel laureate Al Gore). The intention is to provide a unique health check on responsible globalization, in addition to identifying major opportunities for more responsible marketing, taking into account factors such as climate change, human rights, anticorruption, and gender issues.

See Also: Corporate Governance; Corporate Social Responsibility; Corruption.

Bibliography. A. Schedler, "Conceptualizing Accountability," in A. Schedler, L. Diamond, and M. F. Plattner, *The Self-Restraining State: Power and Accountability in*

New Democracies (Lynne Rienner Publishers, 1999); D. G. Woodward, P. Edwards, and F. Birkin, "Organizational Legitimacy and Stakeholder Information Provision," *British Journal of Management* (v.7, 1996).

David G. Woodward
University of Southampton

Accounting Harmonization

Accounting harmonization is the process of minimizing the differences in financial reporting practices across national boundaries. Accounting is a social science, and accounting practice varies across countries due to differences in culture, religion, history, legal and taxation systems, financing and business ownership systems, and level of economic development.

In recent decades, the process of globalization has created the demand for accounting harmonization through investors' awareness that difference in accounting practice due to different rules discourages cross-border investments. Accounting harmonization is also beneficial for multinational corporations operating and raising capital in different countries. Further, accounting harmonization can provide significant cost savings in staff training, and offers mobility and flexibility for public accounting firms.

Attempts to harmonize accounting standards and accounting practice internationally were initiated by the London-based accounting body called the International Accounting Standards Committee (IASC). The IASC was established in June 1973 as a result of an agreement by accountancy bodies in Australia, Canada, France, Germany, Japan, Mexico, the Netherlands, the United Kingdom and Ireland, and the United States. It was created with two key objectives: (1) to formulate and publish accounting standards for global acceptance and observance; and (2) to work for the improvement and harmonization of accounting regulation, standards, and reporting internationally. In the early years of the IASC, its standards were too broad and thus were ineffective in improving comparability of financial statements internationally.

In the late 1980s, the International Organization of Securities Commissions (IOSCO), a body comprising national securities regulators, had realized that having a single set of accounting standards internationally had the potential for significantly reducing the reporting costs for multinational companies wishing to raise capital across national boundaries. Subsequently, the IASC undertook a project to make its standards more restrictive and hence more acceptable to the IOSCO. By 1999 the IASC had revised its core standards, which were accepted by the IOSCO members with the exception of the U.S. Securities and Exchange Commission.

The IASC was superseded by the International Accounting Standards Board (IASB) in 2001. The IASB had adopted all of the IASC standards and embarked on issuing new standards under the name International Financial Reporting Standards (IFRS). The IFRS has since gained widespread acceptance among national regulators permitting or requiring publicly listed companies to comply with them in their financial reporting. As a result, in recent years, adoption of the IFRS has become the dominant trend rather than focusing on harmonization. One of the main obstacles for global adoption of IFRS is the United States's continuing reluctance to give up its own standards on the suspicion that IFRS are of lower quality and less comprehensive than the U.S. standards issued by the Financial Accounting Standards Board (FASB).

In recent years, however, the FASB and the IASB have launched several joint projects in order to minimize differences between the FASB standards and the IFRS. In 2002, at a meeting in Norwalk, Connecticut, the IASB and the FASB agreed to harmonize their agenda and reduce differences between the IFRS and the FASB standards. In 2006 a Memorandum of Understanding was issued by the two standard setters to work toward achieving convergence between the IFRS and the FASB standards. Some progress has been made in this direction, although slowly. For example, since October 2004, the IASB and the FASB have had an ongoing project to develop a common conceptual framework. As of June 2008, these two bodies have several joint projects to develop standards.

A recent development is the concession offered to foreign companies in the United States with regard to their financial reporting. Previously, foreign companies listed on the U.S. stock exchanges were required to issue their financial statements using either FASB standards or local accounting standards or IFRS and reconciling the IFRS- or local standards–based income to the FASB standards. Since 2008 foreign companies that are listed on U.S. stock exchanges and issue financial statements based on IFRS no longer are required to do this reconciliation.

See Also: Auditing Standards; Corporate Accounting; Disclosure Requirements; International Accounting Standards Board; International Financial Reporting Standards; Securities and Exchange Commission.

Bibliography. E. N. Emenyonu and S. J. Gray, "International Accounting Harmonization and the Major Developed Stock Market Countries: An Empirical Study," *The International Journal of Accounting* (1996); J. Fowler, "The Future Shape of Harmonization: The EU versus the IASC versus the SEC," *European Accounting Review* (1997); R. D. Nair and W. G. Frank, "The Harmonization of International Accounting Standards, 1973–1979," *The International Journal of Accounting* (1981); C. Nobes and R. Parker, *Comparative International Accounting* (Pearson Education, 2002).

REZA MONEM
GRIFFITH UNIVERSITY BUSINESS SCHOOL

Accounting Information Systems

The field of accounting information systems (AIS) combines that of accounting with the much newer field of information systems, systems that include people, processes, procedures, and information technology in a flexible resource used to handle data. Specifically, accounting information systems are a subset of management information systems, systems designed to support and supplement the decision-making process at all levels of management. The field of AIS includes the use, design, and implementation of such systems, and their adherence to traditional accounting methods and contemporary standards in accounting practices.

On the technology front, AIS systems usually include computers—ranging from ordinary personal computers, to specialized workstations, to dedicated servers for processing large amounts of data—equipped with scanners (for data entry) and internet access, compatible with electronic data interchange (EDI), and set up to print out various financial reports. Applica-

tions generally cover procedures and reporting areas like budgeting, inventory, assets, purchasing, accounts payable, accounts receivable, and billing, as well as human resources applications like benefits and pension administration, payroll, and time sheets.

AIS systems can cover everything from complicated financial management planning that would take significant man hours to compute and double-check, to basic transaction processing. Generally speaking, everyday business transactions—buying, selling, and producing—will be recorded, summarized, and classified at the time of recording, making it easy to access data for new modules after the time of transaction. Depending on the nature of the business, cost accounting systems may be put in place in order to track production costs of goods or the efficiency of services—or analytical systems may track performance and highlight areas where resource allocation can be improved. Management is typically given greater access to this information than employees.

The development and needs-tailoring of an AIS is a five-stage process. As with all systems development, planning comes first, with the objectives and scope of the system made explicit. The analysis stage documents the processes in use, reviews the types of data generated or recorded by the business, and analyzes what can be automated, streamlined, or otherwise altered. Sometimes most significantly, the analysis stage also registers what sorts of decisions management employees make on a regular basis, often with the result of identifying areas in which AIS can be applied that were not foreseen in the planning stage. The analysis can take a long time, particularly if the nature of the business is such that it must be observed for a lengthy period of time in order to collect a full set of data (businesses subject to seasonal impacts, for instance, like restaurants facing crowds on Valentine's Day or resorts dealing with seasonal slumps, should ideally be monitored for the full year, or incorporate information from a model based on such a set of observations).

The third stage, design, develops elements of the proposed system based on the results of the analysis. Typically, flowcharts or other visual reports are used to present the designs of processes and some other elements. Part of the design stage involves identifying the reports that will be generated by the AIS, and the form they will take. Not all information collected should be present in standard reports, or the critical information will be lost to the casual glance; at the same time, reports should be tailored to their expected audience, not only in content but in presentation. Extensive software options are available to assist in the design stage.

The implementation stage involves the construction and delivery of the system, as well as the testing and security checks thereof. This may require a conversion sub-stage if the AIS is going to replace any processes or systems in use at the business. Finally, the support stage, which continues long after the AIS has been put into use, updates and maintains the AIS, confirms that it is performing as intended and expected, and reevaluates the business to see if further improvements can be made.

See Also: Accounting Software; Cost Accounting; Disclosure Requirements; Information Systems; Management Information Systems; Managerial Accounting.

Bibliography. Nancy A. Bagranoff, Mark G. Simkin, and Carolyn Strand Norman, *Core Concepts of Accounting Information Systems* (John Wiley & Sons, 2008); James A. Hall, *Accounting Information Systems* (South-Western College Publishing, 2008); Marshall B. Romney and Paul J. Steinbart, *Accounting Information Systems* (Prentice Hall, 2008).

Bill Kte'pi
Independent Scholar

Accounting Software

Accounting software is a type of computer program that carries out accounting functions. This software has now largely replaced older paper accounting systems. The software may be in the form of packages or written specially to meet a business's unique requirements. Accounting modules include the general ledger, accounts receivable, accounts payable, payroll, inventory, and fixed assets, and integrated accounting software usually links a number of these modules together. Data from one module are transferred to another module; for example, updating accounts payable automatically updates the general ledger.

The general ledger module is central to the whole accounting system. A small business may find that a general ledger module is adequate. The general ledger module typically produces a chart of accounts, journals, trial balance, general ledger, and financial statements. An accounts receivable module is needed where there are significant amounts of sales transactions. The accounts receivable module assists cash flow and credit policy. Receivables from customers are tracked, reconciled, invoiced, and aged. An accounts payable module is needed only when numerous checks are written. The frequency of the system may be weekly, semi-monthly, or monthly, depending on the availability of cash discounts and the number of transactions. The accounts payable package makes out checks to vendors, assures the receipt of discounts and prepares an aging of payables.

Payroll software aids in determining the payroll deposit and offers needed payroll data at tax reporting time. A good fixed asset package could provide description and categorization of assets; number of assets accommodated; cost, life, and salvage value for fixed assets; allowance for different depreciation methods; pro-rata depreciation calculation and fixed asset cost center.

In purchasing accounting software, compatibility, efficiency, integration, and cost are considerations. It is better to purchase individual modules from one supplier. At the low end, commercial programs are available at around $100. Low-cost accounting software programs focus on cash flow and profitability functions, which small business owners are most concerned with. Two examples of inexpensive small business accounting software are *Quickbooks* by Intuit and *Peachtree* products. They are scalable products that may be upgraded as a business grows. Low-end accounting software can be a fairly good accounting information system solution for businesses with less than $10 million per year in revenues and fewer than 100 employees.

When transaction processing needs grow in volume and complexity, a mid-range software package may be a better solution. Some examples are Microsoft's *Dynamics GP* and Sage Software's *MAS 90, Everest,* and *Accpac.* With these programs, modules cost several hundred dollars each and are usually sold separately. Many international companies do their business globally and need software to handle transactions in multiple currencies. This software can convert transactions from one currency to another and can even write checks in foreign currencies. Another example of a specialized feature that may be included in higher-end accounting software is the ability to split commissions among multiple salespersons.

The number of transactions processed monthly is one important factor in the choice between low-end and high-end software. If a company processes only a few accounts receivable transactions daily, an inexpensive package should handle this processing satisfactory. Transferability is also important: Each time one changes software, employees may need to reenter all transaction data. Cost savings are great when the software vendor offers programs that allow data to be imported automatically into higher-end products.

See Also: Accounting Information Systems; Cost Accounting; International Accounting Standards Board; International Financial Reporting Standards; Managerial Accounting.

Bibliography. Nancy A. Bagranoff, Mark G. Simkin, and Carolyn Strand Norman, *Core Concepts of Accounting Information Systems* (John Wiley & Sons, 2008); James A. Hall, *Accounting Information Systems* (South-Western Cengage Learning, 2008).

TAI MING WUT
INDEPENDENT SCHOLAR

Account Settlement

Account settlement is a non-American term showing the summation of commercial activity of a business during its fiscal year. Companies will use the account settlement to paint a picture that investors use to determine whether they will invest in the company. Some of the key terms of an account settlement are defined below.

Net sales: Gross sales is the total amount in currency (such as euros) of goods sold during a particular period. Normally, this would be the company's fiscal year. This may or may not coincide with the country's calendar year. Net sales is the total amount of sales in currency minus any returns, deductions for damaged goods, or discounts.

Operating income: This figure shows the power of the company to earn money. Operating income is the total amount the company earns before deducting interest payments and taxes. Investors can use year-on-year comparisons to determine whether the company is improving or not improving. Some companies will simply state this as profit before taxation.

Ordinary income: Sometimes companies can beef up their income levels by selling property or other capital holdings. In order to see a "bottom line" of income from the companies' commercial activities, companies will publish their ordinary income, or income from things other than capital gains (selling land, factories, etc.).

Net income: Net income is the bottom line of whether a company is making money. Net income is a company's total revenue minus expenses needed to produce the revenue (salaries, materials, etc.), taxes, depreciation, and interest payments. This figure is one of the key figures (if not the key figure) investors use to determine whether they will invest in a company.

Operating margin: Companies express operating margins as percentages. Operating margin divides operating income by net sales. Operating margin seeks to take out variable costs so that investors can see how well the company can pay off fixed assets like debt or capital investments.

Earnings per share: Earnings per share is another figure used by investors to determine whether the company is profitable and worthy of more investment. While earnings per share can be slightly different depending on how it is defined, generally, earnings per share is income minus dividends of preferred stock (as opposed to an ordinary stock share which we are measuring here) divided by the number of outstanding shares. What makes this tricky is that the number of shares outstanding can fluctuate. Additionally, some overseas companies will remove "minority interests" income from their profit. Minority interests income is income from a company's investment in another company.

In addition to these key terms, the account settlement can be broken down by individual business units for large companies. For instance, if one were to look at British Petroleum's (BP's) account settlement, one would find account settlement for exploration and production, refining and marketing, and other small business units (alternative energy, shipping, treasury, aluminum asset, and other corporate activities) listed as Other Business and Corporate—Financial Statistics.

Finally, the account settlement will offer a narrative of future operations. Included in this narrative can also be a bridge between how recent acquisitions or operational expenses that may have weighed heavily in the current fiscal statement will bring about greater profit/income in future income statements. If a catastrophic event occurred (i.e., Hurricane Katrina), this impact may be mentioned here also.

See Also: Accounting Harmonization; Capital Account Balance; International Accounting Standards Board; Variable Costs.

Bibliography. British Petroleum, *Annual F&OI*, www .bp.com (cited March 2009); "Earnings Per Share," Moneyterms.co.uk (cited July 2008); "Operating Income/ Net Sales/Operating Margin/Net Income," InvestorWords .com (cited March 2009).

Charles R. Fenner, Jr.
SUNY–Canton

Acculturation

Acculturation refers to the adaptation process experienced by individuals or groups when settling into an unfamiliar culture. Whereas some migrating groups may seek to integrate with the host culture, others may choose to maintain their cultural roots and separate themselves from the "new" dominant culture. In a world where both temporary and permanent migration continue to increase it is vital to understand the challenges faced by such individuals and the strategies they employ to survive. Whereas previously migrating groups were not considered as viable segments to target with products and services, increasing immigrant numbers have alerted marketers to the potential profitability of these groups.

Since the term *acculturation* was first formally used by Robert E. Park in 1928 to describe the adaptation of immigrants, the earliest attempts at understanding the acculturation process were conducted in the fields of anthropology and sociology. However, since the 1980s business researchers have shown greater interest in the concept in light of the increasing market value of various immigrant groups. As many of the most prominent acculturation researchers were located in North America, empirical work concentrated on the large numbers of Hispanic immigrants who sought to settle in the United States. Today, the emphasis of most research is still on groups moving away from lesser-developed nations, though researchers have broadened their focus to encapsulate a wider array of migrating groups, including Chinese workers moving to Australasia, Eastern Europeans fleeing their home nations due to civil war, and Italians migrating to Canada.

In the early 1900s the U.S. Immigration Commission was established in response to growing public fears that U.S. culture was under threat from the increasing number and variety of immigrant groups. This uncertainty as to the role of immigrants in U.S. society led to the "melting pot model" (discussed below), which ensured that all immigrants relinquished their previous cultural traits and instead assimilated into everyday U.S. life. This policy led to the term *assimilation* becoming the commonly used term instead of acculturation. Indeed, terms such as *cultural interpenetration* and *ethnic identity* have also been used in studies to address the same process. This myriad of terms that essentially cover similar issues have been thought to have slowed down researchers' attempts to truly understand the process.

The Process
Acculturation typically occurs when two or more cultures are brought into continuous, firsthand contact (be it on an enforced or voluntary basis). The triggers for such cross-cultural interaction have included political unrest between nations, invasion, or even enslavement. More recently, acculturation has also been triggered by international trade agreements, educational or missionary activity, and transnational media. Acculturating groups face a number of obstacles in adapting to a new way of life and these can be particularly challenging in the early stages of their acculturation. Depending on the migrating group, these problems can include language difficulties, financial hardship, homesickness, loneliness, discrimination, and in some cases outright racial abuse. Historically, acculturation has been seen to be a four-step process that includes both positive and negative emotions for an immigrant:

- Honeymoon: Soon after migration, the immigrant enjoys a fascination with the host culture, where there is little firsthand contact or conflict.
- Rejection: In time, the immigrant may feel some homesickness and start to unfavorably compare the host culture with their previous life. This can result in negative and aggressive attitudes to their new home.
- Tolerance: In time, the intensity of these emotions will lessen and the immigrant will begin to acquire the skills and knowledge needed to survive in the new environment.
- Integration: The immigrant develops a confidence in the new culture, conflict decreases, and the new home becomes "another way of life."

Although each individual's experiences will vary, the above process does provide insight into the sorts of emotions experienced by immigrants upon arrival in an unfamiliar culture. The following discussion focuses on two models that describe strategies employed by immigrants to deal with the process.

The Melting Pot Model

Particularly in Western societies, initial reactions to immigrant groups have been very cautious. It was often unclear why such groups had moved to another society and, as a result, they were considered a threat not only by senior politicians but also the general population. In order to ensure that the cultural values of the dominant society were maintained, immigrants were often given no choice but to assimilate into society and lose all connections with their home country. This process became widely known as assimilation or the melting pot model, and was the dominant school of acculturative thought until as recently as the 1960s.

Although such an approach provided security for the host culture, it also meant that immigrants were not contributing to the cultural profile of the country. Immigrants were often considered the underclass of that particular society, and were largely confined to lower-grade employment and ignored by permanent residents. Immigrants were given no formal assistance in how to assimilate, and those who attempted to "integrate" by combining their previous cultural traits with those of the dominant society were deemed to be marginal and faced further sanctions from society.

A common outcome of the assimilation process was "overshooting": in their desperation to become members of the dominant culture, immigrants adopt extreme, overt behaviors they have observed from permanent residents. However, such behaviors were often perceived as artificial and failed to earn the acceptance of the host population.

Given the ethnocentric nature of the melting pot model, it is not surprising that social scientists began to criticize this approach from the 1960s. It has been suggested that as migrating groups became a more common phenomenon, assimilation became a less likely outcome of the acculturation process. Instead, immigrants started to show an increased willingness to retain some if not all of their original culture, particularly in countries such as Canada that are known for their culturally pluralist policies.

The Bi-Dimensional Model

In response to the growing criticism of the melting pot model, social scientists began to search for an alternative acculturation framework that accepted that assimilation was not the only strategy available to immigrants. In 1980 John W. Berry suggested that the choice of an immigrant's acculturation strategy or style could be determined by two questions: first, does the immigrant wish to retain elements of their original culture, and second, are relationships with the host culture to be developed? The answers to these questions led to the development of four acculturation styles that are widely regarded as the most comprehensive means of understanding the acculturation process:

- Assimilation: The traditional acculturation view that immigrants must relinquish their original cultural traits is now regarded as one potential option available to immigrants. This may remain a common outcome of the acculturation process in more mono-cultural societies.
- Integration: Whereas previously immigrants who attempted to combine cultures were regarded as marginal, this bicultural approach to acculturation is now regarded as the most suitable way for an immigrant to adapt. This is characterized by an attempt to forge friendships with members of various cultures, and may result in traits of the immigrant group becoming part of the dominant society's culture.

- Separation: The polar opposite of the assimilation outcome is when the immigrant shows no desire to become part of the host culture and instead retains all elements of their previous culture. This can lead to the development of separate cultural communities and a degree of distance being maintained from the dominant culture, which may result in conflict between various cultural groups.
- Marginalization: A previously ignored outcome of the acculturation process is when individuals become alienated by the whole experience, fail to integrate with the dominant society, and at the same time lose all links with their original culture. This is regarded as the most psychologically damaging acculturation outcome and may be the result of a failed attempt to integrate or assimilate.

This bi-dimensional model offers a number of potential acculturation outcomes and accepts that immigrants may not wish to simply assimilate. More recent research has identified integration as the best outcome in terms of lower stress levels; however, separation has become a particularly common strategy for immigrants in the United Kingdom and the United States.

A number of determinants are relevant in which of the above acculturation strategies are adopted by immigrants. In terms of demographic factors, it has been shown that second-generation immigrants are most likely to integrate: they will be encouraged to maintain their cultural heritage by family at home, but will have regular contact with the host culture through school and friendship networks. In general, later generations are more likely to become involved with the host culture, although this may be a source of intrafamily conflict with older generations. In addition, it is expected that younger, better-educated immigrants will show a greater propensity to integrate into dominant society, largely because they will have greater opportunities to interact with members of other cultures.

Another key issue in acculturation is the language ability of the immigrant. As communication is the primary means by which different cultures interact, those with stronger language skills will find it easier to forge new relationships. An inability to speak the host culture language can result in difficulties in finding employment, being a consumer, and even dealing with the country's welfare system.

The triggers of the acculturation process are also of particular relevance here; if the immigrants have been forced into a new environment because of war or political unrest, this will reduce their desire to assimilate or integrate. However, for those who are moving to another culture for personal reasons (for example, career or educational advancement) this may result in a heightened desire to understand and become involved with the host culture.

The level of cultural distance between the two cultures in question can also be significant in the acculturation process. For example, Chinese immigrants moving to the United Kingdom are more likely to struggle moving from a collectivist to an individualist culture. In some situations, the presence of racial prejudice may also act as a barrier to acculturation: The bi-dimensional model discussed above assumes that the host culture allows the immigrant to choose their preferred acculturation strategy. In reality, the host culture may well impose integration (in the case of a pluralist nation) or even separation if a significant level of discrimination exists.

As well as posing obvious challenges for the migrating groups, acculturation can also put pressures on various elements of the host culture: A substantial number of immigrants can place pressure on public services such as schools, hospitals, and other local amenities. Also, local authorities can face difficulties housing immigrants, and a lack of skills means that many struggle to find employment and depend on the welfare state. National governments have to find a delicate balance between welcoming a culturally diverse society while at the same time implementing measures to ensure such immigration does not cause unrest among the general population.

See Also: Cross-Border Migrations; Culture Shock; Ethnocentrism; Expatriate; Reentry.

Bibliography. W. Flannery, S. Reise, and J. Yu, "An Empirical Comparison of Acculturation Models," *Personality and Social Psychology Bulletin*, (v.27, 8, 2001); R. Maldonado and P. Tansuhaj, "Transition Challenges in Consumer Acculturation: Role Destabilisation and Changes in Symbolic Consumption," *Advances in Consumer Research*, (v.26/1, 1999); M. Novas, M. Garcia, J. Sanchez, A. Rojas, P. Pumares, and J. Fernandez, "Relative Acculturation Extended Model (RAEM): New Contributions with Regards to the Study of Acculturation," *International Journal of Intercultural Relations* (v.29, 2005); A. M. Padilla, ed., *Acculturation: Theory, Models and Some New Findings* (Westview Press, 1980).

David Hart
Newcastle Business School

Achieved Status/ Ascribed Status

Dutch anthropologist Fons Trompenaars and English business professor Charles Hampden-Turner developed seven dimensions of culture that give key insights into successful international trade negotiations. The two researchers studied how people in specific countries resolve dilemmas, and based on an examination of thousands of respondents in over 100 countries, they identified seven basic dimensions for culture. International businesspeople use these dimensions when they design business strategies for different cultures, a task that is particularly important for dealing with emerging markets. One of the dimensions is achieved status versus ascribed status, which is defined below. Applications of the dimension then follow.

The concept of achieved versus ascribed status stems from the work of Talcott Parsons in his studies of social stratification, which Parsons defined as the "differential ranking of human individuals who compose a given social system and their treatment as superior or inferior relative to one another in certain socially important respects." Parsons defines ascribed status as that which results from birth or biological hereditary qualities, such as sex, age, or inherited socioeconomic status. At the other end of the spectrum, Parsons proposes that achieved status results from personal actions, such as that accomplished through talent and hard work.

Achievement Cultures

Trompenaars and Hampden-Turner adapt Parsons' thinking on ascribed versus achieved status to the study of cross-cultural management. Thus, Trompenaars and Hampden-Turner propose that an "achievement culture" is one in which people are accorded status based on how well they perform their functions, while an "ascription culture" is one in which status is attributed based on who or what a person is. Achievement cultures give high status to high achievers, such as the company's top salesperson or the drug researcher who finds a new treatment for controlling blood sugar. In an achievement-oriented culture, the first question someone may ask is "What do you do?" or "What have you done?", thus putting an emphasis on accomplishments.

In achievement cultures, social status can be changed through social mobility, the change of position within the stratification system. Changes in status can be upward or downward. Social mobility is more frequent in societies where achievement rather than ascription accounts for one's social status. Historically, social mobility has been typical of the United States.

Ascription Cultures

Ascription cultures accord status based on age, gender, schools attended, or social connections. Perhaps the most extreme form of ascribed status was the caste system in traditional society in India. Each person's caste group was determined at birth, as children joined their parents' caste group. Moving out of one's caste was virtually impossible as each caste could only perform certain jobs. Unskilled and low-paying jobs were reserved for lower castes, while highly skilled occupations were reserved for other castes.

In organizations in an ascription culture, the person who is part of the "old boys' network" may rise faster in an organization than someone who does not interact with the network. Similarly, an organizational member who has been with the company for 25 years may be listened to more often because of the respect that others have for the person's age and tenure with the firm. Thus, in an ascription-oriented culture, the first question someone might ask is "Where are you from?" or "Who is your family?", focusing on inherent characteristics.

For example, though this is slowly changing, in U.S. culture, males, particularly white males, have a high ascribed status and females have a lower ascribed status. The high ascribed status of males can outweigh many other status and power factors, including high achieved status and high-dominant personality traits in a woman. To counteract the initial ascribed status differences based on sex, research on leadership

Businesspeople from achievement cultures need to be aware of the weight of seniority in contacts with ascription cultures. When Japanese, Koreans, and Singaporeans were polled, 60 percent of respondents felt age alone should confer additional status.

demonstrates that to reduce the power disadvantage experienced by females because of their low ascribed status, women had to be made to appear more competent than men in order to attain the same level within an organization.

To illustrate the influence of achieved status versus ascribed status, Trompenaars and Hampden-Turner asked respondents from different countries whether status should be based on age (an ascribed status). Over 60 percent of American, Australian, British, Canadian, and Swedish respondents disagreed that age should be given special consideration. By contrast, over 60 percent of Japanese, Korean, and Singaporean respondents agreed that age should be given additional status.

Among the ascription cultures are Belgium, Brazil, China, France, Indonesia, Italy, Japan, Singapore, and Venezuela. By contrast, achievement cultures include the United States, the United Kingdom, Argentina, Austria, Germany, Mexico, and Spain. Trompenaars further found that nations' cultural values tend to cluster together. He identified five such clusters—an Anglo cluster, an Asian cluster, a Latin American cluster, a Latin European cluster, and a Germanic cluster. While countries within each culture do not share every dimension in common, there are far more similarities with the clusters than there are differences.

Applications

In achievement cultures, an organizational member's title is only used when it is relevant. In addition, superiors earn respect through job performance. Organizations in achievement cultures often have a diversity of age, gender, and race/ethnicity in management positions.

In ascription cultures, the use of titles is expected as a sign of respect. Furthermore, whether or not the superior has earned his or her position through job performance, respect for the superior is integral to showing commitment to the organization. Finally, managers are often chosen based on their background (such as did they graduate from the "right schools") and age.

Trompenaars and Hampden-Turner recommend that when individuals from achievement cultures do business in ascription cultures, they should be aware that such cultures emphasize seniority in the chain of command. Consequently, individuals from achievement cultures make sure that their group has older, senior, and formal position-holders who can impress the other side, especially by respecting the status and influence of their counterparts in the other group. On the other hand, Trompenaars and Hampden-Turner recommend that when individuals from ascription cultures do business in achievement cultures, they need to be aware that firms emphasize rewards and respect based on skills and accomplishments.

In addition, it is common that managers defer to those who possess expertise in certain technical and functional areas of the company. Thus, businesspeople going into achievement cultures should make sure that their group has the resources (such as data, technical advisers, and additional experts) to convince the other group that they respect the knowledge and information of their counterparts in the other company.

See Also: Culture-Specific Values; Hofstedes Five Dimensions of Culture; Individualism/Collectivism; Universalism/Particularism.

Bibliography. Talcott Parsons, "An Analytical Approach to the Theory of Social Stratification," *American Journal of Sociology* (v.45, 1940); Larry Samovar, Richard Porter, and Edwin McDaniel, *Intercultural Communication: A Reader*, 11th ed. (Thomson Wadsworth, 2005); Fons Trompenaars, *Riding the Waves of Culture* (Irwin, 1994); Fons Trompenaars and Charles Hampden-Turner, *Riding the Waves of Culture: Understanding Diversity in Global Business* (McGraw-Hill, 1997).

RODNEY A. CARVETH
UNIVERSITY OF HARTFORD

Acquisitions, Takeovers, and Mergers

Acquisitions, which include mergers and takeovers, are a part of business strategy involving the combination of two or more businesses, with or without the cooperation of all parties. Once a rare occurrence, these maneuvers became a typical part of doing business on a large scale in the 20th century (though the peak came earlier, in the 19th century's Great Merger Movement). Mergers and acquisitions advisory firms have even developed—sometimes calling themselves transition advisors—although most such guidance is still provided by traditional investment banks.

Mergers and acquisitions (or M&A) are more often referred to collectively than not, but are not synonymous. They simply involve many of the same complications and concerns. Further, many mergers are in actuality acquisitions, but termed mergers in order for the acquired company to save face, a condition frequently included in the written agreement. On the other hand, a hostile takeover, when the purchased company resists being acquired, is never called a merger. At least half of acquisition attempts fail, though companies may try repeatedly, and failed attempts can still leave the attempted acquisitor with significant control of the target company. When NASDAQ abandoned its efforts to acquire the London Stock Exchange (LSE), it sold off the shares of stock it had acquired—nearly a third of the LSE—to the Borse Dubai, a stock exchange holding company of the United Arab Emirates.

Advisory

When a financial adviser says he is "in mergers and acquisitions," he usually means he is in corporate advisory, either with an investment bank or with a specialty advisory firm. M&A is the bread and butter of corporate advisory, but the field includes other maneuvers and transactions, such as the privatization of a public company, the spin-off of a portion of a company into a new business, and the management of joint ventures between businesses. The advisers included in such transactions include legal advisers and financial advisers retained by both sides and looking out for the best interests of their respective clients; financiers who arrange funding and attend to other financial concerns of the transaction; and third-party experts, such as consultants specializing in the industry, intellectual property valuation advisors, public relations firms, and so on. The larger the companies involved, the more advisers will generally be called upon, but at a minimum each company will retain legal services, and nearly always at least one financial adviser.

Investment banks like JPMorgan, Goldman Sachs, Morgan Stanley, and Deutsche Bank offer corporate advisory services around the world, and dozens of other investment banks operate regionally or nationally. The strength of an investment bank is its tendency to have fingers in so many pies, a sort of department store of corporate financial services, and although the 2007–08 economic crisis has demonstrated the way in which this becomes a vulnerability, it renders an investment bank's M&A advice no less useful. But since the end of the 20th century, more and more firms have launched offering corporate advisory services exclusively, and have especially been engaged by businesses concerned about investment banks' potential conflicts of interest. Most such firms are run by senior executives who have left investment banks and have considerable experience, networking contacts, and professional relationships in the financial industry. They are sometimes hired to supplement the advice of an investment bank rather than to substitute for it.

Corporate advisory firms tend to be smaller, and to operate in a smaller area, than investment banks; in Europe they are in a sense the descendants of the merchant banks like Lazard and Rothschild (both of which continue to offer corporate advisory services). Major corporate advisory firms operating multinationally include Evercore Partners (which advised AT&T on its BellSouth acquisition and managed the separation of Viacom and CBS Corporation) and Greenhill & Co. (in the aftermath of the 2008 credit crisis, one of the few remaining independent investment banks operating on Wall Street), both of them based in New York with operations in Europe and Tokyo.

Valuation

One of the services offered by advisory firms and investment banks, engaged when considering an acquisition, is business valuation. There are various ways to value a business, and particular methods or information may be more or less valuable in different industries. "Value" itself is not always a straightforward thing, and can be talked about in terms of fair market value (the price an asset would sell for between informed parties on the current market), fair value (largely similar, a term especially used in Generally Accepted Accounting Principles and legal contexts), an intrinsic value, a more subjective measurement that implicitly perceives a flaw or temporariness in the fair market value.

Public companies are in general easier to value than private ones, because the law and their accountability to shareholders has required them to keep financial records that adhere to a certain standard and are audited regularly. Even well-managed private companies may not do so, particularly smaller ones. Further, while it is in the best interest of public companies to emphasize their profits, it is in the best interest of private companies to minimize them to some degree, for the sake of taxes, and financial records will reflect this. Assets of both companies will probably have their original cost and value recorded, rather than their current market values, and valuing the company will thus require reexamining those assets.

The discounted cash flows method of business valuation values assets not according to their cost or their resale value, but their projected cash flows, discounted to the present value. An immature bond that will be worth $20 when it matures is in the present worth less than that, for instance, but nevertheless more than its original cost. The amount by which that future cash flow value is discounted is the discount rate, expressed as a percentage. The example of the bond is a more clear-cut case than most of those faced by the advisors valuing a business: the risk and predictability of return of a bond is very simple compared to that of a restaurant, for instance, or a patent, or a piece of real estate. Two different advisors may come to different conclusions about the discounted cash flow value of an asset, and presenting their reasoning to the prospective buyer is part of the process of considering an acquisition, especially if the acquisition itself will in any way impact that cash flow.

The guideline companies method of business valuation is a benchmark-based method similar to determining the value of an asset like a car or house: the company is compared to other similar companies that have been acquired, with multiples calculated based on differences in areas like price-to-earnings ratio. This has become a more useful method as acquisitions have themselves become more common, as the number of available benchmarks has increased, in some industries more than others.

Intellectual property, like patents and proprietary processes, are especially difficult to value objectively. Various models have been developed, and there are firms that specialize in the valuation of intellectual property, a specialty that has developed principally since the 1990s. In the United States, the most prominent firms in this subfield are Crais Management Group in New Orleans, Ocean Tomo in Chicago, and Intellectual Ventures in Seattle, all of which have supported the treatment of intellectual property as a security-like class of asset, one that could be bought and sold on an exchange, which would strengthen the reliability of intellectual property valuation thanks to the efficiency of the bid/ask system.

Valuing a business generally requires that business's cooperation, especially if it is a privately-owned company. It is standard for both parties to sign a non-disclosure agreement, though the targeted business could still be at a competitive disadvantage should the other business opt not to go ahead with the acquisition. The valuation report includes an account of the current economic conditions at the time of the valuation date, generally derived from the Federal Reserve's Beige Book and state and industry publications, followed by a detailed financial analysis that discusses both the current situation and past trends of growth and decline. Data is reported in such a way as to make comparison to other businesses in the industry as easy and accurate as possible, and certain other adjustments are made to the report as circumstances demand: non-operating assets (which are assumed to be excluded from the hypothetical sale, such as excess cash) are eliminated from the balance sheet, non-recurring items are adjusted so as not to skew the results of the analysis, and the data of private companies is sometimes adjusted to make it comparable to that of public companies. Executives of private companies often earn a higher salary than those of public companies, for instance.

There are three major business valuation societies in the United States: the American Society of Appraisers, the Institute of Business Appraisers, and the National Association of Certified Valuation Analysts. Each publishes a set of Business Valuation Standards for its accredited members to follow. Common among them are certain minimum requirements for the scope and contents of business valuation reports; the proscription against the appraiser's fee being contingent on the value of the business appraised; and a requirement of full disclosure of the institutions and individuals participating in the valuation report.

Financing

Financing an acquisition is another consideration. If called simply "an acquisition," the transaction was probably financed with cash, the simple purchase of a smaller company by a larger one; because businesses do not like to restrict their cash flow if they can help it, this is most common when the size discrepancy between the two companies is greatest, i.e., a global corporation acquiring a local independent business and bringing it into the fold. Money can also be raised through bonds or loans from a bank, and it is common to finance an acquisition through some combination of these things.

Leveraged Buyouts

A leveraged buyout (LBO) is a special type of acquisition, differentiated by the way it is financed. The acquisition—buyout—of another company is financed by loans (leverage), using the assets of the target company as the collateral. The prevalence of junk bonds in the 1980s was due to the number of high-risk leveraged buyouts financed by bond issuance. Over the course of that decade, over $250 billion of leveraged buyouts were made by "corporate raiders" who acquired a total of 2,000 companies.

An early famous example was the Gibson Greetings acquisition, in which a greeting card company was acquired in 1982 for $80 million, only $1 million of which was contributed by the acquiring group; the other $79 million was easily paid back 16 months later when the company went public with an initial public offering (IPO) of $290 million. It was the sort of success story that launched a thousand ships, at the start of a decade that would soon become known for its bottom-line attitude and glorification of greed. The raider label was as likely to be used by businessmen as the media, as these investors would often—or often enough to feed the perception—embark on a hostile takeover of a company, strip its assets, lay off its employees, and restructure the remains, as much like a virus or group of convert-or-die missionaries as like the Vikings and pirates the label invoked.

The 1987 Oliver Stone movie *Wall Street* combines aspects of investors like Carl Icahn and Michael Milken into the corporate raider Gordon Gekko, played by Michael Douglas; his "greed is good" speech, in turn, was inspired by an address by arbitrageur Ivan Boesky, whose defense of greed in 1986 summarized and polarized much of the decade. Gekko's plans to acquire an airline he promises to restructure, but intends only to liquidate by selling it off piecemeal, are likewise emblematic of much of the corporate raiding activity of the time, even to the choice of an airline as his target. Icahn was best known for his 1985 hostile takeover of Trans World Airlines (TWA) and subsequent reduction of wages and benefits, liquidation of assets, and sale of profitable gates to other competing airlines, while relocating the corporate offices to a building he owned in Westchester County.

The LBO boom peaked with the takeover of RJR Nabisco in 1989, a buyout that cost $31.1 billion—$109 a share, after a prolonged bidding war involving (in one capacity or another) Morgan Stanley, Goldman Sachs, Salomon Brothers, and Merrill Lynch, the most prominent investment banks of the era. When adjusted for inflation, no buyout has been larger, and it was the last of its kind for the era; buyouts slowed, and even the RJR Nabisco deal had to be recapitalized a year later. Milken's firm, Drexel Burnham Lambert, had raised the largest amount of money for the decade's flurry of buyouts, leading the way in the securitization of high-yield debt, for which Milken was called "the junk bond king."

The era symbolically ended shortly after the RJR Nabisco deal, when the firm pleaded no contest to six federal felony charges related to stock manipulation and misdeeds, paying a $650 million fine, the largest ever paid for securities violations. Milken left the firm when he was indicted individually on 98 charges of racketeering and securities fraud (insider trading), for which he was eventually sentenced to ten years in prison. Drexel Burnham Lambert declared bankruptcy less than a year later.

The 21st century saw a rebirth of leveraged buyouts, as lending standards became lax, interest rates declined, and the Sarbanes-Oxley Act altered the regulations affecting public companies. Though no buyout equaled RJR Nabisco's when adjusted for inflation, there were more multibillion-dollar buyouts, totalling significantly more money, in the first decade of the 21st century than in the 1980s. 2006 alone saw 654 companies bought for $375 billion.

The high-yield-debt market enabling this was affected by the subprime mortgage crisis that rippled across the other sectors of the economy in 2007–08; no bankruptcy or indictment was needed to end the boom this time, just general economic malaise and its attendant risk aversion. Many of the buyouts of this recent wave were funded with "cov-lite" loans—covenant light loans, loans with fewer clauses in their agreements protecting the rights of the lender, something more and more banks offered at a time when it was a borrowers' market and lenders had to compete for attention.

Management Buyouts

It is a mistake to conflate leveraged buyouts with the corporate raiding associated with the 1980s; even most buyouts in that decade did not result in negligent handling or opportunistic dismantling of the acquired companies. Management buyouts (MBOs), for instance, are leveraged buyouts instigated by the management of a company, when those managers want to take control of the company—usually, but not always, in order to take the company private. The reasons for this vary, but often management may have a plan for the company that is not going to return a profit to the shareholders quickly, or involves a risk shareholders are not willing to take.

The problem with MBOs when they become a common corporate maneuver is the temptation that is presented for mismanagement: Corporate officers planning an MBO will have to raise less money to buy out the company if they can reduce its worth first.

Takeovers

The 1980s made *hostile takeover* such a common phrase that it can be easy to forget there is any other sort. While it is true that a friendly takeover is more likely to be referred to as an *acquisition*, this is simply a matter of labeling.

A hostile takeover is any acquisition performed without the cooperation of the company—which can mean that the company actively resisted the acquisition (by rejecting initial offers) or can simply mean that its cooperation was not sought. There are different strategies of hostile takeovers, from gathering up enough stock to own a controlling stake in the company to persuading existing shareholders to vote the current management out in favor of managers who will approve the takeover. Hostile takeovers are riskier, insofar as without the cooperation of the targeted company, the business valuation will be less well-informed, and potentially inaccurate.

A reverse takeover is one in which a private company acquires a public company without taking it private—in other words, the private company bypasses the usual process of going public by buying and merging with a public company, which can turn it public in weeks rather than the year or more that a standard IPO usually takes. US Airways, for instance, was acquired by America West Airlines, putting the company in the hands of US Airways' creditors, with the goal of rescuing it from bankruptcy.

Mergers

In a merger, two companies join to form a larger company. There is usually a new name and brand identity for the resulting company, but not always. Mergers may be horizontal—involving companies that produce similar products in an industry, such as Pepsi and Coca-Cola—or vertical, involving two companies involved with different stages of production of the same good or service, like a movie studio and a television network. Conglomerate mergers involve companies from completely separate industries.

Mergers can raise a lot of antitrust red flags, and the busiest period of merger activity in the United States contributed to the speed with which antitrust legislation was adopted. The "great merger movement" took place from 1895 to 1905, a period during which there was a significant national trend toward moving operations and consciousness from the regional level to the national level. For instance, during this same Progressive Era—which historian Robert Wiebe has called the organizational period—the

country's major nationwide professional guilds (such as the American Medical Association and American Legal Association) developed, as did its national labor unions, several of its religious organizations, and a great many of its media organizations. There was a general and pronounced trend since the end of the Civil War to treat institutions in the United States as American institutions first, Alabama and Iowan and Pennsylvanian institutions second, an attitude adopted so successfully that it is taken for granted a century later.

In business, the effect of this trend was for more companies to want to operate nationally rather than in a single state or region. State laws sometimes made this difficult, and trusts were created in order to create legal entities which could then own or merge with smaller regional entities, which would then all be operated uniformly. Hardware stores in 30 states, for instance, could merge into a nationwide hardware chain.

That is not to say that the motivation of the great merger movement was simply to participate in the spirit of cultural change that presided over the day. Economic concerns were foremost. The Panic of 1893 had driven demand and prices down, and mergers allowed costs to come down in order to keep profits stable, or on the increase. When those costs came down because of vertical or horizontal integration, all was well. But when the mergers resembled a form of collusion, with companies joining together in order to keep prices high by removing the need to compete, that is when antitrust legislation had to be enacted in order to limit the circumstances in which mergers could occur, and set out the sorts of companies that, in plain English, are not allowed to exist under American law—companies that represent such a large part of their industry that the industry is rendered noncompetitive.

As an illustration of just how much merging was occurring, in 1900—right in the middle of this period—the value of firms involved in mergers that year was equal to 20 percent of the country's gross domestic product. By contrast, in an ordinary year, it is closer to 5 percent or less.

See Also: Antitrust Laws; AT&T; Economies of Scale; Hostile Takeovers; Investment Banks; Mark-to-Market Valuation; Sarbanes-Oxley.

Bibliography: Bryan Burrough and John Helyar, *Barbarians at the Gate: The Fall of RJR Nabisco* (Harper & Row, 1990); Susan Cartwright and Richard Schoenberg, "Thirty Years of Mergers and Acquisitions Research: Recent Advances and Future Opportunities," *British Journal of Management* (v.17, 2006); Donald DePamphilis, *Mergers, Acquisitions, and Other Restructuring Activities* (Elsevier Academic Press, 2008); Robert F. Reilly and Robert P. Schweihs, *The Handbook of Advanced Business Valuation* (McGraw-Hill Professional, 1999); Thomas Straub, *Reasons For Frequent Failure in Mergers and Acquisitions: A Comprehensive Analysis* (Deutscher Universitatsverlag, 2007).

BILL KTE'PI
INDEPENDENT SCHOLAR

Ad Valorem Duties

Ad valorem duties are duties that are a fixed percentage of the price of the imported good. While conceptually straightforward, the administration of ad valorem duties may be complex, reflecting the practical difficulties in establishing the value of imported goods.

An ad valorem duty, or tariff, is in contrast to the specific tariff, which is a flat rate tariff that is independent of the value of the import. Ad valorem duties, unlike specific tariffs, are flexible and adjust to changes in the price or the value of the import good. If the ad valorem tariff rate is 5 percent and the import price is $100, the tariff revenue would be $5. If the import price increases to $150, then the per unit tariff revenue would be $7.50. With an initial specific tariff of $5 and an import price of $100, the ad valorem tariff and the specific tariff are equivalent. However, once the import price increases to $150, the specific tariff of $5 translates into a tariff rate of 3.3 percent. This reduces the level of protection that domestic producers receive from the tariff structure.

The ad valorem duty regime not only maintains the level of protection that domestic producers receive, it also increases the per unit import tariff revenue that the government receives when import prices are increasing. Ad valorem tariffs are therefore preferable to specific tariffs because they better achieve two of the primary aims of tariffs—namely, protecting domestic firms and rising tariff revenues.

Administration of ad valorem tariffs requires two factors: the first is the ad valorem tariff rate and the second is the value of the import good. Key to answering the first question is the appropriate tariff classification for the import. Tariff classification may be critical as a change in classification may either lower or raise the ad valorem tariff rate. This is the first step in the customs valuation process. The second step in this process is determining the value of the import good.

The value of the import good may be affected by the method used to determine the value of import goods. There are three import valuation methods that are frequently used: Free Along Price (FAS)—the price in the foreign market; Free on Board (FOB)—the price in the foreign market plus the cost of loading the good onto transportation at its port of origin; and Cost, Insurance, and Freight (CIF)—the cost in the foreign market plus insurance and freight costs incurred in delivering the good to its final destination port. In applying ad valorem tariff rates, the United States has traditionally used FOB valuations while European countries have traditionally used CIF valuations.

Determining the import valuation basis does not fully resolve the question of correct import valuation. One further difficulty is that the price of the import good in the foreign market, which affects import prices independently of the valuation method used, may constantly change. This variability in the foreign market price complicates the task of establishing the value of the import good.

With ad valorem tariffs, the tariff rate and import value jointly determine the import duties that are payable. Companies, therefore, have an incentive to shop custom classifications in order to reduce the tariff rate, and to under-invoice their imports in order to reduce the tariff rate. These incentives further complicate the process of administering ad valorem tariffs.

See Also: Duty; Import; International Commercial Terms (Incoterms); Tariff.

Bibliography. Mohamed Hedi Bchir, Sebastien Jean, and David Laborde, "Binding Overhang and Tariff-Cutting Formulas," *Review of World Economics* (v.142/2, July

2006); Robert J. Carbaugh, *International Economics*, 11th ed. (Thomson Southwestern, 2007); W. Charles Sawyer and Richard L. Sprinkle, *International Economics*, 3rd ed. (Pearson Prentice-Hall, 2009).

LAUREL ADAMS
NORTHERN ILLINOIS UNIVERSITY

Advanced Pricing Agreement

An advanced pricing agreement (APA) represents a binding agreement between a multinational corporation and a country's tax authority as to the transfer price for a specified cross-border transaction known as the covered transaction. A typical APA will specify the covered transaction, the agreed transfer price, and an effective time period. Unlike transfer prices that are set in the normal course of business, transfer prices reached under an APA are not subject to further adjustment by either party and as a result avoid the risks of transfer pricing adjustments and associated penalties. In so doing, an APA provides pricing certainty to multinationals.

A transfer price is the price associated with related party transactions, i.e., transactions that take place within a corporation. As per many countries' tax regulations, cross-border transfer prices must satisfy the arm's length standard. This standard requires that related party transactions reflect the price that would have been charged if the parties were independent, i.e., separate companies, and trading at arm's length. Tax legislation details the methods that may be used to determine appropriate transfer prices. Most of these methods rely on the existence of comparable transactions that serve as benchmarks for related party transactions.

Many internal transactions lack satisfactory third-party benchmarks. These internal transactions might be appropriate candidates for APAs. Additional criteria may include the underlying complexity and size of the transaction. One potential complexity is the inability to separate a single transaction into simpler transactions that may be more easily priced. Eligibility criteria for APAs often reflect the demands that they place on the resources of the relevant tax authorities,

as every single APA requires review and approval by the tax authority, and the time commitment to a single APA can be significant. Consequently, not all internal transactions are appropriate candidates for APAs.

APAs may be unilateral, bilateral, or multilateral in scope. Unilateral APAs involve a single tax authority and the multinational corporation. Such APAs protect the multinational from transfer pricing penalties and adjustment in the jurisdiction in which it was negotiated, but confers no transfer pricing risk mitigation in the corresponding jurisdiction where the other end of the transaction takes place. Bilateral APAs involve two taxing authorities and are, by definition, more complex as they require the agreement of multiple taxing authorities with an inherent conflict as to how the associated income from a transaction should be shared between the two countries. Bilateral APAs, as do their unilateral counterparts, require review and approval by the tax authorities and consequently place significant demands on the resources of the relevant tax authorities. Bilateral APAs confer a further advantage to the multinational, however, as bilateral APAs provide transfer pricing certainty in both countries.

Whether unilateral, bilateral, or multilateral in scope, APAs are voluntary and are initiated at the request of taxpayers with a petition to the relevant tax authorities. Taxpayers may petition for an APA for any transaction that falls within the purview of the transfer pricing legislation. Approval for APAs is not always granted, and if they are, the petitioning firm must provide documentation that establishes the arm's length standard of the proposed transactions. APAs are ideally suited to setting transfer prices in advance of transactions. They may also be used to set transfer prices on a concurrent basis.

See Also: Multinational Corporation; Pricing; Taxes; Transfer Pricing.

Bibliography. Internal Revenue Service, "Announcement and Reporting Concerning Advanced Pricing Agreements," March 2008, www.irs.gov (cited March 2009); Organization of Economic Cooperation and Development, "OECD Transfer Pricing Guidelines for Multinational Enterprises and Tax Administrators" (OECD, 1995).

LAUREL ADAMS
NORTHERN ILLINOIS UNIVERSITY

Advertising

Advertising is one of the four primary forms of promotional (or integrated marketing communications) activity employed by marketing organizations to informatively and/or persuasively communicate with consumers and other targeted audiences. Advertising differs from other major forms of promotional activity (i.e., personal selling, sales promotion, and public relations) in that it is a paid, non-personal form of communication typically transmitted through mass media (e.g., television, the internet, radio, newspapers, magazines, and billboards). It is "paid" in that when a marketer, for example, places a full-page ad in *BusinessWeek* or runs a 30-second television ad during a broadcast of *60 Minutes*, the sponsor/marketer pays the media organization for the space or time used to promote itself or its products. Advertising is "non-personal" in that it is not, like personal selling, customized according to the needs, wants, and expectations of individual message recipients. Instead, advertising is typically standardized in that the vast majority of persons seeing and/or hearing any one advertisement receive the exact same message.

When most people think of advertising, what usually first comes to mind are celebrity endorsers, music, and highly creative, attention-grabbing imagery and catchphrases. However, successful advertising entails far more than this. Marketers wishing to effectively—and efficiently—communicate through advertising must first know their target audience and then, typically with the assistance of advertising agencies, carefully choose which media types and vehicles to employ. They, along with their ad agencies, then create messages that not only grab the attention of the target audience but, eventually, inform and/or persuade them in some desired manner. This is never easy.

For the international marketer, performing these challenging tasks is further complicated by the fact that cultural and legal environments often vary significantly from nation to nation. As a result, advertising that works spectacularly in one country may be perceived by the target audience in another nation as irrelevant, ridiculous, and/or offensive. When the latter occurs, not only have international advertisers made themselves look bad; they have, in most cases, also spent a lot of money to do so.

Advantages

The international marketer should be aware that advertising possesses both strengths and weaknesses relative to other forms of promotion. Arguably advertising's main advantage over other forms of promotion is its ability to cost-effectively reach a very large, geographically dispersed target audience. Let us say that a large, global consumer products firm like Colgate-Palmolive is planning on introducing a new brand of toothpaste worldwide. A good way to cost effectively promote the new product to the target audience would be to advertise in a general interest news magazine sold and read in many regions and countries of the world, such as *Time*. This media vehicle is produced in several editions each week—with each edition created for and distributed in a specific region of the world.

Advertisers can, as Colgate-Palmolive would likely want to do with its new toothpaste, purchase advertisements in each edition of *Time*. Running a half-page ad in each edition for three weeks—say one week prior to and two weeks after product introduction—would cost the company a total of approximately US$740,000. Given *Time*'s worldwide (weekly) circulation of nearly 4.4 million people and the fact that roughly three people can, on average, be expected to view each magazine circulated, a total of 39.6 million people—and potential consumers of the new toothpaste—will at least have the opportunity to see and be influenced by Colgate-Palmolive's advertisements.

The US$740,000 may seem like a lot of money to spend on advertising but global companies with large, globally dispersed target audiences—and large ad budgets—like Colgate-Palmolive are more concerned about the cost of reaching each potential buyer (and the return on this investment in advertising). In this case, the cost of reaching each of the nearly 39.6 million consumers with the firm's advertisements in *Time* is approximately US$.02. If only 5 percent—one out of every 20—of the 39.6 million persons seeing the advertisements in *Time* buy the new toothpaste just one time—priced, say, at US$2.00—the $740,000 has been well spent, with a revenue of nearly US$4 million generated.

Related to advertising's ability to cost effectively reach a large, geographically dispersed audience is its ability to also reach a narrowly targeted/niche target audience with minimal waste circulation. A "narrowly targeted" or "niche" audience means a very specific group of people with particular, shared interests or organizations in a specific industry (or group of related industries). "Waste circulation" implies that advertising—particularly when done through magazines and Web pages—can cost-effectively get the marketer's promotional message out to the niche audience with very few people or organizations outside the targeted group also seeing the message. The minimization of waste circulation is very important to marketers because paying to communicate with persons or organizations outside the target market is a waste of money (in that those outside the target market are not very likely to be interested in the message and/or the advertised product).

A good example of a media vehicle that allows advertisers to cost effectively reach a large, geographically dispersed, niche target audience with minimal waste circulation is *The Journal of Commerce* (JOC). The JOC, which began publication in 1827, is a weekly magazine containing content of interest to high-level international trade, transportation, and logistics executives around the globe. Marketers wishing to promote their goods or services to these—and pretty much exclusively these—executive decision makers can run advertisements in the JOC in a variety of sizes up to 52 times per year. For example, international marketers with a relatively small budget could run six quarter-page, black-and-white advertisements over the course of the year in the JOC at a total cost of approximately US$13,620. The advertising would, in this case, be reaching a total of roughly 150,000 readers highly likely to be interested in its message (with a cost-per-reader of slightly over US$.09). An international marketer with a larger ad budget could, for example, place and run 26 of the same quarter-page ads in the JOC (i.e., one every other week over the course of a year) at a total cost of approximately US$44,400. These ads—and the precisely targeted promotional messages they contain—would be reaching a total of about 650,000 readers (with a cost-per-reader of approximately US$.068).

While the cost-per-reader associated with advertising in the JOC is much higher than the previous example of US$.02 to reach consumers worldwide by advertising in *Time* magazine, it should be kept in mind that the JOC is targeted at a very specific and specialized group of organizational managers in

many different countries. It is likely well worth the extra per-reader cost to advertise in the JOC if doing so allows you to reach your target audience—and only your target audience.

Suggested in the latter part of the JOC example above is another strength of advertising. With advertising, the marketer can repeat the message as many times as their budget will allow them to do so. An advertiser could, for example, run ads in the JOC each week it is published (i.e., 52 times in a year). The same marketer could also run dozens of 30-second radio or television advertisements in local markets where their target market members are located. This ability to repeat the message is important because seldom will any one promotional message—run just one time—have the informative and/or persuasive impact desired by the marketer. And, luckily for international marketers with large ad budgets, buying ads in volume typically translates into: (1) lower per-ad cost, and (2) lower per-reader cost.

Finally, advertising, relative to other forms of promotional activity, is also good at both creating a prestige image for the marketer as well as appealing to the target audience in multisensory fashion. With regard to prestige, it enhances the image of the marketer—especially when the marketer is relatively unknown—to be seen advertising: (1) in well-known, well-respected magazines and newspapers, and (2) on major television networks or radio stations. Prestige can also be created or enhanced via the employment of well-known, respected celebrities in advertisements. With regard to the multisensory nature of advertising, television and Web page advertising offer the marketer unmatched potential to grab the attention and inform and/or persuade target audiences through the simultaneous and synergistic use of both sight and sound. Even radio advertising, limited only to sound, offers the creatively inclined international marketer much potential to appeal to the senses of the listener. Radio has been, in this regard, referred to as "the theater of the mind."

Disadvantages

While advertising has some significant advantages over other forms of promotional activity it also has some distinct disadvantages. One primary disadvantage of advertising is its high absolute cost. Earlier, in the context of demonstrating the relative cost-

A roadside fruit peddler waits beneath a large Marlboro billboard on a road into a war-damaged city in Lebanon in 1992. This famous series of ads using images of American cowboys made the Philip Morris (and now Altria) brand a global success.

effectiveness of advertising when communicating with large, geographically dispersed target audiences, a hypothetical example was provided wherein Colgate-Palmolive could possibly generate US$4 million in sales as the result of a US$740,000 investment in advertising. This is, indeed, a good return on investment. However, if a marketer does not have $740,000 to invest in advertising then there is no opportunity to realize this kind of return. While large global firms like Colgate-Palmolive have budgets allowing such large expenditures on advertising many other—particularly smaller—firms do not. Simply put, advertising can be a great investment but the absolute dollar volume required to create and run advertisements on a global—even national or regional or local—scale can be great.

Another relative weakness of advertising is its inability to provide the marketer with timely feed-back with regard to how effective it is (or has been). This weakness is particularly strong when comparing advertising to personal selling (i.e., using salespeople to promote the company or its products). For example, when a salesperson is making a sales presentation to a client, he or she can assess in real time the extent to which their promotional message is: (1) being paid attention to, and (2) having the hoped-for informational and/or persuasive effect. With advertising, due to the fact that the marketer is not present when the message is being received and the fact that multiple exposures to an advertisement are necessary for it to have any impact, it may take weeks or even months to know how effective promotional efforts have been—and it may take a significant investment in marketing research to make this (belated) determination.

Related to the issue of slow feedback on effectiveness is another relative weakness of advertising.

Not only does it take considerable time to judge the effectiveness of advertising, it is also relatively difficult to accurately measure the informational and/or persuasive impact of advertising. Think back again to our hypothetical example of Colgate-Palmolive possibly generating US$4 million in sales as the result of a US$740,000 investment in advertising. Saying that advertising caused this level of sales is not, in practice, easy to do (at least with a great deal of confidence). This is because so many other factors in addition to advertising can effect the sales—and, to an even greater extent, the profits—of an organization. Thus: (1) in order to determine what has caused sales (or profits) all factors having an impact on it must be taken into consideration, and (2) one cannot accurately say to what extent advertising has caused sales (or profits) unless the causal impact of all these other factors has been taken into account. Web page advertising is somewhat an exception here, as far more precise measurement of impact on sales can be discerned (e.g., through tracking how many viewers clicked on links in advertising and then purchased the advertised products).

Finally, it is relatively impractical—if not impossible—to customize promotional messages with advertising. Personal selling, for example, allows the marketer the opportunity to customize each message transmitted to the exact needs, wants, and expectations of every targeted person. Although major magazines do allow some level of customization due to the publication of specialized regional or national editions every one of perhaps hundreds of thousands of persons receiving any one edition of the magazine sees the exact same advertisement. With major broadcast media such as radio and television individualized customization is essentially impossible—even if it were possible it would be very expensive.

The Global Advertising Industry

Advertising's scope is increasingly global. Business organizations large and small and in virtually all industries and countries are using advertising—and increasingly more of it—to promote themselves and their products to prospective and existing consumers. Thus suggested is that the strengths of advertising discussed above generally outweigh its weaknesses—with the latter just placing limits on what can be done with advertising.

According to *Advertising Age*, the preeminent authority on virtually all matters related to advertising, the world's top 100 marketers alone spent nearly US$98 billion on advertising in 2006 (the latest year for which complete data is readily available). For the sixth year in a row, U.S.-based consumer products giant Procter & Gamble—marketer of brands such as Bounty, Camay, Charmin, Gillette, Head & Shoulders, Ivory, Luvs, Max Factor, Mr. Clean, Noxzema, Pampers, Pepto-Bismol, Scope, Tide, and Vicks—topped the list of global advertisers. Rounding out the list of the top five advertisers in the world in 2006 were Unilever, General Motors, L'Oréal, and Toyota. Automotive firms in *Advertising Age*'s Global Top 100 for 2006 spent more on advertising than companies in any other industry and accounted for almost 23 percent of all advertising expenditures by the top 100.

With respect to advertising expenditures by the top 100 global advertisers by region of the world in 2006, the U.S. tops the list with US$46.02 billion. This is followed by Europe (US$31.12 billion), Asia and Pacific (US$14.92 billion), Latin America (US$2.48 billion), Canada (US$2.09 billion), Africa (US$711 million), and the Middle East (US$422 million). The region of the world exhibiting the greatest increase in ad spending was Latin America, with 2006 spending up 12.7 percent from 2005.

Overall, the nearly US$98 billion in global ad expenditures in 2006 represents a 1.1 percent increase over 2005 spending. Interestingly, this growth is in spite of the fact that U.S. marketers ranking among *Advertising Age*'s Global Top 100 cut ad spending by 2.2 percent in 2006. Some of the largest U.S. advertisers were those showing the greatest percentage decrease in expenditures. General Motors tops the list with a 17.4 percent decline, followed by Time Warner (down 13.8 percent) and Johnson & Johnson (down 13.2 percent). This decline in U.S. ad spending was offset by significant increases in advertising by non-U.S. marketers such as Sharp Corporation (Japan), Fiat (Italy), Moët Hennessy Louis Vuitton (France), LG Group (South Korea), and Aldi Group (Germany).

Finally, the large global marketers/advertisers such as those discussed above are not the only "major players" in the global advertising industry. Also heavily involved—albeit not as conspicuously as advertisers—are the media firms that, by virtue of producing magazines, newspapers, and Web sites and running radio and television stations as well as billboard advertising companies, provide advertisers the vehicles through which to reach target audiences worldwide.

A third "major player" in global advertising that is even more "behind the scenes" than media firms are the advertising agencies that provide media planning/buying and creative and production services to marketers/advertisers. It is common, in this regard, for large, international marketers to work with multiple advertising agencies. According to an *Advertising Age* report published in November 2007, the world's largest global advertiser, Procter & Gamble, employs the services of 10 different ad agencies to help it plan for, create, and run advertisements. According to this same report, the three advertising agencies with the largest number of Global Top 100 clients/assignments are: (1) Euro RSCG Worldwide (42 clients), (2) McCann Erickson Worldwide (40 clients), and (3) Ogilvy & Mather Worldwide (35 clients). Euro RSCG Worldwide, the largest ad agency in the world in terms of "global assignments" (i.e., major clients served), is based in New York and has a total of more than 230 offices in 75 countries. Euro RSCG Worldwide, by virtue of working with 10 of the top 20 and 42 of the top 100 global advertisers, exemplifies the global advertising agency.

Cross-Cultural Considerations

It is often said that strategic marketing decisions involving advertising are those most likely to be significantly impacted by cultural variation between nations. It should be of little surprise, then, that failure to carefully consider the appropriateness and likely acceptance of an advertisement through the cultural lens of the targeted audience puts marketers at high risk of—at a minimum—considerable embarrassment. Consider, in this regard, a few "classic blunders" of international advertisers. The United States Dairy Association's successful "Got Milk" advertising campaign was introduced in Mexico. The association was later informed that the Spanish translation used for "Got Milk" could be taken to mean "Are you lactating?" Pepsi's "Come Alive With the Pepsi Generation" advertising slogan translated into "Pepsi Brings Your Ancestors Back From the Grave" in China. And in the United States, Scandinavian vacuum manufacturer Electrolux used the—well-rhymed albeit ill-advised—slogan "Nothing sucks like an Electrolux."

While the validity of several of these "classic blunders" has been debated, they clearly illustrate, at the very least, what can potentially happen when just one cross-cultural factor—language—is ignored or misunderstood by international advertisers. Creating and running just one high-quality television or magazine advertisement can cost an organization hundreds of thousands—perhaps even millions—of dollars. Spending this magnitude of money to make oneself look silly in the eyes of and/or offend members of the target audience—including one's potential and existing customers—is, to say the least, not good strategy.

Language Considerations

Language is, as demonstrated in the "classic blunders" listed above, a particularly perilous cross-cultural domain for international advertisers. In this regard, it is far from enough to have translations be done in literal/"dictionary" fashion by persons who are not fluent in the language of the targeted audience—and, most importantly, the language as actually spoken by the target audience. This is due largely to the fact that literal translations found in most dictionaries fail to adequately account for regional variations, slang, and symbolic meaning in language as spoken by persons in a given country (or region thereof). Further, superficial knowledge of a given foreign language may be more dangerous than no knowledge at all for the international advertiser.

To avoid potentially embarrassing and costly mistakes due to the often subtle yet critical intricacies of cross-cultural language variation, international marketers must take the task of translating what it wants to say in one language into its advertising in another language very, very seriously. At a minimum, translations should be done by persons highly fluent in both focal languages—wherein "highly fluent" with regard to the language of the targeted audience means knowing how the language is actually spoken by members of the audience in their local environments.

In addition, just one translation done by one person is often not sufficient. In this regard, what are known as *back translations* are commonly done. In the process of back translation, advertising content is translated by one bilingual person from one language (e.g., Spanish as spoken in Mexico) into the language of the target audience (e.g., Portuguese as spoken in Brazil) and then translated back—from Brazilian Portuguese to Mexican Spanish—by another competent, bilingual translator. The results of the two translations are then compared to ensure consistency and, ultimately, effective communication through advertising. If, for example, the second translation comes back saying exactly what was meant to be said in the first place—in the same language—then the marketer knows they are on the right track. If, however, the second translation is significantly different than what was originally meant to be said, then the marketer still has much work in translation to be done.

Cultural Considerations

Language is, however, but just one of many potentially arduous cross-cultural hurdles frequently encountered by international advertisers. Indeed, being "culturally fluent" entails far more than being fluent only in the language of a given foreign country or group of people. One prime example of a non-language, culture-based factor that international advertisers must be cognizant of involves what are called *cultural values* (i.e., what is considered appropriate versus not appropriate by persons in a given nation or group of people).

Variation in *cultural values* between one nation and another creates a host of potentially important considerations for marketers wishing to effectively advertise in multiple countries. Take, for example, the appropriateness of certain words used to identify people in two nations that speak the same language—say the United States and Australia. It would, in this regard, generally be acceptable for a U.S. firm to tout itself in domestic—particularly regional or local—advertising as employing "native" persons. This would likely be taken by most recipients of the message to imply that the sponsor of the advertising creates jobs locally and that their employees are not only from the area but are also highly similar to other local persons in many ways (i.e., by virtue of being from the same approximate place and having similar values). Using the word *native* in this manner in advertising in Australia would carry a different meaning. In Australia, *native* usually implies indigenous/Aboriginal persons. This is a mistake that could easily be made by persons working in advertising for foreign firms from countries with less contentious histories with regard

to the plight of indigenous persons. Required in this instance is guidance from Australian locals—including but not limited to Aboriginal persons—well versed in Australian cultural values.

Another potentially critical cross-cultural, value-based consideration for international advertisers involves the use of humor. Simply put, what is considered humorous by members of one target audience in one country may be seen—even if adequately translated—as meaningless, ridiculous, and/or offensive by persons in another country (or region thereof). Again, as with language translations and word appropriateness, successfully using humor across cultures requires the input of persons fluent in the local culture of the targeted audience. Effective international advertising thus requires that the foreign marketer employ persons from the local culture at least as agents or consultants—if not as full-time managerial employees responsible for making key advertising decisions.

Legal Considerations

Just as international advertisers should expect to encounter cross-cultural obstacles so too should they assume that variations in laws across nations may significantly impact their ability to effectively communicate with targeted audiences. Generally, when doing business in foreign countries, the marketer: (1) should not assume that the laws of their home country are applicable abroad, and (2) should be familiar with and abide by the law of the host nation—particularly those laws which impact the ability of the foreign firm to market its specific type of product. These general points reign very true in the context of advertising. The international advertiser should never assume either that: (1) home-country advertising-related law applies abroad, or (2) they will be able to advertise their product in the exact same manner abroad as they do domestically.

A good example of not being legally able to advertise products in a foreign country in the same manner as done in the domestic marketplace is comparative advertising. In this form of advertising, the sponsor directly—and favorably—compares its products to those of a competitor. Comparative advertising law differs significantly from nation to nation. In the United States, it is not only legal to compare your products to those of a competitor but also legal to name the competitor in the advertisement (as long as the comparative statements in the ad can be objectively substantiated). In some Western European nations (e.g., Ireland, Spain, the United Kingdom, and Portugal) comparisons can be legally made but only as long as the comparison is implicit and does not specifically name the competitor. Comparative advertising is illegal, however, in other Western European countries (e.g., Germany, Belgium, and Luxembourg). Comparative advertising is also heavily regulated in other regions of the world. As a result, marketers that commonly (and legally) employ this form of advertising in their home countries must be very careful about using it abroad.

Sometimes an international marketer will find that it cannot advertise its products at all in a given foreign nation. For example, toy, tobacco, liquor, and pharmaceutical drug ads are banned or at least heavily restricted in many nations of the world while advertising these products is perfectly legal in others. Marketers of a product that cannot be legally advertised in a given nation in which the marketer wishes to sell the product must find an alternative means of promotional communication.

At other times, international marketers may discover that they cannot legally advertise via a certain type of media in some countries. Advertising on television, for example, is regulated in many nations. In Kuwait, for instance, only 32 minutes of television advertising per day is allowed on the government-controlled television network. In China, the government has only in the last several years begun to ease some regulations significantly restricting the use of TV advertising. However, the Chinese government has, at the same time, also increased regulation of other aspects of TV advertising (e.g., the required provision of proof of claims made in ads). The bottom line for the international advertiser is to know the law relevant to the marketing of your product in the given country in which you are doing business and to: (1) abide by it, and (2) adapt your advertising efforts accordingly.

See Also: Back Translation; Branding; Buying Motive/Behavior; Consumer Behavior; Consumer Needs and Wants; Cross-Cultural Research; Culture-Specific Values; Global Brand Strategy; Integrated Marketing Communications; International Marketing Research; Marketing; Market Research; Media; Media and Direct Marketing; Promotions.

Bibliography. *Advertising Age*, adage.com/datacenter (cited March 2009); Philip Cateora and John Graham, *International Marketing*, 13th ed. (McGraw-Hill/Irwin, 2007); Ian Dow, "Your Ad Is a Tad Mad!: It's a Marketing Chief's Worst Nightmare When the Catchy Slogan for the Expensive Ad Campaign Translates to Mean Something Hilarious for Foreign Shoppers," *Daily Record* (October 5, 2002); Nadeem Firoz and Taghi Ramin, "Understanding Cultural Variables Is Critical to Success in International Business," *International Journal of Management* (v.21/3, 2004); Ali Kanso and Richard Nelson, "Multinational Corporations and the Challenge of Global Advertising: What Do U.S. Headquarters Consider Important in Making Media-Selection Decisions?," *International Marketing Review* (v.24/5, 2007); Yih Hwai Lee and Elison Ai Ching Lim, "What's Funny and What's Not: The Moderating Role of Cultural Orientation in Ad Humor," *Journal of Advertising* (v.37/2, 2008).

Terrance G. Gabel
University of Arkansas–Fort Smith

Aegon

Aegon (Aegon N.V.) is one of the biggest insurance companies in the world. As a holding company, its main activities include various financial products such as life insurance, non-life insurance, savings, pensions, and investments. Aegon is a Netherlands-based company that was incorporated in 1983 and now employs around 30,000 people (as of January 1, 2008). Its headquarters is located at The Hague, the Netherlands. Aegon owns 17 offices located throughout the United States. Its principal offices are located in Baltimore, Maryland; Cedar Rapids, Iowa; Louisville, Kentucky; Los Angeles, California; Frazer, Pennsylvania; St. Petersburg, Florida; Plano, Texas; Kansas City, Missouri; Purchase, New York; and Charlotte, North Carolina. Aegon is traded on the New York Stock Exchange with the ticker symbol AEG. Aegon has approximately 27,000 shareholders (as of January 1, 2008).

In addition to the Netherlands (13 percent of the 2007 revenues), Aegon operates in the United States and Canada (73 percent of the 2007 revenues), United Kingdom (9 percent of the 2007 revenues), and Slovakia, Czech Republic, Poland, Hungary, Taiwan, and

China (all comprise 5 percent of the 2007 revenues). The core business of Aegon is premium income (69 percent of the 2007 revenues). The second biggest revenue generator is investment income (27 percent of the 2007 revenues), and the commission and fee income makes 5 percent of total revenues in 2007.

Aegon operates in various product segments. These are life for account of policyholders, traditional life, accident and health insurance, fixed annuities, reinsurance, institutional guaranteed products, fee-off balance sheet products, variable annuities, general insurance, banking activities, and holding and other activities. More specifically, Aegon's products and services include permanent and term life insurance, fixed annuities, guaranteed investment contracts, variable universal life insurance, universal life insurance, unit-linked products, variable annuities, accidental death insurance, disability insurance, dismemberment insurance, critical illness insurance, cancer treatment insurance, hospital indemnity insurance, short-term disability policies, automobile insurance, liability insurance, household and fire insurance, investment products, and savings products.

Aegon is the name of the group of companies. It has numerous subsidiary companies. Among them are Aegon USA (agency, direct marketing services, financial markets, institutional products and services, and pension); Aegon Nederlands (both the life and non-life insurance businesses and banking, financial and asset management services); and Aegon UK (manufacturer, fund manager, and distributor of pension, protection and investment products).

Aegon was formed in 1983 as a result of the merger of two Dutch insurance companies, namely AGO Holding N.V. and Ennia N.V., both of which were successors to insurance companies formed in the 1800s. In 1985, the company traded on NASDAQ National Market. Also, its shares were opened to trade at the Amsterdam, London, Basel, Geneva, and Zurich stock exchanges. In the early 1990s, Aegon increased its operations in the United States by acquiring Monumental Corporation and Western Reserve Life. Following these transactions, Aegon started to be listed on the New York Stock Exchange. Since then, Aegon continues its presence in international financial and insurance markets.

The executive team of Aegon comprises Donald J. Shepard (Chief Executive Officer), Jan Nooitgedag (Chief Financial Officer), Alexander R. Wynaendts

While Aegon is based in the Netherlands, 73 percent of its revenues came from its North American operations in 2007.

(Chief Operating Officer). Aegon's board of directors includes Patrick S. Baird, Otto Thoresen, Johan G. van der Werf, Dudley G. Eustace, O. John Olcay, Irving W. Bailey, Rene Dahan, Shemaya Levy, Toni Rembe, Willem F. C. Stevens, Kees J. Storm, and Leo M. Van Wijk.

Aegon's success comes from its strong market position in various countries, which reflects its power in the insurance and pension business. It is one of the biggest insurance companies in the Netherlands and in other European countries and has a substantial presence in the United States. Another reason for its success is the growth performance in new businesses. Moreover, by engaging in new emerging markets, new businesses are expected to increase further, which in return will boost overall financial performance. Third, with its diversified business, Aegon limits its risks and manages stable revenues. By investing in different operations and in different countries, Aegon secures itself as independent of any single market. Its revenues are spread over several product segments; no single business line generates the bulk of revenues.

However, one of Aegon's major weaknesses is that its revenues are declining in the Netherlands, which would adversely affect the performance of the company. Besides, because of higher operating expenses, Aegon faces reduced profits on its investments. Another important setback for Aegon may be its underperformed banking solutions. The company's banking products are sold only in the Netherlands, which combined with market slowdown in the Netherlands, results in fewer earnings.

See Also: Company Profiles: Western Europe; Netherlands.

Bibliography. Aegon, www.aegon.com (cited March 2009); SEC-EDGAR, www.sec.gov (cited March 2009).

GOKHAN TURGUT
HEC MONTREAL

AEON

AEON (or ÆON Co. Ltd.) is a well-known general retail company. AEON is the parent company of a group of companies. The company operates general merchandise stores, supermarkets, specialty stores, drug stores, and convenience stores. AEON is a Japan-based company incorporated in 1926 that now employs around 70,000 people (as of January 1, 2008). Its headquarters is located at 1-5-1 Nakase, Mihama-ku, Chiba, 261 8515, Japan. AEON is traded on the Tokyo Stock Exchange, with the ticker symbol AONN-Y. AEON has 183,000 shareholders (as of January 1, 2008).

AEON generates its revenues through general merchandise and other retail stores (73 percent of its 2007 revenues); service and other operations (13 percent of its 2007 revenues), specialty store operations (12 percent of its 2007 revenues, and other operations (2 percent of its 2007 revenues). The company has operations in Japan, Asia, and North America. Japan is AEON's largest market (89 percent of its 2007 revenues). Asia is the second-largest market for AEON (6 percent of its 2007 revenues). North America is the remaining market and accounted for 5 percent of the total revenues in fiscal year 2007.

In its various stores, AEON offers general merchandise, food and drink, medical care products, and electrical appliances. The division owns Topvalu, the company's private branded range of apparel, food items, leisure goods, and home products. The company operates around 4,200 retail facilities in this division. The company operates 471 general merchandise stores, 765 supermarkets, 2,974 convenience stores, and 197 other stores, which include home centers, discount stores, and department stores.

AEON engages in four business segments: general merchandise stores; specialty stores; shopping center development; and service and other activities. General merchandise stores are operated under the name Jusco, supermarkets under the name Maxvalu, and discount and convenience stores under the name Ministop. AEON operates specialty stores under the names Talbots, Blue Grass, and Sports Authority for women's apparel, family casual fashions, health and beauty-care products, footwear, and other specialty retail activities. Moreover, AEON develops shopping centers and also engages in the leasing and management of these commercial facilities. AEON also engages in the financing of retailing stores, food service, store maintenance, wholesale and other service activities, along with the operation of certain restaurants and amusement parks, namely AEON Fantasy Outlets and AEON Cinemas.

AEON was established in Mie, Japan, on September 21, 1926, as Okadaya Gofukuten Co., Ltd. Its name was changed to its current form in 2001. Some of the biggest events in AEON's history include its 1988 acquisition of Talbots, Inc., of the United States through a subsidiary. In 2005 AEON acquired Carrefour Japan and changed its name to AEON Marche. Also, in 2006, AEON through its subsidiary Talbots, Inc., acquired J. Jill Group, Inc., of the United States.

In January 2009, at the World Economic Forum held in Davos, Switzerland, AEON has been listed in the Global 100 Most Sustainable Corporations in the World.

AEON has a diversified business portfolio. It operates in different forms and also provides several support services. Other than its core business, AEON also provides service and other supportive operations, mainly credit financing. AEON's diversified business portfolio enhances its revenue generating capacity. Also, AEON increased its strength with well-established supermarket operations. The company's decision to focus on private label brand products especially improved the profit margins. Moreover, AEON's financing services enhanced its profits significantly. The opening of new shopping centers contributed to the rise. The credit services operations were another growth-driver for AEON.

The major weaknesses of AEON may be regarded as its geographic concentration. AEON is mainly dependent on the Japanese market. Considering market forecasts with the projection that Japanese

AEON operates around 765 supermarkets and 2,974 convenience and discount stores in Japan under the names Maxvalu and Ministop. Its general merchandise and other stores accounted for 73 percent of 2007 revenues, but they face fierce competition.

buying power will lessen in the near future drives a gloomy overall picture in the coming years. Moreover, AEON's concentration on financing strongly decreases its flexibility for required financial liquidity. That is, whereas AEON enjoys new business growth by offering accessible credit, its debt management causes problems for itself. However, strong geographic diversification gives the rivals of AEON competitive advantage in sourcing and distribution of their operations. Because of intense competition, AEON needs to allocate large quantities of resources to maintain its market share.

AEON's main competitors in Japan include: Takashimaya, UNY, Seiyu, Hankyu Department Stores, and Marui. Its rivals in North America include Wal-Mart Stores, Costco Wholesale, Target, Sears Holdings, BJ's Wholesale Club, Pantry, Family Dollar Stores, Foot Locker, Big Lots, and Dollar Tree.

See Also: Costco Wholesale; Japan; Retail Sector; Sears Holdings; Target; Wal-Mart Stores.

Bibliography. AEON, www.aeon.info (cited March 2009); SEC-EDGAR, www.sec.gov (cited March 2009).

GOKHAN TURGUT
HEC MONTREAL

AEX General Index (Amsterdam)

The desirability of tracking the performance of elite stocks led nations in Eurasia, North and South America, Africa, and Australia to establish stock exchanges in the 20th century. Dating to 1983, the Amsterdam Stock Exchange Index, today the AEX Index, has listed as many as 25 of the most traded Dutch stocks. As an aid to traders the AEX Index posts current data on the performance of its stocks as well as data on the Internet with a 20-minute lag. Several instruments, for example, index reports, serve the AEX Index in its task of sharing with investors the minutia of stock performance. The AEX Index includes Dutch companies that trade on the Euronext Amsterdam.

On January 3, 1983, the AEX-Optiebeurs began compiling the AEX Index. The original 13 stocks totaled 100 points. The AEX Index calculated the value of stocks by multiplying the price of each stock by its weighted factor, 15 percent of a stock's value, summing these amounts and then dividing the aggregate by 100, establishing the value of the index. Among the original 13 companies were the brewer Heineken and the energy company Royal Dutch Shell, both of which have remained on the index to the present. In 1987 investors began trading options and in 1988, futures. To these original 13 companies, the index added five companies, the largest single addition to date, in 1989. The index began on February 18, 1994, to review its composition of stocks, reserving the right to delete stocks from its roster. The AEX Index removed from its list companies whose capital fell below the 25 most capitalized companies in the Netherlands. Subsequently the index established two review dates: March 1 and September 1 of each year.

The index bases its review on the closing price of stocks on the last day of trading in January and June. When the index deletes a company from its roster, it leaves the slot vacant until the next review date, whether in March or September, when it may invite a new company to join. This new company must score in the top 25 in capitalization. If a company has more than one class of stock traded on the Euronext, the AEX Index will accept only the more actively traded class of stock. In addition, in the March and September reviews, the index adjusts the weight of each company, which rises and falls with a company's performance. Following its March and September reviews, the index makes effective any changes in its composition on the next trading day.

On January 4, 1999, the AEX Index began calculating the value of its stocks in Euros. The index's 100 points equals just over €45. Among the index's current holdings is a mix of companies. Banks, life insurance companies, and real estate developers, all of them represented on the index, were the tools for amassing wealth in the 20th century. With the rise of energy prices in the 21st century, companies that process, deliver, and provide equipment for the extraction and distribution of energy have prospered on the index. The petroleum and natural gas supplier Royal Dutch Shell and the petroleum equipment manufacturer Single Buoy Moorings (SBM) Offshore, both of them on the index, have surged in 2008. Also on the index are telecommunications equipment supplier Tom Tom, electronics manufacturer Philips, and semiconductor manufacturer ASML.

Worldwide economic fluctuations affect the index. The frenzied selling of stocks on Black Monday in 1987 sent the AEX Index into decline; conversely, the enthusiastic buying of internet companies in the early 21st century resulted in a bubble. The AEX Index peaked at 703.18 on September 5, 2000, at the height of the bubble. The end of speculation in internet company stocks more than halved the index's value between late 2001 and 2003. During 2007–08 the AEX Index ranged between 374.09 and 559.43, with the lower value only 53 percent of the peak and the higher value 79.5 percent of the peak.

Investors may buy stocks on the index as well as funds that index the AEX Index. Comprising large cap stocks, the index relies increasingly for the value of its portfolio on technology and energy companies. The index balances technology and energy, important as they are, with publishers and the processors of food. The result is a diversity of companies. This diversity hedges against steep losses and rapid ascents, for technology, energy, publishing, food processing, banking, and other classes of companies, whose stocks are not likely all to be up or down on a given day. Rather, gains in one sector offset losses in another. Investors, buying and selling stocks as the opportunity arises, will point the index toward the future. Savvy as they are, investors and pundits are unlikely to pinpoint the future course of the index.

See Also: Netherlands; Stock Exchanges.

Bibliography. NYSE Euronext, www.nyse.com/aex (cited March 2009); H. C. S. Warendorf and R. L. Thomas, *The Netherlands Securities Trading Act and Official Commentary* (Kluwer Law and Taxation, 1986).

CHRISTOPHER CUMO
INDEPENDENT SCHOLAR

Africa

The African continent remains by and large marginalized in the world economy, with over half of the population living on under US$1 a day per person. Its share of worldwide exports has fallen from 6.1 percent in 1960 to 2.4 percent in 2006. The portion of worldwide foreign direct investment inflows to Africa has also declined, from 9.4 percent in 1970 to 2.7 percent in 2006. The continent's labor force was about 370 million strong in 2006.

The continent has struggled to overcome widespread legacies of slavery, colonialism, ethnic tension, and war. Africa became a symbol of Third World underdevelopment as soon as its nations began gaining political independence. Recently, African countries have also been confronted by the challenges of globalization, raising the question of whether some of them could join the ranks of "emerging countries" and create a regional basis of development.

Some have questioned African adaptability to "modern business." First, historians argue that the massive slave trade (more than 10 million people transported abroad from the 1600s to the 1830s in sub-Saharan Africa, but till the 1920s northward to Morocco or the Persian Gulf) deprived Africa of a demographic reserve and, in the long term, of a "normal" evolution of potential elites. Second, numerous northern academics and politicians have considered that the African way of life hindered "modern development." The statutes of ground property remained vague because of collective or religious ownership of land, thus blocking individual intensive investment like in other areas; the social framework that privileged large family networks gave priority to immediate redistribution of income instead of savings that would favor accumulation of capital; the respective position of women and men may have fostered gender gaps; and ethnic and caste considerations added obstacles to social mobility. African wholesale traders seemed unable to rise from short- or middle-term commercial incomes to long-term industrial investments.

Recurrent ethnic tensions and civil war weakened African societies. Geography and demography were involved too, the first because of the influence of climate on development (either drought and deserts, or tropical and subtropical or Mediterranean floods), the second because lack of population or overpopulation conflicted as explanations of economic tensions. Analyses of the evolution of African business continue to stir endless arguments about the causes and duration of African underdevelopment.

Colonial Legacies

Africa's lagging economies have roots deep in the colonial period. One of the more lasting legacies has been the weakness of educational policies. Islands of training comprised mainly Christian missionary schools (Madagascar, Togo, Dahomey/Benin, Liberia) or Islamic schools (northern Africa), but no real comprehensive strategy of mass education took shape during the period. This led to a relatively low level of primary and professional education for Africans, with exceptions in local universities (such as in Egypt, Tunisia, Algeria, and South Africa) or abroad in Europe.

Another long-term policy shaped the framework for the evolution of Africa's economy: Europeans conceived of Africa as a potential reserve for commodities and enticed rural people to develop exports for Europe. That was the case in sub-Saharan Africa for groundnuts, oil palm, gum arabic, rubber trees, coffee, cocoa, and (in the Niger loop and in the Sahel) cotton. Native peasants and plantations owned by European companies became committed to such an expansion. The Lever group (Unilever since 1930) exemplified this approach as the owner of plantations and as an important transformer of commodities in its European manufactures.

This type of "modern" business system involved wholesale trading houses complemented by hundreds of smaller companies and by thousands of African suppliers and transporters. Networks of trading posts collected raw commodities in exchange for European goods, such as clothes, household goods, and agricultural equipment. Warehouses, wharves, and chains of shipping lines facilitated sea transport.

An efficient economy took shape from the 1880s till the 1960s, with the leading big businesses from European countries such as France, the United Kingdom (UK), Switzerland, and Belgium. All over Africa native planters invested their time and skills into commercial agriculture rather than developing more intensively their subsistence crops.

Despite vast programs of modernization, African infrastructure still lagged behind. Colonies generally had to self-finance their investments until World War II or had to borrow in Europe, which slowed the completion of projects. Not until the 1940s and 1950s did construction gather momentum, but it did, leaving several countries with railway networks, ports (such as in Lagos, Abidjan, and Casablanca), dams and hydroelectric power plants (in Algeria and Morocco, and on the Niger River). But this infrastructure was intended mainly for the support of trade with Europe, without enough internal networks of transport through northern Africa or the Sahel. Huge gaps still predominated in the infrastructure programs, thus causing large discrepancies between territories.

Inequity prevailed because European business took hold of wealth almost everywhere. Trade was controlled by big companies or many small ones. Lebanese (sub-Saharan Africa), Chinese (Central Africa), and Indian (South Africa) people were active in the middle ranks of retail trading. Mining was controlled by state entities (in Morocco for phosphates) or big businesses. Africa was perceived as a supplier of raw resources, such as coal, gold, and diamonds (Austral Africa); copper (the Belgian Congo, the British Rhodesias); and phosphates (French North Africa).

In some territories, African natives were deprived of developed agriculture because Europeans had confiscated the richest land, for instance in Austral Africa or in Algeria. This contributed to a phenomenon of "pauperization," with a large reservoir of labor for day-to-day hand tasks, either in agriculture or in transportation. This was sometimes forced labor, which was abolished in French colonies only in 1946, with a Labor Code implemented later in the mid-1950s.

The end of slavery (within Africa itself), "pacification" and military rule on one side, and important healthcare programs on the other side, prompted growth in the African population. Beginning in the 1940s, a rapid growth of towns began, often on the coasts, around harbors, or around economic centers in Central or South Africa. Large numbers of poor people now clustered in shanty towns (called *bidonvilles* in French colonies). In the 1980s and 1990s this trend would begin to reverse as AIDS began crippling several southern African countries.

Dependence

Even after independence, African states were dominated by industrialized countries that influenced technologies, money for investment, and the prices of commodities and ores exported by Africa. Independent states also had to take into account the imbalance of power in favor of ex-colonial countries. Special agreements determined by geopolitical strategies helped ex-colonial states keep privileged positions throughout Africa.

French companies continued to play a key part in the ex-French empire. For example, the French state oil firm Elf-Aquitaine held sway in Central Africa (Gabon, Cameroon, and the Congo), and the UK also had influence, with Shell in Nigeria. The Belgian group Société générale de Belgique was still a force in the Congo, then Zaire, through its dense array of assets in mining, transportation, industry, trading, shipping, and finance. In South Africa under apartheid, big Western industrial groups extended their control over mining.

Socialism and "Mixed Economies"

Some African states wanted to get control over their economies through the nationalization of big business. A turning point came in July 1956 when Gamal Abdel Nasser of Egypt nationalized the Suez Canal, arguing that the revenues of transit should finance the building of the huge Aswan dam and power plant and the modernization of the economy, itself heavily controlled by the state until the mid-1970s. The "socialist model" prevailed in several key countries that nationalized their main resources. In Algeria, the FLN and President Houari Boumédienne nationalized oil assets at the start of the 1970s under the state-owned Sonatrach oil and gas monopoly. Muammar Qadhafi's Libya followed the example, and a few states adopted state-led policies (such as Tunisia, Zambia, Madagascar, Benin, Ghana, and Guinea), with more or less public interventionism and property.

Socialist-minded leaders intended to attain economic take-off with a large accumulation of capital, with revenues from agriculture oriented toward heavy industrialization schemes (as in Algeria) or toward middle-sized industries for consuming goods and light equipment (in Egypt and Tunisia). Subsidies and protectionism countered low productivity or a lack of skilled labor and executives.

All over Africa, pockets of state interventionism were constituted to manage the income of commodities. Marketing boards collected agricultural products, sold them abroad (to multinational trade companies), and shared the revenues between peasants and investments in dams with energy and irrigation schemes, in transportation (ports, roads), or in some forms of welfare state. In these cases, a "mixed economy" prevailed because the state allowed action by private investors, either local or international, thus creating pockets of industrialization (textile, metalworking, car assembly), generally under the umbrella of protectionist customs taxes.

Nigeria and the Ivory Coast were beacons of such policies, and emerged as "rich countries" because of their size, population, natural resources, and, for Nigeria, oil. But a few other experiences of socialist-state countries ended in turmoil because of a paralysis of entrepreneurship (in Ghana and Guinea) and even of foreign direct investment.

Small enterprises, such as this salon advertised on a billboard in Cameroon, have proliferated in Africa, but their impact is slight.

Weak States

Throughout Africa, the results of those various paths were shown to be uncertain in the 1980s. The key issue seems to have been the inability of the state in a majority of countries to fix a guidance framework because of its very weakness. While Western economic administrations were built for decades and through hard political contests ("revolutions," in Britain, the United States, and France), suddenly meager African elites had to steer large areas without administrative tradition, means, or commonly admitted law.

Some states reached some balance between clan interests and general interests, especially where elites were stronger, in northern Africa or in a few sub-Saharan countries, like the Ivory Coast or Senegal. However, a large majority were subject to the rule of ethnic or political groups that used state treasuries as leverage for corruption. Businesses had to face uncertainty of law completion, commonplace extortion forms (at customs posts or through fiscal rackets), and bribery. In a few "kleptocracies," such corruption grew tremendously. Mobutu's Zaire in the 1970s and 1980s was imitated by several oil countries (Nigeria, Gabon, the Congo, and Cameroon, the latter being ranked among the most corrupt countries in the world). All of them benefited from the tolerant support of Western countries because of the Cold War environment and growing business interests.

Military dictatorships (such as in Uganda and Nigeria) provided one explanation, but habits of clan power were also developed in semi-democratic countries (such as Kenya) or socialist ones (Algeria from the 1980s). Meanwhile, the weakness of administrations could also be explained by flawed tax systems and the prevalence of an "informal economy." Lack of budgetary transparency could explain lagging public investments in transportation, education, or health systems, hindering economic growth.

Emerging Entrepreneurship

Several forces helped Africa begin to overcome some of its previous economic challenges. First, international cooperation drove Africans to become conscious of the issues. United Nations (UN) organizations such as the UN Conference on Trade Development (UNCTAD) and the Food and Agriculture Organization (FAO) insisted on investments in agriculture and in manpower training. The World Bank financed infrastructure and was imitated by the African Bank for Development, which was established in 1963. Hundreds of conferences began to forge a shared outlook in favor of "a new economic order," taking into account general interests and the need for infrastructure in rural areas. Many nongovernmental organizations became involved as well. Even business law was cleaned up by more transparent and stable states, or, in about 16 French-speaking countries, thanks to the Organization for the Harmonization of Business Law in Africa (OHADA), created in 1993.

Elites were trained either in African universities or abroad, which, despite the "brain drain" toward developed countries, contributed to creating management executives in economic administrations, local enterprises, or foreign affiliates. The long-term growth and the relative distribution of wealth and income fostered emerging middle classes in a majority of countries (but not in those with lasting civil war).

What was at stake was the emergence of entrepreneurship, mixing traditional African values and capitalist values. Despite water shortages, millions of planters were committed to a "modern" agriculture, either for exports or for local use. The cotton revolution in the Sahel belt from Chad to Mali now involves 15–20 million peasants. Cocoa and coffee, paddy rice, cereals, spices, and vegetables for household consumption have also helped raise standards of living and promote trade.

Huge investments by states into dams and irrigation networks sustained such development (in north Africa, with, for example, the Moroccan program of 1967; and in the Niger loop). The withdrawal of European retail firms eased the growth of native shopkeepers, from petty ones to more specialized ones, while the legacy of commercial cultures benefited ethnic groups, which reinforced their grip in several areas (the Bamileke in Central Africa, Fulas in Sierra Leone, and Ibos in Nigeria, for example).

Middle-sized trade, services, and facilities management houses took shape all over African cities, despite competition, and professional schooling and trading helped sustain the move in the long term. Throughout African or foreign service or industrial firms, middle-class layers of accountants, managers, technicians, and even engineers (for example, at Algerian Sonatrach) were constituted in the 1970s.

The key issue lies in industrialization: Was African entrepreneurship and capital able to fuel initiatives? The transfer of foreign firms to African investors has been a reality in several countries where the law required such reshuffling, for instance, in Nigeria in the 1970s. In South Africa, foreign or local companies from the time of apartheid started following a law in the 1990s imposing buyouts of equity by black investors. But the transfer of manufacturing to private African capital remained hard to achieve because of the trend toward less protectionist rules. These rules were imposed by the General Agreement on Tariffs and Trade (GATT) or by the International Monetary Fund (IMF) in the 1980s and 1990s under the name of "structural adjustment programs." They weakened numerous industries, such as textile production, metalworking, and leather, which, along with gaps in transportation and energy supplies, put the brakes on an industrial emergence. However, tourism and hotel businesses (and real estate linked to them) did emerge in several countries, fostering layers of native mid-sized enterprises.

Globalization

In parallel with the issues of African entrepreneurship, the other issue of the exploitation of resources has been at stake. Could African countries balance their political independence and the call for foreign investors through avoiding "neo-imperialism"? In fact, a new "scramble for Africa" commenced: Big European and American businesses invested massively to develop timber production in tropical Africa, risking overexploitation. They also invested in oil and Africa reached a 12 percent share of world production in 2005. Other investments were in nonferrous metals (such as manganese in Gabon), uranium, diamonds and gold, and phosphates. The United States became a partner to Africa, especially in phosphates or metals—but, in the 21st century, China and India commenced establishing footholds because of their need for ores and energy.

Industrial firms kept momentum up for car assembly plants, light industries, first transformation of commodities (groundnuts, palm oil, and cacao butter), oil refineries, and cement. They did this even though they could not count on a "global African market" because of the lack of integrated transportation systems and because of protectionist positions. In fact, Africa still suffered from a lack of a competitive edge: an untrained workforce; instability in some areas, in particular in Nigeria and the Democratic Republic of the Congo; lack of energy (despite dams in several countries); lack of transparency in governance; and corruption. Such obstacles spurred imports from abroad at the expense of local production.

One key issue remains the use by the state of its income from oil and commodities. Countries benefiting from the oil allowance (100 percent of gross national product for the Republic of the Congo in 2005, 89 percent for Angola and Libya, 64 percent for Chad and Algeria, 52 percent for Nigeria) seemed to insufficiently master its use in favor of general equipment and development, with some even lacking oil refineries and having gas shortages.

Development

Strong pockets of development have increased purchasing power all over the African coasts. Urbanization has contributed to growth, with real estate developments, public works, the engineering of ports, management of energy and healthcare, and even new technologies of information. But the state of capitalist entrepreneurship is still questionable. What is lacking in a majority of countries is a network of complementary industrial and service activities; they are found only in South Africa and perhaps in Algeria. The transformation of primary commodities is still insufficient.

Middle-sized enterprises are fragile because of exposure to recessions, despite the support of national or international "banks of development." Predominant micro and small enterprises employ very few if any people and generate little or no income for the owners, even with the recent support of micro-credit institutions and practices beyond traditional "tontine" uses. States remain a key force in development and investment.

Self-help is another avenue to growth. The New Partnership for Africa's Development (NEPAD) took shape in 2001 to define a strategic framework under the guidance of five advanced countries (Algeria, Egypt, Nigeria, Senegal, and South Africa) within the United Africa Organization. The Southern Africa Development Community arose in 1981 to mobilize capital from rapidly emerging South Africa.

Despite these efforts, if the major UN Millennium Development Goal of reducing poverty by half by the year 2015 is to be achieved in Africa, a major policy shift is required, both at the national and international levels, to help boost growth and development.

See Also: African Development Bank; Algeria; Angola; Botswana; Cameroon; Côte d'Ivoire; Egypt; Ghana; Kenya; Libya; Millennium Development Goals; Morocco; Nigeria; South Africa; Sudan; Suez; Tanzania; Tunisia; World Bank, The; Zimbabwe.

Bibliography. W. M. Adams, *Wasting the Rain: Rivers, People and Planning in Africa* (University of Minnesota Press, 1992); R. Austen, *African Economic History: Internal Development and External Dependency* (J. Currey, 1987); C. Boone, *Merchant Capital and the Roots of State Power in Senegal, 1930–1985* (Cambridge University Press, 1992); W. G. Clarence-Smith, ed., *Cocoa Pioneer Fronts since 1800: The Role of Smallholders, Planters and Merchants* (MacMillan Press, 1996); D. Fick, *Entrepreneurship in Africa. A Study of Successes* (Quorum Books, 2002; D. K. Fieldhouse, *Unilever Overseas* (Croom Helm, 1978); A. G. Hopkins, *An Economic History of West Africa* (Longman, 1973); A. Jalloh and T. Galola, eds., *Black Business and Economic Power* (Rochester University Press, 2002); P. Kennedy, *African Capitalism: The Struggle for Ascendency* (Cambridge University Press, 1990); P. Kibly, *Industrialisation in an Open Economy: Nigeria, 1945–1966* (Cambridge University Press, 1969); M. Lynn, *Commerce and Economic Change in West Africa: The Palm Oil Trade in the Nineteenth Century* (Cambridge University Press, 1997); Gabriël Oosthuizen, *The Southern African Development Community: The Organisation, Its History, Policies and Prospects* (Institute for Global Dialogue, 2006); D. Pallister, S. Stewart, and I. Lepper, *South Africa Inc.: The Oppenheimer Empire* (Yale University Press, 1988); F. Pedler, *The Lion and the Unicorn in Africa. A History of the Origins of the United Africa Company, 1787–1931* (Heinemann, 1974); A. Spring and B. McDade, eds., *African Entrepreneurship: Theory and Reality* (University Press of Florida, 1998); Will Swearingen, *Moroccan Mirages: Agrarian Dreams and Deceptions, 1912–1986* (Princeton University Press, 1987); R. B. Winder, *The Lebanese in West Africa* (Mouton, 1962).

Hubert Bonin
Bordeaux University

African Development Bank

Established in 1964 by 23 African governments, the African Development Bank Group manages the African Development Bank, the African Development Fund, and the Nigeria Trust Fund, to the end of social and economic improvements throughout Africa. Operations began in 1966 from an Abidjan, Côte d'Ivoire, headquarters, which has since been relocated to Tunis.

Current member nations of the African Development Bank, which the African Development Bank Group divides according to region, are: in Central

Africa, Cameroon, the Central African Republic, Chad, Congo, the Democratic Republic of the Congo, Equatorial Guinea, and Gabon; in East Africa, Burundi, Comoros, Djibouti, Eritrea, Ethiopia, Kenya, Rwanda, Seychelles, Somalia, Sudan, Tanzania, and Uganda; in North Africa, Algeria, Egypt, Libya, Mauritania, Morocco, and Tunisia; in Southern Africa, Angola, Botswana, Lesotho, Madagascar, Malawi, Mauritius, Mozambique, Namibia, South Africa, Swaziland, Zambia, and Zimbabwe; in West Africa, Benin, Burkina Faso, Cape Verde, Côte d'Ivoire, Gambia, Ghana, Guinea, Guinea-Bissau, Liberia, Mali, Niger, Nigeria, São Tomé and Príncipe, Senegal, Sierra Leone, and Togo; and the non-beneficiary member countries, Argentina, Austria, Belgium, Brazil, Canada, China, Denmark, Finland, France, Germany, India, Italy, Japan, Korea, Kuwait, Netherlands, Norway, Portugal, Saudi Arabia, Spain, Sweden, Switzerland, the United Kingdom, and the United States. Shareholders thus include 53 African countries, called Regional Member Countries (RMCs) and 24 non-African countries. The Board of Executive Directors that governs the African Development Bank Group is composed of representatives from different member states, with RMC representatives collectively retaining a steady 60 percent of the vote.

The list of RMCs in the African Development Bank Group is almost identical to the member nations of the African Union, and the history of the two entities is intertwined, having emerged in the climate of pan-Africanism that developed in the wake of European imperialism—and amidst strong desire to turn pan-African institutions into Cold War institutions. The African Union, established in 2002, is the successor to the Organization of African Unity founded in 1963, and the spiritual successor to other attempts at African political and economic union. Foreign and economic policy, in particular, are coordinated jointly among the nations of the African Union, which include all of Africa except for Morocco (Guinea and Mauritania are currently suspended in the wake of the 2008 coups d'état). While the Organization of African Unity ostensibly protected African human rights and collective voice in the aftermath of colonialism, the African Union's long-term goals parallel the developments of the European Union, and include an eventual central bank and common currency, as well as a region-wide investment bank and monetary fund.

The African Development Bank employs about 1,000 people, and has funded about 3,000 projects over the last four decades, with a special emphasis on the intersection of social and economic improvement, such as educational funding and attempts to improve and modernize the role of women in the African world. Many of the African Development Bank's loans and grants go to infrastructure projects,

Development Funds

The African Development Fund began operating in 1974, ten years after the founding of the African Development Bank, and provides special interest-free loans to RMCs unable to qualify for African Development Bank loans, usually for projects that will help move those RMCs into a position of economic health that will qualify them for African Development Bank loans in the future. The African Development Fund is a joint operation between the African Development Bank and the governments of its members, and operates from a pool of funds contributed by non-RMC member states, which are generally replenished periodically.

With the Nigerian government, the African Development Bank Group also operates the Nigerian Trust Fund, which has fewer resources than the other African Development Bank Group entities but focuses them solely on the poorest RMCs, where many citizens live on less than a dollar a day.

See Also: Africa; Company Profiles: Africa; Development Assistance.

Bibliography. John Akokpari, Angela Ndinga-Muvumba, and Tim Murithi, eds., *The African Union and Its Institutions* (Jacana Media, 2009); Paul Collier, *The Bottom Billion: Why the Poorest Countries Are Failing and What Can Be Done About It* (Oxford University Press, 2008); K. D. Fordwor, *African Development Bank* (Elsevier, 1981); Samuel Makinda, *The African Union: Challenges of Globalization, Security, and Governance* (Routledge, 2007); Tim Murithi, *The African Union: Pan-Africanism, Peacebuilding, and Development* (Ashgate Publishing, 2005).

BILL KTE'PI
INDEPENDENT SCHOLAR

Agents

Agents are the intermediaries who help to develop and maintain the channels of distribution. Agents arrange for sales between two parties and get paid usually in commission. An agent's duty is to understand the marketer's business model and market objectives so that they can help the marketer to find the suitable partners and routes to the market. They are expected to obtain the best possible deal for the marketer by negotiating with the distributor. The agent's firm may provide different types of mediatory services as necessary for a particular business.

To make a product accessible to the foreign target market is a critical and challenging process for an international marketer. Each foreign market contains unique distribution networks with many channels. Sometimes it is difficult to penetrate the multilayered, complex, and inefficient distribution structure in a new market. The distribution process in any country consists of three main components: the physical handling and distribution of goods, the passage of ownership (title), and, most important from the standpoint of marketing strategy, the buying and selling negotiation between the producers and agents (or middlemen) and the agents and customers. In a distribution structure, the goods pass from producers to the users through the agents whose customary functions, activities, and services reflect existing competition, market characteristics, tradition, and economic development. Distribution structure varies from one country to another. For example, the distribution structure for Japan is very different from the United States or European countries in terms of the density of agents. In Japan, the commodities often pass through three or four intermediaries or agents before reaching customers.

Agents may have different names and functions in foreign countries. It is important for international marketers to thoroughly understand the titles and the type of services the agents provide. The same agent or firm may provide different types of services depending on the job requirement. For example, the functions of a variety of agents namely, a stockist, an exporter, or an importer are different in the markets of England.

The marketer has to be aware of the intent of the agent to maximize his own profit with the least amount of work. Hence, agents sometimes take orders from manufacturers whose products and brands are in demand to avoid any real selling effort to market a new product or a new manufacturer. Frequently, the manufacturer with a new product or a product with a limited market share is forced to bypass the agents until they establish a reasonable market share for their product. Often the manufacturers have to provide adequate inducement to agents to convince the disinterested agents to promote and sell their products.

The services provided by agents are critical to the success of the marketers. Hence the marketers should carefully research the target market in a foreign country while choosing an agent or an agent's firm. The two most important qualities of a successful agent are his personal commitment to the marketer and his product and his superior performance. One way to achieve success in the international market is to work closely with the agent. The manufacturer or marketer has to terminate the agent's contract promptly in case of poor performance, so performance and termination clauses should be clearly documented. Many international businesses have achieved success based on their willingness to terminate all underperforming agents. However, sometimes if unaware of local legalities, the companies may face legal consequences. Sometimes local corruption creates legal adversity. Hence, the agent and the marketer both should understand clearly the rights and the obligations under the agreement.

Agents help marketers eliminate the difficulties involving language, physical distribution, communications, and financing in a foreign country, and their cooperation is crucial to the success of an international marketer.

See Also: Channels; Direct Export; Distribution; Foreign Sales Corporation; Franchising; Gray Market; Indirect Export; Sales; Supply Chain Management; Subsidiary; Vertically Integrated Chain.

Bibliography. Daniel C. Bello and Ritu Lohtia, "Export Channel Design: The Use of Foreign Distributors and Agents," *Journal of the Academy of Marketing Science* (v.23/2, 1995); Philip R. Cateora and John L. Graham, *International Marketing* (McGraw-Hill Irwin, 2007); Warren J. Keegan, *Global Marketing Management* (Prentice Hall, 2006).

Mousumi Roy
Pennsylvania State University

Agreement on Trade-Related Aspects of Intellectual Property Rights

Intellectual Property Rights (IPR) are the rights given to persons over the creation of their minds. Intellectual property includes copyright (for example, the rights of authors of literary and artistic works) as well as industrial property (for example, trademarks and patents). The need to protect IPR was discussed at the Uruguay Round (1986–94) as part of the General Agreement on Tariffs and Trade (GATT). For the first time in the history of GATT, the Uruguay Round established the minimum standards of protection to be accorded to IPR. The Agreement on Trade-Related Aspects of Intellectual Property Rights (TRIPS) came into force in January 1995.

Before the TRIPS Agreement, considerable variation existed between countries in the protection of IPR. These differences became a source for concern among developed industrial countries during the 1970s, because of rapid growth in research and development expenditures and trade in products with a high IPR content (for example, pharmaceuticals, electronics, and computer software). The basic aims of the TRIPS Agreement were to promote protection of IPR and to ensure that international trade was not constrained by the measures that individual countries enforced to protect IPR.

The TRIPS Agreement covers five major issues: the applicability of the basic principles of GATT and relevant international intellectual property agreements; the provision of adequate standards governing the use of trade-related IPR; the provision of effective measures for the enforcement of trade-related IPR; the provision of robust procedures for the settlement of disputes between governments; and the introduction of transitional arrangements during the period when the Agreement was being introduced.

In order to obtain international cohesion in the standards of IPR protection, the agreement built upon the obligations that already existed. For example, in the case of patents and industrial designs, the main international agreement was provided by the Paris Convention for the Protection of Industrial Property. This Convention was held in 1883 and has been subsequently revised. In the case of copyright, the Berne Convention for the Protection of Literary and Artistic Works, 1886, provided the principal protocol on these matters.

A council, which is answerable to the World Trade Organization, was established to oversee the operation of the TRIPS Agreement. Since 1995, the council has reviewed legislation on a wide range of IPR, including, for example: electronic commerce; a multilateral system of notification and registration of geographical indications for wines and spirits; technology transfer; integrated circuits; anticompetitive practices in contractual licenses; and undisclosed information and trade secrets.

Underlying the TRIPS Agreement were a number of general provisions that defined the minimum standards of intellectual property protection: for example, members are not obliged to provide statutory protection beyond that required by the Agreement. Provision was made whereby member countries would treat their own nationals and foreigners equally. It was also stipulated that nothing in the Agreement would absolve members from the existing obligations they had to each other under the various International Conventions for the Protection of Industrial Property. Most-favored-nation treatment was also ruled out; specifically, in the context of the protection of IPR, advantages or privileges granted by a member to the nationals of any other country would immediately and unconditionally be accorded to the nationals of all other members.

A further important principle was that the protection of IPR should contribute to innovation and technology transfer. Finally, public interest considerations were recognized: Members were permitted to exclude from patentability medical treatments for animals and humans.

In addition to these general provisions, the Agreement also provided for the protection of specific IPR. As regards copyright, the Agreement protected computer programs; international copyright rules were expanded to cover rental rights. For example, authors of computer programs had the right to prohibit the commercial rental of such works to the public. Additionally, performers had the right to prevent unauthorized recording and transmission of live performances for up to 50 years. In the case of geographical indications (GIs) of origin, the Agreement was an innovation for many countries. GIs are used to identify the place where a product is made. They are important because a particular product obtains its essential characteristics precisely because it is produced in a particular locality. Classic examples of this are "Burgundy," "Champagne," and "Scotch" in alcoholic beverages. Specific legal provision was also provided whereby interested parties could prevent use of a GI to identify wines if these wines had not originated in the place located by the GI.

Turning to patents, the Agreement provided that protection must be available for inventions for at least 20 years. In the specific case of pharmaceutical products, innovations such as compulsory licensing were introduced to ensure that countries unable to produce pharmaceuticals domestically could import patented drugs.

One of the key factors motivating GATT's interest in the protection of IPR was concern about trade in pirated goods. Accordingly, a further innovation of the Agreement was to strengthen the power of the customs authorities to seize and detain fraudulently marked goods. This led to the creation of the World Customs Organization (formerly Customs Coordination Council) to promulgate customs legislation designed to facilitate the implementation of the Agreement.

See Also: General Agreement on Tariffs and Trade; Intellectual Property Theft; World Trade Organization.

Bibliography. M. Blakeney, *Trade Related Aspects of Intellectual Property Rights: A Concise Guide to the TRIPS Agreement* (Sweet and Maxwell, 1996); C. M. Correa, *Intellectual Property Rights, the WTO and Developing Countries* (Zed Books, 2000).

DAVID M. HIGGINS
UNIVERSITY OF YORK

Algeria

The People's Democratic Republic of Algeria (population 33,769,669 in 2008, GDP $225 billion in 2007) is an industrialized and predominantly Muslim country in North Africa. The largest country on the Mediterranean coast, it is also the second-largest in Africa, and a member of the United Nations, the African Union, OPEC, and the Arab League.

Settled by Berbers thousands of years ago and invaded by both Carthage and Rome in antiquity, Algeria was conquered by Muslims in the Middle Ages, and in 1517 became part of the Ottoman Empire. The Algerian city of Algiers was one of the main ports of operation for the famed Barbary pirates of the 16th through 19th centuries, whose attacks on American ships precipitated the First and Second Barbary Wars. Thousands of European ships were lost to the pirates over the centuries, making them the terror of the north African coast, a reputation that may have contributed to the violence of the French invasion in 1830, when over one million Algerians were killed (a third of the population, under a policy of extermination to prevent revolt). Despite this, it took the rest of the 19th century for the French rulers to stamp out the last of Algerian resistance. In the aftermath of World War II and the collapse of European imperialism around the world, resistance to French rule reignited, and Algerian guerrillas fought a campaign for independence, which was eventually established in 1962.

Since the adoption of its constitution in 1976, Algeria has been a multi-party state, and more than 40 political parties (not all of them active at the same time) have registered with the Ministry of the Interior. The head of state is the president, who is elected to a five-year term (with no term limits) and appoints a prime minister who acts as head of government, and in turn appoints the members of the council of ministers of which the president is head. The legislative branch consists of a bicameral parliament: The 144 members of the upper house, the council of nation, whose members serve six-year terms and are elected by regional authorities or appointed by the president; and the 389 members of the People's National Assembly, who serve five-year terms and are directly elected by their constituencies.

Though Algeria is almost entirely Sunni Muslim, there are small communities of Christians in the larger cities, including a quasi-underground evangelical Christian community operating out of home churches and actively proselytizing new members since the 20th-century rise in worldwide Christian evangelism. The Jewish population since the end of French rule is negligible.

The oasis town of Ghardaïa, in north-central Algeria, is known for crafts and is part of a U.N. World Heritage Site.

accounts for about a quarter of the economy, and the fertile soil of Algeria is ideal for cereal grains, which have been the principal agricultural good since the cotton industry declined in the 19th century. Tobacco, figs, dates, citrus, and olives are all significant exports as well.

See Also: Africa; France.

Bibliography: Charles-Robert Ageron, *Modern Algeria: A History from 1830 to the Present* (Hurst, 1991); Ahmed Aghrout and Redha M. Bougherira, *Algeria in Transition: Reforms and Development Prospects* (Routledge, 2004); Mahfoud Bennoune, *The Making of Contemporary Algeria: Colonial Upheavals and Post-Independence Development, 1830–1987* (Cambridge University Press, 1988); John Ruedy, *Modern Algeria: The Origins and Development of a Nation* (Indiana University Press, 1992); Benjamin Stora, *Algeria: 1830–2000* (Cornell University Press, 2001).

BILL KTE'PI
INDEPENDENT SCHOLAR

Most Algerians speak Arabic, which is the country's official language. The implementation of this official language was tied in with issues of Algerian independence, but has resulted in the derogation of the Berber population, which speaks Tamazight (recently recognized as a national language, which still excludes it from use in official contexts). French remains such a well-known language that some university courses are still taught in it, as they have been since before independence.

Algeria is 14th in the world in petroleum reserves and eighth in natural gas reserves, and fossil fuels account for nearly all exports (95 percent) and 30 percent of the gross domestic product (GDP). The high fossil fuel prices of recent years have resulted in a high and sustained trade surplus for Algeria, and a steady rise in the GDP; since 2006, Algeria's foreign debt has been less than a tenth of its GDP. But unemployment is high—around 12 percent—because this wealth, and especially the foreign investment behind it, does not extend to all sectors of the economy. Agriculture

Allianz SE

The German company Allianz SE, founded in 1890, is now the largest international insurance and financial services organization in the world. The two founders were Carl Thieme, the director of the Munich Rückversicherungs-Gessellschaft (Munich Reinsurance) and Wilhelm Finck, a Munich banker, and its original headquarters were in Munich. Thieme ran the reinsurance company on totally different lines to the original insurers as a market niche. However, his work quickly showed him that there were huge profits to be made from direct insurance, and Allianz was established to do this. It was not long before Allianz was making more profits than Munich Rückversicherungs-Gessellschaft, and Thieme and Finck started concentrating their efforts on Allianz.

The firm started offering transport and accident insurance very soon after the company was established, and as a result of an expansion in business, they moved the company headquarters to Berlin, the German capital, where they also offered fire insurance. In 1904 Paul von der Hahmer was appointed the second head of the company; by this time it had already opened an office in London, enabling it to become more international in its focus. Indeed, by 1913 some 20 percent of the premium income of the company came from outside Germany. During World War I, they assisted the German war effort, and the defeat of Germany in World War I led to a curtailing of the international arms of the company.

From 1921 until 1933 there were many mergers as Allianz, under its new general director Kurt Schmitt, took over Bayerische Versicherungsbank, the Stuttgarter Verein, the Frankfurter Allgemeine Versicherungs-AG, and other companies. It has been alleged that with the rise of the Nazi Party, executives in Allianz started cultivating close relations with some of the German Fascist leadership, although it was certainly not one of the major companies that backed the Nazis. During the Nazi period, Allianz grew and Kurt Schmitt himself served under Adolf Hitler as the Reich economy minister from June 1933 until January 1935. The company continued to expand in the late 1930s. However, with the outbreak of World War II, the company faced problems dealing with insurance in time of war. Much of the infrastructure of the company was destroyed in the war, and when the company's employees met on May 18, 1945, there were about 250 of them.

After the war, it was not until 1950 that Allianz was able to open an office in Paris, later expanding into Italy, and by the 1970s it was operating in Brazil, the Netherlands, Spain, the United Kingdom, and the United States. The expansion into Britain was helped with the takeover of Cornhill Insurance plc of London (which was renamed Allianz Cornhill Insurance plc), and Kleinwort Benson, which it gained when it bought the Dresdner Bank. It also moved further into the Italian market with the buying of a large stake in Riunione Adriatica di Sicurt of Milan. In the United States, Allianz bought Fireman's Fund, and in France it bought Assurances Générales de France. With the fall of communism in Eastern Europe, Allianz expanded into Hungary in 1990, and then into Slovakia, and during the mid-1990s started to become a major presence in China and South Korea.

The company Allianz SE now has its headquarters in Munich, Germany, and has achieved revenue of €102.6 billion (2007), with a net income of €7 billion (2006). It now provides insurance for 60 million customers in more than 70 countries, and has 165,505 employees. The CEO of the company since 2003 has been Michael Diekmann, who took over from Henning Schulte-Noelle, who ran the company for the previous 12 years. The company sponsors the Allianz Arena Stadium in Munich.

See Also: Company Profiles: Western Europe; Germany; Munich Re Group.

Bibliography. Gerald D. Feldman, *Allianz and the German Insurance Business* (Cambridge University Press, 2001); Harold Kluge, "Der Einfluss des Geschäfts der 'Allianz' auf die Entwicklung der 'Münchener Rückversicherungs-Gesellschaft' in deren ersten fünfzig Jahren (1880–1930)" [The Influence of the Business of Allianz on the Development of the Munich Reinsurance Company in its First Fifty Years, 1880–1930], *Jahrbuch für Wirtschaftsgeschichte* (v.2, 2006).

JUSTIN CORFIELD
GEELONG GRAMMAR SCHOOL, AUSTRALIA

All Ordinaries Index

Established in January 1980, the All Ordinaries or All Ordinaries Index (known colloquially as the All Ords) is the oldest stock index in Australia, so called because it contains nearly all ordinary (or common) stock listed on the Australian Securities Exchange (ASX). Its creation coincided with the establishment in September 1987 of the then Australian Stock Exchange (now ASX following a merger with the Sydney Futures Exchange in July 2006) from six separate state-based exchanges in the capital cities of Sydney, Melbourne, Brisbane, Perth, Adelaide, and Hobart.

Like all market indexes, the All Ordinaries is a summary measure of the movement of stock values that result when stock in companies held by individual and corporate stockholders trade on the ASX. It is useful as an indicator of overall share market performance and current trends. It also provides a performance benchmark for invested funds, a record of market cycles, and an indicator of stock market reactions to economic events. As a market index, the All Ordinaries is helpful in the construction of asset pricing models, like the capital asset pricing model (CAPM), where the All Ordinaries serves as the market factor and is used to calculate beta (the sensitivity of a stock's return to market or systematic or nondiversifiable forces). Daily data on the All Ordinaries for these purposes is available since 1980; movements before 1980 have been recalculated using changes in the older state-based indices (mostly the Sydney Stock Exchange). Reconstructed daily observations for the All Ordinaries from January 1958 and backdated monthly data from October 1882 are now available.

When established, the All Ordinaries had a base index of 500—28 years later in December 2007 the All Ordinaries was at 6,421, meaning that it had increased more than twelvefold in nominal terms (that is, not accounting for inflation). This represents an arithmetic return of 1,184 percent and a compound annual return of 9.54 percent. On November 1, 2007, the All Ordinaries hit a record high of 6,873. However, on January 22, 2008, the All Ordinaries plunged 408.9 points (7.26 percent) to 5,222, its fourth-worst day on record and worst performance since October 29, 1987, when it fell 7.52 percent. Since then, it has partially recovered, and as of June 6, 2008, stands at 5,633.

On April 3, 2000, the ASX reconstituted the All Ordinaries from a pool of 229–330 stocks to include the 500 largest companies. Prior to this change, to be included in the All Ordinaries portfolio used for calculating the index a company needed to have a market value of at least 0.2 percent of all domestic equities quoted on the ASX and maintain an average turnover of at least 0.5 percent of its quoted shares each month. The new index now accounts for about 99 percent (up from 90 percent) of the ASX's total market capitalization. This change coincided with the introduction of new benchmark indexes managed by Standard and Poor's (S&P), including the S&P/ASX 300 (i.e., the 300 largest companies listed on the ASX), S&P/ASX 200, S&P/ASX 100, S&P/ASX 50, S&P/ASX 20, and the S&P/ASX Small Ordinaries (i.e., small and medium-sized companies). The importance of the All Ordinaries has diminished with the introduction of the new S&P/ASX indexes.

The All Ordinaries is a market-weighted (or capitalization-weighted) index where stocks are included in the index according to the total market value of their outstanding shares. As a result, the impact of a stock's price change is proportional to the company's overall market value, which is the share price times the number of shares outstanding. Stocks in companies with a larger market capitalization will then exert a proportionally greater influence on the market index. Most stock indexes today are market-weighted; they include the S&P 500 and the Dow Jones Wilshire 5000 in the United States, the Financial Times Stock Exchange (FTSE) 100 in the United Kingdom, and the Tokyo stock Price IndeX (TOPIX) in Japan. Some other indexes are price-weighted where each stock makes up a fraction of the index proportional to its price. This means that stocks are included in proportions based on their quoted prices. Accordingly, higher-priced stock will exert the most impact on the index. Examples of price-weighted indexes include the Dow Jones Industrial Average (DJIA) in the United States and Japan's Nikkei 225.

In terms of calculation, the All Ordinaries represents the aggregate market value of the ASX. The aggregate market value is the sum of the market values (the number of shares on issue multiplied by the current price per share) of all companies included in the All Ordinaries portfolio. Today's movement in the index is then calculated by multiplying yesterday's index by the ratio of today's to yesterday's aggregate market values. Updates to the companies included in the All Ordinaries portfolio are made throughout the month when there are changes in the portfolio companies, including delistings, additions, capital reconstructions, and additions through dividend reinvestment plans and bonus and rights issues. These changes affect the number of shares on issue for each company and mean that the portfolio needs modification to maintain consistency.

The main limitation of the All Ordinaries is that it is a price index: it only includes movements in stock prices. However, investors accrue returns not only through price changes, but also through the receipt of dividends; hence, the All Ordinaries understates the total return to the investor. To resolve this, an All Ordinaries Accumulation Index is available that includes the effects of dividend receipts in its computation by assuming that dividends are reinvested to earn the same returns as the stock already held.

See Also: Australia; Dow Jones Index; FT Index; Nikkei Index; S&P 500; Stock Exchanges.

Bibliography. Australian Securities Exchange, www.asx .com.au (cited March 2009).

Andrew C. Worthington
Griffith University

Alternative Dispute Resolution

Alternative dispute resolution (ADR) is an umbrella term embracing various processes principally designed to overcome some of the alleged weaknesses in litigation. For instance, ADR is generally cheaper, less adversarial, and simpler than litigation, and ADR techniques offer a greater range of remedies than the courts. Contracts can be renegotiated and settlements can include nonlegal concessions such as providing a reference where there is an employment dispute. Moreover, ADR is generally speedier than litigation.

First used extensively in the United States in the 1970s, ADR then spread to other common law countries and is used in many situations; for instance, where there are commercial, accounting, construction, employment, and family disputes. It ranges from morally (and sometimes legally) binding decision making by a third party, such as arbitration, to nonbinding processes such as mediation and conciliation. These processes, which are court annexed in some jurisdictions in some countries, are described below. Arbitration is probably the oldest of ADR processes and can best be described as noncourt adjudication. Procedurally, an arbitration hearing is less formal than a court hearing; for example, the former normally has no formal rules of evidence. Furthermore, arbitration is private unlike a court, and there is finality. Appeals from an arbitrator's decision are severely limited, essentially to questions of procedural fairness and the arbitrator's conduct. Also, arbitration is generally speedier than litigation, and normally the parties choose the arbitrator as well as the time and place.

Arbitration can take various forms. In the most common variant, the arbitrator chooses anywhere between the limits (offers) set by the parties. Alternatively, the arbitrator is restricted to opting for either one party's final offer or the other party's final offer, but nothing in-between. This final offer arbitration is sometimes called flip-flop arbitration. A third variant is where the arbitrator makes a decision and then the offer of the party closest to the arbitrator's decision is the formal arbitration award.

Mediation and conciliation—and the terms are often used interchangeably—are becoming increasingly popular. Both mediation and conciliation are voluntary, nonbinding, confidential, without prejudice, and without precedent processes. Their aim is to assist people to talk to each other in a rational and problem-solving way and to bring realism and objectivity to a dispute. Whereas lawyers focus on *rights*, mediators/conciliators focus on *interests* and the needs of the parties and act as a catalyst to enable the parties to communicate with each other and identify common ground, essentially assisting negotiation. Mediators and conciliators, however, vary in the extent to which their main aim is therapeutic or their main aim is to obtain a settlement and how interventionist they are. Some are mainly messengers, shuttling back and forth with offers. Others not only seek to persuade the parties to settle by giving opinions on facts, law, and evidence but also make recommendations.

Although arbitration, mediation, and conciliation are the most common ADR processes, there are others including med-arb, ombudsmen, and mini-trials. In the United States and South Africa, med-arb is practiced: with the consent of the parties, the same person mediates and, if that is unsuccessful, then arbitrates. Ombudsmen, increasingly available in the United Kingdom, deal with complaints from individuals about public bodies and private sector services such as insurance, banking, and rentals. Once the organization has had an opportunity to deal with the complaint, the complainant can then go to the relevant ombudsman who will investigate the matter and suggest a resolution. As with mediation, the ombudsman procedure does not prevent complainants from entering another ADR process or embarking on litigation. Mini-trials are formalized settlement conferences where representatives of the disputants make short presentations and adjudicator(s) give a decision that, however, is not binding on any party, unless or until they agree to settle.

Although ADR has advantages compared with litigation, it also has disadvantages. First, because there are no precedents, the parties may not be able to weigh accurately the strength of their case. Second, because ADR processes are private, there is no wider message, for instance, about what practices can be viewed as discriminatory on grounds of race or sex or the extent of the duty of care owed by the employer to the worker. Third, a party might embark on conciliation or mediation to buy time, as a party can walk away without reaching a settlement at any time. Nevertheless, ADR is an attractive option for people who are unwilling to risk the complexity and financial reefs of litigation.

See Also: Arbitration; Mediation; Negotiation and Negotiating Styles.

Bibliography. A. Bevan, *Alternative Dispute Resolution*, (Sweet & Maxwell, 1992); M. S. Hermann, ed., *The Blackwell Handbook of Mediation: Bridging Theory, Research, and Practice* (Blackwell's, 2006); R. Smith, ed., *Achieving Civil Justice: Appropriate Dispute Resolution* (Legal Action Group, 1996); S. York, *Practical ADR* (Pearson, 1996).

SUSAN CORBY
UNIVERSITY OF GREENWICH

Altria Group

In the 1950s, a widely publicized article in *Readers' Digest* focused upon the health hazards associated with cigarette smoking. Since then, few companies have endured sustained attacks on their core product as much as has the Altria Group. There have been numerous changes within the Altria Group, many directly in response to health risk and other attacks from varied stakeholder groups.

With corporate headquarters located in Richmond, Virginia, the Altria Group (NYSE; MOS) is a parent company of Philip Morris USA (the largest tobacco corporation in the United States), John Middleton (a leading manufacturer of machine-made large cigars), and Philip Morris Capital Corporation (manager of a portfolio of primarily leveraged and direct-finance lease investments). The Altria Group owns 100 percent of the outstanding stock of Philip Morris USA, John Middleton, and Philip Morris Capital Corporation. Since 2002 the Altria Group has held a 28.6 per-

Between 1998 and 2004, the Altria Group spent $101 million on lobbying the U.S. government.

cent economic and voting interest in SABMiller plc, one of the world's largest brewers.

In 1847 Philip Morris was founded by a London tobacconist of the same name. In 1881 Philip Morris Ltd. went public in London. Later (in 1887) it became Philip Morris & Co., Ltd. In 1902 Philip Morris & Co., Ltd. incorporated in New York and was acquired in the United States in 1919 by a firm owned by American stockholders.

In 1955 Philip Morris established its Overseas Division, and in 1960 renamed it the International Division. In 1968 Philip Morris domestic was renamed Philip Morris USA, and in 2008, the Altria Group completed the spin off of 100 percent of the shares of Philip Morris International to Altria's shareholders. In 1985 Philip Morris incorporated and became publicly traded as a holding company and parent of Philip Morris Inc. That same year, Philip Morris acquired General Foods. In 1988 Philip Morris continued its growth in the food manufacturing industry with the acquisition of Kraft (Jell-O, Kool-Aid, Maxwell House). In 1989 Kraft and General Foods combined to form Kraft General Foods. In 2000 Philip Morris continued to expand with the acquisition of Nabisco, which became part of Kraft. Several years later, in 2001, Philip Morris changed its name to Altria Group, Inc. (The name Altria, derived from the Latin word *altus*, conveys a notion of "reaching ever higher," and emphasizes the company's commitment to peak performance.) In 2007 Altria Group divested its distributed 88.9 percent of Kraft's outstanding shares owned by Altria to Altria's shareholders. As a result, Altria no longer holds any interest in Kraft Foods. In 2008 a similar spin-out of Philip Morris International was carried out with 100 percent of its shares being distributed to Altria's shareholders.

Altria's tobacco subsidiary, Philip Morris, is the world's largest commercial tobacco company in sales. The flagship brand, Marlboro, was first introduced in 1924. Other chief brands include Basic, Black & Mild, L&M, Lark, Parliament, Virginia Slims, and Benson and Hedges. Sales in 2007 in millions were $73,801.0 for this 84,000-employee company that is number 23 on the Fortune 500, one of the Dow Jones Titans, and number 15 on the Financial Times Global 500.

Philip Morris operates in the tobacco industry with an NAICS code of 312. Its top three competitors, according to Hoover's, are Altadis, the product of a Spanish-French merger and since February 2008 owned by Britain's Imperial Tobacco. Altadis had 2006 sales of $16,495.7 (in millions) and 2006 employees of 28,103. A second chief competitor is the London-based British Tobacco Company (AMEX: BTI; London: BATS). This 55,145-employee (in 2006) company had 2006 sales of $49,325.1 (in millions). It is on the FTSE 500 and is number 117 in the Financial Times Global 500. A third major competitor is Reynolds American (NYSE: RAI), with (in millions) 2007 sales of $9,023.0 and 7,800 employees. It is number 28 on the Fortune 500 and is also one of the S&P 500.

Demand for cigarettes is driven by discretionary consumer spending and awareness of the health effects of smoking. According to Hoover's, the profitability of this industry depends upon the strength of its marketing.

In 1999 the U.S. Department of Justice filed a racketeering lawsuit against Philip Morris (now an Altria division). After years of litigation, it was concluded that U.S. cigarette industry members conspired to minimize, distort, and confuse the public about health hazards of smoking, including nicotine's addictive properties. Among other charges, Philip Morris and other industry members were also accused of marketing to young people under the age of 21 as a means to recruit "replacement smokers." Thus, the 2001 name change to Altria was seen by some experts as a means to escape the stigma of selling tobacco products by "repositioning" its image in consumers' minds. Altria has also spent $101 million on lobbying the U.S. government between 1998 and 2004, according to the Center for Public Integrity.

The Altria Group is led by the chairman and CEO of Philip Morris USA, Michael E. Szymanczyk. The company focuses on the development of financially disciplined businesses that are leaders in providing adult tobacco consumers with branded products.

See Also: Acquisitions, Takeovers, and Mergers; Company Profiles: North America; Corporate Governance; Corporate Social Responsibility; S&P 500 Index.

Bibliography. Altria Group, www.altria.com (cited March 2009); Center for Public Integrity: Top 100 Companies and Organizations (Lobby Watch), www.publicintegrity.org (cited March 2009); Hoover's, www.hoovers.com (cited March 2009); Robert H. Miles and Kim S. Camerson, *Coffin Nails and Corporate Strategies* (Prentice-Hall, 1982).

Maria L. Nathan
Lynchburg College

American Depository Receipt

An American Depository Receipt (ADR) is a U.S. dollar-denominated negotiable certificate that represents shares listed on an overseas stock exchange that is traded in the United States. ADRs are issued in the United States by a depository bank that owns the underlying foreign shares and holds them in custody in their country of origin. The issuing bank establishes a ratio of ADRs per each foreign share, ranging from a fraction of one foreign share to a multiple. The price of an ADR reflects the price of the underlying foreign stock adjusted for the exchange rate and the set ratio of ADRs per foreign share. Dividends on ADRs are paid in U.S. dollars. The first ADR was issued in 1927 by J. P. Morgan to allow American investors to invest in United Kingdom shares that were required to remain physically in the country. Subsequently their use has grown dramatically to include Global Depository Receipts (GDRs) that trade in two or more countries outside the issuer's home market. In 2008 there were more than 2,000 depository receipt programs totaling $1.5 trillion in market capitalization.

International diversification and the prospect of higher returns drive U.S. investor interest in foreign shares. ADRs provide a more convenient and less costly means to invest abroad than buying directly in foreign markets, especially for the retail investor. The U.S. investor relies on the depository bank to handle overseas trading and account settlement as well as foreign currency conversion into U.S. dollars, as the U.S. investor in ADRs is exposed to exchange rate risk. Another possible benefit to investors is greater legal protection with securities issued and traded in the United States.

For overseas issuers, ADRs provide effective access to U.S. equity markets, the largest in the world. They increase and diversify the issuer's shareholder base and expand the market for its shares. Several recent studies conclude that cross-listing in the United States increases the liquidity of the issuer's shares. Trading of a foreign corporation's shares in the United States can also increase international awareness of the firm's name. Beyond these benefits, some types of ADRs also allow issuers to raise capital in the United States.

There are several types of ADRs that are distinguishable by their intent, whether solely to expand trading in a firm's shares or to raise capital, and the exchange listing and U.S. Securities and Exchange Commission (SEC) compliance requirements. Level I ADRs are the most basic type. They permit a foreign issuer to have its shares traded in the United States. However, they are not listed on a U.S. exchange and, as a result, need not comply with the reporting standards of an exchange. They trade in the Over-the-Counter (OTC) market via the OTC Bulletin Board or Pink Sheets. They have the least rigorous reporting requirements from the SEC. Their intent is to increase the market for the issuer's shares in the United States. Level II ADRs are listed on a U.S. national exchange, such as the New York Stock Exchange, American Stock Exchange, or NASDAQ, and, thus, are subject to listing requirements of the individual exchange as well as greater SEC compliance requirements. The chief benefit of a Level II program is that listing on a national exchange expands the firm's coverage and visibility in U.S. equity markets. Finally, in addition to the benefits of a Level II program, Level III ADRs allow a foreign firm to raise capital in the United States by issuing new shares in an initial public offering (IPO), which entails stricter SEC compliance requirements but provides even greater exposure in U.S. capital markets. Rule 144(a) ADRs or restricted ADRs (RADRs) also allow foreign firms to raise capital in the United States through private placements to "qualified institutional buyers" as defined under the SEC's Rule 144(a). RADRs are less expensive and require less reporting than do Level III ADRs, but they are less liquid than publicly listed shares.

Another distinction between ADRs is between unsponsored and sponsored certificates. The former are issued by the depository bank without the involvement of the overseas issuer. Unsponsored ADRs are restricted to OTC trading and have become increasingly rare.

See Also: Exchange Rate Risk; Liquidity (or Market Liquidity); Securities and Exchange Commission; Stock Exchanges.

Bibliography. R. Aggarwal et al., "ADR Holdings of U.S.-Based Emerging Market Funds," *Journal of Banking and Finance* (2007); Citigroup, *Depository Receipts Information Guide* (2005); Deutsche Bank AG, *Depository Receipts Handbook* (2003); R. Knight, "Depository Receipts Show Robust Returns," *Oxford Metrica International Equity Review* (2008); B. Solnik and D. McLeavey, *International Investments* (Pearson Addison Wesley, 2003); U.S. Securities and Exchange Commission, *International Investing* (2007).

BRUCE A. CAMPBELL
FRANKLIN UNIVERSITY

American International Group

American International Group (AIG) is a financial services company that provides services in four distinct areas: General Insurance, Life Insurance, Financial Services, and Asset Management. Despite its name, AIG was founded in Shanghai, China, in 1919. Its first business area was selling insurance to Chinese customers. The business expanded throughout Asia, where the company maintains a very high profile throughout the region. AIG's employees in Asia number 62,000, and are located there with offices in the Philippines, Australia, New Zealand, Hong Kong, India, Malaysia, Singapore, China, Japan, Indonesia, Thailand, and Vietnam. AIG also operates in Latin America, Europe, and the Middle East, with a presence in 130 countries.

In 2007 AIG was the 18th largest company in the world and the largest insurance company in the United States. Its revenues for that year totaled over $110 billion with a reported adjusted net income of $9.3 billion. AIG, with 116,000 employees and 700,000 agents, brokers, and sales representatives, serves 74 million customers worldwide.

Although it had lost $5 billion in the last quarter of 2007 and despite warnings of impending problems from AIG's auditor (PricewaterhouseCoopers), Martin Sullivan, AIG's CEO, predicted that 2008 would be a good year. The prediction proved to be inaccurate. AIG suffered a $7.8 billion loss in the first quarter. In May the company would suffer the first of two downgrades from Moody's in that year. Sullivan resigned in June 2008.

Although several parts of the company were profitable, the London branch had been heavily involved in mortgage-backed securities and AIG, like many financial services groups (Lehman Brothers being one of the most visible examples) would suffer for its overextension in this area. The losses as reported by the London branch totaled $25 billion.

In September, the ratings agencies Standard and Poor's and Moody's notified AIG that it would be reviewed and its ratings downgraded again. AIG made attempts to raise capital and failed. The value of its shares would reach $1.25 from a 52-week high of $70.13. At this point, because it was believed that the impact of AIG's bankruptcy on the international finance markets would be too great, the U.S. federal government intervened. It loaned the company money in what would be the largest bailout of a private company in U.S. history. In return for equity and the right to cancel payment of dividends, the United States made an initial loan of $85 billion. Two months later, the U.S. Treasury said that it would provide more funding for a total of $150 billion in assistance.

The financial problems had been preceded by investigations into AIG's business practices. A federal investigation led to the payment of $126 million in fines to the U.S. Securities and Exchange Commission and the Department of Justice. In 2005 the U.S. federal government questioned some financial transactions that had the effect of improving the appearance, but not the substance, of the company's earnings. This issue would be brought up three years later when there were questions about what AIG had done with the money that it had been loaned by the federal government. The following year AIG paid a fine of $1.6 million to the State of New York for being involved in a case in which insurance customers were being steered to AIG on the basis of payoffs.

In October 2008, shortly after AIG had received an additional loan of $37.8 billion, its executives went on a retreat in California that cost $444,000, followed by an executive English hunting trip costing $86,000. These reports were accompanied by estimates that AIG had already spent $90 billion of the first $123 billion. Executive pay and bonuses were another story that was emerging. Joseph Cassano, considered by many to be most responsible for placing AIG in such a poor position, was receiving a $1 million monthly consultant fee. Testifying before Congress, former CEOs Sullivan and Robert Willumstad stated that they would not have done anything differently when they had managed the company. AIG stated that there had been no wrongdoing, that its meetings had been mischaracterized and were necessary for its sales executives to remain competitive. In 2008 AIG was suffering a public relations fiasco along with its financial crisis.

See Also: Accountability; Credit Ratings; Freddie Mac; Mortgage Credit Crisis of 2008; Securities and Exchange Commission.

Bibliography. AIG, *Annual Report 2007*, www.ezodproxy .com/AIG/2008/AR2007/HTML2/aig_ar2007_0018. htm (cited March 2009); AIG, www.aigcorporate.com /corpsite (cited March 2009); Ronald Kent Shelp, *Fallen Giant: The Amazing Story of Hank Greenberg and the History of AIG* (Wiley, 2006); Mary Williams Walsh, "A Question for A.I.G.: Where Did the Cash Go?" *New York Times* (October 30, 2008); Peter Whoriskey, "AIG Spa Trip Fuels Fury on Hill," *Washington Post* (October 8, 2008).

Robert N. Stacy
Independent Scholar

AmerisourceBergen

AmerisourceBergen (AmerisourceBergen Corp.) is one of the largest pharmaceuticals companies in the world. It is engaged in the distribution of generic pharmaceuticals, over-the-counter healthcare products, and home healthcare supplies and equipment. A Pennsylvania-based company formed by the merger of Bergen Brunswig and AmeriSource companies in 2001, AmerisourceBergen now employs around 10,000 people (as of January 1, 2008). The company is traded on the New York Stock Exchange with the ticker symbol of ABC. It has approximately 4,600 shareholders (as of January 1, 2008).

AmerisourceBergen generates revenues mainly through its pharmaceutical distribution business division (98 percent of its revenues in 2007). The pharmaceutical distribution division provides drug distribution and related services. The pharmaceutical distribution division includes the operations of AmerisourceBergen Drug Corporation, Amerisource-Bergen Specialty Group, and AmerisourceBergen Packaging Group. AmerisourceBergen Drug Corporation distributes brand name and generic pharmaceuticals, over-the-counter healthcare products, and home healthcare supplies and equipment to a range of healthcare providers.

AmerisourceBergen Specialty Group provides distribution and other services, including group purchasing services to physicians. It also distributes vaccines, plasma, and other blood products. AmerisourceBergen Packaging Group is one of the leading providers of contracted packaging services for pharmaceutical manufacturers. The company also owns Amerisource Heritage Corporation and PMSI, Inc., as subsidiaries.

AmerisourceBergen's products include generic pharmaceuticals, over-the-counter medicines, home healthcare supplies and equipment, medication, and supply dispensing cabinets. Its services include pharmacy healthcare solutions, pharmaceutical distribution, pharmaceutical consulting, packaging services, inventory management services, pharmacy automation, bedside medication safety software and information services, skilled nursing facilities, assisted living facilities, mail order pharmacy services, consulting services, staffing solutions, and scalable automated pharmacy dispensing equipment.

AmerisourceBergen was incorporated in 1988 as AmeriSource Distribution Corp. The name changed to AmeriSource Health Corporation in 1995. AmerisourceBergen adopted its current name in 2001. AmerisourceBergen preferred to grow by acquiring other companies. As a result, it acquired AutoMed Technologies in 2002; US Bioservices Corporation in 2003; MedSelect, Inc., and Imedex Inc., in 2004; Brecon Pharmaceuticals and Access M.D., Inc., in 2006; Xcenda LLC and Bellco Health in 2007.

As of February 2009, the executive team of AmerisourceBergen includes R. David Yost (President and Chief Executive Officer), Michael D. DiCandilo (Executive Vice President and Chief Financial Officer), Steven H. Collis (Executive Vice President and President, AmerisourceBergen Specialty Group), and the Senior Vice Presidents Antonio Pera, Jeanne Fisher, David W. Neu, John Palumbo, Thomas H. Murphy, John G. Chou, David M. Senior and Denise Shane. Tim G. Guttman and J. F. Quinn are Vice-Presidents. The board of directors includes Richard C. Gozon (Chairman of the Board), Charles H. Cotros, Edward E. Hagenlocker, Jane E. Henney, M.D., J. Lawrence Wilson, R. David Yost, Henry W. McGee, Michael J. Long, and Richard W. Gochnauer.

The success of AmerisourceBergen comes from its position in the U.S. pharmaceutical market. It maintains leading market positions, especially in drug distribution, specialty pharmaceuticals, and packaging. It is also the second largest pharmaceutical distributor in the Canadian market. Its well-positioned strategy of service and support to new biotech companies promises more profits in the future. AmerisourceBergen Packaging Group is one of the leading providers of contract packaging services for pharmaceuticals manufacturers. Therefore, the company is seen as a partner to both suppliers (manufacturers) and dispensers (hospitals or pharmacies). Another reason for its success is its continuous growth, which results in more profits to provide future growth. One important aspect may be the successful financial management of the company. By returning profits into assets efficiently, AmerisourceBergen favors profitable business, resulting in better investor confidence.

On the other hand, one of the major weaknesses of AmerisourceBergen is its high dependence on the operations concentrated in the United States. Any downturn in the demand for its products from the United States will pose significant risks, with severe impacts on the earnings. Another setback for AmerisourceBergen is its single business concentration. It has heavily invested in drug distribution, which is generally regarded as low-margin business. The company's acquisitions are relatively small transactions and concentrated into closely related pharmaceutical distribution. Its competitors, such as Cardinal Health, have diversified into businesses unrelated to drug distribution, such as manufacturing information systems for hospitals. This may have a disadvantageous impact on AmerisourceBergen in the future. Also, AmerisourceBergen may be regarded as a risky company with respect to its dependence on few customers with very large budgets going to AmerisourceBergen. Facing any possible problems with these key clients may result in significant negative impacts on AmerisourceBergen.

See Also: Cardinal Health; Healthcare Benefits/Systems; Supply Chain Management.

Bibliography. AmerisourceBergen, www.AmerisourceBergen.com (cited March 2009); SEC-EDGAR, www.sec.gov (cited March 2009).

Gokhan Turgut
HEC Montreal

Anglo-American

This entry refers to the cultural relationship between peoples who share their origins in the United Kingdom (UK), the United States, and English Canada. It does not refer to the multinational natural resources company (AngloAmerican PLC) headquartered in London, UK, which was originally established in South Africa. Further, the meaning of the term *Anglo-American* varies depending on the context in which it is used, and the boundaries of who is included in the definition change over time.

In its earliest use, the term *Anglo-American* described people originally from England, Scotland, or Wales. Most settled in North America in the late 1700s. The term *Anglo-American* is also used to describe a region in the Americas in which English is the main language or which has significant historical, ethnic, linguistic, and cultural links to England, the UK, or the British Isles in general. For example, political leaders such as Ronald Reagan have used the term to portray the "special relationship" between the United States and the UK.

Anglo-America is distinct from Latin America, a region of the Americas where languages derived from Latin (namely French, Spanish, and Portuguese) are prevalent. *Anglo-American* is sometimes shortened to *Anglo*, which is a much broader term that refers to Americans who are not of Hispanic or French descent, most of whom speak the English language. Thus, in parts of the United States with large Hispanic populations, an American of Polish, Irish, or German heritage might be termed an Anglo just as readily as a person of English descent. However, use of the term *Anglo* generally ignores the distinctions between Anglo Americans, Irish Americans, German Americans, and other northern European descendants. Thus, many people included in the definition do not identify themselves as Anglo, and some may find the term offensive. Consequently, more specific names have been assigned to some ethnic groups who prefer not to be categorized under the much broader term of *Anglo*, resulting in Anglo Americans, Irish Americans, and numerous others.

According to 2005 U.S. Census data, 75 percent of Americans classified themselves as Anglo-American compared to 12 percent as African American, 15 percent as Latin American, 4 percent as Asian American, and 9 percent as multiracial/other. Thus, the term *Anglo-American* is a common expression that encompasses a significant proportion of the U.S. population and has for many centuries profoundly influenced and shaped the legal, economic, healthcare, educational, religious, political, and cultural values of the United States of America. While Anglo Americans remain the majority group in the multiethnic United States society, the proportion of Anglos in the total population is expected to decrease as the population of immigrants from Asia, South America, Africa, and other non-European countries expands.

Past research has shown that Anglo-American cultural values and patterns of thinking and behavior are very different from the cultural heritage of many other ethnic minority groups, each having its own customs and traditions. For example, hamburgers, hot dogs, rock music, fast food, football, sitcoms, and morning coffee are all part of Anglo-American culture. Existing research suggests that most Anglo Americans take their culture for granted as simply part of their life, and thus, may fail to recognize its unique features. Becoming aware of differences between Anglo Americans in relation to other cultures is important so that not all people in America are assumed to be the same, and therefore treated the same. Indeed, as the dominant culture in the United States, Anglo Americans tend to be considered as being all alike with little awareness of any differences between them. Such tendencies have led to cultural clashes, stereotyping, and racism.

Essentially, the English were the first Europeans to colonize the Americas in large numbers even though they were preceded in the southwest by smaller numbers of Spaniards. Anglo Americans had British roots that led to cultural values such as the nuclear family that were largely derived from pre-industrial Britain. There are some common Anglo-American beliefs, values, and practices that are shared and have been passed on to succeeding generations as dominant Anglo-American values, and have been cited by many writers and scientists of Anglo-American culture. Most broadly, Anglo-American culture is described as individualistic (independent, self-reliant) compared to, say, Africans and Latinos, whose culture is more often portrayed as collectivist (interdependent, community focused). Therefore, Anglo Americans are often viewed by these cultural groups as autonomous to the extent that they have difficulty valuing or conforming to group norms and other ways of living. Anglo Americans also value freedom and assertiveness, as well as equal gender roles and rights.

See Also: Acculturation; Ethnocentrism; Latin America; United States.

Bibliography. "Anglo-America," Micropædia, *Encyclopædia Britannica*, Vol. 1, 15th ed. (Encyclopædia Britannica, 1990); "Anglo America," *Wikipedia the Free Encyclopedia*, en.wikipedia.org (cited March 2009); R. N. Bellah, "Is There a Common American Culture?" *Journal of the American Academy of Religion* (v.66/3, 1998); J. A. Hague, ed., *American Character and Culture in a Changing World: Some Twentieth Century Perspectives* (Greenwood Press, 1979); C. P. Kottak, ed., *Researching American Culture: A Guide for Student Anthropologists* (University of Michigan Press, 1982); "North America," *The Columbia Encyclopedia*, 6th ed. (Columbia University Press, 2001–05).

MICHELLE BARKER
GRIFFITH UNIVERSITY

Angola

A country disadvantaged by a 27-year civil war that ended in 2002, Angola is on a rebound with a double-digit gross domestic product (GDP) growth rate and oil production of about 1.9 million barrels per day. The country is resilient; it withstood tribal conflicts and gained independence from Portugal and Brazil in 1975.

Geography contributed to a history of global trade. Angola has a land area of 1,246,700 square kilometers and is located in southern Africa by the South Atlantic Ocean and between Namibia and the Democratic Republic of the Congo. Major ports are in Cabinda, Lobito, Luanda, and Namibe. There are 232 airports in Angola, with an international hub in Luanda.

The 12 million Angolans are diverse, with ethnic groups such as Ovimbundu, Kimbundu Bakongo, Mestizo, European, and others. Portuguese is the official language, alongside Bantu and other African languages. About 47 percent hold indigenous beliefs, 38 percent are Roman Catholic, and 15 percent are Protestant.

The political environment is stable. Unrest in its history resulted from fighting between two rival camps—the Popular Movement for the Liberation of Angola (MPLA) led by current president Jose Eduardo Dos Santos, and the National Union for the Total Independence of Angola (UNITA) led by Jonas Savimbi. When Savimbi died in 2002, UNITA's insurgency ended and the MPLA held power.

Oil Production

Angola's natural resources, primarily oil, contributed to its economic transformation. Oil-related production constitutes about 85 percent of GDP. The country's production includes bananas, sugarcane, coffee, corn, cotton, tapioca, tobacco, vegetables, and forest products. Active industries include petroleum, diamonds, iron ore, phosphates, feldspar, bauxite, uranium, gold, cement, metal products, brewing, tobacco, sugar, textiles, ship repair, and fish and food processing.

Major oil companies and countries trade with Angola. ExxonMobil, Chevron, Total, and China's Sinopec have been oil industry participants. Angola exports over $40 billion worth of products primarily to countries such as the United States, China, Taiwan, France, and Chile. It imports about $11 billion worth of commodities such as machinery and electrical equipment, vehicles and spare parts, medicines, food, textiles, and military goods from the United States, Portugal, South Korea, China, Brazil, South Africa, and France.

Economic indicators suggest economic stability. In 2007 Angola's GDP was $80.95 billion with the real growth rate at 16.3 percent. GDP composition is largely industry and services, and GDP per capita is at $6,500. In 2006 stock of direct foreign investment was about $17.6 billion. Inflation declined from 325 percent in 2000 to 13 percent in 2007. The local currency, "kwanza," had minimal fluctuation against the dollar and was valued at $1 = 76 in 2007.

While the economy is growing, challenges exist. Notable issues relate to poverty, inadequate infrastructure, corruption, unemployment and underemployment, health and environment, and a need for government reforms and transparency. In order to rebuild, billions of dollars in lines of credit were provided by China, Brazil, Portugal, and the European Union.

Despite the challenges, rising oil production, construction, and abundant resources drive growth. In 2007 Angola became a member of OPEC, ensuring long-term participation in the oil trade and global business.

See Also: Africa; BP; OPEC; Portugal.

Bibliography. CIA, "Angola," *World Factbook,* www.cia.gov (cited March 2009); Martin Clark, "Africa," *Petroleum Economist* (v.26/28, October 2005); Embassy of Angola, "History of Angola," www.angola.org (cited March 2009); Martin Quinlan, "Forward, with China," *Petroleum Economist* (v.73/5, May 2006).

J. Mark S. Muñoz
Millikin University

Antiglobalization Movement

Antiglobalization movement is the most recognized term used to describe individuals and a wide variety of social movements that oppose different types of social, economic, and ecological injustice that are believed to be the consequence of globalization. As the ideas within the movement diverge on what globalization is about, who or what caused it, and what the alternatives to it would be, the validity of the term *antiglobalization movement* has been questioned. Alternative names are the global justice movement, the movement of movements, the alter-globalization movement, and the anticorporate-globalization movement. The last expression shows that despite the internal heterogeneity of the movement, a common theme among its members is that corporate-driven global business is part of the problem, not part of any solution.

A "Movement of Movements"

It is often stated that the antiglobalization movement is a child of globalization. First of all the movement brings together different voices that in one way or another speak against the idea and reality of globalization. Second, these voices found each other and promoted their views by the very improvements in transportation and communication that are believed to carry the globalization process. Before dealing with the antiglobalization critiques, it is illuminating to see how the movement grew out of globalization and to review the variety of groups worldwide that are part of the antiglobalization movement.

The antiglobalization movement is a label that was first used by nonparticipants of the movement. During the 1990s, journalists and other observers around the world started to identify different local pockets of resistance in which people spoke out against the social, economic, and ecological injustices in the world. What made these protests remarkable was that many of them were not aimed against the old foes of the Left such as capitalism or the "yuppies" of the 1980s, but against corporate-driven globalization. Although the composition of the agenda and the protesters varied locally, the protests seemed to share the refusal to accept that the economy, before all else, defines the well-being of human society.

An important start for the movement was taken in 1994 when Mexican Zapatistas began their fight

Riot police used pepper spray on this crowd of antiglobalization protestors on November 30, 1999, during the pivotal World Trade Organization convention protests in Seattle, Washington.

against the NAFTA trade agreements. The founding of the World Trade Organization (WTO) in 1995 (as a successor to GATT, the General Agreement on Tariffs and Trade) and the Asian financial crisis in 1997 further fueled the belief that human societies no longer controlled their own fate but were somehow left at the mercy of commercial and financial interests.

The antiglobalization movement as such was perhaps born in 1999, when large protests tried to stop another round of global trade liberalization during the WTO meeting in Seattle. The "Battle of Seattle," as the protests were called, received international media attention and triggered a series of carefully chosen protests against meetings by the WTO, the European Union, the G8, or other associations that were believed to be the leading institutions behind globalization.

The protests brought together politicians, union members, individuals, and activists from a wide variety of social movements, united by slogans such as "the world is not for sale" or "people before profit."

The protests were not organized by any central committee. The movement was very much carried from below and grew on the internet, where Web sites such as Indymedia provided the necessary platform for discussion and informed the public about the critiques against globalization.

The next important steps for the movement were taken in 2001. First of all, the attacks of 9/11 by Al Qaeda against the United States turned the intellectual mainstream away from globalization to global terror, making it harder for the movement to get its message across and be heard by the media. Next to this, the movement faced a public relations problem as the media paid attention to the movement, not so much because of its message, but because of the violent conflicts between protesters and law enforcers that characterized many of the anti-globalist rallies. The attacks of 9/11 made it clear that the movement had to renounce violence as a legitimate means of resistance, alienating perhaps its more militant members while becoming less interesting for the media.

The World Social Forum

Also in 2001, the heyday of the rallies was over. The antiglobalization movements somewhat "settled down" when the first World Social Forum (WSF) took place in Porto Allegre, Brazil, on January 25–30. These dates were not chosen at random, as the WSF wanted to serve as an alternative to the World Economic Forum (WEF) held in Davos, Switzerland, around the same time. The WEF is seen by anti-globalists as an important platform where leading businesspeople and politicians, since 1971, set the agenda for further corporate-driven globalization. The WSF, which does not have a guest list or admission fees, is presented as its democratic substitute.

During the first WSF, some 15,000 participants, among them more than 400 political representatives, searched for alternatives to corporate-driven globalization under the slogan "another world is possible." The second edition in Porto Allegre welcomed more than 50,000 participants. To underline the global outreach of the WSF, the fourth edition was organized in Bombay, India (over 70,000 participants). The sixth edition was polycentric and held in Caracas (Venezuela), Bamako (Mali), and Karachi (Pakistan). The seventh edition in 2007 was held in Nairobi, Kenya, and saw over 1,400 participating organizations from 110 countries, making it the most globally representative WSF so far.

The WSF's International Council organizes the WSF and the yearly event. It is constituted by several organizations working on issues including economic justice, human rights, environmental issues, labor, youth, and women's rights. Important social movements that carry the WSF are, for example, "Via Campesina" from Latin America, the Thailand-based NGO "Focus on the Global South," or France-based "ATTAC." The WSF underscores that it is but a platform for discussion and setting up joint actions. For this end, a "Charter of Principles" was drawn up after the first edition that would guide future ones. A very important principle that characterizes the WSF and the antiglobalization movement is that the WSF is a plural, diversified, nonconfessional, nongovernmental, and nonparty context that, in a decentralized fashion, interrelates organizations and movements engaged in concrete action at levels from the local to the international.

Since 2001 the movement has cherished the idea to "think global but act local." This means that while the antiglobalization movement unites people and protesters by sharing a common critique against the process of globalization, this critique is translated and adapted to the different local settings in which anti-globalists are campaigning around particular issues. To underline this call for "glocalised" action, the 2008 WSF was not organized at a particular place, but took place all over the world through thousands of autonomous local organizations that responded to the "Global Call for Action." Meanwhile the WSF has been complemented by the organizing of many regional social forums, such as the European, United States, and Asian Social Forums, and even Italian, Flemish, and Liverpool Social Forums.

The Antiglobalization Critique

Antiglobalization is of course a reaction to globalization, a concept that gradually came to the front of economic and political analysis after it was first used in *The Economist* in 1959. It took the oil crises of the 1970s, the growth of foreign direct investments during the 1980s, and the fall of the Soviet Union in 1991 before the idea of globalization broke through.

Most definitions of globalization revolve around a common theme of "time and space compression," revitalizing Marshall McLuhan's 1960 idea of a "global village." With regard to the economic sphere, globalization in its broadest sense is generally understood to point to the closer integration of countries and peoples that has been brought about by the enormous reduction in costs of transportation and communication, and the breaking down of artificial barriers to the flows of goods, services, capital, knowledge, and people.

However, the antiglobalization movement believes that this conceptualization is a deceitful one as many people do not have equal access to markets or infrastructure (both in terms of transportation and communication), while probably even more artificial barriers against the movement of people are being put up than broken down. Hence, the idea of globalization rests on the false premise of a closer integration of the peoples of the world. Of course, one could deduce from this that actually more globalization is needed, further bringing down international trade barriers and closing, for example, "the digital divide." The movement in general is, however, skeptical that this will be achieved in a significant and fair way as long as political and economic forces command the globalizing process. A much-referred to person in this respect is Nobel Prize–winning economist Robert Stiglitz, who criticized the way in which the International Monetary Fund (IMF) and World Bank mismanage global development and the financial infrastructure because they primarily serve American and European political, commercial, and financial interests. According to the movement, the globalization process does not lead to a globalized, "flat" world for all, but only to a global level playing field for capital.

The targets for the antiglobalization movement are the major private and public institutions that dominate the global economy. Protests are generally organized around international political meetings by associations such as the WTO or the European Union. Global business is also attacked for hijacking the development of human societies. Building on this critique, the antiglobalization movement believes that beneath the globalization rhetoric is an assumption that globalization is an anonymous and unstoppable force of nature. This implies that peoples and countries have little choice but to accommodate to the new globalizing condition. This has been illustrated by Thomas Friedman, who believes that globalization forces states to follow a particular set of economic policies that he has called "the golden straitjacket."

In a globalizing world in which it is primarily capital that is becoming mobile, countries are forced into competition to attract this capital. To succeed, countries must implement so-called neoliberal policies of privatization, trade liberalization, and business deregulation, while maintaining a low rate of inflation, balanced state budgets, and a small-sized government. According to the antiglobalization movement this view forces states to tailor their economic policies to the wish of mobile capital for total "commodification," meaning the right to do business in every sphere of society (education, health service, public transport, etc.), anywhere, at any time, and at the lowest cost. Meanwhile the state is giving up on the wishes of its citizens for full employment, respectable wages, and decent ecological and other living standards. Seen from this perspective, states have entered in a negative "race to the bottom."

The idea that in the longer run, the policies of the golden straitjacket will indeed benefit the whole of society because attracted capital will create jobs, jobs will create rising incomes, rising incomes create additional demand and this will lead to a diversification of the economy and the development of environmental friendly production processes, is discarded as wishful thinking. According to the movement, this "trickle down effect," as it has been called, is not an automatic process but one that is forced upon capital by political action through taxation and regulation. These are exactly the types of welfare policies that have become difficult to implement under the idea of globalization's unstoppable progress.

Contrary to this, the antiglobalization movement believes that globalization is a process that is instigated, driven, and determined by political decisions. Common opinion is that the golden straightjacket was first put on during the 1980s by Ronald Reagan in the United States and Margaret Thatcher in Great Britain. By stressing the political agency behind globalization, the movement holds political power accountable for the social, economic, and ecological deficits that the politicians themselves ascribe to globalization. Antiglobalists do not accept this excuse and at the same time they remind politicians that the process itself can be altered or reversed.

Alternatives

Whereas it is fairly easy to point to a general critique within the movement against the ideological idée fixe of globalization and who benefits from it, opinions diverge when it comes to fixing the problem and drafting plans for a better world. If anti-globalists are about global justice, much debate concentrates on how to achieve this. The movement is hesitant to come up with a blueprint for development. It refuses to promote its own straitjacket in opposition to the golden neoliberal one, believing that it is exactly this type of doctrinarian thinking that created the problems in the first place. Given the wide variety of individuals and movements that shelter under the umbrella of the movement, no common solution can be presented for all the issues that are discussed. Following this, a lot of the individuals and social movements that are campaigning around particular economic, ecological, and social issues do not feel the need to connect their different agendas or search for the bigger theory. In these cases anti-globalism serves as a metaphor for anti-consumerism, anti-discrimination, anti-war, anti-poverty, or anti-terrorism. The link with the problem of globalization as described above is not always clear, making the antiglobalization movement sometimes look more like an assembly of moral outcries than a movement with a message of its own.

Nevertheless, as the neoliberal and globalization rhetoric is exactly based on the famous TINA doctrine, short for "there is no alternative," the antiglobalization movement had to challenge this idea if it wanted to discredit neoliberalism. As said, the alternative depends on the manner in which the process of globalization needs to be altered or reversed. The belief in the ability to change the commercial and financial interests that drive the present globalization process determines to a large degree the extent to which members of the movement embrace the prefix anti- or alter-. Building on the metaphor of the golden straitjacket, opinions diverge whether the straitjacket should be made to fit more comfortably or should be taken off altogether.

In the anti- option, the exposure of globalization as a profit-driven process that serves the interests of capital implies that globalization itself should be stopped. The economy needs to be tailored to the wishes of the people, and they do not live in a borderless world but in particular societies, sharing particular value systems and cultures. Thought through, this type of reasoning calls for what Walden Bello has called de-globalization, putting up or reinstalling artificial barriers to the economic flows of goods, services, and capital, while reversing the neoliberal agenda by localizing or nationalizing production and regulating business. In practice, complete isolationism or full-fledged protectionism is rarely advocated. Despite its popular label, the movement contains more alter-globalizing than antiglobalizing opinions, especially because in a number of issues, such as migration, it generally favors open over closed borders.

In the alter- option, the general aim is to bring globalization back under democratic control. By and large two options to do so are often discussed. The first option believes that globalization can only be steered in the right direction by global, or at least international, multilateral organizations. The choice can be to reform leading institutions such as the IMF, World Bank, and the WTO, or to give more power to other institutions such as the International Labour Organization (ILO) or the United Nations Conference on Trade and Development (UNCTAD). With

equal and fair participation of all countries in these organizations, globalization could be reshaped by implementing global labor and environmental standards. This way global business would be embedded in a more ethical framework of sustainable development. Global business also has a role to play in this by applying a decent code of conduct, a sign of "good governance." This led to several fair trade agreements and certification programs that indicate that products are labor-friendly and/or respect environmental standards.

The Tobin Tax

A more specific measure that is advocated in this context is the Tobin Tax, a small tax on all international trade in currency. The initiative is named after the Nobel Prize–winning economist James Tobin, who in 1978 suggested such a tax in order to discourage short-term speculation in currencies. This should have a stabilizing effect on the exchange rates by releasing them from the pressures of short-term expectations. Meanwhile the tax would be low enough (between 1 percent and 0.1 percent) to allow for the further financing of international trade and foreign direct investments.

Little attention was paid to Tobin's idea until it was picked up by the antiglobalization movement in the context of the 1997 Asian currency crisis. The crisis was seen as the proof of the destabilizing effects that free capital markets and speculation can bring along. Ignatio Ramonet, chief editor of the French-based *Le Monde Diplomatique,* suggested that the financial market needed to be "disarmed" and he called for a movement that would promote the Tobin Tax in the name of universal solidarity. After this call, ATTAC ["Action pour une taxe Tobin d'aide aux citoyens"] was founded in 1998, one of the driving forces behind the antiglobalization movement. The movement extended the ethical agenda of the Tobin Tax by suggesting that the money that the tax produced could be collected by a global or international organization and be put to use for international development. Of course this was not an end in itself as the tax would actually produce a small amount of money if it had its desired discouraging effect.

To some members of the antiglobalization movement, the fact that the Tobin Tax has not yet been implemented shows the limits of the idea of a "global regulation" of globalization. This option does not work because the building blocks of all these organizations are states and because it depends on the willingness and ability of the different governments to implement the necessary laws that would adjust globalization. Once the Tobin Tax could no longer be discarded as interventionist wishful thinking or as a technical impossibility, it still met with international distrust among national states. As long as one country does not implement the tax, so the argument went, the tax would be futile and that particular country would gain a substantial bonus for its economy. As some countries such as the United States and Great Britain are very much against the tax, other governments refused to operate as an international "avant-garde." By setting an example and implementing the tax, politicians sometimes feared this would hurt the national economy and in the process their own reelection.

Self-Determination

The second option to bring globalization under democratic control is therefore much more "anti-hierarchical." In this option, the basic problem with the present globalization is not so much a lack of global economic and ecological enforceable laws but the very top-down forms of decision making that globalization implies. The problem is not just the "commodification" of everything but the "alienation" of the individual, stripping away sovereignty. Seen from this perspective, the critiques that are raised against global business and capital for being nontransparent and nondemocratic also apply to the state.

Contrary to the actions of large NGOs such as Oxfam or the trade unions, this option leaves less room to use the state as an appropriate channel for change. This option is much more utopian as its fundamental solution is to replace hierarchical institutions such as global business and the state with new politics that again allow for a form of governance that is self-determining. Instead of regulating government in order to regulate capital, the "anti-hierarchical" option wants to come up with a self-organized alternative. This alternative is sometimes sought after in the "civil society," a difficult sociological concept that in its simplest form refers to an organizational sphere between the state and capital. According to some members of the movements, more power should be attributed to this civil society in order to get the economy and politics under democratic control.

Critics have noted that this idea is not only utopian as it aims for long-term change by neglecting the short-term reality of political and economic institutions, but that it is not much of an alternative in itself as the "civil society" is made up of all kinds of self-governing organizations, some with extreme right, other with extreme leftist political ideas. The "anti-hierarchical" option therefore needs to be more specific about its short-term strategy and long-term ideals.

Assessment

Given the heterogenic composition of the antiglobalization movement and its refusal to draft a general program, it is not only hard to define the movement and its message but also to evaluate its success. It is clear that some of the issues that the movement rallied against, such as environmental degradation, climate change, or global poverty, have become political priorities. It is another question if the answers that both political and economic institutions come up with would please all anti-globalists. The trade in carbon gas emission rights, or the international promotion of micro-credits, shows that the leading institutions are far from seeing market forces as a problem, not a solution.

Some members of the antiglobalization movement would support these measures, also believing that the market as such is not a problem, but an unregulated market is. Other anti-globalists would certainly disagree, arguing that none of these measures touches the profit motive behind corporate-driven globalization. The dispute shows that the antiglobalization movement had some strong critiques to offer and for some time it was able to capture the public eye. But now that attention has generally turned away and alternatives need to follow up criticism, the future of the antiglobalization movement seems uncertain.

See Also: Corporate Governance; Corporate Social Responsibility; Cross-Border Migrations; Fair Trade; Global Digital Divide; Globalization; International Labour Office/International Labour Organization; International Monetary Fund; Multinational Corporation; Sustainable Development; United Nations Conference on Trade and Development; World Bank, The; World Trade Organization.

Bibliography. ATTAC, www.attac.org (cited March 2009); Maude Barlow and Tony Clarke, *Global Showdown: How the New Activists Are Fighting Global Corporate Rule* (Stoddart, 2001); Walden Bello, *Deglobalization: Ideas for a New World Economy* (Zed Books, 2005); W. Lance Bennett et al., "Managing the Public Sphere: Journalistic Construction of the Great Globalization Debate," *Journal of Communication* (v.54/3, 2004); William F. Fisher and Thomas Ponniah, *Another World Is Possible: Popular Alternatives to Globalization at the World Social Forum* (Zed Books, 2003); Focus on the Global South, www.focusweb .org (cited March 2009); Thomas Friedman, *The Lexus and the Olive Tree: Understanding Globalization* (Farrar, Straus & Giroux, 1999); Global Justice Movement, www .globaljusticemovement.org (cited March 2009); International Forum on Globalization, www.ifg.org (cited March 2009); David Harvey, *A Brief History of Neoliberalism* (Oxford University Press, 2005); Martin Khor, *Rethinking Globalization: Critical Issues and Policy Choices* (Zed Books, 2001); Hans-Peter Martin and Harold Schumann, *The Global Trap: Globalization and the Assault on Prosperity and Democracy* (St. Martin's Press, 1997); Marshall McLuhan, *The Gutenberg Galaxy: The Making of Typographic Man* (University of Toronto Press, 1962); Heikki Patomäki, *Democratising Globalisation. The Leverage of the Tobin Tax* (St. Martin's Press, 2001); Ignacio Ramonet, *The Geopolitics of Chaos* (Algora Publishing, 1998); John Ralston Saul, *The Collapse of Globalism and the Reinvention of the World* (Atlantic Books, 2005); Joseph Stiglitz, *Globalization and Its Discontents* (W.W. Norton, 2003); Via Campesina, viacampesina.org (cited March 2009); World Social Forum, www.forumsocialmundial.org .br (cited March 2009).

Jan-Frederik J. Abbeloos
Ghent University

Antitrust Laws

Though its earliest forms were enacted by the Roman empire, antitrust law is largely a product of the post–Adam Smith age of capitalism. *Antitrust* is the American term for this form of legislation, referring to the trustbusting of the Progressive Era when legislation was enacted to counter the anticompetitive effects of trusts and collusion, especially in the aftermath of the Panic of 1893 and attendant decline in demand and prices. Internationally, the legislation is better known as competition law, which reflects the broad focus of it: that class of legislation that exists to protect and regulate competition in the marketplace. This includes not only the repression of monopolies, cartels, and industry collusion, but the regulation or criminalization of predatory pricing, price gouging, and other abusive acts performed from a dominant position in the market, as well as the regulation of mergers and acquisitions.

The earliest acts of competition law were aimed principally at the support of local production. Tariffs were imposed on foreign goods to various ends, including offsetting the price difference if those imported goods were significantly cheaper than what could be found locally. This was a common practice in Rome during both the Republic and Empire periods; Rome was also known to seize the property of trade monopolies or collusive trade combinations which acted against the interest of the people or the state.

The rise of trade guilds in the Middle Ages required legislation to prevent their abuse, and in many European countries attempts were made to directly control prices, especially for household necessities like bread or ale, or commodities like grain. Various acts sometimes dictated the wages of specific types of laborers while fixing prices of the common items everyone was expected to purchase, thus preserving for those laborers a specific balance of income and outgo. Traders who overcharged for these items not only faced a penalty from the state, but paid punitive damages to the customer—a concept that was carried through English common law and adopted into American antitrust law in the form of the treble damages paid for certain violations of antitrust law or infringement of intellectual property rights.

Anti-competitive laws of the Middle Ages and Renaissance were called "combination laws," because they regulated or forbade the cooperation between combinations of merchants or businesses. Bohemian mining companies, for instance, were forbidden to cooperate in jointly raising their prices. Other combination laws targeted labor unions, as in the British Combination Act of 1799, which outlawed unions and collective bargaining; the idea of conflating monopolies and labor unions is today a foreign one, demonstrating the degree of change in those two centuries.

Modern Antitrust Law

Modern antitrust law began in the United States, where the Industrial Revolution, the railroads, 19th-century banking panics, and the tendency of the Gilded Age to shift thinking and activity from the regional to the national level—with the institution of nationwide professional organizations like the American Medical Association, nationwide newspaper and magazine distribution, and a growing number of firms attempting to do business nationally—colluded, as it were, to create an environment in which businesses could enjoy tremendous success and had the opportunity to abuse the power they attained.

The period from 1895 to 1905 saw more mergers than any other time in American history. To an extent, this was an organizational activity, as small local stores joined together to form chains and larger firms. There were practical and non-objectionable considerations at work, largely inoffensive to capitalist needs and nonharmful to the consumer. But there were also significant and increasingly common abuses of power, with businesses using these mergers and the creation of trusts in order to gain an advantage and be able to increase prices.

Trusts themselves are not the target of antitrust law, confusingly enough. A trust is simply the management of a property or business by a trustee or trustees, on behalf of the beneficiary—most people are familiar with them through the institution of trust funds, in which money is managed by a trustee, especially if the beneficiary is a minor. Trustees are accountable to their beneficiaries. The trusts formed in the 19th century, though, were legal entities formed in order to engage in anticompetitive practices—they were in essence cartels, groups of businesses colluding for the purposes of monopoly-like behavior.

The Sherman and Clayton Acts, passed in 1890 and 1914 and more or less bookending a particular era of pre-Depression trustbusting, codified and streamlined a body of common law and attempted to clarify various acts of abusive conduct. It was not nearly as effective as hoped, though Presidents Theodore Roosevelt and William Taft got a lot of political mileage out of Sherman Act prosecutions. In the reorganization of European institutions following World War I, American antitrust law was used as the basis for similar bodies of legislation across the west, and after World War II, these antitrust ideas were enforced externally on Germany and Japan, both of which were cartel-friendly during and in the years leading up to the war. In the United States, antitrust laws have been responsible for the break-up of companies like Standard Oil in 1911 and AT&T in 1982, as well as the source of a prolonged battle between the federal government and Microsoft.

The American model of antitrust law has been the essential core of antitrust law adopted around the world, and enforced by organizations like the World Trade Organization.

Because of its origins, antitrust law distinguishes between the actions of an individual company and the actions of companies working together; this in fact was one of its weaknesses in the Progressive Era, when the Sherman Act failed to prohibit the existence of a single-company monopoly, unless the actions taken to create that monopoly were themselves prohibited. Multi-company monopolies, on the other hand, were criminalized so long as intent—in the form of some kind of agreement among the companies, some form of collusion—could be demonstrated. Since the Progressive Era, restrictions of monopolies of any sort have been strengthened, though some exemptions, notably for labor unions and professional sports leagues, have also been granted.

Certain activities attract the attention of the federal government, and an examination of whether there are anticompetitive practices in play. Price fixing is the classic example of this; while goods will tend to reach a particular price because of market forces, the deliberate agreement among companies to set a price is in defiance of those forces. Likewise, agreements between potential competitors to limit their activities to particular geographic areas in order to avoid competing are potential violations of antitrust law.

Since the 1970s, the enforcement of American antitrust law has focused more and more on the effect on the consumer, rather than absolute standards of corporate behavior. The shift is the result of a distrust of government intervention in the economy, as new conservative factions came to power in the aftermath of Watergate's impact on the Republican Party. A particularly influential thinker in the matter is Robert Bork, who reframed the issue as a matter of consumer welfare—and both his supporters and his opponents have largely continued to do so.

Enforcement of antitrust legislation falls to various bodies. At the state level, the state's attorney general can file a suit against a corporation in violation of either state or federal antitrust laws; the Microsoft antitrust case involved various states acting in a coalition with the Justice Department. Private suits can be brought in either state or civil court. Both the Federal Trade Commission and the Antitrust Division of the Department of Justice can bring federal civil suits against companies in violation, but only Justice can bring a criminal suit. The most famous successfully prosecuted federal antitrust case remains the *United States vs. AT&T*, a suit brought by Justice in 1974 and settled in 1982 with the Baby Bell divestiture: effective 1984, in exchange for being allowed to branch out into computers, AT&T retained its long-distance services but divided its local exchange services into the seven Regional Bell Operating Companies.

Criticism

Though Bork's take on antitrust law is still fairly conservative, there are some who go much further than simply reframing the matter. Economist Milton Friedman has changed his mind on antitrust legislation over the course of his career, and believes that they have wrought more harm than good, despite the seemingly sound principles on which they are based. Former Fed chairman Alan Greenspan believes that the subjectivity of antitrust legislation, in particular, has dissuaded a good deal of legal and beneficial business activity out of the fear that it could violate the letter of the law.

One of the targets of antitrust law is predatory pricing, the pricing of a good so low as to constitute an anticompetitive action, with the goal of driving away existing competitors or preventing new ones from entering the market. The problem, antitrust critics point out, is that this is not rational behavior to begin with, and market forces are generally sufficient to prevent irrational business behavior if you give them sufficient time to do so. By its nature, predatory pricing can't be permanent—in order for the company to benefit from driving away its competitors, it has to bring the price back up, and once it has done so, the market is again safe for other companies to participate in. There are few incontrovertible cases of predatory pricing occurring over a significant period of time, and the anticompetitive motive is a difficult one to establish.

As game theory has become a more prominent part of economic thought, it has been used to demonstrate that certain anticompetitive practices like predatory pricing may be beneficial in the long run. The problem here, in part, is that it is difficult to institute a system of law in which the legality of actions depends in part on the expectation of how consequences will turn out "in the long run."

See Also: Acquisitions, Mergers, and Takeovers; AT&T; Barriers to Entry; Capitalism; Competition; General Agreement on Tariffs and Trade; Legal Environments; Microsoft; Monopolistic Advantage Theory; Pricing; World Trade Organization.

Bibliography. Dominick T. Armentano, *Antitrust: The Case for Repeal* (Ludwig von Mises Institute, 2007); Robert H. Bork, *The Antitrust Paradox* (New York Free Press, 1993); Jay Pil Choi, ed., *Recent Developments in Antitrust: Theory and Evidence* (MIT Press, 2007); Einer Elhauge and Damien Geradin, *Global Competition Law and Economics* (Hart Publishing, 2007); Milton Friedman, *Capitalism and Freedom* (University of Chicago Press, 2002); William H. Page, *The Microsoft Case: Antitrust, High Technology, and Consumer Welfare* (University of Chicago Press, 2007); Tony Prosser, *The Limits of Competition Law* (Oxford University Press, 2005); Edwin S. Rockefeller, *The Antitrust Religion* (Cato Institute, 2007); Richard Wilberforce, Alan Campbell, and Neil Elles, T*he Law of Restrictive Practices and Monopolies* (Sweet and Maxwell, 1966).

BILL KTE'PI
INDEPENDENT SCHOLAR

A. P. Møller Mærsk Group

A conglomerate involved in a wide range of business—containers and related activities, energy, shipping and retail—Mærsk is Denmark's largest company, a dominant regional player in the North Sea oil and gas industry and the owner of the world's largest container shipping fleet.

Since its creation in the Danish town of Svendborg in 1904, Mærsk has developed into a multinational corporation, employing approximately 117,000 people in more than 130 countries. Mærsk was established as a privately run shipping business when 28-year-old Arnold Peter Møller together with his father, Captain

Shipping accounts for more than half of Mærsk's revenues, and its containers are a familiar sight at ports worldwide.

Peter Mærsk Møller, bought a secondhand steamer of 2,200 tons dead weight. In 1965 Arnold Mærsk Mc-Kinney Møller, son of Arnold Peter Møller, assumed the leadership of Mærsk. In 1993 Mærsk Mc-Kinney Møller withdrew from the day-to-day management, and today the group is headed by Nils S. Andersen, who took over as the fourth Group Chief Executive Officer and Partner in 2007.

Mærsk's container division is called Mærsk Line. It is one of the leading shipping companies in the world, with a fleet numbering more than 550 container vessels and more than 1,900,000 containers. Mærsk already has twice the overall fleet capacity of its nearest rival. Furthermore, Mærsk owns 50 container ports around the world.

Mærsk Line keeps expanding the economies of scale in shipping, a key driver of trade globalization. Mærsk's container business may play a role in the integration of production processes, not only by moving goods from manufacturers to consumers and coordinating multiple modes of transport, but also by connecting industrial productions that are located in different places. Container shipping and related activities are by far the largest business areas for Mærsk, providing 53 percent of the group total revenue in the first half of 2007. Its container-related activities are under the brand names Mærsk Line, Mærsk Logistics, Safmarine, and APM Terminals.

Mærsk's main competitor in the container shipping industry is the Mediterranean Shipping Company (M.S.C.), based in Geneva, Switzerland, and owned by the Italo-Swiss Aponte family. M.S.C. specializes both in the container and in the cruise business (revenue in 2007 equals US$14 billion and US$1 billion, respectively). It was established in 1970, is not listed, and is not as diversified as Mærsk. Its organizational chart is light and the consequent rapidity of adapting to market changes is M.S.C.'s main advantage. This fact combined with a competitive price policy has led M.S.C. to achieve a consistent market share as the second largest ocean-carrier in the world.

Tankers, offshore, and other shipping activities are part of the main business in which Mærsk operates. It offers solutions for the transport of crude oil, refined products, and gas; drilling with mobile production units; salvage; and towage activities, as well as door-to-door transport, inter-European freight, and passenger transport. All these activities are under the brand names Mærsk Tankers, Mærsk Supply Service, Mærsk Contractors, Svitzer, and Norfolkline. Excluding Svitzer's 600 vessels, they operate more than 260 vessels and rigs. Maersk Oil participates in oil drilling in Denmark, Qatar, United Kingdom, Algeria, and Kazakhstan. In addition, Mærsk Oil leads exploration activities in the North Sea, Africa, the Middle East, Central Asia, South America, and the U.S. Gulf of Mexico.

Retail activity includes supermarkets and hypermarkets in Denmark, Germany, the United Kingdom, Poland, and Sweden. Dansk Supermarked incorporates, among others, the Føtex stores, the Netto stores, and the Bilka hypermarkets. The group extends its interests in shipyards in Denmark and the Baltic countries, in the industrial production of plastic products, and in Star Air, an airways company engaged in contract parcel flying in Europe. In addition to this, the group includes a 20 percent stake in Danske Bank. Total market capitalization by March 2008 equalled DKK217 billion (US$45.4 billion).

See Also: Denmark; Globalization; Transportation.

Bibliography. Majbritt Greve, Michael W. Hansen, and Henrik Schaumburg-Müller, *Container Shipping and Economic Development: A Case Study of A.P. Moller–Maersk,* (Copenhagen Business School Press, 2007).

Michele Caracciolo di Brienza
Graduate Institute of International and
Development Studies

Arbitrage

Arbitrage is the process whereby traders profit from price discrepancies between markets. Certain conditions must be met for arbitrage to occur. The profit opportunity must be a riskless one, meaning that the transactions (buying in one market and selling in the other) must occur as near to simultaneously as possible, and the prices at which the asset is traded are both known with certainty at the time of the trade. If these conditions are met, the trader will gain the profit without tying up any capital.

Arbitrage activities contribute to the "law of one price," a fundamental economic assumption that an efficient market will ensure at any time only one price prevails for a particular asset. Arbitrage drives prices together and is implicit within the concept of a perfect market (another way of describing the "law of one price"). Buying increases demand for the cheaper asset forcing its price up, while the higher price in the other market falls as the cheaper asset is introduced into the supply to that market.

The English word *arbitrage* is derived from the French *arbiter,* meaning to umpire or referee and so, by extension, to resolve differences. Traders who perform these activities are arbitrageurs. In immature markets, opportunities for arbitrage will be greater than in mature markets with widespread access to information.

In practice, all trading activity involves transaction costs, even if only very small. For arbitrage profits, any transaction costs must be less than the difference between the two anomalous prices and known at the time of the trade. The profit will be the net value of the price differences less transaction costs. Examples of transaction costs might be dealing charges, or transaction taxes. There is rarely such a thing as an entirely riskless transaction. Even computerized trades of currencies, for example, will involve a transaction delay, even if only a matter of seconds, during which the opportunity may disappear.

Arbitrage is not speculation. Speculators take risks and expose themselves to changes in price of the assets in which they take a position. Their objective is profit but they are prepared to risk losses to make gains. Speculators back their own judgment and may misjudge the direction markets take. Arbitrageurs take a certain profit from temporary market price anomalies

and in doing so will remove those anomalies. Some arbitrageurs are occasional opportunists, but others engage in the process full time. In efficient markets profits on arbitrage may appear to be small relative to the value of the transaction, but when adjusted to an equivalent annual return and taking into account the riskless nature of the profit, the return may be high. Many financial institutions conduct arbitrage operations on a regular basis. The scale of their operations means that a high volume of operations compensates for the low margins. By conducting their own in-house dealing operations scale economies minimize their transaction costs.

In the real economy, firms may practice price discrimination by segmenting buyers and charging different prices according to their different price elasticities of demand. Arbitrage may not be possible between the price segments because of barriers between them. For example, the recipient of a discount price could not sell at a smaller discount to the normal price to make a profit because of the supplier's customer identity conditions. Thus a student could not sell a discount travel ticket to a full-fare-paying customer who had no student identification.

The principle of arbitrage is central to many important ideas in economics and financial theory. For example, arbitrage provides the logic for the "purchasing power parity" theory of international exchange rates. If prices in different countries are experiencing different rates of inflation, then exchange rates will alter to restore price parity. *The Economist* newspaper publishes a "Big Mac Index" based on the international price of hamburgers that identifies over- or undervaluation of currencies based on this limited purchasing power comparison. Although the theory is inadequate as a full explanation of exchange rate movement, it sheds light on the importance of international price differences for the long-term path of a currency's value.

"Interest rate parity" theory holds that the difference between future and spot (current) exchange rates reflects the differential between interest rates in the countries of the two currencies. Thus the practice of covered interest arbitrage seeks to take advantage of differences in interest rates in different countries while hedging (covering) the exchange rate exposure (risk of change) involved in dealing in a foreign currency. In the foreign exchange market, triangular arbitrage is a trading technique that exploits pricing anomalies between three currencies in different markets.

In markets for forward contracts (where two parties agree to a sale/purchase of a commodity or financial asset at some definite point in the future at an agreed price), the process of arbitrage ensures there is no difference between the current price of the asset and the forward price after allowing for the passage of time. In financial theory, the Modigliani and Miller propositions hold that all firms with the same potential earnings should sell at the same price, regardless of their capital structure, through arbitrage in the stock market. "Arbitrage pricing theory" has developed in recent years in an attempt to more accurately calculate the cost of capital for firms and their true value.

The term *arbitrageur* has been applied to entrepreneurs involved in the business of buying and selling companies or parts of companies and seeking a profit from perceived anomalies between the stock-market valuation of a company and the underlying value of the business. Regulatory arbitrage is the exploitation of variations in market regulations between countries.

See Also: Financial Markets; Purchasing Power Parity; Risk.

Bibliography. J. Madura, *International Financial Management* (Thomson South-Western, 2006); W. L. Megginson and S. B. Smart, *Introduction to Corporate Finance* (Thomson South-Western, 2006); K. Pilbeam, *Finance and Financial Markets* (Palgrave Macmillan, 2005).

TOM CONNOR
UNIVERSITY OF BEDFORDSHIRE

Arbitration

Generally considered a genre of dispute resolution, arbitration is a proceeding used to obviate the litigation process. Arbitration seeks to expedite the resolution of disputes in an uncomplicated and inexpensive manner prior to the filing of a lawsuit. An impartial, private third party—an arbitrator—hears the parties' dispute and makes a final determination that typically binds the parties. Litigation, by contrast, involves a lawsuit and, while also a method used to resolve disputes between parties, for the most part, tends to be lengthy and expensive. There are many benefits associated with arbitration; however, agreeing to submit to arbitration requires one to relinquish his or her right of access to the courts. Still, arbitration has been used more frequently throughout the past decade.

In theory, any contractual agreement may result in a disagreement. Businesses around the world understand that, many times, disputes are inevitable. Generally, disputes can be resolved in several different ways: litigation, mediation, conciliation, and arbitration. Arbitration and mediation are cost-effective alternatives to litigation. Arbitration is the submission of a dispute to one or more impartial persons for a final and binding decision. This is known as an award, which is made in writing and, generally, is final. Usually, awards bind the parties involved.

Non-binding arbitration is conducted similarly to binding arbitration, except that when the arbitrator issues the award after the hearing, it is not binding on the parties, who do not give up their right to a jury trial. In that case, the arbitrator's award is merely an advisory opinion. Many cases go to settlement or binding arbitration after this phase. Alternatively, the parties may choose to go to trial. By contrast, mandatory arbitration, also known as court-ordered arbitration, is a judicial mandate intended to resolve pending court cases, utilizing informal rules of evidence and procedure in an advisory arbitration process ordered by the court at an early stage of a lawsuit. The availability of this process, in large part, depends upon local, state laws or court procedures.

Mediation is a process in which an impartial third party facilitates communication and negotiation and, therefore, promotes voluntary settlements by the parties themselves. This process can be effective for resolving disputes prior to arbitration or litigation. Arbitration, however, offers parties a decisive legal outcome to their dispute without the expense and inconvenience of court proceedings and attorney fees.

Businesses and government departments—even courts themselves—have used arbitration programs to resolve disputes, and there is widespread satisfaction with the process. Because the arbitrator renders a final decision upon hearing both parties' arguments, arbitration is considered to be adjudicatory, not advisory. Similar to litigation, arbitration has a so-called appeals process. In other words, an arbitrator's decision can be challenged under very limited circumstances only, for example, if you can demonstrate an arbitrator was biased; therefore, parties are not always bound by the award. This process is somewhat of a misnomer, however. For the most part, arbitration is considered a binding, adjudicatory process.

Providers of alternative dispute resolution services address areas such as employment, intellectual property, consumer, healthcare, financial services, technology, construction, and international trade conflicts. The largest provider in the United States is the American Arbitration Association (AAA); it plays a vital role in resolving complex matters, especially in such volatile industries as construction. The plans, specifications, site conditions, disciplines involved, construction methods, and goals in each construction project vary. Today's projects, for example, are more intricate, the technology more advanced, and the trades working on them more specialized. Identifying and establishing systems to manage potential business disagreements on construction projects can help parties avoid delays and resolve disputes that could threaten an entire project.

Arbitration Agreements

Arbitration agreements are essentially of two types: (1) a future-dispute arbitration agreement, commonly referred to as an arbitration clause, which is contained in a broader contract between the parties and anticipates arbitration procedures to follow, should a dispute arise under the broader contract; and (2) a present-dispute arbitration agreement, known as a submission agreement, which counsel for the parties craft when the parties desire to arbitrate a dispute, but where there is no pre-existing contract clause.

Arbitration can take place only if both parties have agreed to it, unless of course, the proceeding is court-ordered. For this reason, the parties are obligated to accept the terms of settlement, regardless of whether it is unfavorable. If the parties do not agree in advance to follow the arbitrator's final decision, but merely agree to consider it, the process is termed conciliation. Additionally, parties are able to choose important elements such as the applicable law, language, and venue of the arbitration. In this vein, neither party enjoys home court advantage.

Parties may insert arbitration clauses into contracts to resolve future disputes. An existing dispute can be referred to arbitration by means of a submission agreement between the parties. In contrast to other forms of dispute resolution, specifically mediation, a party cannot unilaterally withdraw from the proceeding. Within the two main types of arbitration agreements, parties must agree on the terms of arbitration.

Terms agreed upon may be as narrow or as broad as the parties desire. For instance, the parties can agree in advance to the parameters within which the arbitrator may render his or her award. If the award is lower than the specified low, the defendant will pay the agreed-upon low figure; but, if the award is higher than the specified high, the plaintiff will accept the agreed-upon high. If, however, the award falls between the high and low, the parties agree to be bound by the arbitrator's decision. The parties' terms may include a form of binding arbitration wherein each of the parties chooses one number only, and the arbitrator may select only one of the figures as the award.

Whether to reveal the figure to the arbitrator is another decision the parties must make. In some instances, the parties exchange their own determination of that value of the case, but the figures are not revealed to the arbitrator. Subsequently, the arbitrator assigns a value to the case and the parties agree to accept the high or low figure closest to the arbitrator's value.

History

Historically, arbitration was practiced by the Greek city-states, and in the Middle Ages high ecclesiastical authorities were called upon to settle controversies. In the first part of the 20th century, some countries—the United States and France—began passing laws that sanctioned and even promoted the use of private adjudication as an alternative to what was perceived to be inefficient court systems. The growth of international trade however, brought greater sophistication to arbitration. As trade grew, so did the practice of arbitration. Ultimately, this led to the creation of international arbitration as a means for resolving disputes under international commercial contracts.

Since then, great advances have been made, notably the establishment of the Permanent Court of Arbitration. Functions analogous to arbitration were performed by the Permanent Court of International Justice under the League of Nations: functions that belong to the International Court of Justice. Today, many treaties contain clauses providing for arbitration or conciliation of disputes. The most notable of these is the Charter of the United Nations.

The last decade has seen an unprecedented increase in professional liability claims, including those brought by businesses and individuals against accounting firms. Typically, those disputes were resolved by litigation that, in more than 90 percent of the cases, results in a settlement.

Increasingly, the international business community is using arbitration to resolve commercial disputes arising in the global marketplace. Supportive laws are in place in many countries that provide a favorable climate for the enforcement of arbitration clauses. International commercial arbitration awards are recognized by national courts in most parts of the world. Arbitration is popular in international trade as a means of dispute resolution because, among other methods used to resolve disputes, it often is easier to enforce an arbitration award in a foreign country than it is to enforce a judgment of the court.

See Also: Bill of Lading; International Law; Mediation; Negotiation and Negotiating Styles.

Bibliography. F. Paul Bland, Jr., Michael J. Quirk, Kate Gordon, and Jonathan Sheldon, *Consumer Arbitration Agreements,* 4th ed. (National Consumer Law Center, 2004); Michael W. Buhler and Thomas H. Webster, *Handbook of ICC Arbitration* (Sweet and Maxwell, 2005); Christian Buhring-Uhle and Gabriele Lars Kirchhof, *Arbitration and Mediation in International Business,* 2nd ed. (Kluwer, 2006); A. Redfern and M. Hunter, *Law and Practice of International Commercial Arbitration,* 4th ed. (Sweet and Maxwell, 2004); Tibor Varady, John J. Barcelo, and Arthur Taylor Von Mehren, *International Commercial Arbitration,* 3rd ed. (West Group, 2006).

DANIEL A. ESPINOSA
ST. THOMAS UNIVERSITY SCHOOL OF LAW

Archer Daniels Midland

The Archer Daniels Midland Company (ADM) is a multinational agribusiness. It engages in process-ing agricultural commodities on a global scale. It uses agricultural produce to make food ingredients, food additives, oils, and other products. Some of the ingredients are used for human consumption, while other ingredients are used as animal feed ingredients. Nutrients are manufactured into digestible foods for both animals and humans.

Agribusinesses like Archer Daniels Midland serve as a vital link between farmers and consumers. Many food products must either be preserved or processed into easily transportable commodities. Many agricultural commodities such as corn are bulky and costly to ship; transporting them in a processed form not only adds value but also serves to start the processing. The processing operations that ADM engages in create thousands of products from the crops produced by farmers all over the globe. Its product line includes a range of products from amino acids to sweeteners and from nutraceuticals (foods with presumed health benefits) to chocolate.

The company was founded in 1902 in the heartland of American agricultural production. It has always sought to work in partnership with the farming communities in locations where it has operations. Its business philosophy recognizes that healthy agricultural sectors in an economy are essential for the overall health of both the national and the global economy. It is currently headquartered in Decatur, Illinois. Since ADM was incorporated in 1923, it has expanded its business activities to include sales and distribution facilities in 40 U.S. states. It also manages a network of grain elevators.

In Canada ADM engages in transporting and processing cereals such as wheat, durum, or oil seeds like canola and sunflower. It has a number of facilities in locations as diverse as Medicine Hat in Alberta and Montreal. It also produces lecithin, malt, and animal feeds across Canada, along with chocolate from its cocoa bean processing facility in the West African country of Côte d'Ivoire and other locations.

Latin American operations in Mexico produce sweeteners, starch, and wheat flour. ADM also has a number of joint ventures in the cornmeal business. Central American plants include several that mill wheat and premix a variety of products. It also has soybean crushing plants and a string of elevators. In South America ADM processes cocoa and maintains storage operations. It also works to promote the production of soybeans and other grains. ADM has also been very active in opening trade with Cuba.

Pacific Rim facilities operated by ADM process cocoa beans and corn, premix feeds, mill wheat, and manufacture vegetable oil. It also packages vegetable oil and many other products across Asia as well as the Pacific Rim. Sales offices are operated in many Asian countries, and ADM has been engaged in developing business exchanges with Vietnam.

The European oilseed crushing operations of ADM are numerous and spread across the continent. It currently has a fermentation plant in Ireland. Cocoa for the production of chocolates is another major part of ADM's European businesses. In the United Kingdom it operates flour mills. It also has meat and dairy alternative production plants.

The emerging biofuels industry is one of ADM's growing business sectors. It engages in biofuel production in Germany. Sales offices are located in all of its principal markets. Gasohol is a mixture of ethanol (grain alcohol) made from corn. Its use has been mandated by governments in a move to reduce dependence on foreign oil. The move has been profitable for ADM and other agribusinesses, but increased the price of corn for many individual consumers.

In mid-1995 ADM was prosecuted for price fixing. Two of its executives served short prison terms for their part, resulting in two sensationalist books about the affair.

See Also: Company Profiles: North America; Multinational Corporation; Nestlé; United States.

Bibliography. Archer Daniels Midland Company, *Nature of What's to Come: A Century of Innovation* (Archer Daniels Midland, 2002); M. James Bovard, *Archer Daniels Midland: A Case Study in Corporate Welfare* (Cato Institute, 1995); E. J. Kahn, *Supermarketer to the World: The Story of Dwayne Andreas, CEO of Archer Daniels Midland* (Warner Books, 1991); James B. Lieber, *Rats in the Grain: The Dirty Tricks of the "Supermarket to the World"* (Basic Books, 2000); Robert Rubovits, *Archer Daniels Midland: A Report on the Company's Environmental Policies and Practices* (Council on Economic Priorities, Corporate Environmental Data Clearinghouse, 1991).

Andrew J. Waskey
Dalton State College

Argentina

Argentina is the second largest country in size in South America after Brazil and ranks as one of the highest in the region on human development indicators for life expectancy, educational attainment, literacy, and gross domestic product (GDP) per capita. The strong agricultural sector, abundance of natural resources, diversified industrial base, and a large middle class have made Argentina a popular target for global business. In addition, the democratic political structure with executive, judicial, and legislative branches operating at the national and provincial level has enhanced the attractiveness of the country. Despite a fragile economy in the past, this upper-middle income country is now flourishing. Nevertheless, the sustainability of the economy in the long term is questionable because of limited investment in infrastructure and in planning growth.

Several sectors are major contributors to Argentina's GDP, including manufacturing, telecommunications, the service industry, and agriculture. Manufacturing is the largest sector operating in areas such as the production of automobiles, farming equipment, cement, and industrial chemicals. The telecommunications, service, and tourism sectors are also important to the country's GDP. Nevertheless, much of the infrastructure in these areas still needs to catch up with the vigorous expansion that the economy has experienced since the beginning of the 21st century. In addition, domestic transportation is limited, and services are localized to major population areas.

Argentina contains an abundance of fertile land in the region covering several provinces known as the Pampas, which has thrived because of easy access to fresh water, low population density, and a mild climate. The primary staples produced for export include soy and vegetable oils as well as fruits and vegetables. These agreeable conditions have also led Argentina to become one of the largest wine producers in the world and enabled a vibrant cattle industry to prosper. This environment coupled with a flexible exchange rate has allowed the country to be extremely competitive in the export market at the turn of the 21st century and to achieve real annual average GDP growth of over 9 percent for five consecutive years. Participation in the free-trade agreement Mercosur with neighboring countries has also facilitated exports in the region.

Crisis

Argentina suffered a political, economic, and financial crisis in 2001, marked by widespread protests, several interim presidents, the collapse of the banking and financial system, and the default on foreign debt. This crisis was long expected, as the country had been undergoing a recession for a number of years. From 1991 to 2001, President Carlos Menem had upheld a fixed currency exchange rate with the U.S. dollar that was initially intended to control the rampant hyperinflation of the 1980s. Unfortunately this exchange policy led to massive imports with the consequent demise of the national industry and generalized unemployment as well as large trade deficits and high levels of foreign debt.

The country has rebounded from the crisis under the leadership of President Nestor Kirchner, who was elected in 2003. He unilaterally restructured the country's foreign debt, took steps to curb political corruption, exponentially expanded social programs and supported policies to increase exports and lower inflation. In 2007 his wife Cristina Fernandez de Kirchner became the first female president of Argentina.

History and Culture

Although indigenous groups lived in Argentina prior to the European conquest, they now make up less than 1 percent of the population. The country Argentina as it is currently known was largely molded by the arrival of the Spaniards in 1516. The Spanish created the Viceroyalty of the Río de la Plata, of which Argentina was a part, by 1776, but by 1816 under the leadership of General Jose de San Martin the country was declared independent from Spain. A large wave of European immigrants primarily from Spain, Italy, and to a lesser extent France arrived in the country at the turn of the 20th century and at the time contributed to making Argentina one of the wealthiest countries in the world by expanding the agricultural sector.

Nevertheless, during the 20th century recurring economic crises, numerous military coups, waves of high inflation, escalating external debt, and capital flight plagued the country. In addition, constant changes in civilian and military factions in power led to many periods of political unrest after independence. An important and controversial figure who shaped the political landscape of the country was President Juan Peron, who from 1946 to 1955 helped develop unions and other policies to protect the working class. Also of note is the military dictatorship that from 1976 to 1983 led a "dirty war" in which thousands of dissidents "disappeared."

Spanish is the official language of the country. Argentina is predominately Roman Catholic, but Arab and Jewish communities are also prevalent. The typical cuisine includes turnovers (empanadas), meat (asado), and pastries (facturas). Argentina is also one of the largest consumers of wine in the world. As in many Latin American cultures, the most popular sport is soccer. Tango, a melancholic style of music, came into being in Argentine brothels at the turn of the 20th century and is enjoyed worldwide.

See Also: Brazil; Latin America; Mercosur/Mercosul.

Bibliography. CIA, "Argentina," *World Factbook*, www.cia.gov (cited March 2009); C. Floria and C. García, *Historia de los Argentinos I and II* (Larousse Argentina, 1971); J. Lanata, *Argentinos* (Ediciones B, 2003); D. K. Lewis, *The History of Argentina* (Palgrave Macmillan, 2003); J. L. Nolan, *Argentina Business: The Portable Encyclopedia for Doing Business with Argentina* (World Trade Press, 1996); L. A. Romero, *A History of Argentina in the Twentieth Century* (Fondo de Cultura Economica, 2006); World Bank, *Argentina Country Brief*, web.worldbank.org (cited March 2009).

Moriah A. Meyskens
Florida International University

Asia

Asian countries have recently become major players in the world economy with the emergence of Japan in the 1960s, India in the 1970s, and China in the late 1980s. Asia covers some 29.4 percent of the world's land mass, and since the 1980s its 4 billion people have made up about 60 percent of the world's population.

From ancient times, there has been significant trade around Asia and also between Asia and other parts of the world. There was contact between Han Dynasty–China and the Roman Empire, but this was through intermediaries, and there were theories that the Romans may have sourced some of their tin from southeast Asia. Archaeologists working at the port of

Oc-Eo in southern Vietnam in the 1930s uncovered two Roman coins in the remains of what was probably the capital of the Empire of Funan, which flourished from about 200 c.e. to 500 c.e. and was a precursor to Cambodia. This shows that there was contact, probably through intermediaries. By this time, Chinese junks sailed around much of the South China Sea, and there were also Arab dhows sailing the Indian Ocean. Trade in spices, other foods, silks, and other precious items took place at sea, and also on land with the emergence of the Silk Road, the land route through central Asia connecting China with Turkey and through Turkey to Europe.

In medieval times, there seems to have been increasing trade around Asia, with most trade with Europe along the Silk Road, although this was reduced with the emergence of the Seljuk and then the Ottoman Turks. Trade continued between China and the Turks, but much of Europe was cut off. There were some intrepid travelers who made the journey, such as Marco Polo (1254–1324). There were also many Christian missionaries, going back to St. Thomas himself, who was said to have gone to India soon after the crucifixion of Jesus.

In early modern times the Chinese were involved in trade with most of Asia, and in the early 15th century the government sponsored a number of massive expeditions under Admiral Cheng Ho. Records of these journeys survive, and it is quite clear from them, as well as from archaeological and other evidence, that there were Chinese communities (and also some Indian and Arab communities) around much of the Indian Ocean, southeast Asia, and the South China Sea. Many of these were trading families. There is also a theory that some ships from Cheng Ho's expeditions may have gone to the Americas, but this is disputed by some scholars. A changed political climate at home and the high expedition costs resulted in the Chinese discontinuing their explorations of the world.

European Trade and Imperialism

By the 1480s, there were Portuguese ships in the Indian Ocean, and in 1497–99, Vasco da Gama (c.1460–1524) sailed from Portugal to India and back again, leading to trade by ship from Portugal to India. This Portuguese trade was largely conducted by the Portuguese government, which financed the expeditions and reaped the rewards. In 1510 Afonso

d'Albuquerque (1453–1515) took Goa for the Portuguese, and in 1511 he took Malacca. It was these successes that encouraged British and Dutch merchants to subscribe money to establish, respectively, the Honorable East India Company, founded in 1600, and Vereenigde Oost-Indische Compagnie (VOC), or the Dutch East India Company, established two years later. Both were chartered companies, operating through a government charter that gave them extraterritorial rights over the lands they captured. The profits they made from their expeditions went to pay their shareholders, which included many important government figures in both countries.

The British East India Company was the main trading company in Asia until the 19th century. It maintained a large army and its own navy, and gradually took over a number of important ports from Aden to many parts of India, Ceylon (now Sri Lanka), and also Penang, Malacca, and Singapore, as well as British Burma. It conducted trade with China, and also later attempted to trade with Japan.

The VOC took over Malacca from the Portuguese in 1642, but swapped it with the British in 1824 for British Bencoolen and other settlements on the west coast of Sumatra. The Dutch had also taken over parts of what was to become the Netherlands East Indies from the 1600s. The British captured them in 1811, but returned them in 1824. Both the British East India Company and the VOC suffered from major political interference and from their servants being involved in private trade. This was to lead to the British East India Company collapsing in 1784 and needing an injection of government money, but being kept afloat until 1858, and then formally dissolving in 1873. For the VOC, their rule over the Netherlands East Indies was replaced by direct rule from the Netherlands in 1801.

Other companies also maintained their own chartered companies in Asia with the Danish East India Company founded in 1616; the Portuguese East India Company founded in 1628; the French East India Company founded in 1664; and the Swedish East India Company founded in 1731. The Danes, at their height, are reported to have imported more tea than the British East India Company, with vast quantities smuggled into Britain. They also managed to establish some settlements in India, but their Danish East India Company had to be refounded in 1732 as Asiatisk Kompagni ("Asiatic Company"), which, in

1779, handed its monopoly to the Danish crown. The Swedish East India Company was actually launched by Scottish merchant Colin Campbell and made a fortune for its investors—paying a 25 percent dividend on the first voyage—but never had any territorial claims in Asia.

19th- and 20th-Century Companies

By the 19th century, many new companies started to become involved in trade in Asia. Many of these were trading companies that specialized in a particular field of business, although a few of them operated as general merchants. Later still, some of these businesses transformed themselves into agency houses whereby they imported items for which they were the agents, selling them in particular markets.

For the British, one of the oldest of the companies operating in Asia was Guthrie & Company. It had been established in 1821 by Briton Alexander Guthrie, who was living in Singapore, and James Guthrie who lived in London. By the 1850s the two had built up the company to become a large trading house that came to dominate British trade with Singapore. James Guthrie retired from the company in 1876 and he then returned to Britain where he died in 1900. By that time the company owned six banks, five insurance companies, two shipping companies and 23 new "general" agencies. It was reorganized in 1903, and by the 1920s and 1930s was heavily involved in oil palm. The company headquarters was destroyed in the Japanese bombing of Malaya, and after World War II, it expanded into Africa and Australia, moving its headquarters to London. There are now a number of companies in the Guthrie Group, as well as subsidiaries and independent companies using the name Guthrie.

Another early British-founded company that is still operating is the Borneo Company, founded in 1846. It operated throughout Southeast Asia, and had extensive lands in Sarawak and North Borneo (Sabah), hence its name, but also was involved in trade in Singapore, Malaya, and Thailand. During the 1960s, the Borneo Company were agents in Singapore and elsewhere for many major companies including Bosch, Bovril, Johnson & Johnson, Rolex, and the Sheaffer Pen Company. It still owns considerable property in Thailand, where much of its operation is still located.

Probably the most famous of the British trading companies of the period were those that centered on the Jardines. In Hong Kong and Shanghai, Jardine Matheson operated selling opium and other products, an event that led to the Opium Wars in 1839–42. Jardines remained a major company in the International Settlement in Shanghai, and also Hong Kong, and was also a major agency house there and in Singapore and Malaya, where they formed a partnership with the Henry Waugh Trading Company to form Jardine Waugh. Their business was involved in handling exports and imports, insurance, sales of airplanes and aviation accessories, mining, and heavy engineering.

Another British company that operated throughout Asia was the Peninsular & Oriental (P&O) Line, which had the contract for some of the Royal Mail and other mail deliveries as well as taking passengers between Asia and Europe. Of the other British companies that operated in Asia, two others were heavily concerned with trade in Malaya and Singapore—Sime Darby, which began operations in Malacca in 1902 and was established in Singapore in 1910, and William Jacks, which was created in 1919. The former is still important in Malaysia where it controls rubber plantations; the latter specializes in engineering equipment and also in exporting tin, copra, rubber, and pineapples as well as running a general agency.

There was also the firm of Boustead's, founded in 1828 by Edward Boustead, which was involved in trading in spices, coconuts, tobacco, tin, tea, and silks as well as being agents for the British companies Johnny Walker and Thomas Cook's. Mention should also be made of Anglo-Thai; Harper Gilfillan (formerly Gilfillan, Wood & Co. founded in 1867); Harrisons, Barker & Co. (founded in 1902); Huttenbach Brothers (founded in 1883); McAlister & Co. (founded in 1857); and H. Wolskel & Co. (founded in 1900). The Danish East Asiatic Company, founded in 1897 in Copenhagen, traded throughout southeast Asia, being particularly involved in trade in Thailand, Malaya, and Singapore. It still retains many interests in Asia, including in shipping. Other European agency houses operating in the region included the German firm Behn Meyer, which had been founded in 1840; the Swiss company Diethelm, founded in 1860; and the French firm Dupire Brothers, founded in 1897.

Mention has already been made of P&O, but there were also many other shipping lines in the region. These included the British companies China Navigation Co., Dominion of Far East Line, and Orient

Line; and in Burma, the Irrawaddy Flotilla Company. Other companies included the U.S. Pacific Far East Line; and the Japanese Nippon Yusen Kaisha, Osaka Shosen Kaisha, and Mitsui-O.S.K. lines. The liners were involved in transporting passengers, mail, and, in times of strife, military supplies and/or soldiers.

Many of the shipping companies had arrangements with local hotels, and this led to extensive tourism—the major hotels in Asia at that time included the Astor (c.1890, Tianjin, China); the Cathay (1931, Shanghai, China); the Eastern and Oriental (1884/1885, Penang, Malaysia); the Grand Hotel de Pekin (1900, Beijing, China); the Grand Oriental Hotel (1837, Colombo, Ceylon/Sri Lanka); the Hotel des Indes (1897, Batavia/Jakarta, Indonesia); the Imperial (1915–22, Tokyo, Japan); the Oriental Hotel (1876, Bangkok, Thailand); the Metropole (1901, Hanoi, Vietnam); the Peninsula Hotel (1928, Hong Kong, China); the Raffles Hotel (1887, Singapore); the Royal (1937, Phnom Penh, Cambodia); the Strand Hotel (1901, Rangoon/Yangon, Burma/Myanmar); and the Taj Mahal (1904, Bombay/Mumbai, India). Many of these have gone through several different management companies. In addition, since World War II, there has been an expansion with many major hotel chains buying up or building their own hotels in major cities in Asia.

There were also a large number of European banks that operated throughout Asia. For the British, Grindlays in India, the Hongkong and Shanghai Banking Corporation (now HSBC), the Imperial Bank of India, the National Bank of India, the Standard Chartered Bank, and many others operated, and some of these still maintain a presence in the region, although many of the smaller ones have since been absorbed by larger concerns. In Australia, the Orient Bank helped many Chinese miners transfer funds back to China during the Gold Rush of the 1850s. The French ran the Banque de l'Indochine; the Germans operated the Deutsche Asiatische Bank; and for the Japanese, the Yokohama Specie Bank had branches throughout Asia (the singer/artist Yoko Ono's father managed the Hanoi branch during World War II).

There were also a number of smaller banks such as the Banco Delta Asia located in Macao that gained worldwide attention in 2005 when it had sanctions placed against it by the U.S. government in connection with its dealings with the North Korean government. Later Chinese-owned and Chinese-run banks were established throughout Asia with the Overseas Chinese Banking Corporation, founded in 1932 from an amalgamation of three other banks; and the United Overseas Bank, formed in 1935, both operating heavily in Singapore, British Malaya, and the Netherlands East Indies.

In addition to the trading companies, there were many European-owned plantation or mining companies that focused on individual sites or ran groups of plantations or mines. Of the plantation companies, the most well known was the British-owned Dunlop, which controlled many rubber plantations in Malaya. The Compagnie du Cambodge, owned by the French nobles the Comtes de Beaumont in Paris, was one of the major rubber companies in French Indochina. The Bombay Burmah Trading Corporation operated in northern Thailand and Burma, mainly in timber. In India, the tea companies such Twining's and Lipton's (now a part of Unilever) were important. Other British companies such as the security printers De La Rue and Waterlow's, and the U.S. firm American Banknote Company, were (and still are) involved in the printing of money and postage stamps. Kelly & Walsh were major publishers of books in English from their offices in Hong Kong and Shanghai.

In addition to the European companies, there have also been large numbers of Chinese trading companies. Many of these were not well known until the 1950s, but some of these included Lee Rubber and Yeo Hap Seng's foods. The "Tiger Balm brothers," Aw Boon Haw (1883–1954) and Aw Boon Par (d.1944) were from Burma and developed the ointment Tiger Balm, making a fortune and operating for most of the time from Singapore. Cheong Fatt-tze also ran an extensive business empire in Penang, Sumatra, and some parts of southern China; and Loke Wan Tho (1915–64) ran the Cathay Organization. The Shaw brothers (Runme, Runje, Runde, and Run Run) ran a film company empire in Shanghai, Hong Kong, and Singapore.

Post-Independence

After independence in many of the countries in Asia, business laws were gradually changed to help the local population gain control of many of the businesses. In Malaysia, laws were introduced to promote Malays in business, and these have been successful with many firms in the country now controlled by Malays;

Malaysian citizenship is a requirement to become a director of a company in Malaysia.

In Cambodia, laws to establish state-owned corporations in the 1960s did reduce the Chinese domination of the businesses in the country but led to stagnation in the economy, which in turn has been blamed for the events leading up to the civil war that broke out in 1970. Since the late 1980s, the circle around Hun Sen has controlled many of the major businesses in the country. In Vietnam, the French tried to maintain their businesses in the country with some success, although their last plantations in the country were nationalized in 1976, a year after the end of the Vietnam War. A relaxation of communist restrictions has seen many people establish businesses, especially in Ho Chi Minh City. In Brunei, Shell Oil has formed a partnership with the local government to form Royal Brunei Shell, and in Indonesia, the local company Pertamina was established in 1957. In the Philippines, economic power is closely linked to political power, with many examples from the leading families such as the Ayalas, Cojuangcos, and Lopez.

Japan

The main transformations in Asian business since the end of World War II have been in the emergence of Japanese capitalism, in the reemergence of China from the 1980s, and in the development of the Indian economy. Mention should also be made of the "tiger" economies of the Pacific Rim, notably Hong Kong, Singapore, South Korea, and Taiwan (Republic of China), all of which have had high levels of economic growth.

There had been Japanese trading companies in early modern times, but the country was closed to most traders from 1635 until the arrival of Commodore Matthew Perry in 1853–54. This was followed by the Meiji Restoration, where the Japanese government actively sought to build up its own businesses. In many cases it encouraged existing businesses run by local landowners to transform into joint-stock companies. Government grants were provided for many of the companies such as the Yawata Steel Works, to develop with help from the Bank of Japan (Nippon Ginko), which had been formed in 1882.

After World War II, with the Japanese nation shattered, plans were introduced to rebuild the country's economy. Before the war, Japan had been the source of many cheap goods and toys; it did not have a good reputation for manufactures. As a result, the engineer and statistician Gen'ichi Taguchi sought advice from the U.S. quality control experts W. Edwards Deming, Joseph Moses Juran, and Walter A. Shewhart. The plan was for Japan to develop its business along strict lines that would ensure that the country gained a reputation for inexpensive but good-quality manufactured products. The newest factories, often "staffed" with robots, were developed for what became an economic "miracle."

In 1945 most of Japan's industry had been destroyed and during the Allied occupation of Japan, the large conglomerates (zaibatsus) were broken up. This allowed many new companies to form, but owing to the economies of scale, a number of these later merged. It was not long before Hitachi, Kawasaki, Mitsubishi, Mitsui, Nippon Electric Company (NEC), Nissan, Sony, and Toshiba became household names around the world. In the 1960s, Honda managed to make huge inroads into the motorcycle industry in the United States so quickly that the "Honda effect" was taught at many management courses in U.S. universities.

China

Before World War II, the Chinese economy had been dominated by foreign companies, although during the late 19th century Li Hung-chang and other officials had tried to develop Chinese companies such as the Kaiping Mines and the Shanghai Cotton Cloth Mill. After 1949, when the communists won the Chinese civil war, Chinese businesses on the mainland were nationalized. However, from the late 1970s, China started to engage more with the West, and this led to the creation of a capitalist economy alongside a communist political structure. The result has been great economic influence wielded by large Chinese companies that have been involved in low-price manufactures, which in turn has seen them dominate the textile industry and be responsible for many manufactured items sold around the world.

China has become wealthy through exports, and has also seen Western expertise and businesses relocate to China, especially to Shanghai, which has reemerged as the commercial capital of China. The return of Hong Kong in 1997, and the peaceful manner in which that took place, has in turn led to renewed confidence in the Chinese economy that has seen unparalleled rates of economic growth in the 1990s and the 2000s.

India

In India, the economy of the country has also been transformed since independence in 1947. For periods of time, India has been dominated by a socialist government, and under Prime Minister Indira Gandhi, large government corporations played a large part in the economy of India. However, gradually more and more private companies have been established, leading to India also having long periods of high economic growth, and the entrepreneurial spirit has seen the emergence of many new companies, especially in the information technology sector—India being able to take advantage of a large English-speaking population.

Globalization

With increasing prosperity in much of Asia, there have been many multinationals investing heavily in the region. Foreign banks have premises in many of the major cities of the region. Foreign banking institutions are involved in trade throughout the region, with many investment arms of foreign corporations being active in the Tokyo, Hong Kong, Shanghai, Singapore, Seoul, and other stock markets. Indeed, it was in Singapore in 1995 that the British bank Baring's lost a fortune on the stock market, causing the bank to be sold for £1.

Asia has benefited hugely from globalization with some countries such as China taking advantage of its vast human resources, many others doing so to a lesser extent, and all being able to draw on entrepreneurial skills; this has seen Asian businesses compete in every part of the world. Of the richest people in the world, Indians Lakshmi Mittal, Mukesh Ambani, and Anil Ambani rank, respectively, fourth, fifth, and sixth, with Kushal Pal Singh, also from India, being ninth. Li Ka-shing from Hong Kong is listed as the 12th richest, the Sultan of Brunei is listed as 17th richest, and the Kwok brothers from Hong Kong are the 25th richest.

See Also: Asian Development Bank; Asian Financial Crisis; Asian Tigers; Bangladesh; China; Hong Kong; India; Indonesia; Japan; Korea, South; Malaysia; Pacific Rim; Philippines; Singapore; Sri Lanka; Thailand; Vietnam.

Bibliography. Robert Blake, *Jardine Matheson: Traders of the Far East* (Weidenfeld & Nicolson, 1999); Sjovald Cunyngham-Brown, *The Traders: A Story of Britain's South-East Asian Commercial Adventure* (Newman Neame, 1970); Emil Hellfferich, *Behn, Meyer & Co.* (Hans Christians Verlag, 1983); Hongkong & Shanghai Banking Corporation, *A Century in Singapore 1877–1977* (The Corporation, 1978); David Howarth and Stephen Howarth, *The Story of P&O* (Weidenfeld & Nicolson, 1986); Frank H. H. King, *The Hongkong Bank in the Period of Imperialism and War 1895–1918* (Cambridge University Press, 1988); Richard Lim, *Building a Singapore Bank: The OUB Story* (Overseas Union Bank, 1999); Henry Longhurst, *The Borneo Story: The First Hundred Years of The Borneo Company Limited* (Newman Neame, 1956); David Shavit, *The United States in Asia: A Historical Dictionary* (Greenwood Press, 1990); *Sime Darby: 75th Anniversary* (Sime Darby, 1985); Poul Westpoll, *The East Asiatic Company Limited* (East Asiatic Company, 1972); Arnold Wright and H. A. Cartwright, *Twentieth Century Impressions of British Malaya* (Lloyds Greater England, 1907).

JUSTIN CORFIELD
GEELONG GRAMMAR SCHOOL, AUSTRALIA

Asian Development Bank

The Asian Development Bank (ADB) is an international organization consisting of 67 members, coming from both within and outside the Asia-Pacific region, with a focus on development, poverty, education, and improving the quality of life of the people of the region. ADB works with various partners to attempt to achieve its goals, including members of the private sector, nongovernmental organizations (NGOs), governments, and other organizations. The headquarters of ADB is in Manila, the Philippines, and ADB has a number of branch offices throughout the region.

The primary methods ADB uses to attempt to accomplish its mission are the issuing of loans and grants as well as supplying technical assistance and advice. The majority of the loans and grants ADB provides are given to the governments of Asian nations; however, the organization also provides direct assistance to some private enterprises in the region and ADB has developed a credit-rating service to assist

The Tarbela Dam in Pakistan, shown above in a photo taken from space, was funded in part by the Asian Development Bank.

private firms in securing private funding that is needed for investment. ADB is currently following a strategic framework entitled *Strategy 2020*, which emphasizes inclusive growth, environmentally sustainable growth, and regional integration.

ADB came into existence on December 19, 1966, with Takeshi Watanabe appointed its first president. As this was prior to the rapid industrialization and economic growth that has been seen in the later parts of the 20th century in much of Asia, ADB initially focused primarily on increasing the efficiency of Asian agricultural and rural development. As the economies of Asia began to grow and shift from a focus on agriculture toward a focus on industrial development, ADB shifted its focus as well to include improvements in education, health, and infrastructure as well as development of specific industries as its key objectives.

Into the 1980s and 1990s, ADB continued to expand both its membership and mission. Newly independent central Asian nations became members and recipients of loans, grants, and technical assistance from the organization. New programs were implemented that dealt with gender issues, micro-finance, urban planning, and environmental concerns. Furthermore, ADB got involved in creating a subregional organization with the creation of the Greater Mekong Subregion.

ADB's lending focuses primarily on funding major projects. In 2007 loans totaling $10.1 billion for 82 projects were approved by ADB. During the same year, ADB spent $243 million in technical assistance and gave grants totalling $673 million.

ADB is governed by a board of governors in which each of the 67 members is represented. The board of governors gathers each year for an annual meeting. The day-to-day operations are managed by the ADB president who is elected for a five-year term by the board of governors. Working with the president is a management team consisting of four vice presidents and the managing director general.

ADB has been active in promoting Asian regionalization in recent years, and the priority of achieving this objective has risen since Haruhiko Kuroda's election as president in 2005 and the creation of the Office of Regional Integration. As ADB is a major player in Asian regionalization, Asian regionalism efforts have been primarily concerned with economic development and trade promotion as opposed to security or political integration issues.

It should be noted that ADB has been the target of criticism from many quarters. Officials of the U.S. and UK governments, both members and financial supporters of ADB, have expressed concerns over the bank's management practices. There have also been concerns over ADB's growing mandate and whether it is necessary to duplicate functions that are already the responsibility of other international organizations such as the World Bank and International Monetary Fund. Furthermore, there have also been concerns expressed by grassroots organizations and environmental activists over ADB funding of projects that are seen to be environmentally unfriendly.

Nevertheless, during the period of ADB's existence, Asia has experienced some of the fastest growth and quickest reductions in poverty in the history of mankind. Whether this progress has been assisted or hampered by ADB is open to debate.

See Also: Asia; Asian Financial Crisis; Asian Tigers; Asia-Pacific Economic Cooperation; Association of Southeast Asian Nations.

Bibliography. Asian Development Bank, www.adb.org (cited March 2009); Christopher Dent, "The Asian Development Bank and Developmental Regionalism in East Asia," *Third World Quarterly* (v.29/4, 2008); Raphael Minder, "Asian Development Bank's Donors Seek Shake Up of Oversight and Staffing, *Financial Times* (January 17, 2008); E. Kumar Sharma, "Grassroot Grumbles," *Business Today* (June 4, 2006); James Simms and Denis McMahon, "Asian Development Bank Debates a Change in Role," *Wall Street Journal* (May 8, 2007).

SCOTT A. HIPSHER
ROYAL MELBOURNE INSTITUTE OF TECHNOLOGY

Asian Financial Crisis

The Asian financial crisis, which led to a wave of currency depreciations and economic recession among many east Asian economies, started in Thailand during the summer of 1997. Thailand, Indonesia, and Korea were the most affected, while Malaysia and the Philippines were affected at a lower, but nonetheless significant scale.

The fact that many of east Asia's currencies were pegged to the U.S. dollar before 1997–98 significantly contributed to the crisis. With the dollar appreciating in the 1990s, most east Asian countries experienced huge balance of payments deficits. The countries' governments used their foreign exchange reserves primarily to support the peg. In a short period of time, the reserves decreased to very low levels, leading to a currency crisis in the region.

Large international debts in the private sector also contributed to the crisis. A number of big corporations (mostly financial institutions) from the region borrowed expensive, short-term, foreign currency denominated, unhedged loans to finance rapid investments in real estate and the stock market. The worsening of economic conditions in 1997 led to a sharp rise in defaults among borrowers, causing a number of banks to become financially distressed. That led to a bank run.

In the early 1990s, Thailand's bigger corporations (mostly financial institutions) borrowed heavily on the international market to finance investments, mostly in real estate and stocks. Following an economic recession in 1997, some of Thailand's banks started missing loan repayments; investors feared the event would kick-start an imminent bank run. Thailand's stock of foreign exchange reserves had been drawn down to such low levels that its government could not afford the dual costs of bailing out its banks and maintaining the foreign exchange rate of the Thai baht simultaneously. A depleted reserve forced the government to allow its currency to float in July 1997. The Thai baht depreciated heavily in the subsequent months. At the same time, the lack of governmental support and/or inability of the government to rescue them caused a number of Thai financial institutions to go bankrupt.

During that time period, the Bank of Indonesia was increasing reserve requirements, increasing interest rates, and making attempts to curb credit expansion. Fearing an appreciation of the rupiah, Indonesia repeatedly widened its currency's trading band, hoping that the increased volatility would discourage speculators. That hope did not materialize, and investors did not put too much faith in Indonesia's ability to reform.

In Malaysia, the current account deficit was widening at an alarming rate as well. The then prime minister Mahathir bin Mohamad's "Vision 2020" led to an unrestrained expansion of credit, leaving the Malaysian central bank, Bank Negara, with few options but to take steps to do the exact opposite, i.e., tighten credit availability. Furthermore, Malaysian interest rates were too high to be ignored and that led to a large inflow of speculative capital.

Financing its ever-increasing current account deficit led to an accumulation of short-term foreign debt in Korea. Its large conglomerates, called chaebols, were heavily in debt; this led to a wave of corporate bankruptcies, causing consequential losses to Korean banks. International lenders did not roll over loans that would have been voluntarily restructured in normal circumstances.

In the Philippines, aggressive lending led to a speculative boom in its real estate market. Lenders were left with nonperforming loans when the boom cycle finally went full circle.

Low reserves and inflated currencies led to a wave of currency depreciations in the region. These depreciations dramatically increased the burden of foreign-currency liabilities. Hence, the costs of bailing out financial institutions were now beyond the fiscal means of these countries. The governments were powerless as their currency, financial institutions, and economic activity collapsed.

Although the International Monetary Fund (IMF) intervened at an early stage of the crisis, as the crisis kept its momentum and kept unfolding, adjustments were needed to some of the institutions' policy recommendations that were already under way. The World Bank, the Asian Development Bank, and bilateral donors also assisted in reform efforts that eventually helped the region to recover. The IMF's handling of the Asian financial crisis has been criticized by many. Nonetheless, it is also acknowledged that many of the affected countries had structural deficiencies (for example, weaknesses in financial systems, governance, and politics) that hampered the successful achievement of IMF recommendations.

See Also: Asia; Asian Development Bank; Asian Tigers; Chaebol; Contagion; Currency; Indonesia; International Monetary Fund; Korea, South; Malaysia; Philippines; Thailand.

Bibliography. Iwan J. Azis, "Indonesia's Slow Recovery after Meltdown," *Asian Economic Papers* (v.7/1, 2008); Andrew Berg, "The Asia Crisis—Causes, Policy Responses, and Outcomes," *International Monetary Fund Working Paper* (October 1999); Peter C. Y. Chow and Bates Gill, *Weathering the Storm: Taiwan, Its Neighbors, and the Asian Financial Crisis* (Brookings Institution Press, 2000); Dilip K. Das, *Asian Economy and Finance: A Post-Crisis Perspective* (Springer, 2005); Stephan Haggard, *The Political Economy of the Asian Financial Crisis* (Institute for International Economics, 2000); Karl D. Jackson, *Asian Contagion: Causes and Consequences of a Crisis* (Westview Press, 1999); David R. Meyer, "Structural Changes in the Economy of Hong Kong since 1997," *China Review—An Interdisciplinary Journal on Greater China* (v.8/1, 2008); Dick Nanto, "CRS Report: The 1997–98 Asian Financial Crisis," *CRS Reports for Congress* (1998); Wing Thye Woo, Jeffrey Sachs, and Klaus Schwab, eds., *The Asian Financial Crisis: Lessons for a Resilient Asia* (MIT Press, 2000).

SURENDRANATH R. JORY
UNIVERSITY OF MICHIGAN–FLINT

Asian Tigers

Asian tigers as a term originally referred to the four economies of Hong Kong, Singapore, Korea (South), and Taiwan, which are all known for their very high growth rates and rapid industrialization following Japan from the late 1960s onward. Although usually reserved for the original four economies, the expression "new tigers" since the 1990s and early 2000s has been used for some other economies in Asia (e.g., India) due to their increased visibility in world high-technology competition.

Similarities between the original four are, first, an export-driven model of economic development, where goods were exported to the highly industrialized nations. At the same time the governments tried to put a brake on domestic consumption by way of, for example, high tariffs against imports. Other common traits are that the governments focused explicitly on improved education levels as a means to increase productivity. All four economies suffered the impact of the Asian financial crisis of 1997, although in slightly different degrees, with Taiwan seemingly suffering the least.

Differences between the original four Asian tigers are depicted in a book by C. Edquist, L. Hommen, and colleagues: Variation in policies and specialization within different kinds of industries, in addition to obvious cultural and historical variations. Korea is the largest economy of the four, and also has a high complexity of industrial structures. Its industrialization process was rapid and remarkable in that it evolved from being a poor, agricultural economy, undergoing exploitation during Japanese colonization, and experiencing devastation during the Korean War, into a full-fledged industrialized state in a very short time. As in Taiwan, Japanese colonial rule resulted in a capitalist basis for the economy and infrastructure such as railways, marine ports, roads, and irrigation systems, whereas post-colonial development has been an interplay between indigenous policies and relations with selected foreign ideas.

According to the *Total Economy Database* (TED), Korean gross domestic product (GDP) per capita for the year 1960 was estimated at US$4,071, increasing to US$9,541 (1975), US$15,457 (1985), US$26,161 (1995), and US$30,568 (1999, compared to US$57,460 for the United States). Korea has a dual structure of firms divided into large firms able to have an international technology and market orientation and a large segment of domestic-oriented smaller firms. Industry networks (chaebol groups) and their affiliated firms are dominant in the country also in terms of research and development (R&D), although there is a significant amount of R&D organized as a large government research institute sector rather than in universities. The financial system has predominantly been a banking system and underwent reforms that are in part a result of the more liberalized environment triggered by the aftereffects of the Asian financial crisis.

In the case of Taiwan, the TED figures for GDP per capita are US$4,976 (1960), US$11,559 (1975), US$21,117 (1985), US$31,256 (1995), and US$37,589 (1999). Taiwan can be characterized as a predominantly government policy–led system, although the actual development obviously has been an interplay between government and private firms. However, Taiwan is a prime case of government playing a key strategic role by changing the economic base itself in order to create new market segments in which Taiwanese firms could compete. The Taiwanese system is strongly focused on specialized production, often in the form of original equipment manufacturing (OEM) and original design manufacturing (ODM). This strength is simultaneously a challenge for the system, since it might be necessary to foster new trajectories of growth in the future. For example, the economic growth of mainland China has in part become a source of competition for Taiwan's existing specializations.

Singapore has experienced rapid development since political independence in 1965. The TED figures for Singapore GDP per capita are US$7,691 (1960), US$17,455 (1975), US$23,847 (1985), US$39,399 (1995), and US$43,986 (1999). Until the late 1990s, this development was largely through reliance on foreign direct investment (FDI), i.e., attracting subsidiaries of foreign multinational corporations. Government played a central role by providing incentives, training programs, and infrastructure.

Unlike the structure in terms of ownership of firms in Korea and Taiwan, where there is a large proportion of indigenous firms, there has been a situation in Singapore in recent years with about three-quarters of the manufacturing output coming from multinational corporations, and where more than 60 percent of equity in its manufacturing sector was foreign. In view of the somewhat recipient-oriented nature of these activities, the recent Singapore policy efforts have been aimed at increasing the innovation intensity of the activities located in Singapore. A challenge similar to Taiwan's is to achieve balance between government guidance and independent entrepreneurial initiative.

Hong Kong was a Crown colony of Great Britain 1847–1997, and developed during the five decades leading up to 1997 into a newly industrialized economy as well as a trade hub between the People's Republic of China and the world. Since 1997 Hong Kong has tried to diversify its role. Hong Kong's production networks have started to become integrated into the Chinese mainland. In addition, Hong Kong was particularly hard hit by the Asian financial crisis. Recent policies regarding Hong Kong have included R&D-related investments and attempts at generating new technologies through public support, thereby trying to transform Hong Kong into an innovation hub with links to and from China.

See Also: Asia; Asian Financial Crisis; China; Hong Kong; Korea, South; Singapore.

Bibliography. Lowell Dittmer, "The Asian Financial Crisis and the Asian Developmental State: Ten Years After," *Asian Survey* (v.47/6, 2007); C. Edquist and L. Hommen, eds., *Small Country Innovation Systems: Globalization, Change and Policy in Asia and Europe* (Cheltenham, 2008); Groningen Growth and Development Centre and The Conference Board, *Total Economy Database, Gross Domestic Product Per Capita in 1990 PPP US$*; E. M. Kim, ed., *The Four Asian Tigers: Economic Development and Global Political Economy* (Academic Press, 1998); P. Krugman, "The Myth of Asia's Miracle," *Foreign Affairs* (November/ December 1994); S. Lall, *Learning from the Asian Tigers: Studies in Technology and Industrial Policy* (Palgrave

Macmillan, 1997); Hugh De Santis, "The Dragon and the Tigers—China and Asian Regionalism," *World Policy Journal* (v.22/2, 2005).

Terje Grønning
University of Oslo

Asia-Pacific Economic Cooperation

Asia-Pacific Economic Cooperation, known also under the acronym of APEC, is an international forum created in 1989 in order to enhance commercial and economic cooperation in the Asia-Pacific region by facilitating economic development, trading exchanges, and investments. APEC's members now include 21 countries of the Pacific Rim: the United States, Australia, Japan, Mexico, Peru, Malaysia, Brunei, Russia, Vietnam, Singapore, Thailand, Indonesia, Hong Kong, Papua New Guinea, New Zealand, the Philippines, Taiwan, Republic of Korea, People's Republic of China, Canada, and Chile. They are usually referred to as "member economies."

APEC's main goals, first set in 1994 at the Bogor (Indonesia) meeting, can be summed up as follows: Promotion of free and open trade in the Asia-Pacific area; facilitation of trading exchanges by the elimination of trade, tariff, and other types of barriers that make difficult economic exchanges across the Pacific; reduction of the costs of business transactions by improving access to trade information; improvement of business facilitations in order to help economic operators conduct business more efficiently; expansion of the Asia-Pacific import-export economy by providing cheaper goods and services and more employment opportunities; and enhancement of technical cooperation. Additionally APEC works toward the creation of an international space for the safe and effective movement of goods, services, and people across its member states through policy alignment on the one hand and economic and technical cooperation on the other.

APEC activities are planned and implemented with the consensual agreement of economic leaders and ministers of its member economies. During the meetings in which the representatives of each member state participate, the guidelines of APEC's activities are outlined. Member economies' representatives meet throughout the year to program future cooperation in the Asia-Pacific region and further already agreed-upon projects.

The inaugural meeting of APEC was promoted by and held in Australia in January 1989. It was the then Australian prime minister who launched the idea to implement more efficient cooperation in the Asia-Pacific area. However, when APEC began it was only an informal forum for the ministers of 12 states of the Asia-Pacific region. The first APEC Economic Leaders' Meeting took place in 1993 at Blake Island in the United States under the presidency of Bill Clinton.

The meeting of the member economies' leaders held in 2007 (in Sydney, Australia), put new issues at the top of APEC's agenda, including climate change, energy security, and clean development. Participants in the meeting also emphasized the Asia-Pacific's vulnerability to natural disasters, recognizing the need for protecting the region from environmental risks. Additional economic integration in the area was also discussed, and new agreements were negotiated to further reduce trade barriers, and institutional and noninstitutional impediments to investments. The enlargement of APEC with the possible entry of more members as a tool to strengthen it was considered as well. The issue of membership, which is particularly important, will be discussed again in 2010.

APEC is financed by contributions of member economies, and the annual budget is used for developing projects and sustaining the activities of the secretariat located in Singapore. Japan is the only member that until now has provided additional funds for specific projects related to trade liberalization.

Unlike other international organizations, APEC works on the basis of nonbinding commitments. There are, in fact, no treaty obligations for its members, and commitments are undertaken on a purely voluntary basis. The fact that there are nonbinding agreements, and the enforcement of any decision depends upon the voluntary commitment of each member, impinges upon APEC's practical efficiency as well as on its real capacity to achieve specific goals.

See Also: Asia; Association of Southeast Asian Nations; Australia; World Trade Organization.

Bibliography. Elek Andrew, *APEC after Busan: New Direction* (Korea Institute for Economic Policy, 2005); Mohammad Ariff, *APEC and Development Cooperation* (Institute of South Asian Studies, 1998); Sandra L. Dawing, ed., *Asia-Pacific Economic Cooperation (APEC): Current Issues and Background* (Nova Science, 2003); Richard E. Feinberg, ed., *APEC as an Institution: Multilateral Governance in the Asia-Pacific* (Institute of Southeast Asian Studies, 2003); Loke Wai Heng, *APEC Trade Liberalisation: Open Regionalism, Non-binding Liberalisation and Unconditional MFN* (University of Sussex, 2006); Richard Higgot, *Cooperation-building in the Asia-Pacific region: APEC and the New Institutionalism* (Japan Research Centre, 1991); John Ravenhill, *APEC and the Construction of Pacific Rim Regionalism* (Cambridge University Press, 2001).

Antonella Viola
European University Institute

Assicurazioni Generali

Assicurazioni Generali is one of the leading financial services group providers of insurance products and services in Europe. With a presence in about 40 countries through 331 subsidiaries, the group primarily operates in Italy, where it is the largest insurance company, followed by Germany, France, Spain, Austria, Switzerland, and Israel. The company was established in 1831 and the headquarters are in Trieste, Italy. During the fiscal year 2007, the group has recorded revenues of €66,217.8 million, a consolidated result of €2,915.6 million, and employs 67,306 people. The main shareholders include Mediobanca Group (15.63 percent), Unicredit Group (4.,66 percent) and Bank of Italy (4.45 percent). Its main international competitors are AXA, Allianz, Fortis, and ING Group.

From the very beginning Assicurazioni Generali has been characterized by the capacity to grow, evolve, and innovate constantly, enhancing its wide presence across various segments and geographies. The business of Generali is concentrated on life and non-life insurance products, financial services, and real estate. The life division is involved in the offer of life insurance products for both individuals and corporate clients. The non-life division is engaged in the provision of motor, personal, accident, and health insurance.

The financial services division provides a range of banking and asset management services such as bancassurance and investment management products and services for individuals and institutional clients. It also provides services in the areas of real estate. The strategic focus of the group is on product and distribution innovation, increasing efficiency and improving standards for products and customer service.

Generali can be defined as a global born-leading company. After only four years from its foundation, Generali had already opened 25 offices in western and eastern Europe. Within a few decades, the group had expanded into Africa and Asia (in the 1880s) and North and South America (from 1950), diffusing around the world the trademark of the lion of St. Mark introduced after the establishment of the Republic of Venice. This symbol, after profound restyling, still identifies the group.

Generali's expansion has continued in recent years with a number of mergers and acquisitions, agreements, and joint ventures that have always characterized the growth strategy of the company, giving a strong brand recognition leveraging a distinctive competitive advantage, especially in high-growth areas. Nevertheless a strong base for the growth initiatives has been always represented, especially in recent years, by the group's robust financial performance.

Recent milestones include, in early 2005, the constitution of Generali China Life, a joint venture between Generali and China National Petroleum, followed a year later by the authorization to set up a joint venture to operate also in the Chinese non-life insurance business. The group expansion in the emerging markets was reinforced in 2006 through a joint-venture agreement signed with one of the leading retailers in India, Pantaloon Retail, to serve both life and non-life segments.

Further acquisitions and partnerships have been recently carried out to enhance the market position of Generali in central and eastern Europe (CEE). An agreement was signed in 2004 between Generali and EBRD (the European Bank for Reconstruction and Development) in order to set up a new real estate fund with the aim of investing in the real estate sector in CEE. Additionally Generali acquired majority shareholding in Delta Osiguranje, Serbia's largest private insurance company. In June 2006, an agreement with the UkrAvto Group was signed for the acquisition of a 51 percent stake in Garant Auto and Garant Life (insurance companies) in the Ukrainian market. In the same year the group continued its expansion with the acquisition of Orel-G Group, a leading player in the Bulgarian insurance market. To enhance the geographical reach of the company and strengthen its market position in the CEE market, in 2007 Generali and PPF Group signed a joint venture creating a new company named Generali PPF Holding. The joint venture combines the CEE businesses of both companies to create one of the region's leading insurers with more than 9 million clients throughout Czech Republic, Slovak Republic, Poland, Hungary, Romania, Bulgaria, Ukraine, Russia, Serbia, Slovenia, Croatia, and Kazakhstan.

With its continuous growth at a global and local level, it is notable to point out that Assicurazioni Generali has always demonstrated a strong commitment in the areas of welfare, culture, and sports, and has recently introduced environmental concerns to its list of commitments.

See Also: Company Profiles: Western Europe; Italy.

Bibliography. Datamonitor, "Assicurazioni Generali S.p.A.," www.datamonitor.com (cited March 2009); Hoovers, www.hoovers.com (cited March 2009); Assicurazioni Generali, www.generali.com (cited March 2009).

Vladimir Nanut
Università di Trieste–Facoltà di Economia
Donata Vianelli
Università di Trieste

Association of Southeast Asian Nations

The Association of Southeast Asian Nations (ASEAN) was established on August 8, 1967, with an initial membership of five countries: Indonesia, Malaysia, Singapore, the Philippines, and Thailand. Its formal establishment was announced by the Bangkok Declaration. The association has subsequently expanded to include Brunei (1984), Vietnam (1995), Laos (1997), Myanmar (1997), and Cambodia (1999). ASEAN aims to promote economic growth and peace in the region.

Nominal Gross Domestic Product was US$1,281.9 billion in 2007, and a total trade of about US$1,400 billion for all 10 members of ASEAN. The total population is over 566 million and the ASEAN member states cover a total area of 4.5 million sq. km.

The Bangkok Declaration incorporates statements concerned with the region's economic growth, cultural development, security, technological, academic, and administrative development. ASEAN members are agreed to solve their differences through dialogue and in the spirit of mutual accommodation.

The highest decision-making body of ASEAN is the meeting of ASEAN Heads of State, the ASEAN Annual Summit. The ASEAN ministerial meeting for foreign ministers and the ASEAN economic ministers' meetings are also held annually. The meetings of these two bodies focus on defense and the environment and the region's economy, respectively. ASEAN also provides a forum for discussion and decision making in the areas of energy, agriculture and forestry, tourism, and transport at a ministerial level. The secretariat was established by the ASEAN foreign ministers during the 1976 Bali Summit. The secretariat's purview is to initiate, advise, coordinate, and implement ASEAN activities, using an annual operational budget funded through equal contribution of all ASEAN member countries.

Specialized bodies within ASEAN include the Agricultural Development Planning Centre, ASEAN-EC Management Centre, Centre for Energy, Earthquake Information Centre, Poultry Research and Training Centre, Regional Centre for Biodiversity Conservation, Rural Youth Development Centre, Specialized Meteorological Centre, Timber Technology Centre, Tourism Information Centre, and the University Network to promote cooperation among member countries.

There are three ASEAN Communities: the Security Community, Economic Community, and Socio-cultural Community. The ASEAN Security Community aims to promote peace and harmony within the region. Its duties include political development, shaping and sharing of norms, conflict prevention, conflict resolution, post-conflict peace building, and implementing mechanisms components. The ASEAN Economic Community works toward establishing ASEAN as a single market and production base, and the ASEAN Socio-cultural Community aims at nurturing a community of nations, with caring societies and a common regional identity.

ASEAN was founded at a time of conflict in southeast Asia and was unavoidably divided by the two prevailing ideologies, exemplified in the two competing political entities, the Communist and the Western blocs. The establishment of ASEAN by five non-Communist countries divided southeast Asia into two parts. However, ASEAN was not an anti-communist regional organization but a geographical body. The enlargement of ASEAN in the 1990s shows that those new members share the association's commitment to regional peace and stability as a prerequisite for economic development, which is the top priority among members. This enlargement coincides with the fall of communism in eastern Europe. Political cooperation stressed the resolution of disputes negotiation and the benefits to be gained through peace and stability in the region.

ASEAN is not a homogeneous group. There are considerable differences among its member states with respect to size, history, and level of industrialization. The four new members—Cambodia, Laos, Myanmar, and Vietnam—are still in the process of adjusting their economic policies. At one end of the scale, the wealthiest state is Singapore, with a per capita income more than 50 times that of Cambodia. In descending order, the per capita income of the other members starts with Brunei, and is followed by the four older members—Malaysia, Thailand, the Philippines, and Indonesia. Bringing up the economic rear are the remaining new members—Cambodia (as previously mentioned), Laos, Myanmar, and Vietnam.

ASEAN aimed to create an ASEAN Economic Community through the ASEAN Free Trade Area in the Fourth ASEAN Summit, and the ASEAN Free Trade Area agreement was signed on January 28, 1992. The agreement is a common, external preferential tariff scheme to promote the free flow of goods within ASEAN. More than 90 percent of the total tariff lines in ASEAN are now included in the Common Effective Preferential Tariff Scheme, which covers manufactured and agricultural products.

From 2005, tariffs on 99 percent of the products in the inclusion list of the ASEAN six older members (Brunei, Indonesia, Malaysia, Philippines, Singapore, and Thailand) have been reduced to less than 5 percent. For the other newer members, tariffs on about 80 percent in the inclusion list have also been reduced to less than 5 percent. Products in the inclusion list are those that have to undergo immediate liberalization through reduction in intraregional (CEPT) tariff rates, removal of quantitative restrictions, and other nontariff barriers. A zero tariff has to be achieved by older members by 2010 and by 2018 for the newer members. The ASEAN Free Trade Area is regarded as a tool to increase ASEAN members' competitiveness in international markets and to attract foreign investment.

Members of ASEAN want to be free to implement independent policies without interference from their neighbors. Thus, noninterference, consensus, nonuse of force, and nonconfrontation became the principles of the organization. ASEAN is a setting in which leaders at the highest levels communicate with each other on regional affairs, prefer consensus decision making, and make nonbinding treaty plans. This kind of new culture is called the ASEAN Way. The ASEAN Way consists of beliefs, practices, structures, responses, and values commonly shared in ASEAN. It relies on the personal, often face-to-face approach in contrast with Western dependence on structures and functions.

International Network

The collective weight of ASEAN has made the association a force as an international bargaining tool. In the ASEAN regional forum and APEC, ASEAN has established its authority. However, ASEAN does face some difficulties in reaching consensus because of existing differences between old and new members.

ASEAN members also take part in discussions with nonmembers, with a view to promoting good external relationships. ASEAN established the Regional Forum in 1994 to maintain peace and stability in the region. The forum is an official dialogue in the Asia Pacific region, consisting of 27 participants—ASEAN members and others, such as Australia, Bangladesh, Canada, China, the European Union, India, Japan, North Korea, South Korea, Mongolia, New Zealand, Pakistan, Papua New Guinea, Russia, East Timor, the United States, and Sri Lanka. There are three stages: confidence-building measures, development of prevention diplomacy, and elaboration of approaches to conflicts. Prevention diplomacy includes efforts to build mutual trust and confidence between states, norms building, and enhancing channels of communication.

See Also: Asia; Asia-Pacific Economic Cooperation; Brunei; Free Trade; Free Trade Zone; Indonesia; Malaysia; Philippines; Singapore; Thailand; Vietnam.

Bibliography. Alexander C. Chandra, *Indonesia and the ASEAN Free Trade Agreement: Nationalists and Regional Integration Strategy* (Lexington Books, 2008); ASEAN Secretariat, "ASEAN Overview," www.asean.org (cited March 2009); Denis Hew, *Brick by Brick: The Building of an ASEAN Economic Community* (Institute of Southeast Asian Studies, 2007); Institute of Southeast Asian Studies, *Know Your ASEAN* (Institute of Southeast Asian Studies Publishing, 2007); Estrella D. Solidum, *The Politics of ASEAN* (Eastern Universities Press, 2003); Mya Than and Carolyn L. Gates, eds., *ASEAN Enlargement: Impacts and Implications* (Institute of Southeast Asian Studies, 2001).

TAI MING WUT
INDEPENDENT SCHOLAR

ATA Carnet

The Anglo-French term *ATA Carnet* is derived from *Admission Temporaire/Temporary Admission*. *Carnet* is a French word long used in English to refer to particular customs documents, presumably resulting from the frequent trade between the United Kingdom and France. Specifically, a carnet is a customs document that allows the item it covers to be imported without paying a customs duty (tax) on it. The ATA Carnet is used for goods that are going to be imported temporarily, and excuses the holder from all taxes that would normally apply.

The Customs Cooperation Council (now known as the World Customs Organization) first adopted ATA Carnet conventions in 1961, which are now issued according to an agreement administered by the International Chamber of Commerce in conjunction with the World Customs Organization and the relevant entities of member nations, which actually issue the carnets. In many nations, the national chamber of commerce is the issuing body. In the United States,

carnets are issued by the United States Council for International Business (USCIB), the business advocacy group that represents American business interests to the United Nations.

Over 150,000 ATA Carnets are issued annually, by 65 participating countries. Various other countries, especially smaller ones, are known to accept ATA Carnets without actually committing to the international guarantee to do so, and without issuing their own. A modified ATA Carnet, which does not cover exhibition goods, is used for trade between the United States and Taiwan: the TECRO/AIT Carnet (named for the Taipei Economic and Cultural Representative Office, in the United States, and the American Institute in Taiwan).

ATA Carnets cannot be used for perishable goods, but the conceivable range of goods that could be covered is otherwise theoretically limitless. The three categories of goods for which such carnets are issued are goods brought into the country for exhibitions or fairs; professional equipment; and commercial samples. What those categories have in common is that all such goods are being brought into the country for some commercial purpose other than their sale or rent, and will be brought back out of the country as a result. Excusing such importation from tax encourages international business activity in the country of import, and in many cases leads to increased customs revenue for the country at a later date—such as if tax-free samples and demonstrations lead to sales of taxed goods.

ATA Carnets are granted by the home country of the exporter, which will have various requirements. The USCIB, for instance, requires a refundable cash deposit or surety bond equal to 40 percent of the value of the goods, as collateral. Similar collateral requirements are common in other countries, and the collateral is used to pay taxes if a claim is filed against the importer because of ineligibility for an ATA Carnet or because the time frame has expired. Such claims are filed by the country of import, the country that would have been collecting the customs taxes.

Other carnets include the Carnet de Passage, which is issued to motor vehicles and is typically used to distinguish (and excuse from customs duties) a vehicle that is the owner's possession from vehicles imported for sale; and the International Road Transport (TIR) carnets used to harmonize the administration of road transport across multiple countries (especially in Europe).

See Also: Import; International Chamber of Commerce; World Customs Organization.

Bibliography. Richard J. Hunter Jr., "The ATA Carnet System," *Review of Business* (March 22, 2001); Thomas E. Johnson, *Export/Import Procedures and Documentation* (AMACOM, 2002).

Bill Kte'pi
Independent Scholar

AT&T

The history of AT&T provides an interesting dialectic of how a firm is created and severely wounded by technology; is aided and hindered by regulation; welcomes and hides from competition; and uses and abuses shareholder and market valuations.

On February 14, 1876, Alexander Graham Bell's patent on the telephone was filed at the Patent Office in Washington, D.C., and on July 9, 1877, the American Bell Telephone Company was formed. Between 1880 and 1894 AT&T had monopoly protection and telephone growth was a steady 33 percent per year. However, after the patent protection expired, independent telecommunication companies (ITCs) were quick to enter the market. As a result, between 1894 and 1907, prices declined 47.5 percent for business customers and 64.9 percent for residential customers in competitive markets.

In 1905 Theodore Vail, AT&T's chairman, embarked on a strategy of rapid acquisition of ITCs. As telecommunications grew domestically and became an increasingly important component in everyday life, federal and state governments began to exercise increasing intervention. The legislative response was the Communication Act of 1934 that created the Federal Communications Commission for the regulation of interstate telecommunications.

The advent of World War II spurred significant technological development by Bell Labs in radio telecommunications. The invention in 1947 of the transistor ushered in the modern era of computers. Bell Labs also did breakthrough research on satellites in 1960, fiber optics in 1977, and cellular technology in 1983; however, the commercialization of each of these innovations was severely limited by a regulatory process that discouraged replacement technologies.

During the 1950s and 1960s, AT&T sparred with government institutions but managed to fend off regulatory interference by providing high-quality and low-priced telephone service to an ever-increasing number of Americans. Beginning in the mid-1970s, competition was introduced into the U.S. long distance telephone market, first with MCI and later with Sprint and resellers. First radio technology and then fiber optics provided a cost-effective technology for competitive entry.

In the early 1980s, the Justice Department and Second Circuit Federal District Court in Washington, D.C., approved the Modification of Final Judgment (MFJ) that required AT&T to divest the 22 regional Bell operating companies (RBOCs) but permitted it to keep Western Electric and Bell Labs. With the new market freedoms, AT&T in 1986 also had a new chairman and corporate unifying "Single Enterprise" strategy. Bob Allen, who took over after Jim Olson's death in 1988, employed a dramatically different strategy, focused on individual business unit profitability and overall corporate shareholder value.

In 1991, AT&T acquired NCR ($7.3 billion) in a hostile takeover to increase its data networking and international presence and in 1993 acquired McCaw Cellular Communications ($11.5 billion)—renamed AT&T Wireless—to enter the rapidly growing cellular market. On September 20, 1995, Chairman Allen surprised almost everyone when he announced that AT&T shareholders would be better served by AT&T restructuring into three separate publicly traded companies: a systems and equipment company (Lucent Technologies), a computer company (NCR), and a communications services company (AT&T).

To increase competition in the telecommunications industry, Congress enacted the Telecommunications Act of 1996 that allowed RBOCs to offer long distance service and allowed long distance carriers to offer local service.

In 1997 the Board chose its first outside CEO, C. Michael Armstrong, who had experience with Hughes Electronics and IBM. Armstrong envisioned AT&T as a full-service communication provider, enabled by cable television providing access and driven by the "convergence" of video, voice, and high-speed internet data. The internet bubble provided AT&T with the financial resources to make a string of acquisitions: Teleport Communication Group ($11.3 billion), Tele-Communications ($48 billion), and MediaOne Group ($54 billion). The strategy was not without doubters; many questioned the "inflated" price AT&T paid for these companies, others questioned performance of the voice-over-cable technology. With long distance revenues dramatically dropping and little incremental revenues accruing from the new acquisitions, the market punished AT&T in October 2000. Similar to Allen, Armstrong announced that he would break AT&T into four separate firms: cable/broadband, cellular/wireless, business, and consumer/residential. Soon after, Comcast bought the cable unit for $52 billion, and Armstrong left AT&T to be its CEO.

In November 2002, when David Dorman assumed leadership of AT&T consumer and business areas, the global telecommunications industry entered an era of chaos and instability—highlighted by oversupply, fraud, a complicated regulatory environment, and nonstop pricing pressures. Once again AT&T tried another strategic transformation, i.e., to evolve from a consumer-oriented voice company to an enterprise-focused company based on global internet protocol networking. In January 2005 the remaining parts of AT&T were sold to SBC Communications for only $16 billion. SBC renamed the combined entity AT&T and hopes to create the industry's premier communications and networking company—what the original AT&T once was. So ends the proud history of arguably one of the greatest 20th-century companies.

See Also: Communication Challenges; Deregulation; Verizon Communications.

Bibliography. AT&T, "Milestones in AT&T History," www.corp.att.com/history (cited March 2009); C. Wymbs, "Telecommunications, An Instrument of Radical Change for Both the 20th and 21st Centuries," *Technological Forecasting & Social Change: North-Holland* (v.71/7, 2004).

CLIFFORD WYMBS
CUNY–BARUCH COLLEGE

Attitudes and Attitude Change

Attitudes could be regarded as the categorization of a stimulus object along an evaluative dimension based upon three general classes of information: (a) cognitive information; (b) affective/emotional information; and/or (c) information concerning past behaviors or behavioral intentions. In this sense, attitudes are evaluations. They denote a person's orientation to some object. All attitudes have an "object of thought," which may be specific and tangible or abstract and intangible (equality, globalization). By denoting the individual's orientation to the object, an attitude conveys the individual's evaluation of the object. Attitudes are expressed in the language of "like/dislike," "approach/avoid," and "good/bad." When the object of the attitude is important to that person, the evaluation of the object produces an affective, or emotional, reaction in that person. Two features are important here. The first feature is that attitudes can be activated and can function automatically, suggesting that attitudes are a part of cognitive life (since they constitute categorizations). The second feature is that attitudes are communicative and social, since they only have sense inasmuch as they convey information from one person to another.

The tendency to evaluate is not directly observable and intervenes between certain attitude objects and certain responses. It is assumed to be grounded in experience and to have many observable manifestations. Both the experiences that lead to a certain attitude and its manifestations are often divided into three components: cognition, affect, and behavior. The cognitive component refers to a person's perception of the object of the attitude, and/or what the person says he or she believes about that object. The affective component entails emotions and feelings elicited by the attitude object, and the behavioral component comprises actions directed at the attitude object as well as behavioral intentions.

Attitudes serve a number of functions. The knowledge function is similar to the common understanding of what an attitude does. Attitudes help us explain and understand the world around us. Attitudes serve a utilitarian function, by which it is meant that they help us gain rewards and avoid punishments. To be "politically correct," for example, is to hold and display attitudes for utilitarian reasons. The third function is the value-expressive one. The expression of an attitude can sometimes be no more than a public statement of what a person believes or identifies with. Finally, attitudes can serve an ego-defensive function. Such attitudes are usually deep-seated, difficult to change and hostile to the attitude object. Attitudes that serve this function project outwardly what are really internal, intrapsychic conflicts.

Work-Related Attitudes

There are two specific work-related attitudes that are crucial in organizations: job satisfaction and organizational commitment. Job satisfaction could be defined as a positive emotional state resulting from the appraisal of one's job or job experiences. It generally refers to a variety of aspects of the job that influence a person's level of satisfaction with it. These usually include attitudes toward pay, working conditions, colleagues and boss, career prospects, and the intrinsic aspects of the job itself.

One of the major determinants of job satisfaction seems to derive from the intrinsic features of the work itself. According to J. Hackman and G. Oldham's model, such features might be skill variety—the extent to which the tasks require different skills; task identity—the extent to which an individual can complete a whole piece of work; task significance—the extent to which the work is perceived as influencing the lives of others; autonomy—the extent to which the individual has freedom within the job to decide how it should be done; and feedback—the extent to which there is correct and precise information about how effectively the worker is performing. In addition, leader behavior is also important in satisfaction at work as well as perceptions of distributive justice. Finally, value theory claims that job satisfaction exists to the extent that the job outcomes an individual receives match those outcomes that are desired. The more people receive outcomes they value, the more satisfied they will be; the less they receive outcomes they value, the less satisfied they will be. Value theory focuses on any outcomes that people value, regardless of what they are.

Organizational commitment has been defined by R. T. Mowday and his colleagues as "the relative strength of an individual's identification with and involvement in an organization." This concept is often thought to have three components: (a) a desire to maintain membership in the organization; (b) belief in and acceptance of the values and goals of the organization; and (c) a willingness to exert effort on behalf of the organization. N. Allen and J. Meyer have divided organizational commitment slightly differently into: (a) affective commitment—essentially concerns the person's emotional attachment to his or her organization; (b) continuance commitment—a person's perception of the costs and risks associated with leaving his or her current organization; and (c) normative commitment—a moral dimension, based on a person's felt obligation and responsibility to his or her employing organization.

Organizations can do several things to enhance employees' commitment. People tend to be highly committed to their organizations to the extent that they have a good chance to take control over the way they do their jobs and are recognized for making important contributions. Thus, job enrichment becomes a significant tool for the enhancement of organizational commitment. In addition, aligning the interests of the company with those of the employees leads to highly committed individuals. Many companies do this directly by introducing profit-sharing plans: By letting employees share in the company's profitability, they are more likely to see their own interests as consistent with those of their company. And when these interests are aligned, commitment is high. Finally, in many ways, the easiest way to enhance commitment—also the most effective and the least expensive—is simply listening to employees. The mere act of listening to employees shows them that the organization cares about what they have to say, and they are more likely to reciprocate in terms of organizational commitment.

Attitudes and Behavior

One of the most enduring enigmas researchers have been concerned with is the relationship between attitudes and behaviors. The common-sense view of attitudes has it that attitudes directly cause a person to act in a particular way. However, the relationship between attitudes and behavior is not as simple as this, since as often as not behaviors appear to be quite unrelated to attitudes, and behaviors can cause attitudes as much as the other way around. A number of possible reasons were suggested for this lack of correspondence between attitudes and behavior. One was social pressures of various kinds: laws, societal norms, and the views of specific people can all prevent a person behaving consistently with his or her attitudes. So can other attitudes, limitations on a person's abilities, and a person's general activity levels. It was also argued that the research on this issue was badly designed, that measures of attitude were often general whereas measures of behavior were specific, reflecting only one of many elements of the attitude. Also, behavior was assessed on only one occasion or even a short time period.

A. Praktanis and Turner suggested a number of factors which could increase the correspondence between attitudes and behavior: (a) When the object of the attitude is both well-defined and salient. Salience concerns the extent to which the object of the attitude is perceived as relevant to the situation at hand. (b) When attitude strength is high—that is, when the attitude comes easily to mind. (c) When knowledge supporting the attitude is plentiful and complex. This increases a person's certainty about what he or she thinks, as well as his or her ability to act effectively toward the object of the attitude. (d) When the attitude supports important aspects of the self.

Icek Ajzen and M. Fishbein developed a model of the relationship between attitudes and behavior designed to overcome these difficulties. This model was called the theory of reasoned action. They argue that attitudes do not predict behaviors per se, but rather behavioral intentions. It is behavioral intentions that directly predict behavior. Behavioral intentions are determined by a person's attitude and his or her subjective norms. Subjective norms refer to what the individual actor believes his or her significant others believe he or she should do. The theory of reasoned action is only applicable to behaviors under volitional control.

As one of the authors of the original model, Ajzen has revised the model to become the theory of planned behavior, to accommodate the fact that behaviors are often not under the volitional control assumed by the theory of reasoned action. The theory of planned behavior retains behavioral intentions as central in the link between attitudes and behavior, and still holds that behavioral intentions are the product of attitudes toward the behavior and subjective norms. However, an important third factor is added—perceived behavioral control. This factor refers to the person's perceptions of the ease or difficulty of performing the behaviors. Perceived behavioral control affects the formation of behavioral intentions, and also directly affects the production of behavior itself, independently of behavioral intentions.

Attitude Change

Changing attitudes is an important part of many people's work in organizations. Attitudes might change by changing behavior more immediately through sanctions and incentives rather than focusing on attitude change per se. Some research indicates that attitude change may often be opposite in direction to a change in behavior. According to the theory of psychological reactance, restricting a person's freedom of choice motivates the person to evaluate the eliminated alternatives more positively. Thus, the application of sanctions against some undesired behaviors may backfire, especially if the freedom to engage in the restricted behavior is highly valued. But offering positive incentives for engaging in desired behaviors may also have opposite consequences on attitudes, especially if those who receive the incentive have already been intrinsically motivated (i.e., held a positive attitude toward the behavior). Even though the frequency or intensity of the behavior may increase while the reward is applied, attitudes toward the behavior may become less positive, a phenomenon known as the overjustification effect.

There are also conditions under which attitudes are assimilated to a prior change in behavior. The investigation of these conditions has been stimulated by the theory of cognitive dissonance developed by L. Festinger. According to the theory, a person's thoughts, attitudes, and beliefs can be consonant, dissonant, or irrelevant to each other. Holding dissonant beliefs creates cognitive dissonance, an unpleasant state of arousal which motivates the person to reduce the dissonance by adding, subtracting, or substituting cognitions. In this sense, behavior change can lead to attitude change via a process of dissonance reduction. There are three conditions that are necessary for attitude-discrepant actions to produce attitude change: (a) the person must perceive that the behavior has negative consequences; (b) the person must take personal responsibility for the behavior; and (c) the person needs to feel physiological arousal and to attribute this arousal to the attitude-discrepant behavior.

Persuasion

Attitudes might also change through persuasion. Persuasion is a method of influence using communicated information and argumentation from a given source that begins with changing beliefs and knowledge, the cognitive component of the attitude system. The suggestion is that the key to understanding why people would attend to, understand, remember, and accept a persuasive message is to understand the characteristics of the person presenting the message, the contents of the message, and the characteristics of the receiver of the message. The communicator variable affects the acceptability of persuasive messages. A high level of expertise, good physical looks, and extensive interpersonal and verbal skills make a communicator more effective.

Other source characteristics include credibility, attractiveness, likeability, and similarity. The credibility of a communicator rests partly on his or her expertness and trustworthiness. Expertness concerns how much the communicator knows about the subject of the communication. Trustworthiness usually depends mainly on whether the communicator has a record of honesty, and on whether he or she appears to be arguing against his or her own interests. Sometimes, however, a low credibility source has as much persuasive effect as a high credibility one. This has been termed the sleeper effect, and is thought to be due to the person remembering the message but forgetting the source.

The amount of attitude change is also directly related to the degree of attractiveness of the change agent. The power of attractiveness may rest on the desire of the message receiver to be like the communicator. There is also evidence that attractiveness is useful when the message is likely to be unpopular, though its power can be undone if the communicator is perceived to be deliberately exploiting his or her attractiveness. Finally, with regard to similarity, because we tend to like people who are similar to us, we are more persuaded by similar than dissimilar sources. However, it is not quite this simple. When the issue concerns a matter of taste or judgment, similar sources are better accepted than dissimilar ones. However, when the issue concerns a matter of fact, dissimilar sources do better.

Is the use of threat effective in changing attitudes? Moderate amounts of fear increase the effectiveness with which people process information, but high amounts of fear tend to immobilize them. The amount of fear depends not only on how scary the message is, but also on how optimistic a person is about his or her ability to deal with the threat described in it.

Finally, R. Petty and J. Cacioppo made a distinction between the central route to persuasion (which involves careful thought and weighing of arguments) and the peripheral route, which relies more on emotional responses but relatively little thought. Peripheral processing of information occurs when the recipient of the persuasive message is unwilling or unable to pay it very much attention. When this is the case, peripheral cues matter more than the strength of arguments, which include communicator attractiveness and expertise, sheer length of the message, and reactions of other recipients of the message.

On the other hand, persuasive messages processed through the central route need to contain strong arguments that stand up to scrutiny. People who enjoy thinking, are able to concentrate, feel involvement in the issues in question, and feel personally responsible for evaluating the message are most likely to process persuasive messages by the central route. It could be argued that attitude change through the central route is longer lasting and more closely associated with behavior than that through the peripheral route.

See Also: Commitment; Compliance; Conformance/ Conformity; Employer–Employee Relations; Motivation; Persuasion.

Bibliography. I. Ajzen and T. J. Madden, "Prediction of Goal-Directed Behavior: Attitudes, Intentions, and Perceived Behavioral Control," *Journal of Experimental Social Psychology* (1986); A. H. Eagly and S. Chaiken, *The Psychology of Attitudes* (Harcourt Brace Jovanovich, 1993); D. T. Gilbert, S. T. Fiske and G. Lindsey, eds., *The Handbook of Social Psychology* (McGraw-Hill, 1998); M. A. Hogg and J. Cooper, eds., *The SAGE Handbook of Social Psychology* (Sage, 2003); P. G. Zimbardo and M. R. Leippe, *The Psychology of Attitude Change and Social Influence* (McGraw-Hill, 1991).

Olivia Kyriakidou
Athens University of Economics
and Business

ATX Index (Vienna)

The Austrian Traded Index (ATX) is the most important market index of Austria's Wiener Börse, also known as the Vienna Stock Exchange, itself one of the most important exchanges in eastern Europe. Almost half of the stock trades in Austria are over-the-counter trades, with the remainder handled on the Wiener Börse. Trades on the Wiener Börse are conducted through the Electronic Quote and Order-driven System (EQOS), and the exchange manages the stock exchange of Budapest (sharing structure, information, and stocks). A similar relationship is being arranged with the exchanges of Bucharest (Romania) and Zagreb (Croatia).

The ATX is one of two indices tracking the Wiener Börse; the other is the Wiener Börse Index (WBI), which tracks all domestic shares traded on the exchange. The ATX tracks a mere 20 stocks:

- Andritz AG, a plant engineering group with 120 subsidiaries.
- bwin, an online gaming company formerly known as betandwin.com. Most of bwin's revenue comes from sports betting and online poker; it operates internationally with a variety of licenses from locations as diverse as Gibraltar and the First Nations reservation of Kahnawake in Canada. Like most online gambling services, it has met and largely adapted to a variety of legal challenges.
- Erste Bank, a bank operating throughout central Europe, offering investment and commercial banking services in addition to private lending.
- EVN AG, a holding company for energy and waste management firms.
- Flughafen Wien, the company that developed and operates the Vienna Airport; half of Flughafen's stock is publicly traded.
- Intercell, a biotech company that focuses on the production of vaccines.
- Mayr-Melnhof Karton, a paper and packaging manufacturer with 40 percent of its stock publicly traded.
- Österreichische Post, a postal savings bank owned by the Austrian Mail. A 1996 act of Parliament turned it into a joint-stock company.
- OMV, Austria's largest oil and gas company.

- Palfinger, a manufacturer of cranes and other heavy machinery.
- Raiffeisen International, a cooperative bank with almost 3,000 branches.
- RHI, a large diversified construction company.
- Schoeller-Bleckmann, a supplier of nonmagnetic components for the oilfield industry.
- Strabag, the fifth-largest construction company in Europe.
- Telekom Austria, a telecommunications giant.
- Verbund, Austria's largest power company, dealing mostly in hydropower.
- voestalpine, an international steel company.
- Wiener Städtische, an insurance company operating throughout central Europe.
- Wienerberger, the world's largest brick producer.
- Zumtobel, a lighting company.

See Also: Austria; Dow Jones Index; Stock Exchanges.

Bibliography. "ATX Index," finance.mapsofworld.com (cited March 2009).

Bill Kte'pi
Independent Scholar

Auditing Standards

Auditing standards are professional guidelines promulgated either by an authorized national or international body. Any standards are based on the universally or generally adopted practices, which should serve as guidelines for auditors undertaking audit. They are usually distilled through years of practice and are of such quality that a professional should in most cases apply them indiscriminately. The aim of auditing standards is to provide guidance to professional auditors in fulfilling their professional duties and responsibilities, primarily in the process of audit of historical financial statements. As a rule, auditing standards give full consideration to professional qualities, like competence and independent reporting requirements and evidence.

The International Standards of Auditing (ISA) are promulgated by the International Federation of Accountants (IFAC) through its Audit and Assurance

Standards Board (AASB). Although the intentional standards are, as a rule, not compulsory, they are considered more or less the best practice which should be upheld. National standards are developed by national bodies, and although in the past have been more associated with professional accounting organizations, in recent times the regulatory activity has been moving from a professional self-regulatory model to the model in which a publicly appointed body (representing a wide variety of stakeholders) will in fact be producing the accounting standards and taking care of their enforcement. This shift toward more government-controlled standard setting is undoubtedly the result of the falling public trust in the accounting and auditing profession following a number of high-profile scandals in the early 2000s, Enron being the most publicly covered.

The promulgation of the Sarbanes-Oxley Act in 2002 has changed the shape of the audit profession, preventing the audit companies to be in other professional relationship with their clients, if they are doing statutory audit of the firm, rotation of accountants, etc. The implementation of audit in public interest has been reemphasized and the auditors are made more aware of their assurance function. The users of financial information are primarily interested in the quality and reliability of information submitted to them by the companies, in order to make the best investment decision.

In the United States, the American Institute of Certified Public Accountants (AICPA) has developed the set of 10 generally accepted auditing standards (GAAS), which in accordance with usual national standard-setting practices focus on: (1) general standards; (2) standards of fieldwork; and (3) reporting standards. The predominant feature of GAAS is the focus on the important personal qualities that an auditor must demonstrate in professional conduct. However, with the changes in regulation, GAAS are now applied only to private companies, while those that are "public" (that is, listed on the stock exchange and whose shares are the object of trading) are required to apply the Public Company Accounting Oversight Board's (PCAOB) standards of auditing.

The general standards require auditors to have adequate technical training to perform the audit, maintain independence in mental attitude in all matters related to the audit, and demonstrate due professional care. Standards of field work define accumulation of evidence and filing all other activities. An auditor must demonstrate adequate planning and supervision, proving that he or she can understand the firm and its environment, and sufficient evidence has to be provided. Standards on reporting require the auditor to prepare a report on the financial statements taken as a whole, including any informative disclosures.

Although IFAC promulgated ISA already in 1991 with the first standard being published, the success in ensuring the adoption worldwide is somewhat less noticed than the drive by the International Accounting Standard Board (IASB) aiming at having the International Financial Reporting Standards (IFRS) endorsed by as many countries in the world as possible (at present over 80 countries have adopted or do not oppose the application of IFRS). In the case of ISA there is more convergence with the U.S. practices than it is the case with IFRS. However, there is a noticeable increase in development and application of national auditing standards, where Anglo-Saxon countries are leading. Transitional and developing economies are more prone to endorse ISA and provide the legal base, through their national legislation, for their full application.

Auditing standards provide a professional and technical framework for actions of professional auditors undertaking auditing and assurance services for their clients. Therefore, technical and professional competence are at the center of attention in auditing standards (standards of audit). As auditors (individuals and audit firms) are to discharge the duties in a professional manner, ensuring at least the minimum level of service, they are to follow the sets of professional rules. Often auditing standards cannot be observed individually, but should be regarded as one of the pillars of professional regulations targeting the accounting and auditing profession. For instance, in the United States the professional accountancy firms (CPA firms) should not only adhere to Statements of Auditing Standards (SAS), but also to fully observe compilation and review standards (Statements on Standards for Accounting and Review Services [SSARS]), other attestation standards, consulting standards, and finally the Code of Professional Conduct. All these regulations are enacted by AICPA, as a professional accountancy body in the United States.

Review and Modification

Audit standards, regardless of which body enacted them, are a living body. They are reviewed almost on a constant, rolling basis, taking into consideration new positive practices, problems in application, acts of rules avoidance, or practices that may be regarded as improper, but are not *stricto lege* against the current rules and regulations. Therefore, they are published on an almost annual basis, and periodically all the standards are reviewed and modified. IFAC's AASB even published the plan of activities on the review and modification of the existing standards, allowing the member organizations, their members, and the general public to influence the processes of modification of accounting standards. In such a manner the assurance function of international professional regulation, especially in accounting and auditing, is particularly strengthened.

It is difficult to say whether there will be further harmonization and/or convergence toward ISA, but following the example of IFRS, it is likely to happen, although probably not in the immediate future. However, this may not be an onerous process, after all, as the synergies between ISA and the U.S. regulation is currently higher than between U.S. Generally Accepted Accounting Principles (GAAPs) and IFRS.

See Also: Accounting Harmonization; International Accounting Standards Board; International Financial Reporting Standards; Nonfinancial Information Reporting.

Bibliography. American Institute of Certified Public Accountants, *Codification of Statements on Auditing Standards; Numbers 1 to 111* (2006); American Institute of Certified Public Accountants, *Codification of Statements on Auditing Standards; Numbers 1 to 114 as of January 1, 2008* (2008); International Federation of Accountants, *2008 Handbook of International Auditing, Assurance, and Ethics Pronouncements* (2008); International Federation of Accountants, *International Standards of Auditing*, redrafted (2006).

Željko Šević
Glasgow Caledonian University

Australia

The only nation to occupy a continent, Australia is a country of approximately 21.5 million people (2008 estimate) and had a gross domestic product in nominal dollars that ranked 14th in the world in 2007. Although less populous than Romania, Australia occupies an area approximately 80 percent the size of the continental United States and is one of the wealthier economies in the world. The country is endowed with substantial natural resources, especially coal and precious metals, which serve as primary exports. Agriculture, though declining in relative importance as in most developing countries, is also an important export sector. The economy is reasonably diversified and post-industrial with services being the leading sector (70.7 percent of total GDP in 2007), followed by industry (25.6 percent) and agriculture (3.7 percent).

Australia shares many similarities, and a few important differences, with Canada, a country that it is often compared to. Both are countries founded by the British and both retain ties to that country through the British Commonwealth. As a result, both have legal and political systems based on English common law and parliamentary government. Both countries have significant mineral, energy, and agricultural export sectors. Both countries have small populations within very large national boundaries that nonetheless concentrate heavily in urban areas outside a largely uninhabitable interior (in Australia, along the coasts away from the hot and dry interior broadly referred to as "the Outback"). Both are federal systems formed out of unions of previously separate British colonies.

The differences, however, are equally telling. In particular, Australia has what is frequently referred to as a "Washminster" political system that rests heavily on the model of the British Parliament but that explicitly borrows elements of the U.S. political system such as a written constitution with clearly delineated powers and an upper house of government called the Senate that has nonproportional representation.

Australia also has a persistent trade deficit and its economic fortunes are particularly, though not exclusively, tied to swings in resource prices. Whereas Canadian economic cycles tend to move much in parallel with those of its neighbor the United States, Australia's booms and busts have tended to diverge quite markedly in timing, rising and falling with resource prices. Because of this close link, the value of the Australian dollar in foreign exchange markets tends to move in a wide range and is very volatile. It is one of the 10 most traded currencies in the world mainly

Environmental issues have recently come to the forefront in Australia, which has one of the highest per capita levels of greenhouse gas emissions in the world. At the same time, its agricultural sector has been burdened by a decade-long drought.

because of its being a perceived proxy for commodities prices and also because of its role in the foreign exchange "carry trade" in which speculators move into and out of a currency to exploit differentials in domestic interest rates across different countries.

Australia is continually defining its role in the greater Asian region in which it is located. Originally setting itself apart from Asia and closely aligning itself with Great Britain and, after World War II, the United States, the country has increasingly drawn closer to its Asian neighbors, though not always smoothly. Economic links with Asian countries have vastly increased (China is now Australia's largest trading partner) and immigration into the country has become more open, in contrast to a long-standing and infamous "White Australia" immigration policy that was ultimately repealed in the 1960s. Although still predominantly European Caucasian, other ethnic groups have grown strongly in relative and absolute

number and the population is increasingly diverse. The country also established in 1989 the Asia-Pacific Economic Cooperation (APEC), a forum for 21 Pacific Rim countries to discuss the regional economy.

Australia is a generally free-market economy with a mostly two-party political system, with the major parties being loosely left-of-center and right-of-center, respectively. However on issues of economic sector reform, especially in the area of privatization and financial deregulation, there is a broad bipartisan consensus at both federal and state levels. There has also been liberalization in the area of labor relations although this is less bipartisan and was interrupted and in the process of a partial reverse with the election of the Australian Labor Party (ALP) to the federal government in 2007 after 11 years out of power.

The natural environment looms large in Australian society and economy. The country is quite dry and has been in a sustained and serious drought for at least a decade, with many thinking the change to be a permanent trend due to climate change. Such a permanent shift would pose serious challenges to both urban drinking water and to the agricultural sector, both of which are under stress as a result. Also, the resources sector is a major contributor to greenhouse gas and other emissions, with Australia having one of the highest per capita levels of emissions in the world. Thus debate about the causes and effects of climate change and policies needed to meet the issue are present throughout the world but have a special resonance (though not necessarily always a clear consensus) in Australia.

Culturally, Australia is ranked according to the cross-cultural scale developed by Geert Hofstede as highly individualistic, very close to the United States, but with a more egalitarian social structure than that country, indicating a communitarian streak.

See Also: Asia; Asia-Pacific Economic Cooperation; Company Profiles: Australia and Pacific; Hofstede's Five Dimensions of Culture; Privatization.

Bibliography. Australian Bureau of Statistics, www.abs.gov.au (cited March 2009); CIA, "Australia," *World Factbook*, www.cia.gov (cited March 2009); International Monetary Fund, *World Economic Outlook Database, April 2008* (2007); Organisation for Economic Development and Co-operation, *Economic Survey of Australia 2006* (2006); J. Singh et al., "A Comparative Study of the Contents of Corporate Codes of Ethics in Australia, Canada and Sweden," *Journal of World Business* (2005); E. Thompson, "The 'Washminster' Mutation," *Australian Journal of Political Science* (1980).

CAMERON GORDON
UNIVERSITY OF CANBERRA

Austria

This European country has a population of 8.3 million (2007), and a land area of 83,872 square kilometers. Although now a relatively small country, historically it was a dominant power in central Europe with Austria and then the Austro-Hungarian Empire being one of the major economic, political, and military forces in Europe from the Napoleonic Wars until the end of World War I in 1918.

Wine was produced in the region since early medieval times, and probably earlier. There has also been a printing industry in the country since 1482, and Austrians have been important in the central European book trade. Vienna and Salzburg were centers of music, and both cities were seen as cultural capitals of Europe. Musical instruments made in Austria were sold throughout Europe. There was also the state tobacco monopoly established in 1784 by which war victims and the disabled were able to earn income from selling tobacco products.

During the 19th century, because of its position in central Europe, the Austrian railways became important for trade just as their waterways had previously seen much international commerce. The Donau Dampfschiffahrts-Gesellschaft (Danube Steam Navigation Company), founded in 1829, flourished with an Imperial Charter, giving them a monopoly on Danube trade for 15 years, and they continued in a monopoly position up to 1880 during which time they had to carry government mail free of charge. In 1847 they were transporting some 850,000 passengers and 200,000 tons a year on their 41 vessels. The company continues to operate to this day, as does Austrian Lloyd Trieste, which used to operate from the Austro-Hungarian port of Trieste. In 1873 Vienna hosted the World's Fair and 10 years later the Austro-Hungarian Postal Savings Bank was established. It introduced the world's first postal check system.

The Austro-Hungarian Empire was broken up at the end of World War I, and most of the German-speaking region, which also included Vienna, the former imperial capital, became the Republic of Austria. The major industrial center of the Austro-Hungarian Empire had been in what became Czechoslovakia, and the Republic of Austria was initially in a perilous economic state. Indeed, it did not have enough coal for its industry and went through shortages of food. This led to the League of Nations establishing a process of helping the country in 1922 as economic reconstruction took place. There was significant hardship and unemployment before the Great Depression, and Austria was badly hit in the early 1930s, leading to Austria being annexed by Germany in March 1938. This led to economic recovery and the establishment of many new industrial complexes, but the economic infrastructure was badly damaged in World War II.

After World War II, Austria was initially divided into four zones run by the Allied forces, and these differences were to lead to major problems for the economy for many years. Its economy had been badly damaged by the war, and the black market flourished. Widespread nationalization took place in 1946 and 1947. This included iron and steel plants, smelting works, factories, and also the three largest credit institutions and the main electrical energy installations. Compensation to the previous owners was paid in 1954 and in 1959, and the economy gradually improved with foreign investment and became a stable economy.

For much of the postwar period, Austria enjoyed a Socialist economic outlook, although mention should be made of the influential Austrian-born economist Friedrich von Hayek (1899–1992). However, the country was badly affected by the oil crisis in 1973–74. Since 1965, the Organization of Petroleum Exporting Countries (OPEC) has had its headquarters in Vienna, and it was there that OPEC oil ministers were conferring in 1975 when the meeting was attacked by Carlos "The Jackal." Some of the major Austrian companies involved in the export trade are Agrana (fruit juices, sugar), AVL (automotive engineering), Plansee (metallurgy), Red Bull (beer), Silhouette (glasses), and voestalpine (steel). There has also been a burgeoning electronics industry.

Many migrant workers came to Austria in the 1960s, and by 1973 they constituted some 227,000 people, about 8.7 percent of the workforce. Many of them were from Eastern Europe, but some were from Turkey and, in recent years, migrants from China have also arrived in Austria. During the 1970s and 1980s, Austria had a good reputation for taking refugees, although during the 1990s there was some resentment toward them. Tourism has been very important to the Austrian economy, with many coming either for music-related events or for skiing. The sale of winter sports equipment is now significant in world terms.

See Also: ATX Index (Vienna); Black Market; Cross-Border Migrations.

Bibliography. Sven W. Arndt, *The Political Economy of Austria* (American Enterprise Institute, 1982); Steven Beller, *A Concise History of Austria* (Cambridge University Press, 2006); International Business Publications, *Austria Banking & Financial Market Handbook* (International Business Publications, 2007); Eugen K. Keefe, *Area Handbook for Austria* (Foreign Area Studies, American University, 1976); Anton Pelinka, *Austria: Out of the Shadow of the Past* (Westview Press, 1998); *The Europa Year Book* (Europa Publications, 2008); Rolf Steininger, Günter Bischof, and Michael Gehler, eds., *Austria in the Twentieth Century* (Transaction Publishing, 2008).

JUSTIN CORFIELD
GEELONG GRAMMAR SCHOOL, AUSTRALIA

Aviva

Aviva is a relatively new transnational corporation that started its international expansion during the last decade through a series of mergers, acquisitions, and strategic alliances such as bancassurance joint ventures. Headquartered in the United Kingdom, Aviva is the world's fifth-largest insurance group, has 57,000 employees, and serves around 45 million customers. With a corporate lineage that dates back to 1696, Aviva's main activities are long-term savings, fund management, and health and general insurance. Known as Aviva since July 2002, the corporation brought together more than 40 different brands and operates in 27 countries, including the United Kingdom (UK), France, Canada, the United States, China, India, Russia, Ireland, the Netherlands, Poland, and Romania.

Aviva is currently creating a new worldwide financial services brand that is expected to be completed by April 2010. The corporation's vision "One Aviva, twice the value" suggests the top management's strategic objective to gain recognition as a world-class financial services provider and maximize Aviva's full potential as a transnational corporation. To fulfill this objective, Aviva enters new markets through acquisition and then brings together relatively autonomous business units. Thus, Aviva targets and gets closer to more customers in these new markets using the structures of the acquired units and deploying resources more efficiently. The corporation offers innovative products, such as "Pay as You Drive" insurance that can be sold across different regions, with a clear growth strategy. This strategy is likely to make Aviva successful in an increasingly global and competitive marketplace.

Much like other transnational corporations, such as General Motors, Aviva has different growth targets and strategies for different geographic regions, and derives a significant part of its profits from new markets. Case in point, Aviva's chief executive Andrew Moss aims for minimum 10 percent annual average growth in new business sales and profits to 2010 in Europe, minimum 20 percent annual average growth in new business sales to 2010 in Asia and the Pacific, and 100 percent growth in new business sales in Aviva USA within three years of the acquisition. Meanwhile, the projected growth in the UK is less specific: "grow at least as fast as the market, subject to at least maintaining margins." Likewise, regional strategies for Europe and the Asia Pacific region emphasize the benefits of scale and capture opportunities arising from increasing wealth, whereas the strategies for the UK address legacy, transformation of business model, synergies, and capital generation. According to the three-month interim management statement issued on April 25, 2008, these regionally diversified strategies seem to be successful, in that long-term savings sales (up 2 percent worldwide), as well as life and pension sales (up 5 percent), have been resilient even in the current tough economic conditions. Among other factors, this management statement attributes the sales increases to Aviva's excellent performances in India and China, resilient performance in Europe, and attractive product design in North America, highlighting positive effects of the geographical diversity and balanced distribution.

In addition to the advantages associated with its global diversity and membership in the global business community, Aviva has drawn on collective resources and services, and increased the use of shared services to realize the benefits of scale and purchasing power. For instance, Aviva has increased efficiency of its marketing function by reducing advertising and sponsorship expenses. Corporate social responsibility efforts in areas such as employee satisfaction, sustainability, community involvement, and environmental protection have also contributed to the positive outlook of the corporation.

A pitfall of its fast international expansion is that Aviva is facing risks associated with direct foreign investment, global consistency, and the need for cultural and managerial integration. As a result of buying existing businesses in many different foreign countries and the tendency to sell similar products and run operations in the same way across these countries, Aviva may find some of these businesses to be less efficient. Aviva must maintain a balance between global consistency and local adaptation.

See Also: Aegon; Allianz SE; American International Group; Assicurazioni Generali; AXA; Company Profiles: Western Europe; Fortis; ING Group.

Bibliography. Aviva, www.aviva.com (cited March 2009); Andrew Moss, *One Aviva, Twice the Value*, www.aviva.com (cited March 2009).

Liviu Florea
Washburn University

AXA

AXA is a France-based financial holding company that specializes in financial protection, insurance, and asset management products and services. It has grown to become one of the world's leading insurance companies, occupying a leading position in France (market share: 10 percent at the end of 2007), the United States (8 percent), and the United Kingdom (7 percent).

The AXA group's origins can be traced back to the 19th century. In 1817 the fire insurance company Compagnie d'Assurances Mutuelles contre l'Incendie was created in Rouen, France. In 1881 France's first mutual life insurer, Mutuelle Vie, was founded. In 1946 these two companies were merged by Sahut d'Izarn, then general manager of Compagnie d'Assurances, to create Groupe Ancienne Mutuelle. A number of further acquisitions followed, including Anciennes Mutuelles Accidents and Ancienne Mutuelle de Calvados in 1946, Ancienne Mutuelle d'Orleans in 1950, and Mutualité Générale in 1953. Under d'Izarn's disciplined management style, Groupe Ancienne Mutuelle prospered during the 1960s and 1970s and was renamed AXA in 1985.

By 2007 AXA was generating revenues in excess of €90 billion per year and employed over 150,000 salaried employees and distribution agents in a total of 47 countries across Europe, North and South America, Africa, the Middle East, and the Asia Pacific region. The company had over 52 million clients around the world.

In 2008 the company had four operating business segments. The life & savings division accounts for roughly two-thirds of company revenues. It offers a range of life and savings products, including individual and group savings retirement products, life, and health products. Products offered by the property & casualty segment include mainly motor, household, property, and general liability insurance for both personal and commercial customers. The segment generates around a quarter of the company's total revenues. The company's remaining revenues are split between its asset management and banking activities (the latter conducted primarily in France and Belgium) and its international insurance division, which offers large national and international corporations insurance products to cover the large risks associated with property, transportation, and financial projects.

The recent growth and success of AXA has been attributed to Claude Bébéar, one of the most highly regarded business leaders in France. Bébéar joined Groupe Ancienne Mutuelle in 1958. Early in his career, he was singled out by d'Izarn as one of his potential successors. He worked in various company divisions, undertook several international assignments, and served as AXA's chief executive officer from 1985–2000. He remained chairman of the supervisory board until 2008.

Bébéar brought a North American management style to the once-genteel practice of business in France. Bébéar pushed AXA to focus not only on organic growth but to expand its operations through a combination of acquisitions and direct investments, which were funded primarily through proceeds earned from the sale of non-core businesses and assets and new share issues.

Under Bébéar's leadership, AXA listed on the New York Stock Exchange in 1996 and embarked on a strategy of acquiring and building up businesses in new markets and re-branding them under the AXA name. Notable acquisitions included Equitable Life (1992), National Mutual Holdings (1995), Compagnie UAP (1997), Guardian Royal Exchange (1999), Nip-

The France-based AXA is one of the world's leading insurance companies and has won an 8 percent share of the U.S. market.

pon Dantaï Life Insurance Company (2000), Sterling and Ipac Securities (2002), the Winterthur Group (2006), and MLC Hong Kong (2006).

Bébéar retired from the Supervisory Board in 2008, but continues to push for economic reforms in France through the Institut Montaigne, an independent think tank that he founded in 2000 to contribute to debates surrounding the major economic and political issues facing contemporary France.

In the post-Bébéar period, concerns have been raised that, despite its international expansion strategy, the group generates too high a share of its total revenues in mature markets. By concentrating its business activities in France, the United States, the United Kingdom, Germany, and Japan, AXA is potentially missing out on opportunities to expand in the emerging financial markets of, for example, China and Brazil, which financial analysts consider to have stronger growth potential. Bébéar's successor, Henri de Castries, now faces the challenge of spreading AXA's revenues more effectively over different geographical markets and providing the group with the stability to shield itself from demand fluctuations in established markets.

See Also: Aegon; Allianz SE; American International Group; Assicurazioni Generali; Aviva; Company Profiles:

Western Europe; Fortis; France; ING Group; Multinational Corporation.

Bibliography. Claube Bébéar, *Le courage de reformer* [The courage to reform] (Editions Odile Jacob, 2002); Datamonitor, *AXA* (Datamonitor, 2007); Bertrand Venard, "The French Insurance Market: Background and Trends," in *Handbook of International Insurance,* J. David Cummins and Bertrand Venard, eds. (Springer, 2007).

ANDREW BARRON
ESC RENNES BUSINESS SCHOOL

Back Translation

The verbal translation of a document or a questionnaire has two principal methods—forward translation and backward translation. While forward translation is a method to convert a document or a questionnaire from the source language to the target (foreign) language, the back translation method is used for translating the same document or the questionnaire back from the target language to the original (source) language.

The back translation method has been traditionally used in educational testing and psychological measurement, and has proven to be an important tool for scientific study, legal or ethical liability reviews, and in marketing research. Moreover, the development of new opportunities in global marketing research in the 21st century has increased the importance of the back translation method as an instrument for assuring the quality of translation between source and target languages in the emerging markets beyond the United States, Europe, and Japan.

This method is used to identify language conversion errors by translating back from the target language to the source language. In other words, the back translation process enables the producer or the owner of the document or questionnaire to see how the forward translation will be read by the target audience. The trouble spots are then identified by comparing the back translation to the original document or questionnaire. A few examples of such trouble spots are the parts in a document where the meanings may have been altered or parts that are not fully comprehensive. These defects are then corrected according to the objective of the project and to the satisfaction of the producer or the owner. There are numerous procedures, judgmental or statistical, to evaluate the equivalence and the quality of translation.

In a verbal translation process, a single translator or a group of translators prepares one or several versions of forward translations of the document or the questionnaire from the source language (S) to the target language. These bilingual translators are native speakers of the target language. These translations in the target language are then translated back to the source language (S') by another translator or group of bilingual translators who are native speakers of the source language. The final translated version (S') and the original document (S) are then compared to detect errors and to evaluate the quality of the translation.

The quality and the accuracy of the back translation depend on the competency of the translator(s). A committee approach using a group of translators, instead of a single translator, is preferred to reduce translation errors in back translation. This is organized either by a parallel or a split translation. In a parallel translation several translators make independent translations of the same document/questionnaire. A final version is then decided after reviewing those translations in a meeting. For example, a project coordinator evaluates two questionnaires, back translated from Hindi to English, and finds some differences in some of the questions. In one of the questions, the first translator used the meaning of the word *Aankho* as "eyes," whereas the second translator used "vision" instead. The project coordinator contacted both translators to resolve the discrepancies before running a pilot test of the final questionnaire. This approach is time consuming and costly, yet more accurate.

The split approach, on the other hand, saves time and requires less effort. In this case, the document/questionnaire is divided among two or more translators in an alternate fashion. Each translator then meets with a reviewer to agree on a joint version. To ensure consistency, the committee, including the translators, reviewers, and an adjudicator, reviews the whole document/questionnaire and decides on the final translation.

The bilingual translators are susceptible to developing a particular language structure and usage, and therefore may translate commonly used idioms incorrectly. There is also the possibility of using words that are difficult for respondents to understand. Often the intended meaning may not be captured properly by using standard rules for translating the nonequivalent terms, for example, *amigo* as *friend*. However, with a thorough knowledge in both languages, the bilingual translators are capable of making sense of a poor translation and thus provide a back translation with acceptable quality.

There is always a possibility of dominance of the source language since back translation starts with the assumptions of the structures and the terms of the source language. A "decentering" approach is used to reduce the dominance of the source language by modifying both source and target document or questionnaire through successive iterations and translations, until both terminologies are equally well understood and equivalent in each language context. This process results in the best translations; however, it is time consuming and tedious. Many international projects have difficulty in decentering due to the lack of resources.

This process becomes almost impossible in the case of translations involving three or more languages.

Verbal translation, including back translation, is an art rather than a science. A word in one language literally may have no equivalent in another language, or could have a completely different "meaning" or effect in the translated language. A skilled translator is capable of conveying the true meaning, instead of verbatim interpretation. An idiomatic phrase can be forward translated and back translated using standard rules without conveying proper meaning. For example, the phrase *Das Leben in vollen Zügen geniessen* in German may be forward translated as "enjoy life in full train" in English and literally back translated. However, the translation methods have failed to convey the proper meaning "live life to the fullest." Another example of how the meaning of a phrase can be changed during the verbal translation process is as follows: In preparation of a questionnaire for Brazil, a part of the questionnaire was forward translated from French *un repas d'affaires* (a business meal) to Portuguese as *jantar de negocios*. When back translated, it became a "*diner d'affaires*" (business dinner).

Back translation is likely to fail to identify formal textual problems, such as those affecting target language syntax, morphology, spelling, orthography, punctuation, parallelism, or consistency. It is also a time-consuming and expensive method. However, if used properly, back translation is an efficient and valuable tool to confirm the integrity of any project involving two or more languages by revealing the accuracy of the translation.

See Also: Consumer Behavior; Consumer Surveys; Cross-Cultural Research; Cultural Norms and Scripts; Ethnocentrism; Focus Groups; Home Country; Host Country; Market Research; Multicultural Work Groups and Teams.

Bibliography. Richard W. Brislin, "Back-Translation for Cross-Cultural Research," *Journal of Cross-Cultural Psychology* (v.1/3, 1970); Donald T. Campbell and Oswald Werner, "Translating, Working through Interpreters and the Problem of Decentering," *A Handbook of Methods in Cultural Anthropology* (Natural History Press, 1970); C. Samuel Craig and Susan P. Douglas, *International Marketing Research* (John Wiley & Sons, 2005); C. Samuel Craig and Susan P. Douglas, "Collaborative and Iterative Translation: An Alternative Approach to Back Translation," *Jour-*

nal of International Marketing (v.15/1, March 2007); Ronald K. Hambleton, "Translating Achievement Tests for Use on Cross-national Studies," *European Journal of Psychological Assessment* (v.9, 1993); J. Harkness, "Questionnaire Translation," in J. Harkness, F. J. R. Van de Vijver and P. Mohler, *Cross-cultural Survey Methods* (John Wiley & Sons, 2003); Charles S. Mayer, "Multinational Marketing Research: The Magnifying Glass of Methodological Problems," *European Research* (1978).

MOUSUMI ROY
PENNSYLVANIA STATE UNIVERSITY

Bahrain

Bahrain is a small Arab state (665 sq. km; estimated population 508,573 in 2007) situated in the Persian Gulf. It is an archipelago consisting of two main islands, Bahrain and Al Muharraq, and more than 30 smaller islands. The country's economy depends on processing crude oil, manufacturing, financial and commercial services, and tourism. Manama, its main port, commercial center, and capital, is located on the northeastern end of Bahrain Island.

About 90 percent of Bahrain's population live in urban areas, mainly in Manama and Al Muharraq. Islam is the religion of almost all Bahrainis and the majority of nonnatives. About 70 percent of native Bahrainis belong to the Shia sect of Islam, while the remaining population, including the ruling al-Khalifa clan, belong to the Sunni sect. Christians and other religious minorities represent about 19 percent of the total population. Languages spoken include Arabic (the official language), English, Farsi, and Urdu.

In 2002 the Emir of Bahrain, Sheikh Hamad bin Isa al-Khalifa, declared himself king and approved plans for a constitutional monarchy. The executive branch consists of the king and an appointed prime minister and cabinet. The National Assembly consists of an appointed 40-member Consultative Council and an elected 40-member Chamber of Deputies. In the 2006 elections, the Shia-dominated opposition secured 18 seats while Sunnis secured 22 seats.

Bahrain's gross domestic product (GDP) is $16.9 billion (official exchange rate) or $34,700 per capita (estimated 2007). Services account for 56 percent of the GDP, industry for 43 percent, and agriculture for less than 0.5 percent. Since the discovery of petroleum in the 1930s, oil production and refining has been a mainstay of the country's economy. However, depletion of oil reserves prompted governmental actions to develop other industries. In the 1970s the government started establishing aluminum smelting as an important industry. In a further effort at diversification, the government has also promoted industries such as ship repair and tourism. Bahrain is a worldwide center of Islamic banking. The country is also home to offshore banking units of large multinational banking companies because of its generous financial regulations and tax rules.

The government controls the oil and gas industry, heavy manufacturing, transportation, and certain other sectors. However, light manufacturing, banking, and commerce are managed by private firms, including multinational corporations. In 2006 Bahrain implemented a free trade agreement with the United States, the first of its kind in the Gulf region. Bahrain was described as the freest economy in the Middle East according to the 2006 Index of Economic Freedom published by the Heritage Foundation/Wall Street Journal.

Because the country's refining capacity is much larger than the domestic production of petroleum, Bahrain imports about 225,000 bbl/d of crude oil from Saudi Arabia for refining and further processing. Other imports include machinery, transportation equipment, food, and chemicals. Exports include petroleum and its products, aluminum, and manufactured goods. Petroleum refining and production account for more than 60 percent of Bahrain's exports, representing about 11 percent of GDP (exclusive of allied industries). Bahrain's major trading partners are Saudi Arabia, India, Japan, the United States, and the United Kingdom.

Of the country's labor force of 363,000 (estimated 2007), 79 percent work in industry, 20 percent in services, and 1 percent in agriculture. The unemployment rate is quite high (about 15 percent), at times contributing to discontent among Shias who are historically less advantaged and more prone to unemployment than Sunnis.

See Also: Free Trade Zone; Globalization; Middle East; Saudi Arabia.

Bibliography. M. Almossawi, "Starting and Sustaining Small Enterprises in the Kingdom of Bahrain: Investors' Needs, Available Incentives, and Obstacles," *World Review of Entrepreneurship, Management and Sustainable Development* (2005); A. Alyousha, "Investigating Bahrain Business Cycles," *Applied Economics* (1997); F. Lawson, *Bahrain: The Modernization of Autocracy* (Westview Press, 1989).

Jawad Syed
University of Kent

Balance of Goods and Services

The balance of goods and services, also known as the trade balance, is part of the Current Account (CA) balance in a nation's Balance of Payments (BoP) statistics. This net measure of a country's position with respect to trade in goods and services is a widely cited statistic in the context of the current U.S. trade deficit and implications for its sustainability in future years.

A country's balance of trade in goods records the difference between exports and imports of merchandise and is therefore also referred to as the merchandise balance. As a category, merchandise (or goods) includes physical items such as cars, steel, food, furniture, clothes, appliances, etc. Merchandise exports record the transfer of ownership, between a country's residents and nonresidents, of all tangible goods (including nonmonetary gold). However, some goods are excluded in this category, such as merchandise purchased by a country's residents abroad and purchases of goods by diplomatic and military personnel. The latter are separately classified under travel transactions in the balance of services.

The standard practice in determining the value of merchandise exports is to include the value of the goods themselves, and the value of outside packaging, and related distributive services used up to and including loading the goods onto the carrier at the customs frontier of the exporting country. This is commonly known as the free on board (f.o.b.) value. The value of all exported goods appears as a credit in a country's CA since payments from foreigners are received in exchange for the exported merchandise. Similarly, imports of merchandise appear as a debit

in the CA since they reflect exchanges of movable goods between residents and nonresidents (also valued f.o.b. at the customs frontier of the country that is exporting them). Thus, the merchandise balance is a net measure of merchandise trade which can be either positive (a surplus of exports receipts over import expenditures) or negative (a deficit showing import expenditures exceeding receipts from exports).

Similarly, the difference between exports and imports of services is known as the balance on services. Trade in services includes exports and imports of transportation services (such as shipment and passenger services), insurance services, travel services (such as hotel and restaurant services), legal services, consulting, etc. Other transactions in the services category include items not separately classified as merchandise, or non-factor services, or transfers. Examples include transactions with nonresidents by government agencies and their personnel abroad and transactions by private residents with foreign governments and government personnel stationed in the reporting country. The balance on trade in services is therefore also a net measure which can be either positive (a surplus of services exports over imports) or negative (a deficit indicating that services imports outweigh exports).

Taken together, the balance on merchandise (goods) and services trade comprise the balance of trade which is itself a net trade measure of a country's trade position. A trade deficit implies that a nation is importing more goods and services than it is exporting. A surplus would indicate that exports of goods and services outweigh imports.

Historically, the United States has experienced both trade surpluses and trade deficits. A long (and almost unbroken) string of trade surpluses prior to, and following, World War II coincided with strong support by the United States for the elimination of barriers to trade and investment. Starting in the 1970s, however, trade deficits not only became the norm but grew quite large in the 1980s and 1990s. Since trade deficits are by definition an excess of imports over exports, such imbalances are often seen as an international trade problem that may be alleviated through trade policy initiatives. For example, opponents to freer trade may point to a burgeoning trade deficit as evidence of declining competitiveness and consequently argue in favor of trade restrictions and protectionist measures. At the same time, economic theory shows that imbalances between savings and investment (both domestic, and in relation to the rest of the world) are the more likely long-term cause of trade deficits and trade policy initiatives are unlikely to eliminate the latter.

Statistics from the Bureau of Economic Analysis show record trade deficits in the United States since 2000. The deficit on goods and services stood at an unprecedented $758.5 billion in 2006 and decreased modestly to $708.5 billion in 2007. By comparison, the trade deficit in 1995 was $96.3 billion. This escalation of the U.S. trade deficit over the past decade has intensified the public debate surrounding sustainability of trade imbalances. Arguably, trade deficits of the late 1990s were relatively benign, since they were viewed as a means to finance higher U.S. investment rates. On the other hand, recent trade deficits are generating new concerns. Unlike their 1990s counterparts, they are seen as representative of high consumption and large government deficits (corresponding to increases in U.S. government budget deficits).

The relationship between government budget deficit and trade deficits (also known as the twin deficits), can be established through a National Income accounting identity, which states that the difference between the two is equal to the difference between private saving and investment. From a policy perspective, therefore, a sizable reduction in the U.S. budget deficit is a credible policy recommendation in view of current trends. In addition, policy initiatives need to promote expansion of market demand in major economies outside the United States, and a gradual and substantial realignment of the U.S. dollar with the currencies of other major trading partners. Global adjustment to U.S. trade imbalances could, alternatively, occur through financial markets. However, the latter may have grave implications for the value of the dollar, and consequently, the health of the world economy and the global trading system.

See Also: Capital Account Balance; Current Account; Invisible Trade Balance; Trade Balance.

Bibliography. P. R. Krugman and M. Obstfeld, *International Economics: Theory and Policy* (Pearson/Addison-Wesley, 2006); M. Obstfeld and K. S. Rogoff, *Foundations of International Macroeconomics* (MIT Press, 1996); U.S. Bureau of Economic Analysis, www.bea.gov (cited March 2009).

Rossitza B. Wooster
Portland State University

Banana Wars

The banana wars were an eight-year trade dispute between the European Union (EU) and the United States that started in 1993. It escalated to include sanctions on the import of a range of other products. By 2008 it still had not been fully resolved.

The European Economic Community (EEC) introduced the European Union Common Market Organisation for bananas in 1992, and the European banana import regime was put in place in 1993. At this time barriers against bananas imported from Latin America were established. The EEC did this to give former banana-producing colonies from Africa, the Caribbean, and the Pacific (ACP) preferential access to European markets by imposing a quota and 25 percent tariff on bananas from Latin and Central America. This was clearly to the detriment of those producers. The objective of the regime was to help smaller farmers from the former colonies compete with large plantations run by U.S. multinationals in Central and Latin America.

In February 1996 the U.S. government along with Ecuador, Guatemala, Honduras, and Mexico filed

The WTO approved U.S. sanctions of up to $191.4 million a year to try to reopen access to outlets like this German fruit market.

a legal complaint to the World Trade Organization (WTO) against the European Union's banana import regime, claiming that it unfairly restricted the entry of their bananas to the EU and favored the former colonies. The action of the U.S. government was partly in response to pressure from one of the big three U.S. banana companies, Cincinnati-based Chiquita Brands International, and its chairman Carl Lindner. (During the period of the banana wars, Chiquita reported that its share of the European market had fallen from 40 percent to 20 percent with estimated revenue losses of $1.5 billion. It said it had been pushed to the brink of bankruptcy.)

In September 1997 the WTO ruled that the EU's banana import regime was inconsistent with WTO rules. Following further consideration in January 1999, the EU introduced a new banana import regime. However, in April 1999 the WTO again ruled that this new regime was still incompatible with the EU's WTO obligations. It was at this stage that the WTO granted the United States authorization to impose sanctions up to US$191.4 million per year on EU products entering the U.S. market. This case is one of only seven out of 315 that have reached the stage where the WTO has authorized retaliatory penalties.

The banana wars then spread beyond the banana market. The U.S. government put in place sanctions on a number of European goods, including cashmere, cheese, French fashions, and Danish ham. In return, the Europeans countered by banning the import of hormone-treated beef from the United States. The situation was intensified still further when in May 2000, the WTO granted Ecuador authorization to impose sanctions up to US$201.6 million per year on EU exports to Ecuador. The so-called carousel legislation, introduced into a 2000 trade bill, also required the United States to implement rotating sanctions against Europe until it lifted its restrictions on imports of bananas and hormone-treated beef.

The carousel sanctions were never enacted. The dispute had dragged on for eight years when in April 2001 the EU, United States, and Ecuador accepted a solution whereby Ecuador and the United States agreed to suspend their sanctions and in return the EU agreed to change its banana import regime from the existing tariff-rate quota system to a tariff-only system by January 1, 2006.

The EU Trade Commissioner, Pascal Lamy, announced that the policy would be changed and assured equal access to the European banana market. The new agreement came into effect in July 2001. Under the agreement Chiquita was allowed immediate access to EU markets. It has been suggested by Dole Food Co., a major competitor, that the preferential treatment accorded to Chiquita may have been a result of the substantial campaign contributions given by the company to Democrats and Republicans during the 2000 election cycle.

Subsequently, at the November 2001 Ministerial Conference in Doha, two Ministerial Decisions were adopted that formalized the agreement. These were for a transitional EU import regime for bananas and for the introduction no later than January 1, 2006, of a tariff-only regime that would result in at least maintaining total market access for MFN (most-favored-nation) banana suppliers. The Ministerial Decision also spelled out the procedures and timetable for possible arbitration in the event the EU was unable to reach an agreement with the banana-supplying countries on the new tariff-only system.

In January 2005 the EU proposed a new tariff of €230 per ton. This was not agreed to by the Latin American countries. A WTO arbitration panel ruled that the tariff would not maintain access for these countries. The tariff was revised to €176 per ton and a 775,000-ton tariff quota on imports of bananas of ACP origin, but the parties could still not agree, so a second arbitration was requested. The arbitrator concluded that the EU had failed to rectify the matter. On January 1, 2006, the EU unilaterally introduced its own regime.

On March 21, 2007, Colombia requested further consultations, stating that the application of the banana import regime still entailed discrimination between ACP bananas and MFN bananas. Subsequently, the Disputes Settlement Body (DSB) has ruled that the EU has maintained measures inconsistent with different provisions of the GATT 1994. The panel recommended that the DSB request the European Communities to bring the inconsistent measures into conformity with its obligations under the GATT 1994.

See Also: Fair Trade; Most Favored Nation Status; Nontariff Barrier; Trade Sanctions; Trade War; World Trade Organization.

Bibliography. P. Borrell, "No One Can Afford a New Banana Drama," *Financial Times* (April 20, 2004); A. Bounos, "Banana Wars," *Latin Trade* (v.9/6, 2001); G. Meyers, *Banana Wars: The Price of Free Trade. A Caribbean Perspective* (Zed Books, 2004); WTO, "Dispute Settlement: Dispute DS361 European Communities—Regime for the Importation of Bananas, 2008," www.wto.org (cited March 2009); WTO, "Hong Kong WTO Ministerial 2005: Briefing Notes. Bananas: Discussions Continue on a Long-standing Issue, 2005," www.wto.org (cited March 2009); WTO, "WT/DS27/RW/USA, 2008," www.wto.org (cited March 2009).

JAMIE WEATHERSTON
NORTHUMBRIA UNIVERSITY

Banco Bilbao Vizcaya Argentaria

An international financial institution, headquartered in Spain and with operations in over 30 countries in Europe, Asia, North and Latin America, Banco Bilbao Vizcaya Argentaria (BBVA) offers personal banking, loans and mortgages, insurance, investment banking, asset management, and wholesale banking.

The bank was born from the merger of Banco Bilbao and Banco Vizcaya in 1988, which formed BBV, and the later merger of BBV with Argentaria in 1999. Banco Bilbao had started its international operations in the early 1900s, opening offices in Paris and London. During the 1960s and 1970s, the bank started its expansion in Latin America with the acquisition of banks in Panama and Puerto Rico. However, it was only after the merger with Banco Vizcaya that the institution began a large-scale expansion in Latin America through gradual acquisitions and partnerships with local banks. Through the 1990s, BBV established banking subsidiaries and pension funds in Argentina, Bolivia, Brazil, Chile, Colombia, Ecuador, Paraguay, Peru, Uruguay, and Venezuela.

BBV strategy coincided with the growth of other Spanish companies in Latin America, such as Banco Santander, Endesa, and Telefónica, a phenomenon dubbed by some journalists as La Reconquista. This expansion is a result of market deregulation both in Europe and Latin America, cultural factors stemming from the two continents' former colonial relationships, and acquisition opportunities created by differences between the performances of banks in the two regions.

In 1999, when BBV merged with Argentaria, the companies unified the Spanish retail banks BBV, Argentaria, Banca Catalana, Banco del Comercio, and Banco de Alicante under the BBVA brand. However, some of the former BBV branches outside Spain have maintained their original names. Because of its strong international presence, BBVA has structured its operations around business areas that mainly reflect the bank's geographic reach: business in Spain and Portugal, Mexico, South America, and the United States. Other business areas—global business, finance, risk, and innovation and development—support all markets and global customers' activities. In addition to the business areas, BBVA comprises two other divisions: support and the chairman's office.

To hedge against the volatility of the Latin American market, BBVA's strategy has turned to the United States, Europe, and Asia. In the United States, the bank focuses on immigrant—particularly Latino—customers, and it is currently structured around five businesses: BBVA Bancomer USA specializes in first-generation immigrants in California; Bancomer Transfer Services (BTS) offers money transfers to Mexico and other Latin American countries, China, India, and the Philippines; and BBVA Finanzia USA provides consumer financial services and credit cards. BBVA's other businesses in the United States include banking business in Texas—a state with a large Hispanic population—and Puerto Rico. In Asia, BBVA has partnered with Hong Kong–based CITIC to take a 5 percent stake in CITIC-China. BBVA also has branches in Japan and Singapore, and representatives in India, South Korea, and Taiwan.

The expansion of Spanish banks like BBVA has been the result of their strong investment in information technology (IT), and the early deregulation of the banking industry in Spain. BBVA's expenditure in IT has allowed the bank to create detailed profiles of its customers and thus more accurately target clients for new products. BBVA expects to use this platform to become a "distribution-service company," offering products in insurance, education, healthcare, and retirement. Moreover, this IT investment and the depth of its management experience after many years of strong competition in the Spanish market allows BBVA to improve the performance of the institutions it acquires at home and abroad. Information technology allows BBVA to coordinate the activities of subsidiaries in many countries in real time.

Lately, BBVA has benefited from national regulations that limited the exposure of Spanish banks to mortgage-backed securities. The Bank of Spain, which regulates all Spanish banks, created a series of requirements concerning leverage and capital reserves that are more stringent than the provisions of the Basel I Accord. Despite its good position in the global financial crisis, BBVA still faces challenging times in Spain as a result of the cooling of the local housing market. However, its international diversification should continue to provide a hedge against falls in any particular market.

See Also: Banco Santander Central Hispano Group; Basel Committee on Banking Supervision; Latin America; Spain.

Bibliography. "Conquistadors on the Beach," *The Economist* (2007); E. Sánchez-Peinado, "The Internationalisation Process of Spanish Banks: Strategic Orientation after the Mergers," *European Business Review* (2003); M. Sebastián and C. Hernansanz, "The Spanish Banks' Strategy in Latin America," *Société Universitaire Européenne de Recherches Financières* (2000).

SUSANA VELEZ-CASTRILLON
UNIVERSITY OF HOUSTON

Banco Santander Central Hispano Group

Banco Santander Central Hispano (BSCH) is a Spanish banking group offering retail and wholesale banking, asset management and insurance service in Europe and Latin America. It is headquartered at the Ciudad Financeria Santander (Santander Financial City) in Madrid and employs around 130,000 people worldwide.

The history of BSCH began in 1857 when Banco Santander was established by royal decree to support trade links between the northern Spanish port of Santander and Latin America. During its early years, Banco Santander grew steadily, building up a network of regional branches around the city of Santander. In the early 1930s, Emilio Botín Sanz de Sautuola y López was appointed managing director and embarked on an expansion program throughout Spain. During the 1940s and 1950s, the bank opened its first international offices in Cuba, Argentina, Mexico, and Venezuela. By the 1960s, Banco Santander had become the seventh-largest Spanish bank. Expansion continued through to the 1980s, with Santander acquiring new businesses in Chile, Puerto Rico, and Uruguay. The CC-Bank was acquired in Germany in 1987, and an alliance was formed with the Royal Bank of Scotland. During the 1990s, Banco Santander developed its business in Brazil, Colombia, and Peru.

In 1999, Banco Santander merged with Central Hispano, a major Spanish banking group created following the fusion in 1991 of Banco Hispanoamericano (created in 1900) and Banco Central (created in 1919), to create Banco Santander Central Hispano. On Santander's 150th anniversary in 2007, BSCH was the largest banking group in the Eurozone and the eighth largest bank in the world in terms of market capitalization. In 2007, it generated revenues of €27.095 million, an increase of 20 percent compared to 2006. The same year, the group's operating profit was €9.060 million, an increase of 19 percent over 2006. With nearly 11,000 branches, the bank also operated the largest retail network in the Western world.

BSCH's recent growth has been achieved through a combination of factors, including a continued program of international expansion. In 2000, it acquired Banespa in Brazil, Grupo Serfín in Mexico, and Banco Santiago in Chile. A further landmark was reached in 2004 when it bought Abbey, Britain's sixth largest retail bank. A year later, BSCH acquired a 19.8 percent stake in Sovereign Bancorp, the 18th largest bank in the United States. Together with the Royal Bank of Scotland and Fortis, BSCH launched a successful takeover of ABN AMRO in 2007. As a result, BSCH obtained Banca Antonveneta, acquiring a long-desired presence in Italy, and Brazil's Banco Real, giving it a leading position in the fast-growing Brazilian market.

Recent growth can also be attributed to its exploration of business opportunities beyond its core retail banking operations. In 2002, for example, the bank created Santander Consumer Finance, a pan-European franchise for financing new and used car sales. Following a strategy of acquisitions, this division now operates in 19 countries around the world and generates nearly 10 percent of BSCH's total profits. Santander Consumer Finance now acts as platform to offer other forms of consumer finance, including credit cards and personal loans.

Moving forward, the bank faces a number of strategic challenges. Financial analysts point to its lack of presence in key emerging markets. Having focused its recent international expansion on the Eurozone and South America, it has not yet expanded its operations in the fast-growing markets of Asia where competitors such as Citigroup and HSBC are already exploring the opportunities presented by high growth in the retail banking sector. In addition, the Santander brand was until recently relatively unknown outside of Spain and Latin America. The bank hopes that a five-year sponsorship agreement signed with the McLaren Mercedes Formula One team in 2006 will raise the international recognition of Santander's brand.

See Also: ABN AMRO; Acquisitions, Takeovers, and Mergers; Branding; Spain.

Bibliography. Luisa Alemany, "Venture Capital in Spain: Evolution, Characterisation and Economic Impact Analysis," *International Journal of Entrepreneurship and Innovation Management* (v.6/4–5, 2006); Kevin Dobbs, "With Sovereign Deal, Santander Plans Light Touch," *American Banker* (v.173/199, 2008); Marcela Espinosa-Pike, "Business Ethics and Accounting Information: An Analysis of the Spanish Code of Best Practice," *Journal of Business Ethics* (v.22/3, 1999); Mauro Guillen and Adrian Tschoegl, *Building a Global Bank: The Transformation of Banco Santander* (Princeton University Press, 2008); Ronald A. Ratti, Sunglyong Lee and Youn Seol, "Bank Concentration and Financial Constraints on Firm-Level Investment in Europe," *Journal of Banking & Finance* (v.32/12, 2008).

ANDREW BARRON
ESC RENNES SCHOOL OF BUSINESS

Bangladesh

Bangladesh (population 150,448,000 in 2007, gross domestic product $208 billion in 2007) is one of the most densely populated countries in the world. A south Asian country, it is almost entirely surrounded by India except for the small Burmese border and the Bay of Bengal to the south.

Bangladesh and the Indian state of West Bengal were once united as the kingdom of Bengal, which became an Indian province under British control in the 19th century. Bengal was instrumental in the Indian independence movement, and when India finally gained that independence, the province of Bengal was divided between Hindu West Bengal and Muslim East Bengal, the latter under the control of Pakistan. Bengal-Pakistan tensions were high from the beginning, and when the Pakistani government failed to respond to the damage caused by the Bhola cyclone that devastated the Bay of Bengal in 1970, outrage helped to motivate the Bangladesh Liberation War, which eventually won the support of India and overlapped with the 1971 Indo-Pakistani War. Independence from Pakistan was successfully declared on March 26, 1971.

Islam is the state religion of Bangladesh, though there is a sizable Hindu minority. A parliamentary democracy, Bangladesh holds direct elections for its 345 members of the Jatia Sangsad. Forty-five seats are always held by women. The president, the head of state, is elected by the members of parliament and appoints the prime minister, the head of government, who is always a member of parliament and who forms the cabinet and is responsible for the day to day business of governance. The president's powers are largely confined to the caretaker government that presides during election periods, but he or she also appoints the justices of the Supreme Court. Bangladesh's legal heritage is a mixture of British common law and local religious traditions, and thus laws vary some from municipality to municipality, in keeping with local customs.

Bangladesh's population density compounds its problems with poverty. Per capita income is $1,400—around 14 percent of the worldwide average. About 65 percent of the labor force works in agriculture, which accounts for only a fifth of the GDP; most agricultural workers are poor, rural, subsistence farmers, producing only enough for themselves and their families to live on. Like other south Asian agricultural economies, Bangladesh's is dependent on the monsoon cycle of floods and droughts, which is erratic and costly—but which does result in especially fertile

A student learning textile production in Bangladesh, where garment exports may reach $15 billion by 2011.

soil. In the years since independence, Bangladesh has made great strides in rice and wheat production, and despite population growth, less of the population is at risk of starvation than it had been.

Industry and infrastructure are limited. There are perennial problems with power and water distribution and telecommunications, and Bangladesh has not been able to take advantage of the adoption of overseas call centers to the extent that India and other Asian countries have. Manufacturing is thus dominated by the textile industry, most of the employees of which are female; this region was known for its silk even centuries ago, and ready-made garments are now the number-one export. The American and European caps on imports of Chinese textiles have helped Bangladesh as well, as have the country's efforts to stamp out child labor in textile factories (thus avoiding foreign boycotts).

Since 1989, Bangladesh has actively sought foreign investment, and the Board of Investment in theory exists to streamline the process of starting up foreign-owned businesses and other investments. In practice, investment has been slow to come. The country has been the recipient of $30 billion in grants since independence, from the West, from Japan and Saudi Arabia, and from various international development programs. Improvements are slow, but steady, even in a climate of global recession.

See Also: Asia, Asian Development Bank, India.

Bibliography. Craig Baxter, *Bangladesh: From a Nation to a State* (Westview, 1998); Richard Sisson and Leo Rose, *War and Secession: Pakistan, India, and the Creation of Bangladesh* (University of California Press, 1991).

BILL KTE'PI
INDEPENDENT SCHOLAR

Bank for International Settlements

The Bank for International Settlements (BIS) is an organization that provides services for many central banks, nations, and other official monetary institutions around the world. However, the bank does not provide financial services to corporations or individuals.

The Bank for International Settlements is responsible for promoting monetary and financial stability in the world, and it meets on a bimonthly basis to discuss monetary and financial matters. The organization is composed of four major committees: the Basel Committee on Banking Supervision, the Committee on the Global Financial System, the Committee on Payment and Settlement Systems, and the Markets Committee. In addition, there are several independent organizations involved in international cooperation in the area of financial stability, and these organizations have their secretariats at the Bank of International Settlements. These organizations are the Financial Stability Forum, the International Association of Insurance Supervisors, and the International Association of Deposit Insurers.

The Basel Committee on Banking Supervision provides an avenue for the banking industry to discuss banking supervisory matters. The overall objective of this entity is to increase knowledge and understanding of key supervisory issues and improve the quality of banking supervision worldwide. In January 1999 the Basel Committee proposed a new concept, which became known as Basel II, and a final version was distributed in June 2004. Basel II has three main principles, which are minimum capital requirements, supervisory review, and market discipline.

The Basel Committee has made two major contributions since its beginning. The first contribution occurred in 1975 when the committee took a lead role in making sure that countries share responsibilities when making international banking transactions. The Basel Concordat was an agreement that established the foundation for this process. The first stipulation was that the parent and host authorities shared responsibility for the supervision of the foreign banking establishments. The second stipulation stated that the host authorities had primary responsibility for supervision of liquidity. The third stipulation suggested that the solvency of foreign branches and subsidiaries was the primary responsibility of the home authority of the parent and the host authority. The second major contribution was a standard that would assist in (1) adequately measuring a bank's capital and (2) establishing minimum capital standards.

Although Basel II became effective in December 2006, it was not as widely embraced as the first Basel. The purpose of Basel II was to achieve the European regulators' goals of addressing shortcomings in the original accord's treatment of credit risk, incorporating operational risk, and harmonizing capital requirements for banks and securities firms. Although the banks in Europe have applied Basel II, regulators in the United States still have not embraced it. Although they share the same goal of addressing shortcomings in the original accord's treatment of credit risk, there is a belief that the existing bank supervision in the United States already addresses operational risk.

In addition, harmonization has never been a priority for U.S. regulators. Their perception is that Basel II is more relevant for international banking activities. Therefore, only 10 of the largest banks in the United States have applied Basel II, and an additional 10 banks have the option to join in. However, the other banks in the United States will remain subject to the current U.S. regulations, especially those rules that were adopted under the original Basel. The future of further implementation of Basel II remains unclear at this time. The Committee reorganized in October 2006, and is being operated by four main subcommittees. These subcommittees are the Accord Implementation Group, the Policy Development Group, the Accounting Task Force, and the International Liaison Group.

The Committee on the Global Financial System is responsible for monitoring developments in global financial markets for the central bank Governors of the G10 countries. The Committee on Payment and Settlement Systems serves as a forum for central banks to monitor and analyze developments in domestic payment, settlement, and clearing systems as well as in cross-border and multicurrency settlement schemes.

The Markets Committee was established in 1962 following the initiation of the Gold Pool. When the Gold Pool arrangements collapsed in 1968, members continued to meet at the BIS in order to exchange views. However, the focus has shifted toward coverage of recent developments in foreign exchange and related financial markets, an exchange of views on possible future trends, and consideration of the short term implications of particular current events for the functioning of these markets.

See Also: Basel Committee on Banking Supervision.

Bibliography. James C. Baker, *The Bank of International Settlements, Evolution and Evaluation* (Quorum Books, 2002); Permanent Court of Arbitration, *Bank of International Settlements Arbitration Awards of 2002 and 2003* (Asser Press, 2007); Gianni Toniolo and Piet Clement, *Central Bank Cooperation at the Bank of International Settlement, 1930–1973* (Cambridge University Press, 2007).

MARIE GOULD
PEIRCE COLLEGE

Bank of America Corp.

Bank of America Corp. is a bank holding company headquartered in Charlotte, North Carolina. As of

December 2007, it had $1,716 billion in assets, and 210,000 employees, more than any other U.S. bank except Citigroup. Ranked by deposits, it is the largest bank in the United States, and by market capitalization, the fourth largest in the world. Although it has operations in over 30 countries, and provides an extensive range of global corporate and investment banking and asset management services, its core business has always been U.S. consumer banking. On revenues of $124 billion, it earned $15 billion in 2007, over half of which came from consumer deposits and credit cards.

Like many banks, Bank of America suffered an earnings decline in 2007 as a result of the subprime mortgage debacle in the United States. The bank was not hit as hard as some of its competitors, however, and used the occasion to continue a long-term process of growth by acquisition, most notably by buying Countrywide Financial, previously the nation's largest mortgage lender.

Between 1984 and 2004 the number of commercial banks in the United States was cut in half, mainly due to mergers. Bank of America is a leading example of this consolidation trend. The current bank was created when Nationsbank of North Carolina acquired San Francisco–based Bank of America in 1998 and adopted its name. The post-1998 group has made further acquisitions, including MBNA in 2005 (by which Bank of America became the country's largest credit card issuer).

Nationsbank was formed in 1991 out of the merger of North Carolina National Bank (NCNB) with Citizens and Southern. Subsequent acquisitions soon made it the largest bank in the American south. During this same time, Bank of America took over two large competitors, Security Pacific (1992) and Continental Illinois (1994).

For three decades after World War II, Bank of America had been the largest bank in the world, measured by assets, a position it achieved more by internal growth than by acquisition. Bank of America was originally formed out of several small southern California banks in the early 1900s, but a more important predecessor was A. P. Giannini's Bank of Italy, which acquired Bank of America and its name in the late 1920s. Among Giannini's signal achievements with Bank of Italy were the provision of financial services for the mass consumer market,

and expansion by development of a branch network, although his ambitions to expand nationwide were thwarted by U.S. regulators. Nevertheless, under the leadership of Giannini and his successors, Bank of America spread rapidly across the large and fast-growing retail financial market in California. The bank also funded Walt Disney movies and the Golden Gate Bridge, and in 1958 introduced Bankamericard (predecessor of VISA), the first credit card widely licensed to other banks.

In the late 1970s and early 1980s, when rising interest rates on monies financing Bank of America's large portfolio of fixed-rate home mortgages weakened it relative to "money center" competitors, and a falling U.S. dollar slowed its growth relative to non-U.S. institutions, the bank fell below the top 10 worldwide. A spate of problem loans added further difficulties. After a period of restructuring in the late 1980s, growth then resumed and was followed by the rapid succession of mergers in the 1990s described above. Hugh McColl, head of NCNB and Nationsbank during these mergers, continued as chairman of the new Bank of America from 1998 until 2001, when he was succeeded by Kenneth Lewis.

In addition to its dominant position in consumer banking, Bank of America in 2007 was also among the top 10 mergers and acquisitions advisers, and one of the 10 largest investment managers in the United States. The bank's commitment to environmentally-friendly business is symbolized by the construction of a new office building in New York in 2008 that includes insulating glass and facilities for recycling water.

See Also: Citigroup; Financial Markets; Merrill Lynch; Mortgage Credit Crisis of 2008.

Bibliography. Bank of America Corp., *Annual Report for 2007*; Bloomberg.com, "Bank of America's Countrywide Purchase Boosts Stocks," www.bloomberg.com (cited March 2009); Gary Hector, *Breaking the Bank* (Little, Brown, 1988); Marquis James and Bessie R. James, *Biography of a Bank* (Bank of America, 1954, 1982); "The League Tables: Will BofA Get a Parting Gift?," *Wall Street Journal* (October 31, 2007).

DREW KEELING
UNIVERSITY OF ZURICH

Bank of China

The Bank of China is one of China's four stated-owned commercial banks. Its businesses cover commercial banking, investment banking, and insurance. The Bank of China (Hong Kong), Bank of China International, and Bank of China Group Insurance are members of the Bank of China Group. It is ranked 187th in *Fortune* magazine's Global 500 companies in 2008 and ranked 9th among the world's top 1,000 banks in *The Banker* magazine in 2007.

In 1905 the government of the Qing Dynasty established the Treasury Bank, the first state bank in Chinese history. In 1908 the Treasury Bank changed its name to the Bank of Great Qing. With the approval of the government of the Republic of China, the Bank of China was formally established in February 1912 to replace the Ta Ching Government Bank. The Bank of China acted as the government treasury and handled the remittances of public funds. It served as the central bank, international exchange bank, and specialized foreign trade bank of the country at that time. It issued banknotes on behalf of the central government with the Central Bank of China, Farmers' Bank of China, and Bank of Communications. In 1928 the national government of the Republic of China set up its own central bank. Thus, the Bank of China became a commercial bank.

After 1949 the Bank of China split into two operations. One part of the bank relocated to Taiwan and was privatized in 1971 to become the International Commercial Bank of China. The other part of the bank became the mainland China state-designated specialized foreign exchange and foreign trade bank. The main functions of the bank include trade settlements and foreign exchange transactions settlements between local and foreign enterprises and banks, extension of credit to foreign currency, and renminbi (RMB) bonds and other marketable securities. It further engages in trust, financial leasing, and consulting businesses. The Bank of China group in Hong Kong and Macao is under supervision of the Bank of China. During the early stages of the reforms in mainland China in the 1980s, the Bank of China played a major role as the main channel through which China raised funds from abroad.

In 1995 the Chinese government introduced the Commercial Bank Law to commercialize the opera-

Personal banking makes up a third of the Bank of China's commercial banking business, and it leads in RMB credit cards.

tions of the four state-owned banks: the Bank of China, the China Construction Bank, the Agricultural Bank of China, and the Industrial and Commercial Bank of China. The Bank of China specializes in foreign-exchange transactions and trade finance but is also a major domestic financial service provider. Its business scope covers commercial banking, investment banking, and insurance. The core business of the bank includes corporate banking, personal banking, and financial markets.

The Bank of China was formally incorporated in Beijing as a state-controlled joint stock commercial bank in August 2004. In 2006 its revenue was US$17,645 billion and its net income was US$5.4 billion. In 2007 the total assets of the mainland China segment were US$674 billion, whereas the assets of the Hong Kong and Macao segments were US$163 billion at the end of the year, contributing about 40 percent of the whole group. Assets for the other overseas segments amounted to US$33 billion. The overseas segment only contributed 2.52 percent of the group's profits for 2007. Commercial banking is the core business of the bank and contributed 90 percent of the operating profit of the year. Corporate banking is the major business in commercial banking, which makes up 60 percent of the operating profit of the total commercial banking business. The personal banking business contributes one-third of commercial banking.

The Bank of China is the most internationalized bank on the mainland. It established its first overseas office, the London branch, in 1929. The bank successively opened branches all over the world. In addition to its mainland offices, it has nearly 700 branches in Hong Kong, Macao, and 26 countries and regions, with over 22,000 employees. The Bank of China listed on the Hong Kong Stock Exchange in June 2006. It raised US$9.7 billion in its H-share global offering.

Bank of China (Hong Kong)

The Bank of China started operations in Hong Kong in 1917 and became a note-issuing bank in 1994. In October 2001 the Bank of China incorporated with the merger of 10 members of the former Bank of China Group in Hong Kong. The Bank of China (Hong Kong) listed on the Hong Kong Stock Exchange in October 2002. The bank's headquarters in Hong Kong are located in the Bank of China Tower. It has an extensive service network of over 280 branches and 450 automatic teller machines, with another 15 branches and sub-branches in the Chinese mainland to provide cross-border services to customers in Hong Kong. It has also maintained its leading position in RMB credit cards.

The Bank of China (Hong Kong) has already been able to provide a comprehensive range of general banking products and services with the low to medium class of customer as its main targeted customer groups. Since Hong Kong's return to Chinese sovereignty in 1997, the Bank of China has further developed as a banking force, standing its ground against only two other note-issuing banks in Hong Kong, the HSBC and the Standard Chartered Bank.

See Also: Central Banks; China.

Bibliography. Bank of China Limited, Annual Report 2007, www.boc.cn (cited March 2009); Weidong Liu, "Development of Local Financial Systems in Mainland China," *Eurasian Geography and Economics* (v.49/2, 2008).

TAI MING WUT
INDEPENDENT SCHOLAR

Bankruptcy

Bankruptcy is the legal state of being unable to make good on one's debts. Originally a crime—the accusatory origins of the word are retained when we refer to someone as "morally bankrupt"—ideas about and practices concerning bankruptcy have evolved over thousands of years, changing as do economic systems. Though the negative connotations of the word remain, it is now a thing that can be entered into strategically, even to the benefit of all concerned parties.

History

The need to deal in some fashion with an individual's inability to pay his or her debts is as old as debt, as old as money. A wide variety of remedies developed in different economies. In ancient Jewish law, the debts of Jews are cleared every seventh year, and every 50th year is the Year of Jubilee, clearing all debts, Jewish and otherwise. At the other extreme, Genghis Khan prescribed the death penalty for anyone who had become bankrupt three times.

More widespread, with a good deal of variation, is the ancient Greek practice of debt slavery, in which families and their servants were forced to labor without recompense in order to pay off the debt of the head of household. Debt slaves were not "sold into slavery"—they had more rights than other slaves, and indentured servitude might be a more accurate term for the practice. "Debt slavery" continues to be used figuratively, to refer to the necessity of continuing to earn a certain amount in order to pay off one's debts—the lifestyle one is locked into when one has had to enter into debt in order to acquire necessary luxuries like a financed car, a mortgaged house, and a college education. However, in that modern figurative use, bankruptcy is the remedy (as it were) to debt slavery, rather than the other way around.

In the Middle Ages, individuals accused of bankruptcy (or operating businesses accused of bankruptcy) could be publicly flogged, a solution that helped no one per se but was intended as a deterrent and to satisfy the public need for the service of justice. In England, they could have their ears cut off, or nailed to a wall—punishments which, while more vicious than sending them to debtors' prison, did not prevent them from continuing to work to try to pay off their debts, nor did it add the cost of their upkeep to the state's bills.

The common thread here is that bankruptcy was a form of fraud. The debtor had agreed to pay a debt he proved unable to pay. The word *bankrupt* comes from the Latin *bancus ruptus*, broken table; a bancus (from which both *bank* and *bench* derive) was a table at which the ancient bankers sat in marketplaces and other public places. When he could no longer do business, he broke the table (or it was broken for him) as a sign that he was no longer doing business. From the start, then, *bankruptcy* has been a figurative term, used to refer to people who were as bereft as these broken bankers.

The modern form of clearing debts through the act of declaring bankruptcy dates from English law in 1705. As economic, political, and technological changes changed the nature of individual economic life, attitudes towards debt and bankruptcy shifted. In various countries, legal systems developed designed to liquidate assets and pay off debts, in part or in whole, when an individual or business went bankrupt; and as businesses became more sophisticated (and publicly held businesses accountable to shareholders came into being), laws and practices had to develop to accommodate them as well.

In the United States, the criminal associations of bankruptcy fell away in the 19th century, when a series of economic crises hastened the repeated softening of state and local laws, in part because of the growing awareness of circumstances in which a debtor could find himself bankrupt through no wrongdoing of his own—the "hard luck case." Chapter 13 bankruptcy was introduced in the aftermath of the Great Depression, in order to allow debtors to retain their property and residence while repaying their debts over a three-to-five-year period. Chapter 11 bankruptcy came in the 1970s during stagflation, designed to reorganize bankrupt businesses, and the farm crisis of the end of that decade brought about Chapter 12 bankruptcy to provide similar options for family farms.

In the 21st century, in most of the Western world the emphasis is neither on punishment nor liquidation, but on finding ways to resolve debts while maintaining the economic health of the debtor, whether a business or individual. Bankruptcy is more often declared than accused, and often is the operative word: the end of the 20th century saw the beginning of a boom time for bankruptcy, with 1 in 76 Americans filing for personal bankruptcy in 1997. Texaco and Continental Airlines, once robust giants, joined them in corporate bankruptcy, with the infamous cases of Worldcom and Enron following at the cusp of the new century.

Title 11 in the United States

In the United States, as in most countries, bankruptcy is a federal matter—in fact, it is specifically mentioned in the Constitution (Article 1, Section 8, Clause 4), which gives Congress the power to adopt "uniform laws on the subject of bankruptcies." Such laws form the Bankruptcy Code, Title 11 of the United States Code, which defines six types of bankruptcy, commonly referred to according to the chapter in which they appear: Chapter 7, Chapter 9, Chapter 11, Chapter 12, Chapter 13, and Chapter 15.

Chapter 7 liquidation or "straight bankruptcy," for which both individuals and businesses are eligible, is the oldest and most common form of bankruptcy filing, accounting for more than half of personal bankruptcies. In such liquidations, a bankruptcy trustee liquidates the debtor's property to create a pool of funds from which to pay the creditors. As long as the debtor is guilty of no fraud or other deceitful behavior, a certain amount of debt is forgiven regardless of the size of the pool of funds, but there are debts that cannot be discharged or reduced at all, such as child support, alimony payments, fines imposed by a court in answer to a crime, property taxes, income taxes less than three years old, and student loan payments. Certain property—typical a residence and vehicle—is exempt from being liquidated.

Though a declaration of Chapter 7 bankruptcy remains on an individual's credit report for 10 years, it is such a tempting maneuver for so many victims of debt that in recent years trustees have been much more aggressive in verifying that the filer is indeed entitled to file Chapter 7 rather than Chapter 13. False filing—declaring Chapter 7 when one is capable of filing Chapter 13—is called "abusive filing," and is contested in order to protect creditors. Anyone who is found to have falsely filed is forced into Chapter 13 bankruptcy. In the case of a business, Chapter 7 liquidation means suspending the business's operations unless the trustee resumes them.

The business is usually dismantled in the course of paying off its debts.

2005 Changes

The 2005 Bankruptcy Abuse Prevention and Consumer Protection Act, passed in response to the rise of bankruptcies, requires that any individual filing for bankruptcy receive a briefing from a credit counseling agency and complete an instructional course in personal financial management, prior to filing; the rationale for this is that it will reduce abusive filings. BAPCPA also made it extraordinarily difficult to discharge student loan debt through appeals, which had previously been uncommon but not unheard-of.

As the above implies, Chapter 13 is increasingly encouraged as the bankruptcy filing for individuals. Rather than a liquidation, this is a reorganization and rehabilitation of debt, creating a plan by which the debtor pays off his or her debts in a short time frame (three to five years). The debtor is responsible for proposing the plan, and there are codified limits—calculated according to an equation that accounts for the cost of living—on how much debt a debtor can possess when filing. A Chapter 13 filing remains on the debtor's credit record for seven years.

Chapter 11 is the equivalent for businesses, a reorganization filing. The business proposes a plan, and a bankruptcy court determines whether it is fair and equitable and complies with the goals of the relevant laws. This can result in canceling contracts the business could not otherwise cancel (such as union agreements) and usually causes it to be delisted from its primary stock exchange, if applicable—though in such cases, stocks always continue to be traded over-the-counter. The final outcome of a Chapter 11 plan often terminates shares in the company.

As of 2009, 12 of the 15 largest Chapter 11 bankruptcies had been filed in the 21st century, a result of the many disastrous misadventures of large corporations. Technically, individuals can file Chapter 11; in practice, this rarely occurs, and there is rarely any advantage to it compared to Chapter 7 or Chapter 13.

Other Types

Chapter 9 bankruptcy is less familiar to most people, and is a debt restructuring made available to municipalities. The most notable case of a Chapter 9 filing is that of Orange County, California, in 1994. Reasons for filing range from that of Millport, Alabama, in 2005, when the close of a factory meant a loss of sales tax revenue and income dropped below that necessary to pay off debts; to the Pierce County (Washington state) Housing Authority's 2008 filing because of a class-action lawsuit over mold. One reason Orange County's filing made headlines was because its losses had been the result of bad investments.

Chapter 12 bankruptcy is quite similar to 11 and 13, but is meant for family farms, which faced a significant economic crisis in the late 1970s and early 1980s when incomes failed to keep up with the massive size of the loans offered to farms, much like the more recent subprime mortgage crisis, albeit with stubbier tendrils of consequence. Compared to the thousands of Chapter 11s and hundreds of thousands of Chapter 7 and 13s filed each year, Chapter 12 filings number in the hundreds.

Chapter 15 codifies into federal law the Model Law On Cross Border Insolvency drafted by the United Nations Commission on International Trade Law, making provisions for dealing with cross-border bankruptcy, when a bankruptcy case involves both American and foreign jurisdictions.

Any of the above can constitute either voluntary or involuntary bankruptcies. Involuntary bankruptcies are filed by the creditors rather than the debtor, but are quite uncommon, particularly in the age of debt collection agencies.

See Also: Debt; Debt Rescheduling; Enron Corporation.

Bibliography. Douglas G. Baird, *The Elements of Bankruptcy* (Foundation Press, 2005); Brian A. Blum, *Bankruptcy and Debtor/Creditor: Examples and Explanations* (Aspen, 2006); Kelly DePonte, *The Guide to Distressed Debt and Turnaround Investing: Making, Managing and Exiting Investments in Distressed Companies and Their Securities* (Private Equity International, 2007); David G. Epstein and Steve H. Nickles, *Principles of Bankruptcy Law* (Thomson West, 2007); Scott A. Sandage, *Born Losers: A History of Failure in America* (Harvard University Press, 2006); James D. Scurlock, *Maxed Out: Hard Times, Easy Credit, and the Era of Predatory Lenders* (Scribner, 2007).

BILL KTE'PI
INDEPENDENT SCHOLAR

Baoshan Iron and Steel

Baoshan Iron and Steel Co., Ltd., is one of China's largest and most strategically important companies. It is the publicly listed subsidiary of Baosteel Group, a Chinese state-owned enterprise headquartered in Shanghai. The subsidiary was established in February 2000. In December of that year, 1.877 billion common shares were issued and Baoshan Iron and Steel Co., Ltd., (abbreviated to "Baosteel" in English) was successfully listed on the Shanghai Stock Exchange, raising just under US$1 billion.

Baosteel is set for significant growth and expansion as a major player in the restructuring of the industry in China. The pace of Baosteel's growth and expansion will depend upon how it deals with the challenges of a slew of anticipated mergers and acquisitions, securing strategic iron ore resources, and developing the product and process innovations necessary to underpin sustainable competitiveness.

Baosteel is the largest and most advanced steel company in China and the sixth largest in the world specializing in high-tech and high-value-added steel products. The company produced approximately 20 million tons of iron and 23 million tons of steel in 2007. Baosteel has become China's main steel supplier to automobile, household appliance, oil exploration, oil and gas transmission, shipbuilding, pressure vessel, and container materials industries.

Baosteel's 2007 results showed an 18 percent increase in revenues to CNY191,6bn (US$27.4 billion) with a 2.7 percent fall in net profit to CNY12.7bn (US$1.8 billion). Sharp increases in the costs of raw materials and weakness in the stainless steel market were cited as the main reasons for the profit decline. In December 2007, Standard & Poor's revised the long-term credit rating of Baosteel from "BBB+" to "A-" with "stable outlook."

China's steel industry is in its golden age; however, it remains highly fragmented with Baosteel, the top producer, contributing only 12 percent of the nation's total output. China's Steel Industry Policy (2007) aims to consolidate the industry into several major players. A flurry of merger activity is imminent with Baoshan Iron and Steel Co., Ltd., expected to be a dominant player in the restructured industry.

Baosteel's dynamic capabilities, critical to its current position and future success, are underpinned by the scale and growth of the domestic market. Its strategy includes product differentiation, with increased focus on high-end products and high-strength value addeds, and cost reduction through increased productivity and improved management systems. Baosteel's strategy for market expansion includes establishing production bases abroad with the objective of increasing the contribution of overseas sales to 10–15 percent of the revenue base (currently around 3 percent) over the next five years.

In recent times, government policy has both helped and hindered Baosteel's operations. In June 2007 export tariffs were levied on more than 80 categories of steel products in order to curb exports and secure domestic supply. Then, in late 2007, Baosteel was said to have benefited from US$52 billion in government subsidies to the industry. The Chinese government is expected to play a key role in determining future mergers and acquisitions related to the new Steel Industry Plan. From Baosteel's perspective, the choice of targets and/or partners will have a significant impact on operations, trading, and global expansion plans.

Baosteel faces two major issues that will continue to place upward pressure on costs. China's exchange rate policy is subject to ongoing examination by the world financial community. Should the Chinese government bow to international pressure for a sharp revaluation of the Chinese renminbi, the consequences could be significant for Baosteel and for the entire Chinese steel industry.

The second cost issue is related to the supply of iron ore, the basic raw material for steel manufacture. In recent years, the three dominant suppliers of iron ore have negotiated price increases of 72 percent (2005), 19 percent (2006), and 30 percent (2007). It is widely anticipated that iron ore mining companies in Australia will achieve an increase of approximately 85 percent in 2008, exceeding the 65 percent rise secured by the key Brazilian mining companies. The Chinese government is currently considering a joint bid, including Baoshan Iron and Steel Co., Ltd., to acquire a key Australian supplier (Rio Tinto Group) in order to protect this strategic supply chain.

See Also: China; Manufacturing Strategy; Supply Chain Management.

Bibliography. Baoshan Iron and Steel Co., Ltd., *Annual Report* (2006); Baoshan Iron and Steel Co., Ltd., *Fact Book* (2006); People's Daily Online, "China's Steel Industry Ready for Change," www.english.peopledaily.com.cn (cited March 2009); Jonathan R. Woetzel, "Remaking China's Giant Steel Industry," *McKinsey Quarterly*, www.mckinseyquarterly .com (cited March 2009).

Terence R. Egan
Central University of Finance and Economics

Barclays

Barclays Bank was founded in 1896, but its precursors date back as far as 1690. The Barclay name became connected to the business when the bankers John Freame and Thomas Gould joined forces with Freame's son-in-law John Barclay in 1736. At the start of the 21st century Barclays, along with Lloyds, is one of the remaining Big Five English banks that previously dominated the City. During the 1980s and 1990s the other three original banks were absorbed by competitors and the merchant banks joined foreign banks. The history of Barclays provides an important case study for business strategies.

Barclays has long had a strong presence in Britain because of its early development as a large retail bank with outlets all over the country. Stiff competition from joint-stock banks equipped with capital and a network of branches drove what was once a small local bank on Lombard Street to merge with 19 other banks (including Bevan, Gurney, Goslings, and Backhouse) to set up a modern joint-stock bank in 1896. Barclay & Co. Limited then had 182 branches. The families who united forces conceived a durable strategy of organic and external growth along rules of steady entrepreneurship, and kept nonexecutive representatives on the board.

Barclays became one of the Big Five joint-stock banks of the City after it merged with several banks (Bolithos in 1905; United Countries Bank in the Midlands in 1916; London, Provincial & South Western Bank in 1918; Union Bank of Manchester in 1919; and, much later, Martins Bank in 1969). Among British banks in 1932 it was first in number of outlets (2,175) and, with Lloyds, second in deposits (£382

million) behind Midland. Its widespread middle-class customer base contributed to a continuous transformation into retail banking, which allowed Barclays to join the rally for mass banking beginning in the 1960s. Such growth fuelled its early innovations: the first British credit card in 1966, the Barclaycard, and then the first world cash machine or automatic teller machine, Barclaycash.

Barclays had taken over three institutions active overseas (Colonial Bank, Anglo-Egyptian Bank, National Bank of South Africa) to form Barclays Dominion, Colonial & Overseas, or Barclays DCO, in 1925. But this move was halted by the decolonization trend, and the bank had to rethink its international strategy. Barclays then expanded through commercial banking operations in continental Europe and the United States. The City had also regained its status in the worldwide banking market thanks to the Euromarket in the 1960s.

In 1976 Barclays tried to build a large investment bank to take profit from the demise of merchant banks. In 1983 it purchased several brokerage houses (De Zoete & Revan, Wedd Durlacher, and Mordaunt) to forge Barclays De Zoete Wedd in 1986; but like its competitors it had difficulty creating a new corporate culture linking commercial banking and investment banking. This led to the amalgamation of the mother and the daughter banks into a new organization where risks were more controlled.

From the 1990s, Barclays designed a diversified strategy. Retail banking was reinforced in the United Kingdom with, for example, the purchase of Woolwich in 2000. Barclays extended to other countries with both success (ABSA, the South African leader, in 2005; Banco Zaragozano in Spain in 2003) and failure (the merger with Dutch leader ABN-AMRO was foiled by rivals). It also asserted itself as a key player in credit cards (Barclaycard and business cards).

Solid investment banking and market banking activities (within Barclays Capital) gathered momentum in wholesale corporate banking and project financing. Barclays moved to compete with a few other European and worldwide banks in asset management (Barclays Global Investors, managing more than $2 trillion) and private banking (Barclays Wealth). While it lacks the financial might of London rival HSBC, Barclays, with 134,000 employees in 2007, still ranks with Halifax-Bank of Scotland, Royal Bank of Scotland, Lloyds, and HSBC, in the top British big banks. In the future, Barclays will have to ponder its strategy within the new frame of globalization, for example in central European or Asian emerging countries.

See Also: HSBC Holdings; Lloyds TSB Group; United Kingdom.

Bibliography. Y. Cassis, *La City de Londres, 1870–1914* (Belin, 1987); Y. Cassis and É. Bussière, eds., *London and Paris as International Financial Centres in the Twentieth Century* (Oxford University Press, 2005); N. Ferguson, M. Ackrill, and L. Hannah, *Barclays: The Business of Banking, 1690–1996* (Cambridge University Press, 2001); D. Kynaston, *City of London: A Club No More, 1945–2000* (Chatto & Windus, 2001); D. Kynaston, *City of London: Illusions of Gold, 1914–1945* (Chatto & Windus, 1999); W. Vander, *Falling Eagle: The Decline of Barclays Bank* (Weidenfeld & Nicolson, 2000).

HUBERT BONIN
BORDEAUX UNIVERSITY

Barriers to Entry

A barrier to entry is any obstacle that prevents potential entrants from enjoying the benefits that accrue to incumbents (established firms). These obstacles may be classified as structural or strategic. The benefits that accrue to the established firms are usually defined in terms of long-run abnormal profits (price set above minimum long-run average cost), but may also include other advantages, for example, in research and development. The key point to emphasize about barriers to entry is that they yield rents that are only available to incumbent firms; such firms earn these rents precisely because they are established in a particular industry.

Structural Barriers

Structural barriers to entry depend on the factors that determine the competitiveness of an industry (for example, demand for a product and technology). Neither incumbent firms nor potential entrants can directly determine the size of these barriers. Examples of structural barriers include economies of scale,

absolute cost advantages, and product differentiation. Economies of scale are defined as the rate at which long-run average costs of production fall as output is increased. The point at which these costs are minimized is the minimum efficient scale of production (MES). If the MES is very large in relation to market demand it may only be viable for one incumbent to exist in this industry.

Absolute cost advantages exist when the incumbent's long run average cost is below that of the potential entrant's for all levels of output. In other words, and unlike the case of economies of scale, the scale at which the potential entrant chooses to enter does not affect the cost disadvantage it experiences with respect to the incumbent. Exclusive access to superior technology via patents is one way in which absolute cost advantages are realized.

Product differentiation means that the output of one firm is not perceived by consumers to be a perfect substitute for the output of other firms. This, too, is another type of structural barrier to entry. For example, if consumers are loyal to established brands it can be very difficult (and expensive) for potential entrants to attract customers. Other factors that influence product differentiation barriers to entry include customer inertia, switching costs, product reputation, and established dealer systems.

Strategic Barriers

The major weakness of structural barriers is that they provide little information on how incumbents would respond if entry occurred. This is important because structural barriers may not in themselves be sufficient to deter entry. For example, a new entrant may be able to undercut the monopoly price of the incumbent and force the latter to exit the industry. To overcome this problem a variety of alternative theories of barriers of entry have been developed, which are classed as strategic. Strategic barriers to entry are the actions taken by incumbents to influence the behavior of potential entrants. A key insight of such theories is that actions taken by the incumbent pre-entry alter the post-entry returns available to the potential entrant. Recognizing that ex post returns are less attractive than was anticipated, the potential entrant does not enter.

Pricing policy and commitment are two types of strategic entry barrier that figure prominently in the literature. Limit pricing was one of the earliest theories used to examine the way in which the pricing decisions of an incumbent could deter entry. The limit price is the highest the incumbent believes it can charge without attracting entry. Two assumptions underlie this theory. First, the incumbent has exhausted economies of scale and therefore produces at the minimum of long-run average cost. Second, potential entrants believe that the incumbent will maintain its output at the pre-entry level even after entry. Effectively, the decision to enter will depend on whether it is profitable for the potential entrant to supply the residual demand function (that not met by the incumbent). However, the belief that the incumbent will not change output after entry has been questioned. For example, if entry occurred there is no guarantee that only the potential entrant would incur losses. Recognizing this, the incumbent may allow entry and collude in a market-sharing agreement with the new entrant. Alternatively, it may be more profitable for the incumbent to sell at the monopoly price and permit entry to occur.

Predatory Pricing

Predatory pricing is a strategy by which the incumbent reduces (or threatens to reduce) price to unremunerative levels when faced with actual (or potential) competition. Such a tactic is predatory because it conflicts with short-run profit maximization. However, if the use of this tactic is successful, the incumbent can continue to earn monopoly profits in the long run. Predatory pricing has a long history: in the United States, for example, one of the most famous cases involved Standard Oil in 1911.

The success of predatory pricing depends on a number of factors. For example, for it to be profitable, short-term losses must be less than long-term monopoly profits, but calculating these accurately is difficult; if the result is positive there still remains the problem of communicating the credibility of such action to a potential entrant. If the incumbent faces just one potential entrant, an aggressive pricing policy may succeed, but this outcome is less certain when a number of potential entrants are encountered: For example, while an aggressive response by the incumbent may deter the first potential entrant and all subsequent entrants, it is also possible that a sequence of costly price wars damage the financial resources of the incumbent to such an extent that the threat of an aggressive response is no longer perceived as credible by potential entrants.

Commitment Strategies and Product Proliferation

The basic premise of commitment strategies is that before entry occurs the incumbent has the opportunity to make irreversible decisions that alter the payoffs in the post-entry game. These commitments affect the incumbent's response post-entry while simultaneously signalling to potential entrants the desirability of entering ex ante. For example, the decision by the incumbent to invest in extra capacity will reduce its unit cost of production and this will allow it to pursue an aggressive pricing/output policy post-entry. Observing this, potential entrants will realize that they cannot profitably enter the industry.

Irreversible decisions involve sunk costs: Costs that cannot be recovered if the decision is made to exit the industry. Examples of these irreversible decisions include advertising, investment in large sunk production capacity, and product proliferation. Advertising is a type of promotional campaign designed to increase the demand for a product. One way in which advertising can act as a barrier to entry is by creating a cost asymmetry between the incumbent and the potential entrant. Advertising helps to create goodwill for a product: An advertising campaign today will continue to generate demand in the future even if no further advertising expenditure is undertaken. This cumulative effect of advertising means that in order to attract the same level of demand as an incumbent, the potential entrant needs to spend more on advertising.

The fact that advertising expenditure is a completely sunk cost may increase the difficulties experienced by potential entrants attempting to raise external funds to finance an advertising campaign: In the event of unsuccessful entry, physical plant has some salvage value that can be used as security for a loan, but a failed advertising campaign has no such value.

The established position of incumbents is reinforced if economies of scale in advertising are important. Such economies can arise from threshold effects (a minimum number of advertising messages are required to influence consumers) and also because as a sunk fixed cost, average costs decline as the volume of advertising increases. With large sunk capacity the incumbent incurs higher fixed costs to obtain lower marginal costs of production, and these, in turn, require larger outputs for profit maximization. Large sunk capacity commits the incumbent to a 'tough' strategy when confronted with entry because large-scale output is the profit-maximizing strategy irrespective of entry. Entry is deterred because the output decision of the incumbent reduces the demand available to the potential entrant. In these models, the barrier to entry is also a barrier to exit.

Product proliferation is the strategic decision by an incumbent to preempt entry by creating brands that satisfy every product niche (meaning there is little demand left for a new brand) and to enter profitable market niches before a potential entrant (which rules out profitable entry). Classic examples of industries in which there is significant product proliferation include laundry detergents, bathroom soap, and toothpaste.

Effects

Judgements on the welfare effects of barriers to entry are difficult and need to take account of a variety of factors. For example, significant scale of economies will mean that only a few firms can exist in an industry and be productively efficient. The fact that high profits are being earned in a concentrated industry might indicate the abuse of monopoly power, but such profits are also consistent with incumbent firms having superior technology compared to potential entrants.

The short-run disadvantages of barriers to entry need to be weighed against long-term benefits. For example, the existence of barriers to entry may allow incumbents to charge higher prices compared to a competitive industry and to make significant profits, but these profits may be used to finance research and development into cures for diseases. In this example, removing barriers to entry will make the industry more competitive and lead to lower prices and competitive rates of profit, but these profits may be insufficient to finance research and development.

In many countries the responsibility for investigating barriers to entry and determining whether they are legal or not rests with official bodies. In the United States, for example, the Federal Trade Commission is responsible for these inquires; in the United Kingdom, investigations have been conducted by the Office of Fair Trade.

See Also: Absolute Advantage; Advertising; Brand Loyalty; Economies of Scale.

Bibliography. D. W. Carlton and J. M. Perloff, *Modern Industrial Organisation* (Pearson/Addison-Wesley, 2005); R. Schmalansee and R. D. Willig, eds., *The Handbook of Industrial Organisation*, vol.1 (North Holland, 1989).

DAVID M. HIGGINS
UNIVERSITY OF YORK

Barter

Barter is a form of countertrade where goods and/or services are exchanged simultaneously without using money or similar monetary instruments. This type of trade refers to a single contract between two parties who are fully compensated by the traded nonmonetary items. This clearly distinguishes barter from other forms of countertrade that may include a third party or allow for partial monetary compensation, such as counterpurchase or buy-back deals. Among all forms of trade, barter can be considered as being the simplest and oldest implementation of it. From an anthropological perspective, barter is seen as a natural tendency of human beings distinguished from gift-giving. While the latter implies trust and credit, which are necessary for future cooperation, barter is seen as a one-off action with no implications for future collaboration.

Through barter, companies can increase their sales volume and sell excess production or resources more easily. In international trade, barter allows circumvention of certain trade barriers such as unfavorable regulations concerning international monetary transactions or overcoming economic restrictions to trade. However, there are also some severe drawbacks related to this type of trade. Barter assumes a double coincidence of wants and needs of the organizations involved. Apart from that, barter assumes that traded goods are arbitrarily divisible in order to match their underlying value. These circumstances may not always be the case. Compared to monetary trade, barter involves negotiations for two goods and/or services and requires two simultaneously concluded and fulfilled delivery contracts. Therefore, barter can be more time-consuming and expensive. It also reduces the flexibility of both companies involved to react quickly to new market conditions. As only a limited range of products can be provided by the contractual parties, goods and services may not be related to one's own business and therefore other markets have to be found where these products can be resold to third parties. This may also take time and cost money.

Generally, barter transactions are not superior to monetary trade and are only implemented if external requirements and circumstances make agents prefer nonmonetary operations. At times of communist power, a bulk of transactions between Western and Eastern countries included barter. Austria played a key role as a mediator in these transactions. In 1993 43 percent of Austria's transit exports were delivered to eastern European countries and 33 percent of them to western Europe. One of the reasons for barter trade was the lack of hard foreign currency and trade barriers. Therefore the direct transaction of goods and services was favored.

For trade with Third World countries, barter also played an important role because they had no cash to pay for the goods needed and imported. As a consequence, their creditworthiness was low. Therefore they gave resources in exchange in order to meet their debts and to overcome their liquidity problems. Compared to money, goods better collateralize future payments/compensations than money, because claims on property rights on physical items can more easily be enforced than claims on future cash flows.

In Russia, an explosive growth of barter dealings was reported in the early 1990s. This trend has been described as "re-demonetization" and was caused by a high rate of inflation. In the 20th century many European and Latin American countries suffered from a devaluation of their currencies. As a result, people engaged in barter transactions as prices increased and trading partners lost their confidence in money. It can be said that high inflation is a driver for barter transactions that limit the effects of a devaluing currency as the intrinsic value of one good/service, in terms of other goods/services, does not change. In other words, barter locks out the exchange rate risk.

Finally, organizations tend to barter if the tax system in a country does not favor their operations. In Russia, tax officials were allowed to block the bank account of those companies or individuals that were in tax arrears. Consequently, it was not possible for those people to withdraw money from their accounts and pay their debts for goods and services received. As a result, nonmonetary trade increased, which enabled circumventing this barrier to trade.

Modern bartering is often conducted through bartering clubs or bartering networks, such as the Swiss Wirtschaftsring (WIR) or the International Reciprocal Trade Association (IRTA). Members of such networks pay fees in order to get listed to be considered for barter transactions. Such clubs increase the likelihood of double coincidence as they match supply and demand.

Counterpurchase and buy-back deals are special forms of barter that may include third parties, such as banks, which reliably arrange payment flows, and traders, who are willing to resell exchanged goods. Import certificates that give the right to import a certain value of goods increase the flexibility of barter operations. They allow separating the import and export transaction from each other. Counterpurchase, buy-back, and import certificates imply cross-subsidization from a foreign exporter to a domestic importer or vice versa. In the former case, the foreign exporter could generate considerable profits that cannot be realized due to low purchasing power in the domestic country. The domestic importer, in contrast, would lack purchasing power without being supported by the foreign exporter. In the latter case, a foreign importer would subsidize a domestic exporter by purchasing import certificates. Otherwise the domestic exporter would not be able to sell its products at the given market price and exchange rate.

See Also: Countertrade; Gift-Giving.

Bibliography. W. E. Buffett, "Why I'm Not Buying the U.S. Dollar," *Fortune* (July 21, 2008); T. Hammond, *Countertrade, Offsets and Barter in International Political Economy* (Palgrave Macmillan, 1990); B. Malinowksi, *Argonauts of the Western Pacific* (Routledge, 1922); P. Mayerhofer, "Change in the Service Trade Regime with CEE Countries," *Austrian Economic Quarterly* (WIFO 1/1999); J. Noguera and S. J. Linz, "Barter, Credit and Welfare, A Theoretical Inquiry into the Barter Phenomenon in Russia," *Economics of Transitions* (2006).

Daniel Dauber
Vienna University of Economics
& Business Administration

Basel Committee on Banking Supervision

The Basel Committee on Banking Regulation and Supervisory Practices (Basel Committee), founded in 1974 by the central bankers from G10 countries, serves as a forum for banking supervisory matters. Current members of the Basel Committee come from Belgium, Canada, France, Germany, Italy, Japan, Luxembourg, the Netherlands, Spain, Sweden, Switzerland, the United Kingdom, and the United States. The committee's secretariat is situated at the Bank for International Settlements in Basel, Switzerland, and consists of 15 people who are mostly professional supervisors on temporary assignment from their home institutions.

The committee does not possess any formal authority, and its developments do not have legal force. Rather, it attempts to formulate broad guidelines and recommends codes of best practices that deal with issues such as capital adequacy, the functioning of payment and settlement systems, and other aspects of banking supervision. Central banks then incorporate these guidelines and practices into national regulations of their respective countries.

The committee includes four main subcommittees, around which the work is organized: the Accord Implementation Group, the Policy Development Group, the Accounting Task Force, and the International Liaison Group. The latter provides a platform for nonmember countries to contribute to the committee's current and new initiatives. The committee circulates the papers in which the results of its research are presented to banking authorities around the world.

The Basel Committee aims to encourage convergence toward common standards and approaches in banking supervision. The need for such unification comes from the increasingly global nature of financial markets and a strikingly broad scale of the recent financial crises. Over the years, the committee has implemented various guidelines on the amount and substance of banking supervision. In 1988 the committee adopted a package of standards related to capital adequacy—the so-called Basel Capital Accord, or Basel I. Basel I has become an important international standard in the field of banking supervision.

In 1999 the committee proposed a New Capital Adequacy Framework, also known as Basel II. It is meant to replace the 1988 document. Basel II Framework emphasizes an incentive-based approach toward financial regulation in contrast to the rule-based regulation that was in place before. Many countries, including nonmembers, have included the Basel standards in some form into their national regulation for various reasons, such as a wish to improve the soundness of their banking systems, to raise their credit ratings and country's standing in the international arena, and to benefit in other ways by complying with a universally recognized standard.

Another important document produced by the Basel Committee is called "Core Principles for Effective Banking Supervision." The document, along with the "Core Principles Methodology," has been used by countries as a benchmark for assessing the strength of their supervision systems and for identifying specific steps to be taken to achieve baseline quality of their practices.

The work of the Basel Committee is largely based on personal contacts and is operated by consensus. The decision-making process is nontransparent. Some criticize the committee for its secrecy and a lack of accountability. Although regulations produced by the committee are voluntary and nonbinding, in practice countries face strong pressure to adopt the Basel proposals. For example, the International Monetary Fund (IMF) often requires compliance with the Capital Accord as a condition for receiving financial aid.

The major obstacle to negotiation of binding international agreements lies within the area of so-called sovereignty costs—potential reduction of national autonomy as a result of entering the agreement. Soft laws, on the other hand, allow sufficient flexibility to take national interests and local context into account. The Capital Accord is meant to be a soft piece of regulation, but does not always work like this in practice.

Recent efforts of the committee have concentrated on the implementation of the Basel II Framework, particularly such issues as the coordination between home and host supervisory authorities (global risk management, diversification effects, risk concentrations). A significant number of countries have already implemented Basel II Framework (fully or partially), whereas others are working on the creation of necessary infrastructure (legal, regulatory, and technical). Basel II significantly influences financial institutions, since they have to create new departments, modeling techniques, policies, and information technology systems.

See Also: Bank for International Settlements; Capital Adequacy; Credit Ratings; Regulation; Risk Management.

Bibliography. Kern Alexander, Rahul Dhumale, and John Eatwell, *Global Governance of Financial Systems: The International Regulation of Systemic Risk* (Oxford University Press, 2006); Bank for International Settlements, www.bis.org (cited March 2009); Marie-Laure Djelic and Kerstin Sahlin-Andersson, eds., *Transnational Governance: Institutional Dynamics of Regulation* (Cambridge University Press, 2006); Steven Sloan, "Basel Guidelines on Calculating Risk," *American Banker* (v.173/141, 2008).

LYUDMILA V. LUGOVSKAYA
UNIVERSITY OF CAMBRIDGE

BASF

BASF AG (Badische Anilin-und Soda-Fabrik) is the world's largest chemical company (in terms of both net sales and number of employees). The company has its headquarters in Ludwigshafen am Rhein (Rhineland-Palatinate, Germany). BASF handles a diverse, yet interrelated, portfolio of products, including chemicals, plastics, agricultural products, fine and specialty chemicals, petrochemicals, and fossil fuels and materials. As of December 2007 BASF had net sales of nearly $70 billion and employed over 95,000 people.

BASF, along with Bayer and Hoechst, was one of the important German chemical companies of the late 19th and 20th centuries. Its history of technological achievement—particularly between the 1870s and the 1940s—is unprecedented. BASF's early achievements revolved around coal-tar processes and high pressure synthesis and catalytic processing. Its successes, through international technology transfer to the United States, helped to revolutionize the modern petroleum refining and petrochemicals industries.

BASF was founded in 1865 by Friedrich Engelhorn in Mannheim, Germany. As with the other major German chemical companies of the late 19th century, BASF's success was based on advanced

scientific and technical research in the synthesis of coal-tar-based organics. BASF's first important commercial products were coal-tar dyes for use in the textile industry. Indigo dye was its first important commercial technology. Profits from its synthetic dyes went into financing expansion of the company into the heavy chemical business. Prior to World War I, BASF employed approximately 10,000 people and had built its largest facility across the Rhine from its Mannheim plant, at Ludwigshafen.

At this time, BASF expanded beyond synthetic dyes to high-pressure synthesis. Under the technical direction of Fritz Haber and Carl Bosch, BASF developed two of the most important technologies of the 20th century chemical industry: a continuous sulfuric acid process and the famous high-pressure synthetic ammonia-methanol method. With these critical innovations, BASF could make the basic heavy chemicals cheaply, in mass quantities, and using inexpensive, abundant raw materials (e.g., nitrogen from the air to make ammonia).

During this period, the United States and European countries considered BASF the world's most important chemical company. BASF leveraged its technological superiority into market growth through strict patent control and predatory pricing strategies. Thus, BASF sold dyes, ammonia, and methanol at "below market prices" to U.S. firms to dissuade the U.S. chemical industry from expanding production at home. BASF played a prominent role for Germany during World War I since its technologies assured Germany of ready supplies of coal-tar dyes and drugs as well as explosives (for weapons and construction) and fertilizers (for food production) to carry on the war effort.

Even following Germany's defeat, it did not take long for BASF to resume production of its prewar product line and reestablish its market networks internationally. Its power and influence would soon grow within Germany when in 1925 it, along with Bayer, Hoechst, and other German-based chemical companies, joined in membership in the giant chemical cartel I. G. Farbenindustrie (IG Farben). By the late 1930s, the Nazis elevated IG Farben as its technical (and financial) right arm. During World War II, BASF remained the technological center of the cartel, developing the field of high-pressure hydrogenation that produced needed supplies of aviation and automotive fuels and synthetic rubber for the war effort. Following the defeat in Germany, members of Bayer's board of directors were convicted of war crimes, but were given relatively lenient sentences of no more than four years. Under Allied supervision for seven years, IG Farben itself was finally broken up by the Allies in 1952 into its component corporate parts.

The post–World War II period presented difficult challenges, and offered unprecedented business opportunities, to the former IG Farben companies. This was certainly the case with BASF, which now had to go it alone, as it had done before the formation of the cartel. In an ironic twist, the economic difficulties of West Germany in the 1950s helped propel the company back into the limelight; without money to import chemicals from the United States and other countries, BASF became an important supplier of chemical intermediates and products domestically. By the late 1950s, the company produced nitrogen, ammonia, and related products very near wartime levels.

BASF deftly steered its way into an impressive growth cycle during the next half century. Indeed, BASF, like Dow Chemical, was one of the larger chemical companies that remained in the field as a competitor to the oil companies, which had integrated backward into petrochemicals. BASF realized its growth by using a strategy similar to that embraced by companies such as the American company Dow Chemical.

Recent Strategies

BASF has continued to embrace an active research and development program and linked this work with an aggressive capital expenditures strategy. BASF has in the past dedicated part its its research and development (R&D) budget for developing new, high-value products, such as pharmaceuticals, crop protection agents, fertilizers, and coatings. However, in the 1990s, the company sharply reduced its activities in consumer product lines. As is the case with Dow, BASF excels in improving economies of production (and finding cheap raw materials and feedstock).

Throughout the period from the 1960s to the present time, BASF R&D worked to design larger, more integrated, high-efficiency plants within Germany and worldwide making existing products—e.g., nylon, polypropylene, the amines, polystyrene, and a variety of petrochemical intermediates—cheaply and in mass quantities that effectively competed in their

BASF

The Chemical Company

In 2007 the German chemical giant BASF had net sales of nearly $70 billion and employed over 95,000 people.

designated markets. The culmination of this strategy came in 2001 when BASF, in partnership with ATOFINA Petrochemicals, completed work on the world's largest steam cracker located in Port Arthur, Texas, to provide a wide range of petrochemical intermediates at low cost to the United States and the global chemical industry.

BASF also has proven itself very flexible in modifying its organizational structure as made necessary by economic circumstances and internal growth. In part, this strategy entailed divestitures of underperforming business units, such as (in the 1990s) flavors and fragrances and advanced materials. It also meant creative reorganization to rationalize operations and streamline the company's operations and to create maximum synergies with its R&D activities. In the 1980s, for example, BASF consolidated all of its North American operations under a newly created subsidiary, BASF Corporation. This consolidation generated substantial economies across the organization. This subsidiary now generates one-fifth of all company sales, with 90 percent of all sales by the corporation coming from plants operating within North America.

In 2001 BASF reorganized its core businesses into its five product segments—chemicals, plastics and fibers, performance products, agricultural products, and oil and gas—and these segments divided into 12 operating divisions. This new organization rationalized and maximized the functioning of value-added chains through the economies arising from "bundling" together products with common properties, production processes, and markets.

Equally important, BASF continually expanded internationally in order to sidestep the problems of restricted markets and cyclical downturns that the German economy as a whole, and the German chemical industry in particular, faced during the 1980s and 1990s. As with its competitor Dow Chemical, BASF internationalized through the strategic use of mergers, acquisitions, and joint ventures. Through the 1970s and 1980s, BASF's strategy was to expand its business and production capacity in North America through the construction of Greenfield plants as well as targeted acquisitions and selected joint partnerships. This expansion culminated in the consolidation in 1986 of all North American operations under a new subsidiary.

This period also saw the company begin operating in other strategic locations as well, including western Europe (Belgium, France, Spain, Denmark, the United Kingdom, Italy), Latin America (Argentina, Brazil, Mexico), Asia (Japan, India, China, South Korea), Australia, Africa (South Africa), and eastern Europe. By 2007 BASF entered into approximately 160 subsidiaries and joint ventures and operated more than 150 plant facilities worldwide.

See Also: Bayer; Dow Chemical; Germany; Research and Development.

Bibliography. F. Aftalion, *A History of the International Chemical Industry,* 2nd ed. (Chemical Heritage Press, 2001); A. Arora, E. Landau, and N. Rosenberg, eds., *Chemicals and Long-Term Economic Growth* (John Wiley & Sons, 1998); BASF, *Annual Report* (2007); J. Beer, *The Emergence of the German Dye Industry* (University of Illinois Press, 1959); A. Findlay, *A Hundred Years of Chemistry*, 3rd ed. (G. Duckworth, 1965); FundingUniverse.com, "BASF, AG" (2007); M. Goran, *The Story of Fritz Haber* (University of Oklahoma Press, 1967); L. Haber, *The Chemical Industry, 1900–1930: International Growth and Technological Change* (Oxford University Press, 1971); P. Hohenberg, *Chemicals in Western Europe, 1850–1914: An Economic Study of Technical Change* (Rand-McNally, 1967); P. Spitz, *Petrochemicals: The Rise of an Industry* (John Wiley & Sons, 1989); F. Taylor, *A History of Industrial Chemistry* (Abelard-Schuman, 1957).

Sanford L. Moskowitz
St. John's University

Basis Points

A basis point is a unit of measurement in the market for loan finance used by the market participants in relation to interest rates and bond yields. One basis point is one percent of one percent. The system of basis points is, therefore, grounded in the decimal system (Base 10). Interest rates are frequently quoted to three or four decimal points. One basis point equals 0.01 percent, 100 basis points equal 1.0 percent. For instance, if an interest rate changes from 4.65 percent to 4.67 percent it has changed by 2 basis points. A change from 4.6525 percent to 4.6757 percent would represent 2.32 basis points.

In relation to large principal sums, the money value of a basis point can be significant. For some transactions involving very large sums and very fine rates, even a basis point may be too large for practical purposes. In some instances hundredths or, even thousandths, of a basis point may be appropriate. For example, in a debt issue of $5 billion a hundredth of a basis point would be worth half a million dollars.

Basis points have become established as a common terminology that is useful for expressing small differences in interest rates, and they indicate the low order of magnitude at which the financial markets work. The term is usually abbreviated in use to BP, bp, or bip. It is more convenient, for example, to talk of 25 basis points rather than 0.25 percent, which offers potential for ambiguity and confusion. Given the small changes in interest rates with which the financial markets deal, it is appropriate to have a suitably calibrated measurement. The change in money value of a bond price in relation to a one basis point change in its yield is referred to as the *basis point value*. The term *basis point* should not be confused with *basis*, which is the term used to describe the difference between a futures contract price and a spot price.

Basis points are used to express a spread over a benchmark interest rate for a particular borrower. For fixed interest rates the benchmark will usually be a government bond rate and for floating (variable) interest rates a benchmark such as LIBOR (London Interbank Offered Rate) will be used. A company might, for example, arrange a 10-year floating-rate loan at LIBOR+ 75 basis points. If LIBOR were 4.375 percent, this would represent a rate of 5.125 percent. The spread in basis points will remain constant but the variability of the rate will be derived from the movement of the benchmark rate, which will change. The floating rate the company pays would vary with movements in LIBOR and the rate would be changed at agreed intervals, perhaps every six months.

Basis points are also used in pricing certain derivative instruments. For example, the premium for a credit default swap (CDS) will be expressed in basis points, representing the annual payment the bondholder will make to the seller of the swap, who assumes in return the default risk on the bond. The premium will be calculated as basis points of the face value of the bond. In the market for exchange-traded interest rate futures contracts, the minimum interest rate movement allowable is expressed in a unit known as a "tick," which is denominated in terms of basis points of interest. The tick size will vary from contract to contract. For example, the tick size for a three-month eurodollar interest rate futures contract traded in Chicago will be one basis point, whereas for a three-month euro LIBOR futures contract traded in London the tick size will be half a basis point.

See Also: Arbitrage; Bid/Ask Spread; Credit Ratings; Debt (Securities); Financial Markets; Futures Markets; Government Bonds; Interest Rates; LIBOR.

Bibliography. D. Blake, *Financial Market Analysis* (John Wiley, 2001); M. Durbin, *All About Derivatives* (McGraw-Hill, 2006); S. Valdez, *An Introduction to Global Financial Markets* (Palgrave Macmillan, 2007).

Tom Connor
University of Bedfordshire

Bayer

Bayer AG is a German chemical and pharmaceutical company founded in Barmen, Germany, by Friedrich Bayer in 1863. Bayer has its headquarters in Leverkusen, North Rhine-Westphalia, Germany. It is currently the third largest pharmaceutical company globally. Bayer was one of the important German chemical companies of the late 19th and 20th centuries. Its signature product was aspirin made from coal tar. The company in 2008 is a considerably different corporate entity. Since a major reorganization in 2003, it has become the strategic management holding company for the Bayer Group.

Bayer AG is composed of five main divisions: Healthcare, Crops Science, Materials Science, Technology Services, and Business Services. Bayer's Healthcare activities involve innovation and development in pharmaceutical and medical products; Bayer Crop Science deals with chemical products and services related to crop protection and nonagricultural pest control; Bayer Materials Science focuses on research and development of advanced and high-performance industrial chemical materials such as polycarbonate, polyurethane, and advanced organic polymers, advanced coatings, and such cutting-edge materials as nanotube systems and technology; Bayer Technology Services is Bayer's process and plant development arm, and includes plant design, engineering, construction, and optimization; and Bayer Business Services is Bayer's center for information technology (IT) design, development, and implementation in such areas as infrastructure and applications, procurement and logistics, human resources and management services, and finance and accounting.

In addition to these activities, Bayer has formed the company Currenta, a joint-venture service company with Lanxess that offers a variety of services dedicated to the chemical industry, including utility supply, waste management, infrastructure, and safety and security. As of December 2007 Currenta operates the CHEMPARK sites in Leverkusen, Dormagen, and Krefeld-Uerdingen, Germany.

Bayer AG has four major sales regions. In descending order of sales, these are Europe, North America, Asia/Pacific, and Latin America/Africa/Middle East. The year 2007 was a profitable year for the company. Sales rose by 12 percent to €32.4 billion. Between 2007 and 2008, Bayer experienced increased sales across all divisions and geographical regions.

History

As with the other major German chemical companies of the late 19th century, the company's success was based on advanced scientific and technical research in the synthesis of coal-tar-based organics. Bayer's first important commercial products were coal-tar dyes for use in the textile industry. Because of the chemical linkages between these compounds and pharmaceutical products, Bayer moved into biochemical research and innovation. By the start of World War I, Bayer, under the technical leadership of chemist Felix Hoffmann, discovered and brought to market such landmark pharmacological products as aspirin, sulfa drugs, and anesthetics.

During this period, Bayer became famous for holding tightly onto its patents to gain commercial advantage or as political leverage for German colonial interests. This policy was criticized by humanitarian groups at that time for the delays it caused in the delivery of life-saving drugs in Europe (e.g., to fight pneumonia) and less developed regions, such as Africa (e.g., to use against cases of sleeping sickness). Bayer also developed "mustard gas" that was used by the German military in World War I. As part of its reparations requirements following the war, Bayer's assets—including patents and trademarks—were confiscated by the United States and its allies. These assets were eventually acquired and freely worked by selected chemical firms in the United States, Canada, and other countries.

In 1925, as nationalistic calls for material self-sufficiency spread, the German chemical industry combined into the conglomerate IG Farbenindustrie (IG Farben), which soon became the technical (and financial) hub of the Nazi regime. Bayer was a central part of IG Farben, which owned 42.5 percent of the company. During World War II, IG Farben in general, and Bayer in particular, became an integral part of the Nazi war machine. As such, it played an active role in Nazi atrocities. It developed the chemical Zyklon B, used in the gas chambers at Auschwitz and other German concentration camps, and made extensive use of slave labor in factories associated with the camps. In 1947, members of Bayer's board of directors, indicted for war crimes, were convicted and sent to prison for up to eight years.

But Bayer, as did other firms of the IG Farben conglomerate, would in a short time rise from the ashes of war. In the postwar years, Bayer underwent significant change and expansion during the decades of globalization. With IG Farben ordered dismantled by the Allies, Bayer was once again an independent company. With the company allowed to continue operating its sites at Leverkusen and Elberfield, Bayer refurbished its plants, replacing outdated equipment and machinery, making full use of the newest American

chemical engineering. The company developed new products, including plastics, fibers, and insecticides and, through acquisition of AGFA, entered into photographic products. Bayer proved itself resilient and grew rapidly through the 1950s. During the decade, American investors, increasing impressed with the company's success, held up to 12 percent of the company's stock. During the 1960s, Bayer's domestic production grew 350 percent.

Recent Strategies

Bayer's success in the postwar period, and especially after 1970, has depended on the adoption of three distinct but closely interrelated strategies. First, it captured competitive differentiation in the market through original R&D through which it achieved "new product development, proprietary product technology, and low manufacturing cost." Second, Bayer has been adept at identifying and negotiating the creation of strategic merger and acquisition deals and, as critically, partnering and joint-venture arrangements. These have been primary instruments by which Bayer has been able to expand its pharmaceutical, healthcare, agrichemical, and advanced materials businesses, which the company considers the major drivers of its present and future growth. Third, and most important, the company has been successful in leveraging its first two strategies to embrace and exploit the globalization movement to maximum advantage.

The 1950s and 1960s ushered in the first wave of international expansion for the company. By the early 1960s, Bayer operated production plants in eight countries in Europe, Asia (India and Pakistan), and North America. The international expansion strategy of Bayer at this time focused on "final stage processing" by which the more expensive ("active") chemicals were made in Germany and then shipped abroad to be mixed in Bayer facilities (or by subcontractors) with less expensive, inert materials that would be prohibitively expensive to transport over long distances. These arrangements meant that Bayer could profitably manufacture and market products such as agrichemicals and pharmaceuticals in developing countries.

The 1960s and 1970s saw rapid growth for Bayer's presence in the U.S. market, not only exports but, even more significantly, foreign direct investments in the form of new and refurbished plants. The postwar economy was booming in the United States and, at the same time, U.S. tariffs were on the rise. Moreover, relatively high costs of labor and energy and limited markets in Europe meant that it made strategic sense for Bayer to dedicate direct investment money in the United States.

Important innovations from Bayer that were crucial for its market growth in the United States were the polyurethanes, dyestuffs, and engineering plastics. Through the 1970s, Bayer's foreign investment in the United States increased from $300 million to over $500 million. In the 1980s as well, Bayer actively pursued the spending of foreign direct investment in South America, taking advantage of the benefits afforded to foreign business by Mercosur, which induced privatization of government-held petrochemical holdings. Overall, by the late 1980s, about three-quarters of Bayer's total sales originated from outside Germany. By the 1990s, Bayer had advanced in Asia. Through the formation of strategic joint ventures and partnerships, Bayer has established a presence in China and Taiwan, as well as other parts of Asia. Beyond 2008, Bayer anticipates continued leveraging of its research and development work in the formation of joint ventures and strategic partnerships within its business areas over a growing number of international markets.

See Also: BASF; Foreign Direct Investment, Horizontal and Vertical; Germany; Research and Development.

Bibliography. F. Aftalion, A *History of the International Chemical Industry*, 2nd ed. (Chemical Heritage Press, 2001); A. Arora, E. Landau, and N. Rosenberg, eds., *Chemicals and Long-Term Economic Growth* (John Wiley & Sons, 1998); Bayer AG, *Annual Report* (2007); J. Beer, *The Emergence of the German Dye Industry* (University of Illinois Press, 1959); A. Findlay, *A Hundred Years of Chemistry*, 3rd ed. (G. Duckworth, 1965); FundingUniverse.com, "Bayer AG," (2007); L. Haber, *The Chemical Industry, 1900–1930: International Growth and Technological Change* (Oxford University Press, 1971); P. Hohenberg, *Chemicals in Western Europe, 1850–1914: An Economic Study of Technical Change* (Rand-McNally, 1967); P. Spitz, *Petrochemicals: The Rise of an Industry* (John Wiley & Sons, 1989); F. Taylor, *A History of Industrial Chemistry* (Abelard-Schuman, 1957).

SANFORD L. MOSKOWITZ
ST. JOHN'S UNIVERSITY

Behavioral Economics

The standard theoretical model of economic behavior presents human beings as calculating, rational agents who (a) are motivated by self interest and make clear and logical decisions based upon their preferences and incentives, and (b) possess an unlimited capability to process information. Although intuitively appealing, this model of consumer decision making has been criticized by many for its highly stylized presentation of reality that systematically fails to explain specific behavior. For some, the rational choice model has simply collapsed under the weight of contradictory evidence. Behavioral economics seeks to provide economic analysis with a more realistic, psychological foundation by examining the ways in which various aspects of individual and collective psychology influence economic decision making.

It is impossible, in the space available, to consider the full range of ideas associated with behavioral economics and its empirical findings. The following will therefore concentrate on outlining a number of key areas. The first point to consider is the notion of "bounded rationality." This refers to the view that economic agents are incapable of fully comprehending the complexity of the world in which they live, implying that they do not possess an unlimited capability to process information. A desire for cognitive simplification leads individuals to employ a number of techniques or rules-of-thumb, sometimes referred to as "cognitive heuristics" or "heuristics rules" in order to process information, evaluate outcomes and so make decisions and choices.

These "heuristics" highlight the human tendency to rely heavily upon specific reference points such as the use of memories, ideas they are familiar and comfortable with, and things that they have seen or heard in everyday life. If an unemployed worker is questioned about the total unemployed labor force in the economy, it is probable he or she will overestimate the figure due to the frequency of their contact with other unemployed workers. "Heuristics" are extremely important in economic decision making as they can lead to systematic errors such as overconfident assessments of future events. A famous example of this is the "gambler's fallacy," which highlights people's intuitions about probabilities and the erroneous belief that because a particular event has not been observed in a number of repeated independent trials it is likely to occur in the future.

Another key feature of behavioral economics is "framing" and the view that decisions or preferences are heavily influenced by the ways in which a choice is presented. This idea contradicts the predictions of the standard model of economic rationality and can be illustrated by means of the following example. Assume than an epidemic is predicted to kill 10,000 people. Two different programs, *A* and *B*, are proposed to deal with the problem, and it is left to the government to decide which to implement. If the government selects program *A*, 4,000 people will survive; if it selects program *B*, there is a 40 percent chance that 10,000 people will survive and a 60 percent that nobody will survive. Based on this information, research suggests that a majority of people would select program *A*. Let us now alter the way in which the choice is "framed" and suggest instead that the selection of program *A* will lead to 6,000 people dying, while under program *B* there is a 40 percent chance that nobody will die, and a 60 percent chance that 10,000 people will die. Even thought the second decision problem is identical to the first, research suggests that people will actually reverse their initial preferences and now select program *B*. By "framing" the decision problem in a different way, individuals have switched from being risk averse to exhibiting risk-seeking behavior.

Behavioral economics deals with other important ideas, ranging from the altruistic aspects of human nature (a view that runs counter to standard economic theory) through to issues involving self-control and willpower. The implications of this latter point are worthy of examination. The rational choice model predicts that economic agents will be better off the more choices and opportunities that are available to them. Yet evidence of the self-control problems faced by many people contradicts this view. One example of this would be addictive behavior (such as over-dependence on alcohol or tobacco) that highlights people making choices and decisions that conflict with their long-term interests. This suggests that people may actually be worse off if the number of choices available to them increases, so indicating an important role for government to impose control mechanisms.

Behavioral economics is a rapidly developing, interdisciplinary discipline that draws heavily on research from, among other areas, anthropology, psychology, and sociology. Of growing interest is the new field of neuroeconomics, which employs brain scan technology to examine how the innate structure of the mind influences decisions. By seeking to gain greater insights into the decision-making process of both individuals and institutions, the study of behavioral economics has important implications for a number of subject and policy areas including the study of financial markets, development economics and international poverty, labor economics, health economics, and policies directed toward tackling environmental catastrophe.

See Also: Behavioral Finance; Neuroeconomics.

Bibliography. C. Camerer, G. Loewenstein, and M. Rabin *Advances in Behavioral Economics* (Russell Sage, 2004); P. Diamond and H. Vartiainen, eds., *Behavioral Economics and its Applications* (Princeton University Press, 2007); D. Kahneman and A. Tversky, "Prospect Theory: An Analysis of Decision under Risk," *Econometrica* (v.47/2, 1979); D. Kahneman, J.L. Knetsch, and R. H. Thaler. "Fairness as a Constraint on Profit Seeking," *American Economics Review* (v.76/4, 1986); A. Lewis, ed., *The Cambridge Handbook of Psychology and Economic Behaviour* (Cambridge University Press, 2008); M. Rabin, "Psychology and Economics," *Journal of Economic Literature* (v.36/1, 1998); R. T. Thaler, *Quasi-Rational Economics* (Russell Sage, 1991); N. Williamson, *An Introduction to Behavioral Economics* (Palgrave Macmillan, 2007).

CHRISTOPHER J. GODDEN
UNIVERSITY OF MANCHESTER

Behavioral Finance

Behavioral finance is closely related to the study of behavioral economics and seeks to integrate cognitive psychology into the study of financial markets and institutions. Due to the availability of data, behavioral finance is the branch of economics were the application of behavioral ideas has had its greatest impact.

Behavioral finance argues that individuals attach different levels of satisfaction to gains and losses (a concept referred to in the literature as "prospect theory"). Strong risk aversion among individuals suggests that they view losses as significantly more painful than equivalent gains. Such behavior may therefore manifest itself in a strong unwillingness to sell failing investments since it would force the individual to realize real losses. A further development on this, referred to as "mental accounting," suggests that people evaluate the effects of financial decisions by separating gains and losses, implying that satisfaction is dependent on the ways in which gains arise rather than their effects on final, overall wealth.

A second aspect of behavioral finance is the belief that investment behavior is heavily influenced by simplifying forecasting strategies ("heuristics") that assist market participants in making investment decisions. Whereas standard theory argues that it is useless to form such decisions based on an extrapolation of past exchange rate movements, stock price movements, or earnings trends, research suggests that investors actually do employ this simple technique. "Heuristics" can lead investors to have a disproportionate view of their abilities, possibly make them believe they can directly influence outcomes, and so make decisions without adequate information. Such cognitive biases have the potential to generate systematic errors and can, in extreme cases, generate stock market bubbles or crashes.

A third aspect is the view that investors do not engage in full portfolio diversification, but overinvest in areas they understand or are comfortable with ("familiarity breeds investment"). Furthermore, individuals who regularly deal with financial risk may be unable to fully comprehend the risks associated with different investments, so leading them to attach higher risk premiums to certain investments. A limited knowledge of foreign markets, for example, may lead investors to place a higher risk premium on foreign investments over domestic investments.

Behavioral finance draws upon a large body of research that highlights the inability of standard models to explain a number of financial phenomena. Historical data has highlighted a dramatic disparity between actual share price movements when compared with those calculated via the dividend discount model (which calculates the value of a share price, at any moment in time, as being equal to the sum of discounting future dividends). Such evidence has led many behavioral economists to conclude that cognitive psychology must play an important role in determining stock market volatility. For example, cognitive biases can exert powerful effects on asset prices, with investors under reacting or over reacting to new information. Research on the behavior of stock prices suggests that investors may push prices too high in response to good news, or push them too low in response to bad news.

Attempts have been made to salvage the idea of rational and efficient capital markets by arguing that the existence of only a few rational agents in the market will negate the effects of behavioral factors. A simple example will illustrate this idea. Assume that there are two kinds of agents in the market, those who conform to the standard model of economic rationality, group R, and those who do not conform to the standard model and who instead employ some heuristic rule in forming their decisions, group H. If, via the use of their heuristic rule, group H drive the exchange rate above its fundamental value, it is argued that group R will response to the profit opportunity and bring to rate back down. The outcome, in other words, is seen to be consistent with the rational economic model even through some of the participants are following simplifying rules-of-thumb to make their decisions. Such arguments do not appear to be borne out by the available evidence however, and some economists have argued that it may take a significant number of group R traders to eliminate the actions of group H traders.

By seeking to place the human element firmly at the center of the investment decision-making process, the study of behavioral finance has important implications for policy regulation of financial markets.

See Also: Behavioral Economics; Neuroeconomics.

Bibliography. W. M. F. De Bondt and R. Thaler, "Does the Stock Market Overreact?" *Journal of Finance* (v.40/3, 1985); P. De Grauwe and M. Grimaldi, *The Exchange Rate in a Behavioral Finance Framework* (Princeton University Press, 2006); A. Schleifer, *Inefficient Markets: An Introduction to Behavioral Finance* (Oxford University Press, 2000); R. Thaler, ed., *Advances in Behavioral Finance* (Russell Sage, 1993).

Christopher J. Godden
University of Manchester

Belarus

The Republic of Belarus (also Byelorussia) is an eastern European country, which was formerly the most western of all Soviet Union republics. It became independent in 1991, although it largely aligns its foreign policy with its eastern neighbor, the Russian Federation. Although the country had a very solid industrial base in the last years of the Soviet Union, it has lost much of its advantage with the breakup of the Soviet Union and the loss of the former Soviet internal market. Its advantage has also weakened under an authoritarian political regime largely dominated by the president.

Belarus regained its independence in 1991 with the agreed breakup of the Soviet Union. It is, however, a member of the Commonwealth of Independent States (CIS), a treaty-based organization bringing together a number of the former Soviet republics. The Russian Federation plays a pivotal role in the CIS leadership. Historically Belarus, as such, was never independent and sovereign in the past. During World War II, there was an attempt to create a Nazi-supported puppet state, but to a large extent the area of Belarus was directly controlled by the Germans, and many people suffered.

It has been reported that every fourth person in Belarus was killed in World War II. The war devastated the national economy, as those factories that were not affected by military operations were relocated to either Russia or Germany. It is estimated that more than half of the pre–World War II economy was destroyed or relocated. Interestingly, Belarus is a founding member of the United Nations (UN), although in 1944 it was a constituent republic of the Soviet Union (together with Ukraine). This inconsistency gave the United States more than one vote in the General Assembly of the UN, but this right has never been exercised.

The economy of Belarus recovered very well in the postwar period, and it became a major industrial base in the region. This was supported by the promotion of immigration to Belarus of professionals and others who would spur economic growth. To a large extent the industrialization plan worked well, and achieved steady positive results until the breakup of the Soviet economy. In the model of a centralized economy, cross-republic (cross-jurisdiction) eco-

nomic collaboration and integration were one of the major tasks. Therefore, the factories in Belarus depended largely on the raw material produced in other Soviet republics, and all the plans were made when energy prices were more or less centrally fixed (capped) regardless of the movements in the international market for energy.

With the breakup of the federal common market and liberalization of input prices, Belarus factories lost regular supplies and most of them are de facto bankrupt, although on paper they may still be in existence and operational. One of the possible solutions is the renting of factory premises (usually fractionally) to individual entrepreneurs, where they accept the obligation to employ some of the de facto laid-off workers of the state-owned factory. However, these attempts have not yielded long-term stability.

The economy of Belarus has recorded high growth rates in the last few years. This is mainly due to the fairly low starting base. The Republic of Belarus is regarded as a nondemocratic country, where elections are not universally recognized. The officially reported growth rates are just below 10 percent, and this certainly would have put Belarus on the map of economic successes if it were not such an isolated country. The regime of President Aleksandr Lukashenka is regarded as extremely autocratic (dictatorial) and stifling of any form of societal innovation. On a few occasions, foreign nationals have been evicted from Belarus, or simply advised to leave.

The major industries in Belarus are production of heavy industrial track, heavy chemical industries (usually the most "dirty" ones), and some energy production. The computing industry is growing, as well as the services sector. Agriculture is still rather intensive. Some attempts have been made to privatize companies, but success was not reported. However, it is possible that silent nomenclature privatization has taken place, although not made public as yet.

In line with countries with similar political regimes, the nomenclature privatization model is most likely to have taken place. This process is usually supported by purposely initiated high (hyper-) inflation, which was recorded in Belarus in the late 1990s and early 2000s. At present, the nominal inflation is still higher than reported economic growth, and overshoots it by about 2 percent. The overall economic climate for entrepreneurs and foreign direct investments is not regarded as very good, and most likely it will remain so in the foreseeable future.

See Also: Russia; Transition Economies; Ukraine.

Bibliography. A. Axell, *Russia's Heroes, 1941–45* (Carroll & Graf, 2002); S. M. Birgerson, *After the Breakup of a Multi-Ethnic Empire* (Praeger/Greenwood, 2002); K. D. Martinsen, *The Russian-Belarusian Union and the Near Abroad* (Norwegian Institute for Defence Studies/NATO, 2002); J. Zaprudnik, *Belarus: At a Crossroads in History* (Westview Press, 1993).

Željko Šević
Glasgow Caledonian University

Belgium

Belgium (11,787 sq. mi., population 10,666,866 in 2008, GDP $377 billion in 2007) is one of the founding members of the European Union (EU), and a key participant in the history and economics of Europe for centuries. Along with the Netherlands and Luxembourg, Belgium is part of the Benelux group of states, which together formed the Low Countries in the Middle Ages and early modern era. The so-called battlefield of Europe, the area that became Belgium was the site of major battles among European powers from the beginning of the 17th century until Belgian independence was declared in 1830.

Due to its location and intermingled history with surrounding nations, Belgium has three official languages: Dutch, French, and German. Flemish is the common term both for the Belgian Dutch dialect and the Belgian Dutch people, and the Flemish masters are among the great Renaissance and Baroque painters. Because the Belgian Revolution that led to the nation's independence began with the poor treatment of French-speaking Catholics in what was then the United Kingdom of the Netherlands, Catholicism has played an important role in Belgian culture and politics since the state's inception.

The country has a number of major political parties—thanks to its linguistic heritage, Belgium's political parties tend to be divided by linguistic lines as well as political ones—among which Christian Democrats have long been prominent. The basic tenets of Christian Democracy call for applying Christian principles to public policy; Christian Democratic parties tend to be socially conservative but otherwise left of center with respect to economic and labor issues, civil rights, and foreign policy. From 1958 to 1999, the Christian Democrats remained in power in Belgium, until public outcry over a food safety scandal mobilized the "rainbow coalition" of the Dutch and Francophone Greens, Liberals, and Social Democrats.

Various party coalitions have been in power in the decade since, and as of 2008 Belgium is in a political crisis due in large part to the disagreement between Dutch and Francophone parties over constitutional reform, after a series of liberal legal reforms decriminalizing certain drugs and legalizing same-sex marriages. Pressure from the king has been insufficient to resolve differences between the parties to form a government coalition.

The king (currently Albert II, b. June 6, 1934) is Belgium's head of state and appoints various governmental ministers who compose the federal government, including the prime minister. The Belgian Constitution preserves an equal ratio of Francophone and Dutch ministers. The bicameral parliament consists of a Senate made up of seven representatives appointed by each of the three language-group community parliaments, 40 directly elected representatives, and 10 "senators by right" (which include the king's children) who by tradition abstain from voting; and a Chamber of Representatives with 150 members elected from 11 electoral districts. Voting in Belgium is compulsory.

Belgium is highly industrialized, with a long tradition of supporting free market policies and an open economy. Compared to other countries, it ranks among the highest in the world in terms of exports per capita, and its principal exports are automobiles, food products (such as the legendary chocolate), metals, textiles, petroleum products, and diamonds, exports that speak both to its industrial and industrious natures and to its long history as one of Europe's cultural epicenters. The Flemish regions historically outpace the Walloon (French-speaking) regions economically and in manufacturing in particular. The first country on the continent to adopt the principles and technologies of the Industrial Revolution, Belgium was riddled with mines and mills throughout the first half of the 19th century, and remained one of the leading industrial nations (behind only the United Kingdom and later the United States) until shortly before World War I. Like much of Europe, it felt the blows of the Great Depression in the 1930s and the oil crises in the 1970s.

In the aftermath of World War II, the Benelux economic union—taking its name from the first letters of Belgium, Netherlands, and Luxembourg—was formed between those three nations for common trade, and is now sometimes used to refer rather more generally to those countries which once were "Low." The precursor to Benelux is the Belgium-Luxembourg Economic Union, an economic and monetary union between those two nations, which now occupies itself with fairly specific points of procedure since its major aims have been subsumed by the EU. The Benelux states were major players in the formation of the EU from the very start.

See Also: European Monetary Union; European Union; Luxembourg; Netherlands.

Bibliography. Paul Arblaster, *A History of the Low Countries* (Palgrave Macmillan, 2005); J. C. H. Blom and Emiel Lamberts, eds., *History of the Low Countries,* James C. Kennedy, trans. (Oxford, 1999); Bernard A. Cook, *Belgium: A History* (Peter Lang, 2005); John Fitzmaurice, *The Politics of Belgium: A Unique Federalism* (Westview Press, 1996).

BILL KTE'PI
INDEPENDENT SCHOLAR

Bel-20 Index (Brussels)

The Bel-20 Index is a real-time (computed in principle every 15 seconds) basket of minimum 10 and maximum 20 stocks (listed on Euronext Brussels and meeting some specific criteria) that exhibits the highest free float adjusted market capitalization. The market capitalization is the public consensus on the value of a company's equity (computed by multiplying the share price by the number of shares outstanding) and the "free float" represents simply the percentage of the stocks that is freely tradable on the market. The stocks composing the Bel-20 Index are also weighted according to their market capitalization adjusted by the free float.

In finance, an index is essentially a virtual portfolio of securities representing a specific (sub-) market.

Each index has its own computation methodology. The index value is meaningless (indeed it is expressed in "points"), but its changes are informative. It is not possible to invest in an index; nevertheless, one can invest in a fund (exchange-traded fund, index fund) that replicates the index (returns) as closely as possible. Different indexes need to be composed to represent the financial markets in diverse ways and to compute risk and performance measures. Indeed, a risk or performance measure alone has no value if it has not been adjusted to a pertinent benchmark.

The Bel-20 Index was launched in late December 1990 at an arbitrary level of 1,000 points (called its base value). The Bel-20 is a market value–weighted index and consists of the stocks of approximately 20 of the leading Belgian companies traded on Euronext Brussels. The Bel-20 Index is the major benchmark index of Euronext Brussels and represents the main part of the Belgian stock market. In fact, the principal objective of this index is exactly the replication of the Belgian equity market.

Its composition is reviewed annually (except for exceptional cases). This review is based on the information as of the end of December and is effective the first trading day of March. However, after a recent reform (2008), the reviewing delay can be reduced to one month (instead of one year) when the index integrates less than 20 stocks. This reform has also relaxed some selection criteria (some stocks taken over by a foreign group can remain in the index) and the weight of a Bel-20 component cannot exceed 12 percent at review time (instead of 15 percent before the reform).

In June 2008 the 20 companies composing the Bel-20 were Ackermans, Agfa-Gevaert, Bekaert, Belgacom, CNP, Cofinimmo-Sicafi, Colruyt, Delhaize Group, Dexia, Fortis, GBL, Inbev (Ex. Interbrew), KBC, Mobistar, Nyrstar, Omega Pharma, Solvay, Suez, UCB, and Umicore. The three main components were Suez (16 percent), KBC (12 percent), and Inbev (12 percent).

To improve the visibility of the Belgian equity market, Euronext Brussels integrated two other benchmarks in 2005: the Bel-Mid (composed of approximately 33 companies) and the Bel-Small (composed of approximately 46 companies) Indexes. Their composition is reviewed each quarter (which is generally more frequent than the Bel-20 Index) and these two indexes are also continuously quoted. Together, the three indexes (Bel-20, Bel-Mid, and Bel-Small) cover about 70 percent of the Belgian listed companies. There are an increasing number of financial products that derive their value from the Bel-20 Index. Indeed, investors can buy futures contracts, options contracts, and other more complex derivatives on the Bel-20 Index.

Euronext Brussels has launched a new index called the "Bel-20 Volatility Index" to measure the implied volatility of the option prices. This index intends to offer the needed tools to monitor the option prices. The markets can use this volatility index as a real barometer: A high level means that the markets will expect more volatility in the underlying, and inversely. The Bel-20 Volatility Index follows the traditional VIX methodology (an American indicator based on the options contracts traded on the S&P 500 Index and quoted on the Chicago Board Options Exchange). The Euronext board hopes that this index integration will improve the accuracy of professionals' perceptions about the Belgian market.

The Bel-20 Index has different reported codes (or ticker symbols) depending on the data provider considered. The main codes are the following: the Mnemonic code is "BEL20," the ISIN code is "BE0389555039," the Reuters code is ".BEL20," and the Bloomberg code is "BEL20."

See Also: ATX Index; Belgium; CAC 40 Index (Paris); DAX Index (Germany); Fortis; S&P 500 Index; Swiss Market Index; Taiwan Weighted Index.

Bibliography. "Consultation Paper: Bel-20 Index" (NYSE Euronext, 2008); "Rules for the BEL-20 Index" (Euronext, August 2006).

Laurent Bodson
University of Liège

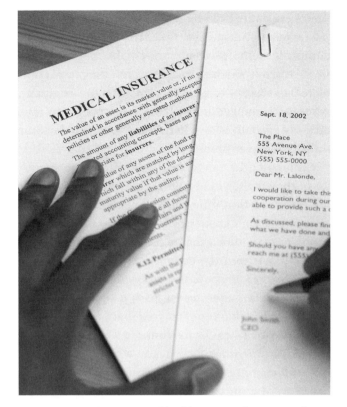

In countries without national healthcare, employers are often burdened with offering health insurance in benefit packages.

Benefits

Benefits are payments or entitlements that are provided by an employer and offered to its employees. Benefits are also referred to as company benefits, employee benefits, and fringe benefits. In most cases, benefits are promised to an employee as part of an employment agreement. Benefits can also be extended via the government. In this situation, people are provided payments or entitlements based on being a citizen of that country.

Some types of benefits include health insurance, life insurance, paid vacation and sick leave, maternity and paternity leave, 401(k) contributions, pensions, profit-sharing, bonuses, and stock options. Companies also provide nonfinancial benefits like employee wellness programs, weight loss programs, and exercise facilities. In many cases, the employer will provide access to the benefit and make payments on behalf of the employee. For example, many companies will provide employees with health insurance. This usually includes providing access to the healthcare and paying a portion of the premiums on behalf of the employee.

The purpose of providing these entitlements or benefits is to attract and retain employees. Typically, companies will offer benefits along with a salary as part of an employment contract. Some companies are able to secure and maintain more qualified employees because of the benefits that they offer. In many cases, the organization will increase the value of the original benefits package over time. For example, in some companies, employees are not eligible to participate in 401k profit-sharing programs until they have completed two years of employment with the company. After an employee is eligible for the program, they are only partially vested in the beginning and become fully vested over time.

Generally, the employer bears all or the majority of the cost for the company benefits. For benefits like paid vacation time and sick leave, the employer bears all of the cost. However, many benefits, like healthcare, require a shared cost that is split between the employer and the employee. For healthcare, the employer typically pays the major portion of the premiums, while the employee pays a smaller portion. Providing benefits to employees can be quite costly. As the cost of healthcare continues to rise in most countries, providing employees with paid vacation time, stock options, healthcare, and other benefits has become quite expensive. Therefore, most companies try to limit these expenses. If not managed properly, the costs associated with company benefits can become a financial burden for the organization.

Company benefits are not always offered to all employees. The cost associated with providing benefits is a major factor influencing why benefits are not extended to all employees. Generally, company benefits are extended to employees who are considered full-time and/or salaried. Although some organizations provide benefits to part-time or hourly employees, these benefits are usually limited and not comparable to the benefits provided to full-time employees. In most cases, part-time or hourly workers are provided very few, if any, benefits at all.

Cultural Influence

Providing employees with company benefits has become customary in many countries around the world. Cultural influences and laws have a direct impact on what benefits a company can and will provide its employees. As a result, the benefits that are offered to an employee can vary significantly from one company to another. Most companies end up offering a unique package of benefits that is based on its country's customs and laws, the size and type of organization, and its financial situation. Some other factors that can directly impact which benefits a company offers an employee can include things related to the employee, like educational background, skill level, job title, and length of time the employee has worked for the company.

Where a company is located has a major effect on the benefits that it offers its employees. That's because a company's location can influence which benefits it can legally provide, the company's culture, and employee expectations. This influence can be significant and tends to vary greatly by country. Countries have laws and cultural norms with different beliefs regarding basic rights and what citizens are entitled to have provided by the government. Some countries have cultures and governments where the government provides very few benefits to its citizens, while some countries have governments that provide a lot of benefits to its citizens. This has a direct impact on the benefits that a company provides to its employees.

Many countries believe that their citizens are entitled to basic healthcare. Therefore, these countries will have national healthcare that provides all or a portion of the healthcare to its citizens. If a company is located in a country that provides healthcare to its citizens, then there is less burden on the company to provide healthcare benefits to its employees. In countries like Great Britain, Canada, and Botswana, the government provides all or some portion of the healthcare for its citizens. As a result, the companies that are located in these countries have less of a burden when it comes to providing basic benefits like healthcare to its employees.

If the company is located in a country where the government does not provide some of these basic benefits to its citizens, then there is typically a greater burden on the company to provide these types of benefits to its employees. In the United States, there is no national healthcare. Therefore, the majority of the people have to work to get access to healthcare. In a country like this, the companies that provide employment tend to provide healthcare as part of the benefits package for employees and bear a greater cost burden.

Some countries provide other benefits to their citizens like social security, pension plans, and disability insurance, which can also impact the benefits that a company offers to its employees. Similarly, a country's laws can have a significant impact on what benefits a company is required to offer its employees. In many countries, there are laws that require the companies to offer benefits like paid time off, paid sick leave, maternity leave, etc. For example, when compared to many other countries, Germany has employment and labor laws that are very favorable to employees, so companies that are located in Germany are required to offer fairly generous benefits because of the employment and labor laws in that country. These laws require the employers in Germany to provide a lot of benefits to the employee; employees are required to receive benefits like generous paid vacation and sick leave. These types of laws place a greater burden on the companies that are located in Germany versus companies that are located in other parts of the world.

As stated previously, benefits are entitlements or payments that are granted to an employee via an employment contract with an employer. The types of benefits that are offered by a company are influenced by many factors, including the laws, culture, and government benefits offered in the country where it is located. Although providing employee benefits is customary, it can be quite costly and create a burden for the company. For this reason, benefits are generally not offered to all employees. However, companies will extend benefits to retain and maintain qualified employees.

See Also: Employer–Employee Relations; Family Leave; Healthcare Benefits/Systems; Holidays; Maternity Leave; Perquisites; Work/Personal Life Balance.

Bibliography. M. Ala and B. Brunaczki, "Online Benefits Solutions—A New Trend in Managing Employee Benefits Programs," *Journal of Health Care Finance* (2003); S. Collins, "Employer-Based Health Insurance Past, Present, and Future," *Healthcare Financial Management* (2007); M. Danis et al., "Low-Income Employees' Choices Regarding Employment Benefits Aimed at Improving the Socioeconomic Determinants of Health," *American Journal of Public Health* (2007); R. Gisonny and S. Douglas, "Nationwide Savings Plan Automatic Enrollment Getting Associates Prepared for Retirement," *Benefits Quarterly* (2008); B. McGuinness, "The Change in Employee Loyalty," *Nursing Management* (1998); "The New Equilibrium: Work/Life Balance," *Benefits Quarterly* (2008); Christopher G. Reddick and Jerrell D. Coggburn, *Handbook of Employee Benefits and Administration* (CRC publishing, 2008).

LYNNE A. PATTEN
CLARK ATLANTA UNIVERSITY

Bent Measuring Stick (or Performance Appraisal)

As perhaps the most central of human resources (HR) systems, performance appraisal has commanded the attention of organizational scientists for many years. In the organizational context, performance is usually defined as the extent to which an organizational member contributes to achieving the goals of the organization. Performance appraisal is defined as the process of identifying, evaluating, and developing the work performance of the employee in the organization, so that organizational goals and objectives are effectively achieved while, at the same time, benefiting employees in terms of recognition, receiving feedback, and offering career guidance. The terms *performance assessment*, *performance evaluation*, and *performance management* are also used to describe the process.

Performance appraisal is an inseparable part of organizational life. Formal performance appraisals are required to justify a wide range of HR decisions such as selection, compensation, promotion, and training. Performance appraisal characteristics include target (individual, team), type (outcome-, behavioral-, or competency-based), and data source (manager or multirater). Especially in team-based organizations there is a critical need for effective leadership in designing and implementing performance appraisal systems. Performance appraisal systems must move from a focus on the outcomes, behaviors, and competencies of teams to those of individuals.

Ineffective appraisal systems can bring many problems including low morale, decreased employee productivity, and a lessening of an employee's commitment and support for the organization. If employees are confident in the fairness of the appraisal process, they are more likely to accept performance ratings, even adverse ones, because they perceive a fair decision making process. On the other hand, if the employees perceive the process as unfair and not systematic, it is unlikely that they will accept the outcome of the appraisal process.

One way to enhance appraisal system fairness, reach organizational justice, and face subjectivity is 360-degree appraisal system design, which requires obtaining information from all sources including supervisors, subordinates, peers, suppliers, clients, and consultants.

In general, anyone who has useful information on how an employee does the job may be a source in the 360-degree appraisal. On another but related issue, participation gives an opportunity to the employees to raise their voices into the appraisal process. Greater employee participation (i.e., goal-setting process, performance standards, qualitative and quantitative evaluation criteria, self-evaluation) increases employee satisfaction and generates an atmosphere of cooperation and support, reducing rater-ratee conflicts, especially during the performance appraisal interview.

The performance appraisal interview is a potentially important part of any organization's performance appraisal system. The appraisal interview might function in several important ways: Providing feedback to employees, developing employees, and discussing compensation, job status, and disciplinary decisions. The interviewer must be sensitive to employee needs for privacy and confidentiality. It is very important to provide undivided attention during the interview and reserve adequate time for discussion.

Management's feedback is essential in gaining the maximum benefits from goal setting. Without feedback, employees are unable to make adjustments in job performance or receive positive reinforcement for effective job behavior. Effective performance feedback is timely, specific, behavioral in nature, and presented by a credible source. Performance feedback is effective in changing employee work behavior and enhances employee job satisfaction and performance.

In general, the superior's knowledge of the subordinate's job and performance, superior's support of the subordinate, and welcoming the subordinate's participation are key factors for producing effective interviews. The appropriate function, frequency, and format of the interview, as well as goal setting and actual subordinate participation, depend on characteristics of the employee and the job.

As stated, most performance appraisal systems depend heavily on subjective ratings of performance provided by supervisors, peers, subordinates, and job incumbents. Despite a heavy reliance on performance ratings, it is generally acknowledged that they are too often contaminated by systematic errors (leniency, central tendency, halo, and contrast errors). Rater training programs can have positive effects on the psychometric quality of performance ratings. Methods used to provide training are lectures, group discussion, and

practice and feedback. In general, the more involved raters become in the training process the greater the outcome. Providing raters with the opportunity to participate in a group discussion along with practice and feedback exercises produces better results than presenting training material to them through a lecture. Practice and feedback exercises appear to be a necessary ingredient for increasing accuracy in ratings.

Today, organizations face environments characterized by increasing dynamism and competition, and sustainable fit can be achieved only by developing a flexible organization. The importance of developing and applying HR practices aimed at achieving fit is crucial. HR systems such as performance appraisal systems have relatively strong universalistic relationships with important measures of organizational performance.

See Also: Commitment; Employer–Employee Relations; Empowerment; Leadership; Motivation.

Bibliography. Amy Delpo, *The Performance Appraisal Handbook: Legal & Practical Rules for Managers* (NOLO 2007); Christoph Demmke, *Performance Assessment in the Public Services of the EU Member States: Procedure for Performance Appraisal, for Employee Interviews and Target Agreements* (European Institute of Public Administration, 2007); Clive Fletcher, *Appraisal, Feedback and Development: Making Performance Review Work* (Routledge, 2008); Margaret Foot and Caroline Hook, *Introducing Human Resource Management* (Prentice Hall/Financial Times, 2008); Martin M. Greller, "Subordinate Participation in the Appraisal Interview," *Journal of Applied Psychology* (v.60/5, 1975); I. M. Jawahar, "The Influence of Perceptions of Fairness on Performance Appraisal Reactions," *Journal of Labor Research* (v.28/4, 2007); Susanne G. Scott and Walter O. Einstein, "Strategic Performance Appraisal in Team-based Organizations: One Size Does Not Fit All," *Academy of Management Executive* (v.15/2, 2001).

Panagiotis V. Polychroniou
University of Patras

BERI

International market entry always warrants a careful assessment of the risk associated with foreign target countries. In evaluating and selecting foreign markets, companies may choose to follow a highly customized country-by-country approach or to work with established country-comparisons. One such established comparison is BERI. BERI, or Business Environment Risk Intelligence, is a company providing ratings, analyses, and forecasts for more than 140 countries. BERI's services are designed to assist executives in risk assessment when making decisions about entering foreign markets or establishing operations abroad. Their most widely known service, Business Risk Service (BRS) is published three times per year. For each country it provides a general outlook outlining opportunities and problems, economic and financial indicators, political information including a future probable scenario, and a composite score, called the Profit Opportunity Recommendation, that consists of the Political Risk Index (PRI), the Operations Risk Index (ORI), and the Remittance and Repatriation Factor (R-Factor).

The PRI provides an assessment of a country's political risk. It is based on the qualitative judgments of 10 political and social factors—six internal causes of political risk (fractionalization of the political spectrum; fractionalization by language, religion, or ethnicity; coercive measures; mentality; social conditions; organization; and strength of forces for a radical government), two external causes of political risk (dependence on a major hostile power; negative influences of regional political forces), and two symptoms of political risk (societal conflict; instability as perceived by nonconstitutional changes, assassinations, and guerrilla wars). Calculated on a scale from 0 to 100 points, countries above 70 points are considered low-risk countries, while countries with a score of less than 40 are considered to be of prohibitive risk.

The ORI is the weighted average of scores on a list of 15 different political, economic, financial, and structural variables. These are policy continuity, attitude toward foreign investors, degree of privatization, monetary inflation, balance of payments, bureaucratic delays, economic growth, currency convertibility, enforceability of contracts, labor cost/productivity, professional services and contractors, communications and transportation, local management and partners, short-term credit, and long-term loans and venture capital. The ORI is provided on a scale from 0 to 100 points with points above 70 indicating stable

countries with a favorable business climate and points below 40 indicating nonacceptable countries.

The R-Factor gives an indication of the risk that profits and capital cannot be transferred out of a country or that access to convertible currencies is barred. It is calculated using a vast amount of data, which are categorized into four sub-indices—Legal Framework, Foreign Exchange Generation, Accumulated International Reserves, and Foreign Debt Assessment. The three indices are then combined into the Profit Opportunity Recommendation (POR). The POR is a measure of general country risk and classifies countries into four categories—fit for foreign direct investment, suitable for medium to long-term contractual relationships, ideal for transaction-by-transaction trade, or not suited for any business activity. It is calculated for the present, for one-year, and for five-year forecasts.

BERI derives its data from two independent expert panels that provide country ratings and qualitative observations. One panel judges political conditions in countries, while the other offers perspectives on the operating environment. The members of each panel are more than 100 senior bank and corporate executives as well as government officials. In addition to BRS, BERI offers other services, including the Financial Ethics Index, the Quality of Workforce Index, Lenders Risk Ratings, and Mineral Extraction Risk Assessment. Founded in 1966 by F. T. Haner, BERI operates globally and is headquartered in the United States.

Other indices similar to BRS, albeit less widely known, include the International Country Risk Guide (ICRG), S. J. Rundt's Country Reports, the Peren-Clement-Index, the Economist Intelligence Unit's Country Risk Service (CRS), Euromoney's Credit Rating Score, Reuters & Oesterreichisches Kontrollbank's CEE Business Climate Index, Institutional Investor's Country Creditworthiness, and the World Bank's Ease of Doing Business Ranking.

See Also: Corruption; Country Screening; Foreign Direct Investment; Risk Management.

Bibliography. Business BERI, "Risk Service," www.beri. com (cited March 2009); Jean-Claude Cosset and Jean Roy, "The Determinants of Country Risk Ratings," *Journal of International Business Studies* (v.22/1, 1991); F. T. Haner and John S. Ewing, *Country Risk Assessment: Theory and Worldwide Practice* (Praeger, 1985); Suhejla Hoti and

Michael McAleer, "An Empirical Assessment of Country Risk Ratings and Associated Models," *Journal of Economic Surveys* (v.18/4, 2004); Llewellyn Howell, *The Handbook of Country and Political Risk Analysis* (PRS Group, 2007); Llewellyn Howell, *Political Risk Assessment: Concept, Method, and Management* (PRS Group, 2001).

GERHARD APFELTHALER
CALIFORNIA LUTHERAN UNIVERSITY

Berkshire Hathaway

Berkshire Hathaway, Inc. (Berkshire) is a holding company incorporated in Delaware that owns a diverse set of subsidiary businesses. Its corporate headquarters is located in Omaha, Nebraska. As of the end of 2007, Berkshire and its subsidiaries employed about 233,000 persons. Berkshire is a unique company in two ways: (1) by its success with its investments in stocks, bonds, and cash equivalents, which are overseen by its chairman, Warren E. Buffett, and its vice chairman, Charles T. Munger; and (2) by its extraordinarily decentralized management style as evidenced by minimal involvement by its corporate headquarters in the day-to-day operations of its subsidiaries.

Berkshire has a portfolio of investment in common stocks with a market value estimated at about $74.9 billion. This group of stocks is closely followed by the financial community. Berkshire has significant holdings (valuations in excess of $4 billion) in the following companies (in descending order of investment): Coca-Cola Company, Wells Fargo & Company, American Express Company, Procter & Gamble Company, Burlington Northern Santa Fe, Johnson & Johnson, and Kraft Foods, Inc.

Berkshire looks to invest in companies that show improvements in earnings and companies that possess superiorities that "make life difficult for their competitors." Berkshire acquires and operates companies based on the following criteria: first, large purchases generating at least $75 million in pre-tax earnings; second, companies with demonstrated consistent earnings power; third, businesses earning good returns on equity while employing little or no debt; fourth, management already in place; fifth, businesses that are simple to understand; and finally, businesses with a known offering price (and a friendly takeover). The following sections describe the business sectors and operating businesses of Berkshire.

Insurance and Reinsurance

Berkshire's 60-some insurance businesses are its most important subsidiaries and operate in both the U.S. domestic market and foreign markets. These subsidiaries compete in both the primary insurance market and in the reinsurance market. Each of its insurance subsidiaries is rated highly for its capital strength, its financial condition, and its operating performance. The insurance operations and their subsidiaries are grouped into one of four units: GEICO, General Re, Berkshire Hathaway Reinsurance Group (BHRG), and Berkshire Hathaway Primary Group.

GEICO, headquartered in Chevy Chase, Maryland, primarily offers private passenger automobile insurance (but also insures other types of vehicles). General Re is a major international reinsurer operating in 56 cities providing insurance and reinsurance services worldwide. General Re's property and casualty operations are headquartered in Stamford, Connecticut, with 16 branch offices serving the United States and Canada. Its large international subsidiary Cologne Re provides property/casualty reinsurance primarily through Faraday, which controls the managing agent of Syndicate 435 at Lloyds of London. The BHRG group, also headquartered in Stamford, Connecticut, primarily provides catastrophe excess of loss reinsurance policies covering property losses that result from terrorism, natural disasters, and aviation risks. The Berkshire Hathaway Primary Group, headquartered in Omaha, Nebraska, and its affiliates primarily underwrite motor vehicle and general liability insurance to commercial enterprises principally in the United States.

Energy, Utilities, and Manufacturing

Berkshire holds a majority interest in MidAmerican Energy Holdings Company, an international energy company. MidAmerican operates two regulated utility companies and two pipelines in the United States, an electricity distribution subsidiary in the United Kingdom, and a hydroelectric facility in the Philippines.

Berkshire owns Shaw Industries, the world's largest carpet manufacturer (revenue and production).

Shaw is headquartered in Dalton, Georgia, and sells its wholesale products throughout the United States, Canada, and Mexico. Shaw also sells hardwood flooring through its Anderson Family of Companies business. Berkshire owns Acme Building Products, a manufacturer and distributor of clay bricks, concrete block, and cut limestone, based in Fort Worth, Texas, that primarily serves the southwestern United States. Berkshire also owns Benjamin Moore & Company, a leading manufacturer and retailer of architectural coatings. Benjamin Moore is headquartered in Montvale, New Jersey, and primarily serves the United States and Canadian markets.

Another major building products business owned by Berkshire is Johns Manville, a manufacturer of a complete line of fiberglass building insulation products and roofing systems and components, headquartered in Denver, Colorado. Johns Manville operates manufacturing facilities in North America, Europe, and China. Berkshire owns Albecca, Inc., headquartered in Norcross, Georgia, that designs, manufactures, and distributes framing products and supplies, serving the United States, Canada, and 15 countries outside North America.

Berkshire is also the owner of Clayton Homes, headquartered near Knoxville, Tennessee, a vertically integrated manufactured housing company operating 41 manufacturing plants in 14 states. Its products are marketed in 48 states through a network of dealers and company-owned sales centers. Clayton also offers various financing and insurance programs for its products.

In addition, Berkshire holds a 90 percent interest in MiTek Inc., headquartered in Chesterfield, Missouri, which is a provider of engineered connector parts, engineering software, and computer-driven manufacturing machinery primarily serving the building components industry. It also produces light-gauge steel framing and specialized assembly line machinery. MiTek has 24 manufacturing facilities in 10 countries, 29 sales/engineering offices in 14 countries, and sales in approximately 90 countries. Berkshire owns an 80 percent interest in ISCAR Metalworking Companies, a manufacturer of consumable industrial precision cutting tools, headquartered in Tefen, Israel, with manufacturing facilities in Israel, the United States, Germany, Italy, France, Switzerland, South Korea, China, India, Japan, and Brazil.

Berkshire is involved in other types of manufacturing not directly related to building, such as the CTB International Corp., headquartered in Milford, Indiana, which designs, manufactures, and markets systems used in the production of poultry, hogs, and eggs. It also owns Forest River, Inc., headquartered in Elkhart, Indiana, a manufacturer of recreational vehicles, utility cargo and office trailers, buses, and pontoon boats for the U.S. and Canadian markets. Berkshire's Scott Fetzer Companies are a diversified collection of businesses that manufacture and distribute a variety of products for residential, industrial, and institutional use.

Service Businesses

Berkshire owns FlightSafety International (FSI) which provides training to operators of aircraft and ships. FSI is headquartered at LaGuardia Airport in Flushing, New York, operates training facilities in 20 states and in Australia, Brazil, Canada, France, and the United Kingdom. FSI also manufactures simulators, visual displays, and other training equipment at facilities in Oklahoma and Missouri. Berkshire owns NetJets, a leading provider of fractional ownership programs for general aviation worldwide with a fleet of some 622 aircraft. NetJets is headquartered in Woodbridge, New Jersey, with its flight operations based in Columbus, Ohio, and its European flight operations based in Lisbon, Portugal. Berkshire owns XTRA Corporation, headquartered in St. Louis, Missouri, a transportation equipment lessor with a diverse fleet of 120,000 units (over-the-road and storage trailers, chassis, temperature-controlled vans, and flatbed trailers) located at 75 facilities in the United States and five facilities in Canada.

Berkshire owns McLane Company, a provider of wholesale distribution and logistics services to discount retailers, convenience stores, quick-service restaurants, drug stores, and movie theaters throughout the United States and in Brazil. Its grocery distribution division is headquartered in Temple, Texas, and operates 22 facilities in 18 states. Its food-service operations are headquartered in Carrollton, Texas, and operate 18 facilities in 16 states.

Other service businesses owned by Berkshire include the following: Business Wire, a San Francisco–based electronic disseminator of full-text news serving 150 countries in 45 languages; Pampered

Chef, the largest direct seller of kitchen tools in the United States; *Buffalo News*, the daily newspaper in Buffalo, New York; International Dairy Queen, a system of about 6,000 stores offering various dairy desserts, foods, and beverages; TTI, an electronic component distributor headquartered in Fort Worth, Texas, operating in more than 50 locations throughout North America, Europe, and Asia. Berkshire also has an 80.1 percent interest in CORT Business Services Corporation, a nationwide provider of rental furniture and accessories.

Apparel, Footwear, and Jewelry

Berkshire owns a variety of apparel and footwear manufacturing companies. Its clothing businesses include Fruit of the Loom (FOL) and Vanity Fair Brands (VFB), a combined business that is a vertically integrated manufacturer and distributor of basic apparel, underwear, and bras, headquartered in Bowling Green, Kentucky. FOL and VFB have labor-intensive manufacturing operations in Central America, the Caribbean, and Morocco, and also contract some third-party manufacturing in Europe and Asia.

Berkshire owns Garan, headquartered in New York, which designs, manufactures, and sells children's apparel in the United States through national chain stores (Wal-Mart represents 90 percent of its business), department stores, and specialty stores. Garan's production facilities are primarily in Central America. Berkshire also owns Fechheimer Brothers headquartered in Cincinnati, Ohio, a firm that manufactures, distributes, and sells uniforms targeted toward the police, fire, postal, and military markets.

Berkshire's footwear businesses, Justin Brands and H. H. Brown Shoe Group, purchase, manufacture, and distribute work shoes, outdoor and casual shoes, and western-style footwear sold principally in the United States but primarily sourced overseas. Berkshire merged two of its acquisitions to create the Richline Group, Inc., a jewelry manufacturing (gold, silver, and gem set) and distribution company selling to mass market merchandisers.

Retailing

Berkshire's retailing businesses primarily consist of several independent home furnishings operations, three jewelry retailers, and a confectionery opera-

tion. Berkshire's home furnishings businesses are an 80 percent ownership of the Nebraska Furniture Mart (NFM) in Omaha, Nebraska, and Kansas City, Missouri, and NFM's Homemakers Furniture in Des Moines, Iowa. Berkshire also owns R. C. Wiley, headquartered in Salt Lake City, Utah, operating 11 retail stores in four states. Berkshire owns Star Furniture Company, with 11 locations in Texas, and Jordan's Furniture, Inc., with four locations in Massachusetts and New Hampshire.

Berkshire owns a 93 percent interest in the single store Borsheim Jewelry Company, Inc., located in Omaha, Nebraska. It also owns Helzberg's Diamond Shops, headquartered in North Kansas City, Missouri, with a chain of 269 stores in 38 states. Its third jewelry operation is Ben Bridge Jeweler, headquartered in Seattle, Washington, with 77 stores in 12 states. Berkshire's confectionery operation, See's Candies, consists of two large kitchens, one in Los Angeles and the other in San Francisco, that produce boxed chocolates and other candies.

For its fiscal year ending December 31, 2007, Berkshire Hathaway reported total revenues of $118.3 billion and valued its total assets at $273.2 billion. Its 2007 net earnings per share was reported at $8,548. As of February 15, 2008, Berkshire Hathaway had approximately 4,600 record holders of its Class A Common Stock that traded in a range from a low $103,800 per share to a high of $151,650 in 2007. Also as of February 15, 2008, Berkshire Hathaway had approximately 13,900 record holders of its Class B Common Stock which traded in a range from a low $3,460 per share to a high of $5,059 in 2007. Since the present management took over Berkshire Hathaway, the company's book value (Class A shares) has grown at a rate of 21.1 percent compounded annually. Berkshire Hathaway has not declared a cash dividend since 1967.

See Also: Acquisitions, Takeovers, and Mergers; Company Profiles: North America; United States.

Bibliography. Berkshire Hathaway, Inc., www.berkshirehathaway.com (cited March 2009); SEC-EDGAR, www.sec.gov (cited March 2009).

FRANK L. WINFREY
LYON COLLEGE

Best Buy

Best Buy was founded in 1966 by Richard M. Schulze and James Wheeler in St. Paul, Minnesota, under the original name "Sound of Music Store." This retailing company, offering mainly consumer electronics, and has more than 150,000 employees. The headquarters are in Richfield, Minnesota, and the Best Buy Co. shares are listed on the New York Stock Exchange. Chairman Schulze is still leading the business, which is focused on consumer electronics, home office products, entertainment software, domestic appliances, and related services. Consumer electronics contribute about 41 percent to current sales, home office products about 28 percent, and entertainment software about 19 percent. Domestic appliances and services are less important, accounting for 6 percent of sales each.

Best Buy manages five private label brands: Insignia (personal computers and accessories), Dynex (low-price computers and home entertainment), Init (storage and portability for technical devices), Geek Squad (best known for its 24-hour on-site technical support services, high-end computer accessories, and cables), and Rocketfish (high-end cables primarily used for home theater installations). Products with these private labels are sold exclusively in Best Buy's own retail outlets. The outlets are identified by the light-brown façade and a "blue box" entrance. The logo is a yellow price label with the name Best Buy printed on it in black letters.

Best Buy, whose 1,150 retail outlets are usually the epitome of the "big box" style, has been ranked 12th among U.S. retailers.

Best Buy has successfully acquired other retail chains, such as Audio Visions, Five Star, Future Shop, Magnolia, Pacific Sales, and Speakeasy. The trust currently ranks 23rd in the Fortune Top 100 and is the leading consumer electronics vendor in the United States and Canada. The company ranks 12th in the list of U.S. retailers and accounts for 17 percent of the North American electronics market. The company has generated an impressive performance: Since the 1990s, their revenue has increased faster than that of Microsoft and the dividend per share was higher than that of Intel, Inc. This is remarkable, considering that Best Buy lost almost all of its profits just 10 years ago. In 1997 an expansion strategy resulted in hypergrowth, overextending technical and financial resources as well as management capacity.

To cope with stagnation of turnover in the U.S. retail industry, Best Buy expanded its business to overseas sites. In a total of 1,150 outlets, Best Buy offers goods and services in the United States, Canada, Puerto Rico, Mexico, and Turkey. By the end of 2008, Best Buy hoped to have eight stores operating in China. The first two were opened in Shanghai.

Best Buy is about to expand to the major European markets. The first step is a joint venture with a British mobile phone provider, Carphone Warehouse. In addition to mobile telephony, this joint venture intends to sell various consumer electronics in the 2,400 outlets in the United Kingdom. Carphone Warehouse also provides this joint venture with stores in other European countries, including 240 Phone House outlets in Germany. Thus, Best Buy could become a credible competitor to the German Metro Group, operating two successful consumer electronics chains, Media Markt and Saturn, in various European countries.

Best Buy's business model differs from those of competitors by emphasizing care for customers' needs. On the one hand, customers can ask for technically skilled employees to install the products in their homes, thus receiving a sophisticated technical solution including planning, financing, all installations, inspections, and repairs. On the other hand, the private label, low-price offerings match the quality of national brands.

Best Buy is currently facing negative publicity because of the computer repair services it provides. Critics focus on lost data stored on notebooks that were left for repair. However, Best Buy is well known for its elaborate corporate responsibility strategy, fitting social and environmental protection aspects into the stakeholders' interest portfolio. Striking elements of Best Buy's corporate relations are the sponsoring of the NASCAR Haas CNC Racing team, the Best Buy Scholarship, and the Best Buy Teach Awards.

See Also: METRO; Retail Sector; Service Level; Wholesale Sector; Wal-Mart Stores.

Bibliography. Best Buy, *Annual Report Fiscal Year 2008*; B. Chakravarthy and P. Lorange, "Continuous Renewal, and How Best Buy Did It," *Strategy & Leadership* (2007); Elizabeth Gibson and Andrew Billings, "Best Practices at Best Buy: A Turnaround Strategy," *Journal of Business Strategy* (2003); Elizabeth Gibson and Andrew Billings, *Big Change at Best Buy: Working through Hypergrowth to Sustained Excellence* (Davies-Black, 2003); G. McWilliams, "Analyzing Customers, Best Buy Decides Not All Are Welcome," *Wall Street Journal Online*, online.wsj.com (2004); H. Salomann, L. Kolbe, and W. Brenner, "Self-Services in Customer Relationships: Balancing High-Tech and High-Touch Today and Tomorrow," *e-Service Journal* (2006).

RALF WAGNER
UNIVERSITY OF KASSEL

Bhopal Disaster

In 1977 Union Carbide India Limited (UCIL) set up a manufacturing facility in Bhopal, a city of some 900,000 inhabitants in Madhya Pradesh, India. It was licensed by the Madhya Pradesh Government to manufacture phosgene, monomethylamine (MMA), methylisocyanate (MIC), and the pesticide carbaryl, also known as Sevin. The plant was located in an urban area in the center of the city, despite the existence of an industrial area that had been set aside for such hazardous undertakings. The site was near a lake that provided an essential water source.

On the night of December 2, 1984, one of the world's worst industrial disasters occurred at the plant. Water inadvertently entered the MIC storage tank. Safety systems could not contain the gases that formed as a result of the heat generated by the chemical reaction. The leak was first detected at 11:30 P.M. by workers whose eyes had begun to burn. The supervisor was informed, but action was not taken immediately. About 40 tons of MIC escaped into the densely populated surrounding area over a period of two hours.

There was no warning because the emergency alarm designed to warn of the rising temperature in the MIC tank had been switched off. Indeed, the temperature and pressure gauges were so unreliable that workers often ignored potential warning signs. The impact on people living in the shanty settlements adjacent to the plant was devastating. Many died in their beds, others choked and vomited in the streets, and many more died later in hospitals. The main cause of death was respiratory failure. The immediate aftermath saw 8,000 people killed.

Following the disaster it was discovered that the plant had been suffering from a number of other technical problems. The freon gas refrigeration unit designed to store MIC had been disconnected and the gas was being used elsewhere on site. The vent gas scrubber designed to neutralize escaping gas had been shut down for maintenance, though it would have been unable to cope with the gas in any event. The flare tower, designed to burn off the gas that escaped the vent gas scrubber, was also turned off, because a piece of corroded pipe needed replacing. The pressure on the water spray system, designed to reach points from which any gas was escaping, was too low and therefore ineffective. Union Carbide's operational procedures also required the MIC tanks to be filled only to 50 percent of capacity. The Bhopal tank was filled to between 75 percent and 87 percent capacity. Another storage tank used to hold excess MIC was already full.

Ironically, a study conducted by a team from Union Carbide in 1982 noted that there was a serious potential for the release of toxic chemicals. Workers may also have been ill equipped to deal with the scale of the problem. Between 1980 and 1984, the crew for the MIC unit had been cut by 50 percent (from 12 to six) and the maintenance crew was cut 66 percent (from six to two). Many workers in key safety positions were not properly trained and the operating manuals were all in English.

Aftermath

Since 1984 more than 20,000 deaths have been attributed to the disaster and the effects are now extending into the next generation—150,000 of the survivors are reported to be chronically ill with long-term health effects ranging from cancer and tuberculosis to birth defects and chronic fevers. Local communities are continuing to drink groundwater contaminated with heavy metals and persistent organic contaminants because the dangerous chemicals left behind still have not been cleaned up.

The Indian government registered more than 600,000 claims against Union Carbide, which did not accept liability for the disaster. Union Carbide used tactics of delay of payment to victims and denial of any responsibility. They spent US$35–40 million on legal fees in connection with Bhopal. They argued that U.S. courts were not the appropriate place to deal with the issues but rather that the Indian courts were better placed to do so. This tied up the litigation for a year. Once back in India, they argued that the Indian courts were unsuitable to try such a complex issue. Union Carbide appealed every decision that went against it. This was essentially a neutralization technique that Union Carbide had previously used in a case brought against them in Long Island (New York) for polluting the local water supply.

Finally, in 1989, the government of India negotiated a $470 million compensation payment for the victims in an out-of-court settlement with Union Carbide. However, owing to bureaucratic inertia and the slowness of India's legal system, in 2004 $325 million was still being held by India's central bank in Mumbai. In July 2004 the Indian Supreme Court accepted the arguments from the victims and ordered the government to release this money. Amnesty International, in its 2004 Clouds of Injustice report, estimates the out-of-court settlement was a fraction of Union Carbide's true liability by international norms.

In February 2001 Union Carbide became a full subsidiary of Dow Chemical, becoming the world's biggest chemical company. In buying Union Carbide, Dow not only bought the company's assets but also its liabilities. However, Dow Chemical continues to deny any liability. India continues to press for the extradition of Warren Anderson, Union Carbide's chief executive at the time of the disaster.

See Also: Corporate Social Responsibility; Dow Chemical; India.

Bibliography. Jackson B. Browning, "Union Carbide: Disaster at Bhopal" in *Crisis Response: Inside Stories on Managing Image Under Siege*, Jack A. Gottschalk, ed. (Visible Ink, 1993); D. Dembo, W. Morehouse, and L. Wykle, *Abuse of Power: Social Performance of Multinational Corporations: The Case of Union Carbide* (New Horizons Press, 1990); Greenpeace, www.greenpeace.org.uk (cited March 2009); Ashok S. Kalelkar, "Investigation of Large-Magnitude Incidents: Bhopal as a Case Study" (Arthur D. Little, Inc., 1988); The Trade & Environment Database, "TED Case Studies: Bhopal Disaster," www.american.edu/ted (cited March 2009); Union Carbide's Bhopal Information Center, www.bhopal.com (cited March 2009).

Jamie Weatherston
Northumbria University

Bid/Ask Spread

The bid/ask spread is also known as the bid/offer spread. In the financial markets the bid price is the price at which a dealer (market-maker) will buy a particular security from an investor. The ask price is the price at which the dealer will sell that security to an investor. The difference between these prices is the spread. This bid/ask spread represents the profit margin for the dealer who trades in a security after allowing for any carrying cost that may be involved if the market is not liquid.

In liquid markets (continual buying and selling) where there are always buyers for the security and trades are quickly concluded, carrying costs will be negligible. However, for some securities it may take a dealer some time to find a buyer and the carrying cost will be the interest earnings foregone by the dealer by tying up money in holding the security. As a general rule, the bid/ask spread for a liquid security, such as shares in a blue-chip company, will be narrower than the spread for a share in a start-up company. In the latter case the spread between bid and ask prices will be wider to compensate for the additional time the dealer will be tying up money in holding the security.

Bid/ask spreads are customary in all financial markets, including shares, bonds, mutual funds, and currencies. The narrowest spreads are found in the currency markets, which are the most liquid. The spreads here will be measured in basis points (hundredths of a percent), whereas the spread for an illiquid company share may be measured in full percentage points of the asset's value.

In addition to volume of trade (liquidity), the spread for a security will be determined by the volatility of the asset's price and also the volatility of the market in general. At times of market volatility all bid/ask spreads will widen. Individual securities with a history of sharp price changes will also have a wider spread than securities with more stable price characteristics. In the stock market the bid/ask spreads for low-priced shares may be wider than for higher-priced shares. The low price may be an indicator of illiquidity in the market for that share. The share prices quoted in newspapers are usually the midpoint of the spread at the previous close of business. For the investor wishing to calculate the return on a security, it is important to ensure that performance is based on an ask-to-bid basis.

A perfectly reversible security would allow the investor to move from cash into the security and back again without loss of value. Any security with a bid/ask spread is, therefore, imperfectly reversible. The market makers are responsible for maintaining an orderly market by providing continuous buying and selling prices. This can only be done by holding inventories of the securities, which requires the market makers to tie up capital. The bid/ask spread is their means of compensation for this essential activity. In open and competitive markets there may be variations in the bid/ask spreads from dealer to dealer for particular securities, but arbitrage will ensure they converge. With an exchange-traded security the client may get a better price than the indicated bid/ask spread as the dealers may improve the transaction price within the spread. With over-the-counter (OTC) deals the client will only deal at the quoted spread.

Bid/ask spreads are not only found in spot markets (immediate trade) but also in forward markets. Thus a bank may quote a bid/ask spread on forward exchange rates. Once again this spread will be wider for currencies that are more difficult to trade. Tourists are familiar with an everyday example of the bid/ask spread when they buy currency for foreign travel. Banks and bureaux de change quote two prices depending on whether the tourist is buying or selling the foreign currency. The difference represents the profit to the dealer. As a general rule in any transaction the dealer gets the more attractive price and the investor/purchaser the less attractive price. The bid/ask spread is a valuable source of information for investment planning, providing insight into the liquidity and potential volatility of a security.

See Also: Arbitrage; Carrying Costs; Credit Ratings; Financial Markets; Foreign Exchange Market; Market Maker.

Bibliography. C. Alexander and E. Sheedy, *The Professional Risk Manager's Guide to Financial Markets* (McGraw-Hill, 2006); D. Connolly, *The UK Trader's Bible* (Harriman House, 2007); R. Vaitilingam, *The Financial Times Guide to Using the Financial Pages* (Prentice Hall, 2006).

Tom Connor
University of Bedfordshire

Big Mac Index

The Big Mac Index compares the prices of McDonald's Big Mac burgers, a fast food item produced and sold in 120 countries worldwide, as an indicator of possible overvaluation or undervaluation of the local currency relative to the U.S. dollar. The tongue-in-cheek analyses give an easily digestible example of the economic theory on purchasing power parity (PPP) and its applicability in the practical sense.

The Big Mac Index is based on the PPP theory, which holds that the price of a certain commodity should be the same in different countries and, if they are not so, that the exchange rate between the currencies of two countries will gradually adjust toward parity, or equality. This notion also extends toward an identical basket of goods and services. If the prices of all components of this basket are the same, then the PPP theory implies that the price for the basket should also be the same among countries.

If the price is not the same, the price difference (called arbitrage) between countries will encourage traders to buy the commodity in the lower-priced country and sell it for a profit in the other country with higher prices. The trade creates demand and induces commodity prices to rise in the lower-priced country; it also increases supply and influences prices

McDonald's standard items and outlets in cities like Bangkok made the Big Mac a lighthearted tool for comparing currencies.

States was $3.41 (the average of prices in four cities: New York, Chicago, Atlanta, and San Francisco). In comparison, the same burger in the United Kingdom (UK) cost £1.99, which was equivalent to $4.00 at the prevailing market exchange rate of $2.01/£1. However, the implied Big Mac PPP is only $1.71 (actual U.S. price in dollars divided into actual UK price in pounds, i.e., $3.41/£1.99). Comparing the Big Mac PPP of $1.71 and the official exchange rate of $2.01, the UK pound has a 17.5 percent advantage and is thus overvalued against the dollar. It can be expected to depreciate in order to reach the PPP rate of £1=$1.71 from the existing £1=$2.01. Put another way, the burger is 17.5 percent more expensive in the UK than in the United States at the existing exchange rate, and is said to be 17.5 percent overvalued versus the dollar.

On the other hand, the same burger in China costs 11.0 yuan, which converts to $1.45 at the prevailing market exchange rate of $1= 7.60 yuan. The implied PPP is 11 yuan/$3.41 or 3.23 yuan per dollar. But the market exchange rate is 7.60 yuan per dollar, and the yuan is therefore undervalued by about 57.5 percent. The yuan can thus be expected to appreciate.

Use of the Big Mac Index

The Big Mac Index was developed by *The Economist* magazine in the UK in 1986. It was not designed to be a precision tool for economic forecasting but simply as a lighthearted test of the PPP. Even *The Economist* acknowledges there are wide divergences in prices across the McDonald's world. Unlike regular commodities, there is no cross-border trade in burgers (as required by PPP). The index, however, has been used as a measure of the costs of living in different countries. Average prices tend to be lower in less-developed countries, making their currencies seem cheaper in comparison to more developed countries.

Goods that are traded across countries will probably be similarly priced, whether in developed or less-developed countries. But products that by their nature are traded only in the domestic market, e.g., labor-intensive services and rents, are usually priced lower in poorer countries. London will have more expensive barbers than Beijing, for example. Price disparities also arise from differences in transportation costs, taxation systems, barriers to trade, and other factors. The level of local wages is also a significant influence on the cost of serving the burgers.

to go down in the high-priced country, until the point is reached when no more price difference exists and there is no more profit to be made.

The Big Mac Index uses the Big Mac burger as the reference commodity, or basket, consisting of its beef patties, cheese, lettuce, spices, and secret sauce on a bun studded with sesame seeds. The index takes the prices of the Big Mac burger in all 120 countries where it is available. The Big Mac PPP refers to the exchange rate that would make the prices of hamburgers in any of the 120 countries identical to prices in the United States (dollars). A currency would be considered undervalued or overvalued when its actual market exchange rate is compared with the Big Mac PPP.

For example, in the last annual publication (every July) of the index in 2007, the burger price in the United

An important implication of the PPP is that the real size of a poor country's economy and the associated standards of living will tend to be understated if the economic figures are converted into dollars using the prevailing exchange rates. The PPP, however, tends to yield higher economic figures for an economy than market exchange rates. China's economy, for instance, will appear more than twice as much when converted at Big Mac PPP than at market exchange rates. The International Monetary Fund also uses more sophisticated models of PPP.

Economic rankings change dramatically when the PPP is used for converting and comparing economic performance. Emerging economies turn out to be greater contributors to global economic output than market exchange rates would indicate. Conversion of economic output using PPP shows that emerging economies contributed nearly half of world output in 2004. But conversion using market exchange rates shows these countries contributing less than one-quarter.

Economists generally acknowledge PPP as descriptive of how international prices are determined in the long run. Over time, similar countries do tend to have smaller price differentials. There is also general recognition that it provides a better idea of relative economic rankings than market exchange rates.

Although it was originally meant to provide a simple, lighthearted means to illustrate the fundamentals of purchasing power parity, the Big Mac index has become an essential feature of the consumer's menu for understanding more complex concepts of currency valuations and exchange rates.

See Also: Arbitrage; Exchange Rate; Purchasing Power Parity.

Bibliography. Gavyn Davies, "Gavyn Davies Does the Maths: The Big Mac Index Says Sterling Should Fall," *The Guardian* (June 8, 2006), www.guardian.co.uk (cited March 2009); Economist Staff, "Food for Thought: The Big Mac Index," *The Economist* (May 28, 2004), www.cfo.com (cited March 2009); Campbell R. McConnell, *Microeconomics: Principles, Problems, and Policies* (McGraw-Hill Professional, 2005); Michael R. Pakko and Patricia S. Polland, "Burger Survey Provides Taste of International Economics," *Federal Reserve Bank of St. Louis–Regional Economist* (January 2004); "The Big Mac Index: Sizzling," *The Economist* (July 5, 2007), www.economist.co.uk (cited March 2009).

Amir Shoham
Sapir Academic College
Miki Malul
Ben-Gurion University

Bilateral Free Trade Agreements

Bilateral free trade agreements (BFTAs) are agreements generally made between two countries or two regions, or one country and one region; it is widely accepted that they lead to economic growth by reducing poverty and increasing standards of living and generating employment opportunity. While some BFTAs can be narrow-range in their dealing of traded goods for a certain time period, some BFTAs can be much more comprehensive and cover other issues including services and investment, and can generally take existing World Trade Organization (WTO) agreements as their benchmark. The free trade agreements are like stepping stones toward international integration into a global free market economy, and they are seen as the manifestation of globalization, which requires governments to implement the liberalization, privatization, and deregulation measures.

The first important general factor for the popularity of BFTAs is the apparent disenchantment with the pace of liberalization at the multilateral level. Another general factor driving the growth of BFTAs can be the snowballing or domino effect. The number of BFTAs thus continued to grow, almost doubling to 109 between 2002 and 2004. By 2007, this number has more than doubled again as countries did not want to be left behind. Finally, it is often claimed that some, if not most, BFTAs are politically motivated. There is no doubt that political economic considerations, political parties, or even individual politicians have played a major role in driving the formation of BFTAs.

Negotiating a BFTA is a serious exercise as the outcome can have major implications for development policy and for social, economic, and development outcomes for many countries. While it can result in some export gains, it can also result in increases in imports, affect the local industries and farms, reduce tariff revenue, and restrict the options and instruments available to a country to institute certain social, economic, and development policies.

Therefore, before negotiating or even contemplating any BFTA, countries should concentrate on three important issues. First, when a proposal is put forward by the BFTA partner or potential partner, it should be evaluated in the context of national development policy framework (plans on local and sectoral levels and issue-based plans like intellectual property). In the absence of such a framework, it would be difficult to determine the objectives of entering any negotiation, or of the advantages/disadvantages of the proposed BFTA.

Second, this framework should also assess the benefits and costs of the BFTAs for the whole nation. By doing that, the gains and losses in terms of trade and jobs, effects of the agreement on the policy space and the degree of flexibility on national plans, effects on social issues such as health, and finally key effects on technology transfers would be examined in detail before the negotiations. The costs and benefits can be applied to the various aspects of the BFTAs, including market access (to the other country, and the partner country's access to one's own market) in goods; services; intellectual property; investment, competition and government procurement; and labor and environment standards.

Third, the country should establish or organize the resources and institutional base for assessing whether or not to enter negotiations for the BFTA. As part of the process, different agencies of the government should be consulted and should be part of the process of the formulation of policy and positions. It is equally important to involve stakeholders, such as local firms, trade unions, farmers, consumers, and groups representing patients and involved in health provision and environmental protection.

Then, the decisions have to be taken nationally whether it is a good idea to enter negotiations in the BFTAs; if the decision is on the side of entering, how to conduct the negotiations; how to manage the process; how to assess the costs and benefits of proposals; and how to conclude the negotiations.

In the context of developing country–developed country negotiations on BFTAs, the costs and benefits might significantly differ in nature whether two developed countries negotiate on BFTAs or one developed and one developing country negotiate on BFTAs. If any developing country contemplates a negotiation with a developed country, then the developing country's production and export capacity should be satisfactory enough for the partner, and the partner should be able to offer significant concessions to the developing country. Otherwise the net cost of having this negotiation will be higher than the benefit. Furthermore, the additional costs of these negotiations can be higher for the developing country, as that country will end up paying more license payments, higher prices of the protected products, less access to medicines, loss in farmer's rights, etc.

Bilateral Versus Multilateral Agreements

It is generally recognized that bilateral agreements, especially between a developing and a developed country, are not the best option, and that multilateral negotiations and agreements are much more preferable. Few reasons can account for that. One of them is that bilateral agreements generally lead to trade diversion that also results in inefficiency in trade. The other reason is that developing countries are usually in a weaker bargaining position due to their undeveloped economies and political instabilities. As a result, they might put themselves in a disadvantaged position. The third reason is that even within the WTO there are flexibilities open to developing countries in interpreting and implementing obligations in trade between countries. Nevertheless, developed countries tend to remove these flexibilities for developing countries in the BFTAs. This attempt would significantly reduce the policy space for developing countries. The proliferation of so many agreements also puts pressure on personnel and financial resources in developing countries and requires technical expertise for the use of limited resources.

There are also some views that BFTAs can even be handicaps in front of multilateral trade negotiations. Philip Levy discussed the position of BFTAs and claimed that BFTAs can undermine political support for further liberalization in the field of multilateral trade, and he suggested that if the BFTAs offer larger gains to some countries than to others, then the multilateral agreements would be blocked and liberalization activities in trade would be prevented. BFTAs can never provide the political support for multilateral free trade for political economic reasons. Similarly, Gene Grossman and Elhanan Helpman also examined BFTAs from the political-agreements point of view and they ask if these negotiations are politically viable due to interaction between special interest groups and an incumbent government. They concluded that if BFTAs are to be followed, then these negotiations should generate substantive welfare gains for voters, and the agreement would create profit gains for actual or potential exporters.

See Also: Free Trade; Regional Trade Agreements; Trade Pact; World Trade Organization.

Bibliography.   Richard   Baldwin,   "Multilateralising Regionalism: Spaghetti Bowls as Building Blocs on the Path to Global Free Trade," CEPR discussion paper (2006); Gene Grossman and Elhanan Helpman, "The Politics of Free-Trade Agreements," *The American Economic Review* (v.85/4, 1995); Mohar Khor, "Bilateral/Regional Free Trade Agreements: An Outline of Elements, Nature and Development Implications," Third World Network, www.twnside .org.sg (cited March 2009); Philip Levy, "A Political-Economic Analysis of Free-Trade Agreements," *The American Economic Review* (v.87/4, 1997).

Dilek Demirbas
Northumbria University

Bill of Lading

Routine business activities often involve contracts known as bills of lading. A bill of lading is a document or receipt issued by a carrier when it receives goods for shipment. Usually, the receipt indicates (1) the particular vessel on which the goods have been placed; (2) destination; (3) cargo weight; and (4) terms of transportation. International sales transactions usually involve sales and transportation contracts; therefore, a seller not only sells goods, but also arranges the transportation of the goods to the purchaser. Under such circumstances, a bill of lading serves as a link between the sales part of the transaction and the transportation portion of it.

Typically, contracts governing carriage of goods by water are evidenced by charter parties or bills of lad-

ing. The term *charter party* is employed to describe three widely differing types of contracts relating to the use of vessels owned or controlled by others. Bills of lading, by contrast, usually fall into one of four categories—inland, ocean, through, and air waybill—and are independent of the vessel used.

An inland bill of lading establishes an agreement between a shipper and a transportation company. It is used to lay out the terms for transportation overland to the exporter's international transportation company. In short, inland bills of lading are necessary for the domestic transportation of goods.

An ocean bill of lading provides terms between an international carrier and an exporter. It deals with the shipment of goods to a foreign location overseas. Ocean bills of lading are usually in order form—that is, they call for delivery to the order of the shipper. These bills of lading can be negotiated similarly to a draft or check. Essentially, this means that a bona fide purchaser of the bill of lading takes it free and clear of any defects that, otherwise, do not appear on its face.

A thorough bill of lading covers specific terms agreed to by a shipper and carrier. It covers domestic and international transportation of export merchandise; further, it provides the details agreed upon for transportation.

Finally, an air waybill is a bill of lading that establishes terms of flights for the transportation of goods, both domestically and internationally. An air waybill can be thought of as a type of through bill of lading because it may cover both international and domestic transportation of goods. Ocean shipments, by contrast, require both inland and ocean bills of lading.

Some bills of lading are negotiable; others are not. But inland and ocean bills of lading may be negotiable or nonnegotiable. If it is nonnegotiable, the carrier must provide delivery to the consignee—the person receiving the goods—named in the document. If, however, it is negotiable, the owner of the bill of lading has the right to ownership of the goods and, thus, has the right to reroute shipment. Depending on the parties' intention, the bill of lading may solely represent ownership of the goods. But the parties may agree that a mere security interest is to be transferred only. Upon receiving the goods, a receipt is issued and later turned in for the bill of lading proper. Apart from proving receipt of the goods to be shipped, the bill of lading incorporates the terms of the contract between the carrier and shipper.

As international trade expands, the quantity of goods transported by water will also continue to grow. Bills of lading will become increasingly important and provide the necessary safeguards to facilitate the expansion of the world economy.

See Also: Export Trading Company; Import; International Commercial Terms (Incoterms); Transportation.

Bibliography. Robert Force, A. N. Yiannopoulos, and Martin Davis, *Admiralty and Maritime Law* (Beard Books, 2008); William McNair, Alan A. Mocata, and Michael J. Mustill, *Scrutton on Charter-Parties and Bills of Lading*, 17th ed. (Sweet and Maxwell, 1964).

Daniel A. Espinosa
St. Thomas University School of Law

Biodiversity Convention

The Convention on Biological Diversity ("Biodiversity Convention" for short) is a treaty signed in 1992 by 150 government leaders who met at the so-called Earth Summit in Rio de Janeiro, Brazil. They pledged to promote sustainable development and to act to protect the natural resources of their respective countries. Business is referred to in the Convention (Articles 10 and 16), both because of the proactive role that the private sector may play, and because of its corporate responsibility toward the environment and global biological diversity.

The Convention is not a long text (42 articles on 20 pages in the English version), yet it represents one of the founding documents of the current agenda for sustainable development, on a par with the "Rio Declaration on Environment and Development" and the "Agenda 21" program. Now a piece of international public law featured in the United Nations (UN) Treaty Collection, it was the first agreement on such a global scale to focus on biological diversity, proclaiming in its preamble that "the conservation of biological diversity is a common concern of humankind" and that "it is vital to anticipate, prevent and attack the causes of significant reduction of loss of biological diversity at source." Since its launch in 1992, over 40 other countries have joined the Convention; only

a very few countries worldwide are not signatory parties yet: Some micro-states such as Andorra and the Vatican, also Iraq as well as the United States (which signed the treaty in 1993 but the U.S. Senate has yet to ratify it).

The Convention provides a global policy framework; national governments remain sovereign to decide and implement the most suitable strategies to achieve, in their own contexts, the three goals of the Convention: "conservation of biological diversity; sustainable use of natural resources; fair and equitable sharing of the benefits" (Article 1). National governments set their own targets, priorities, and action plans. Depending on the country, some industry sectors are more directly concerned, typically forestry, agriculture, fisheries, energy, transportation, and urban planning—but the broad agenda also reaches into other policy areas such as education, health, science, and technology. For the business community, this may translate into a range of opportunities (such as financial measures and incentives for the conservation and sustainable use of biological diversity) but also constraints (such as regulated access to genetic resources or statutory impact assessment).

The Convention is supported by a secretariat operating under the UN Environment Programme and based in Montreal, Canada. The secretariat increasingly regards business as a key stakeholder, on a par with local authorities and nongovernmental organizations. Since 2006 the secretariat has published a regular newsletter on business and biodiversity. The diverse topics in the April 2008 newsletter illustrate the range of challenges that lie at the interface of business and biodiversity: "assessing the economic cost of biodiversity loss," "mainstreaming sustainable agriculture," "catalyzing global corporate ocean responsibility," but also "a mining company perspective." Professional organizations such as the World Business Council on Sustainable Development and the International Chamber of Commerce are also contributing to this agenda.

Although the emphasis has recently shifted from mere environmental issues (reducing waste and avoiding pollution) to commercial objectives (managing biodiversity opportunities in order to provide better products and services and to improve corporate performance), there is also an increasing emphasis on corporate social responsibility and ultimately ethics.

Moreover, the need to engage the business community in biodiversity protection and sustainable development is increasingly recognized by political organizations, as illustrated by the High Level Conference on Business and Biodiversity organized in 2007 by the Portuguese presidency of the European Union Council. One of the outcomes of that conference was the "Message from Lisbon on Business and Biodiversity," which noted that "there is a strong business case for biodiversity, including the competitive advantage gained from conserving biodiversity and using biological resources in a sustainable way."

In 2003 the Biodiversity Convention was supplemented by another international agreement called the Cartagena Protocol on Biosafety. The Convention and the Protocol are now often presented together; most of the countries that signed the Convention have also signed the Protocol, with a few exceptions such as Israel and Russia. The Protocol builds upon the Convention, yet adds a special focus on protecting biodiversity from the potential risks posed by the living modified organisms (LMOs) created by modern biotechnology. Common examples of LMOs include agricultural crops (such as tomatoes, corn, cotton, and soybeans) that have been genetically modified for greater productivity or for resistance to pests or diseases.

Based on the principle of precautionary approach, the Protocol is wary about the impact that such genetically modified organisms may have on other organisms; as a consequence, it promotes biosafety by establishing rules and procedures for the safe transfer, handling, and use of LMOs. Although the Protocol is primarily relevant for businesses involved in agriculture, logistics, the food industry, and biological sciences, the international political will that underpins it further illustrates the global concerns for environmental changes that now frame all business decisions.

See Also: Corporate Social Responsibility; Environmental Standards; Sustainable Development.

Bibliography. Convention on Biological Diversity, *Convention on Biological Diversity* (1992); Earthwatch Institute, IUCN & WBCSN, *Business & Biodiversity: The Handbook for Corporate Action* (WBCSD, 2002); M. J. Epstein, *Making Sustainability Work: Best Practices in Managing and Measuring Corporate Social, Environmental and Economic Impacts* (Berrett-Koehler, 2008); A. Kontoleon, U. Pascual, and T. Swanson, *Biodiversity Economics: Principles, Methods and Applications* (Cambridge University Press, 2008).

Loykie L. Lominé
University of Winchester

Black Market

Black markets are markets that traffic in illegal goods or services. They may exist with the connivance of local authorities. They may be hidden or underground markets found down dark alleyways or they may be openly tolerated. In the shadow economies of the world, commerce is seeking to avoid government regulations or taxes on a vast array of goods and services. The lack of economic freedom in some countries is often a stimulus to the development of black markets. In some cases shadow markets employ people who feel marginalized in a system that favors legal monopolies or has excessive taxes or regulations. Their victimization is seen as a justification for their economic behavior.

Gray markets handle goods that are produced by legitimate firms; however, they are sold through unauthorized dealers. The genuine goods are sold by dealers who are not a part of the producer's distribution system.

Black markets have existed in earlier times as well. For example, in the early 19th century London was a center of medical training. However, there was a shortage of cadavers because many people believed that to enter heaven the body had to be intact. The supply of executed criminals was not sufficient for medical schools. Grave robbers, at times working with church wardens, dug up fresh corpses and sold them to the medical schools. These "body snatchers" were filling the demand illegally. Other types of older black markets included the smuggling of slaves, operating illegal houses of prostitution, and trafficking in drugs or other illegal goods. In general whenever anything is prohibited or priced too high an illegal market can be expected to arise to supply the demand.

Trafficking in human beings is still happening today. Babies can be adopted through back channels for a price. Sometimes the babies are the victims of kidnappings. Smuggling illegal workers into labor markets is a thriving business in the world and one that makes the news in the United States, Canada, or Europe on a frequent basis. Along the border with Mexico authorities have to contend with "coyotes" who are traffickers in humans, as well as with drug smugglers.

After the fall of communism at the end of the Cold War in 1989, criminal gangs arose, in many cases forming the Russian Mafia. They lured women into prostitution, often through deception, as thousands of young, educated women in search of work accepted jobs in western European countries. However, the jobs often were falsehoods told by gangsters to lure their victims into prostitution by force when they arrived at their destination in places such as the Czech Republic. It would have been hard for such activities to operate without the active complicity of the local police.

The demand for goods in contemporary markets evokes all manner of black markets. Pirated goods, knockoff goods, and adulterated goods have been sold in markets around the world. The sale of all of these pirated goods amounts to billions in the black markets even though they are cheap imitations. The cost to the original inventors, designers, manufacturers, wholesalers, and retailers runs into the hundreds of billions of dollars.

Hollywood's sales of DVDs of first-run movies has been especially hard hit by copyright pirates in the Third World. Shanghai before 1937 and the beginning of the Japanese-Chinese War was a city with a reputation for numerous black market operations. Other Chinese cities shared in that reputation. Some of the sales were sales of information in the espionage trade. Other sales were in drugs, or other illegal commodities. Since 1989 and the enormous development of trade in China anyone, and especially foreigners, walking the streets of Shanghai can find black market sales of pirated DVDs selling for less than $1. The DVDs are good quality and are often of first-run movies. In fact they are often on sale in Shanghai and other Chinese cities before the DVDs are released in the United States. Other countries in the Third World also participate in these and many other copyright violations of printed as well as digital materials.

Shanghai is also typical of many other Chinese cities visited by foreigners by the number of street venders selling imitation Rolex watches or knockoffs of famous writing pens. The buyer who asks about the price may well be asked in return how many dozens they want to buy. The traffic in black market goods in many countries has harmed the business of many companies. In some cases the imitation goods show up in the United States or in other countries where they are sold cheaply at a variety of gray market locations. Black market goods are often sold knowingly or unknowingly at flea markets or by street vendors.

Black market pirates may sell goods or services. The goods may be imitations or they may be stolen. The burglar, hijacker, or thief operates in a different type of black market where stolen goods are sold to a middle man who in criminal slang has been called a *fence*. The fence takes possession of the goods and then sells them in some kind of market that may be legitimate or underground. Besides consumer goods art works are continually being stolen and sold to someone who can find a buyer.

Art and Artifacts

Many countries have had to surround their museums or traditional sites with armed security guards in order to protect ancient artifacts. The traffic in stolen artifacts is huge and does serious damage to the integrity of archeological sites around the world. The pieces of ancient art that lose their provenance (record of discovery and ownership) may have commercial value as art, but they lose value as historic pieces.

Museums, libraries, and art institutes have at times willingly purchased items that were excellent pieces but were from the underground market in artifacts. The trade has promoted grave robbing in a great many ancient sites around the world from China to Peru and from India to Arizona. The looted pieces lose archeological value, and then as they move in the underground trade their provenance is also lost. Buyers of artifacts in black markets may be indifferent to the archeological information lost when artifacts are traded in the hidden market.

The illegal trade in ancient art is matched by the traffic in stolen art. From time to time there are news accounts of dramatic robberies of famous works of art that are stolen by thieves. The buyers of such works of art participate in a criminal conspiracy to gain personal pleasure from privately viewing art that was once on public display. To this art should be added the traffic in art that was stolen during World War II by the Nazis and by others. Many of the original owners of these works of art died during the war and left little that could be used to identify the lost property to their possible heirs.

Illegal Drugs

The black market in intoxicating drugs is likely the greatest in the sums of money the trade generates. It also leads to the largest response from law enforcement agencies, many of which have been assigned or created just to deal with it. It is also the most common reason for the imprisonment of people in the United States and in many other foreign countries. However, some countries such as the Philippines and Singapore apply the death penalty to convicted traffickers.

The illegal drugs with the greatest volume are cocaine, marijuana, and opium. Other drugs that are derivatives from these are also widely distributed by the heavily armed criminal organizations that engage in supplying the demand for illicit drugs. The sums of money involved run into the billions of dollars.

Cocaine comes from South America where the Columbian drug cartels have established bases for growing and processing coca leaf into cocaine. The war on drugs has not defeated the trade. Thousands have been killed and perhaps millions imprisoned because of the trafficking in illegal drugs.

Marijuana can be grown around the world and is often grown in the United States in secret locations. These may be in patches of ground in national forests. Or clever growers have bought houses in an area and then staffed them with growers who live on site to tend the plants that are grown under artificial lights in the rooms of the house. Outwardly the house looks normal, but inside it is a pot farm that can produce tens of thousands of dollars in marijuana per year unless detected and suppressed by law enforcement.

Opium and its derivatives have been mostly grown in south Asia. The "Golden Triangle" located in northern Thailand and Burma produces huge quantities of the drug. Afghanistan has also and continues to be a center for growing opium poppies. These and other places are centers for a vast network of drug dealers who sell these toxic chemicals.

At times violence has exploded between rival drug gangs. Jamaican gangs have fought with Columbian and Mexican rivals. The violence in Columbia and Mexico between rival gangs or against the government's efforts to control these gangs has threatened to destabilize these and other countries. Historically Italian gangs known as the Mafia handled the opium trafficking in the United States and elsewhere.

Medicine and Body Parts

The black market trade in recreational drugs is only one type of trafficking in drugs. Many legitimate pharmaceutical products have been copied and sold by illegal manufactures. In addition many cases have been exposed in recent years of companies and consumers who were victims of substitutions. As insulin or some other drug is made and distributed, opportunities for adulteration or substitution occur in the distribution system. The impact for consumers who believe that their medical supplies are secure when they are not has been to adversely affect the health of some and even resulted in deaths. This type of fraud is on a par with the adulteration of products from China or other developing countries. There have been cases where chemicals have been added to such things as baby formula or milk. The adulterant makes it appear that the protein level is higher than it actually is; however, the adulterant in some case could be dangerous for children or even adults to consume. Cases involving the deaths of animals including pets have renewed calls to stopping the trafficking these activities.

The medical field is the scene of a great many black market operations. Not only drugs and medical supplies, whether copied or stolen, enter into the illicit trade—so do body parts. The great development of organ and body part transplant technology has generated a cruel and at times deadly trafficking in body parts. Cases of people who are financially desperate selling a kidney or an eye have received media attention. But for those that make the news, there are others that do not. This is an area were the organs of the poor can be purchased by those with money. It is a trade that is likely to grow unless suppressed with severe penalties.

Plants and Animals

The medical field of modern medicine is not the only area of medicine affected by illegal drug trafficking.

Traditional medical systems in China and India have long used a variety of natural products including teas, herbs, and ointment to treat a variety of ailments. Most of these ancient remedies are supplied with legitimately produced materials. However, there are many products that continue to stimulate a trade in illegally obtained animal organs, or plants that are a threat to the survival of some species. For example, bears are often poached for their bile, which contains ursodeoxycholic acid (UDCA). The chemical has been used in Chinese medicine to reduce fever, act as an anti-inflammatory, and to break down gallstones. It is also believed to protect the liver and to improve eyesight. The active drug is now manufactured from other sources, but tradition and superstition have continued the demand.

Rhinoceros horn is also in wide demand and has been supplied by poaching. In traditional medicine it is believed to be an aphrodisiac. The horn is also used to make traditional handles for knives used by men in Yemen and neighboring countries. The impact upon the rhinoceros populations of the trade has led to a significant reduction in the populations of these famous animals.

Elephant ivory has been sought for centuries for purposes of decoration, as has the ivory of narwhales and other sea mammals. The trafficking in elephant ivory has been successfully suppressed, as has the trafficking in sea mammal ivory. However, there are many other plants and animals that continue to be the victims of black marketers who seek such parts as tiger bones for aphrodisiacs.

The trafficking in animal parts is similar to the illegal trade in rare plants. Illegal logging of rare woods in a common activity in many Third World countries; however, it has been known to occur in the United States, where old Black Walnut trees on abandoned farms in places like Wisconsin are hijacked and sold in legitimate markets to unsuspecting buyers. Other types of commercially valuable trees are stolen from forests around the world in order to sell them for a hidden profit to a buyer who can move them into the legitimate stream of commerce.

Diamonds

Another dangerous and violent type of black market is the trade in diamonds. Most diamonds are sold through legitimate channels. A few diamonds have always been smuggled out of the mines and a few others are taken from people through robbery or by other means. These diamonds are usually smuggled into the legitimate trade. However, far more important is the trade in "blood diamonds" or "conflict diamonds."

Conflict diamonds have developed from the collapse of governments in war-torn Africa. In Angola, Liberia, Sierra Leone, and the Congo, as well as a few other places, the virtual lack of law and order has allowed criminal gangs to pose as guerrilla fighters as a cover for gross criminal conduct. The diamond gangs proceed to capture a mining area and then enslave the local people and force them to do the mining. The diamonds that are found are used to pay for guns and to prosecute more violence. The trade in blood diamonds has also at times involved known terrorist groups such as Al Qaeda seeking a source of funding.

The discovery of new diamond mines in Russia and Canada has not increased the supply enough to make

A diamond miner in Sierra Leone, where in 1999 only $1.5 million out of $300 million in diamond exports was legal.

the conflict diamond operations unprofitable. However, the legitimate wholesalers and retailers have adopted policies that promote selling diamonds with a detailed history of each stone.

Nuclear Technology

Nuclear technology has advanced rapidly since the Manhattan Project produced the first atomic bombs in 1945. There is now a growing fear of nuclear proliferation by many governments around the world. Their concerns about terrorist groups gaining nuclear materials for making a radiological bomb ("dirty bomb") have grown with the piles of nuclear waste and stocks of nuclear materials available for theft or illegal sale.

The fall of the Soviet Union in 1949 left it open to having its military-grade nuclear materials stolen and sold in the Asian region or beyond. Some arrests of this type have been made; however, the sale of "yellow cake," which is uranium ready to process into fissionable material, has been conducted legally or illegally by some Third World countries.

Alcohol

Black markets can be so hidden that wars occur between government agents and the black market operative. However, black markets can also be so widely tolerated that a government openly collects a black market tax on illegal sales. The State of Mississippi until the mid-1960s collected a black market tax on the sale of alcoholic beverages. A large majority of its citizens were Baptist and Fundamentalist members of churches that supported temperance policies prohibiting the sale of alcohol. While it was the case that their preachers supported prohibitions on the sale of alcoholic beverages, significant minorities of these churches did not. In fact many members consumed alcoholic beverages.

In what was a blatant compromise between drinkers of alcohol and opponents, the State of Mississippi began to allow the open sale of beer and wine, for which it collected a black market tax. Citizens could purchase beer stamped with "Mississippi black market tax paid" standing in a cooler beside milk containers. Technically it was illegal to sell the beer, but it was also tolerated. However, in one case the state seized a stock of alcoholic beverages from a bootlegger near Hattiesburg, Mississippi, who then sued to get back his property because he had paid the black market tax. He lost in court on the grounds that the state had the right to seize the contraband even if he had paid the tax. The case demonstrated the hazards of dealing in black markets even when the affected trade is almost legal.

The manufacture, transportation and sale of alcoholic beverages in black markets has a long history. The Whiskey Rebellion of the 1790s began a long American tradition of trafficking in illicit distilling and distributing of untaxed whiskey. During the Prohibition era of the 1920s numerous illegal stills operated, some people made "bathtub gin," while others made home-brewed beer. In the Great Depression there were farmers who were unable to get good returns for their fruit harvests. In some places they fermented the fruit into alcoholic beverages that were sold by local bootleggers in an underground economy. Many of these farmers engaged in a black market trade but were otherwise upstanding citizens. Law enforcement in many places also accepted payments to ignore this black market trade.

Weapons

In contemporary times the illegal sale of alcohol has been supplanted by drug trafficking. Those engaged in illegal drug trafficking often use weapons purchased in the black market in guns. The guns used are often more powerful than those available to the police forces because the police have to operate on a much smaller budget for weapons purchases than do the criminals.

The illegal sale of guns is widespread globally. Following the Cold War many former communist countries had large arsenals of small arms and sometimes larger weapons that were sold to nations-states in Third World countries or to guerrilla groups operating there. In many cases these weapons were stolen from poorly guarded armories, or they were sold to arms dealers who then saw that they were delivered to buyers. The market in guns has continued to be brisk because of the numerous terrorist organizations and conflicts around the world. The numerous small wars that continue to flare up make the demand for weapons virtually constant. Weapons purchased by the various criminal organizations around the world are used to attack the police, rival gangs, or to intimidate civilian populations.

Currency

In the case of the South American drug cartels, huge sums of money flow into their coffers, often making it difficult for them to launder their profits. This leads to illegal currency exchanges, quite often through hidden bank transfers drawing banks into supplying services to black market operations.

Currency transfers in currency black markets are a common feature of many developing countries. Many do not permit free markets in foreign currency exchanges. They often impose a variety of regulations to protect their balance of payments or for other reasons. The various restrictions have different forms from country to country. Among the restrictions are limits on the foreign currency that can be purchased by citizens of their country or restrictions on currency brought into the country. The restrictions often interfere with trade, causing traders to devise ways to gain the currency that is needed for business. In some countries illegal markets in currency are places that attract foreigners seeking a much better exchange rate than the official rate. Such transactions may be openly tolerated, occasionally punished or sometimes severely punished depending upon political needs.

Transportation

Transportation services are another area of underground or shadow market operations. In many places unlicensed cab drivers operate outside of the government regulated system. The unlicensed cabs may be cheaper than the licensed cabs, but riders, especially foreign visitors, may be victimized by thieves or kidnappers if they take one of these cabs. Illegal cab drivers or unlicensed guides are common in Third World countries and they may try to overcharge or to take the fare to places where they are pressured into buying goods from a "cousin."

In many jurisdictions participation in black markets is a criminal offense whether the participant is a seller or a buyer. The illegal nature of these markets puts buyers at greater risk from criminals as well as from government sanctions.

See Also: Copyright Infringement; Gray Market; Money Laundering; Sea Piracy; Smuggling.

Bibliography. Peter Andreas, *Blue Helmets and Black Markets* (Cornell University Press, 2008); Tihomir Bezlov, *Transportation, Smuggling and Organized Crime* (Center for the Study of Democracy, 2004); Gargi Bhattacharyya, *Traffick: The Illicit Movement of People and Things* (Pluto Press, 2005); Ben Davies and Jane Goodall, *Black Market: Inside the Endangered Species Trade in Asia* (Mandala Publishing, 2005); Gianluca Fiorentini and Stefana Zamagni, eds., *Economics of Corruption and Illegal Markets* (Edward Elgar Publishing, 2000); Alan Green, *Animal Underworld: Inside America's Black Market for Rare and Exotic Species* (Public Affairs, 2006); James S. Henry, *The Blood Bankers: Tales from the Global Underground Economy* (Four Walls Eight Windows, 2003); Lora Lumpe, ed., *Running Guns: The Global Black Market in Small Arms* (Zed Books, 2000); Moises Naim, *Illicit: How Smugglers, Traffickers, and Copycats Are Hijacking the Global Economy* (Random House, 2006); Mangai Natarajan and Mike Hough, *Illegal Drug Markets: From Research to Prevention Policy* (Willow Tree Press, 2000); R. T. Naylor, *Wages of Crime: Black Markets, Illegal Finance and the Underworld Economy* (Cornell University Press, 2002); Ramsay M. Ravenel, *Illegal Logging in the Tropics: Strategies for Cutting Crime* (Taylor & Francis, 2005); Peter Reuter, *Organization of Illegal Markets: An Economic Analysis* (University Press of the Pacific, 2004); Friedrich Schneider and Dominik H. Enste, *The Shadow Economy* (Cambridge University Press, 2007); Paul Steege, *Black Market, Cold War* (Cambridge University Press, 2007); Kimberly L. Thachuk, *Transnational Threats: Smuggling and Trafficking in Arms, Drugs, and Human Life* (Praeger Security International, 2007); Sudhir Alladi Venkatesh, *Off the Books: The Underground Economy of the Urban Poor* (Harvard University Press, 2006); Sheldon Zhang, *Chinese Human Smuggling Organizations: Families, Social Networks, and Cultural Imperatives* (Stanford University Press, 2008).

ANDREW J. WASKEY
DALTON STATE COLLEGE

Blame Culture

Blame culture can be defined as the attitude of a person or a group of people of not accepting the responsibility for making a mistake in order to avoid the risk of being criticized or prosecuted. This phenomenon has infiltrated every part of modern society, especially in the Western world in the last 50 years. Cancer patients suing the tobacco companies, obese people blaming the fast food companies for their condition, malpractice cases in the medical practices, etc., are a few of the many examples of blame culture. This is sometimes also referred to as compensation culture. An extreme example of this culture was a burglar suing the household for getting hurt while he was in the act.

The blame culture has become a major nuisance in the healthcare industry. Many millions of dollars are being paid out to patients each year in personal damage cases. It is hard for anyone to report or admit a medical error, especially if it has caused any harm to the patient. The individual involved is afraid of being blamed and punished for the error committed. Often, reporting errors damages professional image, self-confidence, and eventually one's practice in the competitive environment of medical and health services. It is challenging to maintain professional and institutional accountability along with increased public safety and quality of service.

To find a way to reduce the rate of medication error, the government of Great Britain established the National Patient Safety Agency (NPSA) in July 2001. NPSA has launched a nationwide reporting scheme for recording actual medication errors and near misses across the National Health Service to analyze the root causes. The goal of this program is to discourage the blame culture by viewing those who report the errors as heroes. It is, however, important to clarify where and how the professional responsibility fits into the "no blame" culture.

It is not unexpected that when something goes wrong people try to find an explanation and hold someone accountable. But blaming others instead of taking personal responsibility for any misfortune or wrongdoing and trying to obtain compensation has become part of modern culture in the United States and Europe. As a result, the corporations, the institutions, and the general public are all spending an excessive amount of time, energy, and money in innumerable frivolous lawsuits in mostly Western societies. In New Zealand, for example, within the first few years of the introduction in 1974 of the "no fault" principle for accidents, the accident rate increased by 40 percent from people taking advantage of the ACC benefits. Quickly tougher policies were introduced to avoid bankruptcy from the escalating costs.

It is not merely a coincidence that the blame culture is more prominent in the countries with the highest numbers of legal professionals. The United States is at the top of the list of countries with the most lawyers per person (1 lawyer per 265 Americans), followed by Brazil, Spain, Italy, the United Kingdom, Germany, and France in 2007. The increasing numbers of legal personnel have improved accessibility and communications with the public directly, or through media like television ads. They have been very persuasive in encouraging the cultural shift from personal accountability to blaming others.

The financial well-being of the advanced countries is more than ever tied to the rest of the world. Developing countries like China and India are experiencing economic prosperity that was unimaginable in the near past. However, their legal systems and personnel are not yet as established as in the United States and Europe. Hence their societies still focus on personal accountability. It is the obligation of the advanced countries to direct their societies toward "no blame culture," which not only will help to stop the financial bleeding of institutions, government, and corporations in their own countries, but also will prevent the nationals from emerging countries from taking the same path toward "blame culture."

See Also: Cross-Cultural Research; Cultural Norms and Scripts; Culture-Specific Values; Enculturation; Ethnocentrism; Gannon's Cultural Metaphors; Loyalty; Negotiation and Negotiating Styles; Opportunistic Behavior; Silent Language of Hall (Nonverbal Communication).

Bibliography. Michael Bassett, *The Blame Culture* (DOM/PRESS, 2004); Jane Galt, "Lawsuit Culture," www.janegalt.net (cited March 2009); D. McArdle, N. Burns, and A. Ireland "Attitudes and Beliefs of Doctors Towards Medication Error Reporting," *International Journal of Health Care Quality Assurance* (v.16, 2003); Alan Nathan, "Reporting Errors: Can a 'Fair Blame Culture' Really Work for Pharmacists?" *The Pharmaceutical Journal* (v. 272); Jeffrey O'Connell and Joseph R. Baldwin, "(In)juries, (In)justice, and (Il)legal Blame: Tort Law as Melodrama—or is Farce?" *UCLA Law Review* (v.50/2, 2002); Michael Pearn, Chris Mulrooney, and Tim Payne, *Ending the Blame Culture* (Gower Publishing Ltd., 1998); David Pollitt, "Track-Supervisor Training Transforms Attitudes and Culture at Tube Lines," *Training and Management Development Methods* (v.21/3, 2007); Tim van Zwanenberg, "Clinical Governance in Primary Care: From Blind-eye to No-blame Culture in One Short Leap?" *British Journal of Clinical Governance* (v.6/2, 2001).

Mousumi Roy
Pennsylvania State University

Blocked Funds

Blocked funds are capital assets or cash flows generated by a foreign project that cannot be transferred to another country because of restrictions imposed by the host government. Reasons for funds being blocked include political motives, criminal activity, trading violations, or exchange controls on foreign currencies. Some firms specialize in the trading of these securities, but at a sharp discount. Blocked funds are also used in popular media to illustrate any act by a financial institution restricting access to or transfer of funds; this has led to a broader (if somewhat incorrect) use of the term. The use of blocked funds has also led to the emergence of "blocked funds loan scams" on unsuspecting consumers around the world.

Funds are usually blocked for one of four reasons: political motives, criminal activity, trading violations, or exchange controls on foreign currencies. Funds can be blocked for political motives, such as a country being at war or in connection to a national emergency. For example, in 1992, following the Iraqi invasion of Kuwait, Iraqi funds abroad were frozen by the United States to pressure Iraq to stop the invasion as well as for leverage to extract war reparations.

Furthermore, funds can be blocked when the host government suspects the funds are either produced by, or used to generate criminal activities. In those cases, the host government will force the institution to hold the funds until it is satisfied that no illegal activities occurred. If illegal activities are found to have occurred, the host government will demand the funds be turned over to it. One recent example occurred when the U.S. Justice Department requested payment services like Visa and PayPal to block fund transfers to offshore gambling Web sites until which time it could determine the legality of these sites.

Trading violations are a rather uncommon reason for blocking funds; this is usually at the behest of a trading authority, which will ask the financial institution to hold funds because of questionable transactions. Finally, in rare occurrences, currency transfers can be restricted by the host government, forcing financial institutions to block funds until such restrictions are lifted.

Once a host government determines some capital has to be blocked, it will contact the financial institution handling the transaction and will request the institution freeze the funds. The financial institution then places the funds in an interest-bearing account until which time the host government will decide if the funds can be released. During the period when the funds are frozen, the institution makes a reasonable attempt to place the capital in a financial product that generates a commercially acceptable interest rate; interest is returned to the capital holder once funds are unblocked.

It is also possible for funds to be blocked even if they are only transiting in the country hosting the funds. For example, a company in Europe transiting funds through the United States to a country with fund restrictions might have their funds frozen, even if the funds were only in financial transit in the United States. Countries usually reserve the right to verify that funds are not transiting to blocked countries or individuals through its national financial system.

R. D. Ellis has suggested different techniques to prevent having funds blocked by host governments. These techniques include receiving contract payments in dollars, purchasing host country dollar bonds, increasing local purchases, making capital investments with the blocked funds in the host country, and establishing counter trades of equivalent value.

Market Impact

There are a number of brokers and banks that specialize in trading blocked funds. By demanding a deep discount on the blocked funds, these firms take on the risk that the funds may never be released in exchange for potential profits. Some firms specialize in blocked funds due to currency transfer issues; they facilitate the exchange from one currency to the next, making profits on the currency conversion rate they request.

Blocked funds transactions are used in less ethical transactions as well. Some organizations use them for money laundering, exchanging illegally obtained capital for "clean" money. Other scams include individuals purchasing blocked funds for deep discount, only to find that the funds did not exist, or that the transaction has been cancelled by the offering party.

See Also: International Law; Risk Management.

Bibliography. R. D. Ellis, "Recognizing and Avoiding Currency Exchange Problems in International Project Management," *Proceedings of the Project Management Institute Seminar/Symposium* (1988); Young Hoon Kwark, "Risk Management in International Development Projects," *Proceedings of the Project Management Institute Annual Seminars & Symposium* (2001); Zia Ullah, "The Blocking of Funds by OFAC," Pannone LLP, www.pannone.com (cited March 2009).

JEAN-FRANCOIS DENAULT,
UNIVERSITÉ DE MONTRÉAL

The photo shows one of Bloomberg's 2,000 reporters and editors at work in a television studio in London, England.

Bloomberg

Bloomberg L.P. operates the largest privately owned data, news, and financial information network in the world. It provides real-time and historical information on some five million bonds, equities, commodities, currencies, and funds. Its electronic library also holds data on virtually every publicly traded company and has a collection of biographies on more than one million people. Bloomberg's customers include approximately 250,000 subscribers at central banks, investment institutions, commercial banks, insurance companies, corporations, government agencies, law firms, and news organizations in over 150 countries. Bloomberg customers benefit from on-demand multimedia content and communications and extensive electronic-trading capabilities through its network. Bloomberg employs approximately 8,000 people in 55 countries.

The core product of Bloomberg is its subscription service that provides data, news, analytics, multimedia reports and messaging, and trading functions to any personal computer. The service is leased for a flat fee of $1,500 per month paid quarterly in advance on a two-year contract. The Bloomberg network delivers a global securities database with historical pricing data and corporate information from more than 200 exchanges including the New York Stock Exchange, NASD, and the Options Price Reporting Authority (OPRA).

Tools and Services

Bloomberg offers a number of trading tools and services. Its electronic trading products are used by portfolio managers, institutional traders, broker-dealers, market makers, and hedge fund managers for front-to-back execution, clearing and settlement functions on equities, debt, futures, options, and foreign exchange instruments. Bloomberg's trading products are used in over 60 global markets on five continents.

The Bloomberg Terminal is the firm's signature device seen on trading floors around the world, identified by its dual 17-inch flat panels. Users can set up their screens any way they like, typically displaying multiple data and video windows at once. The companion keyboard with its customized keys and biometric security technology provides for the optimal use of Bloomberg information and trading software. The Bloomberg network offers a real-time voice and video system enabling its users to record and send video messages and to participate in one-to-one or multi-caller audio/video conferences.

Bloomberg Law provides law firms a comprehensive source for legal research, including a comprehensive range of case law, codes, statutes, and regulations; dockets, access to pleadings, decisions, adversary proceedings, appeals, and court records;

federal and state securities litigation, SEC enforcement and administrative actions, regulatory guidance, legislative activity, exchange, and rulemaking. It offers specialty services in the areas of bankruptcy, mergers and acquisitions, securities, intellectual property, due diligence, compliance, and litigation. It also provides analytical treatises, proprietary reports, updates on client-development intelligence, news, and research. Bloomberg Insurance is collection of research and analysis applications for insurance underwriters and brokers of commercial lines.

Bloomberg News is a real-time news service that provides definitive coverage of companies, markets, industries, economies, and governments serving readers in more than 130 countries, 24 hours a day, 365 days a year. Bloomberg News offers a wide array of communication services available to the public. These include television and radio programs in seven languages, financial book publishing, an award-winning magazine, and print news carried by more than 400 publications in 70 countries. Bloomberg News employs more than 2,000 reporters and editors in 130 bureaus and publishes more than 5,000 stories on an average day to 400 newspapers worldwide, with a combined circulation of 79 million people.

Bloomberg 1130 (WBBR-AM) is a 24-hour, digital all-news radio station that serves the New York, New Jersey, and Connecticut areas. It syndicates reports to more than 840 radio stations worldwide as well as the Sirius, XM, and WorldSpace satellite radio services. Bloomberg News broadcasts through 11 television networks in seven languages reaching more than 200 million homes. It also maintains an archive of more than 15 million stories and multimedia reports, and a photo library of some 190,000 images.

Bloomberg.com has consistently ranked among top financial Web sites. Bloomberg *Markets* magazine is the largest monthly magazine for financial professionals in the world. Bloomberg Press publishes practical books for financial professionals as well as books of general interest on investing, economics, current affairs, and policy affecting sophisticated investors. More than 140 titles have been released since 1996. The books are written by leading authorities and practitioners and are published in more than 20 languages.

Bloomberg employs a highly trained, multilingual team of technical operators and engineers to provide customer help 24 hours a day, seven days a week.

Bloomberg provides individual and group seminars, special events, and Bloomberg University to train clients and prospects about the information solutions available through its network. It also has a certification program for financial professionals able to demonstrate comprehensive knowledge of its products.

Bloomberg's headquarters are in a seven-story building designed by Cesar Pelli on Lexington Avenue in Manhattan. The open-plan glass building is designed to be a physical manifestation of the 24/7 global marketplace and of information transparency. The building has some 22 fish tanks filled with exotic rare specimens (every office contains a fish tank) and edgy works of art, from a massive aromatic cedar artwork in the first-floor lobby to a large titanium thundercloud over an escalator. The work layout is nonhierarchical with employees stationed every six linear feet in a long row of desks.

Revenues for 2006 were approximately $4.7 billion with operating profits before taxes of about $1.5 billion. In addition to the firm founders, Merrill Lynch holds a 20 percent stake in Bloomberg.

See Also: Market Research; Media; Merrill Lynch.

Bibliography. Bloomberg.com, about.bloomberg.com (cited March 2009); Carol J. Loomis, "The Bloomberg," *Fortune* (April 16, 2007); Aline van Duyn, "News Chief Stays Hungry for Expansion," *Financial Times* (USA) (June 21, 2007).

FRANK L. WINFREY
LYON COLLEGE

BMW

The Bayerische Motoren Werke (BMW Group), a German manufacturer of motorcycles, aircraft engines, and automobiles, producing the three premium products BMW, MINI, and Rolls-Royce, has 23 production plants in 12 countries and representation in more than 140. The BMW Group offers customized luxury cars to an international audience.

BMW is among the world's leading premium manufacturers. In 2007 the net profit of the company for the first time exceeded the €3 billion figure, with more than 1,276,000 BMW brand cars, 222,875 MINI units, and 1,010 Rolls-Royce cars sold. BMW AG, which has more than 107,000 employees (2007), is one of the pillars of the well-known German automobile industry.

Despite its planned downsizing by 8,000 jobs in 2008, BMW remains among the top five companies on the Corporate Trust Index (CTI) of DAX-listed German companies. Despite losing the number one position it had held for several years, BMW remains on this index ahead of fellow German car makers Daimler and Volkswagen.

In a study undertaken of the Sustainable Value of 16 automobile manufacturers, conducted by the Berlin Institute for Futures Studies and Technology Assessment and the Queen's University Management School in Belfast and funded by BMW, BMW ranked second. The study examined the fact that enterprises use not only capital but also ecological and social resources such as water and labor in their production processes. If these resources are employed more efficiently than the market, it is a positive sustainable value. With the provision for ecological and social resources, the study links the value of sustainability with investment decision-making processes.

Following a strategy of local production, this German global player is committing itself to a long-term market penetration strategy while at the same time evading high import duties on importing foreign-produced cars. Another sales and production strategy used by BMW is the completely knocked down (CKD) process in which car parts and components are imported from overseas and locally assembled also using locally produced parts.

Historical Milestones

The aircraft-engine producing company Rapp-Motorenwerke was renamed Bayerische Motoren Werke GmbH on July 21, 1917. Shortly before the end of World War I, on August 13, 1918, the Bayerische Motoren Werke GmbH became a stock corporation. As the Treaty of Versailles forbade German companies to manufacture aircraft engines, in the postwar years the new company specialized in the production of rail vehicle brakes and built-in engines. In 1922 Bayerische Flugzeug-Werke (BFW) purchased the engine production operations and the name BMW. Up to this day, the BFW founding date of March 7, 1916, is considered by BMW as the formation date of the Bayerische Motoren Werke.

In the 1930s, boosted by increasing state subsidies, BMW increased its production of aircraft engines. In 1934 the Aircraft Engines Division was merged with BMW Flugmotorenbau GmbH and later with a joint company of BMW AG and BMW Flugmotorenbau GmbH. This was followed by a period of cooperation with the Brandenburgische Motorenwerke GmbH (Bramo) and the later takeover of Bramo by BMW. The production of aircraft engines rose significantly during the war years.

While BMW's Munich plant was heavily battered by air raids during the last years of World War II, the plant in Allach got off relatively lightly. Production slowly resumed in mid-1945 when BMW was allowed to repair U.S. Army vehicles and to manufacture spare parts, agricultural equipment, and bicycles. However, as the U.S. military government transitionally expropriated BMW from its plants, and in the course of Germany's reparation payments, the company lost control over both assets and machinery.

The slow recovery of the company in the post-war years rendered it vulnerable to takeover bids. In 1959 Daimler-Benz made an offer to BMW, expressing its interest in restructuring the company. BMW rejected the offer and soon afterward restructured itself. Over the next two decades the company, under Board of Management chairman Eberhard von Kuenheim, expanded from a domestic and European brand to an international brand featuring one of the world's most recognized commercial logos.

The expansion strategy included the acquisition of the British Rover Group in 1994 with its brands Rover, Land Rover, MINI, and MG. In 1998 BMW purchased the name Rolls-Royce for cars (with usage not before 2003) that were still being built by the German Volkswagen Group at the time. In 2000 BMW decided to sell Rover, MG, and Land Rover for a very low price as it could no longer cope with high restructuring costs and low profits. Since 2000, BMW has positioned its cars in the premium segment of the international automobile market.

See Also: DaimlerChrysler; DAX Index (Germany); Germany; Volkswagen.

Bibliography. BMW Group, *Corporate News. BMW Group Heading Yowards a Successful Year in 2008* (Bayerische Motoren Werke AG, 2008); BMW Group, *The Fascination* *of Production* (Bayerische Motoren Werke AG, 2007); "BMW Roundel Celebrates 90 Years," www.Motorcycle.com (cited March 2009); Lars Mende, "Vertrauensranking. Stellenabbau—na und?" [Ranking of Confidence. Reduction of Jobs—So What?], www.manager-magazin.de (cited March 2009); Mark C. Schneider, "Nachhaltigkeit. Toyota macht das Rennen" [Sustainability. Toyota Comes Out First], *Wirtschaftswoche*, www.wiwo.de (cited March 2009).

SABINE H. HOFFMANN
AMERICAN UNIVERSITY OF THE MIDDLE EAST

BNP Paribas

One of the most prominent European banks, BNP Paribas was formed in 2000 with the merger of the Banque Nationale de Paris and Paribas, two Parisian banks which, with Crédit Lyonnais (est. 1863) and Société Générale (est. 1864) constitute the "old banks" of France, established in the 19th century and foremost in prestige throughout the 20th. In 2007–08, the bank made headlines as one of several major foreign banks left vulnerable by the American subprime mortgage crisis.

Banque Nationale de Paris had been formed in 1966 by the merger of two 19th-century retail banks, Banque Nationale pour le Commerce et l'Industrie (BNCI) and Comptoir National d'Escompte de Paris (CNEP). Both banks had been nationalized at the end of World War II, along with Crédit Lyonnais and Société Générale, as part of France's postwar reorganization of banking regulations. When the government decided to experiment with re-privatizing these banks decades later, BNP was the second to be privatized, in 1993, after the privatization of Société Générale proved successful. (Crédit Lyonnais followed in 1999.)

Paribas's origins lie with the Banque de Crédit et Depot des Pays-Bas, which was founded in Amsterdam in 1863 and immediately opened a Parisian branch, helping to connect Parisian investors (still recovering from the havoc wrought on the French banking and finance industry by the regime changes of the first half of the century) with private banking throughout Europe. Only nine years after its founding, BCDPB merged with the Banque de Paris (est.

1869) to form the Banque de Paris et des Pays-Bas (BPPB) in January 1872.

BPPB was a public limited company, and began a relationship with Crédit Lyonnais early on, pairing with it to back part of a loan for the French government to repay war debts; a large portion of the funds for the loan was raised from across Europe, through the Pays-Bas connections. This kind of financial intermediation remained a primary pursuit of BPPB through the early 20th century, and it was instrumental in financing the French defense industry during World War I. Because it was not nationalized in the wake of World War II, it was able to become a more prominent commercial bank, and assisted and profited from the reconstruction of French industry.

The bank was eventually renamed Paribas, compressing the "Pari" of Paris and the "bas" of Pays-Bas. It became a focal part of the competition between BNP and Société Générale after both were privatized, as Société Générale attempted to buy out Paribas stock while BNP made attempts to acquire both Paribas and Société Générale. The bid for Paribas eventually succeeded, and BNP Paribas, formed in May of 2000, enjoyed a stronger position in the market. In 2007, when the American subprime mortgage crisis threatened three of BNP Paribas's funds—Parvest Dynamic ABS, BNP Paribas ABS EURIBOR, and BNP Paribas ABS EONIA—the bank suspended their operation, precipitating the intervention of the European Central Bank for the first time since the financial panic following 9/11. A $130 billion loan at 4 percent interest was extended by the ECB in order to keep BNP Paribas's announcement from causing further panic.

BNP Paribas has become the largest bank in the Eurozone by assets, and the second-largest by market cap. Just under half of its 162,000 employees work in Europe, and the bank's branches are spread throughout 87 countries. In its home country, it is most active as a retail bank, having inherited Paribas's extensive coverage—nearly 200 locations in Paris alone, another 2000 throughout the rest of the country, serving 6 million consumers. Its subsidiaries include Bank of the West in the United States, and the Italian bank BNL. The idiosyncratic scholar Nassim Taleb, best known for his writings on finance and the mathematics of rare occurrences—and for his prediction of the failure of Fannie Mae—once worked for BNP Paribas as a proprietary trader.

See Also: CAC 40; France; Mortgage Credit Crisis of 2008; Subprime Loans.

Bibliography. Niall Ferguson, *The Ascent of Money: A Financial History of the World* (Penguin, 2008); James Kanter and Julia Werdigier, "Big French Bank Suspends Funds," *New York Times* (August 10, 2007); Rehan Ul-Haq and Jorg Itschert, *International Banking Strategic Alliances: Reflections on BNP/Dresdner* (Palgrave Macmillan, 2004).

BILL KTE'PI
INDEPENDENT SCHOLAR

Board of Directors

A board of directors is a group of people elected by the shareholders of a corporation to oversee the management of the corporation. Directors are elected at annual general meetings. At this meeting shareholders have the ultimate power to control both their investment and their board of directors. The board of directors delegates authority for day-to-day operations to a group of managers called officers. The primary duty of directors is to act in the best interest of the company and its shareholders.

There are three types of director: executive director, nonexecutive director, and independent nonexecutive director. An executive director is also an employee of the company, whereas a nonexecutive director is not an employee. The standard practice is for the executive director to have an appointment letter, rather than a contract of employment, and to be paid an agreed fee for services rendered. A nonexecutive director usually provides his or her services part-time and is not expected to be involved in the day-to-day running of the company. There is no legal distinction between executive and nonexecutive directors. Independent nonexecutive directors are nonexecutive directors who are free from any connection with the company that might affect their opinions and behavior. An example of a connection is an executive director who manages the same business in which they serve on the board of directors.

A board of directors normally has three committees: nominating, compensation, and audit. The nominating committee selects new candidates to be reviewed for positions on the board. The compensation committee reviews the executives' remuneration. The audit committee examines internal audits and reports from independent audit firms.

The United Kingdom's Financial Reporting Council set up its Combined Code on Corporate Governance in 2003. The code sets out its own view of the role of the board of directors: provide entrepreneurial leadership; set strategy; ensure human and financial resources are available to achieve objectives; review management performance; set the company's values and standards; and satisfy themselves as to the integrity of financial information and robustness of financial controls and risk management. The code also describes the role of chairman of the board of directors: the chairman leads the board, ensures there is a good relationship between the executive and nonexecutive directors, and bears primary responsibility for communications and liaison with shareholders. The code adds that the roles of chairman and chief executive should not be held by the same person. The chief executive is responsible for the day-to-day management of the company and carries out the decisions of the board. The code also requires there to be a balance between the number of executive and nonexecutive directors so that no individual or small group can dominate the board's decision making.

The Sarbanes-Oxley Act is a wide-ranging U.S. corporate reform legislation, coauthored by the Democrat in charge of the Senate Banking Committee, Paul Sarbanes, and Republican Congressman Michael Oxley. The act, which became law in July 2002, lays down stringent procedures regarding the accuracy and reliability of corporate disclosures, places restrictions on auditors providing nonaudit services, and obliges top executives to verify their accounts personally. Under the act, companies should establish an audit committee comprised solely of independent board members.

A good board structure will take into account the board's independence, size, committees and functions, and director development. The combined code states that, in order to qualify as an independent nonexecutive director, an individual must be free of any connections that might lead to conflicts of interest.

The board of an American company may be made up of a large number of nonexecutive directors and only one or two executive directors, whereas a British board has more executive directors. The size of a board can also affect its efficiency. The larger the board, the harder it is to become active and engaged. On the other hand, the board must be large enough to have a range of skills and experience to operate successfully. But directors' free-riding intentions may be higher when the board becomes larger. It has been pointed out that the law of diminishing returns may be applicable here, as companies with small boards have better financial ratios. The loss of value occurs as boards grow from small to medium size.

How a board works and how well it speaks for its shareholders is a key component of a company's performance and financial success. The director may be a senior executive of another company. Many directors also serve on more than one board, in addition to other full-time commitments. A common criticism of this arrangement is the claim that these directors are unable to carry out their directors' duties. The role of directors is largely advisory and does not involve important commercial decision making. When the chairman of the board is also the chief executive officer, the power of directors diminishes.

See Also: Corporate Governance; Decision Making; Management; Sarbanes-Oxley.

Bibliography. William G. Bowen, *The Board Book: An Insider's Guide for Directors and Trustees* (W. W. Norton and Company, 2008); Financial Reporting Council, "The Combined Code on Corporate Governance, June 2008," www.frc.org.uk/corporate (cited March 2009); Scott Green, *Sarbanes-Oxley and the Board of Directors* (John Wiley & Son, 2005); David Yermack, "Higher Market Valuation of Companies with a Small Board of Directors," *Journal of Financial Economics* (v.40, 1996).

TAI MING WUT
INDEPENDENT SCHOLAR

Boeing

The Boeing Airplane Company (originally Pacific Aero Products) was founded in 1916 in Seattle, Washington, by Yale engineer William Boeing and Navy engineer George Westervelt. It was only 13 years since the Wright brothers' successful flight, and

Boeing displayed this extra long-range 777 Worldliner aircraft at the Paris Air Show in 2005.

the aviation industry would go through a number of changes, Boeing changing with it. When the company was folded in with Boeing's airline (est. 1927) and Pacific Air Transport, it became the United Aircraft and Transport Corporation, and went on an acquisition spree of smaller aviation companies. 1933 saw the introduction of the Boeing 247, the first aircraft significantly similar to modern passenger planes, with an autopilot, retractable landing gear, cantilevered wings with wing flaps, deicing boots, and a metal semi-monocoque construction. The modern airplane had arrived. It was also the first model of aircraft to be sabotaged; when a nitroglycerin device was detonated on a 247 over Indiana, the *New York Times* headline put the then-unfamiliar word *bomber* in quotation marks.

United both manufactured airplanes and flew them, and knew the 247 was first in its class—first of a new class—so it kept the first 60, gaining a competitive advantage on other airlines. This was one of the things that led to the 1934 Air Mail Act, in the spirit of trustbusting and the New Deal: Corporations were no longer allowed to both manufacture and fly planes. United was thus split into three companies: United Airlines, the United Aircraft Corporation, and the Boeing Airplane Company. Boeing continued to be at the forefront of aircraft design, building the "flying boat" (the Boeing 314) for the Pan Am airline in 1939. The largest passenger plane of its time, it carried 90 passengers on transoceanic flights.

Boeing also developed the pressurized cabin, allowing planes to travel above the weather, an innovation taken for granted now, but which revolutionized air travel and paved the way for the widespread commercial flights of today. In the early days of the Cold War, Boeing carved out a position in the defense industry, alongside competitors Lockheed Martin and McDonnell Douglas. It remained and remains the leading aircraft manufacturer, especially in passenger planes—introducing the first jet airliner in the early 1950s, the first commercial jet (the 707) in 1958, and the 747 in 1970. The 747 remains Boeing's most successful aircraft, and indeed one of the most famous aircraft by any manufacturer. Development cost over $1 billion, and the final product seated 450 passengers on two decks, on a craft with an intercontinental range. Almost 40 years later, the 747 remains in production, something that can be said of few vehicles of any mode.

Boeing acquired McDonnell Douglas in 1997 when its competitor fell on hard times, giving the company a near-monopoly on intercontinental aircraft. Its main competitor since the 1980s has been Airbus, a European consortium formed in 1970. While Airbus's early successes were in the then-untapped short-to-medium-range aircraft market, it now competes directly with Boeing in the long-range market, and has enjoyed a steadily increasing share of new orders worldwide. Boeing and the American government have disputed Airbus's use of research and development subsidies from the European Union, claiming they violate the World Trade Organization (and when the complaint was first lodged, the General Agreement on Tariffs and Trade); a 1992 agreement limited those subsidies.

In the 21st century, Boeing has lost the coveted Jet Strike Fighter project for the U.S. Defense Department to Lockheed Martin, and continues to battle with Airbus. But it is the principal contractor for the International Space Station and a prominent contributor to NASA's manned Mars mission.

See Also: EADS; Lockheed Martin; Manufacturing; Transportation.

Bibliography. Kenny Kemp, *Flight of the Titans: Boeing, Airbus, and the Battle for the Future of Air Travel* (Virgin Books, 2007); John Newhouse, *Boeing versus Airbus: The Inside Story of the Greatest International Competition in Business* (Vintage, 2008); Joe Sutter and Jay Spenser, *747: Creating the World's First Jumbo Jet and Other Adventures in a Life in Aviation* (Collins, 2007).

Bill Kte'pi
Independent Scholar

Bolivia

A landlocked country in South America, the Republic of Bolivia (population 9,118,000 in 2007, gross domestic product [GDP] $40 billion) is named for Simon Bolivar, the revolutionary and former president of Venezuela, who was instrumental not only in Bolivia's successful war for independence in 1825, but the wars of independence across the Spanish-American colonies. Its history since independence has been tumultuous, marked by long periods of widespread poverty. While many revolutions of the 18th and 19th centuries used independence as an excuse to create democracies, in practice Bolivia remained pseudofeudal until the 20th century, and the terrible living conditions of all but the upper classes provoked the revolution of 1952, which finally resulted in universal suffrage and public education for the rural populace. That government lasted 12 years, and was succeeded by a series of military juntas.

In the 21st century, Bolivian politics are beset by crises. The government's plan, in conjunction with the United States, to eliminate Bolivian cocaine production completely is resisted by much of the population, who have grown coca leaves for centuries, and in some cases enjoyed the profits of the cocaine trade in the last few decades. President Evo Morales has promoted legal coca leaf goods, such as teas and liqueurs, in an attempt to make peace with coca growers. Morales also renationalized Bolivia's oil and natural gas, in 2006.

Bolivia is a democratic republic with a bicameral parliament. The 130 members of the Chamber of Deputies and 27 members of the Chamber of Senators are elected to five-year terms by their constituencies. In practice, the role of the legislature is much weaker than that of the executive branch, and principally discusses legislation introduced by the president. The president also serves a five-year term. The current president is Morales, from the Socialist party, whose term began at the start of 2006.

Despite its natural resources, Bolivia has the lowest per capita GDP in South America, in part because of its lack of a coastline: Transporting natural gas, for instance, most of which is exported to Brazil, requires the use of expensive pipelines that eat into the profits. Inflation and unemployment are high, and the situation is worsened by a long history of corruption at multiple levels of government, with few serious efforts to stamp it out.

The fossil fuels industry is almost solely responsible for Bolivia's trade surplus. The country is energy self-sufficient, with fossil fuels accounting for some 42 percent of energy use and hydroelectric power responsible for most of the rest. Outside of fossil fuels, exports include soy, zinc, and tin; Bolivia's main trading partners are other South American countries (especially Brazil, Argentina, and Chile), the United States, China, and Japan. Foreign investment has been encouraged by various privatization acts since the 1990s, but declines whenever there is political unrest, and Bolivia has yet to demonstrate long-term economic stability.

See Also: Company Profiles: South America; Microfinance; South America.

Bibliography. Benjamin Dangl, *The Price of Fire: Resource Wars and Social Movements in Bolivia* (AK Press, 2007); Rex A. Hudson and Dennis M. Hanratty, eds., *Bolivia: A Country Study*, 3rd ed. (Library of Congress, 1991); Benjamin Kohl and Linda Farthing, *Impasse in Bolivia: Neoliberal Hegemony and Popular Resistance* (Zed Books, 2006); Jeffrey D. Sachs, ed., *Developing Country Debt and Economic Performance, Volume 2: Country Studies: Argentina, Bolivia, Brazil, Mexico* (University of Chicago Press, 1990).

Bill Kte'pi
Independent Scholar

Bonded Warehouse

A bonded warehouse is a public or private warehouse authorized by customs officials to hold goods for which payment of duties and VAT (value added tax) has been deferred until removal. Goods stored in a bonded warehouse can be taken out only after applicable taxes and duties have been paid on them, or when they are moved by a bonded carrier to another bonded warehouse or a customs area. If the goods are destroyed under customs supervision, no duty is payable.

Bonded warehouses are also used to store certain types of finished products on which there are heavy domestic excise taxes, since the producer is not required to pay taxes until the product is taken for distribution. Since a producer may carry substantial inventories of some of these products, a bonded warehouse arrangement helps conserve capital. For example, consider a United Kingdom company trading in spirits that pays £18,000 excise duty and £4,000 VAT per order. Fifteen monthly orders result in £330,000 of duties per month. Two-month average stock turnaround would save the company £660,000 that would otherwise be tied up in prepayment of taxes.

Bonded warehouses sometimes may be used to store goods imported temporarily into a country for transshipment or for consolidation in a shipment going elsewhere. For example, a U.S.-based distributor may be importing products from Europe with the intention of part-exporting to South America. The imported product from Europe would be held at a bonded warehouse until a decision is made about what to import into the United States and what to export. The imported product may be combined with a domestic product and then shipped to South America with the cost benefits of a consolidated shipment. The goods that are imported have the benefit of tax deferral until the time they are withdrawn for consumption, and the exported goods never entered the U.S. economy, so no taxes/duties would be obligated. For the export, the goods would transit from the bonded warehouse to the outbound port by a bonded carrier. Bonded warehouses may also be used to avoid return or destruction of merchandise for which a quota has closed (when the quota opens, stored merchandise may then be withdrawn).

Traditionally, companies have had the choice of delivering the goods through one central point of entry, possibly using a bonded warehouse, where they deconsolidate the cargo, then physically distribute the goods from there, or through a multiple-entry approach, physically transporting products to as many ports of entry as necessary to support their distribution model. Today, through the use of a "virtual bonded warehouse" it is possible for a European Union (EU) importer to separate the physical entry of products from their related financial transactions (for example, physical in Madrid and financial in Amsterdam), thereby improving the ease of transportation throughout the continent.

Cross-border customs warehouses can also be set. If a company has several warehousing facilities in more than one EU country, they can be linked together into a single bonded warehouse system under one license. This offers the advantage that all the customs declarations can be filed in the location where the centralized administration is kept. It is the company's own inventory control system, and not its physical facilities, that is bonded. Transporting goods from one bonded warehouse to another under the same license can be done without customs documents.

In a bonded warehouse simple activities such as cleaning, labeling, and repackaging may be carried out. More substantial activities, such as the completion of manufacturing operations before the finished product is shipped out to another customs jurisdiction, may also be carried out, but require an additional authorization for inward processing relief (IPR) or processing under customs control (PCC).

See Also: Common Market; Customs Broker; Freight Forwarder; North American Free Trade Agreement; Value Added Tax.

Bibliography. Thomas Cook, Rennie Alston, and Kelly Raia, *Mastering Import & Export Management* (AMACON, 2004); Robert Feinschreiber and Charles Crowley, *Import Handbook: A Compliance and Planning Guide* (Wiley, 1997).

Miguel Martins
University of Wolverhampton

Bonds

A form of debt issued by corporations, federal agencies, and local, state, and national governments, a bond is a financial security designed to pay back the bondholder on particular dates. Payments received by the bondholder typically consist of the repayment at the time of maturity of the principal amount borrowed as well as coupon payments (interest pay-

ments) made during the life of the bond (most commonly semi-annually, but often quarterly, monthly, or even once at the time the bond matures and the debt is retired). Because most bonds have a fixed interest payment that the bondholder receives, this form of debt security is also referred to as a fixed-income security.

Interest rates paid by the issuers of bonds can be fixed, can be paid at maturity, or can be variable as is the case with a step-up bond or a floating coupon level bond. The step-up coupon bond is the least complex of the variable rate bonds whereas a derivative bond (derivatives can be tied to an index such as an equity index or a consumer price index or determined by a mathematical equation that links the level of interest payments to an economic variable including market indices, single equities, or even commodity prices) can range from a simple structure to a very complex structure. An example of a fixed-coupon bond would be a bond with a $1,000 denomination (par value) that had a seven percent coupon paying semi-annually with a final stated maturity date of January 15, 2020. In this example, every January 15th and every July 15th until and including January 15, 2020, the investor holding the bond would receive $35 such that his or her annual income from the bond would be $70 (7 percent of $1,000 par value or face value of the bond). In addition, upon maturity of the bond on January 15, 2020, the investor would receive not only the last interest payment of $35, but also the principal par value of the bond, which is typically $1,000.

Some bonds are issued without regular interest payments such that all of the interest is paid at the time the bond matures. These bonds are called zero-coupon bonds; they are issued (or sold) at a deep discount to their face value and they mature at par. The difference between the discounted price and the par value of the bond at maturity is considered accreted interest and represents the return to the investor over a specific time period. Consider the example of a zero-coupon bond that matures January 15, 2020. If the investor bought the bond when it was first issued on January 15, 2010, at a price of $300, then the investor would stand to gain $700 in accreted interest over 10 years time, or $70 a year. Comparing the zero-coupon bond to the previous 7 percent fixed-coupon bond shows that both bondholders would earn $70 per year. The advantage of the 7 percent coupon bond is that the bondholder actually receives current income of $70 each year throughout the life of the bond, whereas the zero-coupon bondholder has to wait to receive his or her income until the bond matures or until he or she sells the zero-coupon bond in the marketplace. The advantage of the zero-coupon bond is that it requires a much smaller initial investment, in this case $300 for the zero-coupon bond versus $1,000 for the 7 percent coupon bond.

Variable Interest Bonds

Examples of variable interest bonds include a simple step-up coupon that will pay a certain coupon or interest rate for a specified period and then increase the coupon payments at a specific point in time. The simplest form of a step-up bond is called a one-time step-up in which the interest rate is fixed for a period of time and then steps-up once to a higher level. The number of times a bond may step-up typically varies from once to five or six times. As an example, the coupon of a one-time step-up bond might have the following characteristics: 4 percent from July 15, 2008, to January 15, 2010, 8 percent thereafter until maturity in January 15, 2020. Typically the step-up bond will be callable at par on the dates on which it is scheduled to have its coupon increased (step-up). When a bond is called by the issuer, the interest due to that point of time along with the principal of the bond at par value is paid to the bondholder in return for the debt being retired.

A step-up bond with several step-ups in coupons might have a coupon schedule that looks like the following: 3 percent from July 15, 2008, to January 15, 2009; 4 percent January 15, 2009, to January 15, 2010; 5 percent January 15, 2010, to January 15, 2012; 7 percent January 15, 2012, to January 15 2014; 9 percent thereafter. As is typically the case with a single step-up bond, the multiple step-up will be callable by the issuer at par on the dates at which the coupon is scheduled to increase. Because the step-up bond is callable, the yield to maturity for the bondholder is typically higher for a step-up then a fixed coupon bond. However, this higher yield will only be realized by the investor if the prevailing interest rate and the borrowing opportunities of the issuing entity are such that the step-up bond is not called.

Another common form of variable (floating) interest rate bonds are bonds issued with coupons tied to a specific interest rate or index including but not limited to examples such as the U.S. Treasury Bill, the 3- or 6-month London Inter-bank Overnight Rate (LIBOR), or the Consumer Price Index (CPI). Many of these types of floating interest rate bonds have coupons that adjust and pay as frequently as monthly such that, for example, the coupon paid for a given month will be 200 basis points (200 bps = 2 percent, pronounced "bips") above the current 3-month LIBOR. So if the 3-month LIBOR is at 3 percent then the coupon for the bond in that month will be 3 percent + 2 percent = 5 percent. The advantage of owning floating interest rate notes is that in the event that interest rates or inflation increases dramatically, then the investors holding these floating rate notes will enjoy increasing coupon payments.

Many more complex forms of floating coupon bonds exist and are typically referred to as structured products or derivatives. A structured product's coupon can be linked to just about any economic variable including but not limited to interest rates, commodity prices, equity indices, single equities, yield curves, inflation indices, or even to other derivatives. In addition, structures may include caps on coupons, be based on averages or weighted averages, and range from a fairly simple one-to-one relationship to a more complex mathematical computation. One example of a derivative would be a bond that paid a fixed 11 percent coupon for one year and then converted to a floating coupon that paid 10 times the difference between the 30-year interest rate and the 10-year interest rate for the duration of the bond until maturity. A derivative like this would likely have a cap on its interest rate (20 percent, for example) and be callable by the issuer in case the difference (spread) between the 30-year and 10-year rates were significant.

Bond Ratings

Bonds are rated by several credit rating agencies including Standard & Poor's (S&P), Moody's, and Fitch. These rating agencies focus on evaluating the credit worthiness of the bond issuers and publish their ratings. Criteria such as the issuer's asset protection, management capabilities, quantity and type of existing debt and its ability to pay the associated interest and principal due, as well as the overall stability of the issuer's cash flow are all assessed to determine the creditworthiness and financial strength of the bond issuer. The best known of the credit rating agencies are S&P and Moody's, each having similar rating scales that range from high-quality investment-grade bonds with little risk through the mid-range investment grade and speculative bonds all the way down to the defaulted bonds that have been issued by organizations that have failed to stay current in the payment of interest and/or principal of their debt.

Typically the defaulted bonds are associated with an organization that is in bankruptcy and going through a process of restructuring. In the process of restructuring, bondholders are treated as general creditors, although bonds have a hierarchy in which secured bonds provide the bondholder with a higher level of claim on the assets of the organization, followed by debentures, subordinated debentures, and finally income bonds.

Ranging from the highest quality ratings to the lowest by S&P/Moody's, the ratings are (1) AAA/Aaa indicates the highest investment-grade rating in which capacity to repay principal and interest is assessed as being very high; (2) AA/Aa indicates a very high quality bond only slightly less secure than the AAA/Aaa ratings; (3) A/A indicates a bond that is slightly more susceptible to adverse economic conditions; (4) BBB/Baa indicates the issuers of these bonds are judged to have reasonable capacity to repay principal and interest, yet they are slightly speculative; (5) BB/Ba indicates that the investment in these bonds is speculative and that there is a significant chance the issuer could miss an interest payment; (6) B/B indicates the issuer has or is likely to miss one or more interest and or principal payments; (7) C/Caa indicates that there is a very high likelihood that the issuer will miss interest and principal payments and go into default, some even consider this rating to mean a technical default; (8) D/D indicates the issuer is in default and that the payment of interest and principal is in arrears.

Each of the above ratings by S&P can be qualified further by a plus sign (+) or a minus sign (−) to indicate relative strength within each rating category. Likewise, Moody's qualifies its rating categories with the numbers 1, 2, and 3. The most positive ratings being "+" and "1," moderate ratings within category being a lack of qualifier for S&P and "2" for Moody's, and the lowest quality rating being a minus sign "−" for S&P and the number "3" for Moody's.

One additional important consideration when judging the creditworthiness of a particular bond issuer is the credit rating trend. The credit rating agencies will issue positive or negative outlooks that indicate potential direction of future credit watches or credit rating changes. Credit watches issued by the rating agencies are a stronger statement of trend and can be either negative or positive. Although a negative credit watch issued by S&P or Moody's indicates a potential future downgrade in the credit rating of a particular issuer, a credit rating downgrade does not always follow the negative credit watch as economic conditions and the financial strength of an issuer is subject to positive changes over time.

The last important aspect of assessing credit rating trend is to analyze the empirical credit ratings over time. It is more common for a troubled firm to undergo a series of downgrades spanning years than for a highly rated investment-grade bond to suddenly become speculative and default, although there are exceptions such as Enron, for example, in which its investment-grade senior secured debt rated Baa3 with a negative credit watch on November 27, 2001, defaulted rapidly and within six days became a Ca rated "junk" bond on December 3, 2001, as evidence of accounting fraud became known.

Bond Yields

The return to an investor in bonds is referred to as yield. There are three important yield calculations for bonds: current yield, yield to maturity, and yield to call. Current yield (CY) is equal to the annual income received from the bond divided by the current market price. For example, a $1,000 face-value bond with a 7 percent coupon trading at a discount of $800 would equal a current yield of 8.75 percent, whereas if the same 7 percent coupon bond was trading at a premium of $1,120 the current yield would be 6.25 percent.

Yield to maturity (YTM) is the annualized rate of return the investor receives if the bond is held to maturity. To calculate YTM, divide either the premium amount paid or the discount by the number of years until the bond's final stated maturity, then subtract this amount from the annual interest paid, and divide the remainder by the price of the bond. Considering the example above, the YTM of a $1,000 face value, 7 percent coupon bond, maturing in 10 years, offered at the discounted price of $800 would be 11.25 percent. Likewise considering the premium-priced bond above, the YTM of a $1,000 face value, 7 percent coupon bond, maturing in 10 years, offered at the premium price of $1,120 would be approximately 5.18 percent. In both of these examples, it is important to understand that an inverse relationship between bond price and bond yield exists such that the higher the price of a bond goes, the lower its yield will be and vice versa.

Calculating yield to call (YTC) is similar to calculating YTM in that the only alteration in the formula is that the "number of years to call" is substituted for "the number of years until the bond's final stated maturity." When comparing YTC and YTM, notice that discount and premium prices for bonds will have a greater impact on the YTC because the number of years to a potential call is always less than the number of years to maturity, thus the amount of discount has fewer years to accrete or in the case of a premium, the amount has fewer years for amortization in the event of the bond being called by the issuer. In the bond market, it is important to make distinctions among the various kinds of yields and to be aware of what the yield in the worst-case scenario will be, which is commonly referred to as yield to worst (YTW). This is of particular importance when callable bonds are being sold at a premium.

The yield curve can be represented by a graph that displays time until a bond's maturity on the x-axis and bond's yield on the y-axis. A "normal" yield curve is upward sloping such that the bonds with longer maturities will tend to yield more than the bonds of the same quality with shorter maturities. A "normal" spread between short-term bonds and long-term bonds is approximately 3 percent or 300 basis points, although spreads between the short end and long end of the yield curve may vary dramatically. An ascending yield curve typically occurs when the economy is growing and tends to predict future increases in interest rates. An inverted, or downward sloping yield curve in which the shorter-term yields are higher than the longer-term yields can occur when the Federal Reserve Board raises short-term interest rates in order to tighten credit and prevent inflation. The inverted curve tends to foretell future decreases in interest rates.

Although a single yield curve depicts bonds of the same quality and type (for instance AAA corporate bonds) it can be informative to view the differences among yield curves representing different types of bonds. For example, as the spread in yields between corporate AAA and U.S. government bonds (AAA) widens, it indicates that there is a "flight to safety" and that investors in the marketplace believe the economy is worsening and that corporate profits will be decreasing, thus in order to be induced to buy corporate bonds investors require a greater differential yield over the lower yield of U.S. Treasuries that are considered to be close to achieving the status of a "riskless" investment.

Bond Pricing

Bond pricing is based on the perceived risk of the bond relative to the risk and return of alternative investments. The majority of investment-grade corporate bonds and agency bonds are priced among bond trade desks based on a negotiated yield spread to the U.S. Treasuries. The lower the investment-grade credit rating for the corporate bond, the greater the negotiated spread will be. For example, a high-quality corporate bond may offer 50 basis points (one-half percent) more yield to the investor when compared to a similar duration U.S. Treasury. As the quality of the corporate bond decreases through the investment-grade spectrum from AAA to the BBB category, the spread of the offered yield to the Treasuries will increase in order to entice investors to take on the additional risk of lending money to a corporation that may be slightly susceptible to variance in economic conditions. So instead of offering a spread of 50 basis points or less, the trade desk may offer a spread of 200 to 300 basis points.

It is important to note that corporate spreads are not only dependent on the bonds' credit ratings, but also on the sector to which the corporation belongs. For instance during the financial sector's troubles of 2008, the spreads were much higher for the bonds issued by financial institutions as compared to corporate bonds of the same quality rating issued by firms within the industrial sector. Corporate bonds that are speculative (rated below BBB) are traded among bond desks based on a dollar price. For instance, a 7 percent coupon bond rated B would be offered for sale at a dollar price such as 95 ($950 per $1,000 face bond) that is expressed in terms of percentage of par value. In general the price will be lower (and the yield higher) the lower the rating of the bond and the longer the period until the bond matures. This lower price and higher yield is meant to compensate the investor for taking on the risk associated with lower creditworthiness and the uncertainty associated with the passage of time.

Similar to investment-grade corporate bonds, agency bonds issued by the Farm Credit System, Federal Home Loan Bank, Federal Home Loan Corporation (Freddie Mac), and Federal National Mortgage Association (Fannie Mae) are offered based on a spread to U.S. Treasuries. In contrast, municipal bonds are offered among trade desks based on yields, although some consideration may be given to the municipal bonds yield as a percentage of similarly maturing U.S. Treasuries.

See Also: Basis Points; Credit Ratings; Debt; Debt Rescheduling; Debt (Securities); Government Bonds; Mortgage Credit Crisis of 2008; Sovereign Borrowing; Spread.

Bibliography. F. J. Fabozzi, *The Handbook of Fixed Income Securities*, 7th ed. (McGraw-Hill, 2005); *Passtrak Series 7: General Securities Representative License Exam Manual*, 15th ed. (Dearborn Financial Publishing, Inc., 2004); Florian Schmidt and Adam Harper, *A Guide to Asian High Yield Bonds: Financing Growth Enterprises* (Wiley, 2008); Securities Industry and Financial Markets Association, www.investinginbonds.com (cited March 2009); Shop4Bonds, www.shop4bonds.com (cited March 2009); Timothy Sinclair, *The New Masters of Capital: American Bond Rating Agencies and the Politics of Creditworthiness* (Cornell University Press, 2008); B. Tuckman, *Fixed Income Securities: Tools for Today's Markets*, 2nd ed. (John Wiley & Sons, 2002).

Dale B. Tuttle
University of Michigan–Flint

Botswana

Sub-Saharan Africa is comprised of 48 countries. Forty-two of these countries are mainland countries and six are island countries that spread across four geographical regions: west Africa (21 mainland and two island countries), central Africa (five mainland countries), east Africa (eight mainland and one island countries), and south Africa (10 mainland and three island countries).

Botswana is a landlocked mainland country in the southern part of sub-Saharan Africa, and was formerly the British protectorate of Bechuanaland. It gained independence from Britain on September 30, 1966. Since independence, the Botswana Democratic Party has dominated the political system of presidential representative democracy; political governance and leaderships have included Seretse Khama (1966–80), Quett Masire (1984–98), and Festus Mogae (1999–present).

The size of Botswana is slightly smaller than Texas in the United States with more than half of the land surface covered by the Kalahari Desert. It borders Angola and Zambia to the north, Zimbabwe to the northeast, South Africa to the south, and Namibia to the west. The climate is semi-arid, with mild winters and hot summers. The population of Botswana is about 1.8 million, ranking 35th in sub-Saharan Africa, with an annual growth rate of about 1.4 percent. The population by age totals about 61 percent between the ages of 15 and 60 years, 35 percent under 14 years, and 4 percent 65 years and over. The life expectancy of the total population is low, about 50 years. Males live slightly longer than females. Infant mortality rates are slightly higher in males than females. The literacy level of the population is somewhat high, with the literacy level of females higher than males.

Diversity in Botswana is less pronounced. Whereas Nigeria and Kenya have 250 and nine ethnic groups, respectively, there are only five ethnic groups in Botswana. The largest ethnic group is Tswana with 70 percent of the population; Kalanga, 11 percent; Basarwa, 3 percent; Kgalagadi, whites, and others, 7 percent. In recent times, there is no evidence that ethnic diversity has promoted instability and corruption. Botswana is one of the most stable countries in sub-Saharan Africa, enjoying an uninterrupted civilian regime and minimal ethnic violence. The level of corruption in Botswana is insignificant. Transparency International ranks Botswana as the least corrupt country in Africa.

The economy of Botswana revolves mainly around the natural resources, tourism, and agriculture (subsistence farming and cattle raising) sectors. The natural resources sector, particularly diamond mining, dominates the economy. Diamond mining contributes between 70 and 80 percent of export earnings and one-third of GDP. Economic performance in

Botswana is remarkable. The GDP grew significantly—at an annual rate of 9 percent—between 1966 and 1999. The economy slowed in 2002 and 2003 due to budget deficits, high military expenditures (4 percent of GDP), and exorbitant healthcare costs resulting from the HIV/AIDS epidemic. However, the GDP per capita income rose from $11,000 in 2006 to $16,450 in 2007.

Though the natural resources policies stimulated growth, sound economic governance was a critical factor that transformed the economy from poor to middle-income. Such economic governance includes responsible fiscal policy devoid of political instability and corruption; investing in education and training; growth and spread of real income throughout the economy; promoting private sector development; and encouraging flow of foreign direct investment through sound microeconomic, macroeconomic, and institutional policy reforms. Botswana ranks as the best credit risk country in Africa.

Nevertheless, the high HIV/AIDS rate and poverty among the rural population remain significant threats to the economy. Botswana has the second-highest HIV/AIDS infection rate in Africa and the world. About 30 percent of the rural population is below the poverty line, a characteristic fact of countries of sub-Saharan Africa.

See Also: Africa; Angola; South Africa; Zimbabwe.

Bibliography. CIA, "Botswana," *World Factbook,* www .cia.gov (cited March 2009); P. Collier, *The Bottom Billion* (Oxford University Press, 2007); M. Umeadi, *A Dark Century for Sub Sahara Africa* (AuthorHouse, 2008); World Bank, *Botswana: Financial Policies for Diversified Growth* (1989); World Bank, *World Development Indicators* (1998); World Bank Group, *Botswana: A Case Study of Economic Policy Prudence and Growth* (August 31, 1999).

MICHAEL UMEADI
SHAW UNIVERSITY

Bottleneck

Bottleneck is the "narrow part of a bottle near the top." The literal meaning aside, the term refers to "a place or stage in a process at which progress is impeded" and was first used sometime between 1895 and 1900. It is used in varied contexts at present: software/internet, road traffic, logistics (of office work), supply chain, even music (to portray the sliding effects on guitar strings). This term is becoming increasingly significant in global business as large businesses and multinational companies (MNCs) are operating around the world, more so now that ever before. Any sort of bottleneck in the global supply chain (of whatever product) hinders the productivity and efficiency of the whole chain.

To conduct business globally, firms work to facilitate coordination to maintain liaisons all over the world. Technology has also made transportation cheaper, allowing the best rates for various steps of production to converge to make the final product. With large MNCs, firm boundaries that once seemed lucid now appear blurry because of the MNCs' multi-layered networks and relationships with many business partners and stakeholders. For instance, different geographic or product divisions in an MNC frequently need to be handled differently to address their varying environmental milieus and strategic frameworks. The interdependence of these very different divisions in the overall production and/or supply chain makes the chain vulnerable to the ever-increased possibilities of bottlenecks. For MNCs pursuing either a global or transnational strategy, hindrances can come in the form of ecological hazard, power failure, political unrest and violence, shipping disaster, etc. This situation in the production or supply chain is akin to shutting down a lane on a highway. It inevitably slows down all other working lanes, just as an obstacle in any major division of an MNC slows the entire chain—creating a global business bottleneck.

One major example of a global business bottleneck can be traced back to the August 2006 closing of London's Heathrow airport. As a precaution to potential terrorist attack, all incoming flights had to be either cancelled or diverted to other airports; all the carry-on baggage had to be checked one by one with the support of a limited number of machines; all passengers on flights leaving the United Kingdom (UK) were searched by hand and their footwear was X-rayed for safety. This led to substantial delay at all UK airports, and subsequently further delays for international travelers who only had transit at Heathrow. Thus, with the shutting down of Heathrow, bottlenecking happened in all other airports.

Yet another global bottlenecking situation can be dated back to September 1999, when Taiwan experienced a 7.6-magnitude earthquake, followed by five strong aftershocks. Serious damage was evident throughout the country, thousands were killed, and infrastructure was damaged. In the days following the earthquake, the computer industry faced troubles internationally, because Taiwan was one of the largest sources of computer chips. The computer chip industry of Taiwan was shut off for weeks, causing a steep rise in silicon chips' prices; and that had adverse consequences on the whole industry. It was estimated right after the quake that while Taiwan's losses could amount to $1–2 billion, another $1 billion of losses would be incurred by the United States. The Taiwan earthquake impacted the Indian computer industry as well. In 1999, 55 percent of computers in India were either purchased from the "gray" market or assembled in India after various parts had been imported from Taiwan and Korea. The trend of lowering prices of personal computers in India (in the pre-quake time) stopped right after the quake; in fact, the prices temporarily moved upward during the post-quake period.

While bottlenecks caused by natural disasters cannot be maneuvered around, troubles such as power failure or communication gaps (due to cultural and even linguistic differences in various locations in an MNC) can be better managed. Obstacles to production caused by power failure simply require having enough backup resources to continue the work. For example, Bangladesh is a developing country with severe nationwide shortages in electricity supply. Despite that, the Square Group of companies decided not to fall prey to the sporadic electricity supply and created a small plant where it generates enough electricity to continue work uninterrupted. It did not take Square Group long to reach the break-even point, and the benefit of a reliable electricity supply remains. With the increasingly diversified locations and production units of large MNCs, communication gaps and disparities in the understanding and evaluating of company strategy cannot be escaped. These gaps, however, may be better bridged as new techniques are incorporated into the workplace.

See Also: Channels; Multinational Corporation; Supply Chain Management; Supply Chain Risks.

Bibliography. *American Heritage Dictionary of the English Language,* 4th ed. (Houghton Mifflin, 2006); Christopher A. Bartlett and Sumanta Ghoshal, "Global Strategic Management: Impact on the New Frontiers of Strategy Research," *Strategic Management Journal* (v.12, 1991); "Heathrow Shut to Incoming Flights Amid Terrorism Fears," Australian Broadcasting Corporation, August 10, 2006, www.abc.net.au (cited March 2009); Navika Kumar, "Taiwan Quake Rattles Indian Computer Industry," *The Indian Express*, November 14, 1999, www.indianexpress .com (cited March 2009); "With U.S. Chip Industry Facing Aftershocks from Taiwan Earthquake, Deloitte & Touche Advises Hi-Tech Companies to Check Insurance Policies for Contingent Business Interruption Coverage—Industry Trend or Event," *Edge: Work-Group Computing Report* (October 11, 1999).

Noushi Rahman
Pace University
Fabiha Naumi
Independent Scholar

Bottom of the Pyramid

"Bottom of the pyramid" (BOP) refers to the persistent dilemma of the world's poorest four billion people subsisting on less than $2 per day in developing countries. According to C. K. Prahalad, this socioeconomic demographic is a relatively untapped commercial market for multinational corporations (MNCs). He calls on MNC chief executive officers to change their long-held beliefs regarding these people as victims to be pitied and instead see them as resilient individuals, skilled entrepreneurs, and consumers demanding value from their products and services.

Prahalad argues that there are business opportunities for MNCs that create innovative products and services for BOP consumers, as he calculates they possess purchasing power parity (PPP) of $13 trillion. Furthermore, these BOP consumers are not necessarily difficult to reach, very brand conscious, and increasingly open to state-of-the-art telecommunications technology. Prahalad and Stuart Hart recommend that these MNCs: (1) build a host country base of political support; (2) reorient research and development efforts to the needs of the poorest consumers; (3) form new alliances with host country organizations; (4) increase host country employment opportunities; and (5) reinvent cost structures.

Aneel Karnani, however, challenges Prahalad's BOP claim of a potential PPP of $13 trillion, since profits are repatriated by MNCs at the financial exchange rate, not the PPP, resulting in a global BOP market of less than $0.3 trillion. With the poor spending nearly 80 percent of their income on food, clothing, and fuel, it leaves little room for the purchasing power needed to acquire brand name luxury goods. Nevertheless, Anand Jaiswal argues that the poor need to be viewed as consumers so that MNCs can offer them increased value products at a lower cost (saving them money), as well as welfare-oriented goods and services, e.g., agricultural inputs enhancing productivity and insurance and microfinance.

Karnani recommends that the best way for MNCs to help eradicate poverty is for them to invest in upgrading the skill sets and productivity of the poor and help create more local employment opportunities. Reflecting Karnani's economic development approach, Erik Simanis, Stuart Hart, and Duncan Duke offer a BOP protocol presenting a new innovative business process model that includes both collective entrepreneurship development and business enterprise co-creation between local communities and MNCs.

See Also: Corporate Social Responsibility; Economic Development; Less Industrialized Countries; Multinational Corporation.

Bibliography. A. K. Jaiswal, "The Fortune at the Bottom or the Middle of the Pyramid?" *Innovations: Technology/ Governance/ Globalization* (v.3/1, 2008); A. Karnani, "The Mirage of Marketing to the Bottom of the Pyramid: How the Private Sector Can Help Alleviate Poverty," *California Management Review* (v.49/4, 2007); C. K. Prahalad, *The Fortune at the Bottom of the Pyramid: Eradicating Poverty Through Profits* (Wharton School Publishing, 2004); C. K. Prahalad and S. L. Hart, "The Fortune at the Bottom of the Pyramid," *strategy + business* (v.26, 2002); E. Simanis, S. Hart, and D. Duke, "The Base of the Pyramid Protocol: Towards Next Generation BOP Strategy" (Center for Sustainable Global Enterprise, Cornell University, 2008).

Thomas A. Hemphill
University of Michigan–Flint

Bouygues

Founded in 1952 by Francis Bouygues (pronounced "bweeg") and run by his son Martin since 1989, Bouygues is a Parisian industrial holding company with two main focuses: construction and telecommunications. One of the largest construction contractors in the world, its over 113,000 employees are employed in 80 countries.

Though Martin oversaw much of the company's diversification, Francis set the ball in motion. "I have no colleagues," he was often quoted as saying, "only competitors." Those competitors called him Monsieur Breton: Mr. Concrete. Mr. Concrete pursued government contracts to build France's roads and motorways, its postwar suburbs, all the while eschewing interactions with the press and his own public relations department.

After his retirement as CEO, Francis stayed involved with the company's motion picture interests, which developed in accordance with his plan to make French cinema more international. Among the movies produced by Bouygues' CiBy subsidiary are *Twin Peaks: Fire Walk With Me*, *Little Buddha*, and *The Piano*, an Oscar-winning commercial success that helped restimulate American interest in the Cannes Film Festival where it first attracted buzz. Francis was also responsible for the acquisition of TF1, the French television network, when it was privatized in 1987; under Bouygues ownership, the network became prosperous, and its nightly news program the most important television program in France.

Martin took control of the company in 1989, having dropped out of the University of Paris in 1974 to work on one of his father's construction sites. Within a few years he was overseeing the construction of the Parisian Les Halles shopping complex, and in 1978 oversaw Maison Bouygues, a Bouygues residential construction subsidiary. Just before Martin became CEO, Bouygues acquired the Screg Group, a holding company that included the highway contracting giant Colas, and began building the Channel Tunnel beneath the English Channel. This was the last major project begun under Francis, who remained on the board until his death in 1993; the Tunnel was completed the following year.

Under Martin, in 1993, the company moved into telecommunications. While acquisitions and ventures in the past had involved what was nominally a construction company in movie financing, flour milling, and frozen foods, the creation of the Bouygues Telecom subsidiary was the first major venture outside the company's wheelhouse. But the company's infrastructure experience and the timing of the move resulted in success; mobile telephony was offered through a joint venture with Telecom Italia, gaining over one million customers in less than two years.

In 2001 Bouygues Telecom was the only cellular service provider in Europe not offering 3G (third-generation) wireless service, because of the licensing fees imposed by the French government; revenues and subscriptions were seemingly unaffected by the decision. Further, Martin Bouygues' comments that such fees would be detrimental to the industry, and that the companies in other countries electing to pay them would face financial consequences for implementing such artificially expensive technology, may have proven prescient, as other companies found themselves struggling with debt. 3G service was eventually added in 2002, when the French government cut their fee from a total of $4.4 billion to $557 million—about an eighth of the original asking price.

Today, Bouygues is run very much according to Martin's philosophies. Employees rotate through different departments, regardless of relevant experience—or more to the point, specifically because of their lack of experience. Martin Bouygues' business approach calls for employees who are smart and quick-witted but do not have significant experience in the industry before coming to Bouygues—ensuring that they do not have preconceptions, or habits to unlearn. The approach has paid off well. Currently the company is organized into five divisions: Bouygues Construction, Bouygues Immobilier (real estate and property development), Colas, TF1, and Bouygues Telecom.

See Also: Euronext; France; Telecom Italia.

Bibliography. "Bouygues Considers Takeover Bids For Its Saur Water Subsidiary," *Europe Agri* (September 16, 2004); John H. Christy, "Clean Slate," *Forbes* (June 12, 2000); Matthew Curtin, "European Trader: Cash Cow: Bouygues Investors Say 'Oui,'" *Barron's* (October 25, 2004); "Special Report: Bouygues," *The Economist* (December 2, 2006); "Tale of a Bubble: How the 3G Fiasco Came Close to Wrecking Europe," *BusinessWeek* (June 3, 2002).

BILL KTE'PI
INDEPENDENT SCHOLAR

BP

The third largest of the six supermajors, British Petroleum (BP) originated when the last Shah of Persia (before that country became known as Iran) granted an oil concession to British land speculator William Knox D'Arcy in 1901. Fittingly, the company that has been so intertwined with modern Middle Eastern history was founded to drill for oil in the first major oil discovery in the Middle East. In the century since, it has expanded to open productions in 22 countries.

The supermajors are the six oil companies that rose to the top of the industry in the 1990s, in the flurry of mergers following the decline in the price of oil. The older term *Big Oil*, used in reference to the cooperative behavior and lobbying of oil companies, is often used now to refer specifically to the supermajors. Each supermajor has revenues in the hundreds of billions of dollars, benefiting from vast stores of petroleum products and natural gas and oil resources. BP currently employs 115,000 workers, with revenues of $274 billion.

D'Arcy found oil in 1908, making the first major oil discovery in the Middle East, and founded the Anglo-Persian Oil Company in order to pursue his claim. The refinery built in Abadan was, until the 1960s, the largest in the world. Nearly as soon as it began operations, the British government "partially nationalized" the company in order to guarantee an oil supply for its ships, which proved even more critical when World War I broke out.

When the D'Arcy concession was first granted, there was no way of knowing if oil would ever be found—indeed, the engineer who eventually found it had been instructed to give up hope, and told that the operation was going to be canceled, but by delaying his response for a matter of weeks he managed to pull the company's fat out of the fire. When the company thus became such an extraordinary success, and the nature of oil wealth became clear to the Persian government, pressure mounted to renegotiate terms. This was a critical time in the nation's history—not long after World War I, in 1925, Reza Khan overthrew the Qatar Dynasty and became Shah, instituting a significant effort at modernization that included railroad construction and nationwide public education.

It was the new Shah's request that the rest of the world refer to once-Persia as Iran, and the Anglo-Persian Oil Company became the Anglo-Iranian Oil Company (AIOC). New terms were negotiated slowly, complicated by the global economic destabilization of the Great Depression. Though the rate of royalty paid to the Iranian government increased, the AIOC's accounting practices saw that the amount paid remained largely the same. Nationalization helped the company survive, with the British government making decisions the private sector could not have—such as refusing to acknowledge the Iranian government's decision to rescind the D'Arcy concession.

Though the Shah was the guiding force behind Iran's demands for better treatment under the agreement, he was still broadly pro-British, and sought to preserve a good relationship with his various European and western allies. Unfortunately, since those connections included both the British and the Germans, as the world approached the precipice of World War II he was forced to make a decision. He abdicated rulership of Iran in favor of his son, Reza Pahlavi, rather than lose British support. However, as far as appeasing British interests, this backfired. Dr. Mohammed Mossadegh was elected prime minister in 1951, and nationalized Iranian oil, a move with widespread approval in the country because of AIOC's refusal to split profits 50-50 with Iran, as was done in Saudi Arabia. Both the communist party and the Islamic fundamentalists supported nationalization as well.

This, then, put Iranian interests at odds with British interests, AIOC's interests, and in the early days of the Cold War, it was perceived that it then put them at odds with American interests as well. Nationalized Iranian oil could become communist oil. In 1953 the United States and newly elected President Eisenhower were persuaded to join the British effort to depose Mossadegh, and the CIA's Operation Ajax was the lever used to dislodge him. Mossadegh was arrested on August 19, 1953, and the Shah's rule was strengthened in order to prevent future prime ministers from being able to do anything so drastic.

Still, public opinion was so strongly turned against AIOC that a new consortium of companies was formed, bearing the name used during the brief period of nationalized oil—the National Iranian Oil Company—of which AIOC, renamed British Petroleum, was given a 40 percent share. The consortium split profits 50-50 with Iran, on an honor basis—in other words, Iran had no authority to conduct an audit, nor access to the consortium's records, no choice but to accept that the amount it was given was correct. The other shareholders in the consortium were European and Western oil companies, including those that became the other supermajors; BP's share, though not a controlling one, was the largest.

The Iranian Revolution

The Shah was now in an untenable position, despite his increased power. Though he was beholden to Western powers for increasing his authority, and for Iran's more or less friendly relationship with the world outside the Middle East, he was at the same time considered too traditional and conservative by those Westerners. As time wore on and the young Shah became the old Shah, his Western allies were embarrassed by the association. When he faced another coup by fundamentalists, he found himself without aid. The Islamic Revolution of 1979 removed him from power, ended BP's 70 year association with Iran, put the Ayatollah Khomeini in power, and—when the United States allowed the Shah entrance to the country in order to have access to medical facilities—resulted in the seizure of American hostages, a crisis that lasted throughout the 1980 presidential campaign and helped to bring conservative Ronald Reagan into power, over conciliatory incumbent Jimmy Carter.

At this point, BP was already operating outside of Iran, and while the loss of Iranian oil hurt it—and the Western world in general—it had been developing oil production in Alaska since 1959, and in the North Sea since 1965. It had also acquired one of the pieces of Standard Oil created by trustbusting: Standard Oil of Ohio. Ironically, while oil was being nationalized again

Oil workers on a BP company drill ship in Angola, one of many locations BP developed to make up for the loss of Iranian oil.

operates along the west coast of the United States, while Air BP provides aviation fuel and Marine BP provides marine fuels.

See Also: Chevron; ConocoPhilips; ExxonMobil; Iran; Royal Dutch Shell; Total; United Kingdom.

Bibliography. R.W. Ferrier and James H. Bamberg, *The History of the British Petroleum Company*, vol. I–III (Cambridge University Press, 2000); Karl E. Meyer and Shareen Brysac, *Kingmakers: The Invention of the Modern Middle East* (W.W. Norton, 2008).

BILL KTE'PI
INDEPENDENT SCHOLAR

in Iran, that same year the British government—under the conservative economic reforms of new Prime Minister Margaret Thatcher—began privatizing BP, selling off its interest in the company in large pieces through 1987. In 1998 the company merged with Amoco, another former Standard Oil company, and was briefly known as BPAmoco until it renamed itself simply BP in 2000, retrofit for a new slogan: Beyond Petroleum.

Both BP and Amoco brands remained in use for a time, as both service stations and branded gasoline, Amoco-branded gasoline having consistently ranked highest in customer satisfaction for years. As of 2008, the Amoco brand is being phased out in much of the United States. BP also owns and operates a number of other store brands: BP Connect is used throughout the world, BP Travel Centres are known for their enormous food courts in Australia, ARCO

Brain Drain

Brain drain is a popular term describing the international migration of highly skilled professionals. Transnational relocation of the highly skilled adheres to general migration patterns, but with some differences. Highly trained migrants are attracted to fast-growing economies from slow-growing economies, from low-wage to high-wage regions, and from political instability, risk, and restriction toward more stability, security, and freedom. Skilled migrants are also drawn toward flexible markets for professional jobs and toward fertile intellectual environments. Brain drains have increased in recent years thanks to the increasing importance of the "knowledge economy," a slowdown or reversal of population growth and concomitant aging of populations around the world, and more mobile and less loyal workforces.

Originally a reference to the movement from post–World War II Europe to the United States in the 1950s and 1960s, "brain drain" has since been applied more widely to describe the phenomenon of trained professionals migrating internationally, but particularly from poorer to wealthier countries. Net recipients of a brain drain, such as the United States, are sometimes said to be experiencing a "brain gain." Some countries having both sizable inflows and outflows, such as New Zealand (losing professionals to Australia but pulling them in from elsewhere in Asia), are regarded as experiencing a "brain exchange." The "draining away" of scientists, computer programmers, nurses, and other such trained professionals is compensated by the knowledge transfers and monetary remittances those professionals send back to their places of origin. The value of such offsets varies across time and place, however. They have also been difficult to measure and difficult for policy makers to agree upon.

The global extent of the brain drain is unclear. Systems for tracking the movement of skilled professionals are incomplete and inconsistent. There are also uncertainties in defining the line between professional and nonprofessional workers, and in assessing the importance of factors, other than the demand for and supply of skilled workers, that also encourage their migration. There is, however, a general consensus on two points. First, the migration of professionals is disproportionately large relative to both the flows of international migrants generally and to the numbers of stay-at-home professionals. Second, this brain drain is likely to remain significant and grow larger in the future.

Information technology and healthcare are two industries most prominently reliant on international imports of trained professionals. India and the Philippines, among many others, are important suppliers of such workers. Leading destination countries include the United States, Canada, and Australia.

Demand for skilled professionals is rooted in growing global needs for "human capital." In 2006 *The Economist* reported that 70 percent of the value of companies making up the United States' "Standard & Poor's 500" was comprised of "intangible assets," much of which derived from technology and the talents of employees. A general ongoing shortage of scientists and engineers further increases their international movement toward places and companies where they are most wanted and best rewarded. The supply of highly skilled migrants also has powerful underpinnings. Compared to other migrants, professional workers are better able to recognize and pursue opportunities abroad, and public policies of recipient countries—and sometimes sending countries as well—have tended to favor skilled over unskilled immigrants.

The increasing globalization of higher education is connected to the brain drain in several ways. Many universities in developed nations now rely heavily on foreign students and teaching assistants who, in turn, often use that education abroad as a stepping stone to a job abroad. The brain drain also fosters the growth of education in developing countries whose citizens seek more advanced training at home as a ticket to a skilled job in a more-developed country. The total number of those obtaining higher education in the less-developed countries has been increasing, however, and some of them do not emigrate, thereby partially compensating developing countries for the skilled workers "drained" away.

Programs

The world's largest official program of international importation of professional migrants is the system of H-1B visas in the United States, created by the Immigration Act of 1990. The number of such visas has been capped at 65,000 annually, although businesses calling for an increased quota succeeded in raising the ceiling to above 100,000 between 1999 and 2003. Foreign university students, often recruited by businesses, do not come under and are thus not limited by the cap of 65,000, however.

A "means test" is required before H-1B visas are approved for workers. Would-be employers have to "attest" that there are not a sufficient number of qualified American citizens to fill the job openings. This test has not proven to be a significant encumbrance, although there have been several controversial cases where the hiring of H-1B workers has been associated with an eventual layoff of local workers. Overall though, the program has been viewed favorably, has remained in effect with minor revisions over the years, and has been emulated by other developed countries. Regularized channels for migrating professionals limit, but do not eliminate, their extra-legal movement internationally.

Multinational corporations have also been active users of skilled migrants, despite a greater capability (than at smaller local firms) for shifting jobs between countries as well. Foreign direct investment is thus a substitute for brain drain but also opens up new channels for it, as workers generally can be moved across borders more easily if they are transferring between units of the same employer, rather than seeking a new job with a new employer abroad on their own. An increasing international diversity in the upper-management ranks of large companies reflects this globalization of talent.

See Also: Cross-Border Migration; Expatriate; Visa.

Bibliography. Showkat Ali et al., "Elite Scientists and the Global Brain Drain," University of Warwick Economic Research Paper (n.825, 2007); H-1B Work Visa Online Information Center, www.h1bvisa.org (cited March 2009); "How to Plug Europe's Brain Drain," *Time Europe* (January 2004); Phillip Martin, Manolo Abella, and Christiane Kuptsch, *Managing Labor Migration in the Twenty-first Century* (Yale University Press, 2006); Babs Ryan, *America's Corporate Brain Drain: Why We Leave, Where We Go, How We Can Reverse the Flow* (Sparks Worldwide, 2008); "The Search for Talent," *The Economist* (October 5, 2006).

DREW KEELING
UNIVERSITY OF ZURICH

Branch

A branch is a part of an organization that is located in a different geographic region than the parent organization. It is also called a branch office and is very similar to a subsidiary. Although it functions autonomously, it is an extension of the corporate headquarters. Authority is granted to the branch or subsidiary to perform the necessary duties to conduct the same business transactions that would normally be conducted at the corporate headquarters.

A typical branch is smaller than the corporate headquarters, but it performs all or many of the same functions. Companies that have branch offices are able to extend the organization's reach into different geographic regions. Establishing a branch office allows the organization to extend its products and services into markets and customer segments far beyond the reach of the corporate headquarters. The additional geographic reach can extend the company's business into different local, regional, or global markets. This allows the organization to conduct business, interact with customers, and perform many of its daily business activities in more than one market. Companies with flatter organizational structures and decentralized decision making will tend to use branch offices more than other types of organizations.

Although many organizations will establish a branch office, some industries tend to use them more than others. This can include companies that are in the mail and/or packaging and shipping industry. Organizations in this industry tend to have a lot of branches so customers can access their services locally. For example, some countries have a national postal service with numerous post office branches, or a shipping company will have numerous branch offices where customers can come to ship packages. Banks will also have branch offices in numerous locations so they can gain access to customer segments in different geographic regions.

In general, the branch office will have: (1) the authority to act on behalf of the organization and (2) the infrastructure that allows it to conduct normal business activities. Similarly, when a company wants to extend its operations into a foreign market, it will sometimes establish a branch office in that country. The branch will have a building, employees, and an infrastructure that allows it to conduct business on behalf of the parent company. It functions autonomously and typically has the authority to spend money, hire employees, and provide service on behalf of the parent organization.

Although a branch office is convenient for the customer and extends the company's business activities into different geographic markets, it generally requires a lot of resources and can be quite costly. The parent organization has to set up a second location that requires many of the same resources as the corporate office, but on a smaller scale. This includes the cost of buying or leasing a building, hiring qualified personnel, and developing an infrastructure that is self-sufficient so that it can function autonomously.

The recent trend has been to reduce or limit the number of branch locations. Many organizations have long desired to limit the number of branch offices because of the costs associated with building and maintaining these offices, but the investment was necessary to extend the company's business activities, and because some business activities required direct or face-to-face contact. However, recent technological improvements allow some organizations to have direct contact and conduct many of these same business activities without face-to-face interaction.

For example, many financial institutions conduct business with customers without face-to-face interaction. With online access and ATMs, these companies can open accounts, check credit, grant credit, transfer funds, and complete numerous other banking activities without having the customer come into a branch or corporate office. It is no longer necessary for a customer to go into a local branch office to complete a business transaction with their bank. In today's environment, there are companies that conduct a lot of business without face-to-face interaction. These organizations do not have customers that access their services at a main office or branch—all or part of the interaction takes place online.

Although a branch is a part of the parent company, it is an autonomous entity that functions separately from the corporate or main headquarters. Branches can be in different local, regional, or global locations than the corporate office. They can perform all or many of the same duties as the main office, as they extend the company's business operations. Because of the cost of maintaining a branch and recent technological improvements, most companies try to limit the number of branches that they have.

See Also: Retail Sector; Service Level; Subsidiary.

Bibliography. B. B. Buchholz, "City To City: When Firms Branch Out," *ABA Journal* (1991); R. Frierson, "Development Order Approving Establishment of a Representative Office," *Federal Reserve Bulletin* (2006); Hazel J. Johnson, *Bank Valuation Handbook: A Market-Based Approach to Valuating Banks & Bank Branches* (Irwin Professional Publishing, 2005); J. Kolari, A. Zardkoohi, T. Santalainen, and A. Suvanto, "Branch Bank Operating Costs: Evidence From Savings Banks in Finland," *Applied Economics* (1992); K. Potvin, "Opening a Regional Office—Not a Choice, A Necessity," *Public Relations Tactics* (1999); Shirley Donald Southworth, *Branch Banking in the United States* (Southworth Press, 2007).

Lynne A. Patten
Clark Atlanta University

Branding

Branding entails much more than simply affixing a clever logo to a product. In fact, the act of branding encompasses a wide range of marketing activities such as product design, name, packaging, advertising, and image projection—all of which are designed with one core purpose in mind: To differentiate a seller's own product from competitors' offerings. When effectively orchestrated, branding enables a product to stand out from a sea of products that otherwise might appear similar to consumers.

If brand managers focus on developing and conveying the points of distinction that matter most to consumers, the brand is likely to thrive and consumers are inclined to pay a premium price to acquire that product. A powerful brand, therefore, is one that commands a large brand premium and engenders a deep level of loyalty among its dedicated users. The best brands, according to marketing guru Philip Kotler, are ones that appeal to consumers on some higher emotional level, not just on the basis of a specific product attribute or benefit sought. While a product feature often can be easily imitated, it is more difficult for competitors to replicate a feeling generated by a compelling brand. Consumers may buy Coke, for instance, not for the taste alone, but also for the positive images and feelings that the product conjures through the company's successful marketing and advertising campaigns.

Indeed, branding is all about good "story-telling," as former English professor James Twitchell emphasizes. He means this not in a derogatory sense—not in the sense of brand managers creating malicious fictions. Rather, by "story-telling," Twitchell means that the best marketers develop convincing and engaging narratives that suffuse their products with such vitality that consumers want to believe in them, use them, and endorse them to others. Consumers enjoy and trust their favorite brands, and the most passionate of them also will act as brand apostles, spreading the word about their brand's perceived strengths.

It is easy to perceive why branding holds such appeal to sellers: Done right, branding offers them significant financial benefits. By eliciting consumers' attention and generating positive interest as well as repeat sales, branding facilitates the selling of a greater number of products. Moreover, sellers generally can command higher prices for stronger brands than weaker ones.

But what about the advantages to branding for buyers? Critics maintain that branding is disadvantageous to consumers. As they argue, the process of creating and maintaining a brand is quite expensive, and those costs are invariably passed on to consumers. Critics also point out that branding, by making an emotional connection with consumers, can encourage irrational purchases, tricking consumers into buying what they do not need or what they cannot truly afford.

A defense of branding, however, also can be made: Branding can be good for consumers. Advocates emphasize that branding, by calling attention to the differences among products, plays a valuable role in helping overwhelmed consumers make decisions in a crowded marketplace. If consumers are pleased with a product's performance, branding also can help consumers identify that product again, facilitating a repeat purchase and a very similar experience as their first time using it. Branding encourages product consistency and uniformity. Viewed in this light, brands therefore may be worth what consumers are willing to pay for them.

Although branding is most frequently associated with the world of consumer products (think, for example, of Coke, Tide, and Apple), it is important to remember that branding also extends to a plethora of other areas, such as nonprofit institutions, services, and ideas. As Twitchell notes, among the many diverse "products" that are branded are museums, churches, and colleges.

Even people can be branded. In fact, in the United States today, some parents are starting to enlist consultants to help them master the art of "branding" their newborn babies with the most effective names—names that allegedly will enable their babies to stand out from the crowd and hence increase their chances of success later in life. Celebrities also are routinely described as being the subjects of brand management. The proper development, cultivation, and maintenance of stars' images can be critical to ensuring their sustained success. Celebrities also frequently engage in brand and line extensions, as they try to leverage their well-known names by attaching them to other product offerings such as perfume, jewelry, and dolls.

The Coca-Cola Conundrum

While it is often tempting for sellers to try to capitalize on a successful brand by expanding it in new directions, brand extension efforts, however, carry the risk of brand dilution. If an extension fails, it may harm the value of the underlying brand. In general, the higher the brand equity, the more risky it is to tamper in any way with the core brand. On a consumer product level, an often cited example of a bungled brand strategy decision was the launch of New Coke in 1984. The taste was supposed to be an improvement and in fact, some consumers did prefer it, yet the alteration in the formula alienated many loyal Coke consumers. Ultimately, in an effort to placate both sides, the company decided to revert to the original formula (renamed "Coca-Cola Classic") but also to retain the updated version ("New Coke").

While the Coca-Cola conundrum seems to illustrate the importance of marketers managing their brands carefully and prudently, a counter school of thought advises marketers to relinquish some of their control and instead empower consumers to help shape the brand. Marketing author and practitioner Alex Wipperfurth maintains that consumers should be encouraged to commit "brand hijack"—an essential takeover of the brand in which end users more than marketers drive the evolution of the product. Wipperfurth perceives this to be a win-win situation: consumers get exactly what they want, and marketers in turn sell more product.

Allowing consumers a relatively free hand in branding, however, can have negative consequences, such as an inconsistent brand image. Moreover, if a brand already possesses high stature, it may be riskier to adopt a more relaxed brand management policy than if the product is new or not yet widely known.

The process of creating a powerful and enduring brand therefore remains a challenging and complex task for marketers. While periodic efforts have been made to reduce branding to a set of rigid rules, branding remains more of an art than a science.

See Also: Advertising; Brand Loyalty; Consumer Behavior; Consumer Needs and Wants; Marketing; Positioning.

Bibliography. Alexander Alter, "The Baby-Name Business," *Wall Street Journal* (June 22, 2007); Del Breckenfeld, *The Cool Factor: Building Your Brand's Image Through Partnership Marketing* (Wiley, 2008); John Gerzema and Edward Lebar, *The Brand Bubble: The Looming Crisis in Brand Value and How to Avoid It* (Jossey-Bass, 2008); Nigel Hollis, *The Global Brand: How to Create and Develop Lasting Brand Value in the World Market* (Palgrave Macmillan, 2008); Philip Kotler and Gary Armstrong, *Principles of Marketing*, 12th ed. (Pearson/Prentice-Hall, 2008); Tengku Chik Melewar bin Tengku Nasir and Elif Karaosmanoglu, *Contemporary Thoughts on Corporate Branding and Corporate Identity Management* (Palgrave Macmillan, 2008); Irving Rein, Philip Kotler, and Marty Stoller, *High Visibility: The Making and Marketing of Professionals into Celebrities* (Dodd, Mead, & Co., 1987); Al Ries and Laura Ries, *The Origin of Brands* (HarperBusiness, 2004); Brian D. Till and Donna Heckler, *The Truth About Creating Brands People Love* (FT Press, 2008); James B. Twitchell, *Branded Nation: The Marketing of Megachurch, College Inc., and Museumworld* (Simon & Schuster, 2004); William D. Tyler, "The Image, the Brand, and the Consumer," *Journal of Marketing* (October 1957); Alex Wipperfurth, *Brand Hijack: Marketing Without Marketing* (Penguin Group, 2005).

Janice M. Traflet
Bucknell University

Brand Loyalty

Brand loyalty is defined as a consumer behavior whereby the consumer prefers to continually purchase the same product over time rather than purchase competing products. This behavior usually occurs when the customer believes the brand he or she is purchasing offers a better product or experience than those offered by competitors. This belief then becomes the basis for future purchases. Brand loyalty is usually attributed to a single product, rather than to the organization; hence, a customer's loyalty to a brand does not automatically imply loyalty to the company's other products.

There are three main reasons why brand loyalty is important: Brand loyalty usually decreases the cost of goods sold (through higher volumes), it allows companies to employ premium pricing, and it increases chances that consumers will recommend the product other consumers. In recent years, retail stores have introduced private labels with great success, but these products are counter-intuitive to the theory of brand loyalty. Whereas brands tend to cultivate image over price, private labels often cultivate the image of homogeneous products that offer lower prices with the same level of comfort.

Development

Most customers make their purchases through a trial-and-error process. If, after a few repeated purchases of the same product, they are convinced that the experience, quality, and features were overwhelmingly better than the products offered by competitors, they will tend to form a purchasing habit where they will favor the product. This happens because to the consumer, the purchase has become safe and familiar and few consumers want to constantly reexamine recurring purchasing decisions (especially for low-value goods). Instead, they choose to stick with the brands that have delivered good results if the product stays within what are perceived as acceptable norms.

Generally, some products are more likely to elicit brand loyalty than others. For example, quickly consumed goods (which imply repeated purchases) are more likely to generate brand loyalty, while other products (such as durable goods) are less likely to do so. Also, brand loyalty is not restricted to physical products, and can occur with online products and other services.

For some researchers, brand loyalty is akin to consumer inertia because the consumer is quite content with his or her current purchasing habit and does not want to explore other product offerings. Others believe that brand loyalty occurs because there is limited competition in the current market structure, existing competing products are sufficiently different that they will not answer current needs, and because customers feel "trapped" with their current purchases.

Nonetheless, building brand loyalty usually requires more effort than just relying on consumer inertia or restrictive market conditions. Companies that want to build brand loyalty must be able to convince customers that there is an advantage in continuing to purchase the product by deploying adequate marketing and sales efforts. Furthermore, a company will try to leverage that customer loyalty onto other company products, or use customer loyalty to spread the advantages of its products by word of mouth.

Importance

There are three main reasons why brand loyalty is important. First, brand loyalty usually decreases the cost of goods sold. Companies that have brand-loyal customers find that they can dedicate less resources and effort to marketing to brand-loyal customers, as they are more likely to look for their brand by them-

Popular sneaker brands are a good example of the way brand loyalty can convince consumers to accept premium pricing.

selves when making a purchase (rather than purchasing the first product they find). Brand-loyal consumers are also less likely to be convinced to change brands by a competitor's marketing effort. Finally, brand loyalty generates a higher sales volume due to higher retention of existing customers. The combination of these three factors usually translates into lower costs on a "per unit" basis.

Second, brand loyalty allows companies to employ premium pricing when selling their wares. Studies have shown that brand-loyal customers are more likely to accept a higher price in light of the higher quality they believe they will get, and are less likely to discriminate because of different costs. They are also less likely to purchase products that are on sale due to the perception of a "unique" premium attribute that competing products do not possess, and are less affected by the phenomenon of private labels as a viable purchasing alternative.

Finally, companies that have a loyal consumer base find that there is an increased chance that current consumers will recommend their favorite brand to other customers. They are far more likely to spread the word to other customers and convince them of the advantages of the product. Because a personal recommendation generates important volumes of sales, it is a desirable effect of brand loyalty.

Decline

The rapid rise of private labels has been pointed to as a prime example of the decline of brand loyalty, because consumers are most likely to purchase cheaper products rather than purchasing their favorite product. In many countries, private labels now account for 20–25 percent of retail sales. Also, studies demonstrate that customers who are satisfied with their brand are less likely to convert into repeat customers than they were just a few years ago.

Some companies have tried to attenuate this decline by increasing line extension, whereas different products (or improvements of an existing product) are sold to customers under the same brand. This strategy has met with mixed results, as customers do not always transfer their loyalty from one product to the next, even if there is an obvious relationship between the old and the new product. In many cases, line extensions disrupt existing purchasing habits and reopen the purchasing decision process.

See Also: Branding; Consumer Behavior; Consumer Needs and Wants; Marketing.

Bibliography. Hsiu-Yuan Tsao and Li-Wei Chen, "Exploring Brand Loyalty from the Perspective of Brand Switching Costs," *International Journal of Management* (September 2005); Miguel Villas-Boas, "Consumer Learning, Brand Loyalty, and Competition," *Marketing Science* (Winter 2004); Mary Werner and Richard Murphy, "On-line Business: Is There Loyalty?" *The Business Review* (December 2007).

Jean-Francois Denault
Université de Montréal

Brazil

The territory of the Federative Republic of Brazil is subdivided into five regions (south, southeast, central west, northeast, and north) and 26 federal states as well as the federal district with its capital Brasília. Counting a population of 189.3 million people and a gross domestic product (GDP) of US$1,295 billion (or US$6,841 per capita), Brazil is the world's fifth most populous country, the largest economy in Latin America, and the 10th largest worldwide in 2007.

After several years of double-digit growth rates in the early 1970s, Brazil's economic development strategy based on import substitution came to an end in the early 1980s. It was followed by the "lost decade" and the default on foreign-currency denominated debt in 1987. Years of hyperinflation reached their peak in 1993. Starting in 1994 a successful stabilization program (*Plano Real*) introduced a new currency, the *real* (R$), which was initially pegged to the dollar and freely floated from 1999 onward. A milestone was achieved when Brazilian foreign-currency denominated debt became investment grade in 2008.

The Brazilian government has conceded operational autonomy to the Central Bank, which has been able to continue its orthodox and highly transparent macroeconomic policy even over the change of government in 2003 from a center right to a center left coalition. Having adopted an inflation target policy, the inflation rate dropped to less than 5 percent in 2006 and 2007. Decreasing foreign debt and rising foreign currency reserves reestablished credibility and permitted the country to become a net creditor in 2008.

Although GDP growth is modest (2003–07 the average was 3.8 percent), it is considerably higher than the long-term (1986–2007) average of 2.7 percent. Increasing domestic demand, one of the key drivers of GDP growth, can be traced back to several factors: (1) nominal interest rates, although the world's highest, fell to 11.5 percent in 2008 after topping 26.5 percent in 2003; together with micro-finance programs, this decrease has fostered lending; (2) higher wages (minimum wage rose to R$415 [US$250] in March 2008), combined with low inflation and currency appreciation have increased purchasing power; (3) a large antipoverty program, *bolsa família* ("family fund"), which conditions payments to children's school attendance and vaccination records, reaches one-fourth of the Brazilian population; (4) formal employment has risen by 15 percent between 2003 and 2007; (5) though a highly unequal country, income distribution has improved over the last decade (the Gini coefficient fell from 0.66 in 1996 to 0.56 in 2006).

Traditionally leading in primary products (iron ore, soy beans, meat, coffee), the economy has increasingly diversified. Brazil is today the world's fourth largest commercial aircraft manufacturer (Embraer) and the sixth largest car producer, with an expected output in 2008 of over 3 million cars. General industrial production has increased since President Luiz Inácio Lula da Silva took office in 2003. Energy supply has been increasing and is mainly provided by

hydro-, thermal, nuclear, and wind power with 76.4 percent, 21.4 percent, 2.0 percent, and 0.2 percent of total energy production, respectively, in 2008. In 2006 Brazil became self-sufficient in oil and in 2007–08, the oil company Petrobras discovered large offshore reserves raising prospects of becoming a future net oil exporter. Oil production was 1.9 million barrels per day in 2007.

Brazil's overall investment rate is low compared to the other countries of BRIC (Brazil, Russia, India, and China) at 17.6 percent of GDP in 2007. However, a fresh investment cycle in new plants with emphasis on the petrochemical, mining, metal and steel, automobile, and agro-industries has been initiated. Investment in manufacturing by the National Social and Economic Development Bank (BNDES) more than doubled since 2003, reaching US$13 billion in 2007. FDI inflows topped US$34.5 billion in 2007 or 2.1 percent of GDP (2003–07 average). Moreover, a public-private partnership scheme has started operating. Portfolio inflows of US$48 billion in 2007 have also fueled the stock exchange BOVESPA. Mentioned factors have contributed to strengthening the economy despite a high corporate tax burden, educational deficits, crime, and inefficiencies in public administration.

Exports

After the *real* was floated in 1999, the trade balance produced surpluses from 2001 onward and exports increased from US$73 billion in 2003 to US$160.6 billion in 2007, while imports increased from US$48 billion in 2003 to US$120.6 billion in 2007. Hence, the Brazilian trade volume equals 21.5 percent of GDP in 2007. Exports are composed of 32 percent basic, 14 percent semi-manufactured, and 52 percent manufactured products. Brazil's export markets are diversified, with the United States, China, and Argentina being the main foreign trade partners (accounting together for roughly one-third of Brazilian trade).

Compared to the 1990s, Brazil has reduced its foreign trade dependence from the Mercosur/Mercosul countries. An increase of commodity prices, attributed to rising demand in Asia, explains part of Brazil's export growth. Brazilian outward investment stock reached US$108 billion in 2006 and is championed by multinationals such as CVRD, Petrobras, Gerdau, Embrae, and Votorantim. Being a medium-income country, Brazil is increasingly becoming an off-shoring destination, due to competencies in the banking, telecommunications, and transportation industries, proximity to the United States, and economic and political stability. Thus, there are signs that Brazil has passed an inflection point in its recent economic and business performance.

See Also: BRICs; Latin America; Mercosur/Mercosul; Petrobras.

Bibliography. P. Arestis and A. Saad-Filho, eds., *Political Economy of Brazil: Recent Economic Performance* (Palgrave Macmillan, 2008); W. Baer, *Brazilian Economy: Growth and Development* (Praeger, 2001); Central Bank, www.bacen.gov.br (cited March 2009); F. V. Luna and H. S. Klein, *Brazil since 1980* (Cambridge University Press, 2006); A. Rodriguez, C. Dahlman, and J. Salmi, *Knowledge and Innovation for Competitiveness in Brazil* (World Bank Publications, 2008).

DIRK MICHAEL BOEHE
UNIVERSITY OF FORTALEZA

Bretton Woods Accord

Toward the end of World War II, there appeared to be a necessity for an international monetary system so as to accomplish meaningful economic coordination between countries, if they were to rejuvenate their economies and live in peace. To attain these goals, delegates from 44 countries led by the United States, Great Britain, and France met at the United Nations Monetary and Financial Conference in Bretton Woods, a small town north of Mt. Washington, New Hampshire, in July 1944.

The location was chosen because most of the European countries were still in the turmoil of war, while the United States was the only major country to remain unscathed and keen to rebuild an international economic system. The dollar was chosen as the index currency over the British pound because the latter had lost considerable luster during the war (because the Nazis undertook a major counterfeiting effort against it). The dollar, on the other hand, had recovered from being a failed currency in 1929 after the stock market crash to being a benchmark currency by which most international currencies were compared, since the United States had emerged as a world power and its economy was thriving.

The major currencies were pegged to the U.S. dollar and allowed to fluctuate by 1 percent of the set standard, and subsequently, the International Monetary Fund (IMF) was founded. The respective central bank intervened to bring the exchange rate back into the accepted range when it fluctuated 1 percent on either side of the set standard. Furthermore, the U.S. dollar was pegged to gold at a price of $35 per ounce. For example, the Deutsche Mark (Germany's currency) was set to one-fortieth of an ounce of gold, implying that it was worth $0.25 ($35/DM140). This was intended to be permanent, and policed by the IMF, and for almost three decades it also brought stability to the world foreign exchange situation.

Another aspect of the Bretton Woods Accord was a commitment not to use devaluation as a competitive trade policy. Nevertheless, a devaluation of up to 10 percent was allowed without the formal approval of the IMF, if a currency became too weak to defend—larger devaluations required IMF approval.

The Bretton Woods system began to gradually collapse in the mid-1960s as national economies moved in different directions. Several realignments kept the system alive until the early 1970s, when President Richard Nixon suspended gold's convertibility in August 1971. Increasing U.S. budgets and trade deficits resulted in the dollar no longer being considered as the sole international currency. By then, however, it had accomplished the important task of reestablishing worldwide economic stability, particularly in Europe and in Japan.

The Smithsonian Agreement was signed in December 1971—it was similar to the Bretton Woods Accord, but allowed greater flexibility and fluctuation bands for the currencies. In 1972 the European Joint Float was formed by West Germany, France, Italy, the Netherlands, Belgium, and Luxembourg, as the European community tried to move away from their dependence on the dollar.

Both agreements collapsed in 1973, signaling the official switch to the free-floating system by default, as no further agreements were signed. Governments were now free to peg, semi-peg, or freely float their currencies. In 1978 the free-floating system was officially mandated by the IMF. Europe, however, created the European Monetary System in 1978, in a final effort to gain independence from the dollar, but in 1993 it too failed, like all of the previous agreements.

The major currencies today move independently from each other. Central banks occasionally intervene to move or attempt to move their currencies to desired levels. The free-floating system is ideal for today's foreign exchange markets—the underlying factor is mostly supply and demand.

See Also: Bretton Woods Institutions; Currency Exposure; Devaluation; Dollar Hegemony; Dollarization; Euro; European Union; European Monetary Union; Exchange Rate; Exchange Rate Risk; Exchange Rate Volatility; Financial Market Regulation; Financial Markets; Fixed Exchange Rate; Flexible Exchange Rate Regime; Floating Exchange Rate; Foreign Exchange Market; Foreign Exchange Reserves; Gold Standard; International Monetary Fund; Managed Float Regime; Monetary Intervention; Money Supply; Pegged Exchange Rate; Terms of Trade; World Trade Organization.

Bibliography. Patricia Clavin and Jens-Wilhelm Wessel, "Trans-nationalism and the League of Nations: Understanding the Work of Its Economic and Financial Organization," *Contemporary European History* (v.14/4, 2005); Forex, "Forex History: The Bretton Woods Accord," www.forexrealm.com (cited March 2009); Laurent L. Jacque, "Management of Foreign Exchange Risk: A Review Article," *Journal of International Business Studies* (v.12/1, 1981); Cornelius Luca, "Should Forex Traders Battle the Banks?" *Futures* (v.34/1, 2005); Ronald I. McKinnon, "The Rules of the Game: International Money in Historical Perspective," *Journal of Economic Literature* (v.31/1, 1993); S. Roden and B. G. Dale, "Quality Costing in a Small Engineering Company: Issues and Difficulties," *The TQM Magazine* (v.13/6, 2001); Oded Shenkar and Yadong Luo, *International Business*, 2nd ed. (Sage, 2008).

Abhijit Roy
University of Scranton

Bretton Woods Institutions

The World Bank and the International Monetary Fund (IMF) are together known as the Bretton Woods institutions. They were created at a meeting of 44 countries in Bretton Woods, New Hampshire, in July 1944. Their goals were to assist in rebuilding the shattered postwar economy and to promote international economic cooperation. The original Bretton Woods Accord also mandated a plan to create an international trade organization, but this was not realized until the formation of the World Trade Organization (WTO) in the early 1990s.

The formation of these two "sister institutions" came at the end of World War II, and was based on the initiatives of a trio of key experts—U.S. Treasury Secretary Henry Morgenthau, Jr., his chief economic adviser Harry Dexter White, and the noted British economist John Maynard Keynes. The goal was to establish a postwar economic order based on consensual decision making and cooperation in the realm of trade and economic relations. A multilateral framework was envisioned to overcome the destabilizing effects of the previous global economic depression and trade wars.

World Bank Group

The goal of the World Bank Group (WBG) was to improve the capacities of countries to trade by lending money to war-ravaged and impoverished countries for reconstruction and development projects. WBG currently lends over $20 billion annually to developing economies worldwide, and is made up of two main institutions—the International Bank for Reconstruction and Development (IBRD) and the International Development Association (IDA)—and three subsidiary organizations: the International Finance Corporation (IFC), the Multilateral Investment Guarantee Agency (MIGA), and the International Center for Settlement Investments Disputes (ICSID). The WBG comprises 185 member countries and is based in Washington, D.C. Membership varies across the institutions—all members of the World Bank are members of the IMF, while IDA has 116 members, the IFC has 174; MIGA has 154, and ICSID has 133 members.

The president of WBG (Robert Zoellick as of June 2008) is the president of all five WBG institutions as well as chairman of the board of the 24 executive directors—five of whom are permanent and represent the United States, the United Kingdom, France, Germany, and Japan, while the remaining 19 are elected by groups of members every two years. The U.S. government has 20 percent of the vote and is represented by a single executive director. In contrast, the 47 sub-Saharan African countries have two executive directors and hold only 7 percent of the votes between them.

Each member state's vote is tied to its level of financial contribution. An 85 percent majority vote is required to pass any supermajority, which gives the United States veto power in all but one of the WBG institutions, the IDA, where it has approximately 13 percent of the votes.

International Monetary Fund

The IMF's original goal was threefold: To promote international monetary objectives, to facilitate the expansion of international trade, and to promote exchange rate stability. The IMF provides several types of loans to member countries. Concessional loans are granted to low-income countries at a concessional interest rate through the Poverty Reduction and Growth Facility (PRGF), while nonconcessional loans are offered with a market-based interest rate through five mechanisms: the Stand-By Arrangements (SBA); Extended Fund Facility (EFF); Supplemental Reserve Facility (SRF); Contingent Credit Lines (CCL); and the Compensatory Financing Facility (CCF).

Members facing a balance of payments problem can immediately withdraw up to 25 percent of their quota in gold or convertible currency. They are further allowed to borrow up to three times their paid-in quota, if the original amount is deemed to be insufficient.

IMF loans are of two major types: Under the Standby Arrangements, member countries are allowed to borrow for a one-to-two-year period to support macroeconomic stabilization programs, and repayments are made within three to five years. The longer-term loan is known as the Extended Fund Facility; countries are allowed to borrow for three to four years and repay the loans five to 10 years down the road.

Criticisms

The criticisms of these two institutions mostly focus on the social and economic impact of their policies on the people of the countries that avail themselves of financial assistance from them. There are questions about governance structures, which are dominated by developed, industrialized countries. Some are also apprehensive about their role in shaping the discourse—through their own research and training—on financial regulation and economic development without participation from poorer and developing economies.

Others have raised the issue of conditions placed by these institutions, which is likely to reduce the authority of the state to govern its own economic policies because these are predetermined under the structural adjustment packages set by Washington-based financial institutions in which they hold insignificant power. Many infrastructural projects financed by the World Bank, such as constructing dams for hydro-electric power, have resulted in the displacement of indigenous people of the area. Finally, there are also concerns that these institutions, in working with the private sector, may undermine the role of the state as the primary provider of essential goods and services, such as healthcare and education, resulting in the underperformance of such services in countries badly in need of them.

See Also: Bretton Woods Accord; European Monetary Union; European Union; Financial Market Regulation; Financial Markets; International Monetary Fund; Monetary Intervention; Money Supply; Pegged Exchange Rate; Trade Bloc; Trade Pact; World Trade Organization.

Bibliography. Bretton Woods Project, www.brettonwoods project.org (cited March 2009); Ariel Buira, ed., *Reforming the Governance of the IMF and the World Bank* (Anthem Press, 2005); International Monetary Fund, www.imf.org (cited June, 2008); Strom Thacker, "The High Politics of IMF Lending," *World Politics* (v.52/1, 1999); World Bank, www.worldbank.org (cited March 2009); Ngaire Woods, *The Globalizers: The IMF, the World Bank, and Their Borrowers* (Cornell University Press, 2006).

Abhijit Roy
University of Scranton

Bribery

Bribery is the practice of enticing people to do something they are otherwise reluctant, unwilling, or legally forbidden to do, with money or gifts. Though that description may sound straightforward, attitudes toward bribery vary widely around the world and across different contexts. A comparison might be to the varying attitudes toward other culture-specific practices, like tipping or haggling—either of which may be taken for granted in one culture while seen as bizarre and frustrating in another, or may be considered a social responsibility in one context (tipping a waiter) and unthinkable in another (tipping a doctor). The mechanism, severity of taboo or illegality, and sometimes language of bribery varies not just from country to country but industry to industry.

Legally speaking, the term *bribery* is applicable only when the transaction is forbidden by law—either explicitly or because it requires one party to break a law or neglect their duties—and typically involves officials and other authority figures. A driver may be pulled over and try to bribe a police officer in order to avoid a ticket, even offering more than the cost of the ticket in order to avoid points on his license. Lawyers may bribe workers in a courtroom for information pertinent to their case.

Gamblers, crime syndicates, or other interested parties may bribe the referees or players in a sports event, in order to influence the outcome so as to profit off of sports betting—this has been a perennial problem in organized sports, from the Black Sox scandal of the 1919 World Series to the charges against NBA referee Tim Donaghy in 2007, and affect even ostensibly "amateur" sports, as in the ice dancing scandal at the 2002 Winter Olympics. While a referee, judge, or other official is an obvious person to target for bribery, athletes can be enticed to throw the game, and coaches may be enticed to exert their influence.

Bribery and International Business

Bribery is an inescapable aspect of doing business internationally. In some countries, bribes are so accepted that they are tax-deductible. The U.S. Foreign Corrupt Practices Act even makes allowances for a limited degree of bribery, permitting "grease payments," which are legally distinguished from the bribery of foreign officials, and which are usually made in order to speed up legal processes rather than to bypass local or international law. This makes it easier to do business, without violating American law, in countries where bribery is a way of life.

The Bribe Payers Index tabulates a rough estimate of how likely businesses from various countries are to pay bribes when doing business abroad. It is based on responses from over 10,000 executives, as part of the World Economic Forum. In 2006, the 30 leading export nations were ranked on a scale of 1 to 10, with 10 being the most likely to pay bribes:

1. Switzerland 7.81
2. Sweden 7.81
3. Australia 7.59
4. Austria 7.50
5. Canada 7.46
6. United Kingdom 7.39
7. Germany 7.34
8. Netherlands 7.28
9. Belgium 7.22
10. United States 7.22
11. Japan 7.10
12. Singapore 6.78
13. Spain 6.63
14. United Arab Emirates 6.62
15. France 6.50
16. Portugal 6.47
17. Mexico 6.45
18. Hong Kong 6.01
19. Israel 6.01
20. Italy 5.94
21. South Korea 5.83
22. Saudi Arabia 5.75
23. Brazil 5.65
24. South Africa 5.61
25. Malaysia 5.59
26. Taiwan 5.41
27. Turkey 5.23
28. Russia 5.16
29. China 4.94
30. India 4.62

One of the interesting things about the list is the low placement of countries like Russia, where the common perception is that bribery is common within the country, which would intuitively lead to the assumption that its businesses would be as willing to pay bribes outside of the country.

Payola and Pay to Play

Pay to play is a phrase used in reference to an assortment of similar activities, some legal, many of them forms of bribery, all of them having in common the transaction of money for some form of access or attention. In its most literal rendering it refers to *payola*, the long-standing and often overlooked practice in the music industry of paying radio stations to play certain songs, without any overt announcement of sponsorship. Many of the most popular, successful, and talented artists in popular music history were given a boost by payola, if only because the practice creates a system into which everyone must buy in.

The institution of independent record promoters arose specifically to try to circumnavigate FCC regulations about payola, after both Alan Freed and Dick Clark—world-famous and influential DJs in the 1950s and 1960s—were subjects of payola scandals. In the independent promoter system, record companies pay independent promoters—separate companies or individuals—who then pay record stations or DJs to play the songs on the list the record company provides. Though blatantly the same essential act as paying the station directly, it was believed that this would honor the letter of the law and at least permit the practice until the law could be rewritten. Instead, the blatancy of the violation of the spirit of the law attracted the attention of state and federal prosecutors, resulting in a federal settlement in which four broadcasting companies—ClearChannel, CBS Radio, Entercomm, and Citadel—paid $12.5 million in fines but were not found guilty of specific charges, nor made to admit to wrongdoing. It was enough to send the message, and the practice has either died off or gone underground.

In politics, *pay to play* refers to the need to pay money—usually in the form of campaign contributions—in order to get special attention from a politician. That attention may be in the form of favorable legislation (which is the essential and legal goal of lobbying), government contracts, appointments to special posts, jobs, et cetera. The potential influence of a newly elected politician is broad, and a good many politicians—especially at the state and local level—elevated their campaign supporters to all the available posts in government, as a reward for their support. Though there are regulations governing campaign contributions from individuals, institutions, and corporations, and the disclosure thereof, pay to play payments are often made with so-called soft money, money that is donated to political organizations (called 527s for the section of tax code governing them) which do not fund advertising promoting the election or defeat of a specific candidate. The abuse and scrutiny of soft money contributions is one of the most prominent issues in campaign finance reform.

Rent Seeking

The reason bribery is so discouraged, beyond the consequences of its specific instances, is because it creates a "rent-seeking" culture, in which those who cannot afford to pay cannot afford to play. The *rent* of *rent-seeking* is derived from Adam Smith's tripartite division of income into wage, profit, and rent, and does not refer specifically to property leasing. A rent-seeking culture is one in which individuals and organizations in that culture seek to increase their incomes through the manipulation of conditions, rather than through production and trade. For instance, it may be cheaper for a manufacturer to preserve or change the regulations affecting its industry and its products than it is to alter those products or practices. If the cost of preserving beneficial regulations allowing for widget production to pollute the environment—whether through lobbying, campaign contributions, illegal bribes, or other illegal activity—is significantly lower than the cost of developing and producing a nonpolluting widget, then on paper it appears that it is in the business's best interest to spend the money on those regulations. In fact, it is in a sense even in the interests of the widget consumer—until one factors in the environmental effects.

In late 2008, a global crackdown on companies using bribery to advance their business interests in foreign nations increased its momentum. In the United States, such investigations went from only three in 2002 to 84 in 2007. Also, in 2007, Baker Hughes, a Houston oil-field services firm, agreed to pay $44 million in fines and return profits associated with bribing Kazakhstan officials, as a penalty under the Foreign Corrupt Practices Act.

See Also: Corruption; Culture-Specific Values; Foreign Corrupt Practices Act; Legal Environments; Lobbying.

Bibliography. Russell Gold and David Crawford, "U.S., Other Nations Step Up Bribery Battle Prosecutions Climb on Tougher Laws Aimed at Businesses," *Wall Street Journal* (September 12, 2008); Gordon Tullock, *The Rent-Seeking Society* (Liberty Fund, 2005); Alexandra Addison Wrage, *Bribery and Extortion: Undermining Business, Governments, and Security* (Praeger Security International, 2007).

Bill Kte'pi
Independent Scholar

BRICs

"The BRICs" refers to Brazil, Russia, India, and China, and specifically to their fast-growing but still developing economies (and, by implication, their similar goals and the mutual benefits to be had from an alliance). The term was coined by Jim O'Neill, head of global economic research at finance corporation Goldman Sachs, and has been rapidly adopted by other parties, to the extent that financial news sources use it with minimal or no explanation, and a 2008 summit between representatives of the four nations was called the BRIC Summit. As O'Neill pointed out, and as Goldman Sachs economists and others have expanded on since, these four economies are not simply rapidly developing. They are rapidly developing and have a great deal of demonstrable potential. One quarter of the world's land and a staggering two-fifths of its population is accounted for by the BRICs.

The BRIC thesis has been a long-term prediction from the start, and its first formal defense was in the 2003 paper "Dreaming with BRICs: The Path to 2050." O'Neill's argument is that these four economies have the capability of being among the dominant economic powers—and collectively, the dominant power—by the year 2050. Specifically, the Goldman Sachs prediction is that by that year, raw materials will be dominated by Russia (particularly petroleum products) and Brazil (particularly soy and iron), and manufactured goods by China and India. This provides a practical reason for cooperation among the BRICs, especially in trade.

The Goldman Sachs scenario postulates a 2050 in which BRIC citizens (apart from Russians) are poorer on average than those of other industrialized nations, but in which the BRIC countries account for the largest share of the global economy and wealth. Commodity prices will change as the global consumer base changes. BRIC currencies will appreciate by 300 percent. Follow-up reports from Goldman Sachs have amplified, rather than contradicted, these predictions. While the predictions are based on economic potential, they do not represent a "best case scenario." They assume the continued adoption of policies that encourage growth, but nothing miraculous or extraordinary—just steady growth as the BRIC countries, having recently adopted favorable capitalist policies, expand their economies to fill the space available to them.

In the wake of the Goldman Sachs conjectures and their popularization, the BRIC term has been adopted by many investment firms and analysts who favor investing in emerging markets. If those countries are expected to rapidly expand, after all, they would seem to offer great investment opportunities. The applications of the conjectures to investing strategies are not immediately apparent, however.

There is a tendency to use the term as shorthand for emerging markets in general, especially in investment contexts. Sometimes this is explained narratively, with the four nations taken as symbolizing developing regions of the world—Latin America, Eastern Europe, South Asia, and East Asia—sometimes the cache of the word, the brand name appeal, is simply used in order to introduce a similar theory about emerging markets. At the same time, the term is sometimes attacked for glossing over the differences among the BRIC nations. Brazil, for instance, is an established full democracy with no recent history of serious disputes with its neighbors. (*The Economist* has called it "the only BRIC without a nuclear bomb.") Russia and China are diminishing in population, while Brazil and India are growing.

Very similar to the BRIC nations are Mexico and Korea, both of which are experiencing economic growth comparable to Brazil's, and have become more devotedly capitalist in the recent past. An early Goldman Sachs BRIC paper explained the exclusion of the two countries as owing to Korea's current political situation—the division between North and South—and the fact that Mexico is already a major economy. But the countries do have BRIC-like potential in the coming decades. Mexico's middle class is growing at a significant rate, while its impoverished class declines, and infrastructure is quickly modernizing. Korea is widely considered likely to reunify before 2050, and has tremendous economic potential if it does so and retains favorable policies. Unlike Brazil, India, and China, Mexico and Korea (unified or just South Korea) are likely to have per capita incomes comparable to the United States and other leading economic powers.

See Also: Brazil; China; Geopolitics; India; Korea, South; Mexico; Russia.

Bibliography. Arindam Banerjee, ed., *Capital Markets in the BRIC Economies* (Icfai University Press, 2007); Marc

Kobayashi-Hillary, *Building a Future with BRICs: The Next Decade for Offshoring* (Springer, 2007); Stefano Pelle, *Understanding Emerging Markets: Building Business Bric by Brick* (Sage, 2007); Dominic Wilson and Roopa Puru-shothaman, "Dreaming With BRICs: The Path to 2050," Goldman Sachs Global Economic Paper no. 99, www2 .goldmansachs.com (cited March 2009).

BILL KTE'PI
INDEPENDENT SCHOLAR

British East India Company

The contribution of the British East India Company (EIC) to the British Empire was considerable. In the closing years of her reign, Queen Elizabeth I (1533-1603) granted a royal charter to the company on December 31, 1600, with rights of trading east of the Cape of Good Hope. Within a span of 150 years, the EIC was the most powerful company trading with India. Gradually Britain established political hege-mony in the subcontinent and from its traders, it became colonial masters.

The EIC, a joint-stock company of 125 sharehold-ers, began with a capital of £72,000. It was adminis-tered by a court of directors, and had a governor and 24 directors elected annually. The EIC got its start in 1601, when merchant ships went to purchase spices from Indonesia. The huge quantities of black pepper brought back resulted in an oversupply in the British domestic market and the company began to diver-sify its trade. Indian textiles were a prized item and a factory (meaning a trading establishment, from the word *factor*, or agent) in Surat was opened on the northwest coast of India in 1608. After three years, a factory was established in Masulipatam on the eastern coast of India. In 1615 the EIC representa-tive Thomas Roe (1581–1644) obtained *farman* (an imperial order) from the Mughal Emperor Jehangir (1605–27) for trading and setting up posts through-out the Mughal Empire. The EIC did brisk trading from major factories such as the walled forts of Saint George in Bengal, Fort William in Madras, and Bom-bay Castle.

An abundance of cotton textiles in the factories resulted in fulfilling global demand for durable and washable Indian textiles. The EIC began to receive concessions from the local rulers of India and in time dabbled in politics. In Bengal, the EIC was enjoying highly profitable trading and in fact, 60 percent of commodities imported from Asia were coming from Bengal. By 1717 it had a free hand in the importing and exporting of goods from Bengal. It did not have to pay any tax and could issue *dastak* (permits) to certify the movement of goods. By adroit diplomacy, warfare, and political conspiracy, the British subju-gated Bengal, and afterward the whole of the Indian subcontinent.

In 1757 the expansion of the EIC began with the Battle of Plassey after the defeat of Mirza Muham-mad Sirajuddaula (1729–57), the *nawab* of Bengal, by Robert Clive (1725–44). The French were defeated in the ensuing Anglo-French conflict. The Carnatic wars eliminated the French from south India. There was further consolidation of the EIC's power in east-ern India after the Battle of Buxar in 1764, which gave the company control over the financial admin-istration of Bengal, Bihar, and Orissa.

With the loss of the American colonies, the "first British Empire" was over by 1783. In the period of the "second British Empire," imperial attention turned toward Asia and the sugar plantations of the Carib-bean. The EIC defeated any power that stood in its way. Mysore and Maratha states came under the British sway. By the middle of 19th century, British authority extended up to present-day Afghanistan in the west and Myanmar (Burma) in the east.

Land revenue was major source of income for the EIC and its collection was a major concern for the company. The commercialization of agriculture increased. With the rise of a new class of manufactures in industrialized Britain, there was an overhauling of the EIC's trading system. The company lost absolute privilege in commerce in 1813. British goods then flowed abundantly to India. The latter was becoming a supplier of raw materials to Britain and a consumer of British finished products. The drain of wealth from India continued, with profits from business being transferred to Britain. The EIC purchased goods from India out of the revenue that was collected from Ben-gal and sent it home. Great Britain drained resources and wealth from India.

The rule of the company had witnessed the revolts of peasants, tribal people, and landowners. The revolt of 1857 (the so-called *Sepoy* mutiny) engulfed large parts of India. It also sounded the death knell for the EIC: Queen Victoria's (1819–1901) proclamation of November 1, 1858, brought the Indian subcontinent under the direct rule of Great Britain.

See Also: Dutch East India Company; India; Pakistan; United Kingdom.

Bibliography. S. Babu, *Merchants of Politics: East India Company and the Dawn of the Raj* (Dominant, 2006); H. V. Bowen, *The Business of Empire: The East India Company and Imperial Britain, 1756–1833* (Cambridge University Press, 2006); H. V. Bowen et al., *The Worlds of The East India Company* (D. S. Brewer, 2002); K. N. Chaudhuri, *The Trading World of Asia and The English East India Company, 1660–1760* (Cambridge University Press, 1978); Brian Gardner, *The East India Company: A History* (McCall, 1972); John Keay, *The Honourable Company: A History of The English East India Company* (Macmillan, 1994); M. S. Naravane, *Battles of the Honourable East India Company: Making of the Raj* (A. P. H. Publishing, 2006); Om Prakash, *Emergence of the East India Company* (Anmol, 2002); K. C. Sharma, *East India Company* (Vista International, 2007); Antony Wild, *The East India Company: Trade and Conquest From 1600* (Lyons Press, 2000).

PATIT PABAN MISHRA
SAMBALPUR UNIVERSITY

Brunei

Brunei (Brunei Darussalam) is an Islamic sultanate located on the northern coast of the island of Kalimantan (Borneo) facing the South China Sea. It is divided into two sections, separated by territory (the Limbang Valley) of the state of Sarawak, Malaysia. The Sultan, His Majesty Sultan Haji Hassanal Bolkiah, is concurrently the prime minister, defense minister, finance minister, and head of religion (Islam) for the country. In the tradition of Islamic sultanates, the government of Brunei is autocratic and is classified as an absolute monarchy.

The Sultanate of Brunei was a major power in the region from the 15th to the 17th centuries, including control over the current Malaysian states of Sabah and Sarawak and north beyond the Sulu Sea. After conflicts with Spain and attacks by pirates, the Sultan eventually gave much of the country (mainly Sarawak) to the Scottish adventurer James Brooke in 1841. Brooke established a raj in Sarawak and installed himself as a "white rajah." Brunei also began ceding territory to Great Britain and eventually became a British protectorate in 1888.

Brunei was occupied by the Japanese during World War II and returned to its British protectorate status in 1945. Brunei was invited to become a part of Malaysia when it was formed in 1963 but refused, mainly on economic grounds, not wanting to grant control to Kuala Lumpur of its extensive oil and natural gas resources. It regained full independence again in 1984, at which time it joined the Association of Southeast Asian Nations (ASEAN), the Organization of Islamic Conference (OIC), and the United Nations.

Brunei has a legislative council but its members are appointed and it has only token power with regard to approving the budget. There is a constitution but it was suspended after an armed rebellion in 1962. When the legislative council was reactivated in 2004, a number of direct restrictions were placed on it by the Sultan. Individual rights remain limited and Freedom House classifies press status as "Not Free."

The economy of Brunei is built around oil and natural gas, which account for more than half of gross domestic product (GDP) and more than 90 percent of exports. The discovery of oil at Seria in 1929 has resulted in development in the country that has kept it ahead of all other Southeast Asian countries except Singapore. It has one of the world's largest liquefied natural gas (LNG) plants. Roughly 90 percent of the LNG produced is sold to Japan. In 2008 cooperation with China in the development of Brunei fisheries was undertaken. Recently, South Korea has also become a major customer. With a per capita GDP of more than US$25,100 (PPP $51,000), Brunei is on a par with the European Union at US$26,300. Life expectancy is more than 75.5 years and the infant mortality rate is low at less than 13 per 1000 live births. An indicator of modern prosperity is the low fertility rate of 1.94.

Brunei has considerable ethnic divisions, with distinct separations between Barunay (including the Sultan and his family line), Iban, Dayak, and other Malays (roughly 60 percent together), plus substantial numbers of Chinese (14 percent), Indians (6 percent),

British (10 percent), and Koreans (9 percent). Citizenship is strictly controlled in favor of Malays, with many Chinese having registration documents but no citizenship. The Chinese and South Asians are a commanding presence in the economy, far outweighing their numbers, while the Malays are heavily represented in government service and in agriculture. The numbers of Chinese in the country may be undercounted.

Vestiges of Brunei's empire remain in its border and island disputes with Malaysia and its claims against China and others in the Spratly Islands. Sea bottom exploration for oil, natural gas, and other minerals continues to be critical to Brunei's economic future.

See Also: Association of Southeast Asian Nations; China; Malaysia.

Bibliography. BP USA, *Brunei: Country Study Guide* (International Business Publications, 2008); Economist Intelligence Unit, "Brunei Country Report" (June 2008); R. H. Hickling, *A Prince of Borneo* (Graham Brash, 1985); G. Saunders, *A History of Brunei* (Oxford University Press, 1994); D. S. Ranjit Singh, *Brunei 1839–1983: The Problems of Political Survival* (Oxford University Press, 1991); Third Point Systems, *Brunei: A Strategic Assessment* (1985).

LLEWELLYN D. HOWELL
THUNDERBIRD SCHOOL OF GLOBAL MANAGEMENT

BSE Sensex Index (Bombay Stock Exchange)

The BSE Sensitive Index (Sensex) is a value-weighted index tracking the performance of 30 stocks on the Bombay Stock Exchange (BSE).

The Bombay Stock Exchange was established in 1875, and in the 21st century it lists more stocks (4,700) than any other exchange in the world. By market capitalization, it is the 10th-largest exchange in the world, and the largest in south Asia. The Sensex was first compiled in 1986, using 1978–79 as its base year, with a starting value of 100 points. The inflation-adjusted rate of return since its base year has been about 9 percent per annum. The index passed the 1,000 point mark in July 1990, doubling in the next year and a half, doubling again in the following two months to pass 4,000 points on March 30, 1992. Growth has been steady, though slower, since then.

Like stock exchanges worldwide, the BSE has suffered from the American subprime mortgage crisis and related credit crisis. The 10 worst single-day falls in the BSE's history all date from 2006 on; most were in 2008. The Sensex was volatile all through that period, experiencing not only its worst falls but its most rapid climbs, with the three fastest 1,000-point climbs in the index's history occurring in the autumn of 2007.

The 30 stocks tracked by the Sensex are the largest and most traded stocks on the exchange, accounting for about one-fifth of the market capitalization of the huge exchange. As of the beginning of 2009, the 30 stocks on the BSE Sensex are:

- Associated Cement Companies Limited, a Mumbai cement company operated by the Swiss corporation Holcim.
- Bharat Heavy Electricals Limited, India's largest infrastructure and energy-related manufacturing company.
- Bharti Airtel, the largest cellular service provider in India.
- DLF India, India's largest real estate developer.
- Grasim Industries, a textile manufacturer that expanded into building materials and chemicals.
- Housing Development Finance Corporation (HDFC), a bank focused on home mortgages.
- HDFC Bank Limited, a commercial bank opened by HDFC after India began allowing private sector banks in 1994.
- Hindalco Industries, an aluminum manufacturer.
- Hindustan Unilever, India's largest consumer products company, a majority stake of which is owned by the Anglo-Dutch company Unilever.
- ICICI Bank, formerly Industrial Credit and Investment Corporation of India, India's largest private bank.
- Infosys Technologies Limited, a multinational IT company headquartered in Bangalore.
- ITC Limited, formerly Imperial Tobacco Company, one of the country's most profitable com-

panies, a conglomerate dealing in everything from cigarettes to hotels to greeting cards.

- Jaiprakash Associates, a housing industry company.
- Larsen and Toubro, a diversified Indian conglomerate with major holdings in construction.
- Mahindra & Mahindra Limited, a conglomerate with operations in IT, infrastructure, automotives, financial services, and farm equipment.
- Maruti Suzuki, one of the largest automobile manufacturers in South Asia.
- National Thermal Power Corporation, the largest power company in the country.
- Oil and Natural Gas Corporation, the company responsible for most of India's natural gas and oil production.
- Ranbaxy Laboratories Limited, the country's largest pharmaceutical company.
- Reliance Communications, a telecommunications company.
- Reliance Industries, a large conglomerate with holdings in petroleum, clothing, and fresh food.
- Reliance Infrastructure, a large power company.
- Satyam Computer Services, an IT company.
- State Bank of India, the nation's largest bank.
- Sterlite Industries, a metals and mining group.
- Tata Consultancy Services, a software and consulting company.
- Tata Motors, a vehicle manufacturer.
- Tata Power, an electricity company with a focus in hydroelectric power.
- Tata Steel, the world's fifth-largest steel company.
- Wipro, an IT company.

See Also: Company Profiles: South Asia; India; Indian Oil; Stock Exchanges.

Bibliography. Gurcharan Das, *India Unbound: The Social and Economic Revolution from Independence to the Global Information Age* (Anchor, 2002); Arvind Panagariya, *India: The Emerging Giant* (Oxford University Press, 2008); Jorge Dige Pedersen, *Globalization, Development, and the State: The Performance of India and Brazil Since 1990* (Palgrave Macmillan, 2008); Robert J. Shiller, *Irrational Exuberance* (Broadway Books, 2006).

BILL KTE'PI
INDEPENDENT SCHOLAR

BT

British Telecom (BT) Group plc is the world's oldest communications company. BT can trace its lineage back to the late 1800s, when, following the Telegraph Act of 1892, the lines of the two private companies that provided the bulk of the then United Kingdom (UK) telephone network were purchased by the government and later in 1912 were run as a government department as part of the General Post Office (GPO) under the Postmaster-General. BT's age means that it has either created or played witness to all of the major events of the global telecommunications industry. The various phases of its development make it an interesting case for those who study trends of privatization and deregulation of nationalized industries and networked utilities.

Until 1969 UK telephony was treated as a natural, statutory monopoly, until following the Post Office Act it became a nationalized industry, becoming "Post Office Telecommunications" (POT). Finally, on April 1, 1984, POT was privatized under the trading name British Telecom (from 1991 "BT"). Today, BT Group is made up of four principal businesses: BT Openreach, BT Retail, BT Wholesale, and BT Global Services. BT is currently a vertically integrated conglomerate offering a range of communication services to domestic and corporate customers based on the strategic resource of its infrastructure and associated services. Although a private company, BT is still expected to act for the public good, for example, connecting consumers to the fixed-line network and providing public call boxes.

In the UK, the degree to which BT can leverage its ownership of the majority of the telecommunications infrastructure is controlled by the UK Government Office of Communications (Ofcom). In response, BT has sought expansion and new markets through global ventures, experiencing mixed results. For example, a joint venture and proposed merger by acquisition with MCI Communication Corporation and the formation of a 50/50 joint venture with AT&T, both to obtain a foothold in the United States, ultimately failed. However, successful acquisitions included the Italian telecommunications operator Albacom and financial infrastructure provider Radianz from Reuters.

The UK government has been keen to stimulate competition in the deregulated telecommunications market; however, efforts to dislodge BT from its virtual monopoly status have been unsuccessful. A distinct example was the government drive to create "Broadband Britain." The government forced BT to allow other broadband providers to use BT exchange equipment to provide commercially viable alternatives for consumers, but the rate at which this was done and ensuing problems with the financial sustainability of early competitors in the immature marketplace led to the government turning to BT to provide leadership and accelerate market development. In the domestic arena, BT is doing this by aggressive pricing, leveraging existing technologies, and its tradition of owning the telecommunications access point in the home, providing a "triple-play" product, bundling broadcasting, telephony, and broadband internet access.

This success is a two-edged sword as broadband internet and mobile communications increasingly negate the BT advantage of ownership of fixed lines and therefore its traditional revenue streams. The international technological and commercial convergence of the telecommunications, information technology, and content industries has created many alternative ways to move voice, data, and video communication. In response, BT is currently developing the 21st Century Network (also known as 21CN), a network based on internet protocol technology, which will replace all existing networks to enable seamless voice, data, and video communication between any static or mobile digital device.

To exploit this infrastructure and entrench BT further into the domestic market, it is making preemptive strategic alliances, for example, with Intel to explore wireless working, outsourcing with Accenture, and multimedia entertainment and online gaming with Microsoft. BT's first-mover advantage in the UK and vast technological, financial, and intellectual resources have become barriers to entry to the UK telecommunications market and a strong platform for global joint ventures and mergers and acquisitions, such that it seems not even the best efforts of the UK government can change this in the short term.

See Also: AT&T; Deregulation; Privatization.

Bibliography. BT, *A Short History of BT's World* (British Telecommunications, 1998); BT, "BT's History," www.btplc .com (cited March 2009); Massimo Florio, "Does Privatisation Matter? The Long-Term Performance of British Telecom Over 40 Years," *Fiscal Studies* (v.24/2, June 2003); John Harper, *Monopoly and Competition in British Telecommunication: The Past, the Present and the Future* (Pinter, 1997); Colin Turner, "Issues in the Mass Market Deployment of Broadband: An Analysis of British Telecommunications' (BT) Strategy," *Info: the Journal of Policy, Regulation and Strategy for Telecommunications, Information and Media* (v.5/2, 2003).

IAN STEWART
BIRMINGHAM CITY UNIVERSITY

Bulgaria

Bulgaria is a country in southeastern Europe that lies south of Romania, north of Greece and Turkey, and has a coastline along the western edge of the Black Sea. Since its reestablishment as an independent country in 1878 after the rule of the Ottoman Empire (from 1422), Bulgaria has faced an economic dilemma: How to raise the standard of living despite a backward rural economy and a meager industrial and savings basis? How to build a balanced society beyond agrarian majorities in favor of entrepreneurial middle classes and bourgeoisies? At first, it relied on export of agricultural commodities to north-central Europe. It called for foreign direct investments to fuel the lean state budget and to finance the basic networks of railroads. Its banking structure took a long time to become efficient, under the aegis of the central bank and inflows of German, Austrian, and French money.

Some signs of take-off occurred at the turn of the 20th century, but Bulgaria failed to enlarge significantly its territory through the Balkan Wars (1912–13) and remained a small country, all the more because it had to submit to reparation payments after having joined Germany and Austria-Hungary in World War I. A predominant agrarian economy and unequal ownership of farms put brakes on growth and diversification, which stopped during the 1930s and 1940s.

After World War II Bulgaria joined the Soviet-controlled economic area Council for Mutual Economic Assistance (COMECON). It benefited from some European globalization thanks to the injection of money by the Soviet Union: The massive land reform transformed agriculture into an efficient sovkhoz-type collectivist sector, exporting wheat and maize to the Soviet Union. The centrally planned industry was specialized into a few segments—with exports of electricity produced by nuclear plants and also of ground resources (lead, zinc), followed by agricultural machinery, truck motors, buses and trucks, and machine tools, thus benefiting from a high level of investment against gross domestic product (GDP) and from the introduction of skills in mechanics and upstream in steel and pig iron. The Black Sea coast welcomed tourists from the entire Communist area. Bulgaria had no genuine margin to maneuver but its standards progressed, thank to this artificial dependency on Soviet money, engineering, customership (75 percent of exports), and energy supplies.

Such rigid dependency was revealed after the fall of the Berlin Wall in 1989, because all of a sudden the Bulgarian economy was swallowed by a crisis of low productivity, while a desperate lack of inner capital and savings became apparent. To counter this chaos, Bulgaria had to rebuild a state economic administration, fight against bribery, and try to stimulate private investment and entrepreneurship for peasants, retail trading, small and medium-sized enterprises in light industry, services, and the hotel and tourism business. The European Bank for Economic Development and the European Union provided financial help. But Bulgaria had to consider whether to open its economy to foreign investors and thus lose economic autonomy or to keep some nationalistic strongholds.

The first strategy took shape in the name of liberalism and moreover of employment. This led to large investments from foreign banks, utilities, and service firms (German ones using Bulgarians as truck drivers throughout Europe). Other investments were made in real estate and tourism and in the food industry. Foreign direct investment was led by Austria (21 percent) in 1996–2007, the Netherlands (16 percent), Greece (9 percent), and Great Britain (9 percent). Such "positive" globalization did not create enough employment, and Bulgarians commenced emigrating to western Europe, mainly to work in construction, sending their earnings to their home country. Bulgaria still needs to determine its "specialization" within the new European economic order and within the European Union, which it joined in January 2007. It has missed out, for example, on the car manufacturing plants welcomed by some other countries.

See Also: Eastern Europe; European Bank for Reconstruction and Development; European Union (EU).

Bibliography. Andy Anderson and Stephane Lambert *Buying a Property: Bulgaria* (Cadogan, 2007); CIA, "Bulgaria," *World Factbook*, www.cia.gov (cited March 2009); Emil Giatzidis, *An Introduction to Post-Communist Bulgaria: Political, Economic, and Social Transformations* (Manchester University Press, 2002); Petia Koleva, *Système productif et système financier en Bulgarie: 1990–2003* [Bulgaria's production and financial systems: 1990–2003] (Harmattan, 2004); John Lampe, *The Bulgarian Economy in the Twentieth Century* (Crown Helm, 1986); John Lampe and Marvin Jackson, *Balkan Economic History, 1550–1950: From Imperial Borderlands to Developing Nations* (Indiana University Press, 1982).

Hubert Bonin
Bordeaux University

Bureaucracy

In its broadest sense, *bureaucracy* means domination through the expertise of the official. A bureaucracy is an organization formally established to fulfill its ends through the determination of the means to guarantee the highest administrative efficiency. Its legitimacy rests on the technical knowledge and the observation of the rules legally set forth that guide its action. It is a machine based on accuracy, calculation, continuity, discipline, rigor, and confidence, which guarantee a stable and certain social order.

The origin of the concept can be traced in the texts of Vincent Gournay and G. W. F. Hegel, which referred to the power of civil servants to service the monarchy. Later, social thinkers like Karl Marx, Ferdinand Tönnies, Emile Durkheim, and Robert Michels analyzed through different approaches the impact of the bureaucratic organization on economic activity and the power structure of modern society. However, Max Weber offers a complete theoretical formulation because, in his intention to understand and characterize the progressive transformation of

Western civilization, he noted the technical superiority of bureaucracy and its consequences.

Attributes

Weber described bureaucracy as the most rational way to exercise domination, because it has certain attributes that are not appreciated in social communities organized around charisma or tradition. The bureaucratic organization is based on the distribution of work and responsibilities, so that the competencies of the officials are precisely defined and are articulated through a hierarchical order in which relations of authority are clearly defined. Each officer complies with the administrative tasks assigned by laws and regulations, and does it with discipline, loyalty, and obedience.

In addition, each position is linked to specific technical qualities, so it can be occupied by anyone who meets the requirements. Bureaucratic work is a remunerated and continuous full-time occupation that enables the realization of a career based on promotion considering expertise and merit. The development of the monetary economy facilitated payment in money to the modern official and the establishment of a tax system allowing the collection of funds to sustain the costs of bureaucratic activities of the state. Accordingly, this model assumes the separation of public service and private life, and distinguishes public property of the heritage of the individuals.

Finally, bureaucracy is associated with modern management techniques based on the documentation and written record of each action, giving rise to the collection, classification, and storage of files. In addition, because bureaucracy operates according to clearly defined general rules, it treats each case avoiding arbitrariness and favoritism.

However, the current operation of bureaucracy does not correspond to the ideal attributes. Robert K. Merton pointed out the relevance of analyzing the tensions produced between the formal structure and the real behavior of officials, which gives rise to phenomena such as trained incapacity, occupational psychosis, and professional deformation of officials. The examination of the dysfunctions inherent to the rational model of bureaucracy shows the ritualism produced by the excessive adherence to formalized procedures; the distortion of information produced by hierarchy, centralization, and specialization; the inhibition of initiative and creativity because of the rigid respect of rules; and the hostility and indifference produced by impersonal treatment based on the record.

Under these approaches, some scholars conducted several empirical studies to demonstrate the displacement of initial commitments of bureaucracy and their unintended consequences, the forces that originate the process of formalization and the latent functions of bureaucracy, the processes of change and innovation in widely formalized organizations, and the disruptive effects of hidden relations of power on the bureaucratic system.

From Bureaucratization to Globalization

Weber considered also the consequences of the generalization of bureaucracy, a process that transformed modern society into an iron cage in which citizens were caught by formal procedures that widely restrict their freedom. The inevitable bureaucratization of the world was appreciated by Bruno Rizzi in the Soviet Union, a centralized state with a huge bureaucratic apparatus that controls economic surplus and any aspect of social life. Capitalist societies were also criticized. James Burnham relied upon the thesis of Rizzi to characterize the process of bureaucratization in the United States, a society increasingly directed by a managerial class that controls the access to the means of production and takes advantage of its position to serve to its own particular interests. These and other experiences have motivated extensive discussions on the effects of bureaucratic power over the freedom of citizens and representative democracy.

Bureaucratization was facilitated by the generalization of division and standardization of work, which led to increased productivity and reduction of costs, encouraging mass consumption. Scientific management, driven by Frederick W. Taylor, and the introduction of the modern assembly line in the Ford Motor Company exemplify this process. These transformations favored the professionalization of management of capitalist companies that were increasingly integrated into conglomerates controlled by professional managers appointed by the board of stakeholders.

In addition, the state created large public enterprises in strategic sectors such as communications, transport, and energy to support private investment and macroeconomic stability. It also created a large bureaucratic system to offer public services demanded by cities and towns, and addressed the needs of education, health, and social security of the most disadvantaged sectors of the population. Finally, in the arena of politics, political parties were impelled to adopt bureaucratic structures to attract the masses and get better conditions for electoral competition. Overall, these trends implied the constant expansion of bureaucracy and the integration of an enormous army of bureaucrats with technical skills acquired by specialized professional training.

The huge size of the state apparatus related with bureaucratization was harshly criticized in liberal thinking, which opposed the growing economic and social action of the state. Ludwig von Mises, Frederick A. Hayek, Milton Friedman, and others argued that Keynesian policies attack individual liberties, disrupting the natural functioning of the economy. From the 1970s, when the failure of the welfare state was evident, liberalism promoted the free market, labor flexibility, and democracy as the antidotes for bureaucratization and state interventionism. Globalization arises then as a stage of reorganization of economic activities of the world under the principles of individual freedom, economic competition, and flexible organization.

The new liberal times have redefined the role of the state, establishing clear limits to government action, and introduced new forms of management and organization based on entrepreneurialism. Managers, consultants, and researchers have spoken increasingly about post-bureaucratic organization and the advantages to adopting flexible and flat structures to promote participatory working groups and the incorporation of dynamic networks of exchange and cooperation. These new organizational forms encourage high value added work, based on knowledge that drives the formation of a new economy of intangibles.

This transformation has been possible thanks to the dizzying development of new information technologies and to the integration of a complex global information network that facilitates transactions in real time and at a distance. As a result, bureaucracy has faced a process of decentralization and delocalization, giving way to more flexible virtual structures, articulated by computer networks and mobile devices for storing, transmitting, and communicating. Thus,

the key question nowadays is whether these changes imply the removal of bureaucracy or its transformation into a "cybercracy" as an emerging organizational design that sustains the exercise of domination through the network.

See Also: Centralization; Management Science; Regulation; Standardization.

Bibliography. Stewart R. Clegg, David Courpasson, and Nelson Phillips, *Power and Organizations* (Sage, 2006); Paul Du Gay, ed., *The Values of Bureaucracy* (Oxford University Press, 2005); Marshall W. Meyer, *Change in Public Bureaucracies* (Cambridge University Press, 2008); Alexander Styhre, *The Innovative Bureaucracy: Bureaucracy in an Age of Fluidity: The Innovative Bureaucracy* (Routledge, 2007).

Eduardo Ibarra-Colado
Universidad Autónoma Metropolitana

Business Cycles

Economists and historians have described a number of different cycles in economic history, patterns that we can see repeated over and over again, from the three-to-five-year Kitchin inventory cycle to the millennia-long cycle of civilization described by futurist Alvin Toffler. These cycles describe fluctuations in various activities or trends; while popular books are often sold on the premise that they are predictable both in frequency and in effect, it's broadly true that the less specific the predictions of such a cycle, the more the data will bear it out.

When we talk about "the business cycle," for instance, or "a business cycle" as a unit of time in American history, we are generally speaking of the theory put forth by Clement Juglar, a 19th-century French economist who posited a 7–11 year business cycle tied to the credit cycle. The modern notion of the business cycle is not purely Juglar's—far from it—but builds on his suggestions and incorporates the work of Friedrich Hayek, Gustav Cassel, Arthur Spiethoff, and others. The idea of cyclical booms and busts, depressions and periods of prosperity, was especially compelling in the years following the worldwide Great Depression, to which many modern schools of economic thought can date their origins.

The easiest and most common statistic to track in discussing business cycles is real gross domestic product (GDP)—the total output produced by an economy. Since 1820, after the nation got on its feet following the expenses of the War of 1812, the United States has shown steady and significant growth in its real GDP, an average increase of 3.6 percent per year. That upward trend alone does not tell the story, however; it doesn't even accurately describe the plot arc. Within that period there have been many short-term fluctuations, contractions of the economy followed by increases.

Those fluctuations, experienced by every capitalist economy and apparently an unavoidable feature thereof, are our business cycles. The two phases of the business cycle are the expansion and the contraction—at any given time, the economy is doing one or the other, though with respect to business cycles we look not at day-to-day trends but longer-term developments. During the expansion, the real GDP increases until it reaches a peak, at which point it declines during the contraction. The contraction reaches a trough, at which point the economy again expands.

Since the Civil War, there have been 29 business cycles in the United States, of varying lengths. The shortest was 17 months (August 1918 to January 1920) with a 10-month expansion, and the longest was a bit over 10 years (July 1990 to March 2001), with an expansion of exactly a decade. The variability of the cycles' duration undermines the appeal of those popular futurism books that claim to be able to tell us what the economy will be like in 2020 or 2030, and at first glance may seem to leave us with nothing but "the economy will get worse, and then better, and then worse, and then better again." However, even that simple fact is interesting—while it may seem obvious that every contraction or expansion must stop eventually, the cyclical nature still sheds light on American economic history, and provides an opportunity to investigate the inciting causes of the phases' cycles.

Business cycles are characteristic of all capitalist economies, a fact that was highlighted after the Great Depression, when all the major capitalist economies of the world experienced contraction and all saw their real GDPs begin to rise again by the end of the decade. A casual read of a history text sometimes misses this fact, as well as the existence of the cycles themselves, because histories will generally use the language of the time—and the phrases that economists and the public have favored for expansions and especially contractions have shifted over time.

Contractions were originally called *panics*, as in the banking panics of the 19th century, but because that word implied a root cause in the hysterical actions (and overreactions) of the public, it was replaced by *crisis*, from which no such things can be inferred. Even *crisis*, though, implies a drastic situation instead of an ordinary part of the economic cycle—and the word sounds overblown for less severe contractions. The familiar *depression* took hold, eventually supplanted by the carefully neutral *recession*, which is the term most commonly used now—ever since the Great Depression, there has been a sense, especially among the public, politicians, and media, that the term *depression* should be reserved for contractionary phases that are long lasting with a deep impact on the American lifestyle. And there are, of course, always euphemistic phrases to be found, like *growth correction* (which even usually clear-headed economist John Kenneth Galbraith used) and *rolling readjustment*. However transparently those terms may be designed to ease the public mind, they are not actually wrong—they do emphasize the cyclical nature of contractions and expansions.

The terms for expansions do not vary nearly as much, because they are not as headline-grabbing, aren't talked about as much. Usually *boom* or *recovery* will suffice, depending on how rapid the expansion is, and how bad the trough of the preceding contraction was. Compatible with the euphemistic tendencies in referring to contractions, though, expansions are often treated as a success, something to be proud of—quite often, expansions are spoken of as something that was accomplished, while contractions were something that happened or were suffered through.

The Great Depression and Beyond

It is not always obvious how to determine the endpoints of a business cycle. The National Bureau of Economic Research defines a recession, for instance, as a period of significant decline in total output, income, employment, and trade, "usually lasting from six months to a year"—but even that definition leaves wiggle room. The most well-known business cycle in American history lasted from August 1929 to May 1937—the Great Depression, minus its last two years (when the economy was expanding, but was still far from recovery). The unemployment rate averaged 18.4 percent and rose as high as 25 percent, while real GDP fell 27 percent and took seven years to recover to its pre-Depression level. Many saw it as the death throes of capitalism, long awaited, long feared. In contrast, more than 50 years after the end of the Depression, the United States experienced its longest expansion, from March 1991 to March 2001, a period of post–Cold War, pre-9/11 stability that was also the nation's longest business cycle.

Since the Depression—when, whether coincidentally or not, presidential administrations began consulting more closely with economists, and the field of economics itself saw a boom—business cycles have been less severe. In the 10 cycles since the end of World War II, contractions have lasted an average of 10 months, while expansions have averaged 57 months—a figure helped, no doubt, by the steady growth of the Clinton years and the general prosperity of the early Cold War. Even in the most severe recession of that period, July 1981 to November 1982, output fell barely 3 percent (versus 27 percent in the Great Depression) and unemployment reached 11 percent (25 percent in the Great Depression). Before World War II, expansions were about half as long, contractions about twice as long.

Inflation has also been a constant since the Depression. In all but three of the years since—and every year since 1954—prices have increased, regardless of the phase of the business cycle. During expansions, prices rise faster—labor costs increase during expansions, which leads to accelerated price hikes; shortly after the expansion peaks, labor prices tend to fall, putting less pressure on rising prices. The rate of inflation, then, tends to follow a cycle that closely shadows the business cycle, while inflation itself more or less persists as a constant.

During the Great Depression, which is part of the best-known business cycle in American history, unemployment in the United States averaged 18.4 percent. The photo shows unemployed men in a bread line under the Brooklyn Bridge in the early 1930s.

Much of the work of economists since the Depression has been the study of recessions and how they might be prevented or minimized. John Maynard Keynes, the foremost economist in the Depression's aftermath, blamed declines in aggregate demand—declines in the number of goods and services sought—for recessions, because such declines lead to businesses reducing production and possibly jobs. His recommendation, issued while the Depression still raged, was for the government to intervene to increase demand, either by reducing taxes (leaving more money in consumers' pockets) or increasing government spending to "pump money into the economy," a prescription that has long since become familiar. This sort of manipulation is called counter-cyclical fiscal policy, because it is designed not only with business cycles in mind but with the explicit aim of changing them. (For his part, Juglar blamed overinvestment, overextension, and rampant speculation for recessions, essentially arguing that they were as bad as they were because the expansions that preceded them were "false" expansions, booms inflated by irresponsible and unsustainable financial behavior. Juglar was writing well before the Great Depression, but nothing about it contradicts him in the broad points.)

World War II seems to have borne out Keynes's theories. The prolonged, high-tech, expensive war, fought with massive amounts of manpower and technology, with extraordinary and unheard-of efforts put into research for the war effort, rejuvenated the American economy—and accustomed many women to the workplace, which helped in the coming years by (in essence) providing more available workers. The existence of the war makes it difficult to say what would have happened to the economy without that massive spending and the historically low levels of unemployment caused by the one-two punch of military enlistment and increased domestic labor demand. Some economists believe the Depression would have ended around the same time without those effects. It is a bit like dropping a brick on a spider and then debating whether it would be just as dead had you only dropped a shoe; it's not that the question is without merit, it's that circumstance has placed a definitive answer out of reach.

See Also: Attitudes and Attitude Change; Buying Motives/Behavior; Consumer Behavior; Contagion; Gross National Product; Mortgage Credit Crisis of 2008.

Bibliography. Samuel Bowles and Richard Edwards, *Understanding Capitalism* (Harper & Row, 1985); Bureau of Economic Analysis, *Survey of Current Business* (v.82/8); John Kenneth Galbraith, *Money: Whence It Came, Where It Went* (Houghton Mifflin, 1975); Angus Maddison, *Monitoring the World Economy 1820–1992* (Development Centre of the Organisation for Economic Co-operation and Development, 1995); U.S. Bureau of the Census, *Historical Statistics of the United States, Colonial Times to 1970* (1975).

BILL KTE'PI
INDEPENDENT SCHOLAR

Business-to-Business

Business-to-Business (B2B) exchanges take place between two or more companies. The overall size of sales revenues attributed to business-to-business transactions is much larger than that of the consumer market. Sectors that are traditionally characterized as business-to-business are institutional, such as healthcare and education, the government, and various commercial enterprises. The products represented are typically intended for use as a manufacturing intermediate, support service, or in the day-to-day business operation.

A powerful segment of commercial enterprises is represented by original equipment manufacturers (OEMs) such as General Motors, John Deere, and Hewlett Packard. Original equipment manufacturers typically make large purchases and may have developed detailed product and vendor specifications. A second commercial enterprise consists of users, who typically purchase products for use in manufacturing other products for sale. They purchase products that support the operations necessary to manufacture their products. John Deere becomes a user when it purchases lubricants for use in its production facilities. It is also a user when it purchases copy machines for use in its corporate offices. Industrial dealers or distributors constitute a third category of commercial enterprises that operate in the business-to-business environment. John Deere may use dealers and distributors who are responsible for handling materials sold directly to the end-user. It is also a consumer supplier when it sells directly online to residential customers.

International business-to-business transactions are defined by the nature of interaction that takes place, the participants involved, and the intended use of the product that is the focus of the trade, while being carried out across country boundaries. Companies may sell to both business-to-business and consumer markets. For example, BP sells products directly to the consumer by selling fuel and motor oil through its retail gasoline outlets. It also sells fuel and lubricants for use in industrial applications such as aviation, mining, construction, and marine operations. GE sells appliances and consumer electronics. It also sells centrifugal compressors to the gas and oil industry and locomotives to the rail industry. John Deere sells residential mowers, along with commercial mowers for lawn services, mowers for golf courses, and agricultural, forestry and construction equipment.

The business-to-consumer market and business-to-business market require very different business and marketing strategies, especially pertaining to communication and sales activities. Business-to-business transactions may be very complex, depending on the size of the business, involving groups from various functional areas, who are very knowledgeable concerning required product performance. Due to the sophistication of business-to-business purchasers, it is necessary for the sales team supporting the customer to also be knowledgeable, not only with the direct customer, but also with the final consumer industry being served.

Business-to-business interactions typically are more complex than business-to-consumer because the expenditures represent large financial outlays and mistakes may result in costly delays or product failures that negatively impact the final end-user performance. For example, the purchase of an automobile from a retail dealer is generally a business-to-consumer transaction. The purchase of the constant velocity joints, used in front-wheel drive vehicles, by the manufacturer for use in the assembly of the automobile is a business-to-business transaction.

Before the automobile manufacturer makes the purchase, a purchasing manager or group of managers may initiate vendor reviews to qualify preferred suppliers, develop product quality and part specification guidelines, and make arrangements for the engineering lab to test parts from various suppliers; a production manager may be involved in the decision

as it relates to delivery times and packaging requirements. Environmental health and safety personnel will be notified to ensure the safety and proper environmental protocols are followed. Detailed shipping and pricing requirements are developed. There may be a bidding process, in which a number of qualified suppliers provide quotes for pricing and service. Business-to-business transactions may occur across many company borders. The rubber for the constant velocity joints may be made in China, the metal made in Japan, the lubricants made in the European Union, for use in a car assembled in Mexico and then shipped to the United States for final distribution.

The consumer purchasing the car may be focused on price, quality, reliability, fuel economy, image, and resale value. The promotional campaign to the consumer may rely on emotional appeals. In the business-to-business transaction, the manufacturer is concerned about conformance to specifications, vendor reliability, shipping options, delivery times, meeting safety requirements, environmental regulations, not just on the finished car, but on every component that goes into manufacturing each part of the product from a variety of suppliers representing a large number of cross-border transactions. The purchaser evaluating a vendor for a multimillion-dollar contract must be more rational and knowledgeable about the product that is being considered. The value of the product to the buyer is an essential part of determining the perceived risk associated with the purchase. The vendor's promotional activities generally revolve around product quality, meeting specification requirements, and support with supply chain issues.

Drivers of Business-to-Business Markets

As they gain more power in the marketplace, consumers are demanding value and quality at an appropriate price. This is a common trend throughout the economy and the business-to-business environment is not immune to this consumer mindset. The key phrase is overall cost. There are many hidden costs associated with using a product. The first is obviously the amount paid for the product, but this is only one aspect. As a product is developed for market introduction, business-to-business suppliers are aware of not only the amount paid for the product, but also the costs to use, store and dispose, the time consumed in the purchasing transaction and usage pattern, and the amount of inconvenience that the customer tolerates throughout the entire process.

Current business market drivers include requirements for extended life, economic benefits, environmental and societal issues, and international product stewardship. In the future, globalization, industry consolidation, and customer-supplier relationships will also impact the manner in which new products are developed and introduced to the business market.

Advancements in technology and the reduction in trade barriers are contributing to the integration and interdependency of businesses, increasing the competitive intensity among businesses that operate in the current economy, therefore elevating the importance of understanding business-to-business transactions as companies build strategy to meet the long-term needs of their global customers. International expansion offers a potential way for companies to increase growth, especially when facing a saturated domestic environment.

The major incentive that motivates businesses to expand into international markets is the saturation of their domestic market; the need to reduce manufacturing costs through either sourcing in cheaper production facilities overseas or increasing volume in the domestic manufacturing facility through exporting is also driving international expansion. External incentives are market driven and are a response to the need to grow beyond the domestic market. Internal incentives focus more on creating a competitive advantage. As the global marketplace increases in size and competitiveness, the initial route to internationalization may be a necessity in order to supply components to a customer that has engaged in foreign direct investment.

The resource-based view of internationalization emphasizes the importance of the accumulation of resources, focusing on the way in which firms can combine resources and create a sustainable competitive advantage. The company begins to feel competitive pressure due to saturation and maturity within its domestic market and starts to consider production offshore to allow cost minimization in many internal areas of operation. Emerging economies, such as those represented by India, China, Brazil, central and eastern Europe as well as other countries in southeast Asia, provide opportunities to improve manufacturing efficiencies due to reduced labor costs and increased resource availability. Cost advantages are achieved through global integration of research and development activities, procurement coordination, and production cost reductions.

Fast-growing emerging markets are also very important to companies operating in the business-to-business arena because, as they develop, there are many infrastructure development needs. Firms operating in the construction, heavy equipment industry, manufacturing consultants, and those in environmental services and technology support represent important business-to-business participants. Companies will also follow their key customers as the larger firms move into emerging markets. For example, as large automobile manufacturers move into China, their component part suppliers may follow in order to meet the production needs of their customer, while maintaining the customer-supplier relationship, creating barriers to competitive entry.

Information technology makes a large contribution to the global expansion of business-to-business activities. The ease of electronic exchange of information across country borders is responsible for improved efficiencies in the coordination of production operations, product development, and purchasing activities. The use of the internet allows suppliers and purchasers to quickly exchange information concerning product performance, industry requirements, and unmet needs. Product development and innovation is improved and the time to market is shortened.

Promotional Activities

The majority of the budget for business-to-business marketing is typically spent on personal selling activities. Face-to-face contact is necessary in order to establish the trust and familiarity necessary to build customer relationships. The majority of promotional activity expenditures for business-to-business promotions are on trade show participation requirements, followed by internet and electronic media costs. There are also costs associated with providing dealer/distributorship support materials. Business consumers are characterized as being educated about their product purchases and therefore seek specification-based information. There is a need for rational justifications and therefore it seems more likely that attributes relating to service, quality, price, reliability, and performance would be stressed in the advertising for a product or company.

However, advertising in specialized trade journals is an important tactic that is playing a greater role in the overall business-to-business marketing communication plan. Business-to-business advertising tends to feature people less often, be less emotional, be facts- and features-focused, and have more informational content than typical consumer ads. The industrial ad has been described as being more rational than the consumer ad. Ads for industrial products also contained more copy discussing product benefits and performance. Informational appeals found in business-to-business advertising center around the needs for removing problems, avoiding problems, reducing incomplete satisfaction, or alleviating normal depletion. Informational advertising seeks to change attitudes or beliefs based on the rational presentation of information concerning the product.

R. Lohtia, W. J. Johnston, and L. Aab have identified four dimensions of a successful business-to-business ad. The dimensions identified were characteristics of the ad, the reader's feelings about their relationship with the ad, the selling proposition, and the company's visibility. The importance of explaining the product and the benefits of using the product in the industrial ad are stressed, as well as providing information concerning product performance and quality. For example, if the product is one that clearly has technical performance advantages, such as a computer, and the audience is an engineering community, then the advertising should encourage information and arguments that make the consumer actively think about that product over the alternative.

On the other hand, if marketing the computer to an audience that does not understand the technical differences, then the advertisement should focus on peripheral cues, such as the spokesperson and the image of computer ownership. For example, Nike uses Tiger Woods as a spokesperson for its golf balls so that the consumer buys Nike golf balls because they want to play golf like Tiger. The golf balls may be made of the same materials, same compression, and same hardness as other balls, but Nike wants the consumer to buy without too much thinking. The golf ball manufacturer is concerned about whether the raw materials it is purchasing will provide the performance necessary to meet the needs of Nike. Given the reported sophistication of industrial buyers and the high financial and operational risk associated with

purchasing decisions, one would expect an advertising strategy for industrial products to consist of producing high involvement, informational messages.

The Buying Process

Overall, the buying process in the industrial setting is more complex and generally more conservative, with a greater reliance on group decision making. The initial step in the buying process consists of need recognition, usually as a result of identification of a problem. For example, specification changes may dictate a change in a raw material that requires investigation into a new supplier.

A decision-making group may form, consisting of production personnel, engineering and product development managers, purchasing representatives, and environmental health and safety members. This group will develop detailed specifications concerning product performance and vendor support requirements. Identification of potential suppliers will be made, and proposals and samples from the qualified vendors will be evaluated. The supplier of choice is then contacted and the supply details relating to delivery, storage, packaging, and pricing are negotiated. A review of supplier and product performance is continually made. The formation of the decision-making unit contributes to the complexity of the business-to-business exchange. Each member brings a different perspective to the purchase decision. The complexity of the decision requires close monitoring by potential suppliers and a focus on personal selling.

Relationship Management

The evolution of competition in a global business arena has led to an increase in the importance placed on interorganizational relationships involving customers, suppliers, competitors, and government agencies. An important factor in establishing the foundation for building customer-supplier relationships is an analysis of the value chain associated with the product. The value chain is defined as the collection of all activities involved in designing, manufacturing, marketing, delivering, and supporting a product.

Value chain analysis considers not only internal linkages, such as the coordination between research and development and marketing, but also external activities, such as relationships with suppliers, agents, or customers across and between countries. Each step in the value chain offers an opportunity for analysis and modification, allowing the firm to increase utility to customers. An extended breakdown of the primary interactions and processes involved at each link of the chain, assessing the responsibilities among all the entities involved is necessary to reach the root activities where modifications can be made to improve the entire process. A thorough analysis of the value chain focuses on answering the question of how customer value will be created. Participants up and down the supply chain are considered important members of the product supply team. Integration is necessary to improving costing and innovative efforts.

Traditionally, customer relationship management developed in the business-to-consumer transactional environment. This may due to the nature of the purchase transaction. As previously noted, the business-to-business purchase appears, on the surface, to be straightforward and technically oriented. Typically, the transaction is handled through the use of personal selling. A salesperson, or a team consisting of a salesperson and a technical support representative, calls on the customer directly. The buyer and seller are very knowledgeable of product requirements. If the product meets the pricing and performance requirements and the vendor is an approved supplier, the decision would appear to be simple. Even though the business-to-business market represents a smaller customer base, the customer purchases are much larger in scale, giving the business-to-business customer more power in the relationship.

The transaction may seem straightforward, void of any personal relationships, but the truth is that people, personalities, cultural aspects, and personal agendas are very important aspects that must be taken into account. The purchaser may be buying for an organization and therefore be more objective in making their decision, but subjective issues will also play a role.

Because of the increase in global competitive intensity, suppliers must find new ways to differentiate and encourage customer loyalty. There is currently a shift in business focus toward recognizing the competitive advantage of strong customer-supplier relationships. Building close customer-vendor relationships is an important strategy to employ while building a competitive advantage, especially when the customer base is small in number but large and powerful in terms of financial importance.

Advancements in information technology have led to the introduction of cost savings processes such as vendor-managed inventory (VMI) and online order processing, all under the umbrella of customer relationship management. The maintenance of two-way communication between the customer and supplier is necessary to ensure the goods and services offered fit the needs of the consumer. Moving the focus from providing products to providing solutions to customers' problems, in some cases, provides value to the customer that may be translated into better profitably, or, in the least, an advantage in the vendor decision process. Working together provides an advantage to the purchaser and the vendor as unmet needs may be discovered earlier and better solutions developed. This improves efficiencies, resulting in lower costs, for both sides of the business equation.

Ethics

With the close working relationship that may develop between the buyer and supplier in business-to-business transactions, breaches in ethical conduct are a serious concern. Ethics are problematic in that there is a general lack of agreement concerning the definition of ethical behavior versus unethical behavior across country borders, especially when there are no clear-cut legal ramifications. In order to create a successful relationship between supplier and purchaser, there has to be an element of trust and freedom to share information.

Shared information concerning product development, pricing, and future plans represent areas in which ethical dilemmas can form. In some cases, proprietary information may be transferred from company to company. It is important to have controls in place to ensure confidential information that is shared does not fall into competitors' hands. In international relationships, this problem may become more pronounced as there may cultural differences with respect to confidentiality. There are also differences in business practices allowed between countries.

Ethics is also an issue concerning product supply and environmental responsibility. Questions arise concerning the quality of products that are sent to unsophisticated markets. The temptation arises to send products of lesser quality to areas where they will not be detected. This is a problem in dealing with underdeveloped countries. Concerns also develop when two countries have different requirements related to the safety and environmental impact of products that enter or leave their borders.

Many companies have developed an internal code of ethics that they require their employees and vendors to follow. For example, international trade within the chemical industry exceeds $500 billion annually, second only to automobiles. The chemical industry is one of the largest and most technically advanced manufacturing sectors engaged in world trade. As such, the industry exerts a positive influence on the health of the world economy only as it maintains its trade performance and strong global competitiveness. The increasing speed of industrialization, urban development, and international growth has placed heavy demands upon antiquated and informal systems of managing environmental and ethical issues. Chemical producers have focused on establishing programs aimed at creating the perception that they are establishing and complying with domestic voluntary environment risk management programs.

Dupont voluntarily spends millions of dollars annually above and beyond the legal requirements on environmental projects. It has a published code of ethics. The company has established a multilingual ethics and compliance hotline, with a specialist, not employed by Dupont, available to discuss with the caller any lack of compliance with the ethical guideline issue around the clock, every day.

Strategic Perspectives

As emerging markets grow and competitive intensity increases, players in business-to-business markets will need to adapt. Two areas that are evolving are building brands and utilizing e-commerce to facilitate global reach. Branding can be defined as the strategy utilized to create a position in the customer's mind. The position provides information to consumers concerning the attributes the product or company represents. The brand relates not only to the naming, symbols, slogans, or other physical aspects associated with the company or product, but also includes psychological factors, such as trust within the relationship and reputation within the industry. The brand represents value to the customer and can be a point of differentiation in a complex, competitive, international business environment.

As discussed earlier, advancements in information technology and e-commerce represent an opportunity for improving supply chain communication and coordination. It allows products and services to be marketed across borders, creating a business environment seemingly without boundaries. It provides another support tool to build customer relationships as teams can conference across borders and exchange information without time constraints in secure sites. E-commerce also acts as an extension to the business-to-business distribution channel. Integration of ordering and supply logistics allows both the supplier and customer to reduce transaction costs. Improvements in international security and the expansion of technology infrastructure will increase the importance of e-commerce in global business-to-business transactions.

The success of any strategy relies on the premise that only a healthy competitive industry can continue to develop and improve its performance and that strategies will be developed based on the needs of the corporation and the geographic location in which it is operating. The customer must find value in purchasing from companies possessing strong integrated customer management programs.

See Also: Branding; Competition; Corporate Social Responsibility; Customer Relationship Management; Globalization; Marketing; Wholesale Sector.

Bibliography. J. C. Anderson and J. A. Narus, *Business Market Management: Understanding, Creating, and Delivering Value*, 2nd ed. (Prentice Hall, 2004); M. D. Hult and T. W. Speh, *Business Marketing Management: B2B*, 9th ed. (Thompson, 2007); J. D. Lichtenthal, "Business-to-Business Marketing in the 21st Century," *Journal of Business-to-Business Marketing* (v.5/1,2, 1998); R. Lohtia, W. J. Johnston, and L. Aab, "Business-to-Business Advertising: What Are the Dimensions of an Effective Print Ad?" *Industrial Marketing Management* (v.24, 1995).

Patricia R. Todd
Western Kentucky University

Buying Motives/Behavior

Buying behavior, a component of consumer behavior, involves how people, in their roles as individual, household, and organizational consumers, seek satisfaction of their needs and wants through product acquisition and use. The focus is also often on the motivating factors that drive consumers to buy a certain brand of product. It can thus be said that buying behavior concerns *how* and *why* consumers acquire products.

Marketers must understand the buying behavior of consumers if they wish to maximize the probability of long-term success. Unfortunately for marketers, understanding buying behavior is much more an art than an exact science. The resultant challenges for marketers can be great in culturally diverse nations. These challenges are compounded when doing business in multiple countries, each with its own norms of behavior, preferences, and way of doing things—not to mention its own unique set of often complex motivating factors—that drive buying behavior.

In recent years, marketing scholars and managers have realized that long-term success is predicated not on making one-time sales to as many customers as possible but rather on the building and maintenance of trust-based relationships with a select group of targeted customers. It is also understood that establishing and maintaining these relationships involves a complex chain of events. This chain of events begins with the marketer consistently meeting customer needs, wants, and expectations. This, in turn, leads to high levels of customer satisfaction.

High levels of satisfaction facilitate the development of customer loyalty—wherein consumers habitually acquire your brand as a result of the experience-based belief that your brand is superior to competitive offerings. Loyalty implies that customers trust you to consistently meet their needs, wants, and expectations—to the point where they do not even consider buying competitive brands. High levels of customer loyalty allow the marketer to build and maintain profitable relationships with customers.

However, building customer relationships is not as easy as suggested above. In order to successfully meet customer needs, wants, and expectations—the first step in the relationship building process—marketers must first understand the multitude of often complex, ambiguous, and even subconscious motivating factors that drive the buying behavior of their targeted customers. When doing business internationally, understanding these motivating factors is predicated first and foremost on understanding the cultural background of targeted customers. This requires that marketers determine which aspects of a given culture most significantly influence buying behavior. They then need to understand how these cultural factors are likely to impact buying behavior.

Although culture is impossible to adequately define in several sentences—even pages—it can be viewed as the collection of shared meanings, rituals, norms of behavior, traditions, and preferences of a given society or subset of its people. Culture surrounds us and impacts all that we do. This includes what we do as consumers—the food we eat, the clothes we wear, the places we shop, and why we prefer one brand of a given product type over others. The chances of marketing success are thus much higher when products are consistent with key cultural aspects of targeted consumers. When this consistency exists, consumers are motivated to at least consider buying your product. When it is not present, consumers may be motivated to avoid your product.

Cross-Cultural Considerations

In the 1980s, it was hypothesized that the forthcoming global diffusion of products and consumption patterns characterizing Western "consumer culture" would necessarily lead to a homogenization of culture around the globe. There was, at that time, considerable debate over whether or not product adaptation would be necessary—based largely on the belief that marketers would be able to create standardized "global products" meeting the needs, wants, and expectations of all consumers worldwide. The homogeneous "global consumer culture" has not yet materialized and the "adaptation vs. standardization" debate has long since ended. Today, business scholars and managers understand that there are still cultural differences from country to country that significantly impact buying behavior. They also realize that this cultural heterogeneity necessitates some level of strategic adaptation.

Consider, in this regard, the United States and Mexico. The two nations are geographically proximate to one another and are also both intimately involved in the global economic system (as close partners by virtue of the North American Free Trade Agreement). Many U.S. marketers do business in Mexico and many Mexican businesses have large operations in the United States. Joint ventures between U.S. and Mexican firms abound. In addition, there has been cultural borrowing between the two countries—witness the popularity of salsa, tortillas, and other food products at least inspired by traditional Mexican food in the United States as well as the conspicuous presence of U.S. movies and fast food restaurants and other retailers in Mexico. In the U.S.-Mexico border region, cultural aspects of the two countries have essentially melded into a culture unique to the area.

However, lurking beneath the surface of these easily observable similarities are cultural differences that significantly impact buying behavior in the two nations. Take, for example, differences in values and time orientation. The United States is a highly materialistic and highly individualistic nation running on linear separable time. This means that U.S. citizens typically: (1) believe that it is appropriate—if not important in defining who and what one is—to accumulate possessions (particularly status goods), (2) define themselves and judge others on the basis of individual achievement, and (3) feel that time is an economic resource that is to be used efficiently and that, therefore, planning for future time expenditures is critical (with precise amounts of time set aside for certain activities, which are ordered in sequential fashion). U.S. consumers are, as a result, often highly motivated to acquire goods that allow them to display status to others and be more efficient and productive with their time.

Mexico is not a highly materialistic culture. It is also very collectivistic in nature. Further, Mexico, like many other Hispanic cultures, runs predominantly on what is known as circular or cyclic time. As a result, compared to their U.S. counterparts, Mexican consumers: (1) do not place as much importance on the possession, accumulation, and display of material goods, (2) are more likely to define themselves and judge others on the basis of how well one plays their role within a group (e.g., the family, the church, or a work group), and (3) see little reason to "hurry all the time" and be as efficient as possible with time. As a result, Mexican consumers are not nearly as motivated as U.S. consumers are to acquire, possess, and display status goods. Further, "saving time" is not the driving force behind product acquisition that it is in the United States.

Consider, within the context of U.S.-Mexico cultural heterogeneity, cellular telephone buying behavior. In the United States, it is estimated that around 85 percent of all people have a cell phone. This should not be surprising—cell phones hold vast potential to use time more efficiently and can be displayed as a status symbol. As one might expect, cell phone penetration rates in Mexico are considerably lower—approximately 66 percent. It can thus be said that cultural factors help drive U.S. consumers, more than their Mexican counterparts, to believe that they "need" a cell phone.

However, it is perhaps more important to understand that cell phones are bought for varying culture-based reasons in the United States and Mexico. As previously stated, primary motivating factors for cell phone acquisition in the United States include desires to "save time" and display status. In Mexico, key reasons for product acquisition include the fact that a relatively high percentage of Mexicans live in large, crowded metropolitan areas and, more importantly, the existence of the often large, extended/multigenerational family as the central organizing unit of highly collectivistic Mexican society. Cell phones are purchased in Mexico not so much to "save time" or display status as they are to organize family-centered activities among family members spread out across large urban landscapes. Smart international marketers understand that cross-cultural differences that impact buying behavior such as these need to be incorporated into marketing strategy.

See Also: Branding; Brand Loyalty; Consumer Behavior; Consumer Needs and Wants; Consumption; Cultural Norms and Scripts; Culture-Specific Values; International Marketing Research; Marketing.

Bibliography. C. Samuel Craig and Susan Douglas, "Beyond National Culture: Implications of Cultural Dynamics for Consumer Research," *International Marketing Review* (v.23/3, 2006); David Luna and Susan Forquer Gupta, "An Integrative Framework for Cross-Cultural Consumer Behavior," *International Marketing Review* (v.18/1, 2001); Michael Solomon, *Consumer Behavior: Buying, Having, and Being*, 8th ed. (Pearson/Prentice Hall, 2009).

Terrance G. Gabel
University of Arkansas–Fort Smith

Buyout

A buyout is a purchase of an entire company or of a controlling interest in a company by another company. The purchase is usually viewed as an investment. A buyout can take a number of forms. Small business buyouts are common in capitalist countries. Most businesses are small entrepreneurial operations. They may be as simple as a "mom and pop" store, a franchise, a motel, or another small business that has been able to produce enough business to gain the owners enough net profit for living and for reinvesting. Sale of their business may be for any number of reasons: health, age, a desire to return to their home country, or to change careers.

The buyouts that usually attract the most public attention are corporate buyouts. These types of purchases have been made since the beginning of corporate capitalism. In some cases, the purchases are of bankrupt companies. In others, the buyouts are of companies in financial distress because of a crisis in its product, financing, or labor relations. Or it may be that the company is an agribusiness that has been broken by a bad harvest.

Corporate buyouts can happen when companies see an opportunity to purchase a company with something of significant value to the buying corporation. The buyout may be to gain market share, or to gain access to technology developed or held by the corporation being sought, or to eliminate technology, or to obtain assets held by the purchased company. In the latter case, a company that owns oil fields may be an attractive buyout target because the buyer can add the assets to its balance sheet. The oil can be pumped and the reduction in the assets value charged against taxes.

Buyouts have been conducted by corporate raiders who seek to capture a company in a hostile takeover and then to use the assets for other purposes. In some cases, buyouts may be made in order to break up a company and sell its units because the parts of the company are worth more than the company as a whole. Leveraged buyouts have been common in recent decades. In some cases, the stock of the company acquired in the acquisition is turned into junk by the wholesale mortgaging of the company, making its own bonds into junk bonds. In other cases, loans that are treated as assets are used to create several layers of borrowing to make the purchase of a company valued in the billions of dollars.

See Also: Acquisitions, Takeovers, and Mergers; Bankruptcy; Corporate Change.

Bibliography. Yakov Amihud, ed., *Leveraged Management Buyouts: Causes and Consequences* (Beard Books, 2002); Stuart C. Gilson, *Creating Value through Corporate Restructuring: Case Studies in Bankruptcies, Buyouts, and Breakups* (John Wiley & Sons, 2001); Rick Rickertsen and Robert E. Gunther, *Buyout: The Insider's Guide to Buying Your Own Company* (AMACOM, 2001); Roy C. Smith, *Money Wars: The Rise and Fall of the Great Buyout Boom of the 1980s* (Beard Books, 2000).

Andrew J. Waskey
Dalton State College

CAC 40 Index (Paris)

The CAC 40 is the foremost of several related French benchmark stock indices tracking the performance of stocks on Euronext Paris (formerly the Paris Bourse), and is one of the most-watched Euronext stock indices.

The index takes its name from the Cotation Assistée en Continu (CAC), the electronic trading system implemented on the Paris Bourse in the late 1980s and used for all listed stocks by 1989. CAC was based on the CATS (Computer Automated Trading System) developed for the Toronto Stock Exchange in the 1970s, and used a double auction algorithm to set prices and match orders, helping to automate and centralize aspects of the exchange over the decades that the open outcry system has gradually fallen out of favor. CAC has itself since been replaced by other systems, as computing and telecommunications have become more sophisticated.

The CAC 40 was established at the end of 1987, with an initial base value of 1000 points, equivalent to a market cap of 370,437,433,957.7 francs. As of December 2003, the basis of the index switched from total market cap to free float market cap, the basis used by most other major indices. At each quarterly review of the index (the third Friday of March, June,

September, and December), the Conseil Scientifique, an independent committee, evaluates the 100 stocks on Euronext Paris with the highest free float market capitalization over the previous 12 months. From that 100, 40 stocks are chosen—not the top 40, but the 40 that, combined, form the most useful benchmark and are suitable as underlying assets for derivatives. Market dominance is often a factor, such that the leading stock in a given industry may be chosen rather than the higher market cap second-place stock in another industry.

The composition of the CAC 40 and related indices listed in this entry is current as of the start of 2009. The stocks of the CAC 40 are:

- Accor, Europe's foremost hotel group.
- Air France, an airline company with a fleet of 622 aircraft.
- Air Liquide, a producer of industrial and medical gas.
- Alcatel-Lucent, a technology, communications, and services company.
- Alstom, an infrastructure manufacturer for the energy and transportation industries.
- ArcelorMittal, the world's leading steelmaker.
- Axa, Europe's largest insurance group.
- BNP Paribas, France's largest banking group.

- Bouygues, an industrial group with media and telecommunications concerns as well as its construction business.
- Cap Gemini, an IT services company.
- Carrefour, a distribution group running thousands of supermarkets and discount stores.
- Crédit Agricole, a European banking group.
- Danone, a food processing group, most of the products of which are dairy or beverages.
- Dexia, a European bank and public finance company.
- EADS, the leading European company (and second-largest in the world) in the aeronautics and aerospace industry.
- EDF, France's leading electric company.
- Essilor, a manufacturer of corrective lenses and optical instruments.
- France Télécom, the leading French telecommunications company.
- GDF Suez, the leading natural gas supplier in Europe.
- Lafarge, a producer of building materials.
- Lagardère, a large media group.
- L'Oreal, the worldwide leader in cosmetics.
- LVMH, owner of luxury brands such as Louis Vuitton, Givenchy, Dom Perignon, Glenmorangie, and Christian Dior.
- Michelin, a tire manufacturer.
- Pernod Ricard, the second largest producer in the world of wines and spirits, including Glenlivet, Seagram's, and Malibu rum.
- Peugeot, the second-largest automobile manufacturer in Europe.
- PPR, a luxury products group that owns brands such as Gucci and Yves Saint Laurent.
- Renault, France's second-largest automobile manufacturer.
- Saint Gobain, a manufacturer of construction materials.
- Sanofi-Aventis, a leading pharmaceutical group.
- Schneider Electric, a manufacturer of electrical distribution equipment.
- Société Générale, one of the "old banks" of France, and one of its largest retail banks.
- STMicroelectronics, a semiconductor maker.
- Suez Environnement, a provider of environmental services like waste treatment and water distribution.

- Total, an oil and gas group.
- Unibail-Rodamco, a commercial real estate group.
- Vallourec, a steel tube manufacturer.
- Veolia, an environmental management services company.
- Vinci, a construction company.
- Vivendi, a media and telecommunications group.

Launched at the end of 2002, the CAC Next 20 is composed of the 20 stocks ranked highest in market capitalization that are not listed in the CAC 40. The stocks of the CAC Next 20 are: ADP, Atos, Origin, Casino Guichard, CGG Veritas, CNP Assurances, Dassault Systemes, Eiffage, Eramet, Hermes, Klepierre, Nataxis, Nexans, NYSE Euronext, Publicis, Safran, SES, Sodexo, Technip, TF1, Thales.

The CAC Mid 100, created in 2005, lists the next 100 largest stocks, after the 40 and 20. The stocks of the CAC Mid 100 are: Alpes, Alten, Altran Technologies, ANF, April Group, Areva CI, Arkema, Bains Mer Monaco, Beneteau, Bic, Biomerieux, Boiron, Bollore, Bonduelle, Bongrain, Bourbon, Boursorama, Bureau Veritas, Camaieu, Canal +, Carbone Lorraine, Cegedim, Ciments Francais, Club Mediterranee, Delachaux, Derichebourg, EDF Energies Nouvelles, Esso, Euler Hermes, Eurazeo, Eurofins Scientific, Eutelsat Communications, Faiveley, Faurecia, Fimalac, Financiere Odet, Foncière des Régions, Foncière des Murs, Gecina, Gemalto, Générale de Santé, Groupe Eurotunnel, Groupe Steria, Guerbet, Guyenne Gascogne, Havas, Icade, Iliad, Imerys, Ingenico, Ipsen, Ipsos, JC Decaux SA, Kaufman et Broad, Korian, Laurent-Perrier, LDC, Legrand, Lisi, Manitou BF, Mauriel et Prom, Mercialys, Metropole TV, Neopost, Nexity, Nicox, Norbert Dentressangle, NRJ Group, Orpea, Pagesjaunes, Pierre Vacances, Plastic Omnium, Rallye, Rémy Cointreau, Rexel, Rhodia, Rubis, S.E.B., Saft, Scor SE, Séché Environnement, Séchilienne Sidec, Sequana, Silic, Sopra Group, Sperian Protection, Stallergenes, Stef TFE, Teleperformance, Theolia, Thomson, Ubisoft, L'union Financière de France Banque, Valeo, Vetoquinol, Vicat, Vilmorin & Cie, Virbac, Wendel, Zodiac.

The CAC Small 90 lists the next 90 stocks after the 40, 200, and 100. The stocks of the CAC Small 90 are: ABC Arbitrage, Affine, Akka Technologies, Alès Groupe, Assystem, Audika, Aurea, Avenir Telecom,

Aviation Latecoere, Bastide Le Confort, Belvedere, Boizel Chanoine, Bull Regpt, Catering International Sces, Cegereal, Cegid Group, Chargeurs, Cnim, CS, Devoteam, Entrepose Contracting, Etam Developpement, Euro Disney, Europacorp, Exel Industries A, Fleury Michon, Foncier, Gameloft, Gascogne, Gaumont, GFI Informatique, Gifi, GL Events, Groupe Crit, Groupe Flo, Groupe Open, Groupe Partouche, Haulotte Group, Hi-Media, High Co, Hiolle Industries, IMS, Infogrames, Inter Parfums, Internationale de Plantations d'Heveas, Lacie S.A., Le Noble Age, Lectra, Linedata Services, Locindus, LVL Medical Groupe, Maisons France, Manutan International, Meetic, Metabolic Explorer, Metrologic Group, Montupet SA, Mr Bricolage, NextRadioTV, Parrot, Pharmagest International, PSB Industries, Radiall, Recylex S.A., Robertet, Rodriguez Group, Samse, Sartorius Stedim Biotech, Seloger.com, SII, SMTPC, Soitec, Spir Communication, Store Electronics, Sucriere de Pithiviers-Le-Vieil, Sword Group, Synergie, Tessi, Thermador Groupe, Tonnellerie Francois Freres, Touax, Toupargel Groupe, Transgene, Trigano, Viel et Compagne, VM Materiaux, Vranken-Pommery, Wavecom.

There are two additional relevant indices. The SBF 120 (Societe des Bourses Francaises) tracks the CAC 40 and 80 additional stocks from the CAC Next 20 and CAC Mid 100. The SBF 250 tracks the CAC 40, CAC Next 20, CAC Mid 100, and CAC Small 90.

See Also: BNP Paribas; Bouygues; Company Profiles: Western Europe; EADS; France; France Telecom; Peugeot; Stock Exchanges.

Bibliography. Benoit Mandelbrot and Richard L. Hudson, *The Misbehavior of Markets* (Basic Books, 2006); Robert B. Reich, *Supercapitalism: The Transformation of Business, Democracy, and Everyday Life* (Vintage Books, 2008).

BILL KTE'PI
INDEPENDENT SCHOLAR

Call Center

Call centers are used by all types of business entities ranging from small telemarketers to large multi-

While outsourced call centers may offer savings of up to 40 percent, backlash over job losses in the West is growing.

national corporations (MNCs) in order to promote, sell, or service their product offerings. The advent of globalization and the intensification of competition worldwide have prompted the necessity to deliver services and respond to inquiries from customers, suppliers, shareholders, and other stakeholders effectively and quickly. Call centers cater to such needs and help firms to promote their products and services from a distance with efficiency, flexibility, and speed. As a consequence, the global call center industry has been growing worldwide at a record pace since the late 1980s. In addition to increased efficiency, the optimization of customers' and shareholders' value is the major motivation behind the worldwide growth of the industry which, to a certain extent, could be seen in the context of cost reductive "global Fordism" strategies.

Typically, a call center can manage a considerable volume of calls simultaneously by screening and forwarding them to the relevant customer service representatives capable of handling the required information. Call center employees receive inbound or make outbound telephone calls using information and communications technologies (ICT). Automatic call distribution (ACD) and remote electronic access (REA) supported by high-speed, high-bandwidth telecommunications are instrumental in managing operations.

As an industry that emphasizes knowledge and e-commerce as the way to do business, the call center does not fit the traditional staged model of internationalization. The traditional model considers a systematic progression through four different stages of firm internationalization beginning with limited exporting activities and culminating with the establishment of foreign production/manufacturing facilities. Indeed, it is an industry that could easily be considered "born global."

Call centers may serve multiple purposes. In addition to business-to-customer (B2C) interactions, call centers may promote business-to-business (B2B) communication, and are a tool to maintain an ongoing relationship with other stakeholders, including suppliers and distributors. Public-sector organizations have started using call centers as a means to improve service delivery to citizens and businesses (G2C and G2B). Call center activities support Dunning's concepts of "alliance capitalism" and the "knowledge economy" somewhat, as call centers enhance the ability of firms to access customers, suppliers, competitors, and collaborators from a distance, reducing the need for face-to-face communication and spatial transactions.

There is a preference among many MNCs to outsource call center operations to developing countries in order to optimize profit and minimize costs. It is argued that outsourced call centers offer significant savings that could jump to a remarkable 40 percent when outsourced to countries such as India, the Philippines, or South Africa.

However, operating costs in places like India are rising. In addition, many consider the jobs created in call centers in developing countries to be at the expense of similar jobs lost in the West. Such controversies are fuelling popular discontent and backlash in the West, resulting in the closure of many call center operations in developing countries. Moreover, some human rights activists consider call centers to have harsh work environments, where staff usually work long hours with poor pay and under strict guidelines and constant surveillance. Accordingly, some activists have dubbed them "electronic sweatshops."

See Also: Globalization; Information Systems; Near-Shoring; Off-Shoring; Outsourcing.

Bibliography. James C. Abbott, *Designing Effective Call Centers* (Robert Houston Smith Pub., 2008); J. H. Dunning, "Regions, Globalization and the Knowledge Economy: The Issues Stated," in J. H. Dunning, ed., *Regions, Globalization and the Knowledge-Based Economy* (Oxford University Press, 2000); B. Garson, *The Electronic Sweatshop: How Computers Are Transforming the Office of the Future Into the Factory of the Past* (Simon and Schuster, 1988); Renee Paulet, "Location Matters: The Impact of Place on Call Centres," *Journal of Industrial Relations* (v.50/2, 2008).

SHARIF N. AS-SABER
MONASH UNIVERSITY

Cameroon

The Republic of Cameroon is a unitary republic of central and western Africa. It is bordered by Nigeria to the west; Chad to the northeast; the Central African Republic to the east; and Equatorial Guinea, Gabon, and the Republic of the Congo to the south. Cameroon's coastline lies on the Bight of Bonny, part of the Gulf of Guinea and the Atlantic Ocean. The country is called "Africa in miniature" for its geological and cultural diversity. Natural features include beaches, deserts, mountains, rain forests, and savannas. The highest point is Mount Cameroon in the southwest, and the largest cities are Douala, Yaoundé, and Garoua. Cameroon is home to over 200 different ethnic and linguistic groups. The country is well known for its native styles of music, particularly makossa and bikutsi, and for its successful national football team. English and French are the official languages.

Cameroon has been recognized as an independent state since 1961, following the integration of separate French and British colonies into one united, bilingual country. Cameroon is improving its governance by adopting a new national governance program and an anti-corruption program. Cameroon's per capita GDP (PPP) was estimated as US$2,421 in 2005, one of the 10 highest in sub-Saharan Africa. Major export markets include France, Italy, South Korea, Spain, and the United Kingdom. Cameroon is part of the Bank of Central African States (of which it is the dominant economy) and the Customs and Economic Union of Central Africa (UDEAC). Its currency is the CFA franc.

Red tape, high taxes, and endemic corruption have impeded growth of the private sector. Unemployment was estimated at 30 percent in 2001, and about 48 percent of the population was living below the poverty threshold in 2000. Since the late 1980s, Cameroon has been following programs advocated by the World Bank and International Monetary Fund (IMF) to reduce poverty, privatize industries, and increase economic growth. Tourism is a growing sector, particularly in the coastal area, around Mount Cameroon, and in the north.

Resources and Infrastructure

Cameroon's natural resources are better suited to agriculture and forestry than to industry. An estimated 70 percent of the population farms, and agriculture comprised an estimated 45.2 percent of GDP in 2006. Most agriculture is done at the subsistence scale by local farmers using simple tools. They sell their surplus produce, and some maintain separate fields for commercial use. Urban centers are particularly reliant on peasant agriculture for their foodstuffs. Soils and climate on the coast encourage extensive commercial cultivation of bananas, cocoa, oil palms, rubber, and tea. Inland on the South Cameroon Plateau, cash crops include coffee, sugar, and tobacco. Coffee is a major cash crop in the western highlands, and in the north, natural conditions favor crops such as cotton, groundnuts, and rice. Reliance on agricultural exports makes Cameroon vulnerable to shifts in their prices. Livestock are raised throughout the country. Fishing employs some 5,000 people and provides 20,000 tons of seafood each year. Bushmeat, long a staple food for rural Cameroonians, is today a delicacy in the country's urban centers. The commercial bushmeat trade has now surpassed deforestation as the main threat to wildlife in Cameroon.

The southern rain forest has vast timber reserves, estimated to cover 37 percent of Cameroon's total land area. However, large areas of the forest are difficult to reach. Logging, largely handled by foreign-owned firms, provides the government US$60 million a year, and laws mandate the safe and sustainable exploitation of timber. Nevertheless, in practice, the industry is one of the least regulated in Cameroon.

Factory-based industry accounted for an estimated 16.1 percent of GDP in 2006. More than 75 percent of Cameroon's industrial strength is located in Douala and Bonabéri. Cameroon possesses substantial mineral resources, but these are not extensively mined. Petroleum exploitation has fallen since 1985, but this is still a substantial sector, such that dips in prices

have a strong effect on the economy. Rapids and waterfalls obstruct the southern rivers, but these sites offer opportunities for hydroelectric development and supply most of Cameroon's energy. The Sanaga River powers the largest hydroelectric station, located at Edéa. The rest of Cameroon's energy comes from oil-powered thermal engines. Much of the country remains without reliable power supplies.

Transport in Cameroon is often difficult. Roads are poorly maintained and subject to inclement weather, since only 10 percent of the roadways are tarred. Roadblocks often serve little other purpose than to allow police and gendarmes to collect bribes from travelers. Road banditry has long hampered transport along the eastern and western borders, and since 2005, the problem has intensified in the east as the Central African Republic has further destabilized. Rail service runs from Kumba in the west to Bélabo in the east and north to Ngaoundéré. International airports are located in Douala and Garoua with a smaller facility at Yaoundé. The Wouri River estuary provides a harbor for Douala, the country's principal seaport. In the north, the Bénoué River is seasonally navigable from Garoua across into Nigeria.

The major radio and television stations are state run, and other communications, such as land-based telephones and telegraphs, are largely under government control. However, cell phone networks and internet providers have increased dramatically since the early 2000s and are largely unregulated. Although press freedoms have also improved since the early 2000s, the press is corrupt and beholden to special interests and political groups.

Government Policies

Cameroon has demonstrated its commitment to improving its economy through its participation in the Economic Community of Central African States, whose 11 members aim to secure economic partnership with the European Union. In April 2003 Cameroon adopted its own poverty reduction program that outlines seven country-led areas of focus: (1) controlling inflation and promoting tax and budget stability; (2) diversifying the economy; (3) revitalizing the private sector's ability to deliver social services; (4) developing basic infrastructure and natural resources, while protecting the environment; (5) creating closer ties with other central African countries on matters of trade, finance, transportation, forestry, education, tourism, and other policies; (6) strengthening human resources and the social sector, and facilitating the integration of vulnerable groups into the economy; and (7) good governance.

This strategy aims to support the government of Cameroon's objective of significantly reducing poverty among Cameroonians. Cameroon is now developing its second poverty reduction strategy paper. The Canadian International Development Agency is increasingly working with the government of Cameroon on matters of economic governance.

See Also: Africa.

Bibliography. CIA, "Cameroon," *The World Factbook*, www.cia.gov (cited March 2009); Igor Oleynik and Natasha Alexander, *Cameroon: Country Study Guide* (International Business Pub., 2005); U.S. Department of State, "Background Note: Cameroon," www.state.gov (cited March 2009).

Sanford L. Moskowitz
St. John's University

Canada

Sprawling across the northern half of North America as the world's second-largest country by land mass with nearly 10 million square kilometers, Canada has a diverse economy that ranks in the top 15 of global standings. The annual gross domestic product is approximately US$1 trillion. A federation and constitutional monarchy whose head of state is Queen Elizabeth II, the national capital is at Ottawa, Ontario. There are 10 provinces that range significantly in size and population (Ontario has 13 million, Prince Edward Island 130,000) and three northern territories. Eighty percent of the population lives in cities, with Toronto the largest (pop. 2.5 million, metro area 5.5 million). A member of the G8 group of industrialized nations, Canada is a founding member of the World Trade Organization (WTO) and its predecessor, the General Agreement on Tariffs and Trade (GATT), and is also a member of the North American Free Trade Agreement (NAFTA) with the United States and Mexico.

Economic History

A nation of approximately 32 million people mostly clustered in cities near the Canada-U.S. border, modern Canada was founded in 1867. Prior to that, the country was first a colonial possession of France, and then of Great Britain. Both powers traded extensively with the aboriginal populations that had lived on the land for thousands of years. As such, the country has always been a source of staple resources, and the region was an important element of both France's and Great Britain's mercantilist empires. Basque fishermen first started coming to Canada in the 1500s. France claimed it as its own and colonized New France, in the area in present-day Quebec, starting in 1608. Furs became a leading export, and the Company of One Hundred Associates, the first business association in Canada, was granted a monopoly on business matters in New France. Meanwhile, in 1670, the British granted the Hudson's Bay Company the rights to trade on all the land that had rivers that flowed into Hudson's Bay. This created a lively imperial competition, especially around the fur trade.

Following the defeat of the French at the Plains of Abraham and the Treaty of Paris in 1763, Britain took possession of the colony. With the independence of Britain's American colonies in 1789, refugees loyal to the British crown flooded northward, precipitating colonial changes and population challenges for the existing French-speaking population. In the 1800s, wheat and timber became leading exports to Great Britain. After an uprising in both the French- and English-speaking colonies in 1837, some local independence was granted. Eventually, the scattered British colonies united to form modern Canada, with complete control over domestic affairs, while Britain retained significant say in Canada's international relations. In the 1867 constitution, the federal government was granted wide-ranging powers over economic concerns, with local matters left to the provinces.

In the 19th century, the federal state utilized its powers as the country expanded westward and was linked by a transcontinental railway, completed in 1885. Immigration and settlement followed, with an emphasis on wheat production. Protectionist policies helped to create infant industry, particularly in Ontario and Quebec where farm implements, steel, railways, and consumer goods became important manufacturing sectors. Banking was also a protected field, and financial services have been a strong area since 1867. An emphasis on building infrastructure (railways, canals, bridges) that was largely government-funded brought the state actively into the economy. A long depression in the 1880s and 1890s was soon eclipsed by a wheat boom that saw the population grow significantly, and the nation's economy improve. By World War I, Canada was a choice destination for British capital and European immigrants, and had developed a solid economy with railways, timber, agriculture, mining, and manufacturing as key sectors. World War I also saw the entry of the federal state into the economy with war mobilization and the creation of new federal regulatory agencies, federally-owned companies, and income taxes.

In the inter-war period, the economy expanded dramatically, with new growth in automobile production (largely fueled by companies from the United States) and other consumer goods, the expansion of wheat production, and urban growth (utilities and infrastructure). The overexpansion of the economy, persistent trade issues, and a general worldwide malaise had a profound effect upon Canada, particularly in the agricultural west, where wheat prices plummeted and natural disasters ravaged farms. By the early 1930s, Canada was among the hardest hit of all nations by the Great Depression, with nearly a quarter of the population on relief.

In World War II, the economy expanded massively to meet the challenges of war, as did the federal state's intervention in the economy. Dozens of new federally-controlled companies were created in fields as diverse as synthetic rubber, to construction to, of course, arms manufacturing. Full employment was reached, and while labor problems persisted during the war, recognition of collective bargaining eventually led to labor peace.

These new federal policies, labor peace, and the return of consumer confidence in the postwar period brought an unprecedented level of prosperity. Between the 1950s and the 1970s, Canada experienced its greatest period of sustained economic growth. The population jumped through natural increase and immigration, from five million in the 1930s to 10 million by the 1960s. Autos, natural resources, consumer goods, and the service economy all developed significantly in this period as Canada became much more urban and suburban. Much of this economic prosperity was fueled by American investment. This was particularly true in natural resources, especially fields such petrochemicals, uranium, and refining, but also in other fields such as forest products, mining, and heavy manufacturing. Much of this was direct investment through branch plant operations of U.S. multinationals. Oil strikes in Alberta profoundly changed the dynamic of Canadian development, and provided a boom in growth in the Canadian Prairie. Interventionist governmental policies that helped to create a welfare state in this period also helped to fuel growth.

By the 1970s, the worldwide economic downturn took its toll on Canada, as inflation increased and growth slowed. With some industrial dislocation and the high cost of energy, the central provinces of Ontario and Quebec lost some of their economic primacy within the federation. The passage of free trade agreements with the United States (1989) and then with Mexico (1993) ended the long-standing protectionism that had existed in the economy, and shifted economic ties from an east-west axis, to a north-south one.

Modern Economy

In the 1990s, restructuring shifted the economy to one even more dependent upon services, particularly high technology, but Canadians still remained largely tied to commodity production and manufacturing. By 2008, Canada ranked sixth place in a global ranking for information-technology competitiveness, according to the Economist Intelligence Unit, behind the United States, Taiwan, Britain, Sweden, and Denmark.

Today, Canada has a diversified economy. Natural resources continue as a key element. Oil and gas production in the western provinces of Alberta and Saskatchewan, and the Atlantic provinces of Nova Scotia, Newfoundland, and Labrador have led to high growth rates in those regions. Continued restructuring in Ontario, particularly in the auto industry (the leading export since the 1960s) have slowed growth in central Canada. Service sectors, such as financial services, health, and education have all grown dramatically. There has been a significant increase in the number of leading Canadian firms purchased by foreigners (mainly Americans), which has been a growing concern of Canadians. This is especially true in the mining and natural resource fields where long-standing Canadian firms such as Alcan (aluminum products), MacMillan Blodel (forestry), Molson (beer), Inco (nickel), and the Hudson's Bay Company (retailing).

Nonetheless, many Canadian firms continue to be leaders in their fields. Leading international and domestic firms include Research in Motion, Nortel, and CAE in technology; Magna International, Wescast, and Linamar in auto parts production; Bombardier in transportation equipment; EnCana, Petro-Canada, and Barrick in oil and gas and mining; TD Canada Trust, BMO, and Royal Bank in banking; Manulife and Sun in insurance; Canadian National and Canadian Pacific in transportation services. Virtually all of these companies are traded on the Toronto Stock Exchange (TSX), the country's largest (and the third-largest in North America).

In terms of its external trade, Canada attributes 40 percent of its gross domestic product to external trade. By far, Canada's main trading partners are the United States and Mexico. Every day more than $1 billion of goods crosses the Canada-U.S. border. Canada's merchandise trade with the United States and Mexico has risen from US$112 billion in 1993 to US$235 billion in 2000. Canadian trade with NAFTA countries has more than doubled, while trade with the rest of the world has grown only by 29 percent, chiefly with the European Union and Japan. Along with the auto trade, lumber, agricultural products, and energy (oil and gas) exports constitute the primary trade for Canada. The currency is the Canadian dollar.

See Also: Hudson's Bay Company; Mexico; North American Free Trade Area (NAFTA); United States.

Bibliography. Michael Bliss, *Northern Enterprise: Five Centuries of Canadian Business* (McClelland and Stewart, 1987); Canadian Statistics Agency, www.statcan.ca (cited March 2009); Diane Francis, *Who Owns Canada Now?: Old Money, New Money and the Future of Canadian Business* (Harper Collins, 2008); Amal Henein and Françoise Morissette, *Made in Canada Leadership: Wisdom from the Nation's Best and Brightest on the Art and Practice of Leadership* (Wiley, 2008); *International Business Publications Canada: Country Study Guide* (International Business Publications, 2008); *International Business Publications Canada Customs, Trade Regulations and Procedures Handbook* (International Business Publications, 2008); *International Business Publications Canada Government and Business Contacts Handbook* (International Business Publications, 2008); Kenneth MacLean, *Out of Control: Canada in an Unstable Financial World* (Canadian Centre for Policy Alternatives/James Lorimer, 1999); James H. Marsh, *The Canadian Encyclopedia*, 2nd ed (Hurtig, 1988); D. McCalla, ed., *The Development of Canadian Capitalism* (Copp Clark Pitman, 1990); W. T. Stanbury, *Business-Government Relations in Canada: Grappling With Leviathan* (Methuen, 1986); Statistics Canada, *Canada Yearbook 2007* (Statistics Canada, 2007); Graham D. Taylor and Peter A. Baskerville, *A Concise History of Business in Canada* (Oxford University Press, 1994).

Dimitry Anastakis
Trent University

Candidate Countries

The term *candidate countries* denotes the countries that are advanced in the accession process with the European Union (EU), and have signed a Stabilization and Partnership Agreement with the European Commission. The countries outside the EU can be either in the group of potential future members or countries that will be regarded as good neighbors. As of 2008 the EU candidate countries are Croatia, (former Yugoslav Republic of) Macedonia, and Turkey. Potential candidate countries, per official documents of the EU, are the countries of the Western Balkans: Albania, Bosnia and Herzegovina, Montenegro, Serbia, and Kosovo (the territory under United Nations [UN] administration following UN Security Council Resolution No. 1244 of 1999).

The accession process and candidature begins with the submission of a request for membership from a potential applicant country to the Council of the European Union. The European Commission (acting de facto as the EU's government) assesses the capacity of the applicant as to whether a country meets the accession criteria. The accession criteria were defined at the meeting of the Council in Copenhagen in 1993 and were modified later at the meeting in Madrid in 1995. If the Commission is of positive opinion and the recommendation of the Commission is unanimously upheld by the Council, the formal negotiation process can begin. In fact the candidate country has a relationship not only with the Commission as the representative of the EU, but also with all the member states.

The negotiation focuses on the endorsement of the entire EU legal framework, known as *Acquis Communautaire*. The negotiations are usually fairly slow and meticulous, with discussions about when and how the candidate country will align its legal system with the EU legal framework, and meet in full the EU expectations. The Copenhagen criteria can be summarized as follows: (1) political: stable institutions guaranteeing democracy, the rule of law, human rights, and respect for/protection of minorities; (2) economic: a functioning market economy and the capacity to cope with competition and market forces in the EU, and (3) the capacity to take on the obligations of membership, including adherence to the objectives of political, economic, and monetary union. The Copenhagen criteria were reinforced by the European Council in Madrid in 1995, with a further one added: (4) adoption of the *Acquis Communautaire* and its effective implementation through appropriate administrative and judicial structures. However, it should also be noted that the EU must be able to absorb new members, so it reserves the right to decide when it will be ready to accept them. This is the reason why the candidate country may make excellent progress toward meeting all four criteria for full membership and still not be invited to join.

The pre-accession strategy is designed to prepare the candidate countries for future membership. It encompasses the following frameworks and mechanisms: (1) Europe agreements—stabilization and association agreements; (2) accession partnerships—European partnerships; (3) pre-accession assistance; (4) co-financing from international, i.e., European, financial institutions; (5) participation in the EU programs, agencies, and committees; (6) national program for the adoption of the *Acquis Communautaire*; (7) regular progress reports; and (8) political and economic dialogue.

The first step in the negotiation process for candidate countries is known as screening, where the EU assesses the candidate country's potential to meet the set criteria, and to identify areas where further assistance from the EU is required in order to bring the capacity of the candidate country in line with the expectations of membership. The Commission pre-

pares the report for each chapter, and each country and the candidate country are expected to submit their position, in order for further rapprochement with the EU, that is the Commission on behalf of the EU. The output of the Commission work is the Draft Common Position (DCP), which is the document outlining the position of the EU and its member states toward the candidate country. The moment the Council adopts the DCP, the formal negotiations may start.

Candidate countries are assessed every year by the Commission, which prepares an annual progress report that is published in all the official languages of the EU. Also, each year the Commission adopts its annual strategy document explaining its policy on EU enlargement. The progress report is produced for all the member countries, and reflects both on their performance and the outlined policy of the EU. The so-called enlargement package also contains proposals to the Council for revised European and Accession partnerships for each country; the Commission also lists areas where further reforms are needed.

Financial Assistance

Candidate countries and to some extent "countries which may become candidate countries," that is, the countries of the Western Balkans, are eligible for financial assistance from the EU in the process of accession or preparation for the accession process. From 2007, these countries (candidate and "pre-candidate" countries) may be recipients of the Instruments for Pre-Accession Assistance (IPA), a program that has replaced the multitude of various programs aimed at these countries.

In order to achieve each country's objectives in the most efficient way, IPA consists of the following five components: (1) transition assistance and institution building; (2) cross-border cooperation (with the EU member states and other countries eligible for IPA); (3) regional development (transport, environment, and economic development); (4) human resources development (strengthening human capital and combating exclusion), and (5) rural development. The first component is more directed toward the potential candidate countries in the Western Balkans where there is a need to build the capacity to develop a fully functional civil society and functioning market economy. It is fully under the administration of the

EU Directorate-General for Enlargement. The second component targets not only the candidate countries and those that are most likely expected to achieve candidateship status in the foreseeable future, but to the countries that are neighbors of the EU and would fall in the category of the countries that may be eligible for support under the European Neighbourhood and Partnership Instrument (ENPI).

The other three components (regional development, human resources development, and rural development) are, generally, exclusively targeting candidate countries, as their aim is to bring the candidate country into line with the EU countries and enable it to reach the status of a functional full member of the EU. These components are managed by the respective Directorate-Generals of the Commission and are integrative measures. Regional development is led by the Directorate-General for Regional Policy, human resources development by the Directorate-General for Employment, Social Affairs and Equal Opportunities, and the rural development is led by the Directorate-General for Agriculture and Rural Development.

Before the IPA program was launched, the EU had an array of financial assistance programs targeting different groups of the countries. The best known program is Phare, initially developed in 1989 to support the transition and rapprochement with the EU of Central and Eastern European Countries (CEECs), but later spreading to some of the countries in the Western Balkans.

From Phare other programs have been developed and evolved out of it, most notably the CARDS program (Community Assistance for Reconstruction, Development and Stability in the Balkans), which focused from 2000 on supporting potential candidate countries in the Balkans, primarily the Western Balkans. From the very outset in 1989, the Phare program was to deal with supporting the process of bringing these (target) countries to the EU. However, the remit was somewhat changed at the Copenhagen criteria, where the Phare program was charged with the following objectives: (1) strengthen public administration and institutions to function effectively inside the European Union; (2) promote convergence with the European Union's extensive legislation (the A*cquis Communautaire*) and reduce the need for transition periods; and (3) promote economic and social cohesion.

Other Programs

Other programs that new member states of the EU enjoyed when they were candidate countries include (1) Instrument for Structural Policies for Pre-accession (ISPA); (2) Special Accession Program for Agriculture and Rural Development (SAPARD); and (3) Community Assistance for Reconstruction, Development and Stabilization (CARDS). The SAPARD component was in operation between 2000 and 2006 and generally marked as a successful one. Similarly, CARDS program was launched in 1999, made operational in 2000 and has to a large extent been replaced by IPA, although the EU agency established to implement the assistance to the Western Balkans is still operational, although its mandate is until the end of 2008; unless another (most unlikely) extension is granted. Interestingly, Turkey as a candidate country has always had a separate program of support, although it has been genuinely developed following the format and experience of other programs targeting other candidate countries. Also, new member states, and the former candidates, have received significant support in the first two years of EU membership, through so-called transition facility, while Bulgaria and Romania enjoyed the extra support during the first year of their EU membership.

To support the candidate countries and potential candidate countries (and recently, countries targeted through good neighbor policies) the EU has launched other related programs, like (1) the Technical Assistance and Information Exchange Instrument (TAIEX); (2) twinning, and (3) SIGMA. The twinning program assumes the appointment of short-term resident twinning advisers who share good practices and facilitate the adoption of EU-endorsed policies and practices. SIGMA is an instrument jointly developed by the EU and OECD that has been focusing on public administration reform and capacity building in the target countries.

Accession Procedure

When all criteria are met in full, the Accession Treaty lays down clearly terms and conditions of the entry (accession), and stipulates any issues of importance for the transitional phase, as the future member may exercise some options, for a number of years, before applying the EU legislation to the letter. The accession procedure requires the positive recommendation of the Commission, which the European Parliament (EP) has to endorse, and all the member states have to ratify the treaty, as well as the democratic bodies in the candidate country (as a rule the parliament or the equivalent). The treaty normally stipulates when the membership of the EU begins and as of that date the candidate country becomes a full member of the EU.

To a large extent the EU has closely followed the criteria stipulated in Copenhagen and developed further at the later summits discussing enlargement, but it is also noted that the enlargement of the EU has been politically motivated, and exercised in groups. The overall economic and political performance of the new member states of the EU demonstrates that there are wide differences in their achievements in either or both economic and political spheres. It is also possible to conclude that the enlargement process that is to include the countries of the Western Balkans is possibly the last logical step in the enlargement of the EU in the foreseeable future, as it may be concluded that the dominant thinking is shifting from "enlargement of Europe" to "completing the process." However, the open question is what will happen with the Turkish application, as now the EU could state that what is important is whether the Union can absorb the new member state or not—not whether the member state meets the criteria.

Historically the EU had waves in which the membership has been expanded and it is most likely that this policy will be extended when it comes to the countries of the Western Balkans, while Croatia may be in a position to join the EU on its own. Although the economic criteria for membership is quite often emphasized (or even overstated), the political factor is the prevalent one and drives the decision-making process notwithstanding some level of sentiment and political alignment between the current member countries and those applying for membership.

See Also: Common Market; Eastern Europe; Economic Union; European Union; Regional Integration; Transition Economies.

Bibliography. E. Brimmer and S. Fruehlich, *The Strategic Implications of European Union Enlargement* (Johns Hopkins University, 2005); N. Nugent, *European Union Enlargement* (Palgrave Macmillan, 2004); M. Sajdik and M. Schwarzinger, *European Union Enlargement: Background, Developments, Facts,* Central and Eastern European Policy Studies, vol. 2 (Transaction Publishers, 2007); S. Trogan and V. N. Balasubramanyam, eds., *Turkey and Central and Eastern European Countries in Transition: Towards Membership of the EU* (Palgrave Macmillan, 2001).

Željko Šević
Glasgow Caledonian University

Canon

Canon, a world leader in the imaging industry, traces its foundation to 1933 with the Precision Optical Instruments Laboratory that sought to compete with Germany in 35 mm cameras. The founders, Goro Yoshida and Saburo Uchida (brothers-in-law) researched German cameras, introducing the "Kwanon" prototype camera in 1934. Takashi Mitarai, Uchida's friend and a gynecologist, provided capital. They trademarked "Canon" in 1935 and subsequently introduced the Hansa Canon, Japan's first 35 mm camera, for ¥275, roughly half the price of a German Leica. The laboratory incorporated as a joint-stock company in 1937 with ¥1 million in capital, listing on the Tokyo Stock Exchange in 1949. The company was renamed Canon Camera Co., Inc., in 1947 to simplify the brand and corporate image, becoming Canon, Inc., in 1969 to reflect the company's broadened product profile.

World War II meant that Canon produced military aircraft cameras and developed X-ray equipment, supported by Mitarai's medical connections. Post–World War II government efforts to support the recovery of the Japanese economy translated into cameras being designated as a key export product in

Now a world leader in cameras and other imaging products, Canon suffered losses in the early 1970s but rebounded.

1947. Canon's emphasis on high-quality precision cameras and lenses became quickly known among professional photographers. Japan's first mass-produced camera, the Canonet (1961), sparked a boom in the industry for its low price (¥19,800) and high quality. Canon's Cine 8T (1956, ¥48,000) was awarded the Good Design "G" mark the following year by Japan's Ministry of International Trade and Industry (MITI). The L1 35 mm camera, Canon's first completely original 35 mm camera that allowed it to break away from a Leica-type design, also won the "G" mark.

In 1959 the Projector P-8 was launched, followed by a zoom-lens 8 mm cine camera in 1960. The Canon F-1, a professional-use single-lens reflex (SLR), was introduced in 1971, positioning Canon as a market leader. In 1976 Canon launched the AE-1 SLR, the world's first computerized camera (¥85,000). Canon introduced the NP-1100 in 1970, Japan's first plain-paper copier (¥880,000), a success story because it did not infringe on Xerox's wall of 600+ patents. Additional successes were the LBP-4000 laser-beam printer in 1975 and the BJ-80 inkjet printer in 1985. Since 2000 Canon's digital camera offerings have ranged from the compact IXY Digital to the professional EOS Digital SLR series.

Global Presence

Overseas sales did not come easily at first for Canon. Despite efforts in 1955 to set up a sales office in New York, Canon was forced to rely on other U.S. sales relationships, first with Scopes Co., Ltd., from 1958–61 and then with Bell Howell. To consolidate sales, Canon dissolved all local sales contracts by 1974 and shifted to direct sales through Canon Sales Co., resulting in $137 million in sales in 1976. In 1971 Canon's first overseas production facility was established in Taiwan, which soon became a world supply hub for the popular Canonet. Today, manufacturing is located in such locations as Oita (Japan), Taiwan, Malaysia, and China to capture nuances in world market demand and keep prices for consumer goods reasonable.

Takeshi Mitarai became president in 1942 and led Canon for 32 years, implementing such innovative management policies as a monthly salary system (1943), employee health examinations, the "San-Ji Spirit" of spontaneity, autonomy, and self-awareness (1952), and Japan's first five-day workweek (1966).

Canon was forced to record its first-ever loss in the early 1970s, citing quality failures with desktop calculators and intense competition. Management took the full blame and offered the 1976 Premier Company Plan as a vision to improve Canon's competitive ability.

Under the leadership of Ryuzaburo Kaku, president from 1977 to 1989, Canon grew quickly. Kaku also helped develop and promote Canon's *kyosei* philosophy of living and working together for the common good. Fujio Mitarai, nephew of T. Mitarai, was named president in 1995 and helped Canon overcome the collapse of Japan's economic bubble via the Excellent Global Corporation Plan announced in 1996. Mitarai was named head of Nippon Keidanren in 2006 and shared leadership of Canon with Tsuneji Uchida.

As of December 31, 2006, Canon recorded net sales of $34,941 million; net income of $3,826 million; 219 consolidated subsidiaries; and 118,499 employees worldwide. Main business areas are business machines, computer peripherals, office imaging products, business information products, cameras, and optical products.

See Also: Hewlett Packard; Japan; NEC; Quality.

Bibliography. Canon, Inc., www.canon.com (cited March 2009); C. E. Dyer, *The Canon Production System* (Productivity Press, 1987); G. Lewis, ed., *The History of the Japanese Camera* (International Museum of Photography, 1990); Kiyoshi Tokuda and Nikkei, *How Canon Got Its Flash Back* (John Wiley & Sons, 2004).

Patricia A. Nelson
Seijo University

Capital Account Balance

The capital account balance measures the net value of transactions involving financial assets between residents and nonresidents of a country. It is equal to the difference between funds acquired from the rest of the world (capital inflows) and funds provided to the rest of the world (capital outflows) in a specific period of time. The capital account balance shows whether a country is a net debtor or a net creditor on a flow basis. If capital outflows are greater than capital inflows, the country in question is a net creditor and runs a capital account deficit. In contrast, being a net debtor means that capital inflows are greater than capital outflows; the capital account is in surplus.

The flow of funds between countries takes various forms. The capital account, under the balance of payments accounting, makes a distinction between direct investment, portfolio investment, reserve assets, and other investment. Direct investment refers to the establishment of a resident enterprise or the acquisition of a lasting interest in a resident enterprise by nonresidents. Portfolio investment denotes transactions in equity and debt securities such as stocks, bonds, and money market instruments. Reserve assets usually consist of foreign exchange reserves held by monetary authorities. The category of other investment covers transactions pertaining to financial assets such as trade credits, loans, and demand deposits. The capital account balance is the sum of net positions in direct investment, portfolio investment, reserve assets, and other investment.

The accounting identity of the balance of payments system implies that the balance on the capital account has a reverse sign of and is equal to the balance on the current account. In other words, the capital account and current account balances sum up to zero. While this accounting identity is true by definition, data collection, reporting, and estimation errors cause a statistical discrepancy between the two. This discrepancy is reported under the category of net errors and omissions.

A further understanding of the capital account balance can be obtained by analyzing its relation to national income. Consider a country where the consumption and investment of its residents and the spending of its public sector are greater than the national income. In a global economy, this excess demand is met by imports, which are financed through funds from the rest of the world. Thus, being a net debtor means that the residents of a country can spend beyond what they produce and can finance this excess spending by borrowing from residents of other countries.

The magnitude of the capital account balance does not—by itself—throw much light on a country's economic strength and health. For example, the absolute size of the funds acquired by the United States in each calendar year is the biggest in the world.

Nevertheless, the stock of the U.S. foreign debt as a percentage of its gross domestic product is small compared to the majority of developing and emerging market economies.

A country can remain as a net debtor as long as private and public economic agents in the rest of the world are willing to provide funds. However, running a capital account surplus increases the stock of foreign debt held in a country. As the stock of foreign debt increases, the willingness of foreign creditors to provide funds diminishes. Thus, a country cannot run a capital account surplus indefinitely.

A stop in the funds acquired from the rest of the world forces an adjustment in national consumption and investment. The severity of adjustment increases if the stop of funds is accompanied and followed by a reversal; that is to say, if a country transitions from receiving funds to sending funds in a relatively short amount of time. In the past, many developing and emerging market economies had to endure severe economic crises as a result of sudden stop and reversal of foreign capital inflows.

See Also: Capital Flight; Currency Exposure; Current Account; External Debt; Foreign Direct Investment, Horizontal and Vertical; Foreign Exchange Reserves; Foreign Portfolio Investment; International Capital Flows; National Accounts; Net Capital Outflow.

Bibliography. Barry J. Eichengreen and Ricardo Hausmann, eds., *Other People's Money: Debt Denomination and Financial Instability in Emerging Market Economies* (University of Chicago Press, 2005); Giancarlo Gandolfo, *International Finance and Open-Economy Macroeconomics* (Springer-Verlag, 2001); International Monetary Fund, *Balance of Payments Manual*, 5th ed. (IMF, 1993); F. Machlup, "Three Concepts of the Balance of Payments and the So-Called Dollar Shortage," *Economic Journal* (v.60, 1950); Jeffrey D. Sachs, ed., *Developing Country Debt and the World Economy* (University of Chicago Press: 1989); Robert M. Stern, *The Balance of Payments: Theory and Economic Policy* (Aldine, 1973); U.S. Department of Commerce, *The Balance of Payments of the United States: Concepts, Data Sources, and Estimating Procedures* (U.S. Government Printing Office, 1990).

Kurtulus Gemici
University of California, Los Angeles

Capital Adequacy

Capital adequacy is a measure of a financial institution's ability to absorb potential losses resulting from various risks to which it is exposed. Financial institutions are required to maintain a certain minimum amount of capital in order to ensure their soundness and the stability of the financial system as a whole. Capital adequacy concerns led to tumbling stock prices of many of the world's largest financial institutions in 2008.

The Basel Committee on Banking Supervision establishes standards for the calculation of minimum capital. The current set of standards was initially published in 2004 and is known as the Basel II Framework. The Framework aims to minimize the difference between regulatory and economic capital. Two types of capital are measured—tier I and tier II capital, with tier I being the most reliable form of capital and consisting primarily of shareholders' equity. Tier II capital is limited to 100 percent of tier I capital. The minimum capital adequacy ratio is 8 percent of the risk-weighted assets. Total capital that banks are required to set aside should cover for three types of risk: credit, market, and operational.

Credit risk is defined as the risk of losses arising from a borrower's nonpayment on its obligations. The Basel II Framework permits banks a choice between two broad methodologies for calculating credit risk: Standardized or Internal Rating–Based, or IRB. Standardized methodology relies on external credit risk assessment by the major rating agencies, whereas the IRB approach uses credit risks systems developed internally by banks, and requires explicit approval of the bank's supervisor. Such approval is subject to certain minimum conditions and disclosure requirements. Under the IRB approach, banks can use their own estimates of risk components that include measures of the probability of default, loss-given default, the exposure at default, and effective maturity.

The IRB methodology is further subdivided into two approaches: foundation and advanced. Under the foundation approach, financial institutions can use their own probability of default and rely on supervisory estimates of other components. Under the advanced approach, banks can also use their own estimates of other risk components.

Market risk refers to the risk of losses that arise from movements in market prices and the resulting decrease in the value of investments. For measuring market risks, banks can use two main valuation methodologies: marking-to-market and marking-to-model. Marking-to-market represents at least daily valuations of positions at current market prices for the same or similar instruments. It means that a security is recorded at its market value rather than book value. The Framework encourages banks to mark-to-market as much as possible. Where it is not feasible, however, banks are allowed to use marking-to-model, which is defined as any valuation that needs to be extrapolated or otherwise calculated based on financial models. Just as with credit risk, for calculating capital requirements for market risks, banks can use either the Standardized methodology that relies on external assessment, or the Internal Measurement approach. Banks that rely on internal models are required to have in place a comprehensive stress-testing system.

Operational risk is defined as the risk of loss resulting from faulty internal processes, from human mistakes or systems failures, or from external events. Legal risks are included in the notion of the operational risk, but strategic and reputational risks are not. For operational risk there are three methods of calculation, listed in order of increased sophistication and risk sensitivity: the Basic Indicator approach, the Standardized approach, and the Advanced Measurement approach. Banks using the Basic Indicator approach must hold capital equal to the average over the previous three years of a certain percentage of positive annual gross income. In the Standardized approach, banks' activities are divided into eight business lines, and the capital requirement for each line is calculated by multiplying gross income by a factor assigned to that business line. Under the Advanced Measurement approach, banks develop increasingly risk-sensitive operational risk allocation techniques.

See Also: Bank for International Settlements; Basel Committee on Banking Supervision; Credit Ratings; Mortgage Credit Crisis of 2008; Risk Management.

Bibliography. Kern Alexander, Rahul Dhumale, and John Eatwell, *Global Governance of Financial Systems: The International Regulation of Systemic Risk* (Oxford University Press, 2006); Bank for International Settlements, www.

bis.org (cited March 2009); Basel Committee for Banking Supervision, *International Convergence of Capital Measurement and Capital Standards: A Revised Framework Comprehensive Version* (Bank for International Settlements, 2006); Atsushi Miyake and Tamotsu Nakamura, "A Dynamic Analysis of an Economy with Banking Optimization and Capital Adequacy Regulations," *Journal of Economics and Business* (v.59/1, 2007); Janine Mukuddem-Petersen and Mark A. Petersen, "Optimizing Asset and Capital Adequacy Management in Banking," *Journal of Optimization Theory and Applications* (v.137/1, 2008); Mansur Noibi, "Prudential Regulation of Islamic Banks: An Analysis of Capital Adequacy Standards," *Journal of Islamic Banking & Finance* (v.24/4, 2007); Hal Scott, *Capital Adequacy Beyond Basel: Banking, Securities, and Insurance* (Oxford University Press, 2005).

Lyudmila V. Lugovskaya
University of Cambridge

Capital Budgeting

Many organizations charge their finance department with overseeing the financial stability of the organization. The chief financial officer (CFO) may lead a team of financial analysts in determining which projects deserve investment. This process is referred to as capital budgeting. It is an example of how an organization may conduct a cost-benefit analysis. There is a comparison between the cash inflows (benefits) and outflows (costs) in order to determine which is greater. Capital budgeting could be the result of purchasing assets that are new for the organization or disposing some of the current assets in order to be more efficient. The finance team will be charged with evaluating (1) which projects would be good investments, (2) which assets would add value to the current portfolio, and (3) how much is the organization willing to invest into each asset.

In order to answer the questions about the potential assets, there are a set of components to be considered in the capital budgeting process. The four components are initial investment outlay, net cash benefits (or savings) from the operations, terminal cash flow, and net present value technique. Most of the literature discusses how the capital budgeting process operates in the traditional, domestic environment. However, as the world moves to a more global economic environment, consideration needs to be given to how multinational corporations will conduct the capital budgeting process when operating in countries outside their home base.

International Capital Budgeting

International capital budgeting refers to when projects are located in host countries other than the home country of the multinational corporation. Some of the techniques (i.e., calculation of net present value) are the same as traditional finance. Financial analysts may find that foreign projects are more complex to analyze than domestic projects for a number of reasons. There is the need to distinguish between parent cash flow and projects cash flow. Multinationals will have the opportunity to evaluate the cash flow associated with projects from two approaches. They may look at the net impact of the project on their consolidated cash flow or they may treat the cash flow on a stand-alone or unconsolidated basis. The theoretical perspective asserts that the project should be evaluated from the parent company's viewpoint since dividends and repayment of debt are handled by the parent company. This action supports the notion that the evaluation is actually on the contributions that the project can make to the multinational's bottom line. There will also be a need to recognize money reimbursed to the parent company when there are differences in the tax system.

The way in which the cash flows are returned to the parent company will have an effect on the project. Cash flow can be returned in the following ways:

- Dividends—it can only be returned in this form if the project has a positive income. Some countries may impose limits on the amounts of funds that subsidiaries can pay to their foreign parent company in this form.
- Intrafirm debt—interest on debt is tax deductible and it helps to reduce foreign tax liability.
- Intrafirm sales—this form is the operating cost of the project and it helps lower the foreign tax liability.
- Royalties and license fees—this form covers the expenses of the project and lowers the tax liability.

- Transfer pricing—this form refers to the internally established prices where different units of a single enterprise buy goods and services from each other.

Among the other factors that analysts must consider are differences in the inflation rate between countries, given that they will affect the cash flow over time. Also, they must analyze the use of subsidized loans from the host country since the practice may complicate the capital structure and discounted rate. The host country may target specific subsidiaries in order to attract specific types of investment (i.e., technology).

Subsidized loans can be given in the form of tax relief and preferential financing, and the practice will increase the net present value of the project. Some of the advantages of this practice include (1) adding the subsidiary to project cash inflows and discount, (2) discounting the subsidiary at some other rate, risk free, and (3) lowering the risk-adjusted discount rate for the project in order to show the lower cost of debt.

Other steps may include determining if political risk will reduce the value of the investment, assessing different perspectives when establishing the terminal value of the project, reviewing whether or not the parent company had problems transferring cash flows due to the funds being blocked, making sure that there is no confusion as to how the discount rate is going to be applied to the project, and, finally, adjusting the project cash flow to account for potential risks.

See Also: Cash Management; Managerial Accounting; Risk Management.

Bibliography. Shahid Ansari, *The Capital Budgeting Process* (McGraw-Hill/Irwin, 2000); Stanley Block, "Integrating Traditional Capital Budgeting Concepts Into an International Decision Making Environment," *Engineering Economist* (Winter, 2000); Adrian Buckley, *International Capital Budgeting* (Prentice Hall, 1995); Neil Seitz and Mitch Elllison, *Capital Budget and Long-Term Financing Decisions* (South-Western College Pub., 2004).

Marie Gould
Peirce College

Capital Controls

Capital controls are measures used by governments to restrict the flow of money in and out of a country. There are many forms of capital controls, ranging from administrative requirements for transactions (e.g., allowing transfers of funds only with permits, prohibitions on certain types of transactions) to market-based controls (e.g., a tax on types of transactions, use of multiple exchange rates to discriminate against a class of transactions).

Almost every nation has relied on some form of capital controls at some point in its history, and capital controls became widespread during World War I and continued to be common through the mid-20th century. More recently, economic crises in the 1990s in Brazil, Chile, Colombia, Malaysia, and Thailand led to short-term impositions of capital controls. Where capital controls exist, they play an important part in business decisions about whether to invest in a country since controls can prevent repatriation of the investment and profits.

In an open economy without exchange or capital controls, money flows into an economy when investors perceive opportunities and out when they perceive risks. For example, if a country has higher interest rates than other countries and a stable currency, money will flow into the economy. On the other hand, if investors perceive a risk that a country will devalue its currency, they will seek to shift their money into a more stable currency. Such transactions limit the ability of governments to set monetary and fiscal policies in accordance with domestic political priorities by subjecting them to market discipline. Capital controls allow governments to avoid this financial market discipline.

The capital controls imposed during World War I enabled the belligerent governments to have a higher inflation rate (effectively a tax on wealth) than they could have sustained had investors been able to shift their wealth into nonbelligerent currencies. Proponents of capital controls also argue that they help countries avoid short-term, destabilizing capital inflows and outflows by speculators and facilitate effective taxation by making it harder for the wealthy to shift substantial assets abroad.

Malaysia's experience in 1998–99 illustrates how capital controls operate. Thailand's devaluation of its currency in 1997 sparked a widespread financial crisis across Asia, as investors sought security by moving their assets out of Asian currencies. To stop capital being withdrawn from Asian economies, the International Monetary Fund pushed governments in the region to raise interest rates. Because higher interest rates would reduce economic growth by making it more costly to obtain capital, the Malaysian government imposed restrictions on withdrawal of capital in September 1998, banning transfers from domestic to foreign bank accounts and otherwise restricting withdrawal of capital from Malaysia for one year. A few months later the government lifted the ban but imposed a heavy tax on capital withdrawals. The government also fixed the exchange rate for the country's currency.

By preventing capital withdrawals, the government was able to prevent financial markets from exerting pressure on the fixed exchange rate. Supporters of the policy argued that it bought the government time, allowing the crisis sparked by the Thai devaluation to recede. Opponents argued that it freed the government to abandon needed financial reforms by insulating it from financial market pressures.

Opponents of capital controls note that controls are costly in five important ways. First, capital controls are costly to implement both for governments and for those subject to the controls. For example, Malaysia's program in the 1990s required highly intrusive financial sector regulations to prevent evasion. Second, controls on capital reduce beneficial transactions as well as harmful ones by making all capital transactions more expensive. Since markets depend on liquidity for their efficient operation, loss of liquidity can result in general welfare losses. Third, the imposition of capital controls itself sends a bad signal to the financial markets about an economy, potentially exacerbating the problems that led to the imposition of the controls in the first place. Fourth, capital controls result in political allocation of valuable rights to make international capital transactions, which can lead to corruption. Finally, by partially insulating economies from financial market pressures, capital controls can undermine efforts at necessary fiscal and monetary policy reforms.

One form of capital control that has gained considerable popular support in recent years is the "Tobin tax," named after James Tobin, the economist who first proposed it. A Tobin tax would tax short-term capital movements across borders, with the aim of discouraging speculation. Antiglobalization activists around the world have embraced the Tobin tax, as have a number of European and Latin American politicians.

See Also: Asian Financial Crisis; Capital Flight; Capital Repatriation; Globalization; International Capital Flows.

Bibliography. Akira Ariyoshi et al., *Capital Controls: Country Experiences with Their Use and Liberalization* (International Monetary Fund, 2000); Barry Eichengreen, *Global Imbalances and the Lessons of Bretton Woods* (MIT Press, 2007); Christopher Neely, "An Introduction to Capital Controls," *Federal Reserve Bank of St. Louis Review* (November/December 1999).

Andrew P. Morriss
University of Illinois

Capital Flight

Capital flight is a phenomenon that occurs when market investors withdraw money from an economy because they have lost confidence in its prospects of growth. International and domestic causes of capital flight are debatable. The monetarist position and the post-Keynesian position mark the boundaries of this debate. The chicken-versus-the-egg problem is preeminent: To garner investor credibility, what should be given priority—growth or equity? Theoretically, growth can create equity in the long run. But, empirically, huge social inequalities (initial or developing) within or between states tend to create social conflict that can decimate growth. Hence, the two camps differ over whether financial globalization and integration of markets is productive for growth and equity. To assess this, they look at macroeconomic fundamentals, i.e., money, output, and consumption that determine supply and demand.

Monetarists tend to emphasize theoretical claims that supply of capital/"sound money" will universally create growth through rational investor actions based on cost-benefit calculations. On the other hand, post-Keynesians tend to emphasize the empirically contingent impact of capital allocation on distributive justice for labor. Hence, they point to irrational market sentiments that misalign capital allocation and productive output and reduce income and consumption demand. Consequently, policy prescriptions differ. Monetarists argue for universal policies of political neutrality of states, auto-regulated/free markets and capital account liberalization. Post-Keynesians prefer historically contingent political intervention in the domestic and global market for purposes of growth and welfare.

Monetarists argue that competitive markets create efficient/rational capital allocation. They claim that equity will occur automatically through trickle down effects of economic growth. Post-Keynesians advocate for politically proactive policies of safety nets to ensure that winners compensate losers. Given that labor engaged in productive output of trade and services is mostly internationally immobile, due to immigration barriers, social insurance would reassure them. It would give them confidence to build capabilities and compromise with capital about wages/income to ensure conflict-free growth. Creating investor credibility is then critical to prevent capital flight, but the difference lies in the focus—capital or labor.

The monetarists posit that it is the lack of long-run macroeconomic fundamentals of growth that generates loss of credibility for international capital and results in capital flight as a form of market discipline. The post-Keynesians point out that it is the lack of market-friendly capital controls that forces governments to take protectionist measures against the short-run excesses of capital mobility that destroy the macroeconomic fundamentals and result in capital flight. The cause and effect, in essence, are reversed in the two arguments.

For monetarists, a stable macroeconomic environment is ensured through low inflation and currency stability to ensure that output and consumption are not affected. Hence, imprudent fiscal and monetary policies of expansion need to be avoided. This can be achieved through political neutrality. For monetarists, governments act expediently to stay in power, and hence, they can never be committed to consistent low inflation. Populist policies of market intervention then result in workers rationally adjusting their wage demands based on future inflationary expectations. Hence, long-term trade-off between inflation and unemployment is impossible. All attempts by government to boost employment, to manage demand and consumption through expansion only result in infla-

tion without real growth. Policies of expansion result in rent-seeking from entrenched interest groups like labor unions. Labor unions demand high wages and, being unrelated to productivity, this leads to increased costs of output. This leads to labor market rigidities and inflationary price spirals. High inflation leads to currency instability. As currency value depreciates in the face of inflation, purchasing power parity falls. This leads to export-import imbalances and balance of payment crisis. As trade deficits and debts increase, loss of confidence by market investors and capital flight occurs.

Other Factors

Monetarists point to other related factors critical to investor confidence and prevention of capital flight. First, the degree of market integration through trade or stock markets will determine the level of development of the domestic economy. Development itself creates confidence in that it creates prospects for growth that draws in capital. Second, the strength of the regulatory environment or the degree of transparency of rules creates confidence. For example, political independence of central banks ensures that monetary policies are geared toward austerity to ensure low inflation as a pre-condition for economic growth and exchange rate stability. Third, the degree of asset-specificity will determine the cost of collecting information about prospects of the economy and create the degree of risk averseness.

For example, foreign direct investment (FDI) is least liquid, and being locally situated, can have more access to information, and hence, is less risk averse. In contrast, bond capital that lends to governments is highly liquid, has difficulty collecting information given the collective action problem of scattered investors, and hence, is highly risk averse. To prevent the flight of risk-averse capital, nonpolitical institutions are critical. Institutional strength increases transparency, reduces transaction costs, enables cost-benefit analyses, and ensures rational behavior.

Counterarguments

The politically normative post-Keynesians offer strong counterarguments to the monetarist claims. They point out that the monetarists' argument is internally inconsistent. If money is neutral in the long run, it cannot also be a source of growth. Why should governments care for "sound money" if there is going to be no fundamental change in the real economy? They indicate that while governments pursue low-inflation orthodoxy there are serious distributive effects in terms of creating inequality by hampering policies designed to rectify unemployment and create growth.

More critically, post-Keynesians point out that the rational expectations assumptions of the monetarists are based on unrealistic expectations of perfectly functioning markets, perfect information, and perfectly rational actors that result in indeterminate predictions about capital flight. They point out that there are market imperfections like concentration of institutional investors that lead to inefficient allocation of capital. Moreover, investors with short time horizons and performance pressures for furthering their own careers are likely to pursue irrational herd-like market behavior rather than individual rational cost-benefit calculus through careful evaluation of available information. This irrationality leads to speculative flows that impact real-time economic decision making within an economy. The sudden expansion of credit leads to asset price bubbles and consumption booms. This leads to currency appreciation "overshoot" as market expectations undergo irrational exuberance about growth expectations.

As consumers start relying on paper wealth in terms of rising asset prices, they engage in risky behavior of borrowing more, consuming more, and saving less. As domestic savings fall and open capital accounts provide the lure of cheap money, investors of local origin undertake unstable, short-term borrowing in hard currency to finance long-term projects. With the economy expanding on the basis of these reflexive asset bubbles—where expectations shape the reality—the outcome is unstable macroeconomic fundamentals. When the economy collapses under negative external shocks, like oil price shocks, currency devaluates drastically. This leads to devalued assets, high debts, and inflation. This causes capital flight as both international investors and domestic savers shift their assets abroad.

The credit crunch impacts further investment and affects local production and exports leading to a contraction of the economy. There is then increasing political demand for protection. With these kinds of market imperfections, growth is hampered, forcing governments to take protective measures to safeguard populations against the harshness of the vagaries of the market through expansionary policies geared to create safety nets. This creates loss of market confidence and results in cumulative capital flight.

Overall, capital flows in disequilibrating ways. "Hot money" flows for quick turnovers and quick profits and there is less productive capital-asset formation in the form of long-term FDI and fixed local capital. However, such market distortions can be corrected through strong political institutional structures—primarily the state undertaking growth measures.

Post-Keynesians point out that capital flight also depends on the capability of states to coordinate and create international regimes and institutions to regulate capital. This regulation would constrain herd-like behavior of investors that spreads contagion of financial crises and weakens economic fundamentals. However, in the current context of an international regime of neoliberalism that delegitimizes capital controls, governments have been forced to open up their economies to generate credibility even if they do not have the necessary domestic institutional strength.

Government Control

International institutions like the International Monetary Fund and the World Bank by advocating capital account liberalization as part of their development package conditionalities have further created an unstable financial system. The system is prone to crises of capital glut or crunch depending upon unstable and irrational market sentiments that lead to capital inflows and capital flight. While the Bank for International Settlements regime has sought to monitor capital behavior through increasing regulations, the regulations lag behind the rapid pace of technological growth that allow capital to evade and exit. Hence, government control of markets is critical.

Mixed economies like China and India that exercise significant government control over their economies have not lost out in terms of growth or ability to attract capital and prevent capital flight (e.g., the Asian financial crisis). Hence, a balance between growth and equity, free market and political intervention is critical.

See Also: Asian Financial Crisis; Bank for International Settlements; Capital Controls; Capitalism; Currency Speculators; Current Account; Free Markets; Globalization;

International Monetary Fund; Labor Standards; Mundell-Fleming Model; Open Economy Macroeconomics; Sustainable Development; World Trade Organization.

Bibliography. Philip Arestis, "Post-Keynesian Economics: Towards Coherence," *Cambridge Journal of Economics* (January 20, 1996); Victor A. B. Davies, "Postwar Capital Flight and Inflation," *Journal of Peace Research* (v.45/4, 2008); European Network on Debt and Development, "Addressing Development's Black Hole: Regulating Capital Flight," www.eurodad.org (cited March 2009); Ilene Grabel and Ha-Joon Chang, "Reclaiming Development from the Washington Consensus," Symposium on "The 15th Anniversary of the Washington Consensus: What Happened? What's Next?" *Journal of Post Keynesian Economics* (v.27/2, 2004–05); Adam Harmes, "Institutional Investor's and Polyani's Double Movement: A Model of Contemporary Currency Crises," *Review of International Political Economy* (v.8/3, 2001); John Harvey, "A Post Keynesian View of Exchange Rate Determination," *Journal of Post Keynesian Economics* (v.14/1, 1991); Andrew Van Hulten, "Capital Flight and Capital Controls in Developing Countries," *Progress in Development Studies* (v.7/4, 2007); Ian Katz, "Capital Flight to South Florida," *BusinessWeek* (June 25, 2007); Jonathan Kirshner, "The Political Economy of Low Inflation," *Journal of Economic Surveys* (v.15/1, 2001).

PALLAB PAUL
UNIVERSITY OF DENVER

Capital Gains Tax

A capital gain (loss) is an increase (decrease) in the value of an asset, such as that realized from the sale of stocks, bonds, precious metals, and property. Since a capital gain is an addition to economic well-being, theoretically it should be included in a comprehensive income tax base. However, in the interest of administrative ease, capital gains are taxed on a realization basis (when the asset is sold) rather than on an accrual basis (when the gain is earned). Deferring taxes in this way makes a big difference in return because the deferral allows the investment to grow at the before-tax rather than the after-tax rate of interest. In effect, the government gives the investor an interest-free loan on taxes due.

Not all countries implement a capital gains tax and most have different rates of taxation for individuals and corporations. In the United States, individuals and corporations pay income tax on the net total of all their capital gains just as they do on other income, but the tax rate for individuals is lower on "long-term capital gains," which are gains on assets that had been held for over one year before being sold, in order to reward long-term asset-holding. The tax rate on long-term gains was reduced in 2003 to 15 percent or to 5 percent for individuals in the lowest two income tax brackets, although in 2011 these reduced tax rates are scheduled to revert to the rates in effect before 2003, which were generally 20 percent. Short-term capital gains are taxed at the higher, ordinary income tax rate. Countries without a capital gains tax include Argentina, Belgium, Hong Kong, Mexico, Netherlands, Germany, and Singapore.

The primary argument for a lower tax or no tax on capital gains is the avoidance of the "lock-in" effect, so called because the tax system tends to lock investors into their current portfolios. The postponement of realization in order to avoid the tax results in a misallocation of capital because it no longer flows to the most economically worthy destination, where its return is highest. Exchange inefficiency results because an asset is not being held by those who value it the most. Further, capital gains tax on owner occupied housing discourages mobility, yet another inefficient outcome, since the after-tax price might not be enough to pay for a new equivalent home. Some research has also shown that a lower tax increases the return to investment, thus encouraging the rate of investment and the start of new businesses, which aids economic growth. However, this result is not universally accepted by all researchers in the field.

From an equity standpoint, since capital gains are among the most unequally distributed sources of personal income, any across-the-board capital gains tax cuts will dramatically reduce the share of all income taxes paid by the very wealthiest taxpayers and will increase the share of taxes paid by lower- and middle-income taxpayers. The large consequences of delaying taxes on investment returns provide further benefits to those high-income taxpayers with capital gains income.

See Also: Taxes; Corporate Income Tax.

Bibliography. L. E. Burman and P. D. Ricoy, "Capital Gains and the People Who Realize Them," *National Tax Journal* (1997); E. Engen and J. Skinner, "Taxation and Economic Growth," *National Tax Journal* (1996); M. K. McKee, "Capital Gains Taxation and New Firm Investment," *National Tax Journal* (1998); H. S. Rosen and T. Gayer, *Public Finance* (McGraw-Hill, 2007).

Donna M. Anderson
University of Wisconsin–La Crosse

Capitalism

Capitalism is an economic system characterized by private property and freely functioning markets without central planning. Prices in capitalist economic systems are determined by the free and open exchanges of buyers and sellers guided by self-interest but constrained by both an ethical consensus and the rule of law. While capitalism is widely viewed as the most effective system for generating wealth and higher material standards of living, capitalist economies also go through periods of instability, some of which have raised concerns about the overall appeal of the system.

In addition to concerns rooted in these periodic cycles, other concerns have been raised regarding broader social issues such as the distribution of income. Most economists believe that the benefits of capitalist systems have far outweighed the costs but this article will present both sides of the argument. To understand capitalism in its present form also requires that we consider the historical developments, both intellectual and material, that gave rise to the modern capitalist system.

Historical Development

Capitalist economic systems are relatively new developments in the broad span of human history and gradually evolved over time in response to previous economic systems. Yet the fundamental driving force of market capitalism, self-interested exchange between buyers and sellers, is as old as humanity itself. M. M. Postan and H. J. Habakkuk described evidence that mammoth hunters of the Russian steppes and the Cro-Magnon hunters of central France both

obtained Mediterranean shells through long-distance trading. The late Robert Heilbroner wrote of how the Tablets of Tell-el-Amarna described lively trade in 1400 B.C. between the Levantine kings and Egyptian pharaohs. Large-scale enterprise, buttressed by financial systems, was a part of Ming China (1368–1644). In addition, Avner Greif has described how the Maghribi traders, a group of Jewish traders from parts of northern Africa and from Muslim Sicily and Spain, were engaged in long-distance trading throughout the Mediterranean by the 11th century. These traders seem to have enforced contracts, a critical requirement for any successful long-distance trading to emerge, through private coalitions composed of merchants and the agents who worked for them.

While there was little formal enforcement of business agreements at the time, these private coalitions enforced contracts themselves through the sharing of information; in effect, they relied on reputation mechanisms and punished those who violated business agreements. Since the emergence of long-distance trading was an important development on the long, slow path toward capitalism, these institutional developments that made distant trading possible are of central importance.

While important stepping stones on the path toward modern capitalism, none of these examples of early exchange were conducted within the economic system we call capitalism. The term itself was first used in the late 19th century and did not become common parlance until the early 20th century. However, most economists would view capitalism as an economic system that emerged out of the demise of mercantilism in the late 18th century. The mercantilist system had emerged alongside the nation-states of Europe and is generally dated to the early 16th century.

These powerful nation-states grew out of the demise of the highly structured medieval feudal society in which economic activity was centered around a manor, which was a district controlled by an elite member of feudal society called a lord. The manorial system was one in which lords owned property that was worked by landless serfs. This system was one of stagnation and lack of exchange, which contrasts nearly completely with the modern capitalist systems that are identified by constant change and the centrality of the free exchange process. Eventually, medieval feudal society broke down in part because of the

Black Death that killed at least one-third of Europe's population beginning in 1348.

The Black Death also intensified social tensions within European feudal society. The sharp declines in urban population (and thus demand) forced down the price of food while wages simultaneously rose because of the shrinking supply of workers. In response, wage controls that sought to prevent wages from rising too far were imposed but these only served to magnify the already rising social tensions. Worker revolts occurred throughout Europe and ultimately altered the economic conditions of feudalism. In the end, these changes gradually brought about freedom for the serfs. If there is any silver lining to the disastrous 14th century in Europe it is that it paved the way for the eventual emergence of capitalism. Yet there was one more step on the path to market capitalism, the economic system known as mercantilism.

Mercantilism

Mercantilism, while not generally viewed as a coherent school of economic thought, can best be described as a system of extensive economic regulations whose purpose was to enhance the power of the nation-state by acquiring as much gold and silver as possible. This was to be done by selling more to foreigners than was purchased from them; that is, the goal was to export as much as possible while importing as little as possible. To accomplish this, the mercantilists established extensive regulations on both international trade and domestic industry. In 1684 Philipp von Hornick enumerated a set of mercantilist policies including those that would promote a large population to drive down wages and thus benefit the merchant class that was most directly engaged in exporting activity.

The mercantilists erroneously viewed international exchange as a zero-sum game; that is, they believed there were winners and losers in international trade and they naturally sought to be on the winning side. Thanks to David Ricardo's seminal work first published in 1817, *Principles of Political Economy*, economists now almost universally believe that international exchange is a positive-sum game; that is, trade benefits both trading partners. Despite its flaws, mercantilism characterized the economic policies pursued by the major European powers from between the 16th and 18th centuries. Indeed,

the original 13 American colonies were established by England as a central component of its mercantilist policy.

The Enlightenment

Eventually, both the internal contradictions of mercantilism and the growing intellectual tide that was part of the Age of Enlightenment (roughly from the Glorious Revolution of 1688 to the end of the French Revolution in 1789) cleared the way for the move toward modern capitalism. The establishment of capitalism, while slowly building over the long term, awaited a powerful and penetrating intellectual argument. This argument would have to convincingly make the case that lack of central direction would not, in fact, result in chaos. It would have to be built on foundations that were seemingly contradictory—that an economy composed of individuals who behaved in ways that were solely consistent with their own personal interests would not degenerate into a chaotic war of all-against-all. This was a high intellectual hurdle to jump and required not just a penetrating argument but an intellectual environment that was a least open to radical ideas. It is thus one of those fortunate coincidences of history that the Scottish philosopher Adam Smith was born into the revolutionary period of Enlightenment that largely defined the western world, at least intellectually, in the 18th century. The Enlightenment thinkers sought to apply reason and systematic, logical thinking to all areas of human activity.

Born in Kirkcaldy, Scotland, in 1723, Adam Smith became the father of modern economics with his monumental treatise *An Inquiry into the Nature and Causes of the Wealth of Nations*, which was published in 1776. If one must place a date on the beginning of capitalism, the publication of Smith's magnum opus is not a bad one to choose. In it, Smith argued that markets could harness the innate self-interest that motivates each human being and exploit it for the common good. In perhaps the most well-known line from the *Wealth of Nations*, Smith wrote,

> It is not from the benevolence of the butcher, the brewer, or the baker, that we expect our dinner, but from their regard to their own self-interest. We address ourselves, not to their humanity but to their self-love, and never talk to them of our own necessities but of their advantage.

The Author of the Wealth of Nations

Adam Smith, whose ideas have been central to capitalist arguments, is depicted in this 1790 engraving.

fare theorem is a mathematical version) and underlie the support afforded free markets by the vast majority of economists. While most economists focus on Smith's *Wealth of Nations*, its predecessor, *The Theory of Moral Sentiments*, is equally important and informs us as to the ethical foundations of capitalism that are often overlooked. Smith's work in fact simultaneously examined both ethics and positive laws in conjunction with market exchange. Smith argued that in the absence of a strong civic ethics we would be forced to rely on increasingly extensive laws which would increase the size and role of the government. This, according to Smith, was the very thing that would stifle economic freedom and prevent the process of growth that he had laid out in the *Wealth of Nations*. Ethical underpinnings were thus central to the success of the capitalist system. Without those underpinnings, the heavy hand of government regulation would be required and would eventually extinguish the very spirit of capitalism.

One of the most counterintuitive ideas that Smith, Hume, and other scholars put forth was how a society that was not regulated from above could still be orderly. The essence of the argument was that the marketplace itself was a form of what the Nobel Prize–winning economist Friedrich Hayek called "spontaneous order." The fundamental problem is that complex social order simply cannot be constructed by a central authority because the information requirement is beyond any person's abilities to manage. The price system, however, aggregates this information and coordinates behavior so efficiently that it seems as if it must be guided or structured in some way. This coordination, while appearing to be the product of some grand design, is actually nothing more than the product of millions of individuals who followed only their own interests. None had any intention of creating overall social or economic order, so the coordination we observe was a beneficial unintended consequence of the pursuit of self-interest. In Adam Smith's words, "man is led to promote an end which was no part of his intention." This is what is known as Adam Smith's concept of the Invisible Hand.

While Smith deservedly gets much of the credit for the intellectual sea change that pushed the Western world toward market capitalism, he was certainly not alone in this. Nor was Smith the first to extol the

Self-interest, commonly thought to be a private vice, could be turned into a public virtue. This notion had earlier been mentioned by Bernard Mandeville in *The Fable of the Bees* but it was with Smith that it was made part of an overall theory of economic development. Both parties, Smith explained, benefited from the process of voluntary exchange that is a defining feature of capitalism. Yet it is less clear what the impact of self-interested behavior is for society at large. Will this pursuit of self-interest lead to a degeneration of society into a war of all-against-all, as the philosopher Hobbes had most notably argued? How, in other words, is capitalism prevented from simply destroying itself?

The echoes of Smith's eloquent description of the benefits of competitive markets are found in modern mathematical economics (the first fundamental wel-

benefits of self-interested market exchange. Intellectually, other schools of thought had long been laying the groundwork for Smith. Arguments defining the benefits of open exchange go as far back as Ancient Greek antiquity. Aristotle most prominently discussed the benefits of private property in the 4th century B.C.

Aristotle also saw the importance of private property rights, which are fundamental to capitalist economies. While the nuggets of economic thought that we find in Ancient Greece were practically lost in the Dark Ages, a group of Catholic Church scholars known collectively as the Scholastics would revive elements of Aristotelian thought from approximately the 9th to the 13th century. While the Scholastics are most remembered for their erroneous views on just price and usury (prohibitions on interest), they also adopted the favorable views of private property rights from Aristotle and reintroduced them to Western thought.

The French Physiocrats, led by Francois Quesnay, the court physician to Louis XV, forcefully argued in favor of laissez-faire free-market principles and were important in developing the case for free-market capitalism. The Physiocrats focused not on the accumulation of gold and silver as the mercantilists had done, but argued that the true wealth of an economy lies in its net product; that is, the surplus produced by the agricultural sector. Their focus on agriculture as the only "productive" class (note they did not view manufacturing as unimportant but did not believe it produced a net product) led them to the free-market principles later expanded on by Smith and others.

The various mercantile regulations in France negatively impacted agriculture in that country according to the Physiocrats. Internal taxes on the movement of grains between regions, for example, were part of the vast mercantilist regulatory structure that hampered the agricultural sector. There were also internal restrictions on the mobility of labor so that farmers in some regions faced labor shortages that could not be corrected by wage movements, so those farmers were forced to reduce production activities. The Physiocrats thus arrived at their free-market views largely through their emphasis on the importance of agriculture, and they subsequently called for lifting restrictions on internal trade and other regulatory burdens that had been hoisted upon the French economy by the mercantilists.

David Hume, a friend and contemporary of Adam Smith, was also a towering figure of the Enlightenment period who helped to usher in the age of capitalism. Indeed, it was Hume who first launched a devastating intellectual attack on the flawed mercantilist trade policy. In what became known as Hume's price-specie flow mechanism, he explained that the inflow of gold and silver (specie) that was central to the mercantilist policies would only generate higher prices throughout the mercantilist economy. As the prices of exported goods were pushed higher, Hume explained that this would make foreign consumers of those exported goods purchase fewer of them. Maintaining a trade surplus indefinitely was therefore not a realistic national economic objective.

Later economists would expand on and modify the principles of market exchange that were laid out in the late 18th century, but the fundamental intellectual shift had been made. England's Industrial Revolution was under way and the transition to modern capitalism was at hand both there and across the ocean in the burgeoning new American states.

The United States

The American economy got its start with a small British outpost in Jamestown, Virginia, in 1607 but was far from a freely functioning capitalist economy at the time. The British colonized America for the purpose of enhancing British economic power in support of its mercantilist interests. Wide-ranging mercantilist restrictions governed the colonial economy, but even the colonists were generally wealthy compared both to other citizens of the world at that time and even compared to some who live in poverty today.

With the emergence of the new nation after successfully breaking away from British rule, modern capitalist institutions began to emerge, setting the stage for the dramatic economic advances of the 19th and 20th centuries. Alexander Hamilton, the first secretary of treasury under President George Washington, was central in the construction of the early American financial and economic system. These pillars of American capitalism helped to create the conditions needed for the dramatic success that was to come. Hamilton worked feverishly to create an American version of the Bank of England, although he was accused by political opponents of harboring British sympathies partly as a result of this.

Hamilton managed to get his wish and the First Bank of the United States was chartered by Congress in 1791. Hamilton also stubbornly insisted on a powerful manufacturing-oriented economy to the dismay of his political opponents (Thomas Jefferson most prominent among them) who favored a rural agrarian economy. Ultimately, the early American financial system that Hamilton helped build proved resilient despite a variety of problems throughout the 19th century. By the end of that century, the American economy was the most powerful in the world.

With the rise of American capitalism came dramatic improvements in the quality of life. Economic historians use not only data on employment, production, and prices to measure economic performance but often use less conventional economic variables such as height, weight, and average lifespan to gauge living standards. According to the Centers for Disease Control, American life expectancy at birth was 47 years in 1900 but had risen to nearly 78 years in 2005. gross domestic product (GDP) per capita was $4,921 in 1900 (measured in 2000 dollars), yet had risen some 6.7 times to $38,291 by 2007. With the material wealth produced by American capitalism comes an improved living standard as measured either by life expectancy, weight, height, or income.

Even more mundane measures of material progress are telling. The U.S. Census Bureau reports that over 70 percent of poor American households (those households below the official poverty level) now have air conditioning; by contrast, only 12 percent of all U.S. households had air conditioners as late as 1960. While some segments of the American population have benefited more than others, there is no denying that all have experienced dramatic improvements in material living conditions over the last century.

Emerging and Transition Markets

Most of the world seems to have accepted that capitalism, despite its flaws, is effective at generating economic prosperity, so countries from Eastern Europe to China have adopted capitalist elements in recent years. In some cases, the market institutions of capitalism have developed spontaneously. In particular, John McMillan described how a tiny clandestine meeting of households in the village of Xiaogang in China's Anhui Province initiated dramatic changes in the economic structure of that country. Embedded in that story is a stark tale of the differences between that singular institution of capitalist economies, private property, and the communal property that had been brought to China by the communists in 1949.

The institution of private property, like all economic institutions, creates incentives to which people respond in predictable ways. Unlike common property rights under which individuals share output equally, private property rights link work effort to reward and thus incentivize people to work hard and produce as efficiently as possible. Private property rights reforms created linkages between effort and reward that were missing under the old common property rights systems of Chinese communism. China has now, as a result of these and other economic reforms, become a major economic powerhouse. The internal changes in the Chinese economy have resulted in a more than tenfold increase in GDP since 1978. According to the *CIA World Factbook*, over 5,000 domestic Chinese enterprises have created direct investments in 172 different countries and regions.

While it holds long-term benefits, transitioning to capitalism is not an easy task. While capitalism is an effective system for generating aggregate wealth, the specifics of the economic institutions that make up an effective system are much more complex. Simply transferring economic institutions that work well in established Western economies to those in the developing world or to transition economies is not sufficient. As such, there are transition economies that have struggled and that continue to struggle. Over time, however, those economies that manage to successfully implement market-based reforms have the potential of reinvigorating their economies and contributing to broad-based increases in the living standards of their citizens.

Critiques

While economists generally see the benefits of free and open exchange in capitalist economic systems, this is not to say that capitalism is a panacea. Historically, the most prominent critic of capitalism was the German economist and philosopher Karl Marx. Marx's critique, like the man himself, was complex and multifaceted but the essence of his objection to capitalism was that it allowed capitalists to exploit labor. The upper-class capitalists (the bourgeoisie) would eventually find themselves in conflict with the free labor force (the proletariat) because of the separation between capital and labor. The conflict is generated by the ever-present push, because of competition among firms in capitalist systems, to replace labor with capital. As the proletariat were increasingly exploited and eventually replaced by capital, they would rise up in revolt and replace the bourgeoisie as the dominant social class. This, in Marx's view, would create a new socialist order. There are, however, a number of contradictions in Marxist theory that have led most economists to reject it as a valid critique of capitalism.

Despite these problems with the Marxist arguments, there are a variety of other critiques of capitalism. For example, capitalist systems are routinely criticized on grounds of inequality. Capitalist economies are structured around a system of rewards and punishments. Those who find better and more efficient ways to produce are rewarded. Henry Ford, for example, became one of America's most successful businessmen by figuring out a better way to manufacture his automobiles through the assembly line. Those who manage to find novel and unique ways of "building a better mousetrap" have incentives to do so because of the potential profits that are realized only with success. Thus, some people in capitalist economies can rapidly acquire enormous amounts of personal wealth. Others are less fortunate and, through either a lack of skill or simply bad luck, end up on the lower end of the income distribution.

Many who object to capitalism point to the wide divergence in economic standing among citizens of capitalist economies and propose policies to try to level out that income distribution. While one might see the benefits of such policies in terms of fairness, there is a risk of destroying or at least reducing the very incentives that make capitalism such a dynamic and powerful system for wealth creation if these policies go too far. Moreover, it is easy to overlook the extent to which the dynamic nature of capitalist economies distorts simple measures of inequality.

There are opportunities to move up the income distribution over time in a capitalist system that may not be available under alternative economic systems. The U.S. Treasury Department has reported that from 1996 to 2005, as in the previous 10-year period, a majority of American taxpayers moved from one income group to another. This study found that about half of taxpayers who began in the bottom quintile of the income distribution moved to a higher income group within ten years. For those in the top income group in 1996, only one-quarter of them remained in that group in 2005, so movement across the income distribution is not always upward. Nonetheless, static portraits of skewed income distributions in capitalist economies are misleading because they fail to capture this income mobility, which is a unique feature of capitalism.

Other Problems

A variety of other problems are associated with economic growth. For instance, China's rapid growth, which resulted from its transition toward market capitalism, has led to some serious concerns about environmental damage. While it may take some time to solve these problems, there are promising market-based solutions to issues of environmental pollution including carbon taxes and cap-and-trade systems.

Even those who are ardent supporters of capitalist economic systems admit that it is a system characterized by the creative destruction described by Joseph Schumpeter. The very dynamism that can generate enormous wealth for individuals can and does destroy old, inefficient methods of production and can thus displace workers in those industries. Yet it is this fundamental dynamism that has made capitalism the most successful economic system for generating material wealth and rising living standards.

Despite the economic growth that finally occurred with the introduction of capitalism, market economies do experience periodic expansions and recessions. Effective government fiscal (tax and spending) and monetary policy may be able to counter these fluctuations, as argued by the economist John Maynard Keynes and by most macroeconomists today. In his classic book *The General Theory of Employment, Interest and Money*, Keynes argued that the government had an important role to play in stabilizing these fluctuations. It could, he argued, "prime the pump" through deficit-spending during economic downturns. By injecting money into the economy through the use of fiscal policy, Keynes believed the government had the ability and obligation to counter the business cycle itself. Keynes was writing in the midst of the greatest challenge to market capitalism ever experienced, the Great Depression.

The "Roaring Twenties" came to an abrupt end in October 1929 when the U.S. stock market crashed. While not the first sign of impending trouble in the economy (the index of industrial production, for example, had turned down in the summer of 1929), the financial market crash was unprecedented and led to widespread consumer pessimism across the country. Whatever its causes, the Great Depression ushered in a serious challenge to capitalism as inflation-adjusted gross national product (GNP) fell by 29 percent between 1929 and 1933 and about one-quarter of the American workforce was unemployed by 1932–33. Waves of bank failures rocked the financial system, wiping out the savings of millions in an era before federal deposit insurance.

Perhaps most important, intellectual challenges to capitalism and its apparent instability threatened to bring down the system altogether. In many ways that are still apparent today, the Great Depression did fundamentally change capitalism. Government did, as Keynes urged, adopt a more interventionist approach to the economy. Both fiscal and monetary policy have been used to counter business cycle fluctuations, although some economists actually blame government intervention for exacerbating the cycles in the economy. Most prominent among those critics was Milton Friedman, whose work with Anna Schwarz on American monetary history blamed monetary policy itself for the downturns. Considerable disagreement remains among economists on the appropriate degree of involvement of the government in the economy.

The Future of Capitalism

True capitalism, in the strictest sense, does not exist; instead, the United States today might be more accurately described as a system of welfare capitalism. That is, we have redistributive income taxes in which the wealthy pay a higher fraction of their income than the poor, along with a wide range of government aid programs. The government itself has become a very large part of economic activity, employing more people than any other sector of the economy (government employment accounts for approximately 16 percent of total nonfarm employment in the United States).

Nonetheless, the basic tenets of free-market capitalism remain in the United States and are emerging in a growing number of countries around the world. Free-trade agreements, robust private enterprise, and sound capitalist institutions all hold promise for the future. Yet there is no reason to think that the very long process of the development of capitalism will stop here. There will undoubtedly be continued challenges and incremental modifications to the system in the years to come.

See Also: Communism; Globalization; Free Markets; Free Trade.

Bibliography. B. Mandeville, *The Fable of the Bees or Private Vices, Publick Benefits* (Clarendon Press, 1732); K. Marx, *Das Kapital* (Penguin, 1992 [orig. pub. 1867]); J. McMillan, *Reinventing the Bazaar: A Natural History of Markets* (W. W. Norton, 2002); M. Postan and H. Habakkuk, *Cambridge Economic History of Europe* (Cambridge University Press, 1967); J. Schumpeter, *Capitalism, Socialism and Democracy* (Harper, 1975 [orig. pub. 1942]); A. Smith, *An Inquiry into the Nature and Causes of the Wealth of Nations* (Modern Library, 2000 [orig. pub. 1776]).

Brandon R. Dupont
Western Washington University

Capital Repatriation

Repatriation is the return of something or someone to its home country, originally referring to the return of soldiers to their homeland at war's end. In economics, it is used to refer to the conversion of money, as when tourists convert their currency back to their native currency when returning from a trip—or when capital from a foreign investment travels back to the country of its source, either through dividends or when a foreign investor sells his holdings.

The repatriation of capital typically refers to the conversion of a foreign investor's earnings into his native currency, which is necessary for him to consider the investment liquidatable. Some governments restrict how much capital can be repatriated in a given time, in order to protect their national economies: If a country that had actively sought foreign investors for a long period were to hit an economic slump, losing that foreign capital to panic selling could be enough to severely exacerbate the slump. Of course, those foreign investors are understandably nervous about investing money they can't get back, and so a balance must be found if investors are to be attracted. Sometimes it is a company trying to attracting the investors, while the government setting the policy remains indifferent—making a compromise position harder to reach.

Countries sometimes temporarily restrict capital repatriation, to prevent such panic or for other reasons. Malaysia suspended capital repatriation in 1998, in the wake of the Asian financial crisis, during which its currency had lost a third of its value and the stock market suffered a 70 percent loss. On the day the ban was lifted a year later, only $328 million was repatriated, of the more than $32 billion that could have been; not only was the attempt to prevent panic selling apparently successful, but the flow of money was delayed to a time when the economy was somewhat more stable. (Many of these foreign investors likely benefited, insofar as in many cases the investments they sold off were worth more in 1999 than they had been at the inception of the ban.) In response to the lift of the ban, the stock market fell less than 2 percent, despite gloomy predictions.

The government at the other end of the repatriation process sometimes enacts special laws, too. When Russia's economy stuttered in the 21st century, a temporary tax amnesty was declared on repatriated capital—meaning that Russians and Russian companies with foreign investments could cash those investments in, turn their money back into Russian currency, and not have to pay taxes on their earnings, if they did so between January and June of 2006. This included previously undeclared income and assets, which in post-Soviet Russia were rampant and had previously been a frequent target of Russian tax authorities. The goal here was simple: To bring money back into the country, for the health of the economy and of the banks (giving them more they can lend out, to the benefit of debtors). Income from repatriating capital is sometimes treated differently from income derived from domestic investments—and when it is, it is usually taxed higher (both to encourage domestic investing and to make up for the lack of tax revenue that would have been generated had the money remained in the country).

In some cases, laws about capital repatriation differ depending on the country to which or from which the capital is repatriated—usually because of treaties between the country in which the investment is made and the country to which the capital is repatriated. Turkey and the United States, for instance, have a bilateral trade agreement protecting the repatriation of capital between the two nations; multilateral trade agreements exist as well. Agreements often also seek to encourage investing by protecting investors from double taxation (in which they are taxed both by their home country and by the country of their investment). In the European Union, investor groups are protected from double taxation but individual investors are not; there are regulations protecting investors within the EU, though, ensuring that tax rates will be uniform.

Developing countries in the midst of reforms or new regimes often encourage capital repatriation for the same reason, as pre-NAFTA Mexico did when it deregulated its economy in the early 1990s, in the attempt to further its recovery from the 1981 financial crisis. Countries wishing to attract foreign investors generally need to offer unrestricted capital repatriation, or at least offer legal guarantees to protect the investors' rights; pursuing a lawsuit in a foreign country is a scenario no investor wants to risk. Often there is a relationship between a country's laws pertaining to capital repatriation and its laws about which domestic companies can be majority foreign-owned; investors typically prefer to deal in countries where foreign control of a company is legal, so that their foreignness doesn't make them a "second-class" investor.

See Also: Asian Financial Crisis; Foreign Direct Investment, Horizontal and Vertical; Investor Protection; Trade Barriers; Trade Liberalization; Trade Sanctions; World Trade Organization.

Bibliography. David F. DeRosa, *In Defense of Free Capital Markets: The Case Against a New International Financial Architecture* (Bloomberg, 2001); Khosrow Fatemi, *Foreign Exchange Issues, Capital Markets, and International Banking in the 1990s* (Taylor and Francis, 1993); Morris Goldstein, *Determinants and Systemic Consequences of International Capital Flows* (International Monetary Fund, 1990); Miles Kahler, *Capital Flows and Financial Crises* (Cornell, 1998); Roger Lowenstein, *When Genius Failed: The Rise and Fall of Long-Term Capital Management* (Random House, 2001); Maxwell Watson, *International Capital Markets: Developments and Prospects* (International Monetary Fund, 1986).

BILL KTE'PI
INDEPENDENT SCHOLAR

Cardinal Health

Nineteenth on the Fortune 500 list, Cardinal Health is one of the leading wholesale drug and health products companies in the world. Ohio businessman Robert Walter founded the company in 1971, as Cardinal Foods, a food wholesaler.

Cardinal Foods expanded its operations throughout the 1970s, ending the decade with its 1979 purchase of the Bailey Drug Company, a regional drug distributor, and reorganization as Cardinal Distribution, distributing both pharmaceuticals and food. In 1983, having expanded to four distribution centers in the Midwest, Cardinal went public. It soon expanded its coverage by buying out the Buffalo-based Ellicott Drug Company in 1984, John L. Thompson Sons & Co. (Peabody, MA) and James W. Daly Inc. (Troy, NY) in 1986, and Leader Drug Stores (Buffalo) in 1987. Most of these acquisitions expanded the pharmaceutical half of Cardinal's business, and the company decided to focus on that exclusively, selling its food distribution operations to Roundy's Inc. Newly reorganized, the company grew rapidly, becoming one of the top two distributors in every region in which it did business by the 1990s.

Expansion from the 1990s on remained within the health services industry. Acquisitions included more drug distributors, but also the Medicine Shoppe pharmacy franchise, the pharmaceutical packing company PCI Services, the surgical product manufacturer Allegiance Corporation, the medical-surgical distribution company Bergen Brunswig, and Owen Healthcare, a hospital pharmacy management company—among others. In 1994 Cardinal Distribution became Cardinal Health Inc., and began to expand beyond its regional coverage to a national focus. By 1996 the company was operating some of its services in England and Germany as well as the United States.

Cardinal.com launched in 2000, the crest of the dotcom boom, and has become the largest healthcare supply online catalogue. After further acquisitions, the company again streamlined, offering its services worldwide under the Cardinal Health brand name, while entering into the pharmaceutical and biotech research field with its acquisition of Magellan Laboratories.

More cutting-edge technologies followed, including the gene insertion techniques developed by 2003 acquisition Gala Biotech. The consultancy firm Beckloff Associates was acquired in 2004 to assist with strategies for bringing biotech and pharmaceutical products to market in the United States, Canada, and the European Union, markets with very specific legal and regulatory concerns.

Increasingly, Cardinal's characteristic approach to doing business and organizing its firm has been to emulate the vertical integration practiced by Andrew Carnegie a century earlier, albeit adjusting for a different industry and different climate. While Pharmacy Benefits Management companies are increasingly affiliated with chains of pharmacies in order to streamline their business, companies like Cardinal go further than that, an approach that could almost be called holistic. As Carnegie controlled the stages of life of steel, and the businesses that shepherded it through them, Cardinal takes a similar approach to pharmaceuticals, maintaining watch over them from their conception and birth through their sale at the point of purchase.

Robert Walter no longer serves as CEO, but has remained on the board of directors, with plans to retire in the summer of 2009.

See Also: Acquisitions, Mergers, and Takeovers; Caremark RX; CVS/Caremark; Vertically Integrated Chain.

Bibliography. Jack W. Plunkett and Michelle LeGate Plunkett, *Plunkett's Health Care Industry Almanac 2009* (Plunkett Research, 2004); S. Rhea, "Cardinal Health Digs Deep," *Modern Healthcare* (April 30, 2007); Robert E. Spekman and Anwar Harahsheh, "Collaborative E-Commerce: Shaping the Future of Partnerships in the Healthcare Industry," papers.ssrn.com (cited March 2009).

BILL KTE'PI
INDEPENDENT SCHOLAR

Caremark Rx

Caremark Pharmacy Services, a subsidiary of CVS Caremark Corporation, is a Nashville-based pharmacy benefit management (PBM) company.

Caremark was the name of a unit of Baxter International (established 1931), a global healthcare company headquartered in Illinois. Baxter's Caremark division (originally an independent company called Home Health Care of America) handled its PBM, the third-party administration of medical prescriptions. Doing business as a Pharmacy Benefit Manager entails processing and paying out prescription claims filed by pharmacies, negotiating with pharmaceutical manufacturers, and acting as the middleman between pharmacies and pharmaceutical companies. This often extends to the PBM being responsible for establishing the formulary: the list of medical prescriptions that will be covered by a given benefits plan (with drugs not on the formulary costing the consumer more). Formularies typically encompass all classes of pharmaceuticals but may not include all brands. While consumers see those elisions in terms of the effect on themselves, from a business perspective there is an important effect on the pharmaceutical company: if a PBM includes Drug X but not Drug Y in its formulary, Drug Y is likely to lose business among the customers affected by the PBM's formulary.

Because of this and the bulk purchases that result from working with a large number of pharmacies, PBMs are able to negotiate lower prices, which can translate into additional services for the customer. As a division of Baxter, Caremark pioneered this style of Pharmacy Benefit Management by offering a mail order pharmacy service in 1985, years before online pharmacies would become a going concern. In the same year, Caremark began offering home care services. In 1991, Caremark acquired what was then the largest PBM in the United States, Prescription Health Services. Baxter spun Caremark off the following year, as a separate publicly held company.

In 1996 Caremark was acquired by MedPartners, a separate company founded by the HealthSouth Corporation. MedPartners went into receivership shortly thereafter, because of difficulties it had managing other operations. By the end of the 1990s it streamlined the company, divested itself of all non-PBM concerns, and renamed the company Caremark Rx. In 2004 Caremark Rx merged with another PBM company, AdvancePCS, retaining key members of management and aspects of its business practices. In 2007 it merged with CVS to form CVS Caremark Corporation.

Caremark Pharmacy Services now operates as one division of CVS Caremark Corporation, managing its PBM operations; the other division is CVS/pharmacy. As a result, Caremark now has an established relationship with the pharmacies with which it does business, further bolstering its bargaining position with pharmaceutical companies. It has become one of the leading PBM companies, working with over 2,000 health plans.

See Also: Cardinal Health; CVS Caremark.

Bibliography. Milt Freudenheim, "Caremark, A Spinoff By Baxter," *The New York Times* (June 13, 1992); Jan Crawford Greenburg, "Healthy Penalties in Caremark Fraud Case," *Chicago Tribune* (June 17, 1995).

Bill Kte'pi
Independent Scholar

Caribbean Community (Caricom)

The Caribbean Community, or Caricom, is a customs union comprised of 15 Caribbean countries. The member states of Caricom are Antigua, Bahamas, Barbados, Belize, Dominica, Grenada, Guyana, Haiti, Jamaica, Montserrat, St. Lucia, St. Kitts, St. Vincent, Suriname, and Trinidad and Tobago. Caricom was established under the Treaty of Chaguramas in 1973 and provides for free trade in goods between member countries and a common external tariff against nonmember countries.

Caricom had its genesis in the failed British West Indies Federation that was established in the late 1950s and represented the first real attempt at Caribbean economic integration. The federation collapsed in 1962, but talks between political leaders in the region on the need to forge closer ties continued at a series of Heads of Government Conferences beginning in July 1963. In December 1965 the

Fishermen in Haiti, where two-thirds of the population work in agriculture and 80 percent live beneath the poverty line. The country is one of the 15 members of the Caribbean Community working toward greater economic integration in the region.

Agreement at Dickenson Bay, Antigua, was executed giving rise to the Caribbean Free Trade Association (CARIFTA). CARIFTA was designed to promote the balanced development of the region by promoting free trade and fair competition. CARIFTA, however, did not function as expected and was replaced by Caricom in 1973.

The Treaty of Chaguramas that established the Caribbean Community and the Caribbean Common Market sets out the following objectives for the Community: (1) the economic integration of the member states by the establishment of a common market regime—referred to as the Common Market, this regime was designed to strengthen trade and economic relations between members, ensure the equitable distribution of the benefits of increased economic activity, and promote economic independence for member countries; (2) the coordination of the foreign policies of member states; and (3)

functional cooperation between people of member states, including greater understanding in the cultural, technological, and social spheres. It should be noted that under the Treaty of Chaguramas the Caribbean Community and the Common Market are distinct legal entities. This institutional arrangement allowed countries to be members of the Community but not the Common Market.

Article 10 of the treaty provides for the establishment of a number of institutions to achieve the objectives set out above. These institutions include (1) the Conference of Ministers responsible for Health; (2) the Standing Committee of Ministers responsible for Education; (3) the Standing Committee of Ministers responsible for Labour; (4) the Standing Committee of Ministers responsible for Foreign Affairs; (5) the Standing Committee of Ministers responsible for Finance; and (6) the Standing Committee of Ministers responsible for Agriculture.

Each member state represented in an institution is entitled to one vote. Recommendations are made by a two-thirds majority that includes at least two of the more developed countries in the region. Recommendations are not, however, binding on member states. Under the terms of the treaty the administrative affairs of the Community are conducted by the Community Secretariat. The Secretariat is based in Georgetown, Guyana, and its duties include facilitating meetings of the Community and its institutions, initiating studies that relate to economic and functional cooperation issues, and undertaking follow-up actions based on decisions taken at meetings.

As noted, the Community and the Common Market are distinct legal entities. In terms of the Common Market, the Common Market Council is the decision-making organ and is comprised of one government minister from each member state. The administrative functions of the Common Market are undertaken by the Community Secretariat.

Under the provisions establishing the Common Market, member states are prohibited, with certain exclusions, from applying import duties on any product of Common Market origin. The agreement also prohibits member states from applying duties or charges on any product exported from their jurisdiction to a member country. Further, under the agreement quantitative restrictions cannot be imposed on any product of Common Market origin.

It should be noted, however, that the agreement does not prohibit a member country from taking appropriate action to address dumping and subsidized imports. A member state of the Common Market is allowed to impose temporary import restrictions on products coming in from other member states if its domestic industry or sector is in difficulty; i.e., is faced with a significant decrease in internal demand. Such restrictions cannot, in general, be imposed for more than 18 months.

Between 1993 and 2000 an intergovernmental task force was mandated to amend the Treaty of Chaguramas with a view to transforming the Common Market and creating the Caricom Single Market and Economy (CSME).

See Also: Common External Tariff; Common Market; Countervailing Duties; Country of Origin; Free Trade; Free Trade Area of the Americas.

Bibliography. Caricom Secretariat, *Treaty Establishing the Caribbean Community* (July 4, 1973); Caricom Secretariat, www.caricom.org (cited March 2009).

CARLYLE FARRELL
RYERSON UNIVERSITY

Carrefour

Carrefour (pronounced kar'fur) is an international hypermarket chain headquartered in Levallois-Perret, France. The name means "crossroads" or "junction" in French. It is the second-largest retailer in the world after Wal-Mart, with 2006 retail sales of $98 billion, income of $2.85 billion, and a compound annual growth rate of retail sales of 2.3 percent over 2001–06. The company reported $1.1 billion net profits during the first two quarters of 2008, a 3.1 percent increase from the year before.

The company was formed by the Fournier and Defforey families in 1959, and opened its first supermarket in Annecy, Haute-Savoie, France, in 1960. In 1963 they created a new store concept, the hypermarket, when they opened in Sainte-Geneviève-des-Bois, France, by selling both food and non-food items in a store with a floor area of 2,500 square meters. It currently operates in over 31 countries using primarily hypermarkets, in addition to other formats such as cash and carry warehouse club, discount department store, supercenter, superstore, and supermarket.

In addition to their presence in France, Carrefour now operates in other countries. In Europe it has opened stores in Spain (1970), Greece (1991), Italy, Turkey (1993), Poland (1997), Belgium (2000), Romania (2001), and Cyprus (2006). In Asia, they operate in Taiwan (1989), Malaysia (1994), China, United Arab Emirates (1995), Singapore (1997), Indonesia (1998), Japan, Oman, Qatar (2000), Jordan, Kuwait (2007), and Pakistan (2008). In the Americas, they have a presence in Brazil (1975), Argentina (1982), Colombia (1998), and in the Dominican Republic (2000). In Africa, their stores are in Tunisia (2001), Egypt (2002), and Algeria (2005).

According to Carrefour's human resources policies, seven specific values are very important to the operations of the company. They include (1) freedom: respecting the customers' freedom of choice by offering a variety of store formats and a diversity of products and brands at various price points; (2) responsibility: fully accepting the consequences of the company's actions on the customers, employees, and the environment; (3) sharing: leveraging the expertise and strengths among these stakeholders to create value; (4) respect: for all parties involved and listening to them and accepting their differences; (5) integrity: dealing honestly and keeping their word; (6) solidarity: helping local economies, businesses, and creating jobs, applying fair trade practices; and (7) progress: encouraging innovation and serving the needs of the people.

Since 2006 the company has continued to consolidate its position in France by opening their 218th hypermarket in the country. In Romania, they continue to solidify their position by the integration of five hypermarkets. In Spain, they have acquired four hypermarkets and two gasoline stations from Caprabo. The group is also involved in developing new concepts, like a mini-hypermarket, Carrefour-Express, and accelerating the pace of organic growth. Overall, this has now created 103 hypermarkets and 1.4 million square meters of new sales floor area in this country.

In Taiwan, they have 45 hypermarkets with the integration of Carrefour Tesco. In Poland, the acquisition of Ahold Polska catapulted the group to second place in the country's grocery retail market, with 194 stores, including 15 hypermarkets. In Great Britain, the company is trying to speed up the information on on-shelf availability through tiered information-sharing with suppliers. They expect to increase the level of integration and enhance collaboration. In the Middle East (including Tehran), Carrefour is in the process of opening shops through Majid al-Futtaim (MAF), its United Arab Emirates–based franchisee.

Despite its successes, Carrefour has also had to withdraw from a few markets, including Chile (2004), the Czech Republic and Slovakia (2005), Hong Kong (1998), Japan (2005), Mexico (2005), Portugal (2007), South Korea (2006), Switzerland (2007), and the United States (1993).

The Carrefour group also owns private labels such as *Produits libres* (free products) used for food products such as oil, biscuits, milk, and pasta sold in unbranded white packages at nominal prices. The

A Carrefour market in a shopping center in Warsaw, Poland, where the company ranks second in the grocery market.

company has also diversified outside the retail market by beginning to offer Carrefour Insurance Services in 1984, and a real estate property company called Carrefour Property in 2004. Carrefour's real estate valuation of its real property holdings is between $29.7 billion and $35.7 billion.

See Also: France; METRO; Wal-Mart Stores.

Bibliography. Carrefour, www.carrefour.com (cited March 2009); N. Bozorgmehr, "Carrefour Aims to Shake Up Iran's Food Industry," *The Financial Times, London*, FT.com (cited March 2009); Katya Foreman, "Carrefour Profits Up," *Women's Wear Daily* (v.196/46, September 2008); Mim M. Spencer, "Earnings Digest: Carrefour Profit Rises, Shares Increase 7.2," *Wall Street Journal* (August 30, 2008).

Abhijit Roy
University of Scranton

Carrying Costs

Carrying cost is an accounting term that refers to the cost of holding a financial position. The position may be purely financial such as the cost of holding securities. Or, it may be the cost of holding physical inventory for manufacturing, for shipping, or for sale. Businesses all over the world have to handle carrying costs in fairly similar ways because they are the natural conditions of business.

In finance the carrying cost of holding a position is determined by whether it is long or short. If the position is long and is on a margin account then the cost of the interest on the margin account is a part of the carrying cost. However, if the position is short then the dividends become a part of the cost to carry that position. Even if the inventory is financial there has historically been a carrying cost between the time of sale and the time of delivery of the security. Computerized transactions may minimize the handling costs but the carrying costs still have to include the costs of transfers.

Another way that carrying costs are figured is in terms of opportunity costs. If an investor takes a position in a market, then other opportunities are excluded from the capital invested or owed because of that position. If the position is in a piece of real estate then the purchase of a house or a building ties up the capital of the investor so that it cannot be used for other investments, thereby creating a carrying cost until the property is sold.

Carrying costs can be viewed as the cost of doing business that may yield a higher rate of return than the return that would accrue from a risk-free interest rate in a security such as a U.S. treasury bill. The investment earns but it is not cost free, even in the case of a treasury bill, because there is the potential for foregone opportunities. In some very secure investments such as money market certificates of deposit there may also be a penalty for early withdrawal.

When the carrying cost of inventory is calculated there are several factors that cost accounting has to consider. These are the investment in the good(s) such as gasoline, or "widgets," or yarn. Then there is the cost of storage of the product. If the product has any significant hazard such as the flammability of gasoline then the cost rises because of the safety requirements that have to be added to the costs. In addition insurance to cover the inventory adds costs.

The cost of storage includes the cost of warehousing goods which in the case of food, furs, or other perishable products means that careful attention has to be given to the care of the product. This means that not only the cost of the storage facilities has to be figured as part of the carrying cost but so is spoilage and the cost of labor to supervise the inventory until it is moved.

In the case of agricultural commodities the cost may be the cost of grain elevator storage or of some other storage facility. The costs of storage are often figured as a percentage of the spot price. If the commodity is some kind of material such as gold or copper the cost of storage is a part of the carrying cost. In the case of perishable goods the carrying cost includes losses due to aging or to shrinkage. For example, bananas may rot or wine may spoil.

Many governments have inventory taxes that go by a variety of names. Many also have an "intangible tax" on positions held in stocks and bonds. In either case the inventory is taxed according to some formula. Taxes also add costs. Some jurisdictions allow goods in transit to be held in a "free port" position, which means they will not be taxed unless consumed or sold locally.

Inventory Models

To avoid carrying costs businesses may use a just-in-time inventory model (JIT). However, this may on occasion cause delays in production, the loss of sales, loss of good will when customers are disappointed, and even the loss of customers. Instead of a JIT model many firms carry excess inventory at a re-order point that keeps a reserve of stock available for production, use, or sale. This is the cyclical stock model for handling excess inventory. This model allows for delivery of the inventory to be restocked even if there are transportation delays. For example an Italian restaurant would be embarrassed if it were to be out of a basic commodity such as olive oil.

The safety stock model for managing inventory used a built-in period of time to account for supplier lead time to manufacture the goods, if necessary, and to deliver them. There may also be variability in the quality controls of supplies that are due to materials and manufacturing methods that can affect sales and later consumption. An example of lead time is the annual manufacturing of influenza vaccine. It has to be manufactured ahead of time and then delivered globally over the flu season.

A third reason for businesses to carry excess inventory is the psychic stock model. When customers, especially at retail businesses, arrive and see only small quantities of stock, they may feel that their choices are too limited and then look elsewhere to make their purchase. An inventory that is excessive will give the perception of plenty, creating a positive attitude among customers that there are plenty of items available from which to choose.

See Also: Cost Accounting; Inventory; Kanban; Manufacturing Strategy; Supply Chain Management.

Bibliography. Edward Frazelle, *World-Class Warehousing and Material Handling* (McGraw-Hill, 2001); Charles T. Horngren, George Foster, and Srikant M. Datar, *Cost Accounting* (Prentice Hall, 2005); Michael R. Kinney and Cecily A. Raiborn, *Cost Accounting: Foundations and Evolutions* (Cengage Learning, 2008); Courtney Smith, *Option Strategies: Profit-Making Techniques for Stock, Stock Index, and Commodity Options* (John Wiley & Sons, Inc., 1996).

ANDREW J. WASKEY
DALTON STATE COLLEGE

Cash Management

In the United States, cash management is actually viewed as a marketing term to describe how businesses promote services to their large customers. When looking at this concept from an international perspective, one could define international cash management as the services provided in the international banking arena to support growth and development of multinationals and developing countries.

As more financial institutions begin to participate in the global economic system, process improvement has led to the reduction of communication and information costs as a result of technology. One of the focal points for many multinational corporations is to have the ability to perform financial transactions outside the United States. It is important for these corporations to have the ability to participate in the international trade process. Some of the key banking services that are needed include letters of credit, wire transfers, collections, and foreign exchange. It is important for an organization to have the ability to wire deposits in a timely manner, have the credibility for banks to provide a letter of credit on its behalf, and collect payments quickly and easily.

Technology has made it possible for financial institutions to offer electronic banking to their customers. Electronic banking, also known as electronic fund transfer (EFT), uses technology as a substitute for checks and other forms of paper transactions. Customers find the service beneficial for several reasons:

- Automated teller machines (ATMs): ATMs are electronic terminals that allow consumers to have access to their funds at any time. Financial institutions provide their customers with a card, which allows them to withdraw money from these machines as well as complete other transactions.
- Direct deposit: Many employers have mandated that employees have their payroll directly deposited into a checking or savings account. Once the funds reach the bank, the bank processes the transactions so that their customers will have access to the funds on the morning of their pay date.
- Pay-by-phone systems: A benefit to consumers is when their banks allow them to pay their bills by calling in the transactions and transferring funds between accounts.
- Personal computer banking: Given the use of technology, many consumers will base their banking selection on whether or not they can perform transactions online using their personal computers.
- Point-of-sale transfers: Consumers can use their ATM cards in many stores to purchase retail items. This process is similar to using a credit card, but the funds will come out of a checking account.
- Electronic check conversions: There are times when a consumer may write a check at a merchant's business and the transaction will become an electronic payment at the point of sale.

With the rise of electronic banking's popularity, financial institutions and consumers must be cautious and protect information that is considered private and privileged. In order to avoid a compromised situation, financial institutions must develop techniques that will assist in authenticating online banking users.

See Also: Currency; Electronic Commerce; Electronic Data Interchange; Globalization.

Bibliography. G. Fest, "Double E-Signatures Double the Security," *U.S. Banker* (v.117/2, 2007); J. Large and W. Large, "Back to Basics: Integrating the Domestic Into the International," in *The 2008 Guide to Technology in Treasury Management* (Euromoney, March 2008); J. Large and W. Large, "International Cash Management Review: Global Solutions to Fit All Sizes," in *The 2008 Guide to Technology in Treasury Management* (Euromoney, March 2008); L. Neville, "After the Crash, Here Comes CASH: Why the World's Biggest Banks Want More From Cash Management," *Euromoney* (v.38/462, 2007).

Marie Gould
Peirce College

While Caterpillar equipment like this is sold in 200 countries, the U.S. market still makes up half of the company's sales.

Caterpillar

Employing nearly 100,000 people all over the world, Caterpillar Inc. is the world's largest manufacturer of equipment for the construction and mining industries, as well as manufacturing turbines and engines. The characteristic yellow paint scheme of much of their equipment is as familiar to people in regions where those industries are dominant as are John Deere green and Coca-Cola red. A Fortune 500 company since the list's inception in 1955, it was ranked 50 in 2008, the most recent ranking. As the leader in its industry, it has been one of the 30 companies of the Dow Jones Industrial Average since 1991.

The innovation with which the company is associated, and has been since its inception, is the caterpillar or continuous track. Such tracks, used instead of wheels, are made of rigid plates connected to each other in a belt, laying flat on the ground as the vehicle moves forward. This allows for a much more efficient distribution of weight, significantly reducing the ground pressure of the vehicle. Caterpillar tracks are most associated with vehicles too heavy to use wheels like cars—such as tanks and construction equipment. Early attempts at making a useful continuous track often referred to them as a type of rail, but unlike rails, they allow for more flexibility of movement, remain with the vehicle, and do not need to be laid down ahead of time. The idea of the continuous track had been in circulation since the 18th century, and became the focus of various inventions during the Industrial Revolution when there was more and more demand for heavy vehicles for which wheels were inefficient or simply unusable.

The first effective model was patented in 1901 by Alvin Lombard, for use with steam-powered log haulers. Two years later, the Holt Manufacturing Company paid Lombard's fees for the right to manufacture equipment using his patented tracks, and subsequently purchased a later British continuous track patent, which included a steering mechanism similar to what's in use today. The designs were combined, the term *caterpillar track* was trademarked, and the Holt Manufacturing Company became the Caterpillar Tractor Company in 1925, through a merger with the C.L. Best Gas Traction Company. Holt tractors using caterpillar tracks were used during World War I, to tow artillery, and the tracks were soon adopted for military tanks.

The Industrial Revolution had permanently changed farming, not only by encouraging larger-scale commercial farms, but by revolutionizing the farm equipment industry. The construction industry was just as affected, and the rise of skyscrapers and other modern building types necessitated the widescale manufacture of equipment. Caterpillar adapted to changing technologies, including the shift to internal combustion engines and diesel engines, and expanded rapidly to meet the construction and manufacturing boom following World War II. Its overseas ventures began in

1950, and it has continued to operate multinationally since. Acquisitions of other companies have fueled Caterpillar's expansion, sometimes into other countries—Hindustan Motors Earthmoving Equipment Division was acquired and renamed Caterpillar India in 2000—and sometimes into new product lines, as with Barber Green (Caterpillar Paving Products since 1991), Elphinstone (Caterpillar Underground Mining since 2000), the acquisitions of many engine and engine component manufacturers, and the 2008 acquisition of LOVAT, a manufacturer of tunnel boring machines. Caterpillar products were responsible for the construction of the Hoover Dam, the tunnel under the English Channel, and the U.S. interstate highway system.

In the 21st century, Caterpillar's products are sold in 200 countries, with about half of its sales accounted for in the United States. Caterpillar dealerships are independently owned and operated, and each dealer has exclusive rights to a given geographical area. Repair and maintenance services are offered by the same local dealerships. Caterpillar's 400 vehicles constitute the bulk of its products, and those for which it is best known, and include both tracked and wheeled vehicles, for construction, excavation, and heavy transport. Many of the engines used in Caterpillar's vehicles are of its own manufacture, and are also sold to other companies for use in locomotives, trucks, and generators.

See Also: Dow Jones Index; Transportation.

Bibliography. Ilan Brat, "Caterpillar Enters Navistar Truck Venture," *Wall Street Journal* (June 13, 2008); "Caterpillar Exits Engine Business, Enters Work-Truck Market," *ENR: Engineering News-Record* (v.260/21, 2008); Tim Kelly, "Squash the Caterpillar," *Forbes* (v.181/8, 2008); Jason Leow, "In China, Add a Caterpillar to the Dog and Pony Show," *Wall Street Journal* (December 10. 2007); Qontro Business Profiles, *Caterpillar Inc.* (Qontro, 2008).

BILL KTE'PI
INDEPENDENT SCHOLAR

CEMEX

One of the largest building supplier companies in the world, Cementos Mexicanos (CEMEX) produces, markets, and distributes cement, ready-mix concrete, and construction aggregates and materials. It is the world's largest trader of cement and clinker, the leading producer of white cement, and the third biggest cement manufacturer, after Holcim Group from Switzerland and French Lafarge. Headquartered in Monterrey, CEMEX employs over 50,000 people and has established a presence in more than 60 countries, mainly in North and South America and more recently in Europe and East Asia.

The history of CEMEX goes back to 1906 with the foundation and opening of one of Mexico's first cement companies, Cementos Hidalgo, the joint effort of an American-born entrepreneur, J. F. Brittingham, and the Garcia family of Monterrey. In these first years of operations, business blossomed and production capacity more than doubled. The Mexican Revolution forced the company to suspend production and distribution in 1912, as energy supplies failed and communications infrastructure was destroyed. Full resumption of activities was delayed until 1921. Meanwhile, Cementos Portland Monterrey was founded in 1920 by Lorenzo H. Zambrano and family. Following the economic crisis of the Great Depression and a regional war of prices, the two companies celebrated a historic merger that, on January 4, 1931, gave birth to a new company: Cementos Mexicanos.

The next four decades witnessed the rise and consolidation of CEMEX in the northeast of Mexico and the beginning of the conquest of the national market. Expansion of production was first driven by successive enlargements and the modernization of the Monterrey plant—new, larger, and more efficient kilns—and the opening of cement mills in Torreon and Ciudad Valles. This, accompanied by an aggressive commercial strategy, positioned CEMEX as market leader in the northern states of San Luis Potosi, Durango, Tamaulipas, Coahuila, and Zacatecas in addition to its home stronghold Nuevo Leon. In the 1960s, the strategy was coupled with plant acquisitions in Guadalajara, Leon, Ensenada, and Yucatan in central and southern Mexico. CEMEX had moved from the local to the multiregional, and by 1970 it produced and sold over 1 million tons per year of Portland cement, which represented more than 10 percent of the Mexican market.

Growing company size and markets posed new challenges. According to business historian Mario Cerruti, CEMEX contracted with the American management-consulting firm Cresap, McCormkick and Paget to effect structural administrative reorganization. Realization of scale and scope economies led to vertical-integration strategies that translated into the acquisitions of concrete, aggregates, and ready-mix firms at the national level. The financial requirements of such integration and plans to buy Cementos Guadalajara—an important rival—led CEMEX to go public on the Mexican stock exchange in 1976. By 1985, productive integration and the inauguration of the Huichapan plant in Hidalgo, the most modern in Mexico at the time, made CEMEX a key player in the domestic market, accruing around 33 percent of total production. The next challenge was the global market.

International Expansion

In the aftermath of the 1982 debt crisis and the trade liberalization and inflow of foreign capital and competition that ensued, CEMEX realized the threats and opportunities that globalization brought about. The strategy to face it was twofold. First, there was a need to dominate the national market effectively, to prevent foreigners from entering CEMEX's historical territory. Second, there was the opportunity to export and to grow in the American and European markets via the acquisition and improvements in the efficiency of foreign plants. To accomplish the former, CEMEX bought Anahuac in 1985 and the other Mexican giant Tolteca in 1989, turning into the sixth largest producer in the world. To achieve the latter, CEMEX increased exports to the United States throughout the 1980s in an effort to meet a surge in demand from the neighboring economy that offered high prices and paid in hard currency. Successful entry into the United States through the construction and purchase of mills and the creation of distribution networks in California, Arizona, Texas, Florida, and New Mexico signaled that CEMEX had competitive prices and supplied good quality products.

In 1992 CEMEX entered the European market, buying Spanish Valenciana de Cementos and Sanson, making it the world leader in white cement production. Two years later it acquired Cementos Bayano in Panama and Vencemos in Venezuela, followed by Diamante and Samper in Colombia in 1996. The buying spree has continued, adding plants in the Philippines, Indonesia, Chile, and Costa Rica. CEMEX maintains

high profit margins and operative efficiency levels. It has become one of the most competitive global firms in the industry.

See Also: Economies of Scale; Economies of Scope; Globalization; Mexico.

Bibliography. Boletín del Colegio de Ingenieros de Ingeniería Mecánica, Eléctrica y Profesiones Afines de León AC, "CEMEX," *En Contacto* (v.10/117, 2007); CEMEX, "CEMEX. Our History," www.cemex.com (cited March 2009); Mario Cerruti and Juan Ignacio Barragán, *CEMEX: Del Mercado Interno a la Empresa Global* (Proceedings of the 5th Brazilian Congress of Economic History, 2003); Datamonitor, "CEMEX, S.A. de C.V. Company Profile" (June 12, 2007).

Carlos Andres Brando
London School of Economics

Central America

Central America is the isthmus connecting North and South America, and though geographically considered part of the North American continent, it is rarely included in cultural, economic, or political mentions of North America. The North American Free Trade Agreement, for instance, does not include any Central American country. Some discussions of Central America include Mexico, which shares a Spanish heritage with the Central American nations that it does not with the bulk of North America (though this glosses over the long Spanish history of much of the United States and the interconnections of American and Mexican history). With the exception of Belize and Panama—neither of which yet existed—the nations of Central America were members of the Federal Republic of Central America, a democratic state that existed from 1823 to 1840, after the region became independent from Spain. Political instability prevented not only the survival of the republic, but the planned construction of an inter-oceanic canal, an idea that was not realized until the construction of the Panama Canal in the 20th century.

That was not the last gasp of Central American integration, though. Throughout the 20th and 21st centuries, region-wide institutions have developed, moving toward the possibility of a European Union–like regional unity. The Central American Court of Justice that was instituted in 1907 was first proposed by Mexico and the United States, and was hashed out at the Central American Peace Conference that was hosted by Secretary of State Elihu Root. Rather than attempt political union at that time, Root and others suggested that they agree to a common court of justice. The experiment lasted 10 years, until Nicaragua terminated its involvement and the other countries decided not to continue without it; member state governments were unhappy with the extent of the court's jurisdiction, while judges were unhappy with their governments' influence on their decisions.

In the aftermath of World War II, as the world reorganized itself in light of the end of European empires and the beginning of European union, and amidst the growing global conflicts of the Cold War, more serious discussions of integration began. Costa Rica, El Salvador, Guatemala, Honduras, and Nicaragua signed a 1951 treaty creating the Organization of Central American States (ODECA) to promote regional cooperation, and reinstituted a regional court, the Corte Centroamericana de Justicia (CCJ). In 1960 the governments of Central America made plans for the Secretariat for Central American Economic Integration, the Central American Bank for Economic Integration, and the Central American Common Market, but when war broke out between Honduras and El Salvador in 1969, integration came to a halt.

It was revived again in 1991, in the aftermath of the Cold War. The Central American Integration System (SICA) was instituted by the countries of Central America with the addition of the Caribbean nation of the Dominican Republic. The CCJ's role was refined to promote peace among member-states, and has jurisdiction over cases between member-states, between member- and non-member states when the latter consents to jurisdiction, between any state and any resident of a member-state, and cases that involve the integration process. Significantly, it also has the power and responsibility to consult with the Supreme Courts of member-states, for the purpose of promoting a common legal philosophy in the region. There is also a Central American Parliament (Parlacen), with directly-elected members, though Costa Rica has not yet ratified its charter and remains a non-participant. Though not as unified as the European Union, SICA certainly represents an intent and goal of Central American unity to a similar degree.

Of the Central American nations, Guatemala is the most populous with about 13 million people, though El Salvador, at half the size, is twice as densely populated. Primarily rural Belize, with 300,000 people, is both the smallest and by far the least densely populated (13 people per sq. km versus the 330 of El Salvador). Critical to the Central American economy is the Panama Canal, which remains one of the most ambitious engineering projects ever undertaken. Proposed for years, not until the advances of the late Industrial Revolution (as well as the resulting adoption of faster ships and impatience at having to travel around the continent) did the canal come to fruition. The canal saves some 8,000 miles of travel, and even today, when air travel has reduced the role of water travel, the canal remains so busy and such an integral part of the international shipping industry that ships over a certain size (the Panamax size, the largest the canal can accommodate) are called super-Panamax ships. In 2008, 14,702 ships passed through the canal, roughly a 10-hour journey.

Country Profiles

Belize is the only Central American country where English is the official language (Spanish, and the local Creole, are "recognized languages"), a reflection of its heritage as a part of the British Empire from 1638 to 1981, during most of which time the country was known as British Honduras. Though one of the least-populated countries in the world, it also has one of the highest population growth rates. The economy is focused on the private sector, especially agriculture; bananas and sugars account for the largest part of the economy. The climate, coast, and Mayan ruins have all contributed to the tourism industry, which grows steadily. The ramifications of the 2006 discovery of oil in the Mennonite town of Spanish Lookout have not yet become clear. The Belize Dollar is pegged to the U.S. dollar at 2:1.

Though Costa Rica has a higher per-capita GDP than many other developing nations, it suffers from rampant inflation (just under 10 percent) and chronic trouble with its infrastructure. Sixteen percent of the country lives below the poverty line, but with the economy growing steadily, it has pioneered social aid and welfare, with its per capita spending on the poor and struggling comparable to that of Western European

Guatemala has an urgent need to develop new exports. In this December 2007 photo, the USAID Director for Guatemala and U.S. Senate Majority Leader Harry Reid tour a vegetable packing plant in Chimaltenango that specializes in nontraditional vegetables.

countries. In an effort to attract foreign investment, tax exemptions have been offered, and companies like Procter & Gamble and Intel have recently opened large facilities. The currency is the colon, which trades at a floating exchange rate, a free market initiative that the government hopes will discourage the long practice of citizens relying on American dollars instead of domestic money.

El Salvador faces significant economic and social problems. More than 30 percent of the population lives below the poverty line, with underemployment widespread (unemployment hovers around 6 percent). One of the poorest Latin American countries, El Salvador is frequently troubled with natural disasters—not only hurricanes, but the earthquakes that result from being on the Caribbean Plate. The government is committed to free market initiatives and has privatized the banking system and much of the infrastructure, including telecommunications. The domestic currency, the Salvadoran colon, was abandoned in 2004, three years after the U.S. dollar was

adopted as legal tender and the unit of currency for all accounting and bookkeeping purposes.

The developing company of Guatemala has 29 percent of its population living below the poverty line, and a trade deficit so significant that remittances from Guatemalan expatriates—sending money back home to their families—outweigh export and tourism revenues combined. The export sector of the country is in flux, struggling to find a successful export good. Currently most exports are agricultural—fruits, vegetables, flowers, coffee, and sugar—with textiles secondary. The currency is the Guatemalan quetzal, previously pegged to the U.S. dollar but currently traded at a floating exchange rate.

Honduras enjoys greater economic growth than most of Latin America, about 7 percent a year—but half the country lives below the poverty line, and unemployment sits at a staggering 28 percent. The country is deeply in debt, with international subsidies necessary to keep the government-operated electrical services operating, and price controls on basic commodities to avoid commodity crises. Nevertheless, there are significant natural resources, especially biological resources, from which the country can benefit once its infrastructure is improved and economy stabilized. The currency is the Lempira, which trades at a floating exchange rate.

Primarily an agricultural country, Nicaragua is known worldwide for its Flor de Cana rum; other sources of revenue include cash crops like coffee, sugar, and tobacco, fisheries, mining, and remittances from expatriates. As much as 28 percent of the population lives below the poverty line, and half of them are either unemployed or underemployed. Most of the indigenous population lives on less than $1 a day. Like much of the region, though, Nicaragua has experienced steady economic growth in the 21st century, though thanks to the infrastructure damage and general problems of the civil war of the 1980s, the economy is best described as "recovering" more than "developing." The cordoba trades at a floating exchange rate.

The fastest growing economy in Latin America after Peru, Panama nevertheless has a 28 percent poverty rate. The presence of the canal plays into the fact that the economy is mainly service-based, but other major services apart from shipping and trading include banking, finance, and tourism. Trade is high and inflation low. The balboa is pegged to the U.S. dollar, but the dollar itself is used as often as domestic currency.

See Also: Caribbean Community (Caricom); Central American Common Market; Company Profiles: Central America and Caribbean; Company Profiles: South America; Costa Rica; El Salvador; Guatemala; Panama.

Bibliography. John A. Booth, Christine J. Wade, and Thomas W. Walker, *Understanding Central America: Global Forces, Rebellion, and Change* (Westview Press, 2005); Eliana Cardoso and Ann Helwege, *Latin America's Economy: Diversity, Trends, and Conflicts* (MIT Press, 1995); Jeffry A. Frieden, Manuel Pastor Jr., and Michael Tomz, *Modern Political Economy and Latin America: Theory and Policy* (Westview Press, 2000); Hector Perez-Brignoli, *A Brief History of Central America* (University of California Press, 1989); Ralph Lee Woodward, *Central America: A Nation Divided* (Oxford University Press, 1999).

Bill Kte'pi
Independent Scholar

Central American Common Market

The Central American Common Market (CACM) is a trade organization originally created for Guatemala, El Salvador, Honduras, and Nicaragua. These four nations signed the General Treaty on Central American Economic Integration on December 13, 1960, in a meeting held in Managua, the capital of Nicaragua. The objective of CACM was to improve the living conditions in Central America by unifying the economies of the four countries and promoting joint development of Central America. The treaty was ratified by Guatemala, El Salvador, and Nicaragua in May 1961 and came into force on June 3, 1961. Honduras ratified the treaty in April 1962 with certain reservations. Costa Rica also joined the CACM in 1963. CACM collapsed in 1969 because of an armed conflict between El Salvador and Honduras, but was reinstated in 1991, when Panama also agreed to cooperate with the association even though it is not a member. The CACM countries cover an area of 163,172 square miles with a population of almost 38 million.

The CACM attempted an import substitution industrialization using protectionist barriers to guard the local industries from global competition. The CACM experiment seemed to be successful as intraregional trade increased significantly, from US$33 million in 1960 to US$1.1 billion in 1980. The intraregional exports as a percentage of total exports grew from 7 percent in 1960 to 26 percent in 1970. By 1967 about 95 percent of the traded goods were duty free. In addition to providing a large protected market for regional goods, CACM also promoted industrial investments and infrastructure development by providing fiscal incentives and creating several organizations for specific infrastructure projects.

Even though CACM made significant progress as mentioned above, the member countries could not carry forward the momentum to take the organization to the next level of economic integration. Several factors led to this stagnation. First, the member states could not undertake structural reforms in their economies, which could have provided a level playing field for all the members and an opportunity to create an economic union. Second, the trade policies were such that they promoted growth of consumer goods industries for which capital-intensive machineries needed to be imported from outside the trade bloc. This meant that CACM countries still faced the foreign exchange problems that they had before the formation of the trade bloc. Third, the member states had some significant differences in terms of their size, economic status, and relations with other countries. The CACM led to further rise in disparities, which resulted in Guatemala, El Salvador, and Costa Rica becoming net creditors and Nicaragua and Honduras becoming net debtors. Besides unbalanced trade, there were also issues related to migration and protection of investment, particularly between Honduras and El Salvador. The disparities were so stark that they led to a four-day war between Honduras and El Salvador in July 1969. In the same year, Honduras quit the CACM, failing to secure concessions from other member states in its favor.

Despite Honduras's exit from CACM, trade continued to grow between other countries in the 1970s. However, a debt crisis and the civil wars in El Salvador and Nicaragua in the 1980s led to a steep fall in intraregional trade. There were no further efforts to revive the organization and the treaty expired in 1982. Efforts were again made to revive the CACM during the eighth summit of Central American Presidents, held in June 1990. The European Economic Community gave active assistance by providing a 120-million European Currency Unit support fund to develop a new payment system for trade. The new payment system was designed to manage creditor-debtor relations on a multilateral basis rather than a bilateral basis. During the 10th summit of Central American Presidents, held in July 1991, the five original signatories to the General Treaty admitted Panama as a nonmember state, but with full privileges in terms of preferential treatment in trade with the member states.

The utility of CACM has been undermined by several other trade agreements in the region, including the North American Free Trade Agreement (NAFTA) between the United States, Canada, and Mexico, and the Dominican Republic–Central America–United States Free Trade Agreement (CAFTA-DR) between the Dominican Republic, Costa Rica, Guatemala, El Salvador, Honduras, Nicaragua, and the United States. CAFTA-DR was signed in August 2004, and ratified by the United States in July 2005 and by all other countries by the end of 2007. All the CACM member countries are also members of CAFTA-DR, making the future role and objective of CACM unclear.

See Also: Central America; Economic Union; Free Trade; Free Trade Zone; North American Free Trade Agreement; Trade Bloc.

Bibliography. CIA, "Appendix B—International Organizations and Groups," *The World Factbook* (cited March 2009); Sebastian Edwards, "Latin American Economic Integration: A New Perspective on an Old Dream," *The World Economy* (v.16/3, 1993); Library of Congress Federal Research Division, "Honduras," *Country Studies*, memory.loc.gov/frd/cs (cited March 2009).

AJAI GAUR
OLD DOMINION UNIVERSITY

Central Banks

Since the establishment of the first central bank in Sweden in 1668, the number of central banks has increased to 178 (in 2008). The emergence of new sovereign states saw a corresponding increase in the number of central banks. Central banks have legitimate power to create national currency, an integral part of monetary sovereignty. These banks play pivotal roles in domestic and international economic management. In the past, they financed government war expenditures and economic development projects. Today, the central banks' main responsibility is to keep the rate of consumer-price inflation low and stable to accomplish and maintain economic and financial stability.

The majority of central banks are state-owned. Thus, a central bank governor is essentially a government official. Politicians and governors may have different and conflicting policy preferences. In times of conflicting views between a governor and politicians, central bank independence (CBI) vis-à-vis political authority becomes significant. The key factor behind the move to increased independence has been the theoretical argument that an independent central bank restricts the avenues for political interference in monetary policy decision making. In doing so, monetary policy making can be insulated from electoral effects (i.e., political business cycles) and partisan politics (i.e., economic growth and employment-oriented policies of leftist parties). Central bankers with legal autonomy from the executive and legislative branches of the government are assumed to have the ability to follow objectives that may conflict with these branches.

Not surprisingly, there has been a significant worldwide trend toward increased central bank independence, transparency, and accountability through legal reforms and actual practices. Introduction of legal reforms granting independence to central banks has been a universal temptation for the majority of sovereign states. Especially from 1990 onward, CBI has become a legal standard, and there has been an international trend toward legal independence. The governments in both developed and developing countries deliberately reformed the statutes of central banks to grant them more autonomy in order to achieve and sustain their primary objective: price stability.

A normative support for CBI revolves around the assumption that central bank governors, who place a greater weight on price stability, are more averse to inflation than politicians. However, the trends toward CBI are built on flawed neoliberal economic theory. It is assumed that inflation is caused by money supply growth, which is determined by the central bank. Conversely, in a world of global finance where financial capital moves freely, money supply increase and credit creation are not solely under the control of the central banks. Further, this view omits other inflationary pressures such as increases in primary goods and energy prices.

In regard to empirical evidence, early studies found that CBI and inflation are strongly negatively correlated in developed economies. These findings are questioned by subsequent studies that there is no correlation and causal link between CBI and inflation. Further, there has been no empirical evidence showing a negative correlation between CBI and inflation in developing economies. Nevertheless, in spite of the questions about the theoretical foundations and the mixed empirical evidence for the merits of CBI, the dominant practice of monetary governance is based on the maintenance of price stability where an independent central bank plays a pivotal role.

Transnational central banking culture is reflected in CBI reforms and promoted by ideational entrepreneurs that include organizations such as the International Monetary Fund (IMF), World Bank, and Bank for International Settlements as well as individuals such as governors who are the members of the translational epistemic community of central bankers. However, the critiques of CBI argue that the delegation of monetary policy to a central bank does not apoliticize monetary policy and has important distributional effects. It is argued that the CBI reflects the interests of international financial capital.

There is also a trend toward greater transparency in central banking. On the theoretical level, it is widely held that transparency in monetary policy can enhance the effectiveness and credibility of monetary policy. Monetary policy is considered effective when central banks influence investors' medium-term expectations about the path of policy rates over time. In doing so, central banks have an impact on long-term bond yields and other securities. Such effectiveness can be achieved with the credibility of monetary policy if central banks' actions match their public statements. On the empirical level, it is widely accepted that there is a cross-country positive correlation between transparency and inflation.

Finally, increased independence of central banks raises concerns about accountability. It is believed that independent central bankers should be accountable to elected politicians, who are accountable to the electorate. In doing so, central bank decisions regarding public goods such as price stability can be fully legitimate. More recently, renewed financial turmoil in global markets brought important questions about the role of central banks to strengthen the global financial system and their appropriate role as the lender of last resort. The financial upheaval of 2008 fostered the belief that central bankers would have to act more globally by introducing easier cross-border borrowing.

See Also: Capital Controls; Discount Rate; Inflation; Interbank Market; Interest Rates; Money Supply.

Bibliography. Sang-Kun Bae and Ronald A. Ratti, "Conservative Central Banks and Nominal Growth, Exchange Rate and Inflation Targets," *Economica* (v.75/299, 2008); C. E. V. Borio, Gianni Toniolo, and Piet Clement, *The Past and Future of Central Bank Cooperation* (Cambridge University Press, 2008); Sven-Olov Daunfeldt and Xavier de Luna,

"Central Bank Independence and Price Stability: Evidence from OECD-Countries," *Oxford Economic Papers* (v.60/3, 2008); J. De Haan, S. C. W. Eijffinger, and S. Waller, *The European Central Bank Credibility, Transparency, and Centralization* (MIT Press, 2005); S. C. W. Eijffinger and P. M. Geraats, "How Transparent Are Central Banks?" *European Journal of Political Economy* (v.22, 2006); Helder Ferreira de Mendonça and José Simão Filho, "Macroeconomic Effects of Central Bank Transparency: The Case of Brazil," *Cato Journal* (v.28/1, 2008); Anne Dolganos Picker, *International Economic Indicators and Central Banks* (Wiley, 2007); Lorenzo Smaghi, "Central Bank Independence in the EU: From Theory to Practice," *European Law Journal* (v.14/4, July 2008); J. Stiglitz, "Central Banking in a Democratic Society," *De Economist* (v.146/2, 1998); M. Watson, "The Institutional Paradoxes of Monetary Orthodoxy: Reflections on the Political Economy of Central Bank Independence," *Review of International Political Economy* (v.9/1, 2002).

CANER BAKIR
KOÇ UNIVERSITY

Centralization

Centralization in the context of an organization relates to the concentration of decision-making authority at the higher levels of management. Its converse, decentralization, is the dispersal of authority from the higher levels to the lower levels of management. If more authority to make decisions is concentrated at the top, we say that the organization is centralized. Real-life organizations do not have absolute centralization or decentralization. The extent of centralization or decentralization varies across organizations, across different divisions and departments, and in the same organization over a period of time. Large organizations generally are believed to allow greater centralization than small organizations, relying on more formalization—the use of rules, procedures, and paperwork. Small organizations can use personal observations and direct contact and so tend to rely on centralization. Thus, there are degrees of centralization and decentralization.

In the contemporary context, there is a bias toward decentralization because it offers several benefits to organizations. Probably the biggest benefit is that decentralization enables delegation of authority from senior managers to middle-level and first-line managers. This makes it possible for the senior managers to concentrate their time and energy on more important tasks of formulating strategies and plans. Delegation of authority to lower levels also allows middle-level and first-line managers to develop their managerial capabilities as they make decisions pertaining to their area of work. This has an added benefit because lower-level managers are in direct contact with the situation requiring decisions. Decentralization speeds up the process of decision making—a vital factor in making organizations respond quickly to emerging situations. An organization that adopts a policy of decentralization could foster a healthy, achievement-oriented organizational climate.

It is not as if centralization is undesirable. Some situations may, in fact, favor centralization. These are situations where the senior managers are required to make decisions and act quickly without waiting for their subordinates' acceptance. Then there are situations where decisions pertaining to the whole organization need to be taken and individual divisions and departments cannot make such decisions. The senior managers also have a better appreciation than the lower level of managers about the external environment, enabling them to make better decisions.

There are many factors that have to be taken into account before an organization centralizes or decentralizes decision making. First of all are the costs involved. If the decision requires heavy investments, then it is more likely that the senior managers would make it. Some organizations also adopt centralization because they wish to have uniformity of policy throughout the organization. How competent the lower-level managers are also determines the degree of centralization and decentralization. The more competent the lower managers, the more likely is the organization to decentralize. Control systems in organizations also often dictate that several aspects of decision making be centralized.

Organizations that operate globally face choices between balancing authority between headquarters and the subsidiaries. When a corporation establishes a subsidiary in a foreign country, its managers must decide how much control they need to maintain over the subsidiary's managers. A headquarters–foreign subsidiary control relationship can be defined in terms of the degree of centralization or decentralization. The question here is how much authority will be retained by headquarters and how much will be delegated to the subsidiary.

Frequently, there has to be a healthy compromise between local autonomy for the subsidiaries and centralized control by headquarters. Such compromise can vary over time depending on the requirements of the overall strategy of the organization. In situations where more authority is decentralized at the subsidiary level, the managers may be able to provide faster response to local conditions but may become too independent and therefore less accountable to headquarters. Where authority is centralized at the headquarters level, there might be better control and uniformity in decision making but this may stifle initiative and prevent empowerment of subsidiary-level managers. For example, Asea Brown Boveri (ABB), a multinational corporation with headquarters in Sweden and Switzerland, attempts a healthy balance between centralization and decentralization by delegating full authority and responsibility for product categories on a worldwide basis to the subsidiaries. ABB headquarters acts as a facilitator of information and knowledge flows between the subsidiaries. Similarly, Honda, Matsushita, Hewlett-Packard, and Dow also grant autonomy to their subsidiaries by empowering their local boards of directors to make decisions and respond to local conditions.

See Also: Accountability; Centralized Control; Control Systems; Empowerment.

Bibliography. Richard L. Daft, *Organization Theory and Design* (South-Western Thompson Learning, 2004); Ricky W. Griffin and Michael W. Pustay, *International Business: A Managerial Perspective* (Pearson Prentice Hall, 2007); Don Hellriegel, Susan E. Jackson, and John W. Slocum, Jr., *Management: A Competency-based Approach* (South-Western Thompson Learning, 2005); Carl. A. Rodrigues, "Headquarters–Foreign Subsidiary Control Relationships: Three Conceptual Frameworks," *Empowerment in Organizations* (v.3/3, 1995).

Azhar Kazmi
King Fahd University of Petroleum & Minerals

Centralized Control

Centralized control, in the context of organizations, means control exercised by a central authority such as top management. Contrary to centralized control, we have the concept of decentralized control where the function of control is delegated to lower levels of management.

In reality, there is no absolute centralized or decentralized control. Having either could be unworkable. Absolute centralized control would keep all decisions related to organizational matters in the hands of the top management, hindering effective functioning of an organization. Extreme decentralization of control, on the other hand, would disperse the decision-making authority within the organization, leaving nothing in the hands of top management. Such a situation would lead to utter chaos as the different units of an organization could work at cross-purposes, each of them not knowing where the other is headed. In practice, therefore, organizations have a combination of centralized and decentralized control.

Organizations need to decide on their optimum level of centralization and decentralization of decision-making authority. Larger organizations would tend to have a higher level of decentralization as such a pattern could facilitate quicker decision making and better responsiveness to the external environment. Older organizations, too, could have a higher level of decentralization as managers have gained enough experience for handling decision-making authority. An organization that has managers of higher-level competence can practice a higher level of decentralization as it has enough confidence to let lower-level managers deal with decision making. Organizations that have managers who have yet to gain the requisite level of competence may have to wait to decentralize the authority for decision making to lower levels.

Controlling is an essential function of management along with planning, organizing, and leading. Controls perform the useful function of ensuring that performance in an organization conforms to the standards so that the objectives of the organization can be achieved. In practice, controls operate through control systems that include rules and regulations, standards, recruitment and selection procedures, and training and development. There are several methods of control that include financial and accounting controls such as budgeting and financial analysis, and physical controls like production control and quality control, and newer methods such as activity-based costing and balanced scorecards.

Any control system operates in the form of a control cycle. This control cycle includes the setting of standards of performance, measurement of performance, comparison of actual performance with standards, and taking corrective action if needed. This is a continuous process and hence called the control cycle.

Centralized and decentralized control has relevance to other aspects of an organization apart from its structure and systems. For instance, information systems within organizations are also designed keeping in view the need for centralization and decentralization of information processing. System design has to deal with the issue of control structure. A centralized information system would thus be a system where information processing is provided by a central facility, while in a decentralized information system such processing would be distributed to various parts of the organization.

Another frequent reference to centralized and decentralized control is found in the case of organizations such as the military, particularly the air force. Centralized control in the context of an air force would mean that the authority to carry out air operations is vested in the hands of a central authority such as an air commodore who provides detailed step-by-step instructions that are to be followed by dispersed air force units. On the contrary, under decentralized control, the authority of decision making related to air operations would be delegated to the front-line airmen on the assumption that they would be best equipped to understand the situation at hand.

Multinational Corporations

Centralized and decentralized control issues also arise in the case of organizations that operate globally. These issues pertain to questions such as: To what extent will the authority for decision making relating to various departments and functions in the organization be centralized at the headquarters or decentralized to the level of subsidiaries? An example of such an issue is that of human resource (HR) management within multinational corporations. From the perspective of headquarters, decentralization may lead to loss of control over subsidiaries while centralization

affords economy of operations. From the subsidiaries' view, centralization at the level of headquarters may stifle initiative, creativity, and innovation. Each corporation has to evolve its own unique balance of centralization and decentralization with regard to its HR management policies depending on its strategies. With the advent of Web-based HR applications, it is now possible to centralize payroll, timesheet administration, performance appraisals, annual leave applications, and virtually every other aspect of HR administration. In a situation where operations are spread all over the world, the availability of the internet is a big benefit to multinational corporations.

The debate over the comparative merits of centralization and decentralization of control as well as some other dimensions of organizations, such as power, authority, decisions, and functions is ongoing and inconclusive. Ultimately, it must be a choice somewhere between the pressures on the organization to innovate or economize.

See Also: Accountability; Centralization; Control Systems; Empowerment.

Bibliography. Richard L. Daft, *Organization Theory and Design* (South-Western Thompson Learning, 2004); Don Hellriegel, Susan E. Jackson, and John W. Slocum, Jr., *Management: A Competency-based Approach* (South-Western Thompson Learning, 2005); Richard M. Hodgetts, Fred Luthans, and Jonathan Doh, *International Management: Culture, Strategy and Behavior* (McGraw-Hill Irwin, 2006); Carl A. Rodrigues, "Headquarters–Foreign Subsidiary Control Relationships: Three Conceptual Frameworks," *Empowerment in Organizations* (v.3/3, 1995).

Azhar Kazmi
King Fahd University of Petroleum & Minerals

Certificate of Origin

A Certificate of Origin is a formal document that authenticates the country of origin of merchandise. The Certificate of Origin (CO) is an import document; the import authority of a country establishes the requirements for it. While Certificates of Origin vary across countries, they have a common set of elements. The certificate has a variety of functions that relate directly to the trade agreements between the importing and the exporting nations: Determining whether merchandise has restricted entry, validating compliance to quota arrangements, or establishing the correct duty of inbound merchandise. Trade regions like NAFTA and the EU require Certificates of Origin to determine whether merchandise should receive the preferential treatment accorded member nations. To be valid, an officially sanctioned organization as determined by the importing country must issue the Certificate of Origin.

Certificates of Origin, despite broad variations across countries, have a set of common elements: Buyer and seller information, an indication whether the exporter is the manufacturer of the goods, the actual country of origin of the goods, a description of the goods, and the Harmonized System (HS) code for the goods. The HS code is a universal commodity code like the standard industrial classification codes (SIC). It functions as a standardized classification system for coding transactions across borders in order to track information and simplify compliance with trade agreements, e.g., collecting tariffs. It is important to note that the descriptions and amounts on the CO must match the comparable entries on the invoice. Discrepancies on certificates can delay or deny entry of goods and result in substantial costs to the exporter.

In order to enforce trade agreements, countries need to have an accounting system for trade. The data for this accounting system comes from trade documents like the Certificate of Origin. There are three common uses for Certificates of Origin. First, they can signal to an import authority that an importer is attempting to bring restricted goods into the country. Restricted entry problems can easily occur when there are more than two countries involved in the trade and when the countries have different trade regimes. Canadians, for example, can import Cuban cigars into Canada; U.S. firms may not import Cuban goods. To prevent a company in Canada from importing Cuban cigars and then reexporting them to the United States, the importer requires a Certificate of Origin. Similarly, import authorities use Certificates of Origin to maintain quota systems. A country may require that a prearranged percentage of an assembled auto may come from foreign parts. This requires a complicated accounting sys-

tem to assure auto assemblers meet this standard. Most commonly, nations use Certificates of Origin as the basic documentation tool for tariffs. For some trade partners, goods may enter the country duty free (U.S. goods enter Canada without duty). It is important to the importing country that only goods from approved trading partners in pre-approved HS codes enter without paying duties.

Some countries participate in complex multilateral trade agreements like the European Union or the North American Free Trade Agreement (NAFTA). In these agreements, internal member nations receive preferential treatment relative to nonmembers. This preferential treatment usually includes the minimization or elimination of tariffs and quotas. These trade agreements often require a specialized form like the NAFTA Certificate of Origin. The NAFTA CO is an especially complicated trade document. It requires delineation of origination materials (raw materials or assemblies that come from within NAFTA), non-originating materials (similar to above but that come from outside NAFTA), and regional value content—in essence, the percentage of a good that comes from origination materials. Companies that purposely provide false information can receive fines from $10,000 to $100,000 in addition to paying the required tariffs.

Each importing country designates an officially sanctioned organization to issue certificates. The official body may be a governmental organization such as a national customs bureau or a nongovernmental organization like a chamber of commerce.

See Also: Export; Harmonized System; Import; North American Free Trade Agreement; Tariff; Trade Pact.

Bibliography. J. Anson et al., "Rules of Origin in North-South Preferential Trading Arrangements with an Application to NAFTA," *Review of International Economics* (2005); P. Brenton and M. Manchin, "Making EU Trade Agreements that Work: The Role of Rules of Origin," *The World Economy* (2003); J. M. Finger, "The Political Economy of Administered Protection," *American Economic Review* (1982); J. Foley, *The Global Entrepreneur*, 2nd ed., (Jamric Press, 2004); E. G. Hinkleman, *International Trade Documentation* (World Trade Press, 2002).

George M. Puia
Saginaw Valley State University

Chaebol

The Korean word *chaebol* is used to refer to the highly diversified business groups contributing to the post–World War II industrialization in South Korea. Family ownership has not been significant in chaebols; despite this, the control of chaebols by founding families is typically due to cross-shareholding. For example, the chairman of a chaebol and his family might hold 10 percent of three core firms, and the three core firms in turn could own equity in some 20 or 30 affiliates. The chaebol family will therefore have effective control of an affiliate when the core firm holds 50 percent of it singly or jointly.

The roots of chaebols can be traced to the Land Reform Bill in 1950, an attempt by the Korean government to compensate the landlords' loss of land with opportunities to invest in former Japanese-owned plants. The chaebols were further involved in Korea's export-led development strategies since the 1960s. By entering into industries selectively targeted by the government, they were able to obtain cheap loans, tax deductions, tariffs, and subsidies that provided the basis for their economic influence in the economy. The top 20 chaebols' shares of Korean manufacturing output increased from 7 percent to 29 percent between 1972 and 1982.

During the 1980s, the Korean government switched to more indirect and functional support of strategic industries. In research and development (R&D), tax deductions were replaced by allowances of tax-free reserves for expenses incurred. Korean chaebols responded to the policy incentives and upgraded themselves; examples of such strategic orientation included Samsung and LG's investment in the forefront of display and semiconductor technology. The chaebols' investment in R&D also enabled them to pursue growth strategies via integration into the technologically sophisticated inputs. By the early 1990s, the chaebols accounted for Korea's significant shares in world exports within categories such as consumer electronics goods; paradoxically, chaebols were having one of the lowest corporate profitability levels in the world. The chaebols' technological capability also paved the way for their expansion abroad during the 1990s.

Overall, chaebols' influence in the Korean economy can be seen in the fact that the top five chaebols accounted for approximately 10 percent of gross national product by 1998. In addition, they had diversified vertically and horizontally, the latter being in unrelated business areas. Hence, the chaebol Samsung consists of affiliates ranging from consumer electronics, electronic components, shipbuilding, insurance, hotels, department stores, public relations, and amusement parks.

The acceleration of liberalization within the Korean economy under its first civilian president, Kim Young Sam, in 1993 had led to a massive inflow of foreign capital into Korea. The chaebols therefore switched from their traditional reliance on government loans to foreign loans in financing, which resulted in a surge of debt/equity ratios before the Asian financial crisis. The top 10 chaebols attained a debt/equity ratio of over 500 percent in 1997, which could be considered unusually high among Asian firms.

The reform program initiated by the Korean government after its consultation with the International Monetary Fund (IMF) led to changes in chaebols; the most notable are the decrease of debt/equity ratios and the use of flexible labor strategies. The financial restructuring was achieved by the public listing of stocks and the sales of affiliates. The flexible labor strategy, on the other hand, derived from the U.S. system and was related to the elimination of non-market based practices such as lifetime employment and a seniority-based system for the first time in chaebols' history. The chaebols practiced mass redundancy among permanent employees; these employees were replaced by temporary employees. The chaebols also required remaining employees to take early retirement.

Other new measures included performance incentives and the use of stock options. The restructuring in chaebols, coupled with the reshaping of corporate cultures, has resulted in profitability among the best achievers. For example, Samsung Electronics is currently one of the most profitable firms in Asia and produces quarterly profit figures to market analysts. Though the conception and growth of chaebols during the postwar period had been intertwined with the policy initiatives of the Korean government, their future growth will depend on their abilities to observe market discipline and compete in the fast-changing environment. Only the most efficient chaebols will survive in the long run.

See Also: Hyundai Motor; Korea, South; LG; Samsung Electronics; SK.

Bibliography. S. J. Chang, *Financial Crisis and Transformation of Korean Business Groups* (Cambridge University Press, 2003); D. K. Chung and B. Eichengreen, *The Korean Economy Beyond the Crisis* (Edward Elgar, 2004); C. Harvie and H. H. Lee, "Export-Led Industrialization and Growth: Korea's Economic Miracle," *Australian Economic History Review* (2003); Heon Joo Jung, "Competition and Corporate Governance in Korea: Reforming and Restructuring the Chaebol," *Journal of East Asian Studies* (v.7/3, 2007); S. H. Jwa and I. K. Lee, eds., *Competition and Corporate Governance in Korea* (Edward Elgar, 2004); Sook Jong Lee, "The Politics of Chaebol Reform in Korea: Social Cleavage and New Financial Rules," *Journal of Contemporary Asia* (v.38/3, 2008); OECD, *Economic Survey* (1994).

DENISE TSANG
UNIVERSITY OF READING

Channels

A channel means a narrow but deep route connecting two entities. Business entities use channels to connect themselves with their customers. Most businesses today use two broad categories of channels: communication channels and distribution channels. They use communication channels to carry various kinds of information and messages to different stakeholders. Some examples of commonly used communication channels are television, radio, texts, e-mail, phone, newspaper, fliers, posters, mail, and billboards. Businesses use distribution channels to take their goods and/or services from their premises to the customer's/end user's premises. This entry focuses on distribution channels. Distribution channels are also known as marketing channels or trade channels. They are constituted by a set of interdependent entities called intermediaries or channel partners. Intermediaries operate primarily at two levels: wholesale and retail.

Wholesale intermediaries are those who sell goods and/or services for resale to other intermediaries such as retailers or for business use to industrial, institutional, governmental, or agricultural firms. They may also sell to other wholesalers but are not supposed to sell to individual consumer end users. Wholesale intermediaries may be owned by producers/manufacturers or could be totally independent business entities. Manufacturer's sales branches or offices are examples of manufacturer-owned wholesale intermediaries. Merchant wholesalers, agents, and brokers are examples of independent wholesalers. Merchant wholesalers use many different names to identify themselves: wholesaler, jobber, distributor, industrial distributor, assembler, importer, or exporter. Wholesalers provide market coverage to producers and manufacturers, develop sales contacts, hold inventories, provide credit, and offer customer support.

Retail intermediaries are those who primarily sell goods and/or services directly to individual consumers for personal or household consumption. Some of them, like Office Depot, also sell for business use. They assume many forms and vary in size and format. Retail intermediaries may also be owned by producers/manufacturers or could be totally independent business entities. They may be as small as a convenience store selling daily necessities in the neighborhood or as gigantic as the mass merchandise chains Wal-Mart and Carrefour.

Retailers offer different levels of services ranging from full service to self service. Some of them have physical as well as virtual presence; others like Amazon.com offer only online shopping. A specialty store like The Body Shop offers a narrow product line whereas a department store like Sears offers many product lines. Other major types of retail intermediaries include supermarkets, superstores, discount stores, category killers, off-price retailers, and catalog showrooms. Charles Y. Lazarus has stated that the role of the retailer, regardless of size or type, is to interpret the demands of customers and to find and stock the goods these customers want, when they want them, and in the way they want them. Retailers' power and influence in marketing channels have significantly increased over the last few decades. Indeed, a few retail intermediaries have grown much bigger than several manufacturers supplying them.

Channel partners are tied together with others in distribution of goods and/or services through the allocation of specific roles and tasks. Such allocation creates a channel structure for the firm. Wide variations in channel structures can be seen across the world due to differences in psychological, social, cultural, political, legal, economic, and other demographic factors. Ensuring that the goods and services efficiently reach the target customers when, where, and how they want them is the real function of channels.

See Also: Advertising; Communication Challenges; Distribution; Marketing; Retail Sector; Wholesale Sector.

Bibliography. A. T. Coughlan, E. Anderson, L. W. Stern, and A. I. El-Ansary, *Marketing Channels* (Pearson, Prentice Hall, 2006); Charles Y. Lazarus, "The Retailer as a Link in the Distribution Channel," *Business Horizons* (1961).

SONJAYA S. GAUR
AUCKLAND UNIVERSITY OF TECHNOLOGY

This 2006 Chevron gas station design in Redwood City, California, incorporates solar panels on its rooftops.

Chevron

Chevron Corporation, one of the world's leading energy companies, is headquartered in San Ramon, California, and operates in more than 100 countries. Among its major business activities are exploration and production of oil and gas, refining, transport, and marketing of oil and oil products, manufacturing and sales of industrial chemicals, as well as power generation.

The company's business is quite diversified, in terms of both production capabilities and geographic spread. For example, in 2007 in crude oil and natural gas production Chevron produced 2.62 billion barrels of net daily oil-equivalent, with approximately 70 percent of the volume coming from more than 20 countries other than the United States. Throughout the years, the company also has invested heavily in various capital development projects in oil and gas production, transportation, and sales all over the world, including such countries as Angola, Bangladesh, Kazakhstan, Indonesia, and Nigeria. In addition, Chevron has a wide marketing network in 84 countries with approximately 24,000 retail sites and 13 power-generating properties in the United States, Europe, and Asia. In 2007 Chevron made around $214 billion in revenues and nearly $19 billion in net income worldwide.

The company emphasizes four main corporate-level strategies that it is pursuing on a global basis:

(1) financial-return objective: aimed at sustainable financial returns that enable Chevron to outperform competition; (2) major business strategies, upstream: aimed at profitable growth in core areas, especially in the natural gas business; (3) major business strategies, downstream: focused on improving returns and selective growth, with a concentration on synergies, and on continuing investment in renewable energy sources; and (4) enabling strategies companywide: focused on investing in people to achieve corporate strategies outlined above, as well as on building organizational capabilities and leveraging technologies.

Chevron, originally known as Standard Oil of California (Socal), was created as a result of the forced breakup of Standard Oil in 1911. After several transformations occurring mainly due to its many concession ventures in the Middle East, by 1980 the company became entirely owned by the Saudi government. In 1984 the cooperation between Socal and Gulf Oil created the largest merger in world business history at the time, and as a part of the merger, Socal changed its brand name to become Chevron Corporation.

Among Chevron's largest business dealings in the next two decades, the merger with Texaco in 2001 was one of the most prominent mergers and acquisitions to date. Although this merger prompted a brief change of name—to ChevronTexaco—the company decided to return to its Chevron name in 2005, with Texaco and its subsidiaries still remaining a brand under the Chevron Corporation. The same year, Chevron entered into another significant deal, a merger with Unocal Corp., which, thanks to Unocal's sizeable geothermal operations in southeast Asia, made Chevron the biggest producer of geothermal energy in the world.

In addition to its core business, Chevron also develops and commercializes advanced and alternative energy sources such as fuel cells, photovoltaic technology, and hydrogen-based fuel. Overall, the company is investing about $300 million a year into alternative fuel sources research and development and has created a biofuels business unit, implicitly indicating that it is becoming a part of Chevron's core business model. In general, all sorts of biofuels and clean technologies are an important part of the company's business.

Similar to other companies in the petroleum industry that are often a target of much criticism for worldwide political influence and environmental damage, Chevron has been particularly blamed for numerous ecological disasters caused by its allegedly unsound exploration and maintenance practices. For instance, the company has been accused of polluting water supplies in several world regions, including North America (dumping a significant amount of toxic waste and illegally bypassing wastewater treatment facilities in Richmond, California), Africa (Angola), and Asia.

Political influence exerted by "big oil" also remains one of the major criticism points, and has recently emerged once again in regard to Chevron's attempts to impact the industry reorganization plans in California. Even though many corporations and various interest groups participated in the reform planning process, mainly Chevron enjoyed tremendous success in affecting the final report through the work of its paid lobbyist and lawyers. To return the favor, the company has contributed more than $700,000 to governor's committees, the California Republican Party, and a governor-controlled political fund.

In order to combat negativity and boost its public image, Chevron, among many other initiatives, pledged to fight global warming and tackle the issues of alternative energy sources. The company has recently created a new public internet-based forum called willyoujoinus.com, where everyone is invited to join the discussion to help find new, clean, and more accessible ways to provide power to the world and its ever-growing demands.

See Also: Downstream; Ecuador; Environmental Standards; ExxonMobil; Total; Upstream; United States.

Bibliography. BBC News, "Chevron Claims Energy Debate," news.bbc.co.uk (cited March 2009); Chevron Corporation, www.chevron.com (cited March 2009); Tom Chorneau, "US: Chevron Donates to Schwarzenegger, Gets Removal of Restrictions on Oil Refineries in California," *Associated Press*, corpwatch.org (cited March 2009); Will You Join Us, www.willyoujoinus.com (cited March 2009).

VLAD VAIMAN
REYKJAVIK UNIVERSITY

Chicago Mercantile Exchange

The Chicago Mercantile Exchange (CME) is an American financial trading place based in Chicago. Often called MERC, it was founded in 1898 as the Chicago Butter and Egg Board. When the CME began it was a not-for-profit organization. Its purpose was to trade futures contracts on agricultural products. In 1919 it became the Chicago Mercantile Exchange.

In 1987 the CME began use of its Globex trading system. It then began operating an electronic trading system in futures contracts in 1992. By 2004 the system recorded its one billionth trade through the Globex system, which is a modified version of the NSC system developed in Europe for European exchanges. In 2006 the CME improved its ability to electronically trade in interest rate swaps with the purchase of Swapstream, a London based company. Electronic trading entered the CME's electronic system on January 13, 2008. Several months prior to this CME was engaged in developing a commodities futures platform with the Singapore Exchange.

A major step in modernizing the corporate organization of the CME occurred in November 2000 when the CME was demutualized and became a joint stock company owned by shareholders. The CME's demutualization was the first time in American financial history that an exchange had demutualized. In December 2002 it went public. In July of 2007 it completed its merger with the Chicago Board of Trade (CBOT) to become the CME Group through an exchange of

$8 billion in stock. On August 18, 2008, CME's shareholders approved a purchase of the New York Mercantile Exchange (NYMEX) for $8.9 billion in cash and CME stock. The CME and NYMEX systems are to be fully integrated by October 1, 2009. With the NYMEX's trade in energy products, metals, and other commodities, the CME's range of commodities and volume will increase dramatically.

The system of trading developed and used by the CME since its beginning was the open outcry system of trading. The system uses humans to stand and cry out bids to buy or sell. It appears chaotic but allows hundreds of auctions to be conducted simultaneously throughout the trading day. The New York Mercantile Exchange, the Chicago Board of Trade, and exchanges in other countries use a similar system.

The outcry system of trading places traders in a trading pit from which they cry out prices and quantities. These are interpreted by other trades as offers to buy or sell specific quantities of the commodity offered. Because the price is "discovered" through the outcry of traders it provides an efficient way to exchange contracts for commodities for future delivery or for speculation. Because of the din created by many traders shouting out orders to buy or sell, a system of complex hand signals called *arb*, short for *arbitrage*, is used.

The open outcry trading floor system of the CME is linked to the electronic trading platform called the "Globe." It allows those who have signed up to trade to do so electronically from anywhere on the globe. The open outcry system is being replaced by the electronic systems because they are cheaper, faster, and can handle larger volumes. They are also not as vulnerable to manipulation of the market by traders, brokers, or dealers who are making a market. Defenders of the open outcry system argue that personal contact allows traders to read the intentions of others in the market and to make position adjustments accordingly. Currently 70 percent of the CME's trade is through its electronic Globe system.

The CME has the world's second largest futures exchange, and the largest in the United States. It provides a marketplace for trading futures and options on futures. Trade on the CME is in equities, stock indexes, foreign exchange currencies, commodities, and interest rates. It also provides a marketplace for trading in weather and in real estate derivatives. The financial instruments that it uses are either cash or primary instruments (loans, deposits, or securities) or derivatives. The derivatives can be traded through the exchange market or through the over-the-counter (OTC) market. Derivatives are financial instruments that derive their market price from an underlying financial instrument. Stock options are derivatives as are interest rate swaps.

On October 7, 2008, the CME partnered with the Citadel Investment Group to create an electronic trading platform (a trading floor) for trading credit default swaps (CDS). The CDS trading will allow banks and others to spread the risk of default by governments, companies or consumers. The move is expected to provide liquidity in the market for standardized contracts and future derivative markets. The Clearing Corporation will provide clearinghouse services with the Depository Trust and Clearing Corporation providing management of assets.

See Also: Futures Markets; Stock Exchanges; Wall Street.

Bibliography. David Griesing and Laurie Morse, *Brokers, Bagmen, and Moles: Fraud and Corruption in the Chicago Futures Markets* (John Wiley & Sons, 1991); B. Joseph Leininger, *Lessons from the Pit: A Successful Veteran of the Chicago Mercantile Exchange Shows Executives How to Thrive in a Competitive Environment* (B&H Publishing, 1999); Jeffrey L. Rodengen, *Past, Present and Futures: Chicago Mercantile Exchange* (Write Stuff Enterprises, Inc., 2008); Robert A. Tamarkin, *MERC: The Emergence of a Global Financial Powerhouse* (Harper Business, 1993).

ANDREW J. WASKEY
DALTON STATE COLLEGE

Chicago School/Chicago Boys

The Chicago School was a group of highly influential economists affiliated with the University of Chicago in the last century. The heyday of this group was in the 1950s when economists teaching in the economics department joined forces with professors in other academic areas in the graduate school of business and the law school to set up a group outlook on economic issues based on monetary theory. More than two-thirds of the members of the faculty agreed on the ideas of the Chicago school of thought. These ideas rest on two pillars: (1) enhancing the Marshallian price theory tradition and (2) developing and applying empirical methods for more rigorous testing of theoretically derived hypotheses.

In the public perception, the Chicago School is frequently associated with antitrust economics, but Edward Chamberlain, among others, made an earlier reference to the "Chicago School of Anti-Monopolistic Competition." Two of the leading researchers of this group were awarded the Nobel Prize in Economics: George J. Stigler (1982) and Milton Friedman (1976). Indeed, the track record of winners of the Nobel Prize in Economics affiliated with the University of Chicago is impressive: in addition to Stigler and Friedman, and up to 2008, the list comprises Paul A. Samuelson (1970), Kenneth J. Arrow (1972), Friedrich A. von Hayek (1974), Tjalling Koopmans (1975), Herbert A. Simon (1978), Theodore W. Schultz (1979), Lawrence Klein (1980), Gérard Debreu (1983), James M. Buchanan, Jr. (1986), Trygve Haavelmo (1989), Harry M. Markowitz (1990), Merton H. Miller (1990), Ronald Coase (1991), Gary S. Becker (1992), Robert W. Fogel (1993), Robert E. Lucas, Jr. (1995), Myron S. Scholes (1997), Robert A. Mundell (1999), Daniel L. McFadden (2000), James J. Heckman (2000), Edward C. Prescott (2004), and most recently, Roger B. Myerson (2007).

Principles

Most of the latter economists contributed to fields other than the antitrust issue. Interestingly, Friedrich A. von Hayek was affiliated with the University of Chicago from 1950 to 1962, but he is acclaimed as one of the most prominent members of the Austrian School. Besides his doctrines, he rejected the empirical evaluation of hypotheses and is, therefore, in conflict with the Chicago School's most important principles, namely

- taking a polar position among economist opinions to advocate an individualistic market economy,
- emphasizing the relevance and usefulness of the neoclassical theory,
- describing both an ideal market and the real markets by expressing the features mathematically,

- seeing and applying economic principles to various aspects of human life, and
- insisting on rigorous empirical testing of all hypotheses.

Particularly the latter principle was not commonly accepted among economists at that time, but was emphasized as a frequently neglected element of Positive Economics by Milton Friedman. This empirical testing, in combination with a sophisticated use of mathematics for describing the markets as well as the (aggregated) behavior of agents within these markets, provided members of the Chicago School with a clear advantage in the competition of scientists. By avoiding economic value judgments and establishing operationally meaningful theorems, Positive Economics advanced the dominating research paradigm, although Normative Economics had prominent supporters, notably the Keynesian School. Thus, the Chicago School's credos that competitive markets are the best way to organize economic activities, that most types of governmental regulations are harmful to economic development, and that the monetary system, particularly the amplitude of money supply, has a substantial impact on a nation's economic conditions, are not an opinion that is integrated into economic analysis, but rather the result of applying formal and empirical methods to issues of interest.

However, the results are grounded in the idea of a market, as described in *The Wealth of Nations* by Adam Smith, including the legitimacy of self-interest as well as the allocation of resources and distribution of income by market mechanisms. Self-interest is a productive force because it provides clear and agreeable guidelines for the behavior of agents in the markets. Contrastingly, if self-interest triggers or enforces regulations of market mechanisms, efficiency will be reduced. By emphasizing the efficiency of market mechanisms, a second value proposition is identified. Both mathematical-formal analysis and empirical testing are restricted to the consequences of decisions made or the market mechanisms under consideration. From an economics point of view, these procedures, which are not based on value judgments, enable a comprehensive understanding of market mechanisms. However, this is a teleological position, disregarding the deontological contents of economic analysis. In terms of philosophy of science, this is a value proposition, but it is not an economics value proposition.

A different thread to the Chicago School is made up by the methodology predominating in the "good old" Chicago School's analysis. In the neoclassical tradition, they simplified the analysis with the "as if" assumptions *as if* they were true. Moreover, their analysis is at the core of a mechanistic conception of economic relations and interactions. Evolutionary simulation casts doubt on this mechanistic conception, and particularly the complexity of real markets is counter to traditional formalism. In addition, the basic assumption of striving for rational decisions in market interactions is being challenged.

Nevertheless, besides its success in economic research, the Chicago Tradition has had a substantial impact on political decisions affecting national and international markets. During the Reagan administration, the economic policy of the United States was broadly in line with the Chicago School's doctrines. Moreover, Thatcherism in the United Kingdom, transforming the British economy from one of the weakest into one of the strongest in Europe, attributes its success to seizing the results and suggestions of the Chicago School. Currently, many of the nations in the European Union are privatizing governmental services, such as the postal service, and aim to shift from governmental pension systems to private pension schemes, as advised by Milton and Rose Friedman in their book *Free to Choose*.

The Chicago Boys

The most prominent impact of the Chicago School has been the policy of the Chicago Boys in Chile. The Chicago Boys were a group of students at the Universidad Católica de Chile, who enthusiastically worked on Milton Freedman's Capitalism and Liberty ideas. In 1957–70, about 25 of them prepared their doctoral degrees at the University of Chicago, mainly under the supervision of Arnold Harberger in the Latin American Finance Workshop and Milton Friedman in the Money and Banking Workshop. During the Pinochet era, the following Chicago Boys made a substantial impact on Chilean economic policy: Pablo Baraona (Minister of Economy, 1976–79), Alvaro Bardón (Minister of Economy, 1982–83), Sergio de Castro (Minister of Finance, 1977–82), Jorge Cauas (Minister of Finance, 1975–77), Martín Costabal (Budget

Director, 1987–89), Sergio de la Cuadra (Minister of Finance, 1982–83), Maria Teresa Infante (Minister of Labor, 1988–90), Miguel Kast (Minister of Planning, 1978–80), Juan Ariztía Matte (Private Pension System Superintendent, 1980–90), Juan Carlos Méndez (Budget Director, 1975–81), José Piñera (Minister of Labor and Pensions, 1978–80, Minister of Mining, 1980–81), and Emilio Sanfuentes (Economic advisor to Central Bank). Another prominent Chicago Boy is Hernán Büchi (Minister of Finance, 1985–89), who studied for his Ph.D. at Columbia University, but agreed with the Chicago School's doctrine and came second in the 1989 Chilean presidential election.

The Chicago Boys attained economic prosperity (the Chilean miracle) in comparison to other Latin American countries and became renowned for the coherence of their political decisions. However, their success was criticized because of income inequality and for admitting foreign companies to reduce profits and related national tax burdens to zero by calculating transfer prices departing from market prices.

The Tradition

The Chicago School is an economic tradition, but one that has also contributed to related disciplines, particularly sociology and law. Not surprisingly, the University of Chicago hosts one of the most prestigious law schools. These are the rules that are still guiding the excellent research process of the Chicago School: (1) they apply their analysis to all parts of (economic) life; (2) they leave no place for prestige, rank, past honor, or personal sensitivities in their economics workshop system; (3) they require strong discipline and methodological rigor. Since these rules are said to be still effective at the University of Chicago Graduate School of Business, this breeding ground will continue to contribute in two ways to contemporary economics and international management. On the one hand, they are likely to come up with path-breaking models. On the other hand, the results of the "good old" Chicago School highly impacts recent discussions of supernational institutions and organizations, including the International Monetary Fund and the World Trade Organization, supporting international trade, environmental protection, and healthcare.

See Also: Antitrust Laws; Chile; Financial Market Regulation; Free Markets; Transfer Pricing.

Bibliography. A. Duhs, "Elegance in Economics," *International Journal of Social Economics* (1994); J. Frank, "Natural Selection, Rational Economic Behavior, and Alternative Outcomes of the Evolutionary Process," *Journal of Socio-Economics* (2003); M. Friedman, "The Methodology of Positive Economics," *Essays in Positive Economics* (University of Chicago Press, 1953); M. and R. D. Friedman, *Free to Choose: A Personal Statement* (Harcourt, 1980); H. Laurence Miller, "On the 'Chicago School of Economics,'" *Journal of Political Economics* (1962); Raza Mir, Ali Mir, and Mehdi Hussain, "Re-Examining Imbeddedness: A Critical Analysis of Global Strategic Management," *Academy of Strategic Management Journal* (2006); M. Nerlove, "Transforming Economics: Theodore W. Schultz, 1902–1998. In Memoriam," *Economic Journal* (1999); J. Van Overtveldt, *The Chicago School: How the University of Chicago Assembled the Thinkers Who Revolutionized Economics and Business* (Agate B2, 2007); R. A. Posner, "Theories of Economic Regulation," *Bell Journal of Economics* (1974); G. Stigler, "The Theory of Economic Regulation," *Bell Journal of Economics* (1971); J. Stiglitz, *Making Globalization Work* (Penguin Books, 2006).

RALF WAGNER
UNIVERSITY OF KASSEL

Child Labor

Children have been used as cheap labor from the earliest times of human existence. Historically children were viewed by parents as a source of labor on farms or in areas of "woman's work." Grown children were the "social security" of their parents for whom they would provide. In a great many areas of the world today this system of children as a labor asset is still the norm. It has only been with the rise of modern industrial societies where the economic surpluses are sufficiently large that a leisure class of children attending school instead of working has been affordable.

Well before 1900 reformers began a campaign to reduce or exclude the labor of children from the economy of the United States and from those in Europe. The Census of 1900 reported that over two million children were working on the streets or employment centers of the United States. The report sparked a national movement to reform child labor practices.

The Keating-Owen Act of 1916 (Wick's Bill) signed by President Woodrow Wilson was declared unconstitutional by the Supreme Court in the case of *Hammer v. Dagenhart* (247 U.S. 251) in 1918. The Court ruled that the law exceeded the authority of Congress to regulate interstate commerce. In December 1918 Congress passed the Revenue Act of 1919, which included a second child labor law. The law known as the Child Labor Tax Law sought to regulate child labor through taxation. However, the Supreme Court ruled the law unconstitutional in *Bailey v. Drexel Furniture Company* 259 U.S. 20 (1922). The Court reasoned that the power of Congress was being excessively widened so that it interfered with the right of the states to regulate local trade.

In 1924 Congress proposed the Child Labor Amendment to the United States Constitution. The Amendment was actively opposed by some business interests. It failed in the 1920s and 1930s; however, today it is in a state of legal limbo because it could be adopted in the future. Ten more states are needed for its adoption. Because the Child Labor Amendment would lodge exclusive jurisdiction over child labor in the Congress of the United States many states have rejected it. The Amendment was a response to decisions of the Supreme Court of the United States that upheld child employment and rejected state legislative efforts to ban or limit child employment practices. The latest case before the Amendment was proposed was the Supreme Court's decision declaring the Child Labor Law unconstitutional. The law sought to regulate the employment of children in canneries, mills, mines, quarries, manufacturing centers or workshops if under the age of 14. In 1941 the Supreme Court reversed its decision on the *Dagenhart Case* in *U.S. v. Darby Lumber Co.*, 312 U.S. 100. The ruling upheld the constitutionality of the Fair Labor Standards Act, which is still in force today.

Child labor opponents were successful in eliminating the labor of small children from the economy by the 1940s. The exclusion of children from the economy as laborers reduced the supply of labor to the benefit of adults and included them in the controls put on labor sought by labor unions. Today the exclusion of children from the labor markets in Western countries is enforced through child labor laws that impose penalties for employing underaged workers. Household chores, family farm work, and work in a business owned by the child's family is generally excluded.

Child labor laws were enacted to achieve several policy goals. The main goal was the protection of children by restricting their hours of work and the type of work they could perform. More specifically child safety was sought by keeping them from working in places or with things that could put them at risk in hazardous or unsanitary conditions; or by protecting them from overly strenuous or immoral working conditions. Occupations that are dangerous to children include work that poses a physical danger. Operating a log shredding machine, or handling explosives in a quarry are such occupations from which children have been excluded. In general child labor legislation has been applied to commercial enterprises. However, in many jurisdictions restrictions are also placed on nonprofit organizations as well.

Child labor legislation applies to minors and not to children who have reached the age of their majority. However, the age of a minor is defined by these laws which can vary from state to state in the United States or from country to country around the world. For example while 18 is the normal age for a young person's majority, some industries like the steel industry have required parental permission for young people under the age of 21 to work in areas that are hazardous.

Laws in many jurisdictions are clear that parents may not contract away their children through a binding employment contract. The law operated on the basis that benefits conferred by law to children many not be nullified by claims to parental rights. In some states for a minor to work in certain businesses not just parental permission is required. In addition there may be specific conditions, supervision, or other conditions and approvals that are required. Child actors are required to have a tutor who teaches them as a requirement of employment. The requirement is one that must be ratified by the parents. For example children who work may not have their compulsory education disrupted by work. They must be enrolled in a school whether public or private or educated by a tutor.

Employer Responsibilities

When children are employed even with a legal permit it is incumbent upon the employer to assume extra responsibilities. Employer responsibilities include seeing that all employment instructions are carefully issued and followed. The delegation of this duty to subordinates is not sufficient in law to absolve the employer of responsibility if an accident were to happen to the child or if the child were to cause some serious damage in the course of employment. If an employer is given legal notice of failure(s) to engage in due diligence in the employment of a child or children then sterner measures can be employed to force compliance. Among the sterner measures may be penalties or stricter regulations of the actions of subordinates.

Employers who are found guilty of employing under aged children or for work proscribed for children can be punished according to law. Those found guilty of technical violations may be held accountable and their certificate of employment for the child(ren) may be nullified. The penalties for which employers found liable for violations of child employment laws can include criminal penalties, or civil penalties including revocation of a license to employ them. The fact that the actual work was performed through a sub-contracting party such as a natural person or a corporation will not be sufficient to excuse an employer from responsibility as the original employer. Some states still hold employers responsible even if the work methods of independent contractors are outside of the control of the child's employer.

Employers who "in good faith" hire a minor are not excused from liability in case of injury to the child. The representation of good faith is not a defense even if the child lied about his or her age. In the case of injury parents are not necessarily to be held liable for the injury. Tort actions initiated against the party causing the injury may be only for the benefit of the child and not for any losses to the parents. This is because they are third parties that the law is not seeking to protect as it is seeking to do for children.

Child Labor in the Third World

In Third World countries where child labor laws are weak or nonexistent it is common to see babies and small children used as beggars. Their pitiful conditions are used to manipulate the sympathies of adults, often tourists or foreigners, in order to gain donations. It is not unusual for children to be deliberately injured in order to add to their wretchedness as objects of pity.

This form of child employment has been observed by Westerners in China, India, and Latin America as well as in other Third World countries.

In Africa child labor has been in such demand that in some countries large numbers of children leave their villages for places to work and never return. In some cases children are sent into the world to work by their parents. In other cases they are simply kidnapped and put to work as virtual slaves. In Brazil it is estimated that there are over two million child workers. Numerous cases of children working to break rocks, carry bricks, do farm work, shine shoes, pound clay, or many other jobs have been observed and documented in some cases. The economy has been growing, but the amount of poverty is such that child labor is tolerated despite the county's laws. The Philippines is estimated to have as many as one million child laborers under the age of 15.

The number of children regularly employed at sustained labor is estimated to be 270 million globally by UNICEF. This figure does not include children employed as domestic help. The United Nations Convention on the Rights of the Child (CRC) holds that child labor is a form of exploitation (Article 32). While it is considered exploitation to employ children before a certain age (excluding home chores and school work), the minimum age for some employment varies between countries. In the United States the minimum age is usually 16. The United States and Somalia were the only countries in the world to not sign the Convention on the Rights of the Child in the 1990s. American conservatives opposed the CRC as a device for the state to take away parental rights and for allowing children to become wards of the state.

Despite the Convention on the Rights of the Child, child labor is common wherever the educational system is weak or non-existent. Among the many occupations performed by children in the Third World are tasks such as factory work, agriculture, selling food or other jobs related to the family business, doing odd jobs on the streets such as polishing shoes, doing repetitive work or in some cases serving as prostitutes. In many countries employers put children to work in hidden locations where they cannot be seen by reformers, the media or labor inspectors. Many are engaged in what have historically been called sweatshops. In the Third World child labor occurs in all types of weather for very small incomes.

One overriding reason for the continued existence of exploitative child labor is the fact that the labor of children supplies poor families with needed income. The short-term income gains for the family may be at the cost of long-term gains from education, but only if it is available. Opposition to limitations imposed by child labor laws is registered at times by youth rights groups. Their claim is that in some cases a child may be eager to earn a living or to provide for the family. In general scholars have concluded that the basic cause of child labor is the poverty of families. Both India and Bangladesh have an estimated 70 to 80 million child workers. Many children who work are below the age of 11. Many work in sweatshops that supply American or European retailers with commodities such as shoes or clothing. Wages usually are limited to a few dollars per week. Child labor in these countries occurs despite Indian and Bangladeshi child labor laws.

There are an estimated 270 million child laborers worldwide, such as this boy working in a tire shop in Gambia in 2008.

Corporate Responses

Retailers and manufacturers accused of ignoring the use of child labor have at times discovered that their accusers were correct and have taken steps to end the use of child labor in their products. In India raids by authorities in 2005 revealed that the embroidery industry in Delhi was employing young children at sweatshop wages. The use of children in the Oriental rug industry is ancient. Rug weaving is performed by young boys from an early age. The work gives then not only income but a future as a weaver. However, the carpet industry in Pakistan has moved beyond the traditional crafts industry of former times. It for at least a time was a center of child labor exploitation.

Companies accused of using child labor have included Wal-Mart, Nike, and the Gap Company. The latter strongly denied the accusation. The Firestone Tire and Rubber Company restructured its operations in its Liberian rubber plantation when it was found that it was involved in child labor practices. A suit brought by the International Rights Fund on behalf of the exploited children was still in court in 2008.

In 2008 Agriprocessors, a kosher meatpacking company in Postville, Iowa, was raided by agents of Immigration and Customs Enforcement. Numerous undocumented workers who were illegal aliens were found, but so were 57 minors. All including those working below the age of 14 were recorded as evidence to be used in prosecuting the company.

Despite decades of progress, child labor is not confined to the Third World. It has been found to continue to exist in Europe and in the United States. In Great Britain a campaign to end child labor sponsored by UNICEF is underway to aid in the elimination of child labor.

See Also: Antiglobalization Movement; Bangladesh; Corporate Social Responsibility; Democratic Globalization; India; Industrialized Countries; Less Industrialized Countries; Off-Shoring; Outsourcing; Sustainable Development; Underdevelopment; Working Hours.

Bibliography. Atenwo Human Rights Center, *Opening Doors: A Presentation of Laws Protecting Filipino Child Workers* (International Labour Office, 2003); Edna Dean Bullock, *Selected Articles on Child Labor* (Kessinger Publishing Company, 2008); Jean-Robert Cadet, *Restavec: From Haitian Slave Child to Middle-Class American* (University of Texas Press, 1998); Holly Cullen, *Role of International Law in the Elimination of Child Labor* (Brill Academic Publishers, 2007); Russell Freedman, *Kids at Work: Lewis Hine and the Crusade Against Child Labor* (Houghton Mifflin, 1998); Christiaan Grootaert and Harry Anthony Patrinos, eds., *Policy Analysis of Child Labor: A Comparative Study* (Palgrave Macmillan, 1999); Wendy Herumin, *Child Labor Today: A Human Rights Issue* (Enslow Publishers, 2007); Gerda Weissman Klein, *All But My Life* (Farrar, Straus and Giroux, 1995); Marvin J. Levine, *Children for Hire: The Perils of Child Labor in the United States* (Greenwood Publishing Group, 2003); Kevin Majors, *Free The Children: A Young Man Fights Against Child Labor and Proves that Children Can Change the World* (HarperCollins, 1999); National Research Council Institute for Medicine, *Protecting Youth at Work: Health, Safety, and Development of Working Children and Adolescents in the United States* (National Academies Press, 1999); Olga Nieuwenhuys, *Children's Lifeworlds: Gender, Welfare and Labour in the Developing World* (Routledge, 1994); Myron Weiner, Neera Burra and Asha Bajpai. *Born Unfree: Child Labour, Education, and the State in India: An Omnibus: the Child and the State in India, Born to Work, and Child Rights in India* (Oxford University Press, 2007); Elizabeth Winthrop, *Counting on Grace* (Random House, 2007); Karin L. Zipf, *Labor of Innocents: Forced Apprenticeship in North Carolina, 1715–1919* (Louisiana State University Press, 2005).

ANDREW J. WASKEY
DALTON STATE COLLEGE

Chile

Chile is a country on the western coast of South America with a distinctive geography and rich natural resources. After decades of import substitution industrialization policies, the country has been pursing an export-led growth strategy since the late 1970s. Its economy is integrated with the rest of the world as a result of high levels of openness in trade and finance. Following a dictatorship that remained in power between 1973 and 1990, Chile has been democratic and politically stable under center-left coalition governments. The center-left coalition, in power since the end of the dictatorship, has followed the market-oriented economic policies of the previous period with an emphasis on lowering income inequality and fighting poverty. Chile has enjoyed one of the strongest economic growth performances in Latin America over the last three decades. The country is the leading producer of copper and nitrates. While its exports are still dominated by copper, Chilean exports have diversified into nontraditional exports such as wine and salmon. Its economy is stable with low levels of public debt and inflation, and a relatively low level of unemployment. Since 2003 the economy has experienced strong economic growth that is partly driven by the extremely favorable copper prices.

Between 1970 and 1973, after a long history of democracy, Chile succumbed to political polarization and economic crisis under the socialist government of Salvador Allende. The military, under the leadership of Augusto Pinochet, intervened in 1973 and established one of the most repressive regimes in Latin America, which lasted until 1990. The military regime implemented radical reforms, transforming Chile into a market-based and capitalist society. Between 1973 and 1990, Chile became highly integrated with the rest of the world; foreign trade's contribution to gross domestic product (GDP) increased substantially. The expansion and diversification of exports, which began in the late 1970s and strengthened in the 1980s, became the engine of growth. The share of exports in GDP reached 33 percent in 1990, while the share of copper in total exports decreased to 45.5 percent (it was 75.5 percent in 1974).

The center-left coalition (La Concertación de Partidos por la Democracia) that took power in 1990 opted for consensus-building in politics, continuing market-friendly policies, and supporting export-led growth. It also aimed to address the massive poverty and income inequality inherited from the previous regime. As a result of further export diversification and remarkable success in agricultural, fishery, and wood products, Chile grew at impressive rates in the 1990s (the average GDP growth rate was above 8 percent between 1991 and 1997). However, despite gains against poverty since 1990, Chile still has a highly skewed income distribution.

During this period, Chilean trade with the European Union and Asian countries such as Japan and South Korea increased considerably. Chilean entrepreneurs were successful in filling particular niches in advanced industrialized countries (e.g., the supply of high-quality fishery products into Asian markets). Chile supported its export industries by enacting trade agreements (preferential and free) with various countries. Currently, Chile has bilateral trade agreements with more than 50 countries, including free trade agreements (FTAs) with the European Union, the United States, China, South Korea, and Japan. Chile is also an associate member of Mercosur.

Following the Asian financial crisis, the Chilean economy slowed down between 1998 and 2002. Economic growth resumed between 2003 and 2007. At the end of 2007, the Chilean GDP was $164 billion and GDP per capita was close to $10,000. Chilean businesses benefit from low levels of taxation compared to other countries in Latin America. Investment has been strong and Chile continues to attract foreign direct investment (especially in mining). The finance sector in Chile is efficient and profitable. Chilean retail chains (e.g., Falabella, Ripley, Ahumada) are major investors in other Latin American countries. Despite these achievements and continuing success of export industries, the stock of human capital is low in Chile, the educational system is plagued by quality problems, and labor force participation is not at desirable levels.

See Also: Bilateral Free Trade Agreement; Chicago School/Chicago Boys; Company Profiles: South America; Import Substitution; Latin America; Mercosur/Mercosul; Trade Pact.

Bibliography. Central Bank of Chile, *Social and Economic Indicators, 1980–2000* (2002); Simon Collier and William F. Sater, *A History of Chile, 1808–2002* (Cambridge University Press, 2004); Economist Intelligence Unit, *Chile Country Profile, 2008* (2008); Ricardo Ffrench-Davis, *Economic Reforms in Chile: From Dictatorship to Democracy* (University of Michigan Press, 2002); Felipe B. Larraín and Rodrigo M. Vergara, eds., *La transformación económica de Chile* (Centro de Estudios Públicos, 2000); Javier Martínez and Alvaro Díaz, *Chile: The Great Transformation* (Brookings Institution, 1996); OECD, *Economic Survey of Chile* (2007); Lois Hecht Oppenheim, *Politics in Chile: Socialism, Authoritarianism, and Market Democracy* (Westview Press, 2007).

KURTULUS GEMICI
UNIVERSITY OF CALIFORNIA, LOS ANGELES

China

China is one of the world's oldest continuous civilizations. The history of China as recorded in traditional historical records extends back as far as 5,000 years. Recorded history is supplemented by archaeological records dating back to the 16th century B.C. Turtle shells with markings reminiscent of ancient Chinese writing from the Shang Dynasty have been carbon dated to around 1500 B.C. Chinese civilization originated with city-states in the Yellow River (Huang He) valley; 221 B.C. is commonly accepted to be the year in which China became unified under a large kingdom or empire. In that year, Qin Shi Huang first united China. Successive dynasties in Chinese history developed bureaucratic systems that enabled the emperor of China to control the large territory.

The entire Chinese landmass tilts from west to east. The Himalayas are a young mountain range, still rising by several feet per century because of the collision of the Indian subcontinent with the Asian landmass. This mountain-building process shapes the entire topography of China, creating a series of mountain ranges that are high and rugged in the west and taper off to low hills in the east. Broadly speaking, the land of China forms three great steps in elevation. The top step is made up of the frigid Tibetan Plateau, which averages more than 4,000 m. above sea level and contains the world's highest mountains. The second step consists of a series of plateaus and basins with an elevation of between 1,000 and 2,000 m. These include the basins in arid northwestern China, the Inner Mongolian Plateau and Loess Plateau in northern China, and the Yunnan-Guizhou Plateau in southwestern China. The third step consists of the plains and low hills of eastern China, where the elevation is generally below 500 m. Even in the east, ranges of relatively low mountains create barriers to north-south transport. The three most important rivers in China, the Yangtze (Changjiang), Yellow (Huang), and Pearl (Zhujiang) rivers, all flow from west to east in accord with the basic topography.

China is the world's most populous nation. About 20 percent of world population is Chinese, down from 30 percent in the 1950s. It is also one of the largest countries, with the third-largest landmass after Russia and Canada. Its land area is 2 percent greater than that of the United States. The western half of China is high and arid, and the population is sparse—only 6 percent of the population lives in the dry, mountainous west; 94 percent of the population lives in the eastern half of the country. China's hilly and complex terrain means that relatively little of the land is suitable for cultivation. The good agricultural land lies in the fertile plains and valleys of the major river systems, separated from one another by hills and mountains. Only 15 percent of China is arable, and there is very little land potentially suited for cultivation that is not already exploited. Over the centuries China has adapted to land scarcity with a labor-intensive agriculture that wrests more total food grain from the soil than any other country.

China has substantial mineral reserves and is the world's largest producer of antimony, natural graphite, tungsten, and zinc. With its vast mountain ranges, China's hydropower potential is also the largest in the world. However, the distribution of mineral and energy resources in China is extremely uneven. The rapidly growing southern coastal regions have virtually no energy resources. Geographic constraints dictate that China must develop in a labor-intensive and, ultimately, knowledge-intensive path. Moreover, unrelenting environmental problems will make economic trade-offs more difficult and complex for the foreseeable future.

The Chinese Economy

The year 1949 appears at first to be a great divide in Chinese history. The government is radically different after 1949, and even more dramatic is the growth performance. Before 1949, China never launched into rapid, modern economic growth. Since 1949, China's economy has grown rapidly, despite sometimes disastrous policies imposed during Maoist times. For more than a century—from the early 19th to the middle of the 20th century—China's economic performance was mediocre at best.

Chinese traditional society was overwhelmingly rural, with over 90 percent of the population living in the countryside. After the People's Republic of China (PRC) was established in October 1949, the Chinese economy was wrenched out of its traditional framework and completely reoriented. China's new leaders turned their backs on China's traditional household-based economy, and set out to develop a massive socialist industrial complex through direct government control. Planners neglected labor-intensive sectors suitable to China's vast population, and instead poured resources into capital-intensive factories producing metals, machinery, and chemicals. The early achievements of coastal enclave industrialization oriented to the Pacific were discarded, and a new inward-directed strategy was adopted. China turned to the Soviet Union as its primary model, as well as its chief trading partner and source of technology. For 30 years, China pursued this vision of socialism and this development strategy shaped virtually every aspect of the Chinese economy.

There were major shortcomings associated with the socialist development strategy. First, the single-minded pursuit of industrial development meant that consumption was neglected. Second, employment creation was relatively slow. Because most industry was capital-intensive and services were neglected, new labor requirements were modest. Third, much of the industrial investment was not only capital-intensive, but also relatively demanding technologically.

Beginning in late 1978, China's leaders viewed China, quite correctly, as a low-income developing country, and the imperative of economic development was constantly on their minds. It was never conceivable to Chinese policy makers that their economy would postpone economic development until after an interlude of system transformation. Since China launched economic reforms at the end of 1978, market transition has extended over almost 30 years. The Chinese leadership has been moving the economy from a sluggish Soviet-style centrally planned economy to a more market-oriented economy but still within a rigid political framework of Communist Party control. Indeed, today China has already spent as long a period building a market economy as under Maoist socialism. China's economy has been transformed by successive waves of economic reform.

China grew fast between 1949 and 1978, but growth really took off after the beginning of reform in 1978. Moreover, the acceleration of economic growth coincided with the slowing of population growth, so per capita growth accelerated even more dramatically. According to official data, the average annual gross domestic product (GDP) growth accelerated from 6 percent in the pre-1978 period to 9.6 percent in the 1978–2006 period. At the same time, popula-

tion growth decelerated from 1.9 percent per year before 1978 to only 1.1 percent after 1978. As a result, per capita GDP growth more than doubled, jumping from 4.1 percent to 8.5 percent annually. China's post-1978 growth experience has been extraordinary by any standard. The comparison of GDP between Chinese and other major economies in Asia and the rest of the world shows that China has maintained its GDP growth at the average of 8 percent since 2000, which is higher than Asia and much higher than the United Kingdom and the United States.

Pattern of Chinese Development

Economic growth has been intertwined with structural changes throughout China's economic development process. The command economy included policies restricting labor mobility and controlling prices, as well as neglecting agriculture and services. These policies all had ramifications for China's growth and structural changes that caused a divergence from the development-process benchmark. Despite these divergences, China has followed general patterns of development found throughout the world.

The one-child policy has shaped China in many important ways and has had important impacts on its economic development. Since the late 1970s, especially since its introduction of the reform and opening program, China has formulated a basic state policy to promote family planning in an all-around way in order to slow population growth and improve its quality in terms of health and education. The government encourages late marriage and late childbearing, and advocates the practice of "one couple, one child" and of "having a second child with proper spacing in accordance with the lay regulations." The Chinese government pays great attention to the issue of population and development and has placed it on the agenda as an important part of the overall plan of its national economic and social development. The government consistently emphasizes that population growth should be compatible with socioeconomic development and be concerted with resource utilization and environmental protection. After nearly 30 years of effort, China has successfully found its own way to have an integrated approach to the population issue with its own national characteristics.

Under the command economy there were no labor markets in China. Each worker was a lifetime member of one of the two vast systems of public employment, urban and rural. This system was slow to change, especially in the cities: employment in state-owned enterprises continued to grow well into the 1990s, nearly 20 years after the beginning of reform. But then, beginning in the mid-1990s, China laid off almost 50 million workers, 40 percent of the public-enterprise workforce. Today the entire system of government-controlled employment has dissolved, and active labor markets have developed nationwide, which create the foundation for a skilled and prosperous economy.

When the old system broke down, unemployment surged, and remains a serious chronic problem. The Chinese government recognized the importance of the issue of employment. It has explored and drawn on international experiences and adapted them for use in the domestic situation, formulating and implementing a number of proactive employment policies. For instance, new forms of employment mushroomed, such as jobs in foreign-invested firms and economic entities of diverse forms, part-time jobs, temporary jobs, seasonal jobs and work on an hourly basis, and jobs with flexible working hours, and became important avenues for the expansion of employment. In recent years, as the employment pressure has been continuously increasing, the Chinese government has adopted many measures to curb the sharp rise of urban unemployment. By the end of 2006, the registered unemployment rate in the urban areas was 4.3 percent, and the number of registered jobless urbanites was eight million.

China and Global Business

China has transformed into a global trade power. In 2005, China was the third-largest trading nation in the world (after the United States and Germany), and its trade is growing far more rapidly than that of any other large economy. China has now achieved a degree of openness that is exceptional for a large, continental economy. In 2005 China's total goods trade (exports plus imports) amounted to 64 percent of GDP, far more than other large, continental economies—such as the United States, Japan, India, and Brazil—which have trade/GDP ratios around 20 percent, the highest being Brazil's 25 percent. Trade liberalization has been an integral part of China's economic reform process since its beginning. The most recent phase

of trade policy reform began with China's formal entry into the World Trade Organization (WTO), on December 11, 2001, which started the clock running on a series of liberalization commitments kicking in between 2001 and 2007. Besides marking a new phase of policy reform, WTO membership symbolizes China's coming of age as a participant in the global economic community.

Investment and trade are closely linked in China and the global economy. For more than a decade China has been one of the world's most important destinations for foreign direct investment (FDI). Investment began to pour into China after 1992, and annual inflows have been over $40 billion since 1996. Trending steadily upward, FDI inflows were at $63 billion in both 2004 and 2005. These inflows are by far the highest of any developing country and have remained remarkably stable and robust despite substantial fluctuations in the Asian and global economies. China has accounted for about one-third of total developing-country FDI inflows in recent years. There is no doubt that the global manufacturing networks created by FDI in China will continue to play a critical role in the world economy.

Future Challenges

For centuries the pressure of population on China's limited natural resources has led to severe environmental degradation. A hundred years ago most of China had already been stripped of forests. Modern economic growth has created another set of challenges, creating massive pollution and apparently unsustainable demands on natural resources. Air and water pollution are damaging to human health, worker productivity, and agricultural output. The growth of industry and the growth of automobile transport are causing an increase in pollutants.

Since 1980 the quality of China's surface water and ground water has deteriorated significantly under the pressure of rapid industrial development, brisk population and urban growth, and increased use of chemical fertilizers and pesticides. As a result, water pollution is now a serious problem for urban and rural drinking water. Moreover, critical environmental problems in China relate to the coordination of enormous demands on China's natural resources. These problems are more difficult to quantify because a large but unknown share of costs is deferred to the future.

While China has enjoyed a phenomenal GDP growth rate averaging 8 percent since 2000, it has come at a steep cost to the environment, especially affecting water quality for both urban and rural populations.

Environmental degradation has imposed serious costs on the Chinese economy and reduced the well-being of the Chinese population. Moreover, there is increasing public concern about environmental issues, and that concern has increasingly been publicly articulated. The government's responsiveness to these protests will be a bellwether of its willingness to let public opinion serve as an input into economic decision making. In its most recent planning exercise, the five-year plan for 2006–11, the Chinese government called for a reorientation of the economic growth model toward sustainable growth with a lighter environmental impact. This shift in viewpoint suggests that government policy has begun to become one positive element in the complex mix of factors that determine China's environmental trajectory. In combination with many other social, technological, and economic factors, that could turn China in the direction of gradual environmental improvement.

See Also: Asia; Asian Financial Crisis; Bank of China; China Life Insurance; China Mobile Communications; China National Petroleum; Communism; Feng Shui; Guanxi; Hong Kong; Socialism; State-Owned Enterprises; Sustainable Development; World Trade Organization.

Bibliography. Institute of Geography, Chinese Academy of Sciences, and China Population and Environment Society, eds., *The Atlas of Population, Environment and Sustainable Development in China* (Science Press, 2000); N. Lardy, "The First Five Year Plan, 1953–1957; The Great Leap Forward and After," in *The Cambridge History of China Vol. 14: The People's Republic, Part 1: The Emergence of Revolutionary China, 1949–1965*, R. MacFarquhar and J. K. Fairbank, eds. (Cambridge University Press, 1987); B. Naughton, *Growing Out of the Plan: Chinese Economic Reform, 1978–1993* (Cambridge University Press, 1995); X. Peng, "Is It Time to Change China's Population Policy?" *China: An International Journal* (v.2/1, 2005); D. Perkins, S. Radelet, D. Snodgrass, M. Gills, and M. Roemer, *Economic Development*, 5th ed. (W. W. Norton, 2001); P. Richardson, *Economic Change in China, c. 1800–1950* (Cambridge University Press, 1999); C. Riskin, *China's Political Economy: The Quest for Development Since 1949* (Oxford University Press, 1991); SEPA, *Analysis Report on the State of the Environment in China* (Ministry of Environmental Protection of the People's Republic of China, 2004); Statistical Yearbook of China, *Zhongguo Tongji Nianjian* [Statistical Yearbook of China] (Zhongguo Tongji, 2006); F. Wang, "Can China Afford to Continue Its One-Child Policy?" *Asia Pacific Issue* (v.77, 2005); World Bank, *China 2020: Development*

Challenges in the New Century (World Bank, 1997); World Bank, *China: Air, Land and Water* (World Bank, 2001); J. Wu, *Understanding and Interpreting Chinese Economic Reform* (Thomson, 2005).

JEAN QI WEI
CITY UNIVERSITY CASS BUSINESS SCHOOL
CHRIS ROWLEY
CITY UNIVERSITY CASS BUSINESS SCHOOL

China Life Insurance

China Life Insurance Company Limited ("China Life") is China's largest life insurance company and the second-largest by market value globally (US$129 billion; RMB 1,032 billion). With a market share of approximately 40 percent with less than 4 percent of the population insured, China Life—and the China insurance market in general—faces substantial growth opportunities. Market liberalization and the consequent entry of the world's largest players represent a considerable challenge, with China Life's future success dependent upon its ability to adapt to the new and dynamic global environment.

China Life was established in Beijing on June 30, 2003, and was listed in New York and Hong Kong in December 2003. In January 2007 the company listed on the Shanghai Stock Exchange, drawing bids for 49 times the volume of stock on offer. The company operates primarily in China and employs approximately 76,000 people. The product mix includes life insurance, annuity products, and accident and health insurance for both individuals and groups.

In 2007 China Life achieved a profit result of US$4.85 billion (RMB 38.9 billion) on revenues of US$23.9 billion (RMB 191.4 billion), an annual increase of 94.8 percent and 29.9 percent, respectively. In 2007 insurance premiums rose by 12.7 percent to US$13.9 billion (RMB 111.4 billion), while net investment income increased 68 percent to US$5.5 billion (RMB 44.0 billion), largely due to rapidly appreciating stock market investments. The company's solvency margin—at 5.25 times the regulatory requirement in December 2007—reflects the company's current financial strength.

China Life maintains a strong leadership position in China with a market share in 2007 of 39.7 percent (2006, 45.3 percent), comprising 93 million individual policies. China Life is also China's largest institutional investor with assets of almost US$125 billion (RMB 1,000 billion) under management. In 2007 Chinese insurance companies were granted the right to invest up to 15 percent of their assets overseas.

In recent years, China Life has maintained its dominant position through scale (specifically, its technical infrastructure and marketing channels) and its strong reputation in a community whose culture has a strong aversion to issues surrounding mortality. China Life's distribution network in China includes more than 3,600 branches, 12,000 field offices, 90,000 bancassurance outlets (financial intermediaries), and 650,000 sales agents.

China Life's history will be sharply delineated by current industry liberalization as China's government seeks to regulate the participation of foreign insurance groups and protect the interests of domestic participants. China Life recognizes that, in order to become globally competitive, it needs to raise the level of its operational management and professionalism at all levels and in all areas. The company has indicated that it will continue to seek strategic foreign investors from whom it can learn advanced investment management systems and risk management, enhance the company's corporate governance, and develop highly competitive sales and marketing strategies and practices.

While the company's current strategy calls for strengthening and increasing its 90,000 bancassurance outlets, industry experts question the ongoing support of these financial intermediaries. In July 2008 four domestic banks applied to invest in China's insurance industry. China Life's ability to develop products tailored to their financial partners' specific needs is critical to maintaining the strength of this valuable marketing channel.

One of China Life's greatest strategic assets is its brand which, in spite of the poor industry penetration of the market (at just 4 percent) still enjoys 92 percent recognition. While this provides considerable leverage in a rapidly developing insurance market, differentiation of its product offerings will be crucial to maintaining a substantial market share into the future.

China Life's investment and risk management skills may also be tested with the volatile domestic stock market. While the company has realized significant profits from stock market investments in recent times, 2008 has seen sharp declines across the board. China Life's future depends on its ability to adapt to the challenges of its new, increasingly dynamic and competitive global environment.

Note: There is no business relationship between China Life Insurance Company in Mainland China and China Life Insurance Co. Ltd. in Taiwan.

See Also: China; Risk Management; Transition Economies.

Bibliography. Stephan Binder, Tab Bowers, and Winston Yung, "Selling Life Insurance to China," *The McKinsey Quarterly* (2004 Special Edition); Olivia Chung, "China's Insurers Look To Looser Shackles," *Asia Times Online*, www.atimes.com (cited March 2009); China Knowledge, "Foreign Strategic Investors for China Life Insurance AMC (HK)," www.chinaknowledge.com (cited September 2008); Research in China, "China Insurance Industry Report, 2007–2008" (August 2007); RNCOS Research Solutions, "China Insurance Sector Till 2010" (December 2007).

Terence R. Egan
Central University of Finance and Economics

China Mobile Communications

China Mobile Limited ("China Mobile") is China's leading mobile services provider, having developed the largest mobile phone network and subscriber base in the world. The combination of continued rapid growth in China's economy, rising consumer purchasing power, the development of the rural economy, and the acceleration of consumer demand for information services is driving remarkable growth in the mobile phone market. Despite rapid growth, however, market penetration in mainland China is still only around 40 percent (2007). China Mobile enjoys a market share of almost 70 percent (2007); however, changing regulations, major industry restructuring, new competitive pressures, and industry convergence will make this level of market domination difficult to maintain.

China Mobile (Hong Kong) Limited was incorporated in Hong Kong in September 1997 and listed in New York and Hong Kong in October 1997. The name change to China Mobile Limited was effected in 2006.

China Mobile's scope as a network provider includes a comprehensive range of voice, data, and value-added services. Value-added voice services include caller identity display, caller restrictions, call waiting, call forwarding, call holding, voice mail, and conference calling. Value-added data services include Short Message Services (SMS), Wireless Application Protocol (WAP), customized ring tones, Multimedia Messaging Services (MMS), Machine-to-Machine and Man-to-Machine applications, as well as many industry-specific applications.

In 2007 China Mobile's subscriber base reached 370 million, an annual net increase of 22.6 percent. Operating revenue increased 20.9 percent to US$44.6 billion (RMB 357 billion), comprising an increase in average subscriber monthly usage (45.3 percent), and strong growth in value-added business (32.2 percent)

China Mobile's network of 307,000 base stations reaches 97 percent of China's population and is the largest in the world.

and SMS usage (42.3 percent). The company's 2.12 million corporate customers also provide an important marketing base for the development of associated individual-user contracts.

China Mobile's competitive advantages are underpinned by the scale of its operations. Its 307,000 base stations provide 97 percent coverage of the population in mainland China. Its sales, marketing, and support systems comprise more than 72,000 sales outlets providing strong representation throughout China including the difficult-to-reach rural, inner, and western markets. China Mobile's GSM roaming services are provided through 350 operators in 231 countries and regions.

While China Mobile is strongly positioned to capture a major share of the continuing growth potential, several strategic challenges lie ahead. In May 2008 the Chinese government announced plans to create three major telecom groups in an effort to rebalance the industry between the highly dynamic and prosperous mobile operators and the recently sluggish fixed-line operators. China Mobile is expected to play a significant part in one of the three groups and is expected to participate in a wave of acquisitions and mergers. Changes to regulations on call tariffs have also required considerable adjustment and an increased focus on productivity and efficiency.

In April 2008 China Mobile began testing its third-generation mobile communication platform (3G) that will allow development of more sophisticated networks with higher data-transmission speeds and capabilities. This is critical to applications such as TV and movie services, music, internet services, and enhanced mobile payment systems. Approximately 60 percent of the company's capital expenditures were dedicated to construction of the GSM network in 2007 with another 55 percent of CAPEX to be allocated to network development in 2008. In June 2008, facing slower than expected adoption of 3G in early technical and marketing trials, China Mobile announced that it would extend the 3G network from the previously planned 10 eastern cities to all 31 provincial capitals.

New competitors are expected to emerge quickly both from within the industry and through cross-industry convergence. In order to maintain competitiveness, China Mobile will seek to leverage strategic alliances such as those currently in place with organizations such as News Corporation, Sun Microsystems, Inc., and Alcatel-Lucent. A highly publicized failed negotiation with Apple, Inc., in 2008 underscores the importance China Mobile places on cross-industry alliances. With rural markets set to provide a substantial part of future growth in the Chinese mobile phone market, the company is well positioned to optimize the geographic advantage of its technical and sales resources.

See Also: Asia; China; Transition Economies.

Bibliography. AFP, "China Plans Three Telecom Giants," www.afp.com (cited March 2009); China Business Services, "Bell (Finally) Rings For Telecoms Reform," www.2chinabusinessservices.com (cited March 2009); China CCM, "2006–2007 Annual Report on Mobile Phone Marketing Channel & Custom Model in China" (2006); Leopoldina Fortunati, Anna Manganelli, Pui-lam Law, and Shanhua Yang, "Beijing Calling ... Mobile Communication in Contemporary China," *Knowledge, Technology, & Policy* (v.21/1, 2008); Jia Lu and Ian Weber, "State, Power, and Mobile Communication: A Case Study of China," *New Media & Society* (v.9/6, 2007); "Telecoms in China," *The Economist* (May 29, 2008).

Terence R. Egan
Central University of Finance and Economics

China National Petroleum

The China National Petroleum Corporation (CNPC) is a state-owned fuel-producing corporation in the People's Republic of China (PRC). CNPC's core businesses include oil exploration and production, natural gas and pipelines, refining and marketing, and chemicals and marketing. The company's origin can be traced to its beginning as a government department of the PRC between 1949 and 1988. In a major initiative to separate government from business, CNPC was formally created in September 1988 as the largest state-owned oil and gas upstream corporation in China to replace the Ministry of Petroleum. In order to establish large-scale Chinese corporations to take on challenges of international competition, CNPC was restructured in July 1998 by the government, which made it China's largest integrated energy corporation. Since then, CNPC has been growing rapidly. It ranked 80th in 2002, 46th in 2005, and 24th in 2007 in the Fortune Global 500. In 2005 it overtook U.S. giant Chevron and France's Total to become the world's seventh-largest oil firm on the basis of six indices, including oil and gas reserves, oil and gas output, and sales volume.

CNPC's growth strategy begins with focusing on its core businesses. Similar to other state-owned organizations in China, CNPC used to run "small societies" of its own, having a work force of 1.56 million in the late 1990s. During the 1998 restructuring, CNPC spun-off two-thirds of its high-quality assets and one-third of its workforce in the core businesses of gasoline and natural gas production and marketing into a separate company, PetroChina, and then had it listed on the Hong Kong and New York stock exchanges in 2000. In this way PetroChina was forced to adopt modern enterprise structure and management systems, and was fast-tracked to international markets. In November 2007 PetroChina became the world's most valuable company, with a market capitalization that topped $1 trillion, the first and only company in the world to do so.

At the time of restructuring in 1998, apart from PetroChina, CNPC had 1.06 million employees and 380,000 retirees, and a large number of subsidiary companies. Without the support of the core businesses, these remaining sections had a loss of 12.8 billion yuan in the first year. For the survival and development of these noncore businesses, CNPC took the following measures: Optimizing resource allocation and organization structure; further restructuring to separate main and servicing businesses; reforming personnel and other management systems; and pushing for the market orientation of businesses. These measures have seen the noncore businesses of CNPC smoothly transformed into a healthy growth mode.

According to Zhou Jiping (2004), the vice president of CNPC, the "Chinese oil industry benefited significantly from the oil science and technology with our own characteristics." With the help of the "continental origin of oil theory," China found large oil fields one after another. The application of the theory of large-scale non-homogenous sandstone development, production by layers, oil-stabilizing by water-cut controlling, as well as tertiary oil recovery had helped the Daqing oilfield achieve an annual oil output of more than 50 million tons for more than 27 years, a miracle by world standards. Sophisticated technologies such as horizontal application, underbalanced drilling, slim hole, cased well, and multiple bottom and multiple branch drilling had also been actively applied. CNPC had close to 18,000 staff working in research and development (R&D) by the end of 2006, with an R&D expenditure of US$396.4 million.

With the rapid development of the Chinese economy and the sharp increase in energy demand, Chinese oil companies have been forced to go overseas since the late 1990s in search of a more diversified and secure energy supply. CPNC started its international operations in 1993 by signing a service contract to manage the Talara oilfield in Peru. In October 2005 CNPC completed acquisition of PetroKazakhstan with US$4.18 billion, despite the attempt by Lukoil to block the sale. It was the largest overseas acquisition by a Chinese company at the time. By 2006 CNPC owned oil and gas assets and interests in 26 countries outside China, forming five major operational regions including Africa, Central Asia, South America, the Middle East, and Asia Pacific. CNPC also provides oilfield services, engineering and construction in 49 countries and regions worldwide. Its engineering and technical services have been expanded to 38 countries, and the petroleum goods and equipment manufactured by CNPC have been exported to 61 countries.

However, CNPC also faces a number of problems and challenges, including a low profit margin (2.4 percent) compared to the industry standard, low technology content in operations, mature production facilities, internal welfare burden (a workforce four to five times larger than those of the super majors), small-scale international operations (lack of bargaining power with host institutions), and lack of presence in high-impact international explorations. It remains to be seen if CNPC can sustain its competitive advantages over the long term.

See Also: China; Kazakhstan; LUKOIL; Sinopec; State-Owned Enterprises.

Bibliography. China National Petroleum Corporation, www.cnpc.com.cn (cited March 2009); F. Carvalho and A. Goldstein, "The 'Making of' National Giants: Technology and Governments Shaping the International Expansion of Oil Companies from Brazil and China," UNU-MERIT Working Papers (n.2008-021, 2008); "Global Blueprint of Energetic CNPC," *China Oil & Gas* (v.14/1, 2007); S. Qiu, "CNPC: Creating a Super Enterprise Aircraft Through Reform," *China Post* (n.6, 2006); D. Roberts, "The Challenges Facing China's Oil Behemoth Abroad," Business-Week Online, www.businessweek.com (cited March 2009); S. Yang and X. Guo, "The Making of the SOE Super Aircraft—An Investigation of the Reform and Development of CNPC," *Qiu Shi* (n.18, 2003).

Xiaohua Yang
Queensland University of Technology
Shan Ma
Queensland University of Technology

Choice of Forum Clause

As global trade increases so does the number of contracts between parties in different countries. If, as may easily happen, a dispute arises out of a contract it is very important to both parties to know which court or body has the authority to decide that dispute. A choice of forum clause is a term in such a contract that specifies that authority. In the case of a lawsuit it stipulates the particular court or jurisdiction where it may be tried. Alternatively it may specify an arbitrator or conciliator to have the authority to decide a dispute. Such clauses have become particularly relevant with the growth of electronic commerce, much of which is cross-border.

If an international contract does not include a choice of forum clause, then a great deal of legal wrangling may be needed in order to determine a competent court or jurisdiction to settle a dispute. In such a situation neither party is likely to be comfortable as different forums may well make different decisions. However, it cannot be assumed that a choice of forum clause will always be respected. In many jurisdictions there is significant difference between business-to-business (B2B) and business-to-consumer (B2C) contracts. For example, within the European Union, in the event of a dispute over a B2C contract, consumers may in general take suppliers to court in their own country, irrespective of any prior agreement. This is an example of an absolute right that takes precedence

over the terms of the contract. The assumption here is that a business is in a more powerful position than a consumer in the formation of a contract; hence, the consumer needs a greater level of protection.

While a choice of forum clause may specify a specific jurisdiction, it does not necessarily specify the corresponding law, although these will usually be the same. The jurisdiction chosen will determine the procedural law that will apply in a particular dispute (e.g., whether or not cross-examination is available to the parties), but not the way in which the contract will be interpreted; this is determined by the "governing" (or "applicable") law, which should be specified in a separate choice of law clause.

Usually a consumer does not have the opportunity to negotiate a choice of forum. However, in the case of B2B, it is normal for negotiation to take place when entering a contract. Issues likely to arise include "hometown advantage" (neither party will normally want to accept the other's home jurisdiction, so they will probably agree a "neutral" jurisdiction), language of the jurisdiction, remedies available in a jurisdiction, and levels of costs and rules relating to them. A particularly important issue in choosing a forum is its power to enforce a judgment; if damages are awarded can the forum enforce their payment?

In the case of B2B contracts it is reasonably common to specify an arbitrator as the forum for dispute resolution, with both parties agreeing that any decision is binding. Advantages of arbitration include faster and cheaper settlement of disputes, the possibility of proceedings being kept secret, and the appointment of technical experts (e.g., in shipping or medicine) as arbitrators. Clauses that specify arbitration are supported in the United States, where compulsory and binding arbitration is permitted by the Federal Arbitration Act.

Care must be taken when entering a contract, either as a consumer or a business, to ensure that any choice of forum clause is understood and is approved by a suitable legal expert; the precise wording is important. In the case of a dispute the clause can, quite literally, have far-reaching effects. Most jurisdictions do recognize the validity of these clauses so long as they were clearly entered into in good faith by both parties.

See Also: Arbitration; Contracts; European Union; International Law.

Bibliography. J. Hörnle, "Legal Controls on the Use of Arbitration Clause in B2C E-commerce Contracts," *Electronic Business Law* (2006).

TIM MUSSON
NAPIER UNIVERSITY

Citigroup

Citigroup is one of the most diversified financial services companies in the world. It was incorporated in 1998 through a merger between Citicorp and Travelers Group. It operates globally and has established competitive advantage in its global presence, broad distribution, valuable brands, unmatched scale, and efficiency and product breadth. The company operates through these operating divisions: global consumer, corporate and investment banking, global wealth management and alternate investments.

Citigroup gained its global presence by aggressively acquiring other organizations, especially in Asia and Latin America. At the same time, Citigroup invested in strategic alliances in order to enter China's emerging credit card market. Citigroup has an asset base of over $1.8 trillion. In 2007 the company was ranked first in Forbes 2,000 global companies and 8th in the Fortune 500. Citigroup has more than 200 million customer accounts. Achieving economies of scale provided Citigroup with competitive advantage and allows it to capitalize on opportunities across geographic markets.

Citigroup has invested in increasing its product portfolio and establishing a strong global brand name. Citigroup offers individual and institutional clients a diversified range of financial products and services. Customers range from small and medium-sized enterprises to fund and securities services as well as government services. This wide range of services enhances the company's cross-selling opportunities and increases its resistance to temporary downturns in demand for one product segment or business. CEO Vikram Pandit claims that the Citigroup brand is unparalleled in the world. Moreover, Citigroup has managed to achieve economies of scale and scope. It claims to have the largest pool of talent in the financial services business. Through continuous investment in talent and human capital, Citigroup has managed to expand its operations globally.

Although Citigroup has established a well-recognized global brand name, it has reported a decrease in profits since 2005. The net profit for fiscal year 2006 was $21,538 million, a decrease of 12.4 percent over 2005. Moreover, the company's net profit margins also declined during the same period. The net profit margin declined from 29.4 percent in 2005 to 24 percent in 2006. This decline in operating profits indicates ineffective cost management as well as problematic leadership in the management of operations. Furthermore, a decline of this value restricts availability of resources and prohibits pursuit of growth projects.

Moreover, Citigroup reported a decline in net interest margins. Citigroup's net interest margin in 2006 was 2.65 percent, down 41 basis points from 2005. This decrease in the margins of the group may show declining profitability of the lending business of the company. Net interest margin declined primarily due to a shift in customer liabilities from savings and other demand deposits to certificates of deposit and e-saving accounts. This decrease in net interest margin caused a decline in the group's net interest revenues during fiscal year 2006.

Citigroup has also been in the news for unethical business behavior. The company was linked to the Enron scandal. Its bankers had advised and assisted Enron along the way to its initial success, and made huge profits. They also advised Enron when it had already started on the slide to bankruptcy, making large sums by organizing the deals that deceived the investing public. Citigroup was also forced to shut down its private banking operations in Japan due to improper trading practices and lax anti–money laundering procedures. The Financial Services Authority said that the bank had brokered deals on such items as artworks without properly informing customers about the possible risks. This had an effect on the reputation of Citigroup in southeast Asia and Citigroup was required to close all its offices in Japan.

Citigroup has managed to overcome these associations with corruption by refocusing the corporation to become a socially responsible organization. This has allowed it to rebrand its name and image to create a competitive advantage in the markets in which it is operating. This strengthened Citigroup's presence globally as it was able to bring its global reach together with its local depth. The transformation of the organizational culture and its detachment from the corruption scandals aims at improving teamwork, encouraging respect, and reinforcing a supportive culture that drives performance in order to enable Citigroup to be the financial services industry's employer of choice.

Citigroup was weakened by but survived the 2008 financial markets tumult.

See Also: Corporate Change: Corporate Social Responsibility; Enron Corporation; Financial Markets; Mortgage Credit Crisis of 2008; Multinational Corporation.

Bibliography. Citigroup, www.citigroup.com (cited March 2009); Louise Cooper, "Scandal-hit Citigroup Rebuilds its Image," *BBC News*, March 14, 2005, news.bbc.co.uk (cited March 2009); Eric Dash, "Blue-Light Specials at Citigroup as its New Chief Plans a Revival," *New York Times* (May 9, 2008); Datamonitor, "Report on Citigroup's Company Profile," March 2008, www.datamonitor.com (cited March 2009); Carol Lomis, "Can Anyone Run Citigroup?" *Fortune* (v.157/9, 2008); Steve Maguire and Nelson Phillips, "'Citibankers' at Citigroup: A Study of the Loss of Institutional Trust after a Merger," *Journal of Management Studies* (v.45/2, 2008); "The Real Scandal at Citi," *Newsweek* (February 26, 2007); Christopher C. York, Andra Gumbus, and Stephen Lilly, "Reading the Tea Leaves—Did Citigroup Risk Their Reputation During 2004–2005?" *Business and Society Review* (v.113/2, 2008).

Efthimios Poulis
Bournemouth University
Athina Vasilaki
Middlesex University Business School
Konstantinos Poulis
IST Studies, Athens

City, The

The City commonly refers to the City of London (a small district within Greater London), and by way of metonymy, to the financial industry operating there, and the culture thereof—just as Wall Street is used to refer to more than simply the street and what is on it. The City is also home to London's legal industry, and use of the phrase may sometimes carry that association

instead or in amplification—a City lawyer being one who works with the financial industry in some way, for instance. Though the City of London is often called the Square Mile, it is less common—though not quite rare—to also use that term for the financial industry.

Greater London consists of the 32 London boroughs (divided among Inner and Outer London) and the City of London. Unlike the boroughs, the City is governed by the City of London Corporation, which is granted with greater-than-usual powers and authority compared to other local governments. The full name of the Corporation, rarely used outside of official contexts, is the Mayor and Commonalty and Citizens of the City of London and the Court of Common Council. The City is divided into 25 wards, which are used as electoral divisions, the largest of which are Farringdon Without, Farringdon Within, Cripplegate, and Bishopsgate, each of which has 8–10 representatives on the Common Council (most wards have 2–5). Each ward also elects one representative to the Court of Aldermen, who serve for six years.

The Lord Mayor of the City of London and two Sheriffs, along with other city officers, are elected by the Common Hall and serve year-long terms. The Common Hall is made up of liverymen, the senior members of the Livery Companies (of which there are over 100) of the City, trade associations that have taken on political and ceremonial duties over the centuries. The Lord Mayor represents the City to foreign dignitaries, and while that is technically the function of many a local politician the world over, London's importance on the global stage brings the Lord Mayor out from the wings more often. The Corporation is heavily criticized by reformers for being outdated, a boys' club with official powers, a single-party microstate that refuses to conform to the practices of the more modern municipal governments surrounding it. This separate administration dates back to 886, when Alfred the Great's son-in-law was appointed Governor of London—but the City at the time was not surrounded by other small municipalities. Given the nature and value of the businesses in the City, it is also worth noting that unlike the boroughs of Greater London, the City maintains its own separate police force.

In the 21st century, the City has a residential population of less than 10,000, and unlike many cities this is significantly less than it has had in the past. Even in 1700, the City's population exceeded 200,000. As

Modern skyscrapers are changing the look of The City—at left is 30 St. Mary Axe, known as the Gherkin, which was developed by the Swiss Re company. Home to one of the largest stock exchanges in the world, The City is a rival to Wall Street.

the boroughs have been developed, though, and as commercial development has become more prominent in the City—since about the middle of the 19th century—the residential population has diminished. It is currently on a mild rise, bouncing back from an all-time low of about 4,200 people in the 1970s.

Important features of the financial industry that so dominates the City include the London Stock Exchange, one of the largest in the world, operating since 1801. The occasional target of takeover attempts, the LSE was most recently subject to takeover bids by NASDAQ from 2005 through 2007, until the latter company finally announced it was abandoning the attempt. Most of the shares NASDAQ accumulated during its takeover attempt—28 percent of the LSE—were sold to the Borse Dubai, in the United Arab Emirates. The Bank of England is also located in the City, as well as Lloyd's of London and offices for Bank of America, Barclays Bank, Citigroup, Credit Suisse, HSBC, and hundreds of other banks.

Outside the City, in the Tower Hamlets borough, but sometimes associated with the City in the international imagination, is the business district of Canary Wharf. Built in the 1980s on the site of the old West India Docks that had been bombed during World War II, Canary Wharf developed as a result of financial deregulation in the United Kingdom, which led to the spread and expansion of many banks and financial institutions, which found themselves stifled by the zoning regulations of the City of London—which sought to preserve its historic and widely-recognized look. Twenty years later, Canary Wharf is part upscale shopping district, part supplemental financial district, with tenants including major investment banks and law firms, as well as offices for the media outlets that cover the City.

See Also: Company Profiles: Western Europe; FT Index; FTSE; Stock Exchanges; United Kingdom; Wall Street.

Bibliography. Alexander Davidson, *How The City Really Works: The Definitive Guide to Money and Investing in London's Square Mile* (Kogan Page, 2008); John Grapper, "Are We No Longer the World's Financial Capital?" *New*

York (v.40/10, 2007); Richard Roberts, *The City: A Guide to London's Financial Centre* (Profile Books, 2008).

BILL KTE'PI
INDEPENDENT SCHOLAR

Clearing House Automated Payments System

A clearing house for Britain's large-value time-sensitive interbank, business-to-business, and home purchase transactions in pound sterling, the Clearing House Automated Payments System (CHAPS) facilitates low-volume, high-value transactions. CHAPS uses a real-time gross settlement (RTGS) process similar to that of Fedwire whereby transactions are quickly cleared and settled across accounts in the Bank of England on the same day. These transactions are final and irrevocable at the time they are made. The system is overseen in the United Kingdom (UK) by the Association for Payment Clearing Services (APACS).

CHAPS is owned by a small number of direct members and used by a large number of direct and indirect members. Direct members include large banks and building societies. Indirect members are smaller banks and building societies with access to CHAPS through direct members. Since 1999 CHAPS had operated as two clearing houses, CHAPS Sterling and CHAPS Euro, clearing and settling transactions in sterling and euros, respectively. However, CHAPS Euro ceased operations in May 2008. Reasons cited for this closure included a change in the UK's stance on the euro and declining volume of euro transactions conducted through CHAPS as other options became available for conducting such transactions (e.g., Trans-European Automated Real Time Gross Settlement Express Transfer, or Target2, and Single Euro Payment Area, or SEPA, for clearing that uses Target2 for settlement).

CHAPS was created in 1984. Initially, CHAPS used a netting settlements process whereby clearing was made throughout the day and a final settlement was made at the end of the day. This exposed the system to settlement risk should a large bank fail during the day. In 1996 CHAPS switched to an RTGS system for nearly instant settlement. This significantly reduces risk in the system. Since CHAPS Sterling payments represent 20–25 percent of annual UK GDP *per day*, there is significant need to keep the system sound. Payments are not made through the system without the funds to back up the payment in the system, thus banks participating in CHAPS use collateral at least equal to the amount of their expected peak payment activities. K. James and M. Willison suspect that this is due to the higher opportunity cost of not being able to make a payment versus the cost of posting collateral and borrowing intraday from the Bank of England.

Typically, individuals wanting to conduct electronic bank transactions in pound sterling had two choices: CHAPS or Bankers Automated Clearing House (BACS). The choice between the two depended on the size, cost, and/or urgency of the transaction. Large urgent transactions were conducted using CHAPS, and smaller, less urgent, and recurring transactions were conducted using BACS. Consumers might use CHAPS to buy a house or car and use BACS to pay their bills online. CHAPS has same day real-time settlement and BACS has an average three-day settlement. However, 50 percent of CHAPS payments are less than £10,000. The recently released Faster Payments Service (FPS) will offer faster, cheaper payments for smaller-value (less than £10,000) transactions. This is expected to draw a significant volume of transactions away from CHAPS, raising its costs and possibly injecting instability into the system. For this reason, FPS will be managed by CHAPS.

See Also: Central Banks; Clearing House Interbank Payments System; Clearing Houses; Interbank Market.

Bibliography. APACS, "CHAPS Euro System to Close After Nine Years of Service," www.apacs.org.uk (cited March 2009); Bank of England, "Payment Systems Oversight Report 2006," February 2007, Issue No. 3, www.bankofengland.co.uk (cited March 2009); Bank of England, "Payment Systems Oversight Report 2007," February 2008, Issue No. 4, www.bankofengland.co.uk (cited March 2009); M. Hughes, "Faster Payments in the UK: What Do Corporates Need to Know?" *Bottomline Technologies*, www.bottomline.co.uk (cited March 2009); K. James and M. Willison, "Collateral Posting Decisions in CHAPS Sterling" (Market Infrastructure Division, Bank of England, November 2, 2004).

CATHERINE CAREY
WESTERN KENTUCKY UNIVERSITY

Clearing House Interbank Payments System

A wire transfer system for large-value wholesale real-time interbank settlements, the Clearing House Interbank Payments System (CHIPS) is the largest private-sector global clearing house for cross-border dollar transactions, accounting for 95 percent of all international payments conducted in dollars. Wholesale payments are large interbank payments for purposes such as commercial transactions, bank loans, and securities transactions. CHIPS engages predominantly in large trade-related transactions and foreign exchange transactions denominated in dollars. CHIPS also accounts for 5 percent of U.S. domestic large-value business-to-business payments. CHIPS is owned by 46 member banks from 22 countries and is operated by the Clearing House, an association that is owned by 22 major U.S. member banks. CHIPS can be used by any banking organization with a regulated U.S. presence.

CHIPS was created in 1970 by the New York Clearing House, and according to former Federal Reserve chairman Alan Greenspan, it represented "the most significant qualitative change in clearing house arrangements." Transfers between banks occur in two parts: clearing and settlement. Clearing is when payment information is sent and received between participants. Settlement is when actual payment occurs. In 1970 CHIPS was the first real-time payments process whereby payments were electronically cleared the same day and then settled the next day. In October 1981 CHIPS added same day settlements. By 2001 settlements became final almost instantly. For banks, this reduces the risk they incur by having any significant amount of time between clearing and settlement.

Banks have two main options when processing interbank payments in dollars: Fedwire, operated by the Federal Reserve Bank, and CHIPS. CHIPS has some distinct advantages over Fedwire. One advantage is that CHIPs uses a patented multilateral netting settlements process. CHIPS keeps track of payments coming in and out of a particular bank's account and releases a single payment whenever the bank is in a positive position so that it will never be in an overdraft position. This is different from Fedwire, which processes transactions individually using a real-time gross settlement process that may leave banks occasionally in overdraft positions that must be settled by the end of the day. The Fed charges fees on those overdraft positions. Thus CHIPS reduces overdraft fees. CHIPS reduces the number of transactions between international and domestic banks during the day and processes more than $2 trillion per day.

While CHIPS and Fedwire are competitors, CHIPS could not operate without Fedwire. CHIPS uses Fedwire to conduct its transactions. Banks participating in CHIPS use a joint CHIPS account at the Federal Reserve to set aside funds for CHIPS transactions. They pre-fund the account to meet settlements throughout the day. Late in the day, there is a second chance to fund any settlements that could not be met with the initial balance. Those settlements are not released unless the bank is in a positive position. If the bank chooses not to be in a positive position, those payments are deleted and the bank can settle them using Fedwire directly. This is one disadvantage to using CHIPS over Fedwire. Payments made via Fedwire are final and irrevocable. Some payments made over CHIPS may not be final until the settlements are made final at the end of the day.

See Also: Clearing House Automated Payments System; Clearing Houses; Electronic Data Interchange; Interbank Market.

Bibliography. Clearing House Interbank Payments System, www.chips.org (cited March 2009); Alan Greenspan, "Clearing and Settlement: Past and Future," Federal Reserve Archival System for Economic Research, fraser.stlouisfed.org (cited March 2009); New York Federal Reserve, www.newyorkfed.org (cited March 2009); "Wholesale Payments Systems," Federal Financial Institutions Examination Council, www.ffiec.gov (cited March 2009).

Catherine Carey
Western Kentucky University

Clearing Houses

Clearing houses are institutions devoted to the exchange of information and the fulfillment of payment processing. A financial clearing house assures that two parties to a transaction do not default. Financial clearing houses include institutions devoted to the clearing of transactions involving the trading of financial securities and the conduct of specific forms of electronic payments.

Albert Bolles describes the clearing house concept as "one of the most useful agencies called into being by the wants of modern commerce ... susceptible to almost infinite expansion." Indeed the clearing house concept has grown dramatically and increased the efficiency of the payments system. The first clearing house in the banking system can be traced back to the London Clearing House, founded in 1775. The first clearing house in the United States, the New York Clearing House, was established in 1853 based on the example set forth by the London Clearing House. The use of checks created a need for clearing houses in the banking system.

When an individual deposits a check in his or her bank that is drawn on another bank, a clearing house ensures that the funds to cover the check flow from the bank the check was drawn on to the bank it was deposited into. Before the clearing house, the depositor's bank would have had to collect payment via messenger to the other bank. Before modern electronic processing, check clearing was largely a time- and paper-laden process. This process is conducted by the Federal Reserve Bank in the United States today. With the aid of wire transfers, check truncation (Check 21), the automated clearing house (ACH), and the electronic data interchange (EDI), payments conducted with paper have been greatly reduced.

The ACH Network

The ACH network was one of the U.S. payments system's first automated paperless answers to the increasing volume of paper checks. (The first was the wire transfer system Clearing House Interbank Payments System.) It was originally designed to clear small-value, recurring paper-check payments such as payroll deposits and mortgage payments. This system performs similar functions to the United Kingdom's Bankers Automated Clearing Service (BACS). For an ACH transaction to occur both the originating and the receiving bank must be members of the ACH network. The first U.S. ACH began in 1972 in California. The network was developed by bankers, but it was run by the Federal Reserve System.

Later, many small ACH associations developed and worked with the Federal Reserve district banks to clear regional electronic payments. By 1974, the National Automated Clearing House Association was formed to oversee and help coordinate the growing ACH network. Currently, the only operators remaining in the ACH in the United States include the publicly owned Fed ACH operated by the Federal Reserve System and the privately owned Electronic Payments Network (EPN), a subsidiary of The Clearing House. In 2007 more than 13.97 billion transactions, worth more than $28.8 trillion, were sent via the ACH network.

The ACH network sends secure electronic funds transfers in the form of debit and credit transactions to handle payments electronically as opposed to using paper checks. Debit transactions are initiated by the payee (e.g., a consumer paying a utility bill, mortgage payment, or fitness facility fee). Credit transactions are initiated by the payer (e.g., the direct deposit of an employee's paycheck or the reimbursement of an employee's travel or health expenses). Business-to-business, or corporate, payments utilize the electronic data interchange (EDI) format with ACH to exchange information and make and receive payments with trading partners, pay tax withholdings to the government, or for intracompany cash management transfers. Governments use the ACH network for such payments as Social Security, tax refunds, and pensions.

Retailers are now getting in on the ACH system through the increasing use of e-check applications. E-checks are checks converted to ACH transactions at the point-of-purchase (when a voided check is returned to the consumer at the time of purchase), at drop and lockbox locations (called accounts receivable checks or ARC—a check converted to an electronic debit), over the internet, and over the phone. In 2007, 40 percent of all noncash payments in the United States went through the ACH network.

In financial markets outside banking, The Clearing Corporation (TCC) purports to be the world's oldest independent clearing house. TCC was created to independently and confidentially clear futures transactions for the Chicago Board of Trade. In that role, TCC became a buyer for every seller and a seller for every buyer. Clearing in the securities industry is more complicated than check clearing since it involves the transfer of ownership along with payment. Efficiency greatly increased with the adoption of computer technology in 1963.

The Depository Trust Company

Similar technology led to the development of the Depository Trust Company (DTC) in 1973. The DTC was created to clear securities trades for the New York Stock Exchange. Prior to the adoption of computer technology, securities trading involved a lot of paperwork from the beginning of the sale to the actual delivery of the physical securities certificate from seller to buyer. As trading volume in the securities industry escalated, the DTC was designated to be a single "house" for the physical securities and then trades of ownership of those securities were conducted electronically rather than physically. This greatly reduced the volume of paperwork and increased the efficiency of the securities exchange system.

Today, the DTC is part of the Depository Trust & Clearing Corporation, or DTCC. The DTCC operates through six subsidiaries and provides clearing services for equities, corporate and municipal bonds, government and mortgage-backed securities, money market instruments, over-the-counter derivatives, mutual funds, and insurance transactions. Similar securities clearing houses in other countries include Euroclear (Belgium), Clearstream (Luxembourg), the Canadian Depository for Securities (CDS Ltd), China Government Securities Depository Trust and Clearing Co, Ltd., and Japan Securities Clearing Corporation.

See Also: Clearing House Automated Payments System; Clearing House Interbank Payments System; Electronic Data Interchange; Interbank Market.

Bibliography. Albert Bolles, *Practical Banking* (Homans Publishing Co., 1884); Terri Bradford, "The Evolution of the ACH," Payments System Research Briefing, December 2007, www.kansascityfed.org (cited March 2009); Electronic Payments Network, *The Electronic Payments Network and the ACH: A History,* www.epaynetwork.com (cited March 2009); NACHA, "ACH Volume Increases 13.4 Percent in 2007," www.nacha.org (cited March 2009); NACHA, "NACHA—The Electronic Payments Association," *Understanding the ACH Network: An ACH Primer,* www.nacha.org (cited March 2009); The Clearing House, "New York Clearing House: A Historical Perspective," www.theclearinghouse.org (cited March 2009).

Catherine Carey
Western Kentucky University

CMA Index (Egypt)

The Capital Market Authority (CMA) is the regulatory body responsible for the Egyptian securities market. Like the Securities and Exchange Commission (SEC) in the United States, the CMA is principally concerned with the protection of investors and the health of primary and secondary securities markets. To this end, it is the licensing authority for new securities companies, reviews and approves prospectuses for new securities issues and memoranda for private placements, and ensures that Egyptian Accounting Standards—derived from international standards—are upheld.

Further, the CMA monitors the securities market for fraud and unfair trading practices, and conducts regular inspections of brokers and other middlemen. Surveillance is planned to be bolstered in the coming years, to build investor confidence and the health of the Egyptian securities market.

The Egyptian securities trade dates to the 19th century, a century bound by the invasion of Egypt by Napoleon at one end and the decades of Egypt's existence as a British colony on the other. The Suez Crisis led to a decades-long experiment in Arab socialism, but after the Camp David Accords in 1978, Egypt's relationship with the United States and the West steadily improved. Ten years after Camp David, the nation was readmitted to the Arab League, and shortly after implemented market reforms. The CMA had been established in 1979, to facilitate the reemergence of Egypt's capital markets; in 1992, the markets began to become fully active again, and have steadily grown since. The electronic trading system was implemented as early as 1995, and since 1999, corporate bond issues have been rated by various agencies. Every year, the CMA has been steadily modifying its structures and regulations, building a stronger market.

Critical to the CMA now is the 2008–12 five-year plan, aimed at attracting foreign investors. The overall strategic mission remains the same—to protect investors and develop the market—while focusing on efficiency and accountability in its regulatory practices. The specific strategic objectives that have been set for the 2008–12 period are as follows:

- The ongoing development of regulatory programs, including the development of necessary legislation and new regulations, and further development of market surveillance.
- The organization and provision of medium- and long-term financial instruments, beginning with an evaluation of the international debt market to inform the development of an Egyptian debt market. A unit at CMA will be established to license and monitor debt issues, and securitization opportunities will be further developed.
- Encouraging and strengthening investors' awareness of Egyptian investment opportunities. This includes the usual public relations, from thrice-annual investor workshops to programs for the media.
- The ongoing development of the CMA's internal work systems to cope with market developments, reorganizing the CMA's administration if necessary.
- The ongoing development of the capital market infrastructure, coordinating with the Ministry of Investment. The CMA will also study derivatives and determine whether they should be introduced to the Egyptian market.

See Also: Bonds; Company Profiles: Middle East; Debt (Securities); Economic Development; Egypt; Financial Market Regulation; Markets; National Regulatory Agencies; Suez.

Bibliography. Hassan Aly, Seyed Mehdian, and Mark J. Perry, "An Analysis of Day-of-the-Week Effects in the Egyptian Stock Market," *International Journal of Business* (v.9/3, 2004); Capital Market Authority, www.cma.gov.eg (cited March 2009); Country Briefs *Financial Times* Survey, "Egypt 2000/Finance and Investment Stock Market: Struggling to Spread Its Wings," specials.ft.com (cited March 2009).

BILL KTE'PI
INDEPENDENT SCHOLAR

CNP Assurances

CNP Assurances is a French personal insurance company that offers both life and nonlife insurance products and services. It is headquartered in Paris, and in 2008 employed 3,200 people. The origins of CNP Assurances can be traced back to three state-owned insurance companies: the Caisse nationale d'assurance en cas d'accident (specialization: accident insurance) was established in 1868; the Caisse nationale d'assurance en cas de décès (death and disability insurance) was formed in 1848; and the Caisse de retraite pour la vieillesse (retirement pensions) was created in 1949.

The French government merged its death and disability and retirement insurance companies in 1949 to form the Caisse nationale d'assurance sur la vie. In 1959, this company was merged with the government's accident insurance company to create the Caisse Nationale de Prévoyance (CNP) and integrated into the Caisse des Dépôts et Consignations (CDC), a financial institution that performs public-interest missions on behalf of France's central, regional, and local governments.

In the early 1990s, the government decided to partially privatize CNP. In preparation for this change, the company was reorganized and renamed CNP Assurances. In an initial move, the state transferred 58 percent of its shares in the company to the CDC, the national postal service (La Poste), and the Caisses d'Epargne banking group. An initial public offering was conducted in 1998, which saw the state selling a further stake in CNP to the general public. The IPO enabled the CDC, La Poste, and Caisses d'Epargne to raise their stakes in the company to their current levels (CDC, 39.88 percent; La Poste and Caisses d'Epargne, 35.48 percent; general public; 23.44 percent: French state, 1.09 percent).

In the mid-1990s, the company began a period of international expansion. In 1996 it purchased a 26 percent stake in Polish life insurer Polisa-Zycie, raising this to 46 percent in 1997. In 2001 CNP moved into the Brazilian market, purchasing a 51 percent stake in the insurer Caixa Seguros. In 2002 CNP partnered with China Post to create the Sino-French Life Insurance Company and offer savings and insurance products in Beijing's post offices. In 2007 CNP Assurances acquired a 94 percent stake in the Spanish insurer Skandia Vida de Seguros y Reaseguros.

In 2008 CNP Assurances consists of three main business divisions. The savings division specializes in retirement savings products and accounts for 80 percent of total revenues. Its personal insurance division provides disability and invalidity coverage, health insurance, and loan insurance and generates 12 percent of total sales. With a market share of over 18 percent and more than 14 million policyholders, CNP is the leading personal insurance company in France.

CNP's pension division offers long-term savings products, designed to provide supplementary pension benefits in addition to the benefits paid under government-sponsored plans. It also manages the pension funds of French civil servants and local elected representatives. Together, the company's pension services make up approximately 8 percent of CNP's total sales.

CNP Assurances has achieved its leading position on the French market by using well-established partners to sell its products. The company has traditionally sold its products primarily through partnerships with state-run financial institutions, including the French Treasury and branches of La Poste, and Caisses d'Epargne. Combined, the 25,000 sales outlets provided by La Poste and the Caisses d'Epargne account for 75 percent of CNP's total sales.

CNP has also developed additional sales channels. In 2003, for example, the company entered into partnership with Mutualité Française, a major health insurance company, to strengthen its position in the mutual insurance market in France. In 2004 the company formed an alliance with the French retailing group Casino to market personal insurance products to the customers of Casino supermarkets in France. CNP has attempted to replicate this strategy abroad, seeking out well-established partners with strong distribution networks.

The company has also benefited from the recent French reforms to develop privately funded pensions alongside the conventional state-sponsored pension system. The further development of French investments in private retirement provision is expected to bring significant growth potential for the private and company pension provision business of CNP Assurances.

See Also: AXA; France; Globalization; Privatization; State-Owned Enterprises.

Bibliography. Gilles Benoist, "Bancassurance—The New Challenges," *The Geneva Papers on Risk and Insurance* (July, 2002); CNP Assurances, "CNP—France's Leading Personal Insurance Company," www.cnp.fr (cited March 2009); Datamonitor, "CNP Assurances SA" (Datamonitor, 2007); Bertrand Venard, "The French Insurance Market: Background and Trends," in *Handbook of International Insurance,* J. David Cummins and Bertrand Venard, eds. (Springer, 2007).

ANDREW BARRON
ESC RENNES BUSINESS SCHOOL

Coaching

Coaching in a sporting context has been used throughout history and has acquired a high status. It was the tool used to enable the athlete to run that bit faster, throw that bit farther: In essence, to win. In the business world, coaching is increasingly seen as one of the tools to enable an organization to achieve winning results. Coaching involves a one-to-one relationship between the coach and the learner, and aims to enhance the performance of the learner. Anyone from new frontline employees to experienced executives can benefit from coaching. Each has different starting points and needs but the outcome is likely to be similar: Overall improvement in performance and increased personal and job satisfaction.

Coaching involves a simple process that helps the learner identify and select the most appropriate course of action. By asking questions and giving support, feedback, and direction when necessary, the coach is able to encourage the learner to think through their own answers and make their own decisions. The following stages are typical: (1) initial fact finding—assessment of the learner's skills, attitudes, and motivation; (2) stage setting—a mutual agreement is established on ways of working together, on goals and desired outcomes for the coaching sessions; (3) defining the challenge/problem—the learner is the best person to define the challenge and to get to the root cause with the coach's help; (4) gaining agreement on facts—discussions are regularly summarized as an aid to understanding; (5) considering options—too often people use the first idea they think of, but the

While mentors are often managers, other approaches include using outside coaches or telephone or computer-based guidance.

coach will encourage the learner to explore a range of options before selecting the preferred solution; (6) action plan development—specific steps are outlined in order to achieve the preferred solution; and (7) evaluation—of how successful implementation was, of the learner's performance, and on what has been learned from the process.

For the learner, the main benefit of coaching is in gaining greater competence and confidence. This should result in better performance, which in turn may lead to greater independence, increased job satisfaction, greater reward, and a higher status. The coach can often be the learner's manager, and where this is the case the coach can benefit from improvements in team performance that result from competent staff. It can also lead to a reduction in management time spent problem solving and increased self-esteem for the coach as they see people blossom under their guidance. For the organization, coaching can result in greater all-around effectiveness, productivity, and quality through more competent staff. It can also lead to increased awareness of the talent within the organization and an enhanced reputation as an employer.

Effective coaching is about relationships. If the coach's and learner's styles or personalities clash, coaching may not be effective. Coach selection is therefore important. The coach needs to have a specific set of skills to be effective. The emphasis in coaching is on giving support and asking questions.

If the wrong person acts as coach, or if solutions are dictated to the learner, then they may not be fully committed to implementing their own learning. Some believe a learner's manager is the best person to be the coach. Depending on the goals and required outcomes of coaching, this may be true, but care needs to be taken with the unequal power relationship that exists and the level of openness and honesty possible. For these reasons, coaches from outside the organization may be preferred. Coaches must also have sufficient skills and experience to have credibility in the learner's and organization's eyes. Another difficulty is the time and cost involved. Coaches most often work one-on-one with people and over a period of time. Telephone or computer-based coaching can sometimes be used to reduce the direct face-to-face contact needed.

Coaching in a business context can be used for a variety of reasons. In business coaching, organizational developments or supporting learners through a change of role or career can often be best achieved through coaching. Executive coaching is targeted to people at board level within the organization, or to people who have the potential to progress to this level. Performance coaching is used to enhance the learner's performance, and it has been shown to be highly successful in this context. Skills coaching focuses on the core skills employees need in their role. Coaches here need to be highly experienced and competent in performing the skills they teach. In personal or "life" coaching, coaches work in supportive roles to learners who wish to make some form of change in their lives. Business coaching is always conducted within the constraints placed on the learner by the organization, but personal coaching takes purely the learner's perspective.

See Also: Empowerment; Management Development; Mentoring; Training.

Bibliography. Ian McDermott and Wendy Jago, *The Coaching Bible—The Essential Handbook* (Piatkus Books, 2007); David Megginson and David Clutterbuck, *Techniques for Coaching and Mentoring* (Elsevier Butterworth-Heinemann, 2005).

Jonathan Smith
Anglia Ruskin University

CoCom

CoCom stands for the "Coordinating Committee on Multilateral Export Controls." CoCom during the Cold War was essentially an economic arm of the alliance of North Atlantic countries. Set up in 1949, it served to prohibit businesses from selling arms and other sensitive products that might have dual civilian and military uses to Soviet-bloc countries. After the fall of communism and the consequent need to provide the newly democratic countries of Eastern Europe with needed technology for economic development, CoCom collapsed and was replaced in 1996 by the so-called Wassenaar's Agreement, named after the Dutch town in which the agreement was signed. Under the CoCom regime, companies were required through their governments to notify other members in advance before exporting a listed item. Under Wassenaar's, the proscriptions are voluntary and much more lenient.

With the rise of the threat of terrorism, particularly after September 11, 2001, governments realized that export restrictions were still critical to prevent so-called rogue states such as Iran, Iraq, North Korea, and Libya from acquiring advanced technology. So Wassenaar became the CoCom for a new century. Its adherents include Argentina, Australia, Austria, Belgium, Bulgaria, Canada, the Czech Republic, Denmark, Finland, France, Germany, Greece, Hungary, Ireland, Italy, Japan, Luxembourg, the Netherlands, New Zealand, Norway, Poland, Portugal, the Republic of Korea, Romania, the Russian Federation, the Slovak Republic, Spain, Sweden, Switzerland, Turkey, Ukraine, the United Kingdom, and the United States. The inclusion of such formerly "inimical" countries as Russia and Ukraine might indicate that this unlikely coalition is actually directed against the economies of the developing world.

The problem for businesses under Wassenaar is determining which product can have unintended impacts. This is especially true for so-called dual-use technologies (DUTs). These are products designed for the commercial market but which can have potential military applications. Many weapons components have legitimate civilian uses. To export DUTs, exporters must apply to national licensing authorities for an export license.

The list of dual-use technologies is seemingly unending. It includes golf equipment (used in missile development), heart pacemakers (useful in nuclear weapons), and even shampoos (for chemical weapons programs). The Japanese government, worried over North Korean missiles, once prohibited for a time the popular Sony PlayStation II home gaming system because of a graphics card that purportedly could drive a cruise missile. Wassenaar turned states like Pakistan to look toward the black market and corporate espionage to advance their nuclear programs. China is a particularly perplexing example. China is a potential Wassenaar ally in the struggle to keep DUTs out of states like India, Pakistan, Iran, and North Korea. But at the same time, the United States distrusts China as a long-time violator and beneficiary of anti-proliferation efforts.

After the U.S. invasion of Iraq, this situation led to a third round of controls, called the Proliferation Security Initiative (PSI). These are designed specifically to prevent North Korea and Iran from acquiring the component parts necessary for weapons of mass destruction and missile development programs. PSI reflects the post-Iraq maturation of a new DUT strategy that emphasizes regulation of core components of weapons of mass destruction (WMDs). This includes uranium and its acquisition by a handful of the world's most dangerous countries. Whereas CoCom and Wassenaar tended to focus on interior controls that kept technologies in a limited number of allied states, PSI reflects an awareness that the multilateral regimes of the future will most likely have to rely on exterior controls that prevent prohibited technologies from passing in or out of relatively confined target regions.

High-tech businesses with defense implications will have to watch Wassenaar's two lists carefully. The Sensitive List includes battle tanks; armored combat vehicles; large calibre artillery systems; military aircraft/unmanned aerial vehicles; military and attack helicopters; warships; missiles or missile systems; small arms and light weapons. The Very Sensitive List includes organic matrix composites; towed acoustic hydrophones' "space-qualified" solid-state detectors; manned, untethered submersible vehicles; ramjet, scramjet, or combined cycle engines; as well as "software" and "technology specially designed for the "development" or "production" of such equipment.

See Also: Black Market; Commerce Control List; Industrial Espionage; Terrorism.

Bibliography. Richard Re, "Playstation2 Detonation: Controlling the Threat of Dual-Use Technologies," *Harvard International Review* (v.25/3, 2003); Wassenaar Arrangement, www.wassenaar.org (cited March 2009).

HOWARD H. FREDERICK
UNITEC NEW ZEALAND

Collateral

Collateral refers to assets given or pledged as security for payment of a loan. Houses, cars, and other types of property are examples of tangible assets used as collateral. A potential problem with collateral arises if one is unable to pay off a loan as scheduled: The collateral assets will be sold, and the money raised by selling the assets will be used to repay the loan. Typically, collateral consists of financial instruments—stocks, bonds, and negotiable paper. Physical goods, however, may be accepted as collateral also.

Collateral items are generally of significant value. But the range varies considerably, depending on the terms of the lending institution's contract with the borrower. A collateral contract is a contract where the consideration is the entry into another contract, and coexists side by side with a main contract. For example, a collateral contract is formed when one party pays another party a certain sum of money for entry into another contract. Still, a collateral contract may be entered into between one of the parties and a third party. In short, many different types of collateral arrangements can be made by companies, whether they are experiencing a financial crunch or making plans for expansion.

Usually, collateral only comes into play when a company needs to make a secured loan—a loan that uses tangible assets as collateral. Contrary to unsecured loans, where a borrower is able to get a loan solely on the strength of its credit reputation, secured loans require a borrowing company to put up a portion of its assets as additional assurance of repayment.

Many start-up businesses often use collateral-based loans. The advantage of such loans is that they have lower interest rates. Unsecured loans, by contrast, have higher interest rates. A problem with many small businesses is that most do not have enough collateral to get a secured loan from a lending institution. Con-

sequently, such businesses often rely on equity financing instead. Notwithstanding the foregoing, borrowers have a broad array of options when using collateral.

A borrower may substitute other collateral for that held by a lender. Such a privilege is particularly useful for borrowers who buy and sell securities. For instance, merchandise collateral, such as negotiable warehouse receipts, bills of lading, and trust receipts are often used. Additionally, personal collateral—deeds, mortgages, leases—is frequently used. Finally, collateral may include bills of sale for crops, machinery, furniture, and even livestock.

When a borrower defaults on a loan, a creditor may sell collateral so it can be liquidated—turned into cash—and apply the money acquired to satisfy the debt. The creditor will charge the debtor with any deficiency remaining but will credit the debtor with any surplus. Accordingly, borrowers usually do not put their biggest asset on the line, unless payment can be made pursuant to the contract.

In today's increasingly complex world of multinational conglomerates, there are several forms of intellectual property that may be pledged as primary sources of collateral—trademarks, patents, derivative royalties. A cologne manufacturing company, for instance, may use its trademarks and future stream of royalties from its trademarks as collateral for millions of dollars in financing.

Because virtually all meaningful companies in almost every industry around the world have intangible and intellectual assets with substantial value, business leaders and entrepreneurs consistently analyze international events and concepts on a daily basis, seeking different ways to apply them to the intricate dynamics at play in the realm of international business. Although increasing globalization among business communities may create international financing options, using appropriate valuation methodologies, coupled with an effective management team, may help maximize the value of assets through sales, securitization, or other forms of monetization.

See Also: Bank for International Settlements; Bill of Lading; Business-to-Business; Contracts.

Bibliography. Fuhito Kojima, "Stability and Instability of the Unbeatable Strategy in Dynamic Processes," *International Journal of Economic Theory* (v.2/1, March 2006); 67

Fed. Reg. 76560, 76608 (2002) (to be codified at 12 C.F.R. § 223.14(e)).

Daniel A. Espinosa
St. Thomas University School of Law

Collateralized Debt Obligations

Collateralized debt obligations (CDOs) are assets that are used as collateral and then pooled together in order to be the basis of new securities that provide cash flows. A company buys the debt instruments, collects the cash from the debts, and then sells securities that are in effect purchases of a portion of the cash flow.

CDOs are used in structured financing operations created through complex legal and corporate entities for the purpose of transferring risk. When pools of assets in the form of debts are securitized it means that a default of one of the debts in the pool will not result in a total loss, but only a minor one that can be overcome by other factors.

When CDO pools are created investors can buy a tranch (from the French word *tranche,* for slice) of the pool. The tranching allows the cash flow from the assets at the bottom of the pool to be allocated to different investor groups in different ways. One goal is to create securities that are rated from the pool of unrated securities. By being rated a market in the securities can be created. There are different levels of tranching, with the most secure usually the senior tranch, followed by mezzanine tranches, followed by the subordinate levels of tranches. Cash flows go to the senior level first, then to the mezzanine level, and then to the subordinate levels. The latter are the least secure and entail the most risk if defaults occur.

CDOs issued as unregulated securities are based upon a portfolio of fixed income assets. The assets are rated by rating agencies that assign the values after each asset is assessed. The senior tranches are typically rated as AAA, while mezzanine tranches are rated from AA to BB. Subordinate tranches are usually unrated.

Investors in CDOs hold a piece of paper that entails risks. Ultimately the risk is based upon the credit risk of the collateral in the pool. CDOs have been unregulated since their introduction in 1987. During the credit crisis that developed rapidly after 2006 they came to be identified as a major source of the crisis. The complex nature of CDOs and their collapse in liquidity were reasons offered for the credit crisis. However, part of the failure to appreciate the risks involved lay in the distribution of financial knowledge. As a result some buyers were not equipped to measure the changing credit ratings and cash flows to the CDOs. In addition the credit rating agencies upon which they relied were also insufficiently skilled at properly valuing the CDOs.

CDOs are typically valued on a mark-to-market basis. This method of valuing an asset marks the asset's value as what it would bring today. However, the future value (as in the case of a futures contract) may be unknown and therefore merely a guess until it is sold at a future time. Because of the complexity of CDOs some businesses have used them to hide debt under the cover of CDOs. In addition many rating agencies failed in 2006 and afterward to accurately assign values to them, causing a loss of confidence in the rating agencies and a retreat from lending.

Drexel Burnham Lambert, Inc., which is no longer in business, was the first company to offer CDOs for Imperial Savings Association. The latter became insolvent by 1990 and was taken over by the Resolution Trust Fund on June 22, 1990. However, by 2000 CDOs had returned and were greatly favored by investment banks, insurance companies, mutual funds, private banks, pension funds, and other financial institutions because they offered a higher rate of return, usually two or three percent higher than corporate bonds with the same credit rating. By 2007 they totaled $2 trillion in investments globally.

See Also: Collateralized Loan Obligations; Mark-to-Market Valuation; Mortgage Credit Crisis of 2008.

Bibliography. Christian Bluhm and Overbeck Ludger, *Structured Portfolio Analysis: Modeling Default Baskets and Collateralized Debt Obligations* (CPR, 2006); Douglas J. Lucas, Frank J. Fabozzi, and Laurie S. Goodman, *Collateralized Debt Obligations: Structures and Analysis* (John Wiley & Sons, 2006); Janet M. Tavakoli, *Structured Finance and Collateralized Debt Obligations: New Developments in Cash and Synthetic Securitization* (John Wiley & Sons, 2008).

Andrew J. Waskey
Dalton State College

Collateralized Loan Obligations

A collateralized loan obligation (CLO) is a debt security, a promissory note, with a pool of commercial loans as its collateral. The backing of the promise of the borrower to repay the loan is guaranteed by debt instruments they own. Historically collateral was some type of asset, such as bank deposits in gold or silver, land, building, businesses, cattle, horses, or other forms of tangible assets. However, contemporary financing has come to accept debt owned by the borrower as an asset (collateral) for new debt. In the case of a CLO, which is a debt security, the debt backing the CLO(s) is a pool of commercial loans.

CLOs are like collateralized debt obligations (CDOs) and collateralized mortgage obligations (CMOs) because they are all debt securities. They differ in the kind of debt that is being used for collateral. Both CDOs and CMOs use a pool of mortgages as assets rather than a pool of commercial loans, which are registered on the CLO's originator's books as receivables.

Banks around the world have, until the credit crisis of 2008, found CLOs to be useful for several reasons. They allow them to avoid the capital requirements demanded by regulators to meet calls on their demand deposits. It also allows them to reduce their risks on their commercial lending because the CLO is a sale of a portion of their commercial loan portfolio.

Investors in CLOs can expect to receive a cash flow from the CLO. However, it is a common practice to securitize the payments into different levels of tranches. This somewhat resembles preferred stock, where the preferred stock is paid a dividend before the common stock. However, with the tranches of CLOs it is more like having several levels of preferred stock getting different levels of dividends and the common stock receiving no dividends but still having an investor appeal because of the speculative risk and rewards that can come from trading the CLOs.

The commercial loans that are used to collateralize CLOs are medium and large business loans. The loans are multimillion-dollar loans commonly called syndicated loans. A bilateral loan is between a bank and a borrower and a participation loan is between a borrower and a group of banks. A syndicated loan is one between a group of lenders and a group of borrowers.

Once they are securitized they are sold to different investors with different tranches.

Loans made though CLOs are usually leveraged loans and involve very short-term loans. They are also leveraged borrowing, where the borrower is borrowing more than could be repaid, but is still accepted as creditworthy because it is more likely that the borrower will succeed than fail. The risk with leveraged loans is that the borrower is using the company as collateral and may be borrowing much more than the company is worth. Lenders receive a return on the loan that is representative of their risk in the case of a default.

Collateral loan obligations were created in order to finance projects with lower interest rates and an increased supply of lenders. The reasoning was that if the risk could be spread it would increase the number of willing business lenders and also reduce the cost of borrowing. The goal was for banks to lend money to businesses and then to use their commercial loans as collateral for the CLOs that were then sold to outside investors. If both financially conservative risk aversive and risk taking lenders could be attracted to the lending action then the supply of lenders could be increased. The outside lenders may be a variety of institutions needing a place for investment. In using the CLO the lending banks could earn fees and also receive some of the tranches. New types of CLOs are being developed for the market after the post-2008 credit crisis. These are being promised as safer investments.

See Also: Collateralized Debt Obligations; Mortgage Credit Crisis of 2008.

Bibliography. Frank J. Fabozzi and Vinod Kothari, *Introduction to Securitization* (John Wiley & Sons, 2008); Frank J. Fabozzi, ed., *Investing in Asset-Backed Securities* (John Wiley & Sons, 2001); Jason H. P. Kravitt, ed., *Securitization of Financial Assets* (Wolters Kluwer Law & Business, 1995).

Andrew J. Waskey
Dalton State College

Colombia

One of the top performers in gross domestic product (GDP) growth in Latin America, Colombia is considered an important emerging market for many foreign direct investors. Economic growth, however, is still hampered by the country's decades-long internal armed conflict. As of 2008, Colombia, which became a republic in 1819, is Latin America's third most populous country after Brazil and Mexico, and the fifth-largest economy in the region according to its GDP measured at purchasing power parity (PPP). The country's economic performance has generally been one of the best in the region, especially under the government of President Alvaro Uribe, who introduced orthodox, market-friendly policies in 2000.

Colombia's decades-long armed conflict involves two leftist insurgencies (the Revolutionary Armed Forces of Colombia—FARC, and the National Liberation Army—ELN), and a right-wing paramilitary organization (United Self-Defense Forces of Colombia—AUC). By 2006, under the leadership of President Uribe, the rates for kidnapping and murder reached their lowest level in over 20 years, and demobilization of ELN and AUC soldiers led to a significant decrease in violence in the country. Despite such progress in violence reduction, the conflict continues to hamper the economy's prospects. According to the World Bank, Colombia's average per capita income would be 50 percent higher than current levels if the country had achieved peace 20 years ago.

In contrast to many other Latin American countries, Colombia benefits from a wealth of natural resources, a diversified economic structure, a relatively developed regulatory environment for business, and stronger institutions. The World Bank even considers Colombia the region's top reformer in 2008 regarding the implementation of new regulations that enhance business activity.

Petroleum, coal, and coffee represent over 40 percent of the country's major exports, while imports are mainly concentrated on intermediate, capital, and consumer goods. Thus, the economy is highly dependent on global commodity prices. In contrast to many other oil exporters, Colombia shows account deficits over the last few years because of higher import growth and increased levels of profit remittances from foreign companies operating in the country. Over 50 percent of exports go to the United States, Venezuela, and Ecuador, whereas suppliers are less concentrated regionally—40 percent of all imports originate from the United States, Mexico, and Brazil.

The economic liberalization of the early 1990s caused a relative deindustrialization, and sectors such as textiles and clothing, leather, and shoes suffered from structural changes, whereas sectors such as chemicals, automotive, food processing, beverages, and printing adjusted more easily to the changing market conditions. Nevertheless, textiles and clothing still contribute significantly to total industrial output and manufactured exports, especially by improved access to the U.S. market under the Andean Trade Promotion and Drug Eradication Act (ATPDEA).

As in most Latin American countries, industrial concentration is high. In the manufacturing sector, two conglomerates dominate the market: the Grupo Empresarial Antioqueño in the sectors of financial services, cement, and processed foods, and the Grupo Ardilla Lülle in the sectors of textiles, sugarcane, and soft drinks. However, such industrial concentration is increasingly challenged by elimination of restrictions on imports and foreign investment.

Foreign investors not only increase local competition, but also contribute significantly to the competitiveness of sectors such as food processing, chemicals, and heavy industry (e.g., automotive). Colombian companies, especially in the sectors of steel, tobacco, processed foods, and beer, increasingly became targets for foreign investors. Since 2003 foreign direct investment (FDI) increased significantly, mainly in the sectors of oil, manufacturing, retail, restaurants, and hotels, with the main investors originating from Spain, the United States, the United Kingdom, and Brazil.

According to the World Economic Forum, Colombia's global competitiveness is positively influenced by factors such as macroeconomic stability, health and primary education, and market size, and negatively impacted by its road and transport infrastructure and technological readiness (i.e., firm-level technology absorption and numbers of internet users and personal computers). Thus, GDP growth can be further positively impacted if Colombia successfully overcomes its infrastructure deficiencies and problems related to the internal armed conflict.

See Also: Emerging Markets; Latin America.

Bibliography. M. E. Porter, X. Sala-i-Martin, and K. Schwab, *The Global Competitiveness Report 2007–2008* (Palgrave Macmillan, 2007); The Economist Intelligence

Unit—ViewsWire, "Colombia," www.viewswire.com (cited March 2009); World Bank Group, "Doing Business in Colombia," www.doingbusiness.com (cited March 2009).

SASCHA FURST
EAFIT UNIVERSITY

Commerce Control List

The Commerce Control List (CCL) is a list maintained by the Bureau of Industry and Security (BIS), an agency of the U.S. Department of Commerce. Similar lists are maintained by other countries. The Bureau of Industry and Security was originally called the Bureau of Export Administration, and references to the BXA are still seen in older texts. The CCL is used to ensure compliance with multinational export restrictions, especially on dangerous goods like munitions or dual-use technologies like computers or propulsion systems.

The body of regulations affecting exports is called the Export Administration Regulations (EAR), for which the BIS is responsible for enforcing and of which the CCL is a subset. Goods are regulated not only according to type, but according to country. Foreign policy severely limits exports to Cuba, Syria, Sudan, and Iran, while nearly anything that is legal to export can be exported to England or Canada. Exports include not only items originating in the United States and sold to foreign customers, but items being returned to their country of origin, items shipped to other countries but not sold, and items passing through the United States from their point of origin to some other final destination.

Certain other agencies outside the Department of Commerce have input into the EAR, whether it is to interpret their own regulations in light of their effect on exports, or to offer technical services in order to assist the BIS in implementing the EAR. The National Security Agency, for instance, is the technical review authority for cryptography and similar technologies. The Department of Agriculture's Foreign Agricultural Service advises on the exports of food and farm goods. The State Department advises on munitions exports. The Food and Drug Administration is involved with the export of American pharmaceuticals, though usually the more important authority in such cases is the analogous agency in the country of destination.

Goods that can be exported are issued a permit, based on the item's Export Control Classification Number (ECCN). The ECCN is an alphanumeric designation identifying the level of export control. There are hundreds of ECCNs, and because the system is organized according to an item's potential for misuse more than its intended use, navigating the list is time-consuming even for those accustomed to it.

The CCL was revised around the turn of the century, following the Wassenaar Agreement. Established in the Dutch town of Wassenaar in 1996, the Wassenaar Agreement is the successor to the Cold War–era Coordinating Committee for Multilateral Export Controls, and is a multilateral export control regime governing export controls on certain technologies. Forty nations are compliant with the Wassenaar Agreement: Argentina, Australia, Austria, Belgium, Bulgaria, Canada, Croatia, the Czech Republic, Denmark, Estonia, Finland, France, Germany, Greece, Hungary, Ireland, Italy, Japan, Latvia, Lithuania, Luxembourg, Malta, the Netherlands, New Zealand, Norway, Poland, Portugal, Romania, Russia, Slovakia, Slovenia, South Africa, South Korea, Spain, Sweden, Switzerland, Turkey, Ukraine, the United Kingdom, and the United States. The agreement governs the export of 22 categories of munitions and 10 categories of "dual-use" technologies (those that have both peaceful and military applications): advanced materials, materials processing, electronics, computers, telecommunications, information security (such as cryptography), sensors, navigation and avionics, marine technology, and aerospace technology.

In addition to the 10 dual-use categories of the Wassenaar Agreement, the CCL (which combines telecommunications and information security into category five) includes "category zero," used for all nuclear technology.

See Also: CoCom; Compliance; Department of Commerce; Export.

Bibliography. UC-Irvine Office of Research, "Export Control Index: Commerce Control List," www.research.uci.edu/ora/exportcontrol (cited March 2009); Wassenaar Arrangement, www.wassenaar.org (cited March 2009).

BILL KTE'PI
INDEPENDENT SCHOLAR

Commercialization of Space

The commercial use of outer space centers around the commercial applications of satellite technology, along with a growing space tourism industry. The exploration of space began with communications satellites—Sputnik, the Soviet satellite launched in 1957, was equipped with radio transmitters, as was the American satellite that followed the next year—and they remain the primary focus of commercialized outer space. The first true communications satellite, Telstar, was launched in 1962 and was used to transmit telephone and data communications. The satellite was launched by a multinational group consisting of NASA, the British General Post Office, the French National Post, Telephone and Telecom Office, Bell Labs, and AT&T, which owned the satellite. It was built at Bell Labs, which earned a NASA contract for work on further satellites.

Telstar orbited the Earth on an elliptical orbit, requiring a ground antenna to track its movements and relay its signals. Today's satellites are geosynchronous (also called geostationary), meaning that their position relative to any spot on the Earth is constant: The satellite, once positioned, orbits at the same speed as the rotation of the Earth. This allows an antenna to be directed at it without needing to track it, which in turn allows for applications that are impractical with elliptical orbit satellites, including consumer satellite dishes (for satellite TV). The first geosynchronous satellite was Syncom 3, used for the first television transmission over the Pacific when the 1964 Summer Olympics were held in Tokyo.

As geosynchronous satellites became more common, and improved in their designs, they helped with the spread of cable television. Early nonbroadcast networks like HBO, the Weather Channel, and Pat Robertson's Christian Broadcasting Network used geosynch satellites to transmit their programming to local cable companies for distribution. Broadcast networks (ABC, NBC, CBS) likewise used them to distribute to local affiliates.

Less expensive than geosynchronous satellites are low-earth orbit (LEO) satellites. Because their position relative to the Earth changes so rapidly, LEO satellites are useful only when there are a lot of them working in concert, in what are called satellite constellations—so that at any given time, one or more

NASA repaired this communication satellite in 1992. Its owner, the Intelsat organization, became a private company in 2001.

of them is accessible from any given spot in the relevant area. This is a more recent approach to satellite technology, and usually used for satellite phones. The Iridium satellite constellation—originally intended to have 77 satellites, and named for the element with the atomic number 77—uses 66 satellites to transfer data to all points of the globe (including the poles and the oceans, where coverage by other means is impossible). Iridium's financial failure, though, discouraged further development of satellite phones and their associated constellations; one of the problems was that the system's benefits (global coverage) could not be seen by customers until the entire system was in place, a hugely expensive venture, which in turn meant a significant price for customers. Both the price and the phone were heftier than customers were used to, at a time when traditional cellular phones were lightening both loads. Less than a year after its 1998 launch, Iridium filed chapter 11. The shriveling of the satellite phone industry is well-illustrated by Teledesic, backed by Microsoft co-owner Paul Allen. Teledesic was supposed to have 840 satellites in orbit, scaled back to 277 satellites because of decreasing projected demand, and only launched one satellite before folding operations.

That said, a decade later Iridium remains in business, with a quarter of a million subscribers, the number of which is growing. Rather than replacing or competing with cell phones, satellite phones like Iridium's have developed a niche among those who need the service's coverage (the U.S. Defense Department is a major customer).

In the 21st century, communications satellites are used for commercial purposes such as telecommunications, television, digital radio (such as Sirius XM Radio), and direct broadcast (such as used by satellite television companies DirecTV, DISH Network, Bell TV, and Sky Digital). The communications satellite industry includes transponder leasers, a growing industry sector of satellite owners who lease access to their satellites; subscription satellite services, such as those used for satellite television and radio; ground equipment manufacturers, who make the telephones, transponders, receivers, and other equipment used for interacting with satellites; and satellite manufacturers themselves. Satellite manufacturing is growing slower in the United States than in the world at large, in part because of strict controls on the export of American-made satellite technology and in part because of the countries now catching up to a space race in which the United States has a decades-long head start.

Commercial uses of other satellites include the sale of satellite imagery from nonmilitary observation satellites and the operation of global navigation satellite systems, which in the United States allows for the world's only fully-functional Global Positioning System (GPS). GPS navigation devices are increasingly popular in the United States, and many automobile manufacturers offer them as an installed option. Similar systems are in the works in Russia, China, India, Japan, and the European Union.

Most of the space transport industry involves the transportation of satellites into orbit. In the United States, the Federal Aviation Administration (FAA)—which governs space as well as air aviation—has licensed four commercial spaceports, in California, Florida, Virginia, and Alaska. Most commercial launches use Boeing's Delta IV rocket system or the Atlas V system developed by Lockheed Martin and built by a joint Lockheed Martin/Boeing venture.

Both are unmanned craft, and are single-use vehicles; development of reusable launch vehicles for commercial purposes has been sporadic, but investment to such ends has increased since the 1990s. Space tourism—manned commercial spaceflights—is a growing commercial interest, though most companies remain in the development stages.

See Also: Barriers to Entry; Private Spaceflight Industry.

Bibliography. Tim Arango, "From the Iron Curtain to the Final Frontier," *Fortune* (May 28, 2007); Jonathan Goodrich, *The Commercialization of Outer Space: Opportunities and Obstacles for American Business* (Quorum Books, 1989); Edward Hudgins, *Space: The Free-Market Frontier* (Cato Institute, 2003); F. Shahrokhi, J. S. Greenberg, and T. Al-Saud, *Space Commercialization: Satellite Technology* (American Institute of Aeronautics and Astronautics, 1990).

BILL KTE'PI
INDEPENDENT SCHOLAR

Commitment

Commitment is the action of committing oneself to a particular course of conduct. In management research the notion is widely used in the sense of organizational commitment, describing an individual's psychological attachment to a group or an organization and desire to remain part of it. High organizational commitment is expected to raise productivity by raising individual and organizational performance.

A number of definitions of organizational commitment have been produced over time. In the historical development of the definition we find three main approaches. An early definition of commitment is based on Howard Becker's notion of side-bet theory. According to this theory committed employees are committed because they have hidden investments, "side-bets," they have made by remaining in an organization that would be lost by leaving the organization.

A second approach was advanced by Lyman W. Porter and his colleagues. Shifting the focus to the psychological attachment of the employee to the organization, commitment was defined as the relative strength of an individual's identification with and involvement in a particular organization. Commitment is here characterized by three criteria: acceptance of organizational goals and values, a willingness to exert considerable effort on behalf of the organization, and a desire to maintain membership in the organization.

A third approach sees commitment as a multidimensional phenomenon, as suggested by John P. Meyer and Natalie J. Allan's three-component model of commitment, distinguishing between affective, continuance, and normative commitment.

Affective commitment refers to the employee's positive emotional attachment to, identification with, and involvement in the organization. Affective commitment is based on affective or emotional attachment to the organization so that the individual identifies with and enjoys membership of the organization. According to this approach, the desire of the employee to remain part of the organization is based on a feeling that he or she "wants to."

Continuance commitment refers to the employee's decision to remain part of the organization because of the perceived costs associated with leaving the organization. The continuance dimension was proposed as a better representation of Becker's side-bet theory. Continuance commitment is based upon an evaluation of the economic costs, as well as the social costs, compared to the economic and social benefits of staying as a member of the organization. The employee decides to remain part of the organization because he or she "has to."

Normative commitment refers to the employee's commitment to an organization because of feelings of loyalty and an obligation to continued employment. The employee has a feeling of moral obligation to stay a member of the organization. These feelings may reflect an internalized norm that one should be loyal to your organization. The employee stays with the organization because he or she "ought to." These three forms of commitment are viewed as components of attitudinal commitment; that is, employees may simultaneously be committed in the affective, continuance, and normative sense in varying degrees. The many different aspects of organizational commitment have been an important topic of research as well as what determines the degree of commitment. Research has indicated that the degree of commitment may depend on personal characteristics, job characteristics, and work experience.

Five foci of commitment have been identified in research on commitment: to work regardless of organization or job; to a specific job; to a union; to a career or a profession; and to an employing organization. Recent research has inquired into the relationships between the foci of commitment and has found four patterns of commitment: to the supervisor or work group (the locally committed); to top management and the organization (the globally committed); to both local and global foci (the committed); and individuals committed to neither global nor local foci.

Commitment is normally measured by attitudinal dimensions, e.g., identification with the goals and values of the organization; desire to belong to the organization; and willingness to display effort on behalf of the organization. Several different scales have been developed to measure organizational commitment, such as the Organizational Commitment Questionnaire (OCQ) developed by Porter and his colleagues. Meyer and Allan developed three scales to measure the three components of commitment they have suggested: the Affective Commitment Scale (ACS), the Continuance Commitment Scale (CCS), and the Normative Commitment Scale (NCS).

High organizational commitment is expected to raise productivity as well as individual and organizational performance. However, the strong positive link between commitment and performance is difficult to demonstrate clearly in empirical studies, indicating that the relationship between individual commitment and organizational performance is rather complex. High organizational commitment may contribute more generally to achieving long-term organizational goals by maintaining the cohesiveness of organizational structures and to aid integration. One of the issues raised that may limit these effects is extent of the homogeneity of employees. A lack of homogeneity of the workforce may lead to competition, disputes, and lack of common values, while a homogeneous workforce may stifle creativity and innovation.

A number of studies have analyzed organizational commitment in a cross-cultural context. One of the results of this type of study is that organizational commitment for Japanese workers was found to be rather low compared to, for example, U.S. workers.

See Also: Attitudes and Attitude Change; Empowerment; Leadership; Motivation.

Bibliography. H. S. Becker, "Notes on the Concept of Commitment," *American Journal of Sociology* (1960); J. R. Lincoln and A. L. Kalleberg, *Culture, Control, and Commitment: A Study of Work Organization and Work Attitudes in the United States and Japan* (Cambridge University Press, 1990); J. P. Meyer and N. J. Allen, "A Three-Component Conceptualization of Organizational Commitment," *Human Resource Management Review* (1991); R. T. Mowday, L. W. Porter, and R, M. Steers, *Employee-Organization Linkages* (Academic Press, 1982); R. T. Mowday, R. M. Steers, and L. W. Porter, "The Measurement of Organizational Commitment," *Journal of Vocational Behavior* (1979); L. W. Porter, R. M. Steers, E. M. Mowday, and P. V. Boulian, "Organizational Commitment, Job Satisfaction and Turnover among Psychiatric Technicians," *Journal of Applied Psychology* (1974); S. Swailes, "Organizational Commitment: A Critique of the Construct and Measures," *International Journal of Management Reviews* (2002).

SØREN JAGD
ROSKILDE UNIVERSITY

Common Agricultural Policy

The European Union system of common agricultural policy (CAP) was introduced in 1962 following the creation of the European Economic Community (EEC, the "Common Market") in 1957 by Belgium, France, the German Federal Republic, Italy, Luxembourg, and the Netherlands. The CAP has remained through the development of the EEC into the European Union (EU) of 12 countries in 1992 and its expansion to 27 countries as of 2008. The initial objectives of the CAP were to increase agricultural production, ensure a fair standard of living for farmers and the agricultural community, guarantee availability of food supplies, provide food at reasonable prices, and stabilize food markets. These objectives were to be achieved primarily by subsidizing agricultural production and maintaining agricultural commodity price levels within the EEC. The CAP has developed in response to a range of factors including overproduction of a range of agricultural products, market pressures, environmental concerns, and expansion of the EEC into the EU.

The CAP is the oldest and most costly common policy of the EU, utilizing approximately 60 percent of the total EU budget in 1992, 40 percent in 2007, and a projected 32 percent in 2013. Initially, the CAP subsidized agricultural production and maintained agricultural commodity prices within the EU by providing a direct subsidy payment for cultivated land, guaranteeing a minimum price to producers and imposing tariffs and quotas on certain goods from outside the EU. These measurements resulted in increased, and subsequently surplus, production of the major farm products in the 1980s. In some cases, goods were stored or disposed of within the EU but, generally, surplus goods were exported to the world market with subsidies given to traders who sold agricultural products to foreign buyers for less than the price paid to EU farmers. Disposal of surpluses had a high budgeting cost. In 1984, the surplus of milk was contained by the introduction of production quotas and in 1988, a limit was set on EU expenditure to farmers.

In 1992, reforms of CAP were established to limit agricultural production of specific products (e.g., wheat and milk) that attracted subsidies in excess of market prices. The prices farmers received for their products were reduced but they were given direct payment compensation for these reductions. Also, "set aside" payments were introduced in which farmers were paid to withdraw land from production and limit stocking rates, the number of animals per unit area. These measures were linked to environment- and rural development–related objectives. For example, reduced production required reduced inputs of agrochemicals such as nitrogen fertilizer that had been shown to have adverse effects on the environment such as the eutrophication of nutrient-poor land habitats and waterways, a decrease in biodiversity inside and outside the agricultural systems, and emissions of greenhouse gases into the atmosphere.

In 1995, in response to the World Trade Organization agricultural agreement, use of export subsidies to exporters was reduced. Also in 1995, rural development aid was introduced with the objective of diversifying the rural economy and making farmers more competitive. In 1999 the "Agenda 2000" reforms set in place reductions in market support prices for several products including wheat and milk. These measures were partially offset by an increase in direct aid payments to farmers. The Agenda 2000 reforms also introduced several rural development/regeneration measures including support for younger farmers and further aid toward the diversification of farms and the implementation of more "environmentally friendly" farming systems.

A major reform of the CAP (Regulation EC No. 1782/2003) which decoupled direct payment from production of particular crops and agricultural commodities was introduced in 2003. A new "Single Farm Payment" was established that is dependent on farmers adhering to environmental, food safety, and animal health standards that were previously in place: This is termed "cross compliance." The bulk of subsidies will be paid independently of the volume of production of specific crops, and farmers' decisions on which crops to produce should be based on market needs. As of 2008, set-aside payments are suspended. The reforms will be phased in from 2005 to 2012. The overall EU and national budgets have been capped and the proportion of the total agricultural budget spent on rural development will increase to around 25 percent over this period.

See Also: Candidate Countries; Common Market; Euro; European Monetary Union; European Union; Maastricht Treaty; World Trade Organization.

Bibliography. EUROPA, "CAP Reform—a Long-term Perspective for Sustainable Agriculture," www.ec.europa.eu (cited March 2009).

MITCHELL ANDREWS
UNIVERSITY OF SUNDERLAND

Common External Tariff

A common external tariff is an agreement among two or more countries to adopt identical tariff schedules for all goods being imported from other trading partners. Having a common external tariff is the central feature of a customs union, which is an agreement among countries to eliminate internal tariffs and establish a common external tariff. A common external tariff may also include the homogenization of nontariff trade barriers such as quotas and other trade preferences.

When countries participate in the process of regional economic integration, they most often begin by forming a free trade area that eliminates all internal tariffs on imports and exports between the partners. A free trade area, however, may provide incentives to nonmember trading partners to engage in the practice of reexportation (also known as entrepôt trade). A company from outside the free trade area may import products into the member country with the lowest external tariff, and then reexport to another member country tariff-free. This situation provides incentives for countries in a free trade area to manipulate external tariffs in order to gain trading advantages. In order to eliminate this activity, countries in a free trade union may form a customs union, in which a common external tariff is instituted.

The European Economic Community (now known as the European Union) established a common external tariff in July 1968. The elimination of most internal tariffs had been completed 11 years earlier with the signing of the Treaty of Rome by member countries Belgium, France, Italy, Luxembourg, the Netherlands, and the Federal Republic of Germany. Just a few weeks after the common external tariff was established in Europe, an agreement to allow the free movement of workers within member states was also adopted. The acceptance of the free movement of labor and capital within member countries is the next stage of regional economic integration and is referred to as a common market.

Mercosur, a trading bloc consisting of Argentina, Brazil, Paraguay, and Uruguay, is another example of regional economic integration that includes a common external tariff. These countries began their formal efforts toward fuller economic integration with the signing of the Treaty of Asunción in 1991. The common external tariff was adopted with the signing of the Treaty of Ouro Preto in 1994. Other examples of economic cooperation initiatives among countries that include a common external tariff are the Caribbean Community (Caricom), the Southern Africa Development Community (SADC), the East African Customs Union, the Andean Community (CAN), and the Gulf Cooperation Council. The European Union has expanded its common external tariff to include San Marino, Andorra, and Turkey, none of which are EU member states.

The North American Free Trade Agreement (NAFTA) eliminated internal trade barriers between Canada, Mexico, and the United States but stopped short of creating a common external tariff. Another prominent trading partnership, the Association of Southeast Asian Nations (ASEAN) Free Trade Area, has also not yet implemented a common external tariff. Countries are sometimes reluctant to adopt a common external tariff because of the loss of flexibility and control over national trade policy that it implies.

See Also: Common Market; Customs Union; European Union; Free Trade; Regional Integration; Regional Trade Agreements.

Bibliography. "A Free-Trade Tug-of-war," *Economist* (2004); K. Bagwell and R. W. Staiger, "Multilateral Tariff Cooperation During the Formation of Free Trade Areas," *International Economic Review* (1997); M. Ghosh and S. Rao, "A Canada–U.S. Customs Union: Potential Economic Impacts in NAFTA Countries," *Journal of Policy Modeling* (2005); B. T. Hanson, "What Happened to Fortress Europe?: External Trade Policy Liberalization in the European Union," *International Organization* (1998); D. E. Hojman, "The Andean Pact: Failure of a Model of Economic Integration?" *Journal of Common Market Studies* (1981); D. Hoy and J. Fisher, "Latin America and the European Common Market," *Geographical Review* (1966).

ROBERT D. STEPHENS
SHIPPENSBURG UNIVERSITY

Common Market

A common market is an advanced stage in economic integration, a process in which two or more countries, usually within a geographic region, agree to reduce barriers to economic transactions among themselves. It goes beyond a preferential trade agreement, in which the countries concerned offer each other lower tariffs than their normal rates, a free trade area, where member countries eliminate trade barriers among themselves, and a customs union, where they also establish common trade polices with respect to non-members. It does not go as far as an economic union, in which all or most economic policies are unified.

In a common market, apart from trade without tariffs or quotas and a common external trade policy, factors of production (labor and capital) can move freely among member countries. Like other forms of economic integration, the motivations are both political and economic. The major political benefit is seen as improved bargaining power with other countries; in some cases, it is also thought that binding the economies of member states closely reduces or eliminates the risk of future wars among them. Economic benefits of a common market go beyond those of free trade among members, which allows them to specialize in products in which they are most efficient. Since labor and capital can move freely, there can be dynamic gains as these factors move from areas where they are in surplus to those where they are scarce, resulting in higher incomes in the common market as a whole. Other benefits include economies of scale, more competition, and increased foreign direct investment because of the larger market.

The term *common market* was also widely used in the English-speaking world in the 1960s and 1970s to refer to the group of countries in western Europe (originally six, with several stages of expansion bringing the number to 27 in 2008) that had embarked on a process of close economic integration, though this group's official name has been the European Economic Community, the European Community, and now the European Union.

A true common market is not easily achieved. Since there are no restrictions on internal cross-border flows of labor and capital, a high degree of cooperation among members is required, particularly in policies about employment, taxation, investment, competition, social security, and immigration, and countries have to give up a considerable amount of sovereignty to supranational institutions. In the European Union, in accordance with the treaty establishing its predecessor, the European Economic Community, in 1957, all internal tariffs and quotas on goods were progressively abolished by 1968, and most formal barriers to the movement of labor and capital were removed by 1970, but in reality, freedom of movement was far from complete.

Differences in technical standards and health and safety regulations often meant products made in one country were not acceptable in another; delays at frontiers imposed considerable costs on trade; preferential treatment for national suppliers often excluded firms from partner countries from government contracts; educational qualifications in fields such as accountancy, architecture, and nursing were not mutually recognized, effectively limiting mobility of skilled labor; and national laws regarding financial services often made it difficult for banks or insurance companies established in one country to operate in another. It was only after the Single European Act of 1987, involving hundreds of directives and regulations aimed at removing these barriers, that the member countries began moving swiftly toward a single market in goods, services, labor, and capital. It is generally agreed that by 1992, the European Union had substantially become a common market.

Several other regional groups, past and present, have had the term *common market* as part of their name, but they have not reached the necessary level of integration. The Central American Common Market, comprising five small economies, was established in 1960, but did not go beyond reducing internal trade barriers before it suspended activity due to disputes among members. It was revived in 1990, with the objective of forming a customs union. The Andean Common Market, which was set up in 1969 and subsequently became moribund, was also revived in 1990 and is moving toward a customs union.

Mercosur ("Common Market of the South") aspires to be a common market, and has become the largest trading bloc in South America, but still has not achieved a full free trade area or customs union, and remains a preferential trade area with some coordination of tariffs on imports from non-members. The East African Common Market, inaugurated in 1967, attempted to coordinate development plans of the member countries, but did not allow free movement of labor and capital; due to disputes about the distribution of benefits, and political differences among leaders, it was officially abandoned in 1977. Subsequently, a large number of African countries have joined COMESA, the common market for eastern and southern Africa that was formed in 1994; as of 2008, it has reduced trade tariffs and quotas and hopes to set up a customs union in the near future. Only Caricom, the Caribbean Community and Common Market, established in 1973, has made substantial progress in eliminating internal trade barriers and some progress toward free movement of labor.

See Also: Caribbean Community; Central American Common Market; Common External Tariff; Customs Union; Economic Integration; Economic Union; European Union; Free Trade; Mercosur/Mercosul; Regional Integration; Regional Trade Agreements; Single Market.

Bibliography. B. Balassa, "Trade Creation and Trade Diversion in the European Common Market: An Appraisal of the Evidence," *Manchester School of Economic and Social Studies* (June 1974); International Monetary Fund, "Central and Eastern Europe: Assessing the Early Benefits of EU Membership," *IMF Survey* (November 20, 2006); Jaime Ros, "Free Trade Area or Common Capital Market? Notes on Mexico-US Economic Integration and Current NAFTA Negotiations," *Journal of Interamerican Studies and World Affairs* (v.34, 2001); D. Swann, *The Economics of the Common Market* (Penguin Books, 1990); J. Viner, *The Customs Union Issue* (Carnegie Endowment for International Peace, 1950).

Animesh Ghoshal
DePaul University

Communication Challenges

Effective communications are vital for success in today's business. Managers need to communicate with those they deal with—their customers, employees, vendors, and the public—in order to give directions, share ideas, motivate and elicit or disseminate needed information. Communicating takes up the majority of the time for managers and business people, and can be in the form of writing, talking, listening, or using the internet.

Communication can be defined as a process in which the sender is transferring meaning to the receiver. This involves coding of the message by the sender and decoding it by the receiver. A medium is involved in the conveyance of the message and can be words, behavior, or material artifacts. Naturally, in the process of communications breakdowns may occur and this is termed as noise. The barriers to effective communication include: semantics, where different words can have different meanings, such as fix and hot; jargon, when technical terms commonly used by various professions, such as military or engineers, are employed; acronyms and abbreviations mainly used by different groups such as the military; perception when one interprets things differently and distortion results; and emotion where one is unable to receive what is conveyed due to the pressures of the mental state.

When communication takes place across cultures, even greater challenges arise. As culture dictates how people view the world, it follows that culture also determines how people encode messages, the meaning they ascribe to the message, and how, when and why the message is transmitted, and finally how it is decoded and interpreted. Culture may be the actual foundation of communication. Hence cross-cultural variables directly affect the communication process and can pose a multitude of challenges. Here are some of the cultural variables that can affect the communication process:

There is a close relationship between language and culture. Language reflects and affects culture directly and indirectly. It is a reflection of the values of the particular community. Language is essentially meaning attached to words in a totally arbitrary way. The vocabulary of a language depicts what is considered important in that culture. There are seven words for bamboo in South India but only one for ice and there is no word for snow. In America there are several words pertaining to the self but only one in Japanese indicating the individualistic and collectivistic approaches of the two cultures.

Poor or limited knowledge of a language is a frequent cause of miscommunication and misinterpretation. When Pepsi Cola's slogan "Come Alive with Pepsi" was introduced in Germany, it was discovered that the literal German translation of "come alive" is "come out of the grave."

A sign in a Romanian hotel informing the English–speaking guests that the elevator was not working read "The lift is being fixed. For the next few days we regret that you will be unbearable." One way of overcoming this is to use back translation, where one person does the translation and another translates the translated version back ot the original language. Knowing a language well does not guarantee communication success. "Yes" when used by Asians usually means that they have heard you and understand what you are saying, while in the West it would be taken as agreement to your viewpoint or proposal.

Stereotyping occurs when a person assumes that all the people in that country or community have the same attributes, characteristics, or personality traits.

Communication problems are bound to arise when we pre-judge individuals based on generalizations. Effective managers are aware of the dangers of cultural stereotyping and make it a point to deal with each person as an individual.

Ethnocentrism is the belief that one's own culture is superior to others and that others are incorrect or defective and that your way is best. There is a tendency to place one's own group or ethnicity in a position of centrality. As such, ethnocentrism negatively affects intercultural communication. This is due to the fact that one's cultural orientation acts as a filter for interpreting messages based on preconceived ideas about one's self and others. One uses one's own cultural standards to evaluate and communicate with others. One may talk down to others assuming that they lack knowledge. Ethnocentric speech may create 'communicative distance' and this would cause indifference, avoidance and disparagement. Managers must make it a point not to judge others based on their own values.

Paralanguage

Paralanguage refers not to what is said but more to how it is said. It is less the content and more the manner it is conveyed—the tone (soft or harsh), the inflection of voice (pitch), the rate of speech (quality), and the sounds that are included in the speech (such as laughing). Paralanguage conveys emotions. Negatives emotions such as impatience, fear and anger may contribute to communication breakdown. In some Asian cultures, silence during communication is acceptable and indicates one is taking in and trying to understand fully what is being conveyed, while in the West silence may cause discomfort and impatience. Arabs have a tendency to speak loudly feeling this shows enthusiasm and sincerity. Thais speak loudly only when they are angry. Filipinos speak softly, as for them this is an indication of respect. Managers need to learn to interpret subtle differences caused by paralanguage.

Context plays an important part in cross-cultural communication in that it is not what the content of the conveyance but the place where it took place. The context in which the communication took place affects the meaning and interpretation of the interaction. In high-context cultures (Asia, Africa, Middle East) feelings are not openly disclosed, and one needs to read between the lines to get to the bottom of what is said.

In these cultures, explicit communication takes place in close personal relationships. In low-context cultures (Western Europe, North America, Australia) feelings are readily displayed. Misinterpretation results when mangers fail to take into account the context in which the message was conveyed. There is need to understand the inherent subtle gestures and nuances when communicating with high-context cultures.

Non-verbal communication is physical behavior that supports oral communication. Included are: posture, gestures, facial expression, interpersonal distance, touch, eye contact, color, and time. Research in communication suggests that many more feelings and intentions are sent and received nonverbally than verbally. These subtle means of communication account for between 65 and 93 percent of interpreted communication.

Posture

The way people hold their bodies frequently communicates information about their feelings, status, and intentions. The way one stands, sits or walks can send positive or negative messages. A stance or posture can signal agreement or disagreement, convey self-confidence, and indicate interest. Posture, when standing or when seated varies with culture. In the West, women when seated cross their legs at the ankle, and men cross with ankle at the knee. Crossing the leg with ankle on the knee would be considered inappropriate by most people in the Middle East. Also, people in Asia and in the Muslim world consider showing the sole of your shoe or pointing your foot at someone unacceptable and insulting. In most cultures, standing when an older person or one of higher rank enters or leaves the room is considered a sign of respect.

Gesture

The use of fingers, hands and arms when communicating varies considerably from one culture to another and is used to add emphasis or clarity to an oral message. Most cultures have standard gestures for daily situations such as for greeting and departing. Americans typically use moderate gestures, while Italians, Greeks and Latin Americans use vigorous gestures when speaking. East Asians tend to keep their hands and arms close to their bodies when speaking. Communication problems arise when these have different meanings in different cultures. The "thumbs up" ges-

ture means "everything is okay" in Western societies but is considered rude in parts of Africa. The "OK" sign with the thumb and forefinger joined in to form a circle is a positive sign in the United States but is in Brazil it is considered obscene. The beckoning gesture with either the fingers upturned or using just the forefinger is used for calling a waiter or to an employee to come hither. To the Filipinos and other Asians it is offensive as serves to beckon animals and prostitutes. Vietnamese and Mexicans also find it offensive.

Facial Expression

The face is very central to the process of communication. It is capable of expressing emotions, attitudes, and factual information instantly. People learn how to control facial expressions to mask emotions to suit their particular needs and in compliance with cultural norms. In the United States a smile means happiness. The Japanese may smile or giggle to cover anger, happiness or sadness. The Chinese people rarely show emotion and may smile or laugh softly when they are embarrassed or to conceal any discomfort. Koreans rarely smile as they consider people who smile a great deal as shallow. They consider it highly desirable to keep an expressionless face. Yet, Thailand is called the "Land of Smiles." The Pacific people are also known for their wide use of smiling and in certain parts of Africa laughter is used to express surprise, wonder and embarrassment and not amusement or happiness. Facial expressions need to be interpreted correctly in the context of the particular culture.

Interpersonal Distance

Communicating by using space is known as proxemics and refers to the physical distance between people when they are interacting and is highly influenced by culture. Researchers have identified four zones from which U.S. people interact. The 'intimate zone' is less that 18 inches and is reserved for very close friends; the personal zone from 18 inches to 4 feet is for working closely with another person; the social zone from 4 to 12 feet is for normal business situations; and the public distance of over 12 feet is the most formal zone. People in America tend to need more personal space that Asians, Arabs, Africans, and some Europeans.

Conversational distance also varies between cultures: for Latin Americans the distance is 15 inches or so, while in the Middle East, this can be as small as 9 to 10 inches. It is common in Asia for very little space to be left between individuals when standing in line.

Touch or haptics may be the most personal form of non-verbal communication. Touching takes place in a variety of ways and for a variety of purposes and includes shaking hands, patting the head or the back, holding hands, hugging, kissing, and linking arms. Each culture has a well defined understanding as to who can touch whom, on what parts of the body, and under what circumstances. High-touch cultures include Mediterranean countries, Arabs, Jews, Eastern Europeans, and South Asians, while the English, Germans, Northern Europeans, Americans, and East Asians are considered low-touch cultures. Touching while dancing is a clear indicator of differences in various cultures—some dance in close proximity in embrace, while others maintain some distance.

Some cultures place more emphasis on gaze or eye contact called oculesics, but all cultures use it when communicating. Direct eye contact is preferred in most Western cultures and is taken as a sign of sincerity, trustworthiness and respect. People who avoid eye contact may be considered insecure, untrustworthy, unfriendly, disrespectful or inattentive. In other cultures there is little direct eye contact and lowering of the eyes is considered a form of respect in China, Indonesia, parts of Africa and the Caribbean. Direct eye contact in East Asia may be construed as being offensive while in the Middle East prolonged and intense eye contact is commonly accepted behavior. In India and Egypt, eye contact is avoided between people from different social backgrounds. Managers need to be aware of the implications of too much or not enough eye contact that each culture and situation demands.

Color or chromatics is a communication tool as it can affect the mood, emotion, and impression. Some colors have positive or negative connotations. Color is often used in symbolism and may also represent an emotional state. Black in many cultures (such as the United States) represents sophistication but also sadness. White is pure and peaceful but in some societies associated with mourning.

In the West, white is worn by brides; in India yellow is preferred and in China it is red. Yellow, and at places purple, is considered the color of royalty. Purple is the color of death in some Latin countries. Red, in many cultures, is associated with romance and in China and Japan represents good fortune. Green is the color of religion in Islamic cultures. In many countries blue represents masculinity and pink femininity. Awareness of such representation is vital when relating to other cultures.

Time or chronemics is a cultural variable that affects business communication directly the most. The way people view time varies from culture to culture. Monochromic societies see time as linear, having a past, present and future. It is considered as something to be spent, saved, or wasted. Most Western countries are monochromic. Other cultures are polychromic in that they do not consider time as a commodity and place less value on it, feeling that there is abundance of time available to all.

See Also: Communication Styles; Culture Shock; Culture-Specific Values.

Bibliography. Helen Deresky, *International Management: Managing Across Borders and Cultures* (Pearson Hall, 2008); Gary P. Ferraro, *The Cultural Dimension of International Business* (Pearson Prentice Hall, 2006); James W. Neuliep, *Intercultural Communication: A Contextual Approach* (Sage, 2009).

Balbir Bhasin
Sacred Heart University

Communication Styles

Global businesspeople often encounter difficulties in cross-cultural communication. These difficulties arise when people from different national cultures have a different understanding of the same concept and different ways to express their thoughts on it. In this backdrop, business people need a better understanding of the factors affecting cross-cultural communication. Communication is effective when the person receiving the message attaches a meaning to the message that is similar to the way the sender intended it. Much of this intention is dependent on one's communication style, which refers to a person's particular pattern of communication.

Communication involves the sharing of information between two or more people, where the information has relevance to at least one of the parties. When this communication occurs between people from different national cultures, the intended meaning of what is being communicated can be distorted by different cultural values. Given the increase in international business, communication across diverse ethnic cultures is becoming increasingly common for many businesspeople.

There are four main communications styles, each style appropriate for different cultural and business settings depending on the objective of the communication. These styles are (1) tell: inform or explain the meaning, (2) sell: persuade or convince, (3) consult: involves high interaction with other parties, and (4) join: collaboration and sharing ideas among parties. The tell and sell communication styles are mainly found in individualistic cultures such as Canada and New Zealand, whereas the consult and join styles are more prevalent in collectivist cultures such as China and Japan.

Cultural Context

All cross-border communication exists in a cultural context. The terms *high context* and *low context* refer to the different rules surrounding the exchange of information and the extent to which the communication is direct or indirect. In high-context cultures such as Japan and Indonesia, communication is slow in getting to the point because consideration is given to people's feelings about what is being said. Therefore what is communicated is as important as how it is communicated. In this context communication is implicit and indirect. In contrast, in low-context cultures meaning is conveyed by rational argument. The explicit, direct use of words conveys the intended meaning.

A strong link exists between how cultures treat time and how cultures communicate. Monochromic or linear temporal-oriented cultures (e.g., the United States and the United Kingdom) tend to "get to the point" in their communications very quickly, with little time for introductions. Conversely, polychromic cultures found throughout Asia and the Middle East might find this linear approach too direct and rude. These cultures prefer a more circuitous approach to communications, because time has neither a beginning nor an end. Time then becomes an important variable in cross-cultural communications.

Other Considerations

Semantics is the study of meaning in language. In cross-cultural communications, semantics is important because many languages have words that do not translate exactly into words in another language. The challenge for global businesspeople is to find substitute words that convey similar meaning without losing the essence of the communication.

The use of a formal tone versus an informal tone is an important consideration in communications. Some cultures require a formal tone in communications whereas others require an informal, relaxed approach. Knowing the appropriate tone requires research into the foreign culture prior to the commencement of any dialogue.

There is a belief that what is not said is as important as what is said. International businesspeople must be aware of nonverbal communication cues such as facial expressions, eye contact, posture, pouting, frowning, and gestures, as these may be offensive in different cultures. Nonverbal communication is a substitute for words. Often there is a contradiction between the verbal and nonverbal communication, where the spoken words convey one meaning and the nonverbal communication (e.g., body posture, facial expression) conveys a different meaning. Usually, nonverbal communication is not consciously observed unless it causes the receiver some confusion or doubt. Thus, businesspeople should be conscious of both forms of communication and align them to communicate one unambiguous meaning.

Effective communication requires as much skill in listening as in speaking. Effective listening improves communication because it involves skills that include asking questions to clarify, empathizing with the speaker (and their point of view), looking at the speaker when they speak, and responding both verbally and nonverbally to the speaker's comments. Effective listening is also useful in conflict resolution. Listening with intent rather than simply hearing what aggrieved parties are trying to communicate is a focal point in conflict resolution.

As businesses look to world markets for growth and profit, the ability to effectively communicate in both a business and social setting with people from different cultural backgrounds will become increasingly important. Businesspeople skilled in intercultural business communications stand to benefit from conducting business across international borders more than those without such training. Communicating effectively across international borders provides both challenges and opportunities for the global business manager. The challenges relate to understanding different communication styles and expectations in different cultures. Given the ethnic diversity that exists even within many countries (e.g., India and China), these challenges require skill, training, and patience to conquer. The opportunities lie in the competitive advantage gained from the awareness of cultural differences and sensitivities that can be leveraged for commercial gain.

See Also: Achieved Status/Ascribed Status; Communication Challenges; Cultural Norms and Scripts; Culture-Specific Values; Diversity; Multicultural Work Groups and Teams; Specific/Diffuse.

Bibliography. William B. Gudykunst and Tsukasa Nishida, "Anxiety, Uncertainty, and Perceived Effectiveness of Communication Across Relationships and Culture," *International Journal of Intercultural Relations* (v.25, 2001); Prue Holmes, "Negotiating Differences in Learning and Inter-Cultural Communication," *Business Communications Quarterly* (v.67/3, 2004); Leon F. Kenman, "Tone and Style: Developing a Neglected Segment of Business Communication," *Business Communication Quarterly* (v.70/3, 2007); Nada Korac-Kakabadse, Alexander Kouzmin, Andrew Korac-Kakabadse, and Lawson Savery, "Low and High Context Communication Patterns: Towards Mapping Cross-Cultural Encounters," *Cross Cultural Management* (v.8/2, 2001); Mohan Limaye and David A Victor, "Cross-Cultural Business Communication Research: State of the Art and Hypotheses for the 1990s," *Journal of Business Communications* (v.28/3, 1991); Mary Munter, "Cross-Cultural Communication for Managers," *Business Horizons* (v.36/3, 1993); Kaylene C. Williams and Rosann L. Spiro, "Communication Style in the Salesperson-Customer Dyad," *Journal of Marketing Research* (v.22, 1985).

Nicholas Grigoriou
Monash College Guangzhou

Communism

The word *communism* is derived from the Latin *communis* meaning common or shared. Communism is a socioeconomic structure and political ideology that aims to replace profit-based economy through the abolishment of private property and the public ownership of the means of production, distribution, exchange, and subsistence. According to the communist view, everything that people produce is a social product; therefore, everyone who contributes to the production of a good is entitled to a share in it. Communism/socialism is opposed to capitalism, which is based on private property and the free market that determines how goods and services are distributed. Karl Marx, like most writers of the 19th century, used the terms *socialism* and *communism* interchangeably. Precisely how communism differs from socialism has been a matter of debate, although the dissimilarity rests mainly on the communists' observance of the revolutionary socialism of Marx. Andrew Roberts (2004) notes that the anthropologist Jan Kubik believed that some political regimes made *communist* and *socialism* ambiguous terms in order to gain legitimacy and confuse the public about who the enemy was.

An earlier definition of communism was introduced by the English humanist Sir Thomas More. More (1516) in his work *Utopia* describes an invented society in which money is eliminated and citizens share in common houses, meals, and other goods. Friedrich Engels (1847) defines communism as "the doctrine of the conditions of liberation of the proletariat." According to *The Communist Manifesto* (1848) by Marx and Engels, the main planks of communism are: (1) the abolition of private property, (2) heavy progressive income tax, (3) confiscation of rights of inheritance, (4) a central bank, (5) government ownership of communication and transportation, (6) government ownership of factories and agriculture, (7) government control over labor, (8) corporate farms and regional planning, and (9) government control of education.

According to Marx, the history of humanity is a series of class struggles from ancient slavery through feudalism, leading ultimately to freedom for all. In each period, a class has dominated the other social classes and has exploited the labor class. For Marx, material production requires material forces and social relations for production. In Marx's view, capitalism is ruled by the bourgeoisie class that owns the means of production and controls the working class or proletariat. Marx recognizes that capitalism has brought remarkable and unprecedented scientific advancement and technological improvements; however, the economic opportunities and political power, in Marx's view, are unfairly distributed. Besides this unequal distribution, Marx found that capitalism alienates workers in the sense that workers are separated from: (1) the product of their labor, (2) the process of production, (3) the sense of satisfaction derived from doing creative work, and (4) other human beings whom workers see as competitors for wages and jobs.

As stated in *The Communist Manifesto*, "the distinguishing feature of communism is not the abolition of property generally, but the abolition of bourgeois property." Marx and Engels summed up communism within a single phrase: Abolition of private property. Marx felt that communism would "supersede" capitalism once the capitalist system of production becomes an obstacle for the development of the forces of production.

In Marx's 1875 *Critique of the Gotha Programme*, Marx recognized two stages of communism that would be pursued after the overthrow of capitalism. The first stage would be a transitional system in which the economy and the government would be controlled by the working class. The second stage would be a fully realized communism, without government or class division. In this second stage, the distribution of goods and the production would be based on the principle "from each according to his ability, to each according to his needs."

According to some authors, there are distinctions to be made between communism and socialism. In general, socialism refers to an economy with considerable public ownership. Communism refers to a country or political system in which a communist party rules. According to J. Kornai (1992), four prototypes of socialist systems can be identified, which seem to refer to consecutive stages in history: (1) the revolutionary-transitional system from capitalism to socialism, (2) the classical socialist system, (3) reform socialism, and (4) the post-socialist system (transition from socialism to capitalism).

Communist States

In the early 20th century, the primary focus of the economy in Russia was agriculture. Most Russians were peasants who farmed land owned by wealthy nobles. Because of land tenancy and labor exploita-

tion, there was discontent in the Russian countryside, and the Russian Social Democratic Party was seen as an opportunity to overthrow the tsarist regime and to replace it with a radically different sociopolitical system. In 1903 the Russian Social Democratic and Labor Party split into the Bolsheviks and the Mensheviks. After the victory of the Bolsheviks in the Russian Revolution in October 1917, Lenin's party became the model for communist parties around the world. Soviet Union countries from Lenin's time to Gorbachev's called themselves socialist countries, and denoting both a revolutionary dictatorship and an evolutionary democracy regime.

In 1985 reform-minded Mikhail Gorbachev became head of the Soviet Union. He allowed freer discourse (*glasnost*) and movement toward more economic diversity (*perestroika*). He made it clear that the Soviet Union would no longer forcefully dominate the communist nations of Eastern Europe, and by 1989, they had largely left communism. In 1991 Boris Yeltsin succeeded Gorbachev and announced the dissolution of the Soviet regime.

Although there are a number of communist parties active around the world, only in China, Cuba, the Democratic People's Republic of Korea, Laos, and Vietnam do they retain power over the state, and therefore these countries are denominated communist states. After the collapse of communism in the Soviet Union and Eastern Europe, communist parties around the world suffered drastically.

Marxism

Karl Marx (1818–83) has been the most influential theorist of communism. He studied law and completed a doctorate in philosophy, and he dedicated his life to radical political activity, theoretical studies in history and political economy, and journalism as a profession. Marx described communism as the "the riddle of history solved." He thought that the gap between private interest and community interest was a feature of a particular stage of human development, rather than an unavoidable characteristic of social existence.

The Marxist tradition is built around three theoretical clusters: (1) a theory of the development and destiny of capitalism, (2) a theory of the contradictions of capitalism, and (3) a normative theory of socialism and communism. Marx as a scholar thought he had discovered the laws of socioeconomic change leading a society toward a communist stage based on historical determinism. Marx described the materialist conception of history as the core of his studies. In his book *Capital*, he presented his economic theories, and he concluded that the capitalist economic system was an alienated form of human life. For Marx, under capitalism workers are forced to sell their labor to the capitalists, who use this labor to accumulate more capital, which further raises the power of the capitalists over workers. In this cycle, capitalists became wealthier, while wages are drained down to the subsistence level; consequently, if capital grows, the domination of capital over workers increases. Furthermore, capital increases its domination by increasing the division of labor. Under Marx's view, labor is a commodity that the worker must sell in order to live. Therefore, wages are determined like the price for any other commodity.

Conservative governments have guided social reforms to undercut revolutionary Marxist movements. Mussolini and Hitler were supported by conservatives who saw their nationalism as the answer to combat the Marxist threat.

Leninism

Vladimir Ilyich Lenin was the leader of the Bolshevik Party in Russia. It built on Marxism and provided the philosophical bases for Soviet communism. In his 1902 publication *What Is to Be Done?* Lenin argued that the revolution against capitalism can be achieved through the disciplined effort of full-time professional revolutionaries. These full-time revolutionaries were paid by the Bolshevik Party, using bureaucratic control as a method of enforcing ideological principles.

In Lenin's 1916 *Imperialism: The Highest Stage of Capitalism*, it is postulated that in the last stage of capitalism, capital is exported in order to pursue higher profit than the domestic market can offer. This is what Lenin named the monopoly finance stage. Lenin argued that

> at a certain stage of their development, the material productive forces of society come in conflict with the existing relations of production, or with the property relations within which they have been at work hitherto.

Maoism

Maoism or Chinese Marxism is a combination of German Marxism, Soviet Leninism, Confucianism, and China's own guerrilla movement. It is referred to as Maoism because Mao Zedong (1893–1976) was the cofounder and the leader of the Chinese Communist Party (CCP) in 1921, which defeated the Chinese Nationalist Party (Kuomintang, or KMT) in the Chinese civil war, establishing the People's Republic of China (PRC) in October 1949. Maoism's ideology was centered in the violent revolutionary potential of the peasantry. It differs from Marxist and Leninist approaches that focused on the potential power of the industrial proletariat.

Mao Zedong promoted a self-reliant, grain-first development repudiating material and market incentives for the people of China. The goals of Maoism included the salvation of China from its foreign enemies, and the reinforcement of the country through modernization. Two of his main socioeconomic pro-

A parade outside the Grand People's Study House in Pyongyang, North Korea, one of the few remaining communist states.

grams—the Great Leap Forward and the Cultural Revolution—focused on the problems of the rural poor.

Evolution of Communist Regimes

Communist systems have five common characteristics that distinguish them from other authoritarian regimes: (1) the monopoly of power of the Communist Party; (2) intra-party relations that were highly centralized and strictly disciplined; (3) state, rather than private, ownership of the means of production; (4) the establishment of communism as the ultimate, legitimizing goal; and (5) a sense of belonging to an international communist movement.

Bartłomiej Kamiński and Karol Sołtan (1989) proposed a political-economic framework to understand change within communism. They distinguish a three-stage typology of development. The first stage is pure communism or totalitarian communism. It is characterized by total control of the economy and society by a political center backed by an extensive and repressive political party apparatus. Therefore, this totalitarian communism is antilaw, antimarket, and antidemocratic. The second stage is late communism, which features the weakening of the main characteristics of totalitarian communism. The authorities in late communism are forced to bargain in order to impose their will. Symptoms of late communism include accepting some degree of autonomy for economic actors. The final stage is constitutional (or juridical) communism, in which the interests of the rulers are imposed. Key components of this tendency include the separation of powers, the institutionalization of bargaining, the institutionalization of freer information flows, and the introduction of clearly defined rules of the state in the economy.

See Also: Capitalism; China; Cuba; Eastern Europe; Russia; Socialism.

Bibliography. Edward Friedman, "Maoism and the Liberation of the Poor," *World Politics* (v.39/3, 1987); Sujian Go, *The Political Economy of Asian Transition from Communism* (Ashgate Publishing, 2006); Nigel Holden, Andrei Kutznetsov, and Jeryl Whitelock, "Russia's Struggle with the Language of Marketing in the Communist and Post-communist Eras," *Business History* (v.50/4, 2008); Bartłomiej Kamiński and Karol Sołtan, "The Evolution of Communism," *International Political Science Review* (v.10/4, 1989); János Kornai, *The Socialist System: The Political Economy of Communism* (Oxford University Press, 1992); Vladimir Ilyich Lenin, *Imperialism: The Highest Stage of Capitalism* (1916); Roderick Martin, "Post-socialist Segmented Capitalism: The Case of Hungary. Developing Business Systems Theory," *Human Relations* (v.61/1, 2008); Karl Marx and Friedrich Engels, *The Communist Manifesto* (1848); Andrew Roberts, "The State of Socialism: A Note on Terminology," *Slavic Review* (v.63/2, 2004); Anna Seleny, *The Political Economy of State-Society Relations in Hungary and Poland: From Communism to the European Union* (Cambridge University Press, 2006); Robert Service, *Comrades!: A History of World Communism* (Harvard University Press, 2007); Dmitry V. Shlapentokh, "Revolutionary as a Career. *Communist and Post-Communist Studies* (v.29/3, 1996); Brooke Skinner and Rosemary B. Bryant, "From Communism to Consumerism," *New Presence: The Prague Journal of Central European Affairs* (v.8/4, 2006); Gabriel Temkin, "Karl Marx and the Economics of Communism: Anniversary Recollections," *Communist and Post-Communist Studies* (v.31/4, 1998).

Maria-Alejandra Gonzalez-Perez
EAFIT University

Company Profiles: Africa

There have long been traders, both African and Arab, working throughout the African continent, but especially along rivers or along its east coast. From the late 15th century, but more particularly in the 16th century, there have been a number of European colonial companies that mainly operated under government charter. Some more recent companies are or have links with mining or agricultural companies that have been on the continent since colonial times; others are agency houses that sell goods and services on behalf of overseas companies. Also, some overseas companies have started operations in Africa since the 1960s, and there are an increasing number of African-owned companies, some government owned or controlled and others created or bought out after independence.

The Chartered Companies

The Portuguese Company of Guinea was involved in trade with West Africa and with the importation of spices to Portugal from 1482 until 1499. Some of the earliest European chartered companies were primarily involved in trade in the East Indies, and so trade with Africa became incidental to their main business. These included the Honorable East India Company (British), which was founded in 1600 and remained in existence until 1858 (being formally dissolved in 1873) and the Dutch Vereenigde Oost-Indische Compagnie (VOC), or Dutch East India Company, which was established in 1602 with an initial 21-year monopoly to carry out trade in Asia. Both companies were involved in establishing trading posts in Africa and had extensive extraterritorial powers, including their own armies and navies.

The Royal African Company, from England, was established in 1660 and was heavily involved in slavery, being responsible for the transportation of 90,000–100,000 slaves between 1672 and 1689. It lost its charter in 1698 and ceased to be involved in the slave trade in 1731, when it started trading in ivory and gold dust. Indeed much of the gold was used in England to make coins, with the result that the English gold coin became known as the guinea. It was succeeded by the African Company of Merchants.

For the Germans, the Kurfürstliche Brandenburgisch-Afrikanische Kompagnie (Brandenburg African Company) was founded in 1682 and occupied two parts of modern-day Ghana, being heavily involved in slavery for much of its existence. Over 100 years later, for the British, the Sierra Leone Company in 1792 founded the first African American colony, helping to settle former slaves from Nova Scotia, Canada. The American Colonization Society set up the Republic of Liberia for similar purposes in 1822. In 1886 the National African Company became the Royal Niger Company—also a British company under Royal Charter—and with its landholdings was, on January 1, 1900, transferred to the British government for a payment of £865,000, thus forming the basis of British landholdings in Nigeria. There were also exploration companies such as the African Association and the Geographical Society, technically under a company structure, which were involved in mapping Africa.

The Deutsch-Ostafrikanische Gesellschaft (German East Africa Company) was founded in 1885 to help establish a German claim to what is now Tanzania, and was heavily involved in plantations and trade prior to selling German East Africa to the German government in 1891. The Deutsch-Westafrikanische Gesellschaft/Compagnie (German West African Company) operated in West Africa but without a central authority.

The Portuguese had tried, for most of their involvement in Africa, to operate through their central government, but found it impossible to raise the capital and as a result established a number of companies, most of which operated in modern-day Mozambique. Of these, the most famous are the Companhia de Moçambique (Mozambique Company), founded in February 1891; the Companhia do Niassa (Niassa or Nyassa Company), which operated from 1891 until 1929; and the Companhia do Zambezia (Zambezi Company). The Mozambique, Niassa, and Zambezi companies remain best known through the colorful stamps they issued during their periods of operation. All three lost their status in 1929 when the Portuguese government took back control of their territories with an attempt to create a bigger home market for the Portuguese Empire.

Regional and Historical Differences

Because of the nature of the creation of colonial powers in Africa and other historical reasons, there have been significant differences between the companies that have operated in various parts of the continent. In north Africa, there had long been connections with the Ottoman Empire, and Turkish companies have had an important role, as have French, Spanish, Italian, and Greek companies. In Egypt, until the late 1950s, many of the companies in the country were controlled by Greeks, with also substantial numbers of Maltese involved in commerce. Under Gamal Abdel Nasser, Greek commercial influence in Egypt declined as he sought to promote Egyptian businesses. Greek companies, however, remained prominent in the Sudan and in Ethiopia, many being run by Greeks who had lived in these countries for many years rather than companies that had any connections with Greece itself. In Ethiopia, this ended with the overthrow of Haile Selassie in 1974, and in Sudan with the emergence of Gaafar al-Nimeiry, who became president in 1969. One of the main streets of traders in Djibouti is called Rue d'Athens, also showing the importance of Greek traders in the Horn of Africa.

In Morocco, Algeria, and Tunisia, French companies had been important in business life since the 19th century, and they continued to dominate the economies of north Africa in the first half of the 20th century. The main commercial telephone directory published in French Africa, the Didot-Bottin, was heavily dominated by north Africa, with French companies being important in the much smaller economies of the countries of former French West Africa (Benin, Burkina Faso, Guinea, Mali, Mauritania, Niger, Senegal, and Togo) and those of former French Central Africa (Central African Republic, Cameroon, Chad, Congo, and Gabon). Prior to independence, most of the companies operating in these areas were registered in Paris, and many of the public services such as telecommunications were under the direct control of the colonial authorities or the French central government.

After independence, some of the former colonies were involved in establishing joint ventures, and a few established their own companies, with newly available capital in some of these countries managing to run rival firms. In addition, some of the countries have subsequently sold off sections of their government corporations to the private sector, in the case of Chad introducing plans for the privatization of the Société des Télécommunications du Tchad, and Congo privatizing the Société des Télécommunications du Congo. In Gabon, the telecommunications sector has the government-owned company providing telephone lines in the country, another company 61 percent owned by the government for overseas telephone lines, and a number of private companies operating mobile-telephone networks.

A few countries, such as Benin and Guinea-Bissau, run numerous para-state companies that are either partly or wholly owned by the state, such as the Société des Ciments du Bénin, the Société Béninoise de Brasserie in Benin, and Ultramaina in Guinea-Bissau. In Benin there were 130 of these in 1980, but only 27 in 1999, with some of these subsequently sold to the private sector.

In British Africa, during the time of colonial rule, British companies dominated the economies, and after independence, a number of these were sold off to local interests, with much of the business in formerly British West Africa (Gambia, Ghana, Nigeria, and Sierra Leone) dominated by companies based in Nigeria. And South African–owned and –based companies tended to dominate—and in fact still dominate—many of the economies of the smaller countries in southern Africa. In east Africa, the economic importance of Kenya also ensured that companies based there often dominated the region, with Indian-owned companies being prominent in Uganda until the expulsion of the Indian community there by Idi Amin in 1972. Lebanese-owned companies remain prominent in trading in parts of British West Africa.

For the Portuguese, apart from their chartered companies that were taken over by the government in 1929, many of the plantations in Lusophone Africa (Angola, Cape Verde Islands, Guinea-Bissau, Mozambique, and Sao Tomé e Principe) were either owned by individuals or by the Portuguese government. As a result, after independence, and with socialist or communist governments taking over the former Portuguese colonies, state industrial enterprises were established. The Spanish government also tended to dominate former Spanish Africa (Spanish Morocco, Spanish Sahara, and Equatorial Guinea).

For transport, most road haulage companies were locally owned, but railways tended to be owned by the colonial government, and after independence, many were controlled by countries other than the ones in which the track was located, such as Rhodesia Railways running the railway line through Botswana until the 1970s. Shared ownership also exists with the Djibouti-Ethiopian Railway. Large numbers of independent countries also established their own airlines, with varying degrees of financial success.

Mining and Plantation Companies

Many European powers were involved in establishing plantation-style agriculture in their colonies in Africa, which led to many cash crops being grown either for consumption in the colonial country or for sale elsewhere. These involved food crops such as cocoa, coconuts, coffee, groundnuts, maize, palm oil, sugar cane, and also other plantation crops such as cotton, tobacco, and some rubber. To this end, there have been a large number of colonial companies involved in establishing and running these plantations. Some of these, such as those operated by the Portuguese, were run by individual wealthy landowners, whereas the British ones were often run through companies listed on the London Stock Market. The U.S. firm Firestone Tire and Rubber Company (now a subsidiary of Bridgestone) ran large rubber plantations in

Liberia from 1926 until it was sold to the Japanese-owned company Bridgestone in 1988.

In addition, there were many smaller operations that were run by individual farmers who owned some of the best farmland in Africa, including the Central Highlands of Kenya, which were parceled out by the British to predominantly British people in the 1920s. It was these farming interests in Kenya and the wealth generated from them that led to a war to prevent independence, leading to thousands of deaths in the Mau Mau insurgency that eventually led to Kenya becoming independent in December 1963. There was certainly a close link between farming and political interests, with the European settlers in Algeria, many of whom were farmers, supporting continued French colonial rule. In Rhodesia, Ian Smith (1919–2007) was a farmer, and Smith's defense minister Pieter van der Byl (1923–99) ran a large tobacco plantation.

The fate of many of these companies essentially depended on how independence was achieved in individual countries. In some of them such as Kenya and Uganda, the governments tried to encourage group farms, with Ghana and Guinea establishing state farms, while others—particularly the former French colonies—recognized the benefits of having private companies, most linked to a particular sector of the economy, such as the Compagnie de Gérance du Coton in Burundi, which controlled the local cotton industry; and the Cameroon Sugar Co., Inc., founded in 1975 for the Cameroon sugar industry.

Although it had been possible in colonial times for individuals to run farms and small plantations, the scale of mining ventures usually required far more capital. As a result, most mining operations were owned by public companies, or by private companies with a range of stock holders. There were obvious exceptions to this; Cecil Rhodes (1853–1902) managed to carve out a large "empire" in southern Africa through good fortune, shrewd deals, links with the governments of both Britain and South Africa (he was prime minister of the Cape Colony from 1890 until 1896), and also force. His company later came together as De Beers, founded in 1888, controlling the diamond business.

Other large diamond companies included Alfred Beit (1853–1906), who struck diamonds at Kimberley and then became an ally of Rhodes. Of the other major mining companies operating from South Africa, the most well known were Anglo American Corporation (founded 1917), Consolidated Goldfields (founded 1887), Gencor Ltd. (founded 1895), and Rand Mines Ltd. Mention should also be made of Billiton, a Dutch mining company with a South African background, which merged with the Australian firm BHP to become BHP Billiton. In other countries, there were many other companies such as the Companhia do Manganes de Angola and the Companhia Mineira do Lobito SARL; in the Central African Republic, the Société Centrafricaine du Diamant in Bangui; and in Ghana, the Ashanti Goldfields Corporation.

Agency Houses and Overseas Companies

Throughout colonial Africa, there were a range of agency houses that sold goods from a range of European firms in Africa, acting as agents and distributors. For the manufacturers this was better than establishing their own operations in African countries where there were always delays in shipping and delivery. In Sudan, the shipping and later trading firm Mitchell Cotts sold a wide range of British goods, especially air conditioning, as did a range of agency houses in other countries.

Although many insurance companies operated through agency houses, some other European insurance companies established their own branches in parts of Africa, particularly those that had large European populations such as South Africa, Egypt, Algeria, and Kenya. There were also a large number of European banking institutions that operated in Africa. The British bank Barclays (founded 1690), was always strong in South Africa, and controversially kept up banking ties with South Africa during the period of apartheid, leading to boycotts of the bank. Two centuries earlier, it had also been associated with financing of the slave trade, although that was far less controversial at the time. Also with long connections to South Africa was the Standard Chartered Bank (founded 1853), which opened a branch in Cape Town in 1862, and runs a subsidiary in West Africa: Standard Chartered Bank (Gambia) Ltd; the Standard Chartered Bank in Lesotho had been bought out by South African businessmen and run as Nedbank, Lesotho. Because of its involvement with India, Grindlays Bank (founded 1828) was favored by many Indian traders in East Africa, and the Bank of India and the Bank of Baroda both operate heavily in Kenya.

French banks such as the Banque Afrique Occidentale and the Crédit Lyonnais operated in French colonies, and retained much of their market share after independence. The Banque des Etats de l'Afrique Centrale operated in the countries of former French Central Africa (and also Equatorial Guinea), and there were also local subsidiaries such as the Bank of Africa-Burkina, and the Crédit Lyonnais Madagascar (which is actually owned by the Malagasy government). There are also other institutions such as the Ecobank-Burkina SA, operating in Ouagadougou, with Ecobank Ghana Ltd. operating in Accra, the Ghanian capital, and Ecobank Guinée in Conakry.

The British security printers De La Rue and Waterlows and the U.S. company, the American Banknote Company, were involved in printing money and postage stamps for many African countries, as well as other important printing contracts such as passports. Foreign and locally owned shipping companies provided mail services and also took passengers around Africa, with many of the colonial powers promoting companies registered in their own countries, such as the Companhia Portuguesa de Transportes Marítimos that still operates in the Cape Verde Islands, with P&O, the White Funnel Line, and other firms operating around the continent.

There were also many engineering companies that were involved in projects throughout Africa. The French company Richier was heavily involved in road construction and other civil engineering projects in French West Africa in the 1960s. As there was not sufficient demand for cars on the African continent, automakers in Europe and North America imported cars to Africa. British Africa was largely involved in importing cars from Britain, and French Africa from France, with car assembly plants in Nigeria and South Africa.

Locally Owned Companies

After independence, many people in Africa were eager to control the economies of their countries and prevent what was seen as the pervading influence of "neo-colonialism," which Kwame Nkrumah of Ghana, and also Julius Nyerere of Tanganyika/Tanzania, saw as a system by which the colonial powers essentially continued to control independent nations through a range of important companies. This saw Ghana and Tanganyika—from British Africa—introduce measures to reduce the importance of these companies. There were also many programs of nationalization, sometimes—as in the case of Namibia, and the Egyptian government taking over the Suez Canal in 1956—with compensation, but many times without any compensation—such as the Algerian government taking over former French businesses after independence in 1962, and the Zimbabwe farm invasions by Robert Mugabe's supporters, the "war veterans" from 1997. The most drastic example of taking over of companies was when Idi Amin in Uganda expelled ethnic Indians in 1972. Some of them were from families that had lived in Uganda for generations, and many of the businesses taken over by Idi Amin and his supporters quickly failed.

One of the major areas of control by foreign multinationals that concerned many governments in independent Africa was that of the oil companies. Shell operated through much of Africa, with the French company Total later making inroads, and Esso was involved in prospecting in Chad. However, after countries became independent, many of them established their own state oil companies such as Sonatrach in Algeria; the Société Congo Gulf Oil in Kinshasa, Congo; the TotalFinaElf Côte d'Ivoire in Abidjan; and the National Oil Corporation in Libya.

Some other governments have had different ways of promoting business in their countries. There have been a number of stock markets; the oldest and most powerful are the ones in South Africa: JSE Securities Exchange, established in 1887; and the AltX, the Bond Exchange of South Africa, and the South African Futures Exchange, all located in Johannesburg. There are also other stock markets in Algeria (1998), Côte d'Ivoire (1976), Botswana (1989), Cameroon (2002), the Cape Verde Islands, Egypt (the Cairo and Alexandria Stock Exchange established in 1888), Ghana (1990), Kenya (1954), Libya (2007), Malawi (1995), Mauritius (1988), Morocco (1929), Mozambique (1999), Namibia (1992), Nigeria (1960 in Lagos, 2001 in Abuja), Rwanda (2008), Sudan (1995), Swaziland (1990), Tanzania (1998), Tunisia (1969), Uganda (1997), Zambia (1994), and Zimbabwe (1993); and there are plans to establish one in Angola. These have helped with raising local capital, and also provided a forum for local investors.

Other countries have insisted on local citizens being directors, which has changed the management of many of the companies operating in Africa and created a large African managerial class. These have transformed the nature of many of the businesses on the African continent, and how they are run, although political problems have interrupted the economic progress in many countries.

See Also: Africa; African Development Bank; Algeria; Angola; Botswana; Cameroon; Côte d'Ivoire; Egypt; Ghana; Kenya; Libya; Morocco; Neocolonialism; Nigeria; South Africa; Sudan; Suez; Tanzania; Tunisia; Zimbabwe.

Bibliography. *Africa South of the Sahara 2008* (Europa Publications, 2008); J. Dickie and A. Rake, *Who's Who in Africa: The Political, Military and Business Leaders of Africa* (African Development, 1973); Raymond E. Dumett, "Sources for Mining Company History in Africa: The History and Records of the Ashanti Goldfields Corporation (Ghana), Ltd.," *Business History Review* (v.62/3, 1988); Ubong Effeh, *Why Sub-Saharan Africa is Mired in Poverty: The Consequences of Misrule* (Edwin Mellen Press, 2008); Adam Jones, *Brandenburg Sources for West African History 1680–1700* (Franz Steiner Verlag, 1985); Louise Fox and Melissa Sekkel Gaal, *Working Out of Poverty: Job Creation and the Quality of Growth in Africa* (World Bank, 2008); Kempe Ronald Hope, *Poverty, Livelihoods, and Governance in Africa: Fulfilling the Development Promise* (Palgrave MacMillan, 2008); Sandra James, Christy Oddy, and Monica Scott, *Major Companies of Africa South of the Sahara, 2009* (Gale-Cengage/Graham & Whiteside, 2008); George Klay Kieh, Jr., *Africa and the New Globalization* (Ashgate, 2008); *The Middle East and North Africa 2008* (Europa Publications, 2008); Godfrey Mwakikagile, *Investment Opportunities and Private Sector Growth in Africa* (New Africa Press, 2007); Geoffrey Wood, *Industrial Relations in Africa* (Palgrave Macmillan, 2007).

JUSTIN CORFIELD
GEELONG GRAMMAR SCHOOL, AUSTRALIA

Company Profiles: Australia and the Pacific

A widely used regional designation for Australia and the Pacific is Australasia, whose broadest scope contains the countries of Australia, New Zealand, Malaysia, the Philippines, Papua New Guinea (PNG), and the many island nations of the Pacific, such as Fiji, Samoa, and Tonga. A more narrow definition contains Australia and New Zealand, countries with close historical, economic and cultural links; and PNG, geographically close and strategically linked to Australia. All three countries are members of the British Commonwealth. The more narrow definition is the focus here.

The largest economy in the region is by far Australia, with a 2007 nominal GDP of roughly US$908 billion in 2007 (according to the International Monetary Fund). New Zealand followed with a GDP of about US$129 billion. PNG's GDP was roughly US$6 billion. This difference in GDP scale is reflected in the relative size of the three countries' corporate equity markets where shares of many of the larger companies trade. Total market capitalization of the Australian Stock Exchange (ASX) as of September 2008 was approximately US$1.2 trillion; of the New Zealand Stock Exchange (NSX), US$36.9 billion (as of July 2008). There are 1,937 domestic companies listed on the ASX while only 149 are listed on the NSX. The Port Moresby stock exchange (POMSoX) is the official stock exchange of PNG. Capitalization of companies listed on POMSoX was approximately US$7 billion in late 2006.

Australia

A company could be considered domestic from a regional point of view either because it is headquartered or domiciled in a local country and/or because its operations are primarily located in the region. From either perspective, Australian companies are the most prominent in the Australasian area. According to IBISWorld (whose database contains both public and private companies), of the top 500 companies in Australasia as defined here, 469 operated in Australia in 2008, with total revenue of approximately A$1.3 trillion. Thirty-one of the remaining companies operated in New Zealand, having total revenue of A$62 billion, while one was in PNG, with total revenue of A$1.4 billion. Many of these Australian corporations were either subsidiaries of foreign multinationals, including companies such as IBM, Coca-Cola Amatil, ING, Nestle, Citibank, Vodafone, Pfizer, and Sony, or large local companies.

Many public-traded and Australian-domiciled firms are not just prominent in the Australasian region but in worldwide markets as well. In 2008, eight of the Fortune Global 500 companies were located in Australia. None were in New Zealand or PNG. Even more Australian firms are represented on the Forbes Global 2000 list (with two from New Zealand and again none from PNG).

Australian financial services firms are especially important in terms of global size. In 2008 the four largest Australian companies on the Forbes Global 2000 list (where companies are ranked in terms of sales) were commercial banks: National Australia Bank, ranking 89, followed by Commonwealth Bank (99), ANZ Bank (117), and Westpac Banking Corporation (130). These constituted the so-called Big Four of Australian banking and had combined total sales that year of over US$110 billion and profits of US$17 billion. Other major Australian financial services firms on the list included QBE Insurance Group (365), Macquarie Group (an investment bank) (410), AMP Australia (435), and St. George Bank (447).

The Macquarie Group also has other listed satellites and affiliates and two of these made the list as well: Macquarie Airports, which takes equity stakes in and operates international airports, including Sydney Airport (1007) and Macquarie Office Trust (1796). Macquarie in particular has a global presence and is known for its financial business model, which involves raising capital on equities markets to invest in various infrastructure and other business enterprises. Its home-grown imitator, Babcock and Brown, was 1353 on the Forbes list. These companies, especially Babcock and Brown, have faced difficulties as a result of the subprime crisis, as sources of inexpensive liquidity to finance leveraged investments have dried up.

As a sector, mining and resources companies are perhaps as significant as financial companies in the overall Australian corporate profile. The Forbes 2000 list included Woodside Petroleum (845), Santos (another energy firm) (1496), Fortescu Metals Group (1633), and Newcrest Mining (1716). Bigger than all of these but jointly domiciled in the United Kingdom and Australia (with primary operations in the latter country) is BHP Billiton, with sales of $39.5 billion and a ranking of 83. These companies have generally been quite profitable but are facing potential challenges as worldwide commodities prices weaken.

Transportation and logistics is also a major corporate sector, mainly because of Australia's large physi-

cal size, which requires long-haul movements of goods and services. Major Australian transport firms included Qantas Airways (719), Toll Holdings (a logistics firm) (985), and Transurban (a major toll road operator and logistics provider) (1786). Outside of these three major sectors, other significant Australian global companies include Telstra, the country's major telecommunications provider (and formerly a government monopoly before being privatized) (215), Westfield Group (a property developer and listed real estate trust) (390), and Woolworths, a major grocery chain (395).

Within Australia, Sydney, in the state of New South Wales (NSW), remains a prime location for many of the largest companies, public or private. In 2008, 45 percent of the IBISWorld top 500 Australasian companies, by revenue, were headquartered in NSW (accounting for 225 companies). This regional dominance was especially striking in the finance sector where 56 of the 58 domestic and foreign authorized deposit-taking institutions were in Sydney. Australia is an especially attractive location for foreign financial services firms seeking to operate in Asia because of its English language, corporate legal system based in English law and time zone that spans the end of the U.S. trading day and beginning of the European trading day while being coincident with the bulk of active trading in most Asian markets. The state of Victoria, which contains Australia's second largest city, Melbourne, accounted for another 27 percent of the top 500 by revenue (133) companies.

One other measure of the size and scope of the Australian corporate sector is a listing of the location of regional headquarters of multinational corporations in the country. As of 2002 Invest Australia indicated that the country was home to 848 Asia Pacific regional headquarters (RHQs), defined as an office located in Australia, whose parent company is located in a country other than Australia and that provides business services on behalf of the parent company to associated companies and customers located in countries other than Australia. The majority of these RHQs were located in NSW. Approximately one-third were involved in the information and communications technology industry, with strong presences in manufacturing, finance and insurance, and research and development.

The Australian Bureau of Statistics (ABS) estimated in its 2001 report on the small business sector (defined as a business employing less than 20 people) that there were 1,233,200 private sector small businesses in Australia during 2000–01, which represented 97 percent of all private sector businesses. These small businesses employed almost 3.6 million people, 49 percent of all private sector employment that year. Overall the industries contributing the highest number of small businesses were the construction industry (21 percent of small businesses), property and business services industries (19 percent) and the retail trade industry (15 percent). Relatively few enterprises were engaged in agriculture but in this sector the majority of enterprises (including Australia's very important wine producing industry) were small.

New Zealand

As noted above, New Zealand's corporate sector is much smaller and less globally prominent with a significantly different sectoral composition. Of the top 10 companies on a list of the country's top 100 companies, the largest is a dairy products manufacturer (Fonterra Co-Operative Group Ltd.) while the sixth largest is a producer of lumber and home interiors (Carter Holt Harvey Ltd.). The second largest firm is a grocer (Progressive Building Limited) and public sector or formerly public sector entities have three places in the top 10 (New Zealand Defence Force, New Zealand Police and New Zealand Post Ltd.). In this last category there are numerous public, quasi-public, or privatized public bodies in the overall top 100 list including local governments, universities, and governmental departments. Only two New Zealand firms are on the Forbes 2000 list for 2008: Telecom of New Zealand (ranked 1095, with sales of US$3.81 billion and profits of US$2.34 billion) and Fletcher Building (ranked 1796 with sales of US$4.58 billion and profits of US$0.37 billion).

New Zealand's corporate sector is also heavily dominated by Australian firms, especially in financial services. Partly this is because New Zealand is much smaller in terms of GDP as noted above and in population (roughly 4 million people versus 21 million in Australia). There are also very close economic links between the two countries, including the Trans-Tasman Travel arrangements of 1973, which allow citizens of the two countries to travel between and live and work without restriction within each other's national borders, and the Australia New Zealand

Closer Economic Relations Trade Agreement (ANZ-CERTA), effective since 1983, which essentially created a common market. As a result Australia is New Zealand's principal trading partner, providing 20 per cent of merchandise imports and taking 21 percent of merchandise exports. New Zealand is the third largest market for total Australian investment, direct and portfolio, and Australia is the largest foreign investor in that country. Australian companies dominate the financial services and transport sectors in New Zealand through foreign subsidiaries. Nearly all banks in New Zealand have parent companies domiciled in Australia and listed on the ASX.

Because of this close integration between the two economies, New Zealand's share market capitalization relative to its economy (42 percent of GDP) was much smaller than Australia's (151 percent of GDP) as of 2005, since it is often more efficient to list on the ASX or raise capital in the much larger Australian funds markets. The countries used to have similar relative levels of capitalization, at roughly 60 percent of GDP for each country in 1994. However, while both countries conducted significant privatizations of government enterprises and deregulation of financial markets, only Australia instituted mandatory retirement savings by employees and employers. The ASX is now the twelfth largest share market in the world and the fourth largest in the Asia Pacific by market capitalization.

By one measure, New Zealand public companies, in any case fewer in number, were more closely held than Australian companies in 1995. However, updated estimates and adjustments for the much smaller size of New Zealand firms (where it takes less capital to accumulate large stakes relative to the total) indicate that both countries' publicly traded firms have relatively broad ownership (with adjustment for size New Zealand's firms are more widely held) with both countries above OECD averages on that metric.

Papua New Guinea

PNG is similar to New Zealand with respect to the fact that it has close ties to Australia. A number of trade and defense treaties bind PNG and Australia, including the Papua New Guinea–Australia Trade and Commercial Relations Agreement (PATCRA II), the Agreement for the Promotion and Protection of Investment (APPI), and, most recently in 2004, the

Joint Agreement on Enhanced Cooperation. These treaties facilitate trade, employment and investment in PNG by Australians. In 2008, 8,000 Australian nationals lived and worked in the country. Australia is PNG's largest source of imports and destination for exports, with Australia purchasing 30 percent of the country's exports in 2006.

However in most other economic respects PNG is quite different from both Australia and New Zealand. The country was administered by Australia under a United Nations trusteeship after the end of World War II. Complete independence was declared from Australia in 1975 at the end of a process of increasing self-government.

Although larger in population terms than New Zealand (6.1 million people in 2008), the country's company sector is much less developed. PNG has a dual economy with a small formal incorporated sector whose employees are engaged primarily in mineral production, public sector services, a small manufacturing industry, and miscellaneous services such as finance, construction, transportation, and utilities. In that formal sector, the largest palm oil company, based in both PNG and the Solomon Islands, floated on the London Stock Exchange in 2007. The Solomon Islands is a major foreign destination of business activity for PNG companies, with 22 operating there in 2008 with investments of US$103 million. The firms operating in the Solomon Islands include names such as Bishop Brothers, Credit Corporation, Daltron, West New Britain Palm Oil Limited, Bank South Pacific, Lamana Hotel Developments, and KK Kingston.

However, the bulk of economic activity and employment in PNG still takes place primarily in the much larger informal sector, which relies heavily on subsistence agriculture. Partly because of that, PNG social indicators put the country well below those of most lower-middle-income countries as measured by the World Bank.

See Also: Australia; New Zealand; Pacific Rim.

Bibliography. Australian Bureau of Statistics (ABS), *Small Business in Australia 2001* (Report 1321.0); Australian Government Department of Foreign Affairs and Trade, *New Zealand Country Brief—January 2008* (2008); Australian Government Department of Foreign Affairs and Trade, *Papua New Guinea Country Brief—June 2008* (2008); Linda Cameron, *Investor Protection and the New Zealand Stock Market*, New Zealand Treasury Policy Perspectives Paper (07/02, October 2007); Forbes Magazine, *The Global 2000* (2008); Fortune Magazine, *The Fortune Global 500* (2008); IBISWorld, *Top 2000 Companies Database* (2008); International Monetary Fund, *World Economic Outlook Database, April 2008* (IMF, 2008); Kompass Company, *Business Profiles of New Zealand's Top 1000 Companies* (2008); Organisation for Economic Development and Co-operation, *Economic Survey of Australia 2006* (OECD, 2006); Pacific Islands Trade and Investment Commission, Sydney, *PNG Investments in Solomon Islands at US$103M* (September 6, 2008); Radio New Zealand International, *Biggest Palm Oil Company in PNG and Solomons to Float on London Stock Exchange* (December 16, 2007); World Federation of Exchanges, *Market Statistics* (July 2008).

CAMERON GORDON
UNIVERSITY OF CANBERRA

Company Profiles: Central America and the Caribbean

Many companies based in Central America and the Caribbean are rapidly becoming integrated into the global economy. The small size of local and regional markets has motivated several companies in this region to pursue business opportunities not only in the more developed countries of North America and western Europe but also in fast-growing emerging countries such as India. The rise of multinational enterprises from Central America and the Caribbean is a relatively new phenomenon and one that has not attracted a great deal of attention in the academic literature or business press.

Central American and Caribbean multinational enterprises (CACMNEs) are operative in a wide range of industries from food and beverage to leisure and tourism and financial services. Companies such as CL Financial (Trinidad), Grace Kennedy (Jamaica), Neal and Massy Holdings (Trinidad), and Goddard Enterprises (Barbados) are examples of companies with significant international and regional operations in a wide range of industries. Other companies such as Nicaragua-based Financiera Arrendadora

Centroamericana (Finarca) continue to focus on their domestic markets but have become targets of regional and multinational firms interested in their assets and markets, while firms such as the Lovable Group (Honduras) have used their domestic competitive advantages to secure major international customers. These firms too find themselves integrated into the global economy.

CL Financial

CL Financial is a Trinidad-based CACMNE that has aggressively pursued extra-regional market opportunities. CL Financial was established in 1993 as the holding company for Colonial Life Insurance Company (Trinidad) Ltd., which at the time was still a relatively small insurance company offering a limited range of products. However, by 2005 CL Financial had grown into a major conglomerate with business operations in insurance, financial services, real estate development, media, medical services, agriculture, manufacturing, methanol, distribution, and retail. The firm now operates in over 28 countries around the world and has assets in excess of $12 billion.

Through its wholly owned United Kingdom–based subsidiary, CI WorldBrands Ltd., CL Financial has become a major player in the global alcoholic beverage industry. In 2004 the company acquired Paragon Vintners Ltd., a London-based wine and spirits distributor, as well as Fassbind Distributors of Switzerland, a company also focused on the distribution of alcoholic beverages. In 2005 the firm acquired ChateauOnLine, a French wine merchant. Also included in the company's wine and spirits portfolio are Burn Stewart, a Scotch whisky producer with three single malt distilleries, 200 employees, and sales operations in Taiwan, South Africa, and the United States. CL Financial also owns Thomas Hine and Company Ltd., a French manufacturer of fine cognacs with a 250-year history. In 2007 the company completed the acquisition of Pernod Ricard's Lawrenceburg facility in Indiana. Pernod is a major producer, importer, and marketer of wine and spirits and is the third-largest company in the U.S. wine and spirits industry.

It is not, however, only in the area of alcoholic beverages that CL Financial has excelled. The company is also a major player in the methanol and biofuels industry. Through its subsidiary, Methanol Holdings (Trinidad) Ltd., CL Financial operates the largest methanol plant in the world with a capacity of 5,400 MT of methanol per day. The company has also, with a German partner, commissioned a methanol plant in Oman that began production in late 2007.

Grace Kennedy Ltd.

Another CACMNE of note is Jamaica-based Grace Kennedy Ltd. This conglomerate was established in the early 1920s as a small trading company. The firm has since grown considerably and now includes some 60 subsidiaries and associated companies and is operative across the Caribbean, North and Central America, the United States, Canada, and the United Kingdom. Grace Kennedy operates in two broad businesses—food and financial services. In the food area, the firm is active in processing, marketing, and distribution across the Caribbean as well as in the United Kingdom and Canada. For example, Grace Foods UK Ltd. is one of Europe's leading suppliers of ethnic foods while Grace Kennedy (Ontario) Ltd. is a major trading company operating in Canada. World Brand Services is a division of Grace Kennedy Ltd. focused on representing a range of international food and nonfood brands. M&M Mars, Lay's, Tostitos, Ziploc, and McCains are among the brands distributed by the company. Grace Kennedy (Belize) Ltd. is also a player in the food distribution business; it is the third-largest food importer in Belize and handles primarily "Grace" branded products.

As previously mentioned, Grace Kennedy is also active in the area of food manufacturing. Grace Food Processors is a manufacturer of Grace branded products including tomato ketchup, canned beans, and juices. Dairy Industries (Jamaica) Ltd., on the other hand, is a manufacturer and distributor of dairy products. This dairy operation is a 50/50 joint venture between Grace Kennedy and Fonterra of New Zealand, which is a leading exporter of dairy products. Grace-branded food products are marketed internationally through Grace Food International, which exports to over 25 countries in Europe, Asia, Latin America, and North America.

In addition to food manufacturing and marketing, Grace Kennedy also operates a portfolio of companies in financial services and nonfood marketing. EC Global Insurance, for example, is a provider of insurance services headquartered in St. Lucia, while FG Fund Management (Cayman) Ltd., is a mutual-fund company based in the Cayman Islands, and Grace Kennedy Remittance Services is based in Guyana and is involved in the wire transfer of funds. Grace Kennedy is also active in the building supplies industry in Jamaica through its ownership of Hardware and Lumber Ltd., which is involved in retailing and wholesaling building materials and home improvement supplies.

Neal and Massy Holdings Ltd.

Neal and Massy Holdings Ltd. (NMH) is one of the largest and most established conglomerates in the region. The company has been in business for over 80 years and has 6,000 employees and over 7,000 shareholders. The firm is operative in a range of industries. The Automotive & Industrial Equipment Business Unit is involved in vehicle sales and service as well as the rental of heavy industrial, construction, and agricultural equipment, and equipment for the petroleum industry. This unit represents a number of world-class brands including Goodyear, Caterpillar, Nissan, Subaru, Hyundai, and Volvo. Associated Industries Ltd. (Guyana) is part of this unit and retails automotive and industrial equipment across Guyana.

NMH also operates the Energy & Industrial Gases Business Unit, which provides a range of products and services to the energy sector, for example, electrical and instrumentation services, and through its associate company, NM Wood Group, has partnered with BP (Trinidad and Tobago) to provide maintenance on the company's onshore plants. The unit also holds a majority stake in Demerara Oxygen Company Ltd., which markets LPG and manufactures and markets oxygen, nitrogen, argon, and acetylene in the Guyana market. Also part of this unit is Industrial Gases Ltd., which is a joint venture between NMH and Air Liquide International of France. This company supplies a range of gas products in cylinders, bulk liquid tanks, and high pressure tubes.

NMH also operates in the financial and related services industry. The company is active in the areas of property development, real estate, construction, security, and financial services. For example, NMH holds a 24.5 percent stake in G4S Holdings (Trinidad) Ltd., which is part of one of the leading manned-security firms in the world, with 400,000 employees and a presence in the United States, Canada, United Kingdom, Germany, and France. Through Nealco Properties Ltd., the firm is also an active player in

the property management, facilities maintenance, and interior architecture and design fields. The NMH group of companies also covers areas such as remittances (NM Remittance Services Ltd.) and leasing, corporate asset financing, and insurance (General Finance Corporation Ltd.).

In 2001 NMH founded Illuminat (Trinidad & Tobago) Ltd., an information technology and communications operation with a presence in Trinidad, Barbados, Jamaica, Cayman Islands, and the Bahamas. Illuminat has more than 400 employees and provides solutions to government, retail, energy, and hospitality clients across the Caribbean. NMH is also involved in the retail, distribution, and logistics business and owns H.D. Hopwood & Company Ltd., a Jamaica-based importer and distributor of consumer and pharmaceutical products as well as Huggins Shipping & Customs Brokerage Ltd., which provides freight forwarding and customs brokerage services. This latter firm has a long history of operation, having been established in 1896. In fiscal 2007 NMH reported total revenues of TT$5 billion.

Goddard Enterprises Ltd.

While CL Financial and Grace Kennedy have taken a decidedly global approach to their international expansion, other Central American and Caribbean firms have opted for a more regional expansion strategy. Goddard Enterprises Ltd. (GEL) is headquartered in Barbados. The firm started in 1921 as a small meat and grocery store in Bridgetown, the capital of Barbados. The company acquired a local bakery in 1939, and by 1943 had expanded into department store retailing and the hotel industry. GEL now operates 50 companies across 23 countries in the Caribbean and Central and South America.

GEL subsidiaries are active in a wide range of industries including airline catering, industrial and restaurant catering, meat processing, bakery operations, automobile retail and automotive parts, real estate, the manufacture of aerosols and liquid detergents, rum distilling, packaging, fish and shrimp processing, and financial services. Countries in which the firm operates include Antigua, Barbados, Bermuda, Cayman Islands, Colombia, Curacao, Grenada, Jamaica, St. Lucia, St. Maarten, and St. Thomas, Trinidad and Tobago, El Salvador, Ecuador, Guatemala, Paraguay, Uruguay, and Venezuela.

The company's airline catering business was established in 1954. In 1972 GEL entered into a joint venture with the Marriott Corporation, and by 1976 the firm had established its first regional catering operation with its expansion into the Antiguan market. GEL quickly expanded into other Caribbean and Latin American markets with catering units established in over 20 countries. The firm also established airport terminal catering operations and negotiated deals to service a number of major regional and international air carriers including KLM, FedEx, United Airlines, Air Jamaica, Air Canada, American Airlines, Delta Airlines, Virgin Atlantic, Cayman Airways, Mexicana, and British Airways. The firm also secured a number of major industrial clients such as British Petroleum PLC, Repsol S.A., BHP Billiton, Esso, Kellogg's, Bayer, and Altria.

Most of GEL's manufacturing and service operations are based in Barbados. For example, Hipac Ltd. is based in Barbados and produces a wide range of meat and seafood products, while the West Indies Rum Distillery, also based in Barbados, is a manufacturer of aged rums, vodka, and gin. Another subsidiary, Purity Bakery, produces baked goods for supermarkets, shops, hotels, and restaurants across Barbados. The company's sole overseas manufacturing operation is BEV Processors Inc., which is a shrimp and fish processor based in Guyana. GEL also manages a number of import and marketing businesses across the Caribbean. Hutchinsons & Brisbane, for example, is a marketing operation based in Antigua that represents a number of major international brands such as Uncle Ben's Rice, Brunswick Seafoods, Lysol, Harpic, Dettol, and Pedigree and Whiskas. GEL also holds a 70 percent stake in Fidelity Motors, which distributes Nissan vehicles in the Jamaican market.

Other Companies

Grace Kennedy, GEL, and CL Financial operate in a range of diverse and unrelated industries. Other CACMNEs are more focused. Digicel Group Ltd. is a privately owned company incorporated in Bermuda. In 2001 the company launched its operations in Jamaica, becoming the first company in that country to offer GSM mobile services. The firm is the largest mobile telecommunications company in the Caribbean with six million subscribers in 23 markets across the region. Digicel serves markets in the Caribbean

and Central America, including Anguilla, Antigua & Barbuda, Aruba, Barbados, Bermuda, Bonaire, the Cayman Islands, Curacao, Dominica, El Salvador, French Guiana, Grenada, Guadeloupe, Guyana, Haiti, Jamaica, Martinique, St. Kitts & Nevis, St. Lucia, St. Vincent and the Grenadines, Suriname, Turks and Caicos, and Trinidad & Tobago. In addition, the company has licenses to operate in Honduras and Panama. The firm has 4,000 employees, operates 1,000 retail stores, and posted revenues of US$1 billion in fiscal 2007.

Nicaragua-based Finarca has become integrated into the global economy, not by expanding internationally but by attracting inbound foreign direct investment from regional and extra-regional firms. This company began operations in 1997 and was the first to introduce the leasing concept to the Nicaraguan market. The company is involved in leasing industrial and agricultural equipment to small and medium-sized companies. With assistance from the Inter-American Development Bank (IDB) Finarca has established a special leasing program for small and medium-sized businesses. As part of this initiative Finarca provides financing to small enterprises of between $3,000–$8,000 for up to four years. Norfund and the IFC injected equity into the company in 1999, and the company has also been successful in raising loan financing from Finnfund, the OVF, SIFEM, and Citibank. In 2003 Interfin, the largest private bank in Costa Rica, acquired a 25 percent stake in Finarca and subsequently increased its ownership to 51 percent in 2005. By 2007, however, Interfin had been acquired by Scotiabank Costa Rica in a $300-million deal that included its 51 percent share of Finarca. In 2008 Scotiabank acquired the remaining 49 percent of Finarca, effectively bringing the Nicaraguan leasing company under the control of the Canadian bank and part of its Latin American and Caribbean network of financial services operations.

The Lovable Group was founded in 1964 in Honduras and has grown to become one of the largest industrial companies in Central America. The firm employs 8,000 people and is active in a number of industries including textile and apparel, the operation of industrial parks, and energy cogeneration. The firm's textile and apparel operation counts among its clients Russell Corporation and Cross Creek, Jockey, Costco Wholesale, and JC Penney. On behalf of these and other clients, the Lovable Group exports products to a number of countries around the world including the United States, Canada, United Kingdom, Japan, Korea, and Taiwan. As part of the textile and apparel operation, Lovable owns and operates a number of companies including Genesis Apparel SA, a sewing operation with 1,000 employees; Pacer Screen Printing and Embroidery; Trueform; and Villatex SA, which produces products for Victoria's Secret and Tommy Hilfiger.

The Lovable Group also operates four industrial parks in Honduras. Zip Buena Vista SA is a 950,000-sq.-ft. facility, while Zip Tex is a 900,000-sq.-ft. operation. These complement two other facilities—Zip Choloma 1 and 11. All four parks provide basic infrastructure services as well as assistance with the recruitment of local workers. The Lovable Group also offers power through its cogeneration facility, established in 2004 to supply its industrial parks. Surplus energy is sold to the local National Energy Company. The Group also provides wastewater treatment as well as food and water laboratory analysis services to industrial clients.

See Also: Canada; Central America; Costa Rica; Inter-American Development Bank; Internationalization; Trinidad and Tobago.

Bibliography. Karen Retana, "Scotiabank Expands Its Nicaragua Presence," *La República* (April 11, 2008); CL Financial, www.clfinancial.com (cited March 2009); Digicel Group, www.digicelgroup.com (cited March 2009); Finarca, www.finarca.com (cited March 2009); Goddard Enterprises, www.goddardenterprisesltd.com (cited March 2009); Grace Kennedy, www.gracekennedy.com (cited March 2009); Lovable Group, www.lovablegroup.com (cited March 2009); Neal and Massy Holdings, www.neal-and-massy.com (cited March 2009).

CARLYLE FARRELL
RYERSON UNIVERSITY

Company Profiles: Central Asia

From ancient times, central Asia had been part of the Silk Road for trade between China and Europe, and this led to the emergence of many small trading

These women sorting raisins for export in 2006 were part of a USAID program to develop small factories in Afghanistan.

companies in the region. It also resulted in Chinese, Turkish, and European businesspeople establishing businesses in Central Asia. Owing to its position in the world, and the history of the region, many of the companies in central Asia have tended to be, in the main, Russian, British, Indian/Pakistani, or Iranian.

The Russian influence in central Asia started in the 16th century, with Russian traders using the region to reach China; later, Russia started annexing parts of central Asia to enlarge the Russian Empire. Under the tsars, many Russian private companies and government corporations operated in central Asia, not only the areas that they directly controlled but also in nearby countries. Under communism, the Soviet Union took over these companies, and also established other trading companies in the region that dominated trade. Most of these were centered on particular cities or towns such as the Chimkent Industrial Amalgamation and the Dzhambul Industrial Corporation, both in Kazakhstan.

Following the end of communism and independence for Kazakhstan, Kyrgyzstan, Tajikistan, Turkmenistan, and Uzbekistan, these former government corporations were taken over by the new governments, some of which embarked on privatization measures. Others like Turkmenistan involved restructuring them and keeping them effectively under state control. Some private companies have also been established in all five countries, especially in the capital cities. However, the dominance of the Russian managerial class was evident throughout the 1990s, and some of the companies in these countries are still dominated by Russians. Some foreign businesses have entered former Soviet central Asia, such as Citibank operating in Almaty.

In Afghanistan, the threat to Soviet investment in the country in the 1970s caused the Soviet leadership to send in troops in 1978, and this kept the communists in power there until 1992. During that time, the economy was modeled on those of the states of Soviet central Asia, with state corporations dominating. Since the end of communism and the fall of Najibullah in April 1992, the economy of the country has become even worse. There are some small businesses operating in the country, and foreign infrastructure companies and security companies have been heavily involved since NATO troops moved into Afghanistan in 2002. However, with a precarious economic climate, few companies are involved in investing in the country. The problem has been that most of these countries, and indeed Pakistan, have large "informal" sectors of the economy with thriving black markets.

British companies were an important part of trade in the region, mainly through their involvement in India/Pakistan until 1947. This saw them fight three wars in Afghanistan, and be heavily involved in the "great game." However, for the most part, business was in the hands of local traders such as the "horse dealer from Lahore" in Rudyard Kipling's story *Kim* (1901). In Pakistan, with a capital free market economy, many British businesses have continued to operate there, usually through locally owned subsidiaries. The sheer size of the population of the country and its connections with Britain have made Pakistan a strong market for British products, and indeed, Britain a market for Pakistani products such as hand-woven carpets that can now be found all around the world. British banks, insurance companies, business advisories, and the like remain popular in Pakistan, and until the mid-1970s, were also popular among the elite in Afghanistan. Indian and Pakistani companies operate throughout the region, and many have seen great opportunities in central Asia, as, have some from Asian countries farther afield such as Thailand and Singapore.

In Iran, many foreign companies—European, North American, and Turkish—were involved in the country in the early 20th century. There was much interest in developing the oil in the region, which saw the signing of the Anglo-Iranian Oil Treaty in 1949. This in turn led to Mohammad Mosaddeq becoming prime minister of Iran in 1951, and he introduced legislation to nationalize the Iranian oil industry soon afterward. A Western economic blockade soon brought the country to the verge of bankruptcy and forced Mosaddeq from power. From 1952, British and U.S. companies managed to make major inroads into the Iranian economy, a situation that changed dramatically with the flight of Shah Mohammad Reza Pahlavi in January 1979. For many years the newly proclaimed Islamic Republic of Iran remained isolated from the West, being immersed in war with Iraq for the next 10 years. There has been a loosening of the economic restrictions in recent years, and this has, once again, led to Western companies working in Iran, and Iranian companies overseas, although there are still restrictions on business dealings between the United States and Iran.

See Also: Iran; Kazakhstan; Pakistan; Russia.

Bibliography. Hooshang Amirahmadi, *Revolution and Economic Transition: The Iranian Experience* (State University of New York Press, 1990); Anders Aslund, *How Capitalism Was Built: The Transformation of Central and Eastern Europe, Russia, and Central Asia* (Cambridge University Press, 2007); Violet Conolly, *Beyond the Urals: Economic Development in Soviet Asia* (Oxford University Press, 1967); Gregory Gleason, *Markets and Politics in Central Asia: Structural Reform and Political Change* (Routledge, 2003); Ali Mohammadi, ed., *Iran Encountering Globalization: Problems and Prospects* (RoutledgeCurzon, 2003); Richard W. T. Pomfret, *The Economies of Central Asia* (Princeton University Press, 1995); Richard W. T. Pomfret, *The Central Asia Economies after Independence* (Princeton University Press, 2006); Boris Rumer, ed., *Central Asia and the New Global Economy* (M. E. Sharpe, 2000); Max Spoor, ed., *Transition, Institutions and the Rural Sector* (Lexington Books, 2003).

Justin Corfield
Geelong Grammar School, Australia

Company Profiles: East Asia

East Asia's roaring economies, led by China, are raising their competitive edge relative to the United States and Europe. The economies of East Asia grew by 9.8 percent in 2006 and those of the United States and Europe rose 2.2 and 1.3 percent, respectively. The entry of multinational corporations (MNCs) has brought the latest technology and advanced management systems to the region. While operating in East Asia, MNCs can use an ethnocentric strategy to transfer their headquarters' practices to their overseas subsidiaries, employ a polycentric strategy to totally adapt to local situations, or adopt a geocentric strategy to balance both global integration and local adaptation.

The economic development of East Asia can also be observed by the international expansion of Asian transnational corporations (TNCs). Globalization, market forces, and technology can push management systems toward uniformity and encourage benchmarking and copying the best practices. TNCs are pressured to adopt some new practices to gain legitimacy. However, embedded customs and idiosyncratic national regimes mediate and reshape the outcome of human resource management (HRM) change.

It is worth examining whether companies operating in East Asia have adopted global HRM practices or customized them to local situations. The discussion is from both sides: Whether MNCs have transferred more global standardized models and whether TNCs have preserved more traditional practices. Eight leading companies operating in East Asia are used to investigate this issue. These companies come from various industries and countries of origin, are well established in the region, and are operating across multiple Asian economies.

Western MNCs: HSBC Holdings

Some management theories assume that a set of "best" management practices can be valid in all circumstances and help organizations perform better and obtain sustainable competitive advantage. To apply "best practices," which are mostly derived from the West, in other countries, such as those in Asia, it is important to understand the background. The following highlights several MNCs' company profiles, their history and involvement in Asia, as well as some of their key HRM practices in the region.

HSBC Holdings plc, number one in the Fortune Global 500 in 2007, is the world's largest company and bank. The Holdings was established in 1991 to become the parent company to the Hong Kong and Shanghai

HSBC's network of 600 offices in 20 countries in the Asia Pacific region includes the famous HSBC building in Hong Kong.

Banking Corporation. It has a significant presence in the major financial markets. Currently, HSBC operates a network of some 600 offices in 20 countries in the Asia Pacific region. Its long history in East Asia can be dated back to the 19th century. It has been the largest note-issuing bank in Hong Kong since the 1880s, handled the first public loan in China in 1874, and was the first bank established in Thailand in 1888.

HSBC's core values of integrity, collegiality, and diversity are reflected in its recruitment practices. A global talent management process was implemented to attract, motivate, and retain employees. Human resources (HR) professionals first visited all countries to describe key principles and nomination guidelines for talent assessment to ensure buy-in for the process. Multiple sources of data, including interviews, panel interviews, and 360-degree feedback were then used to review capability ratings for all talent nominations globally. Potential leaders and specialists were identified to fill future positions in next three to seven years.

HSBC adopts an ethnocentric approach in its rewards practices. Its grading structure, salary adjustment, and bonus scheme are inherited from its head offices. For example, to encourage employees to have a direct interest in the bank, an employee share savings plan was offered in most countries. Global bonus schemes linking employees to the achievement of long-term strategic objectives were introduced in East Asia with limited local adaptation.

Because of its large size and extensive network, HSBC can leverage its training resources across the region. The training programs are organized by regional training teams and launched by local offices. Typically, managers with one to two years' company service would attend fundamental management skills training and those with three to five years' company service would attend advanced courses. Young executives are required to complete a two-month induction course.

Western MNCs: Walt Disney Company

The Walt Disney Company is the third largest media and entertainment company in the world. Founded in 1923 as an animation studio, it now owns 11 theme parks. The first theme park opened in 1955 in Florida. In East Asia, the Hong Kong Disneyland theme park opened in September 2005; Tokyo Disney had opened more than 20 years earlier.

To avoid cultural friction similar to what happened at Disneyland Resort Paris, Disney has taken efforts to make their theme parks in Asia reflect the local culture. For example, in Tokyo Disneyland, "Samurai Land" replaced one of the four compass points of the American parks, creating a ride based on a classic Japanese children's story. In Hong Kong, feng shui advisers were consulted about the layout of the park and the hotels skipped the number four when numbering their floors because four is considered bad luck in Chinese culture.

While these adaptations were made on the surface, at a deeper level, imported Disney values retain their influence and are reflected in HR practices. The same interview questions and selection processes were used in Hong Kong, Tokyo, and the United States. Recruitment of professional and higher positions from the external market are rare; rather, internal promotions and deployments are used. The emphasis of recruitment is on "making" people that fit with Disney tradition.

Most of the managerial training programs stress familiarization with Disney culture. There is also the Disney Site Experience, in which managers are sent to other theme parks for job shadowing, learning the actual operations, and understanding the Disney culture. Disney University provides training courses to all employees (or "cast members") about quality, effectiveness, services, and safety. These courses are modified from, and matched with, its U.S. training modules.

Western MNCs: Cisco Systems

Cisco Systems, Inc., was founded in 1984 and is headquartered in San Jose, California. It designs and sells networking and communications technology and services. In 1990 the company went public and was listed on the NASDAQ exchange. Today, with more than 65,000 employees worldwide and annual sales of US$38 billion as of 2007, Cisco is one of the largest developers of routers (a device that forwards computer traffic between networks) and Internet Protocol (IP) packets. In Asia, it has subsidiaries in China, Hong Kong, South Korea, Malaysia, and some southeast Asian countries.

Cisco recognizes an inclusive and culturally diverse workforce as a business imperative. Its HR strategy aims at developing knowledgeable employees who can move quickly to areas of highest needs, thrive on change, and have strong capabilities in process. To acquire such knowledgeable employees, Cisco uses a "buy" strategy. From 1993 through 2000, it acquired 70 companies worldwide. These acquisitions provided not only technology, but also served as a source of talent needed to support its development in Asia. In terms of selection processes, Cisco uses lengthy processes originated from its U.S. model with multiple rounds of interviews. It is, indeed, company policy to have at least five rounds of interviews; the number of rounds can go as high as 16.

Cisco's rewards schemes in Asia follow its U.S. model. All employees receive stock options, based on company performance and individual performance. Performance-based incentive programs and commission schemes are heavily used.

Cisco University was established to centrally design training programs. For example, it adopted the "3E

Model" (experience, exposure, and education) development framework in early 2003. Similar training programs were subsequently introduced to China and Hong Kong. Several days' managerial training programs were arranged and online e-training was offered. Most of these training materials, however, were written in English with limited translations to local languages.

Western MNCs: KPMG

KPMG originates from an accounting firm founded in 1917. Through a series of mergers and acquisitions, KPMG is now a Big Four auditor employing over 123,000 people in a global network of member firms in 140 countries. In East Asia, KPMG has solid foundations in China, Hong Kong, Japan, South Korea, and Taiwan.

KPMG adopts a geocentric approach in its recruitment practice. It recruits professionals from all over the world who understand Asian culture, attracts overseas graduates to return to Asia to work, and sources international talent. Besides "buying" from labor markets, inexperienced graduates are recruited as trainees and undergo a series of training programs, overseas exchange, and in-house examinations to "make" or train them up.

There are seven hierarchical levels—from top partner to bottom associate. This grading structure is globally applied and there is no local customization. Even in East Asia where people are more concerned about status, the titling system and salary structure remain consistent with headquarters.

KPMG is well known for its training and knowledge management. In Korea, KPMG was named "Best Human Resources Developer 2007." Its training programs are designed to foster multidisciplinary capabilities and support global mobility. Each KPMG employee has their own development program that is complemented by global learning initiatives and linked to global performance management systems.

East Asian TNCs: Hutchison Whampoa Ltd.

As the Asian economies are gaining importance in the global arena, the competition, in both domestic and global markets, encourages Asian TNCs to explore investment opportunities overseas. This has significantly changed the ways in which Asian enterprises are managed and work is performed, creating a new institutional environment.

Hutchison Whampoa Limited (HWL), a Fortune Global 500 company, is a leading international corporation with a diverse array of holdings, including the world's largest port and telecommunications operations. Its business also includes retail, property development, infrastructure, and energy. HWL dates back to the 1800s in the Whampoa area (Pearl River of China) when it provided shipbuilding and ship-repairing services. While its operations now span the globe, it continues to remain based in Hong Kong. HWL's strategy is to focus on global expansion and internationalization while locally managing its services.

With a workforce spanning various East Asian economies, HWL emphasizes diversity in recruitment. Its resourcing practices include tapping domestic and regional labor markets to find the best person for each job regardless of race, color, or gender. Networking across affiliates and cross-function movements are frequently used. HWL also uses the vacant positions of various locations to move high-caliber staff around for retention.

HWL reviews its remuneration scheme annually to ensure that packages are externally competitive. Internally, it rewards employees according to their performance and productivity. Employees enjoy comprehensive medical and insurance benefits and a wide range of product and service discounts offered by various affiliated companies.

Online training and learning resource centers are established through a Web portal. Such e-learning enables more employees to access training in a convenient manner and facilitates organizational knowledge transfer and sharing to geographically dispersed employees across East Asia at relatively low cost.

East Asian TNCs: Bank of Communications

Founded in 1908, the Bank of Communications (BOCM) is one of the oldest banks and the earliest note-issuing banks of China. To operate in line with China's economic reforms, BOCM was restructured in 1986 and thereby became the first state-owned shareholding commercial bank. Its head office was in Shanghai. It has over 2,600 outlets in 148 major cities in China and overseas branches in Hong Kong, Macao, New York, Seoul, Singapore, and Tokyo. It was listed on both the Hong Kong and Shanghai stock exchanges. Foreign investors, like HSBC, were brought in as strategic partners to enhance its organizational structure.

Since then, several changes have been observed in its HRM practices.

BOCM launched a graduate recruitment program a few years ago. Its program contained features similar to those in large foreign banks. However, the program was not successful because it could not attract sufficient graduates from top-tier universities. Subsequently, BOCM reverted to its traditional recruitment methods of taking up government-assigned people.

After the reforms in the 1980s, BOCM commenced a bonus scheme that was mostly discretionary. High staff turnover rates in the banking industry plus fierce competition from foreign banks after China's accession to World Trade Organization means that attraction and retention of people are particularly important. In 2006 BOCM formally introduced an incentive system to improve the attractiveness of its remuneration package. That incentive system has some performance-based features similar to those used in MNCs.

BOCM has tried to upgrade employees' competencies and promote the bank as a knowledge-based learning organization. A series of training courses, such as banking operations and customer relations, are provided to new employees. However, training programs are still narrowly defined in scope and focus mostly on technical aspects and job-related skills.

East Asian TNCs: YKK

The world's largest zipper manufacturer, YKK was founded in Japan in 1934. It was named after its founder, Yoshida Kogyo Kabushikihaisha. Over the years, the letters "YKK" were stamped onto the zippers' pull tabs, and thus YKK became known as the company's trademark. YKK also makes other fastening products, architectural products, and industrial machinery. Its philosophy is to manufacture only high-quality zippers that would benefit the end use goods in which they are installed. Due to this guiding principle, it has evolved into a vertically integrated manufacturing system, that is, it not only produces the zippers, but also produces the machines that make the zippers, and even many of the raw materials (e.g., aluminium) that go into the zippers. Currently, YKK operates more than 123 affiliated companies in more than 70 countries. In East Asia, YKK has several plants in China and Taiwan.

When selecting candidates for its East Asian plants, YKK typically considers technical skills, education of candidates, and culture fit with the company. Young people are recruited to start at the bottom of the organizational hierarchy and climb up it slowly. It is also common to reappoint retired people to join its plants to provide consultant advice. Rewards practice in local plants follows a traditional Japanese model that is largely based on seniority and tenure. Job performance is not truly reflected in salary increases. Promotion is rotated and depends less on individual ability and job performance. Job rotation across the factory floor is common and employees are placed to work in different areas for several years to learn the practices. Quality and knowledge management are highly emphasized in the training courses.

East Asian TNCs: Haier Group

Founded in 1984, Haier Group is headquartered in Qingdao in China's Shandong Province, and is the world's leading white goods home appliance manufacturer. Its products are now sold in over 100 countries. It has 5,000 overseas retail outlets and over 10,000 service centers all over the world. Haier's strategy aims at positioning the company as a local brand in different world markets. Its management philosophy is a blend of international management principles and Chinese tradition. The globalization of best practice means what works best in one subsidiary, e.g., Haier America, is shared with another, e.g., Haier Europe, and then the successful management practices are further introduced to other subsidiaries.

The globalization practice also extends to its recruitment policy. Haier considers both domestic and overseas professions. Since its corporate culture features recognition and participation of all employees, Haier has created an open competitive job bidding system. Employees who have reached the qualified skill level through training are welcome to bid for job openings.

Promotion is based upon excellence. There is a competitive system to review performance and ability. The responsibility of a manager is to establish a "race track," that is, a personal development opportunity for every employee to develop and demonstrate their talents. Haier adopts an open and transparent incentive policy. A point system to check quality problems is set up and the workers receive a higher wage and bonus if they earn more points. Daily evaluation results are announced to all workers in the factory.

Every new employee goes to the Haier University to attend one month of corporate culture and management training before being put to work. In-house training and overseas exchange programs are offered to all employees (including managers, technical experts, and workers) who can register for the courses at will. In order for senior managers to understand the mechanism of the department, they are assigned to work at the bottom level of the department for several months.

Conclusion

In general, most of the eight MNCs operating in East Asia discussed here adopted an ethnocentric approach in rewards and training and extended global incentive schemes and training programs to East Asia. However, transferring global practices without any adaptation to local markets was not without pain. Past success or best practice in one situation did not automatically guarantee an effective transfer and adoption in another. In more recent years, a number of MNCs considered a geocentric recruitment approach to utilize the best people for key jobs throughout the organizations.

On the other hand, some traditional practices predominantly in East Asia (such as seniority-based pay, technical skill training, appointments by government) seem problematic as Asian TNCs expand overseas. Benchmarking best practices and competitive forces have been some key drivers of the reconfiguration of TNCs. However, there is no single management model that shapes the way companies are organized or their people are managed, regardless of whether Asian or Western.

Change in HR management practice involving gradual experimentation of best practices and blending with Asian characteristics will continue. As with most experimentation, the final outcomes may be difficult to predict. Greater appreciation of East Asian contexts as well as understanding the dynamic of HR management change in the region is desirable.

See Also: Asia; China; Ethnocentric Human Resource Policy; Globalization; Hong Kong; Japan; Local Adaptation; Polycentric Human Resource Policy.

Bibliography. Victoria Bentley and Chris Tapster, *Major Companies of Asia and Australasia: South East Asia-*
Brunei, Cambodia, Indonesia, Laos, Malaysia, Myanmar, Philippines, Singapore, Thailand, Vietnam, 24th ed., v. 1 (Gale-Cengage/Graham & Whiteside Ltd,, 2007); J. Chatman, C. O'Reilly, and V. Chang, "Cisco Systems: Developing a Human Capital Strategy," *California Management Review* (v.47/2, 2005); L. X. Cunningham, C. Rowley, and Irene H. F. Poon, "'Globalisation of Asian Firms," in *The Handbook of Technology Management*, H. Bidgoli, ed. (Wiley, 2008); A. Gakovic and K. Yardley, "Global Talent Management at HSBC," *Organisation Development Journal* (v.25/2, 2007); Sandra James and Christy Oddy, *Major Companies of Asia and Australasia East Asia: People's Republic of China, Hong Kong, Japan, South Korea, North Korea, Mongolia, Taiwan*, 24th ed., v. 2 (Gale-Cengage/Graham & Whiteside, 2007); G. S. Lim, "Hutchison Whampoa: A Global 3G Giant in the Making?" *Asian Case Research Journal* (v.9/2, 2005); W. Lin, "Effective OEC Management Control at China Haier Group," *Thomas Strategic Finance* (v.86/11, 2005); C. Rowley and J. Benson, *The Management of Human Resources in the Asia Pacific Region: Convergence Reconsidered* (Frank Cass, 2004); C. Rowley and M. Warner, "The Management of HR in the Asia Pacific into the 21st Century," *Management Revue* (v.18/4, 2007); C. Rowley, J. Benson, and M. Warner, "Towards an Asian Model of HRM? A Comparative Analysis of China, Japan and South Korea," *International Journal of HRM* (v.15/4, 2004); J. Van Mannen, "Displacing Disney: Some Notes on the Flow of Culture," *Qualitative Sociology* (v.15/1, 1992); M. Warner, *The Future of Chinese Management* (Frank Cass, 2003); World Bank Report, "Regional Fact Sheet from the World Development Indicators 2008," www.worldbank.org (cited March 2009).

Irene Hon-fun Poon
Chris Rowley
City University Cass Business School

Company Profiles: Eastern Europe

Because of their location and size, and also the history of the region, Germany and Russia have tended to dominate the countries of eastern Europe, and although there have, obviously, been traders since ancient times, the first evidence of named trading companies comes from the medieval period with the establishment of the Hanseatic League. This was a series of arrangements in ports in the Baltic Sea that helped the traders there to establish a system of trading and credits, and also helped a number of ports establish a trade monopoly. By this time many of the major cities in eastern Europe and all the ports of the Hanseatic League had a system whereby city guilds controlled trades within their region in order to—as they argued—keep up the quality and also prevent competition.

The Early Modern Period

In the early modern period, German trading companies came to dominate many of the ports of the Baltic Sea—indeed, significant German populations started moving to Danzig, Memel, Riga, and Talinn, and also to other cities such as Warsaw and Vilnius. Most of these traders were involved in buying and selling agricultural produce or small manufactured items. Farther south, German companies started to become involved in mining for coal in Silesia. The emergence of the Russian state under Ivan the Great (reigned 1462–1505) and then Ivan the Terrible (reigned 1547–84) also led to some German and Turkish trading companies being involved there.

In 1555 some English capitalists recognized the economic potential of Russia and founded the Muscovy Trading Company (or Muscovy Company), the first major English joint-stock company ever established. It had a monopoly on trade until 1698 and actually continued business operations until 1917, operating as a charity since then. Other countries also started to trade with the Russians, but the isolation of Moscow at the time largely prevented this. Indeed, in Russia, although there were small traders, because the society remained largely feudal until the early modern period, the major construction projects were undertaken by the government. This could be seen by the projects undertaken by Peter the Great, who attempted to modernize the country with the building of St. Petersburg as the new Russian capital. Catherine the Great continued the idea of government initiatives in major engineering projects.

A major problem with the establishment of business in eastern Europe in late medieval and early modern times was the issue of law and order—there often being little exercise of central control except in times of war, when conscription was enforced.

There was one brief respite during the reign of the Romanian medieval ruler Vlad III "the Impaler" (1431–76), who imposed such harsh punishments on malefactors that he terrorized a previously lawless people, and traders soon found that they could operate from his country easily.

At the start of the 18th century, eastern Europe was dominated by Poland, a declining power; Russia; Prussia; Austria; and also Turkey, which dominated the Balkans. There was little industry in much of eastern Europe, but the coal mines and iron ore in Silesia were already attracting the attention of the Prussians who invaded in 1740, sparking the War of Austrian Succession. When the Swedish industrial agent and spy Reinhold Rücker Angerstein (1718–60) went to Bohemia, Carinthia, and Hungary in the early 1750s, he did not find much industrial development in these areas. During the Seven Years' War the Austrians tried to retake Silesia but failed. During the 1770s and 1780s, with Russia keen to develop its industrial potential, Catherine the Great encouraged German artisans to relocate to southern Russia. All these projects were still government funded.

Industrialization

Only gradually did private capital start to help with the development of businesses. These tended to be located in cities, with the emergence, in Russia, of companies in St. Petersburg, Moscow, Riga, Warsaw, Odessa, Kiev, and other places such as Minsk and Smolensk. In Riga and Warsaw, many of these businesses were run by Germans, who also dominated commerce in most of the Baltic Sea. By law, Russian companies needed Russian citizens as directors, but they were allowed some foreign directors provided they did not form a majority on any board of management. During the 19th century, as Russia suddenly embarked on a program of industrialization, joint stock companies were formed and raised money from investors from western Europe, particularly Britain and France. There was also a stock market in St. Petersburg and one in Moscow, both of which raised money for businesses in the Russian Empire. Stock markets were also located in several other Russian towns dealing with locally based companies.

At the same time that Russia was undergoing a program of industrialization, many of the countries in the Balkans were gaining their independence. At the start of the War of Independence from 1821 to 1829, Greece declared itself an independent country, albeit with the British still controlling the Ionian islands (Corfu, Zante, Santa Maura, Ithaca, and Kefalonia), where they operated a number of trading firms. There the companies were registered under British rules until 1862, when the islands were handed over to Greece. Unlike the rest of eastern Europe, Greece operated a capitalist economy throughout the 20th century and were particularly prominent in shipping with magnates such as Stavros Niarchos (1909–96), known as "The Golden Greek" for his manufacture of the first supertankers, and Aristotle Onassis (1906–75) becoming well known for their wealth and power.

Romania, as Wallachia and Moldavia, gained its independence in 1859 and became officially recognized in 1878. It sought to develop its industry by forming a number of companies, including several involved in plans to exploit the oil fields of Ploesti. The oil fields were privately owned until the end of World War II, and their success encouraged the establishment of other companies throughout Romania involved in coal and iron ore. In 1867 Serbia gained its independence from Turkey, and also started developing its business laws to allow the establishment of private companies. Serbia lacked the mineral resources of Romania, but some companies from Germany, Greece, and Russia did establish offices in Belgrade, Serbia's capital. Bulgaria, which became independent in 1878, faced similar problems, but managed to garner some investment from French and British businessmen. Albania, which became independent in 1912, largely on account of its geographical position attracted a number of Italian companies, especially in the port of Durrës.

World Wars I and II

World War I transformed the boundaries of many of the countries in eastern Europe. Yugoslavia was created, incorporating Serbia and (from the Austro-Hungarian Empire) Croatia, Slovenia, and Bosnia-Herzegovina. Also created during this time was Czechoslovakia, which had much heavy industry, especially in the western part of the country. Skoda had been established in 1895 as Laurin & Klement, and by 1924 it had become the biggest single industrial enterprise in the whole of Czechoslovakia, with

Bata shoes having been established a year earlier. There was also a flourishing of Polish commerce.

The creation of Lithuania, Latvia, and Estonia as independent countries after the war led to the establishment and flourishing of many locally owned and also German-owned companies. Latvia in particular, through its enterprise, and also Estonia through the entrepreneurship of its people, were economic success stories for much of the inter-war period. However, for Russia, the takeover by the communists in November 1917 led to the nationalization of all foreign-owned businesses in the country, and the takeover of the vast majority of locally-owned businesses. Many of these were turned into state corporations, remaining as such until 1990.

In World War II, the Germans occupied much of eastern Europe and many businesses were taken over for the German war effort. In particular, the Germans were eager to control the area they called the Upper Silesia Industrial Region. The Skoda Works was renamed the Hermann Goering Works, and many other companies and factories were similarly renamed. The end of the war, however, saw a total transformation of the region as eastern Europe, with the exception of Greece, ended up in the hands of the Soviet Union and its allies.

Under communist and pro-communist governments, all major businesses were quickly nationalized, and gradually the governments in these countries took control of all business life. The most extreme control took place in Albania. Communist government control of eastern Europe lasted until 1989. By that time the economic lives of the countries in eastern Europe were controlled by state corporations that operated at differing levels of efficiency. Through membership of COMECON, with the exception of Romania, the countries were heavily reliant on Soviet oil.

The Fall of Communism

The end of communism in Europe from 1989 led to the establishment of many private companies throughout eastern Europe. Some of these were created by local people who were eager to take advantage of the capitalist society that was forming. Some other companies were formed by expatriates from eastern Europe who returned to help establish a business in their former homeland. Foreign companies also established offices in the capitals and major towns of eastern Europe.

The main problem was the fate of the former communist state corporations, many of which were privatized. Some concerns were sold outright to multinationals, but many more were bought by local Russians and citizens. The way in which some private individuals managed to get control of these large companies immediately attracted much attention as a small group from the Soviet bureaucracy became wealthy. However, by the mid-1980s, the Soviet Union under Mikhail Gorbachev was keen to gain a foothold in worldwide commerce and Gorbachev agreed to pay back the owners of pre-1917 Russian government bonds and holders of stock of companies that were nationalized without compensation by the communist government. Many of these bond and stock certificates were held by collectors rather than the original investors; so few people handed them back that those who did received a large payout.

In Russia, after the end of communism, the period of the 1990s witnessed the rise of very rich businessmen known as the "oligarchs." Some, like Boris Berezovsky, remain extremely crucial not because of the money they made but often because of their involvement in politics. Berezovsky had risen to power under Boris Yeltsin, and in January 1995, he managed to establish ORT, the largest national television channel in Russia, and also large oil concerns that he had bought during the Boris Yelstin presidency for much less than their market values. Berezovsky fled to England, where he has lived ever since. Although much has been made of oligarchs like Berezovsky, some of the men who made fortunes in the privatization process and the period that followed entered Russian politics and have become influential through their business connections. The chess player Kirsan Ilyumzhinov, now president of the Republic of Kalmykia, a part of the Russian Federation, is continuing to use his fortune to promote chess in southern Russia and overseas.

For Russia there were also problems over the state-owned operations in the former constituent parts of the Soviet Union. Most of these were handed over to the newly independent Belarus, Ukraine, Moldova, Lithuania, Latvia, and Estonia, which then embarked on privatization schemes of their own. In most of the other countries in eastern Europe, free enterprise and capitalism has been openly endorsed and the economy of the Czech Republic is little different from many of the countries of western Europe. By contrast, many

Albanians were involved in putting their savings into "pyramid" savings schemes in 1996, and many people continue to view capitalism with suspicion.

Some of the stock exchanges that had operated in eastern Europe from before communism were reopened. The Bucharest Exchange had originally been opened on December 1, 1882, but was closed in 1945. It was reopened on April 21, 1995, as the Bursa de Valori Bucureşti (Bucharest Stock Market). Similarly, the Belgrade Stock Exchange had been founded in 1894, and had remained in operation—except during World War I—as the main method of raising capital, although it was closed down in 1953 by Josip Broz Tito, the leader of the country at that time. It was reopened in 1989 as the Yugoslav Capital Market, and there were also stock markets in other parts of the former Yugoslavia: the Zagreb Stock Exchange, in Croatia; the Ljubljana Stock Exchange in Slovenia; the Macedonian Stock Exchange; the Montenegro Stock Exchange, and the NEX Stock Exchange, also in Montenegro. In spite of the war in many parts of the former Yugoslavia, a stock market was created in Bosnia's capital Sarajevo in 2001 (and commenced trading on April 12, 2002); and in Banja Luka, also from 2001.

In the former Baltic States, the Tallinn Stock Exchange (Estonia), the Riga Stock Exchange (Latvia), and the Vilnius Stock Exchange (Lithuania) are all owned and run by OMX, which also operates the Stockholm Stock Exchange. The Georgian Stock Exchange was opened in 1999 to help provide methods of raising capital to help businesses expand; the Armenian Stock Exchange started operations as early as 2001, although it was officially founded in 2007; and the Baku Stock Exchange in Azerbaijan was established in 2001.

See Also: Bulgaria; Communism; Czech Republic; Eastern Europe; Greece; Hanseatic League; Hungary; Latvia; Lithuania; Poland; Romania; Russia; Slovakia; Slovenia; Turkey; Ukraine.

Bibliography. Frank Bönker, *The Political Economy of Fiscal Reform in Central-Eastern Europe: Hungary, Poland, and the Czech Republic from 1989 to EU Accession* (Edward Elgar, 2006); Robert Deutsch, *The Agriculture Revolution in the Soviet Union and Eastern Europe* (Westview Press, 1986); *Eastern Europe and the Commonwealth of Inde-*

pendent States 1992 (Europa Publications, 1992); *Eastern Europe and the Commonwealth of Independent States 1999* (Europa Publications, 1999); Paul Robert Magocsi, *Historical Atlas of Central Europe: From the Early Fifth Century to the Present* (Thames & Hudson, 2002); Frank Schimmelfennig and Ulrich Sedelmeier, eds., *The Europeanization of Central and Eastern Europe* (Cornell University Press, 2005); David J. Smith and Chris Tapster, *Major Companies of Central and Eastern Europe and the Commonwealth of Independent States, 2008* (Gale-Cengage/Graham & Whiteside Ltd., 2007).

JUSTIN CORFIELD
GEELONG GRAMMAR SCHOOL, AUSTRALIA

Company Profiles: Middle East

Admiral Alfred Thayer Mahan, the American naval strategist, called the region the "Middle East," a name that has stuck though it has negative colonial connotations and is geographically inaccurate. There is no unanimity on which countries constitute the Middle East, with their number varying between 14 and 27 depending on the way the term is interpreted. Today the Middle East is experiencing tumultuous economic changes, with several sectors like real estate, retailing, and telecommunication experiencing explosive growth. This entry presents a broad range of company profiles (in alphabetical order by country) that are representative of the region's economic vibrancy.

Algeria, Bahrain, and Egypt

Sonatrach, Naftal, and Sonelgaz are generally considered Algeria's top three companies, followed by airline carrier Air Algerie. Sonatrach is a state-owned integrated oil and gas company having a capacity of 230 million tons, making it one of the largest corporations in Africa. Established in 1963, its principal activities are research, exploration, production, transport, processing, marketing, and distribution of oil products and derivatives of liquid and natural gas hydrocarbons. The company also operates in Libya, Mali, Niger, and Peru.

Gulf Finance House is a publicly listed company of Bahrain set up in 1999 in the international Islamic

banking industry. It recently became the first Islamic bank to be listed on the London Stock Exchange. During its seven years of operations, Gulf Finance has successfully launched projects and investments worth US$12 billion. Its paid-up capital is US$239 million and authorized capital is US$300 million. Gulf Finance has provided Islamic investment banking services with an emphasis on regional development, capitalizing on an increasing willingness among Islamic investors to back regional opportunities.

Orascom Telecom Holding is considered Egypt's first multinational corporation, operating a large and diversified telecommunications services network in the Middle East, Africa, and Pakistan. It is a part of the Orascom group, which was established in 1976. It had a subscriber base of 74 million in March 2008 in six emerging markets. In 2006 its total revenue was US$44.01 billion, net income was US$7.19 billion, and total assets were US$86.75 billion.

Iran and Iraq

National Iranian Oil Company is a century-old oil conglomerate that boasts of being the inheritor of the first oil discovery in the Middle East, and the fourth largest state-owned oil company in the world. It consists of four companies dealing with oil, gas, petrochemicals, and refining and distribution, and a host of subsidiaries. Nationalized after the Iranian Revolution, the company is responsible for the exploitation of the second-largest natural gas reserves in the world and for helping retain Iran's position as the second-largest oil producer among OPEC countries. Its principal areas of activity include exploration, production, refining, marketing and sale of crude oil, natural gas, and other petroleum products. Its current production level is 4,200 million barrels of oil and 437 million cubic meters of gas per day.

Iraq National Oil Company was founded in 1961 by the government of Iraq. The Oil Ministry of Iraq has 15 operating companies under its control and oversees the nationalized oil industry through the Iraq National Oil Company. There are several autonomous companies under Iraq National Oil such as State Company for Oil Projects, Oil Exploration Company, Northern Oil Company and Southern Oil Company, State Organization for Oil Marketing, and the Iraqi Oil Tankers Company. The Iraqi Hydrocarbon Law of 2007 is controversial legislation under consideration that severely limits the control of Iraq National Oil to just 17 of the country's 80 oilfields, leaving the rest to the provincial governments to award exploration and production contracts to foreign companies.

Israel and Jordan

The biggest Israeli company is generic-drug maker Teva Pharmaceutical, which had a market value of $34 billion in 2008. Teva is among the largest generic pharmaceutical companies in the world. Its business activities are development, production, and marketing of generic and proprietary branded pharmaceuticals and active pharmaceutical ingredients. Headquartered in Israel, 80 percent of Teva's sales of US$9.4 billion in 2007 came from North America and Europe. Teva has production facilities in Israel, North America, Europe, and Latin America. With more than a century of experience in the global healthcare industry, Teva has a dominating presence internationally through its worldwide subsidiaries.

Arab Bank, set up in 1930 by the Palestinian-Jordanian Shoman family group, is one of the largest financial institutions in the Middle East with high credibility and ratings. With headquarters in Amman, it operates 400 branches in 29 countries across 5 continents. By the end of 2007, Arab Bank Group achieved a pre-tax profit of US$10 billion. Its total assets reached almost US$38.3 billion, while shareholders' equity base was US$6.9 billion. The bank is considered a catalyst for Arab economic development. Starting with an emphasis on trade and small scale construction finance, it shifted to large-scale project financing.

Kuwait, Lebanon, and Libya

Kuwait-based Zain (formerly MTC group) is a noteworthy mobile telecommunications provider operating in Middle East and African countries. It aimed to have 70 million subscribers through a strategy termed ACE (Acceleration, Consolidation, Expansion) to realize its 3X3X3 vision—to grow regionally, internationally, and globally, with each phase completed in 3 years. In 2007 Zain claimed 42.2 million active customers providing revenue of US$5.91 billion with net profit of US$1.13 billion.

Solidere is Lebanon's largest company by market value. It was created in 1994 as a unique public-private partnership with the mandate to rebuild the Beirut Central District after the devastation of the civil

war of 1975–90. Besides the Hariri family, who are the principal shareholders, most of Solidere's investment comes from Arabian, European, and North American investment firms. Its principal activities are land development, real estate development, property ownership, property and services management and operations. Solidere's share capital is US$1.65 billion and assets are $8 billion, with 50 projects being developed by private investors. Through Solidere International, the company is set to expand business activities into the United Arab Emirates (UAE), Egypt, and Monaco.

Libyan Iron & Steel Company (Lisco) is one of the largest iron and steelmaking companies in Northern Africa. Established in 1979, it has an annual capacity of 13.24 million tons of liquid steel. Lisco's operations are primarily supplied by imported steel pellets

The Burj Dubai, a project of the UAE conglomerate Emaar Properties, is shown under construction in early 2008.

from Brazil, Canada, and Sweden. Natural gas is used to manufacture sponge iron and hot briquette iron. More than half of the production is exported to European countries including Italy and Spain and some Middle Eastern and southeast Asian countries.

Mauritania, Morocco, and Oman

Mauritania's Société Nationale Industrielle et Minière is the primary African supplier of iron ore to European steelmakers. It has a majority government ownership. Its production capacity is 12 million tons a year. Major investments of US$170 million were made in 2001–02. It has diversified into drainage, civil engineering, transport and maintenance, production and sale of granite and marble, mechanical construction, port handling, iron and steel, gypsum and plaster, and tourism services.

Attijariwafa Bank of Morocco, established in 1911 and headquartered in Casablanca, is the leading financial group in terms of total assets. The bank's principal activities are to provide personal and professional, corporate, investment, and international banking. It also offers real estate, insurance, and banking services through its subsidiaries. The bank operates in North Africa with over 500 branches across Morocco and 35 points of sale in France, Belgium, Spain, Italy, China, Tunisia, and Senegal. It claims to be serving more than 1.5 million customers. Attijariwafa Bank aims to become by 2010 the leading bank for Moroccans living abroad.

Oman Telecommunications Company (Omantel) is the largest communications service provider and public company in Oman. Established in 1980, Omantel provides fixed-line, mobile, internet, and data and other telecommunications services directly and through its subsidiaries. The company's 2007 revenues were US$952 million and profits were US$292 million from 1.87 million subscribers. Omantel completed its first international acquisition in 2008 with a 65 percent stake in Pakistan-based fixed and internet service provider Worldcall for US$200 million.

Qatar

Qatar Airways, the national carrier of Qatar, is widely recognized as one of the fastest-growing airlines in the world with average 35 percent growth year-on-year for the past 10 years. It flies a modern fleet of 60 aircraft to 81 destinations worldwide and has placed large orders for 200 aircraft worth US$30 billion with Airbus and Boeing. It carries nearly 10 million passengers annually. It operates a hub-and-spoke arrangement from Doha International Airport. It acted as the official airline of the 2006 Asian Games, held in Doha.

In a region dominated by state-owned and state-censored mass media, Al Jazeera is a refreshing change. Started in 1996 as an Arabic channel financed by the Qatar government, it began telecasting in English in 2006 and plans to offer programs in other languages. Al Jazeera English is the world's first global English-language news channel to be headquartered in the Middle East. It has four broadcasting centers in Doha, Kuala Lumpur, London, and Washington and supporting bureaus worldwide. The unique selling proposition of the channel is to offer a different perspective from that of the dominating Western media like the BBC and CNN. In doing so, it attempts to become an English-language channel of reference for Middle Eastern events, balancing the largely one-way information flow from the developed world.

Saudi Arabia

Saudi Aramco, a state-owned crude oil producer, has grown from an exploration and production company prior to the 1990s to become an integrated global petroleum enterprise. It owns and operates an extensive network of refining and distribution facilities, and is responsible for the gas processing and transportation installations that fuel Saudi Arabia's industrial sector. It owns a number of international subsidiaries and joint ventures and a large fleet of supertankers, delivering crude oil and refined products to customers worldwide.

Saudi Basic Industries (SABIC) is probably the most globalized of the Middle Eastern corporations. It operates in more than 40 countries and is a leading manufacturer of chemicals, fertilizers, plastics, and metals. SABIC had a net income of US$7.2 billion on sales revenue of US$33.6 billion with total assets of US$68.27 billion in 2007. It has 17 manufacturing affiliates in Saudi Arabia, two manufacturing plants in Europe, and sales offices in Africa, Singapore, and the United States.

Kingdom Holding Company, listed as first among the Gulf's most admired companies by ArabianBusiness.com, is owned by Prince Alwaleed Bin Talal. It holds the distinction of being the largest company in Saudi Arabia. A diversified investment company, its interests include banking, real estate, telecommunications, broadcasting and media, entertainment, hospitality, computers and electronics, agriculture, restaurants, upscale fashion, retailing, supermarkets, tourism, travel, and automotive manufacturing. Kingdom Holding has made rapid strides in its internationalization drive, making investments in several foreign companies. Its assets are valued at US$25 billion and total operating revenue of US$1.23 billion as of December 2006.

Sudan, Syria, and Tunisia

The two biggest companies in Sudan in terms of total revenue are in the telecommunications sector. The top-ranking company is Sudanese Mobile Telephone Company. The second is Sudatel Telecommunications Group, a public company set up in 1994 providing telecommunications and internet service, dial-up access, leased lines, and DSL broadband services. The company is also responsible for the construction and maintenance of Sudan's telecom infrastructure. It has made rapid strides into regional markets. In 2006 it extended its voice and data services in Mauritania. In 2007 it won a telecommunications license to provide mobile services in Senegal and purchased a 70 percent stake in Intercellular, one of Nigeria's leading privately owned telecom operators.

The largest companies in Syria are in the telecommunications sector where each of the top two companies, Syrian Telecommunications Establishment and SyriaTel Mobile Telecom, generated revenues of over US$600 million in 2007. But more exciting are the four new holding companies set up in 2006. Of these, Cham Holding has the largest capital base of US$350 million contributed by over 70 Syrian investors. It has ambitious projects and plans in the pipeline. It is also investing US$1.3 billion in developing several projects in the tourism, housing, banking, energy, industry, health, and transport sectors. These ambitious plans are spurred by changes in statutory regulations facilitating real estate investment activities that jumped up to US$50 billion in 2006.

Petroleum and mining, particularly of phosphates and iron ore, are Tunisia's top two industries and top export commodities. Phosphate-rock production is entirely controlled by the government-owned Com-

pagnie des Phophates de Gafsa (CPG) established in 1896. CPG is the largest company in Tunisia, both in terms of employees and capital investment. It operates several phosphate mines in Gafsa governorate. Annual production of merchant phosphate in 2007 reached 8 million tons, placing Tunisia fifth in the world for phosphate production.

UAE

Dubai-based UAE company Emaar Properties represents one of the growing real estate development companies in a region of the world experiencing fast growth in construction activities. The builder of the world's tallest towers, the Burj Dubai, Emaar is a publicly-listed conglomerate with 60 companies operating in 36 markets aimed at the twin objectives of geographical expansion and business segmentation. In 2007, Emaar had total revenue of US$47.82 billion with net profits of US$17.80 billion and total assets of US$149.17 billion.

UAE-based Emirates group is a popular Middle Eastern holding company that owns the Emirates Airlines and Dnata, which is a ground handling and travel service. The Emirates Group has been consistently profitable. It had a net profit of US$1.45 billion with a turnover of US$11.2 billion in 2007. Increasing fuel costs had a negative impact on the company's financial performance. Emirates Airlines is a fast-growing airline operating services to 90 destinations.

West Bank and Gaza Strip

Palestine Development and Investment Company (PADICO) is a Nablus-based holding company registered in Liberia in 1993. Since 1994, when political control passed from Israel to the Palestinian Authority, PADICO has become the biggest and most influential company in the West Bank and the Gaza Strip. It is a holding company which has 11 subsidiaries in the industrial, real estate, tourism, and capital market sectors. Besides being the largest company traded on the Palestine Securities Exchange, PADICO also owns the Palestinian phone monopoly Paltel. PADICO had a market value of $600 million in mid-2007, about a quarter of the value of all the shares traded on the exchange.

Yemen

Hayel Saeed Anam (HSA) Group of companies is representative of old, established family business groups in the Middle East. HSA of Yemen was established in 1938 and is the largest company in terms of the number of employees—more than 16,000. A diversified conglomerate, its activities include industrial, trading, and services in as many as 25 business areas. The company acts as the agent and partner for nearly 35 international brands. All these activities take place in Yemen as well as several other countries including Egypt, Indonesia, Malaysia, and Saudi Arabia.

See Also: Algeria; Bahrain; Egypt; Emerging Markets; Iran; Israel; Jordan; Kuwait; Lebanon; Libya; Middle East; Morocco; Oman; Qatar; Saudi Arabia; United Arab Emirates; Yemen.

Bibliography. ArabianBusiness.com, "Revealed: Gulf's Most Admired Companies," www.arabianbusiness.com (cited March 2009); DinarStandard, "The 2007 DS100: Top 100 Companies of the Muslim World," dinarstandard.com (cited March 2009); Zawya.com, www.zawya.com (cited March 2009).

AZHAR KAZMI
KING FAHD UNIVERSITY OF PETROLEUM & MINERALS

Company Profiles: North America

Prior to the arrival of the Europeans from the 1490s, little is known about businesses operating in North America, although it is clear that there must have been some system of barter trade between different tribes. The origins of the businesses and firms that operate in North America lie, as with so many other parts of the world, in chartered companies that established settlements on the east coast of North America.

Although some of the early explorers of North America such as John and Sebastian Cabot were financed by wealthy businessmen, and also to a minor extent by King Henry VII and King Henry VIII, most trade with North America was conducted by individual ship captains and their crews. The first major company to be established with the aim of settling in the Americas was put together by English adventurer Sir Walter Raleigh (c.1552–1618) who was keen to settle Roanoke Island off the coast of North Carolina

from 1585 until 1587. This failed, and it was not really until 1606 that two chartered companies, known as the Virginia Companies, were established and given Royal Charters: the Virginia Company of London and the Virginia Company of Plymouth, which had identical charters for different areas of the east coast of North America. The Plymouth Company, as the latter became known, failed after a few years, although it was revived in 1620 as the Plymouth Council for New England. The former, the London Company, which had been established by Royal Charter on April 10, 1606, also failed, but did have one early success when it took over the Somers Isles (modern-day Bermuda) that were settled from 1609.

The establishment of these companies encouraged other European countries, particularly the Netherlands, which saw the founding of the Geoctroyeerde Westindische Compagnie (Dutch West India Company); established by charter in 1621, it was involved heavily in the West Indies but also in the supply of slaves to North America. Eight years later, the Providence Island Company was established in 1629 by some English Puritans who were keen to establish a settlement on Providence Island, off the Mosquito Coast of Nicaragua in Central America. In the same year, the Massachusetts Bay Company was also founded; it was involved in the establishment of the Massachusetts Bay Colony, now the Commonwealth of Massachusetts.

In terms of longevity, the most important chartered company of this period is the Hudson's Bay Company (Compagnie de la Baie d'Hudson), which was founded on May 2, 1670, and is still operating, making it one of the oldest companies in the world still in existence and the oldest commercial corporation in North America. It was started by two French traders, Pierre Esprit Radisson and Médard des Groseilliers, to establish a monopoly over the fur trade in Canada and was, for a time, one of the largest land owners in the world. It currently has 70,000 employees and still owns stores throughout Canada.

French traders had also established the Mississippi Company, which was not successful; a controlling interest in it was bought by Scottish businessman John Law in 1717, establishing a 25-year monopoly. His exaggerated stories of the Louisiana area led to frenzied speculation in the company's shares that rose from 500 livres each in 1719 to a peak of 15,000 livres, falling back to 500 livres in 1721. In many ways it operated in a manner similar to the South Sea Company in England, which also sought to use its shares to take over the debts of, in the case of the Mississippi Company, France.

Industrialization

Gradually during the 18th century, the joint stock company started to become more and more common in North America, with a number of companies able to take advantage of the inventions of the Industrial Revolution in England and Scotland. However, after the American War of Independence, there were restrictions on what could be taken to the United States. This meant that when U.S. industrialist Samuel Slater (1768–1835) decided to leave England for the United States, he had to memorize the information about machinery for cotton because it was illegal to take charts and plans with him. On his arrival in the United States, Slater set up a cotton plant and was later acknowledged as the "founder of the American cotton industry," or even the "founder of the American Industrial Revolution." Soon afterward Francis Cabot Lowell (1775–1817) and Paul Moody (1779–1831) transformed the textile industry in Massachusetts.

The large numbers of migrants who headed to the United States during the 19th century (and indeed since then) brought with them a great amount of entrepreneurial skill that led to the American "can do" attitude shown in the building of the Transcontinental Railroad completed in 1869, and, from 1974 to 1977, the Trans-Alaska Pipeline System. The great inventions of Thomas Alva Edison (1847–1931), and his patenting of so many of them such as the gramophone and the electric light bulb, encouraged many other inventors.

The American Civil War led to major advancements in the use of steel, and the design of weaponry, although it also led to the destruction of many parts of the Southern states. Prohibition in the 1920s and the Great Depression in the 1930s caused major damage to the U.S. economy, but the prosperity from the 1940s and especially in the 1950s led to a number of important U.S. business techniques outlined by people such as Vance Packard in *The Hidden Persuaders* (1957) writing about the mass persuasion of the public, and in his *The Waste Makers* (1961) about the problems of

wastefulness and obsolescence in industry. The Hawthorne experiments from the late 1920s saw studies of the Western Electric factory at Hawthorne, and William H. Whyte, Jr., in *The Organization Man* (1956) described the life of Americans who spent much of their life working for an "organization."

Primary producers dominated the U.S. economy, with large farms in many parts of the country, but also small farms that varied from those in the South that were often able to keep families for generations, and the new soldier-settler blocks in Kansas where the Dust Bowl destroyed the livelihoods of hundreds of thousands of people. In Canada, the large wheat farms and also the breeding of cattle has been important for the global economy. There are also a number of important tobacco companies such as British American Tobacco (founded in 1902) and Philip Morris (renamed Altria Group in 2003).

For processed food, there are many U.S. companies including General Foods (founded from a merger in 1929, now owned by Altria), Heinz (founded in 1869 by Henry J. Heinz), Kellogg Company (founded in 1906 by William K. Kellogg), Kraft Foods (founded in 1903 by James L. Kraft, now owned by Altria), Mars Confectionary (a firm still privately owned by the Mars family), and Nabisco (founded in 1898 as the National Biscuit Company). Frozen foods were produced by Birds Eye, developed by patents of Clarence Birdseye (1886–1956), and founded as General Foods; and by the McCain Foods Limited (founded in 1957). There is increasingly more wine grown in California, and U.S. soft-drink manufacturers include Coca-Cola Company (founded in 1892) and PepsiCo (founded in 1898). For fast food venues, KFC (formerly Kentucky Fried Chicken), McDonald's (founded in 1940), Pizza Hut (founded in 1958), Domino's Pizzas (founded in 1960), and Starbucks (founded in 1971).

Of the many companies connected with heavy industry, some such as Pittsburgh Steel (now the Wheeling-Pittsburgh Steel Corporation) became well known, as did the Bethlehem Steel Corporation that operated from 1857 until 2003, also in Pennsylvania, and the steel mills of Andrew Carnegie's United States Steel Corporation (founded in 1901). Mention should also be made of the Minnesota Mining and Manufacturing Company (founded in 1902), which has diversified to produce stationary and many other products.

Oil Changes Everything

The discovery of oil in Texas led to the United States and U.S. companies dominating the petroleum business around the world. The fortunes of John D. Rockefeller (1839–1937), John Paul Getty (1892–1976), and Howard Hughes (1905–76) came from oil, as did that of the Texan Glenn McCarthy (1907–88), who was nicknamed "King of the Wildcatters." Exxon-Mobil (founded in 1882 as Standard Oil Company and Trust); Chevron (founded in 1926); and Texaco (founded 1902 as the Texas Company) still have a dominant role in the petroleum industry worldwide, and U.S. engineering expertise was crucial to its development in the Middle East.

The largest automakers in the world operated from the United States: Ford Motor Company (founded in 1903), Chrysler (founded in 1913), General Motors (founded in 1931), and also Dodge (founded in 1900; now run by DaimlerChrysler) for trucks and Caterpillar (founded by Benjamin Holt as the Holt Manufacturing Company in 1892) for agricultural and road-building equipment. Detroit, the headquarters of Ford, had, from the early 1900s until the 1960s, one of the largest concentrations of heavy industry in the world. In the field of aerospace and aircraft manufacture, Bell Aircraft Corporation (founded by Larry Bell in 1935), Boeing (founded in 1916 as the Aero Products Company), McDonnell Douglas (founded in 1967 from a merger between the McDonnell Aircraft Corporation and the Douglas Aircraft Company), and Sikorsky (founded by Igor Sikorsky in 1923) provide aircraft and helicopters—both civilian and military—for use in the United States and around the world. U.S.-based airlines Pan American World Airways (founded in 1927; ceased operations in 1991), Trans World Airlines (founded in 1930 from a merger of Transcontinental Air Transport and Western Air Express), and United Airlines (founded in 1929 as the United Aircraft Transport Corporation) have all been important in world aviation.

There have also been many construction and engineering companies that have had a major role in the United States, and are also well known overseas. Bechtel (founded in 1898), now the largest engineering company in the United States, and Halliburton (reorganized in 1920) have been heavily associated with the Ronald Reagan and the George W. Bush presidencies, respectively. Amtrak (formerly the National Railroad Passenger Corporation, established in 1970), the U.S. railroad company, controls nearly all intercity passenger trains in the United States; and from the 1920s to the 1970s, Greyhound buses (founded in 1913) were used by tens of thousands of U.S. travelers on a regular basis.

The large defense expenditure by the United States has resulted in the creation of what President Dwight D. Eisenhower called the Military Industrial Complex, and Father Charles Coughlin in the 1930s denounced the large profits made from World War I. Many of the early designs of guns owe much to U.S. inventors, with Samuel Colt (1814–1862), Dr. Richard Gatling (1818–1903), and Hiram Maxim (1840–1916), being household names. Smith & Wesson has produced handguns since 1852; and Raytheon, founded in 1922 at Cambridge, Massachusetts, is one of the major producers of guided missiles and related technology.

In terms of electrical appliances and white goods, General Electric (founded in 1892) and Westinghouse Electric Corporation (founded in 1886) have been important. Indeed the proliferation of household electrical items in the United States ahead of many other countries in the world owed much to the energy generation from American Light and Traction (founded 1900; merged with DTE in 2001) and Texas Utilities (formed in 1945); and also from schemes such as the Tennessee Valley Authority. Westinghouse was also involved in the design of nuclear power stations. There was increased worry about nuclear power after the accident at Three Mile Island in 1979. Mention also need be made of the energy company Enron that spectacularly went bankrupt in 2001. Kodak (founded in 1888) emerged as one of the largest manufacturers of photographic equipment in the world.

Retail, Media, and Services

With such a large market in the United States, chains of retail stores are very important, with Wal-Mart (founded in 1962) being the most famous. There are also Macy's (founded in 1858), Piggly Wiggly (founded in 1916), and Woolworth's (founded in 1878); and in terms of fashion and more expensive items, in New York, there are Tiffany's (founded in 1837) and Bloomingdale's (founded in 1860), and in Chicago, Marshall Field (founded in 1865).

Although the U.S. postal system is still government-controlled, there are many private courier

Apple, one of the iconic American companies of the Information Age, opened this landmark 24-hour store in New York in 2006.

companies such as UPS (founded in 1907 in Seattle, Washington). Western Union (founded in 1851) was responsible for laying out many of the telegraph lines in the United States, but lost out to Bell—named after Alexander Graham Bell (1847–1922)—which established the first major telephone network in the United States, following George Coy (1836–1915) establishing a telephone exchange in New Haven, Connecticut. Overseas, ITT, whose founders Hernan and Sosthenes Behn were from the Danish West Indies (now the U.S. Virgin Islands), operated since 1920 as a major conglomerate until it was broken up in 1995.

There are many U.S. publishers whose books are sold around the world, including Bantam Books (founded 1945); Doubleday (founded 1897, now a part of Random House); Little, Brown (founded 1837); Random House (founded 1925); and St. Martin's Press (founded 1952 by Macmillan). There is also Reader's Digest, and international newspapers the *International Herald Tribune* and *USA Today*. Australian newspaper owner Rupert Murdoch (b.1931) took up U.S. citizenship in 1985, moving the headquarters of News International to Delaware in 2004. Canadian Conrad Black (b.1944) during the 1980s and 1990s owned many of the world's major newspapers through Hollinger International.

The U.S. higher education sector sees tens of thousands of foreign students coming to study in the United States; the University of California, Columbia, Harvard, Johns Hopkins, MIT, Princeton, Stanford, University of Texas, and Yale, as well as many other universities, attract applications from all over the world. In Canada, the University of British Columbia, McGill University, Montreal University, and other institutions also attract many foreign students. Law schools and medical schools in both countries have also been in the forefront of training lawyers and doctors—the latter resulting in many of the medical companies operating from the United States or with bases or subsidiaries there.

In the entertainment industry, Hollywood has dominated the motion picture industry since the 1920s, the Walt Disney Company (founded in 1923) employing 137,000. U.S. jazz and pop musicians still dominate, with popular singers such as Frank Sinatra, Sammy Davis, Jr., Michael Jackson, and others being responsible for sales of millions of recordings each year. U.S. television documentaries are also sold around the world, and through CNN and CNBC, it has been possible for people around the world to keep up with U.S. and world news. U.S. televangelists have also utilized this technology to reach viewers around the world. Of the major world hotel chains, many have their headquarters in the United States, including Hilton, Intercontinental, Marriott, and Sheraton.

In terms of sports, many of the major players and athletes in the world are from the United States—some of them having their own companies to handle commercial sponsorships and the like. The Summer Olympics have been held in the United States on four occasions, and in Montreal, Canada, in 1976. The Winter Olympics has been held in the United States on four occasions, in Canada once, and are scheduled to be held at Vancouver in 2010. This has meant that there are many manufacturers of sports equipment throughout the United States, the most well known internationally being Nike (founded in 1972).

For financial services, the U.S. Stock Exchange on Wall Street is the largest stock market in the world. NASDAQ (National Association of Securities Dealers Automated Quotations), founded in 1971, allow automated trading and was important in the "tech boom" in the 1990s and early 2000s, and the Chicago Mercantile Exchange has developed large numbers of new financial instruments. There are many large U.S. banking institutions: Chase Manhattan (founded in 1799), Citibank (founded in 1812), CS First Boston (founded in 1932 as First Boston; bought by Credit Suisse in 1988), and Wachovia (founded in 1781) being probably the most well known. U.S. merchant bankers Andrew Mellon and J.P. Morgan in the 1920s and 1930s both presided over important companies.

The Information Age

Companies have defined and ridden the waves of the Information Age. IBM, DEC, and Dell became prominent through providing quality and powerful computers. Apple rose with its focus on user friendly interfaces for its microcomputers. Microsoft became prominent as the provider of the software that ran most personal computers.

The World Wide Web came to prominence in the mid-1990s and soon, companies providing software that helped access it were prominent including Netscape Communications. Companies providing email services such as American Online (AOL) and Yahoo thrived. Improved search engines provided by Microsoft, Google, and Mozilla (Firefox) were important. Social networking sites run by companies such as News Corporation (MySpace), Facebook (valued at more $15 billion in 2008), LinkedIn, and Google (YouTube) appear to provide the means for establishing the collaborations that will be key to business in coming years. Virtual worlds such as Linden Labs' *Second Life* provide three-dimensional augmented reality interfaces that will allow virtual gatherings, enabling rapid and less costly meetings that may be used by the preponderance of large firms by 2012.

Sustainability has come to be increasingly important and it is clear that companies that develop new technologies, products, and services that are more "green" than those of their competitors are likely to be the leaders of coming years. American firms recognized at the 2008 Davos World Economic Forum as among the most sustainable in the world included Alcoa, Eastman Kodak Company, Hewlett-Packard Company, Intel Corp., Nike Inc., and Walt Disney Company.

See Also: Boeing; Canada; Ford Motor; General Motors; Microsoft; Time Warner; United Parcel Service; United States.

Bibliography. William Aspray and Paul E. Ceruzzi, eds., *The Internet and American Business* (MIT Press, 2008); Mansel G. Blackford, *A History of Small Business in America* (University of North Carolina Press, 2003);

Europa Yearbook 2008 (Europa Publications, 2007); Louis Galambos with Barbara Barrow Spence, *The Public Image of Big Business in America, 1880–1940: A Quantitative Study in Social Change* (Johns Hopkins University Press, 1975); Kenneth E. Hendrickson and Glenn Sanford, eds., *The Encyclopedia of the Industrial Revolution 1750–2007* (Facts on File, 2009); William H. Whyte, *The Organization Man* (Doubleday & Anchor, 1956).

Justin Corfield
Geelong Grammar School, Australia

Company Profiles: South America

The storms of history have brought more wreckage than treasure to South American shores. Though pre-Columbian civilizations like the Chavin, the Muisca, the Nazca, the Huari, and the Inca were sophisticated and often technologically superior to their North American neighbors, the continent has been at a disadvantage since European colonization. Native populations were decimated by the infectious diseases introduced by the Spanish and Portuguese colonists and the African slaves they brought with them, and cultures were destroyed as the Spanish went about a religious conversion campaign that far exceeded those attempted by other European settlers. When the wars of independence were fought, they had a racial element missing from that of the United States, where Englishmen sought self-rule apart from other Englishmen; in South America, many of the colonists seeking independence were mestizos, descended from both the natives and the Spanish.

Most of South America gained independence in the 19th century. Guyana did not become independent from the United Kingdom until 1966; Suriname, from the Netherlands, in 1975; and French Guiana remains a French holding. Through the second half of the 20th century, South America was one of the parts of the world where the Cold War was fought. Argentina, Brazil, Chile, and Uruguay had their governments replaced by American-sponsored military dictatorships that detained, tortured, and killed thousands of political prisoners in the name of national security. Colombia continues to exist in a state of unrest, and both it and Bolivia contend with their deeply ambivalent relationships with the coca plant and the illegal overseas cocaine trade, responsible for so much of the trade balance and yet an obstacle in their relations with the rest of the world. For decades, across much of South America, the governments' reputation has been one of corruption, greed, fiscal mismanagement, and diplomatic disaster. Since the end of the Cold War, debt has been a severe problem. Few of these countries have government agencies equipped to deal with their crises, necessitating emergency measure after emergency measure.

The continent suffers from a long and persistent history of high inflation, high interest rates, and difficulty attracting foreign investment money. The economic gap between the rich and the poor is greater than in most parts of the world, the average standard of living lower than that of Europe or North America. Despite the pronounced shift to the left in South American politics, free market policies are still strong and look to remain so, integrated into the new South American liberalism. With the Cold War in the past and the continent no longer used as a battlefield between a North American power and a Eurasian one, there is considerable movement towards continental integration of economies and other spheres. The old customs unions of Mercosur and the Andean Community are being merged into the new UNASUR.

Regional Trade Agreements

Mercosur, the Mercado Común del Sur (Southern Common Market), was a trade agreement signed in 1991 by Argentina, Brazil, Paraguay, and Uruguay, to promote free trade and movement between those countries. It was itself an expansion of the PICE (Programa de Integración y Cooperación. Económica Argentina-Brazil) between Brazil and Argentina, and has since been joined by Bolivia, Chile, Colombia, Ecuador, and Peru as associate members; Venezuela awaits ratification of its member status, applied for in 2006. Unlike the EU agreements, Mercosur provides for no common currency; but with nearly $3 trillion in combined gross domestic product, the Mercosur nations represent the fifth-largest economy in the world.

The Andean Community (Comunidad Andina, CAN) is a similar trade bloc, originally signed into existence as the Andean Pact until 1969 and reorga-

nized in 1996. Member nations are Bolivia, Colombia, Ecuador, and Peru. From 1999 to 2004, Mercosur and the Andean Community negotiated a merger to create a South American Free Trade Area. Venezuela left the CAN and petitioned for membership in Mercosur, with the stated intention of rejoining the CAN, though statements made by the Venezuelan government since then have been unclear, with some of them implying that the CAN is expected to die off to make way for a new integrated trade bloc.

In any case, UNASUR (Union de Naciones Suramericanas, the Union of South American Nations) is the product of those negotiations. Current and former members, full and associate, of both Mercosur and CAN are expected to be integrated into a single customs union modeled after the European Union, joined by Guyana and Suriname. Intent was declared by representatives of twelve governments at the end of 2004, and work has continued since then. Work has been slow, but the success of the European Union after decades of partial measures encourages both participants and onlookers. In addition to trade agreements and the free movement of people among countries, UNASUR is expected to oversee significant infrastructure improvements, such as the construction of the Interoceanic Highway that will run from the Atlantic to the Pacific, better integrating the Pacific nations of Chile and Peru with the highway systems of the rest of the continent. The South American Energy Ring is planned to connect Argentina, Brazil, Chile, Paraguay, and Uruguay with natural gas.

All nations of South America will be part of UNASUR except for French Guiana—a French department, and part of the European Union—and the Falkland Islands, South Sandwich Islands, and South Georgia, contested territories claimed by both the United Kingdom and Argentina. If successful, the UNASUR integration should have considerable positive impact on the free market policies of the continent, providing further business opportunities for the companies in operation.

Argentina

The state-owned Banco de la Nación Argentina is the largest bank in that country, with 616 domestic branches and 15 internationally. Founded in 1891, it employs 16,000 people. A scandal recently damaged the bank's reputation, when it was discovered that in the 1990s, the bank's directors had been bribed in connection with a large IBM contract. The bank was subsequently ranked last of all Latin American banks in an independent survey of banking ethics conducted by Latin Finance magazine.

The Argentinian winery Al Este Bodega y Viñedos was founded in 1999, in the Medanos community of Buenos Aires, where local soil and weather conditions are significantly similar to those of Bordeaux, inspiring a tradition of wine-making that originated with European immigrants in the 1900s. Al Este was founded in 1999 as the first premium winery in the Buenos Aires province, with assistance by Italian winemakers and French and American oak barrels for aging.

Argentinian-based Aluar is one of the largest aluminum smelters in South America, producing over 400,000 tons a year. The company was founded in 1970 and has 2000 employees, and revenues of about $2 million a year.

The most famous of Argentina's recovered factories—businesses taken over by the workers during the Argentinian financial crisis at the start of the 21st century—is Brukman, a textile factory in Balvanera. Half of the employees were fired during the crisis, the remaining workers' salaries cut so severely that few of them could not afford bus fare to get to work. Fifty workers—a third of the remaining workforce—assembled in the factory and demanded a travel allowance in addition to their salaries. The owners agreed to go get the money in order to begin paying out such an allowance, left, and never returned—abandoning the factory. The protesting workers had remained in the factory overnight waiting for their money, and resumed operations on their own. The owners have since attempted evictions, but have been unsuccessful—though the factory has been stormed on their behalf by infantry troops and local police, with dozens wounded. The factory, as a workers' collective, continues to operate, and has raised salaries and paid off old debts.

Colombia

Founded by the merger of two smaller airlines in 1940, Avianca is the largest airline and designated flag carrier of Colombia. It's headquartered in Bogota, and is jointly owned by the National Federation of Colombian Coffee Growers and the Synergy Group multinational conglomerate. Its six subsidiary airlines operate throughout South America (Helicol, SAM Colombia, Tampa Cargo, OceanAIR, VIP, Aerogal) and in Nigeria (Capital Airlines), making it one of the largest airlines in the Americas. International destination cities include Cancun and Mexico City, Fort Lauderdale, Los Angeles, Miami, New York, Washington, D.C., Madrid, and Barcelona. Further European destination cities have been canceled following the adoption of codeshare agreements with Air France and Iberia Airlines; there are also agreements with Air Canada, Delta, Grupo TACA, and SATENA. VIP Lounges are operated throughout the Colombian and Ecuadoran airports.

Brazil

Petrobras (Petroleo Brasileiro) is a semi-public energy company in Rio de Janeiro, Brazil, and the most profitable company in that country. Founded in 1953, it has a monopoly on Brazilian oil until 1997, and continues to produce 2 million barrels of oil a day—its primary oil field, the Campos Basin, produces 80 percent of the country's oil. Between 2007 and the summer of 2008, the company announced the discovery of three megafields in the pre-salt layer of Brazil. The stock actually suffered somewhat upon the discovery of the third megafield, because of investor suspicion: citing the need for trade secrecy, the company has divulged little information about the megafields, and there is concern that they may be overreporting their potential. Still, the company has a longstanding reputation for transparency and fair-dealing, and in the last three years has been commended by Transparency International, the consultancy firm Management and Excellence, and its placement on the Dow Jones Sustainability Index.

The Brazilian videogame company Tectoys was founded in 1987, capitalizing on the lack of competition in the electronic toy market. After producing their own toys for a time, they contracted with Sega Enterprises to become the exclusive distributor of Sega products in Brazil, and thus rode the wave of success that accompanied the video game boom with the Sega Master System, Mega Drive, Saturn, and Dreamcast. Not until 1993 did Nintendo have a Brazilian distributor, which gave Sega (and thus Tectoys) the lion's share of the video game market, an advantage it did not enjoy in many countries. There were even Sega games produced specifically for the Brazilian market—a rarity outside of the United States and Europe. When Sega withdrew from the hardware market, Tectoys was prepared with a diversified product range that included DVD players, mp3 players, and portable karaoke machines, and in 2005 opened Tectoy Mobile, a publisher of cell phone games. Much to the surprise of many, though, they continue to manufacture Sega consoles and games, because demand never completely disappeared; while the video game market in other countries was driven by competition between two to four manufacturers, the almost complete dominance of the Brazilian market by Sega may have superseded the cutting-edge fetishism that in other markets makes older games less marketable.

The economic disparity in South America is well summed-up by Daslu, a Brazilian boutique in Sao Paulo. Opened in a classical-style mansion in 1958, Daslu consists of 30 stores selling 60 designer labels of clothing and accessories, including Louis Vuitton and Jimmy Choo. Recently relocated, the "boutique" now takes up four stories, and is as well known as a place to people-watch—it is a shopping destination for both domestic and international celebrities—as a place to shop. Its relocation placed it immediately next to a shantytown inhabited by some of the city's poorest people, a contrast even more unfortunate in light of the criminal investigation into Daslu's possible tax evasion.

Avibras is a Brazilian defense company, founded in 1961 and headquartered in São José dos Campos. With about 600 employees, it develops and manufactures air-to-ground and surface-to-surface weapon systems, guided missiles, artillery, armored vehicles, aircraft defense systems, and most famously, the Astros II MLRS, the most advanced multiple rocket launcher. Its Tectran division focuses on civilian transportation and telecommunication equipment.

Venezuela

One of Venezuela's largest television networks, Venevision controls a significant portion of the country's entertainment industry. The company was founded in 1961 when businessman Diego Cisneros purchased the assets of the bankrupt Television Venezolana, and expanded to encompass multiple VHF and UHF channels around the country. Much of its content in the 1960s and 1970s was purchased from American tele-

vision network ABC. Since the 1990s, it has broadcast 24 hours a day, 7 days a week, and many of its more popular programs are exported to Spanish-language rebroadcasters in other countries, such as Univision in the United States.

Industrias Pampero, a Venezuelan distillery, makes some of the world's finest rums, and is principally responsible for Venezuela's success in rum exports. Most of the distillery's production is done at the nineteenth-century estate in Ocumare, Hacienda la Guadalupe. The Ron Pampero brand is known for its cowboy on horseback logo—Pampero means "from the Pampas," i.e. a plainsman, a cowboy, a ranger.

Chocolates El Rey, a Venezuelan chocolatier, was established in 1929 and especially since the 1990s has become one of the world's leaders in super-premium chocolate. It is one of the few non-European brands to be mentioned in the same breath as Callebaut and Valrhona, and capitalizes on the many types of cacao native to Venezuela (whereas European companies have to contract with African or South American cacao producers). One of the premium cacao beans, the trintario, is a hybrid of the chocolatey criollo beans and the disease-resistant forastero cultivar.

Uruguay, Ecuador, and Chile

Based in Montevideo (Uruguay), Infocorp is a software company and a local partner with Microsoft. It is best known for financial and business software. Another software company in Uruguay is ARTech Consultores, famous for developing the GeneXus program that has since been sold in dozens of countries. Used mainly for developing applications for Windows and the internet, GeneXus is a software development tool that generates code in Cobol, Visual FoxPro, Ruby, C#, Java, and Visual Basic, with support for standard database management systems like MySQL and Oracle.

Marathon Sports is an international athletic equipment company based in Ecuador, and primarily serving customers in Ecuador, Bolivia, and Colombia. Originally a chain of sporting goods stores, since 1994 it has been producing uniforms for sports teams, and has accumulated a number of exclusive contracts.

Parque Arauco is a real estate holding company based in Chile, and responsible for operating a number of shopping malls in Chile and Argentina. Focusing on the property management of nonresidential properties, the company was founded by Jewish immigrants to Peru who relocated to Chile in the 1940s, originally to work in the textile industry. One of the nine children in the large family, Jose Said, opened Parque Arauco in 1979, and has been principally responsible for it since. By operating in both Chile and Argentina, it was not nearly as badly affected by Argentina's recession as other Argentinian developers were, and it has benefited significantly from its recovery.

Minera Escondida is a Chilean mining company that operates two open pit copper mines in the Atacama Desert in the northern reaches of the country, constituting the largest copper mine in the world. Nearly a tenth of the world's copper production is owed to Escondida, which began operations in 1990 and has reserves of some 34 million tons of copper remaining. Escondida is a significant part of the Chilean economy, accounting for 15 percent of its exports and employing over 6,000 people directly. In 2007 alone, the mining company paid $2.2 billion in taxes to the Chilean government.

Multinationals

The Argentinian multinational Organización Techint is the largest steel manufacturer in South America, and owns stock in over 100 companies in 35 countries, focusing on steel, oil and gas, engineering, and service companies (notably including cable installation, having been responsible for the 1990s upgrade of the Argentinian telecommunications system). Divisions include health care research group Humanitas, oil explorer Tecpetrol, gas transmitter Tecgas, Techint Engineering Construction, steel supplier Ternium, and tube supplier Tenaris.

Responsible for a fifth of Argentina's dairy production, SanCor is responsible for a disproportionate 90 percent of its dairy exports. Founded as a dairy cooperative in 1938 in the "milk basin" around the Cordoba and Santa Fe provinces, the company manufactures a variety of fresh and shelf-stable dairy products available around the world.

See Also: Argentina; Brazil; BRICs; Chile; Ecuador; Inter-American Development Bank; Latin America; Mercosur/Mercosul; Uruguay; Venezuela.

Bibliography. Werner Baer and Donald Coes, eds., *United States Policies and the Latin American Economies* (Praeger,

1990); Leslie Bethell, *Latin America: Economy and Society Since 1930* (Cambridge University Press, 1998); Patrice Franko, *The Puzzle of Latin American Economic Development* (Rowman & Littlefield, 2007); Jeffry A. Frieden, Manuel Pastor Jr., and Michael Tomz, *Modern Political Economy and Latin America: Theory and Policy* (Westview Press, 2000); Robert Patricio Korzeniewicz and William C. Smith, eds., *Latin America in the World Economy* (Praeger Paperback, 1996); Nicola Phillips, *The Southern Cone Model: The Political Economy of Regional Capitalist Development in Latin America* (Routledge, 2004).

BILL KTE'PI
INDEPENDENT SCHOLAR

Company Profiles: South Asia

A term not always immediately familiar to American ears, south Asia consists of the sub-Himalayan countries in a southern region of Asia: Bangladesh, Bhutan, India, the Maldives, Nepal, Pakistan, Sri Lanka—all of which are members of the South Asian Association for Regional Cooperation (SAARC)—as well as the British Indian Ocean Territory. Some discussions and usages include Afghanistan and Tibet; Myanmar, though more properly part of southeast Asia, was part of the British Raj region until 1937 and so is appropriately included in some historical discussions; Iran is included in "southern Asia" by the United Nations. Geographically, the term "Indian subcontinent" may be more familiar, though some parts of some countries of south Asia lie outside the Indian Plate.

SAARC was established in 1985 to strengthen cooperation, social progress, cultural development, and economic growth throughout the region, with a special emphasis on collective self-reliance, no doubt in light of much of the region's history as part of the British empire. The full members as of 2009 are Afghanistan, Bangladesh, Bhutan, India, the Maldives, Nepal, Pakistan, and Sri Lanka; observer members include Australia, the People's Republic of China, the European Union, Iran, Japan, Mauritius, Myanmar, South Korea, and the United States. China, Iran, and Myanmar have all expressed interest in full membership; Russia currently seeks observer status. The granting of observer status to Western nations is a recent phenomenon, dating from 2005. SAARC has created the framework for a South Asian Free Trade Area, eliminating all customs duties on trade within the region, and it is hoped to go into full effect in 2016. Despite SAARC, south Asia is the least integrated region in the world. Only 2 percent of the region's combined gross domestic product (GDP) results from trade within the region, compared for instance to the 20 percent in east Asia.

Sri Lanka

The oldest radio station in Asia is Radio Ceylon, which began broadcasting in 1923, a mere three years after the first European broadcasts; the station is owned by the Sri Lankan government. Briton Edward Harper had popularized amateur radio in Ceylon when he became the chief engineer of the Telegraph Office in 1921, and broadcast music from the Central Telegraphic Office—using a gramophone and a transmitter built from parts scavenged from a captured German submarine.

After radio operations were taken over by the Allies during World War II, the station was handed over to the government and embarked on a serious endeavor of broadcasting. Its senior officers in the postwar era transferred from the BBC, but local on-air talent and off-air professionals were soon developed. Radio Ceylon was instrumental in popularizing Ceylonese music throughout south Asia, as well as broadcasting religious programming—Buddhist, Hindu, Muslim, and Christian—for its listeners. Advertising in Hindi brought enormous amounts of advertising revenue from India, and many Indian announcers went on to become Bollywood stars. The station was also the nexus of the popular trend, from the 1950s onward, of Indian pop stars recording songs in English. One of the station's interesting claims to fame: when Edmund Hillary reached the summit of Mount Everest, Radio Ceylon was the first thing he heard on his transistor radio, and he and his team continued to tune in for the news.

Bangladesh

The Grameen ("villager") family of organizations began with Grameen Bank in Bangladesh. A community development bank founded in 1983 (by Vanderbilt-educated Bangladeshi scholar Muhammad Yunus), Grameen Bank offers small loans—branded as *grameencredit*—to the poor, without requiring collateral. Borrowers recite the "Sixteen Decisions," vows they are expected to follow, notable enough in their difference from western loan applications to be worth reprinting in full:

1. We shall follow and advance the four principles of Grameen Bank: Discipline, Unity, Courage and Hard work—in all walks of our lives.
2. Prosperity we shall bring to our families.
3. We shall not live in dilapidated houses. We shall repair our houses and work towards constructing new houses at the earliest.
4. We shall grow vegetables all the year round. We shall eat plenty of them and sell the surplus.
5. During the plantation seasons, we shall plant as many seedlings as possible.
6. We shall plan to keep our families small. We shall minimize our expenditures. We shall look after our health.
7. We shall educate our children and ensure that they can earn to pay for their education.
8. We shall always keep our children and the environment clean.
9. We shall build and use pit-latrines.
10. We shall drink water from tubewells. If it is not available, we shall boil water or use alum.
11. We shall not take any dowry at our sons' weddings, neither shall we give any dowry at our daughter's wedding. We shall keep our centre free from the curse of dowry. We shall not practice child marriage.
12. We shall not inflict any injustice on anyone, neither shall we allow anyone to do so.
13. We shall collectively undertake bigger investments for higher incomes.
14. We shall always be ready to help each other. If anyone is in difficulty, we shall all help him or her.
15. If we come to know of any breach of discipline in any centre, we shall all go there and help restore discipline.
16. We shall take part in all social activities collectively.

There is no written contract or binding legal arrangement between borrower and lender, but borrowers may only apply in groups of five or more, and while the loans are granted to the group members individually and no member is obligated to make payments on behalf of any other member, no one who has been a member of a group with a defaulting member is eligible for another loan. In other words, instead of depending on legal reprisals or the seizure of collateral, Grameen Bank depends on peer pressure, and manages a 98 percent payback rate (including late payments).

It has been a remarkably effective system, employed in 43 other countries, by Grameen and other institutions. Interestingly, the vast majority of borrowers are women—over 95 percent. The reasons for this are not at all clear, though some argue that women have the most to gain from the system. The bank has been criticized for charging high interest rates, but points out the risks it takes as well as the lack of any alternative for its borrowers. As this argument is similar to that put forth by issuers of secured and high-risk credit cards, the counter-argument is similar as well: when you are poor and given access to debt, it is very easy to become trapped in it perpetually, and to return to it again and again.

Early in Grameen Bank's history, it began to diversify by acquiring fishing ponds and irrigation pumps. In 1989, the non-banking holdings became their own organizations: the Grameen Fisheries Foundation and the Grameen Krishi Foundation (irrigation). More ventures followed. In the 21st century, they include the non-profit Grameen Trust that supports small loan programs all over the world; the Grameen Fund, for small business loans; Grameenphone and Grameen Telecom, providing mobile phones and cellular service for the Bangladeshi poor; Grameen Communications, building Cyber Kiosks to provide internet access in rural areas; and Grameen Danone Foods, a joint venture with the French Groupe Danone, selling highly fortified yogurt to provide rural children with nutrients otherwise missing from their diets.

Aarong is a retail chain in Bangladesh, operated by the Bangladesh Rural Advancement Committee, one of the largest nongovernmental development organizations in the world. First opened in 1978, Aarong has eight outlets in Bangladesh—five of them in the capital city of Dhaka—as well as a franchise in London. Many of the products sold in the outlets are also exported to Europe and North America, and include cloth and silk products, candles, pottery, and wooden goods, produced by 65,000 workers, most of them women, working in 2000 villages.

A major pharmaceutical company in Bangladesh, Amico Laboratories was founded in 1976. Operating out of the industrial district of Dhaka, Amico develops, manufactures, and markets healthcare products sold all over the country.

Nearly half of the residential housing development business in Bangladesh is controlled by Eastern Housing Limited, a real estate developer founded in 1965 by Jahurul Islam to address the housing shortage in Dhaka. It capitalized on the need for low-cost housing in Bangladesh when the country was still East Pakistan, and still focuses on Dhaka projects more than those outside the city. What began as a focus on low-cost houses and mortgages, though, has expanded to include shopping malls, apartment buildings, and commercial plazas. Long a profitable business, it paid its stockholders a 15 percent divided in 2007.

Incepta Pharmaceuticals is a Dhaka pharmaceutical company that began by manufacturing ranitidine (a stomach acid inhibitor) and quickly expanded into other medicines. Incepta's name is derived from its slogan, "Innovative Concept Into Practice," and its stock in trade has been offering a variety of intake methods: not just tablets, capsules, and liquids, but nasal sprays, sustained-release and buffered tablets, quick-dissolving compressed powders, powder inhalers, and flavored liquids.

Sheba Prokashoni is a major publisher based in Dhaka, and focuses principally on Bengali translations of established Western sellers (especially the classics) and novels for young adults and twentysomethings. Most of its books are published as mass-market paperbacks with stylish covers, and it is well known throughout Bangladesh for the *Masud Rana* books, a series of international cloak and dagger adventures published steadily since 1966—a total of 389 books, most of them ghostwritten on behalf of series creator Qazi Anwar Hussain. Other popular series include the Western imprint, which translates (or loosely adapts) classic westerns like those of Louis L'amour and was responsible for introducing the genre to Bangladesh; the *Teen Goenda* series, about a Bangladeshi-American teen detective and his adventures with his two sidekick friends (a white American and a black Muslim American), loosely based on the *Three Investigators* series (by Robert Arthur Jr.) but often borrowing from *The Hardy Boys*; a horror imprint that translated William Peter Blatty's *The Exorcist* and published a three-volume novelization of the Gregory Peck film *The Omen*; and the Kishore Classic series that translates and usually abridges the classic works of Western literature, with a special focus on "boys' stories" (Mark Twain, Sir Walter Scott, Alexandre Dumas, and so on).

Bhutan

Druk Air is the national airline of Bhutan, operating throughout South Asia, with additional flights to Bangkok. Founded in 1981, it remains the only airline with service to Bhutan, and so is an integral part of the nation's trade and modest tourism industry. Recent hikes in the price of jet fuel have constricted the airline's flight schedule, but this is considered a temporary condition; in the 2008–13 period, money is being put aside by the Bhutanese government to further develop the main airport and mull over a feasibility study on a prospective international airport in the southern region of the country.

India

The Tata Group is a Mumbai (India)-based multinational conglomerate founded in 1868 by Jamshetji Tata and run by the Tata family ever since (five generations now). The largest private corporation in India, the Tata Group includes 98 different companies, operating in 85 countries. The companies are divided among seven sectors: engineering (Tata Motors is India's largest commercial vehicle manufacturer), energy (Tata Power is one of the largest power companies in the world), Chemicals, Services (primarily hotels and financial services), Consumer Products (including Tata Tea Limited, which owns the Tetley brand of tea, and Titan Industries), and Information Systems (Tata Consultancy Services is Asia's largest software company). Use of the Tata prefix in company branding is common, but not universal, as is use of the stylized T that serves as the group's logo. Major acquisitions in the 21st century have included Millennium Steel, Eight O'Clock Coffee, the Ritz-Carlton hotel in Boston, Jaguar, Daewoo, and the Corus Group, a $12 billion acquisition of the world's fifth-largest steel producer.

The second-largest conglomerate in India is Reliance Industries Limited, founded in 1966 as the Reliance Commercial Corporation. Primarily an oil and petroleum products company, Reliance was ranked at 206 on the 2008 Fortune Global 500, and the only Indian company to make Forbes' 2008 list of the world's 100 most-respected companies. With three million shares of stock, Reliance is one of the world's most-invested-in companies, and the company claims that a quarter of Indian investors own shares in Reliance. In recent years, the company has diversified from petroleum and oil exploration, adding textiles, the Vimal clothing brand, and the Reliance Fresh supermarket chain to its portfolio.

Another Indian conglomerate is the massive Aditya Birla Group, with over 100,000 employees in 25 countries across southeast Asia, Europe, and North America; though the company of course has a considerable presence in India, half of its revenues come from its overseas operations Primarily a manufacturer, Aditya Birla has subsidiaries that work with fiber, cement, non-ferrous metals, and chemicals, but also operates Idea Cellular (originally a joint venture of the Tata Group and AT&T) and several retail and financial services companies.

Sahara India Pariwar, founded in 1978, is an Indian conglomerate focusing primarily on finance and services company. The Sahara brand is one of the leaders in India in the life insurance, home loan, and real estate sectors, and the diverse equity funds offered by Sahara Mutual Fund are highly ranked by Reuter-owned fund tracker Lipper. Its media subsidiaries control the Filmy movie channel, Samay news channel, 36 city news channels, and Sahara One, one of the country's most popular general entertainment channels, with programming rebroadcast around the world.

India's largest telecommunications company is Bharat Sanchar Nigam Limited, with a 24 percent market share as of 2008. Headquartered in New Delhi, it is India's oldest phone company, founded in the 19th century, and has pioneered both rural telephony and widespread upgrades of broadband connectivity.

Genpact is one of India's leading business process outsourcing (BPO) companies, employing 34,000 people with services available every hour of the day, every day of the year. Its operations are spread out around the world, including its American subsidiary with mortgage services in Irvine, California, and Salt Lake City, and finance services in Wilkes Barre, Nashville, and Parsippany, New Jersey.

Evalueserve, founded at the end of 2000, is an Indian Knowledge Process Outsourcing (KPO) firm, operating out of centers in India, China, Chile, and Romania, with about 2500 employees combined. More than 2100 of those employees work in the New Delhi call center, with a hundred or so in each of the other locations. Evalueserve focuses mainly on investment, market, and business research, with services also available in legal research and data analysis.

Other Companies

Spice Nepal Private Limited is the first company to offer GSM mobile phone services in Nepal, having broken the telephony monopoly of Nepal Telecom. Originally operating only in the capital at the time of its 2004 establishment, SNPL has expanded to every zone of the country and has introduced the full range of standard cellular service features, many of them previously unavailable in the country.

Southern Networks is a Pakistani television network, begun in 1995 as a small system of pay cable channels and pay-per-view services and expanding with the addition of digital broadcasts. It presently offers 50 digital channels and a dozen over-the-air analogue channels, in Pakistani, Hindu, and English.

Micro Cars is a Sri Lankan car company founded in 1995, though thanks to legal issues, the business didn't get healthily underway until 2003, with the introduction of the Micro Privilege, a small car with a 1000cc 4-cylinder engine. The Privilege was the first locally made car in Sri Lanka, and was designed to be more affordable and practical than foreign cars. Vans and hatchbacks have followed, all of them made of flexible composite materials. Currently the company is engaged in producing its first SUVs, in a collaboration with Korean automobile manufacturer SsangYong.

See Also: Bangladesh; India; Indian Oil; Microfinance; Microfinance Institutions; Mittal Steel; Pakistan; Sri Lanka; Tata Group.

Bibliography. Sugata Bose and Ayesha Jalal, *Modern South Asia: History, Culture, Political Economy* (Taylor and Francis, 2007); Ben Crow, *Markets, Class, and Social Change: Trading Networks and Poverty in Rural South Asia* (Palgrave Macmillan, 2001); Meghnad Desai, *Development and Nationhood: Essays in the Political Economy of South Asia* (Oxford University Press, 2006); Barbara Harriss-White,

India Working: Essays on Society and Economy (Cambridge University Press, 2002).

BILL KTE'PI
INDEPENDENT SCHOLAR

Company Profiles: Western Europe

Trading companies had operated in Europe since ancient times, and there is evidence of some of these from Roman times. Perhaps the largest "inter-country" private business operation of the mid third century B.C.E. was the Carthaginian colony on the east coast of Spain, where they extracted silver that was later used to finance the armies of Hannibal in the Second Punic War (218–201 B.C.E.). Prior to that, Phoenicians had been involved in trade in Cornwall in the west of England, where they bought tin. There is a vast amount of archaeological evidence showing extensive trade around the Roman Empire, with quantities of luxury goods and military materiel clearly made in one part of the empire being used in another part. In Rome itself, Marcus Licinius Crassus (115–53 B.C.E.) established a large business in real estate, silver mines, and trading in slaves.

In medieval times, businesses flourished in western Europe, usually within the framework of trade guilds that jealously guarded access to particular trades that kept up the level of quality, the official reason, but also maintained higher wages for members of the guilds. Most cities had a range of powerful guilds, which helped businessmen such as Richard Whittington (1354–1423) of the Mercers Company in London become very wealthy. Indeed, it was the Wool Guild in Florence that was able to finance the building of the dome for Florence Cathedral following the design of Filippo Brunelleschi (1377–1446).

By this time, the wool industry was well developed in England (after the Black Death of the 1340s)—it is still recognized in the "Wool Sack" in the British House of Lords—and in Flanders. Many of the guilds continue to the present day with the Worshipful Company of Mercers establishing schools in England, as have the Worshipful Company of Haberdashers and the Worshipful Company of Merchant Taylors, all from London. Mention should also be made of some of the vineyards, especially in southern France and in the Champagne region, which started producing wine at this time, a few of which continue to the present day. Most, however, date from the 18th and 19th centuries with Moët et Chandon dating from 1743, Veuve Clicquot from 1772, and Champagne Krug from 1843.

As the city and town guilds were building up their strength, the modern banking system emerged. The Knights Templar had a system whereby if a sum of money was left at one of their premises, it could be withdrawn from another if the correct paperwork were provided. This helped with the transfer of large amounts of money—the physical movement of valuables from one city to another was complicated and risky. It was the Lombards who became well known for their banking skills, and the Medici family in Florence under Cosimo de Medici (1389–1464) also established a substantial banking network.

Following from Vasco da Gama (c.1460–1524) and later Christopher Columbus (1451–1506), there was great interest in voyages of exploration, many of which generated massive profits from trade in spices and the like. It was the cost of voyages, as well as the risk in case the ship sank, that led a number of people to own ships, and the advent of shareholding. This allowed investors to spread their risks more widely. This also saw the emergence of the great chartered companies in many European countries, the major ones being the English companies, the Muscovy Company, the Levant Company, the Honorable East India Company (HEIC), and the Dutch East India Company (VOC). Many other countries also had these but few equaled the success of the HEIC and the VOC.

Gradually other companies were established on the same basis, and it was not long before various coffee houses in London, Paris, Lisbon, and elsewhere became central to exchanging news about trade. These in turn led to the establishment of informal stock markets. There were also instances of wild speculation with the emergence of the South Sea Company in London and the Mississippi Company in France in the early 18th century. Both tried to assume the government debt, and both resulted in a spectacular crash in stock prices ruining many people's confidence in stocks for many years.

During this period, there was an increase in agricultural developments through the Agricultural Revolu-

The shops in London's covered Leadenhall Market, built in 1881, stand on the site of a 14th-century market.

tion. Trade between European countries saw countries develop greater specialization, and this was accentuated in recent times when refrigeration allowed for ease of movement of foods. Jersey and Guernsey cows became common in England, horned cattle in Spain, and also cattle bred in Switzerland, pigs bred in Denmark, and sheep in England, were raised on an industrial scale as milking machines, larger abattoirs, and much later, canning of meat resulted in the emergence of a number of agricultural companies. This was replicated in terms of olives from Spain and Italy and citrus fruit from southern Europe, and this later led to the development of apple cider from Kent in southeast England.

Industrialization

More cautious investing started by the middle of the 18th century, and it gradually meant that with the start of the Industrial Revolution in England, Scotland, Flanders, and elsewhere, companies were able to raise capital far more easily than before. This helped finance the establishment of factories, with inventors designing machines to make textiles and other manufactures on a much more extensive level than ever before. People like Richard Arkwright, Samuel Crompton, and the two men called John Kay all became well-known business figures in England. Gradually they and similar businesspeople in Europe started establishing companies which bore their names. How some of these businesses emerged can be seen through the career of John Cockerill (1790–1840) whose father worked in Russia for Catherine the Great, and who then moved to France and later to the southern part of the Netherlands (later Belgium) where he was involved in making steam locomotives and established a company that was involved in heavy arms production up until its capture by the Germans in 1914; the company ran its blast furnaces until 2005.

During the Napoleonic Wars, Napoleon enforced the Continental System that led to the closing of European markets to the British. This allowed for the emergence of numbers of companies in Europe following the joint stock model, which then, in turn, led to the establishment of stock markets around Europe. Some banks emerged from the wars, with men like Samuel Bleichröder running a business exchanging money for the French, and his son Gerson von Bleichröder establishing a banking operation—the Bleichröder Bank—that helped finance German industrialization.

During the 19th century, there was a move toward more and more joint-stock companies in Britain, France, Belgium, Germany, the Netherlands, and elsewhere. The reunification of both Italy and then Germany transformed the political map of Europe, and the various conflicts in Europe and those overseas that involved Europeans led to the emergence of a substantial arms industry and the desire by governments to have a large heavy-industry capacity. With war looming in the early 20th century, several governments in western Europe, particularly those in Britain, France, and Germany, started subsidizing several of their industries, especially shipbuilding, as the three countries built up their merchant navies.

Many of the companies that operated in Britain in the late 19th and early 20th century were named after their founders, and large numbers of these are still household names: the department store Harrod's, also auctioneers Christie's and Sotheby's. A few like Philip Morris had originally been named after their founder—Philip Morris died in 1873, at age 37, and the company ended up in the hands of a relative and

then was bought by totally unrelated people who kept his name. By the late 19th and early 20th century, there were a large number of industrial companies that had the names of their founders: Benz after Karl Benz (1844–1929), Rolls Royce, after C. S. Rolls (1877–1910) and Henry Royce (1863–1933), and Renault after Louis Renault (1877–1944). Some other companies also named after founders were Michelin, founded in 1888, and named after Edouard Michelin (1859–1940) and André Michelin (1853–1931), the German company Krupp Steel run by the Krupp family, the Dutch company NV Philips taking its name from Gerard L. F. Philips (1858–1942), and Citroën founded in 1919, taking its name from André Citroën (1878–1935).

However, from the 20th century, far more companies were involved in naming their companies after the machines made, such as the British firms General Electric Company (GEC), Imperial Chemical Industries (ICI), and the British Oxygen Company (now the BOC Group), the Danish maker of toys Lego, and the German car manufacturer BMW (Bavarian Motor Works). With the exception of Lego, which has a shorter name, the other four companies now use the initials of their name, as do so many other companies including HSBC (formerly Hongkong Shanghai Banking Corporation, now with its headquarters in London), BNP Paribas (formerly two companies, Banque Nationale de Paris and Paribas).

Companies named after people tend to keep the names of the founders such as PSA Peugeot Citroën; there are exceptions such as in the Amsterdam-based KPMG that was formed in 1987 from a merger of Peat Marwick (named after William Barclay Peat and James Marwick) and Klynveld Main Goerdeler (named after Piet Klynveld and Reinhard Goerdeler), becoming KPMG Peat Marwick in 1991, and KPMG four years later. These companies (with the exception of KPMG, which is a partnership) were still reliant on stock markets to raise capital, and the link between them grew stronger as the companies were able to raise capital from these stock exchanges.

World Wars I and II

With World War I, there were major changes in the nature of companies in Europe. Because of the number of men in the war, many factories had to employ women, and working conditions in factories actually improved. After the war, large numbers of women remained in the workforce, so there were now families where both parents worked. The number of jobs open to women remained sharply restricted, but gradually with more and more women in employment, it was only a matter of time before there were numbers of women managers in Britain and Scandinavia, and also in France, the Netherlands, Belgium, and Germany. This coincided with more investment in stocks and shares, and a wider use of banks, with many of them losing money in the Great Inflation of 1923 in Germany and in the stock market crashes from 1929.

The Great Depression affected different countries to varying extents, with Germany, under Hitler from 1933, experiencing an economic boom and quickly regaining its reputation in production of expensive and high-quality manufactures. Germany kept its reputation for technology, Italy for style, and Britain for reliability. With the outbreak of World War II, many of the same needs as during World War I led to far more women in the workforce in many countries.

The Postwar Era

After World War II, the devastation of so much of western Europe saw many companies rebuild their factories, taking advantage of the new developments in industrial design. Some of these were soon able to compete with the established British and Swedish factories undamaged by war. This led to greater prosperity for Germany, and by the 1960s, the British companies were lagging behind. The mid- and late-1970s saw the decline of British Leyland and the British Steel Corporation. This coincided with the Japanese selling far more consumer durables and cars in Europe, eroding the traditional markets of so many companies in western Europe, and resulting in a decline in the manufacturing base in Britain, France, and also later Germany.

With restructuring in the 1980s, many of the companies in western Europe were far more competitive. The economy was far more focused on the services sector—the region attracted far more tourists than ever before, and financial and educational services remained in great demand around the world. A series of bank mergers resulted in the emergence of a number of much larger European financial institutions, many of which had diversified to take in insurance,

loans, and other products. This coincided with a large-scale privatization of government corporations. This was spearheaded by Margaret Thatcher in Britain, and later followed in France, Germany, Belgium, Spain, Italy, and other countries. This dramatically transformed the nature of share ownership in western Europe, with many more small investors.

Soon afterward, many mutual companies, especially the building societies in England, were involved in demutualization, again adding to the number of share owners. Many of the companies privatized or demutualized have been very successful, but some of them, especially telecommunications businesses such as Deutsche Telekom, have seen the prices of their stock fall dramatically.

Since the fall of communism in 1989, some western European companies have spread into eastern Europe, taking advantage of the factories, the workforce, and also the markets. One of these, Thimm in Germany, rapidly emerged as one of the largest makers of cardboard boxes in central Europe. There have been companies that took advantage of the raw materials in eastern Europe, and others, such as the tobacco companies, have preferred the less-regulated business atmosphere of eastern Europe. Many other western European companies have also expanded into west Asia, and especially to east Asia and southeast Asia. In most cases this has been successful, but in one celebrated case, Baring's Bank (which had been established in Britain in 1762) went spectacularly bankrupt over a "rogue trader" based in Singapore, resulting in the sale of the bank to the Netherlands bank ABN for £1 in 1995.

The European Union

In addition to many of the companies becoming larger and more powerful with the European Union (EU) and the economic power of Europe, there have also been many sectors of the economy that have been badly hit in recent years. Westland Aircraft was bought by the U.S. firm Sikorsky in 1986, causing a split in the British government that saw the resignation of Secretary of Defense Michael Heseltine. And although some airlines such as British Airways have flourished, and Air France continues to receive large French government subsidies, many other European airlines have closed down. Sabena, the former national airline of Belgium that had existed from 1923, went bankrupt in 2001. Swissair, the former national airline of Switzerland, founded in 1931, went bankrupt the following year. Neither was able to compete with the "cut price" airlines that appeared in Europe during the 1990s, nor airlines like Air Emirates and Singapore Airlines that have increased their patronage in recent years.

The main development in companies in western Europe over the last 20 years has not been in seeking markets outside Europe, but with the help of the heavy protection barriers provided by the European Economic Community (and from 1993, the EU), they have managed to get more and more sales within the EU, especially with the European Union expanding rapidly into central and eastern Europe. There has also been increased collaboration among European businesses, with the most high-profile example being Airbus, which began as a consortium of various aerospace manufacturers and since 2001 has been a standard joint-stock company.

The Schengen Agreement, initially established at a village in Luxembourg, and enhanced by the Treaty of Amsterdam in 1997, has considerably simplified the workings of the EU, with attempts to change it further in the Treaty of Lisbon in 2007. This has helped continue the standardization of company laws, as well as deal with the more politically high-profile problems of immigration and crime. The introduction of the euro, now used in most of western Europe, has also led to a much greater integration of the economies of the 15 members of the Eurozone: Austria, Belgium, Cyprus, Finland, France, Germany, Greece, Ireland, Italy, Luxembourg, Malta, the Netherlands, Portugal, Slovenia, and Spain.

See Also: European Union; France; Germany; Hanseatic League; United Kingdom.

Bibliography. Derek H. Aldcroft, *The European Economy 1914–2000* (Routledge, 2001); Ivan T. Berend, *An Economic History of Twentieth-century Europe: Economic Regimes from Laissez-faire to Globalization* (Cambridge University Press, 2006); Heather Brewin, *Major Companies of Europe: France* (Gale-Cengage/Graham & Whiteside Ltd., 2007); Heather Brewin and Allison Gallico, *Major Companies of Europe: Benelux Region—Austria, Belgium, Liechtenstein, Luxembourg, Netherlands, Switzerland* (Gale-Cengage/Graham & Whiteside Ltd., 2007); *Europa Yearbook 2008* (Europa Publications, 2007); Allison Gallico, Theresa Rainbird, and Layla Romiti, *Major Companies of Europe: Southern Europe—Cypress, Greece, Italy, Israel, Malta, Portugal, Spain, Turkey* (Gale-Cengage/Graham & Whiteside Ltd., 2007); Susan Hoernig, *Major Companies of Europe: Germany* (Gale-Cengage/Graham & Whiteside Ltd., 2007); Luis Rubalcaba and Henk Kox, *Business Services in European Economic Growth* (Palgrave Macmillan, 2007); Alice Teichova, Herbert Matis, and Jaroslav Pátek, eds., *Economic Change and the National Question in Twentieth-century Europe* (Cambridge University Press, 2000); David J. Smith, *Major Companies of Europe: Central Europe—Bulgaria, Czech Republic, Estonia, Hungary, Latvia, Lithuania, Poland, Romania, Slovakia, Slovenia* (Gale-Cengage/Graham & Whiteside Ltd., 2007); Sue Ward, *Major Companies of Europe: Scandinavia—Denmark, Finland, Iceland, Norway, Sweden* (Gale-Cengage/Graham & Whiteside Ltd., 2007); Katie Wilson, *Major Companies of Europe—United Kingdom and Ireland* (Gale-Cengage/Graham & Whiteside Ltd., 2007).

JUSTIN CORFIELD
GEELONG GRAMMAR SCHOOL, AUSTRALIA

Comparative Advantage

When challenged to provide a nontrivial, nonobvious economic insight, Nobel laureate Paul Samuelson listed comparative advantage. Despite general agreement on the topic in the economics profession since David Ricardo's 1817 formulation in his *On the Principles of Political Economy and Taxation*, comparative advantage remains one of the more difficult economic insights for noneconomists to accept.

A simple example (based on Ricardo's) illustrates the principle. Suppose that Portugal produces both wine and cloth more cheaply than does England. Portugal thus has an absolute advantage in the production of both goods. If Portugal can produce wine more cheaply than it can produce cloth, it will be to the advantage of both countries for England to trade English cloth for Portuguese wine, despite the Portuguese absolute advantage in cloth production.

A numerical example can make the principle clearer. Suppose it takes 15 person-hours to produce a liter of wine in Portugal and 30 to do the same in England, and 10 person-hours to produce a yard of cloth in Portugal and 15 to produce a yard in England. If we arbitrarily assume that England has 270 person-hours available and Portugal 180 person-hours available, the most wine Portugal can produce on its own is 12 liters and the most England can produce is 18 liters. Likewise, for cloth production, the most Portugal can produce is 18 yards and the most England can produce is 18 yards.

The opportunity cost of a liter of wine in Portugal is 1.5 yards of cloth; in England it is 2 yards of cloth. Note that although the Portuguese are more efficient at making both wine and cloth than the English, their advantage is greater with respect to the production of wine. Portugal's opportunity cost of making cloth is thus higher than England's because Portugal must give up a greater amount of wine to produce a unit of cloth. If the countries split their labor between wine and cloth before trade, Portugal would have produced 9 liters of wine and 6 yards of cloth and England would have produced 5 liters of wine and 8 yards of cloth.

With trade, if Portugal specializes in wine production and England in cloth production, world wine production is 12 liters and world cloth production is 18 yards. As a result of comparative advantage, the world ends up with more wine and more cloth than if the two countries each attempted to produce both goods domestically. As this simple example illustrates, comparative advantage is built on the idea that the cheapest way to acquire a good is sometimes not to make the good directly but to make a different good that one trades for the desired good.

Comparative advantage works for individuals as well as countries. Tiger Woods might be an amazing chef as well as one of the world's top golfers, but if he is a better golfer than he is a chef, he'll maximize his income if he devotes himself to golf and eats at restaurants when he wants a fancy meal.

What determines the comparative advantage of a particular person or country? Some individuals and countries have natural advantages in a particular area. Tiger Woods has inherent talents as a golfer; Saudi Arabia has an endowment of crude oil. Other sources are based on investment in education or job training. The United States in the 18th century had a comparative advantage in mechanical inventive skills relative to England because so many Americans worked in jobs that required them to develop such skills, while the structure of English industry did not encourage

individual workers to innovate. Comparative advantage means that a country (or individual) need not have an absolute advantage in anything to reap the rewards of trade. Absolute advantages are beneficial because they lead to higher incomes, but they are not necessary for trade to confer an advantage on the trading partners.

As is common in economics, explanations of comparative advantage typically make a number of simplifying assumptions. The example given above assumes a single factor of production, constant opportunity costs, perfect mobility of labor between sectors within the two countries, negligible transportation costs, and so on. Relaxing these assumptions makes the mathematical proof of comparative advantage more complex but the principle holds true under all reasonable conditions.

When the assumptions are relaxed, however, distributional consequences come to the fore. If labor is imperfectly mobile among sectors of a country's economy, opening the economy to trade is likely to mean that workers in the sectors without a comparative advantage will end up worse off. In the Portugal-England example, both English winemakers and Portuguese weavers may be made worse off. Another criticism of reliance on comparative advantage as a justification for free trade is that it ignores national security or other strategic concerns. For example, many countries believe a domestic steel industry is vital to their national security because steel is an important component of many weapons.

Dependency Theory

The major theoretical challenge to comparative advantage came with the development after the 1940s of dependency theory by theorists including Raul Prebisch and Andre Gunder Frank. Dependency theorists argued that some countries, particularly in Latin America and the Islamic world, fell into the periphery of the world trading system and would remain trapped in the role of exporter of primary commodities. In a related vein of criticism, modern "fair trade" critics of international trade argue that an approach based purely on comparative advantage fails to address the terms on which trade is conducted. They contend that without attention to the terms of trade, developing countries will be unfairly taken advantage of by more advanced economies.

See Also: Absolute Advantage; Dependency Theory; Factor Endowments; Free Trade; Mercantilism; Monopolistic Advantage Theory; Trade Liberalization.

Bibliography. Thomas A. Friedman, *The World Is Flat: A Brief History of the Twenty-First Century* (Farrar, Straus & Giroux, 2005); Douglas A. Irwin, *Free Trade Under Fire*, 2nd ed. (Princeton, 2005); Andrea Maneschi, *Comparative Advantage in International Trade: A Historical Perspective* (Edward Elgar, 1999).

ANDREW P. MORRISS
UNIVERSITY OF ILLINOIS

Compensation

Compensation as a human resources management (HRM) practice is the linkage between reward and employee satisfaction. Modern organizations can adopt various HRM practices to enhance employee satisfaction. The form and structure of an organization's HRM system can affect employee motivation levels in several ways. HRM practices in general and compensation systems in particular have been shown to be highly related to organizational performance. Reward systems are concerned with two major issues: performance and rewards. Performance includes defining and evaluating performance and providing employees with feedback. Rewards include bonus, salary increases, promotions, stock awards, and perquisites.

Organizations have considerable discretion in the design of pay policies and the choices made have consequences for organizational performance. Organizations that are similar in terms of types of employees and jobs, product, market, size, and so on may choose compensation system designs that differ in their effectiveness for attaining similar goals. Also, large corporations with several different businesses may have multiple reward systems. And while they may share some fundamental philosophies and values, they may differ according to particular business setting, competitive situation, and product life cycle. Thus multiple reward systems can support multiple cultures (or subcultures) within one organization.

HRM practices such as profit sharing, results-oriented appraisals, and employment security have relatively strong universalistic relationships with important accounting measures of organizational and financial performance. Pay level and pay structure are each important for understanding the organizational level implications of pay policy. Pay level practices and pay structures interact to affect resource efficiency, employee satisfaction, and financial performance. Different elements of a compensation plan are considered regarding the relationship between pay systems and organizational performance.

The universalistic relationship between the use of compensation and performance also supports both an agency theory and a behavioral theory explanation. Agency theory posits that basing employee rewards on profits ensures that employee interests are aligned with owner interests. Many profit-sharing plans do not distribute profits equally among employees. Instead, profits are distributed differentially according to employee performance. Compensation systems as a major HRM practice can motivate skilled employees to engage in effective decision making and behavior in response to a variety of environmental contingencies.

Alternative Compensation Systems

Employees are one of the most valuable resources companies have to remain competitive. Managerial compensation strategies differ significantly across organizations, particularly with regard to variable pay. Organizations tend to make different decisions about pay contingency, or variability, rather than about base pay, since contingent pay is more associated with financial performance. In general, organizations implement merit pay or incentive compensation systems that provide rewards to employees for meeting specific goals. Fewer employees work under individual incentive plans while greater numbers of individuals work under some type of group incentive system. A substantial body of evidence has focused on the impact of incentive compensation and performance management systems on group performance. In addition, protecting employees from arbitrary treatment, perhaps via a formal grievance procedure, may also motivate them to work harder because they can expect their efforts to be fairly rewarded.

Development of compensation systems other than wages on a monthly basis, benefits required by law, and bonuses is necessary. Compensation in modern organizations should pay more attention to alternative and more sophisticated compensation systems, such as performance-related pay systems, profit-sharing systems, share-ownership systems and stock options, nonfinancial motives, and benefits not required by law. In this way, compensation as a major HRM practice increases the level of satisfaction and enhances fairness perception of employees working at various functional units and different hierarchical levels.

In a dynamic, unpredictable environment, organizations might achieve this by using organic HRM systems that promote the development of a human capital pool possessing a broad range of skills and that are able to engage in a wide variety of behavior. Today, organizations face environments characterized by increasing dynamism and competition and sustainable fit can be achieved only by developing and applying HRM practices, such as sophisticated compensation systems promoting employee financial participation. Organizations that adopt a greater number of prescribed practices are likely to gain a short-term competitive advantage and enjoy superior performance. However, the implementation of these practices is not always an easy task.

See Also: Motivation; Profit-Sharing; Salaries and Wages.

Bibliography. B. E. Becker and M. A. Huselid, "High Performance Work Systems and Performance Systems: A Synthesis of Research and Managerial Implications," *Research in Personnel and Human Resources Management* (1998); M. P. Brown, M. C. Sturman, and M. J. Simmering, "Compensation Policy and Organizational Performance: The Efficiency, Operational, and Financial Implications of Pay Levels and Pay Structure," *Academy of Management Journal* (2003); B. Gerhart and G. T. Milkovich, "Organizational Differences in Managerial Compensation and Financial Performance," *Academy of Management Journal* (1990); J. Kerr and J. W. Slocum, "Managing Corporate Culture Through Reward Systems," *Academy of Management Executive* (2005); D. P. Schwab, "Impact of Alternative Compensations Systems on Pay Valence and Instrumentality Perceptions," *Journal of Applied Psychology* (1973).

Panagiotis V. Polychroniou
University of Patras

Compensation for Expropriated Property

When a multinational firm ("parent company") engages in foreign direct investment, defined here as financially investing in facilities or physical assets—usually through a foreign subsidiary—with the expressed purpose of exploring for, manufacturing, or marketing a product in a foreign country, it does so with the understanding that its property rights are legally recognized by the host country government. It is generally agreed that host country governments may unilaterally engage in nationalization of specific privately owned or public/privately owned industries, whereby industry assets revert to public ownership. The process of nationalization, accomplished with compensation to the parent company, is called expropriation. If nationalization is undertaken by the host government without market-value compensation to the parent company, it is considered a case of confiscation, a recognized political risk associated with foreign direct investment decisions made by multinational executives.

However, there has evolved a general consensus among nations (*Resolution 1803 on Permanent Sovereignty over Natural Resources* by the United Nations General Assembly in 1962) that for a lawful nationalization of industries, it should be accompanied by "appropriate" compensation for private property. This United Nations Recommendation essentially upheld the "Hull Doctrine," generally supported by economically-developed countries, recognizing that under international law compensation should be "prompt, effective and adequate"—although a somewhat weaker term, "appropriate compensation," was substituted for "full value" of the expropriated property.

This United Nations Recommendation substantially rejected the "Calvo Doctrine," supported by many less economically developed countries, which left the question of compensation entirely with the host government, or the view of communist nations, whose ideology did not recognize "private property," thus the right of compensation. From the perspective of how the compensation should be measured, there remain two controversial and interrelated steps. The first step entails agreement on the market value of the expropriated property to ascertain the actual economic loss sustained by the shareholders (or private owners) of the multinational corporation. The second step involves a legal determination of the extent to which the shareholders (or private owners) are entitled to compensation for their economic loss.

One important and widely employed international mechanism for protecting a parent company's foreign direct investment is through the use of a bilateral investment treaty. This trade pact establishes the specific terms and conditions for private investment by corporations, or nationals, of one nation-state in the nation-state of the other treaty signatory. One typical feature addressed in bilateral investment treaties is protection from expropriation or confiscation by the host country. If an expropriation does take place, and insufficient compensation ("less than fair market value") is offered by the expropriating government, the bilateral investment treaty typically allows for the expropriated party to seek arbitration recourse through an alternative dispute resolution mechanism. In lieu of attempting to sue the host country in its domestic courts, or seeking legal recourse in home country courts (a difficult undertaking due to the "Sovereign Immunity Principle"), the leading organization employed to arbitrate such compensation disputes between home and host countries is the International Centre for the Resolution of Investment Disputes (ICSID).

The ICSID, established in 1966 under the World Bank–sponsored Convention on the Settlement of Investment Disputes between States and Nationals of Other States (also referred to as the "Washington Convention"), assists in alleviating noncommercial risks posing an impediment to the free flow of private investment among countries. The ICSID's primary purpose is to provide conflicted parties (subject to their mutual consent) facilities for conciliation and arbitration of international investment disputes. Not surprisingly, the ICSID is often referenced in bilateral investment treaties and international law. As of November 2007, there are 155 nation-states that are signatories to the Washington Convention and are thus eligible to employ the services of the ICSID in matters concerning expropriated or confiscated private property.

See Also: Bilateral Free Trade Agreement; Expropriation; Foreign Direct Investment; International Centre for Settlement of Investment Disputes; Nationalization.

Bibliography. International Centre for Settlement of Investment Disputes, *ICSID Convention, Regulations and Rules* (ICSID/15, 2006); J. L. Knetsch and T. E. Borcherding, "Expropriation of Private Property and the Basis for Compensation," *University of Toronto Law Journal* (v.29, 1979); P. Muchlinski, *International Enterprises and the Law* (Blackwell, 1995); E. L. Richards, *Law for Global Business* (Irwin, 1994).

Thomas A. Hemphill
University of Michigan–Flint

Competition

Competition exists in economic situations whenever two or more actors seek to outperform one another, in pursuit of some commonly identified goal. Markets are the most prominent site of economic competition, employing a price mechanism to connect buyers and sellers, with sellers competing against each other either through cutting prices or through improving the quality of the goods. Markets can experience an absence of competition where monopolies or cartels exist. However, nonmarket forms of economic competition are also significant, especially where technological innovation is concerned, and these are often compatible with monopolistic practices. As a socioeconomic principle, competition is often contrasted with cooperation.

Competitions can be "positive sum," "zero sum," or "negative sum." A positive-sum competition is one in which all parties are better off, in the aggregate, because they are competing against one another. It is one of the founding claims of economic science that markets are positive-sum competitions. This does not mean that some individuals, firms, or communities will not be worse off, but that the net effect of competition is a positive one. A zero-sum competition is one in which the benefits accrued to one party are at the direct and inevitable expense of another party. For example, should two individuals both lay claim to a piece of land, they face a zero-sum competition. A negative-sum competition is one in which all parties are worse off, in the aggregate, because they are competing against one another. Inasmuch as they destroy economic wealth, wars are negative-sum competitions. During periods in which economies contract, capitalism becomes a negative-sum competition.

The concept of competition evokes contrasting political, moral, and emotional responses. Where it is celebrated, it is associated with freedom, fairness, and pursuit of quality. This has tended to be the view of free market liberals and conservative political movements, which gathered momentum in many liberal democracies from the 1970s onward, and arose in former communist countries from the 1990s onward. However, it can also be denigrated, being associated with social atomization, disregard for the weak, and absence of collective direction. Socialists and critics of the free market tend to view competition in this way, and argue that it reduces or ignores the capacity of human beings to collaborate. Finally, a realist view of competition regards it as neither good nor bad, but a symptom of human nature. The Darwinian principle of "survival of the fittest" is commonly identified as operating in a free market economy, but in a more limited, less destructive form.

Even if markets and capitalism are positive-sum competitions, the question of how to treat the "losers" is an important political and economic question. This is exacerbated by the fact that the losers tend to cluster in certain areas of industry and geographic locations. The phenomenon of de-industrialization, for instance, which affected developed economies from the 1970s, meant that regions such as the American midwest and northeast Britain were harshly hit by loss of jobs and wealth. These jobs reappeared in low-wage economies such as China and Mexico, and economists would argue that the aggregate effect was a positive one. Yet the damage to the regions that "lost" in this international competition presents a challenge to the logic of free market economics. The concept of regional or national "competitiveness" refers to the capacity of a location to succeed rather than fail in the global economy, often through investing in public resources such as education and infrastructure.

Markets

A market exists where sellers compete against each other for the custom of buyers. Historically, markets have often been created in specific places, such as town squares or trading floors, meaning buyers and sellers meet each other face-to-face. The presence of multiple sellers competing in one place offers the buyer the freedom to choose the best deal. A physically located market has limits around how many buyers and sellers it can attract, which consequently limits the amount of competition and choice involved.

However, with technological advances and more sophisticated market structures, the number of buyers and sellers involved grows. If a customer is seeking to buy a car, and is restricted to the car dealers in a small town, then competition and choice are limited by geography. However, if the buyer is able to travel and to compare prices from dealers over a large region or internationally, then competition and choice increase. The development of electronic media such as the internet means that markets can become fully "virtual" and global, so competition hits unprecedented levels. Web sites such as eBay connect buyers and sellers around the world.

The fact that markets place sellers in competition with one another is central to why economists believe they are efficient. In an ideal marketplace, consumers judge the rival bargains on offer, and select the one that benefits them the most, taking into account both the utility and the price of the product. Sellers that offer good value for money will attract a lot of custom, whereas those that don't will not. This creates a clear incentive to sellers to cut prices and/or improve quality, which leads them to seek more efficient production techniques, and to shift resources into areas of production that match consumer demand.

It is crucial that the price of a good is allowed to fluctuate (sometimes in the course of a single deal, such as where "haggling" occurs) or else the competitive process stalls and efficiency is not maximized. It is equally crucial that buyers exercise freedom to select the seller who best serves their interests, or else the same problem arises. Where market competition and consumer choice are present, this ought to drive efficiencies throughout the rest of the economy, including into nonmarket spheres such as firms.

A common criticism of economics is that real-world markets are never as competitive as the model suggests. While there may be some markets, such as stock markets, in which prices are constantly changing, with buyers determining where resources are diverted to, there are a large number of markets that do not operate in this fashion. First, sellers may be bound by some informal, psychological, or cultural norms to maintain similar prices. If three tomato salesmen are in a marketplace, and all succeed in finding customers, there is little incentive for any of them to improve their deal to customers. This type of cooperation develops further if the sellers are socially acquainted with one another. Second, buyers often lack the time or the inclination to compare deals and select their preferred one, but buy the same product or brand repeatedly. Advertising and branding exist to build relationships between buyers and sellers, so that consumers do not choose every product as a one-off transaction, and sellers are not constantly operating in a situation of price competition.

Market Power

The significance of the price mechanism is that, in a competitive market, no single seller can control the price of a product. However, as competition reduces, either in quantity or in intensity, the possibility for a seller to control the price of a product arises. Where a seller—or group of sellers—is able to set the price regardless of consumer demand, this is an instance of market power. Market power is one of the four types of "market failure" identified in the tradition of welfare economics, the other three being "information asymmetries," "externalities," and "public goods." These tend to provide the justification for some sort of regulatory intervention.

Markets have a tendency to reduce the quantity of competition contained within them. This is for the simple reason that inefficient firms selling unappealing products will tend to go out of business, whereas efficient firms selling popular products will grow larger. Where markets contain a small number of sellers, they form what is known as an oligopoly. Where all competition is eliminated, the surviving seller has what is known as a monopoly.

Antitrust laws (also known as competition laws) exist to protect competition in the face of oligopolies and monopolies. However, a sharp distinction is now drawn between protecting competition and protecting competitors. The first piece of antitrust legislation ever created was the 1890 Sherman Act in the United States. From the 1940s until the early 1980s, antitrust law in the United States was regularly used to prevent firms from becoming too large, and to protect smaller firms from being squeezed out of markets. Oligopoly

and monopoly were viewed as undesirable in and of themselves, and smaller competitors therefore had to be defended by the state.

Since the 1980s, and the influx of Industrial Organization economics into antitrust policy, policy makers have viewed their role as protecting competition, not protecting competitors. Antitrust authorities now perceive that the presence of competitors in a market is not an automatic indicator of efficiency, and the absence of competitors not an automatic sign of inefficiency. The efficiency or otherwise of an industrial structure becomes a matter for empirical economic analysis. So long as firms are not acting deliberately to exclude potential competitors—for instance, via a cartel—then very large market shares are entirely permissible; indeed, they can be viewed as a sign of efficiency, and therefore beneficial to consumers.

European antitrust authorities have followed a similar path. Although cartels and monopolies were tolerated in many central European countries through the first half of the 20th century, competition authorities emerged in many European nations in the years following World War II. The German economic school of Ordo-Liberalism provided the intellectual foundations for German competition policy. Ordo-Liberalism treats competition as not only a means of achieving efficient economic outcomes, but as an important basis for political freedoms. The legal defense of competitive markets therefore takes on a distinctly ethical and political dimension.

Since the 1980s, the European Commission has become a more active force in European competition policy. Since the late 1990s, it has gradually converged with the American model of employing Industrial Organization economics to defend competition, not competitors. European policy makers use the term "dominance" rather than "market power," and view it as their role to prevent "abuse of dominance," rather than prevent dominance as such.

Anxiety regarding market power has tended to focus on large industrial producers, while political and historical factors also play a role. During periods when the free market is viewed as socially damaging, benign monopolists have been viewed favorably, and almost become an arm of government. When the free market is more in favor, large producers tend to be viewed with greater suspicion, except where they are competing in large, competitive markets. It is worth noting that buyers can also attain market power, where they create "buyers cartels" to fix the maximum price of a product.

Dynamic Competition

The arena of economic competition is never entirely fixed and stable. Where new products and services are being created and sold, they will often create entirely new markets in the process, and destroy previous ones. This process of competing through innovation and the creation of new markets is known as dynamic competition. It is contrasted with the "static competition" that takes place in a stable market, and is closely associated with the ideas of Austrian economist Joseph Schumpeter.

The driving force of dynamic competition is the entrepreneur who helps bridge the gap between technological innovation and buyers. Where a stable market involves several sellers competing to sell similar products, the entrepreneur offers a new product, and therefore initially has no competitors. If this new product somehow renders an existing one obsolete, then the market for that obsolete product is destroyed. This process of "creative destruction" is a different way of understanding the competitive process. Rather than view markets as the organizing frameworks of competition, markets become viewed as internal to competition. Competition becomes a constant remaking of the competitive arena itself.

There are at least two significant implications of this. First, it leads to a very different way of viewing monopolies. In a dynamically competitive environment, monopolies are both inevitable and desirable. The seller who succeeds through dynamic competition has, in all likelihood, taken some substantial risks. Unlike the seller in a stable market who simply reproduces what they (and their competitors) have been doing in the past, the creator of a new product has no certainty that their product will find a market of buyers at all. In order to take this gamble, they need the incentive of a big payoff at the other end. Where their new product succeeds in attracting demand, they will have a monopoly position, which they can exploit as a reward for the gamble. The venture capital industry exists to fuel dynamic competition, and gives an indication of the stakes involved. Venture capitalists expect only a small minority of the businesses they invest in to succeed, but they

also expect the rewards to be very large when success does occur.

In many circumstances, however, the monopoly is not sustainable for very long, which damages the incentives to make risky investments. This introduces a role for intellectual property rights such as patents. A patent is a legally entrenched right to exclusive use of a scientific or technological innovation, for a time-limited period. Intellectual property rights, and patents in particular, exist precisely to nurture innovation and dynamic competition. The individual or firm who makes the effort and takes the risk to produce something new is rewarded with a monopoly, not just in the very short term (what might be called "first mover advantage") but in the medium to long term. This allows them to recoup their investment, before the innovation is released for use by their competitors some years later. Patents are especially important in industries such as pharmaceuticals, in which a large amount of research and development is involved, and a large number of unsuccessful products developed.

This leads to the second significant issue, namely time horizons. As its name suggests, dynamic competition takes place over a period of time, but disputes arise over what are the most appropriate time horizons with which to view it. It is debatable how long an innovator should be permitted to have exclusive rights to their intellectual property. In the realm of competition policy, it is debatable whether (or for how long) an innovator should be permitted to exclude competitors through other nonlegal means.

Those who take a very long-term view argue that monopolies are never permanent, and some new innovation will eventually emerge to destroy the monopolist's power. But those who take a more short-term view would argue that allowing a single seller to have exclusive right to an innovation is still a form of market power, and thus inhibits consumer rights. On balance, antitrust authorities tend to have more sympathy with the latter view. U.S. merger guidelines, for instance, state that monopolistic practices are acceptable only if a new competitor is likely to arrive within two years. The notion that a newcomer will eventually arrive, while true, is not considered a sufficient basis to tolerate market power in the short and medium term.

See Also: Antitrust Laws; Capitalism; Globalization; Markets; Market Share; Patents.

Bibliography. Robert Bork, *The Antitrust Paradox: A Policy at War With Itself* (Macmillan, 1978); David Gerber, *Law and Competition in Twentieth Century Europe: Protecting Prometheus* (Clarendon, 1998); Frank Knight, *Risk Uncertainty & Profit* (Kelly & Millman, 1921); Frank Knight, *The Ethics of Competition and Other Essays* (Chicago University Press, 1935); Joseph Schumpeter, *Capitalism, Socialism & Democracy* (Routledge, 1976); Hans Thorelli, *The Federal Anti-trust Policy: Origination of an American Tradition* (Allen & Unwin, 1955); Harrison White, *Markets from Networks: Socioeconomic Models of Production* (Princeton University Press, 2002).

WILLIAM DAVIES
UNIVERSITY OF LONDON

Competitive Advantage of Nations

The seminal work of Michael E. Porter takes an Industrial Organization (IO) perspective on the management of a nation's assets. This theory aims to explain the reasons for the success of vendors from certain nations in specific branches or industries. Prominent examples are French luxury goods producers, German car manufacturers, Swiss watchmakers, and Japanese fax producers.

By differentiating a nation's production factors in general use factors (infrastructure, financial capital, and skilled labor, which are relevant to all industries) from specialized factors (employees with highly specialized competencies, universities working in specialized fields) and basic factors (land, natural resources, and unskilled labor) from advanced factors (technologies and competencies that make up the knowledge of a nation), Porter's theory challenges both the classic economic wisdom and the IO's conventional Structure-Conduct-Performance (SCP) paradigm:

- Only the basic factors predetermine the structure according to the SCP paradigm. The advanced factors are not inherited, but are created, rather, within a nation in the course of time. Noticeably, the advanced factors are relevant to explain the variance of a vendor's success in most developed industries. For instance, it was not the number of people in the Indian software industry that led to the success of software producers, but the solid mathematical and technical education that many of them possessed.

- In conflict with the classic economic theory, Porter argues that the lack of basic factors is likely to result in a competitive advantage, because it encourages companies to invest in technologies to overcome the disadvantage of scarce, basic resources. An empirical support is given by energy-saving durables created in Japan.

Within this theory, Porter challenges the unidirectional cause/effect relationship inherent to the SCP paradigm. Instead, Porter proposes the "Diamond" of four mutually-reinforcing national determinants. The basic diamond is made up of (1) factor conditions, (2) related and supporting industries, (3) demand conditions, and (4) firm strategy structure and rivalry. Governmental influences (5) and exogenous events by chance (6) are extensions that could reinforce these determinants.

Similar to the factor conditions, the demand conditions are in conflict with the classic economic intuition: A high volume of domestic demand by itself does not provide national vendors with a competitive advantage (which is commonly argued by economies of scale), but needs critical buyers insisting on superior quality of products and services. These customers force vendors always to offer the latest and innovative features and improve the ease of use and availability as well as the value-for-money ratio.

The related and supporting industries provide vendors with a symbiotic environment of strategic, relevant resources. For instance, German car manufacturers owe their success in the international competitive arena to their component suppliers providing them with innovative fuel-injection systems, anti-lock brake controls, etc. These related firms frequently accumulate in industry-specific clusters such as Silicon Valley in computer production or Hollywood in movie production.

The firm strategy, the structure of the industry, and the rivalry is not restricted to the consideration of the number of competing vendors. Instead of striving for monopoly profits by restricting access to the market, Porter claims that competition and rivalry are vital because they encourage both process- and product-related innovations. This argument is in line with the

Austrian School. The existence of intense domestic rivalry provides vendors with an opportunity for "training." Vendors who are used to coping with high levels of domestic rivalry are more likely to succeed in the international competitive arena. In addition, high levels of competition in the domestic market are motivation enough to internationalize or even globalize the business.

In line with this argument, Porter urges national governments to enforce competition rather than protect local vendors by imposing trade barriers. Capital, subsidies, and trade protection might be beneficial in the very early stages of development of an industry, but governments alone cannot foster a competitive advantage of firms in a particular industry. A current example are wind energy plants. Although most of the world's subsidies are granted by the German government, vendors from Denmark, the United States, Spain, and India have achieved substantial market shares in the wind energy industry.

Events of chance are more likely to result in a competitive advantage in nations' well-established diamonds. These events are not restricted to inventions and technological breakthroughs, but include price jumps for basic factors, like the recent rise in oil prices and fluctuations in exchange rates.

The main criticism of this theory stems from the consideration of nations as a demarcation feature of the basic unit of investigation. Thus, the concept does not comprise multinational firms adequately. Moreover, additional determinants such as the influence of national culture have been proposed.

See Also: Absolute Advantage; Comparative Advantage; Economies of Scale; Effective Rate of Protection; Factor Endowments; Leontief Paradox.

Bibliography. H. Davies and P. Ellis, "Porter's Competitive Advantage of Nations: A Time for the Final Judgement?" *Journal of Management Studies* (2000); R. M. Grant, "Porter's 'Competitive Advantage of Nations: An Assessment,'" *Strategic Management Journal* (1991); I. M. Kirzner, "Entrepreneurial Discovery and The Competitive Market Process: An Austrian Approach," *Journal of Economic Literature* (1997); N. J. O. O'Shaughnessy, "Michael Porter's Competitive Advantage Revisited," *Management Decision* (1996); M. E. Porter, *The Competitive Advantage of Nations* (Free Press, 1990); F. A. J. Van den Bosch and A. A. Van Prooijen, "The Competitive Advantage of European Nations: The Impact of National Culture—A Missing Element of Porter's Analysis?" *European Management Journal* (1992).

RALF WAGNER
UNIVERSITY OF KASSEL

Competitive Market Analysis

Competitive market analysis (CMA) is the analysis of the competing companies within a given industry, usually focusing on the top performers. A CMA of the American soft-drink industry, for instance, would usually focus on The Coca-Cola Company, PepsiCo, and the Dr Pepper Snapple Group; an analysis focusing on the New England region might also include Polar Beverages, Adirondack Beverages, and Cornucopia Beverages, the makers of Moxie. CMAs give interested parties—usually one of the companies in the industry—a lay of the land, a sense of the market landscape that goes beyond just the performance of a given company. Depending on the industry and the size of the company, CMAs may be prepared in-house or by outside analysts.

CMAs include, first of all, quantitative data—everything from publicly available information of the sort provided to shareholders (sales figures, capital, number of employees, expenses, et cetera) to figures derived from that data (the biggest sellers in the industry, the fastest-growing companies) to figures derived from both quantitative and qualitative data (ranking and rating the companies). Various metrics may be assessed for each company in the analysis, data that is only of interest when compared laterally among the companies in the field—for instance, in the case of the soft-drink industry, the transportation costs associated with product distribution, or the amount of money spent on sponsorships like Little League scoreboards. In the 21st century, CMAs will usually include search engine data in the analysis, noting the search engine rankings of the included companies with respect to various relevant keywords (which can be an exhaustive list, especially if the CMA concerns an industry that conducts a significant amount of business online, like mail order vendors or domain name services).

Qualitative data forms a significant part of the CMA. This can include everything from visual information—product and logo designs, branded merchandise, Web site screenshots—to consumer surveys. The emphasis of the qualitative data is to examine the points of similarity and difference among competing companies, and to evaluate their strengths and weaknesses relative to one another in as many areas as possible. Efficiency, consistency, and clarity are things looked for in the examination of qualitative data; visual information should convey what the company wants to convey, interactions between the consumer and the company should be consistent and should help to establish user expectations that the company can match, and the overall message should be clear. In the case of large companies or niche markets, these messages are necessarily more complicated than "Coca-Cola is better than Pepsi."

A competitive market analysis provides a business with an understanding of its competitors' strengths, liabilities, goals, and methods of reaching those goals, while putting its own operations in perspective. The business can learn from its competitor's mistakes—avoiding a coffee-cola since there seems to be little market for it, or marketing it differently if they are already committed to it—while also evaluating its competitor's strengths and seeing whether they can be emulated. At the same time, individual corporate identity, what defines competitors in the same field, might be brought into sharper focus. Television networks tend to strengthen their appeal to their existing demographic base, for instance, as well as competing with other networks—and in so doing, they decide which time slots are the most important to them, which audiences they most wish to attract. When fledgling network Fox moved its young animated sitcom *The Simpsons* to a new timeslot to compete directly against NBC's popular and well-respected *Cosby Show*, it was a deliberate move informed not by factors within the company but by factors in the larger market.

The final form of a CMA is a lengthy report that generally places raw data at the back. A summary of findings precedes a list of recommendations or critical findings, followed by less prioritized information organized by category. Analyses can also be conducted on a specific aspect of business operation, such as the popu-larity of soft drinks among senior citizens, or the effectiveness of Web presence for a soft-drink company.

Competitive market analysis can also be used in the process of price-setting, and is a common process in the real estate market (where the term "comparable market analysis" is sometimes used).

See Also: Advertising; Branding; Competition; Electronic Commerce; Industry Information; Market Audit; Marketing; Market Research.

Bibliography. Lee G. Cooper and Masako Nakanishi, *Market-Share Analysis: Evaluating Competitive Marketing Effectiveness* (Springer, 1989); Rainer Michaeli, *Competitive Intelligence: Competitive Advantage Through Analysis of Competition, Markets and Technologies* (Springer, 2009); Adrienne Schmitz, *Real Estate Market Analysis: A Case Study Approach* (Urban Land Institute, 2001).

BILL KTE'PI
INDEPENDENT SCHOLAR

Compliance

Compliance encapsulates numerous obligations that organizations of all types must fulfill. Compliance and the procedures established to meet requirements are becoming a key management concern that is central to running a successful business or organization. In an ever-widening statutory regulatory environment and with commitments to self-regulation, organizations must ensure that they satisfy relevant regulations and guidelines.

The role of compliance is an important area in business management and management in general. Managers and employees within any organization must, where appropriate, respect standards, codes, and regulations. This encompasses all areas of the organization's work that may need to comply with both substantive and modest regulatory conditions subject to the sector and location. Regulatory regimes are not static and evolve with modifications to legislation, which may transform a sector in a positive or negative manner (usually following discussion between the regulators and industry representatives ensuring compliance is reasonable).

Government bodies primarily "regulate" all aspects of economic activity (self-regulation and compliance guidelines can also be included in establishing and adhering to organizational or sector values). Compliance procedures and conditions may be applied to all aspects of the business and organizational behavior, which must be met or negotiated. It is therefore necessary to ensure that acceptable levels of protection and accountability are in place to limit unnecessary damage and harm. With the emergence of an animated global news media, which frequently scrutinizes the activities of companies and organizations in carrying out their responsibilities, good compliance records are essential.

In considering market regulation, compliance concerns may need to address issues of protectionist regulation (to limit monopolies and encourage competition, noticeable in mergers and acquisitions), consumer protection (fair pricing and customer care), systemic integrity (limiting abuses in knowledge differentials), and other organizational practices that impact stakeholders. Competition policies have been introduced by national regulators such as the Competition Commission in the United Kingdom to ensure merger and acquisition activity does not compromise competition.

Emerging Compliance

Emerging compliance is being improved in areas such as digital environments (entertainment and software) where codes of conduct covering intellectual property rights, copyright, and data protection are being abused. At the international level, concerns about protecting intellectual property are noted in the Agreement on Trade-Related International Property Rights (TRIPS) and other international agreements formulated by the World Trade Organization. Compliance demands and procedures vary among countries, which generates a plethora of problems that are difficult to solve (the enforcement issue being the most challenging part of compliance at the international level). The complications associated with the interpretation of regulations and compliance in international business generate further complexities that need to be understood and managed. In the absence of international coordination and sustained harmonization of international regulations, the emphasis for regulation is placed on national and regional regulators.

European Union

Within Europe, the regulatory environment is shaped by membership of the European Union, which seeks and expects a range of compliance with various regulations. Member states also have national regulatory frameworks that may differ from the European model. It is not unusual to find disparities within the state model. Sectors are increasingly regulated; for example, in the United Kingdom market regulation is identifiable in FSA (Financial Services Authority), finance; Oftel, telecommunications; Oflot, lottery; Ofwat, water services; Ofgas, gas services, supply; NICE, drug registration. Compliance practices are frequently amended, modified, and reviewed through monitoring and reviews that are undertaken to ensure that, where possible, regulation and compliance works properly (this frequently includes amendments arising from lobbying and sector concerns). Regulation and compliance is, however, far from simplistic. It can be contentious, unfair, and damaging to all parties.

The lobbying community representing business, most notable in Brussels and Washington, D.C., seeks to influence the conditions within the regulatory framework to reduce the exposure to compliance where unacceptable to a sector. Associations such as the International Chamber of Commerce and its various national and local offices represent business in seeking to reduce unnecessary compliance. This, of course, needs to be studied and assessed on a case by case basis.

Voluntary Codes of Conduct

Corporate governance and corporate social responsibilities have generated interest in voluntary codes of conduct. The desire to become a responsible corporate citizen and instill an effective compliance culture in a positive sense is improving the perception of responsible business behavior. Although far from complete, self-regulation is producing benefits to the company and is improving relations with customers and clients who are demanding responsible internal and external business relations.

Responsibility is increasingly a fundamental in well-managed organizations, for example, internally, health and safety and externally, meeting environmental regulations. The prevalence of risks in various business environments demands a high level of awareness in identifying problems from various sources and the effective management of them through compliance with the regulatory environment.

Compliance and regulation is notoriously complex and costly. Public and private organizations of various size respond in different ways to specific regulation. It is likely that the regulatory regimes in numerous countries will become more stringent in forcing companies and organizations to comply with codes, standards, and legislation. Therefore, companies and organizations need to recognize the full cost of compliance and the intended and unintended consequences of their operations.

See Also: Agreement on Trade-Related Aspects of Intellectual Property Rights; Corporate Social Responsibility; Environmental Standards; Legislation; Regulation; Risk Management.

Bibliography. E. Shea, *Environmental Law and Compliance* (Oxford University Press, 2002); A. Tarantino, *Manager's Guide to Compliance* (John Wiley & Sons, 2006).

PAUL D. SHEERAN
UNIVERSITY OF WINCHESTER

Concession (in Negotiation)

When should you offer something to another party when negotiating, how much should you provide, and in what manner should you do so? These are primary questions in the area of concession in negotiations.

In any type of negotiation, a concession is something that you provide to another party when trying to come to a mutually agreeable deal. Typically, two or more parties approach a negotiation with a list of interests—issues they wish to receive from the other parties involved. These can be tangible goods such as money, raw materials, or finished products. They may also be intangible items such as a confidentiality agreement, information exchange, or even an apology.

Concessions are essential for any negotiation to be successful. Consider a simple barter negotiation over the price for a piece of art. The seller wishes to trade the item for as much as possible, while the buyer wants to spend as little as possible. Their opening offers may be far apart, thus a series of concessions over price will

be necessary to come to a deal. The seller comes down in price while the buyer comes up, but where they ultimately end is a product of the concessions offered by each party. If neither party concedes on price, or if the concessions are inadequate to bridge the gap between the opening offers, then no deal is possible.

In a more complex negotiation, the mix of concessions across multiple issues is critically important. Many negotiations involve several issues, and those issues may be of different importance to each party. For example a job candidate may wish to negotiate over salary, benefits, and vacation days, but she might care more about vacation days than benefits. Conversely, a job recruiter may also wish to negotiate over those same issues, but he may be more concerned about benefits than vacation days. In such a case, negotiators should look for differences in the intensity of preferences in order to concede on items that matter to one party more than another. In addition, such concessions should not be made on individual items one at a time; rather negotiators can make package concessions. In a package concession, a negotiator will offer more or less of multiple items at once, allowing them to use the mix of issues to work toward a deal of mutual value.

The dynamics of concessions are very important in simple or complex negotiations. One example is bilateral versus unilateral concessions. A bilateral concession is when both parties in a negotiation concede something to the other in alternating turns. For example the seller of the piece of art reduces the price slightly followed immediately by the buyer increasing her offer slightly. In contrast, negotiators should be wary of unilateral concessions, where one party adjusts his offer multiple times before the other party makes any concessions. This creates a power imbalance and sends dangerous signals about the resources and skills available to the party making such concessions.

Concession size is also very important. The size of a concession sends an important signal to the other party about willingness to move any further. Utilizing decreasing concession size sends a signal to the other party that you are reaching your reservation point—the lowest or highest you'll go. In contrast, offering consistent concession increments may signal to the other party that you are willing to continue conceding well beyond the current offer. Typically, a negotiator will start with a modest concession, then increasingly cut the size of future concessions to signal when they can go no further.

The dynamics of concessions in negotiations can vary dramatically across cultures. Much research on the topic has shown that negotiation style can be culturally driven. For example, some cultures have a more communal negotiation style, where the overall result is most important. In contrast, other cultures take an individualistic negotiation approach, where the result for a single party is what matters most. Other differences can manifest in the tone of how concessions are offered. In hierarchical cultures, status differences between parties can be critical in how concessions are offered. Typically someone of a lower status will ask for a concession in highly deferential ways in such cultures. In contrast, concessions may be requested similarly in egalitarian cultures, where status differences play less of a role in the dynamics of negotiated outcomes.

See Also: Arbitration; Decision Making; Mediation; Negotiation and Negotiating Styles.

Bibliography. D. M. Kolb and J. Williams, *The Shadow Negotiation* (Simon & Schuster, 2000); D. A. Lax and J. K. Sebenius, *The Manager as Negotiator* (The Free Press, 1986); R. Lewicki, *Decision-Making in Conflict Situations* (National Institute for Dispute Resolution, 1985); William Hernandez Requejo and John L. Graham, *Global Negotiation: The New Rules* (Palgrave Macmillan, 2008).

MICHAEL ALAN SACKS
EMORY UNIVERSITY

Concurrent Engineering

Concurrent engineering (CE) is an approach to new product development, which differs from the traditional approach because new product development tasks are performed simultaneously, instead of in a sequence. Another fundamental difference between CE and traditional product development is the fact that all relevant aspects of product development are considered throughout all phases, from product concept to delivery of the product to customers.

Historically, it is possible to trace the roots of a sequential or relay-like product development process to scientific administration. Roughly, the best way to have a large task (i.e., developing a new product) accomplished is to divide it into smaller tasks and complete them in a timely sequence. The process worked well for many years and still works in less dynamic markets.

In the 1980s, however, American manufacturers were trying to catch up with Japanese manufacturing prowess and they discovered, among other things, an entirely different way of managing product development. Two Japanese researchers, I. Nonaka and H. Takeuchi, published "The New New Product Development Game" in the *Harvard Business Review* in 1986. The article, an instant classic in business literature, exposed the underpinning philosophy of the Japanese way of developing products and sparked a movement that made concurrent engineering a mainstream approach to product development.

From the viewpoint of process, CE is nonsequential with upstream and downstream activities overlapped and generally processed simultaneously. Also, tasks are not distributed over the functional areas independently; commonly, they are interactively performed and managed according to cross-functional teams.

The first characteristic of these teams is that they are formed from individuals from the various areas relevant to product development, therefore holding complementary capabilities. Ultimately, the idea is to develop the product from a multifaceted view of customers' needs. Generally, marketing, design, engineering, manufacturing, logistics, sales, and even partners, suppliers, and customers take part in the process. Second, organization, management, and performance appraisal is generally by project rather than function.

Finally, CE collects all relevant information/knowledge for new product development (NPD) from manufacturability to customer service. That represents an opportunity and a challenge: An opportunity because it is desirable to combine different views of product development to achieve maximum value perceived by customers. In other words, each function might understand well a nuance that is not well perceived by another. It is a challenge because traditionally functional areas focus on different, sometimes conflicting, aspects of a new product; for example, while engineers may be concerned with functionality, designers may be concerned with aesthetics, and finance concerned with the bottom line. Second, technical capabilities and experience naturally diverge among individuals. Team members have received different formal education, and they have experienced NPD from different perspectives. Therefore, communication tends to be a challenge.

Benefits and Drawbacks

Concurrent engineering is generally associated with reducing time-to-market, optimizing overall NPD expenditures, and delivering better target products or services. Concurrent engineering helps organizations reduce time-to-market because development tasks are performed in parallel as opposed to time sequenced, and because transitions between phases of the project are generally smooth and fast; finally, because there are fewer errors and less reworking, when problems are found, they are generally found much sooner.

CE helps to deliver better target products or services because it makes it easier to match tight project timelines and target costs. More importantly, because it takes into consideration various perspectives among functions involved in product development throughout the entire process, a much sharper picture of what customers want is developed and delivered as a product or service.

In terms of shortcomings, CE is not well-suited for extremely large and complex projects with relatively predictable results such as building a bridge. Also, behind concurrent engineering there is an entirely new way of thinking about product development that needs to be in accordance with the organization's culture. CE is better suited to enterprises where there is excellent communication, openness, and a structure organized by project as opposed to hierarchical by functions. Finally, perhaps more than other approaches to product development, concurrent engineering demands excellent project management skills, techniques, and procedures.

See Also: Product Development; Product Life Cycle Hypothesis; Research and Development; Risk Management; Teams.

Bibliography. Chris J. Backhouse and Naomi J. Brookes, *Concurrent Engineering: What's Working Where?* (John Wiley & Sons, 1997); R. Balamuralikrishna, R. Athinarayanan, and X. Song, "The Relevance of Concurrent Engineering in Industrial Technology Programs," *Journal of Industrial Technology* (v.16/3, 2000); R. Handfield and

C. McDermott, "Concurrent Development and Strategic Outsourcing: Do the Rules Change in Breakthrough Innovation?" *The Journal of High Technology Management Research* (v.11/1, 2000); O. Hauptman and K. K. Hirji, "Managing Integration and Coordination in Cross-Functional Teams: An International Study of Concurrent Engineering Product Development," *R&D Management* (v.29/2, 1999); I. Nonaka and H. Takeuchi, "The New New Product Development Game," *Harvard Business Review* (January–February, 1986); P. G. Smith, "Concurrent Engineering Teams," in *Field Guide to Project Management*, D. I. Cleland, ed. (John Wiley & Sons, 1998); K. Umemoto, A. Ando, and M. Machado, "From Sashimi to Zen-In: The Evolution of Concurrent Engineering at Fuji-Xerox," *Journal of Knowledge Management* (v.8/4, 2004).

MARCELO A. MACHADO
KWANTLEN UNIVERSITY COLLEGE

Confidentiality

The confidentiality of personal and business information is an increasingly important issue in international business law. Jurisdictions differ significantly in the scope and depth of protection provided for both personal data (e.g., medical information) and business information (e.g., the details of a person's or company's bank accounts). Failure to comply with a jurisdiction's confidentiality laws can result in criminal penalties in some instances, and businesses operating in multiple jurisdictions must take care to comply with the relevant law in each.

Confidentiality rules have grown increasingly complex since the widespread adoption of generalized confidentiality statutes and regulations in the 1970s. For example, the United Nations Declaration of Human Rights lists privacy as a basic human right, and the European Union (EU) passed a Data Protection Directive in 1995 that requires all data processing to have a "proper legal basis" that incorporates a balance between the vital interests of the data subject, the legitimate interests of those controlling the data, and any contractual obligations. The directive requires that anyone about whom data is collected has a right of access to it, to have inaccurate data corrected, recourse against anyone who unlawfully processes the data, to withhold permission for the use of the data in certain circumstances, and to know the source of the data. Sensitive data concerning ethnicity, religion, political views, sexual history, union membership, or health can only be processed with explicit consent. Further EU rules govern transfer of data from within EU countries to agencies outside the EU. These rules have proven complicated to implement, leading to a lengthy disagreement with the United States over the provision of airline passenger lists in 2005.

One key area of disagreement among jurisdictions is the privacy of financial information. Offshore financial centers like the Channel Islands, the Isle of Man, Switzerland, Luxembourg, Bermuda, the Cayman Islands, the Bahamas, and others tend to have strong confidentiality laws protecting financial information. Governments in larger economies, such as Germany, France, and the United States, tend to view financial confidentiality as a means of tax avoidance and tax evasion and seek to undermine domestic confidentiality rules through international agreements that encourage the sharing of financial information between governments. In 2008 the German government sparked a major international controversy by purchasing stolen confidential financial information from a former employee of a Liechtenstein bank and using the information in tax evasion investigations in Germany.

Confidentiality with respect to financial matters has a long history, with some arguing that it has roots in the Code of Hammurabi in Babylon and biblical texts. More recently, European civil codes incorporated financial privacy provisions and a common law duty in jurisdictions that follow British law from the 1924 case of *Tournier v. National Provincial Bank. Tournier* concerned a bank official who told an employer that one of his employees had bounced checks and that the bank suspected a gambling problem. As a result, the employee was fired. The English court found for the employee, holding that the bank had a duty to protect the employee's financial privacy. Confidentiality should be distinguished from secrecy, associated with anonymous bank accounts, bearer bonds, and the like. Most jurisdictions no longer permit secrecy with respect to financial matters, but confidentiality remains an important legal concept.

Expanding on the historical code provisions and *Tournier*, jurisdictions like Switzerland and the Cayman Islands have created statutory confidentiality regimes that structure the relationship between individuals and financial institutions. For example, under the Caymanian Confidential Relationships (Preservation) Law 1979, information cannot be disclosed without consent or an order from the local court. Like many such laws, the statute goes beyond the specific banking context of *Tournier* to cover:

> confidential information with respect to business of a professional nature which arises in or is brought to the Islands and to all persons coming into the possession of such information at any time thereafter whether they be within the jurisdiction or thereout.

Criminal sanctions, including imprisonment, apply to those who breach the statute.

Although there are statutory exceptions to the requirement of consent, countries concerned with tax issues find these inadequate in many instances. For example, while most jurisdictions' statutes make exceptions for criminal investigations, the exceptions typically only apply to matters that are a domestic crime as well. This precludes disclosure of most information related to income tax evasion investigations in jurisdictions that lack an income tax, such as the Cayman Islands.

Disputes over confidentiality in financial matters are likely to continue to be a major issue between the Organisation for Economic Co-operation and Development (OECD) countries and jurisdictions with economies that specialize in financial transactions. In addition, conflicting confidentiality laws and regulations will continue to be a problem in areas from national security to transportation, as different jurisdictions seek to ensure that businesses operating within their borders comply with local laws.

See Also: European Union; Financial Market Regulation; Global Capital Market; Globalization; Tax Havens.

Bibliography. Rose Marie Antoine, *Confidentiality in Offshore Financial Law* (Oxford, 2002); *Tournier v. National Provincial Bank* (1K.B. 461, 1924); *Toward a Level Playing Field: Regulating Corporate Vehicles in Cross-Border Transactions* (International Tax and Investment Organization, 2002).

ANDREW P. MORRISS
UNIVERSITY OF ILLINOIS

Conformance/Conformity

Conformance or conformity is generally defined as adherence to a standard, specification, or regulation. In literature, this concept usually means adjusting behaviors to align with the norms of the group. Norms are the unwritten rules or standards of behavior for group members that will result in a kind of "equilibrium" pattern of behavior across group members. Usually, the more heterogeneous a group is in its membership (gender, ethnicity, age, etc.), the slower a group will develop stable norms. Norms cover every aspect of our social life, from performance (such as how hard to work for what kind of quality and levels of tardiness), appearance (such as personal dress, when to look busy, when to slack off, or how to show loyalty), social arrangement (such as how team members interact), to allocation of resources (such as pay, assignments, allocation of tools and equipment). In a way, our social life is maintained by implicit or explicit norms.

Homogenous groups tend to establish norms faster; in business, this may affect both decision making and team performance.

To conform is to change or adjust behavior or attitudes to the perceived norms of a certain group so that there is a perceived agreement or correspondence between one's behavior and the behavior of most members in a group. Sometimes conforming is quite automatic, and at other times people feel pressure to fit in with the crowd. Within the above definition, it is important to highlight that the change in behavior or attitude is a result of either a real pressure or an imagined pressure from external sources. Typically, it is because of larger societal understandings and implicit norms (pressure) that one should be, for example, subdued at church, casual at a bar, and patient when in line.

The classic studies done in the area of conformity are both amazing and disturbing in their implications. They give us insight into the willingness to conform at inappropriate times, and what it takes to resist. For example, S. Milgram's obedience experiments are probably one of the classic and infamous sets of studies in social psychology. He studied a dilemma that when following one rule (e.g., following the directions of an expert) means breaking another (e.g., hurting another human being), how are we to know which rule to follow? He found that people are willing to obey an authority figure who instructed them to perform acts that conflicted with their personal conscience. Those of us who read about Milgram's obedience experiments often mistakenly conclude that people are evil and would harm a stranger if given the opportunity. Attributing cruelty to the internal (evil) disposition of the participant misses the whole point of Milgram's experiment—which is that the situational factors, not the individual character, determine behavior in the obedience paradigm.

Another famous study on conformity was conducted by Solomon Asch where he examined the extent to which pressure from other people could affect one's perceptions. In his experiment, he asked the subject to make a judgment of line length (which was designed in such an obvious manner that it was impossible to make a mistake) after the other "subjects" unanimously chose an obvious wrong line (certainly all the other "subjects" were confederates who had been instructed to give incorrect answers). In total, about one-third of the subjects who were placed in this situation went along with the clearly erroneous majority. Why did the subjects conform so readily? When they were interviewed after the experiment, most of them said that they did not really believe their conforming answers, but had gone along with the group for fear of being ridiculed or thought "peculiar."

Apparently, people conform for two main reasons: Because they want to be liked by the group and because they believe the group is better informed than they are. However, not everyone conforms in any situation. A few factors such as group size, unanimity, group composition, cohesion, status, public response, prior commitment, and individual self-confidence will contribute to the likelihood of conformity. For example, social psychologists have been trying to figure out if gender differences play a role in conformity. Possibly because of the stereotype that women are supposed to be submissive, past research about conformity found that women consistently conformed more than did men. However, some researchers found that when women were unfamiliar with the tasks presented in an experiment (such as questions about sports) they were more likely to conform. However, when men were subjected to the same situation (for example, if they were asked questions about fashion) they showed a higher conformity rate. Since many of the studies that showed a gender difference included tasks and topics that were more geared toward men's interests, it should not be surprising that the results showed a gender difference that in reality might not exist.

Another major reason why some people avoid conforming is their desire to be an individual. Individuation is to emphasize one's own uniqueness in order to stand out from the crowd. Most people do not mind conforming most of the time, but still like to think of themselves as individuals, thus not conforming.

Conformity can be destructive, such as when a military unit kills unarmed civilians. Conformity can be constructive, such as when people hurriedly follow each other out of a burning building. Nonconformity can be constructive, such as when a business executive blows the whistle on his corporation's unethical business practices. Yet nonconformity can also be destructive, such as when an antiwar protester decides that violence is the only way to get across his message. Thus, conformity is neither good nor bad in and of itself. It depends a great deal on the context and our values.

See Also: Accountability; Attitudes and Attitude Change; Corruption; Cultural Norms and Scripts; Culture-specific Values; Decision Making; Enculturation; Teams.

Bibliography. S. E. Asch, "Opinions and Social Pressure," *Scientific American* (1955); S. Milgram, *Perils of Obedience* (Harper, 1973).

BING RAN
PENNSYLVANIA STATE UNIVERSITY–HARRISBURG

Confucian Work Dynamism

Confucius was a Chinese philosopher who lived around 500 B.C. and wrote extensively about the pragmatic rules of living. Geert Hofstede and Michael Bond's research on global cultures demonstrated that individuals and firms in China and other Asian countries focused on a dynamic future-oriented mentality and reflected a deep sense of harmony and stable relationships, as recommended in Confucius's writings, and labeled this dimension of culture "Confucian work dynamism."

The interest in Confucian work dynamism and future orientation emanated from a rise in competitive dominance in the latter part of the 20th century of some East Asian countries such as Japan and the "four dragons" (or "tigers")—Hong Kong, Singapore, South Korea, and Taiwan—as well as south Asian countries such as Malaysia, Thailand, and Indonesia. Immigrant Chinese families controlled most of the business and economic operations in many of these countries, and researchers attributed their success primarily to their reliance on the Confucian work ethic, which focused on the quality of relationships a person maintained, as well as their performance of their social and civic duties.

The Confucian work dynamism scale was based on an instrument called the Chinese Value Survey (CVS), which was administered in 23 countries and based on the values as seen by native Chinese social scientists. In addition to the four cultural dimensions identified by Geert Hofstede, Michael Bond discovered a new dimension and labeled it "Confucian work dynamism," to emphasize the importance of practical ethics based on the following principles: (1) the permanence of society is contingent on imbalanced relationships expressing mutual and complementary obligations between father and son, older and younger brother, ruler and subject; (2) "virtuous behavior" toward others entails not treating others as one would not like to be treated by them; (3) the family is the foundation and archetype of all social organizations; individuality should be subdued if it diminishes harmony, and it is very important to maintain everybody's face by preserving others' dignity; (4) virtues in life involve acquiring skills and education, working hard, being thrifty, having a sense of shame, and being patient and persevering;

A group of workers on a tea plantation in China, where the Confucian work ethic may be contributing to economic growth.

Some have argued that Confucian dynamism is also associated with a system of authoritarian pluralism distinguishable from the liberal democracies of the Western world. For example, drug trafficking is heavily penalized in countries such as Singapore, Malaysia, and Thailand. Divorce rates are significantly lower than those of Western societies as family is relied upon as a form of social insurance. Attacks on other beliefs are relentlessly pursued, since most societies are pluralistic as far as religions are concerned. Finally, the press is free, yet not a "fourth estate"—while the freedom of the press is valued as a stipulation for good governance, it has no absolute right and is expected to blend with the national consensus.

Hofstede and others in their later empirical studies observed that the Confucian Dynamism Index taps into only certain aspects of Confucian ethics and excludes others such as filial piety and hence reinterpreted the meaning of this construct as "long-term orientation." This dimension depicts the fostering of virtues oriented toward future rewards, particularly perseverance and thrift. On the other hand, the polar opposite term, short-term orientation, represents cultivation of the virtues related to past and present, in particular, respect for tradition, preservation of face, and fulfilling social obligations.

Certain facets of Confucian societies and their related explanations have been questioned. For example, a high rate of savings, which is considered a distinguishing feature of these societies, may be caused by comparatively high costs of consumption coupled with the high taxes on consumption and the poor availability of social security for the elderly, rather than just long-term orientation.

Second, even though "persistence" and "thrift" are positively loaded on the Confucian Dynamism Index, the index also includes other items that have inconsequential association with long-term orientation, such as "ordering relationships by status and observing this order" and "having a sense of shame." Moreover, some negatively related items, such as "respect for tradition" and "personal steadiness and stability" are not necessarily inversely related to long-term orientation. To the contrary, positive relationships have been shown between taking a long-term perspective and appreciation of how history and tradition define opportunities and capabilities for the future.

and (5) individuals should have a sense of commitment and organizational identity and loyalty.

The Confucian Work Dynamism Index has been shown to be positively correlated with the economic growth of countries as well as to entrepreneurship orientation. Scholars also hypothesized that a high savings rate in east and southeast Asian countries was a consequence of the Confucian ethic that promoted long-term orientation. Predictably, these societies scored high on the Confucian Dynamism Index, while Western societies scored lower. Interestingly, some non-Confucian countries like India and Brazil have also scored high on this dimension.

In other empirical studies, the Confucian Dynamism Index has been shown to be negatively correlated to "this year's profits," but positively correlated to "profits 10 years from now." It has also been shown to be strongly positively related to a measure of "marginal propensity to save."

Finally, William Ouchi's work identified reasons other than the Confucian work ethic as shaping a country's (particularly Japan's) long-term orientation. Because Japan has limited arable land, the planting and harvesting of crops can only be accomplished with the cooperation of 20 or more people. Hence, it is more out of necessity rather than cultural considerations that people in this society have developed the skills to work together in harmony and where individual concerns are outweighed by concerns for group welfare.

See Also: Asian Tigers; China; Cross-Cultural Research; Cultural Norms and Scripts; Culture-Specific Values; Entrepreneurship; Gannon's Cultural Metaphors; Guanxi; Hofstede's Five Dimensions of Culture; Japan; Schwartz Value Theory.

Bibliography. Neal Ashkanasy, Vipin Gupta, Melinda S. Mayfield, and Edwin Trevor Roberts, "Future Orientation," in *Culture, Leadership and Organizations: The Globe Study of 62 Societies*, R. J. House et al., eds. (Sage, 2004); Kuochung Chang and Cherng G. Ding, "An Exploratory Study of the Effects of Chinese Cultural Characteristics on the PRC Governmental Buying Behavior," *Journal of International Marketing and Marketing Research* (v.21, 1996); Richard H. Franke, Geert Hofstede, and Michael H. Bond, "Cultural Roots of Economic Performance: A Research Note," *Strategic Management Journal* (v.12, 1991); Geert Hofstede, *Culture's Consequences: Comparing Values, Behaviors, Institutions and Organizations Across Nations* (Sage, 2001); Geert Hofstede and Michael H. Bond, "The Confucius Connection: From Cultural Roots to Economic Growth," *Organizational Dynamics* (v.16/4, 1988); D. S. Hong, "Dynamics of Asian Workplaces—An Introductory Essay," *Work and Occupations* (v.24/1, 1997); Bih-Shiaw Jaw, Ya-Hui Ling, Christina Yu-Ping Wang, and Wen-Ching Chang, "The Impact of Culture on Chinese Employees' Work Values," *Personnel Review* (v.36/5–6, 2007); David A. Ralston et al., "Eastern Values: A Comparison of Managers in the United States, Hong Kong, and the People's Republic of China," *Journal of Applied Psychology* (v.77/5, 1992); Christopher J. Robertson and James J. Hoffman, "How Different Are We? An Investigation of Confucian Values in the United States," *Journal of Managerial Issues* (v.12, 2000).

ABHIJIT ROY
UNIVERSITY OF SCRANTON

ConocoPhillips

Headquartered in Houston, Texas, ConocoPhillips operates in the energy sector and has operations in 40 countries. Conoco and Phillips merged in 2002 and created ConocoPhillips, which then acquired Burlington Resources in 2006. ConocoPhillips currently employs 33,000 people and has US$183 billion of assets. ConocoPhillips was ranked 9th, 10th, and 12th in 2007, 2006, and 2005, respectively, in the Fortune Global 500 list. ConocoPhillips is the third largest integrated energy company in the United States in terms of market capitalization and oil and natural gas reserves. Among key competitive advantages of ConocoPhillips are reservoir management and exploration, 3-D seismic technology, high-grade petroleum coke upgrading, and sulfur removal.

Conoco, called the Continental Oil and Transportation Co. in 1875 when it was established, was one of the first petroleum marketers in the West. Conoco's founder, Isaac E. Blake, started the company out of his vision of lighting houses using kerosene instead of candles and whale oil. The company introduced many new products such as benzene to clean stoves, candles, ready-mixed paints, hoof oil for horses, and even a popular medicinal ointment.

In 2002 Conoco decided to merge with Phillips Co. Phillips, then called Phillips Petroleum Company, was established in 1907 in Oklahoma. The founders, brothers named Frank and L. E. Phillips, both had an entrepreneurial spirit and were innovative. The Phillips brothers pioneered the natural gas industry by opening in 1917 the first natural gasoline plant for extracting liquid by-products from natural gas, which allowed the liquid by-products to be used in motor fuels. The company continued to research new opportunities, including gas-processing plant technologies. The company formed its research and development group to continue its innovations; its focus on research and development and innovation continues today.

Burlington Resources was established in the 1860s. The discovery of oil and gas on the company's land brought change in the 1980s, and Burlington Resources expanded into the oil and gas industry. During the 1990s, Burlington Resources became the nation's largest independent natural gas exploration and production company. In 2006 ConocoPhillips acquired Burlington Resources.

The operations of ConocoPhillips are as follows. The exploration and production group explores and produces oil, natural gas, and natural liquids around the world; this group has exploration operations in 23 countries and production facilities in 16 countries. Another group is responsible for refining, marketing, and transporting oil, and is the second-largest refiner in the United States, with 12 U.S. refineries, six in Europe, and one in Asia. The natural gas gathering, processing, and marketing group is responsible for the natural gas operations of ConocoPhillips and has 63 natural gas processing plants. The chemicals and plastics group produces chemicals and plastics through Chevron Phillips Chemical Company LLC, a joint venture with Chevron and one of the world's largest producers of many chemical and plastic-related products. In addition to these four groups, ConocoPhillips focuses on developing new energy sources and technologies from conventional to heavy oil and natural gas to alternative supplies of energy. Among its emerging businesses are biofuels, power generation, and proprietary technologies.

Conoco was the first company that established filling stations and constructed refineries, and it developed and received a patent for the Vibrosis method of seismic oil exploration in the United States. Phillips was the first company to develop and market propane for home heating and cooking, built the first long-distance multiproduct pipeline, and invented a process to make high-octane gasoline possible. The acquisition of Burlington Resources enhanced the company's position as a leading producer and marketer of natural gas. ConocoPhillips's recent activities remain innovative and include commercial production of renewable diesel fuel, the first Alpine satellite oil field, a global water sustainability center, and a partnership with Tyson Foods, Inc., to produce renewable diesel fuel.

See Also: Acquisitions, Takeovers, and Mergers; Chevron; Entrepreneurship; ExxonMobil.

Bibliography. D. Carey et al., *Harvard Business Review on Mergers & Acquisitions* (Harvard Business School Press, 2001); ConocoPhillips Company, www.conocophillips.com (cited March 2009).

Serkan Yalcin
Saint Louis University

Consumer Behavior

Consumer behavior is essentially the attitudes, intentions, decisions, and actions of individuals as everyday consumers in the marketplace. The study of consumer behavior is embedded in a host of domains in social and behavioral sciences, such as anthropology, psychology, sociology, economics, and history, with reflection on social psychology, marketing, and management. As explaining and predicting consumer behavior can be very challenging, it becomes more so for marketers doing business globally compared with nationally or regionally. This is because planning and implementing marketing efforts necessitates a profound understanding of consumer motivations and expectations along many cognitive, affective, and behavioral dimensions; consequently, this can differ substantially across country boundaries, given that consumer behavior is subject to cultural, economic, and societal influences. Identifying the extent of consumer deliberation in decision processes is also essential to facilitate efficient and effective marketing communication efforts in international operations.

A prominent view of consumer behavior is how it is embedded in capitalism, marketing, and consumption ideologies. Such consumption ideologies can be traced back to Georg Simmel in the 1900s. Also motivated by scholars such as Max Horkheimer and Theodor Adorno in 1944, this study expanded over time through sociologists, anthropologists, historians, economists, and specialized consumer behaviorists and consumer psychologists. Studies in the area of consumer research in many instances rely on consumption ideologies as a background presumption, where those studies proceed to investigate its corollaries and implications.

The American Marketing Association (AMA), the largest professional marketing association in North America for individuals and organizations involved in the practice, teaching, and study of marketing worldwide, describes consumer behavior as the outcome of two main components: marketing and psychology. This view presents consumer behavior as the dynamic interaction of affect and cognition, behavior, and environmental events by which people conduct the trading facets of their lives. According to this perspective, social psychology (a study of the two-way influence between social groups and an individual's attitudes, motivations, and actions such as reference group influences) and cognitive psychology (a study of all knowledge and mental behavior such as attention, perception, comprehension, memory, and decision making) represent the two main disciplines that the AMA describes as germane to studies of consumer behavior.

Systematic studies of consumer behavior emerged only with the rise in mass production, communication, and sales through big organizations. Advertising and marketing research started earlier in the century in North America and Europe with the objective of practically investigating how to market goods to consumers. Consumer behavior research commenced in the marketing departments of business colleges and universities in the United States in the 1950s. However, it was still tied to economic studies of the consumer as a rational individual having innate needs to be met by produced goods and services, disregarding social and marketing influences. Afterward, motivation research emerged, which involved the use of analytical methods of investigation such as in-depth interviews, focus groups, and projective techniques. It hence started probing into the emotional aspects of consumer attitudes and actions. This path was more psychology-linked, and it was undertaken both in academic research and in the business world.

However, looking into subconscious consumer actions and perceptions as such came to be considered by some as unethical and manipulative, which led to the relative decline of the use of motivational research at that point. Starting in the late 1960s, scientific experimentation spread widely, where studies of the consumer as a rational information processor acquiring and analyzing information in order to make brand choices became dominant. This motivated information processing theories of consumer behavior to dominate related research in the 1960s and 1970s, where they were moderated by psychological processes and also incorporated some individual differences and social and cultural influences. New perspectives of consumer behavior emerged in the 1980s that differed from the earlier positivist philosophies (those based on the notion that only scientific knowledge is genuine knowledge, and the latter can only come from positive verification of theories through strict scientific method and methodologies) that had taken over the field until that period in time.

The new shift that relied on nonpositivist philosophies, involving more qualitative and naturalistic research, caused a stir in the field between supporters and skeptics. However, it broadened studies in the domain of consumer behavior to become multi- and inter-disciplinary, where scientists from other disciplines such as sociology and anthropology engaged with interest in studying "the consumer" alongside psychologists and economists. This more recent consumer behavior perspective addresses the study of consumption and purchase decision processes of products/services as also carrying some symbolic, cultural, and emotional implications, even those decision processes of products once thought to be solely based on rational choice behavior (e.g., the decision to buy a car or a washing machine). Along these lines, consumers are perceived as socially connected human beings constituting part of a network of cultures, and consumption is analyzed as an integral part of human existence.

Behavior Models

Models of consumer behavior depict steps and activities that individuals experience in searching for, evaluating, selecting, purchasing, using, and discarding products/services with the objective of fulfilling needs, wants, and desires. The standard model of the consumer purchase decision process involves a number of steps that basically are problem recognition, information search, evaluation, purchase, and post-purchase evaluation. Consumer buying behavior is largely linked to the consumer's level of involvement and perceived differences among brands offered on the market. These two important criteria distinguish four common characterizations of purchase-related behavior: Complex buying behavior, habitual buying behavior, variety-seeking buying behavior, and dissonance-reducing buying behavior. Complex buying behavior involves a high level of consumer involvement in the purchase, where the consumer perceives many significant differences among available brand choices; an example of this behavior is illustrated in a consumer engaged in the decision to purchase a new car. In habitual buying behavior, involvement in the purchase is low and the consumer perceives a few significant differences among available brands. This can be exemplified in a consumer buying weekly or monthly food groceries such as bread, cooking oil, salt, etc.

In the case of variety-seeking buying behavior, a low level of consumer involvement in the purchase is coupled with the consumer perceiving significant differences among the brands; this can result in the consumer engaging in a great deal of switching among brands in order to experience each and satisfy his/her variety-seeking tendency. An example of this behavior is in the purchase of varieties of cheese, yogurt, or desserts, or in the purchase of a shampoo or liquid hand soap. In such cases, the purchase for the consumer might be characterized by a low level of involvement emanating from habit and routine; however, prior knowledge and/or usage may lead to perceived differences among various brands, motivating the consumer to switch among them in repeat purchases to pursue diversity.

Lastly, dissonance-reducing buying behavior is characterized by a high level of involvement in the purchase but a few significant differences perceived between available brands; in such cases, though the consumer takes time and effort in the purchase process, the purchase action takes place more quickly than expected due to the absence of important differences between alternative brands on the market. An example of this buying behavior is a parent in the process of purchasing an educational toy for his/her child; the parent may decide to look with involvement into a number of options for comparison purposes; however, the planned effort and time may be cut short by a perceived lack of difference in the features exhibited in available alternatives.

Though examination of consumer buying behavior focuses on elements linked to purchase decisions, investigating the behavior of consumers encompasses an extensive set of other phenomena. This includes other facets such as beliefs, inferences, attitudes, preferences, intentions, and memories occurring before and/or after consumption. This is reflected in attempts to understand issues such as customer satisfaction, consumer search and choice, purchase rationalization, regret and returns, brand loyalty, and switching behavior, among many others. Adoption behavior also represents a significant phenomenon exhibited in the consumer adoption decision process (modeled into steps of awareness, interest and information search, evaluation, trial, and adoption/rejection). This links to innovation diffusion and innovative behavior that affects such notions as timing of choice and adoption

The buying process involves problem recognition, information search, evaluation, purchase, and post-purchase evaluation.

and is influenced by consumer-specific and market-related factors.

Consumer behavior embodies a broad formalization of its phenomena through existing consumer behavior theories that evolved over time and continue to develop further; the core objective of such theories is to explore and explain a majority of consumer-related phenomena, where some theories are competitive and others complementary. Emanating from those theories are a number of models used to present and/or predict the why, what, how, when, and where of an individual's behavior in purchasing goods and services. Consumer behavior models may be classified into two types: The monadic models and multi-variable models, which explain market parameters and factors influencing purchases.

Monadic models rely on theories in microeconomics; they are embedded in explaining human beings as economic entities acting to maximize utility within the constraints of income and price. Such models overlook the emotional side of human beings that relates to social satisfaction and desires, and they also fall short of accounting for an imperfect marketplace where knowledge is inadequate and where there are many practical constraints, such as time and effort. On the other side, multi-variable consumer behavior models rely on more diverse theories that retain elements from the behavioral sciences to incorporate psychological effects, social influences as well as individual and cultural ramifications that moderate information acquisition and processing.

Classical and widely used examples of the multivariable models are those proposed by James Engel, Roger Blackwell, and Paul Miniard (EKB), Philip Kotler, Joel Cohen, and others, where further developments on such models are advocated and introduced over time by other researchers. Standard models divide influences on the consumer purchase decision process into internal and external components. The internal component covers individual differences and psychological factors at play in influencing decisions to buy, such as personality, value and lifestyle, motivations, consumer resources, prior knowledge, cognitions, and affections. The external component covers outer environmental influences on consumer purchases, such as demographic, social, economic, cultural, and situational factors.

Focusing on understanding either internal or external factors in isolation results in the critique of an incomplete modeling of the process in consumer research. More recently, though, investigating the intricate relationship between internal and external factors has uncovered more insights into varying behaviors of consumers. For example, studying the influence of social class or family lifecycle/composition on cognitive (thought-based) and affective (emotion-based) choices and expectations of individuals provides a more extensive understanding of purchase decision-making processes and outcomes.

Marketing
Marketers adapt and direct the marketing mix elements (mainly the 4Ps, representing marketing inputs involving product, price, place, and promotion) of a product/service at consumers with the aim of encouraging specific brand choices. In interacting with specific marketing mix elements of a product/service,

consumers are usually bombarded with influences based on their own needs, personal characteristics, culture backgrounds, attitudes, and perceptions. Marketing practitioners may find it particularly insightful to dig deep into relevant theory-based studies in their pursuit of a critical and intense comprehension of various consumer behavior aspects in the marketplace.

Though emanating from academic research, theories do not just stand on hypothetical grounds because, after their development, inherent assumptions and propositions are tested empirically in real life via such vehicles as surveys and experiments. This usually takes place more than once along different perspectives on different samples in different countries, and also through the eye and interpretation of various researchers. As practitioners expose themselves to this rich body of research-based theories and models, they usually identify with consumer behavior that they face in the marketplace, situating it within terms and phenomena long held in academic literature.

Consequently, the process might be easier for marketers who develop early on a richer interest in and engagement with academic marketing literature; this can be undertaken through adopting some theoretical perspectives that may offer marketers a base along which to examine, evaluate, and compare/contrast actual behaviors in the market with those modeled by consumer behavior theories. Such a process can support them in exploring, explaining, and predicting consumer attitudes and actions in different situations, cultures, and countries, a challenge made harder in doing business at the international and global levels.

See Also: Buying Motives/Behavior; Consumer Needs and Wants; Consumption; International Marketing Research; Marketing.

Bibliography. George E. Belch and Michael A. Belch, *Advertising and Promotion: An Integrated Marketing Communications Perspective*, 8th ed. (McGraw-Hill Irwin, 2009); E. K. Clemons and G. G. Gao, "Consumer Informedness and Diverse Consumer Purchasing Behaviors: Traditional Mass-Market Trading Down, and Trading Out into the Long Tail," *Electronic Commerce Research Applications* (v.7/1, 2007); Scott G. Dacko, *The Advanced Dictionary of Marketing* (Oxford University Press, 2008); Del I. Hawkins, David L. Mothersbaugh and Roger J. Best, *Consumer Behavior: Building Marketing Strategy* (McGraw-Hill/

Irwin, 2007); George P. Moschis, "Life Course Perspectives on Consumer Behavior," *Journal of the Academy of Marketing Science* (v.35/2, 2007); Jerry C. Olsen and J. Paul Peter, *Consumer Behavior and Marketing Strategy* (McGraw-Hill/Irwin, 2008); Patricia Mink Rath, *The Why of the Buy: Consumer Behavior and Fashion Marketing* (Fairchild, 2008); Michael R. Solomon, *Consumer Behavior: Buying, Having, and Being* (Pearson/Prentice Hall, 2009).

MARWA S. GAD
UNIVERSITY OF WARWICK

Consumer Needs and Wants

Needs and wants reside within the discipline of motivation and are closely interlinked. Needs are the manifestation of physiological, personal, and/or social motives and wants are the means of fulfilling them. So, taking a simple example, an individual may need to buy a replacement car, and the car they want to buy to solve their transport problems is a brand new Jaguar. This want for a Jaguar will be based on their utilitarian expectations, for example, quality, safety and design, and their hedonic aspirations and fantasies for this brand. Accordingly, needs and wants are important constructs because they help us to understand the "what," "why," and "how" of behavioral choices that people make, individually and collectively.

The Economic Perspective

To understand needs and wants more fully, it is useful to consider them from three interpretative positions, namely (1) economic, (2) psychological, and (3) sociological and anthropological perspectives. The economic perspective maintains that needs are associated with "economic man," whereby individuals act as rational, self-maximizing, economic individuals who engage in limitless goal-orientated consumption that offers them the most satisfaction from the products and services they buy. Examining this through expectancy theory, goal-orientated consumption thus becomes driven by the expectation of achieving a desirable outcome that will satisfy consumers' needs.

In consumption, then, consumers' choice of brands is influenced by their perceptions of what they judge will offer the most positive consequences for them.

Thus, for marketers, the challenge becomes one of persuading consumers that their ongoing consumption of their brands offers the best choice in "feeding" their wants and thus satisfying their needs. Inherent within this perspective is the idea that although needs may be temporarily satisfied, wants do not diminish. Instead, with the choices offered by a plethora of marketing offerings, consumers can continue to accumulate possessions without exhausting their wants. This raises some important ethical questions for marketers, which will be discussed below.

The Psychological Perspective

The psychological perspective is well-represented by the ideas of Abraham Maslow, who urged for the cultivation of higher-order needs in order for individuals to attain self-fulfillment, and, in so doing, to nurture a more caring society. Maslow argued that all human needs are innate and fragile and thus should be protected from social forces that have the potential to destroy them, for example political and economic pressures. In his well-known hierarchy of needs, Maslow makes a distinction between upper- and lower-order needs, where individuals strive toward self-actualization as they move back and forth between their physiological, safety, belongingness, and ego needs. As Maslow argued, individuals are more likely to self-actualize if these needs are cultivated, and, where they are, the contribution of such individuals in helping to create a more empathetic society is significant. In this respect, Maslow maintained that need gratification should be encouraged because of the individual and collective benefits it brings.

Marketing offerings, then, are typically based on this needs hierarchy. However, marketers have typically been selective in what they have extracted from it, which has led to criticisms of marketing that encourages individuals to pursue lifestyles where their individualistic, conspicuous consumption of brands abounds with its transient benefits, with little consideration for others.

Sociological and Anthropological Perspectives

The sociological and anthropological perspectives regard consumption as being socially determined, meaning that the social context of consumption is important. They argue that all needs share a common cultural element and they cannot be separated into physiological (lower) and psychological (upper) need states. Accordingly sociologists examine society, principally differences and distinctions, in order to understand where needs come from. For example, sociologists are interested in material culture, where goods are used as symbols to denote status and membership within a group.

While the advent of credit cards has meant that it has become much harder to judge status, as more people gain access to brands that convey social standing, sociologists are interested in how rank within groups influences need states and thus the satisfaction of wants through consumption. Consequently, fulfilling needs and wants through consumption can act as a cultural indicator, for example, marking differences in society and between groups, i.e., class and gender boundaries.

Behavior

Understanding the influence of consumers' needs and wants on their behavior, then, is inherently complex, yet this is vital for marketers. Summing up these explanations, an economic account of needs and wants would judge all needs as equal, i.e., the need for art is as important as the need for food. The psychological perspective and Maslow in particular disagree, maintaining that the status of needs is dependent on the physiological and psychological state of the individual. For example, if a person in the Western world is literally dying from thirst, then their bodily needs (physiological) and their mental faculties (psychological) will be totally dominated by the urgent need to find any drinkable fluid. In this respect we can begin to appreciate the interdependency between these two types of need states.

Hence we can also begin to understand the complex relationships between mental and physical needs-orientated behavior, for example, compulsive eating and striving to belong, purchasing body-kits for cars and self-esteem. Similarly, anthropologists and sociologists agree, physiological and psychological needs, and their satisfaction, cannot be separated. They conclude that, within a social context, a person in Western society, dying from thirst, would be unthinkable, and therefore if this did happen it would be reflective of a wider Western societal problem, where the needs of an impoverished group were not being recognized

or met. This, in itself, mirrors the status attached to the ability to consume freely in the endless pursuit of needs, contrasted with those who are economically and socially excluded and thus are unable to partake in this cultural ritual.

Ethical Questions

Consumer needs and wants thus raise important ethical questions. Principally, economic growth requires consumption to maintain it, and conspicuous consumption in particular. Consequently mass consumer society has emerged as the major source of economic and social influence. It has been argued that consumers have been socialized into thinking that they want more and more—that they have a right for their needs to be satisfied, and that only though fulfilling their wants, albeit temporarily, will they feel a sense of accomplishment. Yet this focus on needs satisfaction through conspicuous consumption has been charged with undermining the morals of society by encouraging "false values," materialism, unrestrained choice and indulgence, and isolating individuals from their traditional communities as they seek "never-to-be fulfilled" promises from their consumption choices, which, in turn, feeds consumers' anxiety and self-doubt, undermining their sense of subjective well-being, and so reducing their levels of happiness with their lives.

However, this bleak account of needs fulfillment and its consequences for individuals and society assumes that all consumers are passive recipients of marketing messages. It fails to appreciate more contemporary understanding of consumers and their cultures of consumption, where consumerism is regarded as a process of shared, social learning, laden with emotion, symbolic meaning, and identity, and consumers less as culture bearers and more as culture producers. Thus, through marketing offerings premised on needs and wants, consumers possess an assorted repertoire of mythic and symbolic resources that enable them to play with their utilitarian and hedonic aspirations on all levels.

Yet overall, it has to be acknowledged that marketing's emphasis on needs and wants creates a culture that transforms individuals into consumers living in consumption communities, socialized into the mindset of consumerism—where Coca-Cola rather than water is "the real thing."

See Also: Advertising; Branding; Buying Motives/Behavior; Consumer Behavior; Consumption; Lifestyle Research; Marketing.

Bibliography. E. J. Arnould and C. J. Thompson, "Consumer Culture Theory (CCT): Twenty Years of Research," *Journal of Consumer Research* (v.31, 2005); Z. Bauman, *The Individualized Society* (Blackwell, 2001); R. Belk, "Possessions and the Extended Self," *Journal of Consumer Research* (v.15, 1988); A. Borgmann, "The Moral Complexion of Consumption," *Journal of Consumer Research* (v.26, 2000); M. Douglas and B. Isherwood, *The World of Goods: Towards an Anthropology of Consumption* (Allen Lane, 1978); A. H. Maslow, *Motivation and Personality* (Harper Row, 1970 [1954]); M. Poster, ed., *Jean Baudrillard: Selected Writings* (Polity Press, 1988).

JANINE DERMODY
UNIVERSITY OF GLOUCESTERSHIRE BUSINESS SCHOOL

Consumer Surveys

Within consumer-based economies and political systems, the importance of consumer opinion and its role in predicting consumer behavior is often a key factor in decision-making processes within businesses, by providers of services such as healthcare, and by governments. In general, consumer surveys intend to measure consumer attitudes, expectations, and preferences and attempt to predict future consumer behavior. The tendency to measure instead what the surveyed consumers are prepared to admit to—either to the survey team or to themselves—is an ever-present danger, and guarding against this is a key factor in the design of robust, reliable sampling strategies, data collection systems, and analysis. The link between stated consumer opinion and future consumer behavior is not simple and the interpretation of consumer survey data is a key area of expertise.

The identification of an appropriate sample group and/or an understanding of the implications of choosing a particular sample group is key. Sample groups for consumer survey research can be considered in two broad groups: Those designed to provide a quick and relatively inexpensive overview and those that use stratified, sometimes randomized sampling

techniques to provide results that can be generalized to form the basis of conclusions about the population as a whole. In general, this type of consumer survey aims for a representative sample of the consumer group who are likely to be geographically disparate. Both approaches are useful—the key to successful consumer survey work lies in understanding the differences inherent within the two approaches. Conversely, contradictory questions may be included deliberately, specifically to identify consumers whose responses are potentially unreliable.

Either of the major sampling strategies may be used with a variety of data collection methods, focusing around the delivery of direct and indirect questions in person, by telephone, or online. The design of robust questions for the collection of consumer data is the second key factor that influences the validity and reliability of the data and their likely link to future consumer behavior. Avoiding common pitfalls—questions that make assumptions about consumers' knowledge/opinion, double questions, or contradictory questions—is important alongside the design of questions that will accommodate the full range of answers while providing the means to summarize the resultant data.

Direct verbal questioning forms the basis of consumer intercept surveys, typically carried out in the street, within shopping centers or retail parks, or other areas where access to a large group of target consumers is likely. Consumer intercept surveys begin with screening questions to confirm that the respondent is a suitable member of the appropriate sample group, followed by the administration of the full survey instrument, and concluding with thanks and either a small gift or monetary reward as closure. Consumer intercept surveys may be used with simple product testing or comparison techniques, which on occasion offers an advantage over telephone surveys, although the basic premise is similar.

Telephone, postal, and online surveys are commonly used and follow similar principles, being primarily influenced by the sampling strategy, the questions developed, and the response rates, which vary widely. Online consumer survey work is cheap, convenient, and may be appropriate for certain technical areas or where a predetermined sample group is available. The difficulties of obtaining a representative sample online remain a key limitation, however.

Analysis of consumer surveys may include the numerical collation of responses, the cross-linking of responses from different questions or groups, and/or the drawing out of direct quotes to give a feel for the people behind the statistics. In general, the analysis of data from consumer surveys follows the broad, overarching principles of data analysis, based around the identified research questions and the levels of measurement employed. The interpretation of results is also an area where the limitations of the initial target sample merit consideration and the implications of, for example, a self-selecting sample should give perspective to any interpretation of the results.

See Also: Buying Motives/Behavior; Consumer Behavior; Consumer Needs and Wants; Focus Groups; International Marketing Research; Lifestyle Research; Marketing; Market Research.

Bibliography. P. Chisnall, *Marketing Research* (McGraw Hill Higher Education, 2004); J. Collis and R. Hussey, *Business Research: A Practical Guide for Undergraduate and Postgraduate Students*, 2nd ed. (Palgrave Macmillan, 2003); M. B. Davies, *Doing a Successful Research Project: Using Qualitative or Quantitative Methods* (Palgrave Macmillan, 2007): M. Easterby-Smith, R, Thorpe, and A. Lowe, *Management Research*, 2nd ed. (Sage, 2002); D. George and P. Mallory, *SPSS for Windows Step by Step: A Simple Guide* (Allyn and Bacon, 2001); J. Gill and P. Johnson, *Research Methods for Managers,* 3rd ed. (Paul Chapman, 2002); W. Gordon, *Goodthinking—A Guide to Qualitative Research* (NTC Publications, 1999); D. E. Gray, *Doing Research in the Real World* (Sage, 2004).

CLAIRE SEAMAN
QUEEN MARGARET UNIVERSITY

Consumption

The term *consumption* is used in different academic disciplines in different ways. Depending on the specific academic background, people ask how supply and demand and, in other words, production and consumption in economy and society are related to each other. Or they investigate how individual people, social classes, or societies realize their consumption practices. The consumption practices illuminate differing empirical answers concerning how much actors spend for specific goods and services. Furthermore, consumption research inquires into the preference structures of individual actors, households, or classes and their corresponding rationalities that lead consumption behavior. How consistent are preference structures due to changing empirical backgrounds of time, space, and related culture? Finally, consumption research is also concerned with the relationship between earnings and spending. Are observed consumption practices directly related to a specific level of income and other available financial resources and vice versa? Which socioeconomic context variables (historical time, geographical framework) specify the relationship and in which way do attributes such as age, gender, class, occupation, and lifestyle have their own impacts on the way in which consumption is realized?

Economics has a long history of changing concepts dealing with consumption. Adam Smith argued in *The Wealth of Nations* that "consumption is the sole end and purpose of all production" while later, John-Baptiste Say in his so-called law of supply and demand saw production as the real ground-work of wealth or value. Criticizing Adam Smith, John-Baptiste Say argued:

How great, then, must be the mistake of those, who, on observing the obvious fact, that the production always equals the consumption, as it must necessarily do, since a thing can not be consumed before it is produced, have confounded the cause with the effect, and laid it down as a maxim, that consumption originates production.

This statement has evolved to textbook knowledge as "supply creates its own demand," a formulation by which John Maynard Keynes had summarized Say's law, although ongoing voices say that Say's thought was more differentiated than such shorthand definition suggests. Keynes turned previous discussion on its head by strengthening the role of customers at a macroeconomic level, which led to the formulation that demand creates its own supply. What Keynes had in mind was that economic growth can be created best by strengthening incentives for consumption. For Keynes, the sphere of consumption was based upon socio-psychological dispositions of human agents which are remote from the economic theory existing before.

Past Consumption Research

During the last 70 years economic consumption research has moved in many different directions. While Keynes attributed the cognitive dimension of perceptions in combination with issues of uncertainties to consumption, other authors strengthened other aspects. Franco Modigliani stressed the aspect that consumers differ concerning their decisions within their life cycles; J. K. Galbraith linked consumption to a historically new phenomenon of an affluent society, while T. Scitovsky bridged the discussion to human needs. The later points of discussion overlapped clearly with historical and sociological views dealing with consumption.

Historians investigate consumption issues from many different perspectives. They ask which specific goods are used and consumed in different centuries, how and why goods are bought, the evolution of consumption patterns within socioeconomic changes, and how different societies are constituted and portrayed by specific "regimes" of consumption. Historians also produce analytic stories of specific consumption goods (e.g., history of tea consumption) or practices of consumption (e.g., history of cooking or traveling) that serve as pieces of historical change and that are simultaneously items of historical diagnosis where particular elements of analysis stand as examples for the whole. Max Weber discussed the rise of industrial capitalism in relation to Protestant ethics and the inherent consumption ascetics, but in the 20th century historians came up with labels of a "consumer society," which had changed the previous face according to the progress and spirit of changing times.

A pioneer of socioeconomic consumption research was Thorstein B. Veblen, who was a representative of early American institutionalism. Veblen, who also discussed limitations of marginal utility theory and reflected on the organization of science, authored *The Theory of the Leisure Class* (1899), the first and most famous book among his seven book publications. It is now considered a sociology classic, though its focus was as much economic, anthropological, and psychological as sociological. In the book, Veblen coined the term *conspicuous consumption* to describe tendencies of economic activities to be driven by nonutilitarian, even impractical motives that are more akin to tribal and prehistoric behavior than rational economics.

Veblen's discussion of conspicuous consumption went well beyond possession of material objects. He extended his socio-psychological analyses to religious practices, gender relations, sports, the cultivation of accents, manners, and other factors not widely studied at the time. He was highly critical of the leisure class, including its treatment of women. He anticipated the trophy wife phenomenon of the modern leisure class by noting that marriage was largely another acquisitive activity for men of the leisure class. Veblen's discussion was a starting point of subsequent debate, which we find in the interface between consumption studies, and research on lifestyles and social inequalities.

New Research

Current consumption research is increasingly interdisciplinary. Among many specific perspectives, five empirical research areas are of specific significance. First, the links between consumption behavior and social order are of specific research interest. Drawing the landscape of local, regional, national, and international consumption profiles in contrast to different classes, household types, lifestyles and their modifications over time is specifically on the agenda. The work of P. Bourdieu provides an excellent example of how well an empirical study of consumption patterns can serve as background diagnosis of a society. Inequalities become visible in terms of material and cultural disparities within vertical and horizontal disparities through differing consumption patterns.

Microeconomic and microsociological patterns and conditions of consumption behavior also need to be fostered for further exploitation. This research area involves social conditions of learned behavior as well as further investigation into decision-making structures and contextualizing network structures that help to decode the grammar of human behavior relevant for consumption processes, including intentional refusal of consumption by saving or philanthropy.

A topic that is getting more attention is the role of consumers as active agents. What is the role of a consumer in society, how can he/she be protected by legal rights strengthening the autonomy of consumers compared to traders or producers? Further, consumers see themselves increasingly as political decision makers or voters through their own decision for (and against) specific products or labels. Since markets often offer a variety of competing products to satisfy a single need, consumers decide for boycott of specific brands if negative secondary information is available, e.g., discrimination practices at the workplace or negative treatment of the natural environment.

Another area of research explores the social code of consumption processes at a symbolic level, or which signs are transported for which purposes. J. Baudrillard wrote:

Consumption is neither a material practice, nor a phenomenology of "affluence." It is not defined by the food we eat, the clothes we wear, the car we can drive, nor by the visual and oral substance of images and messages, but in the organization of all this as signifying substance. Consumption is the virtual totality of all objects and message presently constituted in a more or less coherent discourse. Consumption, in so far as it is meaningful, is a systematic art of the manipulation of signs.

Consumption processes and their diffusion modes seem to have overlaps to diffusion processes of social trends and social fashions. The research area must integrate elements of thought that have been provided by separate disciplines (e.g., sociology, psychology, consumption behavior, history, economics, anthropology, neurobiology) in order to reintegrate individual aspects for a better theory of diffusion processes of consumption behavior.

Of further interest are those research topics that treat consumption as part of a changing consumption society, which is itself part of international processes of homogenization and heterogenization. An increasing trend toward so-called issues of sustainability and greening of industry and society creates new demands, provides new business opportunities, and changes consumers' profiles and their consumption patterns. Especially, debate on globalization is asking if consumption practices occur at an international level that are elsewhere labeled as phenomena of an ongoing process of "McDonaldization." McDonaldization processes can be highlighted in different fields of consumption practices, e.g., in food industries, textile industries, tourism, entertainment industries, by credit cards, or in many other fields of application.

See Also: Advertising; Branding; Buying Motives/Behavior; Consumer Behavior; Consumer Needs and Wants; Lifestyle Research; Marketing; Status.

Bibliography. J. Baudrillard, *The System of Objects* (Polity Press, 1988); D. Bögenhold, "Social Inequality and the Sociology of Life Style. Material and Cultural Aspects of Social Stratification," *American Journal of Economics and Sociology* (v.60, 2001); P. Bourdieu, *Distinction: A Social Critique of the Judgment of Taste* (Harvard University Press, 1984); J. K. Galbraith, *The Affluent Society* (Houghton Mifflin, 1958); J. M. Keynes, *The General Theory of Employment, Interest and Money* (Macmillan, 1936); F. Modigliani, *The Collected Papers of Franco Modigliani, Vol. 2: The Life Cycle Hypothesis of Saving* (MIT Press, 1980); A. Offer, *The Challenge of Affluence: Self-Control and Well-Being in the United States and Britain Since 1950* (Oxford University Press, 2007); G. Ritzer: *The McDonaldization of Society: An Investigation into the Changing Character of Contemporary Social Life* (Pine Forge Press, 1995); J.-B. Say, *A Treatise on Political Economy* (Lippingcott, Grambo & Co., 1855); T. Scitovsky, *The Joyless Economy: An Inquiry Into Human Satisfaction and Consumer Dissatisfaction* (Oxford University Press, 1976); A. Smith, *The Wealth of Nations* (Dent & Dutton, 1970); N. Stehr, *Moral Markets: How Knowledge and Affluence Change Consumers and Products* (Paradigm Publishers, 2008); T. B. Veblen, *The Theory of the Leisure Class: An Economic Study of Institutions* (Macmillan, 1889).

Dieter Bögenhold
Free University of Bolzano

Contagion

Contagion is related to extremely high levels of international financial co-movements. However, there is not consensus in academic literature about what contagion represents. It denotes an increase in probability that a crisis in one country is caused by a crisis in another country. Second, it involves the asset price spill-over effect from a crisis-stricken country to others. Third, if fundamentals do not provide any justification for a significant increase in cross-country price and quantity co-movements there must a contagion involved. Finally, international transmission mechanisms will have stronger impact during the financial crisis. Nevertheless, the contagion effect must change the level of co-movements and unconditional market volatilities. Otherwise, a strong cross-country conditional correlation during a shock does not constitute contagion.

Recent Crises

The frequent outbreaks of crises in recent financial history have led to a widespread interest in academic circles. The Mexican crisis commenced on December 20, 1994, initiated by a 12.7 percent decline in the national currency's value. The peso was allowed to freely float in order to avoid the depletion of foreign exchange reserves. In addition, the financial system was supported by a $52 billion rescue package provided by the U.S. government. Even though this incident did not have global repercussions, the so-called Asian crisis initiated by the Thai baht's 10 percent devaluation in June 1997 did send a ripple throughout the region. Other currencies in the vicinity were severely hit, with the exception of the Singaporean dollar and the Taiwanese dollar. Due to its currency board policy, the Hong Kong dollar was pegged to the U.S. dollar, but the economy suffered deflation, which was an alternative correction mechanism. The International Monetary Fund (IMF) provided substantial bail-out packages to help these countries restructure economies and introduce more effective market models.

The Malaysian prime minister, Dr. Mahathir bin Mohamad, blamed wealthy speculators like George Soros for destabilizing emerging markets. However, a study conducted in the Korean Stock Exchange (KSE) indicates that during the crisis foreign investors were not buying (selling) stocks based on the previous increase (decrease) in the market. In addition, the stock return of the previous day did not have any predicting power about the foreign investors' trade the next day. By contrast, before the onset of the crisis foreign investors demonstrated positive feedback trading at KSE. The root of the Asian crisis may be found in the short-term lending of banks exposed to these markets. When Korea stopped defending its foreign exchange parity on November 14, 1997, exposed banks had a minus 1.5 percent abnormal return (compared with minus 0.71 percent for unexposed counterparts). When the bailout agreement with IMF became evident on December 1, 2007,

the abnormal return was 2.07 percent (as opposed to 1.22 percent for parties unexposed to the Korean market). Nevertheless, the differences between these bank groups were statistically insignificant.

The impact of the Asian crisis was mainly regional, unlike the subsequently ensuing Brazilian currency and Russian bond crises in 1998. Speculators diverted their attention from Asian currency to the Brazilian real, assuming that the strong currency policy was not matched by appropriate fiscal and monetary austerity.

The doubling of interest rates to 43 percent and belated tax reforms were not sufficient to reverse the decline. Immediate investors' response was capital flight and an apparent loss of confidence in emerging markets. On August 17, 1998, the Russian government devalued the ruble and publicly announced its decision to place a moratorium on debt repayments, which was conducive to an increase in spreads between bond issues in emerging and developed economies, respectively. Foreign investors, such as the Long Term Capital Management (LTCM) hedge funds, were severely affected. In order to counteract the loss of $550 million on August 21, 1998, LTCM decided to seek recapitalization. In view of the size of this fund (notional principal in excess of $1 trillion) the Federal Reserve decided to support the $3.65 billion bailout package provided by 15 financial institutions in September 1998. The Brazilian real crisis did not only have short-term ramifications. As part of efforts to improve deteriorating terms of trade with the largest trade partner in South America and support economic growth, Argentina was forced to devalue its national currency in 2001.

In order to evaluate the ramifications of the LTCM bailout, market participants can be separated into companies that took part in the LTCM bailout, financial companies that were directly exposed to LTCM but never participated in the bailout deal, banks that do not have any exposure to hedge funds, and banks that do have exposure to hedge funds but not LTCM. It was found that following the bailout announcement on September 24, 1998, the largest negative abnormal return was recorded by banks directly involved in the bailouts and those that had been exposed to hedge funds. Financial institutions with either indirect exposure to LTCM or no exposure to hedge funds were not as adversely affected.

See Also: Asian Financial Crisis; Brazil; Currency; Globalization; International Monetary Fund; Mexico; Russia; Tequila Effect.

Bibliography. H. Choe, B.-C. Kho, and R.,M. Stulz, "Do Foreign Investors Destabilize Stock Markets? The Korean Experience in 1997," *Journal of Financial Economics* (1999); K. J. Forbes and R. Rigobon, "No Contagion, Only Interdependence: Measuring Stock Market Movements," *Journal of Finance* (2002); J. M. Halstead, S. Hedge, and L. S. Klein, "Hedge Fund Crisis and Financial Contagion: Evidence from Long Term Capital Management," *Journal of Alternative Investments* (2005); B.-C. Kho, D. Lee, and R. M. Stulz, "U.S. Banks, Crises, and Bailouts: From Mexico to LTCM," *American Economic Review* (2000); M. Pericoli and M. Sbracia, "A Primer on Financial Contagion," *Journal of Economic Surveys* (2003); A. C. Shapiro, *Multinational Financial Management* (John Wiley & Sons, 2006).

Aleksandar Šević
University of Dublin
Željko Šević
Glasgow Caledonian University

Context

The terms *high context* and *low context* were popularized by American anthropologist Edward T. Hall to describe the broad-brush cultural differences that can exist between different societies. During the early 1950s, Hall defined culture as a means of communication that takes place through symbols, or "silent languages." He identified five such languages, including the languages of time, space, material goods, friendship, and agreements. As he continued his research, Hall found common patterns in the ways that people in different cultures and societies used these five different languages: He observed that some people tended to communicate in a relatively explicit fashion, while others communicate effectively with much more implicit information. Drawing on these findings, Hall proposed a distinction between what he called "high context" and "low context" cultures.

In accordance with this classification system, a high-context culture or society is one whose members establish a few close connections among each other over a long period of time. High-context cultures tend to place a great emphasis on friends and intersecting networks of long-term relationships based on trust and mutual understanding. This high degree of shared understanding means that members of high-context cultures are able to communicate with each other effectively without the need for explicit information: Many aspects of cultural behavior are implicit since most members have learned what to do and what to think over their many years of interaction with each other. Since knowledge of how to behave in a high-context culture is hidden, it is difficult for outsiders to understand the rules of a society, and it is often difficult for the insider members of high-context cultures to explain these rules to outsiders. The time needed to create close relationships acts as a further barrier to integration.

By contrast, the members of a low-context culture or society tend to establish many connections with each other. These connections, however, are typically short-lived in duration; they are also comparatively more superficial than relationships in high-context cultures insofar as they are based not on friendship, but often only serve specific purposes. In low-context societies, cultural behavior and beliefs may need to be spelled out explicitly so that members of society know how to behave. Compared to members of high-context societies, people in low-context cultures tend to be more precise, specific, and require more explicit information in order to communicate effectively. Unlike high-context cultures, low-context ones are relatively easier for outsiders to enter: Much of the information that they need to participate is highly visible in the cultural environment, and they can form relationships relatively quickly.

Hall's concepts of high and low context can be helpful in describing the cultural behavior of specific countries. The United States, for example, can be seen as a low-context culture. Americans tend to communicate in explicit terms: They value candor and frank discussion, and are likely to voice disagreement openly. Plain speaking—the act of saying exactly what one thinks—is a virtuous trait in the eyes of many Americans. In the business world, Americans tend to make contacts easily and casually, and negotiate contracts that are explicit, complete, and literal.

Compared to the United States, France is a more high-context culture. In French society, relationship building and social contacts are of great importance. Business negotiations are typically preceded by a lengthy process of establishing trust. This process commonly includes dinners and lunches that are not only opportunities to discuss business but also have a ceremonial quality. The contents of French contracts are typically open to interpretation.

Japan is generally considered to be a very high-context culture where effective communication is possible through relatively little explicit information. An example of high-context Japanese communication is *haragai*, a form of guttural speech that seems incomprehensible to Westerners but that represents for the Japanese an effective medium of communication. Typical of a high-context culture, in which relatively less overt communication is needed, Japanese business negotiations are conducted without explicit statements of agreement and disagreement: To make an overt and blunt statement when subtle communication would suffice is considered abrupt and rude in Japanese society.

Not surprisingly, these different ways of communicating have at times led to cross-cultural problems in communication. Americans often complain that the Japanese are reluctant to voice direct disagreement—they appear never to say no. While it may be true that the Japanese prefer not to say *no* in the explicit fashion preferred by Americans, it is incorrect to say that they do not express disagreement. It would be more precise to say that their high-context expressions of disagreement are difficult for members of low-context cultures to understand.

Some critics of Hall argue that, although it is sometimes useful to describe some aspects of a culture as high or low context, it is misguided to apply the terms to entire cultures because societies can contain both forms of context. "High" and "low," argue the critics, are less relevant as a description of an entire people, and more useful to describe and understand particular situations and environments.

See Also: Acculturation; Cross-Cultural Research; Cultural Norms and Scripts; Culture-Specific Values; Silent Language of Hall (Nonverbal Communication); Space.

Bibliography. Richard R. Gesteland, *Cross-cultural Business Behaviour—Marketing, Negotiating, Sourcing and*

Managing Across Cultures (Copenhagen Business School, 2002); Edward T. Hall and Mildred R. Hall, *Understanding Cultural Differences* (Intercultural Press, 1990); Susan C. Schneider and Jean-Louis Barsoux, *Managing Across Cultures* (Prentice Hall/Financial Times, 2003).

ANDREW BARRON
ESC RENNES SCHOOL OF BUSINESS

Contract Repudiation

Repudiation is a term used to describe circumstances where a party acts or expresses intent not to accept the obligation of a contract, hence the term *contract repudiation*. Repudiation amounts to a breach of contract where the refusal to perform is clear. Refusal to perform may be evidenced by words or voluntary acts, but it must be distinct, unequivocal, and absolute. In today's global economy, business law is a global practice, and the obligations of contracts have become increasingly important; therefore, contract repudiation often leaves at least one party to a contract dissatisfied.

Generally, a definite and unconditional repudiation of a contract by a party, communicated to the other, is a breach of contract, creating an immediate cause of action in a court of law. This is so even if it takes place long before the time prescribed for the promised performance; further, before conditions specified in the promise have even occurred. Ironically, contract repudiation should be encouraged where the promisor is able to profit from his default, so long as he or she places the promisee in as good a position as the promisee would have been in had performance been rendered. Typically, a breach of contract entitles the other party to compensation for the loss sustained as a consequence of the breach. But with the exceptions and subject to express contractual rights of determination, a breach of contract by one party does not discharge the other party from performance of his or her unperformed obligations. Otherwise stated, repudiation by one party standing alone does not terminate the contract. It takes two to end it: Repudiation on one end, and acceptance of repudiation on the other.

There are, however, two circumstances where a breach of contract by one party entitles the other to elect to put an end to all remaining primary obligations of both parties. The first is where the contracting parties have agreed, whether by express words or implication of law, that any breach of the contractual term in question shall entitle the other party to terminate the contract—where there is a breach of condition. The second is where the event resulting from the breach of contract has the effect of depriving the other party of a substantial portion of the benefit as intended by the contract. In other words, where there is a "fundamental breach."

When one party elects to put an end to all remaining primary obligations of both parties, it is referred to as the determination or rescission of the contract, or as treating the contract as "repudiated" or "accepting the repudiation" of the contract breaker. Under Florida law, for example, where an obligor repudiates a duty before he has committed a breach of contract by nonperformance, and before he or she has received all of the agreed exchange for it, his or her repudiation alone gives rise to a claim for damages. The contract is not rescinded as from the beginning, however. But both parties are discharged from further performing obligations under the contract. Still, rights that have already been unconditionally acquired are not divested or discharged, and a full arbitration clause will normally continue to apply to disputes arising upon the acceptance of repudiation. In rare circumstances, advance payment may be recovered—that is, if the contractor has provided no consideration in the nature of part performance. Such an instance is made clear in the realm of anticipatory repudiation.

Anticipatory repudiation is a term in the law of contracts that describes a declaration by one party to a contract, the promising party, that they do not intend to live up to their obligations under the contract. Where such an event occurs, the other party to the contract, the performing party, is excused from having to fulfill their obligations. The repudiation, however, can be retracted by the promising party so long as there has been no material change in the position of the performing party; further, a retraction of the repudiation restores the performer's obligation to perform on the contract.

In the event that the promising party's repudiation makes it impossible to fulfill its promise, then retraction is not possible and no act by the promising party can restore the performing party's obligations. For example, if Willie promises to give Guillermo his new golf clubs in exchange for Guillermo's building him a new residence, but Willie sells his golf clubs to Chuck before Guillermo commences the job, Willie's act constitutes an anticipatory repudiation. Essentially, Guillermo is excused from performing. Once the golf clubs have left Willie's possession, it is impossible for Willie to fulfill his promise to give Guillermo his new golf clubs.

In the global markets of today, contract repudiation can have devastating effects not only on individuals, but also on the local economy. Because business in the United States is very much intertwined with business in several other economies, a strong foreign presence in international markets may help to make up for a downturn in the local economy. As a result, the performance of contractual obligations is of utmost importance.

See Also: Arbitration; Contracts; International Law; Mediation.

Bibliography. Gerald E. Berendt et al., *Contract Law and Practice* (Matthew Bender and Company, 2007); Amy Hilsman Kastely, Deborah Waire Post, and Sharon Kang Hom, *Contracting Law*, 3rd ed. (Carolina Academic Press, 2005); Restatement (Second) Contracts § 253.

Daniel A. Espinosa
St. Thomas University School of Law

Contracts

A contract is an agreement among two or more parties. It includes a promise, or mutual set of promises, freely agreed to and in exchange for something of value. Once properly set in place, the agreement will be enforced by the court. We will now take a closer look at how contracts are formed, how contracts are voided and how contracts are enforced by the courts.

What Makes a Contract?

A contract is formed when the two essential contract elements are in place: mutual assent and consideration. Mutual assent refers to an offer made by one party, plus the acceptance of this offer by the other party. Consideration is something of value: Each party must promise to give something of value to the other in order to bind the contract. When mutual assent and consideration come together, the law claims there has been a "meeting of the minds" and a contract is formed. Memorializing it on paper will make it more certain to be enforced in court, but an oral contract is as legally binding as a written one.

When determining if a party has made or accepted an offer, the courts use an objective interpretation of contract formation. The court considers: Would the reasonable person believe she or he had just entered into an agreement? A defense of "but that's not what I really meant" will not move the court. The court makes no attempt to peer into a person's mind, it looks only at behavior. If Tom behaves in a way to lead Fred to reasonably conclude that Tom and Fred have a contract, the court will likely honor Fred's reasonable belief.

The creation of a contract begins with the offer. In order to fulfill the legal definition of an offer, it must convey that the one making the offer (the offeror) has a serious intention to enter a contract; to be bound to the agreement if the offer is accepted. The courts employ their objective standard here: Was it reasonable to believe that the offer was sincere? When Tom says to Fred, "I'm so sick of repairing my house, I'd sell it for a dollar," Fred has no reasonable expectation that he may now pull four quarters out of his pocket and complete a cash transaction for Tom's home.

The key characteristic of a legal offer is its completeness: It contains all the essential components of the deal and nothing of substance remains to be negotiated. It should be specific in terms of quantity, price, and description. It should state who may accept and spell out the appropriate manner of acceptance, including the time limit for acceptance. And it must be communicated to the potential buyer (offeree). An offer is not an offer until the potential buyer hears it.

The offeror is the master of the offer: She or he is free to revoke the offer at any time prior to a communication of acceptance, even if the offeror has stated that the offer will remain open. For example, let's assume you are a musician and you enter negotiations to sell a recording to Bighits Records. You tell Bighits, "I'll give you the exclusive right to buy my recording for $50,000 at any time in the next 90 days." Later you change your mind, and send a letter to Bighits revoking the offer. The offer is now null and void, even though we are still within the 90 days.

As is often the case within the law, this general rule is subject to certain limits. The offer may not be revoked if Bighits gave something of value in order to hold the offer open. Assume Bighits responds to your initial offer and gives you $5,000 to keep your offer open for the full 90 days. Now you may no longer revoke your offer to sell the recording. This "option contract" is a contract in and of itself: you offered to sell a right; Bighits accepted. Both parties give something of value to bind the deal: Bighits gave cash; you gave up your right to sell to anyone but Bighits. All the elements of a contract are in place and the courts will enforce it as such. Acceptance of the offer will complete the requirement of mutual assent. Again, the courts employ an objective standard: It is the offeree's behavior that matters. The court will not be moved by a statement that one did not intend to accept if the offeror was justified in believing the offer had been accepted.

Just as an offer must conform to certain standards to fulfill the legal definition of an offer, an acceptance also must meet certain standards. As the master of the offer, the offeror sets the specifics of most of these standards. The offeror controls when the offer may be accepted. The offer may normally be accepted until the offer is overtly terminated or until the end of the stated life of the offer (i.e., "this offer is good for the next 90 days").

The offeror also controls how the offer may be accepted, determining what medium should be used to communicate the acceptance, be it fax, mail, or some other means. There is an automatic implication that whatever medium was used to make the offer is an authorized medium. According to the widely adopted "mailbox rule," if the offer is accepted via an authorized medium, that offer becomes binding the instant it is dispatched. If an unauthorized medium is employed, the acceptance is not binding until it is received. Thus, if the U.S. mail is authorized, an acceptance is binding the second it is dropped into a mailbox, and the offer could not be revoked while the letter was in the mail. However, if U.S. mail was not authorized, the offeror could revoke the offer while the letter was in transit. It was delivered via an unauthorized medium and would not become binding until received.

One may not accept an offer while simultaneously attempting to alter the terms of the offer. The "mirror image rule" requires that an acceptance be unequivocal. Any attempt at alteration converts the acceptance into a counteroffer. So, Sam Seller offers to sell four tires to Dave Driver for the sum of $500. Dave replies by stating, "I accept your offer, but I want the tires mounted with no change in price." Legally, Dave has rejected the offer, then made a counteroffer. Sam is now the recipient of an offer that he is free to accept or reject. If Sam rejects, Dave cannot attempt to back up and say, "I now accept your original offer." Sam's original offer disappeared the instant Dave countered.

An acceptance need not be a completely mechanical "I accept" in order to furnish mutual assent. For example, Dave could express dissatisfaction with the deal and it would still be an acceptance. ("I think that is highway robbery, but I accept anyway.") Dave could make an implicit term explicit. ("I accept, assuming that the tires meet U.S. government safety guidelines.") And the inclusion of a request within Dave's acceptance does not automatically convert it to a counteroffer. ("I accept, but I would like you to consider mounting the tires for no additional charge.")

What Is Consideration?

The sine quo non of any contract is consideration. It is the glue that holds the contract together. Consideration is something that is (a) a detriment to the one accepting, (b) induced by the one offering, and (c) given in exchange—it is a promise for a promise. When a court decides if something does or does not act as consideration, the key is the detriment to the one giving the consideration, not the benefit to the one receiving. An example will clarify why the law looks at it this way. August Uncle makes an offer to Neal Nephew: "If you don't drink alcohol until your 25th birthday, I'll give you $10,000." Neal accepts in an unequivocal fashion and follows through on his promise. On Neal's 25th birthday, August states, "I'm not going to give you the $10,000. After all, I derived no benefit from your behavior. Therefore I owe you nothing."

A court will not allow August to weasel out of his obligation because he did not benefit. August was the master of this offer. The law will not allow him to rewrite the terms when the moment comes for him to perform. August also loses if he argues that Neal suffered no loss by abstaining. Neal sacrificed a clear legal right—the right to consume alcohol. Giving up this right is a legal detriment to Neal. Neal's adherence to this obligation and acceptance of this detriment is the glue that holds this entire agreement together. That is the consideration he offered in exchange for $10,000. That consideration makes the entire contract binding on both parties.

What Breaks a Contract?

The issues here fall into two categories. The first deals with the parties involved. The law recognizes that certain people may not form a contract: they lack "contract capacity." The second category deals with the facts involved. The basic suppositions of fact that support the contract may have been misunderstood or may change through no fault of the parties.

As politically incorrect as it may be, every law student is taught to remember that people who may not form a contract are described by the "three i's": infants, idiots, and the intoxicated. The legal adage is that one contracts with an infant (person below the age of 18) at one's own peril. An adult contracting with a child will be held to his promises. Yet the child may disaffirm the same contract at any time prior to his/her 18th birthday and even for a "reasonable period" thereafter.

If you form a contract with one who is mentally incapacitated—either by level of IQ or level of intoxication—the law is not so clear. Generally speaking, if you were reasonable in assuming that the other party had the capacity to contract, the contract will be enforced. But if you knew or should have known that the other party may be compromised, that other party will be able to void the contract. The reasoning is fairly straightforward. The law expects a certain amount of prudence on the part of one forming a contract. For example, it is a simple matter to ensure that you are not forming a contract with a child: You insist on seeing a birth certificate or other proof of age. Not so with mental capacity. It is possible for one who is incapacitated to appear within the bounds of "normal" on some occasions and to some observers. If you formed a contract with the reasonable expectation that the other party had the capacity to contract, the court will support that reasonable expectation.

Mistakes concerning, or alterations in, the basic facts surrounding a contract may void that contract. For a mistake of fact to void a contract, that mistake must demonstrate three qualities: the mistake must be mutual, the mistake must have a material effect on the agreement, and the risk of the mistake must not have been assumed by the one attempting to void the contract. For example, let's assume Ben Buyer agrees to purchase a cow from Dan Dairyman. Dan and Ben negotiate a price based on the number of calves the cow is expected to produce over her lifespan. After the agreement is made, it is discovered that the cow is sterile and incapable of producing offspring. Here, the mistake is mutual: Neither Ben nor Dan had an accurate understanding. The impact is material: A cow capable of breeding is worth several times more than a one that is not. And Ben did not agree to the risk. He did not negotiate to buy an animal "as is," but negotiated specifically to buy breed stock. Under these circumstances, Ben may rescind this contract for "mutual mistake."

Contracts may also be rescinded if a change in the basic facts makes performance of the contract impossible or if the change frustrates the contract's basic purpose. "Impossibility" is exactly what it sounds like: it becomes impossible for one party to perform. Two people contract for the rental of a hall for a gathering. Prior to the day of the gathering, the hall burns down. Performance has become impossible and the contract is rescinded as a matter of law.

"Frustration of essential purpose" refers to a change in basic facts causing the entire agreement to become irrelevant. To use a classic case from England: A royal coronation was scheduled and a parade route established. Many people with homes along the route offered their houses for rent. These rentals were for just a single day—the day of the coronation. When the coronation was postponed, the original purpose for the rental contracts disappeared. The courts voided the contracts using a line of reasoning we have seen before: The renters did not contract to assume this risk. In such a set of circumstances, the court will often void a contract.

Is a Written Contract Required?

The general rule is that an oral agreement is as much a contract as a written agreement. However, the Statute of Frauds, first enacted in England in 1677, requires that certain agreements must be evidenced by writing in order to be enforceable. Every state in the United States has enacted some form of this statute. While the coverage alters from jurisdiction to jurisdiction, common provisions include the following:

- Sale of an interest in land (not only a transfer of ownership of real property, but also leases of over a year; mineral rights; easements; etc.)
- Promises to pay the debts of another; promise by an executor to pay the debts of an estate
- Promises in consideration of marriage
- A promise that cannot be performed within one year
- Sale of goods at a price of $500 or more

It is important to note that courts may be fairly expansive in what is termed "written evidence." A single, formal document labeled "contract" is not required. If one can piece together a paper trail of letters, e-mails, checks, and the like that demonstrate that an agreement was in place, this may fulfill the requirement of written evidence.

How Are Contracts Enforced?

If one party to the contract does not live up to a promise, that party is said to have breached and will likely owe damages to the disappointed party. What the disappointed party often wants—but rarely receives—is specific performance: An order from the court that the breaching party must deliver on the promise. Specific performance is usually reserved for situations where what is bargained for is unique; the classic example is real estate. As each parcel of land is unique, a court will often order specific performance to transfer ownership of a contracted-for piece of real property.

But in most cases the court will order only money damages, which is seen as a replacement for performance. The most common way of calculating damages is "expectation" or benefit-of-the-bargain damages. Herb Homeowner contracts with Bob Builder to build a new home on Herb's lot. Just as Bob is about to begin work, Herb announces that he does not want a house on the lot and will not pay Bob to build one. Clearly, an order of specific performance makes no sense: Bob has little interest in building a home no one wants. What Bob wants is the benefit of the bargain. He wants money damages equivalent to the profit he would have made by completing the home and being paid according to the terms of the contract. The court will subtract Bob's construction costs from the contracted home price to determine Bob's profit and order Herb to pay that amount. Bob has now received the expectation of profits he had when he formed the contract.

Courts will sometimes use an alternative method called "reliance" damages. The goal here is to place the injured party in the same position he or she would be in had the contract never been formed. This is usually done if any estimate of expectation damages would be too speculative for the court to rely upon. In the example above, let's assume that Herb's lot is partially covered with quicksand and many builders feel that it would not be possible to place a stable building on the property. Here, it is impossible to estimate Bob's building costs, thus it is impossible to estimate his profits or even to determine if there would be any profits. So the court will unwind the contract and compensate Bob for any work he may have done or expenses he may have incurred prior to Herb's cancellation.

See Also: Contract Repudiation; Cross-Licensing; Licensing; Warranties.

Bibliography. B. A. Blum, *Contracts: Examples and Explanations*, 2nd ed. (Aspen, 2001); K. W. Clarkson, R. L. Miller, G. A. Jentz, and F. B. Cross, *Business Law: Text and Cases* (South Western, 2009); R. J. Consiver, ed., *Barbri Bar Review: Multistate* (Thompson, 2006); W. McGovern, L. Lawrence, and B. D. Hull, *Contracts and Sales: Contemporary Cases and Problems*, 2nd ed. (LexisNexis, 2002).

CLIFFORD D. SCOTT
UNIVERSITY OF ARKANSAS, FORT SMITH

Control Systems

Control systems are designed to provide corrective action to align actual performance with standard performance. Effective control systems use feedback to determine whether organizational performance meets established standards to help the organization achieve its objectives.

Managers like to be in control; they try to shape their organization's future by formulating and implementing strategies designed to achieve objectives. For this reason, control systems are ubiquitous in organi-

zations. There may be traditional budgetary control systems or the more recent and sophisticated strategic control systems. There may also be management control systems or business control systems.

When the structure of an organization is created, it results in subdivision of responsibility and dispersal of the total managerial task among different organizational units. Since the activities of each of these units are to be coordinated, control systems are necessary. Control systems are, in fact, devices to enforce or facilitate desirable behavior so that the organization, as an entity, moves toward its predetermined goals.

Control systems operate on the basis of the control cycle. This cycle is made up of a process that has four elements: Establishing standards, measuring actual performance, evaluating actual performance against standards, and determining corrective action. The control process works to bring performance in line with the predetermined plan. Standards are in the form of budgeted performance. Measurement of performance is done through an appraisal system. Actual performance is evaluated with reference to the standards, and positive or negative variation is observed. Corrective action follows so that performance corresponds to standards.

Control systems may be classified as preventive or corrective, formal or informal, direct or indirect, or social or individual controls. Preventive controls are mechanisms designed to reduce the possibility of errors and minimize the need for corrective action. Corrective controls are mechanisms to correct errors that have occurred. Formal controls are prescribed in nature and are based on quantitative, objective data; for instance, financial controls are based on accounting data and are used to quantify performance in fiscal terms. Informal controls are emergent in nature and are based on quantitative, subjective data; for example, adherence to ethical standards can only be ensured through informal means. Direct controls are exercised in face-to-face situations such as controlling performance through direct observation. Indirect controls are exercised though the means of mechanisms such as financial statements and information systems. Social controls act through the collective will of groups in organizations. Individual control takes place through direct interventions.

Control systems are also classified as open- and closed-loop systems. Open-loop control systems are those in which the output has no effect on the input. Closed-loop control systems are those in which the output has an effect on the input in such a way as to maintain the desired output value. A closed-loop system includes some way to measure its output to sense changes so that corrective action can be taken.

In organizations that operate globally, control systems assume special importance. The relationship between headquarters and subsidiaries in a multinational corporation, for instance, is determined on the basis of the distribution of authority among them. Where centralization of control systems is preferred, it results in concentration of authority at the headquarters. Where authority is delegated to the level of subsidiaries, decentralization of control systems takes place. Each of these options has its own set of advantages and disadvantages, making it challenging for organizations to decide in favor of one or the other. As an illustration of this dilemma, consider the case of Alfred Sloan of General Motors. When this multinational corporation chose a multidivisional structure, Sloan found that when the headquarters retained excessive power and authority, the subsidiaries having the operating divisions lacked sufficient autonomy to take their own decisions. Conversely, when too much power and authority was delegated to the subsidiaries, they tried pursuing their own set of objectives, ignoring the needs of the greater corporation. The design of control systems in multinational corporations thus has to deal with special challenges not faced by organizations operating domestically.

The term *control systems*, apart from its use in the context of organizations, has several other connotations. For example, there are several references to control systems in the context of technical systems such as power line control systems or lighting control systems. Interestingly, the basic principles of technical control systems are much the same as they are for organizational control systems. In the case of an automatic washing machine or a toaster, for instance, the combination of components that might be electrical, electronic, mechanical, or hydraulic operate together to maintain system performance close to a desired set of performance specifications. That is how washing machines "know" when to stop washing and start rinsing, and toasters "know" when to stop toasting. Control systems play a vital role in making any system work to predetermined specifications. They also pro-

vide feedback that helps in adjustment of systems to keep them working efficiently and effectively.

See Also: Accountability; Centralized Control; Centralization; Empowerment; Management Information Systems.

Bibliography. Alfred P. Sloan, Jr., *My Years with General Motors* (Doubleday Business, 1990); Don Hellriegel, Susan E. Jackson, and John W. Slocum, Jr., *Management: A Competency-based Approach* (South-Western/Thompson Learning, 2005); Ricky W. Griffin and Michael W. Pustay, *International Business: A Managerial Perspective* (Pearson Prentice Hall, 2007).

Azhar Kazmi
King Fahd University of Petroleum & Minerals

Convertibility

A currency is convertible when it can be exchanged freely for other currencies (or, in the past, gold). Restrictions on convertibility act as a barrier to international trade and capital flows; similarly, for convertibility to be meaningful, other barriers to trade must come down. Since the 1980s, convertibility has spread rapidly, as a large number of countries reduced or eliminated these barriers.

Since countries can impose several levels of currency controls, economists distinguish between different kinds of convertibility. The main distinctions are between current and capital account convertibility, and external and internal convertibility. Current account convertibility refers to the use of a currency for current account transactions, i.e., international payments for goods and services, interest and dividend payments, and remittances or gifts. Capital account convertibility means the absence of restrictions on international capital flows. External convertibility refers to transactions between residents of a country and nonresidents, while internal convertibility is the right of residents to hold assets denominated in foreign currency and to carry out transactions with them.

During the international gold standard, the major economies of the world maintained convertibility between their national currencies and gold at fixed ratios, and permitted international movements of gold with little interference. The U.S. dollar, for example, was defined as equivalent to 23.22 grains of gold. Issuers of these currencies were obligated to convert them to gold on demand at the defined rate ("par value"), and therefore the currencies were convertible to each other. The beginning of the period is not clearly defined, as various countries adopted the gold standard at different times (Great Britain in 1821, Germany in 1871, France and Switzerland in 1878, the United States in 1879, Japan in 1897).

Before that, these countries had followed either a silver or bimetallic standard, and in principle their currencies were convertible, but convertibility was frequently suspended during wars or financial crises. At the end of the 19th century, however, convertibility at the par value was considered to be a prime goal of monetary policy. The stability and confidence this provided helped the great expansion of international trade and investment during this period, sometimes regarded as the first age of globalization.

The outbreak of World War I in 1914 saw the belligerent countries impose strict trade and currency controls, and the gold standard and convertibility were suspended. During the inter-war period (1918–39) attempts were made to restore convertibility, but economic instability, high unemployment, and competitive devaluations led to these attempts being less than successful. During World War II, international transactions again came under severe controls, and currencies became inconvertible.

At the end of World War II, the International Monetary Fund (IMF) was established to promote the smooth functioning of the international monetary system. One of its principal objectives was "to assist in the establishment of a multilateral system of payments in respect of current transactions between members and in the elimination of foreign exchange restrictions which hamper the growth of world trade" (Article 1). Specifically, under Article 8 of the IMF charter, members were to remove restrictions on current account transactions (though such restrictions could be maintained on a temporary basis). Article 6, however, allowed members to regulate international capital movements, since they could be disruptive to the fragile macroeconomic stability of most economies in the immediate postwar period.

For many years, most industrial countries other than the United States and Canada maintained some "temporary" restrictions on current account transactions, particularly for nontrade items. Most developing and centrally planned countries had severe foreign exchange restrictions, and their currencies remained inconvertible.

With inconvertible currencies, international trade often took the form of barter or countertrade. Sometimes this was straightforward—for example, Pepsi-Cola's sale of soft drinks to the Soviet Union in the early 1970s in exchange for vodka. Frequently, it was more complex, like a three-way deal in the 1980s involving the export of cars from Germany to Romania, paid for in jeeps that were sold to Colombia, which paid for the jeeps in coffee and bananas, which were sold to a German supermarket. These transactions, of course, were more difficult to arrange than payment in cash, and inconvertibility was a major barrier to trade.

By the end of the 20th century, the situation had changed considerably, as the benefits of integrating national economies into the global economy became apparent to policy makers. Today, the 23 countries considered "industrial" in the IMF's classification have no restrictions on the use of their currencies, which are fully convertible externally. Their residents also have almost complete freedom to hold accounts denominated in foreign currency, and therefore their currencies are internally convertible as well.

A majority of developing countries and former centrally planned countries have also accepted the obligations of Article 8, and dismantled currency restrictions on most current account transactions as part of comprehensive liberalization programs. Capital account convertibility has been given lower priority, and is more controversial. While the gains from free trade in goods and services are clear, free flows of capital are seen to have costs as well as benefits. The major benefits to developing countries are more resources and investment (since capital is expected to flow from developed to developing countries), leading to an increase in the standard of living. However there is a potential cost: As recognized in Article 6 of the IMF, macroeconomic stability can be endangered by large inflows of capital, since these would generate inflationary pressures. A second cost, illustrated in the Asian crisis of 1997, is that capital inflows can be reversed quickly, leading to severe dislocations in an economy, and by contagion, in other economies as well. Developing economies, therefore, are proceeding carefully in establishing convertibility in the capital account. Most also restrict residents' ability to hold foreign currency accounts, because of concerns about dollarization, and thus do not have internal convertibility.

See Also: Barter; Countertrade; Currency; Current Account; Capital Account Balance; Capital Controls; Capital Flight; Dollarization; International Monetary Fund.

Bibliography. J. Bhagwati, "The Capital Myth: The Difference Between Trade in Widgets and Dollars," *Foreign Affairs* (1998); Stanley Fischer, *Should the IMF Pursue Capital-Account Convertibility?* (International Finance Section, Department of Economics, Princeton University, 1998); R. B. Johnston and Mark Swinburne, *Exchange Rate Arrangements and Currency Convertibility: Developments and Issues* (International Monetary Fund, 1999); J. Braga de Macedo, B. Eichengreen, and J. Reis, *Currency Convertibility: The Gold Standard and Beyond* (Routledge, 1996); International Monetary Fund, *Currency Convertibility and the Fund: Review and Prognosis* (IMF, 1996).

Animesh Ghoshal
DePaul University

Cooperatives

Cooperatives are associations freely created by a group of people to meet their shared needs and to achieve their common purposes. They are democratically controlled organizations in which the ownership, benefits, risks, and losses are shared. They constitute the "third sector" representing the social economy paradigm as an alternative to current globalization trends. Cooperatives are based on trust, self-esteem, shared responsibility, the common welfare, solidarity, and mutual assistance—values that contrast with competition, individualism, control, and coercion, which characterize the private enterprise.

Cooperatives are created to meet different economic and social needs and purposes of its members. There are cooperatives of production, consumption, banking, housing, community development, and others to

This Mongolian herders' cooperative gathered to review plans to increase their production of vegetables in 2007.

solve shared problems related to education, health, employment, culture, and recreation. Their economic relevance, though not widely recognized, is unquestionable. Some available data indicate that more than 800 million people worldwide are involved in a cooperative; they are a very important source of employment, redistribution of wealth, and social equity.

The idea of cooperatives is not recent. Their origin can be traced to the beginning of the 19th century, when the utopian socialists began imagining new forms of organization. Robert Owen and Charles Fourier, for example, conceived cooperatives as an alternative organizational arrangement compared to capitalism and competition. The Rochdale pioneers also developed cooperative experiences in the interests of its members under some main principles: Voluntary and open membership, democratic control, economic participation, autonomy and independence, education and training, cooperation with other cooperatives, and concern for the community's interests. One of the most remarkable examples of the 20th century is the successful Mondragón Cooperative Corporation in Spain, which has demonstrated some advantages of cooperatives over traditional capitalist enterprises.

Cooperatives remain an important organizational option in the 21st century to overcome the failures of multinational corporations and the market economy to ensure economic development and to meet the social needs of the majority of the population. Cooperatives formed from the factories recovered in Argentina reaffirms that workers are able to run companies and to design and control their own work. The autonomous Zapatista municipalities in Mexico are also a good example of the possibilities of cooperatives to solve community problems. The cooperative movement is increasingly seen as an important option for social change in favor of economic democracy and social empowerment.

Cooperatives are distinguished from private companies by their purposes, their governance structure and their modes of operation. Their purposes are shared; they protect the interest of the association under a principle of solidarity, instead of individual goals. Management involves the active participation of its members. Decision making is accomplished through an equal distribution of power because each member has a vote regardless of the contribution that he or she has made to capital. Their governance structure can be represented by an inverted pyramid in which the members of the cooperative are the highest authority and the board of directors depends on them. Finally, their mode of operation is collaborative, and is based on mutual aid and shared responsibility.

Some characteristics raise important advantages compared to private enterprise and its traditional bureaucratic structure based on a vertical division of labor and centralized decision making. Members of the cooperative are highly motivated people disposed to collaborate: They appreciate their position as co-owners, so they know everything they do or cease to do has an impact on performance, results, and profits. Cooperatives adopt a flat scale of remuneration to avoid large wage differentials between levels, which means greater internal equality; they attain a greater internal cohesion based on collaborative work to reduce direct control and hierarchical authority. In addition, inter-cooperative collaboration facilitates the creation of tools like mutual support funds to overcome temporary difficulties, producing solidarity economy initiatives that favor local development. Teamwork and participation reduce the required bureaucratic apparatus and, consequently, their operating costs. Finally, benefits produced by the cooperative do not have to be given to external shareholders, which propitiates a greater social distribution of profits.

However, cooperatives also confront some difficulties and problems. On the one hand, globalization of markets increasingly presses cooperatives to compete with private companies, which has led to the need to adopt more entrepreneurial forms that threaten their nature and purposes. Needs of the members of the association are gradually displaced by the imperative of growth and accumulation that all economic enterprises need to survive in highly competitive and dynamic markets. Cooperatives appear to be trapped in a dilemma because economic success seems at odds with social effectiveness.

On the other hand, democratic governance of cooperatives involves more time to make a decision, delaying opportune responses demanded by dynamic markets. In addition, such democratic structures do not imply necessarily the democratization of the production processes and the introduction of participatory arrangements to favor collective solution of problems at work. This contradiction between democratic governance and authoritarian shop practices generates frustration among the members of the cooperative, because they know they can participate in main decisions but, at the same time, they realize they are excluded from the day-to-day decisions in their workplace.

The accumulated experience of cooperatives is very important for the future. Emerging social movements are increasingly demanding greater participation to prevent abuses of the state and corruption of large private corporations; cooperatives reemerged as an alternative that could lead to building a new social project to transcend the current market economy and globalization. This option would be based on a growing social participation to establish new institutions of regulation of state actions as well as private economic freedom, allowing a real economic integration of the world based on the general well-being of society.

See Also: Antiglobalization Movement; Consumer Needs and Wants; Fair Trade; Democratic Globalization; Individualism/Collectivism; Sustainable Development.

Bibliography. David C. Korten, *The Great Turning From Empire to Earth Community* (Berrett-Koehler, 2006); William Foote Whyte and Kathleen King Whyte, *Making Mondragon: The Growth and Dynamics of the Worker Co-operative Complex* (ILR Press, 1991); Kimberly A. Zeuli and Robert Cropp, *Cooperatives: Principles and Practices in the 21st Century* (University of Wisconsin–Extension, 2004).

Eduardo Ibarra-Colado
Universidad Autónoma Metropolitana

Co-Production

Co-production has had various meanings over the years. In the 19th century, for example, the *Oxford English Dictionary* was "co-produced" from volunteer contributions of millions of slips of paper. For many years it referred to film co-production and the co-production of armaments. But today, the most frequent use of co-production is as a Web 2.0 tool where customers actually produce their own products and services. In the past, customers expected companies to do a lot of the work for them. Now, companies are expecting customers to do more of the work themselves.

The changes in the meaning of co-production are astounding. During the Cold War era, co-production meant transferring manufacturing know-how to allies to enable them to produce weapon systems. Co-production has also long meant film companies working together on a movie or a television venture in which more than one broadcaster is providing the funding. In publishing, co-production refers to the process where a book is created and sold to publishers in different countries in a joint production. The firms adapt or translate the book into their local language, sending the digital files for printing back to the originator who co-ordinates the overall production.

In the manufacturing sector co-production refers to a system in which multiple products are produced on the same production run for customers that differ in their product price thresholds or upgrade desires. A more recent definition of co-production is when clients work alongside professionals as partners in the delivery of social services. One refers here to the "co-production sector" where service users are regarded as assets involved in support and delivery of services. Co-production redefines clients as assets with experience, the ability to care, and many useful skills.

One frequently used definition of co-production today emerges from the barriers to entry that many firms face when going into a foreign market. These include physical barriers, political and regulatory barriers, trade sanctions and export controls, market barriers, cultural barriers, and so forth. Many firms overcome these barriers by entering into arrangement such as joint ventures, licensing agreements, franchises, mergers and acquisitions, or greenfield investment. Another way to overcome market barriers is when companies cooperate to produce goods.

This kind of co-production allows firms to share complementary resources, take advantage of unused capacity, shift the location of production, and benefit from economies of scale. Companies may cooperate to make components or even entire products. In cross-manufacturing agreements, companies in different markets can cooperate to manufacture each other's products for their local markets.

The newest definition starts with the notion of customers as the new co-production sector. This ranges from something as mundane as pumping one's own gas or taking cash out of the ATM to something as sophisticated as designing one's own laptop computer. In the internet era of relationship marketing, customer testimonials, and reputation networks, companies are creating goods, services, and experiences in close cooperation with experienced and creative consumers. They tap into their intellectual capital and reward them for what gets produced, manufactured, developed, designed, serviced, or processed. Co-production allows firms to reduce their own costs while giving the customer greater control and value. The net result is a value chain that increases usage, satisfaction, trust, loyalty, and ultimately lifetime customer value.

Co-production in this sense is a dynamic process composed of distinct stages where consumers can become involved. Certain economic, cultural, and technological preconditions have to be met. For example, customers from poorer economies may not be ready to attach greater value to customization in their needs satisfaction. Nor may the threshold of ease and accessibility of Web-based tools have been reached. Nor may customers have much of the determining resource in co-production, their own time. A highly innovative culture will lead to more co-production than a highly standardized or hierarchical culture. Also, the product makes a difference. A washing machine has a limited number of features and offers limited incentives for co-production than does a laptop computer. Situational factors such as trust make a difference (can I trust that my e-ticket will be honored?). Of course, the cost-benefit analysis in a co-creation activity is core.

A good example is the Swedish multinational IKEA. IKEA customers are accustomed to collecting unassembled pieces of furniture from a warehouse on the fringe of a metropolitan area in their own large car. They transport these kits to their own homes and, using tools provided by the manufacturer, they assemble the components into a sofa or a table. Southwest Airlines early on shifted booking to the customer through a simple Web interface for completing transactions. The incentive was the double awards credit (which it has since eliminated without negatively impacting their business).

Benefits

For decades, consumers have been saving up their insights and rants because they didn't have adequate means to interact with companies. The era of co-creation and co-production has led to new forms of business. Customers are the minipreneurs, that is, consumers turned into value-creating entrepreneurs. They are also called e-lancers, micro businesses, Web-driven entrepreneurs, free agents, cottage businesses, co-preneurs, co-creators, eBaypreneurs, ad-sponsored bloggers, PodCasters, and so on.

Changes in the value chain lead to increased company revenue at a lower cost. When customers are given the opportunity of performing tasks themselves, their system usage increases and they are able to capture more value. Operating costs to the firm decrease since the do-it-yourselfer needs less help. This leads to a virtuous circle: Usage contributes to satisfaction, satisfaction leads to trust, trust leads to loyalty, and loyalty leads to an increase in the customer's lifetime value to the company.

The Information Age

Co-production is now powered by Web 2.0 (online tools that enhance creativity, information sharing, and collaboration) and by Generation-C (customers imbued with creativity, content, and control). Generation-C entrepreneurs are multitaskers and they like constructing products rather than being sold to. They want to be interactive and want to customize as they choose. They are the emerging "co-production sector" where customers are regarded as assets, involved in mutual support and the delivery of products and services. Rather than being treated as "end users," they are now seen as untapped potential assets.

Co-production in the Information Age has morphed into a number of new terms such as crowd-sourcing, do-it-yourself advertising, customer product development, mass customization, and customer

ticket clipping. Today's co-producers enjoy a wide range of highly-developed tools, resources, and processes at their disposal. This includes hardware, software, ICT and skills; design, production and manufacturing; ways to monetize assets; new marketplaces; new forms of advertising; and new ways to find talent and manage finance, payment, and logistics. Wikipedia, the free online encyclopedia, is a good example of modern co-production because it allows anyone to change or create an article. Wikipedia content improves over time as more and more accuracy is gained through an exposure of articles to the whole community.

Where this all will lead is probably to the ballot box. Joined-up government, place-based policy making, and co-production with citizens offer exciting new possibilities for creating flexible, dynamic, and democratic governments.

See Also: Consumer Behavior; Entrepreneurship; Focus Groups; Service Expectations; Value Chain.

Bibliography. Seigyoung Auh, Simon J. Bell, Colin S. McLeod, and Eric Shih, "Co-Production and Customer Loyalty in Financial Services," *Journal of Retailing* (v.83/3, 2007); Taco Brandsen and Victor Pestoff, "Co-Production, the Third Sector and the Delivery of Public Services: An Introduction," *Public Management Review* (v.8/4, 2006); S. Carlson, "The Net Generation Goes to College," *Chronicle of Higher Education* (October 7, 2005); Marcia-Anne Dobres, "Inside the Politics of Technology: Agency and Normativity in the Co-Production of Technology and Society," *Technology and Culture* (v.48/1, 2007); M. Etgar, "A Descriptive Model of Consumer Co-production Process," *Journal of the Academy of Marketing Science* (v.36, 2008); Selma Oener and Taner Bilgic, "Economic Lot Scheduling with Uncontrolled Co-Production," *European Journal of Operational Research* (v.188/3, 2008); Tale Skjolsvik, Bente R. Lowendahl, Ragnhild Kvalshaugen, and Siw M. Fosstenlokken, "Choosing to Learn and Learning to Choose: Strategies for Client Co-Production and Knowledge Development," *California Management Review* (v.49/3, 2007); Wei-Feng Tung and Soe-Tysr Yuan, "A Service Design Framework for Value Co-Production: Insight from Mutualism Perspective," *Kybernetes* (v.37/1–2, 2008).

HOWARD FREDERICK
UNITEC NEW ZEALAND

Copyright Infringement

Copyright infringement is the violation of copyright law through the illegal use of protected material. This includes both the reproduction of that material and the creation of derivative works from it. In the case of media (movies, music, books, software, et cetera), reproduction is also called *piracy*—a term that is sometimes contested, but has in fact been used this way with reference to books and documents since at least the beginning of the 17th century, longer than copyright law itself has existed. One of the controversies surrounding copyright has always been that infringement is not exactly theft; while it may impact the copyright owner's profits (as in bootleg DVDs), the law does not require that it do so. And while it may bring to the infringer profits reaped from someone else's property, in the case of derivative works the labor and intellectual contribution of the infringer is still involved—and, again, profit is not necessary to constitute an infringement. Although copyrights can be filed, material is copyrighted regardless of whether a filing was made; the filing is simply helpful in the event of a court case, to provide proof of the validity of the rights-owner's claim.

Enforcing a copyright claim begins with a cease and desist letter, which in many cases is sufficient, because of the fear of legal reprisals or the infringer's previous misunderstanding of the relevant law. If this proves insufficient, the rights-holder can then file a lawsuit, and will often seek a preliminary injunction, which prevents the infringer from continuing the alleged infringement until the trial has completed. This will nearly always be done in cases that the plaintiff expects to be settled out of court, because of the additional hassle for the defendant. If the trial is resolved in the plaintiff's favor, he is entitled to a permanent injunction against the defendant's further infringement, and/or monetary damages, depending on the circumstances of the infringement.

The Doctrine of Fair Use

The doctrine of fair use is a concept in American copyright law that permits certain uses of copyrighted material without requiring permission from the copyright owner, even over the owner's objections. Similar doctrines obtain in the copyright laws of other countries.

There are four factors used to determine if fair use applies, which the Copyright Act of 1976 identifies as, first of all, the purpose or character of the use, including whether such use is of commercial nature or for nonprofit educational purposes. This factor considers, for instance, whether the use of the copyrighted material is merely derivative (not protected under fair use) or transformative (protected). Satire and parody are protected instances of fair use, in theory: in practice it's important to remember that the copyrighted material must be necessary to the parody. Inserting scenes from other movies into your own movie is more likely to be derivative than transformative—and even if the court rules in favor of transformativeness, the legal costs to see that decision through are prohibitive.

Not every educational use is fair use, which stands to reason when one considers the amount of educational material that is copyrighted; if it were permissible to ignore copyright simply because one's use is educational and nonprofit, schools would Xerox their textbooks rather than purchase multiple copies of them, which in turn would lead to textbook publishing being too unprofitable for the industry to persist, a classic (or textbook) example of the process by which copyright infringement can have consequences beyond the impact on a single rights-holder.

The second factor is the nature of the copyrighted work. This expressly does not mean that the extent of protection from copyright infringement is proportionate to the artistic merit of the work. The type of work can be a factor, though. It is in this second factor that the "idea-expression dichotomy" comes into play: facts and ideas cannot be copyrighted. Contrary to what many people think, for instance, you cannot copyright an idea for a movie or novel—you can only copyright the expression of that idea, i.e., the screenplay (and finished film), the novel, and the distinctive characters involved. Even in the case of the characters, trademark is much stronger protection than copyright, which is why major properties like Indiana Jones are trademarked. The name and likeness can be trademarked; every work in which they appear can be copyrighted; but the idea of an archaeology professor having serial-inspired adventures on major digs is fair game for anyone. Likewise, though you can copyright your memoir about your life with your ex-spouse, you cannot prevent her from writing her own book about those events.

Another wrinkle here is the fact that although inclusion of a patentable idea in a copyrighted work does not constitute a patent claim, it does prevent anyone else from making a patent claim on the idea, regardless of whether the copyrighted work is the source of the claim. The famous example of this, well-known in discussions of intellectual property law, is Arthur C. Clarke's description of the idea of geosynchronous communications satellites, which prevented Bell Labs from patenting such satellites they developed in-house. The functionality doctrine likewise prevents patentable ideas from being protected by trademark alone. The fact that we have had to bring up both trademark law and patent claims in a discussion of copyright fair use hints at some of the problems legal reformers have with the body of IP law as it now stands; the difference in protections offered to an idea in a copyrighted work and an idea in a patent claim depends essentially on the paperwork the rights-holder filled out.

As mentioned previously, work is copyrighted at the moment of creation, and the courts have ruled that copyrighted work is treated equally whether it is published or not. An unexpected wrinkle of this, one that may be the object of concern in the 21st century as privacy concerns become prominent, is that fair use applies equally to unpublished work as well, which in a bogeyman slippery slope scenario provides a little brother with the legal right to publish excerpts of his sister's diary, provided his parody is sufficiently transformative.

Another factor is the amount and substantiality of the portion of the copyrighted work used. Both words are important here. Since 1991's *Grand Upright Music v. Warner Bros Records*, use of song samples in music do not constitute fair use if the sample is long enough to be recognizable. There is a commonly held belief that up to 300 words of a written work can be quoted and constitute fair use; there is no legal basis for this belief. Book reviews may not often provide excerpts longer than that, but that is as much because of space concerns—while term papers may well quote more than that, and theses will almost certainly do so, and both of these instances are commonly considered fair use.

The last factor is the effect of the use upon the potential market for or value of the copyrighted work. This includes, but is not limited to, the impact of the usage on the rights-owner's profits. Giving away bootlegged copies of a DVD has a clear impact on the rights-owner's profits, for instance. A *MAD Magazine* parody of that movie that persuades the reader that the movie isn't worth watching—or a review that spoils the ending—has just as much impact but is almost certainly protected as fair use. Another common misconception is that any reproduction of a portion of a copyrighted work is fair use if the source is credited, for which there is no basis in either the letter or the spirit of the law.

Though many of our examples may seem trivial, the significance of the fair use doctrine extends beyond its interest in upholding First Amendment freedoms of speech; a 2007 study by the Computer and Communications Industry found that one-sixth of the American gross domestic product was generated by fair use (search engines, for instance, depend on fair use protections).

Bootlegging

The word *bootlegging* can be hard to nail down, and in its broadest sense simply means the creation of a recording not authorized by the owner of the pertinent rights. This can include illegal copies of albums, movies, and software, and in the 21st century the term "bootleg" has been used, especially in Europe, to refer to bastard pop music, a form of computer-manipulated music in which elements of multiple songs are combined into a new song that retains the familiarity of its source material. (The classic bastard pop formula is A+B: the vocals of one song with the music of another.) But typically, especially in the United States, bootlegging is understood to refer to the recording of concerts, and the subsequent distribution of those recordings.

Though it is possible to buy such recordings, there is a long history—going back to the early days of blues, and especially strong since the advent of touring rock bands—of not-for-profit behavior among bootleggers. Despite the high cost of bootlegging in earlier decades, when recording equipment was costlier and bulkier, the resulting tapes were typically only traded for other tapes, or made available for the cost of reproduction. Though this does not constitute fair use and does not make the copyright any less infringed, it did have the desired effect: because little money was changing hands, record labels had little reason to go after bootleggers after the fact, and in such cases when they did decided to be bothered by the practice, their efforts were confined mostly to the prevention of such recording. Some bands, most famously the Grateful Dead, embraced bootlegging and encouraged taping of their concerts. While the band is not always the rights-holder, this still makes the matter more difficult to pursue in court.

The Digital Millennium Copyright Act

The ambitiously named Digital Millennium Copyright Act was passed unanimously by the Senate and signed into law by President Clinton in October of 1998. Principally, the DMCA updated the language of copyright law to reflect the existence of the internet and digital media, and implemented the two treaties signed by members of the World Intellectual Property Organization in 1996. It explicitly extended the reach of copyright in order to protected copyrighted material from being illegally reproduced electronically—such as through the online sharing of mp3s—and limited the liability of internet service providers. If you put a copy of the new Indiana Jones movie on your Web site, you are the one in trouble—not the cable company through which you connect to the internet, or the company you rent your online data storage from.

An area the courts are undecided on is the legality and liability of linking to copyright-infringing material. While it has not explicitly been found legal, neither has anyone yet been found liable for it yet, except in such cases when the linker was trying to get around an injunction by linking to material they had been forced to remove from their own Web site.

See Also: Intellectual Property Theft; Patents; Trademark Infringement.

Bibliography. Ben Depoorter and Francesco Parisi, "Fair Use and Copyright Protection: A Price Theory Explanation," *International Review of Law and Economics* (v.21/4, 2002); Wendy J. Gordon, "Fair Use as Market Failure: A Structural and Economic Analysis of the 'Betamax' Case and Its Predecessors," *Columbia Law Review* (v.82/8, 1982); Pamela Samuelson, "Copyright's fair use doctrine and digital data," *Publishing Research Quarterly* (v.11/1, 1995); B. Rosenblatt, *Digital Rights Management: Business and Technology* (M&T Books, 2001); Clinton Heylin, *Bootleg! The Rise & Fall of the Secret Recording Industry* (Omnibus Press, 2004).

BILL KTE'PI
INDEPENDENT SCHOLAR

Core

"The core" refers, collectively, to those affluent, heavily industrialized, and highly developed countries from which emanates the majority of global economic activity. Prime examples of "core" nations include the United States, Japan, Germany, France, and the United Kingdom (UK). Understanding the nature of "the core" and how it interfaces with non-core areas of the world is essential to understanding economic development and the global economic system.

From a practical standpoint, the notion of "the core" is useful in accounting for the fact that there is great heterogeneity among the nations of the world in terms of their respective nature and level of involvement in the global economic system. Some countries are very inwardly focused—domestically producing most products consumed and not engaging in extensive exporting. Other countries—the "core" countries—are heavily involved in global economic activity. In this regard, a core nation's role in the global economic system typically involves high levels of both transnational exporting (of domestically produced products) and importing (of foreign-made goods). It should thus be of little surprise that core nations are typically home to the world's largest and most global businesses. For example, 337 of the corporations in the 2007 Fortune Global 500 are headquartered in five core nations (162 in the United States, 67 in Japan, 38 in France, 37 in Germany, and 33 in the UK). Nine of the 10 largest global corporations are headquartered in these five core nations.

The notion of the core also helps account for vast international heterogeneity with regard to level of wealth. Core nations tend to be very wealthy in terms of a host of indicators such as gross domestic product (GDP), per capita income, and average household income. Consider, for example, that although the United States and Japan account, respectively, for only 4.67 percent and 2.09 percent of the world's population, they account for 25.4 percent (United States) and 9.86 percent (Japan) of global wealth and 21.67 percent (United States) and 7.05 percent (Japan) of the world's GDP. The world's seven wealthiest nations, while accounting for only 11.66 percent of the world's population, account for 54.81 percent of global wealth and 43.48 percent of the world's GDP.

Theoretically, the notion of the core formally originated in the context of dependency theory. This theory of economic development was created in the late 1950s and 1960s by development scholars in poor nations who felt that then dominant theories of development failed to adequately account for the fact that the uneven diffusion of technical progress had heavily contributed to the division of the global economy into two types of countries (i.e., affluent, heavily industrialized, and highly developed "core" nations, and less affluent, relatively unindustrialized, and underdeveloped "peripheral" countries [e.g., inwardly focused, agrarian African nations such as Burundi, Rwanda, Tanzania, and Zambia]). Further, these scholars believed that existing conceptualizations of economic development focused far too heavily on understanding "core" nations while also misguidedly laying much of the blame for the underdevelopment of poor countries on these nations and their disadvantaged peoples.

Dependency theory holds, most essentially, that "peripheral" countries may suffer negative (economic, cultural, and developmental) consequences as a result of forming economic bonds with "core" nations heavily involved in the global economic system. Dependency proponents contend, in this regard, that the formation of ties with "the core" may cause "peripheral" nations to become highly dependent on the core and that self-serving, potentially imperialistic core leaders may take advantage of this situation by exploiting key peripheral nation resources (e.g., human labor and water, lumber, minerals, and other raw materials).

However, it should be noted that the hypothesized outcomes of interaction with the core for peripheral countries differ in the two main forms of dependency theory. In the context of "orthodox (or radical) dependency," increased linkage to core nations is viewed as necessarily leading to the "development of underdevelopment" (i.e., worsened economic conditions and quality of life) in "the periphery." In the less extreme "unorthodox" version of dependency theory, development and underdevelopment can occur simultaneously. Here, the level of development in the periphery is viewed as being a function of the manner in which the periphery interacts with the core. It is hypothesized, for example, that interactions with the core involving foreign direct investment (i.e., allowing companies located in the core to purchase or establish wholly owned production facilities in peripheral territory), foreign debt, and export trade lead to a higher level of dependence and less positive and slower peripheral development than interactions based on the acceptance of foreign aid and foreign trade.

From a theoretical perspective, it is also important to understand that the hypothesized role of the core in dependency theory is diametrically opposed to the core's role in (the previously dominant) modernization theory. The latter theory of economic development contends that poor nation development is predicated first and foremost on the establishment of close economic bonds with the core. From this perspective, less-affluent, peripheral nations are necessarily brought up to core-nation standards (i.e., modernized) as a result of increasing involvement in the global economic system—realized perhaps only by forging intimate economic ties to the core. Modernization theorists contend that the developmental benefits of this increased level of involvement in the global economic system necessarily "trickle down" from the core to the periphery.

The Case of China

Consider China's rapid, ongoing ascension toward "core" status. The world's largest country was for many years a relatively isolated, inwardly focused peripheral nation in the background of the modern global economic system. In the last three decades the Chinese economy has not only become very global but has also doubled in size every eight years. In addition, during this same period of time, nearly 400 million Chinese people have emerged from poverty—many of them by personally becoming part of the global economic system as a result of moving from farms in rural areas to manufacturing jobs in large cities.

Although China's amazing rise toward the core can be viewed as at least somewhat supportive of both the unorthodox version of dependency theory and modernization theory, its development defies simple, complete explanation by either theory. Consistent with unorthodox dependency theory, China's (highly uneven and far from completely core-like) development is predicated significantly on high levels of foreign trade—both importing and exporting—with governments and corporations in established core nations. At the same time, more consistent with modernization theory, the growth of China's economy can also be credited to high levels of foreign direct investment from core nations. However, neither theory adequately takes into account other developmental factors including, but not limited to, high levels of personal savings and the leveraging of outsourcing-based partnerships with core-nation manufacturers (to gain access to key technologies that can be used to spawn Chinese firms that eventually compete in the global marketplace against the very same core-nation companies outsourcing their manufacturing to China in the first place).

See Also: China; Dependency Theory; Economic Development; Industrialized Countries; Less Industrialized Countries; Periphery.

Bibliography. James Davies, Susanna Sandstrom, Anthony Shorrocks, and Edward Wolff, "Estimating the Level and Distribution of Global Household Wealth," World Institute for Development Economics Research of the United Nations University, www.wider.unu.edu (cited March 2009); Peter Evans and John D. Stephens, "Development and the World Economy," in *Handbook of Sociology*, N. J. Smelser, ed. (Sage, 1988); Gary Gereffi, "The International Economy and Economic Development," in *The Handbook of Economic Sociology*, N. J. Smelser and R. Swedberg, eds. (Princeton University Press, 1994); Fareed Zakaria, *The Post-American World* (W. W. Norton, 2008).

Terrance G. Gabel
University of Arkansas–Fort Smith

Corporate Accounting

Corporate accounting is the measurement, summary, and interpretation of financial information and events pertaining to a company or organization. More than just bookkeeping, the key word in corporate accounting is the *account* of the name—the tale it tells, the explanation of the numbers.

The core of accounting is the double-entry bookkeeping system, which originated with Luca Pacioli, a Franciscan friar in 15th-century Venice who taught mathematics to Leonardo da Vinci. Pacioli streamlined the system in use among Italian merchants, and included it in his seminal mathematics textbook, from which it was quickly adopted across Europe. In double-entry bookkeeping, every transaction leaves a record in two (or more) accounts—the debit account from which money is leaving, and the credit account

to which it is going. Balancing a personal checkbook, by contrast, is usually done according to a single-entry bookkeeping system.

Double-entry bookkeeping involves multiple copies of the same information. Sales transactions generate receipts for both parties. Deposit slips are collected after making bank deposits. These source documents are saved, with their information recorded into daybooks, of which there are usually multiple types for different types of data—a sales journal, a tax journal, and so on. After a set period of time—usually monthly, weekly, or quarterly—the figures from each journal are tallied to provide a financial picture of the period. Those tallies are further recorded—a process called posting, in accounting terminology—in the book of accounts (or ledger), and balanced to make sure that debits and credits are equal.

Double-checking the ledger is done by producing an unadjusted trial balance, an accounting document usually made in three columns, the first of which contains the names of accounts with non-zero balances. Debit balances are recorded in column two, credit balances in column three. If the respective totals of the two columns aren't the same, an error has either been made during the posting process or revealed by it. Once any such errors have been taken care of, the balance is adjusted according to the needs of the business—typically correcting for inventory amounts—and an adjusted trial balance is produced and used as the basis for a variety of financial statements. Those statements include the P&L—the profit and loss statement—the statement of retained earnings, the balance sheet, and the cash flow statement.

In preparing financial statements, accountants in the United States are bound by Generally Accepted Accounting Principles (GAAP); other countries have other terms for their standards, and an international set of standards is of increasing importance. Common law countries—like the United States and the United Kingdom—do not specifically set their standards in law, though there is growing sentiment that they would benefit from doing so. It is part of the body of common law, required of publicly traded companies by the SEC, set by the Governmental Accounting Standards Board and the Financial Accounting Standards Board according to the type of accounting. The SEC has announced that by 2016, it expects the accounting standards followed by public companies to adhere to those of the International Accounting Standards Board (IASB), reflecting the increasingly global nature of doing business.

The objectives of GAAP are to ensure that financial statements are useful to investors and creditors both actual and potential, in order to help them make financial decisions in which the company is involved. GAAP is organized into four "basic assumptions," four basic principles, and four basic constraints. The assumptions are that the company is a business entity, with a financial identity independent of its owners; that it is a "going concern," expected to remain in business indefinitely; that a stable currency such as the dollar will be the unit used in financial statements; and that the company's economic activities transpire over a time period that can be divided up for the purpose of preparing reports.

The four principles are the cost principle (companies report their actual costs, not the fair market value of their assets), the revenue principle (companies record when revenue is realized or earned, not when cash is received), the matching principle (expenses have to be matched with revenue), and the disclosure principle (sufficient information should be disclosed to allow the readers of financial statements to make informed decisions). The constraints are the objectivity principle (financial statements should be based on objective evidence), the materiality principle (that which would impact a decision is significant and material), the consistency principle (the same accounting methods should be used year to year), and the prudent principle (err on the side of understating the company's success, not overstating it). In the unlikely event that adhering to GAAP would create a misleading financial statement, the accountant is ethically bound to depart from GAAP practices and explicitly note the departure and the nature of the misapprehension that would have resulted.

International standards differ not so much in their objectives as in their specifics; the International Financial Reporting Standards (IFRS) adopted by the IASB specifically lay out the financial statements and documents that are to be produced for a variety of situations and uses. IFRS also explicitly calls for comparability as a qualitative characteristic of a standards-compliant financial statement: the statements produced for any two companies should be similar enough in structure and type of content that it is easy for potential investors to compare the two companies without having to do any "translation." In general, the IFRS reflect the specificity and tendencies of code-law countries such as much of western Europe and Asia. Regardless of the set of accounting standards adhered to, separate standards—again, more specific than GAAP—obtain when preparing reports for tax purposes, where very specific information needs to be identified.

One reason for the switch to IFRS is because of growing dissatisfaction with American corporate accounting practices, as a result of recent accounting scandals. 2002 saw every major accounting firm—Arthur Andersen, Deloitte & Touche, Ernst & Young, KPMG, and PricewaterhouseCoopers—charged with negligence or admitting to other forms of wrongdoing, amid the indictment of Arthur Andersen over the Enron scandal, the bankruptcy of WorldCom only weeks later, and a stock market downturn credited in part to the failure of investor confidence in the accurate reporting of the companies in which they were expected to invest.

See Also: Accounting Harmonization; Accounting Software; Compliance; Cost Accounting; Enron Corporation; International Accounting Standards Board; International Financial Reporting Standards.

Bibliography. Troy Adair, *Corporate Finance Demystified* (McGraw-Hill, 2005); John R. Emshwiller and Rebecca Smith, *24 Days: How Two Wall Street Journal Reporters Uncovered the Lies that Destroyed Faith in Corporate America or Infectious Greed* (HarperInformation, 2003); Bethany McLean and Peter Elkind, *The Smartest Guys in the Room: The Amazing Rise and Scandalous Fall of Enron* (Portfolio, 2004).

BILL KTE'PI
INDEPENDENT SCHOLAR

Corporate Change

Firms, as organizers of productive activities, undergo a continuous process of change. To remain competitive in a world characterized by rapid shifts in technology and resource utilization patterns, firms need to commit themselves to all manner of transition and transformation. However, firms also need to deliver a dynamic response that takes into account all major stakeholders, including customers, suppliers, regulators, and global competition. Corporate change management thus strives to meet customer and market demands by reexamining the relevant processes of production and service delivery. The assumed response may be driven by specific needs of the firm: There could be a felt need for new product-market strategies that fully meet changing market demand or there could be a desire to maximize resources by dealing with managerial and control inadequacies.

One way of managing change is to undertake a merger. Mergers can redraw the boundaries of a firm. It is traditionally assumed that mergers are conducted when a firm with high asset valuations purchases another firm with low asset valuations. It is believed that under the better management of the high-asset purchaser, the assets of underperforming targets will be directed toward more profitable projects. Seen this way, a merger leverages the strengths of one firm by combining with another firm. A number of studies explained the merger waves of the 1980s and 1990s in such terms. However, recent evidence suggests that target valuations are much higher than the average firm, which casts doubt on such a motive for a merger.

A firm's strategic change and rapid growth objectives may also be important in explaining the motive for wanting to merge with another firm. Mergers can be undertaken to allow diversification or vertical integration, help achieve resource sharing and operational efficiencies, or permit access to global markets. Research on organizational change suggests that many such opportunities are more fully exploited by identifying and coordinating complementary products or processes. Strategic complementarities are about how two activities when joined together produce an outcome that is better than when activities are undertaken on their own account. Complementarities associated with new technologies, changes in people-oriented organizational systems, and globalization help make mergers successful and enduring.

The success of the modern corporation is built on possessing unique capabilities or resources. Such capabilities may be related to a product, process, or a way of doing things that meets an existing or potential market need. But any attempt to strengthen firm products, processes, or ways of doing things often carries within it the danger of an inflexibility that ensures operational efficiency but also an inability to build new skills and capabilities. As a result, it becomes harder and harder to anticipate and make changes that assimilate new technologies and processes effectively, turning firms' "core" businesses into "noncore" operations and making "unique" products not very unique. In these situations, firms may experience contraction, which will be noted in the processes of privatization, divestment, or many other types of restructuring programs. Corporate restructuring in the 1980s saw a major realignment of existing firm assets, resulting in divestment and selling off of a large number of activities and assets. The release of resources through the disposal of assets that are unimportant to the main operational areas of a firm is a major plank of the strategic approach to corporate change.

Leveraged buy-outs (LBOs) are a good example of how corporate changes are undertaken in response to the inability or unwillingness of current owners and managers to take the business through to its new stage of development. Businesses sometimes need to inject new capital or attract or warrant the management talent, or introduce financial innovations such as new debt and equity structures, which can more appropriately be achieved through an LBO. LBOs thus serve an important corporate objective.

Corporate change thus manifests itself in many shapes and forms of "restructuring," "reengineering" operations, and "rethinking" strategy and organization. Such initiatives are an essential part of the process of growth in an economy that seeks to make the best use of available resources.

See Also: Acquisitions, Takeovers, and Mergers; Citigroup; Corporate Governance; Privatization; Product Development; Technology.

Bibliography. M. Marks and P. Mirvis, *Joint Forces: Making One Plus One Equal Three in Mergers, Acquisitions, and Alliances* (Jossey-Bass, 1998); R. Miles and C. Snow, *Organizational Strategy, Structure and Process* (McGraw-Hill, 1978); P. Milgrom and J. Roberts, "Complementarities and Fit Strategy, Structure, and Organizational Change in Manufacturing," *Journal of Accounting and Economics* (1995).

Tahir M. Nisar
University of Southampton
School of Management

Corporate Codes of Conduct

Nearly every large domestic and multinational corporation today has a corporate code of business conduct as part of its formal corporate governance system. The nature and content of the codes vary considerably and they are influenced by the national cultures from which they originate and/or are applied. However, in general, corporate codes of conduct are voluntary, self-regulatory statements of business moral standards, legal compliance, organizational policy, and/or civic responsibility that hold those governed or affected by the codes accountable for ethical behavior in accordance with them.

Corporate codes of conduct can be classified into three categories: codes of compliance, codes of ethics, and codes of best practice. Codes of compliance emphasize strict alignment with enacted legal and regulatory requirements. For example, the passage of the Foreign Corrupt Practices Act in 1977, the creation of the 1991 U.S. Corporate Sentencing Guidelines, the implementation of the Sarbanes-Oxley Act of 2002, and other legislative enactments influenced the content of corporate codes of compliance by explicitly criminalizing executive actions that authorized inaccurate accounting and financial reporting to investors, resorting to global bribery to obtain business, and violating workplace health and safety standards. Corporate codes of compliance are designed to prevent criminal misconduct and to protect the firm from the risk of financial and litigation costs due to illegal and/or unethical employee behavior.

Corporate codes of ethics are not designed to prevent criminal misconduct but to enable current responsible corporate action. These codes state the values and principles that form the purpose of the corporation and the current prioritized moral responsibilities that employees have to all company market and non-market stakeholders and for which they are held accountable. For example, the Johnson & Johnson Credo is a corporate code of ethics that identifies and prioritizes the moral responsibilities of company leaders in making ethical strategic business decisions. This corporate code of ethics provided critical moral guidance to global corporate decision makers who took Tylenol off the shelves when product tampering was documented, thereby morally prioritizing the safety needs of current customers over the financial needs of current investors. The corporate code of ethics enabled uniform, timely, principled global business decision making in a crisis situation by providing value prioritization guidance and a comprehensive stakeholder moral frame of reference to exercise responsible business judgment—even when it would have been legally defensible to delay such a business decision.

Corporate codes of best practice are aspirational in nature and geared to the future direction of corporate moral progress. For example, the United Nations Global Compact and the Caux Roundtable's Code delineate moral best practices that would improve future world prosperity and global corporate citizenship relations between business and its many stakeholders worldwide. Such codes of best practice provide direction and incentives for continual corporate moral improvement in the global marketplace.

A corporate code of conduct is, however, only one part of an organization's ethics and compliance system. Its credibility among market and non-market stakeholders depends on the extent of participant drafting, transparency, monitoring and enforcement that were and remain part of its implementation. In general, codes which are drafted with the wide involvement of market and non-market stakeholders rather than narrowly promulgated as directives from top executives and company legal counsel are more likely to be taken seriously since all parties affected have been empowered to "own" the code standards.

Code transparency entails clear understanding, widespread dissemination, distribution within and outside the company, and regular training with compliance sign-off/affirmations regarding its provisions and applications. Codes can be internally and/or externally monitored. Internal monitoring is best conducted by a certified, trained ethics and compliance officer (ECO) with an operational organizational ethics development system that provides for anonymous and/or nonanonymous reporting of ethics and/or legal violations, strong internal control procedures, whistleblower protection from retaliation, with full investigative and resolution power to make both announced and unannounced monitoring visits. External monitoring can be conducted by certified, trained professional auditors, government regulatory officials, certified benchmarking experts, and/or contracted international NGO consultants.

Codes can also be internally and externally enforced. Internal enforcement means that violations of the company standards of conduct will result in appropriate corrective action including discipline. Documented disciplinary measures include but are not limited to counseling, oral and written reprimands, warnings, probation or suspension without pay, demotions, reductions in salary, termination of employment and/or restitution. External enforcement may entail government regulatory intervention, criminal and/or civil legal proceedings, and domestic or international court involvement.

See Also: Accountability; Compliance; Corporate Governance; Corporate Regulation; Corporate Social Responsibility; Johnson & Johnson; Risk Management.

Bibliography. D. Leipziger, *The Corporate Responsibility Code Book* (Greenleaf Publishing, 2003); S. P. Sethi, *Setting Global Standards: Guidelines for Creating Codes of Conduct in Multinational Corporations* (John Wiley & Sons, 2003).

Joseph A. Petrick
Wright State University

Corporate Diplomacy

Corporate diplomacy is the intersection of international business and international relations. Since the days of the East India Company and other joint-stock companies, the role of business in relationships between countries has intensified, and in the 20th century the spread of transnational corporations brought about an awareness of the effects and responsibilities attendant to this larger role. Sony had become, in some sense, the public face of Japan on the international stage, or in the international department store; Coca-Cola and McDonald's had assumed the same role for the United States. With great power, as another transnational icon would have it, came great responsibility. In the 21st century, corporate diplomacy is poised to become a prominent part of public diplomacy.

Public diplomacy, since the Cold War era, has been discussed as the segment of international relations conducted outside of government. Asian exchange students in Midwestern high schools, Peace Corps volunteers working in Belize, European youths backpacking across the continent—these are all examples of public diplomacy. But so are American movies playing in Germany, French comic books in school libraries, and Japanese video games in living rooms around the world. Though the term *public diplomacy* was first coined as a euphemism for propaganda—government-sponsored or at least government-approved—the phrase has uprooted itself from its euphemistic soil and become attached to a living and more literal truth. Public diplomacy is something that simply happens, planned or not—the development of recording media in the late 19th and early 20th century greatly accelerated the exportation of cultural goods like music, movies, and later television, software, video games, and so forth.

Government may not be directly involved in public diplomacy, then, but remains interested in it. In its propagandist use, public diplomacy was associated with the United States Information Agency. When the USIA folded in 1999, the State Department instituted the Award in Corporate Excellence, given to companies that practice and promote social responsibility and pro-American attitudes overseas. There are joint ventures between business and government to counter anti-Americanism abroad, on the theory that such prejudices are bad not only for American foreign relations but for American business interests.

Corporate diplomacy, that component of public diplomacy practiced by corporations, is more deliberate than those cultural exports, which were produced for domestic audiences first (though the international audience is increasingly of concern in the crafting of blockbusters and television shows). Particularly since the end of the Cold War and the fall of communism—and the many fresh and emerging markets that have since been opened to global business—businesses have seen the competitive advantage of working diplomatically rather than trying to do business in the same way all over the world. The simplest example of this is the use of non-beef sandwiches by American fast food chains in India, but corporate diplomacy has advanced far beyond just adapting products to local concerns. Foreign-owned companies stand out less, less likely to be bastions of their home country's values imposed on a local population of employees and customers; American-based oil companies do business with Iran and Russia with a good deal more success than the American government, even while that government often makes their work more difficult.

Corporations are doing more than opening plants in other countries, they're instituting outreach programs, investing in infrastructure, easing the cultural friction where their bubble of culture floats through the sea of the world. One of the classic examples of the difference between corporate diplomacy and government diplomacy is the American embassy in Baghdad ... where only 3 percent of the staff speak Arabic. Business concerns would never let this happen at a Baghdad McDonald's, a Baghdad Gold's Gym. Milton Friedman's famous declaration that the only social responsibility of business is to increase its profits without breaking the rules is either proving outdated or redundant—perhaps there is an extent to which social responsibility is the best way to increase profits.

See Also: Corporate Social Responsibility; Globalization; International Chamber of Commerce; International Marketing Research.

Bibliography. Shaun Riordan, *The New Diplomacy* (Polity, 2002); Robert D. Schulzinger, *U.S. Diplomacy Since 1900* (Oxford University Press, 2001); Ulrich Steger, *Corporate Diplomacy: The Strategy for a Volatile, Fragmented Business Environment* (Wiley, 2003); Robert Trice, Miyako Hasegawa, and Michael Kearns, editors, *Corporate Diplomacy: Principled Leadership for the Global Community* (Center for Strategic and International Studies, 1995).

BILL KTE'PI
INDEPENDENT SCHOLAR

Corporate Governance

While definitions vary, corporate governance can be explained as the set of rules, policies, laws, measures, and instruments that have an effect on the manner in which a company is ruled. These factors can be external to the company, meaning that they are given by the environment in which the company develops its business activity, or internal to the company, such as its board culture. Good corporate governance is appreciated by the market, as investors are more willing to

place their money in those companies with higher governance standards. On the other hand, low-level corporate governance discourages investment, because it is seen as an obstacle to the good performance of the company. Financial scandals involving bad governance practices, such as those at Enron or Parmalat, as well as initiatives in the form of laws or voluntary codes aimed to improve corporate governance, have existed both in the past and in recent times.

The way institutions are governed varies among countries and over time. With the development of large public companies, a separation between ownership and management has occurred. Companies are now owned by a large number of investors who cannot directly rule the company. Therefore shareholders appoint directors and pass on the control of the company to them. These, collectively known as the board of directors, hire the CEO and managers. The main task of the board of directors is to represent the owners and protect their interests in the company. But problems arise because directors and shareholders may have diverging objectives.

In academic literature this is called a principal-agent problem, which finds its theoretical base in the agency theory. According to this theory, a principal, in this case the shareholder, hires an agent, the director, to perform a task on his or her behalf. Once the agent has been appointed to carry out the job, they may not have incentives for seeking the principal's best interest, but their own. In order to avoid this possible situation, measures need to be taken to align the interests of both parties. The instruments used to achieve this target may vary from reward schemes, such as remuneration linked to the company's long-term performance, to enforcement schemes.

The aspiration of any initiative on corporate governance is to have a board made up of directors who make decisions and behave with honesty, diligence, integrity, and commitment to the company and the shareholders. Different measures can be undertaken in order to accomplish this broad and somehow challenging goal. Some countries have passed acts that establish detailed compulsory rules. This has been the path followed by the United States with the Sarbanes-Oxley Act. In other cases, good corporate governance practices are compiled in the form of codes that are of voluntary application. These codes may be issued by professional organizations, international institutions, financial market supervisors, stock exchanges, or other entities. As their application is not compulsory, companies merely explain if they comply or not with the recommendations or principles. Thanks to these disclosures, investors can decide whether to rely on the company's practices.

For its importance and international scope, the Organisation for Economic Co-operation and Development (OECD) initiative must be highlighted. The OECD Steering Group on Corporate Governance has the following mission:

> Co-ordinate and guide the Organization's work on corporate governance and related corporate affairs issues [...] and to guide and support OECD outreach activities in the area of corporate governance.

In order to do so, it issued its Principles on Corporate Governance in 1999, which were revised in 2004, and a methodology for assessing their implementation. These principles address six main areas: legal framework, exercise of shareholders rights, equal treatment of all shareholders, importance of stakeholders, transparency and disclosure, and board structure.

See Also: Board of Directors; Corporate Codes; Enron Corporation; Investor Protection; Organisation for Economic Co-operation and Development; Sarbanes-Oxley.

Bibliography. Gueler Aras and David Crowther, "Governance and Sustainability—An Investigation Into the Relationship Between Corporate Governance and Corporate Sustainability," *Management Decision* (v.45/3–4, 2008); John Colley, Wallas Stettinius, Jacqueline Doyle, and George Logan, *What Is Corporate Governance?* (McGraw-Hill, 2004); Kenneth A. Kim and John R. Nofsinger, *Corporate Governance*, 2nd ed. (Pearson/Prentice Hall, 2007); Chris A. Mallin, *Corporate Governance*, 2nd ed. (Oxford University Press, 2007); Robert A. G. Monks and Nell Minow, *Corporate Governance* (Wiley, 2008); Giles Proctor and Lilian Miles, *Corporate Governance* (Cavendish, 2002); Zabihollah Rezaee, *Corporate Governance and Ethics* (Wiley, 2009); Avanidhar Subrahmanyam, "Social Networks and Corporate Governance," *European Financial Management* (v.14/4, 2008).

BELEN GARCIA-OLMEDO
UNIVERSITY OF GRANADA

Corporate Income Tax

Corporate income tax is the tax paid by business corporations on their corporate profit or income. It is an important consideration in making business decisions such as investing and financing. Differential corporate tax rates among countries are an important factor for multinational companies in choosing their investment locations. Although the significance of corporate income tax as a source of government revenue has gradually declined over time, it is a highly political issue in many countries. Unlike sole tradership and partnership businesses, corporations are recognized as artificial legal entities. Because of their separate legal status apart from the owners of the business, corporations are also required by law to pay income tax.

The history of corporate income tax is quite long and complex in many countries. For example, in the United States, corporate income tax predates personal income tax, although its importance has gradually declined over time. Further, the corporate income tax has implications for personal income tax. In the United States, while corporate income is taxed twice, first at the corporate level and then at the individual level when individuals report dividends as part of income in their tax returns, in Australia shareholders are protected from this "double-dipping" through the imputation tax system, where each dollar of dividend paid out of after-tax profit carries an imputation tax credit.

Low corporate income tax rates and exemption from corporate income tax for several years (also known as a tax holiday) are among the tax incentives used by various countries to attract foreign direct investment (FDI). Corporate income tax plays an important role in corporate financing decisions as well. Because interest paid on borrowed capital is tax deductible, this tax deductibility makes borrowing an attractive option to magnify shareholders' returns. For example, if the interest expense for a corporation is $10 million and the corporate income tax rate is 30 percent, then effectively the corporation pays an interest expense of $7 million. Similarly, in computing cash inflows and outflows in relation to an investment decision, corporations need to measure after-tax cash inflows and outflows to arrive at a correct decision.

Effective corporate income tax rates vary from country to country. For example, in 2007, the corporate income tax rates in some selected countries were as follows:

Country	Effective Corporate Tax Rates
Australia	30.0%
China	33.0%
France	33.3%
Germany	38.4%
India	42.2%
Singapore	20.0%
United Kingdom	30.0%
United States	40.0%

Note: Based on 2007 KPMG and PricewaterhouseCoopers corporate tax surveys.

In many common law countries that also predominantly use outsider systems of finance, income measured for financial reporting purpose (i.e., for reporting to shareholders of the company) can be quite different from tax rules used for determining corporate income tax liability. It is quite legitimate in these countries, for example, to use the straight line depreciation method for financial reporting purposes while using some form of accelerated depreciation method for tax reporting purposes. To the contrary, in many Roman law countries, which predominantly use insider systems of finance, the rules used for financial reporting purposes closely follow the rules used for tax reporting purposes.

When corporate income measured under tax laws differs from corporate income measured using financial reporting standards, the resultant tax difference turns into some kind of asset or liability. Suppose in a common law country like Australia, a corporation reports a profit of $200 million to shareholders. But when the tax laws are applied to this company, the profit turns out to be $170 million. If the corporate income tax rate is 30 percent, the company's tax liability in relation to current year's income will be $170 million x 30% = $51 million. But the income tax expense based on the income statement reported to the shareholders would be $200 million x 30% = $60 million. The difference of $9 million is a deferred tax liability for the company to be reported in its balance sheet. Had the difference been in the opposite direction, that is, tax liability > income tax expense by $9 million, the company would have reported the difference as a deferred tax asset. It would be treated as an asset because it is a tax payment that the company is making now with the expectation of saving an income tax of $9 million in the future. To what extent these tax savings materialize depends on the extent to which the tax rules and the tax rate remain the same. If the tax rate changes in the future before the deferred tax asset or liability is realized, the amount of this deferred tax liability or asset will be required to be restated, reflecting the new tax rate.

When the application of tax rules to a company's revenues and expenses produces a loss for the company, the loss is called a "tax loss." Tax laws in some countries allow tax losses to be adjusted against future tax liabilities or past tax payments.

See Also: Taxes; Tax Havens; Tax Holiday.

Bibliography. S. James and C. Nobes, *The Economics of Taxation: Principles, Policies and Practice* (Financial Times–Prentice Hall, 2000); R. Jankowski, *Profits, Taxes, and the State* (Praeger, 1998); KPMG, *Corporate Tax Rate Survey* (KPMG, 2007); R. La Porta, F. Lopez-de-Silanes, A. Shleifer, and R. W. Vishny, "Legal Determinants of External Finance," *Journal of Finance* (1997); G. A. Plesko, "The Corporate Income Tax: Impact and Incidence," in *Handbook on Taxation*, J. A. Richardson, ed. (Marcel Dekker, 1999); W. B. Hildreth and J. A. Richardson, eds., *Handbook on Taxation* (CRC Press, 1999); PricewaterhouseCoopers, *2007 Worldwide Tax Summaries* (PricewaterhouseCoopers, 2007).

Reza Monem
Griffith University Business School

Corporate Social Responsibility

Corporate social responsibility (CSR) is the concept that business has a set of multidimensional obligations to meet the expectations of society's global stakeholders by fulfilling economic, legal, ethical, ecological, and discretionary philanthropic responsibilities. The belief that modern corporations have a responsibility to society and nature that extends beyond the economic responsibility to make money or profits for investors has become a key element in global corporate governance and a pervasive global expectation in light of the tremendous power exercised by multinational corporations (MNCs). The history and nature of CSR and the business case for it as a new global expectation requiring a strategic corporate response are dimensions of this concept to consider.

History and Nature of CSR

CSR has been discussed throughout the 20th century, but it was Howard R. Bowen's book *Social Responsibilities of the Businessman* (1953) that originated the modern debate on the topic. Bowen reasoned that there would be general social and economic benefits that would accrue to society if business recognized broader social goals in its decisions.

Numerous scholars contributed to the development of the concept, but during the 1970s a number of catalysts accelerated the acceptance of CSR. First, in its 1971 publication *Social Responsibilities of Business Corporations*, the Committee for Economic Development (CED), composed of business practitioners and leading scholars, endorsed CSR as reflecting a changing social contract between business-society and business-government relations. Second, in the early 1970s there was a major expansion of U.S. government social regulation including the creation of the Environmental Protection Agency, the Consumer Product Safety Commission, and the Equal Employment Opportunity Commission, which led to a supportive national context for CSR. Third, in the late 1970s Archie B. Carroll proposed a four-part model of CSR that differentiated CSR from corporate social performance (CSP). He maintained that CSP was an extension of the concept of CSR that focuses on actual performance results achieved rather than the general notion of business accountability or responsibility to society. However, in order for managers to engage in CSP they needed to have a basic definition of CSR, identification of stakeholders to whom the firm had a responsibility, and a pattern of responsiveness to CSR issues.

Carroll noted that the traditional view, advocated by the eminent economist Milton Friedman—that the only social responsibility of business was to legally make a profit for its investors—was inadequate to describe the judgment of many business leaders and did not reflect the changing expectations of domestic and global societies. He proposed that CSR encompass economic, legal, ethical, and discretionary expectations that society has of organizations at a given point in time. This definition provided individuals with categories with which to quantitatively state the nature or kind of obligation that business had toward society.

First, according to Carroll, business has an economic obligation to society. Business has an economic responsibility to supply goods and services that society demands and to sell them at a profit. Unless a business is financially viable, its other responsibilities cannot be fulfilled. To achieve its capitalistic economic responsibilities, business must be effective, efficient, innovative, and strategically adaptive to changing global conditions.

Second, CSR entails meeting legal obligations at the local, state, federal, and international levels. Society charters and allows the business to function and enacts the laws and regulations under which business is expected to operate. These codified rules are the formal framework within which business is expected to generate prosperity; they represent the public boundaries of acceptable business practice.

Third, CSR also entails ethical responsibilities. Ethical responsibilities refer to those activities and practices that are expected, or prohibited, by societal members even though they may not be codified into law. They embody the range of norms, standards, or expectations about business activity that reflect a concern for what major stakeholders such as consumers, employees, owners, the community, and others regard as fair or just. The ethical responsibility of business includes the dictum to "do no harm" by such activities as polluting the environment, discriminating against workers, producing dangerous products, engaging in misleading advertising, and so on. To be sure, some of these practices are governed by the legal responsibility of business but some are not. The ethical responsibility embraces a response to the "spirit" of laws and regulations and helps guide business actions in those decision areas in which regulations are ill-defined or nonexistent. Some view the law as the ethical minimum or "floor" on business behavior, whereas the ethical manager or firm is often expected to operate above the minimum required by law. Ethical leadership would be a manifestation of this kind of business obligation.

Fourth, CSR entails discretionary responsibility. Society expects business to be a good corporate citizen by contributing to the well-being of the community, through business giving or philanthropy. The discretionary category of responsibility might well be named the philanthropic category, because the best examples of business fulfilling this expectation typically are considered philanthropic: giving money or other resources to charitable causes, initiating adopt-a-school programs, employing executive in-house programs in the community, conducting civic events, and so on. The distinction between ethical and discretionary responsibilities is that the latter are typically "desired" by society and not expected in a moral or ethical sense.

In summary for Carroll, the socially responsible corporation should strive to make a profit, obey the law, be ethical, and be a good corporate citizen. Though the social responsibility concept is normative in that it proposes what business ought to do, it is also descriptive because it captures the essence of what socially responsible business organizations are doing today.

In more recent times, CSR has expanded to explicitly include ecological responsibility, not as a discretionary but an expected performance standard. The subfield of corporate ecology focuses on sustainable development, triple-bottom-line accountability, biodiversity, and intergenerational justice as necessary components of modern corporate strategy.

The Business Case for CSR

The business case for CSR includes the following arguments: (1) corporations that pursue CSR defensively avoid the pressures that create costs for them from litigation and/or increased government regulation; (2) corporations that pursue CSR internalize the full costs of doing business, instead of externalizing them onto society, and thereby have a more accurate accounting of their business processes and the data to improve future performance; (3) corporations that pursue CSR form stakeholder partnerships that enhance their social capital so that economic growth opportunities/issues that impact stakeholders can more likely be cooperatively resolved; and (4) corporations that pursue CSR enhance their global citizenship reputation and find it easier to attract and retain high-quality human capital and to gain access to lucrative financial capital opportunities that serve the long term strategic interest of the firm.

In the 2002 Sustainability Survey Report by PricewaterhouseCoopers, the following were the reported reasons why corporations were deciding to be more socially responsible: (1) enhanced reputation, (2) strategic competitive advantage, (3) cost savings, (4) industry trends, (5) CEO/board commitment, (6) customer demand, (7) SRI demand, (8) top-line growth, (9) investor demand, and (10) access to capital.

Among the 100 Best Corporate Citizens identified by *Business Ethics* magazine are numerous corporations engaging in CSR practices, including Cummins, Inc., of Columbus, Indiana, which has reduced diesel engine emissions by 90 percent (far more than legally required); Xerox Corporation of Stamford, Connecticut, which has implemented its Employee Social Service Leave Program for selected employees to take a year off with full pay to work for a community nonprofit organization; and Green Mountain Coffee Roasters of Waterbury, Vermont, which assists developing countries by paying "fair trade" prices, that exceed regular market prices, and offering microloans to indigenous coffee-growing families.

See Also: Bhopal Disaster; Corporate Codes; Corporate Governance; Corporate Social Responsibility; Downstream; Environmental Standards; Fair Trade; Regulation; Social Contract; Sustainable Development.

Bibliography. Archie B. Carroll and Ann K. Buchholtz, *Business and Society: Ethics and Stakeholder Management*, 7th ed. (Cengage Learning, 2008); William B. Werther, Jr., and David Chandler, *Strategic Corporate Responsibility: Stakeholders in a Global Environment* (Sage, 2005).

Joseph A. Petrick
Wright State University

Corporate Social Responsibility and International Business Ethics

Corporate social responsibility (CSR) encompasses the economic, legal, ethical, philanthropic and discretionary expectations that society has of a firm at a given point in time. Until very recently, most firms viewed business ethics only in terms of administrative compliance with legal standards and adherence to internal rules and regulations in international business transactions. In today's environment, it is imperative to pay attention to business ethics around the world and firms must earn the respect and confidence of their customers in order to succeed. Legal and ethical behavior are of paramount importance and companies and individuals alike are being held increasingly accountable for their actions, as demand grows for higher standards of corporate social responsibility.

While business ethics emerged as a field in the mid-19th century, international business ethics did not emerge until three decades ago. Managers and researchers have since then begun focusing on infinitely more complex issues in the international marketplace as value judgments differ widely amongst culturally diverse groups. There are several issues that have become salient such as comparison business ethical transactions from various religious perspectives, varying global standards, e.g., such as the use of child labor, the way multinationals take advantage of international differences, such as outsourcing production and services to low-wage countries, the permissibility of global business transactions with pariah states, and an overall search for universal values as a basis for international business transactions.

The rapid pace of globalization in the last decade has compelled multinational enterprises to leverage their resources to alleviate a wide variety of social problems. The pharmaceutical industries have priced their drugs well below market price in developing nations to avoid negative publicity, whereas those engaged in manufacturing have restricted environmental pollution regardless of the local laws and customs.

Furthermore, multinationals should not adversely disturb the balance of payments or currency exchange rates of the countries in which they do business. They should reinvest some of their profits in the countries in which they operate, and should resolve disputes arising from expropriation by host governments under the domestic laws of those countries. They should also reduce solid waste by incorporating recycling into their manufacturing processes.

Corruption and Bribery

In addition to taking a proactive stance in practicing appropriate business ethics etiquette as described above, businesses should also avoid certain forms of business practices that are a deviation from the sound practices of business policy, such as corruption, bribery, extortion, lubrication, subornation and agent's fees among other undesirable practices.

Corruption involves an illegitimate exchange of power into material remuneration mostly on the part of officeholders who take advantage of their position to grant undeserving favors. Not all forms of corruptions are likely to violate the law, and the semantics of the word can vary considerably around the world. Making profits, individualism, rampant consumerism are considered corruptions in many parts of the world. Transparency International publishes the annual *Corruption Perception Index*, and Nordic countries (e.g., Denmark, Finland, Sweden, Norway, and Iceland), New Zealand and Singapore are typically found to be the least corrupt countries in the world. The organization also publishes the annual *Bribe Payers Index*, and the lowest levels of bribe paying are usually found in Switzerland, Sweden, Australia, Austria, and Canada.

While voluntary offered payment by an individual seeking unlawful advantage is considered bribery, *extortion* refers to payments that are extracted under duress by someone in authority from a person seeking only what he or she is entitled to. Yet another variation of bribery is the difference between *lubrication* and *subornation*. While the former involves a relatively small sum of cash, a gift or a service given to a low-ranking official in a country where such offerings are not prohibited by law, subornation, in contrast, involves offering large sums of money—frequently not properly accounted for—designed to entice an official to commit an illegal act on behalf of the person offering the bribe. A final form of payment, an agent's fee, is paid to an individual to represent the company in that country. This form of payment is not necessarily a bribe, although it may be construed to be one under some circumstances.

Ethical behavior should be the trait of every firm not only in their domestic transactions, but in their international ones as well. Perhaps the best guides to a litmus test of whether or not something is ethical is based on utilitarian ethics, i.e., whether the actions of the company or the individual optimizes the benefits of all constituencies, rights of the parties, i.e., does the action respect the rights of the individuals, and justice or fairness, i.e., does the action respect the principles of justice or fairness to all stakeholders involved? Answers to these questions will shepherd businesses and individuals navigate through challenging international business transactions in the 21st century.

See Also: Biodiversity Convention; Bottom of the Pyramid; Child Labor; Corporate Social Responsibility; International Bank for Reconstruction and Development; Kyoto Protocol; Microfinance; Sustainable Development; U.S. Agency for International Development; World Bank, The.

Bibliography. Stephen Brammer and Andrew Millington, "Does it Pay to Be Different? An Analysis of the Relationship Between Corporate Social and Financial Performance," *Strategic Management Journal* (v.29/12, 2008); Sandro Castaldo, Francesco Perrini, Nicola Misani, and Antonio Tencati, "The Missing Link Between Corporate Social Responsibility and Consumer Trust: The Case of Fair Trade Products," *Journal of Business Ethics* (v.84/1, 2009); Andrew Crane, Abagail McWilliams, Dirk Matten, Jeremy Moon, and Donald S. Siegel, eds., *The Oxford Handbook of Corporate Social Responsibility* (Oxford University Press, 2008); Longinos Marin, Salvador Ruiz, and Alicia Rubio, "The Role of Identity Salience in the Effects of Corporate Social Responsibility on Consumer Behavior," *Journal of Business Ethics* (v.84/1, 2009); Ivan Montiel, "Corporate Social Responsibility and Corporate Sustainability: Separate Pasts, Common Futures," *Organization & Environment* (v.21/3, 2008); Doreen J. McBarnet, Aurota Voiculescu, and Tom Campbell, *The New Corporate Accountability: Corporate Social Responsibility and the Law* (Cambridge University Press, 2008); Terje I. Vaaland, Morten Heide, and Kjell Grønhaug, "Corporate Social Responsibility: Investigating Theory and Research in the Marketing Context," *European Journal of Marketing* (v.42/9–10, 2008).

ABHIJIT ROY
UNIVERSITY OF SCRANTON

Corruption

In general, corruption is defined as the abuse of authority for improper gain. Public corruption refers to the misuse of governmental authority while private corruption indicates a misuse of purely nongovernmental power. Many analysts focus on public corruption. A very standard definition of public corruption, used by the World Bank, is "the abuse of public power for private benefit." A more detailed discussion is offered by Bradhan who notes the violation of an implicit or explicit agreement between a principal and their agent:

> [public] corruption ordinarily refers to the use of public office for private gains where an official (the agent) entrusted with carrying out a task by the public (the principal) engages in some sort of malfeasance for private enrichment which is difficult to monitor for the principal.

A more neutral and legalistic formulation, and one that can apply in both public and private settings is offered by Tanzi; he defines corruption as consisting of "intentional non-compliance with arm's length relationship aimed at deriving some advantage from this behaviour for oneself or for related individuals." There are other types of intentional subversions of processes such as political corruption (e.g., vote-buying in an election) but these meanings will not be considered here.

As to the types of specific actions that may constitute corruption, there are many. A few examples include: bribery and gratuities; influence peddling; offering one's official services for sale; misreporting of financial transactions; fictitious billing and invoicing; fabricating documents, signatures, and approvals; destroying records and evidence; fraud; misrepresentation; and providing special favor to related parties.

However context is critical in judging whether or not any of these actions in a specific instance are, in fact corrupt. For example misreporting may simply be due to negligence and not intentional, therefore not corrupt. Favoring of family members over nonfamily members may be culturally accepted in some cases and therefore not seen as corrupt, especially when the favored party is able to meet a particular obligation, such as a job qualification, even if that party is not the most able available.

Thus two sets of norms help to delimit what might constitute corruption in a given circumstance: morality and legality. Morally, the abuse of authority implies some violation of trust, whether it is the trust of the citizen in their officials or the trust of shareholders in their managers. And abuse that leads to gain is in a general sense doubly immoral, first because it is breaking a commitment (and thus lying to one or more parties, by omission or commission) and second because it implies taking resources that do not belong to the party taking those resources, i.e., stealing. There will be some cultural variation on whether a specific action in a particular context constitutes lying, betrayal, and stealing but these general concepts are in the abstract almost always universally disapproved of.

The law offers a second set of standards by which to judge corruption though these generally will be based on some prior moral precepts, if only loosely. Therefore corruption is not always illegal, nor is illegal behavior always corrupt. For example, gratuities offered by contractors to public agencies are, in most countries, generally legal so long as they are some *de minimus* (i.e., very small) amount. Conversely, misreporting of transactions to protect shareholders from a venal management might be illegal but might be the morally correct thing to do under the circumstances.

International Legal Standards

There are a variety of legal standards pertaining to corrupt behavior, nationally and internationally. National laws generally offer the greatest penalties for corruption and of course the greatest potential enforcement, but they also exhibit the greatest variation across countries. Price-fixing and offering of bribes in particular are not consistently illegal according to national local codes.

Internationally, there is the 1997 OECD Convention on Combating Bribery of Foreign Public Officials in International Business Transactions which has been signed by 30 OECD countries and six non-OECD countries. The Convention deals specifically with bribery and requires that peer-country panels review each signatory country's performance in implementing and applying the Convention. There is also the 2003 United Nations (UN) Convention against Corruption, which has now been ratified by the required minimum number of signatory and is therefore technically binding.

Of course the problem with transnational laws is that there is little ability to enforce them and equally little penalty for breach of them. The OECD Convention offers a self-regulating and peer-accrediting approach to legal regulation of corruption which is only as strong as the commitment of the peers involved and which has no formal sanction beyond moral suasion. The UN Convention has no enforc-

ing authority other than the UN itself which obviously has limited enforcement power. More effective are transnational anti-corruption codes such as those established by the World Bank and which are applied to Bank development assistance. The International Monetary Fund (IMF) applies similar conditions to its loans. Even here however, such codes apply only to aid or loan recipients and are often flouted by those recipients.

Costs

Regardless of subtlety in the understanding and interpretation of corruption, there is certainly a material amount of it taking place in business and government worldwide. The estimates of the cost of corruption, while necessarily rough, are substantial. A 2003 UN conference on corruption estimated such costs as representing 5 percent of the world economy, or more than $1.5 trillion a year. In reviewing the literature on gross corruption costs, the Asian Development Bank (ADB) highlighted some particular sets of costs that illustrate both the magnitude and spread of the problem: as much as $30 billion in aid for Africa ending up in foreign bank accounts; one East Asian country over the course of 20 years estimated to have lost $48 billion due to corruption, surpassing its entire foreign debt of $40.6 billion; in one North American city, businesses cutting $330 million from an annual waste disposal bill of $1.5 billion by removing Mafia domination from the garbage industry; studies that indicate that in several Asian countries governments have paid from 20 percent to 100 percent more for goods and services because of corrupt practices by contractors; and estimates that corruption in a European country has inflated this country's total outstanding government debt by as much as 15 percent or $200 billion.

These are direct costs but equally or more important are the costs that corruption imposes on economic development, poverty and competitiveness. The biggest problem is that corrupt practice distorts implicit and explicit pricing, creates deadweight loss and causes misallocation of resources. Thus investment may be driven to uneconomical projects because of payoffs, and legitimate entrepreneurial activity might be supplanted by higher 'return' sham enterprises. Individuals who might otherwise engage in honest business might decide they have no alternative but to participate in a culture of economic subversion. The poor often suffer the most because they are not well-connected or able to pay bribes. Worst case there might be an undermining of legitimacy of the entire public sector.

Within a purely private setting, a corrupt company will likely become less competitive for the same reasons of resource misallocation and in extreme cases may fail due to malfeasance. There are a significant number of large corporate failures that can be traced at least indirectly to corrupt practices and compromised internal governance. In the United States the failure of Enron was in large part due to a business model that relied on an ever-increasing firm share price which became collateral to finance reckless expansion using accounting irregularities, earnings misreporting, market rigging (as was the case with its energy trading and its abuse of company-owned electricity generating assets in California), and blatantly unethical and illegal structured-finance and derivatives transactions. In Europe, Parmalat collapsed for somewhat similar reasons, namely a rapid expansion that temporarily hid structural financial problems which were covered up by managers through the use of fraud. Even when failure is not the end result, misuse of shareholder resources for the enrichment of specific managers is all too common.

Research bears out the existence and ultimate costs of these processes. In a study of over 70 countries during the late 1970s and early 1980s, Mauro found that corruption is negatively associated with investment rates; according to his model a one standard deviation improvement in the "corruption index" will translate into an increase of 2.9 percent of GDP in the investment rate and a 1.3 percent increase in the annual per capita rate of GDP growth. Research published in the World Bank *1997 World Development Report* found that countries that were perceived to have relatively low levels of corruption were always able to attract significantly more investment than those perceived to be more prone to corrupt or illicit activity. Of course these financial and economic measures such as these do not fully capture the range of deleterious public consequences that corruption can engender, such as a building collapse due to building codes that were unenforced because of bribes or consumer deaths due to tainted food that was not properly inspected.

From a private shareholder perspective corruption is no less costly. Taylor, in reviewing a particularly bad year for US corporate scandals (2002) in which there were failures or soon-to-be failures of Enron, WorldCom, Adelphia and Global Crossing, and scandals at blue chip companies like Xerox and AOL Time Warner estimated that in a total of 23 firms under investigation that year, the CEOs of these firms collectively earned $1.4 billion from 1999 to 2001, laid off 162,000 employees, and saw the reduction in the value of their shares fall by $530 billion, about 73 percent of their market value. While these consequences cannot be completely attributed to corrupt practice, it is nonetheless indicative of what such practices can held lead to.

Prevalence

More general evidence finds that the prevalence of corruption varies both geographically and sectorally although there is little doubt that the problem occurs in some form almost everywhere. Transparency International (TI), the largest international NGO dedicated to monitoring and reporting on global corruption, publishes a Corruption Perceptions Index (CPI), which ranks countries according to the perceived level of their corruption in demanding bribes. The 1999 CPI, to take but one example, ranked Denmark, Finland, New Zealand, Sweden, and Canada in the top five as far as having the least perceived corruption and Uzbekistan, Azerbaijan, Indonesia, Nigeria, and Cameroon as in the bottom five as having the most. Countries such as the United States, UK, Chile, and Australia were included in the top 20 and Kenya, Russia, and Pakistan were in the bottom 20. While there is some shifting across the geography from year to year, the TI rankings are overall generally stable. TI estimates that some US$100 billion annually is paid out worldwide in the form of bribes or some other pay-off.

Another measure of the incidence and cost of corruption is offered by the World Economic Forum Global (WEF), a Europe-based consortium with a large membership of firms, and designed by the Harvard Institute for International Development (HIID). The WEF issues an annual Competitiveness Report which surveys responding firms about various aspects of "competitiveness" in the host countries where they invest. The questions on corruption asks the respondent to rate the level of corruption on a one-to-seven scale according to the extent of "irregular, additional payments connected with import and export permits, business licenses, exchange controls, tax assessments, police protection or loan applications." The corruption index for a particular country is the average of all respondents' ratings for that country, with 7 being the best score. In the 2006/7 survey Iceland, Singapore, Finland, Norway, Sweden, and Denmark all had numerous rankings within the top 10 positions in terms of low corruption. Venezuela is ranked near the bottom with very high corruption. The United States has a somewhat middling rate: the worst rankings for the United States were 111 on the cost of terrorism to business and 102 on the impact of legal contributions to political parties.

There are some criticisms of measures such as these. In particular, these instruments are survey-based and so only indicate perceptions of corruption, not direct observational metrics of it. There can be biases and gaps in such surveys. Survey results may not always be comparable across different instruments that are conducted by different organisations or even across the same instrument across given years given changes in survey questions. However there is a high correlation of national rankings across surveys and relative stability within a given survey from year to year, indicating a basic core stability of the measures.

Besides national variations, some industrial sectors are well known to be more corrupt than others, like oil and gas, construction and armaments. A firm negotiating a deal in one of these sectors, in a country with a generally high corruption level is likely to be doubly hit and there may still be significant corruption in problematic sectors even in relatively 'clean' countries. The scale of sectoral corruption is indicated by the example of such costs in the construction sector, estimated globally at some US$3,200 billion per year according to TI. TI's Global Corruption Report of 2005 presents case studies of large-scale infrastructure projects that have been plagued by corruption, such as bribes paid to secure contracts for the Lesotho Dam in Africa, and the implication of politicians in corruption concerning the purchase of a waste incinerator in Cologne, Germany. Stories such as these are repeated in various reports and studies year after year. It is notable that they take place in both the developed and developing world.

Cause and Effect

A big focus of discussion in the corruption literature revolves around cause and effect. For example, an academic study by Treisman found that countries with Protestant traditions, histories of British rule, more developed economies, and higher imports to be less corrupt; with federal states, more corrupt; and the current degree of democracy not significant, although long exposure to democracy predicted lower corruption.

This broad finding, while by no means incontrovertible, is broadly consistent with other research that focuses on the relationship between governance institutions and corruption. A governance-corruption model generally asserts that corruption affects overall productivity and efficiency by reducing governmental capacity, weakening political institutions and citizen participation, offering more opportunities for rent taking by well-connected parties, reducing overall trust in government and thus leading to a sort of vicious cycle. Conversely transparent and efficient government in a context of well-educated, empowered, and actively participating citizenry will enjoy a virtuous circle of low corruption.

Of course any theory of particular causes of corruption will yield corresponding theories as to how to combat it. To the extent that fundamental social values are important (e.g., "Protestant traditions" as noted by Treisman) corruption will be harder, though not impossible, to change. However, evidence on the role of social and cultural factors is inconclusive. The relatively stable corruption rankings of individual countries on various surveys suggest some role for cultural factors but closer examination of the effect of specific cultural norms on corruption does not seem to carry significant explanatory effect and as Wei notes the costs of corruption do not vary by culture. Since corruption in general is costly it would seem to be undesirable from that standpoint alone, regardless of cultural and social context.

Governance and management can be more readily changed and many proposals to limit corruption focus on these elements. There are a number of common themes across such proposals. Transparency is key since open information about who gets what and who is paying who at least make the participants in the problem apparent and may provide disincentives to corrupt behavior through the threat of prosecution and public disapproval. Accountability is also mentioned frequently, in this context meaning that there are clear lines of authority and responsibility for consequences of actions. Legality is a final plank in which there are clear laws, regulations and codes defining what corruption is and what it is not and spelling out clear and strong penalties for noncompliance. Education underlies all of this since people must be trained in both the values and workings of any anti-corruption system.

The ADB follows these general principles in guidelines that it has developed and which are consonant with much of the anti-corruption literature. The ADB framework focuses on processes for hiring and promotion and remuneration of responsible authorities; regulations on conflicts of interest and conduct in office; regulations concerning gifts and hospitality; guidance and training on ethical conduct; enforcement of codes of conduct; duties to report; e-government and other methods of information dissemination; rotation of officials and division of duties; strong, independent and proper auditing procedures and institutions; criminalization of corrupt activities such as bribery and illicit enrichment; well-funded and well-trained enforcement authority; and public education and building of public support.

Although the ADB framework is focused on public agencies, private corruption will have a set of parallel issues. Thus in private corporations it is generally recommended that there be clear corporate policies governing conduct with clear sanctions spelled out for noncompliance; proper external and internal audit authority; appropriate division between different levels of management and between the board of directors and management; and free flow of information. Classic problems in corporate corruption include boards that are compromised or captured by management (for example through the offer of lucrative company contracts by managers to board members) and internal processes where there is a lack of genuine oversight for critical decisions (for example having a manager responsible for setting an underling's pay and promotion also overseeing that underling's performance as an internal auditor).

There is a school of thought that sees public information and education as primary in effecting a shift towards values that are antithetical to corruption. Once values are changed, so the thinking goes, behavior will follow. Examples of such an approach are offered by TI which compiles a Bribe Payers Index that evaluates the perceived propensity of firms from industrialized countries to bribe in the places where they do business and the Integrity Pact, in which the host government and all would-be bidders for a public contract agree beforehand that no party to the negotiations will offer or accept bribes. TI claims to have achieved success with Integrity Pacts in some of the world's most chronically corrupt countries. Whether such an approach is universally effective remains to be seen.

Of course an alternative approach is creation and enforcement of laws in which acts are clearly criminalized and vigorously prosecuted. Clearly there are many public and private officials who have been heavily fined, jailed and, in some cases, such as China, even executed and such disincentives and penalties no doubt have limited the extent of overall corruption. Nonetheless there are at least as many officials who escape without penalty and the costs of enforcement are very high. Whether worldwide public and private corruption is being reduced, increased, or staying level, there is no question that it remains a significant and costly problem with no one single solution.

See Also: Agents; Black Market; Compliance; Corporate Social Responsibility; Corporate Codes; Enron Corporation; Smuggling.

Bibliography. Asian Development Bank (ADB), *Anti-Corruption Policies in Asia and the Pacific* (2004); Stewart Hamilton and Alicia Mickelthwait, *Greed and Corporate Failure: The Lessons from Recent Disasters* (Palgrave MacMillan, 2006); Seymour M. Lipset and Salman Lenz, "Corruption, Culture, and Markets," in Lawrence Harrison and Samuel Huntington, eds., *Culture Matters: How Values Shape Human Progress* (Basic Books, 2001); Transparency International, *Transparency International Press Release Global Corruption Report 2005* (March 2005); Daniel Treisman, "The Causes of Corruption: A Cross-national Study," *Journal of Public Economics* (v.76, 2000); Shang-Jin Wei, *Corruption in Economic Development: Beneficial Grease, Minor Annoyance, or Major Obstacle?* Harvard University and National Bureau of Economic Research Working Paper (1998); World Bank, *World Development Report: Helping Countries Combat Corruption: The Role of the World Bank* (1997).

CAMERON GORDON
UNIVERSITY OF CANBERRA

Cost, Insurance, and Freight

Cost, insurance, and freight, or CIF, is one of the most frequently used terms in international business. It is a basis on which the exporter or seller quotes the price to the buyer or importer. When the seller quotes the price on a CIF basis, the total price includes the cost of the merchandise for the buyer, the premium for the insurance coverage for the merchandise from the seller's premises to the destination, and the transportation costs from the seller's premises to the destination.

As the distance between the buyer and the seller grows, transportation costs of the merchandise become important. Similarly, both the buyer and the seller need to protect themselves against accidents, loss of property, damages, or other unpredictable events such as the sinking of the ship carrying the merchandise or natural calamities such as cyclones and the consequent damage to the merchandise. For these reasons, quoting a price that includes insurance coverage and freight charges becomes very important.

In a CIF quotation, cost does not refer to the cost incurred by the seller or exporter in acquiring or producing the merchandise. From the seller's perspective, it is the price (without insurance and freight) at which the seller or exporter is willing to sell to the buyer. Obviously, how this price is derived remains entirely at the seller's discretion. Based on the seller's pricing strategies, the seller may choose to charge the full cost or below the full cost of the merchandise plus some markup.

Other terms that are also used in sales contracts include free on board (FOB) and cost and freight only (C&F). FOB quotations imply that the seller is responsible for all the costs up to the point where the merchandise will be boarded on a vessel or airplane and the buyer is responsible for paying the freight and insurance for the merchandise while being transported. C&F excludes insurance coverage and includes only cost of the merchandise and the freight charges. In this case, the responsibility for taking insurance lies with the buyer.

See Also: Freight Forwarder; International Commercial Terms (Incoterms); Landed Cost; Transportation.

Bibliography. V. J. Geraci and W. Prewo, "Bilateral Trade Flows and Transport Costs," *The Review of Economics and Statistics* (1977); Richard Gilbert and Anthony Perl, *Transport Revolutions: Moving People and Freight Without Oil* (Earthscan, 2007); C. Moneta, "The Estimation of Transportation Costs in International Trade," *The Journal of Political Economy* (1959); D. M. Sassoon, *C.I.F. and F.O.B. Contracts* (Sweet & Maxwell, 1995).

Reza Monem
Griffith University Business School

Cost Accounting

Cost accounting is a process that involves accumulating, measuring, analyzing, interpreting, and reporting cost information for the purpose of internal and external decision making. It determines the cost of something through direct measurement, systematic and rational allocation, or arbitrary assignment. Cost accounting is often discussed in the accounting literature as a distinct branch of accounting—however, it should best be thought of as a bridge or overlap between financial and management accounting, since it addresses the demands of both branches of accounting.

The origins of modern cost accounting can be traced to the industrial revolution. During that time, managers recognized that the complexities of managing large-scale operations necessitated that systems be developed to record and track costs to facilitate better decision making. At the beginning of the industrial era, variable costs tended to dominate the interest of managers. However, with the passage of time, managers began to recognize that fixed costs were equally important in decision making. Today, modern cost accounting is no longer considered as mere numbers—rather, cost accounting has become a major player in business decision making.

In theory, accounting is generally classified under three main branches: financial accounting, management accounting, and cost accounting. Financial accounting is concerned with measuring and recording business transactions to produce financial statements for external decision making, while management accounting is concerned with measuring and reporting financial and nonfinancial information for the purpose of internal decision making. In contrast, cost accounting provides information for both internal and external decision making. It provides information to external parties to make investment and credit decisions and for internal parties to manage and control current operations and plan for the future.

Cost accounting is divided into three broad areas: (1) the measurement of cost (e.g., historical cost vs. market value vs. present value, standard cost vs. actual cost); (2) the assignment of cost to the accounting period (e.g., accrual accounting vs. cash basis accounting); and (3) the allocation of cost to cost objectives (e.g., determination of whether costs should be classified as direct or indirect, determination of cost pools and their allocation bases). Cost accounting can therefore be considered as the part of financial and management accounting that collects and analyzes cost information.

In the accounting literature, cost accounting principles, procedures, and practices are generally discussed within the context of manufacturing firms. However, cost accounting is essential for the efficient operations of all business entities: large and small, public and private, profit and nonprofit, and manufacturing, merchandising, and services. In today's dynamic global environment, reliable and timely cost information is the key to business success. Business entities therefore rely heavily on cost accounting to generate knowledge and wisdom about an entity's operations. Cost accounting can provide information for various types of decision making such as: assessing operational performance, reducing costs, determining the price of goods/services, determining the effect of an increase in one or more cost elements on sales revenue, and analyzing the reasons for variances between actual and standards costs, to name a few.

Regardless of size, industry or trade, all business entities need good cost accounting information systems to manage, track and improve their business processes. The traditional cost accounting system—absorption costing—is still used by many manufacturing entities. Under this approach, all manufacturing costs are included in the cost of a product. However, in recent times, a wide variety of service, manufacturing and nonprofit organizations have embraced the use of activity based costing. This approach assigns costs to specific activities (e.g., manufacturing, engineering). Other innovative approaches that have emerged to manage and improve business processes include approaches such as lean production, theory of constraints and six sigma. Lean production is based on the logic that production should be in response to customer orders and that perfection should be continuously pursued. The theory of constraints is based on the observation that every organization has at least one constraint, which should be effectively managed for success. Finally, six sigma relies on customer feedback and fact-based data gathering to drive process improvement.

Today, businesses have an array of cost accounting approaches that they can utilize. However, it is important to note that when information is being provided for financial accounting purposes, it must be developed in compliance with Generally Accepted Accounting Polices (GAAP). In contrast, information provided for management accounting need not be in compliance with GAAP. Notwithstanding, two important bodies, namely the Institute of Management Accountants and the Society of Management Accountants of Canada do issue cost accounting guidelines. Although these guidelines are neither mandatory nor legally binding, they are nonetheless useful to ensure that high-quality accounting practices are followed. A third body—the Cost Accounting Standards Board—has also produced a set of standards to help ensure uniformity and consistency in government contracting. This body was established by the U.S. Congress in 1970. The standards produced by this board are legally binding on companies bidding on cost-related contracts to the federal government.

See Also: Accounting Information Systems; Cost Structure; Fixed Costs; International Accounting Standards Board; Managerial Accounting.

Bibliography. Ray H. Garrison, Eric W. Noreen, and Peter C. Brewer, *Managerial Accounting*, 12th ed. (McGraw-Hill, 2008); Charles T. Horngren, Srikant M. Datar, and George Foster, *Cost Accounting: A Managerial Emphasis*, 11th ed. (Prentice Hall, 2003); Michael R. Kinney, Jenice Prather-Kinsey, and Cecily A. Raiborn, *Cost Accounting: Foundations and Evolutions* (Thomson South-Western, 2006); Edward J. VanDerbeck, *Principles of Cost Accounting* (Thomson South-Western, 2005).

Nadini Persaud
University of the West Indies

Cost Analysis

Cost analysis refers to a specific methodology that can be used to analyze financial decisions. This methodology includes several distinct, but related tools that are useful for calculating costs, particularly of something that is being appraised, assessed, or evaluated. Cost analysis is used by decision makers in both the public and private sectors, and is useful for both for-profit and not-for-profit decision making. It is primarily discussed in the literature as a methodology for optimizing the use of resources in light of economic constraints and limited resources; however, this methodology should be employed to make decisions even if resources are not an issue.

Cost analysis methodologies became popular in the 19th century with the use of cost benefit analysis by the U.S. Corps of Engineers when it began to evaluate federal expenditures on navigation in 1902. Over the next 60 years, this methodology gathered momentum in the United States with the enactment of the Flood Control Act of 1936, use by the U.S. Department of Defense in the 1960s, and promotion by the Office of Management and Budget. In 1981 cost benefit analysis became an official appraisal tool of the U.S. federal government with the signing of Order 12291 by President Reagan.

The term *cost analysis* is often used interchangeably with terms such as *cost benefit analysis, cost effectiveness analysis, cost utility analysis,* and *cost feasibility analysis.* However, each of the aforementioned methodologies has unique characteristics that make each appropriate to specific applications. In cost benefit analysis, costs and benefits are both translated into monetary terms. This methodology can therefore facilitate comparison of alternatives with widely disparate objectives (e.g., health, education, national security) to determine which provides the highest ratio of benefits to costs in order to facilitate overall social analysis for public investment decisions. Cost effectiveness analysis is useful for comparing the costs of different programs that are designed to achieve the same or similar outcomes. It is an appropriate tool for cost appraisals when it is difficult to assess benefits in pecuniary terms, when controversy arises over the valuation of certain types of benefits (e.g., reduced mortality), or where the effort of calibrating benefits into monetary units is unjustifiably great. In cost effectiveness analysis, only costs are translated into monetary units—benefits are expressed in outcome units such as lives saved, percentage of alcoholics abstaining for one year, and so forth. In other words, efficiency is expressed in terms of the costs of achieving a given result.

Cost utility analysis assesses alternatives by comparing costs and utility (satisfaction derived by someone from some outcome) as perceived by users, to determine which option yields the highest level of utility for a given cost. Cost feasibility analysis compares the cost of an investment with the available budget to determine if the investment would be feasible. Other methodologies classified under cost analysis include: net present value, which measures wealth maximization; the internal rate of return, which measures the return on capital; and the payback period, which is the time required to recover the original investment.

Cost analysis methodologies can yield invaluable information for decision making—however, these methodologies can be quite complex and complicated. Cost analysis can be complicated by the following issues, among others: choice of discount rate, selection of the correct costs/benefits for the analysis, duplication/double counting of costs/benefits, measurement of intangible (e.g., reduced stress, cleaner environment) or controversial (e.g., value of lives saved) costs/benefits, and valuation of nonmonetary costs/benefits, indirect costs/benefits, and opportunity costs.

See Also: Cost Structure; Make-or-Buy Decision.

Bibliography. Anthony E. Boardman, David H. Greenberg, Aidan R. Vining, and David L. Weimer, *Cost-Benefit Analysis: Concepts and Practice* 2nd ed. (Prentice Hall, 2001); Henry M. Levin and Patrick J. McEwan, *Cost-Effectiveness Analysis* 2nd ed. (Sage, 2001); Tevfik F. Nas, *Cost-Benefit Analysis: Theory and Application* (Sage, 1996).

NADINI PERSAUD
UNIVERSITY OF THE WEST INDIES

Costa Rica

A Central American nation located between Nicaragua and Panama, Costa Rica had a 2008 population of approximately 4.47 million people. By Central American standards, it is a relatively prosperous nation with a 2008 gross domestic product (GDP) of US$30.5 billion. In per capita terms, at US$6,830, it ranks ahead of all Central American economies except Panama. Costa Rica has one of the most stable democracies in the Western Hemisphere. That, in combination with a relatively well-trained labor force, mild climate, and beautiful countryside, has made the country a popular destination for both direct foreign investment and wealthy retirees.

Macroeconomic trends have been largely favorable in recent years. Between 2000 and 2007, real GDP expanded at an annual rate of 5 percent. That figure implies an impressive seven-year growth rate of 3.1 percent in per capita terms. Monetary policy has allowed liquidity to expand at an even faster clip, however, causing inflation to persist at double-digit rates throughout the new millennium. That circumstance is more manageable than might be expected. Central bank policies have generally kept real interest rates in positive territory and avoided excessively easy credit stances. Similarly, the Finance Ministry has also held the central government fiscal deficit in check during this period.

Foreign Trade

Foreign trade patterns resemble those of many tropical economies wherein the service account takes on added importance via tourism as a key generator of commerce. Traditional exports include bananas, coffee, sugar, pineapples, timber, and beef. Newer important merchandise exports include electronic equipment, medical equipment, and pharmaceuticals. Service sector exports encompass tourism, software development, and financial outsourcing. The latter play critical roles in largely offsetting an annual $3 billion plus merchandise trade deficit. Costa Rica further exports substantial volumes of energy produced by its extensive system of hydroelectric dams. It also imports all of its oil-related energy products, contributing to larger than normal merchandise trade deficits since 2002. Other merchandise import categories include capital goods and food.

Although the current account has tallied negative balances in recent years, the colon has remained remarkably strong against the dollar. That reflects the large volumes of foreign direct investment that have

occurred during this period in each of the manufacturing and service export sectors mentioned above. Those sectors have attracted an impressive list of multinational corporations drawn in part by strategic fiscal incentives. A growing number of European and North American expatriates have also invested in a variety of residential real estate projects throughout the country, also strengthening the capital account.

Infrastructure

From a regional perspective, the economy of Costa Rica is centered around San Jose, the capital and largest city. Beyond metropolitan San Jose, other important metropolitan economies include Liberia, Puerto Limon, and Puntarenas. All three are regional public administrative, agricultural, and tourism centers. As seaports, international commerce plays an important role in the economies of Puerto Limon and Puntarenas. Although not directly located on the Pacific coast, Liberia has an international airport that helps increase its overseas business linkages.

Among the various policy issues facing Costa Rica, one of the most important is physical infrastructure development. The road system has not been maintained very well and also has failed to keep pace with economic growth in recent decades. Public utility systems and municipal street grids suffer from similar difficulties. Information technology also lags behind modern economies elsewhere in the world. Operational efficiencies for in-country business endeavors inevitably suffer as a consequence of these shortcomings. Services trade issues facing Costa Rica include intellectual property rights, telecommunications competition, and insurance competition. Some of those problems are expected to be addressed as the government moves toward implementation of the Central American Free Trade Agreement. As is the case with most Latin American countries, labor market rigidities continue to hamper Costa Rican economic performance. The labor market is also affected by illegal immigration from Nicaragua. Regulatory burdens facing businesses are also relatively heavy.

Future prospects for Costa Rica remain positive. As a very popular tourist and off-shore residential destination, it has met the trend toward increased service sector globalization very effectively. Its growing industrial sector exports are also helping to modernize an economy characterized by one of the best labor forces in Latin America. Overall productivity in this country can also accelerate as the national government addresses the policy areas currently slowing development.

See Also: Central America; Central American Common Market; Company Profiles: Central America and the Caribbean; El Salvador; Guatemala; Panama

Bibliography. Banco Central de Costa Rica, *Informe Mensual de la Situación Económica de Costa Rica* (BCCR División Económica, April 2008); Douglas Belt, Robert Birnbaum, and Lowell Gudmundson, *Some Aspects of Costa Rican Political Economy: Balance of Payments and Foreign Investment* (ACM Central American Field Program, 1972); Thomas Grennes, *Role of Coffee Exports in the Costa Rican Economy—APAP II*, Collaborative Research Report Number 330 (Abt Associates, 1992); International Monetary Fund, *International Financial Statistics* (IMF Publication Services, April 2008); S. Mosquera, "Costa Rica," *Latin America and Caribbean Quarterly Review and Outlook* (Global Insight, First Quarter 2008); Deborah Sick, "Coping with Crisis: Costa Rican Households and the International Coffee Market," *Ethnology* (v.36/3, 1997); World Bank, *Doing Business 2008* (International Bank for Reconstruction and Development, 2007).

THOMAS M. FULLERTON
UNIVERSITY OF TEXAS AT EL PASO

Costco Wholesale

A big-box, no-frills, minimally stocked operation that requires a membership fee to offset low margins on goods and services, Costco was founded in 1983 by James Sinegal and Jeffrey Brotman with a mandate to provide a minimal selection in an extensive range of products that excel in their class and at the same time provide good bargains. The lack of advertising and its associated costs, the low overhead, the negligible markup, the high sales volumes, a respected high-quality signature brand and co-branding with well-known high-end manufacturers, the infrequent and unexpected availability of highly valued and desired goods, and road shows of premium specialty items at affordable prices contribute to Costco's success. How-

One of Costco's 76 Canadian stores; it has other international outlets in Great Britain, Taiwan, Korea, Japan, and Mexico.

ever, Costco's respect and care for its employees as well as its customers has also helped its success.

Costco relies on word of mouth from satisfied customers rather than costly advertising to secure business and loyalty. The use of skylights and reduced lighting on sunny days, the use of shipping pallets to act as displays on the barren concrete retail floor, the lack of shopping bags and other forms of packaging materials contribute to their cost savings. Only one credit card company, American Express, is used exclusively and in return, no fee is charged to Costco on transactions, which magnifies savings to both the consumer and the seller.

Great attention is paid to providing high quality goods that are also sought after by consumers. There is little choice available in the 4,000 core goods that are stocked, only 25 percent of which continually change, but those goods chosen are purchased in large lots to minimize costs and prices. Even in its food court where a limited number of items are available for an extremely reasonable price, a family of five can be fed for less than $10. Costco guarantees a full refund at any time for the products that it sells. Electronic products must be returned within 90 days to secure a full refund; however, to further entice customers, Costco offers a free two-year warranty. Kirkland, its signature brand, is well priced, of good quality, and upgraded frequently. Costco has been innovative in its packaging of goods, its merchandising mixture, and limits its overall markup to 14 percent.

There are also great values in higher-priced merchandise that appears occasionally for a short period of time. Whether the product is diamonds, boutique wines, leather sofas, or exotic cheeses, they are of high quality with never more than a 14 percent markup. These special lots pique shoppers' interest and drive repeated visits. The periodic rotations of unusual goods such as oriental rugs further induce customers to shop frequently.

According to analysts, Costco's unskilled employees in the United States receive an average wage of $17.25 per hour, which is 42 percent higher than the wage paid by its major rival. Costco also covers 92 percent of the cost of the healthcare benefits that are provided to all employees, including part-time workers. High profits result from the respect shown to employees and in return there is low turnover and a higher rate of productivity. The accompanying low rates of theft help propel Costco above its poorly paying rivals. Costco has proven that healthy profits and well-paid employees are not mutually exclusive.

See Also: Retail Sector; Wal-Mart Stores.

Bibliography. Costco Wholesale, www.costco.com (cited March 2009); M. Duff, *A Private Label Success Story* (DSN Retailing Today, 2005); David W. Fuller, Anita Thompson, and Mary-Jane Butters, *Costco Wholesale Household Almanac* (Costco Wholesale, 2007); "Discounters: Costco's Battle to Change Beer and Wine Distribution," *BusinessWeek* (n.4065, December 31, 2007); Euromonitor PLC, *Costco Wholesale Corp.* (Euromonitor, 2003); Institute of Grocery Distribution, *Costco Wholesale* (Institute of Grocery Distribution, 1992); Duane E. Knapp, *The BrandPromise: How Costco, Ketel One, Make-a-Wish, Tourism Vancouver, and Other Leading Brands Make and Keep the Promise That Guarantees Success* (McGraw-Hill, 2008.

Marilyn Cottrell
Brock University

Cost of Living Allowance

A cost of living allowance (COLA) is an adjustment in wages to make up for a change in purchasing power, in order to keep an employee at a certain standard of living or lifestyle. A change in purchasing power is determined with a measure of inflation, or rising prices, facing consumers over time or in different geographic areas, such as the U.S. Consumer Price Index (CPI). Employment contracts, pension benefits, and government entitlements, such as Social Security, often contain annual COLAs. Alternatively, COLAs may also be tied to a cost-of-living index that varies by geographic location if an employee temporarily relocates to a higher cost area within a particular country or to another country, including military personnel stationed overseas.

One controversy surrounding the COLA is that it often does not take into account the effect of higher taxes that must be paid if the recipient is pushed into a higher tax bracket. In that case, the COLA is not enough to keep the person "whole" or at the same after-tax salary level. In addition, the COLA is usually retroactive, or based on the inflation rate of the prior year, meaning recipients have difficulty keeping up with a higher cost of living. However, if the COLA is based on a measure of inflation that overestimates price increases facing consumers, then the recipient's purchasing power is increased rather than just maintained. Because the CPI did not take into account consumer substitution into cheaper goods or stores with better bargains, the U.S. Bureau of Labor Statistics created the Chained CPI to better reflect consumer adjustments and thus the cost of living.

COLAs were under scrutiny during the inflationary 1970s as a possible cause of cost-push inflation, a situation where the cost of production suddenly rises but the demand for the product or service remains the same. This additional cost must be passed on to the consumer in the form of price increases. Wage increases, along with increased costs of inputs, such as oil, were considered the primary culprits. However, further research indicates that sustained cost-push inflation can only occur with an increase in the money supply.

See Also: Compensation; Pension Systems.

Bibliography. C. Burdick and L. Fisher, "Social Security Cost-of-Living Adjustments and the Consumer Price Index," *Social Security Bulletin* (v.67/3, 2007); Shaohua Chen and Martin Ravallion, "Absolute Poverty Measures for the Developing World," *Proceedings of the National Academy* *of Sciences of the United States of America* (v.104/43, 2007); U.S. Bureau of Labor Statistics, "Overview of BLS Statistics on Inflation and Prices," www.bls.gov (cited March 2009); U.S. Social Security Administration, "Latest Cost of Living Adjustment," www.ssa.gov (cited March 2009).

Donna M. Anderson
University of Wisconsin–La Crosse

Cost Structure

Cost structure has traditionally been defined as the relative proportion of fixed and variable costs in an organization and how these costs behave in response to changes in production or sales volume. Additionally, cost structure is generally discussed in the context of long-run and short-run production, with an emphasis on a particular function. Modern definitions of cost structure, however, encompass a much more holistic definition, namely, rethinking business models to reduce costs across entire processes in order for organizations to remain competitive in the globalized business environment.

In economics, cost structure is defined as the relationship between costs and quantity. Embedded in this definition, firms have at least one fixed factor of production in the short run—all other costs are assumed to be variable. In the short run, fixed factors of production are assumed to have no impact on the firm's decisions since they cannot be changed over a short time period. For example, most products require raw materials, labor, machinery, and factory space. If demand increases for a particular product, it is generally quite easy to increase raw materials and labor in proportion to the increased demand. However, adding new machinery and a factory is not as easy since these are capital investments that generally require large financial outlays and a certain amount of time for completion.

In contrast to the short run, the long run is the period over which firms are assumed to be able to vary all factors of production. The implications therefore of the short run/long run at the industry level are that in the short run, firms can increase/decrease production in response to demand, while over the long run, firms can enter/exit the market.

A proper understanding of cost structure hinges on the fundamental distinction between fixed costs and variable costs. Fixed costs can be classified into two categories: (1) committed fixed costs, and (2) discretionary fixed costs. Committed fixed costs are costs associated with investments in basic organizational assets and structure (e.g., depreciation, insurance expenses, property taxes, and administrative salaries). Such costs are long term in nature (several years) and cannot be significantly reduced in the short term even during periods of diminished activity. In contrast, discretionary fixed costs (e.g., advertising, repairs and maintenance, research and development) are short term in nature (one year). Such costs can be altered by current managerial decisions with minimal damage to an organization's long-term goals. As a result, these costs are generally the first to be cut during bad times.

In terms of per unit and total comparisons, fixed costs that are expressed on a per-unit basis will vary inversely with the level of activity. In other words, unitized fixed costs will decrease as volume increases and vice versa. However, in total, fixed costs remain constant within the relevant range. For example, rent will not increase if a factory is working at full capacity or at minimum capacity, or if an outpatient clinic serves one patient or 20 patients daily. The relevant range is the range within which a factory, business, hospital, school, etc. can operate without increasing the size of its operations in the short run. Within this range, assumptions about variable and fixed cost behavior are reasonably valid.

In contrast to fixed costs, variable costs are expenses that vary in total according to the size of the program or in direct proportion to the level of business activity, but which remain constant on a per unit basis within the relevant range. For example, the number of latex gloves used in a hospital will increase with the number of patients; however, the cost per latex glove will not generally change if one glove or 100 gloves are used. Typical variable costs include direct materials, sales commissions, and supplies. Note that variable costs will be zero when business activity is zero. In order for a cost to be variable, it must be variable with respect to some activity base or cost driver. Business activity can be expressed in many ways such as beds occupied, units sold or produced, miles driven, customers served, or products serviced. Knowing what drives cost is crucial in order for cost reduction to be targeted in the right areas. Notwithstanding, it is important to recognize that no cost driver is a perfect prediction of cost. For example, although machine hours may be used as a cost driver to predict electricity consumed in a factory, it has no relationship to the actual price charged per kilowatt hour.

A question that may frequently be asked is "which cost structure is better?" This answer depends on numerous factors including type of industry, long-run sales trend, and flexibility to risk. Firms with higher proportions of variable to fixed costs tend to enjoy greater profit stability and are better protected against losses. In contrast, firms which are characterized by high levels of fixed costs (e.g., the airline industry) experience greater profits in good years. However, the downside to this type of cost structure is that greater losses are experienced in bad years. If demand falls, profits decline swiftly and turn into losses. For example, United Airlines' fixed costs for pilots and flight attendants was so high in comparison to its competitors that the company could not cover its higher operating costs—the airline was forced to file for bankruptcy in 2002. Cost structures with high proportions of fixed costs are therefore quite risky when demand is uncertain and fluctuating.

One option that can help to minimize risk in high-fixed-costs industries is to lease rather than purchase, since leases can be cancelled. In general, decision makers have some flexibility in trade-offs between fixed and variable costs. For example, variable labor costs can often be replaced with automation. However, organizations will not move toward automation unless the long-run sales trend suggests that this may be a viable alternative. These types of decisions can generally be facilitated through the use of cost analytical techniques.

Closely aligned with the term *cost structure* is the concept of operating leverage, that is, a measure of the sensitivity of net operating income to a given percentage change in sales dollars. Operating leverage is computed as contribution margin (sales minus variable expenses) divided by net income. If two firms have identical revenues and expenses but different cost structures, the firm with the higher fixed expenses will have greater operating leverage. The effects of operating leverage can be quite dramatic when a company's sales are near the break-even point. However, as sales and profits rise, operating leverage declines.

Given the dynamics of the 21st century, it is important that organizations recognize that proactive strategic vision on cost structure is the key to business success and survival. Such vision requires that organizations take a holistic view of cost structure, rather than a strictly departmental/functional view. Moreover, this holistic view needs to encompass not only internal issues/factors but also external issues/factors, since the external environment can greatly affect an organization's success. For example, inflation/deflation, that is, fluctuations in money value that cause the price of goods and services to change, and supply/demand conditions that circularly influence price, are all factors beyond the control of management. Nonetheless, these factors can greatly affect profitability.

Profitability can also be affected by external factors that can be controlled to some extent by management. For example, higher oil prices may necessitate using a different transportation route, sourcing from a different vendor, or purchasing in bulk in order to reduce transportation costs. Generally, bulk purchasing is adopted in order to reduce unit costs of either raw materials or products. However, a more holistic vision considers not only the discounts that could result from buying in bulk, but also the savings that could be realized on transportation and handling costs.

Proactive strategic vision may, however, frequently necessitate that organizations make difficult strategic choices about the business model itself, for example, removing organizational or supply-chain layers, embracing outsourcing, or sharing service centers. Nonetheless, today, the key to success hinges on an organization's ability to expeditiously redesign its business model to respond rapidly to changing dynamic economic conditions. Continuous review of cost structures is therefore critical for organizations to maintain a competitive edge and avoid bankruptcy or hostile takeovers.

See Also: Cost Accounting; Cost Analysis; Fixed Costs; Managerial Accounting.

Bibliography. Ray H. Garrison, Eric W. Noreen, and Peter C. Brewer, *Managerial Accounting*, 12th ed. (McGraw-Hill, 2008); Michael R. Kinney, Jenice Prather-Kinsey, and Cecily A. Raiborn, *Cost Accounting: Foundations and Evolutions*, 6th ed. (Thompson, 2006); KPMG International, *Rethinking *Cost Structures: Creating a Sustainable Cost Advantage* (KPMG, 2007); Henry M. Levin and Patrick J. McEwan, *Cost-Effectiveness Analysis*, 2nd ed. (Sage, 2001); Nadini Persaud, *Conceptual and Practical Analysis of Costs and Benefits in Evaluation: Developing a Cost Analysis Tool for Practical Program Evaluation* (Unpublished doctoral dissertation, Western Michigan University, 2007).

NADINI PERSAUD
UNIVERSITY OF THE WEST INDIES

Côte d'Ivoire

This West African country became a protectorate of France in 1843–44, and then a French colony in 1893, gaining its independence in 1960. In spite of its name, "Ivory Coast" in English, the country has depended heavily on the sale of agricultural produce, and about 70 percent of the population still relies on agriculture. The country is one of the largest producers and exporters of cocoa beans, coffee, and palm oil.

Because of its colonial history, French companies tend to have a major role in the country's economy, developing the countryside to establish plantations for cash crops. After World War I, the French imposed a more centralized administration and also started expanding the country's infrastructure. Tropical hardwood was harvested, and the plantations—largely run by French companies—produced cocoa and coffee, but there were also some locals who established their own plantations. To help with the building of roads and railways, the French relied on a system of forced labor by which the locals worked in lieu of payment of taxes.

During World War II, the colony was controlled by the French loyal to the pro-German Vichy regime, After the war the French administration introduced a large number of economic and political reforms including the abolition of forced labor, which had become very unpopular because the system was subject to abuse. Agitation also started for independence and much of this was led by Félix Houphouët-Boigny, a local activist who owned plantations and who had established the Syndicat Agricole Africain (SAA), a union that helped protests for independence. Houphouët-Boigny was able to get elected to the French national assembly, spending two years as a French cabinet minister.

In 1958 protests in Côte d'Ivoire led to French president Charles de Gaulle holding a referendum in which the colony voted against a federation being established, and in 1960 Houphouët-Boigny declared independence. He introduced a socialist economy with central planning in an attempt to build up the country. Politically, the country was stable and this helped encourage foreign investment, especially in the cocoa and coffee industries. In the late 1970s, after the oil crisis pushed up the price of gasoline, Côte d'Ivoire started exploiting its own offshore oil-fields that provided a degree of wealth for the country. The Abidjan Stock Exchange (Bourse de Valeurs d'Abidjan) was created in 1976 and was one of only four stock exchanges operating in Africa during the 1990s. This helped encourage investment—both local

A man runs a conveyor belt at an Ivoirian cooking oil bottling plant. Palm oil is one of the country's top exports after cocoa.

and foreign—in Ivoirian companies, and by 1986 some 30 percent of the shares were owned by Ivoirians. In the early and mid-1990s, Côte d'Ivoire went through a period of austerity and hardship, resulting in a rescheduling of loans in November 1996—it had previously stopped repayments in 1987.

In spite of the discovery of oil, cocoa remains the country's largest export, making up about a third of Côte d'Ivoire's export income. Other exports include coffee, petroleum, tropical hardwoods, cotton, bananas, palm oil, pineapple, and fish. Consumer goods and manufactured items make up much of the imports, with 23 percent coming from France; Nigeria and the United Kingdom are Côte d'Ivoire's other two major trading partners.

See Also: Africa; Company Profiles: Africa.

Bibliography. "Cote D'Ivoire: The Real Rulers," *New African* (n.471, 2008); John Rapley, *Ivoirian Capitalism: African Entrepreneurs in Côte d'Ivoire* (Lynne Rienner, 1993); Michelle Riboud, *The Ivory Coast 1960–1985* (International Center for Economic Growth, 1987); Douglas Rimmer, *The Economies of West Africa* (Weidenfeld & Nicolson, 1984); Francis Teal, "The Foreign Exchange Regime and Growth: A Comparison of Ghana and the Ivory Coast," *African Affairs* (v.85/339, 1986); I. William Zartman and Christopher Delgado, eds., *The Political Economy of Ivory Coast* (Praeger, 1984).

JUSTIN CORFIELD
GEELONG GRAMMAR SCHOOL, AUSTRALIA

Cotonou Agreement

The Cotonou Agreement was signed in Cotonou, Benin, on June 23, 2000, and revised in 2005. It is a cooperation agreement between the European Community and its member states and the 78 African, Caribbean, and Pacific countries (the ACP), most of whom are former European colonies. The Cotonou Agreement builds on a series of similar agreements and includes five interdependent pillars: an enhanced political dimension, increased participation, a more strategic approach to cooperation focusing on poverty reduction, new economic and trade partnerships, and improved financial cooperation. Recent controversy has mainly focused on the trade provisions, which granted the ACP unilateral preferential access to European Union (EU) markets until the end of 2007, after which these had to be replaced by new trading arrangements called Economic Partnership Agreements or EPAs.

Much of the driver for this change in trade policy came from the increasing difficulties the ACP and EU had in justifying to other World Trade Organization (WTO) members the special EU market access in previous agreements. Favoring one group of developing countries over others is incompatible with the principle of Most Favored Nation (MFN) treatment set out in Article I of the General Agreement on Tariffs and Trade (GATT) and the subsequent agreement in 1974 to enable the provision of greater market access for developing countries—the "Enabling Clause." As a result, the EU was forced to seek a series of waivers from other WTO members to enable its special trade regime for the ACP to continue. At the same time a series of complaints was brought to GATT/WTO on the EU-ACP banana regime—in a dispute dubbed the Banana Wars. It was consistently found that the special access for ACP bananas was incompatible with the rules of the international trading system. A final waiver was agreed in 2001 that allowed preferences to continue until EPAs were negotiated in 2007.

Moreover, the special access to the EU market which ACP countries enjoyed did not seem to have been effective in stimulating growth and economic diversification. In spite of the privileged market access, ACP shares of EU trade declined from 6.7 percent in 1976 to 3 percent in 2007, while about 55 percent of their total exports became concentrated in only 5 products. There was broad consensus among the ACP and EU that a more comprehensive approach was required. This led to the decision to create EPAs between the EU and regional groupings of ACP countries. Negotiations at the regional level finally began in 2003 with six regions that broadly speaking cover the Caribbean, the Pacific, eastern Africa, west Africa, central Africa, and southern Africa.

Negotiations on EPAs between the EU and ACP subregions have been long and complex. As negotiations advanced, it became clear that a key issue was the interpretation of requirements to establish reciprocal market access under WTO-compatible free trade areas (FTAs). Fears were widespread among the ACP and many development-oriented nongovernmental organizations (NGOs) that opening ACP markets to EU products would damage domestic industry. This motivated an intense discussion on the extent and timing of ACP liberalization that was complicated by the fact that the requirements for WTO-compatible FTAs are not clearly defined. The rules state that "substantially all trade" be liberalized within "a reasonable period of time." A subsequent understanding by WTO members stated that "a reasonable period of time" could exceed 10 years only in "exceptional circumstances" but there is no clear definition of "substantially all trade." This led to claims that EU exports to the ACP could be liberalized at levels as low as 50–60 percent over periods as long as 20 years, while still qualifying as FTAs under WTO rules. Further controversy surrounded the extent to which services trade and measures covering issues like investment and intellectual property were in the ACP interest.

As the 2007 deadline loomed, several NGOs and academics suggested that the EPAs would be bad for the ACP and that there were other potential means of ensuring WTO-compatible market access. In this context it became difficult to secure an agreement, and by the end of 2007, only the Caribbean region of 15 CARIFORUM countries had reached agreement on a fully fledged EPA with the EU, including a high level of liberalization of goods and services.

Faced with the prospect of increasing tariffs on some of its poorest trading partners, the EU proposed a series of interim agreements with individual countries or subregions (e.g., the East African Community) including WTO-compatible reciprocal goods trade arrangements. These were initialled by 20 countries in late 2007, securing market access in a manner which the EU and ACP hoped would build the foundations for full EPAs. The 10 remaining countries (Nigeria, Gabon, Congo-Brazzaville, and seven small Pacific islands) had no significant preferential trade and declined to sign agreements; 32 are classified as Least Developed by the United Nations and have duty free access to EU markets, and South Africa already has a WTO-compatible free trade agreement with the EU. At the time of writing, negotiations for full EPAs continue with the remaining five ACP regions.

See Also: Africa; Banana Wars; Caribbean Community; Pacific Rim.

Bibliography. S. Bilal and F. Rampa, *Alternative (to) EPAs Possible Scenarios for The Future ACP Trade Relations With the EU* (ECDPM, 2006); Petersmann Ernst-Ulrich, "The European Union and the Developing Countries: The Cotonou Agreement," *Common Market Law Review* (v.44/2, 2007); Adrian Flint, "Marrying Poverty Alleviation and Sustainable Development? An Analysis of the EU-ACP Cotonou Agreement," *Journal of International Relations and Development* (v.11/1, 2008); Commission of the European Communities, "The Cotonou Agreement" (2000); C. Stevens and J. Kennan, Agricultural Reciprocity Under Economic Partnership Agreements, *IIIS Discussion Paper* (n.111, IIIS, Trinity College, Dublin, 2006).

LOUISE CURRAN
TOULOUSE BUSINESS SCHOOL

Countertrade

Countertrade is a system of trading that was developed to enable governments to minimize the economic imbalance of international transactions. Countertrade is not barter trade, although barter may provide an element of countertrade.

A single major international purchase contract may have a negative effect upon a country's balance of trade, particularly for small nations or those with restricted access to hard currencies. To counter this imbalance, governments seek to moderate any trade bias by insisting upon a reciprocal mechanism that balances it, either immediately or in the future.

There are several scenarios that encourage the application of countertrade. The prime motivation appears to be trade facilitation, in that it enables trade that might otherwise be barred by a lack of convertible currency or foreign exchange, or other problems with international commercial credit.

Countertrade may be categorized into several forms that may be applied either discretely or in combination (the use of the term *product* in this article includes primary materials and manufactured goods as well as services):

1. Direct offset: The seller agrees to purchase components or materials used in the manufacture or assembly of the actual products that they will

be selling. This effectively reduces the cost to the buyer. This is commonly used in high-value markets such as military or aerospace. A good example of this was when McDonnell Douglas sold helicopters to the British government, but had to equip them with British Rolls-Royce engines.

2. Indirect offset: This is used in similar market sectors to direct offset, but in this case, the importer requires the exporter to make a long-term investment or other commitment to the benefit of the importer's economic infrastructure.

3. Switch trading: Switch trading, sometimes known as swap, is when a third country uses its position as a trading partner with two other countries whose reciprocal trade is not in equilibrium. For example, the third country C purchases a product from A and sells another product to B to help balance the trade between A and B.

4. Counterpurchase: In this form, the exporter contracts to purchase goods, materials, or services that are not required to be incorporated in their products, thus reducing the effective cost of the products to the importer. This is seldom a direct value for value exchange and may also be for a longer period than that required for the execution of the primary contract.

5. Barter trading: Barter is the straightforward trading of one product against another. The obvious drawback to this is that a product of sufficient commercial value to fulfill a barter contract probably already has a viable export market. Similarly, a product that does not have an export market is unlikely to be of sufficient interest for barter.

It must be remembered that barter trade is seldom in equilibrium, thus a broker will be involved to ensure that there is a terminal market for bartered products. A product that does not have a potential market is of little interest to a broker. The balancing of barter trade usually requires a complex series or "string" of trades. Note two terms that often cause confusion: *agio,* the broker's premium paid by an exporter; and *disagio,* the commission paid by the exporter to the broker to recompense the broker for assuming the countertrade transaction risk. (In effect, the same payment from different points of view.)

Product Tolling

Tolling is the production of goods from raw materials supplied by the eventual buyer. This occurs when raw materials are not available to a production company or state, usually due to financial constraints. This usually comprises the entire content of the finished product, all of which remains the property of the supplier, although the cost of production may be paid in part by the product.

An example would be a fertilizer factory, where the buyer of the finished product supplied raw materials, corrosion inhibitor, and bags to the operator of a factory that was operating below economic output in another country. They would then pay for the processing in either cash or bagged fertilizer, or a combination of both.

This is closely related to buyback. Buyback is when either the whole or part payment is made with products manufactured either by machinery or equipment supplied by the seller, where the buyer of the machinery pays for it through product that is produced by the equipment. Examples might be the supply of agricultural equipment paid for by part of the harvest over a period of time, or a transport facility such as a pipeline, where some of the transported product will be used to pay.

Risks of Countertrade

Countertrade transactions seldom match in terms of value or timing. Obligations acquired by either the importer or the exporter from such transactions are usually outside the scope of their commercial expertise. Thus the successful conclusion of a countertrade contract often depends upon a skilled countertrade broker, who will add cost or decrease the value of the transaction.

Specific risks may include the following:

1. Offset: Risk is low due to this form of countertrade normally being limited to governments and multinational enterprises (MNEs).

2. Switch: Also being at governmental or MNE level, the risk is relatively low.

3. Counterpurchase: Balancing of the trade may not occur until a considerable time after the initial transaction, increasing risk of execution.

4. Barter: Needs brokers with expertise in handling a string of contracts or turning a range of prod-

ucts into cash. They expect a substantial *disagio* for facilitating the deal and taking risk.

5. Tolling: Has the risk that an already underfinanced producer may collapse or divert materials and products to meet conflicting needs.

6. Buyback: Has the risk that the equipment may fail to produce sufficient product for payment in either the agreed or a viable time frame, or else the primary source may fail. However, these risks are to some extent moderated, since the quality of the end product should be improved by better production machinery, thus increasing its value.

See Also: Barter; Swap.

Bibliography. C. G. Bowers and B. Bowers, "The American Way to Countertrade," *Countertrade and Barter Quarterly* (February/March 1988); Barter News, issue 17, www.barternews.com (cited March 2009); Chong Ju Choi, Soo Hee Lee, and Jai Boem Kim, "A Note on Countertrade: Contractual Uncertainty and Transaction Governance in Emerging Economies," *Journal of International Business Studies* (v.30/1, 1999); Global Offset & Countertrade Association, www.globaloffset.org (cited March 2009); London Countertrade Roundtable, www.londoncountertrade.org (cited March 2009); Dorothy A. Paun, Larry D. Compeau, and Dhruv Grewal, "A Model of the Influence of Marketing Objectives on Pricing Strategies in International Countertrade," *Journal of Public Policy and Marketing* (v.16/1, 1997); UNCITRAL, *Legal Guide to International Countertrade Transactions* (United Nations, 1993).

Brian M. W. Clements
University of Wolverhampton
Business School

Countervailing Duties

A countervailing duty is intended to neutralize the competitive advantage that a firm gains when exporting to a foreign market due to the receipt of subsidies from its home government. It is an additional duty that removes the advantage gained by the receipt of the subsidy. Countervailing duties, like their counterpart anti-dumping duties, are intended to correct for

unfair trade practices that create advantages for overseas firms that export products to the domestic market. While anti-dumping duties address unfair trade practices that are caused by dumping, i.e., selling goods in the domestic market below costs, countervailing duties, also known as anti-subsidy measures, are intended to address unfair trade practices that are caused by payment of subsidies to foreign firms. Under World Trade Organization (WTO) rules, subsidies may be countervailed if they cause material injury to the domestic industry.

To better understand what it means to countervail a subsidy, consider the following example with two symmetric firms, one domestic and one foreign, each of which produces goods in its home market. Both firms sell in the domestic market and each earns an operating profit of $25,000. Now suppose that the foreign firm receives a subsidy from its home government, and this subsidy enables it to undercut its competitor's price. With the subsidy, the foreign firm earns a profit of $37,000 while the domestic firm suffers a loss of $8,000. The domestic firm has been materially injured by the subsidy received by the foreign firm as reflected by the change in its profitability. Under these circumstances, a countervailing subsidy may be imposed as the material injury test has been met. Suppose further that the subsidy to the foreign producer is the form of an export subsidy of $1.30 per unit. To countervail this subsidy, the importing country imposes a specific duty of $1.30 per unit. This returns the foreign firm to the position it was in prior to receipt of the subsidy. It also returns the market to its pre-subsidy position with both firms earning an operating profit of $25,000. As a result of the countervailing duties, the material injury suffered by the domestic firm has been eliminated.

The export subsidy used in the example above is a prohibited subsidy under WTO rules because it is specifically designed to distort international trade flows and in the process create winners and losers. Export subsidies and other forms of prohibited subsidies can be countervailed. Actionable subsidies, unlike prohibited subsidies, are not designed to distort international trade flows but may nonetheless cause material injury to the domestic industry. Most subsidies fall into this category. Given that the trade distortion and hence material injury effect of actionable subsidies is no longer definitive, the WTO rules require a detailed investigation prior to the implementation of countervailing duties in these circumstances. Investigations must be conducted in accordance with the procedural requirements set forth in the WTO's Agreement on Subsidies and Countervailing Measures. National legislation in member countries, when adopted, is consistent with these requirements.

Typically, countervailing duty investigations must establish that a subsidy was received, that the domestic industry was materially injured, and that this material injury was a result of the subsidy. The WTO procedures allow for a preliminary determination of material injury. If the preliminary determination is positive, the foreign firm is generally required to post a bond that is equivalent to the estimated subsidy margin on all relevant imports pending final determination. If the final determination is positive, countervailing duties are imposed. Normally, countervailing duties are imposed for five years.

Countervailing duty investigations are normally initiated when companies submit a petition to the relevant national agency. Some critics have argued that although countervailing duty rules are intended to discipline the use of subsidies, the ease with which such investigations can be initiated has led to abuse. Such abuse is a result of companies using the countervailing duty laws to seek administered trade protection.

See Also: Dumping; Subsidies; World Trade Organization.

Bibliography. United States International Trade Commission, *Antidumping and Countervailing Duty Handbook*, 12th ed., April 2007, www.usitc.gov (cited March 2009); World Trade Organization (WTO), "Agreement on Subsidies and Countervailing Measures," www.wto.org (cited March 2009); WTO, "Understanding the WTO," www.wto.org (cited March 2009).

Laurel Adams
Northern Illinois University

Country of Origin

Country of origin is the country of manufacture, production, or growth from which an article or product originates. Designation of the country of origin is implemented for two reasons. The first is that such information is sought by consumers and traders who regard such designations favorably: For example, the engineering products of a particular country may be renowned for their reliability and technical specification; similarly, clothes produced in another country may be especially prized because of their sophistication. Within this category may also be mentioned the administration of "buy national policies." The second reason is administrative. Designation of country of origin is required for the imposition of duties, import restrictions, and for the compilation of national trade accounts. This second category could be extended to include measures to protect local or "infant" industries, and as an extension of political policy where sanctions are applied.

Rules governing country of origin have been longstanding, especially where the imposition of tariffs has been concerned. Examples include the Australian Customs Tariff Act, 1908, which accorded preference to United Kingdom exports; section 304 of the United States Tariff Act, 1930, which required imported products to be marked with the country of origin, and the British Import Duties Act, 1932, by which duties were levied on non–British Empire products. Since 1945, rules of origin marking have become important as a consequence of the spread of regional trading agreements: Between 1947 and 1995, 98 regional trading agreements were notified to GATT (General Agreement on Trade and Tariffs). This meant that accurate designation of country of origin was important if the exports of particular countries were to avoid tariffs.

Global-level awareness of the issues generated by country of origin were raised during the formation of GATT in 1947, but no specific regulation was effected on origin matters and the countries that acceded to this agreement were free to determine their own rules of origin. A GATT proposal required that the nationality of goods resulting from materials and labor of two or more countries would be that of the country in which such goods last underwent a substantial transformation, but it was left to individual countries to determine the processes which would satisfy this condition.

The International Convention on the Simplification and Harmonization of Customs Procedures (Kyoto Convention) was agreed in 1973. This Convention stipulated that the origin of goods should be determined by the last country in which a "substantial transformation" occurred. But the rules determining "country" of origin were nonbinding. Much of the Convention's work was limited to clarifying different criteria to apply in the determination of origin. In fact, the first binding multilateral agreement on country of origin did not occur until the Uruguay Round Agreement on Rules of Origin. This agreement established a three-year program to harmonize rules of origin among GATT (subsequently World Trade Organization) members. This program was not completed by the set deadline of 1998, and currently there is still no global harmonization of country of origin requirements.

Increasing globalization has affected the accuracy of country of origin designations. For example, when all stages of production, from raw material to ready-for-sale product occur in one country, the origin of an import is completely unambiguous. But when the various stages of production occur in different countries (for example, by trade in intermediate products) determining country of origin becomes more complicated. In this case, a single country of origin designation becomes meaningless. A further factor has been the rapid growth in foreign direct investment (FDI): Multinational companies transfer semi-processed products within their global supply chain networks.

Other economic distortions that have arisen from country of origin marking schemes are that they create a bias toward the concentration of final-stage production (usually the highest value-added stage) in particular countries. This issue becomes more intractable in cases where the final production stage is no more than a simple assembly stage and does not, therefore, represent substantial transformation. Where origin rules are predicated on specific components, production according to comparative advantage may be undermined. Restrictive origin regulations can distort investment flows toward major importing countries. These flows can, in turn, undermine indigenous manufacturers.

These economic distortions can also influence the tariff policy adopted by particular countries or countries belonging to a free trade area. For example, it may be more appropriate that a tariff structure should not depend on the price of the imported article but the value outside the free trade area. Alternatively, because vertically related processing occurs in a number of different countries, it may be more accurate to implement multicountry tariffs: In this case the tariff rate to be imposed on a particular product would be the sum of the tariff rates levied on each country component of the value added.

Until there is a binding global agreement on country of origin designations, especially with respect to preferential origin rules (those that determine the duty to be imposed on imported goods from specific countries), the pattern of global trade and the location of production may be distorted. This is further complicated by the fact that different bilateral free trade agreements use different criteria to set rules of origin: Goods processed partly or fully in a third country may obtain duty-free access under a bilateral agreement by being reexported with just enough processing to satisfy rules of origin requirements.

In late 2008 supermarkets in the United States became required to label the country of origin for meat, produce, and certain kinds of nuts. However, it was uncertain what effects that might have.

See Also: Country of Origin Requirements; Export; General Agreement on Tariffs and Trade; Import.

Bibliography. Sadrudin A. Ahmed and Alain d'Astous, "Antecedents, Moderators, and Dimensions of Country-of-Origin Evaluations," *International Marketing Review* (v.25/1, 2008); Greg R. Bell, Curt B. Moore, and Hussam A. Al-Shammari, "Country of Origin and Foreign IPO Legitimacy: Understanding the Role of Geographic Scope and Insider Ownership," *Entrepreneurship Theory and Practice* (v.32/1, 2008); Christian Bluemelhuber, Larry L. Carter, and C. Jay Lambe, "Extending the View of Brand Alliance Effects: An Integrative Examination of the Role of Country of Origin," *International Marketing Review* (v.24/4, 2007); Michael Chattalas, Thomas Kramer, and Hirokazu Takada, "The Impact of National Stereotypes on the Country of Origin Effect: A Conceptual Framework," *International Marketing Review* (v.25/1, 2008); David Kesmodel and Julie Jargon, "Labels Will Say If Your Beef Was Born in the USA," *Wall Street Journal* (September 23, 2008); Hina Khan and David Bamber, "Country of Origin Effects, Brand Image, and Social Status in an Emerging Market," *Human Factors in Ergonomics in Manufacturing* (v.18/5, 2008); E. Vermulst, P. Waer, and J. Bourgeois, eds., *Rules of Origin in International Trade: A Comparative Study* (University of Michigan Press, 1994).

David M. Higgins
University of York

Country of Origin Requirements

At the global level there are no uniform or enforceable guidelines governing country of origin requirements. Apart from treaty obligations, which may be bilateral or multilateral, and excluding any obligations arising as a member of a customs union, for example, the European Community (EC), individual countries have considerable freedom in the following: the way in which a product acquires origin (for example, whether it is wholly, or partly processed); limits on the extent to which value is added in non-preference countries; and documentary requirements to establish origin. Additionally, further restrictions may be imposed on country-of-origin marking in the case of specific products that are being exported (for example, "Swiss" watches and watch movements).

In the EC there exist two broad rules determining rules of origin: preferential rules and non-preferential rules. The former allow most products originating in a preferential-partner country to be imported to the EC after little, if any, common external tariff. Such preferences apply to Norway, Iceland, Switzerland, and Turkey (pan-European partners) as well as to Egypt, Israel, Jordan, and Lebanon (pan-Mediterranean partners). These arrangements have been supplemented by a pan-Euro-Med cumulation agreement that helps manufacturers satisfy relevant origin rules provided they originate within the EC's preferential trading arrangements.

Non-preferential rules apply to imported products originating from countries for which the EC does not extend preferential arrangements. This includes Australia, Japan, and the United States. Products covered by non-preferential rules include those "wholly obtained or produced" in a single country (for example, extracted mineral products), and those whose production involved more than one country (for example, electrical and electronic goods). Where more than one country was involved in the production of a good, the originating country is defined as that in which the final major process was effected.

In the United States, it is a legal requirement that U.S. content must be disclosed on certain types of products, for example, motor cars, textiles, and woollen and fur products. The relevant legislation governing the description to be applied to each of these products is, respectively, the American Automobile Labeling Act, the American Textile Fiber Products Identification Act, the Wool Products Labeling Act, and the Fur Products Labeling Act.

However, in certain cases, North American Free Trade Agreement (NAFTA) override rules can be used if a NAFTA preference is claimed. For example, China is a producer of comforter shells and the down used to fill these shells. Both of these textile products are sent to Canada, where the down is inserted into the shells. Although China is the country of origin of the finished comforter, Canada, which is a NAFTA member, can claim duty preference and if this is successful, the country of origin of the finished comforter is recognized as Canada. However, a product comprising foreign components may be labeled "Assembled in the USA" when its assembly has occurred in the United States and this assembly represents a "substantial transformation." It is also the case that certain qualified "Made in the USA" claims can be made. For example, "Made in the USA of U.S. and imported parts." Such qualified statements are considered appropriate when the products that include U.S. content don't satisfy the criteria for making unqualified "Made in the USA" claims.

Outside of the European Union and North America, countries are free to impose such restrictions as they wish on country of origin requirements, especially when country designations apply to particular products. In the case of watches, for example, Swiss law defines a watch as Swiss made when its movement is Swiss, its movement is cased in Switzerland, and the final inspection of the watch occurs in Switzerland.

A final category of origin requirement to which reference should be made concerns regional appellations that belong to particular countries. For example, "Stilton" cheese (England) and wines from the French regions of Burgundy and Champagne. Misuse of a regional appellation (for example, labeling wine "Burgundy" when it was not made there), can mislead consumers and it can lead to unfair competition (producers who do not have the right to the appellation nonetheless use it to try to capture some of the goodwill attached to genuine appellation products). Rules governing these appellations were promulgated by the International Convention for the Protection of Industrial Property dating back to the later 19th century (for example, Paris, 1883, and Brussels, 1900), and have more recently been covered by the Agreement on Trade-Related Aspects of International Property Rights (TRIPS), which set out the rules governing the registration of these appellations and the methods required to ensure their protection. In the case of wines and spirits, the TRIPS agreement contains special clauses that afford these products even higher levels of protection.

See Also: Agreement on Trade-Related Aspects of Intellectual Property Rights; Country of Origin.

Bibliography. Australian Competition and Consumer Commission, *Country of Origin Claims and the Trade Practices Act* (Australian Competition and Consumer Commission, 2002); Australian Competition and Consumer Commission, *Electrical Goods: Country of Origin Guidelines to the Trade Practices Act* (Australian Competition and Consumer Commission, 2003); Australian Competition and Consumer Commission, *Food and Beverage Industry: Country of Origin Guidelines to the Trade Practices Act* (Australian Competition and Consumer Commission, 2005); United States Congress: House Committee on Agriculture: Subcommittee on Domestic Marketing, *Consumer Relations, and Nutrition, Implementation of Country-of-Origin Labeling Requirements under Florida Produce Labeling Act of 1979: Hearing Before the Subcommittee on Domestic Marketing, Consumer Relations, and Nutrition of the Committee on Agriculture* (House of Representatives, One Hundredth Congress, second session, April 15, 1988); United States Congress, House Committee on Ways and Means, Subcommittee on Trade, *Country-of-Origin Labeling Requirements for Imported Meat and Other Food Products: Hearing Before the Subcommittee on Trade of the Committee on Ways and Means* (House of Representatives, One Hundredth Congress, second session, September 27, 1988); United States General Accounting Office, *Country-of-Origin Labeling Opportunities for USDA and Industry to Implement Challenging Aspects of the New Law: Report to Congressional Requesters* (United States General Accounting Office, 2003); E. Vermulst, P. Waer, and J. Bourgeois, eds., *Rules of Origin in International Trade: A Comparative Study* (University of Michigan Press, 1994).

DAVID M. HIGGINS
UNIVERSITY OF YORK

Country Screening

Country screening is the process of scanning international markets, with the intention of identifying and assessing opportunities for expansion. This process can be carried out through both primary and secondary research. Its main purpose is to answer three questions: Should we enter the country or not? Is there sales potential for our products or services? Where can we best leverage our core competencies? The country screening stage normally precedes the country selection stage and is the first step in the international planning process.

There are around 200 countries in the world. Even large multinational corporations will have problems entering all and every one of these countries. Thus, international markets will have to be screened to remove those that do not offer adequate potential. The criteria used in preliminary and secondary screening are relatively broad and include mainly economic and social data (e.g., income per capita or population) that should be available for most countries and allow for intercountry comparisons. In order to decide if further research may be worthwhile, potential markets have to fulfill three criteria: accessibility, profitability, and market size/growth potential. If a company is unable to enter a market, due to tariffs and non-tariff barriers or legal restrictions, or to reach the customers by means of communication or distribution, if the market is unable to return a profit, sometimes due to exchange regulations, or if its actual and future size is small, then there is no point for the company to pursue this venture.

When information regarding one specific country is sparse, mainly in latent and incipient markets, a company may have to rely on comparative research, between the target country and some other country, normally one that is at a more advanced economic level or that belongs to the same geoeconomic group. Some of the key techniques used are demand pattern analysis, multiple factor indexes, analogy estimation, regression analysis, and macro-surveys.

When screening a country, uncertainty and risk factors are the most pertinent ones and cannot be ignored. Risks can be political, commercial, industrial, or financial, can be evident or latent, and can be spread along a risk scale. Over the past years a range of risk indexes have been developed. The largest country and political risk consultancies are Business Environment Risk Intelligence (BERI), Business Monitor International, The Economist Intelligence Unit, Global Insight/World Markets Research, and Political Risk Services/International Country Risk Guide. These indexes cover different environment factors such as political stability, taxation, infrastructure, and security. They normally come to a score, indicating how the country ranks regarding risk type and level. For example in BERI's operation risk index a score of 55–41 points means "high risk, bad business climate for foreign investors." In their Business Environment Ratings Report for 2006, Switzerland, Singapore, Netherlands, Japan, and Norway were the five least risky countries in the world. The Economist Intelligence Unit's Country Risk service assesses credit risk (based on currency risk, sovereign debt risk, and banking risk) across 120 countries. The latest findings (May 2007) ranked Singapore, Hong Kong, and Chile as the least risky, and Iraq, Zimbabwe, and Myanmar as the riskiest countries.

To facilitate a proper screening process, companies need to follow a methodical approach. One of the most widely used frameworks is the 12C environmental analysis. The twelve Cs are country, concentration, culture/consumer behavior, choices, consumption, contractual obligations, commitment, channels, communication, capacity to pay, currency, and caveats. Some of the elements analyzed comprise SCLEPTE (social, cultural, legal, economical, political, technological, and environmental) factors, structure of the market segments, characteristics of competitors, growth patterns, business practices, trade barriers and incentives, logistics and media infrastructures, and currency stability, among others. The information obtained will help to design a profile for each considered country, including major threats and opportunities, degree of country attractiveness and company competitive advantage, and the most suitable entry mode.

In order to obtain country-related information there are a variety of secondary sources that can be used such as international chambers of commerce, trade organizations, embassies, export councils, or trading companies. With the advent of the internet, online databases have become a good source of information, for example Kompass, Textline, Comtrade, Eurostat, Euromonitor, or Mintel. Web sites of the United Nations, European Union, World Bank, or the World Trade Organization are also very useful sources.

When using secondary data to screen a country, companies must be aware of some of its pitfalls: availability, accessibility, quality, and recency. However, and despite these problems, secondary data may be the only kind available for small and medium-sized companies or even for larger companies in very distant markets. When all secondary data has been collected, companies may need to gather primary data to attain the information considered necessary. Unknown cultures and countries make international data collection a difficult task and key decisions when undergoing it are linked to organizational factors: Should we do it with our own resources (in-house) or through a market research company and, in this case, should it be a domestic agency (from our own country), a local agency (from the host country), or a major global agency? Availability of resources, market/country characteristics, budget, and urgency of the data will determine the final choice.

See Also: BERI; Economic Indicators; Host Country; International Chamber of Commerce; Nontariff Barrier; Risk; Risk Management.

Bibliography. John Daniels, Lee Radebaugh, and Daniel Sullivan, *International Business*, 12th ed. (Pearson, 2009); Isobel Doole and Robin Lowe, *International Marketing Strategy* (South Western, 2008); Office of Fossil Energy/ Argonne National Laboratory, *Potential Markets for Small Coal-Fired Combustors in OECD Countries Country Screening/United States* (U.S. Department of Energy, Office of Fossil Energy, 1988).

Miguel Martins
University of Wolverhampton

Craft Production

Craft production refers to work carried out by a skilled worker. Its aim is to produce not just a commodity but to do something well for its own sake. In craft production, work can be an end in itself, an expression of the individual's talents. It is not simply a means to an end. Craftsmanship means quality. Craft production is often said to be a less-alienated form of production than the machine-based mass production of the factory or office. The ideal of craft production is used as a standard against which other forms of labor are judged and measured. Critics of modern capitalism, from writers like John Ruskin, William Morris, and John Dewey onward, have looked back to craft production as part of a world that is being lost and looked forward to an age yet to come when its principles could be recovered. The acquisition of the output of craft production could then be, not the privilege of the few, but the basis of the life of the many.

All human labor involves some degree of explicit and tacit skill. Historically this has been so important that people have been named after their "craft"—smith, thatcher, fletcher, mason, potter, carpenter, etc. Early craft production is most associated with the urban labor of artisans in medieval cities where production was organized in small workshops and (though not invariably) guilds. Although goods were produced for sale, craft production, in principle, involved strict codes. Craft workers served apprenticeships in which they were introduced to the "mysteries" of their craft. An apprenticeship (often six to seven years) might involve 5,000–10,000 hours of supervised work before it was considered that the craft worker had been trained. The apprentice would then demonstrate his proficiency as journeyman by producing his "masterpiece." The journeymen might hope to progress to be a "master craftsman" in their own workshops, joining the craft guild on their basis of their established "mastership." So powerful was this idea of craft production that what we today consider the artifacts of high culture from this time—art, jewelry, furniture, sculpture—were actually the results of craft workshops under the control of artists, instrument makers, etc. as master craftsmen.

The craft guilds, often supported by legislation and local regulation, negotiated with powerful merchants and helped to set prices to avoid exploitation. They policed the quality of goods, fines for offenses against "honor and solidarity" being a significant element in their disciplinary actions. They oversaw skill development, provided a mechanism for the mobility of labor, and acted as a source of credit. They also formed the social and political basis of the life of the worker in craft production.

A 16th-century Swiss woodcut illustrates the traditional craft process of a small group of shoemakers and assistants.

But the social function of craft production went beyond the workplace. Craft work was seen as the basis of self-respect for the individual. People spoke of "craft pride" and "artisan independence." Craft was also an important source of civic pride. It could even be the basis of political rights. Craft work was also seen as a quasi-religious vocation—craft was a gift from God and its support a celebration of God's gifts. Craft can be analyzed using conventional economics as a form of social capital. But to explain the role of craft production through a narrow economic calculus is to miss the way that craft production developed historically. It cannot explain its wider social resonance nor the way that today the output of earlier generations of craft workers still embodies our ideas of accomplishment and beauty.

In England in the 16th century concern about the impact of economic change, enclosures, vagabondage, and masterless men led to the passing in 1563 of the Statute of Artificers. This supported craft work by requiring apprentices to serve for seven years, terminating at 24 (reduced to 21 in 1778). This created a framework that lasted in England, although unevenly enforced, until the early 19th century. Elements of this were also applied piecemeal in the American colonies.

Measuring the scale of earlier craft production is not easy. In pre-industrial society, peasants and farmworkers predominated and there were many unskilled workers. But one minimum estimate suggests that in England, around 1700, some 11,000–12,000 males completed apprenticeships each year, which would total between 290,000 and 460,000 workmen trained as apprentices at that time in a population of some 5 million.

By this time some urban craft production was already feeling the challenge of the rise of proto-industrialization in the more advanced parts of Europe. Proto-industrialization was the spread of unregulated forms of craft production into the countryside to take advantage of labor surpluses. Methods of production might be formally similar but conditions of work deteriorated as networks of merchant capital became ever more sophisticated. Nevertheless, if skill levels were inferior and the market more pressing in proto-industrial craft production, workers still retained a greater degree of control over the labor process than would be possible in the factories that came with the Industrial Revolution.

Capitalism Changes Production

The development of capitalism, and especially industrial capitalism, led to a change in the nature of craft production and a profound long-term challenge to it. One aspect of this was ideological. As the potential of the division of labor and mass production began to develop, some writers began to attack guilds and craft production as economically irrational and a brake on technical progress. Guilds, they suggested, acted as rent-seeking coalitions that thrived on monopoly rents to the disadvantage of unskilled workers and customers. Craft production would and should give way to not only to industrial production but "freer" market relations.

State action also played a role in the weakening of craft production, if only at the level of removing earlier protections. Artisans saw the defense of the regulation of craft production against "illegal men," whether masters or journeymen, as part of their birthright and a protection of the rights of labor. But in late-18th-century Britain, laissez-faire pressures led to a consolidation of the rights of property while encouraging an ever freer market for hired labor. Not only were workers' combinations banned but the old legislation protecting craft apprenticeship and conditions came under attack. The Statute of Apprentices was repealed in 1814 despite a significant artisan campaign to defend and even extend it. One craft petition numbered 300,000 signatures.

In this shift, our understanding of the past also changed. "Art" began to be separated from "skill" as a higher-order activity and even divided internally into different levels. The artist became in the popular mind a lonely individual with a unique sensibility and an intuitive talent, producing for rich patrons or themselves. The skills of the craft worker were separated and diminished. Since labor was seen as repugnant, the labor in the production of art, and the tools necessary for it, became marginalized when people spoke of art. Even the term "masterpiece" was appropriated to higher art.

These changes also had an impact on our understanding of science and its development as a separate and specialized function. Much early science was rooted in craft production, which has been described as a repository of scientific production technique. The inquiring mind of the artisan craftsman as watchmaker, instrument maker, millwright, or spinner was behind many decisive steps forward. Craft work could sustain a tradition of self-education that could be undertaken to surprisingly high levels—not merely the literacy but the knowledge of other languages of the printer or the mathematical skills of the mechanic.

The effect could also be seen in education. When formal education systems began to develop, they were defined by a tension between education in its broadest sense and the narrower tasks of fitting people, groups, and classes for particular positions. This produced a divided and segmented system where the pressure lower down was to create an impoverished vocationalism which, if it referred to an early tradition of craftsmanship, did so only in name.

More radical accounts attack this diminution of the idea of craft and craft production and the analysis used it support it. Some historians argue that craft guilds survived much later into the 18th and 19th centuries than was previously suggested. The longevity of guilds suggests a rationality that critics missed. Productivity in guild-based craft production may, for example, have been higher than in the equivalent nonguild production. Nor is it clear that invention and innovation was hindered. Even Adam Smith recognized the possible stultifying impact of the division of labor on human ingenuity.

The pressures that new forms of production put on craft production were not, according to this view, a simple product of technical change. Rather, capitalism needed to find a form of work organization in which the employer could dominate and exploit the work. The factory was therefore a socially determined form of technology designed in part to overcome the fact that craft production left too much power in the hands of the craftsman. The skill of the worker had to be appropriated by the system, divided up, reduced, and embodied in organizations and equipment controlled by the employer or their agent. The extreme of this was represented by Frederick Taylor's desire for a system of scientific work control, "in the past the man has been first; in the future the system must be first ..." Sometimes craftwork directly succumbed to this after a struggle. In other cases, craft work degenerated into forms of outwork labor. Both involved a continual process of deskilling.

But formal apprenticeship as the basis of craft production in particular and work more generally had a longer life, albeit to significantly different degrees in different national contexts. In the United States it was difficult to get masters and men to keep to indentures. Here craft work quickly became more open to market influences. There was limited incentive for employers to commit to long-term training of their employees when workers could easily leave and when legal enforcement was costly and difficult. By 1850 there were less than two apprentices per 1,000 employees in the United States. But forms of craft work (in the widest sense) remained widespread; Walt Whitman's poem "Song of the Occupations" is a lyrical invocation of some of them.

In Britain and Europe apprenticeship as an underpinning for craft work survived on a wider basis and became incorporated into trades like engineering. Sometimes this was based on formal indentures, but in Britain the respect attached to a worker's "lines" was so significant as to enable much apprenticeship to be based on informal agreements. In Europe, for-

mal agreements were often supported by the state, and in Germany modernized craft-style apprenticeships became and still are part of the training system. At the end of the 1970s, apprenticeship accounted for only 0.3 percent of civilian employment in the United States compared to 2–3 percent in the United Kingdom and Commonwealth countries and 5–6 percent in West Germany, Austria, and Switzerland.

Post–Industrial Revolution

Several different trajectories for craft work can be identified since the development of the Industrial Revolution. Some craft production simply succumbed to the challenge of factory-based mass production and was eliminated. In other industries, craft production continued to survive but market pressures caused a deterioration of conditions and intensified and impoverished the division of labor, with craft work perhaps degenerating into forms of sweated workshop labor. In a third and smaller group of industries, craft production survived, often based on the production for high-quality and high-cost markets (although beneath the surface conditions might worsen). A fourth trajectory was where "crafts" were able to turn themselves into "professions" through the development of higher-status images and controls. But there was and is a fifth element. Sometimes technical change can generate areas of craft like "responsible autonomy" where within the most advanced elements of the system, elements of craft-like production can survive. This was apparent in the past, for example, in the engineering industry. Today a popular example is the way in which in the computer industry and the development of information technology, supporters of open source software and "the creative commons" collectively work for the common good, sharing their developments. What drives them is less a concern for financial gain or corporate service than the expression of enthusiasm, joy, and creativity in work.

When this happens there is a struggle for control that to some degree parallels earlier struggles that might otherwise be thought of only out of historical interest. Major companies seek to establish property rights in intellectual creativity and to control and discipline what is seen as an unruly and even potentially subversive movement. In this view such a craft ethic has no place in modern capitalism, even though it is to be found in the most modern sector (or perhaps it should be said to have no place unless the results of it can be privately appropriated).

The fate of craft production is not therefore one of straight-line decline. Strong pressures exist in this direction and the best analysis of them remains that of Harry Braverman (1920–76) in his *Labor and Monopoly Capital*, where he described the tendency since the Industrial Revolution for work to be divided up in its component jobs, each of which might require less skill and training, and thus be paid less. However, automation and computerization of a plethora of low skill tasks has led others to observe an upgrading of the skill levels of jobs in developed economies.

Craft production was also the basis of the development of the early labor movement in most countries; the skill of the craft workers and the demand for their labor gave them a stronger bargaining position and made them better able to resist employers than early factory workers. Early unions therefore were associated with better-paid craft workers, were largely male, and a product of the labor aristocracy. Mass industrial unionism was often counterposed to the craft base of traditional unions. But under pressure, craft unions had to look beyond sectionalism. Even Samuel Gompers, the archetypical American craft unionist, warned his members that today's artisan was the unskilled laborer of tomorrow as pressures toward deskilling developed.

But just as there is the reproduction of some elements of craft production in capitalism as a whole, so too can this provide the basis for ongoing craft-like labor organization. However, most such modern craft unions tend to link their fate much more closely to the labor movement as a whole. In these terms the fate of craft production should not be seen as a battle fought and lost. Rather, change in work relationships under capitalism involves a continuing tension over the nature and purpose of production and a continual struggle over its meaning.

See Also: Capitalism; Empowerment; Management Science; Salaries and Wages; Technology.

Bibliography. C. Bina and B. Finzel, "Skill Formation, Outsourcing and Craft Unionism in Air Transport," *Global Economy Journal* (2005); H. Braverman, "Labor and Monopoly Capital: The Degradation of Work in the Twentieth Century," *Monthly Review* (1974); Carl Bridenbaugh, *The Colonial Craftsman* (New York University Press, 1950); A. Briggs, ed., *William Morris: Selected Writings and Designs* (Penguin, 1962); B. Elbaum, "Why Apprenticeship Persisted in Britain but Not in the United States," *The Journal of Economic History* (1989); S. Marglin, "What Do Bosses Do?" *Review of Radical Political Economics* (1974); R. Sennett, *The Craftsman* (Allen Lane, 2008); Izumi Shimada, *Craft Production in Complex Societies: Multicraft and Producer Perspectives* (University of Utah Press, 2007); Carla M. Sinopoli, *The Political Economy of Craft Production: Crafting Empire in South India, c. 1350–1650* (Cambridge University Press, 2003); Anne P. Underhill, *Craft Production and Social Change in Northern China* (Kluwer Academic/Plenum Publishers, 2002); D. Woodward, "The Background to the Statute of Artificers: The Genesis of Labor Policy, 1558–63," The Economic History Review (1980).

MICHAEL HAYNES
UNIVERSITY OF WOLVERHAMPTON
BUSINESS SCHOOL

Credit Ratings

A credit rating is an assessment of the creditworthiness of a debt issuer or a specific debt obligation, together with any additional security attached to it. The rating represents an opinion on the ability and willingness of an obligor to deliver payments due to investors. This opinion usually has a form of a letter-based rating, which corresponds to a certain relative (not absolute) probability of default. The rating is often accompanied by an extensive commentary.

Credit ratings can be assigned to countries, municipalities, various types of organizations, or particular debt issues. Sovereign ratings assess the credit risk of national governments and depend on both political and economic factors. These ratings serve as a benchmark for the ratings of other issuers who operate within the same sovereign jurisdiction and represent a so-called ceiling—normally the ratings of other issuers in the same country cannot be higher than the sovereign rating.

Ratings are assigned by specialized organizations—credit rating agencies. There exist many of them worldwide (roughly 130 to 150 as of 2000), and they vary in terms of size, geographical and industry focus, and the methodology that they employ. However, most of these agencies are rather small, and the field is dominated by two major players: Moody's Investors Service Inc. (Moody's) and Standard & Poor's (S&P). The large credit agencies play an important role in capital markets. First, they provide valuation by disseminating timely and supposedly valuable information to the market participants. Second, they indirectly participate in financial regulation: In some countries letter ratings are viewed as useful credit quality benchmarks, and capital requirements are directly linked to credit ratings. For example, the quasi-regulatory role of the major credit agencies has been increased by the Basel II Framework.

There are two main types of ratings: solicited and unsolicited. A solicited rating means that a company itself expressed a wish to be rated and asked an agency to issue it a rating, usually for a fee. An unsolicited rating implies that it was an agency's own decision to rate a company. In the case of unsolicited ratings, an agency usually has to rely on publicly available information only to come up with an assessment. The rationale for the practice of assigning unsolicited ratings is that it discourages a self-selection process in which only low-risk issuers are rated and all others avoid obtaining a credit rating by not requesting it. Rating agencies also use unsolicited ratings to establish their reputation or expand their business into new markets. When a rating is solicited, an agency relies not only on public information, but also makes extensive use of internal data such as company documents, interviews with the company's executives, etc.

There are several reasons why issuers are interested in acquiring a credit rating. The main one is the access to capital markets—in some countries, having a rating is a de-facto prerequisite. Other reasons include building up market reputation, lowering the cost of funding (an unrated entity usually has to pay a larger risk premium), and distinguishing oneself from competitors.

The rating processes used by different agencies can vary significantly. Large agencies use both quantitative and qualitative criteria to assess an issuer, whereas smaller agencies tend to focus on quantitative criteria only. The rating process consists of the assessment of various factors. One of them is the environment, which can vary considerably depending on the nature of the entity under assessment. Meetings with the issuer constitute an important part of the rating process. During these meetings, comprehensive in-depth information is collected and any questions that came up in previous phases are clarified. The rating process also often includes the analysis of a peer group (a group of comparable entities).

Several points of criticism have been expressed about the credit-rating agencies. They have apparently failed to predict large-scale crises such as the 1997 Asian crisis or notorious corporate scandals such as Enron and WorldCom. Another source of criticism is the secretive nature of the rating process—rating agencies disclose their rating methodologies only partially. Some have expressed concerns about the fact that rating agencies have conflicting incentives connected with their two functions of information dissemination and facilitation of contracts. Another point of criticism has to do with the so-called rating triggers. A rating trigger is a contractual provision that gives lenders certain rights in case a borrower's rating falls below a predefined level. Rating triggers can lead to the loss of investor confidence and the bankruptcy of an issuer.

See Also: Bankruptcy; Capital Adequacy; Regulation; Risk.

Bibliography. A. Duff and S. Einig, *Credit Rating Agencies: Meeting the Needs of the Market?* (Institute of Chartered Accountants of Scotland, 2007); A. Fight, *The Ratings Game* (John Wiley & Sons, 2001); Lita Epstein, *The Complete Idiot's Guide to Improving Your Credit Score* (Alpha Books, 2007); C. Frost, "Credit Rating Agencies in Capital Markets: A Review of Research Evidence on Selected Criticisms of the Agencies," *Journal of Accounting, Auditing and Finance* (2007); Gudrun M. Nickel, *The Credit Repair Answer Book: Your Answer for Raising Your Credit Score* (Sphinx Publishers, 2007); Timothy J. Sinclair, *The New Masters of Capital: American Bond Rating Agencies and the Politics of Creditworthiness* (Cornell University Press, 2005); John Ventura, *The Credit Repair Kit*, 4th ed. (Dearborn Trade, 2004); Steve Weisman, *50 Ways to Protect Your Identity and Your Credit: Everything You Need to Know about Identity Theft, Credit Cards, Credit Repair, and Credit Reports* (Pearson Prentice Hall, 2005); Liz Pulliam Weston, *Your Credit Score: How to Fix, Improve, and Protect the 3-Digit Number that Shapes Your Financial Future* (Pearson Prentice Hall, 2005).

LYUDMILA V. LUGOVSKAYA
UNIVERSITY OF CAMBRIDGE

Credit Suisse

The Credit Suisse Group is a Zurich-based financial services corporation offering investment banking, private banking, and asset management through its three divisions. The Credit Suisse Shared Services division provides services in support of the other three divisions, principally legal and IT service.

Alfred Escher (1819–82) founded the company, then called Schweizerische Kreditanstalt, in 1856. An adept politician from Zurich, Escher had made a nationwide name for himself with his support of railways as the solution to Switzerland's malaise following the brief civil war of the 1840s, a solution that would end the country's economic and geographic isolation. In particular, Escher was instrumental in keeping the railroads in the private sector—benefiting Zurich, since state-supported railroads would centralize the industry and its earnings in Bern, the capital of the new federal government (established in 1848). While continuing his political service, Escher also acted as the Managing Director of the Northeastern Railway Company, and founded the Kreditanstalt to finance transalpine railway lines. He helped develop Swiss Life, now Switzerland's largest insurance company, the following year.

Three million francs of Kreditanstalt stock were issued, valued at over 200 million francs within days. The Swiss Confederation, at risk of falling behind western Europe and its Industrial Revolution, was hungry for industrialization and the railways helped make that possible while the Kreditanstalt helped finance it—and helped Zurich become and remain Switzerland's financial center. As Switzerland industrialized, it entered—until World War I—a golden age that helped it become the banking capital of the world. The first foreign office of Credit Suisse was opened in 1870 (in New York City), and by the end of the 19th century the company had become the principal player in the Swiss underwriting business. Branch offices outside of Zurich began opening in 1905 (the first in Basel), and its underwriting business expanded overseas.

The impact of the Great Depression increased tensions and nationalist sentiment across Europe, and Credit Suisse looked overseas for safer sources of capital. The Swiss American Corporation was founded in 1939 in New York City, as a subsidiary of Credit Suisse's underwriting business and investment consultancy. Years later, it would be discovered that during the war

The Credit Suisse offices in Hong Kong. In 2007 the company employed 50,000 people worldwide.

years, Credit Suisse was one of several banks guilty of improper dealings with Nazi Germany, and mishandling of the "dormant accounts issue" (accounts opened before the end of the war by account holders who became victims of the Holocaust). Like the other banks, Credit Suisse eventually settled by paying money into a pool for reparations as well as to establish a humanitarian fund. In 1964 Credit Suisse was granted a license as a full-service bank in the United States, and in 1982 the bank became the first Swiss bank with a listing on the New York Stock Exchange (via its subsidiary Swiss American Securities).

The American bank First Boston was taken over by Credit Suisse in 1990, becoming Credit Suisse First Boston—now the bank's investment banking division. The acquisition came in fits and starts. Credit Suisse First Boston had been the name of a joint CS/FB venture in 1978, and unhappiness with the terms of the venture along with an unsuccessful stretch of a few years led to the departure of several CSFB executives, some of them leaving for Merrill Lynch.

Credit Suisse's acquisition of First Boston, folding it into CSFB, was part of its response to the change in investment banking in the 80s as Goldman Sachs and Salomon Brothers began to compete with them in the Eurobond market, along with the perception that CSFB and Credit Suisse were in competition with one another for certain services. The 1987 stock market crash and mid-1980s allegations that the bank participated in laundering eastern European drug money had hit Credit Suisse hard, while First Boston suffered from bad loans made for mergers and acquisitions. The acquisition and restructuring was meant to strengthen and redefine both companies.

The 1990s saw more acquisitions and alliances, and the array of banks and services were reorganized in 2002 as the Credit Suisse Group. Several restructurings followed in rapid succession as the company maneuvered to recover from the record losses it had posted in 2002. The current form of the bank, with its three main divisions and shared services division, originated in 2006, in commemoration of the original bank's 150th anniversary. Credit Suisse First Boston provides debt and equity underwriting, securities services, and mergers and acquisitions management. The group is the second largest financial services firm in Switzerland, behind UBS, and operates in 60 countries, with over 200 retail branches in its homeland.

See Also: Gnomes of Zurich; Merrill Lynch; Switzerland; SWX; Transportation.

Bibliography. Edmund L. Andrews, "When the Sure-Footed Stumble: Swiss Banks Stagger After Several Investing Missteps," *New York Times* (October 23, 1998); Paul Beckett, "Credit Suisse and UBS Agree to Open 2.1 Million Holocaust-Era Accounts," *Wall Street Journal* (May 4, 2000); Dieter Fahrni, *An Outline History of Switzerland: From The Origins To The Present Day* (Pro Helvetia, 2003); David Fairlamb, "On the Edge: Will a Radical New Strategy Save the Day for Credit Suisse's CEO?," *Business Week* (July 15, 2002); Joseph Jung, *From Schweizerische Kreditanstalt to Credit Suisse Group: The History of a Bank*, trans. by James Knight (Neue Zürcher Zeitung, 2000); Ian Rodger, "The Enfant Terrible of Swiss Banking," *Financial Times* (January 9, 1993).

BILL KTE'PI
INDEPENDENT SCHOLAR

Croatia

At the beginning of the 20th century, Croatia was part of the Austro-Hungarian Empire. Following the empire's demise in 1918, a kingdom of Slovenes, Croats, and Serbs was established. Croat opposition to the new structure gradually increased, but any attempts to promote democratic change were stifled, and Yugoslavia was established in 1929. An independence movement, led by the Ustase Croatian Liberation Movement, gradually grew. Force was used in an attempt to establish an independent state. However, it was not until the German invasion of Yugoslavia on April 6, 1941, that Ustase leader Ante Pavelic was installed as the leader of an independent state of Croatia. However, by 1943 partisan opposition forces, under Josip Broz (Tito), controlled much of Croatia. On October 20, 1944, Tito became prime minister of Yugoslavia; Croatia became one of six constituent republics of a federal, independent communist state.

The further concentration of power in Belgrade produced further unrest in Croatia, culminating in the Croatian Spring of 1971—a call for greater autonomy and constitutional reform. When Tito died in 1980, Croatia was still a long way from independence. However, 1989 saw political change sweeping across Eastern Europe. Following elections, constitutional changes, and a referendum, Croatia declared independence on June 25, 1991. Fighting broke out. Amid ethnic rivalries thousands were killed and hundreds of thousands were forced to leave their homes. In January 1992 the United Nations negotiated a cease-fire and Croatia was recognized by the European Union (EU), and in April by the United States.

January 1993 saw further fighting in the Krajina region. In June 1993, the Krajinian Serbs voted to join Greater Serbia. Fighting continued, with widespread atrocities on both sides, until the Dayton Accord, recognizing Croatia's traditional boundaries, was signed in Paris in December 1995, establishing the Republic of Croatia as a presidential/parliamentary democracy, with Zagreb as its capital. The last Serb-held enclave in eastern Slavonia was returned to Croatia in 1998. Croatia's bid for membership of the EU received a boost in March 2008 when the European Commission said that it should be possible to complete accession negotiations by the end of 2009.

Croatia is now divided into 20 counties, and in 2008 the population is estimated to be approximately 4.5 million. The president is the head of state, elected to a five-year term. The leader of the majority party or the leader of the majority coalition is usually appointed prime minister by the president and then approved by the unicameral Assembly or Sabor. The Assembly comprises 153 seats; members are elected from party lists, by popular vote, to serve a four-year term. In the elections of November 25, 2007, the center-right Croatian Democratic Union or HDZ was the biggest party, with 66 seats; although not a majority, they were able to hold power through deals with smaller coalition partners that gave them an 83-seat total.

Croatia's economy suffered badly during the 1991–95 war as output collapsed. Since 2000, however, economic fortunes have improved steadily. gross domestic product (GDP) growth has been between 4 and 6 percent (5.6 percent in 2007). This has largely been on the back of a rebound in tourism and credit-driven consumer spending. Croatia registered 53 million tourist nights in 2006, up 36 percent from 2000. Total annual visitors could top 12 million by 2012. Inflation over the same period has remained low, 2.2 percent in 2007, and the currency has been generally stable. The government has also reduced the budget deficit to 2.6 percent of GDP in 2007. On the downside, the unemployment rate remains high at 11.8 percent in 2007, though economic growth should bring this down. There is also a growing trade deficit and uneven regional development.

Incremental reforms have helped the investment climate, as reflected in improved ratings in 2007 from Transparency International, the World Bank, and the World Economic Forum (WEF). The WEF's Global Competitiveness Index for 2006–07, published at the end of October 2007, ranks Croatia 57th out of 122 countries, with strong scores for education and technological readiness, along with weak scores for state administration and corruption.

See Also: Candidate Countries; European Union; Slovenia.

Bibliography. Central Intelligence Agency, "Croatia," *The World Factbook*, www.cia.gov (cited March 2009); Marcus Tanner, *Croatia: A Nation Forged in War* (Yale University Press, 1997); United States, *Croatia. Foreign Labor Trends* (U.S. Department of Labor, Bureau of International Labor Affairs and U.S. Embassy, Zagreb, 2004); Susan Woodward, *Balkan Tragedy: Chaos and Dissolution after the Cold War* (Brookings Institution, 1995).

Jamie Weatherston
Northumbria University

Cross-Border Migrations

The human species has a long nomadic history. The more recent concept of "cross-border migration" emerged from the formation of powerful territorially-based states in Europe. It gained practical importance after developments in transportation, communication, and industrialization enabled Europeans to colonize large parts of the rest of the world, and to relocate both within Europe and overseas in large numbers. By the early 20th century, with the general adoption of passports and border controls, cross-border migration had become a widespread political concern, and foreign workers a major source of labor used by businesses large and small.

In 2007 about 200 million people, or 3 percent of the world's population, lived outside the country of their birth. Likewise, the roughly 100 million migrant workers globally amounted to about 3 percent of the world's workforce. In certain regions, especially Western Europe and North America, and in certain occupations, such as computer programming, nursing, restaurants, and crop harvesting, these percentages have been much higher. International migrant remittances to developing countries totaled about $250 billion in 2005.

Most modern cross-border migration is associated with economic differences between countries. In 1975 per capita gross domestic product was about 40 times greater in high-income countries than in low-income countries; by 2000 this ratio had risen to over 60. Other "pushes" and "pulls" motivating international migration are noneconomic, notably family reunification and mass flight from disaster. Refugees with a "well-founded fear of persecution" have protected status under international conventions and within many national jurisdictions. In practice, however,

A densely populated Mexican city, at right, juts up against the heavily fortified border with the United States. In 2000 per capita gross domestic product was over 60 times greater in high-income countries than in low-income countries.

"economic migrants" and "political refugees" are overlapping categories. Similarly, although a cross-border migrant is generally one who moves internationally and stays at least a year in the new "host" country, it is often difficult to distinguish between "temporary" and "permanent" migrants. A more recent concern is the potential for cross-border refugee flows provoked by natural disasters, particularly catastrophic floods and droughts associated with global climate change.

A considerable fraction of cross-border migration moves without documentation and illegally into receiving countries. This causes practical problems along migratory routes and political problems for governments of sending countries (whose people want to leave) and of receiving countries (which cannot "control" their borders). Undocumented migrants also face the risk of exploitation by smugglers and difficulties of social integration while working "underground." How to deal with illegal immigration has recently been a major political issue in the United States.

Government Policies

Government policies on cross-border migration have been inconsistent. There are far fewer border restrictions on leaving than on entering. Official policies also partly reflect popular ambivalence. Voters in receiving countries are often apprehensive about large numbers of foreigners in their midst, but not opposed to readily available low-cost labor. Migrant workers are usually more productive than they would be at home, but the resulting net benefits of cross-border migration are unevenly distributed. At times, low-skilled workers in richer countries may suffer wage declines due to migration. Movements of migrants, however, are significantly influenced by economic cycles, not just by public policies or popular attitudes.

A "guest worker" program bringing foreigners temporarily to the United States was a key component of the comprehensive "compromise" immigration bill rejected by the U.S. Congress in 2006. Past guest worker programs, such as the "bracero program" of the 1940s and 1950s in North America, and the imports of labor to Western Europe during the 1960s boom, did provide economic benefits. "Temporary" guest workers, however, have often become permanent residents, bringing in relatives through the family network links that have long been central to self-replicating migration. Such networks are also prevalent within the growing migration between developing countries.

Large corporate employers in developed countries have been particularly interested in hiring more high-skilled foreigners. With cross-border flows of goods and finance much less restricted in recent decades than movements of workers, it has been more cost effective to tap the low-skilled labor of poorer countries by "outsourcing" production, assembly, and clerical functions there. Movements of professional workers, especially in science, engineering, and higher education, are a smaller but important form of cross-border migration. The extent and incidence of benefits and costs resulting from this "brain drain" are a matter of considerable interest to scholars and policy makers on which no general consensus has yet emerged.

See Also: Brain Drain; Expatriate; Globalization; Near Shoring; Off-Shoring; Outsourcing; Visa.

Bibliography. Georg Berkemer and Dietmar Rothermund, *Explorations in the History of South Asia: Essays in Honour of Dietmar Rothermund* (Manohar, 2001); Phillip Martin, Manolo Abella, and Christiane Kuptsch, *Managing Labor Migration in the Twenty-first Century* (Yale University Press, 2006); "Senators Back Guest Workers", *Washington Post* (March 28, 2006); Stalker's Guide to International Migration, www.pstalker.com/migration (cited March 2009); "A Turning Tide?" *The Economist* (June 28, 2008).

DREW KEELING
UNIVERSITY OF ZURICH

Cross-Border Trading

The role and importance of international financial markets and the traders who work in the industry has grown during the past decades. Professional traders are highly visible, especially in the media. They tend to be in a position to exploit market imperfections and have access to privileged information, critical mass, or proprietary knowledge and models.

Financial markets can be defined in two ways. The term can refer to organizations that facilitate the trade of financial products or it can refer to the interaction between buyers and sellers to trade financial products. Many who study the field of finance use both definitions, but economics scholars tend to use the second meaning. Financial markets can be both domestic and international.

Financial markets can be seen as an economics term because it highlights how individuals buy and sell financial securities, commodities, and other items at low transaction costs and prices that reflect efficient markets. The overall objective of the process is to gather all of the sellers and put them in one place so that they can meet and interact with potential buyers. The goal is to create a process that will make it easy for the two groups to conduct business.

When looking at the concept of "financial markets" from a finance perspective, one could view financial markets as a way to facilitate the process of raising capital, transferring risk, and conducting international trade. The overall objective is to provide an opportunity for those who want capital to interact with those who have capital. In most cases, a borrower will issue a receipt to the lender promising to pay back the capital. These receipts are called securities and can be bought or sold. Lenders expect to be compensated for lending the money. Their compensation tends to be in the form of interest or dividends.

Traders

Trader activities can be divided into three categories, which are trading on behalf of the customer, market making, and propriety trading. Traders with the least amount of risk are the ones who act on behalf of the customer. At the other end of the spectrum are proprietary traders, who take on the greatest risk. Regardless of the category, traders must utilize a set of strategies and approaches in order to make a profit. Four of the main strategies include the following:

1. Insider strategy: The trader achieves the advantage by exploiting privileged access to information. However, the trader must be cautious because some techniques may be illegal. For example, information about company earnings

and potential takeovers could be considered illegally obtained information. Insider strategies give the trader an opportunity to anticipate market movements.

2. Technical strategy: Some traders attempt to exploit market imperfections by analyzing past price information. One form of technical strategy involves the use of patterns in price data in order to identify potential turning points in price trends. This is referred to as charting. Traders attempt to identify trends early, buy into those trends, and exit before the trend breaks. There are a number of traders who use the technical strategy to complement other techniques.

3. Fundamental strategy: Fundamental strategies focus on the fundamental relationship between the economic value of the underlying asset and the market price. Traders use this strategy to seek expertise and information in order to obtain an accurate valuation of securities. There is an assumption that market values will converge to theoretical values.

4. Flow strategy: This strategy predicts prices as a function of demand and supply for securities in the market.

Swaps

In the world of finance, a swap can be defined as an agreement between two parties, who are referred to as counterparties. The counterparties exchange cash flows over a period of time in the future. The cash flows are calculated based on a notional principal amount, which is not exchanged between the counterparties. As a result, the swaps can be used to create unfunded exposures to an underlying asset. The value of a swap is the net present value (NPV) of all the future cash flows. Most swaps are traded over the counter (OTC) for the counterparties. There are five basic types of swaps: interest rate swaps, currency swaps, credit swaps, commodity swaps, and equity swaps.

An interest rate swap is one in which the counterparties exchange cash flows of a floating rate for cash flows of a fixed rate or vice versa. Although notional principal does not change hands, it is based on a referenced amount against which interest is calculated. Interest rate swaps can be international or domestic. Counterparties may participate in an interest rate swap if (1) there are changes in financial markets that may cause interest rates to change, (2) borrowers have different credit ratings in different countries, or (3) borrowers have different preferences for debt service payment schedules. Interest rate swaps tend to be organized by international banks acting as swap brokers. These transactions allow borrowers to receive a lower cost of debt service payments and lenders can obtain profit guarantees.

A currency swap is one in which one party provides a certain principal in one currency to its counterparty in exchange for an equivalent amount in a different currency. Principal exchange is not redundant with currency swaps. The exchange of principal on the notional amounts is done at market rates, and tends to use the same rate for the transfer at inception as is used at maturity. Currency swaps allow organizations to have extra flexibility in order to take advantage of their comparative advantage in their respective borrowing markets. These swaps start with a net present value of zero. However, over the life of the instrument, the currency swap can go in-the-money, out-of-the-money, or stay at-the-money.

A credit swap occurs when two parties enter into an agreement and one counterparty pays the other a fixed periodic coupon for the specified life of the agreement. The other party does not make any payments unless a specified credit event occurs. Examples of credit events include a material default, bankruptcy, or debt restructuring for a specified reference asset. If one of these types of credit events occurs, the counterparty is required to make a payment to the first party, and the swap is terminated. As a rule, the size of the payment tends to be linked to the decline in the reference asset's market value following the credit event.

A commodity swap is where exchanged cash flows are dependent on the price of an underlying commodity. This is usually used to hedge against the price of the commodity. There are two types of commodity swaps, which are fixed-floating swaps and commodity for interest swaps. Fixed-floating swaps are similar to the fixed-floating swaps in the interest rate swap market. However, both indices are commodity based indices. Two popular market indices in the commodities market are the Goldman Sachs Commodities Index and the Commodities Research Board Index. These two indices place different emphasis on the various commodities in order to meet the swap agent's requirements.

Commodity for interest swaps are similar to equity swaps in which a total return on the commodity in question is exchanged for a designated money market rate. Swap agents using this type of swap must take into consideration (1) the cost of hedging, (2) the institutional structure of the particular commodity market in question, (3) the liquidity of the underlying commodity market, (4) seasonality and its effects on the underlying commodity market, (5) the variability of the futures bid/offer spread, (6) brokerage fees, and (7) credit risk, as well as capital costs and administrative costs.

The last type is the equity swap, exchanges of cash flows in which at least one of the indices is an equity index. An equity index is a measure of the performance of an individual stock or a basket of stocks. Common equity indices include Standard & Poor's 500 Index, the Dow Jones Industrial Average, and the Toronto Stock Exchange Index. Equity swaps makes the index trading strategy easy, especially for the passive investment manager and emerging markets fund managers.

See Also: Custodians; International Capital Flows; Market Maker; Securities Financing; Stock Exchanges.

Bibliography. Sebastian Auguste, *Cross-Border Trading as a Mechanism for Capital Flight: ADRs and the Argentine Crisis* (National Bureau of Economic Research, 2002); Alex Chambers and Jethro Wookey, "Crunch Wakes US to CDS E-trading," *Euromoney* (February 2008); Dennis Davitt, "Handicapping Bank Payouts," *Barron's* (December 2007); Steven Dellaportas, Barry J. Cooper, and Peter Braica, "Leadership, Culture and Employee Deceit: The Case of the National Australia Bank," *Corporate Governance: An International Review* (v.15/6, 2007); Danielle Goldfarb, *Is Just-in-Case Replacing Just-in-Time? How Cross-Border Trading Behaviour Has Changed Since 9/11* (Conference Board of Canada, 2007); Lina Saigol, "Keep Them on Their Toes," *Financial Times* (December 4, 2007); Steven M. Sears, "Traders Tiptoe Back to Banks," *Barron's* (October 2007); "Traders Glimpse Daylight as Fed Rescue of Bear Sinks In," *Euroweek* (March, 2008).

MARIE GOULD
PEIRCE COLLEGE

Cross-Cultural Research

Culture shapes the values, attitudes, and behavior of human beings. In a managerial context cultural differences lead to diverse management activities and processes, which may present barriers to effective decision making and profit orientation in international management. Information and knowledge on cultural differences and their effects on modern management can help overcome these differences and improve and ease business processes.

Cross-cultural research therefore investigates managerial research questions in two or more cultural settings. Cross-cultural management research focuses on comparing management processes in corporations located in different cultures. Its overall aim is to make these differences understandable and allow managers to develop solutions to overcome and bridge cultural differences and challenges in an international business environment.

Cross-cultural research methods can be divided into qualitative and quantitative research methods. Data can either be gathered by getting hold of secondary data sources, which is information that has been collected before, or by collecting primary data, which refers to the researcher conducting his or her own cross-cultural research project to receive the necessary information to answer a specific research question. The main challenges when conducting research in a cross-cultural context are conceptual and functional equivalences of data collected in different cultures.

Culture in International Management Research

Culture is a critical factor in a global economy. While internationalizing, multinational corporations enter markets that differ in economic, legal, political, social, and cultural levels. But whereas economic, legal, and political differences between countries and their citizens can be observed easily, cultural differences between countries are often not so obvious.

Culture can be defined as a set of common values within a certain group or system, which is communicated from older members of the group to younger ones. According to Nancy Adler, culture becomes evident through common values, attitudes, and actions within a group or system. Cultural differences present challenges to perform management processes effectively. In a corporate context, they lead to different managerial actions, different consumer attitudes and buying behavior as well as particular expectations of international negotiation partners, all of which subsequently may lead to misunderstandings or conflict between employees of multinational corporations.

From an international manager's perspective, culture and differences between cultures therefore play an increasingly important role. To avoid mistakes and promote goal-oriented decision making, gaining information on cultural differences and their effect on international management is vital. Cross-cultural research provides this information and refers to any kind of research in which a research question is investigated in two or more different cultures.

The idea of investigating exotic cultures is not new and was originally a research topic of cultural anthropology, a research field that concentrates on culture and involves the investigation of different societies, their cultures and norms. Management studies, on the other hand, has so far not developed a research stream investigating cultures and their particularities from within, but focuses on comparisons between cultures or groups of cultures. This is done through a number of theoretical frameworks on cultural diversity that have been developed.

The most prominent classifications are Hall and Hall's, Kluckhohn and Strodtbeck's, Hofstede's, and Trompenaar's cultural dimensions. All of these authors distinguish culture across several dimensions. E. T. Hall and M. R. Hall identify cultural differences among the following dimensions: structure of space, structure of time, speed of messages, and context orientation (low-context or high-context). F. Kluckhohn and F. L. Strodtbeck defined six different dimensions and classify cultural differences along time orientation, relation to nature, relations with other people, mode of human activity, space, and belief about basic human nature. The most cited author in this area is Geert Hofstede, who developed the following categories to classify cultures: individualism versus collectivism, power distance, masculinity versus feminity, and uncertainty avoidance.

The final classification presented here was developed by Fons Trompenaars and Charles Hampden-Turner. In this classification, cultures are grouped along these dimensions: universalism versus particularism, individualism versus communitarism, neutral culture versus affective culture, specific culture versus diffuse culture, achievement culture versus ascription culture, sequential time orientation versus synchronic time orientation, and inner-directed culture versus outer-directed culture. All these frameworks present the base of cross-cultural research and aim to provide an overview on the complex topic of culture. They also allow cultural comparisons that support managers in understanding differences in managerial practices.

Aims

Cross-cultural research is important at every stage of a corporation's internationalization process. The first stage of entering a foreign market is dominated by the question of which market is the most suitable for the corporation. Researchers need to compare economic, legal, and political information on different countries to assess the business opportunities of each market. Once the host market is decided upon, the conditions of this particular market need to be investigated in greater detail. In this area, cross-cultural research often focuses on the examination of international consumers, their attitudes, behavior, and preferences. Information on consumers helps multinational corporations to adapt their marketing activities and improve profits in international markets.

Cross-cultural management research further examines processes inside the firm. Cultural differences among employees may lead to complications in reaching company goals or to manage efficiently. The overall goal of cross-cultural management research is to compare management processes in different national cultures. Areas investigated include differences in corporate culture, attitudes, values, and behavior of organizational members, as well as culture-related management processes, such as differences in leadership styles, human resources management styles, decision making, and process development. Based on cross-cultural research results, managers can develop effective solutions to overcome these differences and to create effective management processes for multinational corporations.

Cross-Cultural Research Methods

Cross-cultural research can be conducted via collecting secondary or primary data. Secondary sources refer to data that was collected beforehand and is readily available. Primary sources, on the other hand, are data that are collected by the researchers personally to answer a specific research question. Cross-cultural secondary sources can be found at governmental or government-related organizations, trade associations, universities, or market research institutes. Primary sources are collected by the researcher himself and find answers to specific questions that have not been previously investigated. Primary cross-cultural research can be conducted via qualitative and quantitative research methods. Qualitative cross-cultural research methods include observations, experiments, focus groups, and qualitative interviews. Quantitative cross-cultural research methods refer to standardized surveys conducted in two or more countries.

Challenges

The differences in national cultures between corporations, managers, and employees also create challenges for researchers of international management. Researchers engaged in cross-cultural research face problems and research conditions that differ from their traditional research setting. Not only is the research project conducted on more than one market, it is also conducted in environments that have very unique characteristics.

Using secondary sources in cross-cultural research can save on cost and effort. However, secondary data sources may not always be reliable, and may lack in accuracy, comparability, and timeliness. Secondary data must be carefully selected and examined for its usability in a cross-cultural research project.

When conducting primary research in a cross-cultural setting, researchers need to think about how to avoid inequivalence between data collected in different countries or in different cultural settings. Information and data may not be available or comparable to data from other cultures. Jean-Claude Usunier divides equivalence into conceptual and functional equivalence. The researcher must first assure that concepts investigated have an equivalent meaning in each country's setting. Survey translation must be carefully conducted to confirm that all respondents are not only asked the same questions, but also understand these questions in the same way. Sample equivalence, which refers to finding a comparable sample in every culture investigated, is another aspect that ensures that data collected is comparable.

Functional equivalence, on the other hand, refers to similar standards applied when developing measurement and collecting data. Respondents of cross-cultural surveys may show biases and may answer according to their national culture. Accuracy, reliability, precision of measurement, and survey supervision may differ from one country to another and need to be constantly administered and supervised by cross-cultural researchers in order to gain data that can be compared across cultures.

See Also: Context; Culture Shock; Culture-Specific Values; Hofstede's Five Dimensions of Culture; Individualism/Collectivism; Market Research; Monochronic/Polychronic; Silent Language of Hall (Nonverbal Communication); Space.

Bibliography. Nancy J. Adler and Allison Gundersen, *International Dimensions of Organizational Behavior*, 5th ed. (Thomson/South-Western, 2008); E. T. Hall, *Beyond Culture* (Anchor Press, 1976); E. T. Hall and M. R. Hall, *Understanding Cultural Differences* (Intercultural Press, 1990); G. Hofstede, *Culture's Consequences: International Differences in Work-Related Values* (Sage, 1980); Lenard C. Huff and Scott M. Smith, "Cross-Cultural Business Research: Introduction to the Special Issue," *Journal of Business Research* (v.61/3, 2008); Karin Ikas, and Gerhard Wagner, *Communicating in the Third Space* (Routledge, 2009); F. Kluckhohn and F.L. Strodtbeck, *Variations in Value Orientations* (Peterson, 1961); Peter Bevington Smith, Mark F. Peterson, and David C. Thomas, *The Handbook of Cross-Cultural Management Research* (Sage, 2008); J.-C. Usunier, *Marketing Across Cultures* (Prentice Hall, 1996); Jan Pieter Van Oudenhoven and Kenneth Cushner, "Convergence of Cross-Cultural and Intercultural Research," *International Journal of Intercultural Relations* (v.32/2, 2008); Jingyun Zhang, Sharon E. Zhang, and Gianfranco Walsh, "Review and Future Directions of Cross-Cultural Consumer Services Research," *Journal of Business Research* (v.61/3, 2008).

PARISSA HAGHIRIAN
SOPHIA UNIVERSITY

Cross-Hauling

Generically speaking, cross-hauling is the concurrent trade of the same product or service in reverse directions over the same route. For instance, the import and export of an identical product or service by a specific country at the same time is a type of cross-hauling. However, it should be noted that there are different sorts of cross-hauling. There may be cross-hauling of foreign direct investment (FDI) or capital, normally resulting from technological differences or differences in governments' tax and tariff policies; suburb-to-suburb cross-hauling, when residents of the suburbs cross the city in the opposite direction every morning on their way to work; duty-free cross-hauling, when duty-free goods purchased on the outbound journey are brought back for consumption at home; and even cross-hauling of polluting factors. Here we will discuss cross-hauling from a trade perspective.

Cross-hauling of goods can occur for a variety of reasons. For instance, some goods, such as vegetables and fruit, are both imported and exported. Some of this cross-hauling can be explained easily by proximity to a border. For example, it may be cheaper for retailers in the south of France to obtain their vegetables and fruit from Spain, at the same time that producers in the north are sending some of their output to Belgian consumers.

Product differentiation is another reason. While some consumers may prefer Gala apples, others may have a preference for Fuji apples, and because these two varieties have different geographic origins, cross-hauling will occur. If each product were completely homogeneous there would be no reason for cross-hauling to exist. For example, if automobiles were homogeneous, consumers in the United States would buy only Ford and GM cars and consumers in Germany would buy only Mercedes and BMW. In reality, however, automobiles are quite heterogeneous. Mercedes are shipped into the United States and Fords are shipped in the other direction.

In countries where vertical differentiation greatly exceeds horizontal, such as India, China, and Brazil, it is not surprising that these countries are likely to export low-quality apparel and import high quality, for example, or to be part of globally or regionally integrated supply chains. Products with strong brand image and consumer loyalty are implausible candidates for substitution, explaining much of the existing cross-hauling.

Where there are a large number of competing manufacturers serving a small geographic area, each one using a different carrier operating less than truckloads,

on a single road segment containing several stops, the possibility of cross-hauling increases. In the case of a retailer, poor sales forecast per store may imply the removal of surplus stock back to the distribution center. Finally, there are industries in which the range of products is so large that an individual manufacturer or even a cluster of local producers cannot compete effectively in all segments of the industry.

If we accept that cross-hauling is the act of shipping the same good in opposite directions at the same time, then it seems clear that much of it is stimulated by low trade barriers, public policy to promote competition, consumer acceptance, and the interest of transport companies (railroads, haulers) to boost their traffic. Trade between different regions and countries is generally beneficial because it allows for scale economies and makes markets more competitive. An increase in trade of similar products, driven by profit margins perceived by each firm in external markets, is hence expected and cross-hauling is therefore unavoidable in facilitating the permanent adjustment of supply and demand.

On the other hand, the effect of the present-day fight among large manufacturers for the conquest of the global market is no more than a mere exchange of accounts, leading to the increase of unnecessary marketing and transportation costs, as they work farther and farther away from their home territory where they can market their product most economically. Yet we are so amazed by the impressive economies of mass production that we refuse to face the fact that marketing and transportation cross-hauling is eating up all that mass production saves and may also be socially costly because it makes use of real resources, for two-way trade of similar goods and marketing campaigns, and no longer transfers revenues to society.

With computers and centralized buying, it appears the cross-hauling problem should have been reduced. Yet trains today meet other trains loaded with the same products, and empty trucks meet other matching empties. These motorway encounters might be acceptable for perfumes and designer clothes, but it is hardly justified for more commoditized goods. The most unnecessary and wasteful elements of cross-hauling should therefore be discouraged.

See Also: International Capital Flows; Nontariff Barrier; Procurement; Trade Barriers; Transportation.

Bibliography. Benjamin Eden, "Inefficient Trade Patterns: Excessive Trade, Cross-Hauling and Dumping," *Journal of International Economics* (v.23/1, 2007); H. Huizinga, "Foreign-Investment Incentives and International Cross-hauling of Capital," *Canadian Journal of Economics* (v.24/3, 1991); Ronald W. Jones, J. Peter Neary, and Frances Ruane, "Two-Way Capital Flows: Cross-Hauling in a Model of Foreign Investment," *Journal of International Economics* (v.14/3–4, 1983); Carol McAusland, "Cross-Hauling of Polluting Factors," *Journal of Environmental Economics and Management* (v.44, 2002); M. H. Robison and J. R. Miller, "Cross-hauling and Nonsurvey Input Output Models: Some Lessons from Small-Area Timber Economies," *Environment and Planning* (v.20/11, 1988).

MIGUEL MARTINS
UNIVERSITY OF WOLVERHAMPTON

Cross-Licensing

A cross-licensing agreement is a contractual arrangement that allows a group of companies to make use of one another's patents. All firms involved agree to refrain from suing one another for patent infringement, usually for both currently held and future patents. These agreements are sometimes referred to as "patent pools."

Cross-licensing allows the participating firms to design and manufacture new products without fear of being sued for patent infringement. Certain complexities, such as excluding specific patents from the pooled arrangement, are often part of the contract. The concept of cross-licensing has deep roots in certain industries, such as high technology, that rely heavily on patents. While there is some debate, on balance cross-licensing agreements are usually thought to be good for competition and good for the economy.

The key benefit of a cross-licensing agreement is "freedom to design." Consider the situation of an established firm in a rapidly evolving industry where much of the competition is based upon the use of patented technology. Examples would include pharmaceuticals, consumer electronics, and almost any aspect of high technology. Such a firm may hold thousands of patents, and annually apply for hundreds more. Each of its major competitors also holds thousands of patents. Any one of these patents may apply to dozens or even hundreds of individual products, thousands in the case of a particularly important patent.

Thus, each firm in the industry faces enormous risk. With so many patents outstanding, it is not possible to be completely certain that a newly designed product will not infringe on any patent held by any competitor. Even if this new product avoids infringing on an existing patent, it could still infringe upon an applied-for, but not-yet-issued patent. Any patent—currently held or pending—held by any direct competitor represents a potential disaster for the new product. A patent infringement suit could delay the new product, drain the profits out of it, or kill it completely.

This situation makes any research and development (R&D) investment quite risky—unless competitors develop cross-licensing agreements. The arrangement reduces the risk of lawsuits for any participating firm. Thus, the participating firms have greater freedom to design; there is less need to filter each new design element to ensure that it will not violate someone else's patent.

Concept Development

The concept of cross-licensing is not new. Early in the 20th century, new competitors moving into the rapidly evolving field of radio quickly realized that they were at constant risk of infringing on one or another of their competitor's patents. The key competitors in the field formed a company to hold all major patents and license the use of those patents to all founding companies. This newly formed company, the Radio Corporation of America, or RCA, is still a major force in the field of entertainment today.

In the 1950s an antitrust ruling affecting IBM helped create a cross-licensing culture in the computer industry. Under the ruling, IBM was required to enter into a cross-licensing agreement with any firm wishing to enter such an arrangement. As part of the arrangement, the applicant agreed to allow IBM reciprocal patent access and agreed to pay reasonable royalties, similar to a modern cross-licensing contract. This open approach characterizes behavior in much of the computer industry to this day: IBM recently announced that it will allow free access to some 500 software patents considered key to software interoperability. Similar traditions in the communications industry may be traced to a 1950s antitrust ruling concerning AT&T/Bell Labs that mandated behaviors parallel to those required of IBM.

More recently, some firms have taken the entire concept of cross-licensing a step further and made patent licensing their core business. For example, Acacia Technologies Group is in the business of acquiring and licensing pools of patents. They design no products and manufacture no products. They are one of a new wave of patent clearing houses building an entire business on intellectual property (IP) alone. The largest of these firms is Intellectual Ventures (IV), founded by several Microsoft alumni. Some reports indicate that IV garners hundreds of millions in royalties and is seeking an additional investment of $2 billion to continue expansion of its patent portfolio.

Not all cross-licensing agreements are as straightforward as two firms agreeing to refrain from suing one another. First, the agreement would normally be limited to specific portions of either firm's patent portfolio. For example, a diversified firm operating in both the chemical industry and in aviation may not wish to include all patents in any single agreement. If this hypothetical firm made an agreement involving chemical patents only, it might wish to further limit the agreement based on field of application. Such a limitation might allow a partner firm to make use of the patents for fertilizers but not for paints or other industrial applications.

Most important, the agreement will probably recognize that all patent portfolios are not of equal value. A firm with a more valuable portfolio will likely receive royalty payments from a firm with a less valuable portfolio. A valuable portfolio will include patents that enjoy broad application and are not yet nearing the end of their legal viability.

Is cross-licensing good or bad for the economy? While this is a hotly debated topic, there is little doubt that cross-licensing agreements, properly implemented, can facilitate the health of an industry and benefit consumers. By lowering the risk of investing in R&D and providing freedom to design, cross-licensing speeds innovation, accelerates the release of new products, and lowers operating costs.

See Also: Intellectual Property Theft; Licensing; Patents; Risk Management.

Bibliography. T. R. Beard and D. L. Kaserman, "Patent Thickets, Cross-licensing and Antitrust," *Antitrust Bulletin* (2002); V. W. Bratic, S. Webster, S. Matthews, R. S. Harrell, "How Patent Pools Can Avoid Competition Concerns," *Managing Intellectual Property* (2005); R. Buckman, "Patent Firm Lays Global Plans," *Wall Street Journal* (2007); Mark E. Crain, *Intellectual Property Cross Licensing Agreements: Are They Taxable?* (University of Houston Law Center, 2006); P. C. Grindley and D. J. Teece, "Managing Intellectual Capital: Licensing and Cross-licensing in Semiconductors and Electronics," *California Management Review* (1997); J. I. Klein, *Cross-Licensing and Antitrust Law* (U.S. Department of Justice, 1997); Josh Lerner, Marcin Strojwas, and Jean Tirole, "The Design of Patent Pools: The Determinants of Licensing Rules," *Rand Journal of Economics* (v.38/3, 2007); R. J. Mann, "Do Patents Facilitate Financing in the Software Industry?" *Texas Law Review* (2005); R. McMillan, "Developers Voice Mixed Reactions to IBM Patent Policy," *InfoWorld* (2005); Sadao Nagaoka and Hyeong Ug, "The Incidence of Cross-Licensing: A Theory and New Evidence on the Firm and Contract Level Determinants," *Research Policy* (v.35/9, 2006).

CLIFFORD SCOTT
UNIVERSITY OF ARKANSAS

Cross Rate

A cross rate reflects the exchange rate between a foreign currency and another foreign currency. It shows the relationship between two foreign currencies with neither currency being the domestic currency. If the exchange rate between U.S. currency and country X's currency is known, and the exchange rate between U.S. currency and currency of county Y is also known, it is possible to determine the implied exchange rate between the currencies of countries X and Y. The implied exchange rate is what is referred to as a cross rate.

Foreign exchange rates can be quoted in two ways: direct quote and indirect quote. A direct quote is stated in the form of domestic currency per foreign currency. An indirect quote is expressed as the number of foreign currency units needed to acquire one unit of domestic currency. A direct quote is also referred to as a normal quote, while an indirect quote is called a reciprocal quote. An example of a direct quote between the U.S. dollar (USD) and the British pound (GBP) is USD/GBP = 1.90. This means that $1.90 of U.S. currency is needed to purchase a unit (£1) of British currency. The direct quote can be converted into an indirect quote of the form, GBP/USD = 0.53. Again, this means that £0.53 British currency is needed to purchase a unit ($1.00) of U.S. currency.

The cross rate is usually calculated from two other foreign exchange rates. Let the exchange rate between U.S. dollar (USD) and South African rand (ZAR) be stated as USD/ZAR = 7.5. Again, let the exchange rate between U.S. dollar (USD) and Mexican peso (MXP) be stated as USD/MXP = 10.5. From these two quotes, it is easy to determine the implied cross rate between ZAR and MXP. The cross rate is MXP/ZAR = 0.71 (calculated as 7.5/10.5).

In order to understand the rationale for its use, it is important to examine the concept of vehicle currencies. Vehicle currencies are currencies that are actively traded in the foreign exchange market. Examples of vehicle currencies are U.S. dollar (USD), euro (EUR), Japanese yen (JPY), and the British pound (GBP). International transactions are conducted in a few vehicle currencies. The logic for using a few currencies for international transactions is to promote efficiency. If the number of currencies used in international transactions is denoted as N, then there are N(N-1)/2 possible exchange rates. The larger the value of N, the larger is the number of exchange rates to be determined. Therefore, it makes sense to use a few currencies for international transactions and then infer the cross rates from existing relationships among trading currencies of the world. The *Wall Street Journal* publishes a table of cross rates daily.

The foreign exchange market is an integrated market that is made up of a network of large commercial banks in the major financial centers of the world. The existence of modern communication technology means that information is quickly transmitted in the market. Thus, all the markets are linked together. This is the reason why quoted exchange rates are consistent. For example, the USD/GBP rate quoted in New York is not significantly different from the USD/GBP rate quoted by a London bank.

See Also: Arbitrage; Currency Speculators; Exchange Rate; Foreign Exchange Market.

Bibliography. D. Ball and W. McCulloch, *International Business* (Irwin McGraw-Hill, 1999); G. Bekaert and R. J. Hodrick, *International Financial Management* (Pearson Prentice-Hall, 2009); M. Livingston, *Money and Capital Markets* (Kolb, 1993); M. Melvin, *International Money & Finance* (Pearson Addison-Wesley, 2004); T. J. O'Brien, *International Financial Economics* (Oxford, 2005).

O. Felix Ayadi
Texas Southern University

Cultural Norms and Scripts

Cultural norms are sometimes defined as "the way we do things around here," but that merely describes the custom and practice processes or interactions within a particular environment. It does not explain *why* things are done in that way, how those norms gain authority, or what mechanisms ensure that relative compliance occurs. Cultural norms are important because they are the generally accepted way that a society or culture guides and regulates the behaviors of its members. Without them, a societal group would be wholly subject to the self-interest of each individual member.

Many societies share commonalities in respect of the types of behavior that are subject to governance by social standards, but this is by no means universal. Cultural norms are often divided into four main categories with differing degrees of importance: "conventions" or "folkways" are codes of social conduct or a standard of etiquette that is expected but is not morally significant, for example, not taking food from another person's plate; "mores" are more strongly held and breaches carry greater sanctions, for example, one does not walk down the street naked; "taboos" are behaviors that are actually forbidden by a culture, like murder or incest in many societies, and are often enshrined in legislation; "laws" are formalized norms backed by the power of government, containing virtually all taboos, but only the more significant mores. What falls into each category and the prescribed penalties for breaches varies between countries or even within the same country, an example being state variance in U.S. legislation.

For a society or group to function, the majority of participant members must agree upon what is "normal" and desire to conform to the rules. These are invariably internalized through the socialization processes taught to children and reinforced through the educational system. Where an individual or group fails to conform, social control mechanisms are utilized in order to encourage conformity, enforce adherence to rules, and in extreme cases, exclude or segregate those who have broken laws or serious taboos. Social control ranges from disapproval at one end of the spectrum to imprisonment or even execution at the other.

Interestingly, there often tends to be more social acceptance of certain infringements than others: While theft and exceeding the driving speed limit are both illegal in many countries, the former usually carries significantly more disapproval than the latter, in the same way that imbibing too much alcohol (an addictive substance) or smoking cigarettes is often deemed by many people to be more acceptable than using certain drugs.

Within a culture may exist "countercultures," wherein the norms of a group or subgroup differ or run counter to those of the prevailing social group. These often, but not always, manifest themselves in the espoused values, behaviors, dress, and musical preferences of younger members of society, or the norms of those with orientations "other" than those of the societal majority. Examples in Western society from the 1960s onward include Beatniks, hippies, and punks. Norms exist within these groups, but they may not be aligned with recognized and ratified societal norms. This is different from an absence of norms, sometimes referred to as "anomie." It is suggested that a state of anomie is categorized by societal breakdown and psychological dissonance.

Cultural norms are by no means universally similar within the global context. Variance is evidenced not only in external manifestations such as art and music, but in behaviors, nonverbal communication, and eye contact. This is also said to influence how individuals from different countries interact with others and with their environment. Theories exist that explore national cultural dimensions. Some suggest that people may have a "national" tendency, possibly embedded through socializing processes, toward certain orientations and preferences; for example, adherence to rules, respect for authority, assigning of power, emotionality, collectivism, and individuality. These

dimensions may be seen in folkways, mores, taboos, and laws, in varying degrees.

Organizations can be deemed to have cultures, influenced by factors including age, type, leaders, demographics, sector, and size. Although few would attempt to change or merge all aspects of national cultures, this is frequently attempted at the organizational level. Culture change strategies should focus upon creating norms that support desired behaviors and allow for individual choice; therefore, culture change efforts should be directed at making those behaviors norms.

Cultural Scripts

It is generally accepted that speech communities have different ways of speaking, not just in respect to the specifics of language, but also in the form of the interactions. These differences reflect the assumptions that people have about social interaction in that particular environment or the contextual "nuancing" that people bring with them to the interaction. These assumptions influence the form but not the content of the interaction, for example, the degree of formality, directness, and cooperation. While most languages have "universal" words in common, including words for *I*, *there*, and *and*, other aspects of the language are context-specific or culturally nuanced conventions, which may reflect the cultural norms of a country. "Cultural scripts" can be viewed as rules of interpretation and evaluation that indicate more than just the semantic meaning of the actual words. Cultural scripts are not intended to provide an account of real-life social interactions, but are descriptions of commonly held, societal assumptions regarding how members of a particular group think about social interaction, the "norm," and how this transfers into communication.

Changes in speech patterns can often reflect shifts in cultural values or norms. An example of this would be where a country has a language with an informal and formal address: *tu* and *vous* in French; *du* and *Sie* in German. Should there be a decline in the use of the formal address and an increase in the use of the informal, this may indicate within that particular society, a change in how individuals interact with each other, reflecting a move toward a more classless informality.

See Also: Communication Styles; Culture-Specific Values; Culture Shock; Enculturation.

Bibliography. Geert Hofstede, *Culture's Consequences: Comparing Values, Behaviours, Institutions, and Organisations Across Nations* (Sage, 2003); Richard D. Lewis, *The Cultural Imperative: Global Trends in the 21st Century* (Intercultural Press, 2003); Pallab Paul, Abhijit Roy, and Kausiki Mukhopadhyay, "The Impact of Cultural Values on Marketing Ethical Norms: A Study in India and the United States," *Journal of International Marketing* (v.14/4, 2006); David C. Thomas and Kerr Inkson, *Cultural Intelligence: People Skills for Global Business* (Berrett-Koehler, 2004).

ELAINE D. KIRKHAM
UNIVERSITY OF WOLVERHAMPTON

Culture Shock

The term *culture shock* was first introduced in the 1950s to describe the anxiety a person can frequently experience when moving to a different environment, and encompasses feelings of disorientation and not knowing what to do or quite how to do it and, ultimately, what is acceptable or appropriate within the new culture. The discomfort experienced can be physical as well as emotional, and while the term might be used in different contexts (and where it might then have different meanings) *culture shock* is generally interpreted as the process of coming to terms with differences in culture, as these occur through daily interaction in the new context.

The term may be traced to two sources. First of these is Schumann's Theory of Acculturation, which attempts to explain the various stages that an immigrant will go through from initial arrival in the foreign country to eventual assimilation. Schumann envisages a continuum of adaptation along which the immigrant will travel, even accepting that many people will not stay in a foreign country long enough for total "conversion" to occur. The second source is represented by the work of the pioneering and world-renowned anthropologist Kalervo Oberg. Born to Finnish parents in British Columbia, Oberg had an early academic career in universities in the United States (Missouri and Montana), the United Kingdom (London School of Economics), and Brazil (São Paulo). He then worked for various U.S. government agencies as an applied anthropologist with postings to South America, before late in his career returning to academe (then at the universities of Cornell, Southern California, and Oregon State).

The basis of Oberg's developed theory of culture shock was his now famous address to the Women's Club of Rio de Janeiro on August 3, 1954, which outlined the feelings common to people when face-to-face with a cross-cultural situation. The model he developed was a four-stage one, although more recently this appears to have been expanded to five elements; nor is there total acceptance of the relevant nomenclature.

It is important to recognize that while psychology is the study of individual personality, it is the alternative discipline of sociology that is the study of groups and the behaviors they exhibit. Thus the study of culture is not about the study of individuals per se since the development of a particular culture is not something to which the individual can contribute. Culture is developed within a nation over a period of many years and through processes that are largely beyond the awareness of the individual. Culture imbues a country with national characteristics: The concept of "living the American dream" (anything is possible) familiar to a U.S. citizen or the British obsession with the weather are obvious examples. Other frequently cited aspects of culture are the acceptability (or otherwise) of smoking, semi-nudity, drinking or kissing in public (perhaps particularly by women). More specific examples might be, for example, not showing the soles of one's feet in public, or demonstrating appreciation of a meal by belching, or leaving one's shoes outside one's host's house.

Oberg considered that culture shock is precipitated by the anxiety that results from losing all familiar signs of social intercourse. This leads to feelings of frustration and anxiety; the home environment suddenly assumes enhanced significance; and ridicule may be poked at everything that is now encountered that is found strange or unfamiliar. The stages of culture shock that have been identified are as follows:

1. The first stage is generally known as the "honeymoon" stage (although also variously as "incubation" or "stimulation"). The recent arrival is full of hope and excited by everything new that is encountered and this positive (even euphoric) outlook keeps negative feelings at bay.

2. The second stage is the culture shock (or "hostile") stage, when the need to settle into the new culture (probably through now starting work as either a businessperson or student) means coping with day-to-day situations that are different from "back home." Dislike and/or criticism of the host culture surfaces, to be frequently accompanied by homesickness, lethargy, irritability, and even outright hostility to the host culture.

3. The third or "acceptance" stage is when a period of adjustment is gone through, during which the individual begins to perceive value in their new environment. A favorable comparison of "new" and "old" environments may even occur as the new arrival gains understanding. Pleasure and good humor return as empathy with the new environment develops.

4. In the fourth or "enthusiasm" stage, the host country begins to appear more and more like "home" and certain aspects of the adopted culture may well be perceived to be preferable to the native culture. Integration is accompanied by an enhanced sense of belonging.

5. The fifth (and final) stage occurs following return to the native culture (hence "re-entry" or "reverse culture" shock). Things may not be the same as they were upon leaving, so a readjustment process must be gone through all over again.

It is important to recognize that not everyone will be affected to the same extent by culture shock. The state of an individual's physical and mental health, their personality, language familiarity, level of education, and previous travel experience can make the necessary adjustment process easier or more difficult.

See Also: Acculturation; Cross-Border Migrations; Cultural Norms and Scripts; Culture-Specific Values; Expatriate.

Bibliography. Bonnie S. Guy and W. E. "Pat" Patton, "Managing the Effects of Culture Shock on Sojourner Adjustment on the Expatriate Industrial Sales Force," *Industrial Marketing Management* (v.25/5, 1996); John R. Hanson, "Culture Shock and Direct Investment in Poor Countries," *Journal of Economic History* (v.59/1, 1999); M. R. McComb and G. M. Foster, "Kalvero Oberg, 1901–1973," *American Anthropologist* (1974); Jean McEnery and Gaston DesHar- nais, "Culture Shock," *Training and Developmental Journal* (v.44/4, 1990).

David G. Woodward
University of Southampton

Culture-Specific Values

For American companies to conduct successful business globally, cultural values must not be ignored. The attitude of "if it works in America, it will work anywhere" should not prevail. If cultural values are ignored, a businessperson's effort to forge a relationship will be met with resistance, for even though some cultural values are elective and are not deal-killers, some are cultural exclusives and must be honored. Americans conducting business in other countries must be aware of all cultural values, for any disrespect could be a deal-breaker. Singapore and India present two contrasting examples of the role of culture-specific values in business.

Singapore is the smallest country in southeast Asia. The ethnic makeup of Singapore is diverse, with Chinese as the majority, followed by Malay and Indian. When conducting business, English is the preferred language. Singapore is a group-oriented culture; therefore, a businessperson must form personal relationships. Just like in the United States, in Singapore, businesspeople can take their time and work their way into cliques or get in through being introduced.

In comparison to the United States, conducting business in Singapore is more formal; therefore, protocol is valued. Appointments must be made in advance, with writing a letter the number one preferred choice. Punctuality is essential, for being late for appointments is viewed negatively.

Conducting business in Singapore is also more slowly paced than in the United States. Singaporeans frown upon being rushed; therefore, a businessperson must allot adequate time to conduct business. Business is not discussed immediately; small talk always comes prior to the business discussion. Therefore, businesspeople eagerly wanting to make a connection must be cognizant of being too aggressive. In Singapore, upon entering a business meeting, one must never take a seat immediately. One must wait until being told where to sit. This is in sharp contrast to the United States, for in many cases upon entering a business meeting, the businessperson will sit in any available seat.

Singapore, dubbed one of the safest countries in the world, deals with crime differently from the United States. A businessperson must be cognizant of the differences, for Singapore's laws are as applicable to noncitizens as to citizens. For example, crimes such as first-degree murder carry an automatic death sentence; minor offenses are dealt with harshly. A violator on public transit can be fined up to $500 for eating or drinking. Chewing gum is prohibited unless for medical or dental reasons, as is spitting in public.

In contrast, the U.S. legal atmosphere is more lenient than in Singapore. Even though penalized in Singapore, Americans can eat and drink on public transit, chew gum, and spit virtually anywhere. A businessperson must be aware that commercial disputes that may be handled as civil suits in the United States can escalate to criminal cases in Singapore and result in heavy fines and prison sentences.

India, a country in south Asia, has more than 1 billion people. Even though India has a large population of English-speaking people, at times, confusion can arise over words' meanings. Unlike Singaporeans, Indians value punctuality, yet may not be punctual themselves. Even though it is advisable for appointments to be made at least one month in advance, a businessperson should confirm the appointment upon arrival. Business appointments should ideally be made for late morning or early afternoon, between the hours of 11 and four.

Like Singaporeans, Indians do not like to be rushed when making decisions; therefore, a mild, relaxed demeanor is valued, whereas impatience is frowned upon and viewed as being rude and disrespectful to their culture. Unlike the United States, where the purpose of the meeting is stated almost immediately, in India a meeting usually begins with friendly small talk. The talk normally involves questions about the family unit, for in India, the family is highly valued; therefore, discussing the family unit shows respect.

American businesspeople must be aware that even though in the United States disagreements are usually directly expressed, in India disagreements are rarely expressed directly due to the value placed on well-established honest business relationships. Therefore, to avoid hurt feelings, Indians use indirect communication and nonverbal cues. Because of the value placed on structure and hierarchy in Indian companies, senior colleagues are highly respected and obeyed. Therefore, Americans must be sensitive by showing the needed respect.

Even though it may be a company's dream to expand overseas, it is important that cultural values not be ignored. Familiarity with business customs specific to a culture can determine the success or demise of a venture.

See Also: Achieved Status/Ascribed Status; Communication Styles; Cultural Norms and Scripts; Culture Shock; Multicultural Work Groups and Teams.

Bibliography. J. M. Brett, *Negotiating Globally: How to Negotiate Deals, Resolve Disputes, and Make Decisions Across Cultures* (Jossey-Bass, 2001); C. Cellich and S. Jain, *Global Business Negotiations: A Practical Guide* (South-Western Educational Publishing, 2003); L. Chaney and J. Martin, *Intercultural Business Communication* (Prentice Hall, 2005); N. Dresser, *Multicultural Manners: Essential Rules of Etiquette for the 21st Century* (Wiley, 2005); A. Milligan, *Culture Smart!* (Kuperard, 2006); Carlos Noronha, *The Theory of Culture-Specific Total Quality Management: Quality Management in Chinese Regions* (Palgrave, 2002); J. Salacuse, *The Global Negotiator: Making, Managing and Mending Deals Around the World in the Twenty-First Century* (Palgrave Macmillan, 2003).

MARTHA J. ROSS-RODGERS
INDEPENDENT SCHOLAR

Currency

The term *currency* generally refers to the official means and regulations of payment of a country or region, which have been legally introduced and which are accepted (by law) as a compensation for goods and services. Currency includes banknotes and coins and represents a sub-category of money. Money refers to all means of exchange, also gold, whiskey, tobacco, and other commodities. Currencies, however, are means of payment that are produced and regulated by the government and do not represent goods on their own. Their intrinsic value (i.e., the physical value of a currency) does not coincide with its traded value.

The production and issuance of currencies is, in most cases, incumbent on national central banks or a single central bank for a certain currency zone, such as the European Central Bank, which is responsible for the European Monetary Union. Such institutions regulate the money supply in order to guarantee price stability and, thus, avoid inflation.

Today, about 160 different currencies exist which have, according to their name, an ISO 4217 currency code consisting of three alphabetical letters. They are used in international trade, e.g., EUR for the euro or USD for U.S. dollar. In order to buy goods from any other society it may be necessary to have foreign currency. Therefore, currencies can also be subject to trade and the value of one currency in terms of another currency is expressed by the exchange rate. For international trade, very often leading currencies (i.e., currencies that are preferably used in cross-border transactions) are chosen. They can be easily traded internationally and are often chosen to lock out the exchange rate risk, because they are considered more stable than other currencies. Such leading currencies include, among others, the U.S. dollar, the euro, the yen, the pound sterling and the Swiss franc.

Functions and Characteristics

A currency fulfills three main functions: medium of exchange, unit of account, and store of value. As a medium of exchange, a currency allows its holder to exchange it for any good or service that he or she requires. That is, the seller of a product is not confined by the products of his clients, as would be the case in barter transactions, where goods and services are exchanged without money. Therefore, currencies give their owners more flexibility. It is necessary that people trust in a currency as a medium of exchange, i.e., that they can reliably exchange it for other goods or services. This is of special importance if the traded value of the currency does not reflect the real value of the material that the currency is made of; for example, banknotes may indicate a higher value (printed on the surface) than their real, physical value (i.e., the value of the paper) represents. In order to guarantee that the nominal value of a banknote equals the real value of goods and services, its issuer has to hold reserves of com-

modities (such as gold) that guarantee the nominal value. In case of inflation (i.e., a decrease in the value of a currency), market agents may lose their trust in a certain currency and shift to barter transactions to exclude the risk of a devaluing currency.

Currencies, as a unit of account, also facilitate the comparison of unequal goods or services. It may seem difficult to compare a haircut (a service) with a new notebook (a commodity) without having a value of reference. By indicating how much of a currency is needed to buy a haircut and a notebook, it is possible to easily compare these commodities with each other. In addition, this also allows the comparison between countries by using the exchange rate, e.g., how much does a certain notebook cost in country A and how much in country B. Currencies as a unit of account also facilitate the comparison of productivity and success of companies across industries and countries.

Finally, currencies allow their owner to store value for future consumption. In comparison to goods, such as fish or vegetables, currencies are more durable and therefore save value. Historically speaking, however, periods of inflation and deflation have shown that the real value of a currency can considerably be altered, which relativizes this function. Still, the advantages of currencies outweigh other media of exchange or units of account. Currencies also allow the establishment of more complex credit systems, where those who need value to buy certain assets can borrow money from those who have stored it for future consumption. This again improves the efficiency of an economy as money can more optimally be allocated by its participants, in line with their wants and needs.

In order to fulfill all these functions, a currency has to have certain characteristics. A good currency is easy to recognize and can be easily distinguished from other assets. This is definitely true for gold, due to its unique luster, color, and weight. Regarding banknotes and coins, they are unique, because they have special imprints and embossments. Apart from that, they also include several copy protections. It is also important that a currency is divisible and portable. On the one hand, if gold is used as a currency, it can be simply cut into pieces without destroying the value of the broken parts as they reflect their implicit value. As far as banknotes and coins are concerned, there are several subunits of them, indicating different values printed on their surfaces, which do not represent their real

Some of these traditional paper currencies and coins have been supplanted by the euro.

value (see above). On the other hand, the transportation of a currency should be easy, thus increasing the its flexibility and circulation. Finally, it is crucial that a currency is durable. This is necessary to fulfill the function of storage of value as explained above. Today, the use of electronic transactions and electronic credit cards, instead of a physical exchange of currencies for goods or services, makes these characteristics nearly obsolete. Also, bank accounts are denominated in currencies and not in goods or services.

Currency and the Economy

The introduction of a currency facilitates intranational and international trade considerably. David Ricardo's theory of comparative advantage postulates that countries, companies, and individuals should specialize in the production of certain goods or services in order to realize gains from trade. However, this indicates that agents have to buy several other goods or services in order to survive, as they specialize in producing only one particular product and not everything they may need. In simple economies, barter may be eligible, but costs of trade will increase due to higher transportation costs, thus making products more expensive. In more complex economies, trade that is solely based on barter transactions is almost impossible.

Due to the three functions of currencies (see above) it is not necessary to triangulate transactions, i.e., individual A wants to buy goods from individual B, who is only prepared to exchange products for those of individual C, who him/herself needs products

from individual A. As a consequence, currencies even speed up trade and reduce the number of transports as the purchase and sale of goods or services can be separated from each other. This increases efficiency in trade and transaction costs can be cut severely.

Currency Crises

The pressure on global financial markets in the 1990s caused several currency crises. Examples include the Czech Republic crisis in 1997 and the Russian crisis in 1998, which harmed their economy severely. It is worth mentioning that both crises had been triggered by different economic variables. On the one hand, the Czech currency crisis was characterized by a deterioration of macroeconomic fundamentals and political instability, appearance of a speculative attack, an effort to defend the koruna, and finally a depreciation and change in the exchange rate regime from a fixed to a floating one. On the other hand, the crisis in Russia can be seen as the consequence of its fragile and vulnerable economic and political fundamentals and massive capital flight.

So far, three different prevailing models aim at explaining how currency crises come into existence and which variables best describe or even predict them. Krugman's model, developed in 1979, is generally known as the traditional approach concerning currency crises. It is based on balance of payments problems, reflected by a steady but slow reduction in international reserves, in a country with a pegged currency. According to this model, the expansion of domestic credits to finance fiscal deficits or improve a weakening banking system and the increase of money demand reduce international reserves and consequently results in a speculative attack that would force authorities to abandon their fixed exchange rate regime. In following years, Krugman's model was extended by other studies and showed that a real appreciation of a currency often precedes a speculative attack. In addition, domestic interest rates increase if a currency crash is at hand. To sum up, the first-generation models focus on expansionary macroeconomic measures undertaken by a country with a fixed exchange rate regime and therefore are said to be predictable.

Second-generation models refer to countercyclical government policies and take into account uncertainties and features of speculative attacks. Currency crises are also defined as changes from one monetary policy equilibrium to another, caused by self-fulfilling speculative attacks. For example, agents believe that currency A will lose its value in the near future and therefore exchange it for a more stable one. Therefore, the demand for currency A decreases and, as a consequence, its value does as well. The interaction of economic policies and economic agents could allow jumps between multiple equilibria without having an impact on fundamentals. Thus, an economy with a fixed exchange rate regime could find itself in equilibrium, but a turn in expectations of economic agents could trigger policy measures, which cause a breakdown of the exchange rate regime. In other words, speculative attacks are independent of the consistency between the currency policy and an exchange rate fixing. In short, second-generation models imply that currency crashes are far more difficult to predict, but economic fundamentals are still of importance, although there is no strong relation between these indicators and a possible crisis.

While second-generation models assume that all speculators know about each others' intentions, third-generation models eliminate this unlikely assumption in arguing that fundamentals can only be monitored with noise. Moreover, the amount of noise in a signal may vary between speculators, but at the same time results in a new equilibrium. Furthermore it is concluded that economic fundamentals might not signal an upcoming crisis, like in second-generation models, but speculators would still attack the currency, due to the uncertainty of expectations of other economic agents. Apart from that, third-generation models are based on structural weaknesses, e.g., foreign currency debt exposure in the corporate and financial sector. Finally, these models are characterized by moral hazard, imperfect information, and the exorbitant up- and downturns in international lending and asset pricing.

In view of the above, currency crises can be considered to be diverse in their nature and, as a consequence, in their origination. Very often currency crises accompany or are accompanied by banking crises.

See Also: Asian Financial Crisis; Barter; Central Banks; Contagion; Currency Speculators; Currency Zone.

Bibliography. Irving Fisher, *The Purchasing Power of Money: Its Determination and Relation to Credit Interest and Crises* (Gardners Books, 2007); International Organization of Standardization, ISO 4217, www.iso.org (cited March 2009); G. L. Kaminsky, "Currency Crises: Are They All the Same?" *Journal of International Money and Finance* (v.25, 2006); G. L. Kaminsky, S. Lizondo, and C. M. Reinhart, "Leading Indicators of Currency Crises," *IMF 79* (1997); P. Krugman, "A Model of Balance-of-Payments Crises," *Journal of Money, Credit, and Banking* (v.11/3, 1979); Allan H. Meltzer, *A History of the Federal Reserve* (University of Chicago Press, 2003); Emilie Rutledge, *Monetary Union in the Gulf: Prospects for a Single Currency in the Arabian Peninsula* (Routledge, 2009); F. Schardax, "An Early Warning Model for Currency Crises in Central and Eastern Europe," *Focus on Transition 1* (OeNB, 2002); P. J. G. Vlaar, "Currency Crisis Models for Emerging Markets," *DNB Research Reports*, Research Memorandum WO&E (n.595/9928, 2000).

Daniel Dauber
Vienna University of Economics
& Business Administration

Currency Exposure

Firms doing business in more than one currency (i.e., U.S. dollar, euro, yen, etc.) face currency exposure. This exposure arises from the fact that, in the current global environment of floating exchange rates, the value of a currency relative to other currencies (its exchange rate) is constantly changing—rising or falling based on forces of supply and demand, government activity, even currency speculators. There are three main types of currency exposure—transaction, translation, and economic.

Transaction exposure reflects the exposure of the firm to changes in the value of a foreign-currency-denominated transaction (sale or purchase) between when the price is set and when payment is made. For example, say a U.S. aircraft manufacturer contracts to produce and sell 10 airplanes to a German airline for 100 million euros, to be paid upon delivery in six months. Although the dollar/euro exchange rate when the deal is signed is $1.50/euro, the U.S. manufacturer does not know whether the value of the 100 million euros it will receive in six months will be higher or lower than the current value of $150 million (dollars), and is thus faced with transaction exposure. If the dollar/euro exchange rate drops to $1.25/euro in six months, the 100 million euros will be worth only $125 million, whereas a rise to $1.75/euro would result in a better-than-expected $175 million. If the U.S. firm wishes to eliminate variability in the dollar amount, they may enter into a contract on the forward market, which allows them to lock in a future exchange rate. Alternatively, they may purchase a foreign currency option, insuring them against the downside risk of a decline in the value of the euros they will be receiving, while still allowing them to benefit from potential increase in the euro's value.

Translation exposure arises within the firm's accounting function. The financial statements of the firm's foreign units must be translated into the parent currency, then consolidated into the financial statements of the parent. If there has been a shift in the exchange rate between the subsidiary's and parent's currencies since the last consolidation was performed, unrealized "paper" gains/losses may affect the company's books. If the U.S. aircraft manufacturer had purchased a German factory for 10 million euros when the exchange rate was $1.50/euro, it would appear as an asset on the parent's books, valued at $15 million. If the exchange rate were $1.75/euro the following year, that same factory, with a value of 10 million euros (not accounting for depreciation), would translate into the parent's books valued at $17.5 million, a $2.5 million gain based not on increasing real value, but merely driven by rising exchange rates (alternatively, a drop in the exchange rate to $1.25/euro would create a $2.5 million "paper" loss).

It can be risky for firms to make strategic decisions based on "paper" gains/losses; one technique for minimizing translation exposure is to balance foreign currency assets and liabilities. The aircraft manufacturer could borrow 10 million euros to purchase the German factory, resulting in a 10 million euro asset (the factory) and a 10 million euro liability (the loan), which would effectively cancel each other out—whenever the euro rose/fell against the dollar, asset and liability would rise/fall simultaneously.

Economic exposure reflects the degree to which exchange rate shifts affect a firm's future foreign profitability. This exposure has the greatest potential for long-term impact on firm performance, and thus requires greater strategic planning and decision making on the part of the firm. Once the U.S. aircraft

manufacturer owns a factory in Germany, economic exposure could be triggered by a large rise in the value of the euro, say from $1.50/euro to $2.00/euro. Such a shift may hurt the firm (reduced export performance from Germany, as their products will now look pricier on international markets) and/or may have a positive impact on the firm (profits made in euros will translate into more dollars than before). One way firms can manage economic exposure is to diversify production locations internationally, so that large shifts in one currency will not affect their entire business.

See Also: Currency; Currency Speculators; Devaluation; Exchange Rate; Exchange Rate Risk; Floating Exchange Rate; Forward Market.

Bibliography. Saleh Alharbi, *Three Essays on Currency Exposure* (University of Wisconsin, 2004); Naohiko Baba, Kyoji Fukao, Nihon Ginko, and Kin'yu Kenkyujo, *Currency Risk Exposure of Japanese Firms with Overseas Production Bases: Theory and Evidence* (Tokyo Institute for Monetary and Economic Studies, Bank of Japan, 2000); Soehnke M. Bartram, "What Lies Beneath: Foreign Exchange Rate Exposure, Hedging and Cash Flows," *Journal of Banking and Finance* (v.32/8, 2008); David K. Eiteman, Michael H. Moffett, and Arthur I. Stonehill, *Multinational Business Finance*, 11th ed. (Addison-Wesley, 2007); Sanjoy Ghosh, *Hedging Currency Exposure* (University of Pennsylvania, 2000); Philip R. Lane and Jay C. Shambaugh, *The Long or Short of It: Determinants of Foreign Currency Exposure in External Balance Sheets* (Centre for Economic Policy Research, 2008); E. B. Lubach, *Currency Exposure in Mutual Funds: To Hedge or Not to Hedge* (Erasmus Universiteit, 2006).

David M. Berg
University of Wisconsin–Milwaukee

Currency Speculators

A currency speculator is an individual who trades in the foreign exchange market with the sole purpose of making a profit. For example, if the British pound is falling relative to the U.S. dollar, currency speculators will sell pounds, expecting to buy them back again sometime in the near future at a lower price.

This implies that speculators will have an uncovered "open position," which can be difficult to cover if the pound does not fall relative to the U.S. dollar. Currency speculators are willing to take this exchange rate risk when they believe that exchange rates will move to their benefit.

In general, currency speculators trade either on the spot market and/or on the derivatives market. In the first case, a speculator will sell on the spot price if he believes that the asset is overvalued and then wait to buy back the asset in the future when he thinks that the price has fallen by so much that it will generate him a profit after all transaction costs have been paid. In the second case, currency speculators will sell the overvalued currency at the spot market and at the same time they will buy the future price of the same currency. The future price of currencies is traded in the derivatives markets and can be in the form of a forward, a future, or an option contract. In most cases, the currency speculator will "short sell" the asset, that is, she will sell an asset that she does not own hoping to buy it back in the future at a lower value.

The advantage of selling and buying the asset simultaneously is that the potential profit that can be derived from this strategy is secured. However, the downside is that by buying the asset for future delivery the trader binds himself to the future price of the asset. In such a case, the trader discards the opportunity to get an extra profit if the spot price of the currency in the future is much lower than its price of the future contract. Also, speculators, using the purchasing power parity (PPP) rules between two or more currencies, speculate by trading on the price of one currency compared with the value with all the currencies that can be exchanged for one unit of this currency.

Currency speculators predict the future exchange rate prices by analyzing changes in value or by just bluffing about the future price of assets. When speculators analyze changes in the value of assets they do so by estimating the change in the value of assets that is caused by news about their value. For example, if the American interest rate is set at a point higher than the European Union interest rate, speculators will short sell euros as they will expect that investors will start selling euros as well in order to buy U.S. dollars that offer a greater return. The downward pressure will destabilize the euro/U.S. dollar exchange rate and speculators will earn their profits by buying back euros at a lower price. On numerous occasions speculators have been accused of deliberately selling the currency of one country in order to create downward pressure; thus their prediction of a devaluated currency becomes a self-fulfilling prophecy.

The most famous example of a currency speculator is George Soros. Soros is said to be responsible for the "Black Wednesday" when the United Kingdom was forced to withdraw the British pound from the Exchange Rate Mechanism that was designed to keep a number of currencies floating within very small margins. On September, 16, 1992, Soros sold short more than £10 million, putting enormous downward pressure the Bank of England (BoE) either to raise interest rates, so that investors will start buying pounds, or to devaluate the currency. Eventually, the BoE decided to let the currency float freely, leaving the Exchange Rate Mechanism. It is said that, on that day, Soros made more than £1 million from this speculative trade.

However, currency speculators claim that it is on their actions that markets become fully efficient. Their argument is the following; when prices are not fully efficient, i.e., prices do not reflect the true fundamental values of assets, currency speculators trade on those assets, making the prices more informative and as a result the trading prices converge with the fundamental value of assets. Had the currency speculators not traded, the asset prices would have continued to trade in prices different from their optimal. In other words, speculators argue that they help prices to trade at their true value and the absence of speculative trading will have devastating results in the long term. Nevertheless, as with any profit-motivated trader, speculators ask for greater returns in order to accept the exchange rate risk that is associated with trading currencies.

See Also: Currency; Devaluation; Exchange Rate Risk; Exchange Rate Volatility; Fixed Exchange Rate; Foreign Exchange Market.

Bibliography. Brendan Brown, *Bubbles in Credit and Currency: How Hot Markets Cool Down* (Palgrave Macmillan, 2008); L. Copeland, *Exchange Rates and International Finance* (Addison-Wesley, 1994); D. Eiteman, A. Stonehill, and M. Moffett, *Multinational Business Finance* (Addison-Wesley, 1998); C. Goodhart and R. Payne, *The Foreign Exchange Market: Empirical Studies with High-Frequency*

Data (MacMillan, 2000); L. Harris, *Trading and Exchanges: Market Microstructure for Practitioners* (Oxford University Press, 2003); Kathy Lien, *Day Trading and Swing Trading the Currency Market: Technical and Fundamental Strategies to Profit from Market Moves* (John Wiley & Sons, 2009); K. F. Radalj, "Hedgers, Speculators and Forward Markets: Evidence from Currency Markets," *Environmental Modelling and Software* (v.21/9, 2006); K. Pilbeam, *Finance and Financial Markets* (Palgrave, 2005); J. Rutterford, *An Introduction to the Stock Exchange Investment* (Palgrave, 2007); S. Valdez, *An Introduction to Global Financial Markets* (Palgrave, 2007).

THANOS VEROUSIS
ABERYSTWYTH UNIVERSITY

Currency Zone

A currency zone or optimum currency area is defined as a geographical region in which there is a single currency or several currencies that are pegged to each other so that the currencies can fluctuate only against the rest of the world. Currency zones eliminate exchange rate uncertainties and maximize economic stability within that area. The most prominent example of a currency zone is the Eurozone in which the European Union member states have decided to abandon their domestic currencies and adopt the euro as their single currency.

The optimum currency zone theory, first published by R. Mundell (1961), along with the theory of comparative advantage of David Ricardo, are the most cited theories in international economics that have also seen widespread applications in recent decades.

The benefits associated with the adoption of a single currency are twofold: First, the elimination of transaction costs and, second, the minimization of risk originating from exchange rate uncertainties. In particular, it is argued that the most visible gain of a monetary union is the removal of costs associated with exchanging one currency into another. Yet, even though this benefit is relatively small, less than half of 1 percent of the Eurozone GDP, it should be added to the overall benefits of a single currency. These benefits mainly refer to the increased usefulness of money. That is, a currency zone increases price transparency,

decreases price discrimination within the zone, and in general fosters competition. So, a currency zone promotes trade between the member-states of the zone, increases efficiency in the allocation of resources, and endorses cross-area foreign direct investment.

The second major advantage of a currency zone is that it reduces the exchange rate uncertainty risk. Even when two or more currencies are narrow-banded to each other, like in the case of the Exchange Rate Mechanism, there is still some exchange rate risk associated with the individual currencies. This risk is eliminated when a single currency is introduced to replace the old monetary system. The indirect welfare gains that come from a currency zone are said to help firms increase their efficiency by eliminating the uncertainty about the future prices of good and services. This, in turn, should increase economic growth within that area. At the same time, a single currency removes from single countries their ability to print money; thus, inflationary pressures to single countries are eliminated.

However, skeptics of currency zones argue that the loss of the ability of individual countries to conduct a national monetary policy is more important than the benefits of a single currency. That is, a nation joining a single currency loses its ability to change interest rates, to determine the quantity of money, and to change the price of its currency. The key point is that, within a currency zone, the member countries may face the one-size-fits-all problem, which refers to the application of policies that are inappropriate for individual countries. So, for example, combating inflation within the Eurozone might have disturbing consequences for individual member states that have no inflation problems. Further, it has been argued that member states lose their ability to react to asymmetric shocks, that is, shocks that affect one economy differently from others.

The costs and benefits of a currency zone are strongly linked with the assumptions that determine its effectiveness. These assumptions refer to the degree of labor and capital mobility within the currency zone and to price and wage flexibilities that apply across the different member states. In the case of the Eurozone, strong doubts have been raised about the mobility of labor and about the wage and price rigidities that seem to persist for some countries. However, as convergence progresses, these problems are likely to decrease.

In general, the effectiveness of a currency zone relies on the pre-conditions that must be met before the application of a single currency and on the time horizon and the law enforcement tools that are available when the single currency is introduced. The Eurozone has still a long way before it is an optimal currency area in terms of reacting to asymmetric shocks and eliminating the structural differences between the member states.

See Also: Central Banks; Common Market; Comparative Advantage; Currency; Economic Union; Euro; European Monetary Union; European Union; Exchange Rate Risk; Exchange Rate Volatility; Fixed Exchange Rate.

Bibliography. D. Eiteman, A. Stonehill, and M. Moffett, *Multinational Business Finance* (Addison-Wesley, 1998); Charles A. Goodhart, "Currency Unions: Some Lessons from the Euro-Zone," *Atlantic Economic Journal* (v.35/1, 2007); P. De Grauwe, *Economics of Monetary Union* (Oxford, 2007); A. Griffiths and S. Wall, *Applied Economics* (Prentice Hall, 2004); Isamu Kato and Merih Uctum, "Choice of Exchange Rate Regime and Currency Zones," *International Review of Economics and Finance* (v.17/3, 2008); P. Krugman, R. Wells, and K. Graddy, *Economics* (Worth, 2007); R. Mundell, "A Theory of Optimal Currency Areas," *American Economic Review* (1961); D. Salvatore, *International Economics* (John Wiley & Sons, 2000); J. Sloman, *Economics* (Prentice Hall, 2006); Leila Simona Talani, *The Future of the EMU* (Palgrave Macmillan, 2009); G. S. Tavlas, "The New Theory of Optimum Currency Areas," *The World Economy* (1993).

THANOS VEROUSIS
ABERYSTWYTH UNIVERSITY

Current Account

The current account measures transactions in goods, services, and income, as well as current transfers between residents and nonresidents of a country. As such, the current account records the value of real resource transactions (i.e., exchanges involving goods, services, and income) and current transfers (i.e., unilateral transfers such as food donations) in a specific time period between a country and the rest of the world. The balance on the current account and the size of the current account relative to gross domestic product are important indicators of a country's integration and openness to the rest of the world.

The value of transactions recorded in the current account of a country is estimated through periodic surveys of economic exchanges between its residents and nonresidents. In the current account, each transaction is recorded either as a credit or debit entry. A transaction that is a source of foreign exchange leads to a credit entry; a transaction that is a use of foreign exchange generates a debit entry. Thus, exports of merchandise goods are recorded as credit whereas imports are recorded as debit.

The current account is said to be in deficit when the value of real resources and current transfers acquired from the rest of the world exceeds the value of real resources and current transfers provided to the rest of the world. A surplus in the current account indicates that the opposite is true: real resources and current transfers to the rest of the world have a greater economic value than those from the rest of the world. Furthermore, the balance on the current account shows the relationship of national expenditure to national income. A current account deficit indicates that a country spends more than it produces (its income); the difference between what it spends and produces is imported from the rest of the world.

The current account is a primary component of a country's balance of payments. The other major component is the capital and financial account, which records capital flows and transfers. The balance of payments is organized on the basis of the double-entry accounting principle; it records economic transactions between residents and nonresidents of a country in the form of two offsetting entries, a credit and a debit. A credit entry in the current account is a source of foreign exchange, which implies an increase in the financial assets acquired from the rest of the world. It is thus recorded as a debit entry in the capital and financial account. For this reason, a surplus or deficit in the current account is offset by a deficit or surplus in the capital and financial account. In other words, a country running a deficit in the current account is a net debtor from the rest of the world whereas a country running a surplus is a net creditor to the rest of the world. It should be observed that the relationship between the current account and the capital and financial account holds true through accounting identity.

The balance on the current account can be seen as being constituted by the balance on goods trade, the balance on services trade, the balance on income, and the balance on current transfers. While the current account is conceptually different from the balance on goods and services trade, a deficit or surplus in the current account is often driven by a trade deficit and surplus. This is because exports and imports of goods and services are often the biggest—in terms of value—components of the current account.

See Also: Capital Account Balance; Exchange Rate; Export; Import; National Accounts; Terms of Trade; Trade Balance.

Bibliography. Jörg Decressin and Piti Disyatat, "Productivity Shocks and the Current Account: An Alternative Perspective of Capital Market Integration," *Journal of International Money and Finance* (v.27/6, 2008); Giancarlo Gandolfo, *International Finance and Open-Economy Macroeconomics* (Springer-Verlag, 2001); International Monetary Fund, *Balance of Payments Manual*, 5th ed. (1993); Rita M. Maldonado, "Recording and Classifying Transactions in the Balance of Payments," *International Journal of Accounting* (v.15, 1979); Robert M. Stern, *The Balance of Payments: Theory and Economic Policy* (Aldine, 1973); U.S. Department of Commerce, *The Balance of Payments of the United States: Concepts, Data Sources, and Estimating Procedures* (U.S. Government Printing Office, 1990).

KURTULUS GEMICI
UNIVERSITY OF CALIFORNIA, LOS ANGELES

Custodians

The global custody business is the safekeeping of clients' assets. It includes processing cross-border securities trades, keeping financial assets safe, and servicing the associated portfolios. Institutional investors, money managers, and broker/dealers are among those who rely on custodians and other market participants for the efficient handling of their worldwide securities portfolios. The kinds of assets involved include 1) equities, 2) government bonds, 3) corporate bonds, 4) debt instruments, 5) mutual fund investments, 6) warrants, and 7) derivatives.

Custodians effect settlement of trades (that is, completion of a transaction, wherein the seller transfers securities or financial instruments to the buyer and the buyer transfers money to the seller) and provide safekeeping of the assets on behalf of clients. The services also include (1) collection of income arising from the portfolios (dividends and interest payable), (2) application of entitlements to reduced rates of withholding tax at source and reclaiming withheld taxes after-the-fact, and (3) notification and dealing with corporate actions (such as bonus issues, rights issues, and takeovers).

In terms of service offering, custodians have moved far beyond the core services on which the business was founded—safekeeping and settlement, income collection, proxy voting—as companies have sought to add value for an increasingly sophisticated globalizing client base. Securities lending, benchmarking services such as performance measurement and risk analysis, compliance monitoring, fund accounting, and retail transfer agency are today variously or all part of the deal, as custodians seek to recast themselves as information enhancers and global market facilitators.

Many custodians outsource safekeeping of assets in foreign markets to sub-custodians. Sub-custodians use their knowledge and expertise for that particular market and charge a fee for their services. This helps custodians extend their network over a wider region and provides better service irrespective of region of operation.

While much of the work is administrative and repetitive, the role of the custodian has widened to a range of other services. Custodians typically specialize in a particular area. Custodians also have client-focused and technical personnel. Relationship managers, for example, work with clients to reassure them that their assets are safely maintained.

The global custody product was conceived out of changes to U.S. pension laws. In 1974 the Employee Retirement Income Security Act (ERISA) became law, requiring U.S. pension plan sponsors to segregate investment management and custody of the underlying assets. Prior to this, banks had provided settlement and safekeeping services on an international basis. However, these activities were typically provided free of charge—and the functions therefore starved of resources—as part of investment management or other activities. The term *global custody* was coined in 1974. Global custody services include the following:

- Safekeeping activities: Ensure that assets are protected.
- Clearing: Operate in a highly automated environment to ensure accurate records are kept of mutual positions in the exchange of cash and securities between counterparties or among a group of participants and to effect orderly settlement of their obligations on a net basis.
- Settlement activities: Ensure timely, accurate, and secure transmission of trade instructions and timely completion of settlement Straight-through processing (STP); an automated passage of a securities trade from execution to settlement is used for faster turnaround time.
- Derivatives: Ensure timely and accurate accounting for derivatives and associated margin payments.
- Network of markets: Ensure strength and reliability in supporting all required markets.
- Other services such as reporting and record-keeping, cash management, securities servicing, and income collection.

Today technology is also enabling an unprecedented democratization of business. It is now feasible for mid-size and even smaller companies to go global. In the future, global custody is going to be more concentrated, more comprehensive, and more competitive. Relationship management will be crucial: Custody will become commoditized. There will be more products and more consolidation. Only those who extend their product through joint ventures, acquisitions, alliances, and consortiums will survive. Stratification and specialization will continue, and processes will be more transparent. There will be more players, but technology will allow custodians to become more specialized. Their clients will choose the best products from a large group of specialists. Technology is a major driving force. Clients will want the ease of access that already exists on the retail side. Key players are the Bank of New York, Citibank, HSBC, EFG Eurobank, and Mellon group, to name a few.

See Also: Citigroup; Cross-Border Trading; HSBC Holdings; Pension Systems; .

Bibliography. Pierre Agnes, "Embeddedness in Custodial Banking," *Tijdschrift Voor Economische en Sociale Geografie* (v.93/3, 2002); Gregg Miller "Maintenance and Custodial Services: Getting the Most for the Money," *School Business Affairs* (v.59/7, 1993).

Seemantnee Nadgauda
Rutgers University

Customer Relationship Management

Customer relationship management (CRM) is a customer-centric business philosophy, policy, and strategy that focuses on processes and systems that organizations undertake to enhance their relationships with customers. Customer relationship management is based on the premise that a stable customer base is a core business asset, and further, that knowledge of customer behavior and attitudes coupled with effective service delivery at every point of interaction with customers enhances business performance. CRM takes a long-term perspective, focused on customer retention, and the building of multiple levels of relationships between buyer and seller, in pursuit of enhanced levels of customer commitment. Goals of CRM typically include providing better customer service; making call centers more efficient; cross-selling products more effectively; helping staff close deals faster; simplification of marketing and sales processes; discovery of new customers; and increasing customer revenues.

Successful CRM is dependent on the coordination of different players within the organization responsible for delivering customer value (in accordance with Porter's value chain). These include (1) customer facing operations: the people and technologies that interact directly with and deliver service to the customer; (2) internal functional operations: the people and technologies in the back office that support the activities of the customer facing operations; (3) supplier and partner organizations: the people and technologies that support organizational processes; (4) impression management operations: the people and technologies that have responsibility for managing the impression of the brand, brand reputation, and brand experience.

Types of Relationships

Businesses can seek to create different types of customer relationships. These might include (1) basic: where the organization sells the product; (2) reactive: where the organization sells the product and encourages the customer to call with questions or problems; (3) accountable: where the organization contacts the customer a short time after the sale, to check on product performance; (4) proactive: where the organization contacts the customer with suggestions for use improvements, and with details of new products; and (5) partnership: where the organization works continuously with the customer to drive innovation and improved customer value.

The appropriateness of CRM, and more specifically, the choice of relationship type depends upon the product (e.g., level of complexity and uncertainty in purchase, margins); the customers (e.g., tendency to shop around, consumers or businesses); and, the marketing organization (e.g., structure, business process, and core values). In addition, relationships may vary on another dimension—the stage of the life cycle that they have reached with a specific business. The customer development process is concerned with moving customers through this life cycle: suspects (consumers and businesses with a profile that suggests they might become customers); prospects (consumers and businesses who have indicated potential interest in the organization's products); first time customers; repeat customers; clients (who are in a dialogue with the business); members (who have signed up to a contractual membership engagement); advocates (who actively promote the organization); and, partners (who work with the organization to enhance its products and services to the mutual benefit of both parties).

CRM is designed to reduce customer turnover, or churn. Customer switching is determined by relationship strength (the nature and depth of the bond with the organization), perceived alternatives (e.g., competitors offerings), and critical episodes (such as an unsatisfactory experience). Relationships may terminate if the customer no longer has need for the organization's products or services; more suitable providers enter the marketplace; the relationship strength has weakened; the organization handles a critical episode poorly; and/or there are changes in the organization's offering (such as changes in brand reputation or price) that cause the customer to reconsider their behavior.

Types of CRM

There are two main types of CRM. The first is operational CRM, which supports customer facing operations, including sales, marketing, and customer service. Service agents record details of each interaction into a customer contact history, so that staff can retrieve information on customers from the database to support subsequent interactions. Such data is useful in call centers, but also for managing campaigns, and marketing and sales automation. The second type is analytical CRM, which includes applications that analyze customer data generated by CRM applications to provide information to improve business performance. Analytical CRM applications are based on data warehouses that consolidate data from operational CRM systems and mine the data, to, for example, identify buying patterns, create segments for marketing, and identify profitable and less profitable customers.

Businesses need to be able to identify more profitable customers and focus relationship building on those customers. In seeking to optimize their customer portfolio, businesses seek measures of customer worth. A key measure is customer lifetime value, based on consideration of customer interactions in terms of recency x frequency x value. Other measures may be based on estimates of "relationship costs" versus "relationship revenue" for specific customers, or on the balance between the value of a customer and the risk associated with their likelihood of switching. Such analysis complements the effect of the segmenting and targeting undertaken by the organization on the customer portfolio.

See Also: Branding; Brand Loyalty; Consumer Behavior; Consumer Needs and Wants; Consumer Surveys; Customer Responsiveness; Customization; Focus Groups; Marketing.

Bibliography. F. Buttle, *Relationship Marketing* (Chapman, 1996); M. Christopher, A. Payne, and A. Ballantyne, *Relationship Marketing: Creating Customer Value* (Butterworth-Heinemann, 2002); J. Egan, *Relationship Marketing*, 2nd ed. (FT Prentice-Hall, 2004); B. Foss and M. Stone, *Successful Customer Relationship Marketing* (Kogan Page, 2001); Mae Y. Keary, "Electronic Customer Relationship Management," *Online Information Review* (v.31/5, 2007); Stephen F. King, "Understanding Success and Failure in Customer Relationship Management," *Industrial Marketing Management* (v.37/4, 2008); A. Ant Ozok, Kristen Denburger, and Gavriel Salvendy, "Impact of Consistency in Customer Relationship Management on E-Commerce Shopper Preferences," *Journal of Organizational Computing and Electronic Commerce* (v.17/4, 2007); D. Peppers and M. Rogers, *Managing Customer Relationships: A Strategic Framework* (Wiley, 2004); Keith A. Richards, "Customer Relationship Management: Finding Value Drivers," *Industrial Marketing Management* (v.37/2, 2008); Keith A. Richards and Ell Jones, "Customer Relationship Management: Finding Value Drivers," *International Marketing Management* (v.37/2, 2008); D. Rigby, F. F. Reichheld, and P. Schefter, "Avoid the Four Perils of CRM," *Harvard Business Review* (v.80/2, 2002); Rima Tamosiuniene, "Consumer Relationship Management as Business Strategy Appliance: Theoretical and Practical," *Journal of Business Economics and Management* (v.8/1, 2007); Julian Villanueva, Pradeep Bhardwaj, Sridhar Balasubramanian, and Yuxin Chen, "Customer Relationship Management in Competitive Environments: The Positive Implications of a Short-Term Focus," *QME-Quantitative Marketing and Economics* (v.5/2, 2007).

Jennifer Rowley
Manchester Metropolitan University

Customer Responsiveness

Organizations compete in their markets basically in two ways: By offering products and services at lower prices than competitors do and by offering better products and services than competitors do. In the first case, an organization relies on cost leadership business strategy and in the second case on differentiation business strategy. An organization that can outdo its competitors in terms of lower price or differentiation stands to gain competitive advantage.

Charles Hill and Gareth Jones, in their text on strategic management, describe customer responsiveness as giving customers what they want, when they want it, and at a price they are willing to pay so long as the organization's long-term profitability is not compromised in the process. Customer responsiveness can thus be understood as the ability of an organization to take action to identify their customers and react to their needs and wants in a way that will satisfy them. Consequently, customers learn to attribute more utility to the products and services. For example, an automobile company trying to develop customer responsiveness can build cars to order for individual customers, letting them choose from a wide range of colors and options. In doing so, it strives to be better than its competitors and aims to gain competitive advantage.

The purpose of customer responsiveness is to develop customer loyalty—preference of customers for an organization's products and services so that they continue using them. When an organization is successful at creating customer loyalty it can charge a premium price that the customers are willing to pay for that something extra they get and that they do not get elsewhere.

Organizations that provide superior customer responsiveness pay attention to several aspects such as customer response time, superior design, superior service, and superior after-sales support. Customer response time is the time it takes for the product to be delivered to the customer. An organization that takes less time to respond to its customers reaches them earlier than its competitors. In this manner, that organization gains on time beating its competitors and gaining competitive advantage. Superior design and service backed by superior after-sales support is another way organizations try to serve their customers better than their competitors do. For example, mobile phones have evolved from being simple communication device to becoming sophisticated, multiple-feature gadgets, responding to customers' needs as time went by. Those mobile phone companies that have succeeded in offering better mobile phones with more features have consistently outrivaled their competitors. As they did so, they were able to charge a premium price that their customers are happy to pay.

An organization striving to develop customer responsiveness has to start by identifying what its customer needs are. This calls for keeping customers at the forefront when designing products and services. The top management of an organization plays a critical role in creating commitment to customers within the organization. They may design the mission statement of an organization that puts customers first. This gives a clear signal to the employees inside and the customers outside of the priorities of an organization.

When an organization tries to provide customer responsiveness outside it has to take several steps inside. For instance, a company trying to develop customer responsiveness may design newer products with new features that it thinks will serve customers' needs better. It will have to manage its internal processes in such a way that they are attuned to serving customers' needs better. This will require added emphasis to quality and innovation.

When an organization builds products and services around customer needs and wants, the process is called customization. In the example of the automobile company that builds cars keeping in view their individual customer needs, it is trying to customize its cars to satisfy the unique requirements of its customers. Customization usually results in increasing the costs of production, forcing the company to raise the prices. So long as customers are willing to pay those higher prices, customization works. When the costs become prohibitive, companies have to find other ways. This may involve better and faster production methods that save on costs.

Organizations that operate internationally may choose to consider each of their country markets as separate market segments, adapting their products and services to suit the local preferences of customers in those market segments. This approach, often referred to as the polycentric approach, involves customizing the marketing mix in each market segment in order to meet the unique needs and wants of customers in those market segments.

See Also: Brand Loyalty; Competition; Consumer Needs and Wants; Customer Relationship Management; Customization; Local Adaptation; Polycentric; Service Level.

Bibliography. Janet Godsell, Alan Harrison, Caroline Emberson, and John Storey, *Customer Responsive Supply Chain Strategy: An Unnatural Act?* (Taylor & Francis, 2006); Ricky W. Griffin and Michael W. Pustay, *International Business: A Managerial Perspective* (Pearson Prentice Hall, 2007); Charles W. L. Hill and Gareth R. Jones, *Strategic Management: An Integrated Approach* (Houghton Mifflin, 2008); M. Mital, "An Empirical Analysis of Factors Influencing Customer Responsiveness to Mobile Advertising," *Journal of Database Marketing and Customer Strategy Management* (v.15/2, 2008); Michael E. Porter, *Competitive Strategy: Techniques for Analyzing Industries and Competitors* (Free Press, 1980).

Azhar Kazmi
King Fahd University of Petroleum & Minerals

Customization

Customization refers to the efforts of companies to offer goods and services specifically designed or customized according to the needs of a particular customer, a group of customers, or an entire market (country). The core of customization or customization strategy is the focus on specific customer needs. The opposite of customization is standardization, which refers to the efforts of companies to offer a common product or common marketing programs throughout a particular market, region, or the whole world. Therefore, with respect to global business, companies pursuing the customization strategy or view treat each country as having unique features and customize their offerings accordingly instead of offering standardized products. That means that companies will modify their offerings according to differences in market characteristics, culture, industry conditions, legal environment, and marketing infrastructure (distribution channels, advertising agencies, and media) to better serve foreign consumers. Some terms used in the same or similar meaning with customization are *adaptation, personalization, personalized marketing*, and *one-to-one marketing*.

There are two broad strategies regarding international operations of companies: the global and the multidomestic strategy. In companies implementing the global strategy, products are the same across all countries in which the company operates and there is a centralized decision-making and control system. This strategy is appropriate when there are small differences across foreign markets with respect to the product the company offers; this strategy provides cost advantage and flexibility. However, companies pursuing the multidomestic strategy customize their offerings for each market and give these markets autonomy in decision making. This strategy is appropriate when there are significant differences across foreign markets and companies may better serve local customers if local needs and preferences affect buying behavior. Compared to the global strategy, the multidomestic strategy is harder to design and implement due to the existence of different factors to be considered in each foreign market.

From the marketing point of view, companies are expected to serve consumers better through customization than standardization since the ideal market segment size is one for which 100 percent customer satisfaction is needed. Therefore, customization at the individual level is the highest level of customization and assumes that each individual is different from others and thus has unique needs. Therefore, companies need to know the specific needs of each customer to be able to individually customize their offerings. For example, many computer producers now do not offer computers with only standardized configurations; instead, they give consumers the opportunity to configure computers according to their needs. Similarly, companies in many industries such as automobile, clothing, real estate, and tourism offer customization opportunities to best meet the needs of their customers.

However, it may not be possible for some companies to customize products at the individual level since such a high level of customization increases costs and requires additional resources. As a result, some companies implement customization at the consumer group or segment level as well. For example, the needs of children, teenagers, and adults may be different, and thus companies customize their offerings according to the group's needs; in addition to age, customers can also be segmented in many other ways, for example, climate, language group, media habits, education, and income.

In addition to customization at the individual and group level, customization can be done at the country level as well; laws and regulations, traditions, and religion may necessitate such a country level customization. For example, cars with the steering wheel on the right in the United Kingdom and meatless hamburgers in India are examples of customization of products at the country level, resulting from differences in law, regulations, and religion across markets.

Customization is sometimes referred to as mass-customization, which means production and marketing of good and services according to customers' needs at normal or low prices that are close to prices of products produced in large quantities, which is called mass-production. When companies engage in mass-production, they are able to decrease their unit cost, capitalizing on the scale economies; however, with respect to customized production, this is not always the case since companies need to have additional resources to produce customized or somewhat different products. So, how are products not so high priced in mass-customized production? In the past, companies could offer low-priced but similar products through mass-production (having taken advantage of low unit cost), but they used to offer customized or differentiated products at generally higher prices. However, technological developments nowadays have allowed companies to interact with customers easily and effectively and also enabled quick and flexible production that together allow decreases in costs of customized products as well. Therefore, mass-customized products are not priced as high as they once were.

Types

There are four types of customization: collaborative, adaptive, transparent, and cosmetic. In collaborative customization, companies listen to their customers and find out their exact needs. According to this information, companies then produce the product. Customized computers, clothes, and cars are all this type of customization. In adaptive customization, companies produce a standard product but the consumer or the end user can change the product according to his/her needs. For example, think of two chairs. One is not adjustable, whereas the other is adjustable. The latter gives opportunity to the end user to adjust the chair and is an example of a product for adaptive customization. In transparent customization, companies offer individual customers unique products without telling them directly. This kind of customization occurs when companies can foresee customers' specific needs. Companies implementing transparent customization observe consumers without interaction and based on this observation and further analyses, companies forecast the needs of customers and produce accordingly. In cosmetic customization, consumers use a product in a similar way, but they do change the way the product is marketed. For example, through different packaging, advertisement, marketing materials, promotion, placement, terms and conditions, and brand names, a particular product is highly customized psychologically or emotionally but not functionally.

There are several patterns and various degrees of customization that firms can adopt to do business in international markets. The most common of these are obligatory and discretionary product customization. An obligatory or minimal product customization indicates that a company is urged to introduce minor changes or modifications in the product design for either of two reasons. First, customization may be obligatory to enter and operate in a particular foreign market. Second, customization may be forced by external environmental factors, including the special needs of the foreign market. In brief, obligatory customization is related to safety regulations, trademark registration, quality, and media standards. An obligatory customization requires mostly physical changes in a product. Discretionary, or voluntary, product customization reflects a sort of self-imposed discipline and a deliberate move on the part of an international company to build stable foreign markets through a better alignment of product with market needs and/or cultural preferences.

Many factors necessitate customization, and customization may require significant changes in the design, manufacturing system, distribution, and marketing of the product in foreign markets. These changes will no doubt bring additional costs, and if the company has operations in many foreign markets, then the costs will further increase due to the increased number of adaptations. Therefore, if possible, companies usually prefer standardization because it is easier and less costly than adaptation. Others implement customization to meet local customer needs and mandated regulations. In most cases, companies implement standardization and customization simultaneously at varying degrees since it is rarely feasible or practical to follow a one offering–one world strategy across all different markets. Convergence of regional preferences, regional economic integration, harmonization of product standards, and growth of regional media and distribution channels all make regional customization more feasible than pursuing global standardization.

In conclusion, customization offers opportunities to companies to better serve their customers since companies can create greater variety in their products to be sold at competitive prices because products are produced according to customers' specific needs. When companies are able to find opportunities for mass-customization by identifying unique needs of consumer groups, they can gain benefits from offering both unique and relatively low-priced products. Companies may also have to customize their offerings for a foreign country since laws, traditions, life styles, and religion necessitate customization.

See Also: Consumer Behavior; Consumer Needs and Wants; Customer Responsiveness; Local Adaptation; Localization; Marketing; Service Level; Standardization.

Bibliography. R. P. Bagozzi, J. A. Rosa, K. S. Celly, and F. Coronel, *Marketing Management* (Prentice Hall, 1998); Thorsten Blecker, *Innovative Processes and Products for Mass Customization* (Gito, 2007); S. T. Cavusgil, G. Knight, and J. R. Riesenberger, *International Business, Strategy, Management, and the New Realities* (Prentice Hall, 2008); H. M. Hayes, P. V. Jenster, and N. E. Aaby, *Business Marketing: A Global Perspective* (Irwin, 1996); Lars Hvam, Niels Henrik Mortensen, and Jesper Riis, *Product Customization* (Springer, 2008); S. C. Jain, *Marketing Planning & Strategy* (Thomson, 1997); T. Levitt, "The Globalization of Markets," *Harvard Business Review* (May–June, 1983); Haim Mendelson and Ali K. Parlakturk, "Competitive Customization," *Manufacturing & Service Operations Management* (v.10/3, 2008); B. J. Pine II and J. H. Gilmore, "The Four Faces of Mass Customization," *Harvard Business Review* (v.75/1, 1997); B. J. Pine II and S. Davis, *Customization: The New Frontier in Business Competition* (Harvard Business School, 1999); M. M. Tseng and J. Jiao, "Mass Customization," in *Handbook of Industrial Engineering, Technology and Operation Management*, Gavriel Salvendy, ed. (Wiley, 2001).

Serkan Yalcin
Saint Louis University

Customs Broker

A customs broker is a company or individual licensed by the host country to act on behalf of importers and exporters. The broker handles the formal paperwork to assure legal compliance and speed in the importing process. While brokers are involved in expediting imports, they are often hired by the exporter to assure that all work is done in compliance with local law and to speedily meet the conditions needed to receive payment for their products. The broker prepares import documents and calculates client payments for duties, tariffs, excise taxes, and any other special fees. The broker performs this work at the local customhouse—the government specified location where customs duties and import transactions are managed. In the United States, customs brokers are a licensed profession.

When goods reach a foreign destination, the customhouse performs a series of steps before allowing them to enter the country. These steps typically include checking to see if entry documents are properly completed, verifying any necessary markings related to the country of origin, making sure the goods are not on a prohibited item list, checking the goods against the tariff schedule (a price list of tariffs organized according the Harmonized System), checking the inventory of goods, and determining the value of goods in terms of customs duties and tariffs. When all of these steps are completed, the government customs agent clears the goods for entry into the country and posts the results to a public space (typically an electronic space). Because of the sheer volume of goods that pass through a port of entry, shipments without an expediter move more slowly. The slower the goods move through the entry process, the more cost is accrued for warehousing and storage.

The customs broker expedites the customs clearing process, assisting the customhouse to clear goods for entry. The broker, for example, reviews the tariff schedule and prepares a customs invoice for the client. The customhouse need only verify that the broker selected properly. In some ports, the broker certifies that the client has met the obligations for country of origin markings. If markings are incorrect, the customs broker will act as an intermediary, securing the correct documentation and markings and affixing them to the goods while in customs. To accelerate the customs clearing process, clients often provide their customs broker with power of attorney, a legal document that empowers the broker to act on behalf of the client in all customs clearing issues. The customs broker is a valuable source of knowledge for the exporter,

staying current on all issues related to import documentation and duty and tariff changes.

Certain customs clearing tasks require notification and/or approval by government agencies other than the customhouse. For example, aquaculture importers into the United States need approval of the Fish and Wildlife Service of the U.S. Department of Agriculture to ensure that imported fish are not on the invasive species list. Because of these unique requirements, many customs brokers specialize in particular industries. Because of the relationship of customs clearing to overall delivery efficiency, many freight forwarders employ their own customs brokers.

Importing firms often bring in goods that they transform for export. In most cases, the local government allows a refunding of the duties when the goods leave the country after transformation. We call the refunding of duties a "duty drawback." Customs brokers who maintain contractual relations with clients often manage their duty drawback programs to ensure the client receives full refunds for duties paid.

In the earliest days of customs clearing, brokers and customs officials would post their findings on bulletin boards in the local customhouse. Brokers would read the bulletin board and telex their findings to the client. The current state of the art is to have sophisticated electronic data interchange systems (EDI). With each change in status, the broker instantaneously transfers information to the client's account. Brokers also provide document imaging services, scanning processed documents for immediate retrieval by their clients. Similarly, modern brokerage services interlink with freight forwarders to provide documentation that the exporter has met transportation security standards. Often, this includes the sophisticated integration of global position (GPS) data with accounting information.

To become a licensed customs broker in the United States, candidates must meet experience requirements and pass a proctored standardized examination. In developed countries, the preponderance of all import transactions are managed by customs brokers.

See Also: Duty; Freight Forwarder; Harmonized System; Letter of Credit; Tariff.

Bibliography. G. Alexis and M. Pavlos, "On the Development of a Web-Based System for Transportation Services," *Information Sciences* (2006); C. M. J. Carr and M.

R. Crum, "The U.S. Customs Modernization and Informed Compliance Act: Implications for the Logistics Pipeline," *International Journal of Logistics Management* (1995); M. A. Haughton, "Information Technology Projects by International Logistics Services Providers: The Case of Canada's Small Customs Brokers," *Canadian Journal of Administrative Sciences* (March 2006); E. Ianchovichina, "Are Duty Drawbacks on Exports Worth the Hassle?" *Canadian Journal of Economics* (2007); International Business Publications, *US Customs Broker Handbook Regulations, Procedures, Opportunities* (International Business Publications, 2008); Scott W. Taylor, *Introduction to Customs Brokerage* (Boskage Commerce Publications, 2005).

George M. Puia
Saginaw Valley State University

Customs Union

A customs union is a treaty signed between two or more countries to promote trade between participants. The countries in the customs union establish a common free trade market with each other while simultaneously maintaining a common trade barrier for foreign goods. This agreement is the third step in complete trade integration between participating nations, occurring after the "free trade" zone step and before the "common market" step. Trade with outside participants is regulated through a common external tariffs rate and the application of a common trade policy. Some custom unions will be negotiated to allow different import quotas from one country to the next. Current custom unions include the Southern African Customs Union and the East African Community.

Customs unions provide three main advantages for participating countries. They promote the trade of goods between participants; protect industries operating within the protected region; and serve as a source of revenue for participating countries that are less likely to generate trade activities.

Customs unions promote the trade of goods in participating countries due to lower tariffs. Hence, the union increases local competition and lowers costs of goods for consumers while imposing a common barrier for the same goods from nonparticipating countries. This is used to effectively promote intracoun-

try trades. A recent study examined the impact of Turkey's integration in the European Custom Union. It found a positive effect in importations from European Union (EU) countries without overly impacting local industries.

Simultaneously, external tariffs protect regional industries operating inside the protected zone. This is important, as it protects a strategic sector of activity (such as agriculture and fishing). Hence, products that are produced inside the tariff zone have an immediate advantage over products that are from the external zone.

Finally, custom unions can serve as a source of revenue for the participating members, since revenue generated by the external tariff is pooled in a common revenue pool and shared among participants. This allows sharing of import revenues between participants. This is especially beneficial for countries that are insular and are less likely to trade with nonperipheral countries.

There are also have a number of disadvantages that countries must contend with when participating in a customs union. These include some loss of control over fiscal policy, increased competition to local industries, and the inherent advantages customs unions confer to larger participating countries.

One disadvantage a country faces when joining a custom union is that participants have to give up some level of control on fiscal matters. Hence, when a country is unable to unilaterally control tariffs, excise duties, and sales taxes, it loses some level of ability to use these instruments to control internal economic policy and strategy formulation.

Another disadvantage is that while custom unions favor the emergence of some regional industries, they can produce adversity for national companies as they find themselves competing directly with neighboring countries (without the benefit of tariffs to protect them). This often leads to the disappearance of local inefficient industries in favor of more regional competitors.

Finally, customs unions often favor larger countries because they are able to take advantage of economies of scale to produce goods more cheaply than their smaller counterparts. As such, bigger participants usually have the upper hand in these arrangements. While smaller countries get access to cheaper goods, they often find that their local industries are slowly eroding, leaving them unable to compete in their national markets.

Hence, smaller countries have to increasingly depend on market specialization, focusing their local economies on some natural resources or local expertise in favor of a broader diversified industry.

Customs unions are present throughout the world. Examples include the Southern African Customs Union (SACU), which is the oldest customs union in operation. Established in 1910, SACU permits the free movement of goods among five member countries (South Africa, Botswana, Lesotho, Swaziland, and Namibia), and a uniform external tariff regime on goods from outside the region. The East African Community (EAC) is another customs union in Africa, comprised of five east African countries—Kenya, Tanzania, Uganda, Burundi, and Rwanda.

Other examples around the world include the European Union. While not itself a customs union, the EU establishes customs unions with other countries when they are evaluated for membership (like Turkey in 1996). Mercosur is a free trade area that is considering evolving into a full-fledged customs union. Negotiations in the region are ongoing.

See Also: Candidate Countries; Common Market; Economic Union; European Union; Free Trade; Mercosur/Mercosul; Monetary Union; South Africa.

Bibliography. Arzu Akkoyunlu-Wigley and Sevin Ã. Mihci, "Effects of the Customs Union with the European Union on the Market Structure and Pricing Behaviour of the Turkish Manufacturing Industry," *Applied Economics* (v.38/20, 2006); D. K. Brown, K. Kiyota, and R. M. Stern, "An Analysis of a US-Southern African Customs Union (SACU) Free Trade Agreement," *World Development—Oxford* (v.36/3, 2008); Daniel C. K. Chow and Thomas J. Schoenbaum, *International Trade Law: Problems, Cases, and Materials* (Aspen Publishers, 2008); Ian F. Fergusson and Library of Congress: Congressional Research Service, *United States-Canada Trade and Economic Relationship Prospects and Challenges* (Congressional Research Service, Library of Congress, 2008); Laurence W. Gormley, *EU Law of Free Movement of Goods and Customs Union* (Oxford University Press, 2007); Alina Kaczorowska, *European Union Law* (Routledge-Cavendish, 2008); L. Simon and J. Van Der Harst "Beyond the Customs Union: The European Community's Quest for Deepening, Widening, and Completion, 1969–75," *Journal of Common Market Studies* (v.46/4, 2008); Veysel Ulusoy and Ahmet Sözenm, "Trade Diversion and Trade Creation: The Case of Turkey Establishing Customs Union with the European Union," *European Journal of Scientific Research* (v.20/2, 2008).

JEAN-FRANCOIS DENAULT
UNIVERSITY OF MONTREAL

CVS Caremark

Woonsocket, Rhode Island–based CVS Caremark (NYSE:CVS) is the largest U.S.-based integrated pharmacy service provider, combining one of the leading American pharmaceutical benefit management companies (Caremark) with the country's largest pharmacy chain (CVS). The U.S. healthcare system is struggling to manage growing costs as employers shift responsibility for managing costs to employees. In response, CVS acquired Caremark for $26.5 billion in order to become more consumer-centric and responsive to rapid changes in the healthcare delivery system. This 2007 merger of the two entities was expected to permit more fully integrated pharmacy services, including pharmacy benefit management, mail order, specialty pharmaceuticals, an online pharmacy (CVS.com), and the retail-based health clinic subsidiary, MinuteClinic.

CVS Caremark has been making investments in new stores and technology in order to drive future growth both through in-house start-up and acquisitions. Several of their larger recent acquisitions include the 2004 purchase of over 1,200 Eckerd drugstores, primarily in high-growth markets in Florida and Texas, and in 2006 Southern California–based Sav-on and Osco drugstores (700 stores total) that were integrated into CVS/pharmacy. Altogether, CVS Caremark offers end-to-end services from plan design to prescription fulfillment. The company feels that the combination of CVS Caremark helps payers control costs more effectively, improves patient access (through phone, mail, the internet, or face-to-face), and promotes better customer health outcomes.

The lineage of CVS Caremark can be traced back to the Melville Corporation, a large retail holding company incorporated in 1922 as the Melville Shoe Company, and renamed in 1996 as CVS Corporation. (The CVS stands for Consumer Value Stores.)

Caremark was established in 1979 as Home Health Care of America, changing its name to Caremark in 1985. In 1987 Caremark was acquired by Baxter International, but then spun off as a public company, Caremark, in 1992. In 1996 Caremark merged with MedPartners/Mullikin, Inc., and they became MedPartners. In 1998 MedPartners changed its name to Caremark Rx.

CVS Caremark currently employs 136,000 people in two operating segments: CVS/pharmacy and Caremark Pharmacy Services. CVS/pharmacy fills more than one of every seven retail prescriptions in America, amounting to more than 1 billion prescriptions per year, which is more than any other pharmacy service provider. CVS/pharmacy generates over 68 percent of its revenues from its pharmacy business. Their ExtraCare program has enrolled over 50 million cardholders. Caremark Pharmacy Services is one of the nation's leading pharmacy benefit management companies, providing comprehensive prescription benefit management services to over 2,000 organizations' health plans, including corporations, managed care organizations, insurance companies, and government agencies. Caremark also operates a national retail pharmacy network of over 60,000 participating pharmacies, 11 mail service pharmacies, and 70 specialty pharmacies.

Among their initiatives in community involvement are the CVS Caremark Charitable Trust (education and community involvement in cities where the company operates pharmacies), the CVS Samaritan Vans providing free roadside (medical and on-site auto repair) assistance to motorists and communities in numerous cities, and the annual CVS Caremark Charity Golf Classic.

According to CVS Caremark, the average revenue per employee is close to $200,000. Strong future demand is anticipated in response to an aging population, increasing incidence of chronic diseases, and increasing utilization of the Medicare drug benefit.

See Also: Acquisitions, Takeovers, and Mergers; Cardinal Health; Caremark Rx; S&P 500 Index; Walgreen; Wal-Mart Stores.

Bibliography. *Chain Drug Store Review*, www.chaindrug review.com (cited March 2009); CVS Caremark, www .cvscaremark.com (cited March 2009); Hoover's, www .hoovers.com (cited March 2009); National Association of Drug Stores, www.nacds.org (cited March 2009).

MARIA NATHAN
LYNCHBURG COLLEGE

Cyprus

Cyprus is an island in the Mediterranean Sea whose political status is dominated by the division of the country into the Greek-Cypriot southern area (Republic of Cyprus) controlled by the Cyprus government and the northern area that is administered by Turkish-Cypriots. The Greek-Cypriot part of the island enjoys a prosperous economy—it is one of the advanced economies of the world according to the International Monetary Fund.

A large part of the southern part's prosperity is attributed to Cyprus's strategic location at the crossroads of three continents and in close proximity to the Middle East. This position has played a significant role as Cyprus has been a country with a platform of political turbulence for many years. Characteristics like a developed infrastructure, a stable legal framework, and the highly skilled workforce also contribute to the wealth that Greek Cypriots enjoy, and have made Cyprus a popular business center. Moreover, tourism plays a dominant role in growth and wealth generation, which is, however, susceptible to external influences such as fluctuations in the financial conditions of major tourism-producing countries (primarily western European countries such as Germany and the United Kingdom).

The Turkish Cypriot area of the island has about 20 percent of the population and its gross domestic product (GDP) is one-third of the GDP of the southern part of the island. The de facto Turkish-Cypriot administration is recognized only by Turkey, so attracting foreign investment has been a difficult task to accomplish. As a result, the economy of the northern part still relies on agriculture and on the government.

The Republic of Cyprus has been a member of the European Union since May 2004. The beginning of 2008 marked the entry of the country to the Eurozone and thus, Cyprus has adopted the euro at a fixed exchange rate of CYP 0.585274 per EUR 1.00. The introduction to the Eurozone was accompanied by accelerated growth at a rate that is above the European Union average. This growth is largely a result of the activity of traditional, family-owned enterprises with a strong entrepreneurial flair supported by a liberal economy whose backbone is the private sector. In this respect, the public sector has a supervising role monitoring the smooth operation of the economy and providing public utilities. The main economic indicators manifest the country's economic "health," with the inflation rate being less than 3 percent and registered unemployment less than 4 percent.

The services sector is an increasingly important part of the economy, as indicated by its 70–73 percent contribution to GDP and its share in employment. At the same time, the importance of agriculture and manufacturing showcase a steady decline over the years. Key services sectors include banking and financial services, insurance, advertising, legal, architecture and civil engineering, accounting and auditing, consultancy, design, electrical and mechanical engineering, market research, medical, printing and publishing, public relations, education, software development, tourism, and related services. In terms of social life, Cypriots enjoy a high standard of living with no or extremely low levels of homelessness or criminality.

In terms of international trade, the country relies on the importation of energy resources such as oil from the Middle East because of the lack of raw materials and heavy industry. Export-wise, many Cypriot products and services go international, primarily to several European and neighboring Middle Eastern countries. A prime feature of the Cypriot economy is its attractiveness for foreign investment. The strategic location of the country, favorable tax incentives, and a free zone area located near Larnaca airport provide an ideal location for many investing enterprises. Some restrictions on foreign investors are, however, applied in some economic sectors such as broadcasting, land development, education, the press, travel agencies, commercial shipping, and fisheries, since relevant licenses must be obtained.

See Also: Euro; European Union; Greece; Turkey.

Bibliography. CIA, "Cyprus," *The World Factbook*, www .cia.gov (cited March 2009); Maria Krambia-Kapardis and Jim Psaros, "The Implementation of Corporate Governance Principles in an Emerging Economy: A Critique of the Situation in Cyprus," *Corporate Governance: An International Review* (v.14/2, 2006); IBP USA, *Cyprus Business Intelligence Report* (International Business Publications, 2008).

EFTHIMIOS POULIS
BOURNEMOUTH UNIVERSITY
KONSTANTINOS POULIS
IST STUDIES, ATHENS
CELIA HADJICHRISTODOULOU
EUROPEAN UNIVERSITY CYPRUS

Czech Republic

The Czech Republic, capital Prague, is a small landlocked central Eastern European state with a population of 10.2 million. The lands of Bohemia and Moravia were an advanced part of the Austro-Hungarian Empire. When the empire collapsed in 1918, a new Czechoslovak state was formed. This lasted until Nazi expansion in World War II. Liberation led to the re-creation of the state and a short-lived coalition government before integration into the Soviet bloc in still-controversial circumstances in 1948–49. The communist regime was shaken in 1968 by the Prague Spring. Soviet invasion halted this, but in 1989 the communist regime collapsed in the face of popular demonstrations and the peaceful Velvet Revolution. The current Czech state emerged in January 1993 from a Velvet Divorce with Slovakia—hitherto the eastern part of the country.

When the communist regime failed, the Czech Republic was seen as something of a model transition country and its leaders sought to obtain recognition for its strategic location in central Europe. (Czechs were often offended at being considered "east," as Prague is farther "west" than Vienna). The Czech Republic joined NATO in 1999 and the EU in 2004.

Czech leaders, and especially Vaclav Klaus as prime minister from 1992 to 1997 (elected president in 2003 and 2008), were careful to echo the appropriate free market rhetoric, although some skeptics suggested that reality often deviated. Czech privatization was distinguished by the use of vouchers to create popular share ownership. This aim was not achieved but the management quality of Czech privatized firms tends to be relatively high. Early on, a high international credit rating was gained. Czech politics and society were viewed positively despite undercurrents of corruption, crime, racism, and minority oppression. The tourist boom reflects these contradictions, with some attracted to the glories of the past and others by cheap alcohol and prostitution.

Czech industrialization began early, and the country today is 75 percent urban. Agriculture plays a small role (3 percent output). Industry provides around 38 percent, and services the remainder. The Czech arms industry was famous for many decades. Engineering, machinery, and iron and steel along with consumer goods, including the famous Czech beers, are an important part of industrial output. But parts of Czech industry are still in the central European economic "rust belt." There is significant inequality between the 13 different regions of the Czech Republic, with a strong polarization around the capital Prague.

Economic growth has enabled a sustained rise in output per capita. Inflation has been held down and unemployment has been contained. The government has tried to make the Czech economy more market friendly. Staged reductions in corporate taxes are in place, as is the replacement of the progressive income tax with a flat rate. But there is a strong tradition of welfare support and opposition to elements of a neo-liberal agenda. This makes consensus difficult to maintain.

Trade is focused on the West, with Germany having a third share. Trade with Slovakia is relatively small given the history of unity. Manufactured goods make up an important part of commodity trade. The Czech Republic early on attracted significant foreign investment and is one of the more successful cases in the transition states. Brands like Skoda and the Czech beers were still seen to be valuable by Western multinationals.

The Czech population offered a more qualified support for joining the European Union, with a 77 percent yes vote on only a 55 percent turnout. Both as prime minister and president, Vaclav Klaus has been notorious for his skepticism about aspects of the European Union. This has often found him favor in Washington and among those who see the possibility of a more pro-American "new Europe" to set against the "old" western Europe.

See Also: Capitalism; Communism; European Union; Slovakia; Transition Economies.

Bibliography. I. Berend, *Central and Eastern Europe, 1944–1993: Detour from the Periphery to the Periphery* (Cambridge University Press, 1999); *Czech Republic Taxation Laws and Regulations Handbook* (International Business Publications, 2008); Czech Statistical Office, www.czso.cz/eng (cited March 2009); Thomas Dalsgaard, Sònia Muñoz, and Anita Tuladhar, *Czech Republic: Selected Issues.* IMF country report, 08.40 (International Monetary Fund, 2008); M. Dangerfield, *Subregional Economic Cooperation in Central and Eastern Europe: The Political Economy of Cefta* (Edward Elgar, 2001); Datamonitor, *Retailing in the Czech Republic 2008: First Phase of Retail Development Successfully Completed, Tougher Times Ahead* (Datamonitor, 2008) A. Innes, Czechoslovakia: The Short Goodbye (Yale University Press, 2001); P. Kenney, *The Burdens of Freedom: Eastern Europe since 1989* (Fernwood, 2006); Daniel Miller, "Czech Republic," in *Eastern Europe: An Introduction to the People, Lands, and Culture*, vol. 2, Richard Frucht, ed. (ABC-CLIO, 2005); OECD Economic Surveys, *Czech Republic* (2008).

Michael Haynes
University of Wolverhampton